Foundations of Ethics

BLACKWELL PHILOSOPHY ANTHOLOGIES

Each volume in this outstanding series provides an authoritative and comprehensive collection of the essential primary readings from philosophy's main fields of study. Designed to complement the *Blackwell Companions to Philosophy* series, each volume represents an unparalleled resource in its own right, and will provide the ideal platform for course use.

Foundations of Ethics

An Anthology

Edited by

Russ Shafer-Landau and Terence Cuneo

Blackwell Publishing

Editorial material and organization © 2007 by Blackwell Publishing Ltd

BLACKWELL PUBLISHING
350 Main Street, Malden, MA 02148-5020, USA
9600 Garsington Road, Oxford OX4 2DQ, UK
550 Swanston Street, Carlton, Victoria 3053, Australia

First published 2007 by Blackwell Publishing Ltd

1   2007

Library of Congress Cataloging-in-Publication Data

Foundations of ethics : an anthology / edited by Russ Shafer-Landau
        and Terence Cuneo. — 3rd ed.
            p. cm.
        Includes bibliographical references and index.
        ISBN-13: 978-1-4051-2951-0 (hardback : alk. paper)
        ISBN-10: 1-4051-2951-4 (hardback : alk. paper)
        ISBN-13: 978-1-4051-2952-7 (pbk. : alk. paper)
        ISBN-10: 1-4051-2952-2 (pbk. : alk. paper)
            1. Ethics.   I. Shafer-Landau, Russ.   II. Cuneo, Terence.
        BJ1012.F638 2007
        170—dc22

                                                            2006007481

A catalogue record for this title is available from the British Library.

Set in 9 on 11pt Ehrhardt MT
by SNP Best-set Typesetter Ltd, Hong Kong
Printed and bound in Singapore
by COS Printers Pte Ltd

The publisher's policy is to use permanent paper from mills that operate a sustainable forestry policy, and which has been manufactured from pulp processed using acid-free and elementary chlorine-free practices. Furthermore, the publisher ensures that the text paper and cover board used have met acceptable environmental accreditation standards.

For further information on
Blackwell Publishing, visit our website:
www.blackwellpublishing.com

Contents

Contents

Contents

Acknowledgments

In preparing this collaborative volume, we have been aided by the expert advice of two fine philosophers: Jamie Dreier, of Brown University, and Pekka Väyrynen, of the University of California, Davis. We have also benefited greatly from the acute comments of our reviewers: Paul Bloomfield (Connecticut), Jack Bricke (Kansas), Rachel Cohon (SUNY-Albany), Tim Roche (Memphis), Geoffrey Sayre-McCord (University of North Carolina, Chapel Hill), Geoffrey Scarre (Durham), and an additional reviewer who prefers anonymity. The University of Wisconsin's Vilas Trust, and the Calvin Center for Christian Scholarship at Calvin College, provided generous financial assistance to support ·summer work on this project. Finally, Luke Maring and Doug Walters provided help with proof-reading.

We feel very fortunate to have been able to work with such a fine editorial and production team at Blackwell. We are especially grateful to Jeff Dean, philosophy editor at Blackwell, and his assistant, Danielle Descoteaux, who have shown us many kindnesses, have been patient and flexible as needed, and have been unfailingly encouraging during the entire process of putting together this collection. Their sound judgment and continued good will have made what was in all respects an enjoyable undertaking even more so.

RSL   TC
Madison, Wisconsin   *Grand Rapids, Michigan*

Text Credits

The editors and publisher gratefully acknowledge the permission granted to reproduce the copyright material in this book:

1   John Mackie, "The Subjectivity of Values," pp. 15–18, 27–9, 30–43, 45 from *Ethics: Inventing Right and Wrong* (London: Penguin, 1997). Reprinted by permission of Penguin Books Ltd.

2   Richard Joyce, pp. 1–5, 8, 42–4, 49, 51, 80–5, 88–91, 100 from *The Myth of Morality* (Cambridge: Cambridge University Press, 2002). Reprinted with permission of the author and the publisher, Cambridge University Press.

3   A. J. Ayer, "Critique of Ethics and Theology," pp. 102–14 from *Language, Truth and Logic* (Dover Publications, 1952). Reprinted by permission of Dover Publications.

4   Simon Blackburn, "How To Be an Ethical Anti-Realist," pp. 166–81 from *Essays in Quasi-Realism* (Oxford: Oxford University Press, 1993). © 1993 by Simon Blackburn. Used by permission of Oxford University Press, Inc.

ix

5 Terry Horgan and Mark Timmons, "Nondescriptivist Cognitivism: Framework for a New Metaethic," pp. 121–53 from *Philosophical Papers* 29 (2000). Reprinted by permission of Philosophical Papers.

6 Allan Gibbard, "The Reasons of a Living Being," pp. 49–60 from *Proceedings of the American Philosophical Association* 62 (2002). Reprinted by permission of the American Philosophical Association.

7 Gilbert Harman, "Moral Relativism Defended," pp. 3–22 from *Philosophical Review* 85 (1975).

8 Christine Korsgaard, "The Authority of Reflection," pp. 91–4, 96–108, 112–26, 128–30 from *The Sources of Normativity* (Cambridge: Cambridge University Press, 1996). Reprinted by permission of the author and the publisher, Cambridge University Press.

9 Roderick Firth, "Ethical Absolutism and the Ideal Observer," pp. 317–45 from *Phenomenological Research* 12 (1952).

10 Ronald Milo, "Contractarian Constructivism," pp. 181–204 from *Journal of Philosophy* 92 (1995). Reprinted by permission of the author and the Journal of Philosophy.

11 John McDowell, "Values and Secondary Qualities," pp. 110–29 from Ted Honderich, *Morality & Objectivity* (Routledge, 1985). Reprinted by permission of Routledge.

12 David Wiggins, "A Sensible Subjectivism?," pp. 185–211 from *Needs, Values, Truth*, 2nd edn. (Oxford: Blackwell, 1991). Reprinted by permission of Blackwell Publishing Ltd.

13 Richard Boyd, "How To Be a Moral Realist," pp. 182–7, 196–217 from Geoffrey Sayre-McCord (ed.), *Essays on Moral Realism* (Ithaca, NY: Cornell University Press, 1988). © 1988 by Cornell University. Used by permission of the publisher, Cornell University Press.

14 Peter Railton, "Moral Realism," pp. 163–207 from *Philosophical Review* 95 (1986) © 1986 by Cornell University Press. Reprinted by permission of the publisher and the author.

15 Jean Hampton, "The Authority of Reason," pp. 95–7, 111–12, 114, 207–14 from *The Authority of Reason* (Cambridge: Cambridge University Press, 1996). Reprinted with permission of the author and the publisher, Cambridge University Press.

16 Russ Shafer-Landau, "Ethics as Philosophy: A Defense of Ethical Nonnaturalism," from Terence Horgan and Mark Timmons (eds.), *Metaethics after Moore* (Oxford: Oxford University Press, 2006). Reprinted by permission of Oxford University Press.

17 Michael Smith, "The Externalist Challenge," pp. 60–76, 85–91 from *The Moral Problem* (Oxford: Blackwell, 1994). Reprinted by permission of Blackwell Publishing Ltd.

18 Nick Zangwill, "Externalist Moral Motivation," pp. 143–54 from *American Philosophical Quarterly* 40 (2003). Reprinted by permission of the American Philosophical Quarterly.

19 Margaret Little, "Virtue as Knowledge: Objections from the Philosophy of Mind," pp. 59–77, 79 from *Noûs* 31 (1997).

20 Jonathan Dancy, "Acting for a Good Reason," pp. 98–116, 126–37 from *Practical Reality* (Oxford: Oxford University Press, 2001). Reprinted by permission of Oxford University Press.

21 Philippa Foot, "Morality as a System of Hypothetical Imperatives," pp. 305–16 from *Philosophical Review* 81 (1972).

22 Bernard Williams, "Internal and External Reasons," pp. 17–28 from Ross Harrison (ed.), *Rational Action* (Cambridge: Cambridge University Press, 1979). Reprinted with permission of the author and the publisher, Cambridge University Press.

23 Christine Korsgaard, "Skepticism about Practical Reason," pp. 5–25 from *Journal of Philosophy* 83 (1986). Reprinted by permission of the author and the Journal of Philosophy.

24 Russ Shafer-Landau, "Moral Reasons," pp. 176–88, 192–203, 209–13 from *Moral Realism: A Defense* (Oxford: Oxford University Press, 2003). Reprinted by permission of Oxford University Press.

25 Gilbert Harman, "Ethics and Observation," pp. 3–10 from *The Nature of Morality: An Introduction To Ethics* (Oxford: Oxford University Press, 1977). © 1977 by Oxford University Press, Inc. Used by permission of Oxford University Press Inc.

26 Nicholas L. Sturgeon, "Moral Explanations," pp. 49–75 from David Copp and David Zimmerman (eds.), *Morality, Reason, and Truth* (Totowa, NJ: Rowman & Allanheld, 1985).

27 Terence Cuneo, "Moral Facts as Configuring Causes," pp. 141–62 from *Pacific Philosophical Quarterly* 87 (2006). © 2007 by Blackwell Publishing Ltd.

28 Charles L. Stevenson, "The Nature of Ethical Disagreement," pp. 1–9 from *Facts and Values* (New Haven: Yale University Press, 1963).

29 David Brink, "Moral Disagreement," pp. 198–209 from *Moral Realism and the Foundations of Ethics* (Cambridge: Cambridge University Press, 1989). Reprinted with permission of the author and the publisher, Cambridge University Press.

30 Norman Daniels, "Wide Reflective Equilibrium and Theory Acceptance in Ethics," pp. 256–82 from *Journal of Philosophy* 76 (1979). Reprinted by permission of the author and The Journal of Philosophy.

31 Robert Audi, "Intuitionism, Pluralism, and the Foundations of Ethics," pp. 32–51, 55–8 from *Moral Knowledge and Ethical Character* (Oxford: Oxford University Press, 1997). © 1997 by Robert Audi. Used by permission of Oxford University Press, Inc.

32 Margaret Olivia Little, "Seeing and Caring: The Role of Affect in Feminist Moral Epistemology," pp. 117–37 from *Hypatia* 10:3 (Summer 1995). Reprinted with permission of the Copyright Clearance Center.

33 Simon Blackburn, "Supervenience Revisited," pp. 47–67 from Ian Hacking (ed.), *Exercises in Analysis* (Cambridge: Cambridge University Press, 1985). Reprinted with permission of the author and the publisher, Cambridge University Press.

34 Frank Jackson, "The Supervenience of the Ethical on the Descriptive," pp. 118–29 from *From Metaphysics to Metaethics* (Oxford: Oxford University Press, 1988). Reprinted by permission of Oxford University Press.

35 G. E. Moore, "The Subject-Matter of Ethics," pp. 53–5, 57–72 from *Principia Ethica* (Cambridge: Cambridge University Press, 1993). Reprinted with permission of the author and the publisher, Cambridge University Press.

36 Simon Blackburn, "Attitudes and Contents," pp. 501–17 from *Ethics* 98 (1988). Reprinted by permission of the University of Chicago Press and the author.

37 Walter Sinnott-Armstrong, "Expressivism and Embedding," pp. 677–93 from *Philosophy and Phenomenological Research* 61 (2000).

38 Terry Horgan and Mark Timmons, "New Wave Moral Realism Meets Moral Twin Earth," pp. 447–65 from *Philosophy and Phenomenological Research* 16 (1991).

Every effort has been made to trace copyright holders and to obtain their permission for the use of copyright material. The publisher apologizes for any errors or omissions in the above list and would be grateful if notified of any corrections that should be incorporated in future reprints or editions of this book.

General Introduction

Over the course of the past hundred years, it has been customary to divide the realm of moral philosophy into at least two areas: normative ethics and metaethics. Though the boundaries that separate them are sometimes blurred, the division has proved a useful one, and we will rely on it in what follows. Normative ethics is devoted to identifying the conditions under which actions are morally right, or motives and intentions morally good. We might say that normative ethics is concerned with the content of morality, insofar as it seeks to identify the content of the correct standards of morality. Utilitarian theories, deontological and contractarian views, egoistic and virtue theoretic accounts are some of the most prominent contenders within normative ethics. If one wants to know how to live a moral life, one will want to consider each of these options (and others) very carefully.

But suppose that one has larger questions about the very enterprise of normative ethics. Rather than focusing on the intramural debates among these theories, and thus on the content of morality, one might ask about its *status*. Are moral theories and moral judgments a product of human invention? Or do they have some more objective source? If the latter, just what is the nature of that source? How could we gain knowledge of what is right and wrong – if we can? Are moral require-ments (assuming they really exist) rationally authoritative by their very nature, or do they supply reasons for obedience only when they happen to align with what we really care about?

These questions are at the heart of that branch of moral philosophy known as *metaethics*. This book is devoted to these latter issues. The writings that we have selected for inclusion in this volume are not focused on the normative questions that make up such an important part of the moral life. There is no discussion here of weighty moral matters, of life and death decisions, or the specific moral standards that would correctly guide us in their resolution. Rather, the foundational questions that our authors raise concern the legitimacy of normative theories, and theorizing, in the first place.

To get a sense of what this means, consider an analogy with language. One might want to know whether a particular turn of phrase is grammatical or not. The rules of grammar for the language will dictate this. Suppose that these rules are complete – every question of grammar is answered by the rules. These rules are analogous to a comprehen-sive normative ethic – if such an ethic is truly com-plete, then every legitimate moral question will be answered by recourse to the theory.

But we might also wonder about the status of the rules of grammar, or morality. Are they merely

1

conventional? What kind of authority do they have over us, and what is the source of this authority? What diagnosis do we make when people with equally coherent views of the relevant rules disagree with one another? How can we know what the rules are? The rules themselves do not provide us with answers to these questions. In this sense, we have to go beyond (*meta*, in Greek) the rules to determine the answers to our questions *about* the rules. That is what metaethics does for the rules, and judgments, of normative ethics.

In effect, those who do metaethics seek to provide a philosophical account of normative ethics. Metaethicists are concerned about the metaphysics of morality, about its epistemology, its semantics and syntax, its normativity and practical point. These concerns are all reflected in the content of our readings.

We think that a fruitful way to explore the many issues in metaethics is by means of an initial distinction between ontological matters (i.e., matters dealing with questions of what kinds of things really exist) and all others. The first part of this volume is devoted to canvassing the major ontological views in metaethics. The second part contains discussions of a variety of other metaethical issues, each of which has at least some important implications for the relative plausibility of the ontological views represented in part I.

The basic ontological question in metaethics is this: what is the nature of moral reality? At one end of the spectrum we have those philosophers known as *error theorists*. These philosophers are nihilists about morality – according to them, there is no moral reality. The world contains no moral features. Nothing is morally right or wrong, good or bad. We are mistaken if we assert that torture or treachery is immoral. Not that such actions are morally right. Rather, nothing is immoral. And nothing moral.

Error theorists combine this metaphysical thesis with a thesis about what we do when we hold or sincerely express a moral judgment. Such judgments, they claim, are beliefs that seek to represent the way things really are. When we say that torturing children is immoral, we mean just what we say. There is a kind of action (torture), and we attribute a certain feature (that of being immoral) to it. The claim is true just in case the act has the feature we attribute to it. Since, according to error theorists, nothing ever exemplifies these features, our moral judgments are never true. Yet almost all of us believe that they are at least sometimes true. Hence the error.

Expressivists agree with error theorists about the ultimate metaphysical status of morality. When we step back from engaged moral thinking, and ask whether there are any moral facts, really, the answer must be No. The real world is the natural world, the world as described by the natural and social sciences. Moral features are not part of that world. Despite this important point of ontological agreement, expressivists part company with error theorists when it comes to the nature of moral judgment. Where error theorists depict such judgment as expressive of beliefs that try (but fail) to describe reality, expressivists think that there is some other point to moral judgment. We don't invariably land in error when making moral judgments, because we are not trying in the first place to describe a (nonexistent) moral reality. Rather, we are trying (say) to express our emotions, or to prescribe a course of action to others, or to evince a commitment to norms regulating guilt and anger. We can do each of these activities largely successfully, and so we needn't convict people of falling into massive error in their moralizing.

Many people think, however, that there is something more to morality, that our moral views answer to a set of moral standards that are neither pure fictions, as error theorists would have it, nor only expressions of personal commitments, as expressivists believe. *Constructivists* think that there are true moral standards that are in some way the product of an actual or hypothetical constructive process. Moral standards might, for instance, be constructed from the content of social agreements among actual people. This would generate a familiar kind of relativism. Prior to the existence of such agreements, there are no moral standards, and so no moral truths. But once these agreements are in place, they serve to codify the correct moral standards, by reference to which particular moral judgments are rendered true or false. Alternatively, one might opt perhaps for an ideal observer theory, according to which correct moral standards are fixed by reference to the responses of wholly impartial, fully informed, and flawlessly rational individuals – none of whom walk amongst us. Here, types of action are wrong just in case they would be disapproved of by such hypothetical agents. Again, the thought is that we can construct the correct moral standards from the attitudes and activities of the relevant agents of construction.

There are no correct moral standards without such agents. As a conceptual matter, we require reference to their attitudes and activities before we can determine which moral standards are correct.

Sensibility theorists believe that there are correct moral standards not of our own making, though we cannot understand such standards without making essential reference to the reactions of well-situated moral agents. This intriguing mixture of objectivity and subjectivity is ordinarily explicated by relying on an analogy between moral properties and dispositional properties. What makes something blue is its being such as to elicit a certain kind of response from normal observers in normal contexts. In other words, being blue is a dispositional property. According to sensibility theorists, moral properties are also dispositional. We can understand them only by reference to the responses that they do, or should, evoke from agents who are properly situated to appreciate them. Just as a berry may be blue even if one can't be convinced of its color, so too an action may be depraved or immoral, despite our refusal to see that it is. On this sort of view, moral standards are objective (in the sense that anyone might be mistaken about them), and yet in another sense are also subjective (in that their content depends importantly on a set of appropriate human responses).

Having traversed most of the spectrum of moral ontologies, we come finally to *moral realism*. According to moral realists, things are morally right or wrong, good or bad, regardless of how they are viewed by actual or even idealized human beings. The basic principles that specify our moral duties, or dictate the conditions of moral value, are immune to alteration based on the attitudes of those to whom they apply. It isn't as if moral facts are entirely independent of human attitudes. The degree of a criminal's moral culpability importantly depends on what was going on in his mind; the goodness and praiseworthiness of a benefactor will depend crucially on her beliefs and attitudes towards her beneficiaries. So moral realists do not believe that moral reality is entirely mind-independent. But they do believe that there is a set of correct moral standards and claims whose truth does not depend in any way on human endorsement. For moral realists, some moral truths are as objective as those of logic, or the laws of physics. We do not create them, but rather discover them, if we are fortunate. We invent language to refer to them, but we do not invent the truths themselves.

For the intelligent and sensitive among us, we appreciate what is there awaiting our understanding, rather than creating a set of norms from our desires and beliefs.

How does one determine which of these ontological views to accept? A natural thought is that we need first to identify the relevant criteria of theoretical adequacy in metaethics, and then investigate to see how each family of theory fares. Yet this approach can be only partly successful. There are widely accepted criteria of theoretical adequacy in this domain, and we can rely on these to yield that partial success. But there are also two hurdles. First, even where all agree that something should serve as a criterion, there may be disagreement about its relative importance. And, second, there is also (surprise!) a good deal of disagreement about whether some putative criteria deserve the name.

Before discussing the difficulties here, let us first mention the points of agreement.

1 All theorists accept that a plausible metaethical theory must be able to account for moral disagreement. The depth and breadth of moral disagreement, especially as compared to that within the sciences, is striking, and has tempted many people to the error-theoretic end of the spectrum. This subject is taken up in part II.4.

2 There is also widespread acknowledgment of the importance of developing an adequate moral epistemology. If there is anything to be known within morality, there should be an account of how to apprehend it. The error theorist, of course, doesn't need such a thing, and epistemological hurdles have often been seen as major reasons to reject its competitors. This topic is discussed in part II.5.

3 The relation between the moral and the nonmoral world needs to be accounted for. Everyone agrees that the moral status of things depends very importantly on what is happening in the nonmoral world. Further, unlike other familiar relations of dependence – mental states on brain states, color facts on facts about surface reflectance properties, etc. – the reliance of the moral on the nonmoral is a conceptual truth. We can see, a priori, that nothing can change its moral status without a correlative change in the nonmoral world. And two situations that are nonmorally identical must be morally identical. This expresses a relation

of *supervenience*. All theorists agree that any plausible metaethic must have something to say on this subject, which is the focus of part II.6.

4 A semantics of moral discourse is required for any plausible metaethical view. A semantics provides a theory of meaning; all are agreed that it is a serious strike against a metaethic if it is unable to provide one, or unable to reply to criticisms. Readings that represent a variety of semantic puzzles are offered in part II.7.

There are, in addition to these four criteria, other standards of theoretical adequacy that are widely accepted, but whose relative significance is disputed. Perhaps the two most important of these are conservatism and ontological parsimony. Many agree that a theory is more plausible to the extent that it can preserve a greater number of our existing beliefs, especially if these are widely held, are supportive of many other beliefs, and are extremely resistant to alteration after reflection. Error theories score very badly on this front, which is precisely why such theorists downplay the importance of conservatism. They'd much rather focus on ontological parsimony, which counsels us to adopt the view that explains all that needs explaining with the fewest hypotheses, or by means of positing the fewest entities. Here, error theories (and expressivist views) are in the ascendant, as their ontology contains no moral properties, and so is slimmer than those of their competitors.

Finally, there are three disputed criteria of adequacy that are important enough to devote attention to. The first of these is given by what philosophers call *motivational internalism*: other things equal, a metaethical theory is superior to its alternatives to the extent that it can explain why it is that, necessarily, anyone who sincerely holds a moral view is motivated to some extent to comply with it. Whether the connection between moral judgment and moral motivation is as strong as the internalist alleges is a matter of great controversy. Much hangs on the answer, as internalism is a natural ally of expressivist theories, and has posed a perennial challenge to moral realism. In any event, all agree that some accounting must be given of the ordinarily reliable connection between moral judgment and motivation, and of moral motivation quite generally. Issues regarding moral motivation are examined in part II.1.

The second disputed criterion is the *rationalist criterion*: other things equal, a metaethical theory is superior to its alternatives to the extent that it can explain how moral requirements entail excellent reason for compliance. There is no consensus on whether the rationalist criterion is acceptable, because there are such widely divergent popular views about the rational authority of morality. Part II.2 focuses on the many issues in this area, and provides a representative sampling of the different positions nowadays on offer.

Rounding out our agenda is a final, disputed criterion. We can call this the *explanatory criterion*: we have reason to believe that moral facts exist only if they are indispensable to best explaining a range of nonmoral facts. We no longer believe in ghosts, the tooth fairy, or Zeus, and rightly so. That is because these beings do not figure in the best explanation of what we experience in our world. The explanatory criterion has done excellent work in weeding out superfluous entities from our ontology. But it also threatens to abolish moral facts, as they don't, at least initially, appear to be essential to the explanation of why the world works as it does. Some theorists, believing that moral facts will indeed fail this test, reject the explanatory criterion. Others like the criterion, but think that moral facts can pass it. Still others endorse the criterion, and are prepared to jettison moral facts on its account. Discussion of these positions is carried out in part II.3.

This is obviously the merest sketch of the fascinating and very complex realm of metaethics. We have sought to provide much more substantive and informative introductions to each of the dozen sections of this book, and have included suggestions for further reading at their conclusion, for those whose interest is sufficiently piqued by any of the topics represented here.

Suggestions for Further Reading

For those who are new to metaethics as well as to philosophy, we might immodestly recommend Russ Shafer-Landau's *Whatever Happened to Good and Evil?* (Oxford University Press, 2004) as an accessible introduction to the basic questions of metaethics. It is an opinionated book, and very elementary. There are more even-handed introductions to metaethics; the two we'd recommend are both excellent, and more sophisticated than Shafer-Landau's slim book. These are Stephen Darwall's

Philosophical Ethics (Westview, 1998), and Alexander Miller's *An Introduction to Contemporary Metaethics* (Polity, 2003). The latter, especially, will give readers a comprehensive and detailed overview of the major figures and positions in the current literature and debates in the foundations of ethics. Darwall's book is more historically focused and informed. Reading the two of these, in combination with the present anthology, would get any reader well up to speed in metaethics. For those interested in having a look at the latest important work in metaethics, there are the usual philosophy journals to scour, but also an annual book series, *Oxford Studies in Metaethics* (published by Oxford University Press), devoted entirely to new work in the field.

Part I

Moral Ontology

I.1   Moral Error Theories

Introduction

Who among us hasn't felt, at one time or another, that morality is just a fiction, just a set of made-up constraints lacking entirely in real authority? For those who are quite deeply skeptical of the claims of morality, error theories may be just the thing. Error theorists claim that there is some ineliminable mistake that lies at the heart of moral thought and discourse.

Error theorists are not attempting to revamp morality from within. They are not offering criticisms of conventional morality, with an eye towards getting us to embrace a new, improved moral posture. Nor are they leveling parochial charges against various moral theories. They are not faulting Kantianism for its attachment to a principle of universalizability, or criticizing Utilitarianism for its impartiality. Rather, they seek to identify a common presupposition of all serious moral theories, and to show that this presupposition, whatever it may be, is false. If they have done their work correctly, they will have both properly identified this shared foundational element, and also shown that it is corrupt. The edifice of morality rests on these foundations. If they can be shown to be mistaken, the entire edifice comes crashing down.

All error theories are defined by allegiance to three central claims: (1) our moral judgments aim to represent moral facts; (2) there are no moral facts; and so (3) none of our moral judgments are true.[1]

Let us first try to get a handle on claim (1). Consider an ordinary descriptive claim: *Bolivia is a landlocked country*. When people say such a thing, they are expressing a belief, whose content purports to represent reality. That sounds very grand, but it is perfectly ordinary. The belief, like every belief, has a content. In this case, as in all descriptive cases, there is (at the least) a subject and a predicate. Descriptive claims are true just in case the claim about the subject is accurate. In our present example, the claim is true just in case Bolivia really is landlocked. And it is. The content of the claim matches up with reality, because the subject of the claim (Bolivia) really possesses the feature (that of being landlocked) that is predicated of it.

The error theorist sees moral judgments as descriptive judgments. They are true just in case the subjects of such judgments really possess the moral features that are attributed to them. When we make moral judgments, we assert that (e.g.) deliberately flying planes into populated buildings is immoral; that detonating a bomb in a crowded market is gravely wrong; that humiliating and starving a vulnerable child is evil. We express our belief that certain actions, motives, traits, etc. possess certain moral features. We are trying to state the truth, to represent reality aright, to accurately describe the situations we encounter or contemplate.

If claim (2) is correct, however, then all such efforts are bound to fail. Our moral judgments are never true, because there are no moral facts that await our accurate description. Those who sincerely issue moral claims – just about every one of us – are invariably mistaken in those claims. Just as the claim about Bolivia is true if, and only if, Bolivia really is landlocked, so too the claim that suicide bombers are immoral is true if, and only if, suicide bombers really are immoral. But, according to error theorists, nothing is immoral. So this particular claim is untrue.[2] Not that there is anything special about immorality. The same story will repeat itself for all moral qualities: that of being morally permissible or required, morally good, morally admirable or praiseworthy, morally deserving, etc. If error theorists are correct, then any claim that assigns such a feature to a subject is bound to be mistaken.

There have not been many error theorists. Most philosophers, even those highly critical of conventional morality, have thought that there really is such a thing as being immoral, morally praiseworthy, morally required, etc. Of course there has been great disagreement about just what qualifies as such, but that there are such genuine categories of assessment has only rarely been challenged. Error theorists are prepared to issue this sort of challenge directly. They are committed to the view that nothing – not even genocide, not even sadistic torture – is ever immoral; nothing – not even caring for the most vulnerable among us, not even laying down one's life for innocent others – is ever morally right. Error theorists might counsel us to avoid or undertake such actions, but not on the basis of their moral qualities. If the error theorist is right, nothing ever possesses such qualities.

So the central idea is this: in holding and expressing moral views, we are trying to believe and state the truth about what is morally right or wrong, good or bad. But there is no such truth. Therefore our moral views, no matter how considered, no matter how nuanced, are, one and all, mistaken. What is the explanation for this?

The explanation will differ depending on which error theory we are discussing. At the most fundamental level, what distinguishes one such theory from another is the nature of the central error that it imputes to morality. In principle, we can develop an indefinite number of such theories. But in practice, only two versions of the error theory have been advanced. John Mackie (1977) develops both

of them; Richard Joyce (2001) only the latter.[3] We include a representative sampling of the thought of each writer in the present section.

According to Mackie, morality is "queer" – unlike anything else we know of in the universe – because it claims for itself two unique powers. The first is the power, necessarily, to motivate us to compliance. Once we view an act, say, as our moral duty, we are automatically inclined to do it (even if this motivation is outweighed in some cases by other factors). The second special feature of morality is its power to be rationally authoritative – the power, that is, to supply us with excellent reasons for obedience, no matter what our likes and commitments might be. Such reasons, following Kant, are often called "categorical" reasons.

Mackie thinks that morality is founded on an error because nothing in fact possesses such motivational and reason-giving powers. Nothing is morally right or wrong, good or bad, because nothing is motivationally and rationally authoritative in the way that we take moral demands to be. Joyce agrees with Mackie on both counts. But his error theory is confined to an argument about categorical reasons.[4] Morality presupposes the existence of such reasons. They don't, in fact, exist. Therefore morality is founded on an error.

Perhaps a helpful way to appreciate the structure of moral error theory is by an analogy with atheism. Atheists are error theorists about religious claims. According to atheists, religious believers are trying to speak the truth when asserting that there is an omniscient, all-powerful creator of the universe, a unique, immaterial being who exists eternally. Religious adherents make a variety of claims about such a being. But, says the atheist, such claims are never true, because of a relevant failure of presupposition. Such claims presuppose the existence of a being matching this description, and no such being, in fact, exists. The error runs deep, and infects all traditional Western monotheistic discourse. Claims that reflect endorsement of this tradition are uniformly untrue.

We are now in a position to see how a critical assessment of error theories might go. There are two stages to an error-theoretic argument, and so two points of potential success or vulnerability. The first stage focuses on the assignment of a basic commitment or presupposition to morality. And the second argues that this basic presupposition is mistaken. To press the atheism analogy a bit further, one might reject an error theory about religion, either by denying that religious discourse presupposes the existence of an omniscient, omnipotent, eternal being, or by conceding that, but defending the existence of such a being against criticisms. Likewise, those who cast a skeptical eye on moral error theory must either deny that morality commits itself to the existence of special motivational or reason-giving powers, or concede that, but then proceed to argue on behalf of such powers. (These two sets of issues are taken up in this book in part II.1 and part II.2 respectively.)

Suppose that moral error theory is correct. What then? Should we abandon moral discourse altogether? It may well seem so. After all, if the atheist is correct, then it might seem perverse to persist in making claims about a divine being. Abolition, not reform, would be the order of the day. Richard Joyce is the error theorist who has devoted most attention to this matter in the moral arena. In portions of his book that we highly recommend (but were unable to excerpt here – see Joyce 2001, chapters 8 and 9), Joyce argues for *retaining* moral thought and talk, while regarding it as a very useful fiction. In all but our most reflective moments, we should proceed as if our conventional moral beliefs were correct.

The reason for taking such an approach is, at bottom, pragmatic. Belief in morality has done a great deal to enforce altruism and social cohesion throughout the ages. We would be far worse off without our moral commitments – not morally worse off, but worse off in the sense of greatly suffering from the rise in antisocial behavior that would follow the widespread abandonment of moral belief.

It is an interesting question whether it is possible to have the attitude towards morality that Joyce recommends – taking it seriously enough to secure the aforementioned benefits, while thinking, in the back of one's mind, that it's all a baseless fiction. However one comes down on such a question, it is essential to remember that the error theory may be correct, even if one is suspicious of Joyce's particular recommendations about what to do if it is. The plausibility of a moral error theory depends, ultimately, on whether error theorists can correctly identify the common foundation of morality, and whether, in the end, this foundation succumbs to their criticisms.

Notes

1 Technically, this is a bit too strong. Some moral judgments are indicative conditionals with moral claims as antecedents. The error theorist will regard all such antecedent claims as necessarily false. By the logic of such statements, this makes these conditionals turn out to be *true*. But this is the only category of true moral claims that the error theorist allows, and, as it represents something of an oddity, we will pass it over in subsequent discussion.

2 Of course, the error theorist may personally be just as appalled at such actions as anyone else. But he will (if consistent) refrain from sincerely registering any moral condemnation of the behavior he finds so repugnant.

3 One might also class Nietzsche (1966, 1967) as an error theorist. On one reading, he would endorse the error theorist's view that all positive moral judgments are mistaken, based as they are on an allegiance to the vicious commitments of slave morality. It isn't clear whether this is the best way to read Nietzsche. Even if it is, it would remain unclear as to whether Nietzsche is best seen as an error theorist, or rather as a moralist who endorses a minority view in the intramural debate about which moral outlooks are correct. Here we are confident of only this: that the matter cannot be resolved in a footnote.

4 Joyce agrees with Mackie that moral requirements and moral judgments lack any necessary motivating power. But he disagrees with Mackie's assertion that such power is presupposed in our moral thinking. This explains Joyce's decision not to rest his error-theoretic arguments on claims about moral motivation.

Selected Bibliography

Blackburn, Simon. 1985. "Errors and the Phenomenology of Value." In Ted Honderich, ed. *Morality and Objectivity*. London: Routledge.

Burgess, John. 1998. "Error Theories and Values." *Australasian Journal of Philosophy* 76: 534–52.

Garner, Richard. 1990. "On the Genuine Queerness of Moral Properties and Facts." *American Philosophical Quarterly* 68: 137–46.

Garner, Richard. 1994. *Beyond Morality*. Philadelphia: Temple University Press.

Hussain, Nadeem. 2004. "The Return of Moral Fiction-alism." In John Hawthorne, ed. *Philosophical Perspectives 18: Ethics*. Oxford: Blackwell.

Joyce, Richard. 2001. *The Myth of Morality*. Cambridge: Cambridge University Press.

Lillehammer, Hallvard. 2003. "Debunking Morality: Evolutionary Naturalism and Moral Error Theory." *Biology and Philosophy* 18: 567–81.

Lillehammer, Hallvard. 2004. "Moral Error Theory." *Proceedings of the Aristotelian Society* 104: 93–109.

Mackie, John. 1946. "A Refutation of Morals." *Australasian Journal of Philosophy* 24: 77–90.

Mackie, John. 1977. *Ethics: Inventing Right and Wrong*. London: Penguin.

Nietzsche, Friedrich. 1966. *On the Genealogy of Morals*, trans. Walter Kaufmann. New York: Vintage.

Nietzsche, Friedrich. 1967. *Beyond Good and Evil*, trans. Walter Kaufmann. New York: Vintage.

Ruse, Michael. 1998. *Taking Darwin Seriously: A Naturalistic Approach to Philosophy*. Buffalo, NY: Prometheus Publishers.

Shafer-Landau, Russ. 2005. "Error Theory and Normative Ethics." In Ernest Sosa and Enrique Villanueva, eds. *Philosophical Issues, 15, Normativity*. Oxford: Blackwell.

Wood, Allen. 1996. "Attacking Morality: A Metaethical Project." *Canadian Journal of Philosophy*, supp. 21: 221–49.

The Subjectivity of Values

John Mackie

Moral Scepticism

There are no objective values. This is a bald state-ment of the thesis of this chapter, but before arguing for it I shall try to clarify and restrict it in ways that may meet some objections and prevent some misunderstanding.

The statement of this thesis is liable to provoke one of three very different reactions. Some will think it not merely false but pernicious; they will see it as a threat to morality and to everything else that is worthwhile, and they will find the present-ing of such a thesis in what purports to be a book on ethics paradoxical or even outrageous. Others will regard it as a trivial truth, almost too obvious to be worth mentioning, and certainly too plain to be worth much argument. Others again will say that it is meaningless or empty, that no real issue is raised by the question whether values are or are not part of the fabric of the world. But, precisely because there can be these three different reactions, much more needs to be said.

The claim that values are not objective, are not part of the fabric of the world, is meant to include not only moral goodness, which might be most nat-urally equated with moral value, but also other things that could be more loosely called moral

values or disvalues – rightness and wrongness, duty, obligation, an action's being rotten and con-temptible, and so on. It also includes non-moral values, notably aesthetic ones, beauty and various kinds of artistic merit. I shall not discuss these explicitly, but clearly much the same considera-tions apply to aesthetic and to moral values, and there would be at least some initial implausibility in a view that gave the one a different status from the other.

Since it is with moral values that I am primarily concerned, the view I am adopting may be called moral scepticism. But this name is likely to be mis-understood: 'moral scepticism' might also be used as a name for either of two first order views, or perhaps for an incoherent mixture of the two. A moral sceptic might be the sort of person who says 'All this talk of morality is tripe,' who rejects morality and will take no notice of it. Such a person may be literally rejecting all moral judgements; he is more likely to be making moral judgements of his own, expressing a positive moral condemnation of all that conventionally passes for morality; or he may be confusing these two logically incompatible views, and saying that he rejects all morality, while he is in fact rejecting only a particular morality that is current in the society in which he has grown up.

But I am not at present concerned with the merits or faults of such a position. These are first order moral views, positive or negative: the person who adopts either of them is taking a certain practical, normative, stand. By contrast, what I am discussing is a second order view, a view about the status of moral values and the nature of moral valuing, about where and how they fit into the world. These first and second order views are not merely distinct but completely independent: one could be a second order moral sceptic without being a first order one, or again the other way round. A man could hold strong moral views, and indeed ones whose content was thoroughly conventional, while believing that they were simply attitudes and policies with regard to conduct that he and other people held. Conversely, a man could reject all established morality while believing it to be an objective truth that it was evil or corrupt.

With another sort of misunderstanding moral scepticism would seem not so much pernicious as absurd. How could anyone deny that there is a difference between a kind action and a cruel one, or that a coward and a brave man behave differently in the face of danger? Of course, this is undeniable; but it is not to the point. The kinds of behaviour to which moral values and disvalues are ascribed are indeed part of the furniture of the world, and so are the natural, descriptive, differences between them; but not, perhaps, their differences in value. It is a hard fact that cruel actions differ from kind ones, and hence that we can learn, as in fact we all do, to distinguish them fairly well in practice, and to use the words 'cruel' and 'kind' with fairly clear descriptive meanings; but is it an equally hard fact that actions which are cruel in such a descriptive sense are to be condemned? The present issue is with regard to the objectivity specifically of value, not with regard to the objectivity of those natural, factual, differences on the basis of which differing values are assigned.

Subjectivism

Another name often used, as an alternative to 'moral scepticism', for the view I am discussing is 'subjectivism'. But this too has more than one meaning. Moral subjectivism too could be a first order, normative, view, namely that everyone really ought to do whatever he thinks he should. This

plainly is a (systematic) first order view; on examination it soon ceases to be plausible, but that is beside the point, for it is quite independent of the second order thesis at present under consideration. What is more confusing is that different second order views compete for the name 'subjectivism'. Several of these are doctrines about the meaning of moral terms and moral statements. What is often called moral subjectivism is the doctrine that, for example, 'This action is right' *means* 'I approve of this action', or more generally that moral judgements are equivalent to reports of the speaker's own feelings or attitudes. But the view I am now discussing is to be distinguished in two vital respects from any such doctrine as this. First, what I have called moral scepticism is a negative doctrine, not a positive one: it says what there isn't, not what there is. It says that there do not exist entities or relations of a certain kind, objective values or requirements, which many people have believed to exist. Of course, the moral sceptic cannot leave it at that. If his position is to be at all plausible, he must give some account of how other people have fallen into what he regards as an error, and this account will have to include some positive suggestions about how values fail to be objective, about what has been mistaken for, or has led to false beliefs about, objective values. But this will be a development of his theory, not its core: its core is the negation. Secondly, what I have called moral scepticism is an ontological thesis, not a linguistic or conceptual one. It is not, like the other doctrine often called moral subjectivism, a view about the meanings of moral statements. Again, no doubt, if it is to be at all plausible, it will have to give some account of their meanings, and I shall say something about this [. . .] But this too will be a development of the theory, not its core.

It is true that those who have accepted the moral subjectivism which is the doctrine that moral judgements are equivalent to reports of the speaker's own feelings or attitudes have usually presupposed what I am calling moral scepticism. It is because they have assumed that there are no objective values that they have looked elsewhere for an analysis of what moral statements might mean, and have settled upon subjective reports. Indeed, if all our moral statements were such subjective reports, it would follow that, at least so far as we are aware, there are no objective moral values. If we were aware of them, we would say something about them. In this sense this sort of subjectivism entails moral scepticism. But the converse entailment does not hold. The denial that there are objective values does not commit one to any particular view about what moral statements mean, and certainly not to the view that they are equivalent to subjective reports. No doubt if moral values are not objective they are in some very broad sense subjective, and for this reason I would accept 'moral subjectivism' as an alternative name to 'moral scepticism'. But subjectivism in this broad sense must be distinguished from the specific doctrine about meaning referred to above. Neither name is altogether satisfactory: we simply have to guard against the (different) misinterpretations which each may suggest.

[. . .]

Hypothetical and Categorical Imperatives

We may make this issue clearer by referring to Kant's distinction between hypothetical and categorical imperatives, though what he called imperatives are more naturally expressed as 'ought'-statements than in the imperative mood. 'If you want X, do Y' (or 'You ought to do Y') will be a hypothetical imperative if it is based on the supposed fact that Y is, in the circumstances, the only (or the best) available means to X, that is, on a causal relation between Y and X. The reason for doing Y lies in its causal connection with the desired end, X; the oughtness is contingent upon the desire. But 'You ought to do Y' will be a categorical imperative if you ought to do Y irrespective of any such desire for any end to which Y would contribute, if the oughtness is not thus contingent upon any desire.

[. . .]

A categorical imperative, then, would express a reason for acting which was unconditional in the sense of not being contingent upon any present desire of the agent to whose satisfaction the recommended action would contribute as a means – or more directly: 'You ought to dance', if the implied reason is just that you want to dance or like dancing, is still a hypothetical imperative. Now Kant himself held that moral judgements are cat-

egorical imperatives, or perhaps are all applications of one categorical imperative, and it can plausibly be maintained at least that many moral judgements contain a categorically imperative element. So far as ethics is concerned, my thesis that there are no objective values is specifically the denial that any such categorically imperative element is objectively valid. The objective values which I am denying would be action-directing absolutely, not contingently (in the way indicated) upon the agent's desires and inclinations.

[. . .]

The Claim to Objectivity

If I have succeeded in specifying precisely enough the moral values whose objectivity I am denying, my thesis may now seem to be trivially true. Of course, some will say, valuing, preferring, choosing, recommending, rejecting, condemning, and so on, are human activities, and there is no need to look for values that are prior to and logically independent of all such activities. There may be widespread agreement in valuing, and particular value-judgements are not in general arbitrary or isolated: they typically cohere with others, or can be criticized if they do not, reasons can be given for them, and so on: but if all that the subjectivist is maintaining is that desires, ends, purposes, and the like figure somewhere in the system of reasons, and that no ends or purposes are objective as opposed to being merely intersubjective, then this may be conceded without much fuss.

But I do not think that this should be conceded so easily. As I have said, the main tradition of European moral philosophy includes the contrary claim, that there are objective values of just the sort I have denied. I have referred already to Plato, Kant, and Sidgwick. Kant in particular holds that the categorical imperative is not only categorical and imperative but objectively so: though a rational being gives the moral law to himself, the law that he thus makes is determinate and necessary. Aristotle begins the *Nicomachean Ethics* by saying that the good is that at which all things aim, and that ethics is part of a science which he calls 'politics', whose goal is not knowledge but practice; yet he does not doubt that there can be *knowledge* of what is the good for man, nor, once he has identified this as well-being or happiness, *eudaimonia*, that it can

15

be known, rationally determined, in what happiness consists; and it is plain that he thinks that this happiness is intrinsically desirable, not good simply because it is desired. The rationalist Samuel Clarke holds that

> these eternal and necessary differences of things make it *fit and reasonable* for creatures so to act . . . even separate from the consideration of these rules being the *positive will* or *command of God*; and also antecedent to any respect or regard, expectation or apprehension, of any *particular private and personal advantage or disadvantage, reward or punishment*, either present or future . . .

Even the sentimentalist Hutcheson defines moral goodness as 'some quality apprehended in actions, which procures approbation . . .', while saying that the moral sense by which we perceive virtue and vice has been given to us (by the Author of nature) to direct our actions. Hume indeed was on the other side, but he is still a witness to the dominance of the objectivist tradition, since he claims that when we 'see that the distinction of vice and virtue is not founded merely on the relations of objects, nor is perceiv'd by reason', this 'wou'd subvert all the vulgar systems of morality'. And Richard Price insists that right and wrong are 'real characters of actions', not 'qualities of our minds', and are perceived by the understanding; he criticizes the notion of moral sense on the ground that it would make virtue an affair of taste, and moral right and wrong 'nothing in the objects themselves'; he rejects Hutcheson's view because (perhaps mistakenly) he sees it as collapsing into Hume's.

But this objectivism about values is not only a feature of the philosophical tradition. It has also a firm basis in ordinary thought, and even in the meanings of moral terms. No doubt it was an extravagance for Moore to say that 'good' is the name of a non-natural quality, but it would not be so far wrong to say that in moral contexts it is used as if it were the name of a supposed non-natural quality, where the description 'non-natural' leaves room for the peculiar evaluative, prescriptive, intrinsically action-guiding aspects of this supposed quality. This point can be illustrated by reflection on the conflicts and swings of opinion in recent years between non-cognitivist and naturalist views about the central, basic, meanings of ethical terms. If we reject the view that it is the function of such terms to introduce objective

values into discourse about conduct and choices of action, there seem to be two main alternative types of account. One (which has importantly different subdivisions) is that they conventionally express either attitudes which the speaker purports to adopt towards whatever it is that he characterizes morally, or prescriptions or recommendations, subject perhaps to the logical constraint of universalizability. Different views of this type share the central thesis that ethical terms have, at least partly and primarily, some sort of non-cognitive, non-descriptive, meaning. Views of the other type hold that they are descriptive in meaning, but descriptive of natural features, partly of such features as everyone, even the non-cognitivist, would recognize as distinguishing kind actions from cruel ones, courage from cowardice, politeness from rudeness, and so on, and partly (though these two overlap) of relations between the actions and some human wants, satisfactions, and the like. I believe that views of both these types capture part of the truth. Each approach can account for the fact that moral judgements are action-guiding or practical. Yet each gains much of its plausibility from the felt inadequacy of the other. It is a very natural reaction to any non-cognitive analysis of ethical terms to protest that there is more to ethics than this, something more external to the maker of moral judgements, more authoritative over both him and those of or to whom he speaks, and this reaction is likely to persist even when full allowance has been made for the logical, formal, constraints of full-blooded prescriptivity and universalizability. Ethics, we are inclined to believe, is more a matter of knowledge and less a matter of decision than any non-cognitive analysis allows. And of course naturalism satisfies this demand. It will not be a matter of choice or decision whether an action is cruel or unjust or imprudent or whether it is likely to produce more distress than pleasure. But in satisfying this demand, it introduces a converse deficiency. On a naturalist analysis, moral judgements can be practical, but their practicality is wholly relative to desires or possible satisfactions of the person or persons whose actions are to be guided; but moral judgements seem to say more than this. This view leaves out the categorical quality of moral requirements. In fact both naturalist and non-cognitive analyses leave out the apparent authority of ethics, the one by excluding the categorically imperative aspect, the other the claim to objective validity or truth. The ordinary user of moral language means to say something about whatever it is that he characterizes morally, for example a possible action, as it is in itself, or would be if it were realized, and not about, or even simply expressive of, his, or anyone else's, attitude or relation to it. But the something he wants to say is not purely descriptive, certainly not inert, but something that involves a call for action or for the refraining from action, and one that is absolute, not contingent upon any desire or preference or policy or choice, his own or anyone else's. Someone in a state of moral perplexity, wondering whether it would be wrong for him to engage, say, in research related to bacteriological warfare, wants to arrive at some judgement about this concrete case, his doing this work at this time in these actual circumstances; his relevant characteristics will be part of the subject of the judgement, but no relation between him and the proposed action will be part of the predicate. The question is not, for example, whether he really wants to do this work, whether it will satisfy or dissatisfy him, whether he will in the long run have a pro-attitude towards it, or even whether this is an action of a sort that he can happily and sincerely recommend in all relevantly similar cases. Nor is he even wondering just whether to recommend such action in all relevantly similar cases. He wants to know whether this course of action would be wrong in itself. Something like this is the everyday objectivist concept of which talk about non-natural qualities is a philosopher's reconstruction.

The prevalence of this tendency to objectify values – and not only moral ones – is confirmed by a pattern of thinking that we find in existentialists and those influenced by them. The denial of objective values can carry with it an extreme emotional reaction, a feeling that nothing matters at all, that life has lost its purpose. Of course this does not follow; the lack of objective values is not a good reason for abandoning subjective concern or for ceasing to want anything. But the abandonment of a belief in objective values can cause, at least temporarily, a decay of subjective concern and sense of purpose. That it does so is evidence that the people in whom this reaction occurs have been tending to objectify their concerns and purposes, have been giving them a fictitious external authority. A claim to objectivity has been so strongly associated with their subjective concerns and purposes that the collapse of the former seems to undermine the latter as well.

This view, that conceptual analysis would reveal a claim to objectivity, is sometimes dramatically confirmed by philosophers who are officially on the other side. Bertrand Russell, for example, says that 'ethical propositions should be expressed in the optative mood, not in the indicative'; he defends himself effectively against the charge of inconsistency in both holding ultimate ethical valuations to be subjective and expressing emphatic opinions on ethical questions. Yet at the end he admits:

> Certainly there *seems* to be something more. Suppose, for example, that some one were to advocate the introduction of bullfighting in this country. In opposing the proposal, I should *feel*, not only that I was expressing my desires, but that my desires in the matter are *right*, whatever that may mean. As a matter of argument, I can, I think, show that I am not guilty of any logical inconsistency in holding to the above interpretation of ethics and at the same time expressing strong ethical preferences. But in feeling I am not satisfied.

But he concludes, reasonably enough, with the remark: 'I can only say that, while my own opinions as to ethics do not satisfy me, other people's satisfy me still less.'

I conclude, then, that ordinary moral judgements include a claim to objectivity, an assumption that there are objective values in just the sense in which I am concerned to deny this. And I do not think it is going too far to say that this assumption has been incorporated in the basic, conventional, meanings of moral terms. Any analysis of the meanings of moral terms which omits this claim to objective, intrinsic, prescriptivity is to that extent incomplete; and this is true of any non-cognitive analysis, any naturalist one, and any combination of the two.

If second order ethics were confined, then, to linguistic and conceptual analysis, it ought to conclude that moral values at least are objective: that they are so is part of what our ordinary moral statements mean: the traditional moral concepts of the ordinary man as well as of the main line of western philosophers are concepts of objective value. But it is precisely for this reason that linguistic and conceptual analysis is not enough. The claim to objectivity, however ingrained in our language and thought, is not self-validating. It can and should be questioned. But the denial of objective values will have to be put forward not as the result of an analytic approach, but as an 'error theory', a theory that although most people in making moral judgements implicitly claim, among other things, to be pointing to something objectively prescriptive, these claims are all false. It is this that makes the name 'moral scepticism' appropriate.

But since this is an error theory, since it goes against assumptions ingrained in our thought and built into some of the ways in which language is used, since it conflicts with what is sometimes called common sense, it needs very solid support. It is not something we can accept lightly or casually and then quietly pass on. If we are to adopt this view, we must argue explicitly for it. Traditionally it has been supported by arguments of two main kinds, which I shall call the argument from relativity and the argument from queerness, but these can, as I shall show, be supplemented in several ways.

The Argument from Relativity

The argument from relativity has as its premiss the well-known variation in moral codes from one society to another and from one period to another, and also the differences in moral beliefs between different groups and classes within a complex community. Such variation is in itself merely a truth of descriptive morality, a fact of anthropology which entails neither first order nor second order ethical views. Yet it may indirectly support second order subjectivism: radical differences between first order moral judgements make it difficult to treat those judgements as apprehensions of objective truths. But it is not the mere occurrence of disagreements that tells against the objectivity of values. Disagreement on questions in history or biology or cosmology does not show that there are no objective issues in these fields for investigators to disagree about. But such scientific disagreement results from speculative inferences or explanatory hypotheses based on inadequate evidence, and it is hardly plausible to interpret moral disagreement in the same way. Disagreement about moral codes seems to reflect people's adherence to and participation in different ways of life. The causal connection seems to be mainly that way round: it is that people approve of monogamy because they participate in a monogamous way of life rather than that they participate in a monogamous way of life because they approve of monogamy. Of course,

the standards may be an idealization of the way of life from which they arise: the monogamy in which people participate may be less complete, less rigid, than that of which it leads them to approve. This is not to say that moral judgements are purely conventional. Of course there have been and are moral heretics and moral reformers, people who have turned against the established rules and practices of their own communities for moral reasons, and often for moral reasons that we would endorse. But this can usually be understood as the extension, in ways which, though new and unconventional, seemed to them to be required for consistency, of rules to which they already adhered as arising out of an existing way of life. In short, the argument from relativity has some force simply because the actual variations in the moral codes are more readily explained by the hypothesis that they reflect ways of life than by the hypothesis that they express perceptions, most of them seriously inadequate and badly distorted, of objective values.

But there is a well-known counter to this argument from relativity, namely to say that the items for which objective validity is in the first place to be claimed are not specific moral rules or codes but very general basic principles which are recognized at least implicitly to some extent in all society – such principles as provide the foundations of what Sidgwick has called different methods of ethics: the principle of universalizability, perhaps, or the rule that one ought to conform to the specific rules of any way of life in which one takes part, from which one profits, and on which one relies, or some utilitarian principle of doing what tends, or seems likely, to promote the general happiness. It is easy to show that such general principles, married with differing concrete circumstances, different existing social patterns or different preferences, will beget different specific moral rules; and there is some plausibility in the claim that the specific rules thus generated will vary from community to community or from group to group in close agreement with the actual variations in accepted codes.

The argument from relativity can be only partly countered in this way. To take this line the moral objectivist has to say that it is only in these principles that the objective moral character attaches immediately to its descriptively specified ground or subject: other moral judgements are objectively valid or true, but only derivatively and contingently – if things had been otherwise, quite different sorts of actions would have been right. And despite the prominence in recent philosophical ethics of universalization, utilitarian principles, and the like, these are very far from constituting the whole of what is actually affirmed as basic in ordinary moral thought. Much of this is concerned rather with what Hare calls 'ideals' or, less kindly, 'fanaticism'. That is, people judge that some things are good or right, and others are bad or wrong, not because – or at any rate not only because – they exemplify some general principle for which widespread implicit acceptance could be claimed, but because something about those things arouses certain responses immediately in them, though they would arouse radically and irresolvably different responses in others. 'Moral sense' or 'intuition' is an initially more plausible description of what supplies many of our basic moral judgements than 'reason'. With regard to all these starting points of moral thinking the argument from relativity remains in full force.

The Argument from Queerness

Even more important, however, and certainly more generally applicable, is the argument from queerness. This has two parts, one metaphysical, the other epistemological. If there were objective values, then they would be entities or qualities or relations of a very strange sort, utterly different from anything else in the universe. Correspondingly, if we were aware of them, it would have to be by some special faculty of moral perception or intuition, utterly different from our ordinary ways of knowing everything else. These points were recognized by Moore when he spoke of non-natural qualities, and by the intuitionists in their talk about a 'faculty of moral intuition'. Intuitionism has long been out of favour, and it is indeed easy to point out its implausibilities. What is not so often stressed, but is more important, is that the central thesis of intuitionism is one to which any objectivist view of values is in the end committed: intuitionism merely makes unpalatably plain what other forms of objectivism wrap up. Of course the suggestion that moral judgements are made or moral problems solved by just sitting down and having an ethical intuition is a travesty of actual moral thinking. But, however complex the real process, it will require (if it is to yield authoritatively prescriptive conclusions) some input of this

distinctive sort, either premisses or forr ment or both. When we ask the awkward q. how we can be aware of this authoritative p scriptivity, of the truth of these distinctively ethical premisses or of the cogency of this distinctively ethical pattern of reasoning, none of our ordinary accounts of sensory perception or introspection or the framing and confirming of explanatory hypotheses or inference or logical construction or conceptual analysis, or any combination of these, will provide a satisfactory answer; 'a special sort of intuition' is a lame answer, but it is the one to which the clear-headed objectivist is compelled to resort.

Indeed, the best move for the moral objectivist is not to evade this issue, but to look for companions in guilt. For example, Richard Price argues that it is not moral knowledge alone that such an empiricism as those of Locke and Hume is unable to account for, but also our knowledge and even our ideas of essence, number, identity, diversity, solidity, inertia, substance, the necessary existence and infinite extension of time and space, necessity and possibility in general, power, and causation. If the understanding, which Price defines as the faculty within us that discerns truth, is also a source of new simple ideas of so many other sorts, may it not also be a power of immediately perceiving right and wrong, which yet are real characters of actions?

This is an important counter to the argument from queerness. The only adequate reply to it would be to show how, on empiricist foundations, we can construct an account of the ideas and beliefs and knowledge that we have of all these matters. I cannot even begin to do that here, though I have undertaken some parts of the task elsewhere. I can only state my belief that satisfactory accounts of most of these can be given in empirical terms. If some supposed metaphysical necessities or essences resist such treatment, then they too should be included, along with objective values, among the targets of the argument from queerness.

This queerness does not consist simply in the fact that ethical statements are 'unverifiable'. Although logical positivism with its verifiability theory of descriptive meaning gave an impetus to non-cognitive accounts of ethics, it is not only logical positivists but also empiricists of a much more liberal sort who should find objective values hard to accommodate. Indeed, I would not only reject the verifiability principle but also deny the conclusion commonly drawn from it, that moral judgements lack descriptive meaning. The assertion that there are objective values or intrinsically prescriptive entities or features of some kind, which ordinary moral judgements presuppose, is, I hold, not meaningless but false.

Plato's Forms give a dramatic picture of what objective values would have to be. The Form of the Good is such that knowledge of it provides the knower with both a direction and an overriding motive; something's being good both tells the person who knows this to pursue it and makes him pursue it. An objective good would be sought by anyone who was acquainted with it, not because of any contingent fact that this person, or every person, is so constituted that he desires this end, but just because the end has to-be-pursuedness somehow built into it. Similarly, if there were objective principles of right and wrong, any wrong (possible) course of action would have not-to-be-doneness somehow built into it. Or we should have something like Clarke's necessary relations of fitness between situations and actions, so that a situation would have a demand for such-and-such an action somehow built into it.

The need for an argument of this sort can be brought out by reflection on Hume's argument that 'reason' – in which at this stage he includes all sorts of knowing as well as reasoning – can never be an 'influencing motive of the will'. Someone might object that Hume has argued unfairly from the lack of influencing power (not contingent upon desires) in ordinary objects of knowledge and ordinary reasoning, and might maintain that values differ from natural objects precisely in their power, when known, automatically to influence the will. To this Hume could, and would need to, reply that this objection involves the postulating of value-entities or value-features of quite a different order from anything else with which we are acquainted, and of a corresponding faculty with which to detect them. That is, he would have to supplement his explicit argument with what I have called the argument from queerness.

Another way of bringing out this queerness is to ask, about anything that is supposed to have some objective moral quality, how this is linked with its natural features. What is the connection between the natural fact that an action is a piece of deliberate cruelty – say, causing pain just for fun – and the moral fact that it is wrong? It cannot be an entailment, a logical or semantic necessity. Yet it is not merely that the two features occur together. The wrongness must somehow be 'consequential' or

'supervenient'; it is wrong because it is a piece of deliberate cruelty. But just what *in the world* is signified by this 'because'? And how do we know the relation that it signifies, if this is something more than such actions being socially condemned, and condemned by us too, perhaps through our having absorbed attitudes from our social environment? It is not even sufficient to postulate a faculty which 'sees' the wrongness: something must be postulated which can see at once the natural features that constitute the cruelty, and the wrongness, and the mysterious consequential link between the two. Alternatively, the intuition required might be the perception that wrongness is a higher order property belonging to certain natural properties; but what is this belonging of properties to other properties, and how can we discern it? How much simpler and more comprehensible the situation would be if we could replace the moral quality with some sort of subjective response which could be causally related to the detection of the natural features on which the supposed quality is said to be consequential.

It may be thought that the argument from queerness is given an unfair start if we thus relate it to what are admittedly among the wilder products of philosophical fancy – Platonic Forms, non-natural qualities, self-evident relations of fitness, faculties of intuition, and the like. Is it equally forceful if applied to the terms in which everyday moral judgements are more likely to be expressed – though still . . . with a claim to objectivity – 'you must do this', 'you can't do that', 'obligation', 'unjust', 'rotten', 'disgraceful', 'mean', or talk about good reasons for or against possible actions? Admittedly not; but that is because the objective prescriptivity, the element a claim for whose authoritativeness is embedded in ordinary moral thought and language, is not yet isolated in these forms of speech, but is presented along with relations to desires and feelings, reasoning about the means to desired ends, interpersonal demands, the injustice which consists in the violation of what are in the context the accepted standards of merit, the psychological constituents of meanness, and so on. There is nothing queer about any of these, and under cover of them the claim for moral authority may pass unnoticed. But if I am right in arguing that it is ordinarily there, and is therefore very likely to be incorporated almost automatically in philosophical accounts of ethics which systematize our ordinary thought even in such apparently innocent terms as these, it needs to be examined, and for this purpose it needs to be isolated and exposed as it is by the less cautious philosophical reconstructions.

Patterns of Objectification

Considerations of these kinds suggest that it is in the end less paradoxical to reject than to retain the common-sense belief in the objectivity of moral values, provided that we can explain how this belief, if it is false, has become established and is so resistant to criticisms. This proviso is not difficult to satisfy.

On a subjectivist view, the supposedly objective values will be based in fact upon attitudes which the person has who takes himself to be recognizing and responding to those values. If we admit what Hume calls the mind's 'propensity to spread itself on external objects', we can understand the supposed objectivity of moral qualities as arising from what we can call the projection or objectification of moral attitudes. This would be analogous to what is called the 'pathetic fallacy', the tendency to read our feelings into their objects. If a fungus, say, fills us with disgust, we may be inclined to ascribe to the fungus itself a non-natural quality of foulness. But in moral contexts there is more than this propensity at work. Moral attitudes themselves are at least partly social in origin: socially established – and socially necessary – patterns of behaviour put pressure on individuals, and each individual tends to internalize these pressures and to join in requiring these patterns of behaviour of himself and of others. The attitudes that are objectified into moral values have indeed an external source, though not the one assigned to them by the belief in their absolute authority. Moreover, there are motives that would support objectification. We need morality to regulate interpersonal relations, to control some of the ways in which people behave towards one another, often in opposition to contrary inclinations. We therefore want our moral judgements to be authoritative for other agents as well as for ourselves: objective validity would give them the authority required. Aesthetic values are logically in the same position as moral ones; much the same metaphysical and epistemological considerations apply to them. But aesthetic values are less strongly objectified than moral ones; their subjective status, and an 'error theory' with regard to such claims to

objectivity as are incorporated in aesthetic judgements, will be more readily accepted, just because the motives for their objectification are less compelling.

But it would be misleading to think of the objectification of moral values as primarily the projection of feelings, as in the pathetic fallacy. More important are wants and demands. As Hobbes says, 'whatsoever is the object of any man's Appetite or Desire, that is it, which he for his part calleth *Good*'; and certainly both the adjective 'good' and the noun 'goods' are used in non-moral contexts of things because they are such as to satisfy desires. We get the notion of something's being objectively good, or having intrinsic value, by reversing the direction of dependence here, by making the desire depend upon the goodness, instead of the goodness on the desire. And this is aided by the fact that the desired thing will indeed have features that make it desired, that enable it to arouse a desire or that make it such as to satisfy some desire that is already there. It is fairly easy to confuse the way in which a thing's desirability is indeed objective with its having in our sense objective value. The fact that the word 'good' serves as one of our main moral terms is a trace of this pattern of objectification.

[. . .]

Another way of explaining the objectification of moral values is to say that ethics is a system of law from which the legislator has been removed. This might have been derived either from the positive law of a state or from a supposed system of divine law. There can be no doubt that some features of modern European moral concepts are traceable to the theological ethics of Christianity. The stress on quasi-imperative notions, on what ought to be done or on what is wrong in a sense that is close to that of 'forbidden', are surely relics of divine commands. Admittedly, the central ethical concepts for Plato and Aristotle also are in a broad sense prescriptive or intrinsically action-guiding, but in concentrating rather on 'good' than on 'ought' they show that their moral thought is an objectification of the desired and the satisfying rather than of the commanded. Elizabeth Anscombe has argued that modern, non-Aristotelian, concepts of *moral* obligation, *moral* duty, of what is *morally* right and wrong, and of the *moral* sense of 'ought' are survivals outside the framework of thought that made them really intelligible, namely the belief in divine law. She infers that 'ought' has 'become a word of mere mesmeric force', with only a 'delusive appearance of content', and that we would do better to discard such terms and concepts altogether, and go back to Aristotelian ones.

There is much to be said for this view. But while we can explain some distinctive features of modern moral philosophy in this way, it would be a mistake to see the whole problem of the claim to objective prescriptivity as merely local and unnecessary, as a post-operative complication of a society from which a dominant system of theistic belief has recently been rather hastily excised. As Cudworth and Clarke and Price, for example, show, even those who still admit divine commands, or the positive law of God, may believe moral values to have an independent objective but still action-guiding authority. Responding to Plato's *Euthyphro* dilemma, they believe that God commands what he commands because it is in itself good or right, not that it is good or right merely because and in that he commands it. Otherwise God himself could not be called good. Price asks, 'What can be more preposterous, than to make the Deity nothing but will; and to exalt this on the ruins of all his attributes?' The apparent objectivity of moral value is a widespread phenomenon which has more than one source: the persistence of a belief in something like divine law when the belief in the divine legislator has faded out is only one factor among others. There are several different patterns of objectification, all of which have left characteristic traces in our actual moral concepts and moral language.

The Myth of Morality

Richard Joyce

Faulty Frameworks

When European explorers first interacted with cultures of the South Pacific, they found the islanders employing an unfamiliar concept: a type of forbiddenness called "tapu." Europeans developed this into the familiar English term "taboo," but what we mean by "taboo" is quite unlike what the Polynesians meant. (It is to signal this difference that I have chosen the Maori word "tapu" over "taboo.") It is not the case, for instance, that "tapu" may be translated into "morally forbidden," with accompanying understanding that the Polynesians have different beliefs from Europeans concerning which actions are forbidden. "Tapu" centrally implicates a kind of uncleanliness or pollution that may reside in objects, may pass to humans through contact, may be then transmitted to others like a contagion, and which may be canceled through certain ritual activities, usually involving washing. This is not a concept that we employ, though one may find something similar in ancient Roman and Greek texts.

If one of the European explorers had a penchant for metaethics, what would he say about the Polynesians' discourse? He would naturally take them to have a *defective* concept; no judgment of the form "φ is tapu" is ever true (so long as "φ" names an actual action) because there simply isn't anything that's tapu. Saying this implies nothing about how tolerant in attitude the explorer would be of the Polynesian's discourse; his identifying their discourse as "defective" is consistent with recognizing that it serves them well, and choosing not to point out to them their error. It is also consistent with his electing to employ the concept in sincere assertions of the form "φ is tapu," but only when this is an anthropological judgment, elliptical for "For the islanders, φ is considered tapu." It would be strange for him to make non-elliptical judgments of the form "φ is tapu" if he thought, as he naturally would, of the whole framework as mistaken. And in all of this the explorer would be quite correct: "tapu" is certainly not a term that I apply (non-elliptically), and the reason I don't is that reflection on the kind of "metaphysical uncleanliness" that a literal application of the term presupposes leads to recognition that *nothing* is tapu. I treat the Polynesians' discourse – with all due cultural respect – as systematically mistaken.

But how could it be that a discourse that is familiar to a group of perfectly intelligent people – one that they employ every day without running into any trouble or confusion – is so mistaken? After all, the users of the term unanimously apply it to certain types of action, unanimously withhold it from other actions, and perhaps even agree on a range of types of action which count as a "gray area." Doesn't all this amount to the predicate ". . . is tapu" having a non-empty extension? To see that the answer is "No" we might reflect again on the European explorer's own defective concept: *phlogiston* (we'll assume that his travels predated Lavoisier). The chemists Stahl, Priestley, *et al.*, were equally able to agree on the extension of their favored predicate. Indeed, they were able ostensively to pick out paradigm examples of phlogiston: they could point to any flame and say *"There is the phlogiston escaping!"* And yet for all that they were failing to state truths, for there wasn't any phlogiston. Clearly, when speakers used the predicate ". . . is phlogiston" something more was going on than merely applying it to objects. What sentenced the predicate to emptiness, despite its ostensive paradigms, was that users of the term (considered collectively) thought and said certain things *about* phlogiston such as "It is that stuff stored in bodies," "It is that stuff that is released during combustion" and "Soot is made up almost entirely of it," and these concomitant statements are false. It's not that any competent user of the word "phlogiston" was disposed to make these statements – our Pacific explorer, for example, may have had only a rudimentary grasp of the theory, despite being considered perfectly competent with the term. But he would have been willing to defer to the firm opinions of the experts in chemistry of the day, and *they* would have said these things.

Let us say that the above three propositions concerning phlogiston were firmly held by the experts. Let us pretend, further, that these three propositions have a kind of "non-negotiable" status. What I mean by this is the following: Imagine that we were to encounter a population speaking a quite different language to our own, most of which we have translated and tested to our satisfaction, and we find that they have a concept that appears rather like our concept of *phlogiston* (say, it plays a central role in explaining combustion and calcification) – call their term "schmogiston" – but we also find that they don't endorse one of the three propositions about schmogiston. If that would be sufficient for us to decide *not* to translate "schmogiston" into "phlogiston," then the proposition in question must be a non-negotiable part of our concept *phlogiston*. It may not be that any *one* proposition is non-negotiable: perhaps we would be content with the translation if any two of the "schmogiston"-propositions were dissented from, but if the speakers dissented from all three (i.e.,

they said "No" to "Is schmogiston released during combustion?", "Is schmogiston stored in bodies?", and "Is soot made up of schmogiston?") then we would resist the translation – we would conclude that they weren't talking about *phlogiston* at all. In such a case we might call the disjunction of the three propositions "non-negotiable."

This translation test gives us a way of conceptualizing what we mean by a "non-negotiable" proposition, though I don't pretend that it gives us a widely usable decision procedure (involving, as it does, a complex counterfactual about when we would or wouldn't accept a translation scheme). The point is to make sense of a distinction. On the one hand, we might have a discourse that centers on a predicate ". . . is P," involving the assertion of a variety of propositions – "*a* is P," "*b* is not-P," "For any *x*, if *x* is P, then *x* is Q," etc. – and when we discover that we're *mistaken* about one or more of these things – e.g., we discover that some things that are P are not Q – we don't decide that the whole "P discourse" has been a disastrous mistake; we simply change our minds about one aspect of it: we stop making the conditional claim and carry on much as before. On the other hand, there are some discourses regarding which the discovery that one or more of the things we've been assenting to is mistaken leads us to throw in the towel – to stop using the discourse altogether. The latter describes what happened in the phlogiston case: the discovery that we had been wrong in thinking that there is a stuff stored in combustible bodies and released during burning was sufficient for us to decide that there is no phlogiston at all. When Lavoisier gave us the concept *oxygen*, it wasn't available for Stahl to say "Well, this stuff that Lavoisier is calling 'oxygen' just *is* what I've been calling 'phlogiston' all along – I was just mistaken about its being stored and released during combustion." The belief that phlogiston is stored and released was a *non-negotiable* part of phlogiston discourse – the falsity of this belief was sufficient to sink the whole theory.

Now we can see how a smooth-running, useful and familiar discourse, apparently with clear paradigms and foils, could be systematically flawed. The users of the target predicate (or the experts to whom most users firmly defer) assent to a number of non-negotiable propositions – propositions which would play a determinative role in deciding whether or not a translation goes through – and a critical number of these non-negotiable propositions are, in fact, false. This might be how our explorer-cum-metaethicist conceives of the concept *tapu*. If the Polynesians had merely used "tapu" as a kind of strong proscription, and thought, say, that public nudity is *not* tapu but burying the dead is, then (*ceteris paribus*) this would not have prevented the explorer from translating "tapu" into "morally forbidden" while ascribing to the Polynesians some different beliefs about which actions are morally forbidden. But given the kind of robust metaphysics surrounding the notion of tapu – centrally involving supernatural and magical forces – no obvious translation (along with the ascription of different beliefs) was available. The explorer doesn't just attribute to the Polynesians a set of false beliefs – he attributes to them a faulty *framework*. (I don't intend this to sound culturally critical – the eighteenth-century European is certainly no better off with his concept *phlogiston*, and nor, I will argue, are we with our familiar moral concepts.)

The terminology introduced by John Mackie to describe this situation is that the European explorer holds an *error theory* regarding the historical Polynesians' "tapu discourse," just as we now hold an error theory with respect to phlogiston theory (for shorthand we can say that we are "error theorists about phlogiston").[1] We don't hold an error theory about *any* discourse involving the term "phlogiston," of course. People continue to talk about phlogiston long after Lavoisier's discoveries – saying things like "Georg Stahl believed in phlogiston," "Phlogiston doesn't exist" – and *that* phlogiston discourse is just fine. What we don't do is assert judgments of the form "*a* is phlogiston" (or make assertions that imply it). It is only a discourse that made such assertions, such as the one existing through the seventeenth century, regarding which we are error theorists.

An error theory, as we have seen, involves two steps of argumentation. First, it involves ascertaining just what a term *means*. I have tried to explicate this in terms of "non-negotiability," which in turn I understood in terms of a translation test (but there may be other, and better, ways of understanding the notion). So, in artificially simple terms, the first step gives us something roughly of the form "For any *x*, F*x* if and only if P*x* and Q*x* and R*x*." We can call this step *concep-*

tual. The second step is to ascertain whether the following is true: "There exists an *x*, such that P*x* and Q*x* and R*x*." If not, then there is nothing that satisfies ". . . is F." Call this step *ontological* or *substantive*. The concept of *phlogiston* – with its commitment to a stuff that is stored in bodies and released during combustion – and the concept of *tapu* – with its commitment to a kind of contagious pollution – do not pass the test.

[. . .]

The Semantics of an Error Theory

[. . .]

The view that our moral judgments are neither true nor false is often equated with the metaethical position known as "noncognitivism," but the noncognitivist and error theoretic positions are distinct. However, I prefer to understand noncognitivism not in terms of truth values, but in terms of assertion. Assertion is not a semantic category; it is, rather, a purpose to which a sentence may be put: one and the same sentence may on some occasions be asserted, on other occasions not asserted. The question then is not whether "a is F" is an assertion, but whether it is typically used assertorically. The noncognitivist says "No": the sentence "a is F" is typically used to express approval, or as a disguised command.

A moral cognitivist will, by contrast, hold that sentences of the form under discussion are usually used assertorically. But this is not to say that the cognitivist holds that moral sentences are usually either true or false, for (some have argued) there can be assertions that are neither. Strawsonian presupposition failure is one example. According to some views, the assignment of certain vague predicates to "gray area" objects will also result in assertions that are neither true nor false. The difference is brought out by imagining a conversation in which one person utters "The present king of France is wise" and her companion responds "Say that again." A Strawsonian would hold that neither utterance is true or false, but it would be an odd view that held that the former utterance is not asserted (and an odd view that held that the latter utterance *is*

---

[1] J. L. Mackie, *Ethics: Inventing Right and Wrong* (New York: Penguin Books, 1977). See also his "A Refutation of Morals," *Australasian Journal of Philosophy* 24 (1946), pp. 77–90.

asserted). We might say that the former utterance was "in the market for truth," whereas "Say that again," being a command, is never in that market, and is therefore automatically neither true nor false.

An error theory, then, may be characterized as the position that holds that a discourse typically is used in an assertoric manner, but those assertions by and large fail to state truths. (These qualifications of vagueness should not cause concern; to expect more precision than this would be unrealistic.) This is clearly the correct stance to take towards phlogiston discourse. The view that seventeenth-century speakers typically spoke without assertoric force when they uttered sentences of the form "*a* is phlogiston" may be rejected. And such judgments were not true. [. . .]

An Argument for a Moral Error Theory

We now have the resources on the table to deploy a strong argument for a moral error theory. It is best if we state it succinctly, though with the understanding that it will be subject to refinement. For any *x*:

1 If *x* morally ought to φ, then *x* ought to φ regardless of whether he cares to, regardless of whether φing satisfies any of his desires or furthers his interests.
2 If *x* morally ought to φ, then *x* has a reason for φing.
3 Therefore, if *x* morally ought to φ, then *x* has a reason for φing regardless of whether φing serves his desires or furthers his interests.
4 But there is no sense to be made of such reasons.
5 Therefore, *x* is never under a moral obligation.

The structure of the argument is very simple:

	1	If P, then Q
	2	If P, then R
∴	3	If P, then (Q & R)
But	4	Not (Q & R)
∴	5	Not P

Premises (1), (2) and (4) are the ones that require argument (premise (3), following from (1) and (2), requires no independent support). Establishing (4)

is the most complex matter, and is the job of following chapters. In the present chapter I want to make sure that (1) and (2) are understood and settled.

The basic consideration in favor of premise (1) has already been pressed several times. When we morally condemn a criminal we do not first ascertain the state of his desires. Were we to discover that his desires were well-served by his crimes, perhaps even to the point of his wanting punishment, we do not respond "Oh, well I suppose you ought to have done it after all." This simple consideration is enough to show that anyone is mistaken who dismisses categorical imperatives as a bizarre extravagance endorsed only by Kant and his followers. We use them all the time. Just consider our moral condemnation of Nazis. Any offering along the lines of "Well, we wanted to create an Aryan master race, and genocide seemed like an efficient means of accomplishing it" is no defense at all! But, barring an argument that their actions were in some subtle way desire-frustrating, this shows that it is a categorical imperative with which we denounce them. Of course, concerning Nazis we might not *say* "You ought not to have done that," for this sounds altogether too weak to capture the outrage – rather, we appeal to the language of "evil" and "bestiality." But the "ought" statement is implied by the stronger language – evil is, at the very least, something we ought not be.

The manner in which we condemn Nazis, ignoring any unusual desires or interests that they may have, is not a peripheral element of moral discourse; it represents a kind of reprehension that is central. A system of values in which there was no place for condemning Nazi actions simply would not count as a *moral* system. Further, I do not think that this kind of desire/interest-ignoring condemnation is a particularly modern or Western phenomenon. Despite the fact that it required an eighteenth-century Prussian to *label* categorical imperatives, I am confident that they have been with us for a long time. Did, say, ancient Chinese people retract condemnation of their own moral monsters upon discovering their unusual desires? I doubt it. Perhaps Foot is correct that we could get along adequately without such imperatives. After all, we could, in the absence of making such judgments, still be justified in defending ourselves from outlaws and monsters. We might have chosen to hang Nazi war criminals without invoking categorical imperatives at all. But this, in my book, is equivalent to saying that we could get along adequately without morality (the truth of which is investigated in later chapters).

Premise (2) is Mackie's Platitude, specifically for moral prescriptions. I argued that whenever one is speaking from within a normative institution, a willingness to say "X ought to φ" will license saying "X has a reason to φ." So understood, (2) is true. So understood, however, (4) is certainly false, for we have seen that we *can* make sense of such reason: they are merely reflections of weak categorical imperatives, which are expressions of systems of rules – and nobody could doubt the existence of systems of rules.

I mean (2) to be taken in a stronger manner, which thus far I have been able to explicate only in a rhetorical way. Consider again our moral condemnation of a felon. We say (at the very least) "You ought not to have done that." We cannot end matters there, or we have nothing with which to counter the felon's "So what?" Indeed, if *all* we had to say on the matter was "You simply *mustn't!*" – accompanied by some table-pounding – then the felon's query seems positively reasonable. We seek something that might *engage* the criminal. Even if it is something that does not succeed in actually persuading her, we want something the ignoring of which would be in some manner illegitimate on her part. Looking to provide her with a *reason* appears the only possibility. I am mindful of the fact that it sounds a little odd to say that the Nazis "had a reason" to refrain from genocide. But what else are we to say? We certainly think that they *ought* to have refrained (a seriously weak way of putting it, to be sure, but not false for that), and to my ear it sounds no less odd for their moral jury to admit "You ought not to have done it, but we accept that you had no reason to refrain."

However, we do not want the claim "You have a reason not to do that" to be nothing more than an utterance licensed by our having taken the moral point of view, otherwise we've said little more than a reiteration of "You ought not do that," and we may still quite reasonably be ignored. (Nor do we want the reason to be something we *create* in the act of threatening punishment. We morally condemn no less those whom we know can evade our reprisals.) So when premise (2) links "having a reason" with a moral "ought," it is intended to be something other than an institutional reason; it is what I have been calling up until now (rather

deplorably) a "real" reason. The most precise understanding we have thus far gained of "real" reasons is that they are reasons that cannot be legitimately ignored. Thus understanding premise (2) to be referring to *non-institutional* reasons, premise (4) seems far more plausible.

Practical Reasons as Non-Institutional

But a worry remains. The above argument held that questioning morality from an external viewpoint is possible because one may do so employing the concepts of a broader, established framework: practical rationality. But isn't practical rationality just another normative institution? And, if so, aren't we merely questioning morality from a perspective to which we may *or may not* maintain allegiance? It is crucial to see why the answer is "No."

An institution, let us say, is something one may or may not adopt, something which, by its very nature, may be sensibly questioned from the outside. Certain institutions may never, as a matter of fact, be questioned – my point is that questioning them must at least be *intelligible*. The rules of gladiatorial combat are a good example: we have no difficulty imagining Celadus insisting "But what is that to me? – Why should I adopt this set of rules?" Without wanting to beg the question, I think that morality has all the hallmarks of an institution too: someone who says "Yes, I can see that morality requires me to keep that promise, but so what? – Why should I adopt that set of rules?" appears to be asking a perfectly intelligible question. Could practical rationality be just another such institution?

Whatever else it consists of, practical rationality is the framework that tells us what our reasons for acting are. We haven't yet investigated what the internal nature of this framework may be, but we know this much about it. Can we imagine someone questioning practical rationality: "Yes, I recognize that there is a practical reason for me to φ, but what is that to me? – Why should I adopt that set of rules?"? This, it seems to me, is incoherent (perhaps uniquely among these sorts of questions). Even to ask the question "Why should I be interested in practical rationality?" is to ask for a *reason*. Thus even to question practical rationality is to evince allegiance to it. After all, what kind of answer could be provided? If the questioner is already expressing doubts about whether things he acknowledges as "his reasons" should move him, then there would be no point in providing further reasons. Therefore to question practical rationality *is* unintelligible – it is to ask *for a reason* while implying that no reason will be adequate. Practical rationality delivers reasons claims, but practical rationality is not an institution which we may intelligibly question. If in practical rationality we have located the "real reasons" that I have been gesturing at in this chapter, then the vital question is whether one might have such a reason to φ regardless of whether φing serves one's desires or interests. If one might, then premise (4) of the argument is defeated. This, I believe, is the only hope for the opponent of a moral error theory: to defend the thesis that practical rationality delivers categorical imperatives, and then to forge a connection between the imperatives of practical rationality and those of morality. The objective of the next three chapters is to argue that this cannot be done. Practical rationality, I will argue, yields only hypothetical imperatives, and therefore cannot be appealed to as a way of vindicating "moral inescapability."

The Rationalist's Dilemma

Any moral rationalist faces a metaethical dilemma. One horn is the alienation of an agent from her normative reasons, the other horn is moral relativism.

"Moral rationalism" I understand to center on the thesis that moral reasons are a subset of normative reasons, such that moral failing is, necessarily, rational failing. This thesis will not count as sufficient for being a rationalist, for consider if normative reasons turn out – as I think they do – to be in some substantive manner agent-relative. We might still link these practical reasons to moral reasons, to the conclusion that moral reasons are relative to agents (which is close to the conclusion that moral imperatives are hypothetical). This is the basic structure of Gilbert Harman's version of moral relativism . . . but it would be very misleading if Harman turned out to be a moral *rationalist*. In response to this, let us add to the above criterion

for rationalism two further theses: that the imperatives of practical rationality are categorical imperatives; and that there are some true imperatives of practical rationality. The last condition is needed just to cover the unlikely case of an argument linking normative reasons to moral reasons, asserted in conjunction with a denial that there are any true normative reasons claims. . . . "Moral rationalism" had better not permissibly denote a moral error theory!

Let us consider the first horn of the rationalist's dilemma. Normative reasons claims – claims concerning what it is rational for an agent to do – must be something that potentially engage the agent to whom they are applied. This doesn't mean that the presentation of a true normative reason claim immediately results in the agent being motivated; rather, it means that the agent cannot sensibly both acknowledge that something is a normative reason for him to act and ask "But so what?" Any adequate theory of normative reasons must make out reasons to be precisely those things that forestall a "So what?" response. Some theories of reasons threaten to violate this constraint – to "alienate" an agent from his reasons. Roderick Firth, for instance, introduces the concept of *the ideal observer*, who is omniscient, omnipercipient, disinterested, dispassionate, consistent, and otherwise normal (the details need not detain us).[2] The ideal observer will approve of certain things, form desires, etc., and consequently have motivating reasons for performing certain actions. And what for the ideal observer are motivating reasons are for us normative reasons. The problem with such a theory is that it seems perfectly reasonable to say "I accept that the ideal observer would be motivated to φ, but what's that to me?" Why should one care about what a dispassionate person would want any more than one should care about what an enthusiastic philatelist would want? It will not do for Firth to *stipulate* that the question is unreasonable – a "So what?" question cannot be made unreasonable by *ad hoc* linguistic decree. A consequence of Firth's theory that some would count as a virtue is that it implies that every agent has exactly the same normative reasons, for the ideal observer borrows no idiosyncratic features from

---

2 R. Firth, "Ethical Absolutism and the Ideal Observer," *Philosophy and Phenomenological Research* 12 (1952), pp. 317–45. To be fair to Firth, he presents an analysis of *moral goodness* rather than *reasons for action*, but he may be interpreted as providing the basis for an analysis of the latter. See, for example, Paul Moser, *Philosophy After Objectivity* (Oxford: Oxford University Press, 1993), p. 183. [Firth's article is included as chapter 9 of this volume.]

particular agents. Unfortunately, this is attained at the cost of alienating the agent from rationality, of making it perfectly reasonable for her to ignore these reasons claims.

Finding this unacceptable, one might prefer an account of normative reasons which avoids alienation, by tying an agent's normative reasons directly to the things that the agent is interested in. The virtue of such a theory is that it promises to answer any "So what?" demands. Hume would find the grounding ultimately in actual desires that the agent has. If one asked a person why he takes exercise he may reply that it is for the sake of his health; ask him why he desires that, and he may answer:

> that *it is necessary for the sake of his calling.* If you ask, *why is he anxious on that head,* he will answer, *because he desires to get money.* If you demand *Why? It is the instrument of pleasure,* says he. And beyond this it is an absurdity to ask for a reason. It is impossible that there can be a progress *in infinitum*; and that one thing can always be a reason why another is desired. Something must be desired on its own account.[3]

On this occasion Hume makes pleasure the thing that is desired "on its own account," but he does not insist that the final answer must always be an appeal to self-interest. The foundational desire may be a genuinely altruistic one – the desire may be "That my friend ceases to suffer." If asked "And why do you desire the cessation of your friend's suffering?" it is possible (Hume allows) that the correct answer is "I just do!" The only further sense that can be made of the question is that it asks for the *cause* of the desire, rather than one's reason for so desiring (e.g., a reasonable answer would be "Because we go back a long way and so I care about him" which is a different *type* of answer from those of the preceding question-and-answer sequence).

Part of the object of the previous chapter was to reject the Humean view that reasons must always be grounded in present desires. [Michael] Smith's non-Humeanism allows that an agent has reason to φ if a fully rational version of that agent (with all and only relevant true beliefs) would desire that the actual agent φs. This adequately answers any "So what?" question and provides a place for the "And why should I care about *that?*" question-and-answer routine to conclude; in other words, it

avoids alienating an agent from her reasons. This important result is not obvious, so let me explain.

It is quite clear that if an agent, Jill, is simply told "You should φ" she may quite reasonably say "Why?", or if she is told "You have a reason to φ" she can ask "In virtue of what?" Answering the latter question by an appeal to, say, a Firthian ideal observer invites a legitimate "So what?" response. Before considering Smith's alternative, let us examine the Humean's resources. If it were pointed out to Jill that she does want X, and she is told (and believes it) that φing would be the optimal means of obtaining X, then "So what?" seems blocked. For what is "So what?" if not a request for something that is relevant to the questioner, for a demonstration that the proposal ties in with her desiderative set? I realize that insisting that "So what?" must be understood in such a manner is question-begging, but we shall try to do better in due course. Assuming for the moment that "So what?" is precisely a request for evidence that the proposal fits with one's desiderative set, then to acknowledge that some action is a means to desire-satisfaction *is* to accept that the question has been answered. A further "So what?" could only be to question practical rationality itself, and we have already seen that this is incoherent.

What now of the non-Humean instrumentalism that was argued for in the previous chapter? If told that an improved version of herself, Jill+, would want Jill to φ, may Jill acknowledge that this is true, yet reasonably respond "But so what?"? Much turns on the details of the "improvement" in question. We have seen practical rationality is not something that we may legitimately question, for to question it *is* to acknowledge it. Can we use the same kind of transcendental argument to go a little further? I believe so.

To ask "Why should I φ?" (the politer form of "So what?") is to imply that one is in the business of accepting reasons, that one is able (at least sometimes) to recognize reasons, that one can take a potential reason claim and examine it to see if it really is a reason, that one is willing to compare this reason claim with potentially competing reason claims to see which weighs most, that one is disposed to participate in deliberative activity, that one values such things as evidence and truth. Of course, merely saying the words "so" and "what" doesn't imply these things (one can teach a parrot

---

[3] *Enquiry,* appendix 1 (1983), p. 87.

to speak) – but if one is *seriously* asking the question, seriously seeking an answer, then such basic general commitments are evinced. If this is correct, then we are in a position to see that Jill *does* take the desires of Jill+ as reasons, for those desires just are what Jill would desire for herself if she were fully reflective and epistemically successful. In other words, the question "I recognize that if I were to deliberate properly on the matter, armed with all and only relevant true beliefs, I would desire my actual self to φ, but what is that to me?" is not something we need take seriously, for just in asking the question one would be demonstrating one's valuing of deliberation and truth. This is not, to repeat, to say that whenever Jill recognizes that Jill+ would desire her to φ, she automatically will feel motivated to φ; but it is to say that the recognition is tied to her desiderative motivational set in such a way as to silence any reasonable questioning.

It is important to see what a fine line such an argument treads. For were we tempted to add a further feature to our account of "Jill+" – say, that she is *dispassionate* – then it would immediately make a "So what?" question intelligible. Asking a question in no (obvious) way implies an allegiance to dispassionateness. The fact that the non-Humean instrumentalism defended in the last chapter does not fall foul of such a problem – that it attributes to the idealized counterpart of the actual agent pretty much exactly the appropriate attributes (and no more) to forestall "So what?" question; that it, in other words, avoids alienating the agent from her normative reasons – is a theoretical virtue of considerable significance. That is to say, Smith's non-Humean instrumentalism (my label, not his) has the all-important virtue of avoiding the first horn of the metaethical dilemma.

In the process, however, non-Humean instrumentalism lands on the other horn: relativism. Alienation is avoided by tying normative reasons to the agent's desiderative set, but different agents have different desiderative sets (different desires, different projects, different interests) and so what is a normative reason for one person needn't be for another. Thus, claims of the form "There is a normative reason to φ (in circumstances C)" are not properly formed; we must understand them as shorthand for something like "There is a normative reason *for* S to φ in C." Therefore two people who utter the same sentence – "There is a normative reason to φ in C" – may well be expressing different propositions: one about S, the other about S* (thus one speaker may be uttering a truth and the other a falsehood). This is what I understand by "relativism." Someone keen to avoid relativism will need to demonstrate that agents are such that there is necessary *convergence* in their normative reasons, despite their disparate desiderative starting points, such that to claim that S has a normative reason to φ in C implies that S* will have the same reason to φ in C. In other words, the non-relativist (the absolutist) needs to show that careful reflection and full information lead to convergence of motivation. On the face of it, it's a very implausible claim, which we must subject to further scrutiny.

But another possibility beckons. If an agent is not alienated from reasons when those reasons are derived from what a fully informed and flawlessly deliberating agent would desire, but making this idealized agent a counterpart of an actual agent (with all her idiosyncrasies) introduces relativism – then can't we go between the horns? Can't we simply say that an agent has a normative reason to φ if and only if a fully informed and flawlessly deliberating agent would desire her to φ? But this, it seems to me, is a hopeless thought, and leads directly to an error theory of normative reasons. I say this because I very much doubt that a non-actual agent picked out only in such thin terms desires *anything*. It would be like analyzing a property in terms of what tall people would be inclined to choose as their favorite color. There is simply no truth about what tall persons' favorite color is. Similarly, there is no truth about the favorite color of fully informed, flawlessly deliberating agents. Although it may be true that each fully informed, flawlessly deliberating agent has a favorite color, it is a fallacy to conclude that there is a favorite color had by all such agents. Similarly, I submit that there is no truth about what a fully informed, flawlessly deliberating agent would *want*. One might be hoodwinked by the following fallacious reasoning:

> If S were fully informed and deliberated correctly, S would desire to φ
> ∴ If S were a fully informed, correct deliberator, S would desire to φ
> ∴ A fully informed, correct deliberator would desire to φ

But full information and flawless deliberation alone simply do not produce *desires*. They do not even produce a desire that, say, the preconditions for being a fully informed, correct deliberator be satisfied. A rational agent *as such* need not desire to be or to remain a rational agent, any more than a garbage collector *as such* desires being and remaining a garbage collector.

The idealized agent needs something to "work with" – he needs some desires, which may then be coupled with true beliefs, reflected upon properly, etc., thus resulting in "corrected" desires. But whose desires shall he start with? We can't just stipulate which desires. Suppose Jill were told that a fully informed and flawlessly deliberating version of *Bill* (someone she has never heard of) wants her to ϕ. Saying "So what?" is perfectly reasonable! Alienation is avoided only by making the counterfactual agent who provides Jill's normative reasons an idealized counterpart of *Jill*. And doing so threatens to impale one on the horn of relativism.

I have not argued that a theory of normative reasons that avoids alienation *must* stumble into relativism, and vice versa – only that it is a notable danger. If one's interest is in providing only a theory of normative reasons, then there is no real problem. Alienation, to be sure, is something to be avoided: a theory of practical reasons that allows a person legitimately to say "I acknowledge that I have a normative reason to ϕ, but what is that to me?" has gone terribly wrong. However, relativism is not in any obvious way a theoretical cost, and so to be "impaled on the horn of relativism" is in fact no disaster – one should simply embrace normative relativism. But if one is interested not only in presenting a theory of normative reasons, but is out to defend *moral rationalism* – tying moral reasons to normative reasons – then normative relativism will bring moral relativism, and that, I will argue, *is* a problem. Before that discussion, however, we must return to Smith, who thinks he can steer his theory of normative reasons between Scylla and Charybdis.

Smith embarks on the project of demonstrating that normative reasons are non-relative by breaking the question into two. First, there's the conceptual question of whether our concept of a normative reason is a relativistic or absolute concept. But even if, with Smith, we think that it's the latter kind of concept, there remains a substantive question of whether there *are* any such reasons. If the substantive question cannot also be answered in a non-relativistic way, then all Smith's labors will be for the error theorist in the end.

[. . .]

The Relativity of Normative Reasons: The Substantive Question

Ultimately everything turns on the substantive question. (Nevertheless, we will have further cause to discuss the conceptual question below.) To this crucial matter Smith devotes just over a page of his book (roughly, p. 188). The argument depends on mustering support for "the empirical fact that moral argument tends to elicit the agreement of our fellows." To the obvious rejoinder that there simply is no such fact, that moral disagreement is characterized more by its intractable irresolubility than any convergence, Smith makes three points.

1 First, we must remember that alongside such entrenched disagreements as we in fact find we also find areas of entrenched agreement . . .
2 Second, when we look at current areas of entrenched disagreement, we must remember that in the past similarly entrenched disagreements were removed *inter alia* via a process of moral argument . . .
3 [Third], we must remember that where entrenched disagreements currently seem utterly intractable we can often explain why this is the case in ways that make them seem less threatening to the idea of a convergence in the opinions of fully rational creatures.

These are all reasonable observations; the question is whether they jointly get us anywhere near the conclusion required to support the substantive non-relativity of rationality. (2) tells us that where there has been disagreement in the past, it has been solved by, *inter alia*, rational debate. The "inter alia" must be noted, for it tells us that things other than rational debate may also account for convergence. But this, in turn, tells us that observation of convergence of moral opinions does not, in and of itself, provide evidence that rational debate leads to convergence, for an observed convergence of moral opinions might be explained in other ways. And this point, I believe, effectively dismantles Smith's argument. Consider the convergence that the world is undergoing towards driving the same cars, wearing similar clothes, eating the same hamburgers. It would be silly to think that the convergence is driven by *rational* considerations – that rational argumentation has as its output that we should drive *these* cars, wear *these* clothes, and eat *these* hamburgers. Rather, the convergence is explained by (no doubt complex) considerations concerning cultural hegemony. I see no reason to doubt that as with cars, so with tastes, and so with evaluative outlooks. Convergence in moral opinion may be quite well explained by reference to a theory of how cultures interact and influence each other in *arational* ways. The point is that even if there were to be complete and universal convergence of moral opinion, this would not show that normative reasons are non-relative. An extra argument would be needed – presumably *a posteriori* in nature – showing that the convergence was achieved *through rational debate* (in this case, the equivalent of everybody reflecting on and discussing what each of them would desire if fully reflective and armed with true beliefs, and coming to see that their answers are all the same.)

It is also worth noting that convergence *per se* may be considered valuable, and so negotiating parties may aim at it while not caring (within parameters) what they converge *upon*. Analogy: it is valuable that all countries of continental Europe drive on the same side of the road; it doesn't much matter which, so long as they decide upon one or the other. Similarly, a group of people who start out with disparate moral views may see that in order to live together cooperatively they need to adopt a shared moral policy. Let's say that there are a number of policies that are potentially acceptable to all ($P_1, P_2, \ldots P_n$), and through a process of negotiation P_3 is decided upon. Rational debate, in such a case, has led to convergence of moral policy, but it would be wrong to say that rational debate leads to convergence *on P_3* – for it might have easily converged on P_1 or P_2, etc. instead. Now suppose that there were another group which is also seeking a common policy starting from the same balance of disparate opinions among its members as did the first group. Again, rational debate and negotiation leads to convergence – but this time on P_4. If these two groups interact with each other they may decide, for the same reasons as before, that a joint policy will be advantageous, and so another round of negotiations may be entered into. But suppose the two groups *don't* interact, or their interaction does not demand a common policy, and so there is no pressure for them to have the same opinion. Would we say, in that case, that rational debate leads to convergence?

Debate is most likely to lead to convergence when convergence is itself seen to be a value to aim at. But when convergence is not of use – when there are two groups who have little to do with each other, for example – then there are no grounds for assuming that, starting from disparate desiderative points, there will be convergence. In fact, the issue of whether *debate* can lead to convergence is a red herring, for it implies that the two parties are already negotiating, and that they already see a unified settlement as a desideratum. The much clearer question is whether rational reflection, coupled with true beliefs, leads to convergence over what the best course of action is, *even when the parties in question are not interacting with each other*.

We can put this in the terms set in the previous chapter. Imagine two agents, Bill and Jill, who have quite different desires, interests, tastes, etc. Bill wants to φ. Jill wants to refrain from φing. Let's stipulate that Bill+ (the fully rational and fully informed Bill) would want Bill to ψ instead of φ, and so Bill has a normative reason to ψ. I find the claim that we now have all the information needed to conclude what Jill+ would want of Jill to be utterly implausible. Now it's possible that Jill and Bill are partners, say, trying to form a joint policy. We might put it like this: Bill+ would want Bill and Jill to have a joint policy, and so would Jill+. If this were the case, then they will negotiate: Jill+ will take into account what Bill wants; Bill+ will take into account what Jill wants. Perhaps if their starting points are not too far apart, they will come to an agreement. And perhaps if we observe a lot of such partnerships we will observe that agreement is often reached. My complaint is that this is quite beside the point. We need to question whether Bill+ and Jill+ are likely to want the same thing for Bill and Jill respectively, *when Bill and Jill are not in a partnership*. Their being in a partnership just muddies the water, by making convergence something that they are actively seeking. The claim that the non-relativist about normative reasons makes concerning convergence is not restricted to persons or groups who are antecedently committed to a settlement.

As a final comment on Smith's evidence for non-relativism, let us turn to his third point: that some entrenched disagreements are explained because one or more of the parties is not properly participating in rational deliberation.

For example, one or the other parties to the disagreement all too often forms their moral beliefs in response to the directives of a religious authority rather than as the result of the exercise of their own free thought in concert with their fellows. But beliefs formed exclusively in this way have dubious rational credentials. They require that we privilege one group's opinions about what is to be done – those of a religious authority – over another's – those of the followers – for no good reason.[4]

The item to emphasize is that Smith allows that only *some* entrenched disagreements are explained in this way. But what he is committed to, in order to make his point, is that *all* moral disputes that cannot be resolved must be due either to doxastic disagreement or to rational failing such as the kind he describes (though, as we have seen, Smith thinks rational failing includes epistemic failing). In other words, if Smith's three points are to convince us, then they must work, in their pithiest form, as follows:

1   There are moral agreements and disagreements
2   The agreements are sometimes due to rational deliberation
3   The disagreements are due to the failure of rational deliberation or differing beliefs

(1) can be granted. (2) has yet to be shown. No doubt agreements are sometimes due to rational deliberation, but that may occur only when the parties' respective desiderative starting points are already quite close, or when they antecedently value coming to an agreement. Other agreements may simply be due to cultural forces, political pressures, globalization of tastes, etc. Therefore, merely adverting to widespread moral agreement tells us little about the substantive non-relativity of normative reasons. (3) is the crucial thesis, and little has been provided to make it seem compelling. The moral rationalist's position boils down to a simple and surprising claim: that moral failure is rational failure. Given this, the very first thing that can be demanded of such a theorist is a careful description of *how* a moral villain necessarily rationally miscarries (or what false beliefs he has). *Some* disagreement are doubtlessly due to rational failure – after all, if we grant, as we should, that rational failure occurs, then we should expect that its existence will lead to irresoluble disputes. But it takes

little imagination to envisage a dispute that cannot be explained away in such a manner, especially given the account of normative reasons that I have adopted from Smith.

Summary

I argued that moral discourse commits us to reasons-talk. Now, there are all sorts of kinds of reasons, and it has not been my intention to provide a monolithic theory. In particular, I pointed out the existence of institutional reasons: reasons-talk that is legitimated by adherence to an institution. Moral reasons, however, are not presented as institutional in nature. Morality is not presented as something that may be legitimately ignored or begged off. So the question is: What sense can be made of reasons that cannot be evaded, of non-institutional reasons, of "real" reasons? The answer I gave is that *practical rationality* yields non-institutional reasons, for to question practical rationality is self-undermining. "I acknowledge that practical rationality says I should φ, but why should I have any interest in that fact?" fails to express a well-formed skeptical position, and this cannot be upheld if we replace "practical rationality" with the name of any other normative system.

We then investigated what practical rationality may consist in. I adopted a view close to Smith's: that S is practically rational to the extent that she is guided by her subjective reasons, which in turn are understood as follows: S has a subjective reason to φ if and only if she is justified in believing that S+ (S granted full information and idealized powers of reflection) would advise S to φ. The outstanding virtue of this theory is that it accounts for the non-institutionality of practical rationality; it avoids alienating an agent from her normative reasons.

A key point is the realization that the non-institutional reasons that have been located (let us just call them "normative reasons") are not going to "rescue" moral reasons. The explanation is that normative reasons are agent-relative, altering depending on the desiderative profile of the agent in question. We have seen no argument that there must be convergence in agents' normative reasons, and *a fortiori* no argument that there must be convergence towards a view that approves of

4   Michael Smith, *The Moral Problem* (Oxford: Blackwell, 1994), pp. 188–9.

promise-keeping and condemns inflicting harm on innocents, etc. This is what Smith attempts, but I have argued in the present chapter that his attempts fail.

One might complain: "Well, so much the worse for moral rationalism, but there are plenty of alternative programs that purport to vindicate moral discourse." However, if the arguments that I have pressed are correct, then this complaint is mistaken. Of course, there *are* alternative programs, but they are doomed to disappoint, for they will never vindicate that all-important moral *authority* that putatively binds us regardless of our desires. The rationalist at least sees the special sense of "requirement" that requires defense; it is just that his defense fails.

I.2 Expressivism

Introduction

Suppose one were convinced of the following two claims: moral realism commits us to the existence of moral facts and, thus, to metaphysically extravagant entities. Error theories, however, commit us to the view that the moral convictions of ordinary persons are massively mistaken and, thus, to an overly pessimistic view of ordinary moral practice. If one were convinced of these two claims, to which ethical theory would one turn? During the last century, many philosophers disinclined to accept either realism or error theory have found themselves attracted to a view commonly called "non-descriptivism" or "expressivism."

For our purposes here, it will be helpful to divide expressivism into two kinds – what we can call "classic" and "explanatory" expressivism.

To have the rudiments of classic expressivism before us, let's begin with some terminological matters. Let's stipulate that a "moral sentence" is a sentence that has the surface form of explicitly attributing a moral feature to an entity. "Smith's assassination of Jones is wrong" and "Sam is compassionate" are examples of moral sentences. A "moral proposition," as we can think of it, is the content of a moral sentence that purports to represent a moral fact. Finally, let's say that a "moral fact" is a feature of the world that makes the content of moral sentences true and that can be represented by the content of such sentences. *That*

Smith's assassination of Jones is wrong and *that Sam is compassionate* are examples of moral facts. (We can think of such facts either as the realist or the constructivist does.)

"Classic expressivism" is any view that embraces the following two theses – the first regarding moral ontology, the second regarding moral discourse:

There are no moral facts.

When an agent sincerely utters a moral sentence, that agent does not thereby assert a moral proposition, but rather (at least) expresses an attitude of endorsement, approval, condemnation, disapproval, or the like toward a non-moral state of affairs.

Common to both expressivism thus understood and its cognitivist rivals is an affirmation: both positions maintain that ordinary moral discourse *looks* as if it were discourse wherein agents assert moral propositions. For example, ordinary moral discourse appears truth-apt (e.g., "It is true that you ought to give generously to the poor") and embeds in conditionals (e.g., "If you ought to give generously to the poor, then you ought to encourage others to do so as well") and propositional attitude ascriptions (e.g., "I believe that I ought to give generously to the poor"). Unique to classic expressivism, however, is a denial: the classic expressivist denies that the surface form of moral discourse gives us very good reason to believe that it is genuinely assertoric or statement-making moral discourse. We cannot, says the expressivist, read off the linguistic function of some area of discourse simply by gazing at its surface syntax.

Thus described, classic expressivism is a general position that includes among its members such diverse views as emotivism, prescriptivism, norm-expressivism, quasi-realism, and assertoric non-descriptivism. We'll take a closer look at some of these views in just a moment. For present purposes, it is worth emphasizing the attractiveness of classic expressivism. For those disinclined to accept either moral realism or a moral error theory, classic expressivism appears to present a *via media*. On the one hand, classic expressivism avoids putatively extravagant metaphysical claims, such as the claim that there are moral facts. On the other, since expressivism implies that moral discourse is not even in the business of representing moral facts, it is incompatible with the error theorist's contention that moral discourse is systematically mistaken because it fails to represent moral reality aright. Moreover, if one takes seriously the idea that moral judgments are by their nature motivationally efficacious – the view that philosophers call "motivational internalism" – then there is something else to say in favor of expressivism: if moral judgments are really expressions of endorsement, approval, condemnation, and so on, then, arguably, they are exactly the sort of thing that move us to action. (For more on this topic, see part II.1, "Moral Motivation.")

There are, then, clear reasons to be attracted to the expressivist position generally conceived. What, though, divides the various expressivist views from one another? The differences are sometimes fairly subtle, but worth pointing out. We can better appreciate these differences if we distinguish between three "waves" in the expressivist movement.

The first wave of expressivism took place in the early part of the twentieth century with the development of so-called emotivist and prescriptivist views. (For an example of emotivism, see the selection included in this section from A. J. Ayer. Prescriptivist views are best represented by the work of R. M. Hare, cited in the bibliography.) When viewed from seventy years' distance, perhaps the most striking feature of first-wave expressivism is its iconoclastic character. Like all classical expres-

sivists, first-wave expressivists agree that moral discourse appears assertoric in character. Still, first-wave expressivists such as Ayer did little to try to explain why, if moral discourse is really non-assertoric in character, it should appear otherwise. Moreover, first-wave expressivists did little to vindicate central features of ordinary moral discourse. For example, participants in ordinary moral discourse regularly predicate truth of moral claims. And such participants regularly use moral sentences to argue for moral conclusions by plugging such sentences into argument forms such as modus ponens and modus tollens. But it is difficult to see how, according to first-wave expressivists, these practices could be justified. First-wave expressivists flatly deny that truth can be properly predicated of moral claims, for these claims do not express moral propositions. And since expressions of approval, disapproval, and the like fail to obey the laws of truth-functional logic, it is difficult to see how, according to first-wave expressivism, we can make sense of moral arguments. (For more on this latter issue, see the essays by Simon Blackburn and Walter Sinnott-Armstrong in part II.7, "Semantic Puzzles.") In short, whatever popularity first-wave expressivism enjoyed during the early to middle period of the twentieth century – and it was considerable – was not due to its having done a particularly good job of capturing the appearances of ordinary moral thought and discourse!

Second-wave expressivism emerged as a remedy for these difficulties. Beginning with the work of R. M. Hare, and continuing more recently with the work of Simon Blackburn and Allan Gibbard (see, for example, the selection from Blackburn in this section), second-wave expressivists have addressed themselves to two central questions: how, according to a broadly naturalist perspective, can we explain why moral discourse should have all the grammatical and logical trappings of assertoric discourse? And, on the assumption that such discourse is in fact primarily expressive, how can we vindicate our ordinary practices of attributing truth to moral claims, engaging in moral arguments, and claiming to represent moral features? To the first question second-wave expressivists offer a broadly evolutionary answer. There is a need, says Blackburn, "to communicate, revise, and adjust attitude; to rehearse moral scenarios together and to coordinate our responses; to encourage some attitudes and to discourage others." It is this need, so second-wave expres-

sivists claim, that "explains and justifies the propositional surface of our [moral] commitments"
(Blackburn 1996: 84).

To the second question regarding how to vindicate our ordinary moral practices and discourse,
second-wave expressivists offer a two-part answer.
In the first place, second-wave expressivists have
attempted to develop a "logic of attitudes,"
wherein it can be shown that, even though moral
sentences express pro and con attitudes, they too
can feature in something like valid argument forms
such as modus ponens. This has resulted in a small
cottage industry of interesting, but technical, work
in the intersection between moral philosophy and
philosophical logic. (For a sample of such work, see
the readings from Blackburn and Sinnott-
Armstrong in part II.7, "Semantic Puzzles.")
While it is safe to say that second-wave expressivists have focused on the project of developing a
logic of attitudes, they have also employed a second
strategy to vindicate ordinary moral thought and
practice. This strategy consists in deploying so-
called deflationary accounts of truth. The deflationary views accepted by expressivists are of two
kinds, and it is worth identifying them.

"Radical" deflationary views claim that the truth
term is not a genuine predicate and that there is no
truth property. According to these views, the term
"true" does not purport to stand for a property, but
is used to perform actions such as endorsing the
content of a sentence or repeating that very
content. For example, according to one way of
understanding this view, to say that "It is true that
one ought not to steal" is simply to commend not
stealing. "Sober" deflationary views, by contrast,
maintain that the truth term is a logical predicate
and that there is a truth property for which it
stands. As this view has it, the truth term is a logical
device that, among other things, allows us to make
generalizations. Suppose, for example, I want to
attest to Smith's reliability with respect to some
subject matter M. I might reel off a long list of
claims such as "Smith said p and p," "Smith said
q and q," and so on. Or, to keep things simple, I
might simply claim "Everything that Smith says
about M is true." The truth predicate allows us to
make this generalizing maneuver. And, according
to sober deflationists, since for every intelligible
predicate, there is a corresponding property, we can
also claim that there is a truth property. But if such
a position admits that there is a truth property, why
is it characterized as a deflationary view? The

reason this view is deflationary is that it maintains
that the truth property "has no nature." As sober
deflationary theorists see things, this means that
there is nothing informative we can say about that
in which truth consists. The truth property, for
example, does not consist in a proposition's representing a correlative fact, being ideally justifiable,
or any other such thing. At any rate, second-wave
expressivists have found deflationary accounts such
as these very attractive for their purposes. By
deploying such views, we can, according to these
expressivists, vindicate our ordinary practices of
claiming that some moral judgments are true,
without committing ourselves to moral facts that
make these judgments true. As Blackburn says in
one place, if we are deflationists about truth, talk
of moral truth comes "for free."

At the heart of the polemic leveled by moral
realists against classic expressivism is a simple but
attractive argument that rests on three assumptions. The first assumption – what Mark Timmons
calls the "semantic assumption" – tells us that
moral assertions and beliefs (if any there be) are
such that their content aims to represent moral
reality. The second assumption – what Timmons
dubs the "thesis of semantic unity" – tells us that
the grammatical and logical trappings that constitute a discourse are indicative of the real semantics
of that discourse. The third assumption – call it
"the empirical thesis" – says that moral discourse
does in fact manifest the grammatical and logical
trappings of assertoric discourse (see Timmons
1999: 130). Since these three assumptions are
jointly incompatible with expressivism, expressivists have been forced to reject at least one of
them. And almost without exception, second-wave
expressivists have rejected the second assumption,
thereby committing themselves to the view that the
grammatical and logical trappings of moral discourse do not reveal but mask its deep expressive
structure. Distinctive of third-wave expressivism is
the claim that expressivists can plausibly reject the
semantic assumption, but retain both the thesis of
semantic unity and the empirical thesis. (For an
example of this view, see the selection in this
section from Horgan and Timmons.) To defend
this position, third-wave expressivists introduce a
distinction between different types of belief –
those that have "representative content" and those
that don't. In short, beliefs with representational
content purport to represent or accurately map the
world. Beliefs that fail to have this content do not.

Third-wave expressivists claim that moral judgments express bona fide beliefs, but not of the kind endowed with representative content. In so doing, third-wave expressivists claim to even better capture and vindicate the appearances of ordinary moral thought and discourse.

So far, we've divided the classic expressivist movement into three waves, each of which devotes increasing effort to capture the realist-seeming appearances of moral thought and practice. Recently, however, Gibbard has developed an alternative to classic expressivism, which we can call "explanatory" expressivism. (For a sample of this view, see the selection from Gibbard included in this section.) What distinguishes explanatory from classic expressivism? Two features. First, unlike classic expressivism, explanatory expressivism is not, in the first instance, a position about what we are doing when we engage in moral thought and discourse. Nor is it a proposal for how we should revise such thought and discourse. Rather, it is a strategy for explaining how normative concepts (concepts "fraught with ought," as Gibbard (2003: ch. 1) puts it) might work. Indeed, Gibbard calls the expressivist position he develops in his book *Thinking How to Live* a "hypothesis," asking not whether the account offered captures our actual use of normative discourse or even whether it should, but what the consequences would be if it did (Gibbard 2003: xi). Distinctive of the explanatory expressivist style of explanation is the thesis that, at the outset of theorizing at least, we should not describe moral judgments as bona fide beliefs whose content purports to represent moral facts. Instead, they should be described, as Gibbard puts it, "psychologically, as sentiments or attitudes . . . states of norm-acceptance . . . or states of planning" (Gibbard 2003: 181). From a basis that "excludes normative facts" and assumes that moral claims do not purport to represent normative reality, the explanatory expressivist aims to develop a program wherein normative claims progressively mimic genuine beliefs.

Second, unlike classic expressivists, explanatory expressivists do not purport to vindicate a position incompatible with moral realism. (They may, of course, vindicate such a position, but that would be something we discover at the end of theorizing; it is not a constraint on the theorizing itself.) Contrary to critics of expressivism such as Ronald

Dworkin, Gibbard claims that were explanatory expressivism to mimic realist views so closely so as to be indistinguishable from them, that would not be a reason to be suspicious of the program (see Dworkin 1996; Wright 2003: ch. 2). After all, the character of moral claims can be explained in any number of different ways, and if explanatory expressivism explains this character in a way preferable to realism but, at the end of the day, yields a position that is in important respects indistinguishable from realism, then this only speaks in favor of explanatory expressivism. For then the view yields a happy convergence of positions from a more adequate explanatory basis (Gibbard 2003: 184). To which it should be added that fundamental to explanatory expressivism is the thesis that it does explain certain features of the moral domain in a way preferable to broadly nonnaturalist versions of moral realism. For one thing, explanatory expressivism "explains phenomena that non-naturalism, on its own, treats just as unexplained normative facts . . . aspects of warrant and value that otherwise we can attribute to brute features of the normative realm." And, for another, explanatory expressivism "explains why we can't do without normative concepts. It thus vindicates concepts that we might otherwise find raise an inescapable anomaly," for everyone who deliberates must employ normative concepts (Gibbard 2003: 191, 44).

When one scans the landscape in contemporary metaethics, one can find adherents to each of the expressivist views identified. Each expressivist view has been subject to numerous criticisms, ranging from the claim that it commits us to moral subjectivism to the concern that it cannot capture the character of ordinary moral discourse. The fulcrum of debate, however, is whether expressivists can develop a plausible logic of attitudes wherein moral judgments (understood in the expressivist fashion) adequately mimic ordinary moral propositions. (For an outline of this debate, see part II.7, "Semantic Puzzles.") Since this issue is unresolved, expressivism – whether in its classic or explanatory guise – is very much a lively research program. Shorn of the iconoclastic tendencies of its predecessors, however, it becomes increasingly difficult to see what separates sophisticated forms of the view from its realist rivals.

Selected Bibliography

Ayer, A. J. 1936. *Language, Truth and Logic*. London: Gollancz.

Barker, Stephen. 2000. "Is Value Content a Component of Conventional Implicature?" *Analysis* 60: 268–79.

Bennett, Jonathan. 1993. "The Necessity of Moral Judgments." *Ethics* 103: 458–72.

Blackburn, Simon. 1981. "Reply: Rule-Following and Moral Realism." In Steven Holtzman and Christopher Leich, eds. *Wittgenstein: To Follow a Rule*. London: Routledge & Kegan Paul.

Blackburn, Simon. 1984. *Spreading the Word*. Oxford: Oxford University Press.

Blackburn, Simon. 1993. *Essays in Quasi-Realism*. Oxford: Oxford University Press.

Blackburn, Simon. 1996. "Securing the Nots." In Walter Sinnott-Armstrong and Mark Timmons, eds. *Moral Knowledge?* Oxford: Oxford University Press.

Blackburn, Simon. 1998. *Ruling Passions*. Oxford: Oxford University Press.

Blackburn, Simon. 1999. "Is Objective Moral Justification Possible on a Quasi-Realist Foundation?" *Inquiry* 42: 213–28.

Copp, David. 2001. "Realist-Expressivism: A Neglected Option for Moral Realism." In Ellen F. Paul, Fred D. Miller, and Jeffrey Paul, eds. *Moral Knowledge*. Cambridge: Cambridge University Press.

Cuneo, Terence. 2006. "Saying What We Mean: An Argument Against Expressivism." In Russ Shafer-Landau, ed. *Oxford Studies in Metaethics* 1. Oxford: Oxford University Press.

Dreier, James. 2004. "Meta-ethics and the Problem of Creeping Minimalism." In John Hawthorne, ed. *Philosophical Perspectives 18: Ethics*. Oxford: Blackwell.

Dworkin, Ronald. 1996. "Objectivity and Truth: You'd Better Believe It." *Philosophy and Public Affairs* 25: 87–139.

D'Arms, Justin, and Daniel Jacobson. 1994. "Expressivism, Morality, and the Emotions." *Ethics* 104: 739–63.

D'Arms, Justin, and Daniel Jacobson. 2000. "Sentiment and Value." *Ethics* 110: 722–48.

Gert, Joshua. 2002. "Expressivism and Language Learning." *Ethics* 112: 292–314.

Gibbard, Allan. 1990. *Wise Choices, Apt Feelings*. Cambridge, MA: Harvard University Press.

Gibbard, Allan. 2003. *Thinking How to Live*. Cambridge, MA: Harvard University Press.

Hare, R. M. 1952. *The Language of Morals*. Oxford: Oxford University Press.

Hare, R. M. 1963. *Freedom and Reason*. Oxford: Oxford University Press.

Hare, R. M. 1981. *Moral Thinking*. Oxford: Oxford University Press.

Horgan, Terry, and Mark Timmons. 2000. "Nondescriptivist Cognitivism: Framework for a New Metaethic." *Philosophical Papers* 29: 121–53.

Horwich, Paul. 1993. "Gibbard's Theory of Norms." *Philosophy and Public Affairs* 22: 67–78.

Horwich, Paul. 1994. "The Essence of Expressivism." *Analysis* 54: 19–20.

Jackson, Frank, and Philip Pettit. 1998. "A Problem for Expressivism." *Analysis* 58: 239–51.

Joyce, Richard. 2002. "Expressivism and Motivation Internalism." *Analysis* 62: 336–44.

Lenman, James. 2003. "Disciplined Syntacticism and Moral Expressivism." *Philosophy and Phenomenological Research* 67: 32–57.

Miller, Alexander. 2003. *An Introduction to Contemporary Metaethics*. Cambridge: Polity Press, chs. 3–5.

O'Leary-Hawthorne, John, and Huw Price. 1996. "How to Stand Up for Non-Cognitivists." *Australasian Journal of Philosophy* 74: 275–92.

Rosen, Gideon. 1998. "Blackburn's *Essays in Quasi-Realism*." *Noûs* 32: 386–405.

Skorupski, John. 1999. "Irrealist Cognitivism." *Ratio* 12: 436–59.

Smith, Michael. 1994. "Why Expressivists about Value Should Love Minimalism about Truth." *Analysis* 54: 1–12.

Smith, Michael. 2001. "Some Not-Much-Discussed Problems for Non-Cognitivism in Ethics." *Ratio* 14: 93–115.

Stevenson, C. L. 1944. *Ethics and Language*. New Haven: Yale University Press.

Stevenson, C. L. 1963. *Fact and Value*. New Haven: Yale University Press.

Sturgeon, Nicholas. 1995. "Critical Study: Gibbard's *Wise Choices, Apt Feelings*." *Noûs* 29: 402–24.

Thomson, Judith Jarvis. 1996. "Emotivism." In Gilbert Harman and Judith Jarvis Thomson. *Moral Relativism and Moral Objectivity*. Oxford: Blackwell.

Thomson, Judith Jarvis. 2003. "The Legacy of *Principia*." *The Southern Journal of Philosophy* 41: 62–82.

Timmons, Mark. 1999. *Morality without Foundations*. Oxford: Oxford University Press.

Wright, Crispin. 2003. "Realism, Antirealism, Irrealism, Quasi-Realism." In *Saving the Differences*. Cambridge, MA: Harvard University Press.

Zangwill, Nick. 1990. "Quasi-Quasi-Realism." *Philosophy and Phenomenological Research* 50: 583–94.

Zangwill, Nick. 1992. "Quietism." In Peter French, Theodore Uehling, and Howard Wettstein, eds. *Midwest Studies in Philosophy* 17: 160–76.

Zangwill, Nick. 1994. "Moral Mind Independence." *Australasian Journal of Philosophy* 72: 205–18.

Critique of Ethics and Theology

A. J. Ayer

There is still one objection to be met before we can claim to have justified our view that all synthetic propositions are empirical hypotheses. This objection is based on the common supposition that our speculative knowledge is of two distinct kinds – that which relates to questions of empirical fact, and that which relates to questions of value. It will be said that "statements of value" are genuine synthetic propositions, but that they cannot with any show of justice be represented as hypotheses, which are used to predict the course of our sensations; and, accordingly, that the existence of ethics and æsthetics as branches of speculative knowledge presents an insuperable objection to our radical empiricist thesis.

In face of this objection, it is our business to give an account of "judgements of value" which is both satisfactory in itself and consistent with our general empiricist principles. We shall set ourselves to show that in so far as statements of value are significant, they are ordinary "scientific" statements; and that in so far as they are not scientific, they are not in the literal sense significant, but are simply expressions of emotion which can be neither true nor false. In maintaining this view, we may confine ourselves for the present to the case of ethical statements. What is said about them will be found to apply, *mutatis mutandis*, to the case of æsthetic statements also.

The ordinary system of ethics, as elaborated in the works of ethical philosophers, is very far from being a homogeneous whole. Not only is it apt to contain pieces of metaphysics, and analyses of non-ethical concepts: its actual ethical contents are themselves of very different kinds. We may divide them, indeed, into four main classes. There are, first of all, propositions which express definitions of ethical terms, or judgements about the legitimacy or possibility of certain definitions. Secondly, there are propositions describing the phenomena of moral experience, and their causes. Thirdly, there are exhortations to moral virtue. And, lastly, there are actual ethical judgements. It is unfortunately the case that the distinction between these four classes, plain as it is, is commonly ignored by ethical philosophers; with the result that it is often very difficult to tell from their works what it is that they are seeking to discover or prove.

In fact, it is easy to see that only the first of our four classes, namely that which comprises the propositions relating to the definitions of ethical terms, can be said to constitute ethical philosophy. The propositions which describe the phenomena of moral experience, and their causes, must be assigned to the science of psychology, or sociology. The exhortations to moral virtue are not propositions at all, but ejaculations or commands which are designed to provoke the reader to action of a certain sort. Accordingly, they do not belong to any branch of philosophy or science. As for the expressions of ethical judgements, we have not yet determined how they should be classified. But inasmuch as they are certainly neither definitions nor comments upon definitions, nor quotations, we may say decisively that they do not belong to ethical philosophy. A strictly philosophical treatise on ethics should therefore make no ethical pronouncements. But it should, by giving an analysis of ethical terms, show what is the category to which all such pronouncements belong. And this is what we are now about to do.

A question which is often discussed by ethical philosophers is whether it is possible to find definitions which would reduce all ethical terms to one or two fundamental terms. But this question, though it undeniably belongs to ethical philosophy, is not relevant to our present enquiry. We are not now concerned to discover which term, within the sphere of ethical terms, is to be taken as fundamental; whether, for example, "good" can be defined in terms of "right" or "right" in terms of "good," or both in terms of "value." What we are interested in is the possibility of reducing the whole sphere of ethical terms to non-ethical terms. We are enquiring whether statements of ethical value can be translated into statements of empirical fact.

That they can be so translated is the contention of those ethical philosophers who are commonly called subjectivists, and of those who are known as utilitarians. For the utilitarian defines the rightness of actions, and the goodness of ends, in terms of the pleasure, or happiness, or satisfaction, to which they give rise; the subjectivist, in terms of the feelings of approval which a certain person, or group of people, has towards them. Each of these types of definition makes moral judgements into a subclass of psychological or sociological judgements; and for this reason they are very attractive to us. For, if either was correct, it would follow that ethical assertions were not generically different from the factual assertions which are ordinarily contrasted with them; and the account which we have already given of empirical hypotheses would apply to them also.

Nevertheless we shall not adopt either a subjectivist or a utilitarian analysis of ethical terms. We reject the subjectivist view that to call an action right, or a thing good, is to say that it is generally approved of, because it is not self-contradictory to assert that some actions which are generally approved of are not right, or that some things which are generally approved of are not good. And we reject the alternative subjectivist view that a man who asserts that a certain action is right, or that a certain thing is good, is saying that he himself approves of it, on the ground that a man who confessed that he sometimes approved of what was bad or wrong would not be contradicting himself. And a similar argument is fatal to utilitarianism. We cannot agree that to call an action right is to say that of all the actions possible in the circumstances it would cause, or be likely to cause, the greatest happiness, or the greatest balance of pleasure over pain, or the greatest balance of satisfied over unsatisfied desire, because we find that it is not self-contradictory to say that it is sometimes wrong to perform the action which would actually or probably cause the greatest happiness, or the greatest balance of pleasure over pain, or of satisfied over unsatisfied desire. And since it is not self-contradictory to say that some pleasant things are not good, or that some bad things are desired, it cannot be the case that the sentence "x is good" is equivalent to "x is pleasant," or to "x is desired." And to every other variant of utilitarianism with which I am acquainted the same objection can be made. And therefore we should, I think, conclude that the validity of ethical judgements is not determined by the felicific tendencies of actions, any more than by the nature of people's feelings; but that it must be regarded as "absolute" or "intrinsic," and not empirically calculable.

If we say this, we are not, of course, denying that it is possible to invent a language in which all ethical symbols are definable in non-ethical terms, or even that it is desirable to invent such a language and adopt it in place of our own; what we are denying is that the suggested reduction of ethical to non-ethical statements is consistent with the conventions of our actual language. That is, we reject utilitarianism and subjectivism, not as proposals to replace our existing ethical notions by new ones, but as analyses of our existing ethical notions. Our contention is simply that, in our language, sentences which contain normative ethical symbols are not equivalent to sentences which express psychological propositions, or indeed empirical propositions of any kind.

It is advisable here to make it plain that it is only normative ethical symbols, and not descriptive ethical symbols, that are held by us to be indefinable in factual terms. There is a danger of confusing these two types of symbols, because they are commonly constituted by signs of the same sensible form. Thus a complex sign of the form "*x* is wrong" may constitute a sentence which expresses a moral judgement concerning a certain type of conduct, or it may constitute a sentence which states that a certain type of conduct is repugnant to the moral sense of a particular society. In the latter case, the symbol "wrong" is a descriptive ethical symbol, and the sentence in which it occurs expresses an ordinary sociological proposition; in the former case, the symbol "wrong" is a normative ethical symbol, and the sentence in which it occurs does not, we maintain, express an empirical proposition at all. It is only with normative ethics that we are at present concerned; so that whenever ethical symbols are used in the course of this argument without qualification, they are always to be interpreted as symbols of the normative type.

In admitting that normative ethical concepts are irreducible to empirical concepts, we seem to be leaving the way clear for the "absolutist" view of ethics – that is, the view that statements of value are not controlled by observation, as ordinary empirical propositions are, but only by a mysterious "intellectual intuition." A feature of this theory, which is seldom recognized by its advocates, is that it makes statements of value unverifiable. For it is notorious that what seems intuitively certain to one person may seem doubtful, or even false, to another. So that unless it is possible to provide some criterion by which one may decide between conflicting intuitions, a mere appeal to intuition is worthless as a test of a proposition's validity. But in the case of moral judgements, no such criterion can be given. Some moralists claim to settle the matter by saying that they "know" that their own moral judgements are correct. But such an assertion is of purely psychological interest, and has not the slightest tendency to prove the validity of any moral judgement. For dissentient moralists may equally well "know" that their ethical views are correct. And, as far as subjective certainty goes, there will be nothing to choose between them. When such differences of opinion arise in connection with an ordinary empirical proposition, one may attempt to resolve them by referring to, or actually carrying out, some relevant empirical test. But with regard to ethical statements, there is, on the "absolutist" or "intuitionist" theory, no relevant empirical test. We are therefore justified in saying that on this theory ethical statements are held to be unverifiable. They are, of course, also held to be genuine synthetic propositions.

Considering the use which we have made of the principle that a synthetic proposition is significant only if it is empirically verifiable, it is clear that the acceptance of an "absolutist" theory of ethics would undermine the whole of our main argument. And as we have already rejected the "naturalistic" theories which are commonly supposed to provide the only alternative to "absolutism" in ethics, we seem to have reached a difficult position. We shall meet the difficulty by showing that the correct treatment of ethical statements is afforded by a third theory, which is wholly compatible with our radical empiricism.

We begin by admitting that the fundamental ethical concepts are unanalysable, inasmuch as there is no criterion by which one can test the validity of the judgements in which they occur. So far we are in agreement with the absolutists. But, unlike the absolutists, we are able to give an explanation of this fact about ethical concepts. We say that the reason why they are unanalysable is that they are mere pseudo-concepts. The presence of an ethical symbol in a proposition adds nothing to its factual content. Thus if I say to someone, "You acted wrongly in stealing that money," I am not stating anything more than if I had simply said, "You stole that money." In adding that this action is wrong I am not making any further statement about it. I am simply evincing my moral disapproval of it. It is as if I had said, "You stole that money," in a peculiar tone of horror, or written it with the addition of some special exclamation marks. The tone, or the exclamation marks, adds nothing to the literal meaning of the sentence. It merely serves to show that the expression of it is attended by certain feelings in the speaker.

If now I generalise my previous statement and say, "Stealing money is wrong," I produce a sentence which has no factual meaning – that is, expresses no proposition which can be either true or false. It is as if I had written "Stealing money!!" – where the shape and thickness of the exclamation marks show, by a suitable convention, that a special sort of moral disapproval is the feeling which is being expressed. It is clear that there is nothing said here which can be true or false. Another man may disagree with me about the wrongness of stealing, in the sense that he may not have the same feelings about stealing as I have, and he may quarrel with me on account of my moral sentiments. But he cannot, strictly speaking, contradict me. For in saying that a certain type of action is right or wrong, I am not making any factual statement, not even a statement about my own state of mind. I am merely expressing certain moral sentiments. And the man who is ostensibly contradicting me is merely expressing his moral sentiments. So that there is plainly no sense in asking which of us is in the right. For neither of us is asserting a genuine proposition.

What we have just been saying about the symbol "wrong" applies to all normative ethical symbols. Sometimes they occur in sentences which record ordinary empirical facts besides expressing ethical feeling about those facts: sometimes they occur in sentences which simply express ethical feeling about a certain type of action, or situation, without making any statement of fact. But in every case in which one would commonly be said to be making an ethical judgement, the function of the relevant ethical word is purely "emotive." It is used to express feeling about certain objects, but not to make any assertion about them.

It is worth mentioning that ethical terms do not serve only to express feeling. They are calculated also to arouse feeling, and so to stimulate action. Indeed some of them are used in such a way as to give the sentences in which they occur the effect of commands. Thus the sentence "It is your duty to tell the truth" may be regarded both as the expression of a certain sort of ethical feeling about truthfulness and as the expression of the command "Tell the truth." The sentence "You ought to tell the truth" also involves the command "Tell the truth," but here the tone of the command is less emphatic. In the sentence "It is good to tell the truth" the command has become little more than a suggestion. And thus the "meaning" of the word "good," in its ethical usage, is differentiated from that of the word "duty" or the word "ought." In fact we may define the meaning of the various ethical words in terms both of the different feelings they are ordinarily taken to express, and also the different responses which they are calculated to provoke.

We can now see why it is impossible to find a criterion for determining the validity of ethical judgements. It is not because they have an "absolute" validity which is mysteriously independent of ordinary sense-experience, but because they have no

objective validity whatsoever. If a sentence makes no statement at all, there is obviously no sense in asking whether what it says is true or false. And we have seen that sentences which simply express moral judgements do not say anything. They are pure expressions of feeling and as such do not come under the category of truth and falsehood. They are unverifiable for the same reason as a cry of pain or a word of command is unverifiable – because they do not express genuine propositions.

Thus, although our theory of ethics might fairly be said to be radically subjectivist, it differs in a very important respect from the orthodox subjectivist theory. For the orthodox subjectivist does not deny, as we do, that the sentences of a moralizer express genuine propositions. All he denies is that they express propositions of a unique non-empirical character. His own view is that they express propositions about the speaker's feelings. If this were so, ethical judgements clearly would be capable of being true or false. They would be true if the speaker had the relevant feelings, and false if he had not. And this is a matter which is, in principle, empirically verifiable. Furthermore they could be significantly contradicted. For if I say, "Tolerance is a virtue," and someone answers, "You don't approve of it," he would, on the ordinary subjectivist theory, be contradicting me. On our theory, he would not be contradicting me, because, in saying that tolerance was a virtue, I should not be making any statement about my own feelings or about anything else. I should simply be evincing my feelings, which is not at all the same thing as saying that I have them.

The distinction between the expression of feeling and the assertion of feeling is complicated by the fact that the assertion that one has a certain feeling often accompanies the expression of that feeling, and is then, indeed, a factor in the expression of that feeling. Thus I may simultaneously express boredom and say that I am bored, and in that case my utterance of the words, "I am bored," is one of the circumstances which make it true to say that I am expressing or evincing boredom. But I can express boredom without actually saying that I am bored. I can express it by my tone and gestures, while making a statement about something wholly unconnected with it, or by an ejaculation, or without uttering any words at all. So that even if the assertion that one has a certain feeling always involves the expression of that feeling, the expression of a feeling assuredly does not always involve the assertion that one has it. And this is the important point to grasp in considering the distinction between our theory and the ordinary subjectivist theory. For whereas the subjectivist holds that ethical statements actually assert the existence of certain feelings, we hold that ethical statements are expressions and excitants of feeling which do not necessarily involve any assertions.

We have already remarked that the main objection to the ordinary subjectivist theory is that the validity of ethical judgements is not determined by the nature of their author's feelings. And this is an objection which our theory escapes. For it does not imply that the existence of any feelings is a necessary and sufficient condition of the validity of an ethical judgement. It implies, on the contrary, that ethical judgements have no validity.

There is, however, a celebrated argument against subjectivist theories which our theory does not escape. It has been pointed out by Moore that if ethical statements were simply statements about the speaker's feelings, it would be impossible to argue about questions of value. To take a typical example: if a man said that thrift was a virtue, and another replied that it was a vice, they would not, on this theory, be disputing with one another. One would be saying that he approved of thrift, and the other that *he* didn't; and there is no reason why both these statements should not be true. Now Moore held it to be obvious that we do dispute about questions of value, and accordingly concluded that the particular form of subjectivism which he was discussing was false.

It is plain that the conclusion that it is impossible to dispute about questions of value follows from our theory also. For as we hold that such sentences as "Thrift is a virtue" and "Thrift is a vice" do not express propositions at all, we clearly cannot hold that they express incompatible propositions. We must therefore admit that if Moore's argument really refutes the ordinary subjectivist theory, it also refutes ours. But, in fact, we deny that it does refute even the ordinary subjectivist theory. For we hold that one really never does dispute about questions of value.

This may seem, at first sight, to be a very paradoxical assertion. For we certainly do engage in disputes which are ordinarily regarded as disputes about questions of value. But, in all such cases, we find, if we consider the matter closely, that the dispute is not really about a question of value, but about a question of fact. When someone disagrees with us about the moral value of a certain action or type of action, we do admittedly resort to argument in order to win him over to our way of thinking. But we do not attempt to show by our arguments that he has the "wrong" ethical feeling towards a situation whose nature he has correctly apprehended. What we attempt to show is that he is mistaken about the facts of the case. We argue that he has misconceived the agent's motive: or that he has misjudged the effects of the action, or its probable effects in view of the agent's knowledge; or that he has failed to take into account the special circumstances in which the agent was placed. Or else we employ more general arguments about the effects which actions of a certain type tend to produce, or the qualities which are usually manifested in their performance. We do this in the hope that we have only to get our opponent to agree with us about the nature of the empirical facts for him to adopt the same moral attitude towards them as we do. And as the people with whom we argue have generally received the same moral education as ourselves, and live in the same social order, our expectation is usually justified. But if our opponent happens to have undergone a different process of moral "conditioning" from ourselves, so that, even when he acknowledges all the facts, he still disagrees with us about the moral value of the actions under discussion, then we abandon the attempt to convince him by argument. We say that it is impossible to argue with him because he has a distorted or undeveloped moral sense; which signifies merely that he employs a different set of values from our own. We feel that our own system of values is superior, and therefore speak in such derogatory terms of his. But we cannot bring forward any arguments to show that our system is superior. For our judgement that it is so is itself a judgement of value, and accordingly outside the scope of argument. It is because argument fails us when we come to deal with pure questions of value, as distinct from questions of fact, that we finally resort to mere abuse.

In short, we find that argument is possible on moral questions only if some system of values is presupposed. If our opponent concurs with us in expressing moral disapproval of all actions of a given type *t*, then we may get him to condemn a particular action A, by bringing forward arguments to show that A is of type *t*. For the question whether A does or does not belong to that type is a plain question of fact. Given that a man has certain moral principles, we argue that he must, in order to be consistent, react morally to certain things in a certain way. What we do not and cannot argue about is the validity of these moral principles. We merely praise or condemn them in the light of our own feelings.

If anyone doubts the accuracy of this account of moral disputes, let him try to construct even an imaginary argument on a question of value which does not reduce itself to an argument about a question of logic or about an empirical matter of fact. I am confident that he will not succeed in producing a single example. And if that is the case, he must allow that its involving the impossibility of purely ethical arguments is not, as Moore thought, a ground of objection to our theory, but rather a point in favour of it.

Having upheld our theory against the only criticism which appeared to threaten it, we may now use it to define the nature of all ethical enquiries. We find that ethical philosophy consists simply in saying that ethical concepts are pseudo-concepts and therefore unanalysable. The further task of describing the different feelings that the different ethical terms are used to express, and the different reactions that they customarily provoke, is a task for the psychologist. There cannot be such a thing as ethical science, if by ethical science one means the elaboration of a "true" system of morals. For we have seen that, as ethical judgements are mere expressions of feeling, there can be no way of determining the validity of any ethical system, and, indeed, no sense in asking whether any such system is true. All that one may legitimately enquire in this connection is, What are the moral habits of a given person or group of people, and what causes them to have precisely those habits and feelings? And this enquiry falls wholly within the scope of the existing social sciences.

It appears, then, that ethics, as a branch of knowledge, is nothing more than a department of psychology and sociology. And in case anyone thinks that we are overlooking the existence of casuistry, we may remark that casuistry is not a science, but is a purely analytical investigation of the structure of a given moral system. In other words, it is an exercise in formal logic.

When one comes to pursue the psychological enquiries which constitute ethical science, one is immediately enabled to account for the Kantian and hedonistic theories of morals. For one finds that one of the chief causes of moral behaviour is fear, both conscious and unconscious, of a god's displeasure, and fear of the enmity of society. And this, indeed, is the reason why moral precepts present themselves to some people as "categorical" commands. And one finds, also, that the moral code of a society is partly determined by the beliefs of that society concerning the conditions of its own happiness – or, in other words, that a society tends to encourage or discourage a given type of conduct by the use of moral sanctions according as it appears to promote or detract from the contentment of the society as a whole. And this is the reason why altruism is recommended in most moral codes and egotism condemned. It is from the observation of this connection between morality and happiness that hedonistic or eudæmonistic theories of morals ultimately spring, just as the moral theory of Kant is based on the fact, previously explained, that moral precepts have for some people the force of inexorable commands. As each of these theories ignores the fact which lies at the root of the other, both may be criticized as being one-sided; but this is not the main objection to either of them. Their essential defect is that they treat propositions which refer to the causes and attributes of our ethical feelings as if they were definitions of ethical concepts. And thus they fail to recognise that ethical concepts are pseudo-concepts and consequently indefinable.

As we have already said, our conclusions about the nature of ethics apply to æsthetics also. Aesthetic terms are used in exactly the same way as ethical terms. Such æsthetic words as "beautiful" and "hideous" are employed, as ethical words are employed, not to make statements of fact, but simply to express certain feelings and evoke a certain response. It follows, as in ethics, that there is no sense in attributing objective validity to æsthetic judgements, and no possibility of arguing about questions of value in æsthetics, but only about questions of fact. A scientific treatment of æsthetics would show us what in general were the causes of æsthetic feeling, why various societies produced and admired the works of art they did, why taste varies as it does within a given society, and so forth. And these are ordinary psychological or sociological questions. They have, of course, little or nothing to do with æsthetic criticism as we understand it. But that is because the purpose of æsthetic criticism is not so much to give knowledge as to communicate emotion. The critic, by calling attention to certain features of the work under review, and expressing his own feelings about them, endeavours to make us share his attitude towards the work as a whole. The only relevant propositions that he formulates are propositions describing the nature of the work. And these are plain records of fact. We conclude, therefore, that there is nothing in æsthetics, any more than there is in ethics, to justify the view that it embodies a unique type of knowledge.

It should now be clear that the only information which we can legitimately derive from the study of our æsthetic and moral experiences is information about our own mental and physical make-up. We take note of these experiences as providing data for our psychological and sociological generalisations. And this is the only way in which they serve to increase our knowledge. It follows that any attempt to make our use of ethical and æsthetic concepts the basis of a metaphysical theory concerning the existence of a world of values, as distinct from the world of facts, involves a false analysis of these concepts. Our own analysis has shown that the phenomena of moral experience cannot fairly be used to support any rationalist or metaphysical doctrine whatsoever. In particular, they cannot, as Kant hoped, be used to establish the existence of a transcendent god.

4

How To Be an Ethical Anti-Realist

Simon Blackburn

Some philosophers like to call themselves realists, and some like to call themselves anti-realists. An increasing number, I suspect, wish to turn their backs on the whole issue.[1] Their strengths include those of naturalism, here counseling us that there is none except a natural science of human beings. From this it follows that there is no 'first philosophy' lying behind (for instance) physics, or anthropology, enabling the philosopher to know how much of the world is 'our construction' (anti-realism) or, on the contrary, 'independent of us' (realism).

This naturalism bestows small bouquets and small admonishments to each of the previous parties. The anti-realists were right to deny that there exists a proper philosophical (*a priori*) explanation of things like the success of physics, which some people were acute enough to discern from their armchairs, while others did not. A scientist can say that there was a certain result because a neutrino or electron did this and that, but a philosopher has nothing to *add* to this. If she tries to say, 'Not only did the result occur because of the neutrino, but also because neutrino theory depicts

(corresponds with, matches, carves at the joints) the world,' she adds nothing but voices only a vain, and vainglorious, attempt to underwrite the science. This attempt may have made sense in a Cartesian tradition, when the mind's contact with the world seemed so problematical, but its time has passed. On the other hand, anti-realists, sensing the futility of this road, stress instead the dependence of the ordinary world on us, our minds and categories, and again the additions they offer are unacceptable.[2] Characteristically, if realism fails because it is vacuous, anti-realism fails because it strays into mistakes – making things dependent on us when they obviously are not, for example.[3] Again, and perhaps even more clearly, it is plausible to see anti-realism as attempting to theorize where no theory should be – in this case, making the unnatural, Cartesian mind into a source of worlds. These theories are naturally described as 'transcendental', and the word reminds us that for all his hostility to rational psychology, Kant himself failed to escape this trap.

The transcendental aspect can be seen if we put the matter in terms of what I call 'correspondence

---

[1] For example, see Arthur Fine, 'Unnatural Attitudes: Realist and Instrumentalist Attachment to Science', in *Mind*, 1986.

[2] On Putnam in this connection, see Ruth Garrett Millikan, 'Metaphysical Anti-Realism', in *Mind*, 1986.

[3] My favorite example is Putnam, *Reason, Truth and History* (Cambridge: Cambridge University Press, 1981), p. 52.

conditionals.' We like to believe that if we exercise our sensory and cognitive faculties properly and end up believing that p, then p. What kind of theory might explain our right to any such confidence? If p is a thesis from basic physical theory, only the theory itself. To understand why, when we believe that neutrinos exist, having used such-and-such information in such-and-such a way, then they probably do, is just to understand whatever credentials neutrino theory has. That is physics. Any attempt at a background, an underwriting of the conditional from outside the theory, is certain to be bogus.

When considering such global matters as the success of our science or the nature of our world, it seems that naturalism ought to win. But in local areas, it seems instead that the battle can be joined. In this essay I would like to say in a little more detail why I think this is so. The main problem which I leave dangling is that of seepage, or the way in which anti-realism, once comfortably in command of some particular area of our thought, is apt to cast imperialistic eyes on neighboring territory. The local anti-realist faces the problem of drawing a line, which may prove difficult, or that of reneging on naturalism and allowing that global anti-realism must after all make sense. The second part of my essay is an exploration of this specific problem.

Why can battle be joined in local areas? What I said about physics might be retorted upon any area. To understand how, when we believe that twice two is four, we are probably right requires arithmetical understanding. To understand why, when we believe that wanton cruelty is wrong, we are also right requires ethical understanding. Where is the asymmetry?

Let us stay with the example of ethics. Here a 'projective' theory can be developed to give a satisfying way of placing our propensities for values. According to me, the surface phenomena of moral thought do not offer any obstacle to this theory. They can be explained as being just what we should expect, if the projective metaphysics is correct. (I call the doctrine that this is so 'quasi-realism' – a topic I return to later.) I have also argued that this package contains various explanatory advantages over other rival and alleged rival theories. The projectivism is not, of course, new – the package is intended indeed to be a modern version of Hume's theory of the nature of ethics, but without any commitment to particular operations of passions

such as sympathy. Emotivism and Hare's prescriptivism are also immediate ancestors. Anything new comes in the quasi-realism, whose point is to show that, since projectivism is consistent with, and indeed explains, the important surface phenomena of ethics, many of the arguments standardly used against it miss their mark. These arguments allege that projectivism is inadequate to one or another feature of the way we think ethically; the quasi-realism retorts that it is not, and goes on to explain the existence of the features. Such features include the propositional as opposed to emotive or prescriptive form and the interaction of ethical commitments with ordinary propositional attitude verbs, talk of truth, proof, knowledge, and so forth. Here, it is the relationship of that programme to naturalism that is to be determined.

I

The first link is this. I think that naturalism demands this view of ethics, but in any case it motivates it. It does so because in this package the fundamental state of mind of one who has an ethical commitment makes natural sense. This state of mind is not located as a belief (the belief in a duty, right, value). We may *end up* calling it a belief, but that is after the work has been done. In fact, we may end up saying that there really are values (such as the value of honesty) and facts (such as the fact that you have a duty to your children). For in this branch of philosophy, it is not what you finish by saying, but how you manage to say it that matters. How many people think they can just *announce* themselves to be realists or anti-realists, as if all you have to do is put your hand on your heart and say, 'I really believe it' (or, 'I really don't')? The way I treat the issue of realism denies that this kind of avowal helps the matter at all. The question is one of the best theory of this state of commitment, and reiterating it, even with a panoply of dignities – truth, fact, perception, and the rest – is not to the point.

The point is that the state of mind starts theoretical life as something else – a stance, or conative state or pressure on choice and action. Such pressures need to exist if human beings are to meet their competing needs in a social, cooperative setting. The stance may be called an attitude, although it would not matter if the word fitted only inexactly: its function is to mediate the move from features of a situation to a reaction, which in the appropriate circumstances will mean choice. Someone with a standing stance is set to react in some way when an occasion arises, just as someone with a standing belief is set to react to new information cognitively in one way or another. It matters to us that people have some attitudes and not others, and we educate them and put pressure on them in the hope that they will.

So far, two elements in this story are worth keeping in mind, for it will be important to see whether a projective plus quasi-realist story can do without them. These are: (1) the fundamental identification of the commitment in question as something other than a belief and (2) the existence of a neat, natural account of why the state that it is should exist.

Obviously, the emergence of cooperative and altruistic stances is not a mere armchair speculation. It can be supplemented by both theoretical and empirical studies.[4] It is noteworthy that the account will insist upon the nonrepresentative, conative function for the stance. The evolutionary success that attends some stances and not others is a matter of the behaviour to which they lead. In other words, it is the direct consequences of the pressure on action that matter. Evolutionary success may attend the animal that helps those that have helped it, but it would not attend any allegedly possible animal that thinks it ought to help but does not. In the competition for survival, it is what the animal *does* that matters. This is important, for it shows that only if values are intrinsically motivating is a natural story of their emergence possible. Notice, too, the way the evolutionary success arises. Animals with standing dispositions to cooperate (say) do better in terms of other needs like freedom from fleas or ability to survive failed hunting expeditions by begging meals from others. No right, duty, or value plays any explanatory role in this history. It is not as if the creature with a standing disposition to help those who have helped it does well *because* that is a virtue. Its being virtue is irrelevant to evolutionary biology. There is no such naturalistically respectable explanation.

The commitment may have psychological accretions consistently with this being its core or essence. The precise 'feel' of an ethical stance may be a function of local culture in its scope, or of some of its interactions with other pressures and other beliefs. A pressure toward action can be asso-ciated variously with pride, shame, or self-respect, and there is no reason to expect a simple phenomenology to emerge, The essence lies in the practical import, but the feelings that surround that can vary considerably. There is no reason for a stance to feel much like a desire, for example. Consider as a parallel the way in which a biological or evolutionary story would place attraction between the sexes, and the culturally specific and surprising ways in which that attraction can emerge – the varieties of lust and love (whose imperatives often do not feel much like desire either, and may equally be expressed by thinking that there are things one simply *must* do; I say more about this later). So, if a theorist is attracted to the rich textures of ethical life, he need not, therefore, oppose projectivism. No 'reduction' of an ethical stance to one of any other type is needed.

Now contrast the kind of evolution already sketched with any that might be offered for, say, our capacity to perceive spatial distance. Again, what matters here is action. But what we must be good at is acting according to the very feature perceived. A visual-motor mechanism enabling the frog's tongue to hit the fly needs to adapt the trajectory of the tongue to the place of the fly relative to the frog, and an animal using perceived distance to guide behaviour will be successful only if it perceives distances as they are. It is because our visual mechanisms show us far-off things as far-off and near things as near that we work well using them. That is what they are *for*. We can sum up this contrast by saying that although the teleology of spatial perception is spatial, the teleology of ethical commitment is not ethical. The good of spatial perception is to be representative, but the good of ethical stances is not.

The possibility of this kind of theory, then, provides the needed contrast between the general case of science, where an attempt to provide a further, background theory is transcendental, and the local particular case of ethics, where there are natural materials for such a story ready at hand. It also means that philosophers wanting a general realism versus anti-realism issue cannot take comfort from the local case; the materials to generate theory there exist, as it were, by contrast with anything that can be provided in the general case.

These simple naturalistic points are not always respected. Consider, for example, the position

---

[4]   R. Axelrod, *The Evolution of Cooperation* (New York: Basic Books, 1984).

associated with John McDowell and David Wiggins. This goes some way in the same direction as projectivism, at least in admitting that a person's ethical outlook is dependent on affective or conative aspects of his makeup. But it takes those aspects as things that enable the subject to do something else – to perceive value properties. It is only if one is moved or prone to be moved in a certain way that one sees the value of things, just as it is only if one is prone to be moved in some way that one perceives the sadness in a face.[5] This is supposed to do justice to the obvious point that sentiments have something to do with our capacity to make ethical judgements, yet to retain a 'perceptual' and cognitive place for moral opinion.

Let us suppose that this is a substantial theory and different from projectivism (in the light of what is to come, neither supposition is beyond doubt). The view is substantial if it holds that changes in one's sensibilities enable one to do something else: *literally* to perceive ethical properties in things. Or if the 'something else' is not literal perception, then at least its kinship with perception must be very close – so close that it cannot be explained as projection of a stance. For the view is no different from projectivism if this 'something else' is nothing else at all, but merely a different label for reaching an ethical verdict because of one's sentiments. In other words, it is only different from projectivism if this literal talk of perceiving plays a theoretical role, and not just a relabeling of the phenomena. This is not at all obvious. Theoretically low-grade talk of perception is always available. Everyone can say that one can 'see' what one must do or what needs to be done, just as one can 'see' that 17 is a prime number. When I said that it is not what one finishes by saying that is important, but the theory that gets one there, this is one of the crucial examples I had in mind.

Literal talk of perception runs into many problems. One is that the ethical very commonly, and given its function in guiding choice, even typically, concerns imagined or described situations, not perceived ones.[6] We reach ethical verdicts about the behavior of described agents or actions in the light of general standards. And it is stretching things to see these general standards as perceptually formed or maintained. Do I see that ingratitude is base only on occasions when I see an example of ingratitude? How can I be sure of the generalization to examples that I did not see? (I could not do that for colour, for instance. Absent pillar-boxes may be a different colour from present ones; only an inductive step allows us to guess at whether they are.) Or do I see the timeless connection – but how? Do I have an antenna for detecting timeless property-to-value connections? Is such a thing that much like color vision? Perhaps these questions can be brushed aside. But in connection with naturalism, the question to ask of the view is why nature should have bothered. Having, as it were, forced us into good conative shape, why not sit back? Why should this be merely the curtain-raiser for a perceptual system? It seems only to engender dangerous possibilities. It ought to make us slower to act, for we must process the new information perceived. Worse, it might be that someone moved, say, by gratitude comes to see the goodness of gratitude and then has, quite generally, some other (negative) reaction to what is seen. Perhaps typically, the conative pressure opens our eyes to these properties, about which we then have a different, conflicting feeling. Or is it somehow given that what comes back is what went in – that the property perceived impinges on us with the same emotional impact required for perceiving it? How convenient! But how clumsy of nature to go in for such a loop! And why did we not evolve to short-circuit it, as projectivism claims? In other words, we have here the typical symptoms of realism, which not only has to take us *to* the new properties but also has to take us back *from* them, showing how perception of them contrives to have exactly the effects it does.

This extravagance came from taking literally the talk of perception made possible by changes of sensibility. But the theory seems to be meant literally. Wiggins, for example, thinks that although projectivism can be dismissed (values 'put into [or onto, like varnish] the factual world'), the right view is that there are value properties and sensibilities for perceiving them 'made for each other' as 'equal and reciprocal partners'.[7]

---

[5] John McDowell, 'Non Cognitivism and Rule Following', *Wittgenstein: To Follow a Rule*, ed. by S. Holtzman and C. Leich (London: Routledge & Kegan Paul, 1981). Also, Sabina Lovibond, *Realism and Imagination in Ethics* (Oxford: Blackwell, 1983).

[6] John Locke, *An Essay Concerning Human Understanding*, Book IV, chapter IV, pp. 6–7.

[7] D. Wiggins, *Truth, Invention and the Meaning of Life* (British Academy Lecture, 1976), p. 348.

Can this be understood? Projectivism, from which the theory is supposed to be so different, can easily embrace one half of the doctrine – that the properties are made for the sensibility. The embrace ought to be a bit tepid, because we shall see better ways of putting the view that value predicates figure in thought and talk as reflections or projections of the attitudes that matter. But it is the other half, that the sensibilities are 'made for' the properties, that really startles. Who or what makes them like that? (God? As we have seen, no natural story explains how the ethical sensibilities of human beings were made for the ethical properties of things, so perhaps it is a supernatural story.)

Wiggins, I think, would reply that nothing extraordinary or unfamiliar is called for here. Refinement or civilization makes both sensibility and property. It is the process of education or moral refinement that makes sensibilities end up in good harmony with values. 'When this point is reached, a system of anthropocentric properties and human responses has surely taken on a life of its own. Civilization has begun'. The implicit plea that we get our responses to life into civilized shape is admirable, but is it enough to locate a view of the nature of ethics, or is there a danger of confusing uplift with theory? Certainly, it is true that when we have gone through some process of ethical improvement, we can turn back and say that now we have got something *right* – now we appreciate the value of things as they are, whereas before we did not. This Whiggish judgement is often in place, but it is, of course, a moral judgement. Is it not pertinent to explaining *how* sensibilities are 'made for' values. Is it a good theoretical description or explanation of the fact that we value friendship that, first, it is good and, second, civilization has 'made' our sensibilities 'for' the property of goodness? It seems overripe, since it goes with no apparent theory of error (what if our sensibilities are unluckily not made for the properties?), no teleology, and no evolutionary background. Its loss of control becomes clear if we think how easy it is to generate parallels. Perhaps something similar made our arithmetical powers for the numbers, or our tastes for the niceness of things. Or, perhaps, on the contrary, the talk of our sensibilities being made for the properties is theoretically useless and the more economical remainder is all that is really wanted.

Might there still be room for a view that the properties are 'made for' the sensibility, which avoids projectivism? The analogy with colours, for all its many defects, might be held to open such a possibility. But colour at this point is a dangerous example. If we ask seriously what colour vision is made for, an answer can be found – but it will not cite colours. Colour vision is probably made for enhancing our capacities for quickly identifying and keeping track of objects and surfaces, and this asymmetry with, for instance, spatial perception remains the most important point of the primary-secondary property distinction.

Any analogy with colour vision is bound to run into the problem of dependency. If we had a theory whereby ethical properties are literally made by or for sensibilities, ethical truth would be constituted by and dependent on the way we think. This might not repel Wiggins. It agrees with the analogy with colours, and in the course of discussing Russell's worry ('I find myself incapable of believing that all that is wrong with wanton cruelty is that I don't like it'), Wiggins freely asserts that 'what is wrong with cruelty is not, even for Bertrand Russell, just that Bertrand Russell does not like it, but that it is not such as to call forth liking given our *actual* responses.[8] But is it? I should have said not. It is because of our responses that we *say* that cruelty is wrong, but it is not because of them that it is so. It is true that insertion of the 'actual' into the sentence makes it wrong to test the alleged dependence by the usual device of imagining our responses otherwise and asking if that makes cruelty any better. But our actual responses are inappropriate anchors for the wrongness of cruelty. What makes cruelty abhorrent is not that it offends us, but all those hideous things that make it do so.

The projectivist can say this vital thing: that it is not because of our responses, scrutinized and collective or otherwise, that cruelty is wrong. The explanation flows from the way in which quasi-realism has us deal with oblique contexts. It issues an 'internal' reading of statement of dependence, according to which the statement amounts to an offensive ethical view, about (of course) what it is that makes cruelty wrong. Critics of this explanation allow the internal reading, but complain that the quasi-realist is being wilfully deaf to an

8   'A Sensible Subjectivism?', in *Needs, Values, Truth* (Oxford: Blackwell, 1987), p. 210. [This essay appears as chapter 12 below.]

intended 'external' reading, according to which the dependency is a philosophical thesis, and one to which the projectivist, it is said, must assent.[9] The crucial question, therefore, is whether the projectivist wilfully refuses to hear the external reading. According to me, there is only one proper way to take the question 'On what does the wrongness of wanton cruelty depend?': as a moral question, with an answer in which no mention of our actual responses properly figures. There *would* be an external reading if realism were true. For in that case there would be a fact, a state of affairs (the wrongness of cruelty) whose rise and fall and dependency on others could be charted. But anti-realism acknowledges no such state of affairs and no such issue of dependency. Its freedom from any such ontological headache is not the least of its pleasures. A realist might take this opportunity for dissent. He might say, 'I can just *see* that the wrongness of cruelty is a fact (perhaps an external one) that needs an ontological theory to support it – no theory that avoids providing such support is credible'. In that case I gladly part company, and he is welcome to his quest – for what kind of ontology is going to help? The Euthyphro dilemma bars all roads there.

It is tempting to think: on this metaphysics the world contains nothing but us and our responses, so the fact that cruelty is bad *must* be created by our responses. What else is there for it to be dependent upon? The prejudice is to treat the moral fact as a natural one, capable to being constituted, made, or unmade, by sensibilities. The wrongness of wanton cruelty does indeed depend on things – features of it that remind us how awful it is. But locating these is giving moral verdicts. Talk of dependency is moral talk or nothing. This is not, of course, to deny that 'external' questions make sense – the projectivist plus quasi-realist package is an external philosophical theory about the nature of morality. But external questions must be conducted in a different key once this package is brought in. We may notice, too, how this undermines a common way of drawing up the realist versus anti-realist issue, according to which anti-realism asserts that truth in some or all areas is 'mind-dependent' and realism denies this. For here is the projection, as anti-realist a theory of moral-ity as could be wished, denying that moral truth is mind-dependent in the only sense possible.

The point can be made as follows. As soon as one *uses* a sentence whose simple assertion expresses an attitude, one is in the business of discussing or voicing ethical opinion. Such sentences include 'The fact that *cruelty is wrong* depends on . . .' or 'Our refined consensus makes it true that *cruelty is wrong*'. And so on. If one generalizes and says things like 'moral facts depend on us,' the generalization will be true only if instances are true or, in other words, if one can find examples of truths like those. Since these ethical opinions are unattractive, they must be judged incorrect, as must generalizations of them. If one attempts to discuss external questions, one must use a different approach – in my case, a naturalism that places the activities of ethics in the realm of adjusting, improving, weighing, and rejecting different sentiments or attitudes. The projectivist, then, has a perfect right to confine external questions of dependency to domains where real states of affairs, with their causal relations, are in question. The only things in this world are the attitudes of people, and those, of course, are trivially and harmlessly mind-dependent. But the projectivist can hear no literal sense in saying that moral properties are made for or by sensibilities. They are not in a world where things are made or unmade – not in this world at all, and it is only because of this that naturalism remains true.

The charge that projectivism refuses to hear an explanatory demand as it is intended can be returned with, I suggest, much more effect. I was severe earlier with Wiggins's theoretical description of us as indulging in a kind of coordination of responses and properties as we become civilized. But it is telling that the Whiggish appeal to a value ('civilization') is introduced at that point. For the introduction of values into explanatory investigations is echoed in other writings in this tradition, notably in those of John McDowell.[10] The strategy is that in a context purportedly comparing explanations of a practice – the practice of ethical judgement – we allow ourselves to invoke the very commitments of that practice. Why are we afraid of the dark? Because it is fearful. Why do we value friendship? Because it is good and we are civilized.

9 Quassim Cassam, 'Necessity and Externality,' in *Mind*, 1986.
10 For instance in his 'Values and Secondary Qualities', in *Value and Objectivity, Essays in Honour of J. L. Mackie,* ed. T. Honderich (London: Routledge & Kegan Paul, 1985). [This essay is included as chapter 11 in the present volume.]

Why do I dislike sentimentality? Because it merits it. And so on.

The refusal to stand outside ethics in order to place it is supposed to tie in with one strand in Wittgenstein. This is the thought that there is characteristically neither a reduction nor an explanation of the members of any major family of concepts in terms of those of another. Ethical notions require ethical sensibilities to comprehend them. Similarly, why should it not require an ethical sensibility to comprehend an explanation of the views we hold? Only those who perceive friendship as good will understand why we do so, and to them it can be explained why we do so by reminding them that it is good, or making them feel that it is so. The rest – aliens, outsiders, Martians – cannot be given the explanation, but this is as it must be. What I said about the explanation of our spatial capacities will make it apparent that the circularity exists there in exactly the same way. Only those who appreciate distance can understand the distance-centered explanation of visual perception.

This returns us to a theme that has been touched at many points in this essay. The insistence on hearing explanatory demands only in a way in which one can invoke values in answering them had a respectable origin. We agreed earlier that the parallel would be true of thinking about the correspondence conditionals in the case of physics. But I hope I have said enough to show that nature and our theory of nature surround our ethical commitments in a way that gives us a *place* from which to theorize about them. No thing and no theory surround our physics. In other words, the difference in the ethical case comes in the theses I labeled (1) and (2) – the brute fact that an external explanatory story is possible. We already know that in even more local cases, where what is at question is not 'the ethical' in a lump but particular attitudes and their etiologies. Social anthropology is not confined to explaining the rise of puritanism to puritans or the evolution of polygamy to polygamists. Similarly, nothing in Wittgenstein offers any principled obstacle to explaining the general shape and nature of ethical attitudes and their expressions in projective terms.

Indeed, much in Wittgenstein is sympathetic to doing so. Not only is Wittgenstein himself an anti-realist about ethics, he is in general quite free in admitting propositions or quasi-propositions whose function is not to describe anything – the rules of logic and arithmetic, for instance. It is clear that what he wants to do is to place mathematical practice, not as a representation of the mathematical realm, but as 'a different kind of instrument', commitment to which is not like central cases of belief but much more like other kinds of stance. It is also interesting that some of the apparently irritating or evasive answers he gives when faced with the charge of anthropocentricity are exactly those that a projectivist can give if quasi-realism has done its work, and that according to me, no other philosophy of these matters can give. For example, when Wittgenstein approaches the question whether, on his anthropocentric view of mathematical activity, mathematical truth is yet independent of human beings, he says exactly what I would have him say:

> "But mathematical truth is independent of whether human beings know it or not!" – Certainly, the propositions 'Human beings believe that twice two is four' and 'twice two is four' do not mean the same. The latter is a mathematical proposition; the other, if it makes sense at all, may perhaps mean: human beings have *arrived* at the mathematical proposition. The two propositions have entirely different *uses*.[11]

The proposition expresses a norm that arises in the course of human activities, but it does not describe those activities, and it has no use in which the correctness of the norm (the truth of the proposition) depends upon the existence or form of those activities. *That* question simply cannot be posed; it treats what is not a dependent state of affairs belonging at all to the natural world as if it were.

I have tried to show that naturalism, which turns away from realism and anti-realism alike in the global case, turns toward projective theories in the ethical case. This theory is visibly anti-realist, for the explanations offered make no irreducible or essential appeal to the existence of moral 'properties' or 'facts'; they demand no 'ontology' of morals. They explain the activity from the inside out – from the naturally explicable attitudes to the forms of speech that communicate them, challenge them, refine them, and abandon them, and which so mislead the unwary.

So far I have talked of the issue of mind-dependency in fairly abstract terms, and relied upon a relatively subtle move in the philosophy of

---

[11] Ludwig Wittgenstein, *Philosophical Investigations* (Oxford: Blackwell, 1953), p. 226.

language to defend my view. I now want to discuss these points in practical terms. It is evident that a more fundamental mistake underlies some discomfort with projectivism. The mistake is visible in Wiggins's critique of 'non-cognitive theories' in his British Academy Lecture.[12] It results in the charge that projectivism cannot be true to the 'inside of lived experience'. Other writers (I would cite Nagel, Williams, and Foot) seem to illustrate similar unease. The thought is something like this: it is important that there should be some kind of accord in our thinking about ethical stances from the perspective of the theorist and from that of the participant. Our story about ethical commitment is to explain it, not to explain it away. But projectivism threatens to do the latter (many people who should know better think of Hume as a skeptic about ethics, and, of course, John Mackie saw himself as one). It threatens to do so because it shows us that our commitments are not external demands, claiming us regardless of our wills or in direct opposition to our passions. It makes our commitments facets of our own sentimental natures; this softens them, destroying the hardness of the moral must.

From the inside, the objects of our passions are their *immediate* objects: it is the death, the loved one, the sunset, that matters to us. It is not our own state of satisfaction or pleasure. Must projectivism struggle with this fact, or disown it? Is it that we projectivists, at the crucial moment when we are about to save the child, throw ourselves on the grenade, walk out into the snow, will think, 'Oh, it's only me and my desires or other conative pressures – forget it'?

It ought to be sufficient refutation of this doubt to mention other cases. Does the lover escape his passion by thinking, 'Oh, it's only my passion, forget it'? When the world affords occasion for grief, does it brighten when we realize that it is we who grieve? (The worst thing to think is that if we are 'rational', it should, as if rationality had anything to tell us about it.)

There is an important mistake in the philosophy of action that, I think, must explain the temptation to share Wiggins's doubt. The mistake is that of supposing that when we deliberate in the light of various features of a situation we are *at the same time* or 'really' deliberating – or that our reasoning can be 'modeled' by representing us as deliberat-

ing – about our own conative functioning. Representing practical reasoning as if it consisted of contemplating a syllogism, one of whose premises describes what we want, encourages this mistake. But just as the eye is not part of the visual scene it presents, the sensibility responsible for the emotional impact of things is not part of the scene it takes for material. Nor is our sense of humor the main thing we find funny. This does not mean that our sensibility is hidden from us, and when we reflect on ourselves we can recognize aspects of it, just as we can know when we are in love or grieving. But it does mean that its own shape is no part of the input, when we react to the perceived features of things. Furthermore, even when we reflect on our sensibility, we will be using it if we issue a verdict: when we find our own sense of humor funny, we are not escaping use of it as we do so.

This misconstruction leads people to suppose that on a projective theory all obligations must be 'hypothetical' because they are properly represented as dependent upon the existence of desires. But the lover who hears that the beloved is present and feels he must go, or the person who receiving bad news feels he must grieve, has no thoughts of the form 'if I desire her/feel sad then I must go/grieve'. Nothing corresponds to this. The news comes in and the emotion comes out; nothing in human life could be or feel more categorical. In ordinary emotional cases, of course, a third party may judge that it is only *if* he desires her that he must go; this is not so in ethical cases. One ought to look after one's young children, whether one wants to or not. But that is because we insist on some responses from others, and it is sometimes part of good moralizing to do so.

Once these mistakes are averted, is there any substance left to the worry about failure of harmony of the theoretical and deliberative points of view? I think not. Sometimes theory can help to change attitudes. One might become less attached to some virtue, or less eager in pursuing some vice, after thinking about its etiology or its functioning. One might qualify it a little (we see an example in what follows). But sometimes one might become more attached to the virtue, and sometimes everything stays the same. Does the story threaten to undermine the promise that the stances cited in this theory of ethics make good natural sense (does

---

[12]   *Truth, Invention, and the Meaning of Life*, section 4, note 6.

it take something divine to make the claims of obligation so pregnant with authority)? Not at all – I have already mentioned the 'musts' of love and grief, and those of habit and obsession are just as common.

There is one last charge of the would-be realist. This claims that projectivism must lead to relativism. 'Truth' must be relative to whatever set of attitudes is grounding our ethical stances; since these may vary from place to place and time to time, truth must be relative. The very analogies with other conative states press this result: what to one person is an occasion for love or grief or humor is not to another. Consider a young person gripped by the imperatives of fashion. The judgement that people must wear some style, that another is impossible, has its (naturally explicable and perfectly intelligible) function; it appears quite categorical, for the subject will think that it is not just for him or her that the style is mandatory or impossible (it was so in the parents' time as well, only they did not realize it). Yet, surely this is a mistake. The verdict is 'relative', having no truth outside the local system of preferences that causes it. The image is plain: a projectivist may inhabit a particular ethical boat, but he must know of the actual or potential existence of others; where, then, is the absolute truth?

The answer is that it is not anywhere that can be visible from this sideways, theoretical perspective. It is not that this perspective is illegitimate, but that it is not the one adapted for finding ethical truth. It would be if such truth were natural truth, or consisted of the existence of states of affairs in the real world. That is the world seen from the viewpoint that sees different and conflicting moral systems – but inevitably sees no truth in just one of them. To 'see' the truth that wanton cruelty is wrong demands moralizing, stepping back into the boat, or putting back the lens of a sensibility. But once that is done, there is nothing relativistic left to say. The existence of the verdict, of course, depends on the existence of those capable of making it; the existence of the truth depends on nothing (externally), and on those features that make it wrong (internally). For the same reasons that operated when I discussed mind-dependency, there is no doctrine to express relating the truth of the verdict to the existence of us, of our sentiments, or of rival sentiments.

What, then, of the parallel with the other emotions, or with the fashion example? The emotions of grief and love are naturally personal; if the subject feels they make a claim on others, so that those unstricken somehow *ought* to be stricken, then she is nonrelativistically, absolutely wrong. Similarly with fashion: the underlying story includes the need for a self-presentation that is admirable to the peer group, and if what is admirable changes rapidly as generations need to distance themselves from their immediate predecessors, then the teenager who thinks that her parents were wrong to like whatever clothes they did is mistaken in the same way as the subject of an emotion who imputes a mistake to those who cannot feel the same. But the strongest ethical judgements do not issue from stances that are properly variable. They may sometimes be absent, from natural causes, as if a hard life destroys a capacity for pity. But this is cause for regret; it would be better if it were not so. In the variations of emotion, and still more of fashion, there is no cause for regret. In saying these things I am, of course, voicing some elements of my own ethical stances, but, as I promised, it is only by doing this that ethical truth is found.

II

If projective theories have everything going for them in ethics, how much can they jettison and still have *something* going for them? The two ingredients I highlighted are the possibility of identifying the commitment in a way that contrasts it usefully with belief, and a 'neat, natural account' of why the state that it is should exist. In the case of ethics we have conative stances and a visible place for them in our functioning. But what of other cases?

Colour commitments might attract attention, because not everybody will be happy that the agreed story about what colour vision is and why we have it leaves realism as a natural doctrine about colours. Here the second ingredient is present. There is a neat, natural story of our capacity for colour discrimination, and in its explanatory side, both physically and evolutionarily, it makes no explanatory use of the *existence* of colours. But there is no way woefully to contrast colour commitments with *beliefs*. Their functional roles do not differ. So there will be no theory of a parallel kind to develop, explaining why we have propositional attitudes of various kinds toward colour talk, or why we speak of knowledge, doubt, proof, and so forth in connection with them. If anything can be drawn from a realism versus anti-realism debate over colour (which I rather doubt), it would have to be found by different means.

Modal commitments are much more promising. Our penchant for necessities and possibilities, either in concepts or in nature, is not easy to square with a view that we are representing anything, be it a distribution of possible worlds or (in the case of natural necessity) a timeless nomic connection between universals.[13]

First, consider the case of logical necessity. A theory insisting on a nonrepresentative function for modal commitment is clearly attractive. Here, however, although I think the first desideratum is met – we can do something to place the stance as something other than belief in the first instance – the second is not so easy. The kind of stance involved is insistence upon a norm, an embargo on a trespass. Saying that 2 + 2 is anything other than 4 offends against the embargo, and the embargo in turn makes shared practices, shared communication possible. So far so good, but what of a 'neat, natural theory' of the emergence of the embargo? That shared practice should exist is good – but do they so clearly depend upon such policing? If they do, it appears to be because of something else: because we can make no sense of a way of thinking that flouts the embargo. It introduces apparent possibilities of which we can make nothing. This imaginative limitation is, in turn, something of which no natural theory appears possible, even in outline. For when we *can* make sense of the imaginative limitation, we do find it apt to explain away or undermine the original commitment to a necessity. If it seems only because of (say) confinement to a world in which relative velocities are always slow compared to that of light that we find a relativistic view of simultaneity hard to comprehend, then that already shows how we would be wrong to deem the theory impossible. If it is only because of the range of our colour vision that we cannot imagine a new primary colour, then we would be unwise to rule out the possibility that some natural operation might result in our admitting one. Natural explanation is here the enemy of the hard logical must.

It is not obviously so in the case of natural necessity. Once more the paradigm is Hume – not the

Hume of many commentators, but the real Hume, who knew that talk of necessity was irreducible but gave a projective theory of it. The explanation here has us responsive to natural regularity, and forming dispositions of expectation (we might add, of observing boundaries in our counterfactual reasoning), which in turn stand us in good stead as the regularities prove reliable. Here, once we accept the Humean metaphysics, the naturalism seems quite in place. The upshot – talk of causation – is not undermined but is explained by this interpretation. This accords exactly with the case of ethics. There is a difference, however. I do not think metaphysical obstacles stand in the way of the conception of nature that does the explanatory work in the example of ethics. But many writers have difficulty with the conception of nature that is supposed to do it in Hume's metaphysics of causation. Regularities – but between what? Events – but how are these to be conceived, stripped of the causal 'bit' (to use the computer metaphor)? Events thought of as changes in ordinary objects will scarcely do, for as many writers have insisted, ordinary objects are permeated with causal powers. Nothing corresponds to the easy, sideways, naturalistic perspective that strips the world of values.

What is the option? All sides carry on talk of causation in whichever mode they find best. The new realists like to produce apparent ontologies – universals, timeless connections, and the rest. The Humean does not mind, so long as the explanatory pretensions of these retranslations are kept firmly in their place (outside understanding). Is there scope for a debate here? It is a place where the ghosts are hard to lay, and I for one do not like being there alone in the gloom.

Addendum

Since this essay was written, an influential marker in the debate has been its nominal mirror-image, entitled 'How To Be a Moral Realist', by Richard Boyd (in *Essays on Moral Realism*, ed. Geoff Sayre-McCord, Ithaca: Cornell University Press, 1988). [This essay is included as chapter 13 in the present volume.] Readers of that paper may expect this essay to be a reaction not so much to Oxford, Wittgensteinian, realism, but to the newer, naturalistic, Cornell variety. That is unfortunate. I can here add some brief remarks about that theory.

---

[13]   David Armstrong, *What Is a Law of Nature?* (Cambridge: Cambridge University Press, 1983), chapter 6.

Cornell realism highlights the possibility of a property identity: to be good is to be something-or-other natural. The theory may cite sophisticated clusters of natural properties, or whatever natural properties best satisfy some alleged folk theory of The Good, but its essence is equally visible if we consider a simple equation: to be good is to produce human happiness, for instance. The equation is protected from Moore's open question argument, by being presented not as any equation of meaning, but as a substantive metaphysical identity, conceived along the lines of 'water is H_2O' or 'heat in gases is molecular motion'.

I find this approach puzzling, because it is unclear what problems it solves. It does not speak to moral psychology, because it does not tell us what the difference is between those who equate creating human happiness with the good and those who do not. That is, it does not address the question of whether seeing the creation of happiness *under the heading* of the good is possession of an attitude, or a belief, or something else, or whether it connects with action in one way or another, or with emotions such as guilt and shame. It does not speak to issues of meaning, because we do not know whether those who resist the equation flout some (hidden) principle of meaning that governs ethical concepts, and it does not speak to issues of proof and objectivity, because we do not know whether denying the equation is making an objective or cognitive mistake or something else. If the equation does not help with issues of moral psychology, or motivation, or meaning, or epistemology, what good does it do? It seems to be an agreeable after-thought of those particular people whose ethics allows them to accept the creation of human happiness as a standard.

One way of missing these questions is to think that realism, at least so far as a predicate is concerned, is essentially the doctrine that the predicate refers to a property, or a real property. If we have reference to a real property, then any sentence in which the predicate is concerned can be given a standard truth-theoretical semantics; its truth is guaranteed in the way any more straightforward truth is guaranteed, and the contrasts that anti-realism tried to open up are smoothed out. Michael Dummett has expressed this conception of realism, but he himself appears to go on to point out that unless reference plays some role in the theory of meaning, it remains possible that the meaning we give to some set of remarks deserves an anti-realist construction. Here it is a question of what states of mind *end up* with the theorist announcing the identity of reference, and if those states are either covertly or visibly 'noncognitive', no advance in a realist direction is made.

The crucial point, as far as 'reference' goes, is that in ordinary cases it ties with meaning: to understand an expression is to have a grasp, explicit or implicit, of what its reference is. Here, without further argument (which then bears all the burden), there is no such equation, since people with aberrant standards understand ethical terms, yet there is no apparent link to the properties that the naturalist highlights. One might be tempted to think that if there is a real property identity, anyone missing it must be making an objective, metaphysical error. But this is not so, since all it takes to miss it is a defective ethical sensibility.

Once this is understood, property identity drops out of the picture. There is no harm in saying that ethical predicates refer to properties, when such properties are merely the semantic shadows of the fact that they function as predicates. A quasi-realist protection of ethical truth protects ethical predicates, and if our overall semantic picture is that predicates refer to properties, so be it. But ethical *predication* remains an entirely different activity from naturalistic predication, and this is only disguised by thinking of the world of properties as one in which hidden identities may be revealed by the philosopher-as-scientist.

Nondescriptivist Cognitivism: Framework for a New Metaethic

Terry Horgan and Mark Timmons

We propose to break some new ground in metaethics by sketching a view about moral judgments and statements that departs from traditional ways of thinking about them. As the title suggests, our view combines a nondescriptivist account of moral judgments and statements – they are not in the business of describing moral facts – with the cognitivist idea that moral judgments are genuine beliefs and moral statements are genuine assertions. We claim that in addition to descriptive beliefs, there are (moral) evaluative beliefs which are neither reducible to, nor a species of, beliefs of the former type. We think that our kind of metaethical view has obvious advantages over the standard menu of options (versions of realism, rationalism, relativism, error theory, and forms of standard nondescriptivism) – advantages that will become apparent as we proceed.

Our plan is to begin (section I) by questioning a deeply embedded assumption of traditional metaethical thinking which we think has unfortunately and unnecessarily blocked from view the metaethical theory we favor and which, when rejected, opens up some new metaethical territory worth exploring. We then proceed in sections II–VI to outline our positive view by developing a new framework for understanding belief and assertion within which nondescriptivist cognitivism emerges as a consistent and plausible metaethical contender.

In section VII we consider various challenges to our brand of cognitivism, explaining how our view can answer such challenges and also indicating some of the main tasks that lie ahead for any attempt to develop the view further.

Our central focus will be on moral judgments, with much of what we say applying *mutatis mutandis* to moral statements. Sometimes, but not always, we will explicitly extend points made about judgments to the case of statements too.

I. The Semantic Assumption

In order to focus on the semantic assumption that we think ought to be rejected, we distinguish three notions of semantic content.

First, let judgments whose overall content is expressible by declarative sentences be called *declarative* judgments, and let the overall content of such a judgment be called its *declarative content*. Declarative content, then, is possessed simply as a result of grammatical form. Typical moral judgments are expressible by declarative sentences (e.g., 'Slavery is wrong'; 'Himmler was an evil man'), and so in metaethics all competing views – descriptivist and nondescriptivist alike – must grant that moral judgments have declarative content.

Even if all metaethical views recognize that moral judgments have declarative content, they disagree over whether such judgments also have *cognitive content*. Cognitive content is belief-eligible and assertible content, and so to say that a judgment has such content is to say that the judgment is a genuine belief. Correspondingly, to say that a statement has cognitive content is to say that it is a genuine assertion. Although talk of cognitive *content* might be a relatively recent bit of philosophical nomenclature, talk of cognitive *meaning* has a history of use in metaethics, though the two expressions may be used to signify the same thing. Of course, there have been sharp divisions within metaethics over the question of whether or not moral judgments and statements have cognitive content and if so, whether such content is semantically primary. Cognitivists in metaethics affirm that typical moral judgments have cognitive content, while their noncognitivist opponents deny that the declarative content of a moral judgment is cognitive (or primarily cognitive).

But notice that what has been taken for granted in analytic philosophy generally, and metaethics in particular, is the idea that for content to be genuinely cognitive it must be in the business of purporting to represent how the world is. And this brings us to a third notion of content – *descriptive* content. Descriptive content is content that purports to represent the world as being a certain way, and is characteristic of ordinary nonmoral beliefs about the world. The judgment that Clinton was impeached has as its overall cognitive content the descriptive content, *Clinton's having been impeached*.

Now, according to our view, moral judgments are genuine beliefs and moral statements are genuine assertions. Consequently, moral judgments and statements have declarative content that is genuinely cognitive – that is, they have belief-eligible, assertible content. Cognitivism in ethics is the view that moral judgments are genuinely cognitive in their content, and so we are ethical cognitivists. Cognitive content has been assumed, by all parties in these discussions, to be the same thing as descriptive content. Thus, 'descriptivism' and 'cognitivism' have been seen as alternative labels for the same kind of metaethical position. In opposition to the tradition, we maintain that the declarative content of moral beliefs and assertions is not a species of, nor is it reducible to, descriptive content – content that represents the world as being a certain way. We therefore reject metaethical descriptivism; on our view, moral beliefs (and the sentences expressing them) are not descriptive.

This combination of cognitivism and non-descriptivism flies in the face of a deeply embedded assumption that we call the *semantic assumption*:

> SA: All genuinely cognitive content is descriptive content, i.e., way-the-world-might-be content. Thus, mental states like beliefs and linguistic items like sentences that have cognitive content are in the business of representing some (putative) state of affairs or stating some (putative) fact.

This assumption, we claim, is a largely unquestioned dogma of both descriptivist and nondescriptivist views in metaethics, and (we think) is the main culprit that stands in the way of developing a fully adequate metaethical account of moral thought and discourse. Let us briefly review how it figures in traditional metaethical thought.

Suppose one accepts what we call the *thesis of semantic unity*:

> SU: Sentences with the grammatical and logical trappings of assertion have genuine cognitive content. Similarly, judgments whose content is expressible by such sentences have genuine cognitive content.

So now consider a typical (if somewhat simplified) line of thought behind versions of metaethical descriptivism. The descriptivist begins with the following observation about moral thought and discourse:

> M: Moral thought and discourse manifest the relevant grammatical and logical features that are characteristic of genuine belief and assertion.

Now M, together with SU (the view that judgments having grammatical and logical trappings really are genuinely cognitive) and SA (the view that all genuinely cognitive content is descriptive), jointly entail the main descriptivist claim:

> D: Moral thought and discourse have descriptive content, i.e., declarative moral content is descriptive.

By contrast, the traditional nondescriptivist rejects metaethical descriptivism, recognizes that moral discourse has all the grammatical and logical trappings of genuine cognitive content, but then, given the semantic assumption, is forced to reject the thesis of semantic unity. That is, the traditional nondescriptivist reasons as follows: not-D; M; SA; therefore not-SU. And so the nondescriptivist, rejecting the thesis of semantic unity, must distinguish, for moral discourse, between surface features of moral thought and discourse and the supposedly deep features that reveal its true semantical workings. Hence, the project of the traditional nondescriptivist was to characterize the deep semantic workings of moral thought and discourse – often through reductive meaning analyses that essentially equated declarative moral content with some kind of noncognitive content expressible in nondeclarative language. Eschewing descriptive declarative content for moral thought and discourse, the traditionalist embraced some form of noncognitivism (e.g., emotivism).

Our proposal is to break away from all this by rejecting the semantic assumption that weds genuine cognitive content to descriptive content. The line of thought we employ, then, could be expressed this way: we do recognize and take seriously the fact that moral thought and discourse display the grammatical and logical trappings of cognitive content, and along with the traditional descriptivists, we agree that such trappings are indicative of genuine, deep, cognitive content for moral thought and discourse; but since we reject descriptivism in ethics, we must hold (and think there is good reason to hold) that some forms of genuinely cognitive thought and discourse are not descriptive. Our project involves staking out a metaethical position according to which this claim, in connection with moral thought and discourse, is both consistent and plausible.

Here, then, is an initial statement of our nondescriptivist cognitivism (henceforth, NDC):

(1) Declarative judgments with moral content are genuine beliefs, having genuinely belief-eligible, cognitive content. Thus, declarative statements with moral content are genuine assertions – their declarative content is cognitive.

(2) However, the cognitive content of such judgments and statements is not descriptive (way-the-world-might-be) content.

It will perhaps help if we locate our metaethical position vis-à-vis standard views using a visual aid:

METAETHICAL VIEWS ABOUT MORAL JUDGMENTS		
DESCRIPTIVIST COGNITIVISM	NONDESCRIPTIVIST COGNITIVISM	NONCOGNITIVISM
Descriptive Content	Nondescriptive Content	
Cognitive Content		Noncognitive Content
Declarative Content		

Notice that on our diagnosis of what is wrong with traditional metaethics, two levels of content – descriptive/nondescriptive and cognitive/noncognitive – are simply conflated owing to the semantic assumption. Rejecting the assumption and distinguishing these types of content opens up fertile metaethical territory that we plan to explore and cultivate.

II. A Fresh Start

In developing a metaethical theory, one would like to accommodate what seem to be deeply embedded features of moral thought and discourse as plausibly and coherently as possible. One thing that seems clear is that moral judgments and moral statements exhibit many of the characteristics distinctive of genuine belief. First, we have already mentioned that moral judgments have the *logico-grammatical* trappings of genuine beliefs: the content of a moral belief is declarative, and can embed as a constituent of a judgment that has logically complex declarative content (e.g., the judgment that either Jeeves has already mailed Uncle Willoughby's parcel or Bertie ought to mail it). As such, moral judgments can figure in logical inferences. They can combine with other beliefs to yield new beliefs that are content-appropriate given prior beliefs. Second, moral judgments also exhibit *phenomenological* features characteristic of beliefs. They are experienced as psychologically involuntary, and as grounded in reasons: given one's evidence, one cannot help but make certain moral judgments. And because of their reason-based

involuntariness, moral judgments exert a felt rational authority upon us.[1] The belief-like nature of
typical moral judgments is widely enough recognized and uncontroversial enough that we need not
digress here in order to elaborate the case for this
claim.

Moral judgments also seem to play a distinctive
action-guiding role in a person's overall psychological economy that makes them in some ways
unlike ordinary nonmoral beliefs. Typically,
anyway, moral judgments directly dispose us
toward appropriate action, independently of our
pre-existing desires, whereas ordinary nonmoral
beliefs only become action-oriented in combination
with such prior desires. (Thus, the reason-based
authority of moral beliefs typically gives them
motivational force, over and above the motivational
force of our pre-existing desires and often capable
of 'trumping' them.) Associated with this action-
guiding role are certain distinctive phenomenological features too, notably, a felt demandingness, a
phenomenological 'to-be-done-ness'. The action-
oriented nature of typical moral judgments, with
its accompanying typical phenomenology, has led
many moral philosophers to embrace some form or
other of ethical internalism. Despite difficulties in
formulating a plausible form of internalism, we
think the insight behind such philosophical views
is correct – distinctive of moral judgments is their
action-guiding role.

The problem is to plausibly combine these two
dominant features of moral judgments – their
being a kind of belief and yet mainly in the business of action-guidance – into a plausible metaethical view. Many moral philosophers see a tension
here, some opting for nondescriptivist views that
would deny that moral judgments have overall cognitive content, others denying internalism. Of
course, there are those who attempt to defend cognitivism and internalism, but not too successfully
we think.

We are nondescriptivists, and we aim to develop
a strain of this general kind of view that fairly
accommodates both features just mentioned.
Doing so requires that we face three serious
tasks:

First Task:
> Articulate a conception of belief that does
> not require the overall declarative content of
> beliefs to be descriptive content.

Second Task:
> Make a case for the independent plausibility
> of this conception of belief.

Third Task:
> Argue that nondescriptivist cognitivism, for-
> mulated in a way that draws upon the pro-
> posed conception of belief, has significant
> comparative advantages over descriptivist
> forms of cognitivism.

The first task is the most basic, because it is not
antecedently clear how the semantic assumption,
which effectively equates cognitive content with
descriptive content, could possibly be mistaken.
This task is also the most important, because it is
what will open up the new metaethical territory we
seek to occupy. We propose to address this challenge by developing a generic framework for belief
that does not presuppose that all cognitive content
is descriptive content, and therefore is consistent
with the claim that some beliefs have overall cognitive content that is not descriptive. (The framework is also consistent with the denial of this
claim.) This is the business of section III.[2]

Of course it is not enough just to propose a conception of belief that is *consistent* with the claim
that some beliefs have overall content that is not
descriptive. For, the proposal might complicate the
notions of belief, assertion, and cognitive content
in ad hoc, implausible ways, and/or it might seem
theoretically unmotivated (and hence, question-
begging) from the perspective of advocates of the
semantic assumption. The second task, then, is to
show that the framework is theoretically plausible
independently of the fact that it is consistent with
the possibility that some beliefs have overall
content that is not descriptive. We take up this
project in section IV, where we argue that the proposed framework for belief is attractive even for
those who accept the semantic assumption, because it provides a way for descriptivist versions

---

[1]   See for example, Mandelbaum (1955) and Smith (1993) for characterizations of these features and also those we
mention in the next paragraph.

[2]   Unless otherwise indicated, when we speak of the content of a judgment (or assertion) we mean its overall declarative content. Nondescriptivist cognitivism claims that *this* kind of content is cognitive, while also claiming that it is not
descriptive.

of cognitivism to accommodate the internalistic, action-guiding, aspect of moral judgments.

Insofar as the framework turns out to be independently plausible, however, the third task then arises: arguing that nondescriptivist cognitivism, as situated within the framework, is more plausible than descriptivism, and, in particular, is more plausible than the kind of descriptivist cognitivism that is situatable within the same framework (thereby successfully combining descriptivism with internalism). Addressing this issue is the business of section V.

The discussion in sections III–V thus will constitute an articulation of both the metaethical position we advocate and the reasons for embracing it. In section VI we make some observations about the philosophical methodology employed in the preceding sections, in order to underscore how our approach departs from standard metaethical debates not only in substance but also metaphilosophically.

III. A Framework for Belief and Assertion

We will describe a generic approach to belief and assertion that provides the backbone of our brand of nondescriptivist cognitivism. We begin with a characterization of the base-case for understanding beliefs and assertions, or, more precisely, those beliefs and assertions whose declarative content lacks truth-functional or quantificational complexity, and also lacks any embedded deontic operators, and then turn to cases that have that kind of logical complexity.

1. The base case

Speaking most generally, a base-case belief is a kind of psychological commitment state, of which there are two main species: *is-commitments* and *ought-commitments*. Beliefs of both sort have what we call *core descriptive content* – a way-the-world-might-be content. So, for instance, the belief that Bertie will mail the parcel, and the belief that Bertie ought to mail the parcel, share the same core descriptive content, expressible by the nonevaluative that-clause, *that Bertie mail the parcel*. A parallel point applies to assertions, about which we say more below.

An ordinary descriptive belief (purporting to represent how the world is) is an is-commitment with respect to a core descriptive content, and so the belief's declarative content coincides with its core descriptive content. For descriptive base-case beliefs and assertions, then, their overall declarative content is descriptive.

By contrast, an evaluative belief is an ought-commitment with respect to a core descriptive content. Evaluative beliefs differ essentially from descriptive beliefs in the following respect: the core descriptive content of an evaluative belief does not coincide with its overall declarative content. For instance, the belief that Bertie ought to mail the parcel is an ought-commitment with respect to the core content, *that Bertie mail the parcel*; however, its overall declarative content is *that it ought to be that Bertie mail the parcel*, and so its overall declarative content does not coincide with its core descriptive content. Thus, whereas descriptive beliefs involve an is-commitment – a how-it-is-with-the-world commitment with regard to a core descriptive content – moral beliefs involve a different type of commitment – a how-it-ought-to-be-with-the-world commitment with regard to a core descriptive content.[3]

Some observations are in order. First, we previously distinguished three species of content: declarative, cognitive, and descriptive, where we were focusing on an item's *overall* content. Moral judgments certainly have overall declarative content because their overall content is expressible by declarative sentences. Furthermore, within the framework we are proposing, their overall content is also *cognitive* content since they count as genuine beliefs. The framework is officially neutral, however, about whether or not their overall content is *descriptive* content. According to the metaethical position we will be advocating, moral beliefs do not have overall descriptive content, but the framework could be adopted by someone who thinks

---

[3] For simplicity's sake, we focus exclusively on moral beliefs expressible linguistically by the deontic operator 'it ought to be that', thus ignoring those kinds of moral beliefs expressible linguistically by operators like 'it is permissible that' and 'it is good that'. We leave open how exactly to understand these latter beliefs as types of evaluative commitment state, although we expect that our general approach to understanding ought-commitment states can be appropriately adapted to the understanding of evaluative commitment states of these other sorts.

their overall content is descriptive. (More on this below.)

Second, even if one denies that the overall content of moral judgments is descriptive content, there is still a kind of descriptive content that is possessed both by ordinary descriptive beliefs and by moral beliefs (as illustrated above in the pair of statements about Bertie). We introduced our notion of core descriptive content to refer to such content. Once one construes a base-case moral judgment as an ought-commitment with respect to a core descriptive content, conceptual space thereby opens up for the claim that the judgment's overall declarative content is cognitive content on the one hand (so that the state is a genuine *belief*), but is nondescriptive on the other hand. Even though the state is a genuine belief, by virtue of being an ought-commitment with respect to a core descriptive content, it doesn't follow that its overall declarative content is descriptive content.

Third, on standard accounts of these matters, a belief involves a relation between a believer (speaker) and a proposition (or sentence, or whatever) such that what is believed is something having overall descriptive content. This conception of belief presupposes the semantic assumption and makes the very idea of nondescriptivist cognitivism incoherent. By contrast, our framework opens up the possibility that certain genuine beliefs have overall declarative content that is not descriptive. Thus, the framework calls into question the common assumption that a belief is always a relation between a believer (speaker) on the one hand, and on the other hand a *proposition* constituting the belief's overall declarative content.

Fourth, in maintaining that there are two distinct base-case species of belief – is-commitments and ought-commitments – we are maintaining that states of both types exhibit certain generic kinds of functional and phenomenological features that qualify them as genuine beliefs. However, in maintaining that ought-commitments are a distinct kind of commitment, to be distinguished from is-commitments, we are also maintaining that ought-commitments exhibit certain functional and phenomenological features that are distinctive of this sort of judgment. We have noted the action-guiding character of typical moral judgments, and here it is worth mentioning that understanding base-case moral beliefs as essentially ought-commitments with regard to a core descriptive content, helps accommodate the widely shared internalist intuition that there is some intimate relation between having a moral belief and action. That is, the very idea of an ought-commitment suggests a kind of commitment oriented toward appropriate action vis-à-vis the specific core descriptive content of the belief. The way to understand this manner of action-orientation is by way of examining the role of such beliefs in the overall cognitive economy of agents.

Just as beliefs are psychological commitment states with a certain distinctive role in psychological economy, assertions are speech acts that play a certain distinctive sociolinguistic role – a role in interpersonal dynamics. An assertion is a *stance-taking* speech act, an act through which (i) one expresses an is-commitment or an ought-commitment with respect to a core descriptive content, and thereby (ii) one positions oneself, within the context of sociolinguistic dynamics, vis-à-vis that core content. A stance is an orientation thereby occupied, within an interpersonal situation. An ought-stance, in particular, is a distinctively *action-guiding* orientation. For instance, to take an ought-stance with respect to the core descriptive content, *Bertie's mailing the parcel*, is to engage in an action-guiding speech act whose role within interpersonal dynamics is importantly similar to the role of the corresponding psychological ought-commitment (the moral belief) within intrapersonal cognitive economy. This sociolinguistic role involves *reasons* for action, and a preparedness to provide them. By asserting that Bertie ought to mail the parcel, one normally signals one's willingness to defend one's ought-commitment on this matter over and against opposing ought-commitments, including a willingness to give reasons for such a commitment. Normally it is understood that the reasons one is prepared to give are of a certain distinctive kind that, e.g., appeal to impartial considerations bearing on the issue. In general, one enters the space of interpersonal moral discourse and reasoning bound by the sorts of conventions (often unstated and partly inchoate) that govern interpersonal deliberation and discussion about moral issues.

2. The framework continued: logically complex cases

We now generalize our framework, by extending it to beliefs and assertions whose overall declarative content has truth-functional and/or quantificational logical complexity, and/or embedded deontic operators. To begin with, let us restrict the notion of 'core descriptive content' to *atomic* descriptive content – the kind of content expressible by atomic sentences. Given this stipulation, here is the key idea for generalizing our approach: whereas a base-case belief is a *logically simple* commitment-state with respect to a *single* core descriptive content, a non-base-case belief is a *logically complex* commitment-state with respect to *several* core descriptive contents. Whereas base-case beliefs comprise two logically simple commitment-types (viz., is-commitment and ought-commitment), non-base-case beliefs comprise a whole recursive hierarchy of logically complex commitment-types, corresponding to the various logical forms that can be exhibited by logically complex declarative sentences. The essential feature of any given logically complex commitment-type is its distinctive *constitutive inferential role* in an agent's cognitive economy (insofar as the agent is rational), a role involving the relevant core descriptive contents.

First let us consider cases of moral belief exhibiting truth-functional complexity, i.e., complexity involving connectives but not quantifiers. On our view, such a belief is to be understood as a logically complex commitment-state with respect to a *sequence* of core descriptive contents. So, for example, consider the belief that *either Jeeves mailed the parcel or Bertie ought to mail the parcel*. This belief is a logically complex commitment-state of the logical type $[\phi \vee (Ought)\psi]$, with respect to the sequence of core descriptive contents <Jeeves mailed the parcel, Bertie mails the parcel>. The key to understanding this belief, and others of the same logical type, involves understanding their constitutive inferential role in the psychological economy of the agent. In particular, their role is to combine in a distinctive way with other beliefs (other commitment-states) to inferentially yield further beliefs (further commitment-states). One way to put the main idea about such logically complex commitment-states is that the simple constituents of complex commitment-states are logically 'in the offing' in the sense that the complex commitment-state involved in the disjunctive belief, when combined with an appropriate additional belief, rationally-inferentially yields an ought-commitment with declarative moral content. In the example at hand, the embedded

moral constituent, *Bertie ought to mail the parcel*, is in the offing in the sense that the complex commitment-state in question, together with the belief that Jeeves did not mail the parcel, inferentially yields (at least for the minimally rational agent) an ought-commitment with respect to Bertie's mailing the parcel.

Now consider cases of belief with quantificational complexity, i.e., complexity involving quantifiers (and perhaps connectives too). Such a belief is a logically complex commitment-state vis-à-vis a *set* of sequences of core descriptive contents. So, for instance, the belief that *anyone who pinched Uncle Willoughby's parcel ought to mail it*, is a logically complex commitment-state of the logical type $(\alpha)[\Phi\alpha \supset (Ought)\Psi\alpha]$, with respect to a set of sequences of core descriptive contents {<Bertie pinched the parcel, Bertie mails the parcel>, <Aunt Agatha pinched the parcel, Aunt Agatha mails the parcel>, ...}, etc. Again, the essential feature of this type of commitment-state is its constitutive inferential role in the psychological economy of the agent. For someone whose belief has the universally quantified declarative content in question, other beliefs with declarative moral content are 'in the offing' in the sense that the complex commitment involved in the universally quantified belief, when combined with an appropriate additional belief (e.g., the belief that Bertie pinched the parcel) rationally-inferentially yields an ought-commitment with declarative moral content (e.g., the belief that Bertie ought to mail the parcel).

The aspect of logical complexity arising from embedded 'Ought' operators gets accommodated too, within this framework. Each belief-type involving embedded deontic operators will have its distinctive, constitutive, inferential role in the psychological economy of the rational agent. It is the business of deontic logic to systematize these logical roles.

As we said, on this approach there is a whole recursive hierarchy of commitment-types of increasing logical complexity, corresponding to the hierarchy of increasingly complex logical forms exhibited by declarative sentences that can express the overall declarative content of a belief. Each such commitment is directed toward a core descriptive content, or a sequence of core descriptive contents, or a set of sequences of core descriptive contents. And each such commitment has a constitutive inferential role in psychological economy – a role involving the core descriptive content(s) toward which the commitment is directed.

These observations about beliefs with logically complex declarative content can be extended, *mutatis mutandis*, to assertions. Whereas a base-case assertion is a speech act of taking a *logically simple* stance with respect to a *single* core descriptive content, a non-base-case assertion is a speech act of taking a *logically complex* stance with respect to *several* core descriptive contents. A logically complex stance plays a constitutive inferential role in the dynamics of sociolinguistic intercourse that is analogous to the constitutive intra-psychological inferential role of logically complex beliefs. The constitutive inferential role is this: to combine with other sociolinguistic stances, taken by making additional assertions, to generate – often automatically and implicitly – certain further stances that are logically implied by one's overt stance-taking speech act. Implicit is-stances and ought-stances are thus 'in the offing' when one makes a logically complex assertion: such an assertion, in combination with appropriate additional ones, will logically generate implicit is-stances or ought-stances with respect to certain core descriptive contents.

Suppose, for example, that one asserts, *either Jeeves mailed the parcel or Bertie ought to mail the parcel*, and one also asserts *Jeeves did not mail the parcel*. The former assertion is a logically complex stance-taking speech act, of the logical type [ϕ ∨ (Ought)ψ], with respect to the sequence of core descriptive contents, <that Jeeves mailed the parcel, that Bertie mails that parcel>. The latter assertion is a speech act of logical type ~ϕ, with respect to the core descriptive content, that Jeeves mailed the parcel. In performing these two speech acts together, one thereby comes to occupy, as a matter of the logic of speech acts, an ought-stance with respect to the core descriptive content, that Bertie mails the parcel.

3. NDC as a consistent metaethical position

Our main task has been to provide a framework for belief and assertion that renders the basic tenets of NDC consistent. According to NDC, judgments and statements with moral content are genuine beliefs and assertions, having cognitive content, and yet the overall declarative content of such an item is not descriptive. If one accepts the semantic assumption, then such a view is outright inconsis-

tent (since according to that assumption cognitive content just is descriptive content). According to our framework this assumption is not taken for granted; it is quite consistent with our framework to hold that some beliefs and assertions lack overall descriptive content. Consider, once again, base-case moral beliefs and logically complex moral beliefs.

As we have already noted in passing, nothing in the notion of a base-case belief or assertion, construed as an ought-commitment with respect to a core descriptive content, forces on us the claim that the overall declarative content of a such a belief or assertion is descriptive content. And the point generalizes: in light of the previous section, nothing in the notion of a morality-involving logically complex belief (or assertion) – understood as a logically complex commitment with respect to a multiplicity of core descriptive contents (where what is essential about the belief or assertion is its constitutive inferential role) – forces on us the claim that the overall declarative content is descriptive. Thus, the position we call nondescriptivist cognitivism is rendered consistent by our proposed framework.

On the other hand, the framework certainly does not *entail* nondescriptivist cognitivism. Rather, it is neutral with respect to competing metaethical positions that recognize that moral thought and discourse involves genuine beliefs and assertions, that is, competing versions of cognitivism. In particular, our framework is consistent with descriptivist metaethical views. The descriptivist, that is, could grant what we have said about ought-commitments and is-commitments being distinct commitment types, and about beliefs and assertions with complex overall declarative content being logically complex commitments vis-à-vis core descriptive contents, without having to deny that morality-involving beliefs and assertions have overall descriptive content (the fundamental claim of the descriptivist). Our framework, recall, leaves open whether or not the overall declarative content of a moral belief is descriptive.

IV. On the Plausibility of the Framework

A critic might be inclined to say that we are trading in the implausibility of metaethical descriptivism, with its burdensome metaphysical commitments, for a complicated and *ad hoc* framework for belief and assertion, and thus that there is a more or less straight trade off – metaphysical extravagance for semantic complexity. Not so, however, as we will now explain.

Not only is the framework consistent with descriptivism (as already explained), but there is good reason for the descriptivist to embrace our framework: viz., doing so allows the descriptivist to accommodate strongly held and deeply shared internalist intuitions about moral thought and discourse. Adopting the framework, descriptivists would maintain that the belief that, e.g., Bertie ought to mail the parcel is *both* an is-commitment with respect to the overall declarative content (which they understand to be descriptive), *that it ought to be that Bertie mails the parcel*, and an ought-commitment with respect to the core descriptive content, *that Bertie mails the parcel*. Given the specific action-oriented functional role of ought-commitments and their distinctive phenomenology, descriptivists could thereby neatly combine their view with internalism. (The point generalizes to encompass morality-involving logically complex commitments as well, since action orientation is inferentially 'in the offing' for these too.) So descriptivists have no reason to suppose that our framework begs any important metaethical questions against them, and they have good reason to positively embrace it.

An adequate metaethical position should be faithful to the phenomena it seeks to understand. If the phenomena are sufficiently complex, then a corresponding degree of complexity in one's metaethical position is theoretically appropriate – not *ad hoc*. Moral judgment and moral discourse have internalist aspects – a form of complexity in the phenomena whose theoretical illumination evidently requires the kind of complexity exhibited by our proposed framework. So even descriptivists have ample reason to embrace the framework.

V.   Nondescriptivist Cognitivism versus Descriptivist Cognitivism

Although we will not attempt to explain why we think that all of the various traditional metaethical views are unsatisfying, we do want to say something about the plausibility of our view vis-à-vis descriptivist versions of cognitivism. Doing so is especially important because, as just explained, there is a version of internalist descriptivism that draws upon our own proposed generic framework for belief as a way of combining the idea that moral judgments are genuine beliefs (and moral statements are genuine assertions) with the idea that they are action-guiding. Why prefer our nondescriptivist cognitivism to descriptivism? In particular, why prefer our view to the kind of descriptivist cognitivism that accommodates the internalistic aspects of moral judgment and moral discourse?

We will briefly mention three philosophical reasons for doubting that the declarative content of moral beliefs is descriptive. First is what Jackson (1998) calls the *location problem* in ethics – the problem of locating putative moral facts and properties in the natural world. *Pace* Jackson and other moral realists, we do not think that the efforts of philosophers to locate moral facts and properties has been, or ever will be, successful. Here, we refer our readers to some of our past writings in which we show (so we think) that various realist attempts to solve the problem inevitably fail, and are destined to keep on failing. (See Horgan and Timmons 1991, 1992a, 1992b, 1996a, 1996b, and Timmons 1999.) Of course, even if one cannot solve the metaphysical location problem for ethics, one might, like Mackie, hold that affirmative moral judgments purport to describe or pick out worldly moral facts and properties and thus possess genuine descriptive cognitive content, but that there are no such facts and properties, i.e., one can embrace an error theory. So it may be granted that mere failure to solve the location problem is far from decisive evidence against descriptivism. But the location problem viewed in light of the next two problems is part of an overall case against descriptivist views in ethics.

Second, in arguing that moral judgments are a species of belief, part of our plan was to show that construing them as beliefs does not commit one to the further theoretical claim that they possess descriptive cognitive content. The point here is that attributing to such beliefs this sort of content is gratuitous for purposes of understanding them as beliefs and understanding their distinctive action-guiding role in our lives. In light of their psychological role and associated phenomenology, there simply is no apparent need to burden them with a kind of theoretical commitment which, given the location problem, cannot be discharged.

Third, the case against descriptivism receives additional support from considerations of conservatism with respect to the nature and evolution of human concepts. Applied to moral notions the argument would go like this. Moral discourse, and moral concepts employed in such discourse, play an indispensable role in human life that would survive rejection of the idea that there are objective moral facts that moral claims purport to describe. Indeed, after Mackie argued that all affirmative moral sentences are false because they involve (so he thought) metaphysical commitments to ontologically 'queer' properties, he did not advocate eliminating the use of moral concepts and moral discourse; rather, he went on to propose a normative ethical system based on a certain conception of human flourishing. Now if we assume that human concepts tend to evolve in a broadly pragmatic way and are thus not likely to have application conditions that are more demanding than is required for the purposes they serve, then the fact that moral discourse would survive the rejection of objective moral facts and properties strongly suggests that such discourse does not have any such metaphysical commitments.

VI.   Semantic Illumination
by Triangulation

Our main task is completed: we have sketched the rudiments of a new kind of metaethical theory, involving a generic conception of belief and assertion that renders the view a consistent position, and we have indicated briefly what virtues our view has vis-à-vis the more standard metaethical options. Obviously, filling out the theory and defending it against all relevant challenges would require a book or at least a series of articles. However, in the space remaining we will address, if only in a preliminary way, certain questions and matters of detail that have very likely occurred to the attentive reader. In this section we will make some remarks about philosophical methodology in relation to filling out our positive metaethical story about the semantics of moral thought and discourse. Then, in the following section, we will take up more specific questions concerning truth ascription, logical embedding, moral progress, and moral seriousness.

According to our nondescriptivist cognitivism, the contents of moral beliefs and assertions are *sui generis* in the sense that they cannot be reduced to

or analyzed as equivalent to other types of declarative or nondeclarative contents (or even a combination of the two). In this respect, our view is unlike older nondescriptivist views according to which, for instance, moral beliefs and assertions are essentially commands and so have prescriptive content as primary in addition to any descriptive content they may also possess. In rejecting all reductive semantic projects in relation to understanding moral thought and discourse, the appropriate response to questions like 'What is the content or meaning of moral judgment, M?' is simply to repeat the content of the judgment in question. Thus: 'What is the content of *Genocide is wrong?*' Answer: genocide is wrong. However, offering only such a disquotational response to these kinds of questions about content does not mean that our view is deeply mysterious or that we are obscurantists about matters of moral semantics. Quite the contrary. We maintain that one gains sufficient semantic illumination of the nature of nondescriptive cognitive content precisely by coming to understand the psychological states and speech acts that have it, *as* states and speech acts involving a certain distinctive kind of commitment (or stance-taking) with respect to certain core descriptive contents. Such understanding involves coming to appreciate in enough detail the psychological role and associated phenomenology definitive of the relevant psychological states, and, correspondingly, by coming to appreciate in enough detail the sort of sociolinguistic role of the relevant speech act. In short, illuminating the characteristic roles of moral thought and discourse helps one understand the *sui generis* kind of cognitive content moral beliefs and utterances possess. We call this kind of methodology for illuminating content, *triangulation*, which we have employed in sketching our semantic story about both base-case and logically complex moral beliefs and assertions. Thus our break with metaethical tradition involves not only our proposed metaethical theory but our methodology as well.

VII.   Work to be Done

We turn finally to various challenges that may have occurred to our readers, in order to indicate at least roughly how we propose to deal with them. Specifically, we take up issues of truth ascription, logical embedding, moral progress, and moral seriousness.

1.   *Truth ascription*

According to NDC, moral judgments are genuine beliefs, and moral utterances are genuine assertions. But the concepts of belief and assertion are linked by platitudes to the concept of truth: a belief is a psychological state that aims at truth; to assert is to set forth as true. How does our view deal with matters of truth? After all, being nondescriptivists, we claim that moral beliefs and associated speech acts lack overall descriptive content; they are not in the business of representing or purporting to describe the world.

On our view, the proper way to gain illumination about matters of truth in relation to moral thought and discourse is to focus on truth ascriptions to moral statements as metalinguistic speech acts, and ask about the nature of these speech acts. When one thinks or remarks, 'The claim that slavery ought to be stopped is true', what is one doing? The appropriate answer involves noting that such a truth ascription constitutes a *morally engaged* semantic appraisal: one that is infused with one's own moral commitment. The main idea can perhaps be conveyed by saying that truth ascriptions to moral statements involve a kind of appraisal in which semantic and moral are 'fused' – which is to be expected, since ordinary uses of the truth predicate operate in accordance with schema T.

In recent years, so-called minimalist treatments of truth have been developed and defended – views that attempt to make sense of truth ascription without robust metaphysical commitments. Our view is in the minimalist spirit though we would insist on two things. First, to understand truth minimalistically in one discourse does not commit one to minimalism in relation to every mode of discourse. Second, there is an interesting story to be told about moral truth ascription; our view is not a simple redundancy view.

2.   *Logical embedding*

A certain problem involving embedded contexts has been frequently pressed against various forms of nondescriptivism. One common way of raising the embedding challenge is to point out that inferences like the following seem to be valid: (1) one ought not to kill; (2) if one ought not to kill, then one ought not pay someone to kill; thus, (3) one ought not pay someone to kill. The problem for, say, an emotivist is that according to emotivism, the meaning of premise (1) is to be understood in terms of its noncognitive emotive role in thought and assertion, viz., to express one's emotion and influence the attitudes of others. However, in premise (2), where (1) occurs as the antecedent of the conditional, (1) is not expressed with its typical emotive role; one who affirms premise (2) is not thereby committed to affirming its antecedent. But then it appears that one has to say that 'one ought not to kill' differs in meaning in its two occurrences in the argument which implies that, despite appearances, the argument is not valid; it commits the fallacy of equivocation. The critic pressing this objection presumably thinks that only if moral statements have descriptive content, and so can be understood in terms of some set of descriptive truth conditions – something that a statement carries from unembedded to embedded contexts – can we make sense of moral modus ponens and other such valid inferences.

Our reply to this challenge is implicit in our above discussion of logical complexity. In developing our framework in connection with logically complex moral beliefs and assertions, we noted that the declarative content of such beliefs and statements can be triangulated in terms of their constitutive inferential role in modus ponens and other argument forms. Thus, the conditional statement, 'If one ought not to kill, then one ought not pay someone to kill', is to be understood primarily in terms of its role in mediating inference from an affirmation of its antecedent to an affirmation of its consequent, as in the little argument featured above. So on our view, to get a handle on embedded moral claims involves understanding the role of the kinds of logically complex statements that embed them. What one can say about the contents of embedded and unembedded occurrences of some one moral claim is that (1) they share the same core descriptive content, (2) in an embedded context an ought-commitment with respect to that core content is 'suspended', but nevertheless (3) the overall claim containing the embedded context expresses a logically complex commitment state whose constitutive role in inference is such that an ought-commitment with respect to the relevant core descriptive content is 'in the offing'. To make these observations, we think, is to make sense of valid inference involving embedded moral constituents.

Often when the embedding issue is raised, those posing the challenge assume that one must first give an account of the meaning of moral statements, and then show that their meaning (according to the given account) remains constant when the statements are embedded. But, given our proposed framework for belief and assertion, this methodological assumption gets called into question. On our approach, *what it is* for a statement S with nondescriptive cognitive content to have constant meaning, whether unembedded or in various embedded contexts, *just is* for the states and speech acts whose overall declarative content includes S (i.e., whose overall declarative content is expressible by a statement with S as constituent) to figure in certain specific constitutive inferential connections involving S's core descriptive content. This is a dialectical reversal, turning the standard embedding problem on its head. (Remember: on our approach, one explains nondescriptive cognitive content by explaining the psychological states and speech acts that have it, *as* certain distinctive kinds of psychological or sociolinguistic commitments with respect to certain core descriptive contents. Such commitments bear constitutive inferential connections to one another.)

3. Moral progress and taking morality seriously

For a descriptivist-realist, intellectual moral progress is a matter of one's moral beliefs coming to better approximate the moral facts. But if moral belief and assertion are not primarily in the business of describing or representing in-the-world moral facts, then how can we make sense of genuine moral progress? Put another way, how can our view distinguish between mere change in moral belief and genuine progress? And, relatedly, if there is no metaphysical anchor for moral thought and discourse, then why take it seriously, why not construe moral discussion and disputes as being more like disputes about matters of taste?

These challenges focus on our irrealist moral metaphysics, and we consider them to be some of the most difficult for any moral irrealist. Here, then, is an indication of how we would respond to these challenges, though they certainly deserve a more thorough reply than we can offer here.

Of course, on our view, moral progress of the sort in question is not to be understood as a matter of bringing one's beliefs into closer proximity to a realm of moral facts. We propose that, instead, one think of moral progress as something to be judged from within a committed moral outlook: when one makes judgments about moral improvement, one does so from an engaged moral perspective. In judging, for example, that moral progress was made in the United States with the rejection of slavery, we are employing our current moral outlook and not simply registering the fact that one moral reaction to slavery was replaced with another; we are making a moral judgment about slavery which we think is backed by reasons. This way of dealing with moral progress is very much akin to what Wright says about the notion of moral progress available to a minimalist about moral truth.

> [T]he minimalist will have to admit that such ideas of progress, or deterioration, are ones for which we can have use only from *within* a committed moral point of view; and that the refinement of which our moral sensibilities are capable can only be a matter of approaching a certain equilibrium as appraised by the exercise of those very sensibilities. (Wright, 1992: 168–9).

Again, we think the challenge to make sense of moral seriousness does not require some metaphysical backing for moral thought and discourse. Rather, on our view, the challenge regarding moral seriousness is plausibly understood as a *moral* challenge: why ought we take our moral views seriously? And the appropriate response to such a challenge is to give moral reasons – reasons that, for instance, will likely appeal to the important role of morality in people's lives. Like our reply to the moral progress challenge, our reply here is to view the challenge as one to be appropriately dealt with from within a committed moral outlook.[4]

VIII. Conclusion

We think it is time for a change in metaethics, and only by challenging certain pervasive philosophical assumptions is one likely to make progress. Our proposal is to rethink fundamental assumptions about the nature of belief and assertion; specifically, we challenge the idea that all belief-eligible and assertible contents are descriptive – what we

---

[4] For some elaboration of the various challenges and replies featured in this section, see Timmons (1999: ch. 4).

call the semantic assumption. We have set forth a framework for belief and assertion that does not presuppose the semantic assumption, thus allowing for the *possibility* of beliefs and assertions that are not descriptive. Nondescriptivist cognitivism embraces the framework, and also maintains that the overall declarative content of moral beliefs and assertions is *in fact* not descriptive. The virtues of this metaethical position are great. It surely deserves to be taken seriously as a theoretical option in metaethics. Indeed, we submit that it ought to be the default view.

References

Horgan, T. and M. Timmons. 1991. 'New Wave Moral Realism Meets Moral Twin Earth'. *Journal of Philosophical Research* XVI: 447–65. Reprinted in *Rationality, Morality, and Self-Interest*, edited by John Heil, Rowman & Littlefield (1993): 115–33.

Horgan, T. and M. Timmons. 1992a. 'Troubles on Moral Twin Earth: Moral Queerness Revived'. *Synthese* 92: 221–60.

Horgan, T. and M. Timmons. 1992b. 'Troubles for New Wave Moral Semantics: The Open Question Argument Revived'. *Philosophical Papers* 21: 153–75.

Horgan, T. and M. Timmons. 1996a. 'From Moral Realism to Moral Relativism in One Easy Step'. *Critica* 38: 3–39.

Horgan, T. and M. Timmons. 1996b. 'Troubles for Michael Smith's Metaethical Rationalism'. *Philosophical Papers* 25: 203–31.

Jackson, Frank. 1998. *From Metaphysics to Morals*. Oxford and New York: Oxford University Press.

Mandelbaum, Maurice. 1955. *The Phenomenology of Moral Experience*. Glencoe, IL: The Free Press.

Smith, Michael. 1993. 'Objectivity and Moral Realism: On the Significance of the Phenomenology of Moral Experience'. In J. Haldane and C. Wright, eds., *Reality, Representation and Projection*. Oxford: Oxford University Press.

Timmons, M. 1999. *Morality without Foundations: A Defense of Ethical Contextualism*. New York: Oxford University Press.

Wright, Crispin. 1992. *Truth and Objectivity*. Cambridge, MA: Harvard University Press.

6

The Reasons of a Living Being

Allan Gibbard

When I came to the University of Michigan twenty-five years ago, Charles Stevenson had just retired, and I came to occupy his budget line. Over the next few years, this seems to have had a deep effect on me. Previously I had thought hard about moral disputes and what is at issue in them, but I had just been baffled; I hoped some solution would turn up. Now some Stevenson-like ways of tackling the puzzle began to occur to me, and I convinced myself that they have more power than I had previously thought possible. Perhaps I had good reason to be convinced – or perhaps you'll find it was just the subliminal influence of the budget line.

The puzzle about moral issues was Moore's puzzle, the one that G. E. Moore made especially vivid a century ago. As we all learn at our philosophical parents' knees, Moore argued that moral questions concern a non-natural property. When we try to settle a moral question, he maintained, we're not in the same line of inquiry as when we use empirical, scientific methods to inquire into the natural world. Notoriously, Moore had an "open question" argument which seems in retrospect to be dubious, and a "naturalistic fallacy" which he put in many different ways, all of which seem to beg the question. Later on he saw his first book as terribly confused. But he had another line of argument which, it seems to me,

just won't go away; I call it the "What's at issue?" argument.

Jack, imagine, claims that all pleasure is good in itself, but Jill says that guilty pleasures are not in themselves good. So Jack says that all pleasure is intrinsically good, and Jill disagrees. What's at issue in all this? The two disagree about something, sure enough – but what? Jack, imagine, adds that after all, 'good' just *means* pleasant. But if he is right about what 'good' means, then they can't be disputing whether all pleasure is good, for they both agree that all pleasure is pleasant. Take any proferred definition of 'good', Moore argued, and we can construct a similar puzzle for it. Now whether any Moore-like argument can be made to work is still a matter of controversy, but Moore does, with this argument, offer us a broad test for any account of what moral claims consist in: ask what's at issue. What, according to the account, is at issue in moral disputes? What does the disagreement consist in? Some accounts, even today, fail to offer plausible answers to this question.

Charles Stevenson thought that Moore's arguments on this score worked, or at least that he could find arguments like Moore's that worked. And Stevenson had an answer to the "What's at issue?" challenge: Jack's for and Jill's not. What's at issue is what pleasures to aim for. Jack intrinsically favors all pleasure, whereas Jill withholds intrinsic favor from guilty pleasures. The two disagree not in belief about some special property; instead, they disagree in attitude.

Now of course much happened philosophically in Stevenson's three decades at Michigan, and the influence of his budget line wasn't going to reproduce in me exactly Stevenson's original theory. I'm taken also with A. J. Ayer's original way of putting things – and eventually, Ayer and Stevenson each took on board aspects of the other's approach. My own view isn't either of theirs; it isn't a form of emotivism. But devices that Ayer, Stevenson, and others invented in the mid-1930s turn out, I claim, to be more powerful than even they realized.

The issues now seem much broader than just morality. My teacher and colleague Richard Brandt talked of what it's *rational* to do or to support. Wilfrid Sellars talked of the "space of reasons". We can broaden the puzzle the great non-naturalists and emotivists addressed, to one of rationality, or to something grandiose like "the place of reasons in a natural world". Reasons are what weigh toward something's being rational. What's puzzling in moral disputes, then, may boil down to what's puzzling about reasons – reasons to do things, reasons to believe things, and the like. What reasons do you have to help others? Do you have reason to care if they suffer, apart from how their suffering comes to affect you? How do you have reason to feel about someone who preys on others? Is the pleasure something brings you always reason to favor it?

Reasons are puzzling, and one of the puzzles is this: We are living beings, and as such, we are parts of the world of nature. In the natural world, though, clearly we are exceptional. Our species has developed refined and ingenious ways of studying the natural world, and these methods tell us of many ways in which we are exceptional. For one thing, of course, we are living, and life is so unlike anything else in the universe that it long seemed that the only possible explanation was a special vital principle. Since Darwin, though, we begin to see how aeons of natural selection can account for why life, viewed as part of nature, is so different from non-life. Even among living organisms we are exceptional, and the human brain is vastly more complex than anything else we know about. Human history, politics, social life, learning, and the arts are far more complex than anything even in the life of chimpanzees, though the genetic equipment that allows a human child to grow up to participate in

all this is just a last minute evolutionary tinkering, over the past couple of hundred thousand generations, with a tiny proportion of chimp DNA. Biological thinking may give some hints as to how natural selection worked to shape the potentialities of a human infant. We can get some idea of how babies equipped with these potentialities grow up, in interaction with older people who all started out as babies, to become the human adults we know. Lore, literature, and common sense tell us much, and psychology and social sciences at their best can extend this knowledge and help us integrate it into what we know of the workings of the natural world.

We are exceptional, though, in ways that seem to resist incorporation into any such scientific picture. We have thoughts and opinions and we make assertions to each other. We are conscious of colors and feelings. And crucially, we have reasons to do things Imagine a science of humanity so successful that it could explain, in terms of levels of complexity built on fundamental physics, the sound waves that come from my mouth, all the neuronal patterns in your heads as a result, and all the movements of our limbs and fingers for the next week. Such a science would have to show us as exceptional indeed in the universe. But throughout the era of modern natural science, at least since Galileo and Descartes and Hobbes, crucial parts of philosophy have tackled what's exceptional about us and seems to be left out of the picture. Philosophy is always dealing with how to make sense of new findings in science, thinking how they might transform our visions of ourselves and our surroundings, or how they might fit in with things we always thought we knew. That is by no means all that philosophy does, but questions of what to make of the scientific image form a significant part of our job. And so we ask where in a naturalistic picture of ourselves are beliefs, consciousness, and reasons.

Moore thought that moral facts somehow lie outside the world that empirical science can study. We can broaden this to a claim about the space of reasons as a whole, which, we can say, lies outside the space of causes. The "space of reasons" is the whole realm of normativity, to use a less picturesque, more technical term in the philosopher's lexicon. This is the realm of *oughts*, we might say, for what I ought to do is what the reasons that pertain weigh all told toward doing. The reasons to do something, as T. M. Scanlon puts it, are considerations that count in favor of doing it.

Now Stevenson and Ayer devised a cluster of strategies which I want to broaden. (I should warn you that I'll play rather free with their doctrines and motivations, as I've already been doing.) Moral claims, they agreed with Moore, aren't claims that can form part of the empirical sciences. But still, we can understand what we are doing when we make moral claims: according to Ayer, we are expressing emotions or attitudes. There is a broad strategy at work here, a strategy that has come to be known as *expressivism*. (All names that I know of for this strategy are misleading, but this one, I think, is the least unsatisfactory.) To explain the meaning of a term, to explain the concept that the term conveys, don't offer a straight definition. For normative terms, Moore and the non-naturalists are right that no definition in non-normative terms will capture the meaning. Instead, explain the states of mind that the uses of the term *express* – and don't just explain it as the "belief" that so-and-so. Trivially, normative statements express normative beliefs or judgments. Ayer and Stevenson proposed that moral judgments are feelings or attitudes. I have said that we can broaden the question of meanings to cover normative terms in general. Suppose, then, we try the expressivist twist on oughts in general. What kind of state of mind do *ought* claims express?

Ayer stressed the difference between expressing an attitude and saying that one has it. It is, as our pedagogical lore has it, the difference between saying "Boo for lying" and saying "I'm against it." This difference is subtle, since either one of these speech acts gets the hearer to think the speaker is against lying. Stevenson's talk of disagreement, though, lets us get at the difference. If you say "I'm against it," then literally, I disagree if I think you're not against it. If you say "Boo for lying," I disagree only if I disagree with your opposition to lying. What's at issue in the two cases, then, is different: With "I'm against it", what's literally at issue is your state of mind, whereas if you say "Boo!", what's at issue are feelings.

What's at issue with *oughts* in general, then? Jack and Jill need water, imagine, but the hill is slippery. I say that Jack ought now to go up the hill, but you disagree. What's at issue between us? Isn't the issue what to do? It's not an issue of what to do in your case or in mine, but somehow in Jack's, in Jack's shoes. When we explore together what Jack ought to do, we engage in a kind of hypothetical contingency planning. We put our heads together and think the problem through as if on Jack's behalf. Jack himself thinks fleetingly what to do, and decides to follow Jill up the hill. When he falls and breaks his crown and the dangers become more vivid to him, he may come to disagree with that earlier decision. You and I address the same problem as Jack himself rethinks: what to do in his original situation. You disagree, perhaps, with Jack's decision to go up the hill, whereas I agree with it. Switching to normative language, we can describe our states of mind like this: you and Jack both think he ought not to have gone up the hill, whereas I disagree: given the need for water, I conclude, getting the water was, in prospect, worth the danger.

Why should you or I plan, though, for such a fantastic contingency? Why, for that matter, should Jack rethink his decision, when the moving finger has writ and he can't unbreak his crown? It's clear enough why to plan for some contingencies you might face – a traffic jam on the Dan Ryan Expressway, say, when you want to drive south. Why, though, plan for contingencies you know you won't face – such as Jack's choice of whether to go up the hill? Well of course, mostly we don't. Even if I am right that *ought* thoughts are plans, we don't usually worry ourselves with whether, in light of the needs and the dangers, Jack ought to have gone up the hill. But we do do considerable planning for how to cope with needs and dangers; that is a crucial part of life to plan for. Jack reconsiders after the fact because he will face such choices again; he is engaged in a kind of rehearsal for further such choices. You and I might join him in this, considering Jack's plight as an exercise in planning for life. Just as Jack might disagree with his earlier decision and so emerge wiser from the calamity, so might you or I. Of course mostly, when we engage scenarios and the places one might hypothetically occupy in them, we aren't thinking to some aforethought purpose – any more than children play to develop their skills and social knowledge, or you read a novel to sharpen your powers of social apprehension. We humans are just built to engage in such activities, and it's a good thing we are, since doing so functions as rehearsal for later eventualities. We are curious about *oughts* as well as *iss*.

There is a place in our lives, then, for planning even for the wildest of contingencies. Still, does this really vindicate disagreement in plan? Why treat your plans and mine for Jack's plight as anything on which we could disagree with each other?

You have your plans and I have mine; why isn't that just a difference between us as with age, height, or tastes? You have a flatter head than I do, suppose: that's not a disagreement between us; it's just a difference in how we are. You plan, for the contingency of Jack's plight, to stay safe and waterless at the foot of the hill, whereas I plan, as did Jack, to go up the hill with Jill. Isn't this just another difference in our biographies? How is it a disagreement?

What you are to do in Jack's plight and what I am to do are not separate questions: Jack's exact circumstances include everything about him, and our question is what to do if one is *he* – and thus exactly like him in every respect in which we differ. Still, why treat that as something you and I can discuss and agree on or disagree on? That, I say, is because we need to be able to put our heads together. Often we need to think cooperatively, treating each other's thoughts like thoughts that occur to oneself, to be considered and supported or refuted, to be accepted or rejected. It is not always good for a person to think alone.

So let's extend Stevenson to say that there is such a thing as disagreement in plan. You and I can disagree on what to do if in Jack's situation, with all his characteristics. This, note, isn't the same thing as "disagreement in attitude" as Stevenson used the phrase. His disagreement in attitude is disagreement as to what shall happen. Imagine a pacifist who is meek on principle and a bully who takes advantage of this and slaps the pacifist's cheek. When it comes to what shall happen, the two might both favor the same thing: that the pacifist turn the other cheek. On this one point, the two agree in Stevensonian attitude: they both favor the same thing's happening. But they disagree in plan; they disagree on what to do if in the shoes of the pacifist. The bully plans to strike back in such cases, but the pacifist instead turns the other cheek. The bully is planning, to be sure, for the contingency of being someone who is meek on principle, someone who is going, as it happens, to turn the other cheek. But the bully disagrees with the pacifist's plan. The bully's hypothetical preference for the pacifist's situation is to snap out of his pacifism and strike back. The two disagree in plan, then, for the contingency of being the stricken pacifist.

Now the possibility of such disagreement in plan, I claim, has far-reaching consequences. I'll sketch a few of them, though I won't really be able to argue for what I say; I want rather to contemplate what happens if these claims are true. One chief consequence is that we can deal with complex normative claims. We get an answer to the Frege–Geach challenge to expressivism. The mother admonishes, "If lying is wrong, then getting your brother to lie is wrong too." Starting with the notion of disagreement, we can say canonically what the content of such a plan-laden claim is. The mother has come out in disagreement with any plan to shun lying but get one's brother to lie. In general, to get the content of a plan-laden claim, we map all the combinations of pure plans and pure factual beliefs with which the claim is in disagreement. Disagreement is the key to content; content is what there is to agree or disagree with. So allowing for disagreement in plan gives us plan-laden content – normative content.

A second chief consequence will sound surprising, coming from an expressivist. In a sense, it follows, normative terms like 'ought' refer to properties and relations – indeed to properties and relations that are natural, that can figure in an empirical science of humanity. My argument for this is transcendental: As planners, capable of agreement or disagreement in plan, we are each committed to this naturalistic-sounding thesis. Once we establish this thesis as one to which we are all committed, this thesis of natural constitution, we can proceed to assert it: There is a natural property that constitutes being what one ought to do. Thus we are all committed to agreeing, in a way, with normative naturalists: the term 'ought' refers, in a sense, to a natural property.

And what property is this? The question is not linguistic; rather, it's the grand, basic question in ethics, the question of how to live. You accept an answer to this question if you have fully thought out what to live for and have come to a conclusion. Consider a view that fits some aspects of Henry Sidgwick's doctrines: A universal hedonist whom I'll call Henry plans always, in every conceivable contingency, to do whatever holds out maximal prospects for net pleasure in the universe. Henry, then, has a view about the property that constitutes being what one ought to do. It is, he says, the property of being *unihedonic*, as we might call it: the property of holding out maximal prospects for net pleasure in the universe.

Henry, then, accepts this thesis of natural constitution. Indeed not only does he think that there's a natural property that constitutes being what one ought to do; he has a view on what it is. Many of us, though, don't have anything like a complete contingency plan for what to pursue in life, or a formula for constructing such a plan. Still, I claim, we are each committed to the thesis of natural constitution. For suppose you are at least consistent. Then the thesis is something you'd accept if, fantastically, you completely filled out your views on how to live, and did so without changing your mind about anything. Any way of filling out your plans, becoming hyperdecided on how to live, brings with it accepting the thesis of natural constitution. So it's something you are already committed to as you think your way toward a fuller view of how to live. It's something that obtains, you can say, no matter what turns out to be the way to live.

Now I don't mean you to be convinced by this cryptic sketch of an argument. Even if I had succeeded in making the argument clear, it would raise many issues I can't quickly resolve. I want to sketch the possibility, though, of a view of normative concepts that has us sounding like expressivists, like non-naturalists, and like naturalistic realists in important respects – all at the same time. We start out with devices of the classic emotivists: with disagreement in plan reminiscent of Stevenson, and with Ayer's talk of expressing a state of mind. We let the state of mind in question be a kind of contingency planning for living. As Ayer and Stevenson saw, we derive Moore's conclusion that normative concepts aren't naturalistic. Two people might agree, in naturalistic terms, on all the natural facts and still disagree basically in plan. Something is at issue between them, but not something we can put in naturalistic terms. It's a question of *how to live*. Still, as naturalistic realists insist, normative terms like 'ought' do signify natural properties. That's something that Ayer and Stevenson didn't say, but it falls out as a consequence of some of their ways of thinking.

Simon Blackburn coined the term 'quasi-realism' for a program like this one. We start out without helping ourselves to ethical and other normative properties. Then, we earn the right to speak as realists do. Indeed we may be hard pressed to identify any real differences between naturalistic realism, non-naturalistic realism, and expressivism, once these positions are suitably refined. We may have a happy convergence of different approaches to metanormative theory. I think of what I'm sketching as filling out this program that Blackburn proposed. My impression is that Blackburn is skeptical of the extremely metaphysical-sounding claims that I have been sketching here, but if those claims are right, then perhaps they fit Blackburn's program.

Everything I have been saying depends on a distinction that has been in the air in recent decades but which wasn't much around when Ayer and Stevenson were doing most of their work. It's the distinction between properties and concepts. The property of being water, we can say, turns out to be the property of being H_2O, of consisting in molecules of a certain kind. Still, the concepts are different: the prescientific concept of being water isn't the scientific concept of being H_2O. It was a live question at one time whether water was H_2O, a question on which people could coherently disagree. People disagreed as to whether water is H_2O; they didn't disagree as to whether water is water. We can ask what was at issue. Disagreement, then, is a matter of concepts, not properties: it isn't always preserved when we substitute distinct concepts of the same property.

Once we have this distinction, we can say this: All properties are natural, but some concepts of properties aren't descriptive and naturalistic. Some concepts find their place not in naturalistic description but in planning. Suppose, then, that Henry the universal hedonist is right on how to live: the thing to promote in life is the happiness of all. Then the property of being what one ought to do just *is* the property of being unihedonic, of holding out maximal prospects for total net pleasure in the universe. But the concept of ought is distinct from the concept of being unihedonic. For a perfectionist Percella can dispute with Henry: Percella says that the unihedonic thing isn't always what one ought to do. Henry understands her – and nothing about logic or our linguistic conventions by itself settles who is right. Percella and Henry have the same concepts; that's why they can engage each other's claims and not just talk past each other. Henry is right, we are supposing, and so the terms 'ought' and 'unihedonic' refer to the same natural property. But conceptually, Percella is coherent. Once she explains what perfection consists in, on her view, we know what's at issue between her and Henry. It's whether to live for universal happiness or to attain that kind of perfection.

This scheme, as I've been saying, has attractive features. Some tenets of Sidgwick's and Moore's ethical intuitionism seem hard to escape, and the scheme delivers these tenets. The inescapable tenets consist, it turns out, just in what we have to accept if we are to plan our lives coherently and intelligibly. We don't need non-natural properties, just the kinds of non-descriptive, non-naturalistic concepts that would have to figure in planning. Normative concepts do signify natural properties, we can say, but they have their own special way of doing so. The scheme respects normative thinking: it avoids any blanket debunking of it – though we should still debunk certain theories of what normative thinking consists in. And it's a good thing that we can see normative thinking as inescapable in intelligent living. For normative thinking figures in a wide range of areas that we couldn't give up as nonsense. Normative epistemology, for instance, we can now say, consists in contingency plans for forming beliefs. It's a serious question, for instance, whether the evidence supports a Darwinian theory of natural selection, and more broadly, what the canons of scientific evidence are. I take these to be planning questions, questions of how much credence to put in theories given various epistemic contingencies. They are questions of what we ought to believe. Oughts are to be found even in places far from ethics.

Is this picture I have given, though, a naturalistic one? Does it really let us dispense with all mumbo jumbo of a non-natural realm? Not exactly: We can view ourselves as complex products of natural selection and the kind of cultural history that natural selection could make possible. We can see, in these terms, why beings like us might be interpretable as planners who share our planning thoughts. Suppose we view ourselves this way, and suppose furthermore, we interpret such natural beings as keeping track of what disagrees with what. Then we are interpreting ourselves as having normative thoughts. We can see, in short, why natural beings like us would be plausibly interpretable as having normative thoughts.

The scheme I have been sketching has a further happy consequence: If you start out as a non-naturalist, you have to accept certain features of the space of reasons as just brute normative facts: for instance, that the normative supervenes on the natural. Once we see normative facts as plans, we see why this supervenience is something that any planner is committed to. Plans must be couched in empirical, naturalistic terms because we have to be able to recognize the situations the plans address. A plan to do whatever there's most reason to do, for instance, is no plan at all, until it's supplemented by an account of how to recognize what

there's most reason to do. With this supplement, the plan is in effect couched in empirical terms.

On the other hand, the scheme in no way lets us substitute naturalistic thinking for normative thinking. Instead it follows Moore in concluding that there's just no substitute for normative thinking. And moreover, it doesn't tell us how to translate, in strictly naturalistic terms, claims about people's normative states of mind. Take the claim, "Jack is convinced that he ought to go up the hill." I haven't indicated how to translate such a psychological claim into terms that fit a broadly Galilean picture of the universe. Imagine we understood Jack completely as a physical system. Imagine we understood him, at many different levels of explanation, as a product of natural selection and a vastly complex human ecology. This would include grasping the explanatory patterns of his neurophysiology, understanding how evolutionary signaling theory applies to his patterns of neural firings and the sound waves that come out of his mouth, and all sorts of things like that. My hope is that the expressivistic scheme I've sketched would then let us see why Jack, so viewed, is conveniently interpretable as thinking that he ought to go up the hill.

He'd be conveniently interpretable that way, I'm saying. For Jack, viewed as a natural system, is conveniently interpretable as keeping track of his surroundings. (We have some naturalistic idea, for instance, how rats keep track of their position in a maze.) He'll be conveniently interpretable as planning, and we can conveniently interpret him as agreeing and disagreeing with combinations of plan and mundane fact. And that, I'm saying, is all we need if we are to interpret him as having normative thoughts.

I'm speaking of convenient interpretation, how a natural being, viewed naturalistically, might be conveniently interpreted. But how much does this establish if true? For anything I've claimed, a convenient interpretation might be no more than a convenient fiction – like the stupidities we attribute to the computers on our desks. When Jack is conveniently interpretable as thinking he ought to go up the hill, is that what he's really convinced of? Is he really thinking he ought to go up the hill?

That, I have implied, is a question of agreement and disagreement: for issues of meaning and interpretation, as I've been harping, agreement and disagreement are the key. What Jack accepts by way of *ought*s and *is*s, I've been saying, is a question of which possible states of mind he disagrees with and which he doesn't. Now I haven't offered any naturalistic translation of claims about disagreement. And if I did, my translation might be subject to Moore-like challenges. Do Jack and Jill really disagree with each other on whether he ought to go up the hill? Suppose you and I disagree on this question of how to interpret the two. What's then at issue between *us*? That is Moore's challenge, transferred from ethics to the theory of meaning itself. It's a question about the meaning of meaning, or the meaning of claims about mental content, claims about what people are thinking. And I have not said, or even sketched, how to respond.

Issues of meaning and mental content may in part themselves be normative issues. A number of leading philosophers have asserted that they are, and whether meaning is in some sense "normative" is a daunting question. The question has received intensive scrutiny over the past decade or two, and the issues still aren't entirely clarified. Perhaps to understand claims about what Jack really is thinking, you have to understand about commitments, or about correctness – and the concepts of commitment and correctness seem to be normative ones. Take two claims that contradict each other: Jack thinks, imagine, that snow is white whereas Jill thinks that nothing is white. Jack and Jill disagree – and this implies, among other things, that we ought not to accept both these claims at once. We ought not both to accept that snow is white and to accept that nothing is white – that's a normative claim. Claims about states of mind and their content seem themselves, then, to be fraught with ought. Some philosophers argue that this appearance dissolves on close scrutiny, and I'm not claiming to establish this "normativity of meaning" thesis or even urging us to accept it. But I'm not denying it either. Perhaps the right theory of normative thinking must itself be a normative theory. Perhaps Robert Brandom is right, and it's norms all the way down.

If so, then the account we end up with won't be strictly expressivistic or strictly quasi-realistic, by a stringent standard of what qualifies under these terms. That is to say, it won't fit the following pattern: that it starts out helping itself to a purely non-normative reality, and ends up, all on its own, earning our right to realistic ways of talking about oughts.

Still, the account is expressivistic in a weaker sense. It draws on central philosophical devices of Ayer and Stevenson. And if it succeeds in its ambition, it makes clear how natural beings like us would be conveniently interpretable as having *ought* thoughts. As for whether this interpretation would really get things right, perhaps we should take this question with a grain of salt. Suppose none of our uncertainties were scientific: we understood Jack completely in purely naturalistic terms, insofar as beings like him or us can be understood in naturalistic terms. Suppose you and I none the less have competing interpretations of Jack, and that these interpretations both are as convenient as can be. As Moore might ask, what's then at issue between us? Perhaps nothing real at all is at issue. That is a familiar enough conclusion in the past half century of philosophy, with Quine and in his wake. We can perhaps be skeptics about picky questions of meaning that go beyond questions of convenient interpretability.

With normative questions, in contrast, it is hard to be a skeptic; it's hard to take the questions with too many grains of salt. The question of what to do is inescapable. Sartre's man who asks himself whether to join the resistance or take care of his mother can't dismiss the question as nonsense. When he comes to a decision, he has accepted an answer to a normative question, the question of what he ought to do in the circumstance.

Or at least, he has come to a normative view *if* a big if is satisfied. He has reached an ought conclusion *if* there is such a thing as agreement and disagreement in plan, if we can come to agree or disagree with his conclusion. Whether there is such a thing as disagreement in plan, though, is a deep question – as I have indicated. You and I can certainly think what to do if in this Frenchman's exact circumstances, and form a different plan from his. The deep question is why to treat this as any sort of disagreement. Why think there is such a thing as disagreement in plan? My answer has gone in two stages. First, in planning I have to be able to change my mind, and this amounts to disagreeing with things I had concluded earlier. Second, in thinking how to live, we need each other's help.

Disagreement in plan, I have been saying, is the key to explaining normative concepts – that along with Ayer's distinction between expressing a state of mind and saying that one is in it. The concepts we explain with these devices act much as the classic non-naturalists recount. Explanatory devices we get from the classic emotivists Ayer and

Stevenson, then, lead us to crucial aspects of Sidgwick, Moore, Ross, and Ewing. Now if we really get this much convergence, that should be grounds for celebration: perhaps we're really getting at what's going on with *is* and *ought*. Of course, whether we do achieve this convergence is bound to go on being controversial – and legitimately so, as we work to understand better the tangle of issues in play. The convergence also leaves the question, though, whether an expressivism that draws on Ayer and Stevenson tells non-naturalistic normative realists anything they didn't know before.

Let me review, then, some of the ways that Ayer's and Stevenson's devices lead to illumination, if I am right. First of all, Ayer's and Stevenson's devices let us take what comes across a mystery, as Moore presents it, and see it in terms of something familiar and fairly comprehensible. We can explain ought convictions as plans, oughts as deliverances of planning. Second, the brute features of Moore's non-natural realm fall out as things a coherent planner would have to believe in. We get supervenience of the normative on the natural, and get something that fits Moore's talk of "*the* good" as something natural: there's a natural property, I've been saying, that constitutes being what one ought to do.

So do we eliminate the mumbo jumbo of a non-natural realm we can intuit? Not exactly, but we see why a being like you or me would have to be interpretable as committed to this mumbo jumbo. We work toward a naturalistic view of why we'd have to be so interpretable. All this is in a world where all properties are natural – though non-naturalistic concepts apply to it, and we can see why.

We ourselves are parts of the natural world we study, and the moral, perhaps, is that this makes for concepts that aren't just naturalistic classifications of nature. I have been exploring some ways all this might happen – but mostly, I have been musing over the consequences of a philosophical approach, a theory of normative concepts. I went in haste over a number of theses and issues, sketching this approach not so much with an eye to laying out "What does it mean and how do we know?" but to the question "So what?" In particular, what does all this say about whether we live as purely natural parts of a purely natural world? Is what I've been sketching, then, naturalism, non-naturalism, or something else? It's a view that's all three, I answer, in ways we need to distinguish. It's not the classic emotivism of Ayer and Stevenson, but still, devices those thinkers invented help us construct a view that takes in crucial aspects of all three of these classic positions.

I.3 Constructivism

Introduction

Many philosophers accept the claim that there is a ready-made world – a world of mountains, oceans, and animals whose existence and nature owe nothing to our cognitive activity. But hardly any philosophers accept the claim that everything in the world exhibits this kind of mind-independence. Mountains, for example, may exist independently of our cognitive activity, but paperweights don't. Whether the rock on a person's desk is a paperweight is, after all, a function of the attitudes we have toward it, how we treat it, and so forth. Otherwise put, the property of *being a paperweight* is "conceiving-dependent"; it is such that it is conferred on, or imparted to, pieces of glass, stone, wood, and the like by our cognitive activity.

Having acknowledged the plausibility of the view that some properties are conceiving-dependent, it is natural to raise the question of whether moral properties are a species of such a property. Moral constructivists believe that there are powerful reasons for answering in the affirmative.

Consider three aspects of our commonsensical view of morality. In the first place, common sense strongly suggests that moral discourse is (by and large) assertoric or statement-making. Given the trappings of ordinary moral discourse, it appears as if a central aim of such discourse is to represent or describe moral reality. In the second place,

common sense strongly suggests that some moral propositions are true because they represent moral reality aright. Most of us, for example, believe that, at least some of the time, our moral judgments get things right inasmuch as they correctly register the moral facts. Third, common sense appears to tell us that moral reality is to a significant degree objective; it does not seem that we can simply make up the moral facts as we please.

We've seen that both error theorists and expressivists have difficulty capturing these aspects of common sense, for they either deny that moral discourse represents moral reality or maintain that it is not even in the business of doing so. Constructivists think we can do better. For suppose, constructivists suggest, there were conceiving-dependent moral properties. If there were, then we could say that a central function of moral discourse is to represent these properties, that the content of some such discourse is true, and that morality is objective in a fairly robust sense. In these respects, constructivist positions compare favorably with robust versions of moral realism because they too can capture the "objective pretensions" of moral thought and practice. (For a description of the realist's commitments, see part I.5, "Moral Realism.")

In fact, as constructivists see things, not only does their view compare favorably with moral realism, it is also more attractive than realism in significant respects. The worry about realism that animates both error theorists and expressivists is that realism is metaphysically extravagant; the realist, after all, tells us that there is a realm of moral facts. But, according to constructivists, the real worry about realism is not so much that it commits us to the existence of moral facts or even that such facts are normative or reason-giving in character. Rather, the real worry is that realism commits us to a view according to which moral facts are objectionably "brute." After all, we're perfectly familiar with the norms of, say, etiquette or baseball. We don't think that there is anything mysterious about these facts because we can explain their origin perfectly well: they are the product of convention. In short, they are conceiving-dependent facts of a certain kind. However, if moral realists are correct, some moral facts are mind-independent much in the way that mountains or trees or the laws of logic appear to be; their existence and nature owe nothing to our cognitive activity. This, constructivists have urged, is objectionable for two reasons.

First, realists exceed the bounds of theoretical modesty by postulating a realm of conceiving-independent facts when there are other attractive alternatives available – alternatives that offer explanations where the realist offers none. And, second, if we do postulate a realm of conceiving-independent facts, it is difficult to see why we should care about them. How would facts of the sort the realist postulates be relevant to human interests, desires, and capacities? Were we to view moral facts as conceiving-dependent, so constructivists argue, these problems would disappear. If moral facts were a function of our attitudes, we could offer explanations of why things have moral features. Moreover, if moral properties were a function of our rational or social nature, we could explain why, as rational and social beings, we should care about being moral (more on this later).

So far, we've said that distinctive to constructivism is the claim that moral properties or facts are conceiving-dependent. At this point, however, it will prove helpful to state the constructivist position more carefully so as to distinguish it from its realist rivals.

For starters, let's say that something is a conceiving-dependent property just in case if something exemplifies that property, then it does so in virtue of the intentional attitudes taken toward it (or that would be taken toward it) by some actual or idealized (human) agent(s). *Being a paperweight*, we've said, is a good example of such a property. By contrast, let's say that a property is conceiving-independent just in case it is false that, if something displays it, then it does so in virtue of the intentional attitudes taken toward it (or that would be taken toward it) by some actual or idealized (human) agent(s). *Being square* is an example of a property of this kind. On the assumption that facts just are states of affairs in which things have properties, it follows that a conceiving-dependent fact *that x is F* is one in which a thing, x, instantiates a conceiving-dependent property F. Alternatively, a conceiving-independent fact *that x is G* is a fact in which a thing, x, instantiates a conceiving-independent property G. With these definitions in hand, we can state moral constructivism as follows:

> Every moral fact is either itself a conceiving-dependent moral fact or explained by a conceiving-dependent moral fact (and not a conceiving-independent moral fact).

It is worth noting that, according to this definition, a constructivist needn't say that all moral facts are conceiving-dependent. She might hold, for example, that whether an agent has a moral reason to act is a conceiving-dependent moral fact. But she might also maintain that whether an agent is compassionate is not such a fact. For example, she might hold that an agent's being compassionate depends not on the fact that she herself is (or would be) the object of one or another person's attitude, but simply depends on the fact that she is disposed to respond to reasons aright. Nonetheless, according to this view, the fact that an agent is compassionate is *explained* in terms of or is *determined by* her disposition to respond to conceiving-dependent moral facts (viz., moral reasons). So, according to the present account of moral constructivism, this view is a version of constructivism, for it explains conceiving-independent moral facts in terms of conceiving-dependent ones. Otherwise put, this view is a version of constructivism because it implies that there are no *basic* conceiving-independent moral facts – that is, moral facts that are not determined by conceiving-dependent moral facts.

Having identified the general character of constructivism, we can now identify two species of this view. The first type of constructivist view – what we can call a "non-idealized" constructivist position – tells us that moral properties are conferred on things not by ideal agents, but by ordinary, actual agents. Gilbert Harman's moral relativist view, developed in his essay in this section, is a non-idealized constructivist position, for it views morality "as a compromise based on implicit bargaining" between agents (Harman 1975: 13). As Harman views things, morality is like etiquette inasmuch as it is the product of social convention. Likewise, Christine Korsgaard's broadly Kantian view, also defended in this section, is a non-idealized constructivist position. Rather than saying that morality is the product of social convention, Korsgaard maintains that morality is the product of our being rational agents. In Korsgaard's view, in order for someone to count as an agent, she must value her own humanity – that is, her power of rational choice – as an end in itself. By thus valuing her own humanity, Korsgaard contends that an agent thereby confers value on herself. And if an agent values her own humanity in this way – so the claim is – she cannot, on pain of contradiction, fail to value the humanity of others in the same way.

While both Harman's and Korsgaard's views capture much of what is desirable in a moral theory – for example, they both offer explanations of the origin of morality – they clearly differ in the extent to which they imply that morality is objective. If Harman's view is correct, morality is objective in only a very weak sense. True enough, according to his view, there are moral standards to discover. But had we reached different social agreements, these standards would be different from what they are. And, with regard to at least some agreements, it appears as if we can simply opt out of them and, hence, opt out of the moral codes that they generate. Korsgaard's position promises more than this. According to her view, morality is objective in a fairly strong sense. The basic moral standards do not change with shifts in societal agreements. Moreover, according to her view, to fail to act morally is either to fall into contradiction or cease to be a practical agent at all. Since it is difficult to see how one could reasonably desire to suffer such a fate, Korsgaard's view appears to capture the objectively binding nature of morality, because it explains why we should care about being good.

Worries linger about this broadly Kantian approach, however. Mightn't it be possible for an agent not to value her humanity as an end in itself, but nonetheless act because she values other things

as ends in themselves, such as the power and beauty of nature? If so, it follows that such an agent would not have value as an end in herself. And, thus, it follows that whatever obligations we have toward her would not be a matter of respecting her humanity (assuming that respect is reserved only for things that have value as ends in themselves). And mightn't an agent coherently view her own humanity, but not the humanity of others, as somehow special and, thus, worthy of preferential treatment? If so, it is difficult to see why an agent would be rationally obligated to act in ways that we would ordinarily regard as being right, such as treating others with kindness and respect.

The second type of constructivist view alluded to earlier – what we can call an "idealized" constructivist position – is designed to handle these concerns. For suppose we agree that there are conceptual constraints on what could count as a right action. Actions designed to wreak wanton havoc, for example, don't appear to be serious candidates for being right actions. It is also plausible to believe that right actions are generally such that they are either aimed at promoting, honoring, or respecting human well-being or the components thereof. (If one wishes to state this idea in a more Kantian vein, we could say this: right actions are generally such that they are aimed at respecting the worth of persons. If one is inclined toward this view, what is said below can be translated into this Kantian idiom.)

Now suppose we call an agent who confers rightness on acts of certain types by way of having one or another intentional attitude toward acts of those types a "conferring" agent. If we are to honor the idea that there are conceptual constraints on right actions of the sort just mentioned, there are reasons to believe that a conferring agent must have an accurate view of what human well-being consists in and must reason well about how to promote, honor, or respect it. For if she did not – if, for example, she mistakenly believed that actions intended to wreak wanton havoc promote human flourishing – then any position that held that such an agent is a conferring agent would violate the conceptual constraints on what counts as a right action. In short, given the idea that there are conceptual constraints on what could count as a right action, it is plausible to believe that a conferring agent must be sufficiently idealized: she herself must have adequate information regarding human well-being at her disposal, and accurately assess the ways in which acts of various kinds promote or honor well-being, on the one hand, or frustrate or undercut it, on the other.

Idealized constructivist positions, such as those defended by Roderick Firth and Ronald Milo in this section, appear well situated to honor the conceptual constraints on right action. Moreover, when developed, they appear equally suited to explain why we should care about being good. Consider in this regard the type of constructivist view defended by Michael Smith in his book *The Moral Problem*. Smith argues that an act is right for an agent S in circumstances C just in case and because an idealized counterpart of that agent would desire S to act in that fashion when in C. According to Smith, if S believes that it is right that he should act in this fashion when in C, then presumably he believes that his idealized counterpart would desire that he act in that fashion when in C. Suppose, however, S were to fail to act in this fashion when in C, say, because he was overcome by moral listlessness. It follows that S is irrational by his own lights; were he fully rational, he would desire that he do otherwise in C. Smith's constructivist view implies, then, that moral failures are failures of rationality. And, thus, it appears to capture the Kantian intuition that failures of morality are at bottom failures of rationality. And surely, it might be thought, we should care about whether we are rational!

Apparently, then, there are multiple advantages to accepting idealized versions of constructivism. What challenges do these views face? There are several, perhaps the most central of which is a *Euthyphro*-style objection to the position. According to this objection, idealized constructivist views face a dilemma: either they honor the conceptual constraints on what could count as a right action or a virtuous agent, but fail to be constructivist views; or they fail to honor these constraints, and thereby forfeit some of the most powerful reasons for accepting the view in the first place.

One way to run the argument is to assume that, necessarily, idealized agents would exhibit virtues of various kinds such as conscientiousness, open-mindedness, honesty, fairness when evaluating the views of others, and so forth. Displaying traits such as these is what appears to make such agents ideal: were an agent to fail to exhibit these traits, it is difficult to see why we should take her desires for us to be normatively binding. The traits just mentioned, however, look like moral virtues. If so, there seem to be three options for explaining their pres-

ence: either (1) the presence of these virtues is a basic conceiving-independent moral fact (that is, a moral fact not explained by one or another conceiving-dependent moral fact), or (2) the presence of these virtues is a conceiving-dependent moral fact, or (3) the presence of these virtues is explained by reference to conceiving-dependent moral facts (and not conceiving-independent moral facts).

The first option is not promising for constructivists. To accept it is to surrender moral constructivism altogether.

The second option is also not promising for constructivists. After all, it is not plausible to believe that an agent can simply confer a property such as *being conscientious* on herself simply by *taking* herself to be conscientious. To be conscientious, an agent also needs to respond to reasons aright, pay careful attention to the evidence, not jump to snap conclusions, and so on.

If this is right, we're left with the third option. In this case, the aim would be to explain the presence of the moral virtues in terms of a conceiving-dependent moral property, such as *being a moral reason*. But think back to Smith's constructivist account of moral rightness for a moment. It tells us that that an act is right for an agent S in circumstances C just in case and because an idealized counterpart of that agent would desire S to act in that fashion when in C. By hypothesis, we cannot understand S's idealized counterpart in such a way that she already exhibits the virtues, for this is what we are trying to explain. But if your idealized counterpart failed to exhibit traits such as being conscientious, open-minded, honest, or fair, what reason would you have to care about what he or she desires you to do? Further, if your idealized counterpart failed to exhibit these traits, it is difficult to see whether what he or she desired you to do would preserve the conceptual constraints on what counts as a right action. And, so, a variant of the original dilemma surfaces: either we suppose that an idealized agent exhibits moral virtues, in which case we honor the conceptual constraints on what counts as a right action but fail to explain the presence of the virtues in a constructivist fashion, or we suppose that an idealized agent does not exhibit moral virtues, in which case we fail to honor the conceptual constraints on what counts as a right action and surrender some of the most powerful reasons for accepting the view in the first place.

Selected Bibliography

Brink, David. 1989. *Moral Realism and the Foundations of Ethics*. Cambridge: Cambridge University Press, appendix 4.

Carson, Thomas L. 1984. *The Status of Morality*. Dordrecht: Reidel.

Carson, Thomas. 2000. *Value and the Good Life*. Notre Dame: University of Notre Dame Press.

Cohon, Rachel. 2000. "The Roots of Reasons." *The Philosophical Review* 109: 63–85.

Copp, David. 1995. *Morality, Normativity, and Society*. Oxford: Oxford University Press.

Enoch, David. 2005. "Why Idealize?" *Ethics* 115: 759–87.

FitzPatrick, William. 2005. "The Practical Turn in Ethical Theory: Korsgaard's Constructivism, Realism, and the Nature of Normativity." *Ethics* 115: 651–91.

Harman, Gilbert. 1975. "Moral Relativism Defended." *Philosophical Review* 69: 221–5.

Harman, Gilbert. 1977. *The Nature of Morality*. Oxford: Oxford University Press.

Harman, Gilbert. 1984. "Is There a Single True Morality?" In David Copp and David Zimmerman, eds. *Morality, Reason and Truth*. Totowa, NJ: Rowman & Allanheld.

Joyce, Richard. 2001. *The Myth of Morality*. Cambridge: Cambridge University Press, ch. 3.

Korsgaard, Christine. 1996a. *Creating the Kingdom of Ends*. Cambridge: Cambridge University Press.

Korsgaard, Christine. 1996b. *The Sources of Normativity*. Cambridge: Cambridge University Press.

Korsgaard, Christine. 2003. "Realism and Constructivism in Twentieth-Century Moral Philosophy." *The Journal of Philosophical Research*, APA Centennial Supplement, 99–122.

Milo, Ronald. 1996. "Contractarian Constructivism." *Journal of Philosophy* 92: 181–204.

Rawls, John. 1999a. *Collected Papers*. Samuel Freedman, ed. Cambridge, MA: Harvard University Press.

Rawls, John. 1999b. *A Theory of Justice*. Revised edition. Cambridge, MA: Harvard University Press.

Scanlon, Thomas. 1998. *What We Owe to Each Other*. Cambridge, MA: Harvard University Press.

Shafer-Landau, Russ. 2003. *Moral Realism: A Defence*. Oxford: Oxford University Press, ch. 2.

Smith, Michael. 1994. *The Moral Problem*. Oxford: Blackwell.

Van Roojen, Mark. 2005. "Rationalist Realism and Constructivist Accounts of Morality." *Philosophical Studies* 126: 285–95.

Wedgwood, Ralph. 2002. "Practical Reasoning as Figuring Out What Is Best: Against Constructivism." *Topoi* 21: 139–52.

Wong, David. 1984. *Moral Relativity*. Berkeley: University of California Press.

Moral Relativism Defended

Gilbert Harman

My thesis is that morality arises when a group of people reach an implicit agreement or come to a tacit understanding about their relations with one another. Part of what I mean by this is that moral judgments – or, rather, an important class of them – make sense only in relation to and with reference to one or another such agreement or understanding. This is vague, and I shall try to make it more precise in what follows. But it should be clear that I intend to argue for a version of what has been called moral relativism.

In doing so, I am taking sides in an ancient controversy. Many people have supposed that the sort of view which I am going to defend is obviously correct – indeed, that it is the only sort of account that could make sense of the phenomenon of morality. At the same time there have also been many who have supposed that moral relativism is confused, incoherent, and even immoral, at the very least obviously wrong.

Most arguments against relativism make use of a strategy of dissuasive definition; they define moral relativism as an inconsistent thesis. For example, they define it as the assertion that (a) there are no universal moral principles and (b) one ought to act in accordance with the principles of one's own group, where this latter principle, (b), is supposed to be a universal moral principle.[1] It is easy enough to show that this version of moral relativism will not do, but that is no reason to think that a defender of moral relativism cannot find a better definition.

My moral relativism is a soberly logical thesis – a thesis about logical form, if you like. Just as the judgment that something is large makes sense only in relation to one or another comparison class, so too, I will argue, the judgment that it is wrong of someone to do something makes sense only in relation to an agreement or understanding. A dog may be large in relation to chihuahuas but not large in relation to dogs in general. Similarly, I will argue, an action may be wrong in relation to one agreement but not in relation to another. Just as it makes no sense to ask whether a dog is large, period, apart from any relation to a comparison class, so too, I will argue, it makes no sense to ask whether an action is wrong, period, apart from any relation to an agreement.

There is an agreement, in the relevant sense, if each of a number of people intends to adhere to some schedule, plan, or set of principles, intending to do this on the understanding that the others

---

[1] Bernard Williams, *Morality: An Introduction to Ethics* (New York, 1972), pp. 20–1; Marcus Singer, *Generalization in Ethics* (New York, 1961), p. 332.

similarly intend. The agreement or understanding need not be conscious or explicit; and I will not here try to say what distinguishes moral agreements from, for example, conventions of the road or conventions of etiquette, since these distinctions will not be important as regards the purely logical thesis that I will be defending.

Although I want to say that certain moral judgments are made in relation to an agreement, I do not want to say this about all moral judgments. Perhaps it is true that all moral judgments are made in relation to an agreement; nevertheless, that is not what I will be arguing. For I want to say that there is a way in which certain moral judgments are relative to an agreement but other moral judgments are not. My relativism is a thesis only about what I will call "inner judgments," such as the judgment that someone ought or ought not to have acted in a certain way or the judgment that it was right or wrong of him to have done so. My relativism is not meant to apply, for example, to the judgment that someone is evil or the judgment that a given institution is unjust.

In particular, I am not denying (nor am I asserting) that some moralities are "objectively" better than others or that there are objective standards for assessing moralities. My thesis is a soberly logical thesis about logical form.

I. Inner Judgments

We make inner judgments about a person only if we suppose that he is capable of being motivated by the relevant moral considerations. We make other sorts of judgment about those who we suppose are not susceptible of such motivation. Inner judgments include judgments in which we say that someone should or ought to have done something or that someone was right or wrong to have done something. Inner judgments do not include judgments in which we call someone (literally) a savage or say that someone is (literally) inhuman, evil, a betrayer, a traitor, or an enemy.

Consider this example. Intelligent beings from outer space land on Earth, beings without the slightest concern for human life and happiness. That a certain course of action on their part might injure one of us means nothing to them; that fact by itself gives them no reason to avoid the action. In such a case it would be odd to say that nevertheless the beings ought to avoid injuring us or that

it would be wrong for them to attack us. Of course we will want to resist them if they do such things and we will make negative judgments about them; but we will judge that they are dreadful enemies to be repelled and even destroyed, not that they should not act as they do.

Similarly, if we learn that a band of cannibals has captured and eaten the sole survivor of a shipwreck, we will speak of the primitive morality of the cannibals and may call them savages, but we will not say that they ought not to have eaten their captive.

Again, suppose that a contented employee of Murder, Incorporated was raised as a child to honor and respect members of the "family" but to have nothing but contempt for the rest of society. His current assignment, let us suppose, is to kill a certain bank manager, Bernard J. Ortcutt. Since Ortcutt is not a member of the "family," the employee in question has no compunction about carrying out his assignment. In particular, if we were to try to convince him that he should not kill Ortcutt, our argument would merely amuse him. We would not provide him with the slightest reason to desist unless we were to point to practical difficulties, such as the likelihood of his getting caught. Now, in this case it would be a misuse of language to say of him that he ought not to kill Ortcutt or that it would be wrong of him to do so, since that would imply that our own moral considerations carry some weight with him, which they do not. Instead we can only judge that he is a criminal, someone to be hunted down by the police, an enemy of peace-loving citizens, and so forth.

It is true that we can make certain judgments about him using the word "ought." For example, investigators who have been tipped off by an informer and who are waiting for the assassin to appear at the bank can use the "ought" of expectation to say, "He ought to arrive soon," meaning that on the basis of their information one would expect him to arrive soon. And, in thinking over how the assassin might carry out his assignment, we can use the "ought" of rationality to say that he ought to go in by the rear door, meaning that it would be more rational for him to do that than to go in by the front door. In neither of these cases is the moral "ought" in question.

There is another use of "ought" which is normative and in a sense moral but which is distinct from what I am calling the moral "ought." This is the use which occurs when we say that something ought or ought not to be the case. It ought not to be the case that members of Murder, Incorporated go around killing people; in other words, it is a terrible thing that they do so. The same thought can perhaps be expressed as "They ought not to go around killing people," meaning that it ought not to be the case that they do, not that they are wrong to do what they do. The normative "ought to be" is used to assess a situation; the moral "ought to do" is used to describe a relation between an agent and a type of act that he might perform or has performed.

The sentence "They ought not to go around killing people" is therefore multiply ambiguous. It can mean that one would not expect them to do so (the "ought" of expectation), that it is not in their interest to do so (the "ought" of rationality), that it is a bad thing that they do so (the normative "ought to be"), or that they are wrong to do so (the moral "ought to do"). For the most part I am here concerned only with the last of these interpretations.

The word "should" behaves very much like "ought to." There is a "should" of expectation ("They should be here soon"), a "should" of rationality ("He should go in by the back door"), a normative "should be" ("They shouldn't go around killing people like that"), and the moral "should do" ("You should keep that promise"). I am of course concerned mainly with the last sense of "should."

"Right" and "wrong" also have multiple uses; I will not try to say what all of them are. But I do want to distinguish using the word "wrong" to say that a particular situation or action is wrong from using the word to say that it is wrong *of someone* to do something. In the former case, the word "wrong" is used to assess an act or situation. In the latter case it is used to describe a relation between an agent and an act. Only the latter sort of judgment is an inner judgment. Although we would not say concerning the contented employee of Murder, Incorporated mentioned earlier that it was wrong *of him* to kill Ortcutt, we could say that *his action* was wrong and we could say that it is wrong that there is so much killing.

To take another example, it sounds odd to say that Hitler should not have ordered the extermination of the Jews, that it was wrong of him to have done so. That sounds somehow "too weak" a thing to say. Instead we want to say that Hitler was an evil man. Yet we can properly say, "Hitler ought not to have ordered the extermination of the Jews," if what we mean is that it ought never to have happened; and we can say without oddity that what Hitler did was wrong. Oddity attends only the inner judgment that Hitler was wrong to have acted in that way. That is what sounds "too weak."

It is worth noting that the inner judgments sound too weak not because of the enormity of what Hitler did but because we suppose that in acting as he did he shows that he could not have been susceptible to the moral considerations on the basis of which we make our judgment. He is in the relevant sense beyond the pale and we therefore cannot make inner judgments about him. To see that this is so, consider, say, Stalin, another mass-murderer. We can perhaps imagine someone taking a sympathetic view of Stalin. In such a view, Stalin realized that the course he was going to pursue would mean the murder of millions of people and he dreaded such a prospect; however, the alternative seemed to offer an even greater disaster – so, reluctantly and with great anguish, he went ahead. In relation to such a view of Stalin, inner judgments about Stalin are not as odd as similar judgments about Hitler. For we might easily continue the story by saying that, despite what he hoped to gain, Stalin should not have undertaken the course he did, that it was wrong of him to have done so. What makes inner judgments about Hitler odd, "too weak," is not that the acts judged seem too terrible for the words used but rather that the agent judged seems beyond the pale – in other words beyond the motivational reach of the relevant moral considerations.

Of course, I do not want to deny that for various reasons a speaker might pretend that an agent is or is not susceptible to certain moral considerations. For example, a speaker may for rhetorical or political reasons wish to suggest that someone is beyond the pale, that he should not be listened to, that he can be treated as an enemy. On the other hand, a speaker may pretend that someone is susceptible to certain moral considerations in an effort to make that person or others susceptible to those considerations. Inner judgments about one's children sometimes have this function. So do inner judgments made in political speeches that aim at restoring a lapsed sense of morality in government.

II. The Logical Form of Inner Judgments

Inner judgments have two important characteristics. First, they imply that the agent has reasons to do something. Second, the speaker in some sense endorses these reasons and supposes that the audience also endorses them. Other moral judgments about an agent, on the other hand, do not have such implications; they do not imply that the agent has reasons for acting that are endorsed by the speaker.

If someone S says that A (morally) ought to do D, S implies that A has reasons to do D and S endorses those reasons – whereas if S says that B was evil in what B did, S does not imply that the reasons S would endorse for not doing what B did were reasons for B not to do that thing; in fact, S implies that they were not reasons for B.

Let us examine this more closely. If S says that (morally) A ought to do D, S implies that A has reasons to do D which S endorses. I shall assume that such reasons would have to have their source in goals, desires, or intentions that S takes A to have and that S approves of A's having because S shares those goals, desires, or intentions. So, if S says that (morally) A ought to do D, there are certain motivational attitudes M which S assumes are shared by S, A, and S's audience.

Now, in supposing that reasons for action must have their source in goals, desires, or intentions, I am assuming something like an Aristotelian or Humean account of these matters, as opposed, for example, to a Kantian approach which sees a possible source of motivation in reason itself. I must defer a full-scale discussion of the issue to another occasion. Here I simply assume that the Kantian approach is wrong. In particular, I assume that there might be no reasons at all for a being from outer space to avoid harm to us; that, for Hitler, there might have been no reason at all not to order the extermination of the Jews; that the contented employee of Murder, Incorporated might have no reason at all not to kill Ortcutt; that the cannibals might have no reason not to eat their captive. In other words, I assume that the possession of rationality is not sufficient to provide a source for relevant reasons, that certain desires, goals, or intentions are also necessary. Those who accept this assumption will, I think, find that they distinguish inner moral judgments from other moral judgments in the way that I have indicated.

Ultimately, I want to argue that the shared motivational attitudes M are intentions to keep an agreement (supposing that others similarly intend). For I want to argue that inner moral judgments are made relative to such an agreement. That is, I want to argue that, when S makes the inner judgment that A ought to do D, S assumes that A intends to act in accordance with an agreement which S and S's audience also intend to observe. In other words, I want to argue that the source of the reasons for doing D which S ascribes to A is A's sincere intention to observe a certain agreement. I have not yet argued for the stronger thesis, however. I have argued only that S makes his judgment relative to *some* motivational attitudes M which S assumes are shared by S, A, and S's audience.

Formulating this as a logical thesis, I want to treat the moral "ought" as a four-place predicate (or "operator"), "Ought (A, D, C, M)," which relates an agent A, a type of act D, considerations C, and motivating attitudes M. The relativity to considerations C can be brought out by considering what are sometimes called statements of prima-facie obligation, "Considering that you promised, you ought to go to the board meeting, but considering that you are the sole surviving relative, you ought to go to the funeral; all things considered, it is not clear what you ought to do." The claim that there is *this* relativity, to considerations, is not, of course, what makes my thesis a version of moral relativism, since any theory must acknowledge relativity to considerations. The relativity to considerations does, however, provide a model for a coherent interpretation of moral relativism as a similar kind of relativity.

It is not as easy to exhibit the relativity to motivating attitudes as it is to exhibit the relativity to considerations, since normally a speaker who makes a moral "ought" judgment intends the relevant motivating attitudes to be ones that the speaker shares with the agent and the audience, and normally it will be obvious what attitudes these are. But sometimes a speaker does invoke different attitudes by invoking a morality the speaker does not share. Someone may say, for example, "As a Christian, you ought to turn the other check; I, however, propose to strike back." A spy who has been found out by a friend might say, "As a citizen, you ought to turn me in, but I hope that you will not." In these and similar cases a speaker makes a moral "ought" judgment that is explicitly relative to motivating attitudes that the speaker does not share.

In order to be somewhat more precise, then, my thesis is this. "Ought (A, D, C, M)" means roughly that, given that A has motivating attitudes M and given C, D is the course of action for A that is supported by the best reasons. In judgments using this sense of "ought," C and M are often not explicitly mentioned but are indicated by the context of utterance. Normally, when that happens, C will be "all things considered" and M will be attitudes that are shared by the speaker and audience.

I mentioned that inner judgments have two characteristics. First, they imply that the agent has reasons to do something that are capable of motivating the agent. Second, the speaker endorses those reasons and supposes that the audience does too. Now, any "Ought (A, D, C, M)" judgment has the first of these characteristics, but as we have just seen a judgment of this sort will not necessarily have the second characteristic if made with explicit reference to motivating attitudes not shared by the speaker. If reference is made either implicitly or explicitly (for example, through the use of the adverb "morally") to attitudes that are shared by the speaker and audience, the resulting judgment has both characteristics and is an inner judgment. If reference is made to attitudes that are not shared by the speaker, the resulting judgment is not an inner judgment and does not represent a full-fledged moral judgment on the part of the speaker. In such a case we have an example of what has been called an inverted-commas use of "ought."[2]

III.   Moral Bargaining

I have argued that moral "ought" judgments are relational, "Ought (A, D, C, M)," where M represents certain motivating attitudes. I now want to argue that the attitudes M derive from an agreement. That is, they are intentions to adhere to a particular agreement on the understanding that others also intend to do so. Really, it might be better for me to say that I put this forward as a hypothesis, since I cannot pretend to be able to prove that it is true. I will argue, however, that this hypothesis accounts for an otherwise puzzling aspect of our

moral views that, as far as I know, there is no other way to account for.

I will use the word "intention" in a somewhat extended sense to cover certain dispositions or habits. Someone may habitually act in accordance with the relevant understanding and therefore may be disposed to act in that way without having any more or less conscious intention. In such a case it may sound odd to say that he *intends* to act in accordance with the moral understanding. Nevertheless, for present purposes I will count that as his having the relevant intention in a dispositional sense.

I now want to consider the following puzzle about our moral views, a puzzle that has figured in recent philosophical discussion of issues such as abortion. It has been observed that most of us assign greater weight to the duty not to harm others than to the duty to help others. For example, most of us believe that a doctor ought not to save five of his patients who would otherwise die by cutting up a sixth patient and distributing his healthy organs where needed to the others, even though we do think that the doctor has a duty to try to help as many of his patients as he can. For we also think that he has a stronger duty to try not to harm any of his patients (or anyone else) even if by so doing he could help five others.

This aspect of our moral views can seem very puzzling, especially if one supposes that moral feelings derive from sympathy and concern for others. But the hypothesis that morality derives from an agreement among people of varying powers and resources provides a plausible explanation. The rich, the poor, the strong, and the weak would all benefit if all were to try to avoid harming one another. So everyone could agree to that arrangement. But the rich and the strong would not benefit from an arrangement whereby everyone would try to do as much as possible to help those in need. The poor and weak would get all of the benefit of this latter arrangement. Since the rich and the strong could foresee that they would be required to do most of the helping and that they would receive little in return, they would be reluctant to agree to a strong principle of mutual aid. A compromise would be likely and a weaker principle would probably be accepted. In other words, although everyone could agree to a strong principle concerning the avoidance of harm, it would not be true that everyone would favor an equally strong principle of

2   R. M. Hare, *The Language of Morals* (Oxford, 1952), pp. 164–8.

mutual aid. It is likely that only a weaker principle of the latter sort would gain general acceptance. So the hypothesis that morality derives from an understanding among people of different powers and resources can explain (and, according to me, does explain) why in our morality avoiding harm to others is taken to be more important than helping those who need help.

By the way, I am here only trying to *explain* an aspect of our moral views. I am not therefore *endorsing* that aspect. And I defer until later a relativistic account of the way in which aspects of our moral view can be criticized "from within."

Now we need not suppose that the agreement or understanding in question is explicit. It is enough if various members of society knowingly reach an agreement in intentions – each intending to act in certain ways on the understanding that the others have similar intentions. Such an implicit agreement is reached through a process of mutual adjustment and implicit bargaining.

Indeed, it is essential to the proposed explanation of this aspect of our moral views to suppose that the relevant moral understanding is thus the result of *bargaining*. It is necessary to suppose that, in order to further our interests, we form certain conditional intentions, hoping that others will do the same. The others, who have different interests, will form somewhat different conditional intentions. After implicit bargaining, some sort of compromise is reached.

Seeing morality in this way as a compromise based on implicit bargaining helps to explain why our morality takes it to be worse to harm someone than to refuse to help someone. The explanation requires that we view our morality as an implicit agreement about what to do. This sort of explanation could not be given if we were to suppose, say, that our morality represented an agreement only about the facts (naturalism). Nor is it enough simply to suppose that our morality represents an agreement in attitude, if we forget that such agreement can be reached, not only by way of such principles as are mentioned, for example, in Hare's "logic of imperatives,"[3] but also through bargaining. According to Hare, to accept a general moral

principle is to intend to do something.[4] If we add to his theory that the relevant intentions can be reached through implicit bargaining, the resulting theory begins to look like the one that I am defending.

Many aspects of our moral views can be given a utilitarian explanation. We could account for these aspects, using the logical analysis I presented in the previous section of this paper, by supposing that the relevant "ought" judgments presuppose shared attitudes of sympathy and benevolence. We can equally well explain them by supposing that considerations of utility have influenced our implicit agreements, so that the appeal is to a shared intention to adhere to those agreements. Any aspect of morality that is susceptible of a utilitarian explanation can also be explained by an implicit agreement, but not conversely. There are aspects of our moral views that seem to be explicable only in the second way, on the assumption that morality derives from an agreement. One example, already cited, is the distinction we make between harming and not helping. Another is our feeling that each person has an inalienable right of self-defense and self-preservation. Philosophers have not been able to come up with a really satisfactory utilitarian justification of such a right, but it is easily intelligible on our present hypothesis, as Hobbes observed many years ago. You cannot, except in very special circumstances, rationally form the intention not to try to preserve your life if it should ever be threatened, say, by society or the state, since you know that you cannot now control what you would do in such a situation. No matter what you now decided to do, when the time came, you would ignore your prior decision and try to save your life. Since you cannot now intend to do something later which you now know that you would not do, you cannot now intend to keep an agreement not to preserve your life if it is threatened by others in your society.[5]

This concludes the positive side of my argument that what I have called inner moral judgments are made in relation to an implicit agreement. I now want to argue that this theory avoids difficulties traditionally associated with implicit agreement theories of morality.

---

[3] R. M. Hare, *op. cit.* and *Freedom and Reason* (Oxford, 1963).

[4] *The Language of Morals*, pp. 18–20, 168–9.

[5] Cf. Thomas Hobbes, *Leviathan* (Oxford, 1957, *inter alia*), pt. I, ch. 14, "Of the First and Second Natural Laws, And of Contracts."

IV. Objections and Replies

One traditional difficulty for implicit agreement theories concerns what motivates us to do what we have agreed to do. It will, obviously, not be enough to say that we have implicitly agreed to keep agreements, since the issue would then be why we keep *that* agreement. And this suggests an objection to implicit agreement theories. But the apparent force of the objection derives entirely from taking an agreement to be a kind of ritual. To agree in the relevant sense is not just to say something; it is to intend to do something – namely, to intend to carry out one's part of the agreement on the condition that others do their parts. If we agree in this sense to do something, we intend to do it and intending to do it is already to be motivated to do it. So there is no problem as to why we are motivated to keep our agreements in this sense.

We do believe that in general you ought not to pretend to agree in this sense in order to trick someone else into agreeing. But that suggests no objection to the present view. All that it indicates is that *our* moral understanding contains or implies an agreement to be open and honest with others. If it is supposed that this leaves a problem about someone who has not accepted our agreement – "What reason does *he* have not to pretend to accept our agreement so that he can then trick others into agreeing to various things?" – the answer is that such a person may or may not have such a reason. If someone does not already accept something of our morality it may or may not be possible to find reasons why he should.

A second traditional objection to implicit agreement theories is that there is not a perfect correlation between what is generally believed to be morally right and what actually is morally right. Not everything generally agreed on is right and sometimes courses of action are right that would not be generally agreed to be right. But this is no objection to my thesis. My thesis is not that the implicit agreement from which a morality derives is an agreement in moral judgment; the thesis is rather that moral judgments make reference to and are made in relation to an agreement in intentions. Given that a group of people have agreed in this sense, there can still be disputes as to what the agreement implies for various situations. In my view, many moral disputes are of this sort. They presuppose a basic agreement and they concern what implications that agreement has for particular cases.

There can also be various things wrong with the agreement that a group of people reach, even from the point of view of that agreement, just as there can be defects in an individual's plan of action even from the point of view of that plan. Given what is known about the situation, a plan or agreement can in various ways be inconsistent, incoherent, or self-defeating. In my view, certain moral disputes are concerned with internal defects of the basic moral understanding of a group, and what changes should be made from the perspective of that understanding itself. This is another way in which moral disputes make sense with reference to and in relation to an underlying agreement.

Another objection to implicit agreement theories is that not all agreements are morally binding – for example, those made under compulsion or from a position of unfair disadvantage, which may seem to indicate that there are moral principles prior to those that derive from an implicit agreement. But, again, the force of the objection derives from an equivocation concerning what an agreement is. The principle that compelled agreements do not obligate concerns agreement in the sense of a certain sort of ritual indicating that one agrees. My thesis concerns a kind of agreement in intentions. The principle about compelled agreements is part of, or is implied by, our agreement in intentions. According to me it is only with reference to some such agreement in intentions that a principle of this sort makes sense.

Now it may be true our moral agreement in intentions also implies that it is wrong to compel people who are in a greatly inferior position to accept an agreement in intentions that they would not otherwise accept, and it may even be true that there is in our society at least one class of people in an inferior position who have been compelled thus to settle for accepting a basic moral understanding, aspects of which they would not have accepted had they not been in such an inferior position. In that case there would be an incoherence in our basic moral understanding and various suggestions might be made concerning the ways in which this understanding should be modified. But this moral critique of the understanding can proceed from that understanding itself rather than from "prior" moral principles.

In order to fix ideas, let us consider a society in which there is a well-established and long-standing tradition of hereditary slavery. Let us suppose that everyone accepts this institution, including the slaves. Everyone treats it as in the nature of things that there should be such slavery. Furthermore, let us suppose that there are also aspects of the basic moral agreement which speak against slavery. That is, these aspects together with certain facts about the situation imply that people should not own slaves and that slaves have no obligation to acquiesce in their condition. In such a case, the moral understanding would be defective, although its defectiveness would presumably be hidden in one or another manner, perhaps by means of a myth that slaves are physically and mentally subhuman in a way that makes appropriate the sort of treatment elsewhere reserved for beasts of burden. If this myth were to be exposed, the members of the society would then be faced with an obvious incoherence in their basic moral agreement and might come eventually to modify their agreement so as to eliminate its acceptance of slavery.

In such a case, even relative to the old agreement it might be true that slave owners ought to free their slaves, that slaves need not obey their masters, and that people ought to work to eliminate slavery. For the course supported by the best reasons, given that one starts out with the intention of adhering to a particular agreement, may be that one should stop intending to adhere to certain aspects of that agreement and should try to get others to do the same.

We can also (perhaps – but see below) envision a second society with hereditary slavery whose agreement has no aspects that speak against slavery. In that case, even if the facts of the situation were fully appreciated, no incoherence would appear in the basic moral understanding of the society and it would not be true in relation to that understanding that slave owners ought to free their slaves, that slaves need not obey their masters, and so forth. There might nevertheless come a time when there were reasons of a different sort to modify the basic understanding, either because of an external threat from societies opposed to slavery or because of an internal threat of rebellion by the slaves.

Now it is easier for us to make what I have called inner moral judgments about slave owners in the first society than in the second. For we can with reference to members of the first society invoke principles that they share with us and, with reference to those principles, we can say of them that they ought not to have kept slaves and that they

were immoral to have done so. This sort of inner judgment becomes increasingly inappropriate, however, the more distant they are from us and the less easy it is for us to think of our moral understanding as continuous with and perhaps a later development of theirs. Furthermore, it seems appropriate to make only non-inner judgments of the slave owners in the second society. We can say that the second society is unfair and unjust, that the slavery that exists is wrong, that it ought not to exist. But it would be inappropriate in this case to say that it was morally wrong of the slave owners to own slaves. The relevant aspects of our moral understanding, which we would invoke in moral judgments about them, are not aspects of the moral understanding that exists in the second society. [...]

Let me turn now to another objection to implicit agreement theories, an objection which challenges the idea that there is an agreement of the relevant sort. For, if we have agreed, when did we do it? Does anyone really remember having agreed? How did we indicate our agreement? What about those who do not want to agree? How do they indicate that they do not agree and what are the consequences of their not agreeing? Reflection on these and similar questions can make the hypothesis of implicit agreement seem too weak a basis on which to found morality.

But once again there is equivocation about agreements. The objection treats the thesis as the claim that morality is based on some sort of ritual rather than an agreement in intentions. But, as I have said, there is an agreement in the relevant sense when each of a number of people has an intention on the assumption that others have the same intention. In this sense of "agreement," there is no given moment at which one agrees, since one continues to agree in this sense as long as one continues to have the relevant intentions. Someone refuses to agree to the extent that he or she does not share these intentions. Those who do not agree are outside the agreement; in extreme cases they are outlaws or enemies. It does not follow, however, that there are no constraints on how those who agree may act toward those who do not, since for various reasons the agreement itself may contain provisions for dealing with outlaws and enemies.

This brings me to one last objection, which derives from the difficulty people have in trying to give an explicit and systematic account of their moral views. If one actually agrees to something, why is it so hard to say what one has agreed to? In response I can say only that many understandings appear to be of this sort. It is often possible to recognize what is in accordance with the understanding and what would violate it without being able to specify the understanding in any general way. Consider, for example, the understanding that exists among the members of a team of acrobats or a symphony orchestra.

Another reason why it is so difficult to give a precise and systematic specification of any actual moral understanding is that such an understanding will not in general be constituted by absolute rules but will take a vaguer form, specifying goals and areas of responsibility. For example, the agreement may indicate that one is to show respect for others by trying where possible to avoid actions that will harm them or interfere with what they are doing; it may indicate the duties and responsibilities of various members of the family, who is to be responsible for bringing up the children, and so forth. Often what will be important will be not so much exactly what actions are done as how willing participants are to do their parts and what attitudes they have – for example, whether they give sufficient weight to the interests of others.

The vague nature of moral understandings is to some extent alleviated in practice. One learns what can and cannot be done in various situations. Expectations are adjusted to other expectations. But moral disputes arise nonetheless. Such disputes may concern what the basic moral agreement implies for particular situations; and, if so, that can happen either because of disputes over the facts or because of a difference in basic understanding. Moral disputes may also arise concerning whether or not changes should be made in the basic agreement. Racial and sexual issues seem often to be of this second sort; but there is no clear line between the two kinds of dispute. When the implications of an agreement for a particular situation are considered, one possible outcome is that it becomes clear that the agreement should be modified.

[. . .]

Finally, I would like to say a few brief words about the limiting case of group morality, when the group has only one member; then, as it were, a person comes to an understanding with himself. In my view, a person can make inner judgments in relation to such an individual morality only about himself. A familiar form of pacifism is of this sort. Certain pacifists judge that it would be wrong of them to participate in killing, although they are not willing to make a similar judgment about others. Observe that such a pacifist is unwilling only to make *inner* moral judgments about others. Although he is unwilling to judge that those who do participate are wrong to do so, he is perfectly willing to say that it is a bad thing that they participate. There are of course many other examples of individual morality in this sense, when a person imposes standards on himself that he does not apply to others. The existence of such examples is further confirmation of the relativist thesis that I have presented.

My conclusion is that relativism can be formulated as an intelligible thesis, the thesis that morality derives from an implicit agreement and that moral judgments are in a logical sense made in relation to such an agreement. Such a theory helps to explain otherwise puzzling aspects of our own moral views, in particular why we think that it is more important to avoid harm to others than to help others. The theory is also partially confirmed by what is, as far as I can tell, a previously unnoticed distinction between inner and non-inner moral judgments. Furthermore, traditional objections to implicit agreement theories can be met.

8

The Authority of Reflection

Christine Korsgaard

Introduction

[. . .]

3.1.2

In this lecture and the next I will lay out the elements of a theory of normativity. This theory derives its main inspiration from Kant, but with some modifications which I have come to think are necessary. What I say will necessarily be sketchy, and sketchily argued. In this lecture, I will argue for two points: first, that autonomy is the source of obligation, and in particular of our ability to obligate ourselves; and second, that we have *moral* obligations, by which I mean obligations to humanity as such. However, it will be no part of my argument – quite the contrary – to suggest either that *all* obligations are moral, or that obligations can never conflict, and at the end of this lecture, I will say a little about that.

[. . .]

I will have little to say about the content of any of these obligations. I believe that the view suggests, although it does not completely settle, what that content should be, but I have made no attempt to work that out here. My aim is show where oblig-

ation comes from. Exactly which obligations we have and how to negotiate among them is a topic for another day.

Finally I will address another worry. The argument of this lecture is intended to show that if we take anything to have value, then we must acknowledge that we have moral obligations. Because that conclusion is conditional, you might think that I have not answered the sceptic. At the end of the lecture 4, I will discuss this objection.

The Problem

3.2.1

The human mind is self-conscious. Some philosophers have supposed that this means that our minds are somehow internally luminous, that their contents are completely accessible to us – that we can always be certain what we are thinking and feeling and wanting – and so that introspection yields certain knowledge of the self. Like Kant, and many philosophers nowadays, I do not think that this is true. Our knowledge of our own mental states and activities is no more certain than anything else.

But the human mind *is* self-conscious in the sense that it is essentially reflective. I'm not talking about being *thoughtful*, which of course is an individual property, but about the structure of our minds that makes thoughtfulness possible. A lower animal's attention is fixed on the world. Its perceptions are its beliefs and its desires are its will. It is engaged in conscious activities, but it is not conscious *of* them. That is, they are not the objects of its attention. But we human animals turn our attention on to our perceptions and desires themselves, on to our own mental activities, and we are conscious *of* them. That is why we can think *about* them.

And this sets us a problem no other animal has. It is the problem of the normative. For our capacity to turn our attention on to our own mental activities is also a capacity to distance ourselves from them, and to call them into question. I perceive, and I find myself with a powerful impulse to believe. But I back up and bring that impulse into view and then I have a certain distance. Now the impulse doesn't dominate me and now I have a problem. Shall I believe? Is this perception really a *reason* to believe? I desire and I find myself with a powerful impulse to act. But I back up and bring that impulse into view and then I have a certain distance. Now the impulse doesn't dominate me and now I have a problem. Shall I act? Is this desire really a *reason* to act? The reflective mind cannot settle for perception and desire, not just as such. It needs a *reason*. Otherwise, at least as long as it reflects, it cannot commit itself or go forward.

If the problem springs from reflection then the solution must do so as well. If the problem is that our perceptions and desires might not withstand reflective scrutiny, then the solution is that they might. We need reasons because our impulses must be able to withstand reflective scrutiny. We have reasons if they do. The normative word 'reason' refers to a kind of reflective success. If 'good' and 'right' are also taken to be intrinsically normative words, names for things that automatically give us reasons, then they too must refer to reflective success. And they do. Think of what they mean when we use them as *exclamations*. 'Good!' 'Right!' There they mean: I'm satisfied, I'm happy, I'm committed, you're convinced me, let's go. They mean the work of reflection is done.

Scepticism about the good and the right is not scepticism about the existence of intrinisically normative entities. It is the view that the problems which reflection sets for us are insoluble, that the questions to which it gives rise have no answers. It is the worry that nothing will count as reflective success, and so that the work of reflection will never be done. It is the fear that we cannot find what Kant called 'the unconditioned'.

3.2.2

The problem can also be described in terms of freedom. It is because of the reflective character of the mind that we must act, as Kant put it, under the idea of freedom. He says 'we cannot conceive of a reason which consciously responds to a bidding from the outside with respect to its judgments'.[1] If the bidding from outside is desire, then the point is that the reflective mind must endorse the desire before it can act on it, it must say to itself that the desire is a reason. As Kant puts it, we must *make it our maxim* to act on the desire. Then although we may do what desire bids us, we do it freely.

[. . .]

We do not need the concept of 'freedom' in the first instance because it is required for giving scientific explanations of what people do, but rather to describe the condition in which we find ourselves when we reflect on what to do. But that doesn't mean that I am claiming that our experience of our freedom is scientifically inexplicable. I am claiming that it is to be explained in terms of the structure of reflective consciousness, not as the (possibly delusory) *perception* of a theoretical or metaphysical property of the self.

The Scientific World View is a description of the world which serves the purposes of explanation and prediction. When its concepts are applied correctly it tells us things that are true. But it is not a *substitute* for human life. And nothing in human life is more real than the fact we must make our decisions and choices 'under the idea of freedom'. When desire bids, we can indeed take it or leave it. And that is the source of the problem.

3.2.3

'Reason' means reflective success. So if I decide that my desire is a reason to act, I must decide that on reflection I endorse that desire. And here we run

---

[1]   Kant, *Foundations of the Metaphysics of Morals*, p. 448; in Beck's translation, p. 66.

into the problem. For how do I decide that? Is the claim that I look at the desire, and see that it is intrinsically normative, or that its object is? Then all of the arguments against realism await us. Does the desire or its object inherit its normativity from something else? Then we must ask what makes that other thing normative, what makes it the source of a reason. And now of course the usual regress threatens. What brings such a course of reflection to a successful end?

Kant, as I mentioned, described this problem in terms of freedom. He defines a free will as a rational causality which is effective without being determined by any alien cause. Anything outside of the will counts as an alien cause, including the desires and inclinations of the person. The free will must be entirely self-determining. Yet, because the will is a causality, it must act according to some law or other. Kant says: 'Since the concept of a causality entails that of laws . . . it follows that freedom is by no means lawless . . .'[2] Alternatively, we may say that since the will is practical reason, it cannot be conceived as acting and choosing for no reason. Since reasons are derived from principles, the free will must have a principle. But because the will is free, no law or principle can be imposed on it from outside. Kant concludes that the will must be autonomous: that is, it must have its *own* law or principle. And here again we arrive at the problem. For where is this law to come from? If it is imposed on the will from outside then the will is not free. So the will must make the law for itself. But until the will has a law or principle, there is nothing from which it can derive a reason. So how can it have any reason for making one law rather than another?

Well, here is Kant's answer. The categorical imperative, as represented by the Formula of Universal Law, tells us to act only on a maxim which we could will to be a law. And *this*, according to Kant, *is* the law of a free will. To see why, we need only compare the problem faced by the free will with the content of the categorical imperative. The problem faced by the free will is this: the will must have a law, but because the will is free, it must be its own law. And nothing determines what that law must be. *All that it has to be is a law.* Now consider the content of the categorical imperative, as represented by the Formula of Universal Law. The

categorical imperative merely tells us to choose a law. Its only constraint on our choice is that it has the form of a law. And nothing determines what the law must be. *All that it has to be is a law.*

Therefore the categorical imperative is the law of a free will. It does not impose any external constraint on the free will's activities, but simply arises from the nature of the will. It describes what a free will must do in order to be what it is. It must choose a maxim it can regard as a law.[3]

3.2.4

Now I'm going to make a distinction that Kant doesn't make. I am going to call the law of acting only on maxims you can will to be laws 'the categorical imperative'. And I am going to distinguish it from what I will call 'the moral law'. The moral law, in the Kantian system, is the law of what Kant calls the Kingdom of Ends, the republic of all rational beings. The moral law tells us to act only on maxims that all rational beings could agree to act on together in a workable cooperative system. Now the Kantian argument which I just described establishes that *the categorical imperative* is the law of a free will. But it does not establish that *the moral law* is the law of a free will. Any law is universal, but the argument I just gave doesn't settle the question of the *domain* over which the law of the free will must range. And there are various possibilities here. If the law is the law of acting on the desire of the moment, then the agent will treat each desire as a reason, and her conduct will be that of a wanton. If the law ranges over the agent's whole life, then the agent will be some sort of egoist. It is only if the law ranges over every rational being that the resulting law will be the moral law.

Because of this, it has sometimes been claimed that the categorical imperative is an empty formalism. And this has in turn been conflated with another claim, that the moral law is an empty formalism. Now that second claim is false. Kant thought that we could test whether a maxim could serve as a law for the Kingdom of Ends by seeing whether there is any contradiction in willing it as a law which all rational beings could agree to act on together. I do not think this test gives us the whole content of morality, but it is a mistake to think that

---

[2]   Ibid., p. 446; in Beck's translation, p. 65.

[3]   This is a reading of the argument Kant gives in *Foundations of the Metaphysics of Morals*, pp. 446–8; in Beck's translation, pp. 64–7; and in *Critique of Practical Reason* under the heading 'Problem II', p. 29; in Beck's translation, pp. 28–9.

95

it does not give us any content as all, for there are certainly some maxims which are ruled out by it. And even if the test does not completely determine what the laws of the Kingdom of Ends would be, the moral law still could have content, For it tells us that our maxims must qualify as laws for the Kingdom of Ends, and that is a substantive command as long as we have *some* way of determining what those laws would be. And there are other proposals on the table about how to do that: John Rawls's to name only one.

But it is true that the argument that shows that we are bound by the categorical imperative does not show that we are bound by the moral law. For that we need another step. The agent must think of *herself* as a Citizen of the Kingdom of Ends.

The Solution

3.3.1

Those who think that the human mind is internally luminous and transparent to itself think that the term 'self-consciousness' is appropriate because what we get in human consciousness is a direct encounter with the self. Those who think that the human mind has a reflective structure use the term too, but for a different reason. The reflective structure of the mind is a source of 'self-consciousness' because it forces us to have a *conception* of ourselves. As Kant argued, this is a fact about what it is *like* to be reflectively conscious and it does not prove the existence of a metaphysical self. From a third-person point of view, outside of the deliberative standpoint, it may look as if what happens when someone makes a choice is that the strongest of his conflicting desires wins. But that isn't the way it is *for you* when you deliberate. When you deliberate, it is as if there were something over and above all of your desires, something which is *you*, and which *chooses* which desire to act on. This means that the principle or law by which you determine your actions is one that you regard as being expressive of *yourself*. To identify with such a principle or way of choosing is to be, in St Paul's famous phrase, a law to yourself.[4]

An agent might think of herself as a Citizen of the Kingdom of Ends. Or she might think of herself as someone's friend or lover, or as a member of a family or an ethnic group or a nation. She might think of herself as the steward of her own interests, and then she will be an egoist. Or she might think of herself as the slave of her passions, and then she will be a wanton. And how she thinks of herself will determine whether it is the law of the Kingdom of Ends, or the law of some smaller group, or the law of egoism, or the law of the wanton that will be the law that she is to herself.

The conception of one's identity in question here is not a theoretical one, a view about what as a matter of inescapable scientific fact you are. It is better understood as a description under which you value yourself, a description under which you find your life to be worth living and your actions to be worth undertaking. So I will call this a conception of your practical identity. Practical identity is a complex matter and for the average person there will be a jumble of such conceptions. You are a human being, a woman or a man, an adherent of a certain religion, a member of an ethnic group, a member of a certain profession, someone's lover or friend, and so on. And all of these identities give rise to reasons and obligations. Your reasons express your identity, your nature; your obligations spring from what that identity forbids.

Our ordinary ways of talking about obligation reflect this connection to identity. A century ago a European could admonish another to civilized behaviour by telling him to act like a Christian. It is still true in many quarters that courage is urged on males by the injunction 'be a man!' Duties more obviously connected with social roles are of course enforced in this way. 'A psychiatrist doesn't violate the confidence of her patients.' No 'ought' is needed here because the normativity is built right into the role. But it isn't only in the case of roles that the idea of obligation invokes the conception of practical identity. Consider the astonishing but familiar 'I couldn't live with myself if I did that.' Clearly there are two selves here, me and the one I must live with and so must not fail. Or consider the protest against obligation ignored: 'Just who do you think you are?'

The connection is also present in the concept of integrity. Etymologically, integrity is oneness, integration is what makes something one. To be a thing, one thing, a unity, an entity; to be anything at all: in the metaphysical sense, that is what it

---

[4]   Romans 2: 14.

means to have integrity. But we use the term for someone who lives up to his own standards. And that is because we think that living up to them is what makes him one, and so what makes him a person at all.

It is the conceptions of ourselves that are most important to us that give rise to unconditional obligations. For to violate them is to lose your integrity and so your identity, and to no longer be who you are. That is, it is to no longer be able to think of yourself under the description under which you value yourself and find your life to be worth living and your actions to be worth undertaking. It is to be for all practical purposes dead or worse than dead. When an action cannot be performed without loss of some fundamental part of one's identity, and an agent could just as well be dead, then the obligation not to do it is unconditional and complete. If reasons arise from reflective endorsement, then obligation arises from reflective *rejection*.

3.3.2

Actually, all obligation is unconditional in the sense that I have just described. An obligation always takes the form of a reaction against a threat of a loss of identity. But there are two important complications, and both spring from the complexity of human identity. One is that some parts of our identity are easily shed, and, where they come into conflict with more fundamental parts of our identity, they should be shed. The cases I have in mind are standard: a good soldier obeys orders, but a good human being doesn't massacre the innocent. The other complication, more troublesome, is that you can stop being yourself for a bit and still get back home, and in cases where a small violation combines with a large temptation, this has a destabilizing effect on the obligation. You may know that if you always did this sort of thing your identity would disintegrate, like that of Plato's tyrant in *Republic* IX, but you also know that you can do it just this once without any such result. Kant points out that when we violate the laws of the Kingdom of Ends we must be making exceptions of ourselves, because we cannot coherently will their universal violation.[5] In one sense, a commitment to your own identity – that is, to your integrity – is

supposed to solve that problem. But as we have just seen, the problem reiterates within the commitment to your own integrity. The problem here does not come from the fragility of identity, but rather from its stability. It can take a few knocks, and we know it. The agent I am taking about now violates the law that she is to herself, making an exception of the moment or the case, which she knows she can get away with.

This is why it is best if we love our values as well as having them. [. . .] Obligation is always unconditional, but it is only when it concerns really important matters that it is *deep*. Of course, since we can see that the shallowness of obligation could give rise to problems, we must commit ourselves to a kind of second-order integrity, a commitment to not letting these problems get out of hand. We cannot make an exception 'just this once' every time, or we will lose our identities after all. But the problem will reiterate within that commitment, and so on up the line.

That, by the way, is why even people with the most excellent characters can *occasionally* knowingly do wrong.

3.3.3

To get back to the point. The question how exactly an agent *should* conceive her practical identity, the question which law she should be to herself, is not settled by the arguments I have given. So moral obligation is not yet on the table. To that extent the argument so far is formal, and in one sense empty.

But in another sense it is not empty at all. What we have established is this. The reflective structure of human consciousness requires that you identify yourself with some law or principle which will govern your choices. It requires you to be a law to yourself. And that is the source of normativity. So the argument shows just what Kant said that it did: that our autonomy is the source of obligation.

It will help to put the point in Joseph Butler's terms, the distinction between power and authority. We do not always do what upon reflection we would do or even what upon reflection we have already decided to do. Reflection does not have irresistible power over us. But when we do reflect we cannot but think that we ought to do what on

[5] Kant, *Foundations of the Metaphysics of Morals*, p. 424; in Beck's translation, p. 42.

reflection we conclude we have reason to do. And when we don't do that we punish ourselves, by guilt and regret and repentance and remorse. We might say that the acting self concedes to the thinking self its right to government. And the thinking self, in turn, tries to govern as well as it can. So the reflective structure of human consciousness establishes a relation here, a relation which we have to ourselves. And it is a relation not of mere power but rather of *authority*. And *that* is the authority that is the source of obligation.

Notice that this means that voluntarism is true after all. The source of obligation is a legislator. The realist objection – that we need to explain why we must obey that legislator – has been answered, for this is a legislator whose authority is beyond question and does not need to be established. It is the authority of your own mind and will. So Pufendorf and Hobbes were right. It is not the bare fact that it would be a good idea to perform a certain action that obligates us to perform it. It is the fact that we *command ourselves* to do what we find it would be a good idea to do.

3.3.4

With that in mind, let me return to the example I used in lecture I to illustrate the voluntarist conception of the motive of duty: the example of a student who takes a course because it is a required. In lecture I I said that acting on the motive of duty as Pufendorf and Hobbes understood it seems appropriate in this kind of case. Although the student might appreciate the reasons why it is a good idea that the course should be required, it would be a little odd to say that that is his motive, since he has a decisive reason for taking the course whether he understands those reasons or not. I had in mind a story like this: you are visiting some other department, not your own, and fall into conversation with a graduate student. You discover that he is taking a course in some highly advanced form of calculus, and you ask him why. With great earnestness, he begins to lay out an elaborate set of reasons. 'Philosophers since the time of Plato', he says, 'have taken mathematics to be the model for knowledge: elegant, certain, perfect, beautiful, and utterly *a priori*. But you can't really understand either the power of the model or its limits if you have an outsider's view of mathematics. You must really get in there and do mathematics if you are to fully appreciate all this . . .' And just when you are

about to be really impressed by this young man's commitment and seriousness, another student comes along smiling and says 'and anyway, calculus is required in our department'.

In that story, the first student seems like a phony. Since he has *that* motive for taking the course, all the rest seems a little irrelevant. But now I am saying that when we are autonomous, we bind ourselves to do what it seems to us to be a good idea to do. So isn't the first student, after all, more autonomous than the student who takes the course merely because it's required? And isn't the first student's action therefore more authentically an action from duty?

If he weren't required to take the course, and he took it for the reasons he gives you, then in one sense he would be more autonomous than the student who takes it merely because it is required. He would be guided by his own mind, not that of another. But if he is required to take it, the reasons he gives should not be his motive. This may seem odd, since in a sense they are better reasons. But even if he understands them, they are excluded by his practical identity. Because his practical identity, in this case, is being a student. And this has two implications. First, to the extent that you identify yourself as a student, you *do* act autonomously in taking a course that is required. And second, it is an essential part of the idea of being a student that you place the right to make some of the decisions about what you will study in the hands of your teachers. And that means that when one of those decisions is in question, you are not free to act on your own *private* reasons any more, no matter how good those reasons are in themselves.

This is not just because there is an inherent element of subordination in the position of a student. For exactly similar reasons, a good citizen cannot pay her taxes because she thinks the government needs the money. She can *vote* for taxes for that reason. But once the vote is over, she must pay her taxes because it is the law. And that is again because citizenship is a form of practical identity, with the same two implications. To be a citizen is to make a certain set of decisions in company with the other citizens – to participate in a general will. In so far as you are a citizen, you do act autonomously in obeying the law. And for exactly that reason, in so far as you are a citizen, you aren't free to act on your own private reasons any more.

Some will be tempted to say that the student who understands the reasons why a course is required, and who therefore would take it even if it weren't required, is somehow *more* autonomous than the student who takes the course *just* because it is required. If a student understands why the course is required, his taking it is endorsed both from the point of view of his identity as a student and from the point of view of his identity as a rational being with a mind of his own. So he seems to be more autonomous. But we shouldn't be too quick to jump to the conclusion that this is the way things work in general. The student's autonomy may be augmented in this case, because his understanding of the reasons for the requirement also helps him to make sense to himself of his *being* a student. It helps him to endorse his identity as a student, for it gives him confidence in his teachers' judgment. But other cases are different. The reason for participating in a general will, and so for endorsing one's identity as a citizen, is that we share the world with others who are free, not that we have confidence in their judgment. A citizen who acts on a vote that has gone the way she thinks it should may in one sense be more wholehearted than one who must submit to a vote that has not gone her way. But a citizen in whom the general will triumphs *gracefully* over the private will exhibits a very special kind of autonomy, which is certainly not a lesser form. Autonomy is commanding yourself to do what you think it would be a good idea to do, but that in turn depends on who you think you are. That's what I've been saying all along.

3.3.5

One more step is necessary. The acting self concedes to the thinking self its right to govern. But the thinking self in turn must try to govern well. It is its job to make what is in any case a good idea into law. How do we know what's a good idea or what should be a law? Kant proposes that we can tell whether our maxims should be laws by attending not to their matter but to their form.

To understand this idea, we need to return to its origins, which are in Aristotle. According to Aristotle, a thing is composed of a form and a matter. The matter is the material, the parts, from which it is made. The form of a thing is its func-

tional arrangement. That is, it is the arrangement of the matter or of the parts which enables the thing to serve its purpose, to do whatever it does. For example the purpose of a house is to be a shelter, so the form of a house is the way the arrangement of the parts – the walls and roof – enables it to serve as a shelter. 'Join the walls at the corner, put the roof on top, and that's how we keep the weather out.' That is the form of a house.[6]

Next consider the maxim of an action. Since every human action is done for an end, a maxim has two parts: the act and the end. The form of the maxim is the arrangement of its parts. Take for instance Plato's famous example of the three maxims:[7]

1   I will keep my weapon, because I want it for myself.
2   I will refuse to return your weapon, because I want it for myself.
3   I will refuse to return your weapon, because you have gone mad and may hurt someone.

Maxims one and three are good: maxim two is bad. What makes them so? Not the actions, for maxims two and three have the same actions; not the purposes, for maxims one and two have the same purposes. The goodness does not rest in the parts; but rather in the way the part are combined and related; so the goodness does not rest in the matter, but rather in the form, of the maxim. But form is not merely the arrangement of the parts; it is the *functional* arrangement – the arrangement that enables the thing to do what it does. If the walls are joined and roof placed on top *so that* the building can keep the weather out, then the building has the form of a house. So: if the action and the purpose are related to one another *so that* the maxim can be willed as a law, then the maxim is good.

Notice what this establishes. A good maxim is good in virtue of its internal structure. Its internal structure, its form, makes it fit to be willed as a law. A good maxim is therefore an *intrinsically normative entity*. So realism is true after all, and Nagel, in particular, was right. When an impulse presents itself to us, as a kind of candidate for being a reason, we look to see whether it really is a reason, whether its claim to normativity is true.

---

[6]   These views are found throughout Aristotle's writings, but centrally discussed in books VII–IX of *Metaphysics* and in *On the Soul*.
[7]   Plato, *Republic*, I, 331C., p. 580.

But this isn't an exercise of intuition, or a discovery about what is out there in the world. The test for determining whether an impulse is a reason is whether *we* can will acting on that impulse as a law. So the test is a test of endorsement.

[. . .]

3.3.7

This completes the first part of my argument, so let me sum up what I've said. What I have shown so far is why there is such a thing as obligation. The reflective structure of human consciousness sets us a problem. Reflective distance from our impulses makes it both possible and necessary to decide which ones we will act on: it forces us to act for reasons. At the same time, and relatedly, it forces us to have a conception of our own identity, a conception which identifies us with the source of those reasons. In this way, it makes us laws to ourselves. When an impulse – say a desire – presents itself to us, we ask whether it could be a reason. We answer that question by seeing whether the maxim of acting on it can be willed as a law by a being with the identity in question. If it can be willed as law it is a reason, for it has an intrinsically normative structure. If it cannot be willed as a law, we must reject it, and in that case we get obligation.

[. . .] What I have established so far is that obligation in general is a reality of human life. That we obligate ourselves is simply a fact about human nature, and our maxims can be seen as intrinsically normative entities. But there is still a deep element of relativism in the system. For whether a maxim can serve as a law still depends upon the way that we think of our identities. And as I've said already, different laws hold for wantons, egoists, lovers, and Citizens of the Kingdom of Ends. In order to establish that there are particular ways in which we *must* think of our identities, and so that there are *moral* obligations, we will need another step.

Moral Obligation

3.4.1

There is another way to make the points I have been making, and in approaching the problem of relativism it will be helpful to employ it. We can take as our model the way Rawls employs the concept/conception distinction in *A Theory of Justice*. There, the *concept* of justice refers to a problem, or, if you prefer, refers in a formal way to the solution of that problem. The problem is what we might call the distribution problem: people join together in a cooperative scheme because it will be better for all of them, but they must decide how its benefits and burdens are to be distributed. A *conception* of justice is a principle that is proposed as a solution to the distribution problem. How are we to distribute the benefits and burdens of cooperative living ? 'So that aggregate happiness is maximized' is the utilitarian conception of justice. 'So that things are as good as possible for the least advantaged, in so far as that is consistent with the freedom of all' is Rawls's. The concept names the problem, the conception proposes a solution. The normative force of the conception is established in this way. If you recognize the problem to be yours, and the solution to be the best one, then the solution is binding upon you.

In the same way, the most general normative concepts, the right and the good, are names for problems – for the normative problems that spring from our reflective nature. 'Good' names the problem of what we are to strive for, aim at, and care about in our lives. 'Right' names the more specific problem of which actions we may perform. The 'thinness' of these terms, to use Bernard Williams's language, comes from the fact that they are, so far, only concepts, names for whatever it is that solves the problems in question. We need *conceptions* of the right and the good before we know what to do.

3.4.2

How do we get from concepts to conceptions? As suggested above, what mediates is a conception of practical identity. This conception both embodies the problem and serves as an aid in finding the solution. For example, in Rawls's argument, we move from concept to conception by taking up the standpoint of the pure liberal citizen, who has only the attributes shared by all the citizens of a well-ordered liberal state: a willingness to abide by whatever principles of cooperation may be chosen in the original position, and her own conception of the good. We ask what laws such a citizen has reason to adopt. And in so far as we regard ourselves as such citizens, those are laws which we have reason to accept. In Kant's argument, we move from concept to conception by taking up the standpoint of a legislative Citizen in the Kingdom of Ends, and asking what laws that kind of citizen has reason to adopt. Again, in so far as we regard ourselves as Citizens of the Kingdom of Ends, those laws are ones we have reason to accept. Citizen of the Kingdom of Ends is a conception of practical identity which leads in turn to a conception of the right.

3.4.3

If this is correct, then Williams is wrong to say that reflection is not inherent in, or already implied by, what he calls 'thick ethical concepts'. Thick ethical concepts stand to thin ones as conceptions to concepts. Since they are normative, they are essentially reflective, and that means they embody a view about what is right or good.

And there is another implication. Williams concluded that our ethical concepts, unlike the ones we employ in the physical sciences, need not be shared with members of other cultures. But our thin ethical concepts, although not necessarily our thick ones, will be shared, even with the alien scientific investigators that his argument invokes. For the fact that they are scientific investigators means that they have asked themselves what they ought to believe, and that they have decided that the question is worth pursuing. And that in turn means that they are rational and social beings, who face normative problems like our own, and sometimes solve them. The exact shape of their problems may be different from ours, and so they may have different conceptions. But they will have views about what is right and what is good, and their language will have terms in which these views are expressed. So we will be able to translate our own terms into their language, and to talk to them about the right and the good. And if we can come at least to see their conceptions as solutions to the normative problems that *they* face, there will even be a kind of convergence.

But neither the fact that we will share thin ethical concepts with the aliens nor the way in which reflection is inherent in thick ones suggests that we are converging on an *external* world of objectively real values. Value is grounded in rational nature – in particular in the structure of reflec-

tive consciousness – and it is projected on to the world. So the reflection in question is practical and not theoretical: it is reflection about what to do, not reflection about what is to be found in the normative part of the world.

3.4.4

But this does not eliminate the element of relativism that Williams has sought to preserve. The mediation between concepts and conceptions comes by way of practical identity. A view of what you ought to do is a view of who you are. And human identity has been differently constituted in different social worlds. Sin, dishonour, and moral wrongness all represent conceptions of what one cannot do without being diminished or disfigured, without loss of identity, and therefore conceptions of what one must not do. But they belong to different worlds in which human beings thought of themselves and of what made them themselves in very different ways. Where sin is the conception my identity is my soul and it exists in the eyes of my God. Where dishonour is the conception my identity is my reputation, my position in some small and knowable social world. The conception of *moral* wrongness as we now understand it belongs to the world *we* live in, the one brought about by the Enlightenment, where one's identity is one's relation to humanity itself. Hume said at the height of the Enlightenment that to be virtuous is to think of yourself as a member of the 'party of humankind, against vice and disorder, its common enemy'.[8] And that is now true. But we coherently can grant that it was not always so.

3.4.5

But this is not to say that there is nothing to be said in favour of the Enlightenment conception. This sort of relativism has its limits, and they come from two different but related lines of thought.

We have already seen one of them set forward by Bernard Williams. We could, with the resources of a knowledge of human nature, rank different sets of values according to their tendency to promote human flourishing. If values are associated with ways of conceiving one's identity, then the point will be that some ways of thinking of our identity are healthier and better for us than others. The

---

[8] Hume, *Enquiry Concerning the Principles of Morals*, p. 275.

basic claim here would be that it is better for us to think of ourselves, and more essentially to value ourselves, just as human beings than, say, as men or women, or as members of certain religious or ethnic groups, or as the possessors of certain talents. Or at least it is better if these other conceptions are governed by a value one places on oneself as simply human, a member of the party of humanity.

Obviously, without the resources of psychoanalytic and sociological theory we cannot envision what this kind of argument would look like in any detail. But it is a striking fact that philosophers who promote the adoption of Enlightenment liberal ideas have often appealed to arguments of this kind. In *The Subjection of Women*, for example, Mill points out the damaging effects on *men* of identifying themselves in terms of gender.[9] In *A Theory of Justice*, Rawls argues that the view of human talents as a kind of shared social resource, which he thinks would result from the just society he envisions, would make it easier for people to maintain a sense of self-worth.[10] Both of these arguments are meant to show that societies which accord equal value to human beings as such are better *for* people and that this is one reason to have them.

Of course there are also different ways of thinking of what it means to be valuable as a human being, or as a member of the party of humanity. Citizen of the Kingdom of Ends, participant in a common happiness, species being, one among others who are equally real, are different conceptions of the human-being-as-such among which further sorting would have to be done.

3.4.6

But it is also important to remember that no argument can preserve any form of relativism without on another level eradicating it. This is one of the main faults with one well-known criticism of liberalism, that the conception of the person which is employed in its arguments is an 'empty self'.[11] It is urged by communitarians that people need to conceive themselves as members of smaller communities, essentially tied to particular others and traditions. This is an argument about how we human beings need to constitute our practical iden-

tities, and if it is successful what it establishes is a *universal* fact, namely that our practical identities must be constituted in part by particular ties and commitments. The liberal who wants to include everyone will now argue from that fact. And the communitarian himself, having reflected and reached this conclusion, now has a conception of his own identity which is universal: he is an animal that needs to live in community.

And there is a further implication of this which is important. Once the communitarian sees himself this way, his particular ties and commitments will remain normative for him only if this more fundamental conception of his identity is one which he can see as normative as well. A further stretch of reflection requires a further stretch of endorsement. So he must endorse this new view of his identity. He is an animal that needs to live in community, and he now takes *this* to be a normative identity. He treats it as a source of reasons, for he argues that it matters that he gets what he needs.

And this further stretch of endorsement is exactly what happens. Someone who is moved to urge the value of *having* particular ties and commitments has discovered that part of their normativity comes from the fact that human beings need to have them. He urges that our lives are meaningless without them. That is not a reason that *springs from* one of his own particular ties and commitments. It is a plea on behalf of all human beings, which he makes because he now identifies in a certain way with us all. And that means that he is no longer immersed in a normative world of particular ties and commitments. Philosophical reflection does not leave everything just where it was.

3.4.7

So we may begin by accepting something like the communitarian's point. It is necessary to have *some* conception of your practical identity, for without it you cannot have reasons to act. We endorse or reject our impulses by determining whether they are consistent with the ways in which we identify ourselves. Yet most of the self-conceptions which govern us are contingent. You are born into a certain family and community, perhaps even into a certain profession or craft. You find a vocation, or

---

9   Mill, *The Subjection of Women*. See especially chapter IV, pp. 86–8.
10   Rawls, *A Theory of Justice*, especially sections 67 and 81.
11   See for instance Michael Sandel, *Liberalism and the Limits of Justice*.

ally yourself with a movement. You fall in love and make friends. You are a mother of some particular children, a citizen of a particular country, an adherent of a particular religion, because of the way your life has fallen out. And you act accordingly – caring for your children because they are your children, fighting for your country because you are its citizen, refusing to fight because you are a Quaker, and so on.

Because these conceptions are contingent, one or another of them may be shed. You may cease to think of yourself as a mother or a citizen or a Quaker, or, where the facts make that impossible, the conception may cease to have practical force: you may stop caring whether you live up to the demands of a particular role. This can happen in a variety of ways: it is the stuff of drama, and perfectly familiar to us all. Conflicts that arise between identities, if sufficiently pervasive or severe, may force you to give one of them up: loyalty to your country and its cause may turn you against a pacifist religion, or the reverse. Circumstances may cause you to call the practical importance of an identity into question: falling in love with a Montague may make you think that being a Capulet does not matter after all. Rational reflection may bring you to discard a way of thinking of your practical identity as silly or jejune.

What is not contingent is that you must be governed by *some* conception of your practical identity. For unless you are committed to some conception of your practical identity, you will lose your grip on yourself as having any reason to do one thing rather than another – and with it, your grip on yourself as having any reason to live and act at all. But *this* reason for conforming to your particular practical identities is not a reason that *springs from* one of those particular practical identities. It is a reason that springs from your humanity itself, from your identity simply as *a human being*, a reflective animal who needs reasons to act and to live. And so it is a reason you have only if you treat your humanity as a practical, normative, form of identity, that is, if you value yourself as a human being.

But to value yourself just as a human being is to have moral identity, as the Enlightenment understood it. So this puts you in moral territory. Or at least, it does so if valuing humanity in your own person rationally requires valuing it in the persons of others. There's an objection to that idea, which I will take up in the next lecture. For now, I will assume that valuing ourselves as human beings involves valuing others that way as well, and carries with it moral obligations.

If this is right, our identity as moral beings – as people who value themselves as human beings – stands behind our more particular practical identities. It is because we are human that we must act in the light of practical conceptions of our identity, and this means that their importance is partly derived from the importance of being human. We must conform to them not merely for the reasons that caused us to adopt them in the first place, but because being human requires it. You may give up one of your contingent practical roles. But so long as you remain committed to a role, and yet fail to meet the obligations it generates, you fail yourself as a human being, as well as failing in that role. And if you fail in all of your roles – if you live at random, without integrity or principle, then you will lose your grip on yourself as one who has any reason to live and to act at all.

Most of the time, our reasons for action spring from our more contingent and local identities. But part of the normative force of those reasons springs from the value we place on ourselves as human beings who need such identities. In this way all value depends on the value of humanity; other forms of practical identity matter in part because humanity requires them. Moral identity and the obligations it carries with it are therefore inescapable and pervasive. Not every form of practical identity is contingent or relative after all: moral identity is necessary.

3.4.8

This is just a fancy new model of an argument that first appeared in a much simpler form, Kant's argument for his Formula of Humanity.[12] The form of relativism with which Kant began was the most elementary one we encounter – the relativism of value to human desires and interests. He started from the fact that when we make a choice we must regard its object as good. His point is the one I have been making – that being human we must endorse our impulses before we can act on them. He asked what it is that makes these objects good, and, rejecting one form of realism, he decided that the

---

[12] Kant, *Foundations of the Metaphysics of Morals*, pp. 427–8; in Beck's translation, pp. 45–7.

goodness was not in the objects themselves. Were it not for our desires and inclinations – and for the various physiological, psychological, and social conditions which gave rise to those desires and inclinations – we would not find their objects good. Kant saw that we take things to be important because they are important to us – and he concluded that we must therefore take ourselves to be important. In this way, the value of humanity itself is implicit in every human choice. If complete normative scepticism is to be avoided – if there is such a thing as a reason for action – then humanity, as the source of all reasons and values, must be valued for its own sake.

3.4.9

The point I want to make now is the same. In this lecture I have offered an account of the source of normativity. I have argued that human consciousness has a reflective structure that sets us normative problems. It is because of this that we require reasons for action, a conception of the right and the good. To act from such a conception is in turn to have a practical conception of your identity, a conception under which you value yourself and find your life to be worth living and your actions to be worth undertaking. That conception is normative for you and in certain cases it can obligate you, for if you do not allow yourself to be governed by any conception of your identity then you will have no reason to act and to live. So a human being is an animal who needs a practical conception of her own identity, a conception of who she is which is normative for her.

But you are a human being and so if you believe my argument you can now see that that is *your* identity. You are an animal of the sort I have just described. And that is not merely a contingent conception of your identity, which you have constructed or chosen for yourself, or could conceivably reject. It is simply the truth. It is because we are such animals that our practical identities are normative for us, and, once you see this, you must take this more fundamental identity, being such an animal, to be normative as well. You must value your own humanity if you are to value anything at all.

Why? Because now that you see that your need to have a normative conception of yourself comes from your human identity, you can query the importance of that identity. Your humanity requires you to conform to some of your practical identities, and you can question this requirement as you do any other. Does it really matter whether we act as our humanity requires, whether we find some ways of identifying ourselves and stand by them? But in this case you have no option but to say yes. Since you are human you *must* take something to be normative, that is, some conception of practical identity must be normative for you. If you had no normative conception of your identity, you could have no reasons for action, and because your consciousness is reflective, you could then not act at all. Since you cannot act without reasons and your humanity is the source of your reasons, you must value your own humanity if you are to act at all.

It follows from this argument that human beings are valuable. Enlightenment morality is true.

3.4.10

The argument I have just given is a transcendental argument. I might bring that out more clearly by putting it this way: rational action exists, so we know it is possible. How is it possible? And then by the course of reflections in which we have just engaged, I show you that rational action is possible only if human beings find their own humanity to be valuable. But rational action is possible, and we are the human beings in question. Therefore we find ourselves to be valuable. Therefore, of course, we are valuable.

You might want to protest against that last step. How do we get from the fact that we find ourselves to be valuable to the conclusion that we are valuable? When we look at the argument this way, its structure seems to be like that of Mill's argument, which proved that if there were any utilitarians, they would find their morality to be normative, and invited us to think that therefore utilitarianism is normative.

But my argument, unlike Mill's, will not fail to find its target. For Mill's readers were not already utilitarians, or did not acknowledge themselves to be so, but you are already human beings, and do acknowledge yourself to be so.

And there's a good reason why the argument must take this form after all. Value, like freedom, is only directly accessible from within the standpoint of reflective consciousness. And I am now talking about it externally, for I am describing the nature of the consciousness that gives rise to the perception of value. From this external, third-person perspective, all we can say is that when we are in the first-person perspective we find ourselves to be valuable, rather than simply that we are valuable. There is nothing surprising in this. Trying to actually see the value of humanity from the third-person perspective is like trying to see the colours someone sees by cracking open his skull. From outside, all we can say is why he sees them.

Suppose you are now tempted once more to say that this shows that value is unreal just as colour is unreal. We do not need to posit the existence of colours to give scientific explanations of why we see them. Then the answer will be the same as before. The Scientific World View is no substitute for human life. If you think colours are unreal, go and look at a painting by Bellini or Olitski, and you will change your mind. If you think reasons and values are unreal, go and make a choice, and you will change your mind.

Morality, Personal Relationships, and Conflict

3.5.1

The argument I have just given is, as I said a moment ago, a transcendental argument. What it is really intended to show is this: that if you value anything at all, or, if you acknowledge the existence of any practical reasons, then you must value your humanity as an end in itself. Or, I might put it, if you are to have any practical identity at all, you must acknowledge yourself to have moral identity – human identity conceived as a form of normative practical identity – as well. And this identity like any other carries with it obligations.

I take this argument to show that any reflective agent can be led to acknowledge that she has moral obligations. What makes morality special is that it springs from a form of identity which cannot be rejected unless we are prepared to reject practical normativity, or the existence of practical reasons, altogether – a possibility about which I will say more in the next lecture. Our other practical identities depend for their normativity on the normativity of our human identity – on our own endorsement of our human need to be governed by such identities – and cannot withstand reflective

scrutiny without it. We must value ourselves as human.

But I do not take the argument to show that all obligations are moral, or that moral obligations always trump others. In fact the argument requires – and our nature requires – that we do have some more local and contingent identities, which provide us with most of our reasons to live and to act. Moral identity does not swamp other forms of identity: no one is simply a moral agent and nothing more. Bernard Williams is right when he says that if morality demanded that of us, it would be incoherent.[13] But it would be wrong to conclude that therefore either moral obligation, or our other obligations, can't be unconditional. To conclude that would not be to affirm the possibility of conflict, but rather to remove its sting. Conflicting obligations can both be unconditional; that's just one of the ways in which human life is hard.

To clarify the point, we should distinguish between two kinds of conflict. One may have a practical identity that is in and of itself contradictory to the value of humanity – say, the identity of an assassin. Or, one may have a practical identity that is not by its nature contrary to moral value, but that leads to a conflict with it in this or that case. The first kind of identity, and the conflicts it generates, is, I think, ruled out by the course of reflection I have tried to describe. In so far as the importance of having a practical identity comes from the value of humanity, it does not make sense to identify oneself in ways that are inconsistent with the value of humanity. But the second kind of conflict cannot be ruled out in this way. Conflict between the specific demands of morality and those of some more contingent form of identity may still exist.

[. . .]

Conclusion

3.6.1

In this lecture I have tried to establish two points. First, the reflective structure of human consciousness gives us authority over ourselves. Reflection gives us a kind of distance from our impulses which both forces us, and enables us, to make laws for ourselves, and it makes those laws normative. To make

---

[13]   See Williams, 'Persons, Character, and Morality' and 'Moral Luck' [in his *Moral Luck*].

a law for yourself, however, is at the same time to give expression to a practical conception of your identity. Practical conceptions of our identity determine which of our impulses we will count as reasons. And to the extent that we cannot act against them without losing our sense that our lives are worth living and our actions are worth undertaking, they can obligate us.

Being human, we may at any point come to question the normativity of one or another of our practical identities, to ask why we must live up to them and conform to their laws. Why should it matter whether I live up to the demands imposed upon me by citizenship, or motherhood, or my profession? Most of the ways in which we identify ourselves are contingent upon our particular circumstances, or relative to the social worlds in which we live. How can we be bound by obligations which spring from conceptions of our identity which are not in themselves necessary?

This leads to the second point. The course of reflection to which this kind of question gives rise leads us to recognize the form of identity which stands behind the others: our identity as human, that is, as reflective animals who need to have practical conceptions of our identity in order to act and to live. To treat your human identity as normative, as a source of reasons and obligations, is to have what I have been calling 'moral identity'.

In one sense, moral identity is just like any other form of practical identity. To act morally is to act a certain way simply because you are human, to act as one who values her humanity should. Among the many things that you are, you are a member of the party of humanity, or a Citizen of the Kingdom of Ends. And this identity like any other carries certain obligations. But moral identity also stands in a special relationship to our other identities. First, moral identity is what makes it necessary to have other forms of practical identity, and they derive part of their importance, and so part of their normativity, from it. They are important in part because we need them. If we do not treat our humanity as a normative identity, none of our other identities can be normative, and then we can have no reasons to act at all. Moral identity is therefore inescapable. Second, and for that reason, moral identity exerts a kind of governing role over the other kinds. Practical conceptions of your identity which are fundamentally inconsistent with the value of humanity must be given up.

The view as I have presented it so far leaves three important worries unaddressed. First, you may think that I have shown only (or at most) that you must place a value on your own humanity, but not yet that you therefore have obligations to other human beings. Valuing your own humanity does not require valuing the humanity of others. Second, you may object that moral concern should not be limited to human beings at all: animals and other parts of nature should have moral standing. And third, you may worry that I have not really answered the sceptic, for I have several times said that we must value our humanity if we are to value anything at all, but I have not said why we must value anything at all. In the next lecture, I will develop my account further by responding to these objections.

Bibliography

Aristotle. *The Complete Works of Aristotle*. Edited by Jonathan Barnes. Princeton: Princeton University Press, 1984.

Hume, David. *Enquiry Concerning the Principles of Morals* (1751), in *David Hume: Enquiries Concerning Human Understanding and Concerning the Principles of Morals*. 3rd edition edited by L. A. Selby-Bigge and P. H. Nidditch. Oxford: Clarendon Press, 1975.

Kant, Immanuel. *Grundlegung zur Metaphysick der Sitten* (*Foundations of the Metaphysics of Morals*, 1785). Translated by Lewis White Beck. New York: Macmillan Library of Liberals Arts, 1959.

Kant, Immanuel. *Kritik der praktischen Vernunft* (*Critique of Practical Reason*, 1788). Translated by Lewis White Beck. New York: Macmillan Library of Liberal Arts, 1956.

Mill, John Stuart. *The Subjection of Women* (1869). Edited by Susan Moller Okin. Indianapolis: Hackett Publishing Company, 1988.

Plato. *The Collected Dialogues*. Edited by Edith Hamilton and Huntington Cairns. Princeton: Princeton University Press, 1961.

Rawls, John. *A Theory of Justice*. Cambridge, MA: Harvard University Press, 1971.

Sandel, Michael J. *Liberalism and the Limits of Justice*. Cambridge: Cambridge University Press, 1982.

Williams, Bernard. *Moral Luck*. Cambridge: Cambridge University Press, 1981.

9

Ethical Absolutism and the Ideal Observer

Roderick Firth

The moral philosophy of the first half of the twentieth century, at least in the English-speaking part of the world, has been largely devoted to problems concerning the analysis of ethical statements, and to correlative problems of an ontological or epistemological nature. This concentration of effort by many acute analytical minds has not produced any general agreement with respect to the solution of these problems; it seems likely, on the contrary, that the wealth of proposed solutions, each making some claim to plausibility, has resulted in greater disagreement than ever before, and in some cases disagreement about issues so fundamental that certain schools of thought now find it unrewarding, if not impossible, to communicate with one another. Moral philosophers of almost all schools seem to agree, however, that no major possibility has been neglected during this period, and that every proposed solution which can be adjudged at all plausible has been examined with considerable thoroughness. It is now common practice, for example, for the authors of books on moral philosophy to introduce their own theories by what purports to be a classification and review of all *possible* solutions to the basic problems of analysis; and in many cases, indeed, the primary defense of the author's own position seems to consist in the negative argument that his own position cannot fail to be correct because none of the others which he has mentioned is satisfactory.

There is one kind of analysis of ethical statements, however, which has certainly not been examined with the thoroughness that it deserves – the kind of analysis, namely, which construes ethical statements to be both absolutist and dispositional. In a paper entitled "Some Reflections on Moral-Sense Theories of Ethics,"[1] Broad has discussed a number of the most important features of this kind of analysis, and has even said that most competent persons would now agree that there are only two other theories about the meaning of ethical terms which are worth as much serious consideration. Yet there are many moral philosophers who leave no place for this kind of analysis in their classification of ethical theories, and many others who treat it unfairly by classifying it with less plausible proposals which are superficially similar. And what makes such carelessness especially unfortunate, is the fact that this kind of analysis seems to be capable of satisfying the major demands of certain schools of ethical thought which are ordinarily supposed to be diametrically opposed to one another. It is a kind of analysis, moreover, which

[1] C. D. Broad, *Proceedings of the Aristotelian Society*, N. S. vol. XLV, pp. 131–66.

may have been proposed and defended by several classical moralists;[2] and this is perhaps one good reason for giving it at least a small share of the attention which is now lavished on positions which are no more plausible.

The following discussion of absolutist dispositional analyses of ethical statements, is divided into two parts. In the first part I have discussed some of the important characteristics which are common to all analyses of this general form. In the second part I have discussed some of the problems which would have to be solved in working out a concrete analysis of this kind, and I have made certain proposals about the manner in which such an analysis can best be formulated.

Part One: Characteristics of the Analysis

1.   It is absolutist

To explain the precise sense in which a dispositional analysis of ethical statements may be absolutist rather than relativist, it is helpful to begin by defining the two terms "relative statement" and "relativist analysis."

Speaking first about statements, we may say that any statement is relative if its meaning cannot be expressed without using a word or other expression which is egocentric. And egocentric expressions may be described as expressions of which the meaning varies systematically with the speaker. They are expressions which are ambiguous in abstraction from their relation to a speaker, but their ambiguity is conventional and systematic. They include the personal pronouns ("I," "you," etc.), the corresponding possessive adjectives ("my," "your," etc.), words which refer directly but relatively to spatial and temporal location ("this," "that," "here," "there," "now," "then," "past," "present," "future"), reflexive expressions such as "the person who is speaking," and the various linguistic devices which are used to indicate the tense of verbs. All of these egocentric expressions can apparently be defined in terms of the word "this."[3]

A moral philosopher is commonly called a relativist, and his analysis of ethical statements is said to be a relativist analysis, if he construes ethical statements to be relative. We may thus say, derivatively, that an analysis of ethical statements is relativist if it includes an egocentric expression, and if it is incompatible with any alternative analysis which does not include an egocentric expression.

It follows, therefore, that relativist analyses, no matter how much they may differ from one another, can always be conveniently and positively identified by direct inspection of their constituent expressions. Thus, to give a few examples, a philosopher is an ethical relativist if he believes that the meaning of ethical statements of the form "Such and such a particular act (x) is right" can be expressed by other statements which have any of the following forms: "*I* like x as much as any alternative to it," "*I* should (in fact) feel ashamed of myself if *I* did not feel approval towards x, and *I* wish that *other people* would too," "Most people *now* living would feel approval towards x if they knew what they really wanted," "If *I* should perceive or think about x and its alternatives, x would seem to *me* to be demanding to be performed," "x is compatible with the mores of the social group to which *the speaker* gives his primary allegiance," and "x will satisfy a maximum of the interests of people *now* living or who *will* live *in the future*." Each one of these possible analyses contains an egocentric expression (which I have italicized). And it is evident that if any of these analyses were correct, it would be possible for one person to say that a certain act is right, and for another person (provided, in some cases, that he is not a member of the same social group, nor living at the same time) to say that that very same act is not right, without logically contradicting each other. This familiar characteristic of all relativist analyses is not *definitive* of relativism; it is, however, a necessary *consequence* of the fact that relativist analyses contain egocentric expressions.

We may now define an absolutist analysis of ethical statements as one which is not relativist. The kind of analysis which I propose to discuss in this paper, therefore, is one which does not include an egocentric expression. It is a kind of analysis, I suspect, which is closely associated with relativism in the minds of many philosophers, but it is

---

[2]   Adam Smith comes immediately to mind, but Hume can likewise be interpreted as accepting an absolutist dispositional analysis of "right."

[3]   *Vide* Bertrand Russell, *An Inquiry Into Meaning and Truth* (London: G. Allen & Unwin, 1940), p. 134, and *Human Knowledge, Its Scope and Its Limits* (New York: Simon & Schuster, 1948), p. 92.

unquestionably absolutist and implies that ethical statements are true or false, and consistent or inconsistent with one another, without special reference to the people who happen to be asserting them.

2. It is dispositional

I shall say that a proposed analysis of ethical statements is dispositional if it construes ethical statements to assert that a certain being (or beings), either actual or hypothetical, is (or are) disposed to react to something in a certain way. To say that a certain being is disposed to react in a certain way is to say that the being in question would react in that way under certain specifiable conditions. Thus a dispositional analysis of an ethical statement may always be formulated as a hypothetical statement of the kind which is commonly called a "contrary-to-fact conditional." A dispositional analysis of statements of the form "x is right," for example, might have the form: "Such and such a being, if it existed, would react to x in such and such a way if such and such conditions were realized."

During the past fifty years moral philosophers have given a good deal of attention to the evaluation of dispositional analyses which are *relativist*, and a comprehensive defense of one such relativist analysis can be found in the writings of [Edward] Westermarck.[4] Westermarck believes, if I understand him, that the meaning of statements of the form "x is wrong," can be expressed by other statements of the form "The speaker tends to feel towards x (i.e., *would* feel in the absence of specifiable inhibiting factors), an emotion of disinterested moral disapproval which would be experienced by him as a quality or dynamic tendency in x." Although this analysis is considerably more sophisticated than many of the analyses which relativists have proposed, it is typical of a position to which absolutists have raised a number of closely-related, and by now very familiar, objections.

A dispositional analysis of ethical statements which was *absolutist* would not, of course, be open to the same objections. It would construe ethical statements in one of the following three ways: (1) as assertions about the dispositions of all *actual* (past, present, and future) beings of a certain kind; (2) as assertions about the dispositions of all *possible* beings of a certain kind (of which there might in fact exist only one or none at all), or (3) as assertions about the dispositions of a majority (or other fraction) of a number of beings (actual or possible) of a certain kind. It is evident that an analysis of any of these three types would include no egocentric expression, and would therefore construe ethical statements in such a way that they would be true or false, and consistent or inconsistent with one another, without special reference to the people who happen to be asserting them.

It is only the second of these three kinds of analysis which I propose to examine in this paper, for analyses of the other two types, it seems to me, are open to obvious and yet insuperable objections. An analysis of the first type would construe ethical statements to entail that there actually exists a being (perhaps God) whose dispositions are definitive of certain ethical terms. But this would mean that all ethical statements containing these ethical terms are necessarily false if such a being does *not* exist – a consequence which seems to be incompatible with what we intend to assert when we use ethical terms. And in my opinion an analysis of the third type would be even less plausible, because it would imply that ethical statements express judgments which can only be verified or refuted, at least theoretically, by statistical procedures. I shall not amplify these familiar arguments, however, since much of what I shall say about ethical analyses of the second type can be equally well applied to analyses of the other two types, and anyone who so wishes may easily make the necessary translations in reading the second part of this paper.

It will be convenient, throughout the following pages, to use the term "ideal observer" in speaking about a possible being of the kind referred to in an absolutist dispositional analysis. The adjective "ideal" is used here in approximately the same sense in which we speak of a perfect vacuum or a frictionless machine as ideal things; it is not intended to suggest that an ideal observer is necessarily *virtuous*, but merely that he is conceivable and that he has certain characteristics to an extreme degree. Perhaps it would seem more natural to call such a being an ideal *judge*, but this term could be quite misleading if it suggested that the function of an ideal observer is to pass judgment on ethical issues. As an ideal observer, of course, it is sufficient that he be capable of reacting in a manner which will determine by definition whether an ethical judgment is true or false. And it is even

---

[4] *Vide* especially *Ethical Relativity* (Patterson, NJ: Littlefield, Adams, 1960), ch. V.

conceivable, indeed, that an ideal observer, according to some analyses, should lack some of the characteristics which would make it *possible* for him to pass judgment on ethical issues – which would mean, of course, simply that he would not be able to judge the nature of his own dispositions.

Using the term "ideal observer," then, the kind of analysis which I shall examine in this paper is the kind which would construe statements of the form "x is P," in which P is some particular ethical predicate, to be identical in meaning with statements of the form: "Any ideal observer would react to x in such and such a way under such and such conditions."

This formulation may draw attention to the fact that a dispositional analysis which is absolutist may nevertheless be extensionally equivalent to one that is relativist. For the egocentric expression in a relativist analysis is often qualified by reference to ideal conditions (described in if-clauses), and it is evident that each of these qualifications limits the respects in which one speaker could differ from another if the reactions of each were relevant to the truth of his own ethical statement. Westermarck, for example, analyzes ethical statements not by reference simply to the feeling which the speaker would actually have if confronted with a particular act or situation, but by reference to the feelings which he would have *if* he were impartial and *if* certain inhibiting factors (e.g., fatigue) were absent. And if a relativist were to continue to add such qualifications to his analysis, he might eventually reach a point at which *any* speaker who met all these qualifications would have all the characteristics which an absolutist might wish to attribute to an ideal observer. In that case ethical statements, when analyzed, would be contrary-to-fact conditionals of the form: "If I were an ideal observer I would react to x in such and such a way under such and such conditions." And if the specified characteristics of an ideal observer were sufficient to insure, in virtue of the laws of nature, that all ideal observers would react in the same way, it is evident that the truth value of ethical statements, so interpreted, would not differ from their truth value if interpreted absolutistically as statements about *any* ideal observer. Intensionally, however, the two analyses would still differ: the relativist, unlike the absolutist, would still maintain that the egocentric reference is essential, and by this he would imply, as we have seen, that two different speakers cannot make ethical assertions which are logically incompatible.

Let us now consider briefly some of the derivative characteristics of an analysis which is both absolutist and dispositional.

3.   *It is objectivist*

The adjectives "subjectivist" and "objectivist" are often used in a *logical* sense, and as synonyms, respectively, of the terms "relativist" and "absolutist"; in this sense, as we have seen, an analysis of the kind that we are discussing is objectivist. To avoid duplication of meaning, however, I shall use the terms "subjectivist" and "objectivist" in a traditional *ontological* sense – in the sense in which Berkeley's analysis of all physical statements is subjectivist, and Descartes's analysis of some physical statements is objectivist. We may say, in this sense, that a proposed analysis of ethical statements is subjectivist if it construes ethical statements in such a way that they would all be false by definition if there existed no experiencing subjects (past, present, or future). An analysis may be called "objectivist," on the other hand, if it is not subjectivist. Thus it is evident that in this ontological sense, as well as in the logical sense, an analysis of the kind which we are discussing is objectivist: it construes ethical statements to be assertions about the reactions of an *ideal* observer – an observer who is conceivable but whose existence or non-existence is logically irrelevant to the truth or falsity of ethical statements.

This fact that a dispositional analysis is objectivist, is obviously a reflection of the fact that ethical statements, according to such an analysis, may always be formulated as conditional statements in the subjunctive mood; they may always be construed, in other words, as asserting that if such and such *were* the case, such and such *would* be the case. Hypothetical statements of this kind are commonly called "contrary-to-fact conditionals," but since they are sometimes used in such a way that they may be true even though they are not contrary to fact, they are perhaps more aptly referred to as "independent-of-fact conditionals." As used in an absolutist dispositional analysis, for example, such statements are not intended to imply *either* that there exists, *nor* that there does not exist, a being who satisfies the description of an ideal observer; they are intended to imply, on the contrary, that the existence or non-existence of such a being is *irrelevant* to the truth of the statement. Since the subjunctive conditional has exactly the same function whether the analysis is absolutist or relativist, it is evident that objectivism and absolutism are logically independent characteristics of an analysis of ethical statements; thus Westermarck's analysis is objectivist and relativist, whereas the one which we shall be examining is objectivist and absolutist.

The fact that an analysis of ethical statements is objectivist, moreover, is independent of all questions concerning the kinds of things to which ethical terms can be correctly applied. Thus it might in fact be true that the term "good" can be correctly applied only to conscious states, and hence that all ethical statements of the form "x is good" would in fact be false if there existed no experiencing subjects. And similarly, it might in fact always be false to say that a given act is wrong if neither that act, nor any of its alternatives, has any effect on the experience of conscious beings. But such facts would be entirely compatible with an objectivist *analysis* of ethical statements, for to say that an analysis is objectivist is to say merely that the existence of experiencing subjects is not essential *by definition* to the truth of ethical statements. This distinction is important because the term "subjectivist" is sometimes applied to hedonism and to certain forms of pluralistic utilitarianism, on the ground that these theories attribute value only to states of consciousness, or that they regard actual productivity of these valuable states as the sole determinant of the rightness or wrongness of an act. It is evident, however, that philosophers who support these theories should not be said to accept a subjectivist analysis of ethical statements unless they believe – as some of them, of course, do not – that ethical terms must be *defined* by reference to the experience of actual beings.

4. It is relational

An analysis of ethical statements is *relational* if it construes ethical terms in such a way that to apply an ethical term to a particular thing (e.g., an act), is to assert that that thing is related in a certain way to some other thing, either actual or hypothetical. There is no doubt that an absolutist dispositional analysis is relational, since it construes ethical statements as asserting that a lawful relationship exists between certain reactions of an ideal observer and the acts or other things to which an ethical term may correctly be applied. But to avoid misunderstanding, this fact must be interpreted in the light of certain qualifying observations.

It should not be overlooked, in the first place, that if an absolutist dispositional analysis were correct, ethical statements would have the same form that statements about secondary qualities are often supposed to have. Not only phenomenalists and subjectivists, but many epistemological dualists, would agree that to say that a daffodil is yellow is to say something about the way the daffodil would appear to a certain kind of observer under certain conditions; and the analysis of ethical statements which we are considering is exactly analogous to this. Thus the sense in which an absolutist dispositional analysis is relational, is the very sense in which a great many philosophers believe that yellow is a relational property of physical objects; and to say that a statement of the form "x is right" is relational, therefore, is not necessarily to deny that the terms "right" and "yellow" designate equally simple properties.

But the analogy can be carried still further if a distinction is drawn between a relational and a nonrelational sense of "yellow." Many philosophers believe that the adjective "yellow" has two meanings; they believe that it designates both a relational property of physical objects and a non-relational property of sense-data – a distinction corresponding roughly to the popular use of the terms "really yellow" and "apparently yellow." And it is quite possible not only that the term "right" is similarly ambiguous, but also that in one of its senses it designates a characteristic of human experience (apparent rightness) which in some important respect is just as simple and unanalyzable as the property of apparent yellowness. And thus we might even decide by analogy with the case of "yellow," that "really right" must be defined in terms of "apparently right" – i.e., that the experiencing of apparent rightness is an essential part of any ethically-significant reaction of an ideal observer.

And finally, it must be remembered that to call an absolutist analysis "relational," is not to imply that it construes the ethical properties of one thing to be dependent by definition on the *existence* of any other thing, either natural or supernatural. Since an ideal observer is a *hypothetical* being, no changes in the relationships of existent things would require us, for logical reasons alone, to attribute new ethical properties to any object, nor to revise any ethical judgment which we have previously made. For this reason an absolutist dispositional analysis is not open to one of the most familiar objections to relational analyses, namely, that such analyses construe the ethical properties of an object to be dependent on facts which seem quite clearly to be *accidental* – on the fact, for example, that certain actual people happen to have a certain attitude toward the object.

5.   *It is empirical*

If we define the term "empirical" liberally enough so that the dispositional concepts of the natural sciences may properly be called empirical, there is no doubt that an absolutist dispositional analysis of ethical statements *might* be empirical. Such an analysis would be empirical, for example, if the defining characteristics of an ideal observer were psychological traits, and if the ethically-significant reactions of an ideal observer were feelings of desire, or emotions of approval and disapproval, or some other experiences accessible to psychological observation.

It might be somewhat less evident, however, that an absolutist dispositional analysis *must* be empirical. For most of the philosophers who maintain that ethical properties are non-natural, and that ethical truths are known by rational intuition, have admitted that ethical intuitions may be erroneous under certain unfavorable conditions, or else, if this is regarded as self-contradictory, that under certain conditions we may appear to be intuiting an ethical truth although in fact we are not. And it might seem that to recognize the possibility of error in either of these two ways is to recognize a distinction between the property of apparent rightness and the property of real rightness – a distinction, as we have seen, which is sufficient to permit the formulation of an absolutist dispositional analysis

[. . .]

Even though we conclude that an absolutist dispositional analysis must be empirical, however, there is still considerable room for disagreement about the precise nature of the ethically-significant reactions of an ideal observer. It seems clear that these reactions, if the analysis is to be at all plausible, must be defined in terms of the kind of moral experience which we take to be evidence, under ideal conditions, for the truth of our ethical judgments. It is important to observe that experiences of this kind – which we may properly call "moral

data" – cannot be states of moral *belief.* An absolutist dispositional analysis, like any other analysis which grants cognitive meaning to ethical sentences, would permit us to say that we *do* have moral beliefs, and even that moral consciousness is *ordinarily* a state of belief. But if the ethically-significant reaction of an ideal observer were the belief (or judgment) that a certain act is right or wrong, it is evident that an absolutist dispositional analysis would be circular: it would contain the very ethical terms which it is intended to define.

In order to define an absolutist dispositional analysis, therefore, it is necessary to maintain that moral data are the moral experiences to which we appeal when *in doubt* about the correct solution of a moral problem, or when attempting to *justify* a moral belief. For the epistemic function of moral data, when defined in this way, will correspond to the function of color sensations in determining or justifying the belief that a certain material object is "really yellow." And in that case moral data could play the same role in the analysis of "right" that color sensations play in the analysis of "really yellow."

Now there are many debatable questions concerning the nature of moral data, and until these questions are answered it will not be possible to explain precisely what is meant by the "ethically-significant reactions" of an ideal observer. These questions are primarily psychological, however, and can easily be separated from other questions concerning the content of an absolutist dispositional analysis. And if it is possible to provide a satisfactory formulation of the other components of an absolutist dispositional analysis (epecially the definition of "ideal observer") this formulation will be compatible with *any* phenomenological description of moral data.

[. . .]

Whatever conclusion we might reach concerning the phenomenal location of moral data, it will still be necessary to distinguish very carefully between moral data themselves, which, under ideal conditions, are the *evidence* for moral beliefs, and the very similar experiences which may be the *consequences* of moral beliefs. This distinction would not be difficult to make if we were content to say that moral data are simply feelings of desire (or, correlatively, that moral data are "demand qualities" of *all* kinds). For there seems to be little reason to doubt that feelings of desire may occur in the absence of moral beliefs. But if we should wish to maintain, as many philosophers have done, that moral data are the emotions of moral approval and disapproval, it would be much harder to make the necessary distinction. As Broad has pointed out, those emotions of approval and disapproval which we think of as specifically *moral* emotions, are the very ones "which appear *prima facie* to be felt towards persons or actions in respect of certain moral characteristics which they are believed to have."[5] So if these emotions are said to be the evidence for moral beliefs, there appears to be a vicious circle in the process by which moral beliefs are justified. And there appears to be a similar vicious circle in an absolutist dispositional analysis. For if moral emotions are experienced only as a consequence of moral beliefs or judgments, and if we refuse to attribute moral beliefs to an ideal observer in our analysis, then there is no reason to think that an ideal observer would experience any moral emotions at all. But if, on the other hand, we do attribute moral beliefs to an ideal observer, we should have to employ the very ethical terms (e.g., "right") which we are attempting to analyze. This fact, in one form or another, has provided the basis for many arguments in support of non-naturalist ethics.

But the difficulty, I believe, has been highly exaggerated. It cannot plausibly be denied that moral emotions are often (perhaps usually) felt as a consequence of moral beliefs – that we often feel approval, for example, toward those acts which we believe to be right. But this is merely to say, if an absolutist dispositional analysis is valid, that we often feel approval toward those acts which we think would produce approval in an ideal observer. The crucial question is whether it is possible to feel an emotion of moral approval toward an act when we are *in doubt* about whether it is right or wrong. And surely this *is* possible. It is not uncommon, for example, to find ourselves feeling moral approval toward an act, and then to begin to wonder whether our reaction is *justified*: we might wonder, for example, whether we are sufficiently familiar with "the facts of the case" or whether our emotions are being unduly influenced by some selfish consideration. At such times we may continue to experience the emotion of moral approval although in doubt about the rightness of the act. We may even

attempt to rationalize our emotion by persuading ourselves that the act is right. In rare cases, indeed, we may even continue to experience the emotion although convinced that our reaction is *not* justified. (This is sometimes the case, for example, when people feel approval toward an act of retribution.) Consequently, unless apparent facts of this kind can be discounted by subtle phenomenological analysis, there is no epistemological objection to defining the ethically significant reactions of an ideal observer in terms of moral emotions.

Whether or not this is the correct way to define these reactions, however, is a psychological question which I shall not consider in this paper. There are other, more fundamental, questions concerning the content of an absolutist dispositional analysis, and it is these to which the remaining part of this paper will be devoted.

Part Two: The Content of the Analysis

If it is possible to formulate a satisfactory absolutist and dispositional analysis of ethical statements, it must be possible, as we have seen, to express the meaning of statements of the form "x is right" in terms of other statements which have the form: "Any ideal observer would react to x in such and such a way under such and such conditions." Thus even if we are not to discuss the nature of the ethically-significant reactions of an ideal observer in this paper, it might seem that we are nevertheless faced with two distinct questions: (1) What are the defining characteristics of an ideal observer? and (2) Under what conditions do the reactions of an ideal observer determine the truth or falsity of ethical statements? I believe, however, that the second of these questions can be treated as part of the first. For it is evident that the conditions under which the ethically-significant reactions of an ideal observer might occur, could be relevant to the meaning of ethical statements only if they could affect an ideal observer in such a way as to influence his ethically-significant reactions. And since the influence of any such relevant conditions must therefore be *indirect*, it would always be possible to insure precisely the same reactions by attributing suitable characteristics directly to the ideal observer. If, for example, the absence of certain emotional stimuli is thought to be a relevant and

---

[5] "Some of the Main Problems of Ethics," *Philosophy*, vol. XXI. no. 79, p. 115.

favorable condition, this fact could be taken into account simply by specifying that the ideal observer is by definition unresponsive to such emotional stimuli. I think it will soon become clear, moreover, that this procedure yields a type of analysis which comes closer to expressing what we actually intend to assert when we utter ethical statements. But even if I am mistaken about this, it will not be prejudicial to any basic problem if we assume, for simplicity, that the second question may be reduced to the first, namely, What are the defining characteristics of an ideal observer?

Before attempting to answer this question, however, there are a few remarks which I think should be made about the implications and methodology of any such attempt to define an ideal observer.

It is important, in the first place, to view any attempt of this kind in proper perspective. It would undoubtedly be difficult to arrive at a rational conclusion concerning the plausibility of absolutist dispositional analyses in general, without first experimenting with various concrete formulations. At the present stage in the history of moral philosophy, however, it would be especially unfortunate if the inadequacies of some particular formulation were to prejudice philosophers against absolutist dispositional analyses in general. Any plausible formulation is certain to be very complex, and there is no reason to suppose that philosophers could ever reach complete agreement concerning all the details of an adequate analysis. But this in itself should not prevent philosophers from agreeing that this general *form* of analysis is valid. Nor would it necessarily be irrational for a philosopher to decide that this general form is valid, although he is dissatisfied even with *his own* attempts to formulate a concrete analysis.

Ethical words, moreover, like all other words, are probably used by different people, even in similar contexts, to express somewhat different meanings; and a correct analysis of one particular ethical statement, therefore, may not be a correct analysis of another statement which is symbolized in exactly the same way but asserted by a different person. This kind of ambiguity is a familiar obstacle to all philosophical analysis, but it causes unusual difficulties when we attempt to evaluate a proposed dispositional analysis of ethical statements. Any such analysis, if it is at all plausible, is certain to assign a number of complex characteristics to an ideal observer, and to refer to complex

psychological phenomena in describing the nature of his ethically-significant reactions. And assuming that ethical statements *can* be analyzed in this manner, there is no good reason to believe that all human beings, no matter what the extent of their individual development, and no matter what their past social environment, could analyze their ethical statements correctly by reference to precisely the same kind of ideal observer and precisely the same psychological phenomena. If there *are* any irreducible differences in the intended meaning of ethical statements, some of these differences might not be discoverable, and most of them might be so slight that they could not be held responsible for differences of opinion concerning the proper analysis of ethical statements. Some of these differences in meaning, on the other hand, might be sufficiently large to be reflected in the formulation of philosophical analyses of ethical statements. And there is consequently a clear sense in which philosophers may appear to disagree about the analysis of ethical statements, although in fact, because ethical words are somewhat ambiguous, they are analyzing different statements and hence not disagreeing at all.

[. . .]

It should also be kept in mind that the kind of analysis which we are seeking is one which would be an analysis of ethical statements in the sense (and probably only in the sense) in which hypothetical statements about the way a daffodil would appear to a "normal" observer are said to constitute an analysis of the material object statement "This daffodil is yellow." To attempt an analysis of this sense of the word "analysis" would lead to difficult problems far beyond the scope of this paper. But two points may be mentioned. First, an analysis in this sense of the word is not required to be *prima facie* or "intuitively" equivalent to the analyzandum, and for this reason the surprising complexity of a proposed analysis is not a sufficient reason for rejecting it: thus the fact that a proposed analysis of "This daffodil is yellow" happens to refer to white light, a transparent medium, a neutral background, and a variety of physiological conditions of an observer, is not ordinarily thought to make the analysis unsatisfactory. And second, an analysis in this sense of the word is an analysis of the so-called "cognitive meaning" of ethical statements, and thus is not required to have the same emotive meaning as the analyzandum. Even if we should find a satisfactory analysis of ethical statements, therefore, we should still have to supplement this analysis by a theory of emotive meaning if we wished to take account of all the functions of ethical statements in actual discourse.

The method employed in formulating dispositional analysis – whether of "soluble" or "yellow" or "right" – is the method most aptly described as "pragmatic." In analyzing ethical statements, for example, we must try to determine the characteristics of an ideal observer by examining the procedures which we actually regard, implicitly or explicitly, as the rational ones for *deciding* ethical questions. These procedures, to mention just a few, might include religious exercises, the acquisition of certain kinds of factual information, appeals to a moral authority, and attempts to suppress one's emotions if they are thought to be prejudicial. Each of these procedures will suggest certain characteristics of an ideal observer, and there is reason to believe that the characteristics suggested by these various procedures will not be incompatible with one another: some of the characteristics which are likely to be attributed to a moral authority, for example, seem to be the very ones which we try to produce or to approximate in ourselves when we engage in religious exercises, or seek for factual information, or attempt to suppress emotions which we think are prejudicial.

[. . .]

Characteristics of an Ideal Observer

1. *He is omniscient with respect to non-ethical facts*

We sometimes disqualify ourselves as judges of a particular ethical question on the ground that we are not sufficiently familiar with the facts of the case, and we regard one person as a better moral judge than another if, other things being equal, the one has a larger amount of relevant factual knowledge than the other. This suggests that an ideal observer must be characterized in part by reference to his knowledge of non-ethical facts. I say "non-ethical" because, as we have seen, the characteristics of an ideal observer must be determined by examining the procedures which we actually take to be the rational ones for deciding ethical questions; and there are many ethical questions (*viz.*,

questions about "ultimate ethical principles") which cannot be decided by inference from ethical premises. This does not mean, of course, that an ideal observer (e.g., God) *cannot* have knowledge of ethical facts (facts, that is to say, about his own dispositions); it means merely that such knowledge is not *essential* to an ideal observer.

A difficulty seems to arise from the fact that in practice we evaluate the factual knowledge of a moral judge by reference to some standard of relevance, and regard one judge as better than another if, other things being equal, the one has more complete knowledge of all the facts which are *relevant*. But it is evident that a concept of relevance cannot be employed in *defining* an ideal observer. To say that a certain body of factual knowledge is not relevant to the rightness or wrongness of a given act, is to say, assuming that an absolutist dispositional analysis is correct, that the dispositions of an ideal observer toward the given act would be the same *whether or not* he possessed that particular body of factual knowledge or any part of it. It follows, therefore, that in order to explain what we mean by "relevant knowledge," we should have to employ the very concept of ideal observer which we are attempting to define.

Fortunately, however, we do not seem to think that a person is to any extent disqualified as a moral judge merely because he possesses factual information which we take to be *superfluous*. Our difficulty would be overcome, therefore, if we were simply to stipulate that an ideal observer is *omniscient* with respect to non-ethical facts, and so far as I can see the term "omniscient," when employed in this way, is neither extravagant nor mysterious. We apparently believe not only that the "facts of the case" are relevant to the objective rightness or wrongness of a particular act, but also that there is no point at which we could be logically certain that further information about matters of fact (e.g., further information about the consequences of the act), would be irrelevant. A satisfactory ethical analysis must be so formulated, therefore, that no facts are irrelevant *by definition* to the rightness or wrongness of any particular act. And this is the intent of the term "omniscient," for to say that an ideal observer is omniscient is to insure that no limits are put on the kinds or the quality of factual information which are available to influence his ethically-significant reactions.

[. . .]

2.   *He is omnipercipient*

We sometimes disqualify ourselves as judges of certain ethical questions on the ground that we cannot satisfactorily imagine or visualize some of the relevant facts, and in general we regard one person as a better moral judge than another if, other things being equal, the one is better able to imagine or visualize the relevant facts. Practical moralists have often maintained that lack of imagination is responsible for many crimes, and some have suggested that our failure to treat strangers like brothers is in large part a result of our inability to imagine the joys and sorrows of strangers as vividly as those of our siblings. These facts seem to indicate that the ideal observer must be characterized by extraordinary powers of imagination.

The imaginal powers of the ideal observer, to be sure, are very closely related to his omniscience, and the word "omniscience" has sometimes been used to designate an unlimited imagination of perception. But however we may decide to use the word "omniscience," the important point is simply that it is not sufficient for an ideal observer to possess factual knowledge in a manner which will permit him to make true factual judgments. The ideal observer must be able, on the contrary, simultaneously to visualize all actual facts, and the consequences of all possible acts in any given situation, just as vividly as he would if he were actually perceiving them all. It is undoubtedly impossible for us to imagine the experience of a being capable of this kind of universal perception, but in making ethical decisions we sometimes attempt to visualize several alternative acts and their consequences in rapid succession, very much *as though* we wished our decision to be based on a simultaneous perception of the alternatives. And in view of this fact, and the others which I have mentioned, it seems necessary to attribute universal imagination to an ideal observer, thus guaranteeing that his ethically-significant reactions are forcefully and equitably stimulated.

3.   *He is disinterested*

We sometimes disqualify ourselves as judges of certain ethical questions on the ground that we cannot make ourselves impartial, and we regard one person as a better moral judge than another if, other things being equal, the one is more impartial than the other. This suggests that one of the defin-

ing characteristics of an ideal observer must be complete impartiality. But it is difficult to define the term "impartial" in a manner which will not make our analysis circular or be otherwise inconsistent with our purpose.

[. . .]

Now it seems to me that a large part of what we mean when we say that an ideal judge is impartial, is that such a judge will not be influenced by interests of the kind which are commonly described as "particular" – interests, that is to say, which are directed toward a particular person or thing but not toward other persons or things of the same kind; and in so far as this is what we mean by "impartiality," we can define the term without falling into error. For to say that an ideal observer is not influenced by particular interests, is to attribute to him a certain psychological characteristic which does not refer, either explicitly or implicitly, to a moral standard. Nor does it logically entail, on the other hand, either that an ideal observer would react favorably, or that he would react unfavorably, to an act which benefits one person at the expense of a greater benefit to another.

The term "particular interest," to be sure, is a difficult one to define, and raises problems about the nature of particularity which are beyond the scope of this paper; but I think that for present purposes it is not unreasonable to pass over these problems. Since ethical judgments are concerned, directly or indirectly, with acts, let us use "x" to denote the performance of a certain act by a certain agent. Let us first draw a distinction between the "essentially general properties" of x and the "essentially particular properties" of x. The properties of x which are essentially particular are those properties which cannot be defined without the use of proper names (which we may understand, for present purposes, to include egocentric particulars such as "I," "here," "now," and "this"); thus one of the essentially particular properties of x might be its tendency to increase the happiness of the citizens of the U.S.A. All other properties are essentially general; thus one of the essentially general properties of x might be its tendency to increase happiness. We may then say that a person has a positive particular interest in x if (1) he desires x, (2) he believes that x has a certain essentially particular property P, and (3) he would not desire x, or would desire it less intensely, if, his other beliefs remaining constant, he did not believe that x had this property P.

It may seem that this definition makes a variety of logical and ontological assumptions, some of which can be questioned. But I think that the intent of the definition is clear enough, and that the distinctions which it requires must be made, in one form or another, by any adequate logic and ontology. The definition is intended to represent the characteristic which we have in mind when we say that a moral judge who lacks impartiality is one who is tempted to "sacrifice principle" – i.e., to judge one act in a manner in which he would not wish to judge other acts which he thought to be of the same kind. And the definition proposes, in effect, that to say in this context that two acts are thought to be "of the same kind," is to say that they are thought to have the same essentially general properties. It is quite likely, of course, that we never actually believe that any two acts *do* have the same essentially general properties; it is for this reason, indeed, that we find it so easy to rationalize and "make exceptions" when judging acts which affect ourselves, our children, or our country. But this fact does not affect the usefulness of the definition, because part (3) is formulated hypothetically in the subjunctive mood: whether or not a person has a particular interest, is something to be decided by inferring, as best we can, how he *would* react *if* his beliefs were altered in certain ways.

[. . .]

Assuming now, that we have found a satisfactory definition of "particular interest," we must still decide how to use this term in our analysis. Shall we say that an ideal observer is completely lacking in particular interests? Or shall we say simply that his ethically-significant reactions are uninfluenced by such interests, leaving open the possibility, so far as our analysis is concerned, that such interests might be present but in some sense "suppressed"? At first thought the latter statement seems to be adequate to represent our concept of an impartial moral judge, for we often admire such a judge precisely because we believe that he does have particular interests but that his desire to be impartial has counteracted their influence. On further reflection it will be discovered, however, that we cannot explain what it means to say that a judge is uninfluenced by particular interests, except by reference, directly or indirectly, to the manner in which he *would* react *if* he had no particular interests. And this seems to imply that the first alternative is ultimately unavoidable if our analysis

is to be complete. I think we must conclude, therefore, that an ideal observer is entirely lacking in particular interests – that he is, in this sense, *disinterested*.

4.   He is dispassionate

The concept of impartiality cannot be exhaustively analyzed in terms of interests, for an impartial judge, as ordinarily conceived, is a judge whose decisions are unaffected not only by his interests, but also by his emotions. This suggests that an ideal observer must be defined as a person who is in some sense dispassionate as well as disinterested. It is possible, to be sure, that the supposed effects of an emotion on our ethically-significant reactions, are always the effects of an accompanying or constituent interest; and if this were proved to our satisfaction, our conception of an ideal observer might be somewhat simplified. For our present purpose, however, this is irrelevant so long as it is generally believed that moral nearsightedness or blindness can be caused by the typically passional features of an emotion. We are searching for an analysis of ordinary ethical statements, and it is not to be expected that such an analysis will reflect all those distinctions, or just those distinctions, which would be required for an adequate system of psychology.

It is possible to construct a definition of the term "dispassionate" which will correspond, point by point, with our definition of the term "disinterested." Thus we can define a "particular emotion" as one which is directed toward an object only because the object is thought to have one or more essentially particular properties. And we can say that an ideal observer is dispassionate in the sense that he is incapable of experiencing emotions of this kind – such emotions as jealousy, self-love, personal hatred, and others which are directed towards particular individuals as such. At present this seems to me to be the most satisfactory way of defining the term "dispassionate" as applied to an ideal observer.

[. . .]

5.   He is consistent

Consistency is ordinarily regarded as one of the characteristics of a good judge, and this fact suggests that a ideal observer must be described in part as a being whose ethically-significant reactions are perfectly consistent with one another. But there are obstacles, as we shall see, to defining the relevant kind of consistency in a manner which avoids circularity and yet makes consistency an independent characteristic of an ideal observer.

When we say that the ethical decisions of a judge in two different cases are consistent with one another – or, correspondingly, that in two different situations the ethically-significant reactions of an ideal observer are consistent – we are evidently not passing judgment on the logic of any actual process of thought. There is an obvious sense, to be sure, in which a judge might accept consistent or inconsistent *premises* or use consistent or inconsistent *arguments* (either in reaching his decisions or in attempting to justify them); but when we assert that the two decisions of the judge are *themselves* consistent with one another, we intend to say something about a particular relationship between the two ethical statements which express the judge's final conclusions, and nothing, unless perhaps by insinuation, about the judge's processes of thought.

But it is also clear that we do not intend to say merely that these two ethical statements are *logically* consistent with one another. For since the two statements express ethical decisions about two different cases, they necessarily refer to different acts or events, and of course *any* two self-consistent statements are logically consistent with one another if they refer to different acts or events. Thus the kind of consistency which we have in mind must be "stronger" than logical consistency: we must mean to say that it is in some sense *possible* that the two statements are both true, but not merely that it is *logically* possible.

If this is so, however, the consistency or inconsistency of two ethical decisions must depend on the relationship of these decisions to certain general ethical principles which are conceived as restricting the "possible" combinations of ethical statements. And this conclusion is supported, I believe, by examination of the kind of reasoning which actually leads us to conclude that two decisions are consistent or inconsistent with one another. We might assert, for example, that a moral judge is inconsistent because in one case he decided in favor of act x rather than x′, whereas in another case he decided in favor of y rather than y′; and if we assert this, an analysis of our reasoning would probably show that we are assuming that it is possible for x to be the right act only if a certain ethical principle (*P*) is true, whereas it is possible for y to

be the right act only if *P* is false. Our judgment that the two decisions are inconsistent, therefore, is based on the assumption that there is no *other* valid ethical principle (a certain principle *Q*, for example) which could in some way take precedence over *P* in one of the two cases. We are not, to be sure, committing ourselves either to the belief that *P* is true or to the belief that *P* is false. But we *are* assuming that the facts of the two cases are not different in some respect which is ethically crucial. And to assume even this is to presuppose at least one ethical proposition, namely, that there is no valid ethical principle (e.g., *Q*) which, together with *P*, could be used to justify *both* decisions.

I think we must conclude, therefore, that whenever we assert that the decisions of a moral judge in two different cases are consistent with one another, we are presupposing a certain amount of ethical knowledge. And this implies that our analysis would be circular if we made consistency of this kind one of the defining characteristics of an ideal observer.

There is, however, a much more limited kind of consistency which we might wish to attribute to an ideal observer. For if we agree that his ethically-significant reactions are stimulated by his imagination of a possible act, then, since an act may be imagined at any number of different times, there is nothing in our analysis up to this point which would logically require that an ideal observer always react in the same way even when he imagines one *particular* act (i.e., an act occurring at a particular time and place and hence having a certain particular set of alternatives). And if this appears to be a deficiency in our analysis, we could easily correct it by attributing a limited consistency to an ideal observer: we could define him, in part, as a being whose ethically-significant reactions to any particular act would always be exactly similar.

If we decide to do this, however, it is important to notice that consistency, when interpreted in this way, has a status very different from that of omniscience, disinterestedness, and the other defining characteristics of an ideal observer which we have so far considered. For according to the kind of absolutist analysis which we have been examining, ethical statements, as we have previously observed, are statements which depend for their truth or falsity on the existence of certain psychological laws; and if ethical statements are ever true, they are true only because we have defined an ideal observer in such a way that, in virtue of the relevant psychological laws, *any* ideal observer would react in the same way to a particular act. Thus in attributing omniscience, disinterestedness, and other such characteristics to an ideal observer, we are doing something of crucial importance for the kind of analysis which we are considering: we are eliminating from the personality of the ideal observer, so to speak, various factors which actually cause certain people to differ in their ethically-significant reactions from other people – such factors, for example, as selfish desires and ignorance of the facts of the case. And assuming that ethical statements *are* sometimes true, an absolutist dispositional analysis can be adequate only if such factors are completely eliminated from the personality of an ideal observer.

The characteristic of consistency, however, unlike omniscience, disinterestedness, and the others which we have discussed, does not eliminate some particular source of disagreement in ethical reactions. It is, on the contrary, a *consequence* of eliminating such disagreement, since any factor which could cause two different ideal observers to react in different ways to a particular act, could also cause one and the same ideal observer to react in different ways at different times. And this means, to put the matter bluntly, that if it is necessary to attribute consistency to an ideal observer in order to insure that he is psychologically incapable of reacting to the same act in different ways at different times, then we have simply failed to find all the *other* characteristics of an ideal observer which are necessary for the formulation of an adequate analysis. Thus an ideal observer will indeed be consistent if an adequate dispositional analysis can be formulated; but his consistency will be a derivative characteristic – a consequence of his other characteristics together with certain psychological laws.

6. *In other respects he is normal*

An examination of the procedures by which we attempt to decide moral questions, reveals that there are a great many conditions which we recognize, though not always explicitly, to be favorable or unfavorable for making valid moral judgments. Mild bodily exercise such as walking, the presence of other people trying to make similar decisions, and certain kinds of esthetic stimuli, have all been regarded by some people as favorable conditions, whereas mental fatigue, distracting sensory stimuli, and lack of experience, are generally regarded as unfavorable. It seems likely, however, that our analysis will take all these special conditions into account if we attribute such general characteristics as omniscience and disinterestedness to an ideal observer.

It seems fairly clear, on the other hand, that no analysis in terms solely of such general, and highly ideal, characteristics, could be fully adequate to the meaning of ethical statements. For however ideal some of his characteristics may be, an ideal observer is, after all, a *person*; and whatever may be true of the future, our conception of the personality of an ideal observer has not yet undergone the refining processes which have enabled theologians, apparently with clear conscience, to employ the term "person" in exceedingly abstract ways. Most of us, indeed, can be said to have a conception of an ideal observer only in the sense that the characteristics of such a person are implicit in the procedures by which we compare and evaluate moral judges, and it seems doubtful, therefore, that an ideal observer can be said to lack any of the determinable properties of human beings.

The determinate properties of an ideal observer, however, except for the ideal characteristics which we have so far discussed, are apparently not capable of precise definition. We may employ the customary linguistic device, to be sure, and say that the properties of an ideal observer cannot vary beyond the limits of "normality," but there are a number of reasons why it does not seem to be possible to define these limits satisfactorily. It is evident, for example, that normality is a gestalt concept, and that a certain trait which in abstraction might properly be called abnormal, could nevertheless contribute to a total personality which falls within the bounds of normality. And this fact by itself is sufficient to destroy any hope of defining the term "normal" by continuing to add specific characteristics to the ones which we have already attributed to an ideal observer. This difficulty, however, and the others which prevent us from formulating a satisfactory definition of "normal," are practical rather than theoretical, and they do not tend in the slightest degree to disprove the thesis that ethical statements are statements about an ideal observer and his ethically-significant reactions. There are analogous difficulties, moreover, in formulating a dispositional analysis of the statement "This is (really) yellow"; and I have yet to find any convincing reason, indeed, for believing that "yellow" can be defined dispositionally although "right" cannot.

Contractarian Constructivism

Ronald Milo

The focus of metaethical theory has shifted recently from a preoccupation with questions about whether moral judgments make factual claims and can therefore be said to be true or false, to a concern with questions about the nature of moral truths and facts. Today, even the most recalcitrant emotivists are willing to admit that truth can be predicated of moral judgments. This does not imply, however, that there is some independently existing state of affairs that makes these judgments true, since noncognitivists claim that alleged moral facts are nothing more than hypostatizations of our affective/conative reactions toward the world. Hence, moral judgments may be said to be true only in a pleonastic sense. To say, for example, that it is true (or is a fact) that lying is wrong is just to endorse whatever attitude or prescription one expresses (according to the particular noncognitivist theory in question) when one says that lying is wrong.

This separation of moral truth from reality is vigorously opposed by contemporary moral real-ists, who insist that truth can be predicated of moral judgments in a more substantial sense. Some argue that moral truths and facts are no different from scientific truths and facts in the most important sense. Moral facts are part of an independently given natural order, and we are justified in postulating their existence because this is necessary in order to provide the most plausible explanation of our observations and experiences. This is a very robust form of moral realism.[1] Other contemporary moral realists are more modest in their pretensions about a moral reality. While agreeing that true moral judgments represent correct cognitive responses to a reality that obtains independently of, and is capable of explaining, these responses, they nevertheless do not insist on grounding moral truths in what I shall call a *stance-independent* reality – that is, a reality that obtains independently of how we are disposed to respond to the world in terms of our affective or volitional responses. Although they acknowledge that moral facts are response dependent, they argue that only an

---

[1] This kind of view has been defended by a number of contemporary moral realists. See, for example: Nicholas Sturgeon, "Moral Explanations," in D. Copp and D. Zimmerman, eds., *Morality, Reason and Truth* (Totowa, NJ: Rowman and Allanheld, 1985), pp. 49–78 [included as chapter 25 of this volume]; Peter Railton, "Moral Realism," *Philosophical Review*, XCV (1986), 163–207 [included as chapter 14 of this volume]; Richard Boyd, "How to Be a Moral Realist," in G. Sayre–McCord, ed., *Essays on Moral Realism* (Ithaca: Cornell, 1988) [included as chapter 13 of this volume]; and David Brink, *Moral Realism and the Foundations of Ethics* (New York: Cambridge, 1989).

impoverished conception of reality excludes such facts.[2]

Although I would like to think that moral judgments can be true in a more substantial sense than noncognitivists allow, I find the alternatives so far proposed implausible. The more radical form of moral realism proposed by contemporary American philosophers, which treats moral principles as causal/explanatory hypotheses, seems to me to rest on a misconception of the nature of moral principles (and therefore of moral truths). Moral principles are designed to regulate and direct human behavior, not to help us explain and predict actions and social events. On this score, the noncognitivists seem to me clearly correct. They also seem to me correct in denying that there are any stance-independent moral facts. Indeed, I take this to be the essential truth in their antirealism about morality. Thus, insofar as the more modest form of moral realism proposed by recent British philosophers concedes this point, this counts in its favor. But these moral realists also embrace a "Wittgensteinian" conception of truth, according to which the truth conditions (or at least, assertability conditions) of moral judgments are determined by the social consensus that underwrites a community's moral practices. This, together with their denial that we can have access to an objective point of view that transcends particular social practices, creates an undesirable undertow pulling one in the direction of moral relativism.

My aim in this paper, however, is neither to demonstrate the inadequacies of these forms of moral realism nor to refute noncognitivism. Criticisms of these views are already abundant in the literature, and they are convincing enough, in my view, to make one look for another option. My purpose, therefore, is to propose an alternative conception of the nature of moral truths and facts. *Contractarian constructivism*, as I shall call it, holds that moral truths are most plausibly construed as truths about an ideal social order, rather than the natural (or some curious nonnatural) order of things. It is true (or is a fact) that a certain kind of act is wrong, for example, just in case a social order prohibiting such acts would be chosen by rational contractors under suitably idealized conditions.

This conception was suggested – but then quickly backed away from – by John Rawls[3] in his John Dewey lectures. According to the view there elaborated, what the moral facts are – for example, which social institutions are just and unjust – is the product of a process of construction in which rational agents, under idealized conditions, seek to reach an agreement on principles for regulating their relationships and behavior toward one another. The objectivity of the moral principles so constructed consists not in their being grounded in an independently existing moral order that explains why the process of construction leads to an agreement on these principles. Rather, the objectivity of these moral principles consists simply in their rational acceptability from an impartial social point of view.

I believe that this conception of the nature of moral truths and facts has not received the development it deserves. Rawls's disinclination to become embroiled in metaphysical/metaethical issues, and his preference for addressing more practically oriented normative questions, prevented him from developing this conception himself. This is unfortunate because, as I hope to show, it has a number of important advantages over other accounts of moral truths and facts. After setting out the essential elements of the theory (in part I), I explain (in part II) the sort of ontological status it gives moral facts and the sense in which it underwrites the possibility of objective moral truths. Finally (in part III), I defend the theory against expected objections.

I

Contractarian constructivism conceives of moral truths as truths about an ideal social order rather than truths about the natural order of things. This social order consists in a set of norms and standards specifying that certain kinds of acts are required (duties and obligations) and/or that certain traits of character are to be exemplified (virtues), and it is ideal in the sense that it is rationally preferable to alternative social orders. It is rationally preferable from a social point of view, that is, from the

---

[2]   John McDowell has proposed this kind of moral realism in a series of articles that includes: "Virtue and Reason," *Monist*, LXII (1979), 331–50, and "Values and Secondary Qualities," in T. Honderich, ed., *Morality and Objectivity* (New York: Routledge, 1985), pp. 110–29 [included as chapter 11 of this volume].
[3]   "Kantian Constructivism in Moral Theory," *Journal of Philosophy*, LXXVII, 9 (September 1980), 515–72.

point of view of a collection of individuals seeking to reach an agreement on limits to be placed on the pursuit of their individual aims and interests in the context of social interaction and on reasonable terms for ongoing social cooperation. The moral principles that define this ideal social order are rationally preferable when viewed as specifying terms for mutually acceptable social interaction which are to be publicly acknowledged and advocated, and inculcated by various means of social internalization. They are not necessarily rationally preferable from the point of view of an individual seeking to adopt personal action guides that will enable one best to promote one's own well-being, although it can be argued that it is rational for individuals to prefer that these principles be generally observed in the society in which they live and to support this general observance in various ways.

According to contractarian constructivism, the ideal social order described by moral truths is a product of construction, not an independently given moral order. What the moral facts are – for example, which acts are wrong – is determined by which principles would be chosen by the hypothetical agents of construction. It must be noted, however, that the moral principles chosen by the hypothetical contractors are viewed by them as *action guides*, not as *truth claims*. The agents of construction are not to be conceived of as trying to reach an agreement on which moral principles are true, since apart from their agreement there are no antecedently given moral truths for them to discover. Rather, they determine through their choices which moral principles are true – although, as I shall now explain, only indirectly. In order to understand the relationship between the truth of moral principles and the choices made by the hypothetical contractors, we must note that moral principles have a dual nature in that any moral principle can be construed either as an action guide or as a truth claim. For example, the principle that lying is wrong can be understood as expressing a prescription against lying: do not tell lies. And it can also be understood as asserting that acts of lying have a certain character – namely, that of being wrong. Contractarian constructivism views this latter assertion as the claim that a prohibition of lying would be included in any set of norms agreed upon by the hypothetical contractors. The moral principle characterizing lying as wrong (the moral principle qua truth claim) is true just in case a

moral principle prohibiting or condemning lying (the principle qua action guide) is the object of a certain kind of rational social choice.

Thus, contractarian constructivism views moral truths as truths about what norms and standards hypothetical contractors would have reason to choose. It is true that lying is wrong just in case there is reason for human beings, from an idealized social point of view, to choose norms that prohibit lying. This is to conceive of moral truths as practical truths rather than theoretical truths that we are justified in accepting because of the explanatory necessity of positing them. Practical truths are truths about what there is reason, for some individual or group of individuals, to prefer, choose, or do, from some point of view. The relevant point of view will generally be indicated by the context of discussion. It may be a fairly specific point of view, such as that of satisfying certain interests or aesthetic tastes, choosing among objects designed to serve a particular function, or adopting the appropriate means by which to pursue some chosen goal. Or it may reflect more general prudential concerns, such as the interests we have in preserving our economic security and our physical and psychological well-being. There is also such a thing, I shall suggest, as the moral point of view.

The following are examples of practical truths in this sense: Fyodor Dostoyevsky's novels are worth reading; knives that easily lose their edge are no good; if one is overweight, one ought to diet and exercise; smoking is bad for one; kindness is a virtue; lying is wrong. Notice that practical truths need not directly assert the existence of reasons for preferring, choosing, or doing something. They are truths about practical reasons only in the sense that the existence of such reasons is included in their truth conditions. A novel is worth reading only if there is reason for anyone who enjoys literature to read it. That smoking is bad for one entails that there is reason for one not to smoke. Moral truths, however, are only indirectly about practical reasons, according to contractarian constructivism. Considered directly, they are truths about the conformity or nonconformity of actions, persons, and institutions with certain norms and standards – namely, those which individuals taken collectively have reason to choose (when subject to certain idealizing conditions), for regulating their relations and interactions with one another.

Those who embrace an internalist view about the connection between moral requirements and reasons for action might also want to insist that moral truths entail that individuals have reason to comply with the requirements described by such truths. The practical conception of moral truths, however, is not committed to this kind of strong internalism. The most that need be said is that individuals have reason to conform their behavior to certain norms from *the moral point of view* – here defined as the point of view of intending to comply with the regulatory constraints and live up to the ideals of character that individuals collectively have reason to choose (under idealized conditions). In this respect, contractarian constructivism may be said to endorse a weak form of internalism regarding the connection between moral requirements and ideals and reasons for choosing and acting.

Practical truths are discovered through practical reasoning. Whereas theoretical reasoning aims at determining what to believe, practical reasoning aims at determining what to choose. Because theoretical reasoning is largely preoccupied with attempting to discover the causal relations that explain why things happen as they do when they do, it typically takes the form of an inference to the best explanation. Such inferences appeal to considerations of coherence between the proposed explanatory hypothesis and other beliefs, and the attempt to preserve such a coherence involves mutual adjustments and revisions necessary to achieve a reflective equilibrium among these beliefs. Theoretical reasoning in the empirical sciences is primarily controlled by the constraint of coherence with our observational beliefs, because the aim here is to improve our understanding of the world and because (we believe) such observations involve a causal interaction with the world. Practical reasoning is primarily controlled by the constraint of coherence with our intrinsic (that is, unmotivated) desires, because our aim here is to improve the satisfactoriness of our lives. Intrinsic desires play a role in practical reasoning analogous to that played by observational beliefs in scientific reasoning: though by no means immune from revision, they nevertheless play a dominant role in such reasoning. Intrinsic desires, together with causal beliefs, lead to the formulation of intentions and plans of action for realizing our desired ends. But these plans may have to be abandoned or revised if they are found to frustrate or interfere with the satisfaction of other desires. And if no acceptable means can be found for achieving a particular desired end, practical reasoning may lead us to abandon this end and perhaps even to extinguish or suppress the desire. Thus, practical reasoning may be said to take the form of an "inference to the best means" that involves an attempt to achieve a reflective equilibrium among our beliefs and our desires.

We discover that there would be reason for the hypothetical contractors to choose a set of norms that prohibits lying (and hence discover that the belief that lying is wrong is true) by constructing a warranted pattern of practical reasoning resulting in such a choice on their part. As we have seen, the construction of such a practical inference must observe certain coherence constraints that require one to preserve a reflective equilibrium among the beliefs and desires of the hypothetical contractors. Notice, however, that this practical inference will not include any moral beliefs. It will include certain desires that all (normal) human beings can be presumed to share, such as the desires to be free from pain and to be one's own master, and it may also include certain beliefs about what constitutes a good life for a human being (beliefs which are sometimes included in the class of moral beliefs on a broader conception of morality). But it will not include any moral beliefs about what is right and wrong in our interactions with others or about which traits of character are other-regarding virtues. The hypothetical contractors are not presumed to have any such beliefs. Nor is it necessary to include these beliefs in the reasoning that would lead them to choose, for example, a norm that prohibits causing pain to others when this serves no purpose other than one's own amusement, or a norm that prohibits both individuals and social groups from enslaving others.

II

Contractarian constructivism is a metaethical theory about the subject matter of moral judgments, about what sort of facts makes them true. It is not intended as a normative theory that tells us which general moral principles are true; nor does it specify a method for determining this (although, as we have seen, it has obvious implications concerning this). In order to understand the difference between contractarian constructivism and contractarianism as a normative theory, consider the following contractarian principle: an act is wrong if and only if it would be prohibited by any set of norms chosen by (suitably idealized) hypothetical contractors. When this principle is viewed as expressing a normative ethical theory, the second half of the biconditional – call this the C condition – specifies a criterion for determining when (it is true that) an act is morally wrong. So interpreted, the principle does not commit one to any particular metaethical theory about the nature or ontological status of moral wrongness. It is compatible with the view that moral wrongness is an irreducible, nonnatural property, and it is even consistent with a metaethics that views attributions of moral wrongness as ways of projecting one's disapproval onto actions. (For the projectivist, asserting the contractarian principle expresses one's approval of condemning acts just in case they satisfy the C condition.) These are the kinds of metaphysical/metaethical issues with respect to which Rawls, as a normative contractarian, declines to take sides. But what I am calling contractarian constructivism *is* a theory about the ontological status of moral wrongness. It holds that acts that satisfy the C condition are wrong simply because that is what moral wrongness consists in.

The antirealism espoused by noncognitivists argues that alleged moral facts are nothing more than reflections of the judger's affective/conative reactions to nonmoral states of affairs; hence they have no substantial existence. Insofar as contractarian constructivism proposes a conception of moral facts as more substantial than this, it seems to endorse moral realism. But the issue is complicated by its insistence that moral facts are constructed by the hypothetical contractors and have no existence independently of this. For this reason, classifying it as a form of moral realism may be misleading.

There is one sense, however, in which its conception of moral facts is clearly realistic. Some recent moral realists have defined the view they wish to endorse as holding that there are moral truths that obtain independently of our having any reasons or evidence for believing them. Since contractarian constructivism makes moral facts evidence independent in this sense (it may be, for example, that the norms chosen by the hypothetical contractors would prohibit capital punishment even though no one has been able to construct a convincing argument to establish this), it counts as a form of moral realism on this definition. It should be noted, however, that if moral realism is defined in this way, some theories will count as examples of

moral realism which traditionally have been understood as denying that there are any objective moral truths. Consider, for example, a crude subjectivism according to which something is good relative to a particular person just in case he happens to desire it, or a naive relativism that holds that what is right and wrong is determined for each individual by conformity or nonconformity with the social conventions of the group in which she regularly participates. Such theories entail that moral judgments are objectively true or false, since whether a given object is desired by a particular person and whether a given act conforms to the social conventions of the agent's society are objectively determinable matters. Nevertheless, such theories are considered to be antirealistic because they deny that there are any moral truths that obtain independently of the psychological stances adopted toward the world by human beings. This suggests that moral realism requires that moral truths be not only evidence independent but mind independent as well.

The notion of mind independence is ambiguous, however, because moral truths and facts can be mind *dependent* in two ways. Let us say that moral facts are *weakly* mind dependent if they are constituted by states of affairs that include mental states as essential components. Thus, hedonistic utilitarianism takes moral facts to be weakly mind dependent, since it makes feelings of pleasure or pain essential ingredients of all moral facts. But hedonistic utilitarianism does not construe moral facts as mind dependent in another sense. Let us say that moral facts are *strongly* mind dependent if moral facts supervene on other facts (including psychological facts) only as a consequence of these other facts being made the object of some intentional psychological state, such as a belief or an attitude (perhaps under idealized conditions). Thus, the ideal-observer theory (or one version of it) claims that moral facts are strongly mind dependent because, according to it, moral facts supervene on other facts only in virtue of the fact that an ideal observer would have a certain psychological reaction toward these other facts. According to this theory, if hedonistic utilitarianism is true, this is because an ideal observer would have a certain psychological response (such as disapproval) toward acts insofar as they fail to maximize pleasure and the absence of pain. But although one who accepts hedonistic utilitarianism as a normative ethical theory *might* accept an ideal-observer theory as providing the correct metaethical account of why (or, perhaps better, how) wrongness supervenes on the failure to maximize pleasure, one could also claim that this supervenience is simply part of the natural order of things – that is, one could adopt hedonistic utilitarianism not just as a normative theory about what makes acts right or wrong, but also as a metaethical theory about the ontological nature of moral facts. According to the latter view, the moral wrongness of acts is directly constituted by their failure to maximize pleasure, rather than by an ideal observer's disapproval of such acts.

This would be to adopt a realistic account of the connection between the failure to maximize pleasure and wrongness. Thus, moral realism is compatible with holding that moral facts are weakly mind dependent. To hold that moral facts are strongly mind dependent, on the other hand, seems incompatible with genuine – or, at least, a robust form of – moral realism. Insofar as the moral wrongness of acts that fail to maximize pleasure is taken to be constituted by an ideal observer's disapproval of such acts, we have a form of moral idealism rather than realism. For in that case the connection between failure to maximize happiness and moral wrongness is not a *real* connection in nature, but rather one that we (under idealized conditions) *project* onto it. Henceforth, I shall refer to facts that are not strongly mind dependent as *stance independent*. A fact will be said to be stance *dependent* just in case it consists in the instantiation of some property that exists only if some thing or state of affairs is made the object of an intentional psychological state (a stance), such as a belief or a conative or affective attitude. Conversely, a fact will be said to be stance *independent* just in case it is not dependent in this way on some psychological stance. Contractarian constructivism and the ideal-observer theory make moral facts evidence independent but not stance independent. Theories of this sort are allied with the more robust forms of moral realism in opposing the kind of antirealism endorsed by noncognitivists, who deny that moral judgments may be conceived of as genuine cognitive responses even to stance-dependent moral facts. Thus, they might be considered weak forms of moral realism. Nevertheless, the acknowledgement of the stance-dependent nature of moral facts seems to constitute an important concession to noncognitivist antirealism. In any case, the sig-

nificance of the differences between these theories and the more radical forms of moral realism suggests that they deserve a label of their own. I suggest *moral constructivism*.

As here conceived of, moral constructivism holds that moral facts are the product of human volition (broadly conceived), in that they obtain only as a consequence of the fact that human beings do, or would under idealized conditions, adopt certain attitudes or preferences or make certain choices or decisions with respect to (possible) states of affairs. Thus, insofar as Immanuel Kant suggests that the rightness or wrongness of an act is constituted by whether or not a rational person can will its maxim to be a universal law, he may be viewed as another example of a moral constructivist. The dispositional, or response-dependent, theories of moral facts proposed by recent British moral realists also count as moral constructivism.

The versions of moral constructivism so far mentioned are all designed to provide a basis for the distinction between right and wrong that is capable of grounding objective moral truths. Notice, however, that moral constructivism can also take a subjectivist or relativist form. R. B. Brandt proposes this kind of constructivism when he suggests that rightness or wrongness is to be determined, for each individual, by whether the act in question is permitted by the moral code which that individual would, if fully informed and rational, prefer to see adopted in the society in which she expected to live. Gilbert Harman's version of moral relativism can also be considered a form of constructivism insofar as he claims that what is right is determined, for the members of each social group, by the conventions to which they intend to (and therefore have reason to) adhere.[4] These versions of moral constructivism allow that moral judgments can be said to be true or false insofar as they are relativized to a particular judger or set of social conventions. But they do not allow that there are any nonrelativized truths about what is right and wrong that must be accepted by all persons and social groups regardless of their particular attitudes and preferences, even when they are fully informed and reasoning correctly. This is because they deny that there is any objective basis for the application of moral categories. The applicability

---

[4]   See Brandt, *A Theory of the Right and the Good* (New York: Oxford, 1979), p. 194; and Harman, *The Nature of Morality* (New York: Oxford, 1977), pp. 131–2 [also see Harman's contribution – chapter 7 of the present volume].

of the categories of right and wrong is determined, for each individual or society, by which set of social conventions that individual or society happens to prefer. Objectivist versions of moral constructivism support the view that there are objectively grounded universal moral truths because, according to them, that a moral category applies to a certain kind of act is determined by the outcome of its being made the object of an objective (that is, impartial), rather than a merely personal or parochial, stance. Although they do not attempt to ground moral truths in an external (that is, stance-independent) reality, they view them as objective because they are (1) evidence independent and (2) grounded in an objective psychological stance.

On a constructivist interpretation, moral facts and truths are not, however, capable of the kind of objectivity that characterizes scientific facts and truths – at least, not if scientific realism is true. On that view, the objectivity of scientific truths consists in the fact that recognition of them is imposed on us by an external reality. It is external because it is what it is no matter what we believe, or have reason to believe, about it and because it has the character it has even if we should prefer it to be otherwise. Thus, the objectivity of scientific truths derives from the fact that they describe a stance-independent reality. This reality imposes itself on us through the causal control it exercises over our experiences and beliefs. We feel compelled to recognize certain truths about it because we find it necessary (insofar as we choose to be guided by reason and evidence) to postulate these truths in order to provide the most plausible explanations of our experiences and observations (which are also largely independent of our will). This is how the objectivity of scientific reality manifests itself.

According to contractarian constructivism, moral truths derive their objectivity from the fact that they describe an objectively preferable social order. Their objectivity does not derive from their describing an externally imposed reality; for the "reality" they describe is a (hypothetical) social creation. Like scientific objectivity, however, moral objectivity can be said to manifest itself as a constraint on our beliefs – although it constrains our moral beliefs only in virtue of constraining our (hypothetical) wills. What constrains our choice (insofar as we imaginatively adopt the point of view of the hypothetical contractors) is the necessity of adopting an objective (that is, impartial) point of view. Instead of allowing our beliefs to be con-

strained by an objective reality, we allow our will (and, through it, our moral beliefs) to be constrained by an objective point of view.

Attempts to account for the objectivity of moral truths by grounding them in an external moral reality have not been successful. The nonnaturalism proposed by the British intuitionists led to the postulation of queer entities whose relationship to natural facts and to human motivation remains mysterious, if not inexplicable. Traditional (analytical) ethical naturalism faces all the problems associated with reductionism and, in particular, the charge that it substitutes definition for argument in the defense of substantive moral principles. And the nonreductionist version of ethical naturalism proposed by recent American moral realists falsely assimilates moral truths to scientific truths by construing moral principles as causal hypotheses intended to explain individual actions and social events, instead of normative principles intended to regulate human behavior. The most plausible version of traditional ethical naturalism is, in my view, the ideal-observer theory. But that is because, like contractarian constructivism, it makes moral facts and truths evidence independent without requiring them to be stance independent. Thus, I am inclined to share the skepticism expressed by noncognitivists about the existence of a stance-independent moral reality.

I do not think this means, however, that we must abandon the attempt to show that moral truths can be objectively grounded in a stronger sense than any noncognitivist account of moral truth and objectivity is able to accommodate. The antirealism espoused by noncognitivists does not allow the postulation of alleged moral facts and truths any role at all in explaining the formation of moral beliefs. Thus, our moral beliefs cannot be controlled or regulated by a moral reality (not even a stance-dependent moral reality). There is in this sense no external constraint on the formation of our moral beliefs according to noncognitivist antirealism. Insofar as contractarian constructivism does propose such an external constraint, it attempts to account for the genuine objectivity of true moral beliefs while avoiding the difficulties facing more robust forms of moral realism.

III

Considered simply as a metaethical theory about the nature of moral truths, contractarian constructivism is not committed to providing a specific method for determining *which* moral principles are true. Nevertheless, it does imply that, in general, the correct way to discover which principles (qua propositions) are true is by determining which principles (qua prescriptions) would be chosen by the hypothetical contractors. Thus, it might be thought to be vulnerable to many of the same objections that have been raised against contractarianism as a normative ethical theory. For example, critics have complained that contractarians fail to provide any good reason for thinking that acts prohibited by the norms agreed on by the hypothetical contractors must be wrong. It would be absurd, they argue, to suggest that this is because hypothetical contracts (that is, contracts that one has not in fact made but would have made under certain circumstances) are somehow morally binding.[5] Contractarian constructivism is clearly not committed to such an absurd view. Although it makes the wrongness of lying a consequence of the fact that lying would be prohibited by the norms agreed on by the contractors, this is not because an obligation to refrain from lying is created by such an agreement in the way that promises create obligations. Rather, the wrongness of lying (like the wrongness of breaking a promise) is a consequence of this agreement simply in the sense that being prohibited by such an agreement is what its moral wrongness consists in.

It is not so obvious, however, that contractarian constructivism can avoid the chief objection leveled against contractarianism. This is that no normatively neutral description of the contractors and their circumstance is sufficient to make it seem plausible that a particular set of moral principles would be agreed on by them. The latter can be accomplished, it has been argued, only by subjecting the contractors to normatively loaded idealizing constraints. Thus, critics have charged that Rawls is able to make it seem plausible that the contractors would agree on his two principles of justice only because he characterizes them as cautiously rational (employing a maximin strategy), mutually self-interested (rather than, for example, having a concern for the common good), and desiring certain "primary goods" (but not others, such as friendship). Such a characterization of the contractors, it is said, prejudices the theory in favor of Rawls's particular conception of justice, and, more generally, in favor of nonconsequentialism and a rights-centered rather than a virtue-centered moral theory.

Before considering whether this sort of objection has force against contractarian constructivism as well, let me frankly acknowledge that I do not think it is possible for a metaethical theory about the subject matter of morality to be completely normatively neutral, although it is possible, I think, to avoid begging any *controversial* moral questions. (I shall return to this issue later.) In order to remain as normatively neutral as possible, the contractarian constructivist will want to propose idealizing conditions that ensure only (1) that the contractors adopt a genuinely objective, that is, impartial, point of view and (2) that whatever norms or standards would be chosen by them do not make obviously wrong acts right, or vice versa. Here one may appeal to certain moral paradigms, such as that lying, rape, and torture are wrong. Insofar as they guide us in attempting to discover the nature of moral wrongness, these paradigms may be thought of as fixing the reference of 'morally wrong'. If they are not observed, one might argue, there is no guarantee that one's theory will be a theory about the nature of *morality*. The question then is whether a contractarian metaethical theory can remain at least minimally normatively neutral, while at the same time giving the hypothetical contractors sufficient reason to choose moral principles (qua prescriptions) that make our paradigm moral principles (qua propositions) true. What sort of characterization of the contractors and their circumstances will suffice for this purpose? One will want to require that the contractors be rational and fully informed about the relevant general facts. And it will also be necessary to impose some kind of constraint on them that captures the traditional conception of morality as consisting in a set of impartial constraints on individuals in the pursuit of their particular aims and interests. Different versions of contractarianism may attempt to accomplish this in different ways, however. For example, Rawls imposes a veil of ignorance on the contractors, whereas T. M. Scanlon[6] imposes instead the

[5]   See, for example, Ronald Dworkin, "The Original Position," in Norman Daniels, ed., *Reading Rawls* (Stanford: University Press, 1989), p. 17.
[6]   "Contractualism and Utilitarianism," in A. Sen and B. Williams, eds., *Utilitarianism and Beyond* (New York: Cambridge, 1982).

constraint of having to choose only those rules which "no one could reasonably reject as a basis for informed, unforced agreement" (*ibid.*, p. 110). Insofar as these kinds of constraints prejudice the theory against ethical egoism, it must be acknowledged that contractarian constructivism cannot be neutral in this regard either. But this, I for one am prepared to accept, since I view "ethical" egoism as a theory about what makes acts rational, rather than moral.

If the contractors are to have any basis for choosing some social action guides rather than others, it will also be necessary to give them certain desires and preferences. But the contractarian cannot allow their choice of norms and ideals to be influenced by idiosyncratic or culturally shaped desires and preferences. This would be incompatible with holding that these norms are rationally preferable from an objective point of view. It may well be that the best way of ruling out the influence of such desires is with a Rawlsian veil of ignorance. This would allow the contractors to have only those desires shared by virtually all human beings, such as aversions to pain, injury, disability, and death, and longings for love, respect, economic security, and freedom. It is plausible to suppose, however, that any group of human beings motivated by such universal human desires would have reason to choose norms prohibiting such things as lying, rape, and torture. This much is admitted even by some who are otherwise inclined to adopt a relativist position. If so, it would follow, according to contractarian constructivism, that principles stating that such acts are wrong constitute objective moral truths.

It will be objected, however, that such a thin characterization of the contractors will not give them reason to choose anything at all like a moral code detailed enough to provide guidance in everyday life. They would have reason to choose only a few highly general prima facie moral principles. Even if it is admitted that certain moral principles form a common core that would be shared by the moral code rationally preferred by any group of contractors motivated by these universal human desires, it can still be argued that the extent of this core is limited and that the core principles are indeterminate in their application. Even if all such moral codes contained, for example, requirements to refrain from lying and to aid those in distress, these moral norms may be interpreted quite differently, especially with regard to their stringency.

Granted that there are circumstances under which one is not morally required to avoid lying, how are these to be defined? Just how great a sacrifice in terms of one's own interests is one required to make in order to prevent a serious harm to someone else? There may also be significant differences of opinion concerning how conflicting moral norms are to be weighed. Thus, trustworthiness may be considered such an important value by some people that they are willing to tolerate a considerable amount of suffering before permitting a lie or the breaking of a promise. It is difficult to see how such issues could be resolved by contractors choosing behind a Rawlsian veil of ignorance; for their resolution would seem to depend on an appeal to basic preferences with respect to which people are known to differ.

Although contractarian constructivism does not purport to provide a procedure for deciding which moral principles to accept as true or justified, let alone a method for resolving hard moral cases, it does intend to underwrite the possibility of objective moral truths. It is not necessary, however, for a moral objectivist to hold that there must be a determinate answer for *every* moral question. It seems perfectly acceptable to acknowledge that there may be no correct answer to questions about some hard moral cases. For borderline cases (for example: Just how great a sacrifice of one's own interests must one make in order to prevent the death of another?) and especially in cases of moral dilemma (for example: Ought one to tell the truth or prevent a certain amount of suffering in cases where these conflict?) there may simply be no truth or fact of the matter. With respect to such issues, the hypothetical contractors might decide (it could be argued) to allow these matters to be resolved by social conventions to be adopted by particular social groups, after the veil of ignorance is at least partially lifted and they come to know their own particular preferences concerning how to weigh the conflicting values. This would allow for some degree of cultural relativity. This minimal concession to relativism will not undermine moral objectivity, however; for moral objectivism requires one neither to insist that there is only one true morality (that is, only one complete moral code that is rationally preferable for all social groups) nor to claim that bivalence holds for all moral judgments. It suffices if it seems plausible that certain moral principles (qua action guides) constitute a common core that would be part of any social order chosen by suitably constrained hypothetical contractors.

But, it might be objected, will such a common core include anything beyond the paradigmatic but highly general prima facie moral principles whose truth is assumed in order to help us identify the subject matter of morality? Do we have reason to suppose that the contractors would choose more particular moral principles which specify what circumstances constitute acceptable exceptions to these general but defeasible moral principles, and which specify also how conflicts between such principles are to be resolved? Although some hard questions will remain irresolvable, it seems plausible to suppose that the contractors could resolve *some* of the issues relevant to making the paradigmatic moral principles more specific. It seems plausible, for example, that the contractors would choose a norm regarding promise keeping which permits promise breaking when necessary to prevent serious harm (such as the risk of injury or death) but which does not permit promises to be broken just whenever this would result in somewhat better consequences. Thus, insofar as a form of utilitarianism does permit the latter, it is at odds with contractarian constructivism as well as common sense. Even if we adopt the kind of formal, or substantively neutral, conception of practical rationality I have proposed, it seems plausible to suppose that rational contractors would not choose a norm that permits promise breaking simply on act-utilitarian grounds, because in that case promises could not fulfill their purpose. This is another respect in which contractarian constructivism cannot remain completely normatively neutral.

Although, as I shall later argue, contractarian constructivism should adopt a thin conception of practical rationality that remains neutral on such issues as whether practical rationality involves adopting a maximin strategy (or constrained maximizing, as David Gauthier suggests),[7] such a minimal conception of practical rationality seems sufficient to give the contractors reason to choose a norm requiring some minimal degree of mutual aid. Moreover, it seems plausible to suppose that they would agree that saving a human life at the cost of getting one's clothes wet is morally required (even if doing this at the cost of risking one's life or limbs is not). (Here I must simply disagree with

those rugged individualists or libertarians who would deny this.) Thus, although some hard cases will persist, the moral principles whose objective truth is underwritten by contractarian constructivism go well beyond the highly general paradigmatic moral principles.

Still, it might be objected, does not contractarian constructivism succeed in underwriting the objective truth of certain moral principles only because it assumes their truth to begin with? If, as I acknowledged earlier, we must appeal to certain paradigmatic moral principles to help us identify the subject matter of moral judgments, and if the contractarian constructivist's characterization of the hypothetical contract situation is designed to ensure that these principles will be made true by the contractors' choices, is not this just a covert form of intuitionism – an appeal to the self-evidence of these moral principles?

In considering this objection, it is important to note that contractarian constructivism does not pretend to provide a proof of the truth of the paradigmatic moral principles. The hypothetical contract is not proposed as a way of testing and establishing the objective truth (or justifiability) of certain moral principles, but rather (assuming their truth) as a way of explaining what their truth and objectivity might be thought to consist in. Here again contractarian constructivism differs markedly from contractarianism as a normative theory. The question posed for the latter kind of theory is: Why suppose that the contract device provides us with a test for moral truth? A normative contractarian might attempt to defend the use of this device on the ground that employing this criterion yields moral beliefs that cohere with our considered moral judgments, the general moral principles that explicate them, and certain relevant background theories – insofar as these are brought into a relationship of reflective equilibrium with one another. This is problematic, however, since it is unclear why we should think that this sort of coherence constitutes evidence for the truth of a moral belief. The solution would seem to require a plausible theory about the reliability of considered moral judgments (those made under conditions known to be generally conducive to the formation of true beliefs) which requires us to postulate their truth as the best explanation for our having these beliefs. Such a theory has recently been proposed

---

[7]   *Morals by Agreement* (Oxford: Oxford University Press, 1986).

by the more radical contemporary moral realists discussed above. But for reasons mentioned briefly above, and which cannot be elaborated on here, I do not find this appeal to explanatory necessity convincing.

Contractarian constructivism avoids this problem because it does not view the hypothetical contractors' choice of certain social norms as an infallible (or even a reliable) indicator of the moral wrongness of the acts prohibited by such norms. Viewed in that way, it would be appropriate to try to establish their reliability by showing that the moral principles made true by their choices are in reflective equilibrium with our considered moral judgments and other relevant beliefs and theories. Contractarian constructivism claims, however, that the moral wrongness of acts is *constituted* by their being prohibited by the norms chosen by the hypothetical contractors. The fact that an act violates such a norm is not just evidence of its wrongness; it is the truth maker for the claim that it is wrong. Thus, the contractarian constructivist's use of paradigmatic moral principles to fix the reference of 'moral wrongness' should not be construed as an appeal to the method of reflective equilibrium in order to determine which moral principles to accept as true. It must be acknowledged that, if the moral principles made true by the contractor's choices conflict with our moral paradigms, then there is reason to revise the characterization of the contractors and their circumstances. The moral paradigms themselves, however, are not similarly subject to revision. That is because the truth of these moral principles must be assumed in order to ensure that the theory is focused on the right subject matter (moral wrongness, for example). In this respect, I have acknowledged, metaethical theory cannot remain normatively neutral. A theory of this sort must, nevertheless, strive to be as normatively neutral as possible. This requires that the substantive constraints provided by moral paradigms be kept to a minimum and that controversial moral questions not be begged. Thus, one will want to ensure that torturing another human being merely for the sake of the torturer's amusement is wrong. But one will not want to ensure that torturing an infant is wrong when necessary to prevent the agonizing deaths of a million people. That would be prejudicial toward consequentialism.

Unlike a normative contractarian theory, contractarian constructivism does not need to take

sides on the controversial issues that separate consequentialists from nonconsequentialists and those who prefer a rights- (or duty-) centered ethics from proponents of a virtue-centered ethics. In order to develop such a normative contractarian theory, a much fuller description of the contractors will be necessary. The normative contractarian will need to embrace a particular conception of practical rationality, choosing, for example, between an instrumentalist conception and one that recognizes certain ends as ends that everyone has reason to promote regardless of her particular desires and preferences (or perhaps between these and some third alternative). One will also need to decide whether there is only one conception of the good life that must be accepted by all rational persons, or whether, as Rawls suggests, there is a plurality of equally rational conceptions of the good. Should the contractors be conceived of as purely self-regarding or as having at least some direct concern for others (say, a Kantian respect for persons) or a concern for their common good? All of these issues will have to be settled before one can use the contractarian device to justify a particular normative ethical theory (or a full range of moral principles). A normative contractarian will have to provide independent arguments in defense of all of these normative stands (something which critics charge has not been done).

Fortunately, the contractarian constructivist need not worry about all of this. A thin characterization of the contractors that remains neutral on these issues seems all that is required to ensure the selection of social norms that make the noncontroversial paradigmatic moral principles true. The contractarian constructivist need only constrain the contractors in such a way (for example, by a veil of ignorance) as to guarantee the truth of our moral paradigms – and this only to ensure that the theory is focused on the right subject matter, not to provide a proof of the truth or justifiability of these principles.

Concluding Remarks

Contractarian constructivism proposes a conception of the nature of moral truths that has some important advantages. Insofar as it conceives of them as truths about what sort of social order hypothetical contractors would have reason to choose for regulating their interactions with one another, it suggests a plausible explication of the traditional conception of morality (endorsed by virtually all moral philosophers) as consisting in a set of impartial constraints that constitute mutually acceptable terms for social interaction. It also provides a basis for arguing that there are objective moral truths without committing one to dubious metaphysical assumptions. It does not require one to postulate the existence of a stance-independent moral reality, no matter how naturalized and purged of queer entities. Nor does it require a false assimilation of moral truths to scientific truths which deprives them of their essentially practical character. Because contractarian constructivism

makes the truth of moral principles depend directly on the rational preferability of certain social norms or standards, it draws a much closer connection between the truth of moral principles and their acceptability as action guides (at least from a social point of view) than do other forms of moral objectivism. Thus, contractarian constructivism provides a plausible account of what moral thought and talk is really about that captures the essentially action-guiding function of moral principles without depriving them of their aspirations to substantive truth or the dignity of a cognitive status. These are, it seems to me, important virtues in a metaethical theory.

I.4   Sensibility Theories

Introduction

Central to John Mackie's celebrated "argument from queerness" against moral realism is the claim that "if there were objective values, then they would be entities or qualities or relations of a very strange sort, utterly different from anything else in the universe" (Mackie 1977: 38; see the selection from Mackie that comprises chapter 1 of this volume). Some philosophers sympathetic to a broadly realist view in ethics have thought that Mackie's contention contains both genuine insight and error. If we think of moral values as being akin to Plato's Forms – necessarily existing, immutable objects independent of human cognition and will – then Mackie appears to have a point: for if moral values were like Plato's Forms, then they would be utterly unlike ordinary objects of which we are aware such as Mount Rainier and the Taj Mahal. But, these philosophers contend, Mackie seems to be wrong to suppose that, were moral facts to exist, they would have to be like Plato's Forms. For it is plausible to suppose that moral features are not like Plato's Forms, but rather are akin to ordinary objects of which most of us are aware, namely, colors. This is the driving idea behind what are sometimes termed "sensibility theories."

Sensibility theories have been with us since the Scottish Enlightenment, in the work of philosophers such as Hutcheson and Hume. To understand these views in their contemporary guise,

however, it is useful first to mark a distinction between two different ways to understand them.

In the first place, sensibility theories are sometimes understood to offer an account of the nature of moral *concepts* or the way we think of the moral realm. According to this way of understanding the position, there is a difference between what we can call a "response-independent" and a "response-dependent" account of a concept C. A response-independent account of the concept C tells us that one can understand the nature of the members of its extension without making essential reference to the types of human response they evoke. (We can think of the extension of a concept C as the set of all the actual things that have the property of *being C*.) For example, the concept of 'being square' is arguably response-independent; we can understand the nature of the members of its extension (i.e., square items) in purely mathematical terms, without making any appeal to the propensity of its members to evoke certain kinds of, say, visual experiences in humans. According to some philosophers, moral concepts are like the concept of squareness. This is because we can understand the nature of the members of their extension without regard to the responses they elicit in human beings.

In contrast, a response-dependent account of the concept C tells us that we can understand the nature of its extension only if we make essential reference to the types of human response that its members evoke. The concept of 'being red,' for example, is arguably response-dependent: to grasp its extension, we must understand red things to be such as to evoke responses of certain kinds in human beings, namely, experiences of redness. Some moral philosophers believe that moral concepts are like the concept of redness, for, as they see things, to think that something has a moral property is to think that it is appropriate to respond in certain ways to that thing.

The second way to understand sensibility theories is not as a view about the character of moral concepts, but about the nature of moral *properties*. A response-independent theory of a property F tells us that it is false that something exemplifies F in virtue of the fact that it elicits responses of certain kinds in human beings. To return to the previous example, the property of *being square* is arguably response-independent because it is false that a thing is square in virtue of the fact that it affects, say, our visual capacities in certain ways. Some philosophers think that moral properties are also response-independent in character. According to them, the property of, say, *being just* does not consist in its instances being such as to elicit (or being such as to merit) responses of certain types on our part.

In contrast to this – and to stick with our previous example – the property of *being red* is arguably a response-dependent property. For, according to a popular way of thinking about colors, something is red in virtue of the fact that it evokes responses of certain kinds – namely, experiences of redness – in human agents under the appropriate conditions. Some moral philosophers believe that moral properties are response-dependent. As the view is usually described, the claim is that something displays a moral property F if and only if and because it is such as to elicit (or such as to merit) responses of certain types on our part. A little more exactly, prominent defenders of this position hold that moral qualities are *dispositions* to elicit certain types of responses from suitable subjects in appropriate environments – where the responses in question may include the formation of moral judgments or emotions of certain types. According to this view, an action's *being wicked*, for instance, is simply a disposition of that action to affect agents in such a way that they strongly disapprove of or express indignation toward that action.

There are several reasons why this distinction between response-dependent concepts, on the one hand, and response-dependent properties, on the other, is important for understanding sensibility theories. Although the examples that we used regarding squareness and redness may have suggested otherwise, the first thing to see is that it is possible for a concept C to be response-dependent, but for the property of *being C* to which it applies to be response-independent. If this is right, it is possible for moral concepts to be response-dependent, even if moral properties are not. So, for example, even if we can understand the property of *being just* only by viewing those things that display it as thereby being such as to merit responses of certain types on our part, this does not imply that things are just *in virtue* of affecting (or being such as to merit affecting) us in these ways. Indeed, despite what numerous philosophers appear to claim, it is arguable that embracing a suitably nuanced response-dependent view about moral concepts is entirely neutral with regard to whether one is a realist or not concerning moral features; this position about moral concepts (as it is usually stated) has no ontological ramifications. (This is not to suggest, however, that it is easy to offer a compelling account of response-dependent moral concepts!)

The second thing to see – and this follows from the first point – is that a response-dependent account of moral properties is a much more ambitious philosophical view than a response-dependent account of moral concepts. While it is plausible to believe that a response-dependent account of moral concepts is ontologically innocuous, it would not be plausible to say the same about a response-dependent account of moral properties. To say that moral properties existentially depend on our (potential) responses is a daring metaethical view.

There are, then, several questions to raise about response-dependent views: which of these positions have sensibility theorists defended – a response-dependent account of moral concepts or of properties? The answer is that it is not always easy to tell. In some cases, the position is framed in terms of concepts; in others, it isn't. But, on the assumption that it is the response-dependent view of moral properties that is of most interest to those working in metaethics, we probably cannot go too wrong by assuming that sensibility theorists have meant to defend this position (see McDowell 1985;

Wiggins 1991a: 195; both essays are included in this section). So, our next question is: why have some philosophers found this position attractive?

For two main reasons: first, sensibility theorists have wanted at once to defend the objectivity of moral values while ensuring that these values are not alien to us. Plato's picture gives us objective values, to be sure, but arguably at the price of making it difficult to see any interesting connection between them and us: moral values sit there as brute givens, potentially beyond our cognitive grasp. But several philosophers have thought this is unintelligible because, at least in principle, the practically important features of reality cannot outstrip our grasp of them. Viewing moral features as response-dependent, however, promises to avoid these alleged Platonic excesses, while preserving the objectivity of morality. The view avoids the excesses of Platonism because inasmuch as moral qualities depend on us – and inasmuch as our concepts of them capture this – they cannot (in principle) outstrip our cognitive grasp. But the view also preserves the objectivity of morality. For if moral features are like colors, there is a legitimate sense in which they are objective: they are there in the world to be experienced independent of any of our particular sensibilities. Moreover, we have (as with color judgments) developed practices of evaluating our moral judgments and holding them up to critical scrutiny. According to the advocates of sensibility theories, it is difficult to see how we could desire more objectivity in the moral realm than this.

Second, like many of those working in metaethics, sensibility theorists have been concerned to forge a close link between moral judgment and motivation. That is to say, sensibility theorists have defended a strong version of motivational internalism according to which it is conceptually necessary that, if an agent judges that she ought to act in a certain way, then she is thereby motivated to act in that way. (For more on this view, see part II.1, "Moral Motivation.") According to the Platonic picture, however, it is difficult to see how motivational internalism could be defended. As John McDowell puts the matter:

For it seems impossible . . . to take seriously the idea of something that is like a primary quality [i.e. a response-independent quality] in being simply *there*, independently of human sensibility, but is nevertheless intrinsically (not conditionally on contingencies about human sensibility) such as to elicit some "attitude" or state of will from someone who becomes aware of it . . . (McDowell 1985: 111)

But suppose moral qualities were dispositions not simply to elicit merited moral judgments on our part, but to motivate us to act appropriately. If that were the case, then the sensibility theorist would have a pleasant explanation of the tight link between moral judgment and motivation: moral features are just the sort of things that, when grasped under appropriate conditions, motivate agents to act appropriately.

The desire not to accept an account of moral features that implies that we are "alienated" from moral reasons and the wish to defend motivational internalism are common considerations offered for rejecting robust forms of moral realism. Both moral constructivists and expressivists, for example, cite them as reasons to favor their own views over robust moral realism. Of course whether these considerations should move us to accept sensibility views rather than, say, constructivist or expressivist positions is a complicated issue, calling for detailed comparison of the various positions. While this sort of comparison would lead us too far afield for present purposes, it is probably worth indicating some challenges that sensibility theories face.

In the first place, both error theorists such as Mackie and sensibility theorists such as McDowell believe that motivational internalism is true. However, when Mackie and McDowell articulate this position, they do so in a way that is, on the face of things, puzzling. Both thinkers maintain that moral *properties* or *facts* are intrinsically motivating inasmuch as they are the sort of thing that, when grasped, move us to act. But it is plausible to believe that, properly understood, the issue regarding moral motivation concerns not whether moral properties or facts are intrinsically motivating, but whether moral *judgments* are.

To see the point, suppose we grant that there is an intimate connection between moral judgment and motivation. Notice, however, that it is not simply the apprehension of moral properties or facts that is so intimately linked with motivation. After all, *false* moral judgments, which involve no such apprehension, are also intimately linked with motivation. So, it cannot be that the motivational magnetism of moral properties or facts is what explains moral motivation across the board, for in many cases an agent's judgments are intimately linked with motives, but the judgment itself does not consist in the apprehension of such a property or fact. In these cases, at least, something else has to be doing the motivational work. If this is true, then sensibility theories have not given us a general explanation of the tight connection between moral judgment and motivation. But this, presumably, is what we aspire to.

Second, there is the worry that the account offered by sensibility theorists is uninformative. As the view is sometimes presented, we are told that for any moral feature F:

> X exemplifies F if and only if and because X is disposed to elicit response R in subjects S in conditions C.

Suppose F stands for the property *being a moral reason to Φ* or *being such that one morally ought to Φ*. However, thinkers such as McDowell and David Wiggins – the most prominent sensibility theorists, whose influential papers are presented in this section – maintain that the response in question is not merely one that the property of being F is disposed to elicit, but one that the property *merits*. According to these thinkers, then, sensibility theorists should say something like:

> X exemplifies F if and only if and because X is disposed to elicit a merited response R in appropriately situated subjects S in appropriate conditions C.

Given this schema, we can understand R to stand for a response-type that has the property of *being*

such as to be merited. But it is difficult to know how to understand the expression "R has the property of being such as to be merited" except as a variant of "R is favored by moral reasons" or "R is such that one morally ought to form it." (If the reasons in question are not moral, but practical reasons of some sort, it would seem that the sensibility theorist should also think of them as being response-dependent. After all, the very same motivations for being a sensibility theorist with regard to moral features would also appear to be motivations for being a sensibility theorist with respect to non-moral, practical reasons. For example, it is plausible to believe that we have just as much reason to believe that non-moral practical reasons cannot exceed our cognitive grasp as we do to believe that moral reasons cannot exceed our cognitive grasp.) Now Wiggins and others emphasize that schemata such as the one just stated do not purport to offer a definition of moral properties; they are supposed to offer informative elucidations – albeit circular elucidations of the nature of these properties. But even if the view does not purport to furnish a definition of moral properties, it is difficult to see how it offers an informative elucidation of the property being F. The explanandum (the thing to be explained) in this instance is the property of *being a moral reason to Φ*. But we cannot explain the nature of this property by appealing to that self-same property in the explanans (the thing that is explaining). And, thus, there is the worry that appealing to appropriate responses when explicating the nature of moral qualities cannot furnish a general explanation of the nature of those qualities.

Selected Bibliography

Blackburn, Simon. 1985. "Errors and the Phenomenology of Value." In Ted Honderich, ed. *Morality and Objectivity*. London: Routledge & Kegan Paul. Reprinted in *Essays in Quasi-Realism*. Oxford: Oxford University Press, 1993.

Campbell, John, and Robert Pargetter. 1986. "Goodness and Fragility." *American Philosophical Quarterly* 23: 155–65.

Cuneo, Terence. 2001. "Are Moral Qualities Response-Dependent?" *Noûs* 35: 569–91.

Dancy, Jonathan. 1993. *Moral Reasons*. Oxford: Blackwell, ch. 9.

D'Arms, Justin. 2005. "Two Arguments for Sentimentalism." In Ernest Sosa and Enrique Villanueva, eds.

Philosophical Issues 15: Normativity. Oxford: Blackwell.

D'Arms, Justin, and Daniel Jacobson. 2000. "Sentiment and Value." *Ethics* 110: 722–48.

D'Arms, Justin, and Daniel Jacobson. 2006. "Anthropocentric Constraints on Human Value." In Russ Shafer-Landau, ed. *Oxford Studies in Metaethics* 1. Oxford: Oxford University Press.

Darwall, Stephen, Allan Gibbard, and Peter Railton. 1992. "Toward Fin de Siècle Ethics: Some Trends." *Philosophical Review* 101: 115–89.

Holland, Sean. 2001. "Dispositional Theories of Value Meet Moral Twin-Earth." *American Philosophical Quarterly* 38: 177–95.

Johnston, Mark. 1989. "Dispositional Theories of Value." *Proceedings of the Aristotelian Society*, supplementary volume 63: 139–74.

Johnston, Mark. 1993. "Objectivity Refigured: Pragmatism without Verificationism." In John Haldane and Crispin Wright, eds. *Reality, Representation, and Projection*. Oxford: Oxford University Press.

McDowell, John. 1983. "Aesthetic Value, Objectivity and the Fabric of the World." In Eva Schaper, ed. *Pleasure, Preference and Value*. Cambridge: Cambridge University Press. Reprinted in *Mind, Value, and Reality*. Cambridge, MA: Harvard University Press, 1998.

McDowell, John. 1985. "Values and Secondary Qualities." In Ted Honderich, ed. *Morality and Objectivity*. London: Routledge & Kegan Paul. Reprinted in *Mind, Value, and Reality*. Cambridge, MA: Harvard University Press, 1998.

McDowell, John. 1998. "Truth and Projection in Ethics." In *Mind, Value, and Reality*. Cambridge, MA: Harvard University Press.

McGinn, Colin. 1983. *The Subjective View*. Oxford: Clarendon Press, ch. 8.

McGinn, Colin. 1997. *Ethics, Evil, and Fiction*. Oxford: Oxford University Press, ch. 2.

Miller, Alexander. 2003. *An Introduction to Contemporary Metaethics*. Cambridge: Polity, ch. 7.

Pargetter, Robert. 1988. "Goodness and Redness." *Philosophical Papers* 17: 113–26.

Pettit, Philip. 1993. "Realism and Response-Dependence." *Mind* 100: 587–626.

Railton, Peter. 2003. "Red, Bitter, Good." In *Facts, Values, Norms*. Cambridge: Cambridge University Press.

Sosa, David. 2001. "Pathetic Ethics." In Brian Leiter, ed. *Objectivity in Law and Morals*. Cambridge: Cambridge University Press.

Strandberg, Caj. 1999. "Dispositional Moral Properties and Moral Motivation." *Theoria* 65: 171–92.

Wedgwood, Ralph. 1998. "The Essence of Response-Dependence." *European Review of Philosophy* 3: 31–54.

Wiggins, David. 1991a. "A Sensible Subjectivism?" In *Needs, Values, Truth*. 2nd edn. Oxford: Blackwell.

Wiggins, David. 1991b. "Truth, Invention and the Meaning of Life." In *Needs, Values, Truth*. 2nd edn. Oxford: Blackwell.

Wright, Crispin. 1988. "Moral Values, Projection, and Secondary Qualities." *Proceedings of the Aristotelian Society*, supplementary volume 62: 1–26. Reprinted in *Saving the Differences*. Cambridge, MA: Harvard University Press, 2003.

Wright, Crispin. 1992. *Truth and Objectivity*. Cambridge, MA: Harvard University Press, ch. 5.

Zangwill, Nick. 2003. "Against Response-Dependence." *Erkenntnis* 59: 285–90.

II

Values and Secondary Qualities

John McDowell

1 J. L. Mackie insists that ordinary evaluative thought presents itself as a matter of sensitivity to aspects of the world.[1] And this phenomenological thesis seems correct. When one or another variety of philosophical non-cognitivism claims to capture the truth about what the experience of value is like, or [. . .] what we mean by our evaluative language, the claim is never based on careful attention to the lived character of evaluative thought or discourse. The idea is, rather, that the very concept of the cognitive or factual rules out the possibility of an undiluted representation of how things are, enjoying, nevertheless, the internal relation to 'attitudes' or the will that would be needed for it to count as evaluative. On this view the phenomenology of value would involve a mere incoherence, if it were as Mackie says – a possibility that then tends (naturally enough) not to be so much as entertained. But, as Mackie sees, there is no satisfactory justification for supposing that the factual is, by definition, attitudinatively and motivationally neutral. This clears away the only obstacle to accepting his phenomenological claim; and the upshot is that non-cognitivism must offer to correct the phenomenology of value, rather than to give an account of it.

In Mackie's view the correction is called for. In this paper I want to suggest that he attributes an unmerited plausibility to this thesis, by giving a false picture of what one is committed to if one resists it.

2 Given that Mackie is right about the phenomenology of value, an attempt to accept the appearances makes it virtually irresistible to appeal to a perceptual model. Now Mackie holds that the model must be perceptual awareness of *primary* qualities (see *HMT*, pp. 32, 60–1, 73–4). And this makes it comparatively easy to argue that the appearances are misleading. For it seems impossible – at least on reflection – to take seriously the idea of something that is like a primary quality in being simply *there*, independently of human sensibility, but is nevertheless intrinsically (not conditionally on contingencies about human sensibility) such as to elicit some 'attitude' or state of will from someone who becomes aware of it. Moreover, the primary-quality model turns the epistemology of value into

---

[1] See *Ethics: Inventing Right and Wrong* (Penguin, Harmondsworth, 1977), pp. 31–5; hereafter *E*. I shall also abbreviate references to the following other books by Mackie: *Problems from Locke* (Clarendon Press, Oxford, 1976: hereafter *PFL*); and *Hume's Moral Theory* (Routledge & Kegan Paul, London, 1980; hereafter *HMT*).

mere mystification. The perceptual model is no more than a model: perception, strictly so called, does not mirror the role of reason in evaluative thinking, which seems to require us to regard the apprehension of value as an intellectual rather than a merely sensory matter. But if we are to take account of this, while preserving the model's picture of values as brutely and absolutely *there*, it seems that we need to postulate a faculty – 'intuition' – about which all that can be said is that it makes us aware of objective rational connections: the model itself ensures that there is nothing helpful to say about how such a faculty might work, or why its deliverances might deserve to count as knowledge.

But why is it supposed that the model must be awareness of primary qualities rather than secondary qualities? The answer is that Mackie, following Locke, takes secondary-quality perception, as conceived by a pre-philosophical consciousness, to involve a projective error: one analogous to the error he finds in ordinary evaluative thought. He holds that we are prone to conceive secondary-quality experience in a way that would be appropriate for experience of primary qualities. So a pre-philosophical secondary-quality model for awareness of value would in effect be, after all, a primary-quality model. And to accept a philosophically corrected secondary-quality model for the awareness of value would be simply to give up trying to go along with the appearances.

I believe, however, that this conception of secondary-quality experience is seriously mistaken.

3   A secondary quality is a property the ascription of which to an object is not adequately understood except as true, if it is true, in virtue of the object's disposition to present a certain sort of perceptual appearance: specifically, an appearance characterizable by using a word for the property itself to say how the object perceptually appears. Thus an object's being red is understood as obtaining in virtue of the object's being such as (in certain circumstances) to look, precisely, red.

This account of secondary qualities is faithful to one key Lockean doctrine, namely the identification of secondary qualities with 'powers to produce various sensations in us'.[2] (The phrase 'perceptual appearance', with its gloss, goes beyond Locke's unspecific 'sensations', but harmlessly; it serves

simply to restrict our attention, as Locke's word may not, to properties that are in a certain obvious sense perceptible.)

I have written of what property-ascriptions are understood to be true in virtue of, rather than of what they are true in virtue of. No doubt it is true that a given thing is red in virtue of some microscopic textural property of its surface; but a predication understood only in such terms – not in terms of how the object would look – would not be an ascription of the secondary quality of redness.

Secondary-quality experience presents itself as perceptual awareness of properties genuinely possessed by the objects that confront one. And there is no general obstacle to taking that appearance at face value. An object's being such as to look red is independent of its actually looking red to anyone on any particular occasion; so, notwithstanding the conceptual connection between being red and being experienced as red, an experience of something as red can count as a case of being presented with a property that is there anyway – there independently of the experience itself. And there is no evident ground for accusing the appearance of being misleading. What would one expect it to be like to experience something's being such as to look red, if not to experience the thing in question (in the right circumstances) as looking, precisely, red?

On Mackie's account, by contrast, to take experiencing something as red at face value, as a non-misleading awareness of a property that really confronts one, is to attribute to the object a property which is 'thoroughly objective' (*PEL*, p. 18), in the sense that it does not need to be understood in terms of experiences that the object is disposed to give rise to; but which nevertheless resembles redness as it figures in our experience – this to ensure that the phenomenal character of the experience need not stand accused of misleadingness, as it would if the 'thoroughly objective' property of which it constituted an awareness were conceived as a microscopic textural basis for the object's disposition to look red. This use of the notion of resemblance corresponds to one key element in Locke's exposition of the concept of a primary quality.[3] In these Lockean terms Mackie's view amounts to accusing a naive perceptual consciousness of taking secondary qualities for primary qualities (see *PEL*, p. 16).

---

[2]   *An Essay Concerning Human Understanding*, II. viii. 10.
[3]   See ibid. II. viii. 15.

According to Mackie, this conception of primary qualities that resemble colours as we see them is coherent; that nothing is characterized by such qualities is established by merely empirical argument (see *PFL*, pp. 17–20). But is the idea coherent? This would require two things: first, that colours figure in perceptual experience neutrally, so to speak, rather than as essentially phenomenal qualities of objects, qualities that could not be adequately conceived except in terms of how their possessors would look; and, second, that we command a concept of resemblance that would enable us to construct notions of possible primary qualities out of the idea of resemblance to such neutral elements of experience. The first of these requirements is quite dubious. (I shall return to this.) But even if we try to let it pass, the second requirement seems impossible. Starting with, say, redness as it (putatively neutrally) figures in our experience, we are asked to form the notion of a feature of objects which resembles that, but which is adequately conceivable otherwise than in terms of how its possessors would look (since if it were adequately conceivable only in those terms it would simply be secondary). But the second part of these instructions leaves it wholly mysterious what to make of the first: it precludes the required resemblance being in phenomenal respects, but it is quite unclear what other sense we could make of the notion of resemblance to redness as it figures in our experience. (If we find no other, we have failed to let the first requirement pass; redness as it figures in our experience proves stubbornly phenomenal.) I have indicated how we can make error-free sense of the thought that colours are authentic objects of perceptual awareness; in face of that, it seems a gratuitous slur on perceptual 'common sense' to accuse it of this wildly problematic understanding of itself.

Why is Mackie resolved, nevertheless, to convict 'common sense' of error? Secondary qualities are qualities not adequately conceivable except in terms of certain subjective states, and thus subjective themselves in a sense that that characterization defines. In the natural contrast, a primary quality would be objective in the sense that what it is for something to have it can be adequately understood otherwise than in terms of dispositions to give rise to subjective states. Now this contrast between objective and subjective is not a contrast between veridical and illusory experience. But it is easily confused with a different contrast, in which to call

a putative object of awareness 'objective' is to say that it is there to be experienced, as opposed to being a mere figment of the subjective state that purports to be an experience of it. If secondary qualities were subjective in the sense that naturally contrasts with this, naive consciousness would indeed be wrong about them, and we would need something like Mackie's Lockean picture of the error it commits. What is acceptable, though, is only that secondary qualities are subjective in the first sense, and it would be simply wrong to suppose that this gives any support to the idea that they are subjective in the second.

More specifically, Mackie seems insufficiently whole-hearted in an insight of his about perceptual experiences. In the case of 'realistic' depiction, it makes sense to think of veridicality as a matter of resemblance between aspects of a picture and aspects of what it depicts. Mackie's insight is that the best hope of a philosophically hygienic interpretation for Locke's talk of 'ideas', in a perceptual context, is in terms of 'intentional objects': that is, aspects of representational content – aspects of how things seem to one in the enjoyment of a perceptual experience. (See *PFL*, pp. 47–50.) Now it is an illusion to suppose, as Mackie does, that this warrants thinking of the relation between a quality and an 'idea' of it on the model of the relation between a property of a picture's subject and an aspect of the picture. Explaining 'ideas' as 'intentional objects' should direct our attention to the relation between how things are and how an experience represents them as being – in fact identity, not resemblance, if the representation is veridical. Mackie's Lockean appeal to resemblance fits something quite different: a relation borne to aspects of how things are by intrinsic aspects of a bearer of representational content – not how things are represented to be, but features of an item that does the representing, with particular aspects of its content carried by particular aspects of what it is intrinsically (non-representationally) like. Perceptual experiences have representational content; but nothing in Mackie's defence of the 'intentional objects' gloss on 'ideas' would force us to suppose that they have it in that sort of way.

The temptation to which Mackie succumbs, to suppose that intrinsic features of experience function as vehicles for particular aspects of representational content, is indifferent to any distinction between primary and secondary qualities in the representational significance that these features supposedly carry. What it is for a colour to figure in experience and what it is for a shape to figure in experience would be alike, on this view, in so far as both are a matter of an experience's having a certain intrinsic feature. If one wants, within this framework, to preserve Locke's intuition that primary-quality experience is distinctive in potentially disclosing the objective properties of things, one will be naturally led to Locke's use of the notion of resemblance. But no notion of resemblance could get us from an essentially experiential state of affairs to the concept of a feature of objects intelligible otherwise than in terms of how its possessors would strike us. (A version of this point told against Mackie's idea of possible primary qualities answering to 'colours as we see them'; it tells equally against the Lockean conception of shapes.)

If one gives up the Lockean use of resemblance, but retains the idea that primary and secondary qualities are experientially on a par, one will be led to suppose that the properties attributed to objects in the 'manifest image' are all equally phenomenal – intelligible, that is, only in terms of how their possessors are disposed to appear. Properties that are objective, in the contrasting sense, can then figure only in the 'scientific image'.[4] On these lines one altogether loses hold of Locke's intuition that primary qualities are distinctive in being both objective and perceptible.

If we want to preserve the intuition, as I believe we should, then we need to exorcize the idea that what it is for a quality to figure in experience is for an experience to have a certain intrinsic feature: in fact I believe that we need to reject these supposed vehicles of content altogether. Then we can say that colours and shapes figure in experience, not as the representational significance carried by features that are – being intrinsic features of experience – indifferently subjective (which makes it hard to see how a difference in respect of objectivity could show up in their representational significance); but simply as properties that objects are represented as having, distinctively phenomenal in the one case and not so in the other. (Without the supposed intrinsic features, we should be immune to the illusion that experiences cannot represent objects as having properties that are not phenomenal – properties that are adequately conceivable otherwise

than in terms of dispositions to produce suitable experiences.) What Locke unfelicitously tried to yoke together, with his picture of real resemblances of our 'ideas', can now divide into two notions that we must insist on keeping separate: first, the possible veridicality of experience (the objectivity of its object, in the second of the two senses I distinguished), in respect of which primary and secondary qualities are on all fours; and, second, the not essentially phenomenal character of some properties that experience represents objects as having (their objectivity in the first sense), which marks off the primary perceptible qualities from the secondary ones.

In order to deny that a quality's figuring in experience consists in an experience's having a certain intrinsic feature, we do not need to reject the intrinsic features altogether; it would suffice to insist that a quality's figuring in experience consists in an experience's having a certain intrinsic feature *together with* the quality's being the representational significance carried by that feature. But I do not believe that this yields a position in which acceptance of the supposed vehicles of content coheres with a satisfactory account of perception. This position would have it that the fact that an experience represents things as being one way rather than another is strictly additional to the experience's intrinsic nature, and so extrinsic to the experience itself (it seems natural to say 'read into it'). There is a phenomenological falsification here. (This brings out a third role for Locke's resemblance, namely to obviate the threat of such a falsification by constituting a sort of intrinsic representationality: Locke's 'ideas' carry the representational significance they do by virtue of what they are like, and this can be glossed both as 'how they are intrinsically' and as 'what they resemble'.) In any case, given that we cannot project ourselves from features of experience to non-phenomenal properties of objects by means of an appeal to resemblance, it is doubtful that the metaphor of representational significance being 'read into' intrinsic features can be spelled out in such a way as to avoid the second horn of our dilemma. How could representational significance be 'read into' intrinsic features of experience in such a way that what was signified did not need to be understood in terms of them? How could a not intrinsically

---

[4]   The phrases 'manifest image' and 'scientific image' are due to Wilfrid Sellars; see 'Philosophy and the Scientific Image of Man', in Science, *Perception and Reality* (Routledge & Kegan Paul, London, 1963).

representational feature of experience become imbued with objective significance in such a way that an experience could count, by virtue of having that feature, as a direct awareness of a not essentially phenomenal property of objects?

How things strike someone as being is, in a clear sense, a subjective matter: there is no conceiving it in abstraction from the subject of the experience. Now a motive for insisting on the supposed vehicles of aspects of content might lie in an aspiration, familiar in philosophy, to bring subjectivity within the compass of a fundamentally objective conception of reality. If aspects of content are not carried by elements in an intrinsic structure, their subjectivity is irreducible. By contrast, one might hope to objectivize any 'essential subjectivity' that needs to be attributed to not intrinsically representational features of experience, by exploiting a picture involving special access on a subject's part to something conceived in a broadly objective way – its presence in the world not conceived as constituted by the subject's special access to it. Given this move, it becomes natural to suppose that the phenomenal character of the 'manifest image' can be explained in terms of a certain familiar picture: one in which a confronted 'external' reality, conceived as having only an objective nature, is processed through a structured 'subjectivity', conceived in this objectivistic manner. This picture seems to capture the essence of Mackie's approach to the secondary qualities. What I have tried to suggest is that the picture is suspect in threatening to cut us off from the *primary* (not essentially phenomenal) qualities of the objects that we perceive: either (with the appeal to resemblance) making it impossible, after all, to keep an essentially phenomenal character out of our conception of the qualities in question, or else making them merely hypothetical, not accessible to perception. If we are to achieve a satisfactory understanding of experience's openness to objective reality, we must put a more radical construction on experience's essential subjectivity. And this removes an insidious obstacle – one whose foundation is summarily captured in Mackie's idea that it is not simply wrong to count 'colours as we see them' as items in our minds (see the diagram at *PFL*, p. 17) – that stands in the way of understanding how secondary-quality experience can be awareness, with nothing misleading about its phenomenal character, of properties genuinely possessed by elements in a not exclusively phenomenal reality.

4   The empirical ground that Mackie thanks we have for not postulating 'thoroughly objective features which resemble our ideas of secondary qualities' (*PFL*, pp. 18–19) is that attributing such features to objects is surplus to the requirements of explaining our experience of secondary qualities (see *PFL*, pp. 17–18). If it would be incoherent to attribute such features to objects, as I believe, this empirical argument falls away as unnecessary. But it is worth considering how an argument from explanatory superfluity might fare against the less extravagant construal I have suggested for the thought that secondary qualities genuinely characterize objects: not because the question is difficult or contentious, but because of the light it casts on how an explanatory test for reality – which is commonly thought to undermine the claims of values – should be applied.

A '*virtus dormitiva*' objection would tell against the idea that one might mount a satisfying explanation of an object's looking red on its being such as to look red. The weight of the explanation would fall through the disposition to its structural ground. Still, however optimistic we are about the prospects for explaining colour experience on the basis of surface textures, it would be obviously wrong to suppose that someone who gave such an explanation could in consistency deny that the object was such as to look red. The right explanatory test is not whether something pulls its own weight in the favoured explanation (it may fail to do so without thereby being explained away), but whether the explainer can consistently deny its reality.

Given Mackie's view about secondary qualities, the thought that values fail an explanatory test for reality is implicit in a parallel that he commonly draws between them (see, for instance, *HMT*, pp. 51–2; *E*, pp. 19–20). It is nearer the surface in his 'argument from queerness' (*E*, pp. 38–42), and explicit in his citing 'patterns of objectification' to explain the distinctive phenomenology of value experience (*E*, pp. 42–6). Now it is, if anything, even more obvious with values than with essentially phenomenal qualities that they cannot be credited with causal efficacy: values would not pull their weight in any explanation of value experience even remotely analogous to the standard explanations of primary-quality experience. But reflection on the case of secondary qualities has already opened a gap between that admission and any concession that values are not genuine aspects of reality. And the point is reinforced by a crucial disanalogy between values and secondary qualities. To press the analogy is to stress that evaluative 'attitudes', or states of will, are like (say) colour experience in being unintelligible except as modifications of a sensibility like ours. The idea of value experience involves taking admiration, say, to represent its object as having a property which (although there in the object) is essentially subjective in much the same way as the property that an object is represented as having by an experience of redness – that is, understood adequately only in terms of the appropriate modification of human (or similar) sensibility. The disanalogy, now, is that a virtue (say) is conceived to be not merely such as to elicit the appropriate 'attitude' (as a colour is merely such as to cause the appropriate experiences), but rather such as to *merit* it. And this makes it doubtful whether merely causal explanations of value experience are relevant to the explanatory test, even to the extent that the question to ask is whether someone could consistently give such explanations while denying that the values involved are real. It looks as if we should be raising that question about explanations of a different kind.

For simplicity's sake, I shall elaborate this point in connection with something that is not a value, though it shares the crucial features: namely danger or the fearful. On the face of it, this might seem a promising subject for a projectivist treatment (a treatment that appeals to what Hume called the mind's 'propensity to spread itself on external objects').[5] At any rate the response that, according to such a treatment, is projected into the world can be characterized, without phenomenological falsification, otherwise than in terms of seeming to find the supposed product of projection already there. And it would be obviously grotesque to fancy that a case of fear might be explained as the upshot of a mechanical (or perhaps para-mechanical) process initiated by an instance of 'objective fearfulness'. But if what we are engaged in is an 'attempt to understand ourselves',[6] then merely causal explanations of responses like fear will not be satisfying anyway. What we want here is a style of explanation that makes sense of what is explained (in so far as sense can be made of it). This means that a technique for giving satisfying explanations of

cases of fear – which would perhaps amount to a satisfactory explanatory theory of danger, though the label is possibly too grand – must allow for the possibility of criticism; we make sense of fear by seeing it as a response to objects that *merit* such a response, or as the intelligibly defective product of a propensity towards responses that would be intelligible in that way. For an object to merit fear just is for it to be fearful. So explanations of fear that manifest our capacity to understand ourselves in this region of our lives will simply not cohere with the claim that reality contains nothing in the way of fearfulness. Any such claim would undermine the intelligibility that the explanations confer on our responses.

The shared crucial feature suggests that this disarming of a supposed explanatory argument for unreality should carry over to the case of values. There is, of course, a striking disanalogy in the contentiousness that is typical of values; but I think it would be a mistake to suppose that this spoils the point. In so far as we succeed in achieving the sort of understanding of our responses that is in question, we do so on the basis of preparedness to attribute, to at least some possible objects of the responses, properties that would validate the responses. What the disanalogy makes especially clear is that the explanations that preclude our denying the reality of the special properties that are putatively discernible from some (broadly) evaluative point of view are themselves constructed from that point of view. (We already had this in the case of the fearful, but the point is brought home when the validation of the responses is controversial.) However, the critical dimension of the explanations that we want means that there is no question of just any actual response pulling itself up by its own bootstraps into counting as an undistorted perception of the relevant special aspect of reality. Indeed, awareness that values are contentious tells against an unreflective contentment with the current state of one's critical outlook, and in favour of a readiness to suppose that there may be something to be learned from people with whom one's first inclination is to disagree. The aspiration to understand oneself is an aspiration to change one's responses, if that is necessary for them to become intelligible otherwise than as defective. But

---

[5] *A Treatise of Human Nature*, I. iii. 14.

[6] The phrase is from page 165 of Blackburn, 'Rule-Following and Moral Realism', in Steven Hollzman and Christopher Leich, eds., *Wittgenstein: To Follow a Rule* (Routledge & Kegan Paul, London, 1981).

although a sensible person will never be confident that his evaluative outlook is incapable of improvement, that need not stop him supposing, of some of his evaluative responses, that their objects really do merit them. He will be able to back up this supposition with explanations that show how the responses are well-placed; the explanations will share the contentiousness of the values whose reality they certify, but that should not stop him accepting the explanations any more than (what nobody thinks) it should stop him endorsing the values. There is perhaps an air of bootstrapping about this. But if we restrict ourselves to explanations from a more external standpoint, at which values are not in our field of view, we deprive ourselves of a kind of intelligibility that we aspire to; and projectivists have given no reason whatever to suppose that there would be anything better about whatever different kind of self-understanding the restriction would permit.

5   It will be obvious how these considerations undermine the damaging effect of the primary-quality model. Shifting to a secondary-quality analogy renders irrelevant any worry about how something that is brutely *there* could nevertheless stand in an internal relation to some exercise of human sensibility. Values are not brutely there – not there independently of our sensibility – any more than colours are: though, as with colours, this does not stop us supposing that they are there independently of any particular apparent experience of them. As for the epistemology of value, the epistemology of danger is a good model. (Fearfulness is not a secondary quality, although the model is available only after the primary-quality model has been dislodged. A secondary-quality analogy for value experience gives out at certain points, no less than the primary-quality analogy that Mackie attacks.) To drop the primary-quality model in this case is to give up the idea that fearfulness itself, were it real, would need to be intelligible from a standpoint independent of the propensity to fear; the same must go for the relations of rational consequentiality in which fearfulness stands to more straightforward properties of things. Explanations of fear of the sort I envisaged would not only establish, from a different standpoint, that some of its objects are really fearful, but also make plain, case by case, what it is about them that makes them

so; this should leave it quite unmysterious how a fear response rationally grounded in awareness (unproblematic, at least for present purposes) of these 'fearful-making characteristics' can be counted as being, or yielding, knowledge that one is confronted by an instance of real fearfulness.

Simon Blackburn has written, on behalf of a projectivist sentimentalism in ethics, that 'we profit . . . by realizing that a training of the feelings rather than a cultivation of a mysterious ability to spot the immutable fitnesses of things is the foundation of how to live'.[7] This picture of what an opponent of projectivism must hold is of a piece with Mackie's primary-quality model; it simply fails to fit the position I have described. Perhaps with Aristotle's notion of practical wisdom in mind, one might ask why a training of the feelings (as long as the notion of feeling is comprehensive enough) cannot *be* the cultivation of an ability – utterly unmysterious just because of its connections with feelings — to spot (if you like) the fitnesses of things; even 'immutable' may be all right, so long as it is not understood (as I take it Blackburn intends) to suggest a 'platonistic' conception of the fitnesses of things, which would reimport the characteristic ideas of the primary-quality model.

Mackie's response to this suggestion used to be, in effect, that it simply conceded his point. Can a projectivist claim that the position I have outlined is at best a notational variant, perhaps an inferior notational variant, of his own position?

It would be inferior if, in eschewing the projectivist metaphysical framework, it obscured some important truth. But what truth would this be? It will not do at this point to answer 'The truth of projectivism'. I have disarmed the explanatory argument for the projectivist's thin conception of genuine reality. What remains is rhetoric expressing what amounts to a now unargued primary-quality model for genuine reality. The picture that this suggests for value experience – objective (value-free) reality processed through a moulded subjectivity – is no less questionable than the picture of secondary-quality experience on which, in Mackie at any rate, it is explicitly modelled. In fact I should be inclined to argue that it is projectivism that is inferior. Deprived of the specious explanatory argument, projectivism has nothing to sustain its thin conception of reality (that on

---

[7] 'Rule-following and moral realism', p. 186.

to which the projections are effected) but a contentiously substantial version of the correspondence theory of truth, with the associated picture of genuinely true judgment as something to which the judger makes no contribution at all.

I do not want to argue this now. The point I want to make is that even if projectivism were not actually worse, metaphysically speaking, than the alternative I have described, it would be wrong to regard the issue between them as nothing but a question of metaphysical preference. In the projectivist picture, having one's ethical or aesthetic responses rationally suited to their objects would be a matter of having the relevant processing mechanism functioning acceptably. Now projectivism can of course perfectly well accommodate the idea of assessing one's processing mechanism. But it pictures the mechanism as something that one can contemplate as an object in itself. It would be appropriate to say 'something one can step back from', were it not for the fact that one needs to use the mechanism itself in assessing it; at any rate one is supposed to be able to step back from any naively realistic acceptance of the values that the first-level employment of the mechanism has one attribute to items in the world. How, then, are we to understand this pictured availability of the processing mechanism as an object for contemplation, separated off from the world of value? Is there any alternative to thinking of it as capable of being captured, at least in theory, by a set of principles for superimposing values on to a value-free reality? The upshot is that the search for an evaluative outlook that one can endorse as rational becomes,

virtually irresistibly, a search for such a set of principles: a search for a *theory* of beauty or goodness. One comes to count 'intuitions' respectable only in so far as they can be validated by an approximation to that ideal. (This is the shape that the attempt to objectivize subjectivity takes here.) I have a hunch that such efforts are misguided; not that we should rest content with an 'anything goes' irrationalism, but that we need a conception of rationality in evaluation that will cohere with the possibility that particular cases may stubbornly resist capture in any general net. Such a conception is straightforwardly available within the alternative to projectivism that I have described. I allowed that being able to explain cases of fear in the right way might amount to having a theory of danger, but there is no need to generalize that feature of the case; the explanatory capacity that certifies the special objects of an evaluative outlook as real, and certifies its responses to them as rational, would need to be exactly as creative and case-specific as the capacity to discern those objects itself. (It would be the same capacity: the picture of 'stepping back' does not fit here). I take it that my hunch poses a question of moral and aesthetic taste, which – like other questions of taste – should be capable of being argued about. The trouble with projectivism is that it threatens to bypass that argument, on the basis of a metaphysical picture whose purported justification falls well short of making it compulsory. We should not let the question seem to be settled by what stands revealed, in the absence of compelling argument, as a prejudice claiming the honour due to metaphysical good taste.

A Sensible Subjectivism?

David Wiggins

1. Usually – if only for the purpose of having the position summarily dismissed as soon as possible – the doctrine of subjectivism is reported as claiming that '*x* is good' or '*x* is right' or '*x* is beautiful', as uttered by speaker S, says that S approves of *x*, or that *x* induces in S a certain sentiment of approbation.

The first and perhaps most obvious objection, that 'good', 'right', and 'beautiful' do not themselves mean the same, might be countered by distinguishing different species of approbative sentiment. But there is a more familiar and more considerable second objection: at least when it is given in this form, subjectivism makes a difficulty for itself about disagreement. If, where John says *x* is good, Philip denies that *x* is good, Philip is not on this account necessarily disagreeing with John. Certainly, if they are disagreeing, the purported subjectivist analysis of '*x* is good' does not really bring out what they are disagreeing about.

To attend to this fault, the doctrine might be modified, by a shift from *me* to *us*, so as to claim that '*x* is good', as uttered by John, says that *x* is approved of by those whom John calls 'us'. If Philip is one of these persons, there can then be disagreement between John and Philip. But now the risk is that the disagreement in question will appear as merely sociological, whereas the disagreement that always needed to be accounted for

and made room for was not disagreement about what we value, but disagreement *in valuation*. Rival attempts to speak for us as a community (if that is how the subjectivist ought to see disagreement) cannot be plausibly reduced to rival accounts of what, if anything, the community does already say.

2. Emotivists may be expected to butt in at this point to suggest that disagreement in valuation can be seen as disagreement in attitude *expressed* (Stevenson). But this suggestion, and the whole idea of an emotive meaning reckoned separately from cognitive content, does insufficient justice to our feeling that divergence of attitude must itself be founded in something, and reflect a prior or coeval disagreement in something not itself reducible without residue to emotive attitude (*i.e.* in something the sentence is *about*, which is not so far accounted for). Even if it were plainer what emotive meaning was and clearer how it could work in concert with ordinary meaning (and more evident that in the end one will have to settle for it), there would still be something deeply unsatisfying about the suggestion.

3. At this point I think we ought to feel the need to look again at the subjectivists who wrote before G. E. Moore's celebrated and influential critique of subjectivism – and especially at Hume, an author

whom Moore cautiously refrains from mentioning by name in this connexion.[1]

In so far as Hume ever came anywhere near to suggesting a semantical account of '*x* is good/right/beautiful' (which is not, one may think, very near – even at the points where he speaks of 'defining' this or that), it may seem that the best proposal implicit in his theory of valuation is that this sentence says that *x* is the kind of thing to arouse a certain sentiment of approbation. This is not my approbation, or your approbation, or Hume's or society's approbation. If we want a form of words that can be the focus of real valuational disagreement as it was open to Hume to conceive this, then we do best *not to specify* whose approbation. *x* is simply such as to arouse that sentiment. (Note that it can still count against '*x* is good' that *x* in fact arouses a sentiment of approbation in nobody. Just as the claim that *x* is desirable falls into difficulty if nobody at all desires *x*. This is a point that one may register without making the error John Stuart Mill is often accused of making about 'desired' and 'desirable'.)

Not only is such subjectivism free from Moore's well-worn criticism about disagreement. It comes close to escaping Moore's earlier 'open question' argument. If *x* is such as to merit a certain feeling of approbation [when taken as one among the fs], the question is not *wide* open whether or not *x* is [a] good [f]. (For if *x* is such as to arouse that sentiment, this surely need not be without influence upon the will.)

Hume might have been easier to satisfy on this point than Moore would have been. But since the escape is still a rather narrow one, perhaps we should consider another suggestion that Hume could have made. If he had considered a question he does not consider and if he had disclaimed any intention to provide analyses of the ordinary terms of approbation, then Hume could have said that *x* is good/right/beautiful if and only if *x* is such as to make a certain sentiment of approbation *appropriate*.

4.   It may appear that this second account of Hume's theory makes it viciously circular in a way that it previously was not. But I reply that, on a proper understanding of the point of subjectivism and its having no need to supplant valuational by non-valuational language, the circularity is benign (see below and §9); and that in any case no *new* circularity has been introduced. There was already a kind of circle before this adjustment was made. What after all is a sentiment of approbation? (Or if the point of the word 'certain', sometimes inserted by Hume, is that there are different, phenomenologically distinguishable kinds of approbation, numerous enough to differentiate the good, right, and beautiful, then what *are* sentiments of approbation?) Surely a sentiment of approbation cannot be identified except by its association with the thought or feeling that x is good (or right or beautiful) and with the various considerations in which that thought can be grounded, given some particular item and context, *in situ*.

Whether such circularities constitute a difficulty for subjectivism depends entirely on what the subjectivist takes himself to be attempting. If we treat it as already known and given that '*x* is good' (or 'right' or 'beautiful') is *fully analysable*, and if '*x*' is such as to arouse the sentiment of approbation' (or '*x* is such as to make that sentiment appropriate') is the subjectivist's best effort in the analytical direction, and if this equivalent fails to deliver any proper analysis, then subjectivism is some sort of failure. Certainly. But, even if classical subjectivists have given this impression to those who want to conceive of all philosophy as analysis, analysis as such never needed to be their real concern. What traditional subjectivists have really wanted to convey is not so much definition as commentary. Chiefly they have wanted to persuade us that, when we consider whether or not *x* is good or right or beautiful, there is no appeal to anything that is more fundamental than actually possible human sentiments – a declaration that seems both contentious and plausible (but more plausible when we take into account the intentionality of the sentiments, cp. §§14–15). Circularity as such is no objection to it, provided that the offending formulation is also *true*. But what use (I shall be asked) is such a circular formulation? My answer is that, by tracing out such a circle, the subjectivist hopes to elucidate the concept of value by displaying it in its actual involvement with the sentiments. One would not, according to him, have sufficiently elucidated what value is *without* that detour.

[1]   See *Philosophical Studies* (Routledge, 1922), pp. 329–39; *Ethics* (Home University Library, Thornton Butterworth, London, 1912), chapters III, IV.

5.   In all these matters, an analogy with colour is suggestive. '*x* is red if and only if *x* is such as to give, under certain conditions specifiable as normal, a certain visual impression' naturally raises the question 'which visual impression?' And that question attracts the answer 'an impression as of seeing something red', which reintroduces *red*. But this finding of circularity scarcely amounts to proof that we can after all appeal to something beyond visual impressions to determine colour authoritatively. It only shows that 'red' stands for something not in this sort of way *analysable*. Surely it is simply obvious that colour is something subjective; and just as obvious that the unanalysability of colour words represents no difficulty in that claim. The mere unanalysability or indefinability of colour terms does not release us from the task of finding means to elucidate these terms in a way that will bring out their subjectivity. Until one has done this much, one has not even reminded anyone of what he or she already knows about what colours are.

How then, without traducing it or treating it unfairly as a definition or an analysis, are we to develop and amplify the subjectivist claim that *x* is good if and only if *x* is such as to arouse/such as to make appropriate the sentiment of approbation? There are two main ways.

6.   The first way is to follow Hume's lead and say that, just as in the colour case 'the appearance of objects in daylight to the eye of a man in health is denominated their real and true colour, even while colour is . . . merely a phantasm of the senses',[2] so value is merely a phantasm of the feelings or a 'gilding or staining' of 'natural objects with the colours borrowed from internal sentiment',[3] (or in terms alien to Hume but in one way illuminating, value is the intentional object of *une certaine folie à presque tous*); and that to the extent that there is a standard of correctness in morals, this is determined by the verdicts of whoever judges 'most coolly',[4] 'with the least prejudice', and on the basis of the fullest information – all of which, 'if we consider the matter aright', is 'a question of fact, not of sentiment'.[5] When men argue and dispute in valuation, and when they succeed in instructing one another, what they are really seeking to do is to approximate to the verdicts of that judge.

What is remarkable here, among many other merits in Hume's explicit defence of this position as it applies in the case of aesthetic taste, is his anxiety to describe and make room for something that an ordinary or vulgar sceptic would simply deny or explain away. This is the remarkable degree of consensus that is sometimes achieved in the view that is reached about works of art and literature that survive the test of time:

> The same Homer, who pleased at Athens and Rome two thousand years ago, is still admired at Paris and at London. All the changes of climate, government, religion, and language have not been able to obscure his glory. Authority or prejudice may give a temporary vogue to a bad poet or orator; but his reputation will never be durable or general. When his compositions are examined by posterity or foreigners, the enchantment is dissipated and his faults appear in their true colours. On the contrary, a real genius, the longer his works endure, and the more wide they are spread, the more sincere is the admiration which they meet with.[6]

Hume contends that for a subjectivist simply to declare that 'all sentiment is right because sentiment has reference to nothing beyond itself' – which might seem a little close to the position he had himself taken up in the *Treatise* – is for him to invite charges of advancing an 'extravagant paradox, or rather a palpable absurdity'.

It is one of the strengths of Hume's subjectivism that he distances himself from this paradox and works so hard to show how a standard of correctness is possible in taste and morals and to explain our many and frequent lapses from it. No plausible or life-like subjectivism can do less. It is however a difficulty in his execution of the task – and a further difficulty in extending Hume's account of the aesthetic case to the general case and the moral case in particular – that he has to place so much weight at certain points on an analogy between aesthetic taste and ordinary sensory (gustatory, *etc.*) taste:

---

2   'Of the Standard of Taste', in Hume, *Essays Moral, Political, and Literary*, ed. E. F. Miller (Indianapolis: Liberty Classics, 1985), paragraph 12.
3   *Inquiry concerning Principles of Morals*, Appendix I.
4   See (*e.g.*) Hume's essay 'Of the Delicacy of Taste and of Passion', in *Essays*.
5   Cp. 'Standard', in Hume, *Essays*, paragraphs 24–5.
6   Paragraph 11.

Some particular forms or qualities, from the original structure of the internal fabric, are calculated to please, and others to displease, and if they fail of their effect in any particular instance, it is from some apparent defect or imperfection in the organ. A man in a fever would not insist on his palate as able to decide concerning flavours; nor would one affected with the jaundice pretend to give a verdict with regard to colours. In each creature there is a sound and a defective state; and the former alone can be supposed to afford us a true standard of taste and sentiment. If, in the sound state of the organ, there be an entire or a considerable uniformity of sentiment among men, we may thence derive an idea of the perfect beauty.

For the pleasures of the table such claims might just pass. But our chances of making the requisite analogy with an organ of perception, or of something a bit like an organ of perception (a sound judge, or organism or whatever) first weaken and then disappear altogether as we pass with Hume from the gustatory to the aesthetic-perceptual and thence to the aesthetic in general and the moral. And it is not enough, so long as we take the problem on Hume's official terms, to respond to this problem as Hume does (in effect) when he answers the question where the true judges and critics are to be found 'whose joint verdict is the true standard of taste and beauty', by saying that:

Where doubts occur men can do no more than in other disputable questions which are submitted to their understanding: they must produce the best arguments that their invention suggests to them; they must acknowledge a true and decisive standard to exist somewhere, to wit real existence and matter of fact; and they must have indulgence to such as differ from them in their appeals to this standard. It is sufficient for our present purposes if we have proved that the taste of all individuals is not upon an equal footing, and that some men in general however difficult to be pitched upon will be acknowledged by universal sentiment to have a preference above others.[7]

For one happy to speak the language of objects and their properties (as well as of their judges) such a stance may be sustainable. (See below §8.) But for Hume's own purposes the answer is not good

enough – not so much because of the epistemological difficulty (which here, as always, one must learn to live with), but because, in the absence of any possible story about something comparable to sound organs of perception, it leaves us with insufficient grasp, and an insufficient account of our actual grasp (which I take to have regard for the properties attributed to objects within the critic's or judge's sentiment of approbation) of what *constitutes* a good critic or judge.

7.   If Hume holds true to his doctrine that values are merely phantasms of the feelings, or gildings or stainings with colours borrowed from internal sentiment, then strictly speaking, he must never look to objects and properties themselves in characterizing the difference between good and bad judgments in taste and morals. (If he could do this then we should not need the independent standard, or the 'sound organ' story.) So Hume looks instead to the *condition of the judge* (his 'strong sense, united to delicate sentiment, improved by practice, perfected by comparison, cleared of all prejudice'), and this he then takes himself to need to see as (in his terms) a real existence or matter of fact. So that it suddenly appears that, if we pass over the properties of the object itself, then a life-like philosophical subjectivism requires a *non*-subjective foundation as well as the support of a substantial conception of a nearly homogeneous human nature.

This paradox deserves to be conjoined with another kind of puzzle. Our subjective reactions to objects or events will often impose groupings upon them that have no purely naturalistic rationale. (That, in a way, is the point of subjectivism – cp. §8 below.) But, at least for subjectivists who are serious in the fashion of Hume, there are good and bad ways of effecting such groupings. We are not simply to fire off *at random* in our responses to things. A feeble jest or infantile practical joke does not deserve to be grouped with the class of things that a true judge would find genuinely funny. How then in the case of a responsible judge are we to envisage Hume's process of gilding and staining? When the mind of such a judge spreads itself upon objects, does it first determine that *x* really belongs in the non-natural[8] class of genuine specimens of

---

[7]   Paragraph 25.

[8]   For 'non-natural' cp. the explanation given by G. E. Moore in *Principia Ethica*, pp. 40–1 ('By nature then I do mean . . . that which is the subject matter of the natural sciences, and also of psychology'); also my *Sameness & Substance* (Oxford: Blackwell, 1981), p. 183 with note 40.

the funny – first determine the similarity-link of *x* with items a true judge would find funny – and then [. . .] 'gild and stain' *x*, or 'project' or 'discharge itself' upon *x*?[9] That seems a ludicrous suggestion. Is it not rather that there is something in the object that is *made for* the sentiment it would occasion in a qualified judge, and it brings down the sentiment upon the object as so qualified? Surely this feature of *x*, whatever it is, impinges on perception and sentiment simultaneously; and the time has come to enrich our ideas about what can fall under *each* of perception and sentiment in their engagement with the object.

8. Does the subjectivism that we found reason in §4 above to search after admit of some alternative formulation? Let us seize for this purpose upon a Humean suggestion that has no clear place in his official theory:

> It must be allowed that there are certain qualities in objects which are fitted by nature to produce particular . . . feelings.[10]

In Hume's official theory, this is not meant to count against the Humean denial that virtue, viciousness, merit, *etc.* are in the object itself. But let us now abandon Hume's aspiration to secure the standard of correctness in valuation from outside the domain of values, or by sole reference to the qualified judge. And let us restore to its proper place the ordinary idea in its ordinary construal that the criterion for a good judge is that he is apt to get things right. (If questions of value were not questions of real existence or matters of fact, then how could the criterion for being a good judge have that status?)

Suppose that objects that regularly please or help or amuse us . . . or harm or annoy or vex us . . . in various ways come to be grouped together by us under various categories or classifications to which we give various avowedly anthropocentric names, and suppose they come to be grouped together as they are precisely *because* they are such as to please, help, amuse us, . . . or harm, annoy, vex us . . . in their various ways. There will be then no saying, very often, what properties these names stand for independently of the reactions they provoke. (The point of calling this position sub-

jectivism is that the properties in question are explained by reference to the reactions of human subjects.) But equally – at least when the system of properties and reactions diversifies, complicates and enriches itself – there will often be no saying exactly *what* reaction a thing with the associated property will provoke without direct or indirect allusion to the property itself. Amusement for instance is a reaction we have to characterize by reference to its proper object, via something perceived as funny (or incongruous or comical or whatever). There is no object-independent and property-independent, 'purely phenomenological' or 'purely introspective' account of amusement. And equally there is no saying what exactly the funny is without reference to laughter or amusement or kindred reactions. Why should we expect there to be such an independent account?

Of course, when we dispute whether *x* is really funny, there is a whole wealth of considerations and explanations we can adduce, and by no means all of them have to be given in terms simply synonymous or interdefinable with 'funny'. We can do a little better than say that the funny is that which makes people laugh. (Since laughter can come about in quite other ways, no doubt that is just as well.) What is improbable in the extreme is that, either singly or even in concert, further explanations will ever add up to a *reduction* of the funny or serve to characterize it in purely natural terms (terms that pull their weight in our theoretical-cum-explanatory account of the mechanisms of the natural world). If so, the predicate 'funny' is an irreducibly subjective predicate. These diverse supporting considerations will however serve another purpose. By means of them, one person can improve another's grasp of the concept of the funny; and one person can improve another's focus or discrimination of what *is* funny. Furthermore, the process can be a collaborative one, without either of the participants to a dialogue counting as the absolutely better judge. The test of improvement in this process of mutual instruction and improvement can be at least partially internal to the perceptions of its participants. For, as Protagoras might (almost) have said, after the process has begun, those who participate in it may report not only that they discriminate more keenly, make more decisions and are better satisfied with the

---

[9] Cp. *Inquiry* (appendix I).
[10] Hume, *op. cit.*, paragraph 16.

classifications and subclassifications they now effect, but also that they get more and more cognitive-cum-affective satisfaction in their own responses. Finer perceptions can both intensify and refine responses. Intenser responses can further heighten and refine perceptions. And more and more refined responses can lead to the further and finer and more variegated or more intense responses *and* perceptions.

9.   When this point is reached, a system of anthropocentric properties and human responses has surely taken on a life of its own. Civilization has begun. One may surmise that at any stage in the process some <property, response> pairs will and some will not prove susceptible of refinement, amplification and extension. One may imagine that some candidate pairs do and some do not relate in a reinforceable, satisfying way to the subjectivity of human life at a given time. Some pairs are such that refinement of response leads to refinement of perception and *vice versa*. Others are not. Some are and some are not capable of serving in the process of interpersonal education, instruction and mutual enlightenment. Those pairs that do have this sort of advantage, we may expect to catch on and survive, and then to evolve further, generate further <property, response> pairs and make room for the discovery of yet further properties that lie at a progressively greater distance from specific kinds of affect. Those pairs that do not have this sort of viability will no doubt fall by the wayside.

If we see matters in this sort of way, we are surely not committed to suppose that the properties that figure within these <property, response> pairs will bear to natural properties any relation of supervenience that could be characterized in terms that were both general and illuminating of the particular properties in question. Rather they will be primitive, *sui generis*, incurably anthropocentric, and as unmysterious as any properties will ever be to us.

Now, however, in order to embrace the great majority of the valuational predicates in common use, there is need to make room in the story for at least one further complication. Suppose that a point has been reached where a <property, response> pair is well established, the response is corrigible by reference to the question whether whatever is required for the presence of the property is present, and various supplementary considerations have become available that make possible

the criticism, explanation, and vindication of attitudes and responses to a given thing. Suppose therefore that we are past the stage at which the critics of classical subjectivism like to see the position as stuck, where the non-accidental occurrence of some simple response is seen as simply sufficient for the presence of the property. (That is the stage where it can be said that any actual nausea caused by x suffices to prove that x is nauseating, and the claim may be preserved against doubt or difficulty by simple restriction – 'x is nauseating *for John* even if not *for Philip*', or as in Heraclitus' example 'Sea water is good *for fishes* and most poisonous *for men*'.) Suppose then that the language of evaluation is past the point at which some semi-valuational predicates (such as the predicates like 'nauseating' that we can qualify by explicit relativization) have stuck. Then something else also becomes possible. Instead of fixing on an object or class of objects and arguing about what response or responses they are such as to evoke, we can fix on a response – one that we value or disvalue for itself or value or disvalue for what it is a response to – and then argue about what the marks are of the property that the response itself is made for. And without serious detriment to the univocity of the predicate, it can now become essentially contestable what a thing has to be like for there to be any reason to accord that particular appellation to it and correspondingly contestable what the extension is of the predicated. (This was part of the point of the end of §3.)

Once we have the possibility of an attitude's being held relatively fixed, the attitude's being paired with some reciprocally appropriate property that is made for it, and its being essentially contestable what the marks are of the property, we shall have a sketch for an explanation of something that cognitivists have said too little about. We can explain the phenomenon that Stevenson (who was not the first to notice it – cp. Plato *Euthyphro* 8d, Aristotle *Nicomachean Ethics* 1107a, though Stevenson was first to see it so speech-functionally) called the 'magnetism' of value terms. This is the same phenomenon as Hume notices in the second and third paragraphs of 'Of the Standard of Taste'

> There are certain terms in every language which import blame, and others praise, and all men who use the same tongue must agree in their application of them. Every voice is united in applauding elegance, propriety, simplicity, spirit in writing, and in blaming

fustian, affectation, coldness, and false brilliancy. But when critics come to particulars, this seeming unanimity vanishes; and it is found that they had affixed a very different meaning to their expressions. In all matters of opinion and science it is different . . . The word *virtue*, with its equivalent in every tongue, implies praise: as that of *vice* does blame; and no man without the most obvious and grossest impropriety could affix reproach to a term which in general acceptation is understood in a good sense or bestow applause where the idiom requires disapprobation . . .

No philosophy of value can ignore this phenomenon. Stevenson tries to account for it by his doctrine of emotive meanings. Richard Hare would approach the phenomenon by characterizing the meaning of value words in terms of their commendatory function. If what I have just been saying is anywhere near right, however, perhaps we need not go to these lengths or involve ourselves in the difficulties they involve. If a property and an attitude are made for one another, it will be strange for one to use the term for the property if he is in no way party to the attitude and there is simply no chance of his finding that the item in question has the property. But if he is no stranger to the attitude and the attitude is favourable, it will be the most natural thing in the world if he regards it as a matter of keen argument what it takes for a thing to count as having the property that the attitude is paired with.

10.   If we imagine that what the moralist or aesthetician always confronts is the end-product of a long and complicated evolutionary process of the sort I have described, we shall certainly find ethical naturalism an unattractive position (at least if we mean by naturalism what Moore started out meaning), and we may well find subjectivism an overwhelmingly attractive one. If so, then I think we ought to prefer the second of our two formulations, that is the one described in §§8–9 above. There is still place for the sentient subject in our subjectivism – this is a subjectivism of subjects and properties *mutually* adjusted. But if we despair of letting the whole matter of correctness depend on the analogy between a sound, healthy sense-organ and a sound judge or organism, then we shall need to give up the idea of achieving any simple or single statement of the standard of correctness along the lines envisaged by Hume (or the lines sometimes envisaged by Aristotle, cp. *NE* 107a2). In which

case we must keep faith in another way with Hume's desire to maintain the sovereignty of subjects simultaneously with the distinction between sound and mistaken judgment. We shall do this by insisting that *genuinely* [funny/appalling/shocking/consoling/reassuring/disgusting/pleasant/delightful/ . . .] things are things that not only [amuse/appal/shock/console/reassure/disgust/please/delight/ . . .] but have these effects precisely because they *are* [funny/appalling/shocking/consoling/reassuring/disgusting/pleasant/delightful/ . . .] at the same time insisting that this 'because' introduces an explanation that both explains and justifies. (In *something like* the way in which 'there is a marked tendency for us all to think that $7 + 5 = 12$, and this tendency exists because there is really nothing else to think about what $7 + 5$ is' explains a tendency *by* justifying it. On request, the justificatory aspect can be made yet more evident by filling out the explanation with a calculation, or a proof. [. . .] A similar complement for the valuational case could consist in an argued vindication of the claim that x is indeed funny, shocking . . .)

If this is how we work out the second approach, then the subjectivist who is committed to prefer the more Humean formulation of the subjectivist position will ask by what right I characterize the funny/appalling/shocking/consoling/reassuring/disgusting/pleasant/delightful . . . in these terms, and how I can propose to extend this method of elucidation to the good, the right and the beautiful. If he accepts Hume's own criterion of plausibility, however, then there is now a prospect of replying to him as follows: Hume has given the only imaginable external standard of correctness, but it appears more and more implausible the further we move from the gustatory and olfactory cases. If the only other standard we can imagine is an internal one, that is a subject-involving *and* property-involving, piecemeal standard, then we must conclude that what makes possible those discriminations that Hume insists upon our being properly impressed by is just what we think it is, *viz.* the properties of objects as they impinge on us. Such a standard must be essentially contestable and internal to the thoughts and practices it relates to – indeed all of a piece with the practice of criticism, and vulnerable to anything that that can establish. But then (as Hume says, and we have the better right to say this) when critical doubts occur, 'men can do no more than in other disputable questions which are submitted to the understanding; they must produce the best arguments that their invention suggests to them'. The practices and the standards stand or fall (or, having fallen, are shored up again) together. Perhaps it is a shame that nothing vindicates the standard once and for all. But, conceiving the standard in these humble terms, at least we can prefer the obvious to the devious in stating it, and in doing so speak boldly of objects and their subjective properties. Either we hold our ground in making the discriminations that Hume insists that we contrive to make or (cp. §17 below) we don't. If we do, the standard itself – for that sort of evaluation – is surviving another day, and we can continue to employ it in distinguishing between what is really φ and what is not really φ. It is not inevitable that the standard will withstand criticism. But it does not need to be inevitable that it will. So the response to the objection I envisaged at the beginning of this paragraph is that if there is a problem about this 'really', or if its natural link with the ideas of truth and objectivity ought to be severed, then the onus is on him who prefers the first, more Humean formulation of subjectivism to say what the problem is, to make out the case against these natural appearances, and also to show how, even if talk of objects were only a *façon de parler*, Hume's criteria of adequacy could be satisfied. For the following possibility has now become visible: that we should characterize the *subjective* (and then perhaps the valuational) positively, in terms of a subjective judgment's being one that is however indirectly answerable for its correctness to the responses of conscious subjects; that we should characterize the *objective* positively, in terms of an objective judgment's being one that is a candidate for plain truth: and that, having characterized each of these categories of judgment positively and independently, we need to be ready for the possibility that a judgment may fall into both, may both rest upon sentiment *and* relate to a matter of fact.

I should not for my positive preference call such a position *realism*, as if to contrast it with *mentalism* or whatever. Nor should I claim that this preliminary elaboration and defence can go anywhere near to showing the final tenability of the position itself. What is much more urgent than any final assessment of the position is some fuller appreciation of its motivation and commitments. In this essay I attempt little more than this.

11.   (a) Whether we prefer the first or the second of the two ways of expounding subjectivism, it will be appropriate and natural to declare with Protagoras the sophist, the first systematic subjectivist,

> Man is the measure of all things,

restricting the Protagorean doctrine to valuational things, and taking 'man' to mean not 'this man' or 'that man' or 'any man' but 'men in so far as we can reach them or they can reach us and are not alien to us'.

(b) Given our development of the position at sections 8 and 9 it will be equally natural to say that, where the ascription of value is concerned, *finding x to be φ is prior to (or at least coeval with) thinking x to be φ*.

(c) It will also be natural to say that what is φ (simply, not 'φ for us' or 'φ here') is *relative*, in a special sense to be explained. An object's or person's or event's being φ – or φ in our sense, if you will (but that of course is what the predicate will mean in this sentence, the sentence being our sentence) – consists in its being such as to evoke in the right way or such as to make appropriate some response, call it A, – still no relativity so far, but now it comes – where A is *our* response, or the response that *we* owe to it if it really is φ. The relativity to us that is here in question consists in the fact that it is we who owe *x* the response A and owe it that even though one who is not party to the set of associations of paired <property, response> associations to which the <φ, A> association belongs may fail to respond in that way. What this relativity imports is the possibility that there may be simply no point in urging that a stranger to our associations owes the object this response. Even if a stranger can, by an imaginative effort, get himself some idea of what the property φ is and what the associated reaction A is, this may not suffice to effect the connexion between his discerning φ in a thing and his participating fully in A. It may not result in his identifying or associating himself with that sort of response. Even when the response A becomes possible for him, then, this may not trigger any readiness on his part to participate in all the collateral aesthetic or practical responses normally associated with A. (It is for investigation whether that means that he has an imperfect grasp of what φ is.)

A relativity of this kind was always to have been expected if it is by the process speculatively reconstructed in §§8–9 above that we get our value terms. For this process was a historical and particular one, and it comprised some contribution by the mind unlike that which is postulated in Kantian epistemology. What imports the relativity is a contribution that need not be everywhere the same or similar in its content. There is the possibility (at least) of distinct and different moral and aesthetic worlds whose inhabitants need to struggle long and hard to appreciate the differences. They must understand not only the nature and extent of these differences, but also something of the way in which these differences are shaped substantively by the conditions of human life, before it is even an option for them to come properly to disagree with one another in their valuations. (And when they disagree they are not thereby committed to dwell on the Humean question whether the differences are 'blameless' or 'not blameless'. The various circumstances that make up the differences may condition the sense and proper understanding of judgments.)

12. At this point I should expect the intuitionist objectivist and the champion of Hume's version of subjectivism (and several other parties perhaps, *e.g.*, the emotivist) to combine forces in a joint protest: 'In something like the way we each expected, you have now talked yourself into a really impossible position: you are trying to ground a distinction that you like to describe as the distinction between what is really φ and not really φ upon what are by your own account mere responses – upon a convergence in the inclinations various people feel or do not feel to say that x is φ or that x is not φ. Surely this distinction between the really φ and not really φ, like everything else that is distinctive of your subjectivism, is either plain bluff or a mere *façon de parler*. (No wonder you disclaimed the title 'realist'.) In a phrase Williams uses in criticism of intuitionism, you are confusing resonance with reference. Surely the relativity you have now deduced from your subjectivism and described in terms that are both object-involving and blatantly metaphorical ('owing an object a response' and the rest) precisely demonstrates the necessity to treat all such talk as a *façon de parler*. It is no less a *façon de parler* for sounding like the natural continuation of the ordinary language of evaluation.'

It would be a defeat if this were so. We were trying to formulate a variant upon classical subjectivism both positively and literally. Pending a more challenging statement of the objection, however, I believe that I can defend the subjectivist position as we now have it by pointing out that these responses we have been speaking of are not 'mere' responses. They are responses that are correct when and only when they are occasioned by what has the corresponding property φ and are occasioned by it because it *is* φ. If the objector persists: 'How can human agreement in these responses decide what *really* is φ or not φ?' I reply that the sort of agreement that is in question here is only agreement in *susceptibility* to respond thus and so to φ things. It is agreement at most (as one might say, evoking a very familiar passage of Wittgenstein) in what property/response associations we are able to catch onto and work up into a shared way of talking, acting, and reacting. Since this agreement is not in itself agreement in *opinions* about what is φ or not φ (even thought the existence of the shared language presupposes the possibility of such agreement), there is no question of the agreement in the belief that x is φ being the *criterion* for x's really being φ. x is only really φ if it is such as to evoke and make appropriate the response A among those who are sensitive to φ-ness. That is a far cry from agreement about the φ-ness of x simply constituting the actual φ-ness of x.

Agreement figures in the story of the formation of the *senses* of value predicates, not in any story about their references.

13. The response is likely to excite another sort of objection: 'You have spoken of morality's depending, at least in part, upon agreement in susceptibility to respond thus and so to certain things. But what if these susceptibilities changed? Could that make what is now right wrong, what is now good bad . . . ? Again, you suggested at the very outset that Hume could be read as proposing that x is good if and only if x is such as to arouse or make appropriate a certain sentiment of approbation. But whether x is such depends not only on the condition of x but on the nature and range of susceptibilities of the subjects of the sentiments. What sentiment is appropriate to a thing of a given character will depend at least in part upon what the range is of the sentiments themselves. But how can

goodness, goodness itself, depend on anything of this sort?'

The objection is instructive and demonstrates the importance of detaching any development of Humean or Protagorean subjectivism from the Moorean conception of philosophy. I believe it also casts further light upon relativity.

The objection would be dead right if the subjectivist were saying that '*x* is good' may be paraphrased as '*x* is such as to arouse or make appropriate [a certain] sentiment of approbation', and if he were saying that this paraphrase could then be intersubstituted with 'good' *salvo sensu* (or more or less *salvo sensu*). But the subjectivist need not be saying that. His distinctive claim is rather that *x* is good if and only if *x* is the sort of thing that calls forth or makes appropriate a certain sentiment of approbation *given the range of propensities that we actually have to respond in this or that way*; or generalizing a little, and still disclaiming the attempt to provide an equivalent, his claim is that, for each value predicate φ (or for a very large range of such), there is an attitude or response of subjects *belonging to a range of propensities that we actually have* such that an object has the property φ [. . .] if and only if the object is fitted by its characteristics to bring down that extant attitude or response upon it and bring it down *precisely because it has those characteristics*.

To take the matter any further would involve an articulation of the response or attitude and of the associated marks that are annexed to particular value predicates. This articulation would have to be given in a way that threw into relief the organizing point of applying the predicate to anything or withholding it. The existence of a substantial body of attempts at what used to be called the theory of laughter (see the instructive review of these in D. H. Munro's *Argument of Laughter*),[11] all devoted to the understanding of just two or three such predicates, is evidence of the potential difficulty and of the interest of this sort of work. But such a theory need not promise to carry us even one inch nearer to an intersubstitutable equivalent for the predicates that stand for the properties that it studies. It may or may not succeed in this.

14.   But does the subjectivist want to remain perfectly satisfied with the actual condition of our actual response to the objects of moral and aesthetic attention? What of criticism and progress?

It was for this reason that I tried to secure the irrelevance of a change in human nature and susceptibilities, by stressing not the relativity of value to the *totality of our actual responses* but its relativity to our *actual propensities*, these being propensities that are answerable to criticism, *etc.*, to respond in this or that way to this or that feature of things. But to fill out this answer, I must hark back to the claims in §9 about the essential contestability of valuational language, and also to the claim that the standard of correctness for each predicate is all of a piece with the day to day practice of using it and criticizing or vindicating the uses that are made of it. In prosecuting that practice [. . .] we shall reach wherever we reach, for such reasons as seem good and appropriate. Subjectivism itself prescribes no limit to the distance that reflection [. . .] can carry us from the starting point in the sentiments. [. . .] It does not imprison us in the system of evaluations we begin with; nor does it insulate from criticism the attitudes and responses that sustain glib, lazy or otherwise suspect predications.

15.   But someone will now ask: what if, by a sequence of minute shifts in our responses, an evil demon were to work us round to a point where we took what is actually evil to be good? Perhaps the demon might do this without our even noticing it. Yes, I reply, he might. But this is not an objection to sensible subjectivism. It would not follow from our not noticing the magnitude of the shift and everything that went with it that the very same thing that once told the presence of good was now fastened constitutively upon evil. For the subjectivism we have envisaged does not treat the response as a criterion, or even as an indicator. In the full theory of the last stage of the processes we have been describing, it counts as nothing less than an act of judging a content; it is a judgment indispensably sustained by the perceptions and feelings and thoughts that are open to criticism that is based on norms that are open to criticism. It is not that *by which we tell*. It is part of the telling itself.

What the objection does do, however, is to point clearly at the thing that has given subjectivism a bad name. This is all the associations that are commonly imputed to subjectivism with the thought

---

[11]   *The Argument of Laughter* (London and Melbourne, 1951).

that evaluative judgments may be assimilated to 'mere responses' and with the idea that the responses the subjectivist interests himself in are autonomously inner states – or states such that, if you are in one of them, you can tell and tell infallibly, without looking outward, whether you are in it or not. (These really would be states that 'have no reference to anything beyond themselves'.) These associations are made explicit by the objection. But they were already under acute pressure in Hume's more mature statement of ethical subjectivism, and none of them is maintained in the position as we have defended it.

16.   What needs to be emphasized again at this point is that subjectivism ought not to be represented as offering any guarantee that for most (or for any) of the predicates and properties we put our trust in, the very best judgments that we can make involving them *will* gather a consensus such that the best explanation of the consensus is that those who take x to be φ do so precisely because *x is* φ. [. . .] Of course our shared linguistic practice commits us strongly to that belief. But our practice can operate without any special or philosophical guarantee that truth and correctness *will* stay around in this way. Our practice can even continue to operate in full awareness of the flimsiness and contingency of the natural facts that it reposes upon, in the awareness that so often impinges upon valuation as we know it of our proneness to error and self-deception, even in awareness of the theoretical possibility that our minds and nervous systems may have been poisoned or perverted. What we can do about that danger is only to take ordinary precautions, and to have ordinary regard (regard not insulated from thoughts about the subject matter itself) for the credentials with which and conditions from out of which people's judgments are made. Better, we can take ordinary precautions, and then, in deference to the inherent difficulty of the subject matter, a few more. And it is well worth remembering that, by preferring over Hume's subjectivism a subjectivism that was object and property-involving, we did not disqualify ourselves from insisting upon its also being *conscious subject*-involving. If there is something fishy in either the agreements or the disagreements that we encounter, then we must investigate their etiology case by case, and as best we can, having proper regard for everything, not excluding the characters and sensibilities of those participating in the agreements and disagreements.

17.   If nothing can exclude in advance the possibility that the very best judgments we can arrive at involving this or that predicate will fail to gather any consensus, let alone underwrite a consensus such that the best explanation of the consensus is that those who take x to be φ do so because *x is* φ, then what is to be said about such failure? Well. Where we seem to encounter such a thing, it may be that what we call φ-ness is different things to different people. That is one possibility. If so, these is less strict *disagreement* than may appear. But it may be that there is no escape by that route. It may not be possible to establish any sufficient difference in the 'value-focus' of those who appear to be in disagreement.

In that case there are two other possibilities. We may simply give up on the predicate; or we may remain undeterred. [. . .] Sometimes, of course, where the latter seems to be the right attitude Hume's formulation of subjectivism may seem superior to the cognitivist formulation of subjectivism that I have advocated (especially if the Humean version can be freed of the difficulties I have claimed there are in it). It is strange, however, that the pull towards Hume's formulation should be at its strongest precisely where the sense of the predicate gives the appearance of being in danger of the kind of collapse from which Hume himself believed that he needed our shared human nature and our shared proclivity towards certain sentiments to protect it. So long as it is Hume's struggle to make the sovereignty of moral subjects consist with the distinction he wanted between sound and unsound judgments that remains at the centre of Hume's theoretical concern, I think there is no clear advantage for him in the shift back to the first formulation.

In truth, whatever difficulties there are in the possibility of irresoluble substantive disagreement, no position in moral philosophy can render itself simply immune from them. We should not tumble over ourselves to assert that there is irresoluble substantive disagreement. We should simply respect the possibility of such disagreement, I think, and in respecting it register the case for a measure of cognitive underdetermination. [. . .] Some have wished to find a philosophical position that ruled out this possibility in advance, by espousing some anti-subjectivist theory – a Kantian or intuitionist or utilitarian or dogmatically realist theory. But how can such a possibility be simply ruled out? And why on the other hand should the subjectivist be deemed to have *ruled it in*? In this matter the subjectivist really has to do the same as everyone else: he can only urge that, in spite of the possibility of irresoluble substantive disagreement, but in a manner partially conditioned by that possibility, we should persevere as best we can in the familiar processes of reasoning, conversion, and criticism – without guarantees of success, which are almost as needless as they are unobtainable.

18.   In 1960, Bertrand Russell wrote 'I cannot see how to refute the arguments for the subjectivity of ethical values, but I find myself incapable of believing that all that is wrong with wanton cruelty is that I don't like it.' How close have our prosubjectivist efforts carried us to the answer to this difficulty? First, reverting to Hume, we can drop the first person. What is wrong with cruelty is not, even for Bertrand Russell, just that Bertrand Russell doesn't like it, but that it is not such as to call forth liking given our *actual* collectively scrutinized responses. Those responses are directed at cruelty, and at what cruelty itself consists in on the level of motive, intention, outcome . . . To be sure, we should not care about these things, these things would not impinge as they do upon us, if our responses were not there to be called upon. In the presence of a good reason to call them in question, we should not be able to trust them or take too much for granted about the well-foundedness of the properties they are keyed to. But, in the total absence of such a reason, it will not be at all question-begging for Russell simply to remind himself as thoroughly and vividly as he can of just what it is that he dislikes, abhors, detests . . . about cruelty and its ancient and hideous marks.

I.5 Moral Realism

Introduction

According to moral realism, some moral judgments are objectively true, and this in a very strong sense. Let us work our way toward understanding this sense by considering a specific, and hopefully uncontroversial, moral claim: that raising a child's hopes, for the sole purpose of gaining malicious pleasure by later disappointing her, is immoral. What such a person does is wrong. What explains the immorality of this person's behavior?

Well, in one sense, the basis of the immorality has just been identified – the wrongness of the malefactor's behavior consists precisely in raising expectations so that they may be dashed, and pleasure gained thereby. There's nothing mistaken with this account – indeed, it will likely seem clearly true to all but error theorists. Yet we might ask – what *makes it the case* that raising expectations in this way is constitutive of wrongness? Why are actions that raise such expectations immoral?

One way to answer these questions is by invoking a more general moral principle, from which it follows that behavior of this kind is immoral. Raising expectations in this way is wrong because . . . you wouldn't like it if it were done to you; it would diminish overall happiness; it is forbidden by God's decrees, etc. Now it is a contested matter among ethical theorists about whether there is, at the bottom of ethics, just a single, fundamental principle that can explain and unify all correct moral judgments.[1] Advocates of the Golden Rule, or Utilitarianism, or Divine Command Theory, are all involved in efforts to identify and defend such a principle. Let's assume that some such effort will be successful one day – a big assumption. And, while we're making such large assumptions, assume as well, just for purposes of illustration, that the Utilitarian principle turns out to be the correct one. Then what?

Well, we can still ask our earlier question: what *makes it the case* that actions that maximize happiness are morally right? Why is this feature – that of maximizing happiness – selected, from among all possible candidates, as the one that uniquely confers moral rightness on the actions that possess it? And here, at last, we can see the special reply that moral realists offer. For realists deny that a feature makes things morally right (or good, or virtuous, etc.) just because of any person's attitudes towards it. Maximizing happiness is not determinative of moral rightness just because I approve of actions that generate such happiness. That the larger society approves of such actions is neither here nor there. In fact, that the maximization of happiness gets to play this elevated moral role (if it does) does not hinge on the endorsement of *any* group of people, no matter how smart, no matter how kind or sympathetic. *No one* gets to make up the moral laws. Of course we each have our views

157

about what these laws are. But, because we don't have the final authority to create the moral laws, our moral opinions are all fallible. In moral matters, our say-so doesn't make it so.

We can rely on a helpful notion taken from the discussion of constructivism (see the introduction to part I.3) to give a complementary characterization of moral realism. Recall the notion of a conceiving-dependent property: something is a conceiving-dependent property just in case if something exemplifies that property, then it does so in virtue of the intentional attitudes taken towards it by some actual or idealized (human) agent(s). *Being a ten dollar bill*, or *being illegal*, are examples of such properties. A conceiving-*independent* property, by contrast, is just a property that is not conceiving-dependent. *Being square*, *being negatively charged*, and *being symmetrical* are instances of such properties.

Facts are just states of affairs in which things have properties. So moral facts are states of affairs in which moral properties are exemplified. A conceiving-independent moral fact is a state of affairs in which a conceiving-independent moral property is exemplified. And now, with this set-up in place, we are in a position to offer a definition. Moral realism is the claim that every moral fact is either a conceiving-independent moral fact, or is explained by such facts. (For more on the need for this latter disjunct, see the introduction to part I.3, "Constructivism.")

This characterization may seem to commit the moral realist to theism. For if the attitudes of human beings do not determine which things are morally right or good, then whose attitudes can do the trick? The obvious answer is: God. Now some moral realists are theists, and do believe that divine decrees are what make (say) killing, lying, and stealing immoral. But many moral realists do not rest their views on divine authority. These moral realists have no answer to the question of what makes (say) the maximization of happiness the all-important feature that determines whether actions are morally right or wrong. This (or some other candidate) *just is* the relevant feature. Whatever the content of a fundamental moral norm, its status as such cannot be explained by reference to anything more general or basic.

That can sound awfully fishy, but moral realists do have a reply that tries to deflect suspicion. Here, moral realists will point to their counterparts in other domains – logic and physics, for instance.

The fundamental facts of logic or physics are not determined by our attitudes. And, though many believe that they are determined by God's attitudes, there are as many others who are content to allow that these basic facts are, in a sense, inexplicable.

The basic laws in any area (logic, physics, morality, etc.) explain other, subsidiary, principles. Explanation in an area must stop somewhere. If you are a theist, it may terminate in some reference to the divine. If you are not, then there is no alternative but to invoke, at some point, a set of brute facts for which no further explanation is available. Moral realists will claim that some of these facts are moral ones.

This very strong conception of moral objectivity has naturally attracted a broad set of criticisms. One of the most prominent of these is epistemological. If moral principles are not of our own making, then how can we know them? This worry has been developed in a number of ways, but perhaps the line of argument with the longest pedigree is one that can trace its roots to Hume, and was given a modern touch-up in arguments that date from the 1930s, when noncognitivists began to criticize G. E. Moore's realist views. (See the Ayer selection in chapter 3 of this volume for a representative criticism of this sort. Moore's views are excerpted in chapter 35, and are discussed at greater length in the introduction to part II.7.)

In its most compressed form, the antirealist argument can be expressed as a dilemma: either moral realism will be a form of ethical naturalism, or a form of ethical nonnaturalism, and neither version yields a remotely plausible moral epistemology. Obviously, to appreciate this argument, we need to have a handle on the relevant terms. *Ethical naturalism* models ethics on the natural sciences – its subject matter is real, and its truths as objective as those revealed by physics, chemistry, or biology. If we want to know how to discover ethical truths, we look first to the ways in which it is done in other scientific domains, and then apply the same methods of discovery and justification to the moral realm. *Ethical nonnaturalism* rejects this assimilation, and insists that ethical inquiry is quite unlike that of any natural science. Further, properties such as moral rightness, goodness, desert, and praiseworthiness are not naturalistic, scientific features of the world. According to nonnaturalists, any effort to restrict the whole of reality to the confines of scientific understanding is bound to misrepresent the nature of morality. The readings in this section from Richard Boyd and Peter Railton represent naturalistic versions of moral realism. The offerings from Jean Hampton and Russ Shafer-Landau provide a sampling of nonnaturalist views.

Taking a page from Hume, contemporary critics argue that one cannot deduce (or in other ways infer) a moral claim solely from descriptive claims. If we grant (e.g.) that moral rightness consists in maximizing pleasure, we can *then* apply ordinary empirical methods to determine whether an action is morally right. But how can we determine the truth of the original principle, the one linking rightness with the maximization of pleasure? Not scientifically, according to critics – we can investigate the natural world in all of its complexity, and still not be able to vindicate the truth of this (or any other) moral principle. Such investigations will reveal a world of gases and liquids, atoms and molecules. But no matter how acutely we use our five senses, we won't be able to scientifically confirm the existence of our moral duties. Such an investigation will tell us what is the case; to know what ought to be the case, we must leave the natural sciences – and with it, ethical naturalism – behind.

But once we do that, there is no clear path to gaining moral knowledge. The sciences have provided our primary model of how to gain knowledge of the world. If we abandon scientific methods of inquiry in ethics, then just how are we supposed to discover the ultimate ethical principles? Nonnaturalists usually have had to recur to *intuitionism*, the view (discussed at greater length in part II.5) that we are justified in believing some moral claims solely on the basis of adequately understanding their content. We can just see, for instance, that it is wrong to kill children for the fun of it. We don't discover such a thing via empirical confirmation, but instead can know such a truth through an a priori consideration of the proposition itself. Critics, of course, will say that the alleged intuited truths of one age are the outmoded conventions of another. For if we really could intuit moral truths, then why is there so much disagreement about what morality requires of us?

This focus on disagreement forms the basis of an obviously related, though distinct, argument against moral realism. Since this concern is given its own section in part II.4, here we will only briefly summarize the state of play. Anti-realists claim that

any body of objective truths will be accessible to those who are very smart, work diligently at acquiring them, and are more or less free from emotional and computational impediments that cloud good judgment. The problem, say critics, is that people who meet this description invariably end up disagreeing about moral issues. If moral realism were true, then we should expect to see intelligent inquirers converge in their moral opinions as much as they do in (say) mathematics or physics. But they don't. And therefore we have excellent reason to think that moral realism is false. In the articles we have reprinted here, both Boyd and Shafer-Landau attempt a reply to this perennial antirealist criticism.

Moral realism has also been the target of criticisms, leveled mostly over the past thirty years, that it cannot explain the special relationship that obtains between the moral realm and the nonmoral world. John Mackie, in the course of developing his error theory (excerpts from which appear in chapter 1, and are discussed in its introduction), raises the worry in the following way:

> What is the connection between the natural fact that an action is a deliberate piece of cruelty – say, causing pain just for fun – and the moral fact that it is wrong? It cannot be an entailment, a logical or semantic necessity. Yet it is not merely that the two features occur together. The wrongness must somehow be "consequential" or "supervenient"; it is wrong because it is a piece of deliberate cruelty. But just what *in the world* is signified by this "because"? (Mackie 1977: 41; italics in original)

The way things are morally depends very closely on the way things are in the natural world. Indeed, if we imagine two worlds that are identical in all natural respects, then it seems impossible that there is any moral differences between the two. Further, it doesn't seem possible for something to change its moral status without some correlative change in the nonmoral world. This special relation between the moral and the nonmoral worlds is an instance of *supervenience*. Critics of moral realism charge that it has no adequate account of the supervenience of the moral upon the natural or nonmoral world.

The most straightforward way to render such an accounting would be to adopt the line of reductive ethical naturalism. This approach states that moral features are identical to natural features of the world. Our language may mask this fact, but these different vocabularies really end up referring to the same things. Just as "the morning star" and "the evening star" are different ways of designating just one thing – the planet Venus – "moral rightness" and "the maximization of informed preferences" are (on one naturalist account) just different ways of conceptualizing or referring to one and the same feature of the world.

Though this traditional view is making something of a comeback (see, e.g., Peter Railton's article, reprinted here, and Frank Jackson's selection in chapter 34), it is nowadays rejected by many naturalists, who prefer to align themselves with *nonreductive ethical naturalism*. (See Richard Boyd's selection in this section for a prominent example of this view.) These moral realists believe that moral properties are multiply realizable – there are many different non-moral properties that can make it the case that something is (e.g.) immoral.[2] An act can be immoral in virtue of its being coercive, or deceptive, or sadistic, etc. The property of being immoral is not identical to any single natural property. If it were, then something could be immoral if, *and only if*, it exemplified this feature. But acts can be immoral even if they are not coercive; immoral even if they are not sadistic, etc. So the property of *being immoral* is not the very same thing as that of *being coercive*. Nor is it the same thing as *being sadistic*. And so on. Nevertheless, an act's immorality can, in a particular case, be entirely a matter of its sadism, or its coercive or deceptive qualities. The moral property stands to the natural properties that in a given instance realize it, as the property of being a family stands to the various configurations that can constitute it. Something's being a family is sometimes a matter of its being a set of two parents and a daughter. But that is only one among many ways to compose a family. The many ways in which a group might constitute a family make the property of *being a family* multiply realizable.

It must be admitted that philosophers have failed quite spectacularly in their efforts to vindicate reductive ethical naturalism – there has been very little consensus on any candidate identification of moral and natural properties. This is part of the impetus for the recent developments of nonreductive naturalism. But if realists give up on reductive naturalism, then, whether they align themselves with nonreductive naturalism, or opt for ethical nonnaturalism, they owe us a response to Mackie's charge. If moral properties are different in kind from any other, and yet vitally depend on other properties for their instantiation, just how are moral properties related to the other ones? Part II.7 is given over entirely to a discussion of this concern. Read its introduction for a more in-depth presentation of what is at stake in this area.

To believe that there is a distinct set of moral properties that somehow supervenes on other properties is to invite a further skeptical challenge. There is always pressure to minimize one's ontological commitments, i.e., one's inventory of the kinds of things that exist in the universe. Moral realists have often been criticized for having an inflated ontology. Consider two pictures of the world's contents – two ontologies – that are identical but for one thing. And that is the inclusion, in one, of moral properties. In all other respects – the location and identity of every person, every action, every building, every molecule, every atom – these ontologies are identical. Why should we regard the larger list – the one that includes moral features – as the correct one? What could decide which of these two pictures accurately captures reality?

Following in the extremely influential footsteps of philosopher Gilbert Harman (see his selection in chapter 25), many philosophers endorse a causal-explanatory test as a way to determine an answer to this question. The basic idea is quite simple: something earns its way into the ontology just in case it is required to best explain what we experience of the world. Moral realists can take issue with this very popular test (as Russ Shafer-Landau does in his article in this section), but most philosophers, including many moral realists, embrace it.

For those who do, the fate of moral realism hinges on whether moral facts can pass it. Many moral realists (see, e.g., the Boyd and Railton papers here, and the articles by Nicholas Sturgeon and Terence Cuneo in chapters 26 and 27) believe that they can. For these philosophers, the *injustice* of a social order such as apartheid can explain why citizens ultimately revolted against it, and explain this phenomenon better than any other cause that makes no mention of its injustice. By contrast, critics of moral realism claim that reference to moral features is, in every case, explanatorily otiose. That an act was unjust, or immoral, or morally condemnable, doesn't add anything to an explanation of why things in the world occur as they do. All of the relevant explaining can be done without citing any moral features. *If* that were so, and *if* the causal-explanatory test is a good one, then we would have excellent grounds for thinking that moral realism is false. Is it so? Is the test a good one? Interested readers are advised to pursue this debate in part II.3.

In the very first selection of this book, John Mackie lays out the case for a moral error theory. That case includes succinct, and extremely influential, presentations of the skeptical arguments discussed above that focus on moral epistemology, disagreement, and supervenience. Mackie is also responsible for the current popularity of two other prominent antirealist arguments. Since these were discussed in the introduction to our section on error theory above, we will here be brief. Mackie first claims that moral realists are committed to the existence of a kind of fact (moral facts) that necessarily motivate those who sincerely believe in them. But, says Mackie, no facts possess such power. Therefore there are no moral facts. Realists have responded in two ways. Some have denied that moral facts must possess such power, and so their failure to possess it does not impugn moral realism. Others have agreed that this power is required of moral facts, but then have argued that such a power does, indeed, exist. Details of this debate can be found in the introduction and readings in part II.1, "Moral Motivation."

Mackie's other argument starts from the assumption that moral facts would have to supply categorical reasons for action – reasons that obtain no matter what a person's interests, desires, or plans happen to be. If an action is unjust, for instance, then *everyone* has excellent reason to refrain from it – even if that is what a person most wants to do; even if perpetrating the injustice will bring him fabulous wealth and undying fame. Mackie doesn't believe that there are categorical reasons, and so rejects moral realism, which he believes is committed to their existence. Realists again have pursued two avenues of response. (Details here can be found in the introduction and readings in part II.2.) Some have denied that realism is committed to categorical reasons – sometimes, these realists say, we don't, in fact, have good reason to do as morality says. (Peter Railton offers a brief defense of this view in the paper we have included in the present section.) Others have pursued the ancient quest of showing how objective moral facts do, indeed, provide each and every one of us, regardless of our inclinations and interests, with reasons for obedience.

It must be clear by now that the second half of this volume is taken up with an extended series of debates that have been sparked by criticisms, and defenses, of moral realism. These issues are at the heart of metaethics, interesting in their own right, and very wide-ranging. A full assessment of moral realism's (de)merits can't really be undertaken until one familiarizes oneself with this additional literature. We thus commend to your attention part II of this collection, where the lines of argument developed in the various debates receive more extensive coverage.

Notes

1 So-called ethical particularists, though typically moral realists, either deny that there are any moral principles, or insist that those few that do exist are nevertheless both metaphysically and practically unimportant. See Dancy (2004) for such a view. The discussion here will assume the existence (and importance) of moral principles, but those with particular-ist sympathies are invited to replace talk of moral principles with talk of irreducible moral facts.

2 There is a sense in which even a reductionist such as Jackson allows for the multiple realizability of moral properties. See the introduction to part II.6, "Moral Supervenience," n. 2, for more details.

Selected Bibliography

Adams, Robert. 1999. *Finite and Infinite Goods*. Oxford: Oxford University Press.

Bloomfield, Paul. 2001. *Moral Reality*. Oxford: Oxford University Press.

Brink, David. 1989. *Moral Realism and the Foundations of Ethics*. Cambridge: Cambridge University Press.

Copp, David. 2003. "Why Naturalism?" *Ethical Theory and Moral Practice* 6: 179–200.

Cuneo, Terence. Forthcoming. *The Normative Web: An Argument for Moral Realism*. Oxford: Oxford University Press.

Dancy, Jonathan. 1986. "Two Conceptions of Moral Realism." *Proceedings of the Aristotelian*

Society, supplementary volume 60: 167–87.

Dancy, Jonathan. 1993. *Moral Reasons*. Oxford: Blackwell.

Dancy, Jonathan. 2004. *Ethics without Principles*. Oxford: Oxford University Press.

Foot, Philippa. 2001. *Natural Goodness*. Oxford: Oxford University Press.

Little, Margaret. 1994a. "Moral Realism I: Naturalism." *Philosophical Books* 35: 145–53.

Little, Margaret. 1994b. "Moral Realism II: Non-Naturalism." *Philosophical Books* 35: 225–33.

Mackie, John. 1977. *Ethics: Inventing Right and Wrong*. London: Penguin.

McGinn, Colin. *Ethics, Evil and Fiction*. Oxford: Oxford University Press, ch. 2.

McNaughton, David. 1988. *Moral Vision*. Oxford: Blackwell.

Miller, Alexander. 2003. *An Introduction to Contemporary Metaethics*. Cambridge: Polity, chs. 8–10.

Nagel, Thomas. 1986. *The View from Nowhere*. Oxford: Oxford University Press, chs. 8 and 9.

Nagel, Thomas. 1997. *The Last Word*. Oxford: Oxford University Press, ch. 6.

Parfit, Derek. 2006. "Normativity." In Russ Shafer-Landau, ed. *Oxford Studies in Metaethics* 1. Oxford: Oxford University Press.

Railton, Peter. 1996. "Moral Realism: Problems and Prospects." In Mark Timmons and Walter Sinnott-Armstrong, eds. *Moral Knowledge?* Oxford: Oxford University Press.

Railton, Peter. 2003. *Facts, Values and Norms*. Cambridge: Cambridge University Press.

Sayre-McCord, Geoffrey, ed. 1988. *Essays on Moral Realism*. Ithaca: Cornell University Press.

Sayre-McCord, Geoffrey. 2006. "Moral Realism." In David Copp, ed. *Oxford Handbook of Ethical Theory*. Oxford: Oxford University Press.

Shafer-Landau, Russ. 2003. *Moral Realism: A Defence*. Oxford: Oxford University Press.

Smith, Michael. 2000. "Moral Realism." In Hugh LaFollette, ed. *Blackwell Guide to Ethical Theory*. Oxford: Blackwell.

Strandberg, Caj. 2004. *Moral Reality: A Defence of Moral Realism*. Lund: Lund University Press.

Sturgeon, Nicholas. 1986. "What Difference Does It Make Whether Moral Realism Is True?" *Southern Journal of Philosophy*, supplementary volume 24: 115–42.

Tannsjo, Torbjorn. 1989. *Moral Realism*. Totowa, NJ: Rowman & Littlefield.

Thomson, Judith. 1996. "Moral Objectivity." In Judith Thomson and Gilbert Harman, *Moral Relativism and Moral Objectivity*. Oxford: Blackwell.

How To Be a Moral Realist

Richard N. Boyd

1. Introduction

1.1. Moral realism

Scientific realism is the doctrine that scientific theories should be understood as putative descriptions of real phenomena, that ordinary scientific methods constitute a reliable procedure for obtaining and improving (approximate) knowledge of the real phenomena which scientific theories describe, and that the reality described by scientific theories is largely independent of our theorizing. Scientific theories describe reality and reality is "prior to thought" (see Boyd 1982).

By "moral realism" I intend the analogous doctrine about moral judgments, moral statements, and moral theories. According to moral realism:

1. Moral statements are the sorts of statements which are (or which express propositions which are) true or false (or approximately true, largely false, etc.);
2. The truth or falsity (approximate truth . . .) of moral statements is largely independent of our moral opinions, theories, etc.;
3. Ordinary canons of moral reasoning – together with ordinary canons of scientific and every-day factual reasoning – constitute, under many circumstances at least, a reliable method for obtaining and improving (approximate) moral knowledge.

It follows from moral realism that such moral terms as 'good', 'fair', 'just', 'obligatory' usually correspond to real properties or relations and that our ordinary standards for moral reasoning and moral disputation – together with reliable standards for scientific and everyday reasoning – constitute a fairly reliable way of finding out which events, persons, policies, social arrangements, etc. have these properties and enter into these relations. It is *not* a consequence of moral realism that our ordinary procedures are "best possible" for this purpose – just as it is not a consequence of scientific realism that our existing scientific methods are best possible. In the scientific case, improvements in knowledge can be expected to produce improvements in method (Boyd 1980, 1982, 1983, 1985a, 1985b, 1985c), and there is no reason to exclude this possibility in the moral case.

Scientific realism contrasts with instrumentalism and its variants and with views like that of Kuhn (1970) according to which the reality which scientists study is largely constituted by the theories they adopt. Moral realism contrasts with non-cognitivist metaethical theories like emotivism and with views according to which moral principles are largely a reflection of social constructs or conventions.

[. . .]

163

1.2. Scientific knowledge and moral skepticism

One of the characteristic motivations for anti-realistic metaethical positions – either for non-cognitivist views or for views according to which moral knowledge has a strong constructive or conventional component – lies in a presumed epistemological contrast between ethics, on the one hand, and the sciences, on the other. Scientific methods and theories appear to have properties – objectivity, value-neutrality, empirical testability, for example – which are either absent altogether or, at any rate, much less significant in the case of moral beliefs and the procedures by which we form and criticize them. These differences make the methods of science (and of everyday empirical knowledge) seem apt for the *discovery* of facts while the 'methods' of moral reasoning seem, at best, to be appropriate for the rationalization, articulation, and application of preexisting social conventions or individual preferences.

Many philosophers would like to explore the possibility that scientific beliefs and moral beliefs are not so differently situated as this presumed epistemological contrast suggests. We may think of this task as the search for a conception of 'unified knowledge' which will bring scientific and moral knowledge together within the same analytical framework in much the same way as the positivists' conception of 'unified science' sought to provide an integrated treatment of knowledge within the various special sciences. There are, roughly, two plausible general strategies for unifying scientific and moral knowledge and minimizing the apparent epistemological contrast between scientific and moral inquiry:

1. Show that our scientific beliefs and methods actually possess many of the features (e.g., dependence on nonobjective 'values' or upon social conventions) which form the core of our current picture of moral beliefs and methods of moral reasoning.
2. Show that moral beliefs and methods are much more like our current conception of scientific beliefs and methods (more 'objective', 'external', 'empirical', 'intersubjective', for example) than we now think.

The first of these options has already been explored by philosophers who subscribe to a 'con-structivist' or neo-Kantian conception of scientific theorizing (see, e.g., Hanson 1958; Kuhn 1970). The aim of the present essay will be to articulate and defend the second alternative. [. . .]

2. Some Challenges to Moral Realism

2.1. Moral intuitions and empirical observations

In the sciences, we decide between theories on the basis of observations, which have an important degree of objectivity. It appears that in moral reasoning, moral intuitions play the same role which observations do in science: we test general moral principles and moral theories by seeing how their consequences conform (or fail to conform) to our moral intuitions about particular cases. It appears that it is the foundational role of observations in science which makes scientific objectivity possible. How could moral intuitions possibly play the same sort of foundational role in ethics, especially given the known diversity of moral judgments between people? Even if moral intuitions do provide a 'foundation' for moral inquiry, wouldn't the fact that moral 'knowledge' is grounded in intuitions rather than in observation be exactly the sort of fundamental epistemological contrast which the received view postulates, especially since peoples' moral intuitions typically reflect the particular moral theories or traditions which they already accept, or their culture, or their upbringing? Doesn't the role of moral intuitions in moral reasoning call out for a 'constructivist' metaethics? If moral intuitions don't play a foundational role in ethics and if morality is supposed to be epistemologically like science, *then what plays, in moral reasoning, the role played by observation in science?*

2.2. The role of "reflective equilibrium" in moral reasoning

We have already seen that moral intuitions play a role in moral reasoning which appears to threaten any attempt to assimilate moral reasoning to the model of objective empirical scientific methodology. Worse yet, as Rawls (1971) has reminded us, what we do with our moral intuitions, our general moral principles, and our moral theories, in order to achieve a coherent moral position, is to engage in 'trading-off' between these various categories of moral belief in order to achieve a harmonious 'equilibrium'. Moral reasoning *begins* with moral *presuppositions*, general as well as particular, and proceeds by negotiating between conflicting *presuppositions*. It is easy to see how this could be a procedure for rationalization of individual or social norms or, to put it in more elevated terms, a procedure for the 'construction' of moral or ethical systems. But if ethical beliefs and ethical reasoning are supposed to be like scientific beliefs and methods, then this procedure would have to be a procedure for *discovering* moral facts! How could any procedure so presupposition-dependent be a *discovery* procedure rather than a *construction procedure*? (See Dworkin 1973.)

2.3. Moral progress and cultural variability

If moral judgments are a species of factual judgment, then one would expect to see moral progress, analogous to progress in science. Moreover, one of the characteristics of factual inquiry in science is its relative independence from cultural distortions: scientists with quite different cultural backgrounds can typically agree in assessing scientific evidence. If moral reasoning is reasoning about objective moral *facts*, then what explains our lack of progress in ethics and the persistence of cultural variability in moral beliefs?

2.4. Hard cases

If goodness, fairness, etc. are real and objective properties, then what should one say about the sorts of hard cases in ethics which we can't seem *ever* to resolve? Our experience in science seems to be that hard scientific questions are only *temporarily* rather than permanently unanswerable. Permanent disagreement seems to be very rare indeed. Hard ethical questions seem often to be permanent rather than temporary.

In such hard ethical cases, is there a fact of the matter inaccessible to moral inquiry? If so, then doesn't the existence of such facts constitute a significant epistemological difference between science and ethics? If not, if there are not facts of the matter, then isn't moral realism simply refuted by such indeterminacy?

2.5. Naturalism and naturalistic definitions

If goodness, for example, is a real property, then wouldn't it be a *natural* property? If not, then isn't moral realism committed to some unscientific and superstitious belief in the existence of non-natural properties? If goodness would be a natural property, then isn't moral realism committed to the extremely implausible claim that moral terms like 'good' possess naturalistic definitions?

2.6. Morality, motivation, and rationality

Ordinary factual judgments often provide us with reasons for action; they serve as constraints on rational choice. But they do so only because of our antecedent interests or desires. If moral judgments are merely factual judgments, as moral realism requires, then the relation of moral judgments to motivation and rationality must be the same. It would be possible in principle for someone, or some thinking thing, to be entirely rational while finding moral judgments motivationally neutral and irrelevant to choices of action.

If this consequence follows from moral realism, how can the moral realist account for the particularly close connection between moral judgments and judgments about what to do? What about the truism that moral judgments have commendatory force as a matter of their meaning or the plausible claim that the moral preferability of a course of action always provides a reason (even if not an overriding one) for choosing it?

2.7. The semantics of moral terms

Moral realism is an anti-subjectivist position. There is, for example, supposed to be a single objective property which we're all talking about when we use the term 'good' in moral contexts. But people's moral concepts differ profoundly. How can it be maintained that our radically different concepts of 'good' are really concepts of one and the same property? Why not a different property for each significantly different conception of the good? Don't the radical differences in our conceptions of the good suggest either a noncognitivist or a constructivist conception of the semantics of ethical terms?

[. . .]

3.   Realist Philosophy of Science

3.1.   *The primacy of reality*

By "scientific realism" philosophers mean the doctrine that the methods of science are capable of providing (partial or approximate) knowledge of unobservable ('theoretical') entities, such as atoms or electromagnetic fields, in addition to knowledge about the behavior of observable phenomena (and of course, that the properties of these and other entities studied by scientists are largely theory-independent).

Over the past three decades or so, philosophers of science within the empiricist tradition have been increasingly sympathetic toward scientific realism and increasingly inclined to alter their views of science in a realist direction. The reasons for this realist tendency lie largely in the recognition of the extraordinary role which theoretical considerations play in actual (and patently successful) scientific practice. To take the most striking example, scientists routinely modify or extend operational 'measurement' or 'detection' procedures for 'theoretical' magnitudes or entities on the basis of new theoretical developments. This sort of methodology is perfectly explicable on the realist assumption that the operational procedures in question really are procedures for the measurement or detection of unobservable entities and that the relevant theoretical developments reflect increasingly accurate knowledge of such "theoretical" entities. Accounts of the revisability of operational procedures which are compatible with a non-realist position appear inadequate to explain the way in which theory-dependent revisions of 'measurement' and 'detection' procedures make a positive methodological contribution to the progress of science.

This pattern is quite typical: The methodological contribution made by theoretical considerations in scientific methodology is inexplicable on a non-realist conception but easily explicable on the realist assumption that such considerations are a reflection of the growth of *theoretical* knowledge. (For a discussion of this point see Boyd 1982, 1983, 1985a, 1985b.) Systematic development of this realist theme has produced developments in epistemology, metaphysics, and the philosophy of language which go far beyond the mere rejection of verificationism and which point the way toward a distinctly realist conception of the central issues in the philosophy of science. These developments include the articulation of causal or naturalistic theories of reference (Kripke 1971, 1972; Putnam 1975a; Boyd 1979, 1982), of measurement (Byerly and Lazara 1973) of 'natural kinds' and scientific categories (Quine 1969a; Putnam 1975a; Boyd 1979, 1982, 1983, 1985b), of scientific epistemology generally (Boyd 1972, 1979, 1982, 1983, 1985a, 1985b, 1985c), and of causation (Mackie 1974; Shoemaker 1980; Boyd 1982, 1985b).

Closely related to these developments has been the articulation of causal or naturalistic theories of knowledge (see, e.g., Armstrong 1973; Goldman 1967, 1976; Quine 1969b). Such theories represent generalizations of causal theories of perception and reflect a quite distinctly realist stance with respect to the issue of our knowledge of the external world. What all these developments – both within the philosophy of science and in epistemology generally – have in common is that they portray as *a posteriori* and contingent various matters (such as the operational 'definitions' of theoretical terms, the 'definitions' of natural kinds, or the reliability of the senses) which philosophers in the modern tradition have typically sought to portray as *a priori*. In an important sense, these developments represent the fuller working out of the philosophical implications of the realist doctrine that reality is prior to thought. (For a further development of this theme see Boyd 1982, 1983, 1985a, 1985b.) It is just this *a posteriority* and contingency in philosophical matters, I shall argue, which will make possible a plausible defense of moral realism against the challenges outlined in Part 2.

In the remaining sections of Part 3 I will describe some of the relevant features of these naturalistic and realistic developments. These 'results' in recent realistic philosophy are not, of course, uncontroversial, and it is beyond the scope of this essay to defend them. But however much controversy they may occasion, unlike moral realism, they do not occasion incredulity: they represent a plausible and defensible philosophical position. The aim of this essay is to indicate that, if we understand the relevance of these recent developments to issues in moral philosophy, then moral realism should, though controversial, be equally credible.

3.2.   *Objective knowledge from theory-dependent methods*

I suggested in the preceding section that the explanation for the movement toward realism in the philosophy of science during the past two or three decades lies in the recognition of the extraordinarily theory-dependent character of scientific methodology and in the inability of any but a realist conception of science to explain why so theory-dependent a methodology should be reliable. The theoretical revisability of measurement and detection procedures, I claimed, played a crucial role in establishing the plausibility of a realist philosophy of science.

If we look more closely at this example, we can recognize two features of scientific methodology which are, in fact, quite general. In the first place, the realist's account of the theoretical revisability of measurement and detection procedures rests upon a conception of scientific research as *cumulative by successive approximations to the truth.*

Second, this cumulative development is possible because *there is a dialectical relationship between current theory and the methodology for its improvement.* The approximate truth of current theories explains why our existing measurement procedures are (approximately) reliable. That reliability, in turn, helps to explain why our experimental or observational investigations are successful in uncovering new theoretical knowledge, which, in turn, may produce improvements in experimental techniques, etc.

These features of scientific methodology are *entirely* general. Not only measurement and detection procedures but all aspects of scientific methodology – principles of experimental design, choices of research problems, standards for the assessment of experimental evidence, principles governing theory choice, and rules for the use of theoretical language – are highly dependent upon current theoretical commitments (Boyd 1972, 1973, 1979, 1980, 1982, 1983, 1985a, 1985b; Kuhn 1970; van Fraassen 1980). No aspect of scientific method involves the 'presupposition-free' testing of individual laws or theories. Moreover, the theory dependence of scientific methodology *contributes* to its reliability rather than detracting from it.

The only scientifically plausible explanation for the reliability of a scientific methodology which is so theory-dependent is a thoroughgoingly realistic explanation: Scientific methodology, dictated by currently accepted theories, is reliable at producing further knowledge precisely *because, and to the extent that, currently accepted theories are relevantly approximately true.* For example, it is because our current theories are approximately true that the

canons of experimental design which they dictate are appropriate for the rigorous testing of new (and potentially more accurate) theories. What the scientific method provides is a paradigm-dependent paradigm-modification strategy: a strategy for modifying or amending our existing theories in the light of further research, which is such that its methodological principles at any given time will themselves depend upon the theoretical picture provided by the currently accepted theories. If the body of accepted theories is itself relevantly sufficiently approximately true, then this methodology operates to produce a subsequent dialectical improvement both in our knowledge of the world and in our methodology itself. Both our new theories and the methodology by which we develop and test them depend upon previously acquired theoretical knowledge. It is not possible to explain even the instrumental reliability of actual scientific practice without invoking this explanation and without adopting a realistic conception of scientific knowledge (Boyd 1972, 1973, 1979, 1982, 1983, 1985a, 1985b, 1985c).

The way in which scientific methodology is theory-dependent dictates that we have a strong methodological preference for new theories which are plausible in the light of our existing theoretical commitments: this means that we prefer new theories which relevantly resemble our existing theories (where the determination of the relevant respects of resemblance is itself a theoretical issue). The reliability of such a methodology is explained by the approximate truth of existing theories, and one consequence of this explanation is that *judgments of theoretical plausibility are evidential.* The fact that a proposed theory is itself plausible in the light of previously confirmed theories is evidence for its (approximate) truth (Boyd 1972, 1973, 1979, 1982, 1983, 1985a, 1985b, 1985c). A purely conventionalistic account of the methodological role of considerations of theoretical plausibility cannot be adequate because it cannot explain the contribution which such considerations make to the instrumental reliability of scientific methodology (Boyd 1979, 1982, 1983).

The upshot is this: The theory-dependent conservatism of scientific methodology is *essential* to the rigorous and reliable testing and development of new scientific theories; on balance, theoretical 'presuppositions' play neither a destructive nor a conventionalistic role in scientific methodology. They are essential to its reliability. If by the 'objectivity' of scientific methodology we mean its capacity to lead to the discovery of *theory-independent reality*, then scientific methodology is objective precisely because it *is theory-dependent* (Boyd 1979, 1982, 1983, 1985a, 1985b, 1985c).

3.3. Naturalism and radical contingency in epistemology

Modern epistemology has been largely dominated by positions which can be characterized as 'foundationalist': all knowledge is seen as ultimately grounded in certain foundational beliefs which have an epistemically privileged position – they are a priori or self-warranting, incorrigible, or something of the sort. Other true beliefs are instances of knowledge only if they can be justified by appeals to foundational knowledge. Whatever the nature of the foundational beliefs, or whatever their epistemic privilege is suppose to consist in, it is an a priori question which beliefs fall in the privileged class. Similarly, the basic inferential principles which are legitimate for justifying non-foundational knowledge claims, given foundational premises, are such that they can be identified a priori and it can be shown a priori that they are rational principles of inference. We may fruitfully think of foundationalism as consisting of two parts, *premise foundationalism*, which holds that all knowledge is justifiable from an a priori specifiable core of foundational beliefs, and *inference foundationalism*, which holds that the principles of justifiable inference are ultimately reducible to inferential principles which can be shown a priori to be rational.

Recent work in "naturalistic epistemology" or "causal theories of knowing" (see e.g., Armstrong 1973; Goldman 1967, 1976; Quine 1969b) strongly suggest that the foundationalist conception of knowledge is fundamentally mistaken. For the crucial case of perceptual knowledge, there seem to be (in typical cases at least) neither premises (foundational or otherwise) nor inferences; instead, perceptual knowledge obtains when perceptual beliefs are produced by epistemically reliable mechanisms. For a variety of other cases, even where premises and inferences occur, it seems to be the reliable production of belief that distinguishes cases of knowledge from other cases of true belief. A variety of naturalistic considerations suggests that there are no beliefs which are epistemically privileged in the way foundationalism seems to require.

I have argued (see Boyd 1982, 1983, 1985a, 1985b, 1985c) that the defense of scientific realism requires an even more thoroughgoing naturalism in epistemology and, consequently, and even more thoroughgoing rejection of foundationalism. In the first place, the fact that scientific knowledge grows cumulatively by successive approximation and the fact that the evaluation of theories is an ongoing social phenomenon require that we take the crucial causal notion in epistemology to be reliable *regulation* of belief rather than reliable belief *production*. The relevant conception of belief regulation must reflect the approximate social and dialectical character of the growth of scientific knowledge. It will thus be true that the causal mechanisms relevant to knowledge will include mechanisms, social and technical as well as psychological, for the criticism, testing, acceptance, modification, and transmission of scientific theories and doctrines. For that reason, an understanding of the role of social factors in science may be relevant not only for the sociology and history of science but for the epistemology of sciences as well. The epistemology of science is in this respect dependent upon empirical knowledge.

There is an even more dramatic respect in which the epistemology of science rests upon empirical foundations. All the significant methodological principles of scientific inquiry (except, perhaps, the rules of deductive logic, but see Boyd 1985c) are profoundly theory-dependent. They are a reliable guide to the truth *only* because, and to the extent that, the body of background theories which determines their application is relevantly approximately true. The rules of rational scientific inference are not reducible to some more basic rules whose reliability as a guide to the truth is independent of the truth of background theories. Since it is a contingent empirical matter which background theories are approximately true, the rationality of scientific principles of inference ultimately rests on a contingent matter of empirical fact, just as the epistemic role of the senses rests upon the contingent empirical fact that the senses are reliable detectors of external phenomena. Thus inference foundationalism is radically false; there are no a priori justifiable rules of nondeductive inference. The epistemology of empirical science is an empirical science (Boyd 1982, 1983, 1985a, 1985b, 1985c).

One consequence of this radical contingency of scientific methods is that the emergence of scientific rationality as we know it depended upon the logically, epistemically, and historically contingent emergence of a relevantly approximately true theoretical tradition. It is not possible to understand the initial emergence of such a tradition as the consequence of some more abstractly conceived scientific or rational methodology which itself is theory-independent. There is no such methodology. We must think of the establishment of the corpuscular theory of matter in the seventeenth century as the beginning of rational methodology in chemistry, not as a consequence of it (for a further discussion see Boyd 1982).

3.4. Scientific intuitions and trained judgment

Both noninferential perceptual judgments and elaborately argued explicit inferential judgments in theoretical science have a purely contingent a posteriori foundation. Once this is recognized, it is easy to see that there are methodologically important features of scientific practice which are intermediate between noninferential perception and explicit inference. One example is provided by what science textbook authors often refer to as 'physical intuition', 'scientific maturity', or the like. One of the intended consequences of professional training in a scientific discipline (and other disciplines as well) is that the student acquire a "feel" for the issues and the actual physical materials which the science studies. As Kuhn (1970) points out, part of the role of experimental work in the training of professional scientists is to provide such a feel for the paradigms or 'worked examples' of good scientific practice. There is very good reason to believe that having good physical (or biological or psychological) intuitions is important to epistemically reliable scientific practice. It is also quite clear both that the acquisition of good scientific intuitions depends on learning explicit theory, as well as on other sorts of training and practice, *and* that scientists are almost never able to make fully explicit the considerations which play a role in their intuitive judgments. The legitimate role of such 'tacit' factors in science has often been taken (especially by philosophically inclined scientists) to be an especially puzzling feature of scientific methodology.

From the perspective of the naturalistic epistemology of science, there need be no puzzle. It is, of course, a question of the very greatest psychological interest just how intuitive judgments in science work and how they are related to explicit

theory, on the one hand, and to experimental practice, on the other. But it seems overwhelmingly likely that scientific intuitions should be thought of as trained judgments which resemble perceptual judgments in not involving (or at least not being fully accounted for by) explicit inferences, but which resemble explicit inferences in science in depending for their reliability upon the relevant approximate truth of the explicit theories which help to determine them. This dependence upon the approximate truth of the relevant background theories will obtain even in those cases (which may be typical) in which the tacit judgments reflect a deeper understanding than that currently captured in explicit theory. It is an important and exciting fact that some scientific knowledge can be represented tacitly before it can be represented explicitly, but this fact poses no difficulty for a naturalistic treatment of scientific knowledge. Tacit or intuitive judgments in science are reliable because they are grounded in a theoretical tradition (itself partly tacit) which is, as a matter of contingent empirical fact, relevantly approximately true.

3.5. Non-Humean conceptions of causation and reduction

The Humean conception of causal relations according to which they are analyzable in terms of regularity, correlation, or deductive subsumability under laws is defensible only from a verificationist position. If verificationist criticisms of talk about unobservables are rejected – as they should be – then there is nothing more problematical about talk of causal powers than there is about talk of electrons or electromagnetic fields. There is no reason to believe that causal terms have definitions (analytic or natural) in noncausal terms. Instead, 'cause' and its cognates refer to natural phenomena whose analysis is a matter for physicists, chemists, psychologists, historians, etc., rather than a matter of conceptual analysis. In particular, it is perfectly legitimate – as a naturalistic conception of epistemology requires – to employ unreduced causal notions in philosophical analysis (Boyd, 1982, 1985b; Shoemaker 1980).

One crucial example of the philosophical application of such notions lies in the analysis of 'reductionism'. If a materialist perspective is sound, then *in some sense* all natural phenomena are 'reducible' to basic physical phenomena. The (prephilosophically) natural way of expressing the relevant sort of reduction is to say that all substances are composed of purely physical substances, all forces are composed of physical forces, all causal powers or potentialities are realized in physical substances and their causal powers, etc. This sort of analysis freely employs unreduced causal notions. If it is 'rationally reconstructed' according to the Humean analysis of such notions, we get the classic analysis of reduction in terms of the syntactic reducibility of the theories in the special sciences to the laws of physics, which in turn dictates the conclusion that all natural properties must be definable in the vocabulary of physics. Such an analysis is entirely without justification from the realistic and naturalistic perspective we are considering. Unreduced causal notions are philosophically acceptable, and the Humean reduction of them mistaken. The prephilosophically natural analysis of reduction is also the philosophically appropriate one. In particular, purely physical objects, states, properties, etc. need not have definitions in "the vocabulary of physics" or in any other reductive vocabulary (see Boyd 1982).

3.6. Natural definitions

Locke speculates at several places in Book IV of the Essay (see, e.g., IV, iii, 25) that when kinds of substances are defined by 'nominal essences', as he thinks they must be, it will be impossible to have a general science of, say, chemistry. The reason is this: nominal essences define kinds of substance in terms of sensible properties, but the factors which govern the behavior (even the observable behavior) of substances are insensible corpuscular real essences. Since there is no reason to suppose that our nominal essences will correspond to categories which reflect uniformities in microstructure, there is no reason to believe that kinds defined by nominal essences provide a basis for obtaining general knowledge of substances. Only if we could sort substances according to their hidden real essences would systematic general knowledge of substances be possible.

Locke was right. Only when kinds are defined by natural rather than conventional definitions is it possible to obtain sound scientific explanations (Putnam 1975a; Boyd 1985b) or sound solutions to the problem of 'projectibility' in inductive inference in science (Quine 1969a; Boyd 1979, 1982, 1983, 1985a, 1985b, 1985c). Indeed this is true not only for the definitions of natural kinds but also for the definitions of the properties, relations, magnitudes, etc., to which we must refer in sound scientific reasoning. In particular, a wide variety of terms do not possess analytic or stipulative definitions and are instead defined in terms of properties, relations, etc., which render them appropriate to particular sorts of scientific or practical reasoning. In the case of such terms, proposed definitions are always in principle revisable in the light of new evidence or new theoretical developments. Similarly, the fact that two people or two linguistic communities apply different definitions in using a term is not, by itself, sufficient to show that they are using the term to refer to different kinds, properties, etc.

3.7. Reference and epistemic access

If the traditional empiricist account of definition by nominal essences (or 'operational definitions' or 'criterial attributes') is to be abandoned in favor of a naturalistic account of definitions (at least for some terms) then a naturalistic conception of reference is required for those cases in which the traditional empiricist semantics has been abandoned. Such a naturalistic account is provided by recent causal theories of reference (see, e.g., Feigl 1956; Kripke 1972; Putnam 1975a). The reference of a term is established by causal connections of the right sort between the use of the term and (instances of) its referent.

The connection between causal theories of reference and naturalistic theories of knowledge and of definitions is quite intimate: reference is itself an epistemic notion and the sorts of causal connections which are relevant to reference are just those which are involved in the reliable regulation of belief (Boyd 1979, 1982). *Roughly*, and for nondegenerate cases, a term t refers to a kind (property, relation, etc.) k just in case there exist causal mechanisms whose tendency is to bring it about, over time, that what is predicated of the term t will be approximately true of k (excuse the blurring of the use-mention distinction). Such mechanisms will typically include the existence of procedures which are approximately accurate for recognizing members or instances of k (at least for easy cases) and which relevantly govern the use of t, the social transmission of certain relevantly approximately true beliefs regarding k, formulated as claims about t (again excuse the slight to the use-mention distinction), a pattern of deference to experts on k

with respect to the use of t, etc. (for a fuller discussion see Boyd 1979, 1982). When relations of this sort obtain, we may think of the properties of k as regulating the use of t (via such causal relations), and we may think of what is said using t as providing us with socially coordinated *epistemic access* to k; t refers to k (in nondegenerate cases) just in case the socially coordinated use of t provides significant epistemic access to k, and not to other kinds (properties, etc.) (Boyd 1979, 1982).

3.8.   *Homeostatic property-cluster definitions*

The sort of natural definition in terms of corpuscular real essences anticipated by Locke is reflected in the natural definitions of chemical kinds by molecular formulas; 'water = H_2O' is by now the standard example (Putnam 1975a). Natural definitions of this sort specify necessary and sufficient conditions for membership in the kind in question. Recent *non*-naturalistic semantic theories in the ordinary language tradition have examined the possibility of definitions which do not provide necessary and sufficient conditions in this way. According to various property-cluster or criterial attribute theories, some terms have definitions which are provided by a collection of properties such that the possession of an adequate number of these properties is sufficient for falling within the extension of the term. It is supposed to be a conceptual (and thus an a priori) matter what properties belong in the cluster and which combinations of them are sufficient for falling under the term. Insofar as different properties in the cluster are differently "weighted" in such judgments, the weighting is determined by our concept of the kind or property being defined. It is characteristically insisted, however, that our concepts of such kinds are 'open textured' so that there is some indeterminacy in extension *legitimately* associated with property-cluster or criterial attribute definitions. The 'imprecision' or 'vagueness' of such definitions is seen as a perfectly appropriate feature of ordinary linguistic usage, in contrast to the artificial precision suggested by rigidly formalistic positivist conceptions of proper language use.

I shall argue (briefly) that – despite the philistine antiscientism often associated with 'ordinary language' philosophy – the property-cluster conception of definitions provides an extremely deep insight into the possible form of *natural* definitions. I shall argue that there are a number of sci-

entifically important kinds, properties, etc. whose natural definitions are very much like the property-cluster definitions postulated by ordinary-language philosophers (for the record, I doubt that there are any terms whose definitions actually fit the ordinary-language model, because I doubt that there are any significant 'conceptual truths' at all). There are natural kinds, properties, etc. whose natural definitions involve a kind of property cluster *together with* an associated indeterminacy in extension. Both the property-cluster form of such definitions and the associated indeterminacy are dictated by the scientific task of employing categories which correspond to inductively and explanatorily relevant causal structures. In particular, the indeterminacy in extension of such natural definitions could not be remedied without rendering the definitions *un*natural in the sense of being scientifically misleading. What I believe is that the following sort of situation is commonplace in the special sciences which study complex structurally or functionally characterized phenomena:

1.   There is a family F of properties which are 'contingently clustered' in nature in the sense that they co-occur in an important number of cases.

2.   Their co-occurrence is not, at least typically, a statistical artifact, but rather the result of what may be metaphorically (sometimes literally) described as a sort of *homeostasis*. Either the presence of some of the properties in F tends (under appropriate conditions) to favor the presence of the others, or there are underlying mechanisms or processes which tend to maintain the presence of the properties in F, or both.

3.   The homeostatic clustering of the properties in F is causally important; there are (theoretically or practically) important effects which are produced by a conjoint occurrence of (many of) the properties in F together with (some or all of) the underlying mechanisms in question.

4.   There is a kind term t which is applied to things in which the homeostatic clustering of most of the properties in F occurs.

5.   This t has no analytic definition; rather all or part of the homeostatic cluster F together with some or all of the mechanisms which underlie it provides the natural definition of t. The question of just which properties and

mechanisms belong in the definition of t is an a posteriori question – often a difficult theoretical one.

6. Imperfect homeostasis is nomologically possible or actual: some thing may display some but not all of the properties in F; some but not all of the relevant underlying homeostatic mechanisms may be present.

7. In such cases, the relative importance of the various properties in F and of the various mechanisms in determining whether the thing falls under t – if it can be determined at all – is a theoretical rather than an conceptual issue.

8. In cases in which such a determination is possible, the outcome will typically depend upon quite particular facts about the actual operation of the relevant homeostatic mechanisms, about the relevant background conditions and about the causal efficacy of the partial cluster of properties from F. For this reason the outcome, if any, will typically be different in different possible worlds, even when the partial property cluster is the same and even when it is unproblematical that the kind referred to by t in the actual world exists.

9. Moreover, there will be many cases of extensional vagueness which are such that they are not resolvable, even given all the relevant facts and all the true theories. There will be things which display some but not all of the properties in F (and/or in which some but not all of the relevant homeostatic mechanisms operate) such that no rational considerations dictate whether or not they are to be classed under t, assuming that a dichotomous choice is to be made.

10. The causal importance of the homeostatic property cluster F together with the relevant underlying homeostatic mechanisms is such that the kind or property denoted by t is a natural kind in the sense discussed earlier.

11. No refinement of usage which replaces t by a significantly less extensionally vague term will preserve the naturalness of the kind referred to. Any such refinement would either require that we treat as important distinctions which are irrelevant to causal explanation or to induction or that we ignore similarities which are important in just these ways.

The reader is invited to assure herself that 1–11 hold, for example, for the terms 'healthy' and 'is healthier than.' Whether these are taken to be full-blown cases of natural property (relation) terms is not crucial here. They do illustrate almost perfectly the notion of a homeostatic property cluster and the correlative notion of a homeostatic cluster term. [. . .]

The paradigm cases of natural kinds – biological species – are examples of homeostatic cluster kinds in this sense. The appropriateness of any particular biological species for induction and explanation in biology depends upon the *imperfectly* shared and homeostatically related morphological, physiological, and behavioral features which characterize its members. The definitional role of mechanisms of homeostasis is reflected in the role of interbreeding in the modern species concept; for sexually reproducing species, the exchange of genetic material between populations is thought by some evolutionary biologists to be essential to the homeostatic unity of the other properties characteristic of the species and it is thus reflected in the species definition which they propose (see Mayr 1970). The *necessary* indeterminacy in extension of species terms is a consequence of evolutionary theory, as Darwin observed: speciation depends on the existence of populations which are intermediate between the parent species and the emerging one. Any 'refinement' of classification which artifically eliminated the resulting indeterminacy in classification would obscure the central fact about heritable variations in phenotype upon which biological evolution depends. More determinate species categories would be scientifically inappropriate and misleading.

[. . .]

4.   How To Be a Moral Realist

4.1.   Moral semantics, intuitions, reflective equilibrium, and hard cases

Some philosophical opportunities are too good to pass up. For many of the more abstract challenges to moral realism, recent realistic and naturalistic work in the philosophy of science is suggestive of possible responses in its defense. Thus for example, it has occurred to many philosophers (see, e.g., Putnam 1975b) that naturalistic theories of reference and of definitions might be extended to the analysis of moral language. *If* this could be done successfully *and if* the results were favorable to a realist conception of morals, then it would be possible to reply to several anti-realist arguments. For example, against the objection that wide divergence of moral concepts or opinions between traditions or cultures indicates that, at best, a constructivist analysis of morals is possible, the moral realist might reply that differences in conception or in working definitions need not indicate the absence of shared causally fixed referents for moral terms.

Similarly, consider the objection that a moral realist must hold that goodness is a natural property, and thus commit the "naturalistic fallacy" of maintaining that moral terms possess analytic definitions in, say, physical terms. The moral realist may choose to agree that goodness is probably a physical property but deny that it has any analytic definition whatsoever. If the realist's critique of the syntactic analysis of reductionism in science is also accepted, then the moral realist can deny that it follows from the premise that goodness is a physical property or that goodness has any physical definition, analytic or otherwise.

If the moral realist takes advantage of naturalistic and realistic conceptions in epistemology as well as in semantic theory, other rebuttals to anti-realist challenges are suggested. The extent of the potential for rebuttals of this sort can best be recognized if we consider the objection that the role of reflective equilibrium in moral reasoning dictates a constructivist rather than a realist conception of morals. The moral realist might reply that the dialectical interplay of observations, theory, and methodology which, according to the realist, constitutes the *discovery* procedure for scientific inquiry *just is* the method of reflective equilibrium, so that the prevalence of that method in moral reasoning cannot *by itself* dictate a non-realist conception of morals.

If the response just envisioned to the concern over reflective equilibrium is successful, then the defender of moral realism will have established that – in moral reasoning as in scientific reasoning – the role of culturally transmitted presuppositions in reasoning does not necessitate a constructivist (or non-cognitivist) rather than a realist analysis of the subject matter. *If* that is established, then the moral realist might defend the epistemic role of culturally determined intuitions in ethics by treating ethical intuitions on the model of theory-

determined intuitions in science, which the scientific realist takes to be examples of epistemically reliable trained judgments.

Finally, if the moral realist is inclined to accept the anti-realist's claim that the existence of hard cases in ethics provides a reason to doubt that there is a moral fact of the matter which determines the answer in such cases (more on this later), then the scientific realist's conclusion that bivalence fails for some statements involving homeostatic cluster kind terms *might* permit the moral realist to reason that similar failures of bivalence for some ethical statements need not be fatal to moral realism.

In fact, I propose to employ just these rebuttals to the various challenges to moral realism I have been discussing. They represent the application of a coherent naturalistic conception of semantics and of knowledge against the challenges raised by the critic of moral realism. But they do not stand any chance of rebutting moral anti-realism unless they are incorporated into a broader conception of morals and of moral knowledge which meets certain very strong constraints. These constraints are the subject of the next section.

4.2. *Constraints on a realist conception of moral knowledge*

Suppose that a defense of moral realism is to be undertaken along the lines just indicated. What constraints does that particular defensive strategy place on a moral realist's conception of morals and of moral knowledge? Several important constraints are suggested by a careful examination of the realist doctrines in the philosophy of science whose extension to moral philosophy is contemplated.

In the first place, the scientific realist is able to argue that 'reflective equilibrium' in science and a reliance on theory-dependent scientific intuitions are epistemically reliable *only* on the assumption that the theoretical tradition which governs these methodological practices contains theories which are relevantly approximately true. Indeed, the most striking feature of the consistently realistic epistemology of science is the insistence that the epistemic reliability of scientific methodology is contingent upon the establishment of such a theoretical tradition. Moreover, the possibility of offering a realist rather than a constructivist interpretation of reflective equilibrium and of intuition in science rests upon the realist's claim that observations and theory-mediated measurement and detection of 'unobservables' in science represent epistemically relevant causal interactions between scientists and a theory-independent reality. Were the realist unable to treat observation and measurement as providing 'epistemic access' to reality in this way, a constructivist treatment of scientific knowledge would be almost unavoidable.

Similarly, the scientific realist is able to employ a naturalistic conception of definitions and of reference only because (1) it is arguable that the nature of the subject matter of science dictates that kinds, properties, etc. be defined by nonconventional definitions and (2) it is arguable that actual scientific practices result in the establishment of 'epistemic access' to the various 'theoretical entities' which, the realist maintains, are (part of) the subject matter of scientific inquiry.

Finally, the realist can insist that realism not only can tolerate but implies certain failures of bivalence only because it can be argued that homeostatic cluster kinds (properties, etc.) must have indeterminacy in extension in order for reference to them to be scientifically fruitful. These considerations suggest that the following constraints must be satisfied by an account of moral knowledge if it is to be the basis for the proposed defense of moral realism:

1. It must be possible to explain how our moral reasoning *started out* with a stock of relevantly approximately true moral beliefs so that reflective equilibrium in moral reasoning can be treated in a fashion analogous to the scientific realist's treatment of reflective equilibrium in scientific reasoning. Note that this constraint does not require that it be possible to argue that we started out with close approximations to the truth (seventeenth-century corpuscular theory was quite far from the truth). What is required is that the respects of approximation be such that it is possible to see how continued approximations would be forthcoming as a result of subsequent moral and nonmoral reasoning.

2. There must be an answer to the question "What plays, in moral reasoning, the role played by observation in science?" which can form the basis for a realist rather than a constructivist conception of the foundations of reflective equilibrium in moral reasoning.

3. It must be possible to explain why moral properties, say goodness, would require natural rather than conventional definitions.

4. It must be possible to show that our ordinary use of moral terms provides us with epistemic access to moral properties. Moral goodness must, to some extent, regulate the use of the word 'good' in moral reasoning. Here again examination of the corresponding constraint in the philosophy of science indicates that the regulation need not be nearly perfect, but it must be possible to show that sufficient epistemic access is provided to form the basis for the growth of moral knowledge.

5. It must be possible to portray occasional indeterminacy in the extension of moral terms as rationally dictated by the nature of the subject matter in a way analogous to the scientific realist's treatment of such indeterminacy in the case of homeostatic cluster terms.

In the work of scientific realists, the case that the analogous constraints are satisfied has depended upon examination of the substantive findings of various of the sciences (such as, e.g., the atomic theory of matter or the Darwinian conception of speciation). It is very unlikely that an argument could be mounted in favor of the view that moral knowledge meets the constraints we are considering which does not rely in a similar way on substantive doctrines about the foundations of morals. What I propose to do instead is to *describe* one account of the nature of morals which almost ideally satisfies the constraints in question and to indicate how a defense of moral realism would proceed on the basis of this account.

It will not be my aim here to defend this account of morals against morally plausible rivals. In fact, I am inclined to think – *partly* because of the way in which it allows the constraints we are considering to be satisfied – that *if* there is a truth of the matter about morals (that is, if moral realism is true), then the account I will be offering is close to the truth. But my aim in this paper is merely to establish that moral realism is plausible and defensible. The substantive moral position I will consider is a plausible version of nonutilitarian consequentialism, one which – I believe – captures many of the features which make consequentialism *one* of the standard and plausible positions in moral philosophy. If moral realism is defensible on the basis of a plausible version of consequentialism, then it is a philosophically defensible position which must be taken seriously in metaethics; and that's all I'm trying to establish here.

[. . .]

4.3.   Homeostatic consequentialism

In broad outline, the conception of morals upon which the sample defense of moral realism will rest goes like this:

1. There are a number of important human goods, things which satisfy important human needs. Some of these needs are physical or medical. Others are psychological or social; these (probably) include the need for love and friendship, the need to engage in cooperative efforts, the need to exercise control over one's own life, the need for intellectual and artistic appreciation and expression, the need for physical recreation, etc. The question of just which important human needs there are is a potentially difficult and complex empirical question.

2. Under a wide variety of (actual and possible) circumstances these human goods (or rather instances of the satisfaction of them) are homeostatically clustered. In part they are clustered because these goods themselves are – when present in balance or moderation – mutually supporting. There are in addition psychological and social mechanisms which when, and to the extent to which, they are present contribute to the homeostasis. They probably include cultivated attitudes of mutual respect, political democracy, egalitarian social relations, various rituals, customs, and rules of courtesy, ready access to education and information, etc. It is a complex and difficult question in psychology and social theory just what these mechanisms are and how they work.

3. Moral goodness is defined by this cluster of goods and the homeostatic mechanisms which unify them. Actions, policies, character traits, etc. are morally good to the extent to which they tend to foster the realization of these goods or to develop and sustain the homeostatic mechanisms upon which their unity depends.

4. In actual practice, a concern for moral goodness can be a guide to action for the morally concerned because the homeostatic unity of moral goodness tends to mitigate possible conflicts between various individual goods. In part, the possible conflicts are mitigated just because various of the important human goods are mutually reinforcing. Moreover, since the existence of effective homeostatic unity among important human goods is part of the moral good, morally concerned choice is constrained by the imperative to balance potentially competing goods in such a way that homeostasis is maintained or strengthened. Finally, the improvement of the psychological and social mechanisms of homeostasis themselves is a moral good whose successful pursuit tends to further mitigate conflicts of the sort in question. In this regard, moral practice resembles good engineering practice in product design. In designing, say, automobiles there are a number of different desiderata (economy, performance, handling, comfort, durability, . . .) which are potentially conflicting but which enjoy a kind of homeostatic unity if developed in moderation. One feature of good automotive design is that it promotes these desiderata within the limits of homeostasis. The other feature of good automotive design (or, perhaps, of good automotive engineering) is that it produces technological advances which permit that homeostatic unity to be preserved at higher levels of the various individual desiderata. So it is with good moral practice as well.

I should say something about how the claim that the nature of the constituents of moral goodness is an empirical matter should be understood. I mean the analogy between moral inquiry and scientific inquiry to be taken *very* seriously. It is a commonplace in the history of science that major advances often depend on appropriate social conditions, technological advances, and prior scientific discoveries. Thus, for example, much of eighteenth-century physics and chemistry was possible only because there had developed (a) the social conditions in which work in the physical sciences was economically supported, (b) a technology sufficiently advanced to make the relevant instrumentation possible, and (c) the theoretical legacy of seventeenth-century Newtonian physics and corpuscular chemistry.

Via somewhat different mechanisms the same sort of dependence obtains in the growth of our knowledge of the good. Knowledge of fundamental human goods and their homeostasis represents basic knowledge about human psychological and social potential. Much of this knowledge is genuinely *experimental* knowledge and the relevant experiments are ('naturally' occurring) political and social experiments whose occurrence and whose interpretation depends both on 'external' factors and upon the current state of our moral understanding. Thus, for example, we would not have been able to explore the dimensions of our needs for artistic expression and appreciation had not social and technological developments made possible cultures in which, for some classes at least, there was the leisure to produce and consume art. We would not have understood the role of political democracy in the homeostasis of the good had the conditions not arisen in which the first limited democracies developed. Only after the moral insights gained from the first democratic experiments were in hand, were we equipped to see the depth of the moral peculiarity of slavery. Only since the establishment of the first socialist societies are we even beginning to obtain the data necessary to assess the role of egalitarian social practices in fostering the good.

It is also true of moral knowledge, as it is in the case of knowledge in other 'special sciences', that the improvement of knowledge may depend upon theoretical advances in related disciplines. It is hard, for example, to see how deeper understanding in history or economic theory could fail to add to our understanding of human potential and of the mechanisms underlying the homeostatic unity of the good.

Let us now consider the application of the particular theory of the good presented here as a part of the strategy for the defense of moral realism indicated in the preceding section. I shall be primarily concerned to defend the realist position that moral goodness is a real property of actions, policies, states of affairs, etc. and that our moral judgments are, often enough, reflections of truths about the good. A complete realist treatment of the semantics of moral terms would of course require examining notions like obligation and justice as well. I will not attempt this examination here, in part because the aim of this essay is merely to indicate briefly how a plausible defense of moral realism might be carried out rather than to carry out the defense in detail.

Moreover, on a consequentialist conception of morals such notions as obligation and justice are derivative ones, and it is doubtful if the details of the derivations are relevant to the defense of moral realism in the way that the defense of a realist conception of the good is.

In the remaining sections of the essay I shall offer a defense of homeostatic consequentialist moral realism against the representative anti-realist challenges discussed in Part 2. The claim that the term 'good' in its moral uses refers to the homeostatic cluster property just described (or even the claim that there is such a property) represents a complex and controversial philosophical and empirical hypothesis. For each of the responses to anti-realist challenges which I will present, there are a variety of possible anti-realist rebuttals, both empirical and philosophical. It is beyond the scope of this essay to explore these rebuttals and possible moral realist responses to them in any detail. Instead, I shall merely indicate how plausible realist rebuttals to the relevant challenges can be defended. Once again, the aim of the present paper is not to establish moral realism but merely to establish its plausibility and to offer a general framework within which further defenses of moral realism might be understood.

4.4. Observations, intuitions, and reflective equilibrium

Of the challenges to moral realism we are considering, two are straightforwardly epistemological. They suggest that the role of moral intuitions and of reflective equilibrium in moral reasoning dictate (at best) a constructivist interpretation of morals. As we saw in Section 4.2, it would be possible for the moral realist to respond by assimilating the role of moral intuitions and reflective equilibrium to the role of scientific intuitions and theory-dependent methodological factors in the realist account of scientific knowledge, but this response is viable only if it is possible to portray many of our background moral beliefs and judgments as relevantly approximately true and only if there is a satisfactory answer to the question: "What plays, in moral reasoning, the role played in science by observation?" Let us turn first to the latter question.

I propose the answer: 'Observation'.

According to the homeostatic consequentialist conception of morals (indeed, according to any naturalistic conception) goodness is an ordinary natural property, and it would be odd indeed if observations didn't play the same role in the study of this property that they play in the study of all the others. According to the homeostatic consequentialist conception, goodness is a property quite similar to the other properties studied by psychologists, historians, and social scientists, and observations will play the same role in moral inquiry that they play in the other kinds of empirical inquiry about people.

It is worth remarking that in the case of any of the human sciences *some* of what must count as observation is observation of oneself, and *some* is the sort of self-observation involved in introspection. Moreover, *some* of our observations of other people will involve trained judgment and the operation of sympathy. No reasonable naturalistic account of the foundations of psychological or social knowledge *or* of our technical knowledge in psychology or the social sciences will fail to treat such sources of belief – when they are generally reliable – as cases of observation in the relevant sense.

It is true, of course, that both the content and the evidential assessment of observations of this sort will be influenced by theoretical considerations, but this does not distinguish observations in the human sciences from those in other branches of empirical inquiry. The theory dependence of observations and their interpretation is simply one aspect of the pervasive theory dependence of methodology in science which the scientific realist cheerfully acknowledges (since it plays a crucial role in arguments for scientific realism). It is possible to defend a realist interpretation of the human sciences because it is possible to argue that actual features in the world constrain the findings in those sciences sufficiently that the relevant background theories will be approximately true enough for theory-dependent observations to play a reliable epistemic role.

In the case of moral reasoning, observations and their interpretation will be subject to just the same sort of theory-dependent influences. This theory dependence is one aspect of the general phenomenon of theory dependence of methodology in moral reasoning which we, following Rawls, have been describing as reflective equilibrium. We will be able to follow the example of scientific realists and to treat the observations which play a role in moral reasoning as sufficiently reliable for the

defense of moral realism just in case we are able to portray the theories upon which they and their interpretation depend as relevantly approximately true – that is, just in case we are able to carry out the other part of the moral realist's response to epistemic challenges and to argue that our background moral beliefs are sufficiently near the truth to form the foundations for a reliable empirical investigation of moral matters. Let us turn now to that issue.

What we need to know is whether it is reasonable to suppose that, for quite some time, we have had background moral beliefs sufficiently near the truth that they could form the basis for subsequent improvement of moral knowledge in the light of further experience and further historical developments. Assuming, as we shall, a homeostatic consequentialist conception of morals, this amounts to the question whether our background beliefs about human goods and the psychological and social mechanisms which unite them have been good enough to guide the gradual process of expansion of moral knowledge envisioned in that conception. Have our beliefs about our own needs and capacities been good enough – since, say the emergence of moral and political philosophy in ancient Greece – that we have been able to respond to new evidence and to the results of new social developments by expanding and improving our understanding of those needs and capacities even when doing so required rejecting some of our earlier views in favor of new ones? It is hard to escape the conclusion that this is simply the question "Has the rational empirical study of human kind proven to be possible?" Pretty plainly the answer is that such study has proven to be possible, though difficult. In particular we have improved our understanding of our own needs and our individual and social capacities by just the sort of historically complex process envisioned in the homeostatic consequentialist conception. I conclude therefore that there is no reason to think that reflective equilibrium – which is just the standard methodology of any empirical inquiry, social or otherwise – raises any epistemological problems for the defense of moral realism.

Similarly, we may now treat moral intuitions exactly on a par with scientific intuitions, as a species of trained judgment. Such intuitions are *not* assigned a foundational role in moral inquiry; in particular they do not substitute for observations. Moral intuitions are simply one cognitive manifestation of our moral understanding, just as physical intuitions, say, are a cognitive manifestation of physicists' understanding of their subject matter. Moral intuitions, like physical intuitions, play a limited but legitimate role in empirical inquiry *precisely because* they are linked to theory *and* to observations in a generally reliable process of reflective equilibrium.

It may be useful by way of explaining the epistemic points made here to consider very briefly how the moral realist might respond to one of the many possible anti-realist rebuttals to what has just been said. Consider the following objection: The realist treatment of reflective equilibrium requires that our background moral beliefs have been for some time relevantly approximately true. As a matter of fact, the overwhelming majority of people have probably always believed in some sort of theistic foundation of morals: moral laws are God's laws; the psychological capacities which underlie moral practice are a reflection of God's design; etc. According to the homeostatic consequentialism which we are supposed to accept for the sake of argument, moral facts are mere natural facts. Therefore, according to homeostatic consequentialism, most people have always had profoundly mistaken moral beliefs. How then can it be claimed that our background beliefs have been relevantly approximately true?

I reply that – assuming that people have typically held theistic beliefs of the sort in question – it does follow from homeostatic consequentialism that they have been *in that respect* very wrong indeed. But being wrong in that respect does not preclude their moral judgments having been relatively reliable reflections of facts about the homeostatic cluster of fundamental human goods, according to the model of the development of moral knowledge discussed earlier. Until Darwin, essentially all biologists attributed the organization and the adaptive features of the physiology, anatomy, and behavior of plants and animals to God's direct planning. That attribution did not prevent biologists from accumulating the truly astonishing body of knowledge about anatomy, physiology, and animal behavior upon which Darwin's discovery of evolution by natural selection depended; nor did it prevent their recognizing the profound biological insights of Darwin's theory. Similarly, seventeenth-century corpuscular chemistry did provide the basis for the development of modern chemistry in a way that earlier quasi-animistic 'renaissance naturalism' in

chemistry could not. Early corpuscular theory was right that the chemical properties of substances are determined by the fundamental properties of stable 'corpuscles'; it was wrong about almost everything else, but what it got right was enough to point chemistry in a fruitful direction. I understand the analogy between the development of scientific knowledge and the development of moral knowledge to be very nearly exact.

There may indeed be one important respect in which the analogy between the development of scientific knowledge and the development of moral knowledge is *in*exact, but oddly, this respect of disanalogy makes the case for moral realism stronger. One of the striking consequences of a full-blown naturalistic and realistic conception of knowledge is that our knowledge, even our most basic knowledge, rests upon logically contingent 'foundations'. Our perceptual knowledge, for example, rests upon the logically contingent a posteriori fact that our senses are reliable detectors of certain sorts of external objects. In the case of perceptual knowledge, however, there is a sense in which it is nonaccidental, noncontingent, that our senses are reliable detectors. The approximate reliability of our senses (with respect to some applications) is explained by evolutionary theory in a quite fundamental way (Quine 1969a). By contrast, the reliability of our methodology in chemistry is much more dramatically contingent. As a matter of fact, early thinkers tried to explain features of the natural world by analogy to sorts of order they already partly understood: mathematical, psychological, and mechanical. The atomic theory of matter represents one such attempt to assimilate chemical order to the better-understood mechanical order. In several important senses it was highly contingent that the microstructure of matter turned out to be particulate and mechanical enough that the atomic (or 'corpuscular') *guess* could provide the foundation for epistemically reliable research in chemistry. The accuracy of our guess in this regard is not, for example, explained by either evolutionary necessity or by deep facts about our psychology. In an important sense, the seventeenth-century belief in the corpuscular theory of matter was not reliably produced. It was not produced by an antecedent generally reliable methodology: reasoning by analogy is *not* generally reliable except in contexts where a rich and approximately accurate body of theory *already* exists to guide us in finding the right respects of analogy (see Boyd 1982).

By contrast, the emergence of relevantly approximately true beliefs about the homeostatic cluster of fundamental human goods – although logically contingent – was much less strikingly 'accidental'. From the point of view either of evolutionary theory or of basic human psychology it is hardly accidental that we are able to recognize many of our own and others' fundamental needs. Moreover, it is probably not accidental from an evolutionary point of view that we were able to recognize some features of the homeostasis of these needs. Our initial relevantly approximately accurate beliefs about the good may well have been produced by generally reliable psychological and perceptual mechanisms and thus may have been clear instances of knowledge in a way in which our initial corpuscular beliefs were not (for a discussion of the latter point see Boyd 1982). It is *easier*, not *harder*, to explain how moral knowledge is possible than it is to explain how scientific knowledge (in both the seventeenth- and the twentieth-century senses of the term) in a way that we are not so fitted for scientific knowledge of other sorts.

4.5.   Moral semantics

We have earlier considered two objections to the moral realist's account of the semantics of moral terms. According to the first, the observed diversity of moral concepts – between cultures as well as between individuals and groups within a culture – suggests that it will not be possible to assign a single objective subject matter to their moral disputes. The divergence of concepts suggests divergence of reference of a sort which constructivist relativism is best suited to explain. According to the second objection, moral realism is commited to the absurd position that moral terms possess definitions in the vocabulary of the natural sciences. We have seen that a moral realist rebuttal to these challenges is possible which assimilates moral terms to naturalistically and nonreductively definable terms in the sciences. Such a response can be successful only if (1) there are good reasons to think that moral terms must possess natural rather than stipulative definitions and (2) there are good reasons to think that ordinary uses of moral terms provides us with epistemic access to moral properties, so that, for example, moral goodness to some extent regulates our use of the word 'good' in moral contexts.

The homeostatic consequentialist conception of morals provides a justification for the first of these claims. If the good is defined by a homeostatic phenomenon the details of which we still do not entirely know, then it is a paradigm case of a property whose 'essence' is given by a natural rather than a stipulative definition.

Is it plausible that the homeostatic cluster of fundamental human goods has, to a significant extent, regulated the use of the term 'good' so that there is a general tendency, of the sort indicated by the homeostatic consequentialist conception of the growth of moral knowledge, for what we say about the good to be true of that cluster? If what I have already said about the possibility of defending a realist conception of reflective equilibrium in moral reasoning is right, the answer must be "yes." Such a tendency is guaranteed by basic evolutionary and psychological facts, and it is just such a tendency which we can observe in the ways in which our conception of the good has changed in the light of new evidence concerning human needs and potential. Indeed, the way we ('preanalytically') recognize moral uses of the term 'good' and the way we identify moral terms in other languages are precisely by recourse to the idea that moral terms are those involved in discussions of human goods and harms. We tacitly assume *something like* the proposed natural definition of 'good' in the practice of translation of moral discourse. I think it will help to clarify this realist response if we consider two possible objections to it. The first objection reflects the same concern about the relation between moral and theological reasoning that we examined in the preceding section. It goes like this: How is it possible for the moral realist who adopts homeostatic consequentialism to hold that there is a general tendency for our beliefs about the good to get truer? After all, the error of thinking of the good as being defined by God's will persists unabated and is – according to the homeostatic consequentialist's conception – a very important falsehood.

I reply, first, that the sort of tendency to the truth required by the epistemic access account of reference is not such that it must preclude serious errors. Newtonians were talking about mass, energy, momentum, etc. all along, even though they were massively wrong about the structure of space-time. We might be irretrievably wrong about some other issue in physics and still use the terms of physical theory to refer to real entities, magnitudes, etc. All that is required is a significant epistemically relevant causal connection between the use of a term and its referent.

Moreover, as I suggested earlier, it is characteristic of what we recognize as moral discourse (whether in English or in some other language) that considerations of human well-being play a significant role in determining what is said to be 'good'. The moral realist need not deny that other considerations – perhaps profoundly false ones – also influence what we say is good. After all, the historian of biology need not deny that the term 'species' has relatively constant reference throughout the nineteenth century, even though, prior to Darwin, religious considerations injected profound errors into biologists' conception of species. Remember that we do not ordinarily treat a theological theory as a theory *of* moral goodness at all unless it says something about what we independently recognize as human well-being. The role of religious considerations in moral reasoning provides a challenge for moral realists, but exactly the same challenge faces a realist interpretation of biological or psychological theorizing before the twentieth century, and it can surely be met.

The second objection I want to consider represents a criticism of moral realism often attributed to Marx (see, e.g., Wood 1972; for the record I believe that Marx's position on this matter was confused and that he vacillated between an explicit commitment to the relativist position, which Wood discusses, and a tacit commitment to a position whose reconstruction would look something like the position defended here). The objection goes like this: The moral realist – in the guise of the homeostatic consequentialist, say – holds that what regulate the use of moral terms are facts about human well-being. But this is simply not so. Consider, for example, sixteenth-century discussions of rights. One widely acknowledged 'right' was the divine right of kings. Something surely regulated the use of the language of rights in the sixteenth century, but it clearly wasn't human well-being construed in the way the moral realist intends. Instead, it was the well-being of kings and of the aristocratic class of which they were a part.

I agree with the analysis of the origin of the doctrine of the divine right of kings; indeed, I believe that such class determination of moral beliefs is a commonplace phenomenon. But I do not believe that this analysis undermines the claim that moral terms refer to aspects of human well-being. Con-

sider, for example, the psychology of thinking and intelligence. It is extremely well documented (see, e.g., Gould 1981; Kamin 1974) that the content of much of the literature in this area is determined by class interests rather than by the facts. Nevertheless, the psychological terms occurring in the most egregiously prejudiced papers refer to real features of human psychology; this is so because, in other contexts, their use is relevantly regulated by such features. Indeed – and this is the important point – if there were not such an epistemic (and thus referential) connection to real psychological phenomena, the ideological rationalization of class structures represented by the class-distorted literature would be ineffective. It's only when people come to believe, for example, that Blacks lack a trait, *familiar in other contexts as 'intelligence'*, that racist theories can serve to rationalize the socioeconomic role to which Blacks are largely confined.

Similarly, I argue, in order for the doctrine of the divine right of kings to serve a class function, it had to be the case that moral language was often enough connected to issues regarding the satisfaction of real human needs. Otherwise, an appeal to such a supposed right would be ideologically ineffective. Only when rights-talk has *some* real connection to the satisfaction of the needs of non-aristocrats could this instance of rights-talk be useful to kings and their allies.

Once again, when the analogy between moral inquiry and scientific inquiry is fully exploited, it becomes possible to defend the doctrines upon which moral realism rests.

4.6.   *Hard cases and divergent views*

Two of the challenges to moral realism we are considering are grounded in the recognition that some moral issues seem very hard to resolve. On the one hand, there seem to be moral dilemmas which resist resolution even for people who share a common moral culture. Especially with respect to the sort of possible cases often considered by moral philosophers, there often seems to be no rational way of deciding between morally quite distinct courses of action. Our difficulty in resolving moral issues appears even greater when we consider the divergence in moral views that exists between people from different backgrounds or cultures. The anti-realist proposes to explain the difficulties involved by denying that there is a common objective subject matter which determines answers to moral questions.

We have seen that – to the extent that she chooses to take the difficulties in resolving moral issues as evidence for the existence of moral statements for which bivalence fails – the moral realist can try to assimilate such failures to the failures of bivalence which realist philosophy *predicts* in the case, for example, of some statements involving homeostatic cluster terms. Such a response will work only to the extent that moral terms can be shown to possess natural definitions relevantly like homeostatic cluster definitions. Of course, according to homeostatic consequentialism, moral terms (or 'good' at any rate) just are homeostatic cluster terms, so this constraint is satisfied. What I want to emphasize is that a moral realist *need not* invoke failures of bivalence in every case in which difficulties arise in resolving moral disputes.

Recall that on the conception we are considering moral inquiry is about a complex and difficult subject matter, proceeds often by the analysis of complex and "messy" naturally occurring social experiments, and is subject to a very high level of social distortion by the influence of class interests and other cultural factors. In this regard moral inquiry resembles inquiry in any of the complex and politically controversial social sciences. In such cases, even where there is no reason to expect failures of bivalence, one would predict that the resolution of some issues will prove difficult or, in some particular social setting, impossible. Thus the moral realist can point to the fact that moral inquiry is a species of social inquiry to explain much of the observed divergence in moral views and the apparent intractability of many moral issues.

Similarly, the complexity and controversiality of moral issues can be invoked to explain the especially sharp divergence of moral views often taken to obtain between different cultures. For the homeostatic consequentialist version of moral realism to be true it must be the case that in each culture in which moral inquiry takes place the homeostatically clustered human goods epistemically regulate moral discourse to an appreciable extent. On the realistic and naturalistic conception of the growth of knowledge, this will in turn require that the moral tradition of the culture in question embody some significant approximations to the truth about moral matters. It is, however, by no means required that two such cultural traditions have started with initial views which approximated the truth to the same extent or along the same dimensions, nor is it required that they have been subjected to the same sorts of social distortion, nor that they have embodied the same sorts of naturally occurring social experimentation. It would thus be entirely unsurprising if two such traditions of moral inquiry should have, about some important moral questions, reached conclusions so divergent that no resolution of their disagreement will be possible within the theoretical and methodological framework which the two traditions *currently* have in common, even though these issues may possess objective answers eventually discoverable from within either tradition or from within a broader tradition which incorporates insights from both.

In this regard it is useful to remember the plausibility with which it can be argued that, if there were agreement on all the nonmoral issues (including theological ones), then there would be no moral disagreements. I'm not sure that this is exactly right. For one thing, the sort of moral agreement which philosophers typically have in mind when they say this sort of thing probably does not include agreement that some question has an indeterminate answer, which is something predicted by homeostatic consequentialism. Nevertheless, careful philosophical examination will reveal, I believe, that agreement on nonmoral issues would eliminate *almost all* disagreement about the sorts of moral issues which arise in ordinary moral practice. Moral realism of the homeostatic consequentialist variety provides a quite plausible explanation for this phenomenon.

It is nevertheless true that, for some few real-world cases and for *lots* of the contrived cases so prevalent in the philosophical literature, there does appear to be serious difficulty in finding rational resolutions – assuming as we typically do that an appeal to indeterminacy of the extension of 'good' doesn't count as a resolution. In such cases the strategy available to the moral realist *is* to insist that failures of bivalence do occur just as a homeostatic consequentialist moral realist predicts.

Philosophers often suggest that the major normative ethical theories will yield the same evaluations in almost all actual cases. Often it is suggested that this fact supports the claim that there is some sort of objectivity in ethics, but it is very difficult to see just why this should be so. Homeostatic consequentialist moral realism provides the basis for a satisfactory treatment of this question. Major theories in normative ethics have almost always sought to provide definitions for moral terms with almost completely definite extensions. This is, of course, in fact a mistake; moral terms possess homeostatic cluster definitions instead. The appearance of sharp divergence between major normative theories, with respect to the variety of possible cases considered by philosophers, arises from the fact that they offer different putative resolutions to issues which lack any resolution *at all* of the sort anticipated in those theories. The general agreement of major normative theories on almost all actual cases is explained both by the fact that the actual features of the good regulate the use of the term 'good' in philosophical discourse *and* by the homeostatic character of the good: when different normative theories put different weight on different components of the good, the fact that such components are – in actual cases – linked by reliable homeostatic mechanisms tends to mitigate, in real-world cases, the effects of the differences in the weights assigned. Homeostatic consequentialism represents the common grain of truth in other normative theories.

4.7. Morality, motivation, and rationality

There remains but one of the challenges to moral realism which we are here considering. It has often been objected against moral realism that there is some sort of logical connection between moral judgments and reasons for action which a moral realist cannot account for. It might be held, for example, that the recognition that one course of action is morally preferable to another *necessarily* provides a reason (even if not a decisive one) to prefer the morally better course of action. Mere facts (especially mere *natural* facts) cannot have this sort of logical connection to rational choice or reasons for action. Therefore, so the objection goes, there cannot be moral facts; moral realism (or at least naturalistic moral realism) is impossible.

It is of course true that the naturalistic moral realist must deny that moral judgments necessarily provide reasons for action; surely, for example, there could be nonhuman cognizing systems which could understand the natural facts about moral goodness but be entirely indifferent to them in choosing how to act. Moral judgments might provide for them no reasons for action whatsoever. Moreover, it is hard to see how the naturalistic moral realist can escape the conclusion that it

would be *logically possible* for there to be a human being for whom moral judgments provided no reasons for action. The moral realist must therefore deny that the connection between morality and reasons for action is so strong as the objection we are considering maintains. The appearance of an especially intimate connection must be explained in some other way.

The standard naturalist response is to explain the apparent intimacy of the connection by arguing that the natural property moral goodness is one such that for psychologically normal humans, the fact that one of two choices is morally preferable will in fact provide some reason for preferring it. The homeostatic consequentialist conception of the good is especially well suited to this response since it defines the good in terms of the homeostatic unity of fundamental human needs. It seems to me that this explanation of the close connection between moral judgments and reasons for action is basically right, but it ignores – it seems to me – one important source of the anti-realist's intuition that the connection between moral judgments and rational choice must be a necessary one. What I have in mind is the very strong intuition which many philosophers share that the person for whom moral judgments are motivationally indifferent would not only be psychologically atypical but would have some sort of *cognitive* deficit with respect to moral reasoning as well. The anti-realist diagnoses this deficit as a failure to recognize a definitional or otherwise necessary connection between moral goodness and reasons for action.

I think that there is a deep insight in the view that people for whom questions of moral goodness are irrelevant to how they would choose to act suffer a cognitive deficit. I propose that the deficit is not – as the anti-realist would have it – a failure to recognize a necessary connection between moral judgments and reasons for action. Instead, I suggest, if we adopt a naturalistic conception of moral knowledge we can diagnose in such people a deficit in the capacity to make moral judgments somewhat akin to a perceptual deficit. What I have in mind is the application of a causal theory of moral knowledge to the examination of a feature of moral reasoning which has been well understood in the empiricist tradition since Hume, that is, the role of sympathy in moral understanding.

It is extremely plausible that for normal human beings the capacity to access human goods and harms – the capacity to *recognize* the extent to which others are well or poorly off with respect to the homeostatic cluster of moral goods and the capacity to *anticipate correctly* the probable effect on others' well-being of various counterfactual circumstances – depends upon their capacity for sympathy, their capacity to imagine themselves in the situation of others or even to find themselves involuntarily doing so in cases in which others are especially well or badly off. The idea that sympathy plays this sort of cognitive role is a truism of nineteenth-century faculty psychology, and it is very probably right.

It is also very probably right, as Hume insists, that the operation of sympathy is *motivationally* important: as a matter of contingent psychological fact, when we put ourselves in the place of others in imagination, the effects of our doing so include our taking pleasure in others' pleasures and our feeling distress at their misfortune, and we are thus motivated to care for the well-being of others. The psychological mechanisms by which all this takes place may be more complicated than Hume imagined, but the fact remains that one and the same psychological mechanism – sympathy – plays *both* a cognitive *and* a motivational role in normal human beings. We are now in a position to see why the morally unconcerned person, the person for whom moral facts are motivationally irrelevant, probably suffers a *cognitive* deficit with respect to moral reasoning. Such a person would have to be deficient in sympathy, because the motivational role of sympathy is precisely to make moral facts motivationally relevant. In consequence, she or he would be deficient with respect to a cognitive capacity (sympathy) which is ordinarily important for the correct assessment of moral facts. The motivational deficiency would, as a matter of contingent fact about human psychology, be a cognitive deficiency as well.

Of course it does not follow that there could not be cognizing systems which are quite capable of assessing moral facts without recourse to anything like sympathy; they might, for example, rely on the application of a powerful tacit or explicit theory of human psychology instead. Indeed it does not follow that there are not actual people – some sociopaths and con artists, for example – who rely on such theories instead of sympathy. But it is true, just as the critic of moral realism insists, that there is generally a cognitive deficit associated with moral indifference. The full resources of naturalistic epistemology permit the moral realist to acknowledge and explain this important insight of moral anti-realists.

4.8. Conclusion

I have argued that if the full resources of naturalistic and realistic conceptions of scientific knowledge and scientific language are deployed and if the right sort of positive theory of the good is advanced, then it is possible to make a plausible case for moral realism in response to typical anti-realist challenges. Two methodological remarks about the arguments I have offered may be useful. In the first place, the rebuttals I have offered to challenges to moral realism really do depend strongly upon the naturalistic and nonfoundational aspects of current (scientific) realist philosophy of science. They depend, roughly, upon the aspects of the scientific realist's program which make it plausible for the scientific realist to claim that philosophy is an empirical inquiry continuous with the sciences and with, e.g., history and empirical social theory. I have argued elsewhere (Boyd 1982, 1983, 1985a, 1985b, 1985c) that these aspects of scientific realism are essential to the defense of scientific realism against powerful empiricist and constructivist arguments.

If we now ask how one should decide between scientific realism and its rivals, I am inclined to think that the answer is that the details of particular technical arguments will not be sufficient to decide the question rationally; instead, one must assess the overall conceptions of knowledge, language, and understanding which go with the rival conceptions of science (I argue for this claim in Boyd 1983). *One* important constraint on an acceptable philosophical conception in these areas is that it permit us to understand the obvious fact that moral reasoning is not nearly so different from scientific or other factual reasoning as logical positivists have led us to believe. It is initially plausible, I think, that a constructivist conception of science is favored over both empiricist and realist conceptions insofar as we confine our attention to this constraint. If what I have said here is correct, this may well not be so. Thus the successful development of the arguments presented here may be relevant not only to our assessment of moral realism but to our assessment of scientific realism as well. Here is a kind of methodological unity of philosophy analogous to (whatever it was which positivists called) 'unity of science'.

My second methodological point is that the arguments for moral realism presented here depend upon optimistic empirical claims both about the organic unity of human goods and about the possibility of reliable knowledge in the 'human sciences' generally. Although I have not argued for this claim here, I believe strongly that any plausible defense of naturalistic moral realism would require similarly optimistic empirical assumptions. I am also inclined to believe that insofar as moral anti-realism is plausible its plausibility rests not only upon technical philosophical arguments but also upon relatively pessimistic empirical beliefs about the same issues. I suggest, therefore, that our philosophical examination of the issues of moral realism should include, in addition to the examination of technical arguments on both sides, the careful examination of empirical claims about the unity and diversity of human goods and about our capacity for knowledge of ourselves. That much of philosophy ought surely to be at least partly empirical.

Bibliography

Armstrong, D. M. 1973. *Belief, Truth and Knowledge*. Cambridge: Cambridge University Press.

Boyd, R. 1972. "Determinism, Laws and Predictability in Principle." *Philosophy of Science* 39: 431–50.

Boyd, R. 1973. "Realism, Underdetermination and a Causal Theory of Evidence." *Noûs* 7: 1–12.

Boyd, R. 1979. "Metaphor and Theory Change." In A. Ortony, ed., *Metaphor and Thought*. Cambridge: Cambridge University Press.

Boyd, R. 1980. "Materialism without Reductionism: What Physicalism Does Not Entail." In N. Block, ed., *Readings in Philosophy of Psychology*, vol. 1. Cambridge, Mass.: Harvard University Press.

Boyd, R. 1982. "Scientific Realism and Naturalistic Epistemology." In P. D. Asquith and R. N. Giere, eds., *PSA 1980*, vol. 2. East Lansing: Philosophy of Science Association.

Boyd, R. 1983. "On the Current Status of the Issue of Scientific Realism." *Erkenntnis* 19: 45–90.

Boyd, R. 1985a. "Lex Orendi Est Lex Credendi." In Paul Churchland and Clifford Hooker, eds., *Images of Science: Scientific Realism Versus Constructive Empiricism*. Chicago: University of Chicago Press.

Boyd, R. 1985b. "Observations, Explanatory Power, and Simplicity." In P. Achinstein and O. Hannaway, eds., *Observation, Experiment, and Hypothesis in Modern Physical Science*. Cambridge, Mass.: MIT Press.

Boyd, R. 1985c. "The Logician's Dilemma: Deductive Logic, Inductive Inference and Logical Empiricism." *Erkenntnis* 22: 197–252.

Boyd, R. *Realism and the Moral Sciences* (unpublished manuscript).

Brink, D. 1984. "Moral Realism and the Skeptical Arguments from Disagreement and Queerness." *Australasian Journal of Philosophy* 62.2: 111–25.

Brink, D. 1989. *Moral Realism and the Foundation of Ethics*. Cambridge: Cambridge University Press.

Byerly, H., and Lazara, V. 1973. "Realist Foundations of Measurement." *Philosophy of Science* 40: 10–28.

Carnap, R. 1934. *The Unity of Science*. Trans. M. Black. London: Kegan Paul.

Dworkin, R. 1973. "The Original Position." *University of Chicago Law Review* 40: 500–33.

Feigl, H. 1956. "Some Major Issues and Developments in the Philosophy of Science of Logical Empiricism." In H. Feigl and M. Scriven. eds., *Minnesota Studies in the Philosophy of Science*, vol. I. Minneapolis: University of Minnesota Press.

Field, H. 1973. "Theory Change and the Indeterminacy of Reference." *Journal of Philosophy* 70: 462–81.

Gilbert, A. 1981a. *Marx's Politics: Communists and Citizens*. New Brunswick, N.J.: Rutgers University Press.

Gilbert, A. 1981b. "Historical Theory and the Structure of Moral Argument in Marx," *Political Theory* 9: 173–205.

Gilbert, A. 1982. "An Ambiguity in Marx's and Engel's Account of Justice and Equality," *American Political Science Review* 76: 328–46.

Gilbert, A. 1984a. "The Storming of Heaven: Capital and Marx's Politics." In J. R. Pennock, ed., *Marxism Today*, Nomos 26. New York: New York University Press.

Gilbert, A. 1984b. "Marx's Moral Realism: Eudaimonism and Moral Progress." In J. Farr and T. Ball, eds., *After Marx*, Cambridge: Cambridge University Press.

Gilbert, A. 1986a. "Moral Realism, Individuality and Justice in War." *Political Theory* 14: 105–35.

Gilbert, A. 1986b. "Democracy and Individuality." *Social Philosophy and Policy* 3: 19–58.

Gilbert, A. 1990. *Democratic Equality*. Cambridge: Cambridge University Press.

Goldman, A. 1967. "A Causal Theory of Knowing." *Journal of Philosophy* 64: 357–72.

Goldman, A. 1976. "Discrimination and Perceptual Knowledge." *Journal of Philosophy* 73: 771–91.

Goodman, N. 1973. *Fact, Fiction, and Forecast*. 3rd edn. Indianapolis: Bobbs-Merrill.

Gould, S. J. 1981. *The Mismeasure of Man*. New York: W. W. Norton.

Hanson, N. R. 1958. *Patterns of Discovery*. Cambridge: Cambridge University Press.

Kamin, L. J. 1974. *The Science and Politics of I.Q.* Potomac, Md.: Lawrence Erlbaum Associates.

Kripke, S. A. 1971. "Identity and Necessity." In M. K. Munitz, ed., *Identity and Individuation*. New York: New York University Press.

Kripke, S. A. 1972. "Naming and Necessity." In D. Davidson and G. Harman, eds., *The Semantics of Natural Language*. Dordrecht, Netherlands: D. Reidel.

Kuhn, T. 1970. *The Structure of Scientific Revolutions*. 2nd edn. Chicago: University of Chicago Press.

Mackie, J. L. 1974. *The Cement of the Universe*. Oxford: Oxford University Press.

Mayr, E. 1970. *Populations. Species and Evolution*. Cambridge: Harvard University Press.

Miller, R. 1978. "Methodological Individualism and Social Explanation." *Philosophy of Science* 45: 387–414.

Miller, R. 1979. "Reason and Commitment in the Social Sciences." *Philosophy and Public Affairs* 8: 241–66.

Miller, R. 1981. "Rights and Reality." *Philosophical Review* 90: 383–407.

Miller, R. 1982. "Rights and Consequences." *Midwest Studies in Philosophy* 7: 151–74.

Miller, R. 1983. "Marx and Morality." *Nomos* 26: 3–32.

Miller, R. 1984a. *Analyzing Marx*. Princeton: Princeton University Press.

Miller, R. 1984b. "Ways of Moral Learning." *Philosophical Review* 94: 507–56.

Putnam, H. 1975a. "The Meaning of 'Meaning'." In H. Putnam, *Mind, Language and Reality*. Cambridge: Cambridge University Press.

Putnam, H. 1975b. "Language and Reality." In H. Putnam, *Mind, Language and Reality*. Cambridge: Cambridge University Press.

Putnam, H. 1983. "Vagueness and Alternative Logic." In H. Putnam, *Realism and Reason*. Cambridge: Cambridge University Press.

Quine, W. V. O. 1969a. "Natural Kinds." In W. V. O. Quine, *Ontological Relativity and Other Essays* New York: Columbia University Press.

Quine, W. V. O. 1969b. "Epistemology Naturalized." In W. V. O. Quine, *Ontological Relativity and Other Essays* New York: Columbia University Press.

Railton, P. 1986. "Moral Realism." *Philosophical Review* 95: 163–207.

Rawls, J. 1971. *A Theory of Justice*. Cambridge, Mass.: Harvard University Press.

Shoemaker, S. 1980. "Causality and Properties." In P. van Inwagen, ed., *Time and Cause*. Dordrecht, Netherlands: D. Reidel.

Sturgeon, N. 1984a. "Moral Explanations." In D. Copp and D. Zimmerman, eds., *Morality, Reason and Truth*. Totowa, N.J.: Rowman and Allanheld.

Sturgeon, N. 1984b. "Review of P. Foot, *Moral Relativism and Virtues and Vices*." *Journal of Philosophy* 81: 326–33.

van Fraassen, B. 1980. *The Scientific Image*. Oxford: Oxford University Press.

Wood, A. 1972. "The Marxian Critique of Justice." *Philosophy and Public Affairs* 1: 244–82.

Wood, A. 1979. "Marx on Right and Justice: A Reply to Husami." *Philosophy and Public Affairs* 8: 267–9.

Wood, A. 1984. "A Marxian Approach to 'The Problem of Justice.'" *Philosophica* 33: 9–32.

Moral Realism

Peter Railton

Among contemporary philosophers, even those who have not found skepticism about empirical science at all compelling have tended to find skepticism about morality irresistible. For various reasons, among them an understandable suspicion of moral absolutism, it has been thought a mark of good sense to explain away any appearance of objectivity in moral discourse. So common has it become in secular intellectual culture to treat morality as subjective or conventional that most of us now have difficulty imagining what it might be like for there to be facts to which moral judgments answer.

Undaunted, some philosophers have attempted to establish the objectivity of morality by arguing that reason, or science, affords a foundation for ethics. The history of such attempts hardly inspires confidence. Although rationalism in ethics has retained adherents long after other rationalisms have been abandoned, the powerful philosophical currents that have worn away at the idea that unaided reason might afford a standpoint from which to derive substantive conclusions show no signs of slackening. And ethical naturalism has yet to find a plausible synthesis of the empirical and the normative: the more it has given itself over to descriptive accounts of the origin of norms, the less has it retained recognizably moral force; the more it has undertaken to provide a recognizable

basis for moral criticism or reconstruction, the less has it retained a firm connection with descriptive social or psychological theory.

In what follows, I will present in a programmatic way a form of ethical naturalism that owes much to earlier theorists, but that seeks to effect a more satisfactory linkage of the normative to the empirical. The link cannot, I believe, be effected by proof. It is no more my aim to refute moral skepticism than it is the aim of contemporary epistemic naturalists to refute Cartesian skepticism. The naturalist in either case has more modest aspirations. First, he seeks to provide an analysis of epistemology or ethics that permits us to see how the central evaluative functions of this domain could be carried out within existing (or prospective) empirical theories. Second, he attempts to show how traditional nonnaturalist accounts rely upon assumptions that are in some way incoherent, or that fit ill with existing science. And third, he presents to the skeptic a certain challenge, namely, to show how a skeptical account of our epistemic or moral practices could be as plausible, useful, or interesting as the account the naturalist offers, and how a skeptical reconstruction of such practices – should the skeptic, as often he does, attempt one – could succeed in preserving their distinctive place and function in human affairs. I will primarily be occupied with the first of these three aspirations.

One thing should be said at the outset. Some may be drawn to, or repelled by, moral realism out of a sense that it is the view of ethics that best expresses high moral earnestness. Yet one can be serious about morality, even to a fault, without being a moral realist. Indeed, a possible objection to the sort of moral realism I will defend here is that it may not make morality serious enough.

I.   Species of Moral Realism

Such diverse views have claimed to be – or have been accused of being – realist about morality, that an initial characterization of the position I will defend is needed before proceeding further. Claims – and accusations – of moral realism typically extend along some or all of the following dimensions. Roughly put: (1) Cognitivism – Are moral judgments capable of truth and falsity? (2) Theories of truth – If moral judgments do have truth values, in what sense? (3) Objectivity – In what ways, if any, does the existence of moral properties depend upon the actual or possible states of mind of intelligent beings? (4) Reductionism – Are moral properties reducible to, or do they in some weaker sense supervene upon, nonmoral properties? (5) Naturalism – Are moral properties natural properties? (6) Empiricism – Do we come to know moral facts in the same way we come to know the facts of empirical science, or are they revealed by reason or by some special mode of apprehension? (7) Bivalence – Does the principle of the excluded middle apply to moral judgments? (8) Determinateness – Given whatever procedures we have for assessing moral judgments, how much of morality is likely to be determinable? (9) Categoricity – Do all rational agents necessarily have some reason to obey moral imperatives? (10) Universality – Are moral imperatives applicable to all rational agents, even (should such exist) those who lack a reason to comply with them? (11) Assessment of existing moralities – Are present moral beliefs approximately true, or do prevailing moral intuitions in some other sense constitute privileged data? (12) Relativism – Does the truth or warrant of moral judgments depend directly upon individually- or socially-adopted norms or practices? (13) Pluralism – Is there a uniquely good form of life or a uniquely right moral code, or could different forms of life or moral codes be appropriate in different circumstances?

Here, then, are the approximate coordinates of my own view in this multidimensional conceptual space. I will argue for a form of moral realism which holds that moral judgments can bear truth values in a fundamentally non-epistemic sense of truth; that moral properties are objective, though relational; that moral properties supervene upon natural properties, and may be reducible to them; that moral inquiry is of a piece with empirical inquiry; that it cannot be known *a priori* whether bivalence holds for moral judgments or how determinately such judgments can be assessed; that there is reason to think we know a fair amount about morality, but also reason to think that current moralities are wrong in certain ways and could be wrong in quite general ways; that a rational agent may fail to have a reason for obeying moral imperatives, although they may nonetheless be applicable to him; and that, while there are perfectly general criteria of moral assessment, nonetheless, by the nature of these criteria no one kind of life is likely to be appropriate for all individuals and no one set of norms appropriate for all societies and all times. The position thus described might well be called 'stark, raving moral realism', but for the sake of syntax, I will colorlessly call it 'moral realism'. This usage is not proprietary. Other positions, occupying more or less different coordinates, may have equal claim to either name.

II.   The Fact/Value Distinction

Any attempt to argue for a naturalistic moral realism runs headlong into the fact/value distinction. Philosophers have given various accounts of this distinction, and of the arguments for it, but for present purposes I will focus upon several issues concerning the epistemic and ontological status of judgments of value as opposed to judgments of fact.

Perhaps the most frequently heard argument for the fact/value distinction is epistemic: it is claimed that disputes over questions of value can persist even after all rational or scientific means of adjudication have been deployed, hence, value judgments cannot be cognitive in the sense that factual or logical judgments are. This claim is defended in part by appeal to the instrumental (hypothetical) character of reason, which prevents reason from dictating ultimate values. In principle, the argument runs, two individuals who differ in ultimate values could, without manifesting any rational defect, hold fast to their conflicting values in the face of any amount of argumentation or evidence. As Ayer puts it, "we find that argument is possible on moral questions only if some system of values is presupposed."[1]

One might attempt to block this conclusion by challenging the instrumental conception of rationality. But for all its faults and for all that it needs to be developed, the instrumental conception seems to me the clearest notion we have of what it is for an agent to have reasons to act. Moreover, it captures a central normative feature of reason-giving, since we can readily see the commending force for an agent of the claim that a given act would advance his ends. It would be hard to make much sense of someone who sincerely claimed to have certain ends and yet at the same time insisted that they could not provide him even *prima facie* grounds for action. (Of course, he might also believe that he has other, perhaps countervailing, grounds.)

Yet this version of the epistemic argument for the fact/value distinction is in difficulty even granting the instrumental conception of rationality. From the standpoint of instrumental reason, belief-formation is but one activity among others: to the extent that we have reasons for engaging in it, or for doing it one way rather than another, these are at bottom a matter of its contribution to our ends. What it would be rational for an individual to believe on the basis of a given experience will vary not only with respect to his other beliefs, but also with respect to what he desires. From this it follows that no amount of mere argumentation or experience could force one on pain of irrationality to accept even the factual claims of empirical science. The long-running debate over inductive logic well illustrates that rational choice among competing hypotheses requires much richer and more controversial criteria of theory choice than can be squeezed from instrumental reason alone. Unfortunately for the contrast Ayer wished to make, we find that argument is possible on scientific questions only if some system of values is presupposed.

However, Hume had much earlier found a way of marking the distinction between facts and values without appeal to the idea that induction – or even deduction – could require a rational agent to adopt certain beliefs rather than others when this would conflict with his contingent ends.[2] For Hume held the thesis that morality is practical, by which he meant that if moral facts existed, they would necessarily provide a reason (although perhaps not an overriding reason) for moral action to all rational beings, regardless of their particular desires. Given this thesis as a premise, the instrumental conception of rationality can clinch the argument after all, for it excludes the possibility of categorical reasons of this kind. By contrast, Hume did not suppose it to be constitutive of logic or science that the facts revealed by these forms of inquiry have categorical force for rational agents, so the existence of logical and scientific facts, unlike the existence of moral facts, is compatible with the instrumental character of reason.

Yet this way of drawing the fact/value distinction is only as compelling as the claim that morality is essentially practical in Hume's sense. Hume is surely right in claiming there to be an intrinsic connection, no doubt complex, between valuing something and having some sort of positive attitude toward it that provides one with an instrumental reason for action. We simply would disbelieve someone who claimed to value honesty and yet never showed the slightest urge to act honestly when given an easy opportunity. But this is a fact about the connection between the values *embraced by* an individual and his reasons for action, not a fact showing a connection between moral evaluation and rational motivation.

Suppose for example that we accept Hume's characterization of justice as an artificial virtue directed at the general welfare. This is in a recognizable sense an evaluative or normative notion – "a value" in the loose sense in which this term is used in such debates – yet it certainly does not follow from its definition that every rational being, no matter what his desires, who believes that some or other act is just in this sense will have an

---

[1]   A. J. Ayer, *Language, Truth, and Logic* (New York: Dover, 1952), p. 111.

[2]   Neither these remarks, nor those in subsequent paragraphs, are meant to be a serious exegesis of Hume's arguments, which admit of interpretations other than the one suggested here. I mean only to capture certain features of what I take Hume's arguments to be, for example, in book III, part I, section I of *A Treatise of Human Nature*, edited by L. A. Selby-Bigge Oxford: Clarendon, 1973), esp. pp. 465–6, and in appendix I of *An Inquiry Concerning the Principles of Morals*, edited by C. W. Hendel (Indianapolis: Bobbs-Merrill, 1957), esp. pp. 111–12.

instrumental reason to perform it. A rational individual may fail to value justice for its own sake, and may have ends contrary to it. In Hume's discussion of our "interested obligation" to be just, he seems to recognize that in the end it may not be possible to show that a "sensible knave" has a reason to be just. Of course, Hume held that the rest of us – whose hearts rebel at Sensible Knave's attitude that he may break his word, cheat, or steal whenever it suits his purposes – have reason to be just, to deem Knave's attitude unjust, and to try to protect ourselves from his predations.[3]

Yet Knave himself could say, perhaps because he accepts Hume's analysis of justice, "Yes, my attitude is unjust." And by Hume's own account of the relation of reason and passion, Knave could add, "But what is that to me?" without failing to grasp the content of his previous assertion. Knave, let us suppose, has no doubts about the intelligibility or reality of "the general welfare," and thinks it quite comprehensible that people attach great significance in public life to the associated notion of justice. He also realizes that for the bulk of mankind, whose passions differ from his, being just is a source and a condition of much that is most worthwhile in life. He thus understands that appeals to justice typically have motivating force. Moreover, he himself uses the category of justice in analyzing the social world, and he recognizes – indeed, his knavish calculations take into account – the distinction between those individuals and institutions that truly are just, and those that merely appear just or are commonly regarded as just. Knave does view a number of concepts with wide currency – religious ones, for example – as mere fictions that prey on weak minds, but he does not view justice in this way. Weak minds and moralists have, he thinks, surrounded justice with certain myths – that justice is its own reward, that once one sees what is just one will automatically have a reason to do it, and so on. But then, he thinks that weak minds and moralists have likewise surrounded wealth and power with myths – that the wealthy are not truly happy, that the powerful inevitably ride for a fall, and so on – and he does not on this account doubt whether there are such things as wealth and power. Knave is glad to be free of prevailing myths about wealth, power, and justice; glad, too, that he is free in his own mind to pay as much or as little attention to any of these attributes as his desires and circumstances warrant. He might, for example, find Mae West's advice convincing: diamonds are very much worth acquiring, and "goodness ha[s] nothing to do with it."

We therefore must distinguish the business of saying what an individual values from the business of saying what it is for him to make measurements against the criteria of a species of evaluation that he recognizes to be genuine.

To deny Hume's thesis of the practicality of moral judgment, and so remove the ground of his contrast between facts and values, is not to deny that morality has an action-guiding character. Morality surely can remain prescriptive within an instrumental framework, and can recommend itself to us in much the same way that, say, epistemology does: various significant and enduring – though perhaps not universal – human ends can be advanced if we apply certain evaluative criteria to our actions. That may be enough to justify to ourselves our abiding concern with the epistemic or moral status of what we do.

By arguing that reason does not compel us to adopt particular beliefs or practices apart from our contingent, and variable, ends, I may seem to have failed to negotiate my way past epistemic relativism, and thus to have wrecked the argument for moral realism before it has even left port. Rationality does go relative when it goes instrumental, but epistemology need not follow. The epistemic warrant of an individual's belief may be disentangled from the rationality of his holding it, for epistemic warrant may be tied to an external criterion – as it is for example by causal or reliabilist theories of knowledge.[4] It is part of the naturalistic realism that informs this essay to adopt such a criterion of warrant. We should not confuse the obvious fact that in general our ends are well served by reliable causal mechanisms of belief-formation with an internalist claim to the effect that reason requires us to adopt such means. Reliable mechanisms have costs as well as benefits, and successful pursuit of some ends – Knave would point to religious ones, and to those of certain moralists –

---

[3]   See the *Inquiry Concerning the Principles of Morals*, sec. IX, pt. II, pp. 102–3.

[4]   Such theories are suitably externalist when, in characterizing the notions of *reliability* or *warrant-conferring causal process*, they employ an account of truth that does not resolve truth into that which we have reason to believe – for example, a nontrivial correspondence theory.

may in some respects be incompatible with adoption of reliable means of inquiry.

This rebuttal of the charge of relativism invites the defender of the fact/value distinction to shift to ontological ground. Perhaps facts and values cannot be placed on opposite sides of an epistemological divide marked off by what reason and experience can compel us to accept. Still, the idea of reliable causal mechanisms for moral learning, and of moral facts "in the world" upon which they operate, is arguably so bizarre that I may have done no more than increase my difficulties.

III.   Value Realism

The idea of causal interaction with moral reality certainly would be intolerably odd if moral facts were held to be *sui generis*,[5] but there need be nothing odd about causal mechanisms for learning moral facts if these facts are constituted by natural facts, and that is the view under consideration. This response will remain unconvincing, however, until some positive argument for realism about moral facts is given. So let us turn to that task.

What might be called 'the generic stratagem of naturalistic realism' is to postulate a realm of facts in virtue of the contribution they would make to the *a posteriori* explanation of certain features of our experience. For example, an external world is posited to explain the coherence, stability, and intersubjectivity of sense-experience. A moral realist who would avail himself of this stratagem must show that the postulation of moral facts similarly can have an explanatory function. The stratagem can succeed in either case only if the reality postulated has these two characteristics:

(1) *independence*: it exists and has certain determinate features independent of whether we think it exists or has those features, independent, even, of whether we have good reason to think this;

(2) *feedback*: it is such – and we are such – that we are able to interact with it, and this interaction exerts the relevant sort of shaping influence or control upon our perceptions, thought, and action.

These two characteristics enable the realist's posit to play a role in the explanation of our experience that cannot be replaced without loss by our mere *conception* of ourselves or our world. For although our conceptual scheme mediates even our most basic perceptual experiences, an experience-transcendent reality has ways of making itself felt without the permission of our conceptual scheme – causally. The success or failure of our plans and projects famously is not determined by expectation alone. By resisting or yielding to our worldly efforts in ways not anticipated by our going conceptual scheme, an external reality that is never directly revealed in perception may nonetheless significantly influence the subsequent evolution of that scheme.

The realist's use of an external world to explain sensory experience has often been criticized as no more than a picture. But do we even have a picture of what a realist explanation might look like in the case of values? I will try to sketch one, filling in first a realist account of non-moral value – the notion of something being desirable for someone, or good for him.[6]

Consider first the notion of someone's *subjective interests* – his wants or desires, conscious or unconscious. Subjective interest can be seen as a secondary quality, akin to taste. For me to take a subjective interest in something is to say that it has a positive *valence* for me, that is, that in ordinary circumstances it excites a positive attitude or inclination (not necessarily conscious) in me. Similarly, for me to say that I find sugar sweet is to say that in ordinary circumstances sugar excites a certain gustatory sensation in me. As secondary qualities, subjective interest and perceived sweetness supervene upon primary qualities of the perceiver, the object (or other phenomenon) perceived, and the surrounding context: the perceiver is so constituted that this sort of object in this sort of context will excite that sort of sensation. Call this complex set of relational, dispositional, primary qualities the *reduction basis* of the secondary quality.

We have in this reduction basis an objective notion that corresponds to, and helps explain, subjective interests. But it is not a plausible foundation for the notion of non-moral goodness, since the

---

[5]   Or if moral facts were supposed to be things of a kind to provide categorical reasons for action. However, this supposition is simply Hume's thesis of practicality in ontological garb.

[6]   A full-scale theory of value would, I think, show the concept of someone's good to be slightly different from the concept of what is desirable for him. However, this difference will not affect the argument made here.

subjective interests it grounds have insufficient normative force to capture the idea of desirableness. My subjective interests frequently reflect ignorance, confusion, or lack of consideration, as hindsight attests. The fact that I am now so constituted that I desire something which, had I better knowledge of it, I would wish I had never sought, does not seem to recommend it to me as part of my good.

To remedy this defect, let us introduce the notion of an *objectified subjective interest* for an individual *A*, as follows. Give to an actual individual *A* unqualified cognitive and imaginative powers, and full factual and nomological information about his physical and psychological constitution, capacities, circumstances, history, and so on. *A* will have become *A*+, who has complete and vivid knowledge of himself and his environment, and whose instrumental rationality is in no way defective. We now ask *A*+ to tell us not what *he* currently wants, but what he would want his non-idealized self *A* to want – or, more generally, to seek – were he to find himself in the actual condition and circumstances of *A*.[8] Just as we assumed there to be a reduction basis for an individual *A*'s actual subjective interests, we may assume there to be a reduction basis for his objectified subjective interests, namely, those facts about *A* and his circumstances that *A*+ would combine with his general knowledge in arriving at his views about what he would want to want were he to step into *A*'s shoes.

For example, Lonnie, a traveler in a foreign country, is feeling miserable. He very much wishes to overcome his malaise and to settle his stomach, and finds he has a craving for the familiar: a tall glass of milk. The milk is desired by Lonnie, but is it also desirable for him? Lonnie-Plus can see that what is wrong with Lonnie, in addition to homesickness, is dehydration, a common affliction of tourists, but one often not detectable from introspective evidence. The effect of drinking hard-to-digest milk would be to further unsettle Lonnie's stomach and worsen his dehydration. By contrast, Lonnie-Plus can see that abundant clear fluids would quickly improve Lonnie's physical condition – which, incidentally, would help with his homesickness as well. Lonnie-Plus can also see just how distasteful Lonnie would find it to drink clear liquids, just what would happen were Lonnie to continue to suffer dehydration, and so on. As a result of this information, Lonnie-Plus might then come to desire that were he to assume Lonnie's place, he would want to drink clear liquids rather than milk, or at least want to act in such a way that a want of this kind would be satisfied. The reduction basis of this objectified interest includes facts about Lonnie's circumstances and constitution, which determine, among other things, his existing tastes and his ability to acquire certain new tastes, the consequences of continued dehydration, the effects and availability of various sorts of liquids, and so on.

Let us say that this reduction basis is the constellation of primary qualities that make it be the case that the Lonnie has a certain *objective interest*.[9]

[7]   It was some work by Richard C. Jeffrey on epistemic probability that originally suggested to me the idea of objectifying subjective interests. I have since benefited from Richard B. Brandt's work on "rational desire," although I fear that what I will say contains much that he would regard as wrong-headed. See *A Theory of the Good and the Right* (Oxford: Clarendon, 1979), part I.

[8]   We ask this question of *A*+, rather than what *A*+ wants for himself, because we are seeking the objectified subjective interests of *A*, and the interests of *A*+ might be quite different owing to the changes involved in the idealization of *A*. For example, *A*+ presumably does not want any more information for himself – there is no more to be had and he knows this. Yet it might still be true that *A*+ would want to want more knowledge were he to be put in the place of his less well-informed self, *A*. It may as a psychological matter be impossible for *A*+ to set aside entirely his desires *in his present circumstances* with regard to himself or to *A* in considering what he would want to want were he to be put *in the place of* his less-than-ideal self. This reveals a measurement problem for objective interests: giving an individual the information and capacities necessary to "objectify" his interests may perturb his psychology in ways that alter the phenomenon we wish to observe. Such difficulties attend even the measurement of subjective interests, since instruments for sampling preferences (indeed, mere acts of reflection upon one's preferences) tend to affect the preferences expressed. For obvious reasons, interference effects come with the territory. Though not in themselves sufficient ground for skepticism about subjective or objective interests, these measurement problems show the need for a "perturbation theory," and for caution about attributions of interests that are inattentive to interference effects.

[9]   'Interest' is not quite the word wanted here, for in ordinary language we may speak of a want where we would not speak of a corresponding interest. See Brian Barry, *Political Argument* (London: Routledge and Kegan Paul, 1965), especially chapter X, for discussion. A more accurate, but overly cumbersome, expression would be 'positive-valence-making characteristic'.

That is, we will say that Lonnie has an objective interest in drinking clear liquids in virtue of this complex, relational, dispositional set of facts. Put another way, we can say that the reduction basis, not the fact that Lonnie-Plus would have certain wants, is the truth-maker for the claim that this is an objective interest of Lonnie's. The objective interest thus explains why there is a certain objectified interest, not the other way around.

Let us now say that X is *non-morally good for A* if and only if X would satisfy an objective interest of A.[10] We may think of A+'s views about what he would want to want were he in A's place as generating a ranking of potential objective interests of A, a ranking that will reflect what is better or worse for A and will allow us to speak of A's actual wants as better or worse approximations of what is best for him. We may also decompose A+'s views into *prima facie* as opposed to "on balance" objective interests of A, the former yielding the notion of '*a* good for A', the latter, of '*the* good for A'. This seems to me an intuitively plausible account of what someone's non-moral good consists in: roughly, what he would want himself to seek if he knew what he were doing.[11]

Moreover, this account preserves what seems to me an appropriate link between non-moral value and motivation. Suppose that one desires X, but wonders whether X really is part of one's good. This puzzlement typically arises because one feels that one knows too little about X, oneself, or one's world, or because one senses that one is not being adequately rational or reflective in assessing the information one has – perhaps one suspects that one has been captivated by a few salient features of X (or repelled by a few salient features of its alternatives). If one were to learn that one would still want oneself to want X in the circumstances were one to view things with full information and rationality, this presumably would reduce the force of

the original worry. By contrast, were one to learn that when fully informed and rational one would want oneself *not* to want X in the circumstances, this presumably would add force to it. Desires being what they are, a reinforced worry might not be sufficient to remove the desire for X. But if one were to become genuinely and vividly convinced that one's desire for X is in this sense not supported by full reflection upon the facts, one presumably would feel this to be a count against acting upon the desire. This adjustment of desire to belief might not in a given case be required by reason or logic; it might be "merely psychological." But it is precisely such psychological phenomena that naturalistic theories of value take as basic.

In what follows, we will need the notion of intrinsic goodness, so let us say that X is *intrinsically non-morally good for A* just in case X is in A's objective interest without reference to any other objective interest of A. We can in an obvious way use the notion of objective intrinsic interest to account for all other objective interests. Since individuals and their environments differ in many respects, we need not assume that everyone has the same objective intrinsic interests. *A fortiori*, we need not assume that they have the same objective instrumental interests. We should, however, expect that when personal and situational similarities exist across individuals – that is, when there are similarities in reduction bases – there will to that extent be corresponding similarities in their interests.

It is now possible to see how the notion of non-moral goodness can have explanatory uses. For a start, it can explain why one's actual desires have certain counterfactual features, for example, why one would have certain hypothetical desires rather than others were one to become fully informed and aware. Yet this sort of explanatory use – following as it does directly from the definition of objective

---

[10] More precisely, we may say that X is non-morally good for A at time t if and only if X would satisfy an objective interest of A the reduction basis of which exists at t. Considerations about the evolution of interests over time raise a number of issues that cannot be entered into here.

[11] The account may, however, yield some counterintuitive results. Depending upon the nature and circumstances of given individuals, they might have objective interests in things we find wrong or repulsive, and that do not seem to us part of a good life. We can explain a good deal of our objection to certain desires – for example, those involving cruelty – by saying that they are not *morally* good; others – for example, those of a philistine nature – by saying that they are not *aesthetically* valuable; and so on. It seems to me preferable to express our distaste for certain ends in terms of specific categories of value, rather than resort to the device of saying that such ends could under no circumstances be part of anyone's non-moral good. People, or at least some people, might be put together in a way that makes some not-very-appetizing things essential to their flourishing, and we do not want to be guilty of wishful thinking on this score. (There will be wishful thinking enough before we are through.)

interest – might well be thought unimpressive unless some other explanatory functions can be found.

Consider, then, the difference between Lonnie and Tad, another traveler in the same straits, but one who, unlike Lonnie, wants to drink clear liquids, and proceeds to do so. Tad will perk up while Lonnie remains listless. We can explain this difference by noting that although both Lonnie and Tad acted upon their wants, Tad's wants better reflected his interests. The congruence of Tad's wants with his interests may be fortuitous, or it may be that Tad knows he is dehydrated and knows the standard treatment. In the latter case we would ordinarily say that the explanation of the difference in their condition is that Tad, but not Lonnie, "knew what was good for him."

Generally, we can expect that what $A+$ would want to want were he in A's place will correlate well with what would permit A to experience physical or psychological well-being or to escape physical or psychological ill-being. Surely our well- or ill-being are among the things that matter to us most, and most reliable, even on reflection. Appeal to degrees of congruence between A's wants and his interests thus will often help to explain facts about how satisfactory he finds his life. Explanation would not be preserved were we to substitute 'believed to be congruent' for 'are (to such-and-such a degree) congruent', since, as cases like Lonnie's show, even if one were to convince oneself that one's wants accurately reflected one's interests, acting on these wants might fail to yield much satisfaction.

In virtue of the correlation to be expected between acting upon motives that congrue with one's interests and achieving a degree of satisfaction or avoiding a degree of distress, one's objective interests may also play an explanatory role in the _evolution_ of one's desires. Consider what I will call the _wants/interests mechanism_, which permits individuals to achieve selfconscious and unselfconscious learning about their interests through experience. In the simplest sorts of cases, trial and error leads to the selective retention of wants that are satisfiable and lead to satisfactory results for the agent.

For example, suppose that Lonnie gives in to his craving and drinks the milk. Soon afterwards, he feels much worse. Still unable to identify the source of his malaise and still in the grips of a desire for the familiar, his attention is caught by a green-and-red sign in the window of a small shop he is moping past: "7-Up," it says. He rushes inside and buys a bottle. Although it is lukewarm, he drinks it eagerly. "Mmm," he thinks, "I'll have another." He buys a second bottle, and drains it to the bottom. By now he has had his fill of tepid soda, and carries on. Within a few hours, his mood is improving. When he passes the store again on the way back to his hotel, his pleasant association with drinking 7-Up leads him to buy some more and carry it along with him. That night, in the dim solitude of his room, he finds the soda's reassuringly familiar taste consoling, and so downs another few bottles before finally finding sleep. When he wakes up the next morning, he feels very much better. To make a dull story short: the next time Lonnie is laid low abroad, he may have some conscious or unconscious, reasoned or superstitious, tendency to seek out 7-Up. Unable to find that, he might seek something quite like it, say, a local lime-flavored soda, or perhaps even the _agua mineral con gaz_ he had previously scorned. Over time, as Lonnie travels more and suffers similar malaise, he regularly drinks clearish liquids and regularly feels better, eventually developing an actual desire for such liquids – and an aversion to other drinks, such as milk – in such circumstances.

Thus have Lonnie's desires evolved through experience to conform more closely to what is good for him, in the naturalistic sense intended here. The process was not one of an ideally rational response to the receipt of ideal information, but rather of largely unreflective experimentation, accompanied by positive and negative associations and reinforcements. There is no guarantee that the desires "learned" through such feedback will accurately or completely reflect an individual's good. Still less is there any guarantee that, even when an appropriate adjustment in desire occurs, the agent will comprehend the origin of his new desires or be able to represent to himself the nature of the interests they reflect. But then, it is a quite general feature of the various means by which we learn about the world that they may fail to provide accurate or comprehending representations of it. My ability to perceive and understand my surroundings coexists with, indeed draws upon the same mechanisms as, my liability to deception by illusion, expectation, or surface appearance.

There are some broad theoretical grounds for thinking that something like the wants/interests mechanism exists and has an important role in desire-formation. Humans are creatures motivated primarily by wants rather than instincts. If such creatures were unable through experience to conform their wants at all closely to their essential interests – perhaps because they were no more likely to experience positive internal states when their essential interests are met than when they are not – we could not expect long or fruitful futures for them. Thus, if humans in general did not come to want to eat the kinds of food necessary to maintain some degree of physical well-being, or to engage in the sorts of activities or relations necessary to maintain their sanity, we would not be around today to worry whether we can know what is good for us. Since creatures as sophisticated and complex as humans have evolved through encounters with a variety of environments, and indeed have made it their habit to modify their environments, we should expect considerable flexibility in our capacity through experience to adapt our wants to our interests. However, this very flexibility makes the mechanism unreliable: our wants may at any time differ arbitrarily much from our interests; moreover, we may fail to have experiences that would cause us to notice this, or to undergo sufficient feedback to have much chance of developing new wants that more nearly approximate our interests. It is entirely possible, and hardly infrequent, that an individual live out the course of a normal life without ever recognizing or adjusting to some of his most fundamental interests. Individual limitations are partly remedied by cultural want-acquiring mechanisms, which permit learning and even theorizing over multiple lives and life-spans, but these same mechanisms also create a vast potential for the inculcation of wants at variance with interests.

The argument for the wants/interests mechanism has about the same status, and the same breezy plausibility, as the more narrowly biological argument that we should expect the human eye to be capable of detecting objects the size and shape of our predators or prey. It is not necessary to assume anything approaching infallibility, only enough functional success to hold our own in an often inhospitable world.

Thus far the argument has concerned only those objective interests that might be classified as needs, but the wants/interests mechanism can operate with respect to any interest – even interests related to an individual's particular aptitudes or social role – whose frustration is attended even indirectly by consciously or unconsciously unsatisfactory results for him. (To be sure, the more indirect the associ-

ation the more unlikely that the mechanism will be reliable.) For example, the experience of taking courses in both mathematics and philosophy may lead an undergraduate who thought himself cut out to be a mathematician to come to prefer a career in philosophy, which would in fact better suit his aptitudes and attitudes. And a worker recently promoted to management from the shop floor may find himself less inclined to respond to employee grievances than he had previously wanted managers to be, while his former co-workers may find themselves less inclined to confide in him than before.

If a wants/interests mechanism is postulated, and if what is non-morally good for someone is a matter of what is in his objective interest, then we can say that objective value is able to play a role in the explanation of subjective value of the sort the naturalistic realist about value needs. These explanations even support some qualified predications: for example, that, other things equal, individuals will ordinarily be better judges of their own interests than third parties; that knowledge of one's interests will tend to increase with increased experience and general knowledge; that people with similar personal and social characteristics will tend to have similar values; and that there will be greater general consensus upon what is desirable in those areas of life where individuals are most alike in other regards (for example, at the level of basic motives), and where trial-and-error mechanisms can be expected to work well (for example, where esoteric knowledge is not required). I am in no position to pronounce these predictions correct, but it may be to their credit that they accord with widely-held views.

It should perhaps be emphasized that although I speak of the objectivity of value, the value in question is human value, and exists only because humans do. In the sense of old-fashioned theory of value, this is a relational rather than absolute notion of goodness. Although relational, the relevant facts about humans and their world are objective in the same sense that such non-relational entities as stones are: they do not depend or their existence or nature merely upon our conception of them.

Thus understood, objective interests are supervenient upon natural and social facts. Does this mean that they cannot contribute to explanation after all, since it should always be possible in principle to account for any particular fact that they purport to explain by reference to the supervenience basis alone? If mere supervenience were grounds for denying an explanatory role to a given set of concepts, then we would have to say that chemistry, biology, and electrical engineering, which clearly supervene upon physics, lack explanatory power. Indeed, even outright reducibility is no ground for doubting explanatoriness. To establish a relation of reduction between, for example, a chemical phenomenon such as valence and a physical model of the atom does nothing to suggest that there is no such thing as valence, or that generalizations involving valence cannot support explanations. There can be no issue here of ontological economy or eschewing unnecessary entities, as might be the case if valence were held to be something *sui generis,* over and above any constellation of physical properties. The facts described in principles of chemical valence are genuine, and permit a powerful and explanatory systematization of chemical combination; the existence of a successful reduction to atomic physics only bolsters these claims.

We are confident that the notion of chemical valence is explanatory because proffered explanations in terms of chemical valence insert explananda into a distinctive and well-articulated nomic nexus, in an obvious way increasing our understanding of them. But what comparably powerful and illuminating theory exists concerning the notion of objective interest to give us reason to think – whether or not strict reduction is possible – that proffered explanations using this notion are genuinely informative?

I would find the sort of value realism sketched here uninteresting if it seemed to me that no theory of any consequence could be developed using the category of objective value. But in describing the wants/interests mechanism I have already tried to indicate that such a theory may be possible. When we seek to explain why people act as they do, why they have certain values or desires, and why sometimes they are led into conflict and other times into cooperation, it comes naturally to common sense and social science alike to talk in terms of people's interests. Such explanations will be incomplete and superficial if we remain wholly at the level of subjective interests, since these, too, must be accounted for.

IV.   Normative Realism

Suppose everything said thus far to have been granted generously. Still, I would as yet have no right to speak of *moral* realism, for I have done no more than to exhibit the possibility of a kind of realism with regard to non-moral goodness, a notion that perfect moral skeptics can admit. To be entitled to speak of moral realism I would have to show realism to be possible about distinctively moral value, or moral norms. I will concentrate on moral norms – that is, matters of moral rightness and wrongness – although the argument I give may, by extension, be applied to moral value. In part, my reason is that normative realism seems much less plausible intuitively than value realism. It therefore is not surprising that many current proposals for moral realism focus essentially upon value – and sometimes only upon what is in effect non-moral value. Yet on virtually any conception of morality, a moral theory must yield an account of rightness.

Normative moral realism is implausible on various grounds, but within the framework of this essay, the most relevant is that it seems impossible to extend the generic strategy of naturalistic realism to moral norms. Where is the place in explanation for facts about what *ought* to be the case – don't facts about the way things *are* do all the explaining there is to be done? Of course they do. But then, my naturalistic moral realism commits me to the view that facts about what ought to be the case are facts of a special kind about the way things are. As a result, it may be possible for them to have a function within an explanatory theory. To see how this could be, let me first give some examples of explanations outside the realm of morality that involve naturalized norms.

"Why did the roof collapse? – For a house that gets the sort of snow loads that one did, the rafters ought to have been 2×8's at least, not 2×6's." This explanation is quite acceptable, as far as it goes, yet it contains an 'ought'. Of course, we can remove this 'ought' as follows: "If a roof of that design is to withstand the snow load that one bore, then it must be framed with rafters at least 2×8 in cross-section." An architectural 'ought' is replaced by an engineering 'if . . . then . . .'. This is possible because the 'ought' clearly is hypothetical, reflecting the universal architectural goal of making roofs strong enough not to collapse. Because the goal is contextually fixed, and because there are more or less definite answers to the question of how to meet it, and moreover because the explanandum phenomenon is the result of a process that selects against instances that do not attain that goal, the 'ought' containing account conveys explanatory information. I will call this sort of explanation _criterial_: we explain why something happened by reference to a relevant criterion, given the existence of a process that in effect selects for (or against) phenomena that more (or less) closely approximate this criterion. Although the criterion is defined naturalistically, it may at the same time be of a kind to have a regulative role in human practice – in this case, in house-building.

A more familiar sort of criterial explanation involves norms of individual rationality. Consider the use of an instrumental theory of rationality to explain an individual's behavior in light of his beliefs and desires, or to account for the way an individual's beliefs change with experience.[12] Bobby Shaftoe went to sea because he believed it was the best way to make his fortune, and he wanted above all to make his fortune. Crewmate Reuben Ramsoe came to believe that he wasn't liked by the other deckhands because he saw that they taunted him and greeted his frequent lashings at the hands of the First Mate with unconcealed pleasure. These explanations work because the action or belief in question was quite rational for the agent in the circumstances, and because we correctly suppose both Shaftoe and Ramsoe to have been quite rational.

Facts about degrees of instrumental rationality enter into explanations in other ways as well. First, consider the question why Bobby Shaftoe has had more success than most like-minded individuals in achieving his goals. We may lay his success to the fact that Shaftoe is more instrumentally rational than most – perhaps he has greater-than-average acumen in estimating the probabilities of outcomes, or is more-reliable-than-average at deductive inference, or is more-imaginative-than-average in surveying alternatives.

Second, although we are all imperfect deliberators, our behavior may come to embody habits or strategies that enable us to approximate optimal rationality more closely than our deliberative defects would lead one to expect. The mechanism is simple. Patterns of beliefs and behaviors that do not exhibit much instrumental rationality will tend to be to some degree self-defeating, an incentive to change them, whereas patterns that exhibit greater instrumental rationality will tend to be to some degree rewarding, an incentive to continue them. These incentives may affect our beliefs and behaviors even though the drawbacks or advantages of the patterns in question do not receive conscious deliberation. In such cases we may be said to acquire these habits or strategies because they _are_ more rational, without the intermediation of any _belief_ on our part that they are. [. . .] Criterial explanation in terms of individual rationality thus extends to behaviors beyond the realm of deliberate action. And, as with the wants/interests mechanism, it is possible to see in the emergence of such behaviors something we can without distortion call learning.

Indeed, our tendency through experience to develop rational habits and strategies may cooperate with the wants/interests mechanism to provide the basis for an _extended_ form of criterial explanation, in which an individual's rationality is assessed not relative to his occurrent beliefs and desires, but relative to his objective interests. The examples considered earlier of the wants/interests mechanism in fact involved elements of this sort of explanation, for they showed not only wants being adjusted to interests, but also behavior being adjusted to newly adjusted wants. Without appropriate alteration of behavior to reflect changing wants, the feedback necessary for learning about wants would not occur. With such alteration, the behavior itself may become more rational in the extended sense. An individual who is instrumentally rational is disposed to adjust means to ends; but one result of his undertaking a means – electing a course of study, or accepting a new job – may be a more informed assessment, and perhaps a reconsideration, of his ends.

The theory of individual rationality – in either its simple or its extended form – thus affords an instance of the sort needed to provide an example of normative realism. Evaluations of degrees of instrumental rationality play a prominent role in our explanations of individual behavior, but they simultaneously have normative force for the agent. Whatever other concerns an agent might have, it

---

[12] Such explanation uses a naturalized criterion when rationality is defined in terms of relative efficiency given the agent's beliefs and desires. A (more or less) rational agent is thus someone disposed to act in (more or less) efficient ways. There is a deep difficulty about calling such explanation naturalistic, for the constraints placed upon attributions of beliefs and desires by a "principle of charity" may compromise the claim that rational-agent explanations are empirical. Although I believe this difficulty can be overcome, this is hardly the place to start _that_ argument.

surely counts for him as a positive feature of an action that it is efficient relative to his beliefs and desires or, in the extended sense, efficient relative to beliefs and desires that would appropriately reflect his condition and circumstances.

The normative force of these theories of individual rationality does not, however, merely derive from their explanatory use. One can employ a theory of instrumental rationality to explain behavior while rejecting it as a normative theory of reasons, just as one can explain an action as due to irrationality without thereby endorsing unreason.[13] Instead, the connection between the normative and explanatory roles of the instrumental conception of rationality is traceable to their common ground: the human motivational system. It is a fact about us that we have ends and have the capacity for both deliberate action relative to our ends and nondeliberate adjustment of behavior to our ends. As a result, we face options among pathways across a landscape of possibilities variously valenced for us. Both when we explain the reasons for people's choices and the causes of their behavior and when we appeal to their intuitions about what it would be rational to decide or to do, we work this territory, for we make what use we can of facts about what does-in-fact or can-in-principle motivate agents.

Thus emerges the possibility of saying that facts exist about what individuals have reason to do, facts that may be substantially independent of, and more normatively compelling than, an agent's occurrent conception of his reasons. The argument for such realism about individual rationality is no stronger than the arguments for the double claim that the relevant conception of instrumental individual rationality has both explanatory power and the sort of commendatory force a theory of *reasons* must possess, but (although I will not discuss them further here) these arguments seem to me quite strong.

*   *   *

Passing now beyond the theory of individual rationality, let us ask what criterial explanations involving distinctively moral norms might look like. To ask this, we need to know what distinguishes moral norms from other criteria of assessment. Moral evaluation seems to be concerned most centrally with the assessment of conduct or character where the interests of more than one individual are at stake. Further, moral evaluation assesses actions or outcomes in a peculiar way: the interests of the strongest or most prestigious party do not always prevail, purely prudential reasons may be subordinated, and so on. More generally, moral resolutions are thought to be determined by criteria of choice that are *non-indexical* and in some sense *comprehensive*. This has led a number of philosophers to seek to capture the special character of moral evaluation by identifying a *moral point of view* that is impartial, but equally concerned with all those potentially affected. Other ethical theorists have come to a similar conclusion by investigating the sorts of reasons we characteristically treat as relevant or irrelevant in moral discourse. Let us follow these leads. We thus may say that moral norms reflect a certain kind of rationality, rationality not from the point of view of any particular individual, but from what might be called a social point of view.

By itself, the equation of moral rightness with rationality from a social point of view is not terribly restrictive, for, depending upon what one takes rationality to be, this equation could be made by a utilitarian, a Kantian, or even a non-cognitivist. That is as it should be, for if it is to capture what is distinctive about moral norms, it should be compatible with the broadest possible range of recognized moral theories. However, once one opts for a particular conception of rationality – such as the conception of rationality as efficient pursuit of the non-morally good, or as autonomous and universal self-legislation, or as a noncognitive expression of hypothetical endorsement – this schematic characterization begins to assume particular moral content. Here I have adopted an instrumentalist conception of rationality, and this – along with the account given of non-moral goodness – means that the argument for moral realism given below is an argument that presupposes and purports to defend a particular substantive moral theory.[14]

---

[13]   To recall a point from section II: one may make assessments relative to particular evaluative criteria without thereby valuing that which satisfies them.

[14]   It also means that the relation of moral criteria to criteria of individual rationality has become problematic, since there can be no guarantee that what would be instrumentally rational from any given individual's point of view will coincide with what would be instrumentally rational from a social point of view.

What is this theory? Let me introduce an idealization of the notion of social rationality by considering what would be rationally approved of were the interests of all potentially affected individuals counted equally under circumstances of full and vivid information.[15] Because of the assumption of full and vivid information, the interests in question will be objective interests. Given the account of goodness proposed in section III, this idealization is equivalent to what is rational from a social point of view with regard to the realization of intrinsic non-moral goodness. This seems to me to be a recognizable and intuitively plausible – if hardly uncontroversial – criterion of moral rightness. Relative moral rightness is a matter of relative degree of approximation to this criterion.

The question that now arises is whether the notion of degrees of moral rightness could participate in explanations of behavior or in processes of moral learning that parallel explanatory uses of the notion of degrees of individual rationality – especially, in the extended sense. I will try to suggest several ways in which it might.

Just as an individual who significantly discounts some of his interests will be liable to certain sorts of dissatisfaction, so will a social arrangement – for example, a form of production, a social or political hierarchy, etc. – that departs from social rationality by significantly discounting the interests of a particular group have a potential for dissatisfaction and unrest. Whether or not this potential will be realized depends upon a great many circumstances. Owing to socialization, or to other limitations on the experience or knowledge of members of this group, the wants/interests mechanism may not have operated in such a way that the wants of its members reflect their interests. As a result they may experience no direct frustration of their desires despite the discounting of their interests. Or, the group may be too scattered or too weak to mobilize effectively. Or, it may face overawing repression. On the other hand, certain social and historical circumstances favor the realization of this potential for unrest, for example, by providing members of this group with experiences that make them more likely to develop interest-congruent wants, by weakening the existing repressive apparatus, by giving them new access to resources or new opportunities for mobilization, or merely by dispelling the illusion that change is impossible. In such circumstances, one can expect the potential for unrest to manifest itself.

Just as explanations involving assessments of individual rationality were not always replaceable by explanations involving individual *beliefs about* what would be rational, so, too, explanations involving assessments of social rationality cannot be replaced by explanations involving *beliefs about* what would be morally right. For example, discontent may arise because a society departs from social rationality, but not as result of a belief that this is the case. Suppose that a given society is believed by all constituents to be just. This belief may help to stabilize it, but if in fact the interests of certain groups are being discounted, there will be a potential for unrest that may manifest itself in various ways – in alienation, loss of morale, decline in the effectiveness of authority, and so on – well before any changes in belief about the society's justness occur, and that will help explain why members of certain groups come to believe it to be unjust, if in fact they do.

In addition to possessing a certain sort of potential for unrest, societies that fail to approximate social rationality may share other features as well: they may exhibit a tendency toward certain religious or ideological doctrines, or toward certain sorts of repressive apparatus; they may be less productive in some ways (for example, by failing to develop certain human resources) and more productive in others (for example, by extracting greater labor from some groups at less cost), and thus may be differentially economically successful depending upon the conditions of production they face, and so on.

If a notion of social rationality is to be a legitimate part of empirical explanations of such phenomena, an informative characterization of the

---

[15] A rather strong thesis of interpersonal comparison is needed here for purposes of social aggregation. I am not assuming the existence of some single good, such as happiness, underlying such comparisons. Thus the moral theory in question, although consequentialist, aggregative, and maximizing, is not equivalent to classical utilitarianism. I *am* assuming that when a choice is faced between satisfying interest X of A vs. satisfying interest Y of B, answers to the question "All else equal, would it matter more to me if I were A to have X satisfied than if I were B to have Y satisfied?" will be relatively determinate and stable across individuals under conditions of full and vivid information. A similar, though somewhat weaker, form of comparability-across-difference is presupposed when we make choices from among alternative courses of action that would lead us to have different desires in the future.

circumstances under which departures from, or approximations to, social rationality could be expected to lead to particular social outcomes – especially, of the conditions under which groups whose interests are sacrificed could be expected to exhibit or mobilize discontent – must be available. Although it cannot be known *a priori* whether an account of this kind is possible, one can see emerging in some recent work in social history and historical sociology various elements of a theory of when, and how, a persisting potential for social discontent due to persistently sacrificed interests comes to be manifested.

An individual whose wants do not reflect his interests or who fails to be instrumentally rational may experience feedback of a kind that promotes learning about his good and development of more rational strategies. Similarly, the discontent produced by departures from social rationality may produce feedback that, at a social level, promotes the development of norms that better approximate social rationality. The potential for unrest that exists when the interests of a group are discounted is potential for pressure from that group – and its allies – to accord fuller recognition to their interests in social decision-making and in the socially-instilled norms that govern individual decision-making. It therefore is pressure to push the resolution of conflicts further in the direction required by social rationality, since it is pressure to give fuller weight to the interests of more of those affected. Such pressure may of course be more or less forceful or coherent; it may find the most diverse ideological expression; and it may produce outcomes more or less advantageous in the end to those exerting it.[16] Striking historical examples of the mobilization of excluded groups to promote greater representation of their interests include the rebellions against the system of feudal estates, and more recent social movements against restrictions on religious practices, on suffrage and other civil rights, and on collective bargaining.

Of course, other mechanisms have been at work influencing the evolution of social practices and norms at the same time, some with the reverse effect. Whether mechanisms working on behalf of the inclusion of excluded interests will predominate depends upon a complex array of social and historical factors. It would be silly to think either that the norms of any actual society will at any given stage of history closely approximate social rationality, or that there will be a univocal trend toward greater social rationality. Like the mechanisms of biological evolution or market economics, the mechanisms described here operate in an "open system" alongside other mechanisms, and do not guarantee optimality or even a monotonic approach to equilibrium. Human societies do not appear to have begun at or near equilibrium in the relevant sense, and so the strongest available claim might be that in the long haul, barring certain exogenous effects, one could expect an uneven secular trend toward the inclusion of the interests of (or interests represented by) social groups that are capable of some degree of mobilization. But under other circumstances, even in the long run, one could expect the opposite. New World plantation slavery, surely one of the most brutally exclusionary social arrangements ever to have existed, emerged late in world history and lasted for hundreds of years. Other brutally exclusionary social arrangements of ancient or recent vintage persist yet.

One need not, therefore, embrace a theory of moral progress in order to see that the feedback mechanism just described can give an explanatory role to the notion of social rationality. Among the most puzzling, yet most common, objections to moral realism is that there has not been uniform historical progress toward worldwide consensus on moral norms. But it has not to my knowledge been advanced as an argument against *scientific* realism that, for example, some contemporary cultures and subcultures do not accept, and do not seem to be moving in the direction of accepting, the scientific world view. Surely realists are in both cases entitled to say that only certain practices in certain circumstances will tend to produce theories more congruent with reality, especially when the subject matter is so complex and so far removed from anything like direct inspection. They need not sub-

[16]   See, for example, Barrington Moore, Jr., *The Social Origins of Dictatorship and Democracy: Lord and Peasant in the Making of the Modern World* (Boston: Beacon, 1966) and *Injustice: The Social Bases of Obedience and Revolt* (White Plains, NY: M. E. Sharpe, 1978); E. P. Thompson, *The Making of the English Working Class* (New York: Pantheon, 1963); William B. Taylor, *Drinking, Homicide, and Rebellion in Colonial Mexican Villages* (Stanford: Stanford University Press, 1979); Charles Tilly, *From Mobilization to Revolution* (Reading, Mass.: Addison-Wesley, 1978); and Charles Tilly, et al., *The Rebellious Century, 1830–1930* (Cambridge, Mass.: Harvard University Press, 1975).

scribe to the quaint idea that "the truth will out" come what may. The extended theory of individual rationality, for example, leads us to expect that in societies where there are large conflicts of interest people will develop large normative disagreements, and that, when (as they usually do) these large conflicts of interest parallel large differences in power, the dominant normative views are unlikely to embody social rationality. What is at issue here, and in criterial explanations generally, is the explanation of certain patterns among others, not necessarily the existence of a single overall trend. We may, however, point to the existence of the feedback mechanisms described here as grounds for belief that we can make qualified use of historical experience as something like experimental evidence about what kinds of practices in what ranges of circumstances might better satisfy a criterion of social rationality. That is, we may assign this mechanism a role in a qualified process of moral learning.

The mechanisms of learning about individual rationality, weak or extended, involved similar qualifications. For although we expect that, under favorable circumstances, individuals may become better at acting in an instrumentally rational fashion as their experience grows, we are also painfully aware that there are powerful mechanisms promoting the opposite result. We certainly do not think that an individual must display exceptionless rationality, or even show ever-increasing rationality over his lifetime, in order to apply reason-giving explanations to many of his actions. Nor do we think that the inevitable persistence of areas of irrationality in individuals is grounds for denying that they can, through experience, acquire areas of greater rationality.

The comparison with individual rationality should not, however, be overdrawn. First, while the inclusion-generating mechanisms for social rationality operate through the behavior of individuals, interpersonal dynamics enter ineliminably in such a way that the criteria selected for are not reducible to those of disaggregated individual rationality. Both social and biological evolution involve selection mechanisms that favor behaviors satisfying criteria of relative optimality that are collective (as in prisoner's dilemma cases) or genotypic (which may also be collective, as in kin selection) as well as individual or phenotypic. Were this not so, it is hardly possible that moral norms could ever have emerged or come to have the hold upon us they do.

Second, there are rather extreme differences of degree between the individual and the social cases. Most strikingly, the mechanisms whereby individual wants and behaviors are brought into some congruence with individual interests and reasons operate in more direct and reliable ways than comparable mechanisms nudging social practices or norms in the direction of what is socially rational. Not only are the information demands less formidable in the individual case – that is the least of it, one might say – but the ways in which feedback is achieved are more likely in the individual case to serve as a prod for change and less likely to be distorted by social asymmetries.

Nonetheless, we do have the skeleton of an explanatory theory that uses the notion of what is more or less rational from a social point of view and that parallels in an obvious way uses of assessments of rationality from the agent's point of view in explanations of individual beliefs and behaviors. Like the individual theory, it suggests prediction- and counterfactual-supporting generalizations of the following kind: over time, and in some circumstances more than others, we should expect pressure to be exerted on behalf of practices that more adequately satisfy a criterion of rationality.

Well, if this is a potentially predictive and explanatory theory, how good is it? That is a very large question, one beyond my competence to answer. But let me note briefly three patterns in the evolution of moral norms that seem to me to bear out the predictions of this theory, subject to the sorts of qualifications that the existence of imperfections and competing mechanisms would lead one to expect. I do so with trepidation, however, for although the patterns I will discuss are gross historical trends, it is not essential to the theory that history show such trends, and it certainly is not part of the theory to endorse a set of practices or norms merely because it is a result of them.

Generality. It is a commonplace of anthropology that tribal peoples often have only one word to name both their tribe and "the people" or "humanity." Those beyond the tribe are not deemed full-fledged people, and the sorts of obligations one has toward people do not apply fully with regard to outsiders. Over the span of history, through processes that have involved numerous reversals, people have accumulated into larger social units – from the familial band to the tribe to the "people" to the nation-state – and the scope of moral categories has enlarged to follow these expanding boundaries Needless to say, this has not been a matter of the contagious spread of enlightenment. Expanding social entities frequently subjugate those incorporated within their new boundaries, and the means by which those thus oppressed have secured greater recognition of their interests have been highly conflictual, and remain – perhaps, will always remain – incomplete. Nonetheless, contemporary moral theory, and to a surprising degree contemporary moral discourse, have come to reject any limitation short of the species.

Humanization. Moral principles have been assigned various origins and natures: as commandments of supernatural origin, grounded in the will or character of a deity, to be interpreted by a priesthood; as formalistic demands of a caste-based code of honor; as cosmic principles of order; as dictates of reason or conscience that make no appeal to human inclinations or well-being; and so on. While vestiges of these views survive in contemporary moral theory, it is typical of almost the entire range of such theory, and of much of contemporary moral discourse, to make some sort of intrinsic connection between normative principles and effects on human interests. Indeed, the very emergence of morality as a distinctive subject matter apart from religion is an instance of this pattern.

Patterns of variation. In addition to seeing patterns that reflect some pressure toward the approximation of social rationality, we should expect to see greater approximation in those areas of normative regulation where the mechanisms postulated here work best, for example, in areas where almost everyone has importantly similar or mutually satisfiable interests, where almost everyone has some substantial potential to infringe upon the interests of others, where the advantages of certain forms of constraint or cooperation are highly salient even in the dynamics of small groups, and where individuals can significantly influence the likelihood of norm-following behavior on the part of others by themselves following norms. The clearest examples have to do with prohibitions of aggression and theft, and of the violation of promises. By contrast, moral questions that concern matters where there are no solutions compatible with protecting the most basic interests of all, where there exist very large asymmetries in the capacity to infringe upon interests, where the gains

or losses from particular forms of cooperation or constraint are difficult to perceive, and where individual compliance will little affect general compliance, are less likely to achieve early or stable approximation to social rationality. Clear examples here have to do with such matters as social hierarchy – for example, the permissibility of slavery, of authoritarian government, of caste or gender inequalities – and social responsibility – for example, what is the nature of our individual or collective obligation to promote the well-being of unrelated others?

Given a suitable characterization of the conditions that prevailed during the processes of normative evolution described by these patterns, the present theory claims not only that these changes could have been expected, but that an essential part of the explanation of their occurrence is a mechanism whereby individuals whose interests are denied are led to form common values and make common cause along lines of shared interests, thereby placing pressure on social practices to approximate more closely to social rationality.

These descriptions and explanations of certain prominent features of the evolution of moral norms will no doubt strike some as naive at best, plainly – perhaps even dangerously – false at worst. I thoroughly understand this. I have given impossibly sketchy, one-sided, simple-minded accounts of a very complex reality. I can only hope that these accounts will seem as believable as one could expect sketchy, one-sided, simple-minded accounts to be, and that this will make the story I have tried to tell about mechanisms and explanation more plausible.

Needless to say, the upshot is not a complacent functionalism or an overall endorsement of current moral practice or norms. Instead, the account of morality sketched here emphasizes conflict rather than equilibrium, and provides means for criticizing certain contemporary moral practices and intuitions by asking about their historical genesis. For example, if we come to think that the explanation of a common moral intuition assigns no significant role to mechanisms that could be expected to exert pressure toward socially rational outcomes, then this is grounds for questioning the intuition, however firmly we may hold it. In the spirit of a naturalized moral epistemology, we may ask whether the explanation of why we make certain moral judgments is an example of a reliable process for discovering moral facts.

V.   Limitations

[...]

A teacher of mine once remarked that the question of moral realism seemed to him to be the question whether the universe cares what we do. Since we have long since given up believing that the cosmos pays us any mind, he thought we should long since have given up moral realism. I can only agree that if this were what moral realism involved, it should – with relief rather than sorrow – be let go. However, the account offered here gives us a way of understanding how moral values or imperatives might be objective without being cosmic. They need be grounded in nothing more transcendental than facts about man and his environment, facts about what sorts of things matter to us, and how the ways we live affect these things.

Yet the present account is limited in another way, which may be of greater concern from the standpoint of contemporary moral theory: it does not yield moral imperatives that are categorical in the sense of providing a reason for action to all rational agents regardless of their contingent desires. Although troubling, this limitation is not tantamount to relativism, since on the present account rational motivation is not a precondition of moral obligation. For example, it could truthfully be said that I ought to be more generous even though greater generosity would not help me to promote my existing ends, or even to satisfy my objective interests. This could be so because what it would be morally right for me to do depends upon what is rational from a point of view that includes, but is not exhausted by, my own.

In a similar way, it could be said that I logically ought not to believe both a proposition p and a proposition that implies not-p. However, it may not be the case that every rational agent will have an instrumental reason to purge all logical contradictions from his thought. It would require vast amounts of cogitation for anyone to test all of his existing beliefs for consistency, and to insure that every newly acquired belief preserves it. Suppose someone to be so fortunate that the only contradictions among his beliefs lie deep in the much-sedimented swamp of factual trivia. Perhaps his memories of two past acquaintances have become confused in such a way that somewhere in the muck there are separate beliefs which, taken together, attribute to one individual logically incompatible properties. Until such a contradiction rears its head in practice, he may have no more reason to lay down his present concerns and wade in after it than he has to leave his home in suburban New Jersey to hunt alligators in the Okefenokee on the off chance that he might one day find himself stranded and unarmed in the backwaters of southeast Georgia.[17] What an individual rationally ought to do thus may differ from what logic requires of him. Still, we may say that logical evaluation is not subjective or arbitrary, and that good grounds of a perfectly general kind are available for being logical, namely, that logical contradictions are necessarily false and logical inferences are truth-preserving. Since in public discourse and private reflection we are often concerned with whether our thinking is warranted in a sense that is more intimately connected with its truth-conduciveness than with its instrumentality to our peculiar personal goals, it therefore is far from arbitrary that we attach so much importance to logic as a standard of criticism and self-criticism.

By parallel, if we adopt the account of moral rightness proposed above we may say that moral evaluation is not subjective or arbitrary, and that good, general grounds are available for following moral 'ought's, namely, that moral conduct is rational from an impartial point of view. Since in public discourse and private reflection we are often concerned with whether our conduct is justifiable from a general rather than merely personal standpoint, it therefore is far from arbitrary that we attach so much importance to morality as a standard of criticism and self-criticism.

The existence of such phenomena as religion and ideology is evidence for the pervasiveness and seriousness of our concern for impartial justifica-

---

[17]   It is of no importance whether we say that he has *no* reason to do this or simply a vanishingly small one. I suppose we could say that a person has a vanishingly small reason to do anything – even to expend enormous effort to purge minor contradictions from his beliefs or to purge alligators from distant swamps – that might *conceivably* turn out to be to his benefit. But then we would have no trouble guaranteeing the existence of vanishingly small reasons for moral conduct. This would allow naturalized moral rightness to satisfy a Humean thesis of practicality after all, but in a way that would rob the thesis of its interest.

tion. Throughout history individuals have sacrificed their interests, even their lives, to meet the demands of religions or ideologies that were compelling for them in part because they purported to express a universal – *the* universal – justificatory standpoint. La Rochefoucauld wrote that hypocrisy is the tribute vice pays to virtue,[18] but 'hypocrisy' suggests cynicism. We might better say that ideology is the respect partisans show to impartiality. Morality, then, is not ideology made sincere and general – ideology is intrinsically given to heart-felt generalization. Morality is ideology that has faced the facts.

I suspect the idea that moral evaluations must have categorical force for rational agents owes some of its support to a fear that were this to be denied, the authority of morality would be lost. That would be so if one held onto the claim that moral imperatives cannot exist for someone who would not have a reason to obey them, for then an individual could escape moral duties by the simple expedient of having knavish desires. But if we give up this claim about the applicability of moral judgment, then variations in personal desires cannot license exemption from moral obligation.[19]

Thus, while it certainly is a limitation of the argument made here that it does not yield a conception of moral imperatives as categorical, that may be a limitation we can live with and still accord morality the scope and dignity it traditionally has enjoyed. Moreover, it may be a limitation we must live with. For how many among us can convince ourselves that reason is other than hypothetical? Need it also be asked: How many of us old find our sense of the significance of morality or the importance of moral conduct enhanced by a demonstration that even a person with the most thoroughly repugnant ends would find that moral conduct advanced them?

One implication of what has been said is that if we want morality to be taken seriously and to have

an important place in people's lives – and not merely as the result of illusion or the threat of repression – we should be vitally concerned with the ways in which social arrangements produce conflicts of interest and asymmetries of power that affect the nature and size of the gap between what is individually and socially rational. Rather than attempt to portray morality as something that it cannot be, as "rationally compelling no matter what one's ends," we should ask how we might change the ways we live so that moral conduct would more regularly be rational given the ends we actually will have.

VI.   Summary and Conclusion

I have outlined a form of moral realism, and given some indication of how it might be defended against certain objections. Neither a full characterization of this view, nor full answers to the many objections it faces, can be given within the present essay. Perhaps then I should stop trying to say just a bit more, and close by indicating roughly what I have, and have not, attempted to show.

I have proposed what are in effect reforming naturalistic definitions of non-moral goodness and moral rightness. It is possible to respond: "Yes, I can see that such-and-such an end is an objective interest of the agent in your sense, or that such-and-such a practice is rational from an impartial point of view, but can't I still ask whether the end is good for him or the practice right?" Such "open questions" cannot by their nature be closed, since definitions are not subject to proof or disproof. But open questions may be more or less disturbing, for although definitional proposals cannot be demonstrated, they can fare better or worse at meeting various desiderata.

I have assumed throughout that the drawing up of definitions is part of theory-construction, and

---

[18]   François (duc de) la Rochefoucauld, *Réfléxions, ou sentences et maximes morales suivi de réfléxions diverses*, ed. Jean Lafond (Paris: Gallimard, 1976), p. 79. La Rochefoucauld apparently borrowed the phrase from the cleric Du Moulin. I am grateful to a remark of Barrington Moore, Jr. for reminding me of it. See his *Injustice*, p. 508.

[19]   Contrast Harman's relativism about 'ought' in *The Nature of Morality*. Harman adopts the first of the two courses just mentioned, preserving the connection between an individual's moral obligations and what he has (instrumental) reason to do. He defends his approach in part by arguing that, if we suppose that Hitler was engaged in rational pursuit of his ends, an "internal" judgment like 'Hitler (morally) ought not to have killed six million Jews' would be "weak" and "odd" compared to an "external" judgment like 'Hitler was evil' (see pp. 107 ff). I would have thought the opposite, namely, that it is too "weak" and "odd" to give an account of morality such that Hitler can be judged to be consummately evil (which Harman claims, without explanation, his brand of relativism *can* do) but in which 'Hitler (morally) ought not to have acted as he did' is false.

criteria

so is to be assessed by asking (1) whether the analyses given satisfy appropriate constraints of intelligibility and function, and (2) whether the terms as analyzed contribute to the formulation and testing of worthwhile theories. How do my proposals fit with these criteria?

(1)   Beyond constraints of intelligibility, such as clarity and non-circularity, specifically naturalistic definitions of evaluative terms should satisfy two further analytic constraints arising from their intended function. (a) They should insofar as possible capture the normative force of these terms by providing analyses that permit these terms to play their central evaluative roles. In the present setting, this involves showing that although the definitions proposed may not fit with all of our linguistic or moral intuitions, they nonetheless express recognizable notions of goodness and rightness. Further, it involves showing that the definitions permit plausible connections to be drawn between, on the one hand, what is good or right and, on the other, what characteristically would motivate individuals who are prepared to submit themselves to relevant sorts of scrutiny. (b) The naturalistic definitions should permit the evaluative concepts to participate in their own right in genuinely empirical theories. Part of this consists in showing that we have appropriate epistemic access to these concepts. Part, too, (and a related part) consists in showing that generalizations employing these concepts, among others, can figure in potentially explanatory accounts. I have tried to offer reasonably clear definitions and to show in a preliminary way how they might meet constraints (a) and (b).

(2)   However, a good deal more must be done, for it remains to show that the empirical theories constructed with the help of these definitions are reasonably good theories, that is, theories for which we have substantial evidence and which provide plausible explanations. I have tried in the most preliminary way imaginable to suggest this. If I have been wholly unpersuasive on empirical matters, then I can expect that the definitions I have offered will be equally unpersuasive.

It is an attraction for me of naturalism in ethics and epistemology alike that it thus is constrained in several significant dimensions at once. One has such ample opportunities to be shown wrong or found unconvincing if one's account must be responsive to empirical demands as well as normative intuitions. Theorizing in general is more productive when suitably constrained; in ethics especially, constraints are needed if we are to have a clearer idea of how we might make progress toward the resolution of theoretical disputes. Of course, not just any constraints will do. A proposed set of constraints must present itself as both appropriate and useful. Let me say something about (1) the utility of the constraints adopted here, and then a final word about (2) their appropriateness.

(1)   Consider three classes of competitors to the substantive moral theory endorsed above, and notice how criticisms of them *naturally* intertwine concerns about normative justification and empirical explanation. *Kantian* conceptions of morality are widely viewed as having captured certain intuitively compelling normative characteristics of such notions as rationality and moral rightness, but it seems they have done so partly at the expense of affording a plausible way of integrating these notions into an empirical account of our reasons and motives in action. Moreover, this descriptive difficulty finds direct expression on the normative side. Not only must any normative 'ought' be within the scope of an empirical 'can', but a normatively compelling 'ought' must – as recent criticisms of Kantianism have stressed – reach to the real springs of human action and concern. *Intuitionist* moral theories also enjoyed some success in capturing normative features of morality, but they have largely been abandoned for want of a credible account of the nature or operation of a faculty of moral intuition. It is too easy for us to give a non-justifying psychological explanation of the existence in certain English gentlemen of something which they identified upon introspection as a faculty of moral insight, an explanation that ties this purported faculty more closely to the rigidity of prevailing social conventions than to anything that looks as if it could be a source of universal truth. *Social choice theories* that take occurrent subjective interests or revealed preferences as given fit more readily than Kantian or intuitionist theories with empirical accounts of behavior, and, unlike them, have found a place in contemporary social science. But they suffer well-known limitations as normative theories, some of which turn out to be bound up with their limitations as explanatory theories: they lack an account of the origin or evolution of preferences, and partly for that reason are unable to capture the ways in which we evaluate purportedly rational or moral conduct by criticizing ends as well as means.

(2)   However, the issues at stake when we evaluate competing approaches to morality involve not only this sort of assessment of largish theories, but also questions about which criteria of assessment appropriately apply to definitions and theories in ethics, and about whether definitional systematization and largish theorizing are even appropriate for ethics. I am drawn to the view that the development of theory in ethics is not an artificial contrivance of philosophers but an organic result of the personal and social uses of moral evaluation: time and again individuals and groups have faced difficult questions to which common sense gave conflicting or otherwise unsatisfactory answers, and so they have pressed their questions further and pursued their inquiry more systematically. The felt need for theory in ethics thus parallels the felt need for theory in natural or social science. It does not follow from this alone that ethical theorizing must run parallel to or be integrable with theorizing in the natural and social sciences. Ethics might be deeply different. Although initially plausible and ultimately irrefutable, the view that ethics stands thus apart is one that in the end I reject. We are natural and social creatures, and I know of nowhere else to look for ethics than in this rich conjunction of facts. I have tried to suggest that we might indeed find it there.

The Authority of Reason

Jean Hampton

The Psycho-Social Thesis

[. . .]

Some theorists believe that _all_ norms, including all moral norms, are culture-dependent. Those who believe this explain the authority of all norms as (what I will call) a "psycho-social" phenomenon. Of course, a sophisticated version of this account is going to want to explain why "common sense" tells us there is a difference between (what clearly seem to be) "artificial" norms such as monopoly rules, dressage standards, and codes of etiquette on the one hand, and moral norms such as "do not murder" and "treat all people as equals." There are a number of ways to construct such a sophisticated view, and each of these I take to be a variant of the psycho-social thesis about normative authority.

First, there is the "expressivist" variant of the psycho-social thesis, a version of which has recently been propounded by Allan Gibbard. In this view, the apparently "special" authority of moral norms is (in some way) a function of how people accept them. That is, our sense of their necessity is a product of our commitment to them (but not the other way around), and thus something that we understand by investigating human psychology (including, perhaps, its socio-biological

origins) and the way it attracts us to the construction of and commitment to norms of a certain content. In this view, our sense that reasons emanating from norms have a certain compelling rightness that takes either a mandatory or a permissive form is a (mere) feeling that is attached to directives, such that we accept them, feel compelled by them, and are motivated by them. (The emotive nature of authority, on this view, allows the expressivist a natural link between authority, so understood, and motivational force.) Everything that I have said here about the authority of norms is therefore explicable in terms of theories of human psychology, sociology, and biology, which explain how our feelings become engaged by norms that are socially useful and perhaps also biologically inevitable.

Second, there is a cognitive version of the psycho-social thesis. Imagine a theorist who postulated the existence, in human brains, of a special kind of thinking. Call this "normative" thinking. In this view, characteristic of our mental life are not only desires and beliefs, but also norms and the reasons they generate. Hence, to think "I ought to do x" is to be in a distinctive cognitive state. In particular, one engages a part of the brain that "invests" normativity into a possible action, so that this authority is not a feeling but something more like a form of thought. Someone attracted to this view might also contend that usually (albeit not always) this normative state has a connection to our motivational structure, in a way that explains the sense in which we feel we can act *from* our belief that we ought to perform a certain action.

Third, there is what I will call the "error theory" variant of this view. This view, a variant of which is propounded by J. L. Mackie, explains the authority of reasons as deriving from people's acceptance of a certain kind of theory. As normative language develops, this view says that people come to develop a theory about what it means. The theory that has been current in our society is the objectivist's account of authority, as something that is independent of human psychology and culture. Because they accept such a theory, people in many cultures take what they identify as reasons to be innately compelling, such that they direct us (either via mandates or via permissions) to act in certain ways "objectively." But in fact this theory is in error, because there is no such objective authority, so that all norms and reasons are human inventions. Hence, in this view, people believe that the authority of many norms is objective because they accept a false theory – a theory whose acceptance may nonetheless be highly attractive to them (for psychological reasons). Because of this error, they behave as if they are compelled to follow what they take to be reasons, but they do so because of a deep-seated and metaphysical mistake.[1] Clearly, this version of the psycho-social thesis requires an explanation of why this mistake is so common across cultures, and why it seems to persist despite the efforts of so many naturalists (such as Mackie) to "expose" it.

All these versions of the psycho-social thesis accept the same basic strategy for explaining the authority of reasons – that authority is understood to be merely in the head (explicated as a feeling, or a cognitive state, or a theoretical belief), and its origins are explicable by virtue of human psychology, human biology, and/or human sociology.

The Objectivist Thesis

[. . .]

The moral objectivist maintains that the authority of a moral norm does not merely consist in you or your society *thinking* that you have such a reason.

Nor does she believe that you only "have" the reason if you happen to be aware of, or know about it. Instead, she will insist that its authority is "objective," which means that the reason it gives you in the circumstances that it specifies holds for you no matter the social or psychological conditions. Hence it is a reason applicable to your deliberations, a consideration relevant to your acting, choosing, and believing, and a decisive consideration in the circumstances it specifies. It is at this point that the objectivist resorts to the term 'necessity' to describe the nature of the authority of such a norm. To say that this reason holds, no matter the social or psychological contingencies, is, one might think, to say that it holds necessarily. To put it more precisely, for as long as we are moral agents – that is, subjects to whom moral reasons apply (leaving aside for now the criteria specifying moral agency) – the moral objectivist claims that the reasons given us by moral norms are reasons that we have necessarily, no matter the state of our psychology, our profession or interests, the views of our society, or our metaphysical or religious commitments. Whether or not we also have motives by virtue of knowing these reasons, whether or not they are decisive in the circumstances, and whether or not we have committed ourselves to them so thoroughly that we find it is impossible not to comply with them, these reasons direct us, or oblige us. Note that this thesis is separate from a thesis about motivation. When a moral objectivist says that someone "has" a moral reason, he is not saying that ipso facto this person has a motivation sufficient to move him to act from that reason if he knows of it. As I have discussed in the last chapter [Omitted here. Eds.], moral objectivists can disagree on the extent to which reasons have motivational efficacy.

[. . .]

How the Objectivist's 'Ought' Violates the Strictures of Science

[. . .]

What does a moral objectivist have to say about reasons in order to have a theory that is genuinely objectivist? As I pointed out in the last section, she must say, first of all, that there exist norms gener-

---

[1]   See J. L. Mackie *Ethics: Inventing Right and Wrong* (New York: Penguin, 1977), chapter 1.

ating reasons to act that are directives applying to her no matter the contingencies of her situation. Second, she must say that these reasons, along with their authority, can be known by agents (for what would be the point of a theory that recognized these reasons, but despaired of our ability to know them)? Third, she must say that it is at least possible for us sometimes to act "on" or "for the sake of" the reason, as when we say that "Elizabeth acted on her duty to visit Aunt Ethel in the Hospital" or "Jane interfered with Albert's behavior because she thought it was her duty to stop cruelty to animals." To quote Kant, "Everything in nature works in accordance with laws. Only a rational being has the power to act *in accordance with his idea of* laws – that is, in accordance with principles – and only so has he a will."[2] As Kant appreciates, acting on a (moral) law is not like being caused to act by a (physical) law. One might say that a reason is not a causal push, but a "compelling pull," which compulsion is nonetheless something that an agent can choose to resist or defy.

[. . .]

So does science permit explanations that rely on the idea of objective normative authority? As I reviewed in chapter 1 [Omitted here. Eds.], there is no consensus at all in the philosophical community on any substantive conception of the natural, nor any consensus on what science is, such that this enterprise, so defined, could be taken to define the natural. But I want to propose a very basic tenet that is at least a necessary (albeit perhaps not a sufficient) condition of a theory such that it can be considered scientific – which is that such a theory never invoke the Aristotelian idea of final causes in any way. The explanations of science, even though they can take many forms (sometimes causal, sometimes not, sometimes mathematical, sometimes not) nonetheless do not take, and cannot take (on pain of being unscientific), a form that relies on the idea that any object in the world acts for the sake of something else, or has a goal or proper place, to which it tends in its motion.

An explanation in terms of final causes has three components. First, it assumes that there is a certain place, state of affairs, or kind of motion that is appropriate or "fitting" for an object. This place, state of affairs, or movement is thought to have

some kind of compelling rightness. The world is therefore conceived to be so arranged that there are states of being that are appropriate or right for various sorts of objects.

Second, this explanation assumes that the object whose movement or state is to be explained is in some way able to respond to this compelling rightness. This response needn't take the form of being conscious of that rightness, and thus does not assume any agency on behalf of the object. So, for example, the Aristotelians didn't think that when stones fell to the earth (which was thought to be their proper place), they consciously sought the earth because they understood that it was their proper place. Nonetheless, the fact that this was the place where they belonged was assumed to be something that the stones were constructed to be sensitive to. Similarly, planets were thought to be constructed such that they were sensitive to the requirement that their movement be circular, yet without being conscious of this requirement.

Third, a final-cause explanation assumes that the object's state or movement could be explained by appealing to its sensitivity to this compelling rightness. The object was thought to move or change, for the sake of attaining that state, or undertaking that movement, which was appropriate or fitting for it.

In rejecting all manifestations of Aristotelian science, naturalists in the modern era insist that we understand the behavior of any object in the world in a way that rejects the possibility of Aristotelian final causes. This eschewal is consistent with more than one way of conceptualizing the kind of explanation that is characteristic of science. Some will believe that it is an eschewal that is best understood in terms of a cause-and-effect model of scientific explanations (perhaps best realized in mechanistic explanations). Others (often for Humean reasons) dislike the idea of causation, and seek to understand scientific explanations so as to avoid this term (and in a way that will accommodate the strange and very nonmechanistic scientific theories of the twentieth century, such as quantum mechanics). *But both groups are committed to explanations that deny the possibility that an object moves for the sake of something else that compels it to do so by virtue of its "rightness" that it can somehow sense.* I take this to be definitive of the scientific point of view.

---

2   Kant, *Groundwork of the Metaphysics of Morals* (1785), chapter 2, p. 80.

[. . .]

As I noted, this rejection is only a necessary and not a sufficient condition of something's being a scientific explanation. I will not attempt to articulate sufficient conditions here, nor is there any widely accepted list of such conditions extant in the literature at present. But this one necessary condition is enough to rule out any moral objectivist's explanations that rely on moral reasons held to have objective authority. This is because an explanation of an agent's behavior that appeals to objectively authoritative reasons is an instance of a final-cause explanation. Such an appeal assumes, first, that there is a course of action that "ought to be"; second, that the human being can sense the rightness of that course of action; and third, that she can act for the sake of this rightness. So, if to be scientific, one must repudiate final cause explanations, then one must also repudiate the moral objectivist's explanations that invoke the objective authority of moral reasons. Thus, if Sally visits Aunt Ethel in the hospital because, as she puts it, "I have a duty to do so," we cannot think that it is an adequate explanation of her behavior to posit a compelling rightness in the world for the sake of which she acted, any more than we could think that there was a compelling rightness to iron filings' being close to magnet that explained why they were attracted to the magnet.

This doesn't mean that naturalists have to give up the language of reasons. Given the serviceability of this language in our daily lives, naturalists will probably want to find a place for talk of reasons and goals, and "for the sake of" explanations. (They may or may not believe that such talk is compatible with the idea that human beings have free will; that depends on other philosophical commitments they have.) But to be consistent with the assumptions of science, such an accommodation has to be made in a way that rejects the idea that there could be culture-independent authoritative directives for the sake of which we act, since science rejects the possibility of final-cause explanations. (So, for example, reasons might be construed as a type of belief with a "felt" rightness traceable to the operation of psychology or culture, but they cannot be construed as directives whose authority exists independent of this psychology or culture.

A moral objectivist might protest that science is only justified in rejecting final–case explanations for the movement of objects other than human beings.

By this view, human beings are different – uniquely nonmechanistic elements in an otherwise mechanized universe. The naturalist will, however, reject what he will regard as a hubristic picture, on the grounds that there are no reasons to justify treating ourselves as exceptions. Particularly because the science of biology struggled, and eventually succeeded, in ridding itself of the language of final-cause explanations in the nineteenth century, naturalists will argue that this exception is unjustified. If the operation of every other living creature on earth can be explained without resorting to final causes, why shouldn't such explanations suffice for human beings? The moral objectivist's plea to think of us as different and special looks like a plea for using an outmoded and ultimately unsuccessful pattern of explanation in the face of a new and far more successful way of conceiving of ourselves.

One last aside: The idea of objective authority also clashes with methodological naturalism. For how could such authority be detected by the empirical methods of science? We can probably explain how we could think such a thing, but how could we *find* it in the world? Using what tool or scientific device? It isn't difficult to understand this authority as *felt*, but the idea that there is something beyond what is felt, to which we are responding when we say we have a reason, presupposes that we have a tool by which to find it. But what tool or human sense could that be? Even those whose naturalism is purely methodological seem to have good reason to reject the idea of objective moral authority.

Conclusion

At last we have located the idea within the moral objectivist's theory that cannot pass scientific muster. It is the idea that there exist reasons with objective authority, about which we can know, and for the sake of which we can act. Such an idea cannot be developed with any precision, because neither the source of these directives nor their authority over us can be plausibly explained. Even more importantly, explanations that invoke the idea of objective authority violate science's strictures against final cause explanations. So for anyone who is committed to offering only explanations that are both consistent with the assumptions of science and rigorously intelligible in their own right, the moral objectivist's explanations will clearly not do.

Ethics as Philosophy: A Defense of Ethical Nonnaturalism

Russ Shafer-Landau

Ethical nonnaturalism has long been out of favor. I believe that it is due a re-appraisal.

The nonnaturalism that I endorse is a brand of moral realism. As I understand it, moral realism is the view that says that most moral judgments are beliefs, some of which are true, and, when true, are so by virtue of correctly representing the existence of truth-markers for their respective contents. Further, and crucially, true moral judgments are made true in some way other than by virtue of attitudes taken towards their content by any actual or idealized human agent.

Not all nonnaturalisms are realistic – Kantian views, for instance, reject the assimilation of moral to natural properties, and yet also reject realism. I will proceed on the assumption (unargued here) that realism is the best path for nonnaturalists.[1] After describing nonnaturalism, and identifying the most serious worries that face it, I will undertake a partial defense against a number of those problems. My preferred strategy for doing so invokes a parallel between philosophy in general, and ethics in particular. My contention is that once we pay special attention to this relationship, a number of the traditional concerns about nonnaturalism begin to seem less pressing than they have for a long while.

I. The Nature of Nonnaturalism

Ethical nonnaturalism is, first and foremost, a metaphysical doctrine. It claims that there are instantiated moral properties that are not natural properties.

There are instantiated moral properties: this element distinguishes nonnaturalism from all forms of moral nihilism.[2] Moral nihilism is the view that either there are no moral properties, or there are, but none that are ever exemplified. Nonnaturalism asserts the existence of moral properties – there really is such a thing as being (e.g.)

---

[1] I argue against alternatives to realism in part I of *Moral Realism: A Defence* (Oxford: Clarendon Press, 2003). Many of the ideas that appear in this essay receive much fuller development in that book. I have also appropriated a couple of sentences from my *Whatever Happened to Good and Evil?* (New York: Oxford University Press, 2004). My thanks to the Press for permission to rely on this material here.

[2] The following, in my book, all qualify as versions of nihilism: emotivism (e.g., Ayer 1936; Stevenson 1937, 1948), prescriptivism (Hare 1952, 1963, 1989), expressivism (Blackburn 1993, 1998; Gibbard 1990), assertoric nondescriptivism (Timmons 1999; Skorupski 1999), and error theories (Mackie 1977; Garner 1994; Joyce 2001).

morally forbidden, or morally good – and asserts, too, that these properties are sometimes realized by actions, motives, states of affairs, etc.

Nonnaturalism *per se* is, in two respects, neutral as to the exact nature of moral properties. It is first of all ecumenical regarding the conditions under which these properties are instantiated. Many substantive normative ethical theories are compatible with a nonnaturalistic metaphysics. And, second, nonnaturalism is compatible with any number of specific views about what a property is. Nonnaturalists can await a verdict from the metaphysicians on this question, and incorporate their best answer into a comprehensive metaethic.

Ethical nonnaturalism is true only if moral properties are not natural properties. There is no agreement on what makes a property a natural one. The criteria that immediately come to mind – a property is natural in virtue of its being instantiated nonconventionally, materially, or tangibly, or being describable without reliance on evaluative vocabulary – will not do. If nonnaturalists are right, then morality is not conventional. That doesn't make them naturalists. Some paradigmatically natural properties are realized nonmaterially (e.g., being a vacuum). Not every realization of a natural property is tangible – one can't literally touch a muon or a gluon. And, as Nicholas Sturgeon rightly points out in a recent essay (2003), one can't always tell a natural property by the vocabulary in which it is described. If naturalists are correct, then moral worth, virtue and rightness are natural properties, though all are surely also evaluative notions. The debate between naturalists and nonnaturalists cannot be solved just by noting salient features of the terms we use to describe it.

I suggest that we take a different tack, that of offering a disciplinary conception. The natural is whatever is the object of study by the natural sciences. The obvious problem of having just pushed the definitional problem back a step is usually solved by defining the natural sciences ostensively: something is natural just in case it figures inelimiminably in true propositions that emerge from (on some accounts, the perfected versions of) physics, chemistry, molecular biology, astronomy, etc. Leave astrology off that list. Film studies, too.

It would be nice to have an account of what makes a natural science natural. This for two reasons. First, we'll want to know how to fill in that 'etc.', especially for contentious cases. And ethics is likely to be among the most contentious. But,

second, we presumably don't want to limit the natural domain to the things studied by (even perfected versions of) the sciences we now recognize – we want to allow for the emergence of natural sciences that we haven't yet dreamed of.

I don't think that ethics is a natural science. Its fundamental principles are not inductive generalizations. It is not primarily concerned with causal efficacy. Its central principles are not descriptive of historical contingencies. The phenomena it does describe are supervenient as a matter of conceptual requirement. It allows for a much greater degree of indeterminacy and vagueness than is found in typical natural sciences. It has only a very little concern for mathematical quantification and precision. Unlike any of the recognized sciences, its truths are normative truths that direct, guide, and evaluate, rather than (in the first instance) predict the course of future events or explain what has already occurred. Moral truths provide justifying reasons that are often ignored. Physics and geology and hydrology don't do that.

Of course, ethical naturalism may be correct even if ethics is not a science. Ethical naturalism is true so long as moral properties are the proper object of natural scientific study. They might be, even if ethics isn't the science that does the studying.

But if ethics isn't the relevant science, then what is? Sociology and psychology, if we admit them into the pantheon, might do yeoman's work – they will be required to aid us, for instance, in determining how many people are made happy by various actions, or what it was that actually motivated agents to do what they did. All quite helpful information. But neither sociology nor psychology, nor any other science that I know of, will do much to fix the content of our fundamental moral principles. That is the job of ethics proper.

Suppose my truncated case against the scientific status of ethics is way off base. So let us grant, provisionally, that ethics is a science. Still, is it a natural science? We might, for instance, also allow mathematics to qualify as a science. But not many think of it as a natural science. What explains this, it seems to me, is the nature of mathematical investigation. Mathematics is done in a largely *a priori* fashion. And this leads us to the following thought: a science is a natural science just in case its fundamental principles are discoverable *a posteriori*, through reliance primarily on empirical evidence.

Any definition of naturalism is bound to be to some extent stipulative. Yet this characterization is true to all instances of avowed ethical naturalism that I know of, and does seem to capture what many have thought to be essential to the classification. But notice, now, that the difference between naturalists and nonnaturalists, usually taken to be a metaphysical one, turns out on this accounting to be epistemological. Ethical nonnaturalists are those who claim that moral properties are not natural ones. This means, on the present understanding, that fundamental moral truths are discoverable *a priori*. If I am right, prospects for nonnaturalism depend crucially on the possibility of gaining such knowledge.

It isn't my intention here to offer a direct defense of *a priori* moral knowledge.[3] Instead, I will present some ancillary arguments that constitute an invitation to see ethical inquiry as importantly dissimilar from empirical, natural scientific investigation. The rationale and the structure of these supporting arguments is best appreciated by noting the similarities between philosophy and one of its subdisciplines – ethics.

II.   Ethics as Philosophy

Ethics is a branch of philosophy. Few would dispute that. Yet this fact has significant, wide-ranging implications, many of which have gone little noticed in debates about the status of ethical judgments. My central claim is that there are very close parallels between ethical investigation and that pursued in philosophy quite generally. These parallels provide excellent reason for rejecting some of the perennial criticisms that ethical nonnaturalism has faced.

I locate the central claim within a central argument. Here it is:

1   Ethics is a species of inquiry; philosophy is its genus.
2   A species inherits the essential traits of its genus.
3   There are (among others) two essential traits of philosophy: the realistic status of its truths, and its status as something other than a natural science.
4   Therefore nonnaturalistic ethical realism is true.

Both premise (1) and premise (2) strike me as extremely plausible – so plausible, in fact, that I will proceed here by assuming, rather than arguing for, their truth. As for (3), I will say something (but not nearly enough) to defend the claim that philosophy is something other than a natural science. I will say a good deal more about why we should construe philosophical truths realistically.

To see ethics as philosophy is to appreciate a certain kind and degree of methodological similarity. Philosophy is not primarily an empirical discipline, but an *a priori* one. Its truths are ordinarily discoverable, when they are, not exclusively by appeal to what our senses can tell us. We don't bump into such things as universals, free will, or modalities; we can't see them, or hear or touch them. We may have reason to deny the existence of such things, but not because we aren't sure what they taste like. Dismissing such things from our ontology, or ratifying their inclusion in it, is something that no scientist is able to do. Such things are dealt with in an *a priori* way.

Substantiating the claim that fundamental philosophical truths are *a priori* is work for a paper unto itself (at the least). This isn't that paper. Yet this claim about philosophy, while contentious, isn't on the face of it that implausible. Of course there are those who deny the very possibility or existence of *a priori* knowledge. But for all others, basic philosophical principles should be quite attractive candidates. Philosophy must run a close second to mathematics as an exemplar of an *a priori* discipline (if indeed there are any such exemplars). Part of this is explicable by reference to the metaphysically or conceptually necessary status of the principles that are the object of philosophical investigation. And part of this is explicable by reflection on cases. Consider for a moment Leibniz's law of the indiscernibility of identicals, or the modal principle that anything that is necessary is possibly necessary. These certainly don't seem to be inductive generalizations, or conclusions of inferences to the best explanation. The role of sensory evidence in establishing such claims is peripheral, at best. I might be mistaken about this, and nothing to come will absolutely protect against this possibility. But the view that makes the justification of such principles a matter of empirical confirmation is (much) more contentious than the one I am prepared to rely on.

---

[3]   I offer a somewhat programmatic defense in *Moral Realism*, ch. 11. See also Audi 1997, 1999, 2004, and the fine collection edited by Stratton-Lake (2002).

As ethics is a branch of philosophy, we have excellent reason to think that fundamental ethical principles share the same status as fundamental philosophical principles. When we want to know whether something is right or wrong, admirable or vicious, we will certainly want to know what's going on in the world. The evidence of our senses may tell us that happiness has been maximized, or that the words of a promise have been uttered, but that's only the beginning, not the end, of our ethical investigations. When trying to verify the basic standards that govern the application of moral predicates, we will only secondarily (if at all) advert to what the physicists and botanists and hydrologists say. The conditions under which actions are right, and motives and characters good, aren't confirmed by the folks with lab coats. They are confirmed, if at all, by those who think philosophically. And much of that thinking, especially when focused on nonderivative, core principles, is undertaken without clear reliance on what we can see, or hear, or touch.

Since doing ethics is doing a kind of philosophy, we shouldn't be surprised at the similarities just mentioned. In what follows, I will rely on the parallels between the species (ethics) and its genus (philosophy) in a way that aids nonnaturalist realists in answering three of the most pressing objections against their views.

The first objection says that the intractability of ethical disagreement sustains an antirealist diagnosis of ethical thought and talk. The second criticism claims that this disagreement in any event undermines any justified belief we may have for our moral views, provided that they are meant to tell us about how the world really is. The third asserts that the causal inefficacy of moral facts provides excellent reason to deny their existence. These aren't the only criticisms that nonnaturalists have faced,[4] but they are among the most important. I think that they can be met. That is work enough for a day, if it can be accomplished.

III.   Moral Disagreements as a Metaphysical Objection

Nonnaturalism stands for the idea that there are nonscientific moral properties. But if there are such things, why is there so much disagreement about them? Many believe that objective properties of any kind must be such as to garner consensus about (the conditions of) their instantiation, at least among people who are well situated to appreciate such things. But it doesn't take an expert to realize that such consensus is extremely elusive in ethics. So persistent moral disagreement presents us with a choice. Perhaps there are no (instantiated) moral properties at all. Or there are, but ones that are not objective – rather, they are constituted by partial or parochial human attitudes. As such, the conditions of their instantiation, and the instantiations themselves, would presumably be empirically verifiable, at least in principle. Either way, the nonnaturalist loses.

There are really two ways to run this skeptical argument, though they usually remain entangled in the literature. One is as an argument that seeks to draw an inference to the best explanation, the explananda being the scope of actual ethical disagreement we see in our world. The second is as an a priori argument, that has us anticipating persistent disagreement even among hypothetical, idealized moral deliberators. In both cases, the presence of intractable disagreement is said to be sufficient to draw an antirealist conclusion: there are no real, objective moral standards that could serve as guideposts to our moral investigations. In ethics, we make it all up.

The first version of the argument, as an inference to the best explanation, is inconclusive at best. Certainly there is intractable moral disagreement – plenty of it. But just as surely, such disagreement might be well explained as a product of insufficient nonmoral information, or adequate information insufficiently "processed." Such processing failures cover a wide range of cases, from errors of instrumental reasoning, to a failure of nerve, sympathy, empathy, or imagination. One explanation (not the only one) of these errors is that there's typically much more personally at stake in ethical matters than in scientific ones, and these stakes tend to introduce biasing factors that skew correct perception. It may be that for any given real-world ethical disagreement, we could cite at least one of these failings as an explanation for its continued existence.

I think that one's expectation of (lack of) consensus is largely an expression of one's antecedent metaethical commitments, rather than anything

---

[4]   See the introduction to this section of the book for discussion of other such criticisms.

that could serve as an independent argument in this context. Imagine away all of the failings mentioned in the previous paragraph: will there or won't there be any disagreement left to threaten moral realism? I'm not sure. If not, then the realist can rest easy. But suppose disagreement persists, even in the counterfactual situation in which we rid our agents of the flaws that impede correct moral reasoning. Even here, however, realists can sustain their view with a minimum of damage. They will have to say that impeccable reasoning may nevertheless fail to land on the truth. There can be a gap between epistemic accessibility and truth. If we are to posit an absence of consensus even among perfected inquirers, then the idealized picture of moral inquirers will fail to guard against their fallibility.

At this point we can introduce the ethics–philosophy parallel and use it to defend nonnaturalism from the argument from disagreement. The breadth and depth of philosophical disagreement is just as great as that found within ethics (perhaps greater). There's still no consensus on the merits of compatibilism, the analysis of knowledge, or the relation of the mental and the physical. Nor is there broad agreement about which methods are needed to unequivocally confirm the right answers for us.

If the intractability of disagreement in an area is best explained by antirealist assumptions about its status, then we must be global philosophical antirealists. The judgments we render, and the arguments we offer on their behalf, must all be seen either as incapable of truth, as expressions of conative commitments only, or as claims whose truth is contingent on personal or interpersonal endorsement. But that's not a very plausible take on the status of our philosophical views. There is a truth – a real, objective truth – about whether the mental is identical to the physical, or about whether certain kinds of freedom are compatible with determinism. Once we are sure of terms and concepts, the judgments that affirm or deny the existence of such things are literally either true or false, in as robust a sense as we can imagine. We don't have the final say about the truth of such judgments, and the content of these judgments is indeed something other than whatever conative or practical commitments contingently accompany them.

I invite you to reflect on the status of the philosophical judgments you hold most dear, and have worked most carefully to defend. Do you imagine that your views, and their supporting arguments, are either untrue, or possessed of only the sort of minimal truth that is attainable by having been sincerely endorsed from within a parochial perspective? No matter how skeptical you might be about some alleged philosophical entities (universals, free will, or moral facts), you presumably take your confident opinions about such matters as having registered a real truth, one that is a function neither of your attitudes towards it, nor of the language you have used to comprehend it. That truth, you believe, is independent of the circle you inhabit, the agreements you've entered, the conventions you are part of, and the era in which you find yourself.

And yet one's philosophical views are bound to be as controversial as one's ethical views. Disagreements in core (and peripheral) philosophical areas are apparently intractable. Empirical evidence hasn't yet been able to solve any major philosophical problem, and any prediction that it someday might is as likely to divide philosophers as any other philosophical question. If intractable disagreement about verdicts and methods is enough to warrant an antirealist diagnosis of an area, then the whole of philosophy must be demoted. That simply is implausible: there really is (or isn't) such as thing as probabilistic causation, numbers without spatio-temporal location, actions that are both free and determined, etc. My say-so doesn't make it so. Neither does anyone else's.

The philosophical stance that denies the existence of nonnatural moral properties is itself the subject of intractable disagreement. If such disagreement is sufficient to undermine the realistic status of the controversial judgments, then the views of the ethical naturalist or moral antirealist cannot be objectively correct. They are either untrue, or are true reports of the attitudes they themselves take toward nonnaturalism, or are noncognitive expressions that reflect their own practical commitments. If they are *any* of those things, then they cannot rationally command the allegiance of their detractors. Nonnaturalists needn't be making any error when rejecting such views.

The alternative is to see our beliefs about such matters as aspiring to, and possibly succeeding in, representing a philosophical reality not of our own making. This reality is constituted by a set of truths whose alethic status is independent of our endorsement of their content. And this despite the presence of intractable philosophical disagreement.

Of course, one might say that were we free of the shortcomings that beset all of us actual inquirers, we would converge on a set of philosophical claims about free will, causation, etc. The disputes that seem to us so intractable would vanish with more information, more efficient and comprehensive application of that information, etc. That may be so. But then we have every reason to render the same verdict in the ethical case. Since ethics is a branch of philosophy, it would be very surprising to come to any other conclusion.

In other words, even if, at the end of the day, there is (much) more disagreement within ethics than there is in science, this is hardly probative evidence for the falsity of nonnaturalism. For there is just as likely to be (much) more disagreement in philosophy generally than there is in science. That doesn't license a verdict of global philosophical antirealism. It certainly doesn't license us in the claim that philosophy is a natural science. So long as it is true (as almost every working philosopher presupposes) that there is an objectively correct view about central philosophical puzzles, then we have just as much reason to accord the same status to ethical matters. We will have our opinions about such matters, but they are ultimately answerable to a truth not of our own making. Things are no different in ethics.

IV.   Moral Disagreement as an Epistemic Defeater

For any nontrivial moral view one holds, there are bound to be others who disagree with it. This very fact is probably not enough to undermine any epistemic justification one may have for the belief. One might, after all, be unaware of the disagreement, and this ignorance might be non-culpable. Yet what of the ordinary situation, where we realize that our own moral views fail to command universal allegiance? Suppose not only that you know of such disagreement, but that you also rightly believe that your opponents, reasoning correctly from their own incompatible but justified beliefs, will never come over to your side. What does that do to the status of your own beliefs?

As I see it, such awareness does not, by itself, constitute a defeater of one's views. It does not entail that one ought to suspend judgment about what one believes. For one may well think – and this is the usual case – that one has justifying reasons that the other is failing to appreciate. That she is reasoning impeccably from her own starting points does not mean that her beliefs must be true, for her starting points may be way off base. And, as you will see things, they almost certainly are.

Surely it is possible that any defense you offer of your contested views will invoke other beliefs that are as controversial as the ones you are intending to support. In fact, this happens all the time in moral discussions. Perhaps, for many such cases, there is nothing one can do but beg the question. And question-begging arguments never confer justification.

There are two things to say here. First, one's belief might continue to be justified, even if defending it to others has one begging questions. A belief's justification is distinct from an agent's ability to justify it to others. So long as the belief was initially justified, it is possible that its justification survives, despite an agent's inability to advance considerations that an audience finds compelling. (Someone rightly convinced that tomatoes are fruits might be justified in her belief, even if she's unable to bring others around to the idea.) Second, there is excellent reason to believe that the presence of another's incompatible, justified belief doesn't always undermine justification; indeed, there might even be a case for thinking that question-begging arguments can supply positive justification for one's contested beliefs.

We can see this with the help of a series of examples. Suppose that you are engaged in conversation with a principled fanatic. He thinks that the fundamental ethical imperative is to gain power over others; everything else is subsidiary to this primary goal. Any argument you offer for beneficence is bound to be treated as the product of an effective brainwashing. Nothing you can say will convince him. Moreover, suppose that he's not contradicting himself, and isn't making any false empirical claims to support his ultimate principle. In the context of your conversation, you are bound to beg the question.

But you might be justified in your beliefs anyway. For the presence of an intelligent, consistent, and indefatigable opponent does not necessary undermine a belief that one is otherwise justified in holding. This is a general point. It holds for one's ethical views, but also for perceptual, memorial, and philosophical ones, as well.

To simplify, consider a case in which one's perceptual beliefs later form the basis of a memorial belief. I saw and remember talking to my hated nemesis Smith the moment before he made that fatal misstep that no one else witnessed. I try to convince others of what I have seen, and am met with disbelief. They know of our rivalry, and they think I killed him. (Suppose I've done just that in other, similar cases.) That others have excellent reason to doubt my word is compatible with my original belief, and its memorial descendant, both being highly justified. In this case, not only do the incompatible, well-justified beliefs of others fail to undermine my justification, but my own question-begging attitudes (e.g., regarding my own innocence in this case) do appear to be enough to constitute positive justification for the beliefs I hold.

We can broaden the picture in an obvious way. Informed, rational, and attentive skeptics, possessed of internally consistent and coherent attitudes, might remain unconvinced by any of our empirical claims. According to this version of the argument from disagreement, that resistance defeats any justification we might have for our empirical beliefs. Though we can't absolutely discount that possibility, the conclusion is so drastic as to call into question the soundness of the argument that generated it. If we assume, as everyone reading this will, that we do have some positively justified empirical beliefs, then, so far as I can tell, it follows that question-begging grounds can confer positive justification. For anything one might cite as evidence on behalf of one's empirical beliefs will surely be regarded as question-begging by the skeptic.

A similar story can be told regarding all of our philosophical beliefs. The most brilliant philosophers, rational, open-minded, and well-informed, have failed to agree amongst themselves on just about every key philosophical issue. If pervasive and intractable disagreement signaled an absence of justification, this would mean that none of those philosophers (much less the rest of us) would be at all justified in holding the philosophical views that they (we) do. But this seems false; it's certainly belied by anyone who actually undertakes sincerely to argue philosophically. One who has developed a theoretically sophisticated take on some philosophical issue, coming to grips with deep criticisms

and developing novel and integrated positive proposals, is surely justified to some extent in thinking her views correct. Of course such a person will see that some others will fail to be convinced – even some others who are as smart, ingenious, and imaginative as she is. She will recognize her fallibility and appreciate a salient feature of philosophical history – namely, the failure of greater minds to attract even near-unanimity on most of the major points that they had advanced. Still, awareness of this history, and the skepticism of some of her contemporaries, is not enough to force her to suspend judgment on the views that she has so skillfully defended.

I see no reason to register a different verdict for ethics. Deep disagreement there, as elsewhere, should give one pause. It can sap one's confidence, and if it does, then that (but not the disagreement *per se*) may be sufficient to undercut one's justification. But this is no different from the general case. Provided that one brings to a dispute a moral belief that is justified, then exposure to conflicting belief needn't defeat one's justification, even if one is unable to convince an intelligent other of the error of his ways.

The present argument against the epistemic justification of moral belief relies on the following principle (or something very like it):

(E) If (i) S believes that p, and R believes that not-p, and (ii) S and R know of this disagreement, and (iii) S and R have formed their beliefs in rational and informed ways, then S is not justified in a belief that p, and R is not justified in a belief that not-p.

(E) may be true. But no one could be justified in believing it. (E) itself is the subject of intractable disagreement – there are informed and rational people who endorse it, and equally qualified agents who reject it. By its own lights, then, we must suspend judgment about (E). Having done that, however, we are no longer epistemically forbidden from positively embracing a contested belief, even if our opponents are as smart we as are.

We can reveal another kind of skeptical self-defeat if we renew our emphasis on establishing a parity between ethical investigation and philosophical investigations generally. A familiar skeptical line is that there isn't, really, any adequate evidence that can be called upon to support our ethical opinions. Unlike empirical investigations, we haven't anything tangible that can, at the end of the day, finally settle a disputed moral question. All the sensory evidence at our disposal will underdetermine an ethical verdict. And what's left? Only our emotional responses and our moral convictions, both of which are traceable to accidents of birth and upbringing. Their genesis marks them as unreliable indicators of any truth there might be. But there's nothing else to rely on in ethics. And therefore our moral views lack justification, one and all.

The problem with such an argument should by now be apparent. There is a striking equivalence between the nature and source of our evidence in philosophy, and in ethics. We have no choice but to rely on our intuitions and considered judgments in both. What tells us, for example, that many proposed analyses of knowledge are no good is not some empirical finding that scientists have unearthed. It is instead our conceptual intuitions about counter-examples. If we want to know whether determinism is compatible with free will, we will consult arguments that invariably appeal to our intuitive responses to hypothetical cases. If such convictions and responses have no evidential credibility, then we should have to regard all philosophical beliefs as unjustified. Perhaps they are. But then those of the ethical naturalist, and the moral antirealist, are similarly undone.

V. The Causal Inefficacy of Moral Facts

Gilbert Harman (1977: ch. 1 [included as chapter 25 in the present volume]) has famously charged that moral facts are causally inert, and are therefore best construed antirealistically. His brief remarks have inspired a minor cottage industry, most of whose workers, it seems to me, are headed in the wrong direction. Rather than try to establish that point with a survey of the literature, I will try for the larger picture, with the aim of arguing that Harman's basic line of attack is misdirected.

Harman doesn't put things in quite this way, but I think his position, and that of many who take his lead, can be accurately captured in the following argument:

1 If something exists, and its existence is best construed realistically, then it must possess independent causal powers.

2 Moral facts possess no independent causal powers.

3 Therefore either moral facts don't exist, or their existence isn't best construed realistically.

Harman himself believes in moral facts, though he regards them as artifacts of social agreements. He is an ethical relativist, not a realist.

Since the argument is valid, any realist must choose either or both of the premises to come in for criticism. I opt for (1), because I suspect that (2) is true. A property has independent causal powers only if its instantiation by itself has causal implications, apart from the instantiation of any other properties it may in an instance depend on or be realized by. I'm not confident that moral facts possess such powers.

I won't try to vindicate my lack of confidence here. If it is misplaced, then so much the better for moral realism. Moral properties would possess independent causal power, and thereby pass the most stringent test for ontological inclusion. But let's instead imagine that my suspicion is correct, and that we are thus placed in what many have considered a worst-case scenario: trying to defend the existence of moral properties, realistically construed, while acknowledging that they are fundamentally different in kind from the properties whose existence is ratified by the natural sciences. If I am right, then such things as a benefactor's generosity, a regime's injustice, a friend's thoughtfulness, are causes (if they are) only by virtue of inheriting the causal powers of the properties that realize them at a time. Any causal power they have is exhausted by that of the subvening properties that fix a situation's moral character. Nothing follows from this admission unless we are also prepared to insist on a causal test of ontological credibility, of the sort espoused in Harman's first premise.

Such a test is powerfully motivated, but is ultimately resistible. This test is an application of Occam's razor, and is responsible for our having pared down our ontology in many sensible ways. We're quite finished with explanations that invoke Osiris or golems or centaurs, and Occam's razor is responsible for that. All that these entities were once invoked to explain can be more parsimoniously explained by relying on properties whose existence is vindicated through scientific confirmation. And such confirmation makes essential reference to a putative entity's causal powers.

So out with the trolls, the ancient pantheon, and the vampires. That's not so bad, is it? Such things aren't required to explain the goings-on in our world. But then, by my admission, neither are moral facts. So, by parity of reasoning, either we keep moral facts, but at the expense of a bloated ontology that implausibly lets these minor supernatural agents sneak back in, or we abolish the lot of them. Why should morality get special treatment here, when, as we all agree, the causal test has done its good work in so many other areas? Very conveniently for me, I don't have the time in this context to provide the full answer to this question.[5] But in lieu of that long story, let me offer a brief reply, and then a longer one that invokes the ethics–philosophy parallel that I have already relied on.

The brief reply: application of the causal test has highly counter-intuitive implications. This is so on two assumptions: first, that only physical properties possess independent causal powers, and second, that at least most of the properties of the special sciences are not identical to, but only supervenient upon, those of physics. From these assumptions, allied with the causal test, it follows that nothing exists but (roughly) atoms and the void. There certainly won't be any such things as atmospheres, rock strata, newts, and dandelions, if we grant that such things are not type-identical to anything referred to in a physics journal. It seems to me that such things do exist, and are multiply realizable by, rather than identical to, particular physical properties. Thus the causal test eliminates too much from our ontology.

Suppose that doesn't faze you – you can live with such a parsimonious ontology, or you don't endorse one of the two assumptions that got us there.[6] Still, we can invoke the ethics–philosophy parallel in the service of a further argument that should worry proponents of the causal test. By way of introduction, we can note that moral facts are a species of *normative fact*. Normative facts are those that tell us what we *ought* to do; they rely on norms, or standards, for conduct within a given realm. Normative facts cause nothing of their own accord.

We can be helped to see this by comparing ethics, not to philosophy as a whole, but to one of its close philosophical cousins. In my opinion, moral facts are *sui generis*, but they are most similar to another kind of normative fact – epistemic facts. Epistemic facts concern what we ought to believe, provided that our beliefs are aimed at the truth. Once one understands the concept of logical validity, then if confronted with a modus ponens argument, one *ought to* believe that it is logically valid. This is a true epistemic principle.

It's also the case that you oughtn't believe things that you have no evidence for, and much evidence against. What does this epistemic truth cause? Nothing. Nor are particular, concrete epistemic duties – duties had by agents at a time – at all independently causally efficacious. Epistemic facts have as their primary function the specification of standards that should or must be met. We can say, if we like, that such standards are descriptive – they describe the conditions under which agents are (e.g.) appropriately sensitive to evidence, justified in their beliefs, warranted in their views. But, unlike natural scientific principles and facts, such normative standards may be perfectly correct even if they are honored only in the breach. The epistemic requirement that we proportion our beliefs to the evidence can be true even in a world populated wholly by spell-casters and astrologers. The normative facts that specify the conditions under which we ought to believe the truth, or behave morally, lack the ability to explain the workings of the natural order. Our epistemic and moral duties cannot explain why apples fall from trees, why smallpox takes its victims, why leopards have their spots. But they may exist for all that.

Nor is this failure something specific to the moral or epistemological realms. Consider prudential or instrumental duties – those that require us to enhance self-interest or efficiently satisfy our desires. Such normative demands do not explain what goes on in the world. Alternatively, if they are thought, for instance, to be powerful enough to explain why agents act as they do, then surely moral and epistemic requirements are capable of doing so as well. I see no basis for distinguishing the causal powers of any of these normative types from one another.

---

[5] I try my hand in *Moral Realism*, pp. 98–114.

[6] Beware: arguments for rejecting either assumption may well allow moral facts to pass the causal test (though any sound argument rejecting the second assumption would generate a naturalistic, rather than a nonnaturalistic, moral realism).

I don't mean to suggest for a moment that the causal test is useless. Rather, I think we should recognize its limits. The causal test fails as a general ontological test: it doesn't work when applied to the normative realm.

Scientific principles are vindicated, when they are, because they are able to do two closely related things: cite the causes of past events, and accurately predict the nature and occurrence of future events. Their claim to be genuinely explanatory depends almost entirely on their ability to discharge these two tasks.

But moral rules are not like that. We *can* construe rules in this way: Brink, Sturgeon, and others manage this feat.[7] But it's not a very natural way to regard them. Moral principles aren't viewed in the first instance as hypotheses that predict the actions of agents, but rather as requirements that everyone knows will encounter predictive failures. True, moral principles will reliably predict the doings of good and bad agents. But that presupposes the reality of moral properties (goodness and badness), and there's no reason to make such a concession at this stage, especially given the seriousness of antirealist charges, and the proper aim (given a naturalistic vantage point) of beginning from a neutral perspective and relying on the causal test as a way to determine the nature of reality.[8] Yes, we can enshrine moral predicates within true counterfactuals, even (in some cases) counterfactuals of greater generality than those describable at the physical level. But that is no proof of moral realism, as we can do the same for the predicates of etiquette and the civil law, which obviously cannot be construed realistically. Moral principles and facts aren't meant to explain behavior, or anticipate our actions, but rather to *prescribe* how we ought to behave, or *evaluate* states or events. They don't cite the causes of outcomes, but rather indicate what sort of conduct would merit approval, or justify

our gratitude, or legitimate some result. Science can't tell us such things.

If I am right, then an allegiance to the causal test entirely eliminates the normative realm. But this is highly implausible. There *are* reasons to believe things, reasons to satisfy one's desires, reasons to look out for oneself. There are also moral duties to aid others and refrain from harming them, even if doing so isn't going to improve one's lot in life. The standards that supply such reasons are not capable of causing anything. Nor, it seems, are the reasons or obligations themselves. (Again, if they are, all the better for moral realists.[9]) If there is any such thing as a genuine reason, the test must fail. Alternatively, if the test is retained, then such reasons must be capable of passing it. And then the causal argument against moral facts evaporates.

Maybe we can have our cake and eat it, too? Why not retain the causal test, allow that normative facts exist, but view them, as Harman does moral facts, as by-products of human choice and election? The causal test is a realist's test. Failure to pass it doesn't mean that a putative fact doesn't exist. It just means that the fact cannot be construed realistically. Normative facts may be like this. If so, we could retain the test, and also retain a global normative antirealism. Perfectly in keeping with the physicalist leanings of so many of our contemporaries.

The animating spirit behind the causal test is the ontological principle that the real is limited to what is scientifically confirmable, and the epistemic principle that we have good reason to believe in something only if it impinges on our experience, or is required in the best explanation of that which does. The causal test obviously supports, and derives support from, both the ontological and the epistemic principle. Yet both principles are dubious. The case for the causal test is considerably diminished once we see why.

---

[7]   See, e.g., Brink 1989: 182–97, Sturgeon 1986 [included as chapter 26], Boyd 1988, and Railton 1986 [chapters 13 and 14 in this volume].

[8]   So in this respect I think that Harman was wrong to concede to his opponents the existence of moral facts. The proper starting point for an antirealist is one in which we suspend judgment on the existence of such facts, and demand of the realist some positive arguments for believing in them. Harman instead was willing to grant the existence of moral facts, but claimed that even so they possessed no independent causal powers, and so could not be construed realistically.

[9]   One natural line of thinking seems mistaken. This is the one that attributes causal power to normative facts by noting that they, as mediated by an agent's beliefs and desires, can explain a great deal of why agents act as they do. That something is *seen by an agent as* (prudentially, epistemically or morally) obligatory is often enough to get one going. But that sort of mediation undermines the independence of the causal potency that the test requires. (This is one of Crispin Wright's points (1992: 196).)

The epistemic principle is problematic because it invokes an entity – a good reason – whose existence is not itself scientifically confirmable. It's like saying that God sustains a universe that contains no supernatural beings. There's a kind of internal incoherence here: the claim discounts the existence of the kind of thing that is presupposed by the claim itself.

Further, a belief's being justified is not the sort of thing that we can empirically detect. Nor, seemingly, is reference to its epistemic status required to explain anything that we have ever observed. But then, by the epistemic principle under scrutiny, we have no good reason to think that there is any such thing as the property of being epistemically justified. But if there is no such property, then the principle that implies such a thing cannot itself be justified. And so we can be rid of it.

Here's another way to get to the same result. We needn't make essential reference to this epistemic principle to explain why we see or hear or feel the things we do. Nor, so far as I can see, is any epistemic principle required in the best account of why various observable events have occurred in the world. So if the principle is true, then we lack a good reason for thinking it so. This principle, like normative standards quite generally, seeks to regulate and appraise conduct, rather than to describe its causal antecedents or powers. If that's sufficient to render it unreal, or sufficient to remove any justification we might have for believing it, then it can't rightly be used to constrain our epistemic findings or practices.

And the ontological view? The relevant ontological principle tells us that the only existential truths there are (i.e., truths about what exists) are those that are scientifically confirmed. This is certainly false if we are concerned with science as it stands, as some existential truths have yet to be discovered. Yet the view is no more plausible if we are envisioning the edicts of a perfected natural science. Here's why. Consider this existential claim:

(O)   There are no existential truths other than those ratified by perfected natural sciences.

Either (O) is true or false. If false, let's drop it: our ontology wouldn't then be entirely fixed by the natural sciences. But if it's true, then it must be false: it's self-referentially incoherent. For (O) cannot itself be scientifically confirmed. If it were true, it would be an instance of a non-scientifically confirmable existential truth. Thus either way we go, (O) must be false.

(O) is a thesis from metaphysics, not physics. Philosophers, not natural scientists, are the ones who will end up pronouncing on its merits. This is another application of the general idea that there are specifically philosophical truths that escape the ambit of scientific confirmation. There might be abstract entities, or such a thing as conceptual necessity, justified belief, or goodness. Bring your beakers, your electron microscopes, your calculators and calipers – you'll never find them. You can't abolish such things just because they lack independent causal power, and so escape empirical detection. After all, the principle calling for such abolition isn't itself scientifically confirmable.

In the end, the absence of independent causal power is not a good reason to deny the existence of moral facts, realistically construed. Of course, nothing I've said in this section supplies any argument for thinking that there are such things. I doubt that causal considerations could do that. But undermining their role in antirealist arguments can go some ways towards removing a familiar barrier to justified belief in the sort of nonnaturalism that I find appealing.

VI.   Conclusion

Once we attend to the fact that ethics is a branch of philosophy, the plausibility of nonnaturalistic moral realism is greatly enhanced. Philosophy is not a natural science. Basic, fundamental philosophical principles are realistic in nature. And central ethical principles are philosophical ones. This combination of claims gives us excellent reason to suppose that fundamental ethical truths are best construed realistically, and nonnaturalistically.

This seems to me to be a very powerful argument that can aid the nonnaturalist realist in replying to a number of perennial criticisms. One such criticism – that persistent, intractable moral disagreement is best explained as antirealists would do – can be met once we avail ourselves of the ethics–philosophy parallel. Moral disagreement shares all structural features with philosophical disagreement generally, and yet a global philosophical antirealism is very implausible. Moral disagreement also fails to provide a strong epistemic defeater for one's own already justified moral beliefs. Controversial philosophical beliefs might be justifiedly held; things are no different in the specifically moral domain. And the causal inefficacy of moral facts can be admitted without threatening moral realism, since the causal test is too restrictive a standard for ontological credibility. Alternatively, if (contrary to my suspicions) moral facts do manage to pass that test, then retaining the test will entitle moral facts to admission into our ontology.

Once we attend to the fact that ethics is a branch of philosophy, a defense of nonnaturalistic moral realism becomes a bit easier than it otherwise might be. Which is not to say that it's at all easy – the many promissory notes scattered throughout this essay will attest to that. Still, reliance on the ethics–philosophy parallel enables us to plausibly respond to *some* of the critical obstacles to the development of a plausible ethical nonnaturalism. We can hardly hope to vindicate a complex metaethical theory in one fell swoop. We can, if the preceding arguments are any good, manage to dust off a neglected view and show that some of the sources of its unpopularity have been overrated. I hope to have done that here.

References

Audi, Robert. 1997. *Moral Knowledge and Ethical Character*. Oxford: Oxford University Press.

Audi, Robert. 1999. "Self-Evidence." *Philosophical Perspectives* 13: 205–26.

Audi, Robert. 2004. *The Good in the Right*. Princeton: Princeton University Press.

Ayer, A. J. 1936. *Language, Truth and Logic*. London: Gollancz.

Blackburn, Simon. 1993. *Essays in Quasi-Realism*. Oxford: Oxford University Press.

Blackburn, Simon. 1998. *Ruling Passions*. Oxford: Oxford University Press.

Boyd, Richard. 1988. "How to Be a Moral Realist." In Sayre-McCord 1988.

Brink, David. 1989. *Moral Realism and the Foundations of Ethics*. Cambridge: Cambridge University Press.

Copp, David, and David Zimmerman, eds. 1984. *Morality, Reason and Truth*. Totowa, NJ: Rowman & Littlefield.

Garner, Richard. 1994. *Beyond Morality*. Philadelphia: Temple University Press.

Gibbard, Allan. 1990. *Wise Choices, Apt Feelings*. Cambridge, MA: Harvard University Press.

Hare, Richard. 1952. *The Language of Morals*. Oxford: Oxford University Press.

Hare, Richard. 1963. *Freedom and Reason*. Oxford: Oxford University Press.

Hare, Richard. 1989. "The Structure of Ethics and Morals." In his *Essays in Ethics*. Oxford: Oxford University Press.

Harman, Gilbert. 1977. *The Nature of Morality*. Oxford: Oxford University Press.

Jackson, Frank. 1998. *From Metaphysics to Ethics*. Oxford: Oxford University Press.

Joyce, Richard. 2001. *The Myth of Morality*. Cambridge: Cambridge University Press.

Mackie, John. 1977. *Ethics: Inventing Right and Wrong*. New York: Penguin.

Railton, Peter. 1986. "Moral Realism." *Philosophical Review* 95: 163–207.

Sayre-McCord, Geoffrey, ed. 1988. *Moral Realism*. Ithaca: Cornell University Press.

Skorupksi, John. 1999. "Irrealist Cognitivism." *Ratio* 12(4): 436–59.

Stevenson, Charles L. 1937. "The Emotive Meaning of Ethical Terms." In Stevenson 1963.

Stevenson, Charles L. 1948. "The Nature of Ethical Disagreement." In Stevenson 1963.

Stevenson, Charles L. 1963. *Facts and Values*. New Haven: Yale University Press.

Stratton-Lake, Philip, ed. 2002. *Ethical Intuitionism: Reevaluations*. Oxford: Oxford University Press.

Sturgeon, Nicholas. 1984. "Moral Explanations." In Copp and Zimmerman 1984.

Sturgeon, Nicholas. 2003. "Moore on Ethical Naturalism." *Ethics* 113: 528–56.

Timmons, Mark. 1999. *Morality without Foundations*. Oxford: Oxford University Press.

Wright, Crispin. 1992. *Truth and Objectivity*. Cambridge, MA: Harvard University Press.

Part II

Problems in Metaethics

II.1   Moral Motivation

Introduction

Since roughly the publication of David Hume's *A Treatise of Human Nature*, a debate has swirled among moral philosophers concerning the "practicality" of morality. Although a variety of issues fall under this general topic, when philosophers discuss it they are ordinarily concerned with at least this question: what is the nature of the relation between moral judgment and moral motivation? Few doubt that there is a fairly intimate connection between moral judgment and motivation. But is it one of conceptual necessity, such that if an agent sincerely judges that she morally ought to act in a certain way, then she is motivated to act that way? Or is the connection looser than this? And when an agent is motivated to act in a certain way upon judging that she morally ought to so act, is it her judgment itself that motivates her? Or does a separate psychological state, such as a desire, work in tandem with this judgment to produce the motivation? Or is there some other model better suited for thinking about what motivates agents to act?

These questions have generated a lively discussion among moral philosophers because it is frequently thought that how one answers them determines whether one opts for a realist or antirealist view regarding morality and, also, what *kind* of realist or antirealist view one accepts. For example, expressivists ordinarily assume that there

is a very intimate connection between moral judgment and moral motivation. Since their view implies that moral judgments just are expressions of "pro-attitudes" or desires, they have no difficulty accounting for the close connection between moral judgment and motivation. By contrast, expressivists claim that realists have no plausible explanation of this intimate connection, since, according to the realist view, moral judgments merely express ordinary beliefs, which are not intrinsically motivating. And this, so it is urged, is a powerful reason to reject moral realism.

The concern that moral realist views cannot account for the practicality of morality can be expressed in the form of two challenges. The first challenge is that moral realists cannot explain why moral judgment implies moral motivation. As it is sometimes formulated, the challenge rests on the claim that there are three attractive positions that realists cannot simultaneously accept (see McNaughton 1988: ch. 2; Smith 1994: ch. 1). The first is "moral cognitivism," or the view that moral judgments express moral propositions that purport to represent moral facts.[1] The second is "motivational internalism" – the position, roughly, that there is a (conceptually or logically) necessary connection between moral judgment and motivation such that, for any case in which an agent is motivated to act by her moral judgment, it is this moral judgment itself that generates the motivation in question. (It is not generally assumed that the motivation need be overriding.) The third is the "Humean theory of motivation," which is a position comprised of three commitments: first, that motivational states are comprised of judgments and desires; second, that judgments themselves neither are nor generate desires; and, third, that judgments and desires are "separate existences" or modally separable – roughly, any judgment being such that it needn't be accompanied by any particular desire.[2] Stated more precisely, the challenge can be put in the form of the following argument, which we can call "the Internalist Challenge":

1 **Moral Cognitivism.** Moral judgments of the form "I ought to do X" express a moral proposition about a matter of fact, viz., what an agent morally ought to do.
2 **Robust Motivational Internalism.** Necessarily, if someone sincerely judges that she ought to X, then her judgment itself motivates her to X.
3 If Moral Cognitivism is true, then it is possible that an agent sincerely judges that she ought to X and her judgment itself does not motivate her to X.
4 But it is not possible that an agent sincerely judges that she ought to X and her judgment itself does not motivate her to X (from premise 2).
5 So, Moral Cognitivism is false.
6 Moral realism is true only if Moral Cognitivism is true.
7 So, moral realism is false.

This argument rests on a sub-argument for its third premise, which can be stated thus:

1a **The Humean Theory of Motivation.** Judgments themselves neither are nor generate desires.
2a If The Humean Theory of Motivation is true, then it is possible that an agent sincerely judges that she ought to X and her judgment itself does not motivate her to X.
3a So, it is possible that an agent sincerely judges that she ought to X and her judgment itself does not motivate her to X.

If, however, we assume (for conditional proof):

1 **Moral Cognitivism**: Moral judgments of the form "I ought to do X" express a moral proposition about a matter of fact, viz., what an agent morally ought to do.

Then we can affirm the argument's third premise:

3 If Moral Cognitivism is true, then it is possible that an agent sincerely judges that she ought to X and her judgment itself does not motivate her to X.

This argument has received three types of response. The first line of response is broadly "internalist" in character, as it is eager to vindicate the intuitions that the connection between moral judgment and motivation is very close and that moral judgments themselves generate correlative motivational states. The second line of response is broadly "externalist" in character; it holds that a plausible account of moral motivation needn't forge a close connection between moral judgment and motivation, and that moral judgments themselves do not generate motivational states. The third type of response is the most radical of all, for it claims that so-called motivating reasons are not mental states at all, but states of affairs in the world.

While these three responses to the argument differ in important ways, they all share the following feature: all three agree that the second premise of the argument stated above is false. After all, it is said, any plausible position regarding moral motivation has to take into account various maladies of the spirit – such as severe depression, cognitive malfunction, or disenchantment with morality – that can sever the link between moral judgment and motivation. However, the second premise of the argument appears unable to handle these types of case because it tells us that there is a conceptually or metaphysically necessary connection between sincere moral judgment and motivation. But beyond this point of agreement, there are important points of disagreement between the three views just sketched, for each position takes a rather different view about *what* motivates us to action. Let's consider each response in more detail.

The first response – what we can call "non-Humean internalism" – makes a pair of moves in response to the argument stated above. In the first place, it rejects Robust Motivational Internalism in favor of what we can call "Weak Motivational

Internalism." For our purposes, we can think of this chastened internalist position as one that embraces the following thesis:

Weak Motivational Internalism: Necessarily, if someone judges that she ought to X, then either (i) her judgment itself motivates her to X or (ii) she fails to be motivated and thereby suffers from a normative defect.

In a moment, we'll see how non-Humean internalists interpret this thesis (and, in particular, how they understand the notion of a "normative defect"). For now, let's note the second move made by non-Humean internalists, which is to reject the Humean claim that moral judgments themselves cannot generate motivational states. According to the non-Humean internalist view, then, there is an important sense in which motivation is "internal" to moral judgment, as it does not find its source in a desire external to moral judgment itself.

One way to be a non-Humean internalist is to follow the lead of Michael Smith in his book *The Moral Problem*. (For Smith's position, see the selection of his included in this section.) According to Smith's view, the normative defect an agent displays when she fails to be appropriately motivated upon judging that she morally ought to act in a certain way is *practical irrationality*. In particular, Smith thinks the type of irrationality in question is a type of incoherence. This is because Smith holds that for an agent to judge that she ought to act in a certain way just is for her to judge that an ideally rational version of herself would desire her to act in that way. Thus, in such a case, an agent's failure to be motivated, Smith claims, is a matter of her not behaving in a way that she believes she has most reason to. Moreover, Smith holds that when an agent is motivated to act in a given way upon judging she ought to so act, it is her moral belief itself that generates the desire to perform that type of act. For suppose, asks Smith, this were false. How would one explain the fact that when virtuous agents have radical shifts in moral conviction, change in motivation is reliably correlated with change in moral judgment? If we say that it is because the agent generally desires "to do the right thing" and this desire links up with her moral judgments, then we've misdescribed the motivations of the virtuous agent. The virtuous agent is not, at bottom, motivated by a general desire to do what is right, but by concerns for the welfare of partic-

ular people, love of justice, and so on. And, argues Smith, only an account of moral motivation according to which moral beliefs themselves generate motivational states can capture this truth.

A different way to be a non-Humean internalist is to draw inspiration from the work of John McDowell. Fundamental to McDowell's view is the conviction that there is more to moral belief than the mere acceptance of a moral proposition or the apprehension of a moral fact. (See McDowell 1979, and Margaret Little's essay in this section.) There are, after all, ways of holding, construing, or conceptualizing the subject matter of one's belief that are not exhausted by that subject matter itself. To use Margaret Little's example (which is inspired by Wittgenstein), we are well acquainted with the phenomenon of perceiving elements of a picture under different gestalts: the experience of seeing a picture as a duck is, for instance, a different experience from seeing it as a rabbit. Arguably, however, part of what distinguishes the virtuous agent from the non-virtuous one is that she construes or "perceives" her environment differently from the non-virtuous agent. (As an analogy, think about how differently the connoisseur of jazz and the musical know-nothing hear John Coltrane's music.) And, the suggestion goes, it is plausible to believe that the way in which an agent construes a situation has ramifications for moral motivation: it is precisely because an agent's judging that she ought to act in a certain way involves construing her environment in a way that a virtuous agent would that accounts for the tight connection between that agent's moral judgment and appropriate motivation. So, according to this view, it is possible for an agent to judge that she ought to act in a certain way and still fail to be motivated to so act. But this agent's failing to be so motivated is a normative failure – a failure to construe her environment in a way that a virtuous agent would. Understood thus, this view is, according to its advocates, clearly non-Humean. For it implies that in any case in which an agent's moral judgment involves her construing the world as a virtuous agent would, her judgment itself implies appropriate motivation.

Non-Humean internalists, then, reject both the second premise of the Internalist Challenge and the Humean rationale offered in favor of the third premise, for they believe that there are "desire-entailing" beliefs. What we can call "Humean externalists," by contrast, believe that Hume (according to certain interpretations, at least) was right to claim that "reason is inert" and, thus, that there are no desire-entailing beliefs. (A defense of the externalist view is found in Nick Zangwill's paper included in this section.) For a belief to motivate an agent, it needs to link up with an appropriate desire that is not itself generated by a belief. The following three theses characterize this externalist view.

First, we should not be overly optimistic about moral agency, as there are a multitude of cases in which agents either fail to be motivated by their moral beliefs or fail to intend to do what they believe they ought to do. Second, contrary to what many internalists claim, we should not deny that a hardened moral cynic such as Thrasymachus in Plato's *Republic* really does believe that he morally ought to act in certain ways. Nor, finally, should we accept the claim that Thrasymachus' failure consists simply in the fact that he holds an incoherent combination of beliefs or fails to see the world as does the virtuous agent. Rather, the better explanation of Thrasymachus' failure to be motivated by his moral beliefs is that he simply doesn't care about acting in a morally appropriate fashion. To this it should be added that externalists divide on the question of whether an agent such as Thrasymachus suffers from a normative defect such as irrationality. Zangwill, for example, holds that there both is and is not a sense in which Thrasymachus is irrational. Thrasymachus is not irrational according to the canons of instrumental rationality, for his indifference to morality does not frustrate any of his aims. But Thrasymachus, suggests Zangwill, is irrational in the sense that he does not respond appropriately to reasons – in this case, the moral reasons in play.

If this is right, the Humean externalist rejects the second premise of the Internalist Challenge, but accepts the broadly Humean rationale for accepting its third premise. At this point, however, it will be noticed that once motivational internalism and externalism are qualified in the ways just detailed, the issue that divides them appears to be slight. The main difference between these views is that internalists hold that there are desire–entailing beliefs, while externalists deny this. But why should this issue in philosophical psychology provoke such a storm of controversy among moral philosophers?

There are several reasons, two of which it is worth mentioning. (For an additional reason, see the piece by Michael Smith included in this section.) Some philosophers have thought that the Humean theory of motivation implies that there are no categorical imperatives. The argument for this claim runs something like this: the Humean theory of motivational reasons says that an agent cannot be motivated to act in a morally appropriate fashion without having a desire to act in that fashion. But what sorts of desire agents have is a contingent matter; hence, it is possible that an agent lack a desire to act in a morally appropriate fashion. It follows that, according to the Humean theory, if an agent fails to desire to act in a morally appropriate fashion, then she has no reason to act in that fashion.

It is now widely thought that this argument rests on a failure to keep separate two types of reason. On the one hand, there are what we can call "motivational reasons." These, according to the Humean, are mental states comprised of beliefs and desires. On the other hand, there are what are commonly called "normative reasons" – considerations that count in favor of or which justify acting in certain ways. Realists commonly claim that normative reasons are not mental states but facts or truths. At any rate, once we draw this distinction, those sympathetic with the Humean view can claim that the argument just offered implies that there is a sense in which an agent who lacks the relevant desires fails to have a reason to act: the agent does not have a *motivational* reason to act in a morally appropriate way. But this, Humeans contend, does not imply that she does not have a normative reason to so act regardless of what she desires.

Predictably, not all philosophers have been persuaded by this line of response. This brings us to the second reason why philosophers have thought that something important hangs on whether we are Humeans or non-Humeans about motivation – and, indeed, to the second challenge leveled against moral realist views mentioned earlier. We've seen that defusing a common objection leveled against Humean views requires distinguishing motivating and normative reasons. But consider what we can call "the Explanatory Constraint." This principle, articulated by Bernard Williams in several influential essays, tells us that normative reasons cannot be explanatorily inert. (One of these essays is included as chapter 22; the others are cited in the bibliography to part II.2.) A normative reason, so the claim goes, must be capable of contributing to the explanation of an action that is done for that reason. But if normative reasons are facts, it is difficult to see how this could be true. Facts do not explain why we act. Rather, beliefs coupled with desires do. Since moral realism (at least in its non-naturalistic guise) is committed to the idea that moral reasons are facts that are not constituted by our desires, it fails to satisfy the Explanatory Constraint.

Let's call this second challenge to moral realism "the Explanatory Challenge." Some philosophers, such as Richard Joyce (see Joyce 2001: ch. 5), take this argument to be reason enough to reject moral realism, for they hold that inasmuch as realists are committed to categorical normative reasons, realists are thereby committed to facts that fail to explain what we do. Others, such as Jonathan Dancy, draw a different conclusion (see Dancy 1995, and his contribution to this section). They suggest that the Explanatory Challenge is evidence that the debate between Humeans and non-Humeans about motivation has been misconceived. The debate has assumed that motivating reasons are mental states. But – so proponents of this view have suggested – why not think of motivating

reasons as the objects of such states, such as states of affairs or propositions? The advantages of doing so are arguably multiple.

In the first place, this view allows us to reject the second premise of the Internalist Challenge and, in so doing, captures the way we ordinarily describe our reasons for acting. When asked a question such as: "Why did you save the child who was drowning in the pond?" we ordinarily appeal not to our desires, but to features of the world such as the fact *that the child was in need*. In the second place, this type of answer allows a moral realist to honor the Explanatory Constraint. If motivating reasons are states of affairs in the world, they can be both what favors our acting in certain ways and what motivates us to act in those ways. And, finally, if motivational reasons just are that in light of which an agent acts, then it is plausible to hold that some such reasons can count in favor of an agent's acting. Holding that motivational reasons are not mental states, but states of affairs or propositions, then, promises to make good on the claim that one and the same reason can both be motivating and normative.

Notes

1 Philosophers distinguish judgments understood as enduring mental states, on the one hand, and mental acts of judging in which an agent consciously assents to a proposition, on the other. In what follows, the term "judgment" is used in the second sense just specified.

2 As it is described here, the Humean theory of motivation differs from how it is sometimes presented. For

in some presentations (see Smith 1994, a portion of which is reproduced in this section) it refers merely to the position that beliefs and desires are modally separable. So, in order to forestall confusion, it should be emphasized that, although Smith (1994) calls his view "Humean," it is a non-Humean view according to the present way of using the term.

Selected Bibliography

Blackburn, Simon. 1998. *Ruling Passions*. Oxford: Oxford University Press, ch. 1.

Brink, David. 1989. *Moral Realism and the Foundations of Ethics*. Cambridge: Cambridge University Press, ch. 3.

Brink, David. 1997. "Moral Motivation." *Ethics* 108: 4–32.

Clark, Philip. 2000. "What Goes without Saying in Metaethics." *Philosophy and Phenomenological Research* 60: 357–79.

Copp, David. 1995. "Moral Obligation and Moral Motivation." *Canadian Journal of Philosophy*, supplementary volume 21: 187–219.

Copp, David. 1997. "Belief, Reason, and Motivation: Michael Smith's *The Moral Problem*." *Ethics* 108: 33–54.

Cuneo, Terence. 1999. "An Externalist Solution to the 'Moral Problem.'" *Philosophy and Phenomenological Research* 59: 359–80.

Cuneo, Terence. 2002. "Reconciling Realism with Humeanism." *Australasian Journal of Philosophy* 80: 465–86.

Dancy, Jonathan. 1993. *Moral Reasons*. Oxford: Blackwell.

Dancy, Jonathan. 1995. "Why There Really Is No Such Thing as the Theory of Motivation." *Proceedings of the Aristotelian Society*, supplementary volume 95: 1–18.

Dancy, Jonathan. 2000. *Practical Reality*. Oxford: Oxford University Press.

Dreier, James. 1990. "Internalism and Speaker Relativism." *Ethics* 101: 6–26.

Dreier, James. 2000. "Dispositions and Fetishes: Externalist Models of Moral Motivation." *Philosophy and Phenomenological Research* 61: 618–38.

Frankena, William. 1976. "Obligation and Motivation in Recent Moral Philosophy." In Kenneth E. Goodpaster, ed. *Perspectives on Morality: Essays by William K. Frankena.* Notre Dame: University of Notre Dame Press.

Garrard, Eve, and David McNaughton. 1998. "Mapping Moral Motivation." *Ethical Theory and Moral Practice* 1: 267–91.

Gibbard, Allan. 1990. *Wise Choices, Apt Feelings.* Cambridge, MA: Harvard University Press.

Gibbard, Allan. 2003. *Thinking How to Live.* Cambridge, MA: Harvard University Press, ch. 1.

Hampton, Jean. 1998. *The Authority of Reason.* Cambridge: Cambridge University Press, part I.

Hare, R. M. 1952. *The Language of Morals.* Oxford: Oxford University Press.

Jackson, Frank, and Philip Pettit. 1995. "Moral Functionalism and Moral Motivation." *Philosophical Quarterly* 45: 20–39.

Joyce, Richard. 2001. *The Myth of Morality.* Cambridge: Cambridge University Press, ch. 1.

Joyce, Richard. 2002. "Expressivism and Motivation Internalism." *Analysis* 62: 336–44.

Mackie, J. L. 1977. *Ethics: Inventing Right and Wrong.* London: Penguin, ch. 1.

McDowell, John. 1978. "Are Moral Requirements Hypothetical Imperatives?" *Proceedings of the Aristotelian Society,* supplementary volume 52: 13–29. Reprinted in *Mind, Value, and Reality.* Cambridge, MA: Harvard University Press, 1998.

McDowell, John. 1979. "Virtue and Reason." *Monist* 62: 331–50. Reprinted in *Mind, Value, and Reality.* Cambridge, MA: Harvard University Press, 1998.

McNaughton, David. 1988. *Moral Vision.* Oxford: Blackwell.

Mele, Alfred. 1996. "Internalist Moral Cognitivism and Listlessness." *Ethics* 106: 727–53.

Nagel, Thomas. 1970. *The Possibility of Altruism.* Oxford: Clarendon Press.

Parfit, Derek. 1997. "Reasons and Motivation." *Proceedings of the Aristotelian Society,* supplementary volume 71: 99–130.

Schueler, G. F. *Desire.* Cambridge, MA: MIT Press.

Shafer-Landau, Russ. 2003. *Moral Realism: A Defence.* Oxford: Oxford University Press, part III.

Smith, Michael. 1994. *The Moral Problem.* Oxford: Blackwell.

Smith, Michael. 1995. "Internalism's Wheel." *Ratio* 8: 277–302.

Smith, Michael. 1997. "In Defense of the Moral Problem: A Reply to Brink, Copp, and Sayre-McCord." *Ethics* 108: 84–119.

Smith, Michael. 2002. "Evaluation, Uncertainty, and Motivation." *Ethical Theory and Moral Practice* 5: 305–20.

Solomon, W. David. 1998. "Moral Realism and the Amoralist." In Peter French, Theodore Uehling, and Howard Wettstein, eds. *Midwest Studies in Philosophy* 12: 377–93.

Stocker, Michael. 1979. "Desiring the Bad: An Essay in Moral Psychology." *Journal of Philosophy* 76: 738–53.

Stratton-Lake, Philip. 1999. "Why Externalism Is Not a Problem for Ethical Intuitionists." *Proceedings of the Aristotelian Society* 99: 77–90.

Svavarsdóttir, Sigrún. 1999. "Moral Cognitivism and Moral Motivation." *The Philosophical Review* 108: 161–219.

Van Roojen, Mark. 2002. "Humean and Anti-Humean Internalism about Moral Judgments." *Philosophy and Phenomenological Research* 65: 26–49.

Wallace, R. Jay. 2005. "Moral Motivation." In James Dreier, ed. *Contemporary Debates in Moral Theory.* Oxford: Blackwell.

Wedgwood, Ralph. 2004. "The Metaethicists' Mistake." In John Hawthorne, ed. *Philosophical Perspectives 18: Ethics.* Oxford: Blackwell.

Wiggins, David. 1990. "Moral Cognitivism, Moral Relativism and Motivating Moral Beliefs." *Proceedings of the Aristotelian Society* 91: 61–85.

Zagzebski, Linda. 2003. "Emotion and Moral Judgment." *Philosophy and Phenomenological Research* 66: 104–24.

17

The Externalist Challenge

Michael Smith

3.1 Internalism vs. Externalism

Suppose we debate the pros and cons of giving to famine relief and you convince me that I should give. However when the occasion arises for me to hand over my money I say 'But wait! I know I *should* give to famine relief. But you haven't convinced me that I have any *reason* to do so!' And so I don't.

I suggested earlier that such an outburst would occasion serious puzzlement. Having convinced me that I should give to famine relief you seem to have done everything you need to do to convince me that I have a reason to do so. And having convinced me that I have a reason to give to famine relief – absent weakness of will or some other such psychological failure – you seem to have done everything you need to do to motivate me to do so. Puzzlement would thus naturally arise because, having convinced me that I should donate, you would quite rightly expect me to hand over my money. *Believing I should* seems to bring with it *my being motivated to* – at least absent weakness of will and the like.

This idea, that moral judgement has a practical upshot, is generally referred to as 'internalism'.

Unfortunately, however, 'internalism' is a vague label in the philosophical literature, used to refer to several quite different claims about the connection between moral facts or judgements on the one hand, and having reasons or being motivated on the other. Let me begin by spelling out some of these rather different claims.

Sometimes the idea behind internalism is that there is the following conceptual connection between moral judgement and the will.

> If an agent judges that it is right for her to φ in circumstances C, then she is motivated to φ in C.

In other words, moral judgement brings motivation with it *simpliciter*. This is a very strong claim. It commits us to denying that, for example, weakness of the will and the like may defeat an agent's moral motivations while leaving her appreciation of her moral reasons intact. And for this very reason it is, I think, a manifestly implausible claim as well. However I will not have anything more to say about it here.

[...]

More plausibly, then, the idea behind internalism is sometimes that though there is a conceptual connection between moral judgement and the will, the connection involved is the following *defeasible* one.

> If an agent judges that it is right for her to ϕ in circumstances C, then either she is motivated to ϕ in C or she is practically irrational.

In other words, agents who judge it right to act in various ways are so motivated, and necessarily so, absent the distorting influences of weakness of the will and other similar forms of practical unreason on their motivations. I will have more to say about this idea in what follows.

And sometimes the idea behind the internalism requirement is not, or at least is not primarily, that there is a conceptual connection of some sort between moral judgement and motivation, but that there is the following conceptual connection between the content of a moral judgement – the moral facts – and our reasons for action.

> If it is right for agents to ϕ in circumstances C, then there is a reason for those agents to ϕ in C.

In other words, moral facts are facts about our reasons for action; they are themselves simply requirements of rationality or reason.

This last internalist claim might be offered as an explanation of the previous one, for it plausibly entails the previous claim. The proof of this will be spelled out in some detail later, but in general terms the idea can be put like this. It is a platitude that an agent has a reason to act in a certain way just in case she would be motivated to act in that way if she were rational (Korsgaard, 1986). And it is a consequence of this platitude that an agent who judges herself to have a reason to act in a certain way – who judges that she would be so motivated if she were rational – is practically irrational if she is not motivated to act accordingly. For if she is not motivated accordingly then she fails to be rational by her own lights (Smith, 1992). But if this is right then it is clear that the third form of internalism entails the second. For, according to the third form, the judgement that it is right to act in a certain way is simply equivalent to the judgement that there is a reason to act in that way.

The reverse does not hold, however. The second internalist claim does not entail the third. Expres-

sivists, for example, agree that someone who judges it right to act in a certain way is either motivated accordingly or practically irrational in some way, but deny that moral requirements are requirements of rationality or reason. They thus accept the second internalist claim because they think that a moral judgement is the expression of a preference, or perhaps the expression of a disposition to have a preference; but they reject the third because they think that fully rational creatures may yet differ in the preferences that they have, or are disposed to have.

Let me give the second and third internalist claims names. I will call the second, the one that may be accepted even by those who deny the third internalist claim, 'the practicality requirement on moral judgement'. And, for obvious reasons, I will call the third internalist claim 'rationalism'. These two forms of internalism allow us to distinguish corresponding forms of externalism.

One form of externalism amounts to a denial of rationalism. This kind of externalism is consistent with the practicality requirement. Expressivists are typically both externalists and internalists in this sense. They are externalists in so far as they are anti-rationalists, and yet they are also internalists in so far as they accept the practicality requirement on moral judgement. But the other kind of externalism, the stronger form, amounts to a denial of the practicality requirement. Since rationalism entails the practicality requirement, this form of externalism therefore excludes rationalism as well. Many of those who think, against the expressivists, that moral judgements purport to be descriptive are externalists in this stronger sense.

My task in the present chapter is to defend both these forms of internalism – both rationalism and the practicality requirement – against two recent externalist challenges. The first comes from David Brink (1986). Brink's challenge is directed primarily against the weaker internalist claim: that is, against the practicality requirement. The second comes from Philippa Foot (1972). Her challenge is directed primarily against the stronger internalist claim: that is, against rationalism.

In what follows I will begin by clarifying the kind of rationalism to which we are committed by the stronger internalist claim. I then consider Brink's and Foot's challenges in turn. As a matter of fact both Brink and Foot accept the stronger form of externalism, the form that excludes both rationalism and the practicality requirement. However, as we will see, being an externalist of either kind involves far more controversial and counter-intuitive commitments than either Brink or Foot seem to realize.

3.2 Rationalism as a Conceptual Claim vs. Rationalism as a Substantive Claim

John Mackie draws a distinction between two quite different claims a rationalist might make (Mackie, 1977: 27–30). As I see it, it is Mackie's apprecia-tion of this distinction that allows him to argue for his 'error theory': the view that all moral thought and talk is infected with an error of presupposition; the presupposition that the world contains objec-tively prescriptive features.

We can best introduce this distinction by way of an analogy. Suppose we are interested in whether or not there are any witches. How are we to go about answering our question? First we must ask a *conceptual question*. What is our concept of a witch? Let's suppose we answer this conceptual question as follows. Our concept of a witch is the concept of a person who exploits his or her relationship with a supernatural agency in order to cause events to happen in the natural world. Then, second, we must ask a *substantive question*. That is, having now fixed on what our concept of a witch is, we must ask whether there is anything in the world instan-tiating our concept of a witch. If we do not think that there are any supernatural agencies for anyone to have a relationship with, then we will answer this substantive question in the negative. We will say that there are no witches.

Mackie's idea is that, when we ask whether there are any moral facts, we have to follow exactly the same procedure. We must first of all ask a concep-tual question. What is our concept of a moral fact? Mackie answers that our concept of a moral fact is the concept of an 'objectively prescriptive' feature of the world. And then, according to Mackie, we must go on to ask a substantive question. Is there anything in the world answering to our concept of a moral fact? Mackie's answer to this question is, famously, that once we are clear about what it is that we are looking for, we see that there are no moral facts. For we see that our concept of an objectively prescriptive feature is not instantiated anywhere in the world.

I said that Mackie draws our attention to two dif-ferent claims a rationalist might make. This is because, in light of his distinction between con-ceptual claims and substantive claims, rationalism might now be taken to be a conceptual claim: the claim that our concept of a moral requirement is the concept of a reason for action; a requirement of rationality or reason. Or alternatively, rational-ism might be taken to be a substantive claim. That is, rationalists might be telling us that there are requirements of rationality or reason correspond-ing to the various moral requirements. Taken in the first way, rationalism is a claim about the best analysis of moral terms. Taken in the second way, rationalism is claim about the deliverances of the theory of rational action.

As I see it, when Mackie tells us that our concept of a moral fact is the concept of an objectively pre-scriptive feature of the world, he is telling us that the rationalists' conceptual claim is true. And when he tells us that there are no objectively prescriptive features in the world, he is telling us that the rationalists' substantive claim is false. That is, as I see it, Mackie's argument for the error theory may be reconstructed as follows.

Conceptual truth: If agents are morally required to φ in circum-stances C then there is a requirement of rational-ity or reason for all agents to φ in circumstances C

Substantive claim: There is no requirement of rationality or reason for all agents who find themselves in circum-stances C to φ

Conclusion: Agents, are not morally required to φ in circum-stances C

That we are able to reconstruct Mackie's argument in this way is important, for it shows that in defending the rationalists' conceptual claim we do not thereby beg any questions. Even if we accept the rationalists' conceptual claim, we must still go on to defend the rationalists' substantive claim. And conversely, even if we deny the rationalists' substantive claim, we must still engage with the rationalists' conceptual claim.

This distinction between rationalism as a con-ceptual claim and rationalism as a substantive claim is to be central in what follows. For note that the stronger internalist claim – what I have called 'rationalism' – is simply a claim about our concept of rightness: it is a claim about the content of an agent's judgement that her action is right, not a claim to the effect that judgements with such contents are *true*. Moreover, note that it is this conceptual claim that entails the practicality requirement. The *truth* of the substantive claim is simply not required for that entailment to hold.

It is thus rationalism as a conceptual claim that is to be at issue in the present chapter, not rationalism as a substantive claim. Rationalism as a substantive claim will come up for discussion in later chapters, but for now the focus is to be purely conceptual.

3.3 Brink's 'Amoralist' Challenge

In 'Externalist Moral Realism' David Brink argues that we must reject the practicality requirement. Since the rationalists' conceptual claim entails the practicality requirement, his argument thus threatens to refute rationalism as well. Here is Brink.

> Much moral skepticism is skepticism about the objectivity of morality, that is, skepticism about the existence of moral facts. But another traditional kind of skepticism accepts the existence of moral facts and asks why we should care about these facts. Amoralists are the traditional way of representing this second kind of skepticism; the amoralist is someone who recognizes the existence of moral considerations and remains unmoved.
>
> The . . . [defender of the practicality requirement] . . . must dismiss the amoralist challenge as incoherent . . . We may think that the amoralist challenge is coherent, but this can only be because we confuse moral senses of terms and 'inverted commas' senses of those same terms . . . Thus . . . apparent amoralists . . . remain unmoved, not by what they regard as moral considerations, but only by what others regard as moral considerations.
>
> The problem . . . is that . . . [this] . . . does not take the amoralist's challenge seriously enough . . . We can imagine someone who regards certain demands as moral demands – and not simply as conventional moral demands – and yet remains unmoved . . . [If] . . . we are to take the amoralist challenge seriously, we must attempt to explain why the amoralist should care about morality. (1986: 30)

Brink's argument is simple enough.

According to defenders of the practicality requirement, it is supposed to be a conceptual truth that agents who make moral judgements are motivated accordingly, at least absent weakness of will and the like. But far from this being a conceptual truth, it isn't any sort of truth at all. For amoralists use moral terms to pick out the very same properties we pick out when we use moral terms. Their use of moral terms may therefore be reliably guided by the moral facts in the same way as our uses of those terms. But amoralists differ from us in that they see no reason at all to do what they thus take to be morally required. In other words, amoralists make moral judgements without being motivated accordingly, and without suffering from any sort of practical irrationality either. The practicality requirement is thus false.

As Brink notes, defenders of the requirement have generally not responded to this challenge by boldly denying that amoralists exist. And nor could they with any credibility, for amoralists are among the more popular heroes of both philosophical fantasy and non-philosophical fiction. Brink mentions Plato's Thrasymachus and Dickens's Uriah Heep. But nor are amoralists confined to the world of make-believe. There are, after all, real-life sociopaths like Robert Harris, the thrill-killer whose story is faithfully retold and analysed by Gary Watson (1987). Harris claims that he knew that what he was doing was wrong and that he simply chose to do it anyway; that he felt no conflict. It therefore seems quite wrong to suppose that he suffered from weakness of will, or, perhaps, from any other kind of practical irrationality either.

What defenders of the requirement have tended to deny is therefore rather that, properly described, the existence of amoralists is not inconsistent with the practicality requirement. For, they claim, amoralists do not *really* make moral judgements at all. Even if they do use moral words to pick out the same properties that we pick out when we use moral words, they do not really judge acts to be right and wrong; rather they judge acts to be 'right' and 'wrong'. That is to say they use moral words in a different sense; in the inverted commas sense Brink mentions.

According to Hare, for example, the sentence 'φ-ing is right' as used by an amoralist does not mean 'φ-ing is right'; but rather means 'φ-ing is in accordance with what other people judge to be right' (Hare, 1952: 124–6, 163–5). And, as such, the fact that an amoralist may judge it 'right' to ϕ without being either motivated to ϕ or suffering from weakness of will is no counter-example to the requirement. For the requirement tells us that those who judge it right to ϕ are motivated accordingly, absent weakness of will, not that those who judge it 'right' to ϕ are motivated accordingly, absent weakness of will.

Now Brink thinks that this inverted commas response doesn't take the amoralist challenge 'seriously' enough. And I must confess that I share his misgivings, at least as regards the details of Hare's version of the response. For, as Brink points out, there seems to be nothing incoherent about the idea of an amoralist who claims to have special insight into what is *really* right and wrong; an amoralist whose judgements about what it is right and wrong to do are therefore, even by her own lights, out of line with the judgements of others. But if this is right, then the judgements of amoralists can hardly be thought of as judgements about what other people judge to be right and wrong.

Despite these misgivings, however, I think that the inverted commas response to the amoralist challenge is along exactly the right lines. In what follows I want therefore to give a two part reply to Brink. First I will say what the inverted commas response really amounts to; how it differs from what Hare says. And second I will say why defenders of the requirement are right to think that the requirement is a conceptual truth.

3.4 Reply to Brink's Claim that Amoralists Really Make Moral Judgements

As I see it, defenders of the practicality requirement are right to say that amoralists do not really make moral judgements, they simply go wrong in trying to say more than this. The point is not that amoralists really make judgements of some other kind: about what other people judge to be right and wrong, for example. The point is rather that the *very best* we can say about amoralists is that they try to make moral judgements but fail. In order to see why this is not *ad hoc*, consider an analogy.

There is a familiar problem about the conditions under which we should say of someone that she really makes colour judgements. The problem can be brought out by reflecting on the case of someone, blind from birth, who has a reliable method of using colour terms. We might imagine that she has been hooked up to a machine from birth that allows her to feel, through her skin, when an object has the appropriate surface reflectance properties.

Now such a person certainly has a facility with colour terms, a facility that allows her to engage in many aspects of the ordinary practice of colour ascription. For she uses terms with the same extension as our colour terms, and the properties of objects that explain her uses of those terms are the very same properties as those that explain our uses of colour terms. (This is similar to what we said earlier about the amoralist's use of moral language.) And we can even imagine, if we like, that her colour judgements are far more accurate and reliable than those made by sighted folk. When she makes colour judgements, she is therefore not appropriately thought of as making judgements about what other people judge to be red, green and the like. (This is again similar to what we have said about the amoralist.)

However, despite the facility such a blind person has with colour language, many theorists have thought that we should still deny that she possesses colour concepts or mastery of colour terms. For, they say, the ability to have the appropriate visual experiences under suitable conditions is partially constitutive of possession of colour concepts and mastery of colour terms (Peacocke, 1985: 29–30, 37–8). And what such theorists thereby commit themselves to saying is that, despite her facility with colour terms, such a blind person does not *really* make colour judgements at all. They do not have to say that she is really making judgements of some other kind, of course. Rather they can insist that though she is trying to make colour judgements, because she doesn't count as a possessor of colour concepts, she fails. When she says 'Fire-engines are red', 'Grass is green' and the like, she is therefore best interpreted as using colour terms in an inverted, commas sense: she is saying that fire-engines are 'red', grass is 'green' and so on.

It is, I hope, clear that the structure of this debate over the conditions for mastery of colour terms is in crucial respects identical to the structure of the debate we are engaged in with Brink. One side says that a subject has mastery of colour terms (moral terms), and thus really makes colour judgements (moral judgements), only if, under certain conditions, being in the psychological state that we express when we make colour judgements (moral judgements) entails having an appropriate visual experience (motivation). The other side denies this holding instead that the ability to use a term whose use is reliably explained by the relevant properties of objects is enough to credit her with mastery of colour terms (moral terms) and the ability really to make colour judgements (moral judgements). Having the appropriate visual experience (motivation) under appropriate conditions is an entirely contingent, and optional, extra. The debate is a real one, so how are we to decide who wins?

Imagine someone objecting that those who say that the capacity to have certain visual experiences is partially constitutive of mastery of colour terms do not take 'seriously' enough the challenge posed by people who can reliably say 'Grass is green', 'Fire-engines are red', and so on, while yet being completely blind. Suppose the objector insists that since blind people can reliably use colour terms in this way, it just follows that they have full mastery of colour terms. Would the objection be a good one? I do not think so. For the objection simply assumes the conclusion it is supposed to be arguing for. It assumes that blind people have mastery of colour terms, something that those who think that mastery requires the capacity to have the appropriate visual experiences under the appropriate conditions deny.

It seems to me that Brink's amoralist challenge is flawed in just this way. He puts a prejudicial interpretation on the amoralist's reliable use of moral terms. He assumes that the amoralist's reliable use is evidence of her mastery of those terms; assumes that being suitably motivated under the appropriate conditions is not a condition of mastery of moral terms. But those who accept the practicality requirement do not accept the account of what it is to have mastery of moral terms that makes this prejudicial interpretation of the amoralist's use of moral terms appropriate.

What this suggests is that, in order to adjudicate the debate with Brink, what we really need is an independent reason for accepting one or the other account of mastery. In what follows I want therefore to provide such an independent reason. The argument is to be that the account of mastery offered by those who defend the practicality requirement is to be preferred because it alone is able to provide a plausible explanation of the reliable connection between moral judgement and motivation in the good and strong-willed person.

3.5 An Argument for the Practicality Requirement

All we have said so far about the strong externalists' account of moral motivation is that, by their lights, it is a contingent and rationally optional matter whether an agent who believes that it is right to act in a certain way is motivated to act accordingly. But more quite evidently needs to be said.

By all accounts, it is a striking fact about moral motivation that a *change in motivation* follows reliably in the wake of a *change in moral judgement*, at least in the good and strong-willed person. A plausible theory of moral judgement must therefore explain this striking fact. As I see it, those who accept the practicality requirement can, whereas strong externalists cannot, explain this striking fact in a plausible way.

Suppose I am engaged in an argument with you about a fundamental moral question; a question about, say, whether we should vote for the libertarian party at some election as opposed to the social democrats. In order to make matters vivid, we will suppose that I come to the argument already judging that we should vote for the libertarians, and already motivated to do so as well. During the course of the argument, let's suppose you convince me that I am fundamentally wrong. I should vote for the social democrats, and not just because the social democrats will better promote the values that I thought would be promoted by the libertarians, but rather because the values I thought should and would be promoted by libertarians are themselves fundamentally mistaken. You get me to change my most fundamental values. In this sort of situation, what happens to my motives?

Though the precise answer to this question will of course depend, *inter alia*, on the very point at issue, this much at least can be accepted by defenders of the practicality requirement and strong externalists alike. If I am a good and strong-willed person then a new motivation will follow in the wake of my new judgement. So let's add in the assumption that I am a good and strong-willed person. Then, since I no longer judge it right to vote for the libertarians, I will no longer be motivated to do so. And since I have come to judge it right to vote for the social democrats, I will now be motivated to do that instead. The question is: how are we to explain the *reliability* of this connection between judgement and motivation in the good and strong-willed person? How are we to explain why, under a range of counterfactual circumstance, the good and strong-willed person's moral motivations will always fall in line behind her newly arrived at moral judgements?

As I see it, there are only two possible answers. On the one hand we can say that the reliable connection between judgement and movitation is to be explained *internally*: it follows directly from the content of moral judgement itself. The idea will then be either that the belief that an act is right *produces* a corresponding motivation (this is the rationalists' alternative), or perhaps that the attitude of accepting that an act is right is itself *identical* with the state of being motivated (this is the expressivists'). Or, on the other hand, we can say that the reliable connection between judgement and motivation is to be explained *externally*: it follows from the content of the motivational dispositions possessed by the good and strong-willed person. Those who defend the practicality requirement opt for the first answer, strong externalists opt for the second.

Consider the first answer. Since those who defend the practicality requirement think that it is in the nature of moral judgement that an agent who judges it right to φ in circumstances C is motivated to φ in C, at least absent weakness of will or some other such psychological failure, they will insist that it comes as no surprise that in a strong-willed person a *change* of moral motivation follows in the wake of a *change* in moral judgement. For that is just a direct consequence of the practicality requirement.

Moreover, and importantly, note that defenders of the requirement are in a position to insist that what an agent is thus motivated to do when she changes her moral judgement is precisely what she judges it right to do, where this is read *de re* and not *de dicto*. Thus, if an agent judges it right to φ in C, and if she has not derived this judgement from some more fundamental judgement about what it is right to do in C, then, absent weakness of will and the like, defenders of the practicality requirement can insist that she will be motivated non-derivatively to φ in C. This is because, on the rationalist alternative, a non-derivative desire to φ in C is what her judgement that it is right to φ in C causes in her, or because, on the expressivist alternative, the judgement that it is right to φ in C is itself just the expression of such a non-derivative desire. In the example under discussion,

then, in deciding that it is right to vote for the social democrats, defenders of the practicality requirement can insist that I acquire a non-derivative concern for social democratic values.

But now consider the second answer, the answer favoured by the strong externalist. She will say that the defender of the practicality requirement has conveniently overlooked a crucial part of the story: namely, the stipulation that I am a *good* and strong-willed person. She will therefore insist that what explains the reliable connection between judgement and motivation is a motivational disposition I have in virtue of which I count as a good person. In other words, what explains the reliability of the connection is the *content of my moral motivation*. But what exactly *is* the content of my moral motivation, according to the strong externalist?

Before the argument began I was motivated to vote for the libertarians. Could it be that it was my having a non-derivative concern for libertarian values that made me count as a good person, when I judged it right to vote for the libertarians? Evidently not. After all, as a result of the ensuing argument I have come to reject my earlier judgement that it is right to vote for the libertarians in favour of the judgement that it is right to vote for the social democrats. But since, on this way of seeing things, my initial motivation was not itself rationally mandated by my earlier judgement – since it was just a wholly contingent and rationally optional extra – so the mere fact that I have found reason to change my judgement gives me no reason to change this motive. I may therefore quite rationally continue to have a desire to vote for the libertarians; though of course I would have to judge that in so doing I am motivated to do something that I now judge wrong. Having a non-derivative concern for libertarian values while judging it right to vote for the libertarians is thus not what makes me a good person. For it cannot explain why I change my motivation when I change my judgement.

What this forces the strong externalist to admit is that, on their way of seeing things, the motive in virtue of which I am to count as a good person must have a content capable of explaining not just why I am motivated to vote for the libertarians when I judge it right to vote for the libertarians, but also why I stop being motivated to vote for the libertarians when I give up judging that it is right to do so. And the only motivational content capable of playing this role, it seems to me, is a motivation to do the right thing, where this is now read *de dicto* and not *de re*. At bottom, the strong externalist will have to say, having this self-conciously *moral* motive is what makes me a good person.

Note that if this were the content of the good person's motivations, then the strong externalist would indeed be able to explain the reliability of the connection between moral judgement and motivation. A change in the good person's motivations would follow a change in her moral judgements because her motivations would be derived from her judgements together with her self-conciously moral motive. Thus, according to this story, when I no longer believe that it is right to vote for the libertarians, I lose a *derived* desire to vote for them, and when I come to believe that it is right to vote for the social democrats, I acquire a *derived* desire to vote for them. But my motivations are in each case derivative because they are derived from my current judgement about what the right thing to do is together with my basic moral motive: a non-derivative concern to do what is right.

However, if this is the best explanation the strong externalist can give of the reliable connection between moral judgement and motivation in the good and strong-willed person then it seems to me that we have a straightforward *reductio*. For the explanation is only as plausible as the claim that the good person is, at bottom, motivated to do what is right, where this is read *de dicto* and not *de re*, and that is surely a quite implausible claim. For commonsense tells us that if good people judge it right to be honest, or right to care for their children and friends and fellows, or right for people to get what they deserve, then they care non-derivatively about these things. Good people care non-derivatively about honesty, the weal and woe of their children and friends, the well-being of their fellows, people getting what they deserve, justice, equality, and the like, not just one thing: doing what they believe to be right, where this is read *de dicto* and not *de re*. Indeed, commonsense tells us that being so motivated is a fetish or moral vice, not the one and only moral virtue.

It is worthwhile underscoring the present objection by comparing it to a related objection of Bernard Williams's to the kind of moral philosophy that emphasizes impartiality (1976). Williams asks us to consider a man who, when faced with a choice between saving his wife or a stranger, chooses to save his wife. Many moral philosophers think that, even in such a case, a morally good person would be moved by impartial concern; that this man's motivating thought would therefore have to be, at best, 'that it was his wife, and that in situations of this kind it is permissible to save one's wife'. But, Williams objects, this is surely wrong. It provides the husband with 'one thought too many'. And in order to see that this is so he asks us to consider matters from the wife's perspective. She would quite rightly hope that her husband's 'motivating thought, fully spelled out' is that the person he saved was *his wife*. If any further motivation were required then that would simply indicate that he doesn't have the feelings of direct love and concern for her that she rightly wants and expects. He would be alienated from her, treating her as in relevant respects just like a stranger; though, of course, a stranger that he is especially well placed to benefit (Williams, 1976: 18).

The present objection to externalism is like Williams's objection to the kind of moral philosophy that emphasizes impartiality, only more powerful still; for it does not require the assumption, controversial by the lights of some, that morality itself embraces partial values like love and friendship. For the objection in this case is simply that, in taking it that a good person is motivated to do what she believes right, where this is read *de dicto* and not *de re*, externalists too provide the morally good person with 'one thought too many'. They alienate her from the ends at which morality properly aims. Just as it is constitutive of being a good lover that you have direct concern for the person you love, so it is constitutive of being a morally good person that you have direct concern for what you think is right, where this is read *de re* and not *de dicto*. This is something that must be conceded even by those moral philosophers who think that the only right course of action is one of impartiality. They too must agree that a morally good person will have a direct and non-derivative impartial concern; her concern for impartiality must not itself be derived from a more basic non-derivative concern *de dicto* to do the right thing.

We have therefore found a decisive reason to reject the strong externalists' explanation of the reliable connection between moral judgement and motivation in the good and strong-willed person. For, in short, the strong externalists' explanation commits us to false views about the content of a good person's motivations; it elevates a moral fetish into the one and only moral virtue. And the remedy, of course, is to retreat to the alternative, internalist, explanation of the reliability of the connection between moral judgement and motivation. But if we do that then, of course, we have to accept that the practicality requirement is a constraint on the content of a moral judgement after all.

The conclusion is important. For it means that we now have the independent reason we needed for giving an account of mastery of moral terms according to which the practicality requirement is itself a condition of having mastery. Only so can we explain the reliable connection between moral judgement and motivation in the good and strong-willed person. Brink's 'amoralist' challenge thus collapses. For despite the facility they have with moral language, amoralists do not have mastery of moral terms, and they therefore do not really make moral judgements. The fact that they make 'moral' judgements without being motivated or suffering from practical irrationality thus provides us with no challenge to the practicality requirement.

[. . .]

3.9   An Argument for the Rationalists' Conceptual Claim

It seems to me that there is a single, powerful, line of argument in support of the rationalists' conceptual claim. The argument trades on the truism that we expect agents to do what they are morally required to do. The argument can be stated as follows.

Moral requirements apply to rational agents as such. But it is a conceptual truth that if agents are morally required to act in a certain way then we expect them to act in that way. Being rational, as such, must therefore suffice to ground our expectation that rational agents will do what they are morally required to do. But how could this be so? It could be so only if we think of the moral requirements that apply to agents as themselves categorical requirements of rationality or reason. For the only thing we can legitimately expect of rational agents as such is that they do what they are rationally required to do.

The crucial step in this argument is the premise that we expect rational agents to do what they are morally required to do. It might be thought that this premise trades on a pun on 'expect'; that to say we expect someone to do something can mean either that we believe that they *will*, or that we believe that they *should*. For the argument to work, the premise has to be interpreted in the former way; but, it might be said, for the premise to be true it has to be interpreted in the latter way. However I think that this is just a mistake. The premise is true when we interpret the claim that we expect rational agents to do what they are morally required to do as the claim that we believe they will.

In order to see this, note that we certainly expect rational agents to do what they *judge* themselves to be morally required to do: that is, we certainly believe not just that they should, but that they will, other things being equal. For this follows directly from the practicality requirement, and, as we have seen, we have no alternative but to accept that: absent practical irrationality, agents will do what they judge to be right, at least other things being equal. However it might be thought this is also the most that we can expect in that sense, and that, because of this, the argument doesn't go through. For even if, other things being equal, rational agents will do what they judge themselves morally required to do, the argument provides us with no reason to think that rational agents will all come up with the same judgements about what they are morally required to do. Rational agents may therefore differ in their moral judgements, differ without being in any way subject to *rational* criticism. But if agents may differ in their moral judgements without being subject to rational criticism, then it cannot be that their judgements are about what they are required to do by the categorical requirements of rationality. This is the view taken by expressivists. It is the reason why, even though they accept the practicality requirement, they none the less reject the rationalists' conceptual claim. It is, if you like, the reason why they are expressivists.

In fact, however, the objection backfires. For, as we have seen, it is a platitude that our moral judgements at least purport to be objective. Thus if A says 'It is right to φ in circumstances C' and B says 'It is not right to φ in circumstances C' then we take it that A and B *disagree*; that at most one of their judgements is true. And that means, in turn, that we take it that we can fault at least one of A's and B's judgements from the rational point of view, for it is false. But if this is right then it follows that, just as the argument says, we do in fact expect *rational* agents to do what they are morally required to do, not just what they judge themselves to be morally required to do. For we can and do expect rational agents to judge *truly*; we expect them to *converge* in their judgements about what it is right to do. Our concept of a moral requirement thus turns out to be the concept of a categorical requirement of rationality after all.

Indeed, to the extent that we do not expect an agent to do the right thing, but perhaps only what she believes to be right, it can now be seen that our lesser expectation reflects our view of the agent as to some extent irrational; as someone who fails to live up to the requirements of reason to the extent that she should. For it reflects our view of her as someone who will not correct her false belief about what she is morally required to do before she acts. And this in turn suggests a range of other reasons why we might not expect an agent who is morally required to φ in fact to φ. For there are all sorts of ways in which agents can fail to live up the requirements of reason; all sorts of ways in which they can be practically irrational. They may suffer from weakness of will, or compulsion, or any of a range of other forms of practical unreason. Importantly, however, none of these reasons for modifying our expectation shows that there is anything wrong with the crucial premise in the argument: the premise that we expect *rational* agents to do what they are morally required to do, in the sense of believing that they will, at least other things being equal. Indeed, all of these reasons for modifying our expectations *presuppose* the truth of that crucial premise, for they suggest that a modification of our expectation requires some form of practical irrationality or unreason.

As I see it, the argument given is therefore sound. Our concept of a moral requirement is indeed the concept of a categorical requirement of rationality or reason. Moreover, note that we can reach this same conclusion from another direction. For, as I see it, the appropriateness of a whole range of moral attitudes depends upon the truth of the rationalists' conceptual claim. Approval and disapproval, for example, must lie somewhere close to the heart of any account of morality. For it is a datum that we approve and disapprove of what people do when moral matters are at stake: we approve of those who do the right thing and disapprove of those who do the wrong thing. But, as I will now go on to argue, such attitudes themselves presuppose the legitimacy of our expectation that rational people will act rightly, and so, in turn, presuppose the truth of the rationalists' conceptual claim.

In order to see why this is so, we need to remind ourselves of the difference between approval and disapproval on the one hand, and mere liking and disliking on the other. Foot herself makes the following remarks about the difference.

> What anyone can want or like is not restricted, logically speaking, by facts about his relationship to other people, as for instance that he is a friend or a parent of one, and engaged in a joint enterprise with another. Such facts can, however, create possibilities of approving and disapproving that would otherwise not exist. (Foot, 1977: 194)

In other words, whereas we can like and dislike more or less what we please, we cannot just approve and disapprove of what we please. Certain relationships between those who approve or disapprove on the one hand, and those who are approved or disapproved of on the other, are presupposed by the attitudes of approval and disapproval.

> [T]he attitudes of approval and disapproval would not be what they are without the existence of tacit agreement on the question of who listens to whom and about what. (Foot, 1977: 198)

> [A]pproval and disapproval can, logically speaking, exist only against a background of agreement about the part that other people's views shall be given in decision making. (Foot, 1977: 199)

Thus, according to Foot, it makes sense to say that I disapprove of your behaviour only if we presuppose that you are to take account of that fact in deciding what to do. But in order for it to make sense that I merely dislike your behaviour, we need to presuppose no such thing. Consider an example by way of illustration.

Suppose you eat peppermint ice-cream, and that I just can't stand it when people do that. What would it be appropriate for me to say: that I dislike your eating peppermint ice-cream, or that I disapprove of your eating peppermint ice-cream? According to Foot, it only makes sense to say that I disapprove if you are to take account of that fact in deciding what to do. For to say that I disapprove of your behaviour, as opposed to merely dislike it, signals the fact that, as I see it, your behaviour transgresses the standards in terms of which you and I both acknowledge your behaviour is to be judged. In other words, disapproval presupposes that your behaviour is contrary to my legitimate expectations; my beliefs about how you will behave.

Disliking your behaviour presupposes no such thing.

However, if this is right, then it follows immediately that approval and disapproval are only ever in place when there exist *grounds* for legitimate expectations about how someone will behave. One obvious area in which approval and disapproval are in place is therefore the area of rational decision-making. For we all expect of each other that we will decide what to do on rational grounds. As Foot notes, however, this is not the only area in which approval and disapproval are in place. The members of a chess club may well disapprove of a fellow member who moves his castle on the diagonal, for instance, and their disapproval may survive the discovery that, in the context, this is not an irrational thing for him to do. For even if he has good reasons for doing what he does, he still acts contrary to their legitimate expectations, for he acts in violation of an agreement he either tacitly or explicitly entered into by becoming a member of the club, the agreement to move his chess pieces in accordance with the rules. Their legitimate expectation is thus that those who do not want to play by the rules will not play at all.

I began by saying that it is a datum that we approve and disapprove of what people do when moral matters are at stake. But now, in light of our account of the preconditions for approval and disapproval, an obvious question presents itself. Consider, for instance, disapproval of those who act contrary to moral requirements. Such disapproval is ubiquitous. Yet how can this be? For, as we have seen, disapproval of those who do not do what they are morally required to do presupposes the legitimacy of our expectation that they will act otherwise; it presupposes that, as we see it, their decision is a bad one in terms of the commonly acknowledged standards by which their decisions are to be judged. But what provides grounds for the legitimacy of this expectation? In virtue of what are there commonly acknowledged standards by which their decisions are to be judged?

Note how implausible it would be to suppose that what grounds the legitimacy of this expectation is the fact that rational creatures have each entered into an agreement to act morally, an agreement on a par with the agreement the chess player either tacitly or explicitly enters into by becoming a member of a chess club. For no such agreements have ever been made. Perhaps we should say

instead that what grounds our expectation is not an agreement rational creatures have in fact made, but rather an agreement they would make if they were . . . If they were what? If they were rational, of course! But in that case we have abandoned the idea that what grounds the legitimacy of our expectation is the fact of agreement in favour of the alternative. What grounds the legitimacy of our expectation is the mere fact that people are rational agents. Being rational suffices to ground the expectation that people will do what they are morally required to do. Given that moral approval and disapproval are ubiquitous, the truth of the rationalists' conceptual claim thus seems to be entailed by the fact that the preconditions of moral approval and disapproval are satisfied.

It is worth remarking that Foot acknowledges that her views about the preconditions for moral approval and moral disapproval are in apparent conflict with the institutional account of moral requirements she favours. She asks, for example:

> What . . . are we to say about those who altogether reject morality? Surely we think it possible to disapprove of their actions, although they do not agree to take any account of what we say? This is true, and it is an important fact about the phenomenon that we call 'morality' that we are ready to bring pressure to bear against those who reject it. But this no more shows that moral attitudes do not depend on agreement within human society than the possibility of asserting other kinds of authority against those who do not accept it shows that authority requires no agreement . . . [W]e will confront them with the confidence that we have the world with us – the world that pays at least lip service to morality. (Foot, 1977: 205)

But her reply entirely misses the point. For even if, on Foot's institutional account of morality, we in the special sub-group who get to set the standards, change them and enforce them, can in some way be said to enter into an agreement to make our decisions on moral matters in a certain way, those who reject morality are, by her account, not a party to this agreement. The 'world' we have with us when we confront 'them' is thus, for them, simply a mob forcing its commonly agreed standard on another group whose agreement they do not have. The institutions that Foot thinks suffice to undergird a shared standard of decision-making thus undergird no such thing. They provide no basis at all for the expectation that those who reject morality will make their decisions in the way 'we' will.

That requires the truth of the rationalists' conceptual claim, a claim that Foot is in no position to endorse.

3.10   Summary

My aim in this chapter has been to consider and defend two forms of internalism: the practicality requirement on moral judgement and the rationalists' conceptual claim. [. . .]

If my arguments in this chapter have been on the right track, then it follows that [. . .] our judgements about what we are morally required to do are simply judgements about what the categorical requirements of rationality or reason demand of us.

References

Brink, David O. 1986. 'Externalist Moral Realism', *Southern Journal of Philosophy*. Supplement. 23–42.

Foot, Philippa. 1972. 'Morality as a System of Hypothetical Imperatives' reprinted in Foot 1978. 157–73.

Foot, Philippa. 1977. 'Approval and Disapproval' reprinted in *Virtues and Vices*. University of California Press (1978). 189–207.

Hare, R. M. 1952. *The Language of Morals*. Oxford University Press.

Mackie, J. L. 1977. *Ethics: Inventing Right and Wrong*. Penguin.

Nagel, Thomas. 1970. *The Possibility of Altruism*. Princeton University Press.

Peacocke, Christopher. 1985. *Sense and Content*. Oxford University Press.

Watson, Gary. 1987. 'Responsibility and the Limits of Evil' in Ferdinand Schoeman, ed., *Responsibility, Character and the Emotions: New Essays in Moral Psychology*. Cambridge University Press. 256–86.

Williams, Bernard. 1976. 'Persons, Character and Morality' reprinted in *Moral Luck*. Cambridge University Press (1981). 1–19.

18

Externalist Moral Motivation

Nick Zangwill

"Motivational externalism" is the view that moral judgements have no motivational efficacy in themselves, and that when they motivate us, the source of motivation lies outside the moral judgement in a separate desire. Motivational externalism contrasts with "motivational internalism," which is either the view that our moral judgements are partly constituted by motivation, or else that they would be if we were rational. The major problem for motivational internalism – in either guise – is that it flies in the face of common observation and first-personal experience of the fact that we can, without irrationality, be indifferent to morality. Philippa Foot pioneered this argument (Foot 1972). The phenomenon of indifference encourages motivational externalism.

This paper will not revisit this difficulty for internalism, but will travel in the opposite dialectical direction. The aim is to expound and defend externalism, not to argue against internalism. This paper will address, and try to soothe away, the reluctance of many philosophers to embrace motivational externalism. Internalists might reasonably complain that it is all very well to argue against internalism, but no one is going to think about accepting externalism until they see more of what such a theory would be like. The mere possibility of such a theory is not sufficiently reassuring, even given strong arguments against the opposite position. For there may also be objections to externalism.

Moral philosophers have not spent much effort spelling out the details of an externalist model of moral motivation. Those who have endorsed externalism include Philippa Foot, Michael Stocker, David Brink, Al Mele, Sigrún Svavarsdóttir, and myself (Foot 1972, Stocker 1979, Brink 1989, 1997, Mele 1996, Svavarsdóttir 1999, Zangwill 1999). But even these philosophers concentrated mostly on arguing against internalism or defending moral realism rather than articulating the externalist alternative. As a consequence, it is not clear how the externalism that can be gleaned from these writings can be defended against various objections to externalism. This paper is concerned to fashion an attractive version of externalism, and show how it evades objections.

In section I, a particular version of motivational externalism will be presented. In section II, that account will be filled out in the course of dealing with six superficial objections, which are dispatched rather briskly. Then, in section III, the account will be elaborated further by reflection on the distinction between moral and non-moral motives. In sections IV, V, and VI, three deep objections will be tackled and disposed of. That leaves externalism looking attractive and flaw-free.

And, given the problems for internalism, it means that we should believe externalism.

I. Moral Content Externalism: Exposition

In order to state an attractive form of externalism, the traditional conception of the main issue about our moral thought needs recasting. This conception has set the terms of the debate for a long time. However, we should question those terms. On this conception, we want to know whether moral thought is *cognitive* or *non-cognitive*. But casting the debate in such terms has significant drawbacks, especially when we are trying to formulate an acceptable externalism.

We do better to frame the issue in terms of the "representational content" of propositional attitudes of *all* sorts – whether cognitive or non-cognitive. The issue, so characterized, is whether or not we have propositional attitudes, *the contents of which represents mind-independent moral states of affairs*. Let us call such content "realistic moral content." A "moral state of affairs" would be the possession, by a person or their actions or passions, of a real and mind-independent moral property.[1] We can call someone who thinks we have realistic moral contents, a "realist about moral thought," and let us call someone who thinks we don't, a "non-realist about moral thought."

Why should we prefer this characterization of the issue? The reason is that this distinction cuts across the distinction between cognitive and non-cognitive states. There is no reason why someone who thinks that our moral *judgements* are cognitive with realistic moral content should not allow that we also have *non-cognitive* states with realistic moral content – consider guilt, remorse, and the feeling of moral horror. And, conversely, some varieties of cognitivism do not involve the idea that we represent mind-independent moral states of affairs; an example is "subjectivism" – the theory that moral judgements are beliefs about attitudes. It is still true that a realist about moral thought thinks that our moral *judgements* are cognitive, while for most non-realists about moral thought, they are non-cognitive. It is just that there is more to be said than that. Another significant advantage of this alternative characterization of the issue over

moral thought is that we no longer have to face quite the same crippling difficulty over saying exactly what the distinction between cognitive and non-cognitive states amounts to (Schueler 1991, Humberstone 1992, Zangwill 1998).

Given this preliminary, we are in a position to see that the following externalist account of moral motivation is available to realists about moral thought. Moral motivation, on this account, is to be explained by appealing to the existence of *specifically moral motives*. A realist about moral thought can say that when we act on a moral belief, the content of the independent desire which motivates us is moral – that is, its content represents a mind-independent moral state of affairs, where a moral state of affairs is the instantiation of a moral property by something. The motivating desire is the desire to do the morally preferable thing – or perhaps to do the right thing. (Moral goodness is something we can *lust* after!) Moral motivation, on this view, is a matter, first, of believing that some act of ours would have the property of being morally better than some alternative, plus second, there is an independent desire to do actions with that property. These two may combine, in the right circumstances, and perhaps in the light of rational reflection and an act of will, to yield action. Let us call this *Moral Content Externalism* – "MCE" for short.

It is easy to see why those who are in the grip of the traditional cognitive vs. non-cognitive picture are likely to overlook the fact that someone who thinks that we represent a range of moral facts in our judgements can appeal to desires with moral contents. For the assumption is that in giving an account of moral thought, we either appeal only to cognitive states or else we appeal only to non-cognitive states. This is why the "cognitivist" is likely to posit self-motivating moral beliefs, which incur the difficulties mentioned at the outset.

II. Six Relatively Superficial Objections and Replies

Objection (a): Motivational externalism implies that the motivation for conforming to morality derives from a source quite alien to morality. (See for example, McDowell 1978, pp. 25–6.)

---

[1] I discuss the problem of distinguishing real from quasi-properties in Zangwill 1992; I discuss mind-independence in Zangwill 1994.

Reply: This objection rests on a truth. This truth is that when we act on a moral judgement, the motivation is a moral motivation and not a non-moral motivation. *One* way to account for this thought would be the internalism view that motivation springs from the moral judgement alone. But this is not the only way. This insight is also preserved on the externalism account defended here, since the motivating desires have moral content.

Objection (b): If actions are always the result of desires in addition to beliefs, then they are motivated by *selfish* considerations. But moral and selfish motivations are diametrically opposed. So the motivating force of moral judgements cannot be external to them. (Kant seems to endorse this in 1997.)

Reply: The view that actions always result from desires in addition to beliefs, does not imply that we are motivated by selfish considerations. Not all motivating desires are selfish. The fact that the agent must have *some* desire, does not mean that it must be a desire *for* some state of the agent (Williams 1973). There is no reason to think motivational externalism implies psychological egoism. The two issues are quite unconnected.

Objection (c): Our grounds for attributing moral judgements to people are what they do. Hence whether a person has made a moral judgement is not independent of whether he acts on it. So moral judgements cannot be motivated by extrinsic desires. (See, for example, Hare 1952.)

Reply: What people do is indeed *evidence* for their moral beliefs. But one can admit that without embracing internalism. An externalist can admit an evidential relation, so long as an independent motivating desire is usually present. What we do will be evidence for our moral beliefs so long as we typically also have a standing moral desire of sufficient strength. Given a moral desire, we will act on our moral beliefs, unless there are competing motivations or unless there is some failure of rationality. This evidential argument could only be attractive given some very strong and implausible behaviorist premise.

Objection (d): All right, perhaps externalism can explain the connection between judgement and motivation so long as the desire is present. But what if it is not? Externalism about moral motivation leaves open the possibility that someone has strong moral beliefs about some particular matter, but who is not motivated *at all*. This seems objectionable.

Reply: It is not obvious that it is counter-intuitive or impossibly problematic to admit this as a bare possibility – in an extreme case. The bare possibility of someone who has moral beliefs but no moral desires at all is unlikely to be realized, but it is not unthinkable. Perhaps psychopaths are like this. Given that it is in some sense natural for human beings to have a standing general moral desire, this possibility would rarely be realized.

Objection (e): If moral motivation were contingent on an independent desire, it would seem to follow that moral obligations would not apply to someone who lacked such a desire. But to say that would make it too easy to escape the demands of morality.

Reply: We should not confuse the view that moral judgements *motivate* us only on condition that we have some independent desire with the dubious view that the *truth* or *correctness* of a moral judgement depends on the existence of that desire. That would imply that the most obnoxious actions are perfectly all right so long as we feel like doing them! What makes our moral judgements true or correct is one thing, and what motivates us is another. There is no reason why one should not hold that the moral *truth* is independent of our desires, while moral *motivation* is dependent on them.

Objection (f): Moral judgements cannot be externally motivating because if they were, we could be obligated to do things that we are incapable of doing. But we must be capable of doing our duty. Surely "ought-implies-can." But people who know what their duty is but have no desire to do it, not only will not, but cannot do their duty.

Reply: The scope of the ought–implies–can principle is contestable. We can distinguish external and internal constraints on action. Someone cannot be obligated to jump over the moon since there are factors preventing him jumping over it which are outside his control. But it is not clear that internal, psychological constraints always defeat an obligation (Dennett 1984). Suppose someone is utterly indifferent to morality. He has no desire to do what he knows morality enjoins him to do. Then, in a sense, he cannot do what he ought to do. But in that sense this is also true of many quite ordinary cases of free action. Suppose someone has no desire at all to raise his right arm. Then it might be argued that he cannot raise his right arm since he has no desire to do so. But this is obviously too quick, which shows that the ought-implies-can principle is being applied too crudely. (A Kantian might step in at this point and say that the rational will, determined by a judgement of duty, can act counter to all desires; but, of course, that move begs the question at issue, since it is an internalist model.)

III. Sympathy and the Motive of Duty

Let us now flesh out the MCE account by contrasting the motivational role of moral and nonmoral desires. What will emerge is an attractive and intuitive model of moral motivation.

It is sometimes assumed that *if* we are motivated to act on our moral beliefs by independent desires, then they must be desires with *non-moral* content, such as sympathy or benevolence. This is the line Foot takes (Foot 1972), but it is at this point that she errs (from the point of view of MCE). She is right to think that the motivational force of moral judgements is contingent on desire, but she is wrong in her assumption about the content of the motivating desires. If the motivational force of moral judgement were contingent on sympathy or benevolence, as Foot says, then the source of moral motivation would be non-moral, which would be unsatisfactory. But the cognitivist need not say that.

This point about the content of moral desire is crucially important because if a moral belief is to figure in the rational causation of action, then it must combine with a desire with similar content – the contents of the belief and the desire must match each other. (This may underlie the thought that the source of our being motivated by our moral judgements cannot be alien to morality.)

Since MCE is the view that the contents of the desires that motivate us to act on moral judgements are specifically moral, it has the consequence that we can distinguish those motivating moral desires from the ordinary non-moral desires with which the moral desire may conflict. For example, we may desire not to perform some onerous moral duty, but do so all the same. This is because in that situation, we have the moral belief that we ought to do the act, and we desire to do our duty, even though we also don't want to do it for other reasons. On other occasions, such non-moral desires are not opposed by moral desires, and then we will probably fail to do our duty. The presence or absence of the moral desire would explain the difference. And even when a moral judgement *reinforces* what we ordi-narily want to do, the *extra* motivational force is explained as springing from the independent moral desire.

Hence, from the point of view of MCE, Kant was absolutely right to distinguish "the motive of duty," from "melting compassion" (Kant 1998, section I). In contemporary language, this translates into the distinction between moral and altruistic motivation – between our concern with duty and our concern with the welfare of others. Some actions are indeed motivated by sympathy and benevolence, but Kant was right to insist that "acting out of duty" or moral motivation is quite different. To describe actions that are motivated by duty or moral goodness as motivated by sympathy or benevolence is intuitively inaccurate. (Perhaps it is even at variance with the relevant phenomenology.) The difference lies in the *contents* of the desires: one employs moral concepts, the other does not. The person motivated by duty has the thought "It is morally good that I do this thing," whereas the person motivated by altruism has the thought "So and so needs such and such." Altruistic acts are not done for the sake of duty, but for the sake of others. Acting out of altruism is one thing, acting "out of duty" is another.

Despite this agreement between moral content externalism and Kant's view, MCE need not be lumbered with one of Kant's more unpalatable doctrines – that the *only* motives which are good are moral motives (Kant 1998, section I). Kant *may* be right to think that actions done out of duty are of special worth; perhaps they are superior to those done out of altruism. But this is not obvious. It can only be a matter of first-order moralizing. The MCE model of motivation does not commit us to this first-order moral view. We *may* want to say that altruism is morally good and that malice is bad. But that would be a substantial moral claim, not a matter of definition. Altruism may be something which we think is morally good, without itself involving mental states with moral contents. That mental states can be valuable even though they do not have moral content is illustrated by the fact that many moralists of a utilitarian inclination have thought that bodily pain is bad even though it has no content at all or else its content is that a part of the body is damaged. They may have been wrong, but they were not confused. Similarly, the value of the motive of duty is a first-order matter, not a matter of definition. This first-order doctrine of Kant remains unpalatable even if we realize that

Kant is not saying that actions done out of respect for duty are better when sympathy is lacking. Although commentators like Barbara Herman and Richard Galvin are within their rights when they point out that Kant does not say that the moral person lacks sympathy and is unfeeling and unsympathetic (Herman 1981, Galvin, 1991), they are quite mistaken if they think that that negative point is sufficient to remove the moral doubt that surrounds Kant's doctrine that sympathy counts for nothing in itself. Nevertheless, this error on Kant's part should not lead us to lose sight of the important truth in Kant's distinction between the motive of duty and sympathy – between moral and non-moral motives.

IV. Fetishism and the Motive of Duty

Michael Smith complained that motivational externalism, which seems to me to be attractive and intuitive, is in fact unattractive and unintuitive. His objection is that externalism implies that the "virtuous agent" is ultimately motivated by the fact that he possesses a moral property rather than by the natural features of the situation in which he acts (Smith 1994, pp. 72–6; Smith 1997, pp. 112–17).

One thing that seems to have gone wrong here, which we should note straightaway, is that Smith's objection unfairly saddles the externalist with the idea that the moral desires which *motivate* a person to act on a moral belief would have to be what *makes* a person morally good (see especially Smith 1994, pp. 74–6, and Smith 1996). But there is no reason why an externalist need accept this. That specifically moral desires are needed if we are to be *moved* to act on a moral belief does not mean that we *gain our moral virtue* from such motivations.

What Smith has in mind is the persuasive thought that the moral agent should not have "one thought too many," in Bernard Williams's memorable phrase (Smith 1994, p. 73; Williams 1981; see also Brink 1997, pp. 27–8). Smith thinks that he can use Williams's point for anti-externalist ends. In Williams's story a man's wife is in a burning building and he desires ("inclines") to save her. Of course, Williams is right that his wife would have a right to complain if the man – call him Harold – felt no inclination to save her just because she is his wife and if he were motivated to save her *only* out

of a sense of duty. Suppose, however, that there is time for reflection before saving-time arrives. Harold is in a car on the way to the burning building where he knows that his wife is in danger. He might reflect and judge not only that is he inclined to save her, but also that saving her is his duty because she is his wife. (That is, he might reflectively morally endorse acting on his particular inclinations.) These two thoughts do not compete in this case (although in other cases they might). The car arrives at the building; the time comes for Harold to act; and he can happily act on both motivations. The moral motivation is that it is his duty to save her because she is his wife, and the non-moral motivation is his intrinsic concern for her welfare. But Smith assumes that he either acts on one motivation or the other.

More important, though, is Smith's less than ideally charitable analysis of the specifically moral motivation. Someone like Harold is not, as Smith alleges, motivated by some kind of solipsistic moral fact about himself – a narcissistic concern with his own moral standing (Smith 1997, pp. 114–15). He is motivated not only by the non-moral Williamsian though "It's my wife," but also by the thought that that is a morally appropriate motivation. Why do we have to choose between them? What Smith overlooks, quite generally, is the fact that when a person acts out of duty, the ordinary natural features of the act that impose the duty remain significant. Those natural properties play a role in moral motivation because we take those natural properties to determine a moral property and we are motivated by the fact that the act, with its natural properties, has that moral property. So the natural features are essential. They do not drop out of the picture as Smith alleges. It is true that the agent is acting on the moral properties he possesses; but he possesses them in virtue of having an intrinsic concern with other's needs. *Those* needs do not motivationally disappear in the motive of duty. They are part of the motive of duty.

Where there are two sources of motivation, they can come apart. Imagine someone with the misguided moral belief that blue-eyed children should be put to death, and who also desires to do his duty. However, fortunately, when he comes to act, he feels an upsurge of compassion and he fails to act on his moral belief and instead acts on compassion. That is, he thinks that he is morally obligated to kill blue-eyed children, but when he is confronted with the opportunity to do so, he has an attack of weak will and spares them out of compassion. What should we say about him? We should say that he should be morally credited for his "virtuous" action and compassionate motives despite his misguided moral beliefs. We should eschew too intellectualist a picture of the *bearer* of moral value. Contrary to Smith's understanding of the externalist view, we can surely gain moral credit from our non-moral motivations, even if it takes a specifically moral motive to get us to act on our moral judgements. There is no tension here.

What seems to be generating the trouble is Smith's over-inclusive conception of what he calls the "virtuous agent." (This confusion may be traceable to John McDowell's writings.) He thinks that he is not motivated by moral considerations, but by considerations such as other's welfare. Smith's "virtuous person" would be someone who acted merely on "melting compassion" and not at all "out of duty" (in Kant's terms). But we can grant Smith that it is often the fact that a person is concerned with another's welfare that *determines* his moral goodness (or the rightness of his action). So *we* ought to judge that *he* is virtuous because of his non-moral desires. But that has nothing to do with the moral judgements that *he* makes. Of course, *he* might also judge that his own motivations or actions are morally appropriate, but that is another matter. In most cases, *what makes us good* is one thing; and *what motivates us to act on moral judgements about ourselves* is another. Non-moral motivations may make us good but they cannot (by themselves) motivate us to act on our moral beliefs. For that we need a moral desire. Thus Smith's fetishism argument is ultimately ineffective. But addressing it has been worthwhile.

V. Appropriate Moral Motivation

R. Jay Wallace has challenged the externalist to explain why, even though we are not necessarily moved by a moral judgement, nevertheless, being motivated is *appropriate* to our moral judgements (Wallace 2001). There is, Wallace thinks, a *normative* connection between moral judgement and motivation. Wallace concedes that people can deny that moral judgements give us reasons for action. He concedes that motivation does not necessarily accompany a moral judgement. Nevertheless he thinks that (positive) motivation is appropriate to a (positive) moral judgement. A moral cynic,

(Svavarsdóttir's example of Patrick, for example [Svavarsdóttir 1999]), may not desire to do the morally right thing. But moral judgements do in fact *give* reasons for action, even if the cynic, in Wallace's language, does not *take* moral considerations to be normative for him. The moral judgement counts in favor of acting in accordance with it. It is a reason to act. The moral cynic may deny this. He may not *take* moral judgements to give him reasons. But he is wrong. They do. Furthermore, the fact that *non*-cynics think that morality does give them reasons explains why they have moral desires. But externalist moral realists cannot have that explanation of why those who have moral desires do in fact have them. Wallace asks: on an externalist account, why isn't the desire to do what is good quite arbitrary? Why isn't it like "a taste for clams or the color azure" (Wallace 2001, p. 6). A moral desire would be an irrational attachment to something that is not intrinsically worthy of desire. But surely, Wallace argues, the moral desire is appropriate to a moral judgement. The goodness of the action is a reason in favor of desiring it; and if a person sees this, they ought to be motivated by what is right, even if they are not. And when someone *is* motivated, he is motivated because he sees that morality gives him reason to act. This is a *somewhat* internalist thought – and Wallace thinks that externalists will have trouble explaining it. Wallace concludes that moral desires would be "fetishistic" for the externalist, not quite in Smith's sense, but in the more ordinary sense in which they are a desire for something that does not intrinsically warrant desire.

This is an interesting objection, but it can be defused. For it is not plausible that moral judgements give reasons in the way that Wallace says. We can see this very quickly if we think about *false* moral judgements. Suppose someone has a false moral judgement that he should kill red-haired people. Should he desire to kill them? Surely not! So moral *judgements* do not give reasons in themselves. Wallace's fetishism challenge remains. But there is clearly something wrong with his blanket normativity claim.

In what sense, and in virtue of what, is moral desire "appropriate"? For an externalist moral realist, the only normativity here is *moral* normativity. The fact that someone morally ought to do an act, means (determines) that he morally ought to desire to do it. After all, how could he do it without desiring to do it or without intending to do it? This nicely explains Wallace's difficulty over false moral judgements. It is the *moral facts* that make moral desires appropriate. The externalist moral realist can easily explain the normative connection between moral *judgements* and moral motivation when those judgements are *true*. But when they are *false*, there is no such connection to be explained! When a moral judgement is false, there is *no* requirement to act, or to desire to act, or to intend to act, on such a moral judgement.

What of the generic general background desire to do the right thing? That desire is indeed appropriate to the fact that there are some moral facts, which include moral facts about what one should do. We all ought to have such a generic moral desire, even if not everyone does. That's because there *are* moral facts about what one ought to do, and thus about what one ought to desire and intend to do. This generic moral desire, together with particular moral judgements, generates particular desires to do what particular moral judgements prescribe (Zangwill 1999). And when such particular moral judgements are true, that's what we ought to do, and intend to do, and desire to do.

Hence Wallace's challenge poses no insurmountable difficulty for the externalist moral realist.

VI.   Externalism and Deliberation

Let us lastly turn to consider what practical reasoning about morality looks like on the MCE view. Surely, if we are motivated to act by moral desires, these desires must also play a role in the practical deliberation that produces action. Otherwise, practical reason will not connect with the sources of motivation. And if moral desires play a role in practical reasoning, it would be means–end instrumental reasoning. But many will find this objectionable. Surely – it will be objected – however valid a means–end model of "practical reasoning" is as a model of *much* of our deliberation, it cannot be extended to morality. For *moral* deliberation, if it is about anything, is about what *ends* we ought to have. Moreover if we were to apply a means–end model to deliberation about our ends, we would start a bottomless regress. It seems that a quite different account of moral deliberation is needed.

However, it is open to MCE to admit, unashamedly, that moral deliberation *is* plain old-fashioned means–end instrumental deliberation!

An externalist model of moral motivation is indeed committed to a means–end model of practical reasoning about morality – and that is perfectly acceptable. For we can be motivational externalists *and* instrumentalists about practical reason. It is just that when we deliberate about morality, our ends are moral ends. We are interested in moral truth as a means to satisfying our moral desires; we deliberate about morality because we have moral desires. Some will find this idea unsettling. But it is perfectly satisfactory so long as we realize that it does not imply the dubious view that moral *truth* depends on those desires. The fact that we are obligated stands whether or not we care about morality. But only if we care about morality will our awareness of moral truths feed into our practical deliberation. And indeed, only if we care about morality *should* it do so, in the sense that it would be rational to do so. Someone who took account of morality even though they had no moral desires would be irrational. That would be good perhaps, but irrational nonetheless. That's okay though, since moral goodness and rationality are different kinds of evaluative properties (well – for everyone apart from Kantians).

If someone *insists*, we can translate this point into "reason-for-action" language as follows – although talking in these terms invites unnecessary complications and confusions. We could distinguish a notion of someone's *having* a reason to act from *there being* a reason for someone to act (Smith 1994, pp. 94–8 is helpful here; see also Brink 1989, p. 40). There might *be* reasons that we do not *have*. If one is subject to a moral duty, then perhaps there is a sense in which *there* is a certain kind of reason for one to do something – a moral reason for action. By contrast, *having* a reason to act might be a matter of *thinking* that there is a certain kind of reason to act, where one might be entirely mistaken. Or having a reason to act might be a matter of being *justified* in thinking there is a reason to act, given one's "internal" states, in the sense of "internal" which is operative is epistemology (Bonjour 1985; Pollock 1987). So one could have a justified false belief about reasons for action. Or having a reason could be a matter of having a desire that an act would satisfy. These various "subjective" notions of "reason for action" contrast with the sense of "reason for action," where that is just an "objective" matter of what one ought to do, whatever internal states one is in. Since one's moral duties are (for the most part) independent of one's judgements about reasons or of one's desires or "inclinations," they provide "objective" reasons for action. But in the sense of "subjective" reasons, people do not *have* a reason unless they want to do their duty and have a view about what their duty is. In *this* sense, facts about moral obligations do not generate reasons for action in the absence of moral desires. One cannot be instrumentalist about "objective" reasons for action. But one can be instrumentalist about "subjective" practical rationality, where that is a matter of how *responsibly* one practices given one's internal states, or given one's "subjective set" (Williams 1978). Note that having a reason, in this "subjective" sense will connect directly with motivational efficacy if rational deliberation about action presupposes some desire, since that desire will have motivational force.

Given motivational externalism, what if someone asks, in an undiscriminating way, whether we "have reason" to follow the dictates of morality? Does motivational externalism bring an unpalatable view about moral reasons for action in its train, which implies that an "amoralist," who does not give a fig for morality, can be as beastly as he pleases without our being able to say that he has reason to be moral? It is easy to see that this line of reasoning is confused. It is true that the requirements of morality bear on us regardless of our desires. But we should be wary of putting this in terms of "reasons for action." If someone insists on talking that way, we can distinguish two notions of "reason for action." The amoralist lacks the relevant desire. So he would be instrumentally irrational to heed moral requirements. In *that* sense, he has *no* reason to be moral. But the requirements of morality still apply to him. And in *that* sense, there *is* a reason for him to be moral. In inelegant terms, "reasons

of morality" apply but not "reasons of rationality." But this is surely a messy way of putting things. It is simpler and more elegant to say that the amoralist is subject to a moral requirement but not a rational requirement.

Of course, it is far from uncontroversial that instrumentalism is correct as a general theory of practical rationality. Kantians also have theories of rationality, and those theories are not instrumentalist. They have their rational categorical imperatives. The point is merely the defensive one that if motivational externalism is committed to an instrumentalist view of practical reasoning about morality, that is not a problem. Given MCE, an instrumentalist conception of practical rationality delivers a respectable view of moral deliberation.

Coda

In sum, MCE can evade many objections that are thought to threaten motivational externalism. Ironically, the realist about moral thought can and should accept Hume's view that beliefs motivate us to act only on condition that there are independent desires, which combine with beliefs in means–end deliberation. It is just that in morality, those desires have moral content. In Hume's terms, reason can never move the will without enlisting some passion on its side, but the realist about moral thought should pin his faith on the moral passions. Hume was right about motivation in general but he was wrong about the consequences for morality. A realist about moral thought should happily accept Hume's dictum that "Reason is, and ought only to be, the slave of the passions." For in morality, reason is, and ought only to be, the slave of the moral passions.

References

Bonjour, Lawrence. 1985. *The Structure of Empirical Knowledge.* Cambridge, MA: Harvard University Press.

Brink, David. 1989. *Moral Realism and the Foundations of Ethics.* Cambridge: Cambridge University Press.

Brink, David. 1997. "Moral Motivation," *Ethics,* vol. 108, pp. 4–32.

Dennett, Dan. 1984. *Elbow Room.* Cambridge, MA: MIT Press.

Foot, Philippa. 1972. "Morality as a System of Hypothetical Imperatives" In *Virtues and Vices.* Oxford: Blackwell, 1978.

Galvin, Richard. 1991. "On the Alleged Repugnance of Acting From the Motive of Duty." *Mind,* vol. 100, pp. 221–36.

Hare, R. M. 1952. *The Language of Morals.* Oxford: Oxford University Press.

Herman, Barbara. 1981. "On the Value of Acting From the Motive of Duty." *Philosophical Review,* vol. 90, pp. 359–82.

Humberstone, Lloyd. 1992. "Direction of Fit." *Mind,* vol. 101, pp. 59–83.

Hume, David. 1888. *Treatise.* Selby-Bigge edition. Oxford: Oxford University Press.

Kant, Immanuel. 1997. *Critique of Practical Reason.* Trans. Mary Gregor. Cambridge: Cambridge University Press.

Kant, Immanuel. 1998. *The Groundwork of the Metaphysics of Morals.* Trans. Mary Gregor. Cambridge: Cambridge University Press.

McDowell, John. 1978. "Are Moral Requirements Hypothetical Imperatives?" *Aristotelian Society* supplementary volume 52, pp. 13–29.

McDowell, John. 1979. "Virtue and Reason." *Monist*, vol. 62, pp. 331–50.

Mele, Al. 1996. "Moral Cognitivism and Listlessness." *Ethics*, vol. 106, pp. 727–53.

Pollock, John. 1987. "Epistemic Norms." *Synthese*, vol. 71, pp. 61–95.

Schueler, Fred. 1991. "Pro-attitudes and Directions of Fit." *Mind*, vol. 100, pp. 277–81.

Smith, Michael. 1994. *The Moral Problem.* Oxford: Blackwell.

Smith, Michael. 1996. "Reply to Miller." *Analysis*, vol. 56, pp. 175–84.

Smith, Michael. 1997. "In Defence of the *Moral Problem*." *Ethics*, vol. 108, pp. 84–119.

Stocker, Michael. 1979. "Desiring the Bad." *Journal of Philosophy*, vol. 76, pp. 738–53.

Svavarsdóttir, Sigrún. 1999. "Moral Cognitivism and Motivation." *Philosophical Review*, vol. 108, pp. 161–219.

Wallace, Jay. 2001. "Commentary on Svavarsdóttir's 'Moral Cognitivism and Motivation.'" *Brown Electronic Article Review Service*, Jamie Dreier and David Estlund, editors <http://www.brown.edu/Departments/Philosophy/bears/homepage.html>. Posted August 10, 2001.

Williams, Bernard. 1973. "Egoism and Altruism." In *Problems of the Self.* Cambridge: Cambridge University Press.

Williams, Bernard. 1978. "Internal and External Reasons." In *Moral Luck.* Cambridge: Cambridge University Press.

Williams, Bernard. 1981. "Persons, Character, and Morality." In *Moral Luck.* Cambridge: Cambridge University Press.

Wolf, Susan. 1992. "Morality and Partiality." *Philosophical Perspectives*, vol. 6, pp. 243–59.

Zangwill, Nick. 1992. "Quietism." *Midwest Studies in Philosophy*, vol. 17, pp. 160–76.

Zangwill, Nick. 1994. "Moral Mind-Independence." *Australasian Journal of Philosophy*, vol. 72, pp. 205–19.

Zangwill, Nick. 1998. "Direction of Fit and Normative Functionalism." *Philosophical Studies*, vol. 91, pp. 173–203.

Zangwill, Nick. 1999. "Dilemmas and Moral Realism." *Utilitas*, vol. 11, pp. 75–90.

Virtue as Knowledge: Objections from the Philosophy of Mind

Margaret Olivia Little

1. Recently, a number of philosophers have advocated theories reviving the idea that virtue is moral knowledge. To apprehend the Good aright, on this picture, *is* to love it. When we do not act morally, as all too often we do not, it is because we suffer a kind of "moral blindness": to put it metaphorically, our moral vision is clouded, our attunement to the ethical superficial, our moral grasp vague or distorted. The idea, which has an ancient and impressive pedigree, has found renewed advocacy in the works of John McDowell (1978, 1979, 1981), Martha Nussbaum (1986), Mark Platts (1979), and David McNaughton (1988).[1]

Such a view clearly involves contentious claims. After all, it advocates some brand of moral realism or objectivity, in the sense that it claims there are moral truths we can come to know. Further, it forwards a philosophy of action according to which agency is at least sometimes found in cognition. In ideal cases of moral motivation, at least, authorship of intentional, responsible action involves no distinct faculty of noumenal will, say, or inference of practical reasoning: to be moved is to discern things in a particular way. Debates over the view, it would thus seem, should take us to the very heart of deep – which is to say messy – issues about the

possibility of moral truth, the nature of agency, and whether an adequate account of normative authority can be found in their juncture.

In fact, though, there has lately been a tendency to regard the idea of equating virtue and moral knowledge as one that can be cleanly and quickly dismissed on grounds that sidestep such contentious issues. A number of philosophers, but most notably Michael Smith, have argued that such a theory contravenes certain basic, shared tenets of our philosophy of mind and moral psychology (Smith, 1987, 1988a, 1988b, 1994). The virtue theory states, in essence, that certain belief states *are* desire states, or alternatively, that possession of certain belief states *entails* possession of certain desire states. But the very natures of belief and desire, it is claimed, stand in the way of such connections. Beliefs and desires are so fundamentally different – designed to perform such different functions, governed by such disparate rules, assessed by such different standards – that they are simply unsuited as conceptual bedfellows.

This suspicion, which could be fairly labeled Humean in spirit, has been fleshed out in terms of beliefs' and desires' respective "direction of fit." Belief and desire are defined by different and

---

[1] Socrates and Aristotle, of course, advanced some version of the theory, as did 18th-century Rationalists such as Richard Price (1974).

opposing directions of fit, it is said, but the moral theory under question posits a mental state with both directions of fit, or, alternatively, a mental state with a belief direction of fit whose possession entails possession of a mental state satisfying a desire direction of fit. Both such states, we are told, are of questionable coherence. At the very least, they would be "hybrids" of an odd and unfamiliar nature, and hence deserving of our deep suspicion. This background suspicion is borne out, it is urged, when we turn our attention to the lived experiences of human morality: the idea that moral knowledge guarantees moral motivation simply flies in the face of actual moral motivational failures. It is at once too intellectualist and too thin a theory to capture the rich array of cases – outlined by Michael Stocker (1979) among others – in which we fail to have the slightest urge to do as we ourselves believe we should.

I think that these arguments from the philosophy of mind and moral psychology, narrowly construed, are simply barking up the wrong tree. The considerations they advance give us no reason on their own to dismiss or even look skeptically on the suggestion that virtue is moral knowledge. For starters, I hope to make clear that there is nothing in the mere idea of belief and desire that constrains, even presumptively, the conceptual relations that might obtain between them. One may accept analyses of direction of fit as capturing what it is to be a belief and a desire, but such definitional issues provide a remarkably thin wedge for exerting leverage over proposals such as the one under consideration. Arguments that seem to count in the Humean's favor rely, it turns out, on further, smuggled, *substantive* assumptions – assumptions, moreover, about issues that lie well outside the philosophy of mind. Further, it is a mistake to think that the sort of mental state posited by those who equate virtue with moral knowledge represents a radical, odd, or even unfamiliar addition to our common taxonomy of mental states. Our shared philosophy of psychology is both richer and more supple than those who present the above objection would have us think. Finally, while reflections in moral psychology are a welcome addition to the rather more armchair ruminations found in the philosophy of mind, deciding what they show is the $64,000 question. The fact that we experience extensive moral motivational failure does not turn out to be a counterexample to the theory under consideration. Quite to the contrary, I argue, it is

something the virtue theorists take themselves to be explaining; and in the final section of the paper, I provide a sketch of that explanation that shows just how misplaced the objection really is.

Of course, those who advocate virtue as moral knowledge need to explain why we should accept their theory. In the end, we may feel unconvinced by their case, and hence unconvinced of the need to acknowledge the mental states they discuss. What I want to argue is that, if we are wary of those mental states, it will not be in virtue of their conceptual oddity or because of plain facts of moral psychology; it will be in virtue of further substantive disagreements on familiarly contentious issues outside of mind and psychology. To decide whether the theory has merit or is misguided, we will in the end have to tackle the messy task of working through the particular arguments its advocates offer, and to confront the deep issues it raises about the objectivity of morality, conceptions of normative authority, and the nature of agency.

2.   Let me begin by briefly outlining the analysis of belief and desire in terms of directions of fit, and then outlining how the theory equating virtue and moral knowledge translates into these terms. Familiarly, beliefs and desires are each intentional mental states in which a particular kind of attitude is directed toward a proposition. A believing-attitude, we might say, is an attitude of "regarding as true" some proposition, while a desiring-attitude is one of "regarding as to be brought about." Following G. E. M. Anscombe (1957), we can amplify what it means to direct each sort of attitude toward its content by speaking of the resultant mental state's "direction of fit" with the world: crudely put, beliefs are to be changed to fit the way the world is, while the world is to be changed to fit the content of desires. This rather metaphorical notion can be parsed out more concretely in terms of the functional, normative, and counterfactual properties exemplified by the mental states.

To say that beliefs have a mind-to-world direction of fit is to say that the falsity of a belief is a mark of its failure. This means, for one, that the norms by which we evaluate the reasonability of holding beliefs are norms of evidence concerning the proposition toward which the believing attitude is directed: in expressing a belief, we regard ourselves as obligated to offer and respond to considerations that seem to bear on the truth of its propositional content, and we evaluate the reasonability of others' accepting or rejecting the belief by reference to the evidence they have about its truth. It also means that, to count as a belief, a mental state must display some level of counterfactual sensitivity to evidence about its propositional content. Too much stubbornness in the face of evidence indicates that the agent, despite first appearances, is not really committed to advancing the truth. Obviously, this demand must be a fairly weak one, for irrational and fanatical beliefs still count as beliefs. At some point, however, disregard for evidence about the truth of one's assertions – abnegation of one's epistemic responsibilities – indicates that one is not actually in the game of claiming what the world is like.

Desires, on the other hand, have a world-to-mind direction of fit: they don't try to match the world, they try to change it. The falsehood of the desire's propositional content is no mark against the desire, nor is possession of evidence about its falsehood a mark against the reasonability of possessing the desire: the normative strictures governing possession of desires, that is, whatever they may be, are by definition not such as to make the desire beholden to evidence concerning the truth or falsity of the proposition toward which the desiring attitude is directed. Further, because desires aim at making the world match their propositional contents, they counterfactually tend to persist, not disappear, in the face of evidence that their contents are false; and they ground dispositions to act in ways the agent believes will lead to their realization.

Now, at its most general, the view that equates virtue and moral knowledge states that there are certain aspects of reality we cannot clearly and completely discern without thereby having certain desires, indeed, without being moved to act as we see we ought. As Mark Platts puts it, ". . . to recognize the obtaining of, say, some desirable moral feature in a possible state of affairs *is* to desire the obtaining of that state of affairs (though not just that). One cannot see the loyal, the courageous, and so forth *as* the loyal, the courageous, etc., without desiring them" (1980, p. 80).

This quotation from Platts actually helps to illustrate that there are two ways of interpreting the theory's claimed relation between moral knowledge and moral motivation. As both advocates and challengers agree, one might interpret the theory as claiming that the clear apprehension of a moral requirement *is* at one and the same time a motivational state (as the quotation's first sentence seems to indicate); alternatively, one might interpret it as claiming, more simply, that the clear apprehension *guarantees* the motivational state (as the second sentence implies). On the first interpretation, the theory posits the existence of a mental state that is both a belief and a desire – what some have (in rather ungainly fashion) dubbed a "besire" – and that thus has both directions of fit. On the second interpretation, the theory posits the existence of a state with a belief direction of fit whose possession entails possession of a state with a desire direction of fit – what has been called a "desire-entailing belief."[2]

For many, the first is the most natural interpretation. David McNaughton, an advocate of the idea that clear discernment of moral requirements necessarily moves us to act as they recommend, puts the point this way:

> To be aware of a moral requirement is, according to the realist, to have a conception of a situation as demanding a response. Yet to conceive of a situation as demanding a response, as requiring one to do something, is to be in a state whose direction of fit is: the world must fit this state. The requirement will only be satisfied if the agent changes the world to fit it. But the realist also wishes to insist that the agent's conception of the situation is purely cognitive. That is, the agent has a belief that he is morally required to act and so his state must have the direction of fit: this state must fit the world. . . . For his belief will only be correct if it fits the world, if it accurately reflects the way things are. . . . He is committed therefore to the claim that the awareness of a moral requirement is a state which must be thought of, Janus-like, as having directions of fit facing both ways. The agent's conception reveals to him both that the world is a certain way and that we must change it. (1988, p. 109)

The theory need not be read in this way, however. After all, even if we believe that the desire varies perfectly with the belief – coming into and going out of existence as the latter does – it does not necessarily mean that the desire inherits all the properties of the belief. In particular, certain properties defining of directions of fit seem to have explanatory overtones (such as "having an aim" or

---

[2] Smith and Pettit sometimes use 'desires = beliefs' to refer to desire-entailing beliefs.

"grounding a disposition"), and these, of course, do not automatically transfer across extensional contexts such as covariation. In the end, it may simply be a matter of decision how we individuate the mental states – when to talk about one state that has two directions of fit, and when to talk about two states that are tied in an intimate relation.

We will be returning to this interpretational issue later. In any event, those who have objected to the theory have claimed that it suffers under either interpretation, though seemingly more egregiously under the interpretation that there actually are mental states with doubled directions of fit. Let us turn to the various objections advanced.

3.   One persistent charge is that a *literal* interpretation of the idea of a mental state with doubled direction of fit is "just plain incoherent" (Smith, 1994, p. 118; 1987, p. 56). To go forward, then, a theory that posits such a state must rely on some more "relaxed" (1987, p. 56) – perhaps more "subtle" (1994, p. 118) but perhaps more "mysterious" (1987, p. 57) – interpretation of its nature, in which the mental state is conceived of as being a "quasi-belief" (1987, p. 56) or "belief- and desire-like" (1994, p. 118) Despite its concessionary tone – allowing as it does the possibility of pursuing a non-literal interpretation – such a charge saddles the discussion from the start with a sense that something dubious or problematic is in the works. (Indeed, if the charge were innocent of such effect, one wonders why objectors such as Smith continue to raise it before moving on to the more "subtle" interpretation.) I want to take the time, then, to lay to rest this train of thought. For the idea that a fully literal interpretation involves any incoherence at all is a plain red herring: it rests either on a compositional fallacy or on smuggled substantive claims about the best theory of rationality.

We should be clear about what it would take for a literal interpretation to involve incoherence. Note that agreeing to the slogan, "Beliefs and desires have different directions of fit," is simply agreeing that there are different defining properties of being a belief and being a desire. It does not on its own commit us to agreeing that a belief cannot also be a desire, for it leaves open the formal possibility that a mental state could instantiate the properties defining of each. This formal idea is incoherent just in case those sets of properties have incompatible or conflicting instantiation conditions, like the properties being square and being circular.

Of the member properties that together define directions of fit, the culprit most often cited as the locus of incoherence is the property concerning beliefs' and desires' evidential sensitivity. Beliefs, we are reminded, are partially defined in terms of their counterfactual dependence on evidence about the truth or falsehood of the propositional content that is believed; but desires are understood as persisting independently of evidence concerning the truth or falsehood of the propositional content that is desired. Thus, it has been argued, a literal reading of the claim that a mental state has two directions of fit means that such a state instantiates conflicting counterfactual properties: it would both have to track and not track certain specified evidence (Smith, 1994, p. 118; 1987, p. 56). We are left with a state pulling, as it were, in opposing directions at one and the same time.

Now it is certainly true that a mental state cannot satisfy the conditions of tending to disappear and to persist in the face of evidence about a given proposition. It is certainly true, that is, that a mental state cannot have both a belief-direction of fit and a desire-direction of fit with respect to one and the same proposition. But the idea that a fully literal interpretation of doubled direction of fit requires both directions to concern the same proposition rests on a compositional fallacy. The properties of being a belief and of being a desire, we should remember, are complex properties, involving in each case a propositional attitude and a propositional content. Now some people seem to assume that where there is one mental state there is one propositional content; when then confronted with the possibility of a state with doubled directions of fit, they wonder what "its" propositional content could be. But there is no one propositional content of a mental state with doubled directions of fit, anymore than there is one propositional attitude involved in such a state. It is a state with two *complex* properties: it is a believing-attitude directed toward one proposition, and it is a desiring-attitude directed toward another. There is nothing formally odd in saying that a belief(p) can also be the desire(q), just as there is nothing formally odd in nothing that the mathematical operation "add(2)" is also the operation "subtract(–2)."

Put schematically, a mental state will count as having a belief-direction of fit just in case it satisfies the properties defining of that direction with respect to some proposition – for instance, it meets the minimal standards of counterfactual dependence on evidence regarding the proposition's truth – and a mental state will turn out to have a desire-direction of fit just in case it satisfies the properties defining of that direction with respect to some proposition – for instance, it grounds the disposition to bring it about that the proposition is true. Just as this schema is silent about which proposition must be involved for a mental state to count as a belief or a desire, it is silent about which propositions – the same or different – must be involved for a mental state to count as both.

There will, then, be no counterfactual tension in literal interpretation of a mental state having two opposing directions of fit just in case the directions of fit concern different propositions. And, of course, this is precisely what the theory equating virtue with moral knowledge cares to advance: it connects a kind of belief that *p is good* with a desire that *p*, claiming that the mental state responds to and is judged in terms of evidence that *p is good*, while it grounds a disposition to make it the case that *p*. As far as the counterfactual property of evidential sensitivity is concerned, then, we can stay with a fully literal, and fully coherent, notion of a mental state with doubled directions of fit.

A further complaint focuses on the normative strictures that govern the reasonability of possessing or abandoning beliefs and desires.[3] Mental states cannot have both directions of fit, it is charged, because beliefs and desires are governed by opposing sorts of normative rules. Normative assessments of beliefs, it is urged, are assessments that deal with truth and evidence, but normative assessments of desire are insulated from these issues. Of course, given what we have just rehearsed, we know that the accusation here cannot be that the besire would have both to be and not to be evaluated by the evidence concerning one and the same proposition – as we've seen, the mental state is supposed to be a belief-attitude directed toward *p is good* and a desire-attitude directed toward *p*. The complaint must be that desires are immune in some broader fashion from evidential assessment, while beliefs, of course, are not: we measure the rationality of a person's holding a belief relative to her pool of evidence, the thought goes, but we do not appraise her desires by looking at the sort of evidence she might have – desires are simply not the sort of mental state whose posses-

sion is made reasonable or unreasonable by the norms of theoretical reason. To claim then that some one mental state could have two directions of fit, it is concluded, would be to claim that it both does and does not have allegiance to the way the world is, that its possession both is and is not judged by reference to the agent's evidence about the world.

Now, one can certainly forward this view, and many do. The point I want to make, though, is that it does not follow from the definitions of belief and desire. It reflects the acceptance of a particular, substantive, and contested picture about the nature of rationality. Let me illustrate what I mean by returning first to the case of belief. The definition of a belief specifies the properties such a mental state will have with respect to the content toward which the believing attitude is directed: here, we have noted, it is normatively beholden to evidence concerning the truth or falsehood of that proposition. The definition of belief itself is silent about the properties the mental state might, must, or should manifest with respect to other propositions. This is not, I hasten to add, to say that *we* are silent about these relations. For instance, it is commonly held these days that epistemic justification is holistic, rather than foundational, which means it is commonly held these days that the reasonability of accepting or retaining a belief ends up being properly assessed relative to *all* of one's evidence. Beliefs, it turns out on this view, are normatively beholden to evidence about the widest range of propositions. But this claim, obviously, is a piece of epistemological theory. It is a substantive view about the nature of theoretical rationality, a view which can be debated, disputed, agreed upon or rejected. It is not part of some neutral, formal characterization of what it takes to count as a belief.

Just so, the *definition* of desire tells us only about the properties such a mental state has with respect to the proposition towards which the desiring-attitude is directed. This, of course, includes the fact that we do not evaluate the reasonability of one's holding a desire by reference to one's evidence about that proposition. The premise of the complaint outlined above, though, is that we do not evaluate the reasonability of holding a desire by reference to any evidence, about any proposition. But the claim that desires have normative im-

---

[3]   Smith alludes to this sort of worry when speaking of the fact that beliefs are such that their contents are "supposed" to fit the world, while desires are not (1988b, pp. 250–1).

munity to *any* evidential consideration is a further, substantive claim, this time in the theory of practical, rather than theoretical, rationality. It is, of course, an eminently familiar theory of practical rationality – indeed, it is a central tenet of any Humean conception of practical rationality, so it is not surprising to find it invoked in the context of a worry that traces its inspiration to Hume. But it is also, and not accidentally, precisely the conception of practical rationality disputed by those who equate virtue and moral knowledge: on their theory of practical rationality, the reasonability of holding a desire has everything to do with whether one has adequate evidence that its end is good. Clearly, the debate here involves a contested issue about the proper substantive conception of practical reason. It is not a matter that is settled by defining what it is for a mental state to count as a desire.

4. The literal idea of a mental state with two directions of fit, then, is neither incoherent nor mysterious – controversial, certainly, but not conceptually puzzling. Of course, demonstrating that an idea doesn't transgress conceptual constraints provides no assurance it will not transgress one's sensibilities about what is theoretically palatable. A second charge is that besires would be "hybrids" of radical departure from the beliefs and desires recognized by "standard" psychology. For some, the point here is that presumption weighs against acknowledgment of besires because they are sufficient outsiders to our conventional repertoire of mental states.[4] For others, though, the sense seems to be, not simply that advocates of besires, as with any advocates of a positive theory, owe us reasons for accepting their view, but that besires are of such a strange nature that we have reason against invoking them even in advance of looking at the phenomena they are meant to capture. This stronger charge, in short, is that besires are bizarre.

In fact, though, these are odd charges to issue from the Humean camp, for reflection shows that any number of Humeans advance taxonomies that include besires – and without anyone thinking they have become radical outliers in the philosophy of mind. We can start, in fact, with none other than Hume himself.

On one plausible and popular interpretation of Hume's metaethical theory, moral verdicts are "pronouncements" about the instantiation of moral properties such as good and evil; but these pronouncements come about as a result of the agent's having projected her own desires or "sentiments" onto the world. As he puts it, "[T]aste . . . has a productive faculty, and gilding or staining all natural objects with the colours, borrowed from internal sentiment, raises in a manner a new creation" (1975, p. 294). Greatly simplified, Hume's view states that we take in the salient natural facts of a situation – we see, for instance, that torture causes pain – and, in a accordance with our human psychology, we feel some approving or disapproving sentiment in response. Instead of simply experiencing the sentiment, though, we project it onto the action of torturing, and, reading off the world what we ourselves have put there, we come to the conclusion that torture has the property 'evil.'

Possession of such a "projectivist state," as we might call it, is not simply equivalent to possession of the naturalistic belief and desire that together form its genesis. After all, the thrust of the story is that we *do* something with the desire: we project it onto the apprehended state of affairs, and thereby think we discern the instantiation of a further, moral property which in some (perhaps inarticulable) sense "answers to" this desire or sentiment. One who engages in this projection differs from one who merely holds the naturalistic belief and desire. She comes to have a further concept, for one thing, and will regard her state as beholden to different pieces of evidence. (For instance, the fact that Mother Teresa regards lying as wrong provides some modest measure of evidence that lying is indeed wrong, given her status as a moral authority. Her believing it wrong, however, does not lend the same measure of evidence to conclusions about any natural property of lying, such as its propensity to cause pain – her reasons for eschewing lying, after all, may be of some intricate deontological variety that has only distant connection to a given natural property.)

And in fact, the projectivist state looks like nothing so much as a mental state with doubled directions of fit. It necessarily has a desire direction of fit, for one cannot project what is not in one's heart, and what is in one's heart grounds a disposition to act in certain ways. Moreover, the

---

[4] Smith issues this more modest charge, emphasizing repeatedly that acknowledgment of besires is acknowledgment of a "hybrid" mental state requiring "revision" to the standard "austere" psychology offered by the belief-desire model (1987, section 7; 1988a, p. 593).

propositional attitude directed toward *p is good* looks to fit the criteria of the believing-attitude. The result of projecting sentiments, after all, is our making a claim about the way the world is – the claim that some state of affairs, say, is good or bad. We put the claims forward as true, we regard ourselves as obligated to offer and respond to considerations that seem to bear on their truth, and we judge others who put them forward in terms of how responsive they are to such considerations. If we are tempted to question how responsive the mental states are to that evidence, we should beware of importing too high a standard of epistemic responsibility. After all, irrational, crazy, superstitious, even fanatical beliefs still count as beliefs; we would be hard-pressed to conclude that moral verdicts have less evidential sensitivity than the average church member's belief in God or the avid fan's belief about the quality of her football team. This is just to remind ourselves that, while it is ambitious to try to qualify as a justified or a true belief, it is in the end a rather modest enterprise simply to count as a belief.

Of course, Hume didn't think that there was any *adequate* evidence for anything's goodness or badness, or any truth to such verdicts (indeed, he thought the verdicts couldn't be true, since on his account they have no meetable truth-conditions). But such contentions argue against the success of the verdicts, not against their status as beliefs. One might disagree, and insist that such considerations are grounds for disqualifying the verdicts as beliefs. But if this is the objection, let me point out, then it is not the philosophy of mind that serves as leverage against the virtue theory after all. That is, if the reason for disqualifying a state as a belief lies in its failure to meet some substantive epistemic standard or in suspicion about the truth-conditions of its propositional content, then the objection, far from being an argument from the philosophy of mind that skirts contentious questions in epistemology and metaphysics, will turn out to be nothing more than a hidden version of familiar battles in these areas.

Now certainly, not every theorist in the Humean camp is tacitly committed to the existence of besires. In particular, some Humeans have argued that we can account for the belief-like elements of moral verdicts without admitting that they are moral beliefs – without admitting, that is, that they involve a belief direction of fit toward evaluative propositions such as *p is good*. The moral verdicts

display some evidential sensitivity, they agree, but it is only sensitivity toward evidence concerning the natural state of affairs onto which the sentiments were projected (for instance, sensitivity to evidence about whether pain is caused). Thus, it is claimed, while we must mention both a desire and a belief (the naturalistically-specified one) in order to individuate moral verdicts, the verdicts themselves are neither besires nor desire-entailing beliefs.

One point is usually overlooked here: even if this is correct, it is still an admission that Hume's psychology of mind is populated by states other than beliefs and desires. For again, possessing the projectivist state, on Hume's story, is not equivalent to possessing the natural belief and desire, though they do form the projection's genetic components. Having engaged in projection, one ends up with an attitude of *some* variety toward a *further* proposition (for it invokes a further concept) than is involved in either the natural belief or desire. If it is not a believing attitude, it is certainly not a desiring attitude, and must hence be something over and above the supposedly "standard" Humean psychology. Even this conservative version of Humean psychology, then, turns out to be richer than those resisting besires would have us believe. Whose taxonomy is the most satisfying – and least mysterious – is a good question, but one that won't be settled by measuring candidates against some phantom default in which beliefs and desires exhaust the field.

In fact, the conservative view just outlined is actually quite difficult to defend. As many – including many who side with other aspects of Hume's metaethics – agree, it is simply very unlikely that the evidential sensitivity of moral verdicts can be fully accounted for as sensitivity to evidence concerning any naturalistically specified proposition. Whether moral verdicts are amply or poorly responsive to evidence, that is, the contours of the evidence they *do* respond to are unlikely to match precisely the contours of evidence concerning nonmoral states of affairs. As Hume himself discusses, once a practice of moralizing begins, it develops a life of its own, and that life is in part constituted by a distinct, substantive conception of the sorts of things that count as evidence for *moral* as opposed to nonmoral conclusions (think again of the example invoking Mother Teresa's testimony). Indeed, reducing moral verdicts' evidential sensitivity to evidence concerning naturalistically specified states of affairs requires that the concepts invoked in the moral verdicts map onto some natural concepts. It requires, that is, that the items grouped together under the moral classification, say, "courageous," form a kind recognizable as such at the nonmoral level, in the way that color concepts map onto concepts about microphysical structure and light-waves. But many, from a variety of philosophical persuasions, have become persuaded that at least some of our moral claims involve concepts that cannot be mapped onto nonmoral ones (McDowell, 1981; Nussbaum, 1986; Williams, 1985, chapter 8; Blackburn, 1981). If some moral concepts are indeed "shapeless" with respect to nonevaluative concepts, then the evidential sensitivity displayed by the mental state could not be reduced to sensitivity about some other specifiable proposition: we could describe it only as sensitivity to evidence that *p is good*. The last barrier to calling such a state a belief would disappear.

One final point. Assume for the moment that the argument just presented is nonsense. Assume that all moral concepts do in fact map onto some natural properties, that we can thereby reduce the projectivist state's evidential sensitivity to evidence about naturalistically specified propositions, and that we can thereby deny that the propositional attitude directed toward *p is good* qualifies as a believing attitude. Notice how *little* now separates this projectivist, desire-entailing state from a besire. The only difference between the two states has to do with the kinds of concepts they involve – more particularly, with the sort of relations these concepts have with concepts from other domains: one involves a concept that can be mapped onto natural properties, the other involves a concept that cannot. But surely, a mental state involving a concept that is shapeless with respect to certain others is not more peculiar *as a mental state* than one involving a concept that bears mapping relations to certain others. The only difference between besires and states already recognized by the most reductionist of projectivists, then, is not a difference that makes besires suddenly outlandish. The step from their mental state to a besire adds no mysterious element to our psychological repertoire: while the step is an important one, it is not a step onto foreign ground.

5.   So far, I have cast suspicions about equating virtue and knowledge as suspicions about the coherence and palatability of besires – of states with doubled directions of fit. I have done so because I wanted to emphasize that even this ambitious interpretation of the virtue doctrine in fact involves nothing conceptually outré or mysterious. Let me now shift that focus. As we saw earlier, the virtue theorist need not be interpreted as positing besires. The theorist may with integrity confine her claim to the assertion that there are certain belief-states whose possession guarantees possession of certain desire-states. Without claiming, that is, that any one individuated mental state is both belief and desire, she can claim that there are desire-entailing beliefs.

While this is a less ambitious claim, Humeans such as Michael Smith are no less disturbed by it. Indeed, Smith (1994, section 4.7; 1988a) and Philip Pettit (1987) have isolated it as the claim that truly separates the non-Humean from the Humean about moral motivation. According to Smith (1994, pp. 119–20), what deservedly draws Humean fire about the equation of virtue and moral knowledge is its strong modal claim that possession of moral beliefs cannot be pulled apart from the possession of certain desires. One could imagine moral beliefs and moral desires co-travelling as a matter of empirical fact, he says; and one could well assert that possession of moral beliefs entails possession of moral desires in those who are rational (Smith himself is committed to the latter, for the simple reason that he demarcates rational agents as those whose desires match up with their evaluative beliefs). What is implausible, he states, is the claim that there exist cognitive states whose possession entails possession of certain desire states as a matter of conceptual necessity.

For clarity, let me separate out two different sorts of objection here, both of which, I think, contribute to the aura of difficulty many seem to think surrounds the idea of equating virtue and knowledge. The first is an objection still located squarely within the formal philosophy of mind. The idea here is that the very natures of belief and desire stand presumptively against the idea of such conceptual connections between the two. Reflection on belief- and desire-directions of fit, it is thought, have at least revealed them to be sufficiently different that a conceptual entailment from something satisfying the first to something satisfying the second (as opposed to an empirical entailment, or the normatively bounded one Smith outlines), while not incoherent, seems simply out of place. The second objection involves an important shift to concerns in moral psychology. Even if nothing generic stood in the way of positing desire-entailing beliefs, it is thought, reflection on actual lived experiences reveals that such a story would not fit the particular case of moral motivation. Moral belief and moral desire, it is urged, do not even co-travel empirically: they all too often come apart.

Let me start with the first, more theoretical, objection. It is important to point out just how wrong-headed it is: for even if besires remain controversial, the plain idea of a desire–entailing belief is positively mundane. Assertion of plain entailment can simply mean that the entailed desire is a persisting background condition to the entailing belief – in the same way my believing that Washington was our first President entails my being alive. And *no one* sensibly denies that beliefs and desires can be interconnected in this way. We routinely posit all sorts of rich, conceptual interconnections between beliefs and desires, often for interpretive reasons concerning what it takes to count as having a given concept. To give just one example, it's likely that possession of any belief necessarily entails possession of the desire that one's beliefs are true, for it is hard to see how one could count as a believer if one entirely gave up the regulative ideal of aiming at truth. There is quite obviously nothing in the notion of direction of fit that renders such conceptual connections problematic, nothing in the notion that automatically renders suspect the cognitive status of a mental state that counts desires amongst its preconditions.

Obviously, when theorists skeptical of equating virtue and knowledge have discussed desire-entailing beliefs, they have tended to assume that the desire at issue must be one whose possession would be *explained* by the reasons that led to adoption of the belief at issue – to assume, that is, that their adoption is the result of reflection on evidence about *p*'s goodness. In his discussion of the debate, for instance, Pettit understands the question of whether there are desire-entailing beliefs as the question of whether desires can be produced by Reason (1987, p. 531). I have already argued that suspicions over this sort of entailment cannot be justified simply by reflections in the philosophy of mind: they reflect certain substantive views about the natures of theoretical and practical reason, not merely formal consideration about the natures of belief and desire. The further point here, though, is that one needn't interpret the entailment

involved as one that carries this explanatory direction. The virtue theorist's claim may simply be that possession of certain desires is a necessary condition for possession of certain moral beliefs.

And indeed many versions of virtue theory include appeal to this notion of desire-entailment as part of their story. It is argued that one cannot come to have, and cannot count as maintaining, a truly autonomous understanding of, say, good, without having some desire to pursue it. One may have a sort of parasitic grasp on the concept, to be sure, mimicking the classifications others make, but one will be forever glancing sideways, as it were, rather than relying on one's own judgments about the goodness of various situations. Notice further that, if such claims were made good, they would provide a more plausible context in which to invoke the more ambitious claim that desires can be produced or explained by reflection on evidence. According to theories that make use of both interpretations of desire-entailment, we start our moral development with protean versions of certain desires, and these stand as preconditions to developing the rudiments of moral concepts. Our understanding of the concepts, though, deepens in response to theoretical reflection and evidential considerations, and the contours of the desires come to change in tandem. Newly specific desires arise in response to this evidence, that is, as the proto-desires come to be "educated."

Let me turn then to the second objection, the one located in moral psychology. Reflection on the realities of human life, it is claimed, show that the theory simply isn't true to the facts. In contrast to Hume, who, in some moods at least, seemed to advance a very strong internalist connection between moral verdicts and moral motivation, here it is insisted that the two often come apart. It is outlandish to claim that possession of a moral belief guarantees the presence of a desire to act as the verdict recommends, much less to claim that such beliefs guarantee presence of a desire strong enough to trump others. As Michael Stocker (1979) has indicated, all too many things – depression, ennui, weak will – can stand in the way of our being moved to do as we ourselves think we ought.

To think that this is an objection, though, is to misunderstand the nature of the virtue theory's claim. For far from denying that that we can reach moral beliefs without having the desire or motivation to act as they recommend, the theory takes its purpose to be providing a framework in which to locate this fact. Let me clarify.

When virtue theorists assert that there are desire-entailing beliefs, they need not and in fact do not mean that all moral beliefs belong to this category. Rather, they claim that within the broad genus of states that qualify as moral beliefs, there is a particular species whose possession does indeed guarantee the presence of certain desires. Beliefs, after all, constitute a broad class. They come in different shapes and sizes, distinguished by a variety of further cognitive features – some are irrational, some may be self-evident, some are experiential. The virtue theorist's claim is that a kind of cognitive state – a kind of state that does satisfy a belief direction of fit – necessarily brings with it the motivation to act as it says we ought. There are certain *ways* of seeing or of conceiving the world, as many have put it, that one cannot have without reacting affectively in a certain way.

More specifically, the claim is that certain ideal, clear, or complete ways of seeing or conceiving the situation guarantee one will be moved to act morally. Those who are not motivated in the face of moral truths, that is, suffer some kind of "moral blindness," as Mark Platts puts it: if we are not moved, we must not "see sufficiently" (1979, p. 262). At its worst, this blindness prevents agents from even reaching a moral verdict: the agent sees the suffering of war, perhaps, but not the *evil* of war; or again, the agent understands that her neighbor is grieving for his dead son, but she fails to understand the simple *kindness* contained in keeping up everyday chitchat. But often the blindness infects the cognitive quality or mode of the moral conclusion that is reached. To put it metaphorically (more rigorous exposition obviously must follow), our motivation fails because the moral discernment is "cloudy" instead of "clear" (McDowell, 1979), "shallow" instead of "deep" or "formal" instead of "experientially-enriched" (Platts, 1979, p. 262).

The claim advanced by the virtue theorist, then, is not that there are no failures of moral motivation; the claim is that every such failure necessarily involves or signals a cognitive failure. Notice that this needn't even imply that every difference of motivation is attributable to a cognitive difference. McDowell, for instance, states that the difference between continence and incontinence (roughly, the difference between successfully and unsuccessfully battling temptation) need not be

explained as a difference between two ways of conceiving the situation (1979, section 3). On his view, what must be explained as a difference in the agents' cognitive grasp is the difference between virtuous motivation, on the one hand, and the motivational states involved in either continence or incontinence, on the other – the difference, that is, between experiencing the pull of temptation and experiencing competing concerns as "silenced." This having been noted, the point remains that, on any version of the view that virtue is moral knowledge, all motivational failures do involve a cognitive failure, for the simple reason that, since the virtuous person's ideal conception of a situation guarantees proper motivation, any who are not moved cannot be enjoying that conception (McDowell, 1978).

In considering this interpretation of the virtue theory, Smith responds with what he regards as a "knockdown" argument (1994, pp. 123–5). He begins by noting, fairly, that such a theory is committed to finding a cognitive difference between the state a person occupied while virtuous and the state she would occupy if she fell from virtue: such a theory must contend that the person "no longer appreciates" what she once knew. But he then interprets this to mean that the virtue theory regards such people as having "forgotten something that they used to know all too well." The loss of virtue, he thinks, is thought to be a loss of belief in a special type of proposition – namely, propositions which are such that, "if they are entertained at all," must dispose one to act in a certain way. Such a view, he states, is overall "surely quite incredible."

Now obviously, in order to fill in the details of their account, virtue theorists are under obligation to cash out the cognitive difference between the state that guarantees motivation and those that do not. But Smith's objection here is based on a misunderstanding of what that difference is supposed to be. He reads the change from virtue to nonvirtue as constituted by the literal loss of moral belief or propositional knowledge, as if the fall from virtue is tantamount to having one less proposition in the set of what one holds true. But the difference between the virtuous and non-virtuous person's appreciation of the situation is not meant to be a difference in what proposition is believed or known. Indeed, it is not claimed to be a difference that can be captured in propositional terms at all. The point of the virtue theorists' allusion to "ways of perceiving" or "ways of conceiving" moral situations is to make reference to the fact that there are cognitive differences not reducible to differences in propositional content.

Take first the allusion to ways of perceiving. We are all familiar with the fact that the elements of a picture can be organized under different gestalts, and that different gestalts make for differences in one's experience of a picture. The experience of seeing a picture as a duck, say, is simply different than seeing it as a rabbit or as a jumble of lines. Now gestalt shifts certainly can bring with them shifts in propositional belief: the elements of a story, for instance, may suddenly drop into place, and one comes to understand that it shows, say, that pride goeth before a fall. But gestalt shifts are not reducible to differences in what proposition is believed or known, and propositional knowledge can survive shifts or losses in experiential gestalts. One can suddenly lose the ability to find the face in the pointillist painting – to see the dots *as* Marilyn Monroe's visage – without thereby forgetting that it is indeed a painting of Marilyn Monroe. Or again, one can believe that a Magic Eye picture is a picture of an elephant because one has been told on excellent authority, without ever being able to see it oneself in the array of colors. Still, the fact that one who is personally perceiving the Magic Eye elephant can share a propositional belief with one who is not perceiving it does not mean there is no difference in their cognitive states: not all cognitive differences can be captured as differences in propositional content.

Virtue theorists appeal to this perceptual model as an illustrative analogy for understanding what they believe to be involved in the discernment of moral saliences. When we confront a situation and try to assess for ourselves its moral nature, the process involves discerning which of the situation's myriad nonmoral properties have moral relevance, and sizing up what sort of moral import these individual elements together carry. The virtue theorist's claim is that this notion of "taking as morally salient" is not reducible to believing or knowing the proposition that a given feature or set of features has such-and-such moral significance. Rather, they argue, "taking as salient" is akin to having a kind of experience. Analogous to the way in which certain features occupy the foreground in a perceptual gestalt, certain features are experienced or taken as occupying a moral prominence; and, analogous to the way in which the individual elements

of a gestalt come together to form a certain shape, the individual elements of the situation are experienced or taken as adding up to form a given moral whole. Differences in such experiences can ride on top of common propositional belief – on top of the belief that cruelty is bad, say, or that charity is called for in the present case. For one thing, one can come to such moral beliefs, and indeed come in a justified way, without coming to them by "seeing them in" the details of the situation (one is told on reliable authority, for instance). Or again, more to the present point, one can retain the beliefs from occasions when one was able to see them in the details for oneself – just as one can remember that the picture is of Marilyn Monroe despite a temporary inability to see for oneself the face in the dots.

The experience of "taking as salient" also has certain distinguishing features. Unlike merely perceptual gestalts, it can proceed conceptually, as when the details of a narrative resolve into a moral conclusion. But most importantly, while the experience of "taking as salient" is clearly cognitive, constituting as it does a manner of taking the world to be a certain way, it is also regarded as being irreducibly practical. We have noted that, according to the virtue theorist, one is doing more than simply coming to a propositional conclusion when one autonomously takes some feature as morally relevant and organizes such elements into moral wholes. The theorist further claims that, just as the residue of what is involved in having a particular perceptual gestalt cannot be understood except in sensory terms, the residue of what is involved in having a particular "salience" gestalt cannot be understood except in practical terms. What it is to "take" elements as having, separately or together, a kind of moral relevance, is or entails having one's will or motivation oriented in a certain way.

The point of saying that the virtuous person has a special "way of perceiving" the situation, then, is not to say that the virtuous person has hold of some moral belief or propositional knowledge that another may not. It is to say that the virtuous person takes in saliences aright, taking all and only relevant features of the situation as relevant, and accurately taking them to have the moral shape they together form. This gestalt represents the clearest and most complete vision – one that is most true to what is there to be apprehended in moral reality; and this accurate gestalt, it is claimed, is identical to or necessarily entails the practical orientation of taking those features as constituting overriding, and perhaps silencing, reasons for action.

The virtue theorist also alludes to "ways of conceiving" a moral situation. Properly understood, this, too, is not a notion that can or is meant to be captured in purely propositional terms. The knowledge that a virtuous person has is knowledge that would reliably issue in right and only right verdicts. But a central claim of virtue theory is that there is no codifying morality into an exhaustive set of principles (Nussbaum, 1986; McDowell, 1981). This means that the knowledge a virtuous person has is not equivalent to knowing some bounded set of propositions. It is, instead, to have an understanding or broad conception of the moral terrain, a "conception of how to live," as McDowell puts it (1979), that is at one and the same time a cognitive and a practical stance. It is a skill in judging which situations fall under various rich moral classifications such as kind, cruel, obligatory, evil; and what it takes to count as having such a skill, it is claimed, cannot be understood independently of one's having a practical orientation to be identified, if you like, with its judgments.

The difference between the virtuous and nonvirtuous person's cognitive states is the difference between having and failing to have this sort of broad conception. The difference will show itself over time (given the irreducible complexity of the moral terrain and the independent shape of moral concepts, those who lack it will at some point go wrong), but it need not show up in any particular case as a difference in the specific propositions believed or known. The virtuous and nonvirtuous can alike believe that cruelty is bad, or conclude that some particular action is now called for. The virtuous person, however, holds the belief as part and parcel of the broad, uncodifiable, practical conception of how to live, while the nonvirtuous person holds it without so subsuming it. The two differ, if you like, in their conceptual gestalts of the situation. Just so, one who tragically falls from virtue need not be described as having forgotten any of these particular beliefs. The point is that she currently does not situate them into a broader conceptual framework. As when a detail from a story randomly floats to mind, unattached to the narrative to which it belongs, she does not conceive of the element in the same way, for it is not conceived as part and parcel of a certain broad conception. Virtue theory, then, does indeed claim that the vir-

tuous person is in a cognitive state – a state satisfying a belief direction of fit – that guarantees moral motivation. But the guarantee is not located in any particular belief or piece of propositional knowledge. It is, instead, located in a way of conceiving a situation under the auspices of a broad conception of how to live.

To claim that it is something *cognitive* that guarantees motivation has struck some as egregiously ad hoc. Such a complaint needs careful treatment, however. Of *course* the account needs filling in. In particular, it obviously must provide a sufficiently rich and substantive criteria of "cognitive" to enable us to know what is at stake in the classification, and to determine what mental features belong to it in ways that satisfy relative independence constraints. But there is nothing specially gratuitous in the virtue theorist's claim. Crudely speaking, there are three main camps of how to account for moral motivational failure: the Aristotelians place the failure in cognition, Kantians locate it in a failure of will, Humeans attribute it to the absence of a functionally-understood pro-attitude. Fancy as each may sound, they are all of them invocations of some rather empty variable until they are developed into detailed accounts. (Worse yet, think of that favorite all-purpose modern explanation of what bridges motivational failure: the "drawing of a practical inference." Rarely is the advocate of this answer asked what it is to draw a practical inference, other than to become moved – much less whether those criteria satisfy relative independence constraints.)

6.   All of the above, of course, is simply to clarify the form the virtue theory takes. It is not to present any of the arguments virtue theorists have offered for the various steps enumerated; indeed, the claims themselves remain drawn in broadest outline only. My goal has been to argue that objections purporting to dismantle the theory based solely on considerations about direction of fit or plain facts of moral psychology gain little mileage on their own terms. Shared formal conceptions of belief and desire offer little leverage: if we have intuitions pulling for or against the theory equating virtue and moral knowledge, it will be because of substantive background commitments in other areas. And while it is certainly important to attend to the reality of lived moral experiences, one cannot simply read off these experiences a conclusion about whether the virtue theory makes sense or not. The virtue theorist tries to offer an *account* of

familiar motivational phenomena, and any account of such phenomena is going to be a deeply theoretic matter, involving forays into an array of interconnected themes on agency, responsibility, and normativity.

Whether it is plausible in the end to equate virtue and moral knowledge is a complicated matter that can be settled only by assessing how well the theory fills in the details, argues for key moves, and whether it does justice to a broad range of deep issues, not just those in the philosophy of mind and moral psychology. Does a cognitive account of agency relegate us to a heteronomous

understanding of normative authority? Do we have sufficiently rich criteria of "getting it right" to justify a realist interpretation of morality? Does the understanding of moral concepts require a certain orientation of the will or a certain affective sensibility? The virtue theorist has offered arguments on these issues and more, arguments that often turn on tremendously complicated questions which cannot be settled by anything as thin as the objections offered above. There is no shortcut through the philosophy of mind and psychology to rejecting the equation of virtue and knowledge.

References

Anscombe, G. E. M. 1957. *Intention.* Basil Blackwell.

Blackburn, Simon. 1981. "Reply: Rule-Following and Moral Realism." In Steven Holtzman and Christopher Leich, eds., *Wittgenstein: To Follow a Rule.* Routledge, 163–87.

Hume, David. 1975. *An Enquiry Concerning the Principles of Morals.* Clarendon Press.

Hume, David. 1978. *A Treatise of Human Nature.* Clarendon Press.

McDowell, John. 1978. "Are Moral Requirements Hypothetical Imperatives?" *Proceedings of the Aristotelian Society,* supplement, 13–29.

McDowell, John. 1979. "Virtue and Reason." *The Monist,* 331–50.

McDowell, John. 1981. "Non-Cognitivism and Rule-Following." In Steven Holtzman and Christopher Leich, eds., *Wittgenstein: To Follow a Rule.* Routledge, 141–62.

McNaughton, David. 1988. *Moral Vision.* Basil Blackwell.

Nussbaum, Martha. 1986. "The Discernment of Perception: an Aristotelian Conception of Private and Public Rationality." *In Proceedings of the Boston Area Collo-*

quium in Ancient Philosophy, vol, 1, ed. John Cleary. University Press of America, chapter 6.

Pettit, Philip. 1987. "Humeans, Anti-Humeans and Motivation." *Mind,* 530–3.

Platts, Mark. 1979. *Ways of Meaning.* Routledge & Kegan Paul, chapter 10.

Platts, Mark. 1980. "Moral Reality and the End of Desire." In Mark Platts ed., *Reference, Truth and Reality.* Routledge & Kegan Paul.

Price, Richard. 1974. *A Review of the Principal Questions in Morals.* Clarendon Press.

Smith, Michael. 1987. "The Humean Theory of Motivation." *Mind.* 36–61.

Smith, Michael. 1988a. "On Humeans, Anti-Humeans and Motivation: A Reply to Pettit." *Mind.* 589–95.

Smith, Michael. 1988b. "Reason and Desire." *Proceedings of the Aristotelian Society.* 243–56.

Smith, Michael. 1994. *The Moral Problem.* Basil Blackwell.

Stocker, Michael. 1979. "Desiring the Bad: An Essay in Moral Psychology." *Journal of Philosophy,* 738–53.

Williams, Bernard. 1985. *Ethics and the Limits of Philosophy.* Harvard University Press.

Acting for a Good Reason

Jonathan Dancy

5

I. Psychologism: The Three-Part Story and the Normative Story

Psychologism is a view about motivation; it is the claim that the reasons for which we act are psychological states of ourselves. Nagel's claim, by contrast, was that if we explain actions by appeal to the beliefs and desires of the agent, we will have to abandon any suggestion that agents act for reasons. We explain an intentional action by specifying the reasons that motivated the agent. So Nagel is claiming that if we adopt psychologism, we might as well give up talking about acting for a reason altogether. The present chapter is intended to provide support for this view of Nagel's. In writing it, I will be assuming that the form of psychologism to be attacked is the best form, namely pure cognitivism. This has the great advantage that we do not have to introduce complicating considerations about desires. The only psychological states relevant are beliefs, and we can discuss the matter entirely in terms of the relation between the belief (the believing, that is) and the thing believed.

In this chapter, I will operate with a terminology which I have been largely avoiding up to now. This is the terminology of motivating reasons and normative reasons. I have tried in earlier chapters to speak rather of the reasons that motivate us, as contrasted with good reasons – the latter being reasons for being motivated or for doing the action. My purpose was to avoid even appearing to commit myself to the view that there are two *sorts* of reason: the motivating sort and the normative or good sort. Instead I stressed the idea that we use one and the same notion of a reason in answer to two distinct sorts of question, the question why someone acted and the question whether there was good reason so to act. All the issues I have discussed could have been discussed in terms of the contrast between motivating reasons and normative reasons, had it not been for the unwanted implication carried by that terminology. [. . .] Now, however, I want to relax my ban on that terminology for a while. This is because the positions that I am here working to reject are best formulated in its terms. Those positions do hold that though we speak of motivating *reasons* and normative or good *reasons*, we are genuinely dealing with two distinct *sorts* of reason, in a way that raises the question whether the word 'reason' is not awkwardly ambiguous. I am going to allow this way of speaking in the course of an attempt to argue that it is incoherent.

So are any motivating reasons psychological states of the agent? As I said before in chapter 1 [Omitted here. Eds.], the sorts of reason we actually give, in explaining either our own actions or those of others, seem to be characterized sometimes in terms of a psychological state of the agent, and sometimes not. I might say that we are sending our child to this school because we believe it will suit her better; and I might say that I am taking my car down to the garage because it is time for it to be serviced. Admittedly, in the second sort of case, I must believe that it is time for a service if I am to act in the light of that fact. But still it seems to be not so much my believing this as what I believe that is being offered as my reason for doing what I propose to do. So, we may say, some reason-giving offers a belief of the agent as a reason, and some offers what is believed by the agent instead; and there is a world of difference between these. If our motivating reasons are all 'what is believed', no reasons are psychological states of the agent. If those reasons are all psychological states of the agents, none are properly, fully specifiable in the form 'A acted because p'. The proper, philosophically revealing form will be 'A acted because A believed that p'; and we will understand this sort of explanation as specifying a psychological state of the agent as *explanans*.

Psychologism has a large and enthusiastic following. But any complete theory of practical reasons has to deal not only with motivating reasons but also with normative reasons. With that in mind, three possibilities are available for us. We can understand both normative and motivating reasons as psychological states of the agent. We can understand all reasons as what the agents believe, rather than as their believings of those things. Or, finally, we can hold that motivating reasons are psychological states of the agent, while normative reasons are what agents (we hope) believe.

Of these three possibilities, I think that the first is clearly implausible. It is implausible because it is so extreme. It is not the view that all normative reasons are *grounded in* psychological states of the agent. The desire-based view, which holds that all practical reasons derive their normative status from a relation to some desire of the agent, is of that sort; and it is worth arguing against. But the view we are currently considering is that all normative reasons *are* psychological states of the agent. This would rule out any such reasons as that she asked me to do it, that this is an opportunity I have long been waiting for, and that I will be too busy to have time to do it next week. There would have to be an amazingly strong argument to persuade us that

considerations like these are altogether of the wrong sort to count as reasons in favour of an action. The only argument that I can see in the offing is that all motivating reasons are psychological states of the agent, and that normative reasons must be a subset of motivating reasons. Whatever the merits of such an argument (and I confess that it would seem to me to vindicate Nagel's view that psychologism should cause us to abandon the very idea of acting for a reason), it returns us to the question whether motivating reasons are or are not psychological states.

What I want to examine, then, are the respective merits of the second and the third possibilities. I am interested in promoting the second alternative, under which no reasons at all, neither motivating nor normative, are psychological states of the agent. But this requires me to argue against a position that appears well entrenched. It is worth taking a moment to build up an initial version of this third theory, as follows.

We have already noticed that when we speak of reasons for action, the little word 'for' cloaks an ambiguity, or at least a distinction. There are reasons in favour of acting, and reasons why we acted. Favouring is one thing; it is a normative relation, and the reasons that favour actions can include such things as normative states of the world, for certainly they are unlikely to be psychological states of the agent. The reasons why we act, however, are not themselves things that favour actions; they are things that explain them. These are all psychological states of the agent – believings, if pure cognitivism is the truth; pairs of believings and desirings, if it is not. Now there is a constraint on any theory about the relation between normative and motivating reasons. This is that the theory show that and how any normative reason is capable of contributing to the explanation of an action that is done for that reason. Call this the 'explanatory constraint'. There is a way in which it is easy to meet that constraint. The believings that explain the action can themselves be explained, of course, and on occasions at least we do so by appeal to their truth. He believed that there was a rhinoceros before him because there was one there; she believed that he needed her help because he did. So the reasons that favour an action can explain the reasons that explain the action. So though normative reasons do not explain actions directly, they explain them indirectly. The explanatory constraint is met by appeal to the transitivity of explanation. We emerge with a three-part story in which everything has its place, and nothing is missed out. The story is: normative reason → motivating reason → action. The arrows in this story indicate relations of explanation, though of course there is more to the matter than those explanatory relations alone.

Opposed to this three-part story is one which denies the existence of motivating states as reasons of any sort, and tries to make do with normative reasons. These normative reasons are also able to play the role of motivating reasons; that is, in ordinary English, the reason why we should act is to be (at least able to be) the reason why we do act. What is believed is what motivates us as well as what makes it the case that what we did was the right thing to have done. The believing, which of course occurs (though even this will be questioned), does not play the role of a motivating reason; some other role must be found for it. Motivating reasons are what is believed; and some of the things believed are normative reasons as well.

Let us call this alternative story the 'normative story', because it takes its start from normative reasons. It is obviously going to be hard to develop, let alone sustain. In order to gain it some credibility, as it were, I am now going to run through a list of potential objections to the three-part story. For if the three-part story collapses under attack, the prospects for the normative story are obviously much better.

2.   Against the Three-Part Story

I start by considering a standard argument *for* the claim that motivating reasons are psychological states of the agent, specifically believings, which runs as follows:

The statement
(1)   *A*'s reason for ɸ-ing was that *p*
can only be true if
(2)   *A* believed that *p*.
Therefore
(3)   *A*'s reason for ɸ-ing was that *A* believed that *p*.

This argument is of course rather peculiar and not obviously valid. But I want to say two further things about it. The first is that it is not an argument for psychologism. Its conclusion is not that

A's reason for ɸ-ing was his believing that *p*, but that his reason was that he believed that *p*. That is to say, the motivating reason it 'discovers' is not itself a psychological state of the agent but the 'fact' that the agent was in such a state. That *A* believed that *p* is not itself a psychological state of *A*'s. If it were, *A* could be in it; but the sense in which *A* is *in* the fact that *A* believed that *p* is surely not the sense in which *A* is *in* a psychological state.

We could of course rewrite the argument with, as its conclusion, not (3) but the genuinely psychologistic

(3*)   *A*'s reason for ɸ-ing was *A*'s believing that *p*.

The point I am trying to make, however, is directed at those who have become psycholog*ists*, in my sense, by arguing for (3) and then misunderstanding their own conclusion as the psychologistic (3*) – a train of thought which I take to be fairly common.

Second, the argument as I have given it above says nothing about how it is to be interpreted. In particular, it does not say whether its 'conclusion' is to be understood as replacing its first premiss, or as related to that premiss in some other way. I don't want to suggest that there would be any incoherence in an argument whose conclusion is inconsistent with one of its premisses. We are all used to such things. The point is rather that, for all the argument tells us, it may be that the conclusion is intended as a sort of philosophical explication of, rather than a replacement for, the premiss. In general, as will emerge, I have no quarrel with the ideal that (1) and (3) are somehow more or less equivalent, i.e. that (3) is a restatement of (1). It is true that we move without strain from the simple form of action-explanation (1) to the psychologized form (3) and back again. We should accept this and cater for it in our overall account of the explanation of action. Problems only arise when it is supposed that (1) is an incomplete specification of a reason that is only fully characterized by (3) – something on which the argument given above is officially silent. In my view, if there is a difference between (1) and (3), it speaks entirely in favour of (1) as the normal form in which to give a reason. But I have still to argue for this view.

It is one thing, however, to undermine supposed arguments for a position, and another to show the position itself to be false. So I now make three direct objections to the three-part story. The first is one that I have already offered in print.[1] This objection amounts to the introduction of a further constraint, which we can call the normative constraint, in addition to the explanatory constraint that we have already seen. This requires that a motivating reason, that in the light of which one acts, must be the sort of thing that is capable of being among the reasons in favour of so acting; it must, in this sense, be possible to act for a good reason. The explanatory constraint held that all normative reasons should be the right sort of thing to contribute to motivation, since that is what they must be if they are to be capable of contributing to the explanation of action in the right sort of way. The normative constraint goes in the other direction, claiming that motivating reasons should be the right sort of thing to be normative reasons.

The three-part story fails the normative constraint in a very blatant way, for it renders us more or less incapable of doing an action for any of the reasons that make it right. It makes it impossible, that is, for the reasons why we act to be *among* the reasons in favour of acting. If I am trying to decide what to do, I decide which action is right, noticing (we hope) the reasons that make it right; and then I act in the light of those reasons. They are the reasons why I do what I do (my motivating reasons). According to the three-part story, this is impossible. For the three-part story announces that motivating reasons are psychological states and that normative reasons are quite different, including even such things as normative facts about the world. The three-part story has set itself up in such a way that it is bound to breach the normative constraint; which is to say that it has introduced far too great a gap between the explanatory and the normative. And this makes the three-part story paradoxical at its core.

It is not just that, by thinking of motivating reasons as psychological states of the agent, the three-part story breaches the normative constraint. I want to agree with psychologism that we should not be looking among psychological states of the agent for the normative reasons that favour the action. The psychologists are right about this. For no – or only very few – psychological states of the agent are normative reasons; it is not normally psychological states of the agent that make his

action the right one to do. In a way I expect this point to be obvious. What makes my action wrong is that she badly needed help and I just walked away from her. What makes overtaking on the wrong side of a bend not a very sensible thing to do is that there may well be something coming the other way. Once one has started in this vein one can go on for ever. Psychologism must be right to think of normative reasons as facts, as states of affairs, or as features of the situation, and must be wrong, therefore, to think of motivating reasons as psychological states of the agent.

What confuses the issue is that it is possible to think that the agent's mental states do make a difference to the question whether he acted rightly. And so they do, in a way; for that he believed she would welcome his advances surely makes him (or his action) less reprehensible than he (or it) would have been if he had believed the opposite, especially if his belief was reasonable. But, first, that belief, even if reasonable, need not make the action right. As we saw in Chapter 3 [Omitted here. Eds.], his believing this can serve as some defence or excuse for his doing what he did, without making that action right. The normative relevance of the belief lies primarily at the evaluative level, rather than at the deontic level where reasons lie. And, second, there remains the awkward difference between the suggestion that it is his belief, conceived as a mental state that he is in, that is the reason and the suggestion that it is that he so believes that is the reason. For that he so believes is not a mental state that he is in, but a state of affairs; just as his nervousness is a mental state that he is in, but that he is nervous is a state of affairs rather than a mental state. At the moment we are only discussing the less plausible view that the normative reason is a mental state of the agent.

In these matters, I am mindful of the results reached in Chapters 2 and 3 [Omitted here. Eds.], when, having tried to understand the requirements of rationality and morality as somehow relative to the beliefs (and the desires) of the agent, we were forced first to allow that some requirements cannot be so expressed, and second to accept that all requirements (of either sort) are objective rather than relative in the way suggested. If this result was correct, it cannot be the case that all normative reasons consist in psychological states of the agent.

---

[1] See Dancy (1995a, 1996, 2000a).

I have been trying to show that the three-part story is committed to the paradoxical claim that it is impossible to do an action for the reason that makes it right. As I put it earlier, the reasons why we act can never be among the reasons in favour of acting, if the three-part story is true. This paradox is even more marked in the theory of theoretical reasons (reasons for belief) than in the theory of practical reasons. We could tell a three-part story there too: the reasons why we believe things are always other beliefs of ours – other believings, that is – and the reason why we are right to adopt those beliefs is the evidence available, or something like that. The evidence available explains our believings, and those believings explain our adopting this new belief. This three-part story has the same paradoxical consequence, that none of the reasons why we believe something is ever a reason in favour of believing it. The reasons why we believe something will always be other psychological states of ours, never anything like the evidence available to us.

In my now fairly wide experience, the normal response of those attracted to the three-part story is to say, when accused of paradox in this sort of way, that the matter is wildly exaggerated. The normative reason, they say, can perfectly well be thought of as a motivating reason in any case where its being the case that p makes right an action that is done because of the belief that p. For if A explains B and B explains C, A is part of the explanation of C; and motivating reasons include anything that contributes to the explanation of the action. But this seems to me not so much to defend the story as to abandon it. The core of the three-part story is the claim that normative reasons cannot be motivating ones, a claim that rests on psychologism about motivating reasons and a (correct) sense that normative reasons are in general nothing like psychological states of the agent. The sorts of thing that are normative reasons are things like the pain the other is suffering, the wrong I will be doing her if I persist, and other features of the world that call for certain responses from us. These normatively significant states of affairs are metaphysically different beasts from psychological states of the agent. Having insisted on this difference, the three-part story cannot then go on to ignore it, and to say in spite of it that we can perfectly well speak of those normative states of affairs as motivating reasons, even though their official view (indeed, the core of their position) is that only psychological states of the

agent can play that role. This would be far too much like trying to have one's cake and eat it.

Despite this, there may be some truth in the complaint that my attack on the three-part story involves some exaggeration, and for this reason I am not sure quite how much to rest on it. In some moods it seems to me to be annihilating; in others it seems more like nitpicking. The problem is that the attack rests an enormous amount on the possibility that motivating and normative reasons should be capable of being identical. The appeal is to such expressions as 'The reason for which he did it was a very good one' or, more philosophically, 'It must be possible for the reasons in the light of which one acts to be *among* the reasons in favour of doing what one does'. If someone said that these expressions do not need to be taken *au pied de la lettre*, it is not obvious what I have to say in reply.

So I turn now to my second criticism of the three-part story. This is just a slightly different and simpler way of making the point that the separation it introduces between the explanatory and the normative is too sharp. We normally try to explain an action by showing that it was done for good reason, or at least for what might reasonably have been thought to be good reason at the time. But psychological states of the agent are the wrong sorts of thing to be good reasons. A believing cannot be a good reason for acting, because a good reason for acting is a reason that favours acting, and such things, according to the three-part story, are states of the world, not psychological states of the agent. What is more, the three-part story is right about this. What makes my action right in the circumstances is very rarely any psychological state of mine, as we have seen.

Here we see again why it is important to speak of normative reasons rather than, as is common, of justifying reasons. For one's having reasonably believed that p is often offered as a justification of one's action in cases where it turns out that it was not the case that p. And it may indeed succeed in *justifying* one's having acted as one did, that is, in defending one against certain charges, without this meaning that it is able to play the role of a normative reason. As I have suggested several times now, my having (reasonably) believed that p is only able to justify my action if, had it been the case that p, I would have been acting rightly, doing the right thing. The normative reason here would be that p, not my having believed that p. My believing that p is not a reason for action in either sense (or of either sort); it is at best a justification for my having acted as I did.

Perhaps this criticism of the three-part story is not in the end distinct from the first; on any account it is not much more than a generalization of it. It amounts to little more than the claims that a reason for acting (a motivating reason) must be the right sort of thing to be a good reason, and that a good reason is a normative reason. Again, the three-part story meets the explanatory constraint but fails the normative constraint. The important point for present purposes is that this second criticism seems less vulnerable to the charge that it involves a certain exaggeration. There is not so much hanging on the demand for potential *identity* between motivating and normative reasons – at least nothing is hanging on that alone. The need for the potential identity is itself supported by the need for motivating reasons to be of the right sort to be good reasons. If only normative reasons can be good reasons, and if reasons (of whatever sort) must be able to be good or less good, then only the sorts of thing that are normative reasons can be motivating reasons.

The crucial point here is that believing that p is never (or hardly ever) a good reason for ϕ-ing. It is what is believed, that p, that is the good reason for ϕ-ing, if there is one.

Finally, I want to stress one feature of this argument. This is the constant stress on the phrase 'right *sort of* thing'. A motivating reason must, I claimed, be the right sort of thing to be a normative reason. This is really a metaphysical point. Some motivating reasons cannot be good reasons. Perhaps the downfall of others cannot be a good reason for satisfaction. Perhaps, as some hold, the rightness of an action cannot be among the reasons for doing it. But these features are still, metaphysically speaking, the right sort of thing to be a good reason. They are ruled out, if they are indeed ruled out, not by being the wrong sort of thing, but by being wrong ones of the right sort.

These, then, are my first two arguments against the three-part story. My third argument is much more controversial. Arthur Collins has argued that the three-part story makes possible something that is in fact impossible, namely for the agent to explain his action in a way that makes no commitment to the truth of the beliefs that he cites in that explanation (Collins 1997).

The aim of the explanation of action is to give, so far as possible, the agent's own perspective on

things, so as to reveal the light in which the action was done. The subject-matter of the explanation is not the agent's perspective; that perspective is the one from which the explanation is made, but that it is so made is not itself part of the explanation. The subject-matter of the explanation is 'the objective circumstances' (as Collins puts it) as apprehended by the agent, not the agent's apprehension of those circumstances.

Consider now an explanation as offered by the agent; he says 'I am doing this because I believe that p'. Collins calls this sort of explanation, with which as such he has no quarrel, a 'psychologizing restatement' of the briefer explanation that runs 'I am doing this because p'. The agent might move, or be forced to move, to the psychologized explanation because he recognizes that he might well be mistaken in his belief that p. He might even go so far as to say 'I am doing this because, though I may be wrong about this, I believe that p'. What then is the relation between these variously expressed explanations? The simple explanation 'I am doing this because p' clearly expresses the speaker's endorsement of or commitment to the claim that p. No explanation that obliterated that endorsement would be the correct explanation of the action, since it would fail to give the agent's perspective on things, and hence fail to capture the light in which the action was done. The psychologizing restatement offered by the agent must therefore be understood as retaining that endorsement (as discussion of Moore's Paradox encourages us to suppose), and its effectiveness as an explanation depends on this fact. Further, in accepting the psychologized restatement of his reason, the agent is not supposing that the subject-matter of the explanation has thereby been changed from the (supposed) objective circumstances to the subjective nature of the agent. So we have it that the psychologizing restatement of the original explanation must satisfy the following conditions:

1 It does not introduce a new subject-matter;
2 It does not somehow delete the agents' endorsement.

But these two conditions are not met by the way in which the three-part story understands what is going on in what it takes to be the move from the original briefer explanation to the psychologizing restatement. The two stages in the three-part story may be understood as two parts of a complex explanation. First there is the 'proximal' explanation of the action, given by specifying the psychological state of the agent. Then there is the 'distal' explanation of the action, given by specifying what is responsible for the agent getting into that state. The distal explanation of the action is the proximal explanation of the psychological state. So the three-part story takes there to be considerable differences between the subject-matters of the two explanations. We can easily imagine saying of another that he acted because he believed that p, though it was not in fact the case that p, and his believing that p has to be explained in another way. Here we avoid committing ourselves to the things that the agent was committing to, things his commitment to which explains his action. We take ourselves, supposedly, to be giving a proximal explanation of the action in a way that avoids any commitment on the appropriate distal explanation. The point that Collins makes here is that this form of uncommitted explanation is never available to the agent, for reasons to do with Moore's Paradox. The agent himself cannot explain his action by appeal to a belief he currently has without committing himself to the truth of that belief. He cannot say 'I am doing it because I believe that p' in any way that stands back from his commitment to its being the case that p. So the distinction between proximal and distal explanation, which is a central element in the three-part story's understanding of what is going on, distorts the nature of the explanation of action.

This argument of Collins's is extraordinarily difficult to grasp clearly. Here is another attempt to make his point, more briefly. The agent takes 'I am doing it because p' and 'I am doing it because I believe that p' as equivalent explanations. The second explanation does not have a new and quite different subject-matter, the psychology of the agent rather than its being the case that p. And it does not in this or any other way cancel the agent's endorsement of or commitment to its being that case that p. It is not, for the agent, as if the second explanation does something very different from the first. It is not, in particular, as if the second explanation mentions an intermediate stage in the explanatory flow, not alluded to by the first explanation. Nor does the second explanation enjoy other advantages, such as that by a change of subject-matter it specifies something that the agent is less likely to have been wrong about. *It is really the same explanation both times.* Any difference

between them affects not so much the nature of the explanation offered as the form in which it is presented. So much from the agent's point of view. Now since our third-person explanation of the action should be, so far as possible, the agent's explanation, we too should not take the psychologized restatement of the original explanation to be doing a different job from that done by the unpsychologized reasons-statement. In particular, we should not see it as specifying a proximal as opposed to a distal stage in the explanatory flow. We have to understand the psychologizing restatement in some other way – in a way that somehow respects the fact that for the agent the psychologized and the non-psychologized explanations are effectively identical.

We might reply that the distal–proximal distinction is forced upon us by the existence of cases where things are not as the agent conceives them to be. Where the agent says 'I am doing it because p' and it is not the case that p, we cannot offer for ourselves the explanation that he offers. His explanation is mistaken. The truth of the matter is that he is doing it because he believes that p. Since it is not the case that p, that p cannot explain anything; the explanation must lie in the fact that he believes, mistakenly, that p.

I shall return to this matter [. . .] but it is worth quoting here Collins's reply to this objection. 'It is his reason, and in case he is wrong he acts because he makes this error. No claim asserting some other matter about which he is not in error [e.g. that he believes that p] can be substituted in rendering his reason for acting' (1997: 123). One might paraphrase this as follows. If he is wrong, still he acts because of the way in which he takes things to be, a matter on which he is mistaken. It would distort things to suppose that his reason for acting was something else about which he is not wrong, such as that he so takes things to be. Even more simply: either the reason for which he acts is something that is the case, or it is something that is not the case. In the second instance, we do not need to locate something else that is the case to be the reason for which he acts.

This argument of Collins's is much more radical than the two I offered before. He is disputing the standard understanding of the belief-attributions that are supposed to specify motivating reasons. In my first two criticisms on the three-part story I saw no reason to deny that belief-attributions characterize psychological states of the agent, while

Collins eventually denies that beliefs are psychological states at all. They are stances but not states. For if they were states, the statement 'I believe that p' would have to be thought of as alluding to the existence in me of such a state, and so have quite a different subject-matter from that of the simple statement that p. In slightly more detail, Collins's argument here is as follows:

1 If there are inner states of belief that p, then the existence of such a state does not require it to be true that p. This is guaranteed by the fact that some beliefs are false.
2 Therefore, to say that the inner state of belief that p is present in A is not to say it is true that p. It does not express any stand on whether it is the case that p or not, something that is a different and independent matter of fact.
3 (2) obtains even if it is A himself who says (reports) the presence of the inner state.
4 If believing that p is an inner state, A can state that he believes that p (the inner state is present) without expressing a stand on whether it is the case that p.
5 Since A cannot do this, believing that p is not an inner state.[2]

For this reason it does not seem that Collins's views can be seen as an expansion of Nagel's point, unless that point has ramifications that Nagel was not aware of.

A question then arises whether the attack on the three-part story can stop short of this more radical claim. And this question becomes more pressing when we recognize that there are powerful reasons to hold that beliefs are not psychological states at all, not especially for reasons to do with Moore's Paradox, but more for reasons to do with the duration of belief and other features in which belief differs from standard or paradigm examples of psychological states.[3] If this more radical position were sound, the whole of the three-part story would be blown apart. For the three-part story to work, motivating reasons must be states of the agent, caused in certain ways and causing intentional actions. If there are no such things in the first place, the story collapses.

3. Explanation by Appeal to Content

One aspect of the three-part story that I did not criticize concerns the way in which it sought to meet the explanatory constraint. It did this by announcing that the belief which explains the action, the belief that p, is itself to be explained by its being the case that p. That p, therefore, can be understood as a part of the explanation of the action, even though properly it is only contributing to the explanation at one remove, distally, as it were.

Against this we might say that it is actually quite rare for a belief to be explicable by appeal to things being as they are believed to be. To be sure, there are cases in which this is appropriate. But in many, perhaps most, it is not. That it is about to rain may explain why everyone is coming in. Is their belief that it is about to rain to be explained by its being about to rain? Or is it rather the blackness of the clouds and the sudden drop in temperature? These are not themselves to be explained by its being about to rain. The clouds are not black *because* it will shortly rain. The same is very often true in the case that really concerns me, the explanation of moral action. Suppose I act as I do because I believe it to be my duty. Is it at all convincing to suggest that my belief may itself be explained by appeal to the fact that it is my duty? More convincing explanations seem to be available, such as my moral upbringing. That things are as I take them to be does not seem likely to enter into *these* explanations.

We do not have to agree with all these points to wonder whether the three-part story was really the strongest version of psychologism. The appeal to the transitivity of explanation was nice; but perhaps it turns out to be more of a liability than a strength – a liability to be added to the weaknesses already exposed. There may be other ways of constructing a psychologistic account of motivating reasons. The one that suggests itself most forcibly involves the notion of content. The idea here is that the motivating reason is the psychological state of the agent, the believings he is currently engaged in, and the normative reason is the content of those believings. The content of a belief is here being understood as (and only as) *what is believed*. Since

---

[2] Thanks to Arthur Collins for this perspicuous representation of the main argument of Collins (1987).
[3] See Hacker (1992); Hunter (1980); Malcolm (1991).

I have tied myself to the view that normative reasons are what is believed, e.g. that she needs my help, I should be happy about this. But it is further suggested that what is believed can contribute to the explanation of the action, since the believing comes *with* a content, and needs to do so if it is to explain anything. So it is psychological state *plus* content that together constitute the motivating reason, and the content alone that constitutes the normative reason, if there is one.

It is worth pressing the question whether the content-based approach does really meet our two constraints: the explanatory constraint that a normative reason must be at least capable of contributing to the explanation of an action that is done in the light of that reason, and the normative constraint that motivating reasons must be at least capable of being good reasons. One might say, I suppose, that the appeal to content does succeed in meeting both constraints, more or less. The normative reason contributes to the explanation of action by being a vital part of the motivating reason. The motivating reason is capable of being a good reason in the sense that its content is so capable. Still, if I am to stick to my two constraints, the fact remains that we are here trying to conceive of motivating reasons as psychological states of the agent, with real reasons, as one might put it, as content. The sort of motivating reason we are offering is itself incapable of being a good reason (except in certain very special cases). What is more, it will not be the sort of reason we specify when we lay out the light in which he acted, for that light will not consist in certain psychological states of his.

Psychologism, as a theory of motivating reasons, holds that only states can motivate. Contents, however conceived, cannot do it. Equally, a content can be a good reason for action but a psychological state cannot (at least not normally). We do not achieve theoretical equilibrium by amalgamating these two remarks, eliding the bits that we do not want, and hoping that they will thereby be able to make up a conception of how we can do an action for the reason that makes it right. The combination of state and content is torn apart in its attempt to be (able to be) both normative and motivating. If the problem is how to get one thing that can do both, this form of conceptual cookery is not the solution.

None the less, I know that many will think that, in these remarks, I am taking my two constraints, especially the normative one, far more literally than can be justified. We agree that literally speaking the motivating reason is not itself capable of being a normative reason. But it is close enough to what *is* capable of being a normative reason, we may say, for all practical (and indeed theoretical) purposes. And indeed, despite these initial misgivings, I do find the content-based approach much more persuasive than the three-part story. But I am going to suggest that the philosophy of mind that is needed to make it work is going to have to be pretty outlandish. In glossing the content of a belief simply as 'what is believed', I was trying to make it appear that the content-based form of psychologism was not committed to any particular philosophical account of what content is to be. But the fact remains that if this content-based version is to be successful, it must give some account of content that shows how the contents of our beliefs are capable of doing what is here required of them. This really means that we must abandon the standard understanding of the contents of beliefs as propositions believed. For what we are now counting as contents must be capable of playing two roles:

1   They must be able to be good reasons for action (and for belief);
2   They must be the sort of thing that can be believed and be not believed, and can be believed both truly and falsely.

I want to suggest that propositions, even true ones, are incapable of playing at least the first of these roles. Propositions are incapable of being good reasons for action. So if they do indeed count as what we believe, the content-based strategy in its present form is broken-backed.

My first and simplest point here is that intuitively it seems to be not so much propositions as states of affairs that are our good reasons. It is her being ill that gives me reason to send for the doctor, and this is a state of affairs, something that is part of the world, not a proposition. Those who announce that all good reasons are propositions (e.g. Scanlon 1999: 57) seem thereby to lose contact with the realities that call for action from us.

In case this point should not be persuasive, I support it by considering in more detail what sort of thing a proposition is supposed to be, and asking whether anything like that could be a good reason. There are many different understandings of what propositions are, but I will just look at the two leading accounts, or perhaps groups of accounts. The first of these understands a proposition as what is expressed by an assertoric or indicative sentence, and what such a sentence expresses is itself understood in terms of a distinction between two sets of possible worlds, those in which the sentence is true and those in which it is false. We can define the proposition expressed by the sentence 'Canberra is hot in February' as the class of worlds in which that sentence is true.[4] The second understanding of propositions sees them as abstract objects that have the sort of structure that an assertoric sentence has. So the proposition that Canberra is hot in February is a structured object with constituents that correspond to the elements of the sentence 'Canberra is hot in February'. It is an abstract object that consists of Canberra, of being hot, and of certain times of the year, perhaps, and of the relation between these things that would make it the case that Canberra is hot in February, all placed in a suitable structure analogous to that of the relevant sentence. Now the question is whether on either account (remembering that both accounts are hotly disputed) propositions are the right sort of thing to be good reasons for action. It seems just obvious that they are not. For a class of worlds is hardly the right sort of thing to make an action sensible or right. And an abstract object with a structure that mirrors that of a sentence seems to be no better off. On either understanding, propositions are, as we might say, too thin or insubstantial to be able to make an action wrong. They are the wrong sort of beast. Reasons for action are things like his self-satisfaction, her distress, yesterday's bad weather, and the current state of the dollar. They cannot be abstract objects of the sort that propositions are generally supposed to be.

Of course we do, or at least can, say such things as 'That she is in distress is what made his action callous, and that she is in distress is a proposition'. But this should not persuade us that the very thing that made his action callous is a proposition. We also say things like 'That the cliff was unstable was a consequence of the heavy rain, and that the cliff was unstable is a proposition', but we would surely be unwise to conclude from this that a proposition was a consequence of the heavy rain. It may be that by her action she ensured that she would not run

out of petrol before reaching London; but what she ensured was not a proposition. In general, though we use that-clauses to specify propositions, not all uses of such clauses are in the proposition-specifying business; and the ones that specify reasons cannot be in that business at all, for otherwise they would subvert their own purpose.

[. . .]

6

2. The Role of Belief in the Psychologizing Restatement of a Reason

Whenever the agent acts in the light of the fact that p, the agent must take it that p, and I understand this sort of 'taking it that' as a weak form of belief. And ordinarily, we have claimed, the psychologized explanation of the action is to be understood as the same explanation as the non-psychologized one. Sometimes the psychologized explanation is inappropriate, even misleading. The opportunities for use of the explanation 'I am doing this because I think I am married' are rare, one might say; to use this form of words definitely gives one to understand that there is something odd about the situation (as if one might not be quite sure whether the divorce had come through). None the less, if I act in the light of the fact that I am married, I must believe that I am. So what role does 'that I believe I am married' play in the explanation? It seems as if the belief must be there but is not allowed to make much of a contribution, and this is very odd. So what role can the normative story assign to the belief?

Collins's view is that I insert an 'I believe that' into the explanation of my action (actual or intended) when I am in some doubt about whether I am right; the phrase signals that uncertainty. Equally, in the third-person case we move to the psychologized explanation when we take it that the matter is dubious or that the agent is mistaken. In the first-person case, the transaction as a whole is to be understood in terms of a Gricean conversational implicature. The implication of uncertainty

---

[4] Stalnaker suggests that propositions are functions from possible worlds to truth values (1984: 2); I would say the same about propositions understood in this way as I say about propositions as sets of worlds in the main text.

can be cancelled, as when one says, perhaps, 'The reason why I am going to do it is that I believe that p, though I have to say that I am not in any doubt about the matter'. There is clearly much truth in this, but it seems to me not to be an answer to our question. The question is not one about when we do and when we don't adopt the psychologized form of explanation. It is about the role of the belief in the story as a whole if it is not playing the focal role normally attributed to it.

What other account of the role of belief is available to the normative story? I can think of two. The first involves a structural distinction in the theory of explanation. There is a difference between a consideration that is a proper part of an explanation, and a consideration that is required for the explanation to go through, but which is not itself a part of that explanation. I call the latter 'enabling conditions'. For instance, that England is not sinking beneath the waves today is a consideration in the absence of which what explains my actions would be incapable of doing so. But that does nothing to show that England's not submerging today is part of the explanation of why I do what I do (or more generally of my doing what I do). It is therefore an enabling condition in this case, though of course it is a proper part of the explanation of some other things, for instance of why the parts are not disappearing under water. The suggestion therefore is that the believing, conceived traditionally as a psychological state, is an enabling condition for an explanation which explains the action in terms of the reasons for (i.e. in favour of – the good reasons for) doing it. This condition is required for that explanation to go through. That is, in the absence of the believing, what in fact explains the action would not then explain it, either because the action would not then have been done at all, or because, if it had, it would have been done for another reason and so been explained in another way. But the believing does not contribute directly to the explanation.

The difficulty that I see with this move is not so much that the notion of an enabling condition requires theoretical support that I have not provided here. It is rather that there is no clear account of where the line that it draws is to come, case by case. It is not clear what one is to say to someone who insists that the believing is a proper part of the explanation. And so we can have no confidence that there won't be plenty of occasions in which the believing will end up within the explanation

rather than outside it, returning us to our starting-point.

I have something of a reply to this point, which is that the appeal to enabling conditions is made after we have established that motivating reasons must be able to be normative ones, to be good reasons, and shown therefore that motivating reasons do not standardly include psychological states of the agent. It is also made after we have established that explanations of the form 'that I believe that p' are not normally the correct way of specifying the light in which I act, if they are conceived of as distinct in style from the simpler explanation they are intended to replace. Having got this far, however, we have a principled reason for insisting that the believing, or that the agent so believed, is not to be taken as a proper part of the relevant explanation. We were looking for a way of recognizing the fact that it is never wrong to admit a reference to the agent's belief in the story; we can do this, consistently with the results we have already accepted, only by allowing that the believing, or that the agent believes, counts as an enabling condition rather than as a part of the motivating reason. We could not, for instance, say that the believing is part of the motivating reason, the rest being constituted by the normative reason. For this would return us to the point that the (now complex) motivating reason is incapable of being the normative reason. Nor could we say that 'that the agent believes that p' is really the agent's reason, or among the agent's reasons; for to insist on this would be to distort our account of the light in which the agent acted. So there is a principled explanation of the fact that the believing must be seen as an enabling condition rather than as a proper part of the explanation on each occasion.

However, I do not feel confident enough in this reply to rely on it entirely. This motivates me to look for another account of the reference to belief in 'He is doing it because he believes that p'. The one that appeals to me is what I call the appositional account. This hears 'He is doing it because he believes that p' as 'He is doing it because p, as he believes'. The 'as he believes' functions paratactically here, attaching itself to the 'p'. Again, it is not part of the specification of his reason, but is a comment on that reason, one that is required by the nature of the explanation that we are giving. That explanation specifies the features *in the light of which* the agent acted. It is required for this sort of explanation that those features be present to the agent's consciousness – indeed, that they be somehow conceived as favouring the action; so there must always be a way of making room for this fact, in some relation to the explanation that runs from features as reasons to action as response. It is not required, however, that the nature of the agent's consciousness itself either constitute, or even be part of, the *explanans*. The appositional account tells us how to hold all these things together in a coherent whole.

More needs to be said about this paratactic comment. How, for instance, are we to understand statements like 'If I had not believed that p, I would not have done it'? Is there any possibility of running some paraphrase such as 'If it had not been the case, as I believed, that p, I would not have done it'? This seems strained to me, at best; on its most natural hearing, it sounds equivalent to 'If it had not been the case that p, I would not have done it', which is not at all what we want. But we are not here in the business of contributing to the famous Davidsonian research programme. There is perhaps a harder question whether we can, understanding the phrase 'I believe that p' appositionally, retain the validity of *modus ponens* and other inference schemata. In general, however, I offer the appositional account as a philosophical explication of the sense of 'I believe that p', rather than as a contribution to formal philosophy of language. It is only if it is taken in the latter way that these hard-edged questions get a bite.

There are interesting questions here about the relation between the appositional account and the enabling conditions account. One view is that they are distinct. For the enabling conditions account may seem to be committed to the existence of the belief as a psychological state, while the appositional account is consistent with the more radical suggestion that belief is more a stance or commitment than a state. The appositional account, that is, leaves it open what sort of philosophical story we should tell about belief, in a way that the enabling condition account does not. So the appositional account enjoys a considerable strategical advantage, and we should adopt it in preference to the enabling conditions account.

Still, we can never deny that the agent believes that p, if we once explain his action by saying that he did it for the reason that p, as he supposes. Indeed, as I see it, the two sentences at issue:

His reason for doing it was that p, as he supposed

His reason for doing it was that he supposed that p

entail each other.[5] What is more, the second of them is to be understood as entailing that the agent supposed or believed that p. So on either account, appositional or enabling conditions, we have to allow that, had the agent not believed that p, he could not have acted for the reason that p. And this is really all that it amounts to to say that his belief that p is an enabling condition for his acting for the reason that p. What is more, if there is sufficient reason to deny that belief is a psychological state, that reason must be compatible with some positive account of what is going on in ordinary belief-attributions. It is not as if we are forced to allow that the reference to belief in the appositional clause is a reference to a psychological state, just because the appositional clause entails the straightforward claim that the agent believed that p. So perhaps the correct view is that there are two versions of the enabling condition account, one that takes the belief as a psychological state and the other that does not. The appositional version of things is not committed to either version as such.

Why not just say that what explains the action is that p and that the agent believed that p? Because this just opens the door for those who want to argue that the 'that p' is redundant – for in cases where what the agent believes is not the case, we just drop the first conjunct without our explanation being at all damaged or diminished thereby. And we have already seen that this is wrong. Psychologized explanations give the wrong explanation of action, if we conceive of them as somehow preferable to the simpler non-psychologized ones. That the agent believed that p is not the sole correct explanation of the action, even in a case where the belief was false.

---

[5] Except in the special sorts of case discussed in sect. 1 above. [Ed. note: omitted here. See pp. 121–6 of *Practical Reality*.]

3.   Factive and Non-Factive Explanations

The previous section concerned the difficulties thought to arise because of the universal insertability of the 'I believe that', and the admission that if the agent does not believe that p, his reason for acting cannot be that p. This new section concerns the relevance of the claim that, if it is not the case that p, the reason why the agent acted cannot be that p and *must* be that he believed that p. The case of the false belief, as we might put it, drives a wedge between the psychologized and the non-psychologized explanation, in favour of the former. And once this point has been made about cases where the relevant belief is false, we will have to say the same thing about cases where it is true. For we are allowing that the true–false distinction should not affect the form of the relevant explanation.

It is at this point that we return to matters raised early in Chapter 1 [Omitted here. Eds.]. I originally distinguished between the reasons why we do what we do and the good reasons for acting in that way. But I suggested that explanation of action in terms of the reasons that motivated the agent is only one way of explaining why the agent did what he did. All explanations can be given in terms of reasons, after all, even those that are not explanations of action. We can ask for the reason why the sun goes down the sky towards evening, even though we know perfectly well that the sun does not do this for a reason of its own, as it were. We are not, impossibly, supposing that the trajectory of the sun is something intentionally chosen by the sun in the light of these and those considerations. Even when we restrict ourselves to the explanation of intentional action, which will still be offered in terms of reasons, we need not always suppose that the reasons we offer in explanation of why the agent did what he did are among what we have been calling 'the agent's reasons', or that the agent acted in the light of those reasons. Explaining in terms of the reasons that motivated the agent is a special case of explaining (giving the reason) why he acted as he did.

Now one form of pressure in favour of the psychologized explanation of intentional action derives from the simple thought that all explanation is factive. What this means is that from an explanation of the form 'The reason why it is the case that p is that q' we can infer both that p and

that q. This is no different from the relation between 'He knows that p' and 'p', or between 'He has forgotten that p' and 'p'. For him to know that p or to have forgotten that p or indeed to have remembered that p, it must be the case that p. In this sense, we say that knowledge and remembering are factive; and so is forgetting. Equally, various locutions in which we characteristically give explanations are factive. As I said above, 'The reason why it is the case that p is that q' is doubly factive, entailing both that p and that q. So is 'The explanation of its being the case that p is that q'. The question then arises whether all explanations are factive in this sense. Suppose that my question 'What were his reasons for doing that?' is a request for explanation, and that the explanation can be given by laying out the considerations in the light of which he determined to do what he did. Suppose also that, in those considerations, the agent was mistaken. Things were not as he supposed them to be in relevant respects. Does this mean that we cannot base our explanation on those considerations? Is explanation in terms of motivating reasons always factive, like other explanation, or is it non-factive? If it is non-factive, it is different from other sorts of explanation. But we should not beg the question by assuming that such a thing is impossible, though no doubt it will affect our general conception of explanation should things so turn out. The question, then, is whether there is a way of explaining an action by laying out the considerations in the light of which the agent acted without committing ourselves to things being as the agent there conceived them to be.

I take it that the answer to this question is yes. I suggest that locutions such as

> His reason for doing it was that it would increase his pension
>
> The ground on which he acted was that she had lied to him

are not factive. To test this, we only need to consider whether it is possible without contradiction to continue by denying that things were as the agent took them to be. Consider the following sentences:

> His reason for doing it was that it would increase his pension, but in fact he was quite wrong about that.

The ground on which he acted was that she had lied to him, though actually she had done nothing of the sort.

Neither of these sentences sounds self-contradictory to me. Not everyone's ears agree with me about this, I know. But there seems to be no reason why there should not be a way of revealing the light in which the agent saw things as a way of explaining why he did what he did, but without asserting that he was right to see things that way. I think that the two locutions above are ways of doing that. They are not, of course, the only ways of doing it. We can achieve the same thing by saying:

> He did it because he took it that it would increase his pension.

> What explains his doing it was that he thought it would increase his pension.

> The reason why he did it was that he fondly imagined that it would increase his pension.

> He did it for the reason that, as he imagined, it would increase his pension.

> He did this because, as he supposed, she had lied to him.

In the first two of these five cases, we have apparently recognized the factive nature of the locution we are using, in offering after the 'because' and 'explains' a sentence that is true. The same is true of the third. In the last two cases, matters are a little more delicate. Suppose that she had not lied to him, but that he thought that she had. Is it true that, as he supposed, she had lied to him? No. It is not quite clear what truth value this sentence now has, but it does seem clear that it does not have the truth value true. So the insertion or the apposition 'as he believed' does not take us from a falsehood to a truth in the way that the insertion of 'he believed that . . .' does, or at least can do. What it does is to remove the speaker's commitment to things being as the agent supposed. So the appositional use is a sort of halfway house. The relevant context is not factive, since any commitment to the truth of the contained clause can be removed without incoherence, but it has something of the style of a factive explanation, for if you take the apposition out, there is a strong *suggestio veri*.

It may be that there are some forms of action-explanation that are factive and some that are not.

I see no need to decide this issue; my main point is that the purposes of explanation of action in terms of the agent's reasons do not require such explanation to be factive. (Do we, for instance, find forms of inference to the best explanation at all tempting in this case?) Where we are dealing with a non-factive form, there is no real need to include the apposition in order to avoid commitment to things being as the agent supposed. If the explanation is not factive, it is not factive. Any commitment there may be will be more in the style of a conversational implicature than an entailment. So we might want to include the apposition in order to guard ourselves against the implicature otherwise carried by some forms of explanation, that the agent was right about the matter. Some hear 'He did this because she had lied to him' as factive, and so as the wrong explanation of his action if she had not lied to him. Others hear it as carrying a *suggestio veri*, but a cancellable one, so that where the agent is mistaken, we can still explain his action by saying 'He did this because, as he supposed, she had lied to him'. And this pattern of choices repeats with the other styles that our action-explanation can take, e.g. 'His reason for doing this was that *p*'.

What conclusions can we draw from all this? The most general conclusion is in line with what was claimed in Chapter 1.2: that there are explanations of action that do not succeed simply by laying out the agent's reasons for action in the terms that the agent would have done if asked. Restricting ourselves now to attempts to specify the agent's reasons, in the sense that we have given to that phrase, we have decided that though some such attempts may involve a factive context, others do not. The ones that do not are ones that involve a contained intensional context, such as that introduced by 'he believes that . . .', so that the whole can be true *as an explanation*, though the contained part, the thing doing the explaining, is not. There are, then, both factive and non-factive ways of laying out the considerations in the light of which the agent acted.

If this is so, it seems to me that the difference between the factive and the non-factive cannot be of any real significance when it comes to the explanation of action. We can phrase our explanation as we like, and that is the end of the matter. So it cannot be that the very notion of explanation drives us to the use of the phrase 'because he believed that . . .' in order to live up to the factive demands associated with the explanation of events. In this sense, a thing believed that is not the case can still explain an action.

It follows from this that if we do decide to use the factive turn of phrase in giving our explanation of his action, this cannot be because we are driven by the need to find a factive explanation. We do not need to do this, and there are available plenty of effectively equivalent turns of phrase that would have enabled us to do things differently. If the agent's conception of the situation is mistaken, there are some ways of explaining his action that are now ruled out. But this does not show that only factive ones are left in, forcing us towards the phrasing 'He did it because he believed that p'. If we do use the factive ones, this will be a comparatively arbitrary choice.

The picture that is emerging here is one that is very congenial to Collins's basic point: for the agent the psychologized and the non-psychologized explanations are effectively equivalent. We tend to suppose that, once we move to the third-person perspective, things are very different in this respect, on the grounds that the purposes of explanation force us to move to a *different* explanation of the action – one whose general structure consists in a relation between the action and the psychology of the agent *rather than* in a relation between the action and the light in which the agent saw it. But this is a distortion of what is going on when we move from one form of explanation to the other. The distinction between first and third person does not allow us to suppose that in the third-person case, there is a radical distinction between the psychologized and the non-psychologized forms of explanation, when there is no such radical difference in the first-person case. There is only one sort of explanation, though the form in which we may choose to give that explanation may vary according to the circumstances. What is more, the most revealing form, perhaps I should say, the form least likely to mislead philosophers, is the simple form which contains no visible reference to belief at all.

I close this section with a summary of the position so far, and an analogy. The fact that the agent would not have performed the action had he not believed that p should not persuade us that the proper way of specifying the reason in the light of which he acted was as 'that he believed that p'. This sort of counterfactual test takes us in the wrong direction, since it invites us to ignore the differences between two relations: first, the special rela-tion that holds between the reason for which the action was done and the action done for that reason, and second the more general relation that holds between the action and any other condition in the absence of which it would not have been done for the reason that it was. And anyway, there are examples that show the need to distinguish between those special cases of reasons that involve the agent's belief and those that don't. The counterfactual test invites us to blur that distinction. One may feel some unease about saying 'His reason was that p' when we don't ourselves believe that p. But this too should not drive us to saying 'His reason was that he believed that p', supposing that by this device we are respecting the factive nature of explanation; we can avoid any apparent commitment on our part to things being as the agent supposed by use of one of a number of special constructions such as 'as he supposed'.

The analogy that follows I owe to Lloyd Humberstone, and I give it largely in his words. Let us think of what we might call the 'grounds' for a punishment, where the notion of a ground is being used stipulatively for whatever fills the for-phrase in such sentences as 'He was sentenced to six years for armed robbery'. In crime fiction, or in talk-back radio from callers who pride themselves on a certain kind of cynicism, one sometimes hears people say such things as 'Nobody ever got sent to prison for robbing banks, only for getting caught robbing banks'. This can be thought of as another misinvocation of the counterfactual test. The idea is that since you wouldn't be sentenced to imprisonment unless you had been caught, what you are being sentenced for is: having been caught. There would be a similar mistake if being convicted were cited instead of being caught as (what we are calling) the grounds for punishment. What we want to say is that the prisoner is serving time for robbing a bank, rather than for being caught (etc.). But what happens when we think the prisoner has been wrongly convicted, or even when we just don't want to commit ourselves to the correctness of the conviction, because of the factive ring to 'He is serving ten years for robbing a bank'? In these cases we need a decommitment operator, which normally amounts to slipping in the word 'allegedly' before 'robbing a bank', in appositional style. There is indeed no offence of allegedly robbing a bank, and one cannot be accused of that, nor convicted of it. But one can be punished for it, and put in prison for it, in a sense. The explanation of this is that there is no factive pull in the notion of accusation, nor in that of conviction, but there is in the notion of 'punishment for'.

It seems, then, that the explanation of action, at least that of intentional action, can always be achieved by laying out the considerations in the light of which the agent saw the action as desirable, sensible, or required. If things were as the agent supposed, there is no bar against the agent's reasons being among the reasons in favour of doing what he actually did. That is to say, the reasons that motivated the agent can be among or even identical with the good reasons in the case, those that favour acting as he did. Equally, the good reasons can motivate him, since they can be the considerations in the light of which he acted, and citing them can explain the action directly rather than only being able to do so indirectly as part of the content of a suitable psychological state. Good reasons explain action in any case where the agent chose to do that action in the light of those reasons. The psychological state that the agent is in is not, of course, simply irrelevant to the explanation. But neither is it the focus of that explanation. Equally, that the agent has the relevant beliefs is not irrelevant, but is not the focus of the explanation either.

One contentious aspect of the picture that has been developed here is that something that is not the case can explain an action. Another is that a normative fact (for instance, that I owe it to her to do what she asks) can explain an action. Explanations by appeal to the normative or to the non-obtaining are not what we are used to. Nor, even, are we used to the idea that a simple matter of fact can explain an action; we are too used to hearing about beliefs and desires. But these things are things that I think we should countenance without too much reluctance. In doing so, we will be giving one sense to the idea that reality is practical. The reasons that motivate us can be things that are the case.

The other sense to the idea that reality is practical is that good reasons can be, or be grounded in, considerations other than those concerning the psychology of the agent. Here I have especially in mind the desires of the agent. If [. . .] few if any reasons are either desire-based or belief-based, we are a long way towards establishing on the normative side too that reality can be practical. Features of our surroundings can be, or at least can give us, reasons in favour of acting in one way rather than another.

References

Collins, A. W. 1987. *The Nature of Mental Things.* Notre Dame, IN: University of Notre Dame Press.

Collins, A. W. 1997. 'The Psychological Reality of Reasons', *Ratio*, 10/2: 108–23.

Crisp, R. and Hooker, B. W., eds. 2000. *Well-Being and Morality: Essays in Honour of James Griffin.* Oxford: Oxford University Press.

Dancy, J. 1995. 'Why there is Really No Such Thing as the Theory of Motivation', *Proceedings of the Aristotelian Society*, 95: 1–18.

Dancy, J. 1996. 'Real Values in a Humean Context', *Ratio*, 9/2: 171–83.

Dancy, J. 2000. 'Recognition and Reaction', in Crisp and Hooker (2000).

Hacker, P. M. S. 1992. 'Malcolm and Searle on "Intentional Mental States"', *Philosophical Investigations*, 15/3: 245–75.

Hunter, J. 1980. 'Believing', in P. A. French et al., eds., *Midwest Studies in Philosophy*, v: *Epistemology*. Notre Dame, IN: University of Notre Dame Press, 239–60.

Malcolm, N. 1991. '"I believe that *p*"', in E. Lepore and R. van Gulick, eds., *John Searle and his Critics*. Oxford: Blackwell, 159–67.

Scanlon, T. 1999. *What We Owe To Each Other.* Cambridge, MA: Harvard University Press.

Stalnaker, R. 1984. *Inquiry.* Cambridge, MA: MIT Press.

II.2   Moral Reasons

Introduction

Why be moral? It is a question we have all asked ourselves, at one point or another. We might ask such a question out of pure curiosity, but much more likely is a scenario in which we perceive a conflict between what we want, and what morality demands of us. In such cases, why forsake the former for the latter?

To ask such a question is to seek an account of the rational authority of morality. We want to know whether moral requirements supply good reasons for obedience, and if so, how strong such reasons are. A reason's strength is its power to outweigh or extinguish the reasons provided by competing considerations.

Imagine, for instance, a person who is very tempted to cheat on his taxes, because he knows that the chances of getting caught are quite small, and the benefits of keeping all that money are substantial. What reason is there for him to pay his taxes in this case?

Though there might, in fact, be many reasons on both sides, we can simplify things by identifying the two basic replies to such a question. According to the first, the only reasons a person has to do *anything* stem from his own commitments. This view is known as *instrumentalism about reasons* (henceforth, *instrumentalism* for short). You have a reason to do something just because doing it will aid in the achievement of what matters to you. The person

in our example has some reason not to cheat, because there is a chance he will land in jail if he does, and that's something he very much wants to avoid. But on this view, he also has excellent reasons to go ahead and cheat, since, of all options now available, that will get him what he most wants. Indeed, this first view says that the strength of one's reasons is directly proportioned to the likelihood that they will maximize the satisfaction of one's deepest desires. Thus the instrumentalist will deny that there is always best reason to do as morality says.[1] One's strongest reasons are given by one's own ultimate commitments; if these assign priority to considerations other than morality, then, in cases of conflict, morality must go by the board.

A very important feature of instrumentalism is that the reason-giving power of moral considerations is always *contingent*. Whether you have reason to act rightly always depends, on this account, on whether doing so will get you what you most want. Moral considerations are never, all by themselves, reasons for action. That some action is morally admirable, or required, is no reason at all for a person to do the action – unless its admirability is something she cares about, or unless the action, no matter how admirable, will get her something else that she wants.

Moral rationalism is the name of a view that is opposed to instrumentalism. Moral rationalism asserts that there is an entailment, a necessary connection, between moral duties and excellent reasons for action. On this view, there is always very good reason to do as morality says.

Moral rationalists divide on the issue of the strength of moral reasons. Some believe that morality always supplies overriding reasons – reasons that uniformly take precedence over competing considerations. Others believe that morality, though always providing strong reasons for action, can sometimes be overridden in unusual, extreme circumstances. This debate is very hard to settle, because its resolution depends on first determining just what it is that morality requires of us. If, with Kant, we believe that it is always immoral to tell a lie, then we might also be more inclined to think that morality must sometimes take a back seat to other considerations. On the other side, those who regard morality as inviolable tend to believe that it is also not quite so demanding. If moral reasons are always of paramount importance, then there will be only a relatively few occasions on which it genuinely calls on us (say) to risk our lives or our livelihoods.

The question of the rational authority of morality is very often posed by reference to the figure of Gyges, a Lydian shepherd whose story was first recounted by Herodotus, and then later made use of by Plato in his *Republic*. While following his sheep into a cave, Gyges discovered a magic ring which, when turned, made him invisible. He soon realized that this ring made him invulnerable to his enemies. It wasn't long before he put this ring to use, killing the king by stealth, acquiring vast wealth, and consolidating near-absolute political power.

If possessed of such a ring, what would you do? What *should* you do? Instrumentalism and rationalism will give you different advice. If instrumentalism is true, such a person may have no reason at all to do his duty. If a person is very immoral, and also very secure in his power, he may have nothing to gain by acting morally. And so he will have no reason to comply with moral demands. Rationalists will insist that such a person does indeed have excellent reason to be moral. But this reason needn't stem from what he wants – that an act is right is, or entails, a reason to do it. Perhaps, as Plato believed, this is because virtue *always* enhances self-interest, and one always has reason to promote self-interest. Other rationalists, who find this alleged connection between virtue and

self-interest a bit difficult to swallow, must find some other explanation of why, in every case, one has excellent reason to comply with moral requirements.

This has been moral rationalism's Achilles' heel. For if we deny that doing good is always going to benefit us, or get us what we want, then what possible reason could there be to do it? It is very hard to see an answer to this question. And the instrumentalists are in the clear here. They appeal to considerations – namely, a person's own commitments – that everyone thinks of as supplying good reasons. Something has gone wrong, for instance, with the person who acknowledges that an act will gain him what he most wants, and yet denies that he has any reason to do it. But the person who will be the loser for doing as morality says is someone who might, it seems, be perfectly reasonable in refusing to comply with those demands.

The debate between instrumentalists and rationalists is often characterized as one about the existence of categorical imperatives – instrumentalists deny their existence, and rationalists defend them. However, in her seminal (1972) article (reprinted in this section), Philippa Foot shows that the notion of a categorical imperative is ambiguous. This ambiguity has hindered progress in discussions of morality's rational authority, and Foot seeks to set it right. Foot properly draws our attention to two senses of "categorical" that have long been in play in such debates. First, a moral duty might be categorical in the sense of *applying to* persons independently of their ends (i.e., their desires or interests). Second, a duty might be categorical in that it *supplies a reason* for all to whom it truly applies.

To aid us in appreciating this distinction, Foot has us consider the rules of etiquette, which apply to us in categorical fashion, but which do not supply us with categorical reasons for obedience. Whether we like it or not, spitting food in our guest's face is a breach of etiquette – the rules that denounce such behavior apply even to those who reject the prevailing customs. But whether we have reason to refrain from spitting depends, says Foot, on whether so refraining will further our ends. Those who don't care about conforming to etiquette, and who are comfortable living with the consequences of their disregard, will have no reason whatever to comply with them. The rules of etiquette are categorically applicable, without being categorically reason-giving.

As far as Foot can tell, things are precisely the same when it comes to reasons to be moral. Most people have such reasons, but that is only because most people either care about morality directly, or care about the rewards that moral behavior may bring. But those who lack either care have no reason to be moral.

While Foot's discussion put the rationalist on the defensive, it does so by way of assuming, rather than arguing for, the truth of instrumentalism. Just about a decade after the appearance of her article (whose instrumentalism she later repudiated), Bernard Williams published a very influential paper of his own, whose central thesis defends a view quite similar to Foot's. This (1979) paper (reprinted in this section) seeks to defend internalism about reasons, or *reasons internalism* for short. This view claims that all of a person's reasons for action must bear some special link with the considerations that are capable of presently motivating her. These considerations are *internal* to her mental make-up – hence the name.[2] Specifically, Williams argues that something can be a reason for a person to act only if it presently motivates her, or would motivate her, were she to deliberate soundly from her existing commitments (her beliefs, desires, long-range projects, loyalties, etc.). If, after reasoning well on that basis, a person would be left completely cold by the prospect of doing something, then she has no reason to do it.

Instrumentalism and internalism about reasons are related as species and genus. Instrumentalism is the most popular form of internalism. Instrumentalism cites one's desires as the sole relevant internal source of reasons. Other forms of internalism, such as Williams's, allow that things other than desires can motivate people, and also allow that forms of reasoning other than identifying means to desired ends can serve to locate and generate the reasons that genuinely apply to us.

Williams's internalism has clear implications for the moral realm. Some people – those who are extremely powerful, or those who are deeply malevolent – may have no reason to heed morality's call, since sensitive deliberation on the basis of their existing commitments would not justify moral action. As with instrumentalism, internalism here leaves morality's authority contingent on what happens to be "inside" of a person. Moral duty, all by itself, is incapable of supplying anyone with a reason to obey its decrees.

Christine Korsgaard, in her much-discussed (1986) paper (also reprinted here), endorses internalism about reasons, but rejects Williams's conclusion. Her line of argument has been variously interpreted, but the basis of her disagreement with Williams can be reduced to one of two interesting alternatives. Everyone, says Korsgaard, has excellent reason to be moral, even though everyone's reasons are derivable from sound deliberation based on an agent's existing commitments. (This is the internalism at play.) To resist William's conclusions, Korsgaard must say one of two things. Either everyone has, of necessity, at least one shared commitment that serves as the common basis for generating universal requirements of reason. Or there is a picture of sound deliberation that will yield the same requirements of reason for everyone, regardless of their motivational starting points. Readers are encouraged to consider both of these interpretative options when reading the Korsgaard piece.

Korsgaard's defense of internalism is squarely within the Kantian tradition, which stands for the idea (among many others) that there are moral requirements that are categorical in both of the senses that Foot has identified. The Kantian project, to simplify greatly, is to show that some basic commitment of being an agent – someone capable of forming goals, deliberating as to the wisdom of pursuing them, and acting accordingly – entails a commitment to being moral. (A recent attempt to vindicate this kind of Kantian argument is given by Korsgaard in her other piece in this collection, which appears as chapter 8 in this volume.) So if one were to deliberate well on the basis of this initial commitment, one would appreciate the rational requirement to adhere to moral constraints. Indeed, for Kant, and for Kantians, moral constraints just are a subset of the constraints of rationality. So those who behave immorally act irrationally. Those in a broadly Humean tradition, such as Williams, have always thought that this Kantian maneuver was an effort to pull a rabbit out of a hat.

At bottom, the Kantian seeks to show that immoral agents act inconsistently. Different Kantians interpret the inconsistency differently. But it is fair to say that only a relatively small number of philosophers nowadays regard this kind of argument as a success. As Foot writes in her selection, one can accuse an evil man of villainy, but not necessarily of inconsistency. Though we frown on the goal that he has set himself, he may be perfectly efficient in achieving it, without thereby sacrificing any of his other goals. To think this impossible, or to think that he must be acting contrary to his own commitments if he behaves immorally, is, according to most, just wishful thinking.

Now it may be that either the Platonic or the Kantian position is the correct one. We may, at the end of the day, be able to show that virtuous conduct always promotes self-interest, or we might be able to identify that essential commitment, shared by everyone, that entails a reason to be moral. But suppose these projects fail. Must we then reject moral rationalism, and so give up the hope of showing that every agent has categorical reasons to be moral?

In the final entry in this section, Russ Shafer-Landau argues against Foot, Williams, and Korsgaard, and tries to show how, without endorsing either Platonism or Kantianism, moral requirements necessarily supply every agent with excellent reasons for action. In the end, after criticizing the most prominent internalist and anti-rationalist arguments, he comes perilously close to announcing that there is no satisfying explanation for the (alleged) fact that moral duties supply reasons for action. But that, he claims, is not as damaging a position as one might think. There is no explanation for why self-interest generates reasons for action. It just does. There is no explanation for why we have reason to satisfy our desires. We just do. Why couldn't it be the same for morality?

Suppose that a person is dying, right there in front of you, and all you have to do to save her is give her a pill. The woman is a decent person. She's

not a terrorist. She's not going to become a Nazi commandant. She's just a regular person who needs help, right now. As far as you know, if you save her now, she'll go on and live a fulfilling life for many years. That pill is at her bedside, two feet away from you. She's too weak to reach out and take it. All you have to do is pick it up and feed it to her.

Error theories aside, it seems clear that you (morally) must go and help this person. The downside, let us suppose, is that you really don't feel anything for her, or her plight. Offering such help would only be a nuisance to you, and wouldn't earn you anything but the woman's gratitude, which leaves you cold. Yes, you'd want her to feed the pill to you were the positions reversed – but they're not. You'd rather just walk away and forget about the whole thing. Still, isn't there *some* reason for you to give the woman the pill? Isn't it a very good one? Isn't it, in fact, the *best* one in the circumstances?

If you are attracted by this last idea, then you will have begun to see the appeal of moral rationalism. For only moral rationalism can vindicate such a thought.

Yet this points only to the stakes in the debate. It reveals what we must give up if we decide to abandon moral rationalism. Though such examples are easily multiplied, it isn't clear how powerful an argument they provide. For even if we agree that, in the case just presented, there is excellent reason to give the woman the pill, we will still want to know why, and how that reason comes to be. Until we have a satisfying defense of Platonism or Kantianism, or some other general answer to such questions, moral rationalism will remain under a cloud of philosophical suspicion.

Notes

1 Here, and throughout this introduction, we shall simply assume that morality sometimes requires things that neither get us what we want, nor promote self-interest. If morality always best served self-interest, then so long as there is always good reason to promote self-interest, there would be a ready answer to why we should be moral. If morality always got us what we wanted, and if there is always good reason to satisfy our desires, then again the perennial question would be straightforwardly answered. These views may be correct, but we (like most philosophers) have our grave doubts about them, and so will proceed on the assumption of their falsity.

2 Reasons internalism should be distinguished from motivational internalism, which is discussed in the previous section (see the introduction to part II.1). Motivational internalism is a claim about the power of moral judgments to motivate. If it is true, then sincere moral judgments do motivate, and necessarily so. Reasons internalism is a theory not about the motivational power of moral judgments, but rather about the requirements of being a good reason. This sort of internalism says that a good reason must be able to motivate those for whom it is a reason. In short, motivational internalism says that something qualifies as a sincere moral judgment only if it

motivates the one who holds the judgment. Reasons internalism says that something qualifies as a good reason only if it is capable of motivating the agent whose reason it is.

Selected Bibliography

Brink, David. 1989. *Moral Realism and the Foundations of Ethics*. Cambridge: Cambridge University Press, ch. 3.

Brink, David. 1992. "A Puzzle about the Rational Authority of Morality." In James Tomberlin, ed. *Philosophical Perspectives 6*: Ethics. Atascadero, CA: Ridgeview.

Cohon, Rachel. 1993. "Internalism about Reasons for Action." *Pacific Philosophical Quarterly* 74: 265–88.

Cullity, Garrett, and Berys Gaut. 1997. *Ethics and Practical Reason*. Oxford: Oxford University Press.

Dancy, Jonathan. 2000. *Practical Reality*. Oxford: Oxford University Press.

FitzPatrick, William. 2004. "Reason, Value and Particular Agents: Normative Relevance without Motivational Internalism." *Mind* 113: 285–318.

Foot, Philippa. 1972. "Morality as a System of Hypothetical Imperatives." *Philosophical Review* 81: 305–16.

Gauthier, David. 1986. *Morals by Agreement*. Oxford: Oxford University Press, ch. 2.

Gert, Bernard. 1998. *Morality: Its Nature and Justification*. Oxford: Oxford University Press.

Hampton, Jean. 1998. *The Authority of Reason*. Cambridge: Cambridge University Press.

Hubin, Donald. 1999. "What's Special about Humeanism." *Noûs* 33: 30–45.

Hume, David. 2000. *Treatise of Human Nature*. David F. Norton and Mary Norton, eds. Oxford: Oxford University Press, book III, part 1.

Johnson, Robert. 1999. "Internal Reasons and the Conditional Fallacy." *Philosophical Quarterly* 49: 53–71.

Kavka, Gregory. 1984. "The Reconciliation Project." In David Copp and David Zimmerman, eds. *Morality, Truth and Reason*. Totowa, NJ: Rowman & Allanheld.

Korsgaard, Christine. 1986. "Skepticism about Practical Reason." *Journal of Philosophy* 83: 5–25.

McDowell, John. 2001. *Mind, Value and Reality*. Cambridge, MA: Harvard University Press, chs. 4 and 5.

Millgram, Elijah. 1996. "Williams' Argument against External Reasons." *Noûs* 30: 197–220.

Nagel, Thomas. 1970. *The Possibility of Altruism*. Oxford: Clarendon Press.

Parfit, Derek. 1997. "Reasons and Motivation." *Proceedings of the Aristotelian Society*, supplementary volume 71: 99–130.

Quinn, Warren. 1995. "Putting Rationality in its Place." In Rosalind Hursthouse, Gavin Lawrence, and Warren Quinn, eds. *Virtues and Reasons*. Oxford: Oxford University Press.

Railton, Peter. 2003. *Facts, Values and Norms*. Cambridge: Cambridge University Press, part III.

Scanlon, Thomas. 1998. *What We Owe to Each Other*. Cambridge, MA: Harvard University Press, ch. 1 and appendix.

Stroud, Sarah. 1998. "Moral Overridingness and Moral Theory." *Pacific Philosophical Quarterly* 79: 170–89.

Velleman, David. 1996. "The Possibility of Practical Reason." *Ethics* 106: 694–726.

Williams, Bernard. 1979. "Internal and External Reasons." In Ross Harrison, ed. *Rational Action*. Cambridge: Cambridge University Press.

Williams, Bernard. 1995. "Internal Reasons and the Obscurity of Blame." In his *Making Sense of Humanity*. Cambridge: Cambridge University Press.

Morality as a System of Hypothetical Imperatives

Philippa Foot

There are many difficulties and obscurities in Kant's moral philosophy, and few contemporary moralists will try to defend it all. Many, for instance, agree in rejecting Kant's derivation of duties from the mere form of the law expressed in terms of a universally legislative will. Nevertheless, it is generally supposed, even by those who would not dream of calling themselves his followers, that Kant established one thing beyond doubt – namely, the necessity of distinguishing moral judgements from hypothetical imperatives. That moral judgements cannot be hypothetical imperatives has come to seem an unquestionable truth. It will be argued here that it is not.

In discussing so thoroughly Kantian a notion as that of the hypothetical imperative, one naturally begins by asking what Kant himself meant by a hypothetical imperative, and it may be useful to say a little about the idea of an imperative as this appears in Kant's works. In writing about imperatives Kant seems to be thinking at least as much of statements about what ought to be or should be done, as of injunctions expressed in the imperative mood. He even describes as an imperative the assertion that it would be 'good to do or refrain from doing something'[1] and explains that for a will that 'does not always do something simply because it is presented to it as a good thing to do' this has the force of a command of reason. We may therefore think of Kant's imperatives as statements to the effect that something ought to be done or that it would be good to do it.

The distinction between hypothetical imperatives and categorical imperatives, which plays so important a part in Kant's ethics, appears in characteristic form in the following passages from the *Foundations of the Metaphysics of Morals*:

> All imperatives command either hypothetically or categorically. The former present the practical necessity of a possible action as a means to achieving something else which one desires (or which one may possibly desire). The categorical imperative would be one which presented an action as of itself objectively necessary, without regard to any other end.[2]

> If the action is good only as a means to something else, the imperative is hypothetical; but if it is thought of as good in itself, and hence as necessary in a will which of itself conforms to reason as the principle of this will, the imperative is categorical.[3]

---

[1] *Foundations of the Metaphysics of Morals*, sec. II, trans. L. W. Beck.
[2] Ibid.
[3] Ibid.

The hypothetical imperative, as Kant defines it, 'says only that the action is good to some purpose' and the purpose, he explains, may be possible or actual. Among imperatives related to actual purposes Kant mentions rules of prudence, since he believes that all men necessarily desire their own happiness. Without committing ourselves to this view it will be useful to follow Kant in classing together as 'hypothetical imperatives' those telling a man what he ought to do because (or if) he wants something and those telling him what he ought to do on grounds of self-interest. Common opinion agrees with Kant in insisting that a moral man must accept a rule of duty whatever his interests or desires.[4]

Having given a rough description of the class of Kantian hypothetical imperatives it may be useful to point to the heterogeneity within it. Sometimes what a man should do depends on his passing inclination, as when he wants his coffee hot and should warm the jug. Sometimes it depends on some long-term project, when the feelings and inclinations of the moment are irrelevant. If one wants to be a respectable philosopher one should get up in the mornings and do some work, though just at that moment when one should do it the thought of being a respectable philosopher leaves one cold. It is true nevertheless to say of one, at that moment, that one wants to be a respectable philosopher,[5] and this can be the foundation of a desire-dependent hypothetical imperative. The term 'desire' as used in the original account of the hypothetical imperative was meant as a grammatically convenient substitute for 'want', and was not meant to carry any implication of inclination rather than long-term aim or project. Even the word 'project', taken strictly, introduces undesirable restrictions. If someone is devoted to his family or his country or to any cause, there are certain things he wants, which may then be the basis of hypothetical imperatives, without either inclinations or projects being quite what is in question. Hypothetical imperatives should already be appearing as extremely diverse; a further important distinction is between those that concern an individual and those that concern a group. The desires on which a hypothetical imperative is dependent may be those of one man, or may be taken for granted as belonging to a number of people engaged in some common project or sharing common aims.

Is Kant right to say that moral judgements are categorical, not hypothetical, imperatives? It may seem that he is, for we find in our language two different uses of words such as 'should' and 'ought', apparently corresponding to Kant's hypothetical and categorical imperatives, and we find moral judgements on the 'categorical' side. Suppose, for instance, we have advised a traveller that he should take a certain train, believing him to be journeying to his home. If we find that he has decided to go elsewhere, we will most likely have to take back what we said: the 'should' will now be unsupported and in need of support. Similarly, we must be prepared to withdraw our statement about what he should do if we find that the right relation does not hold between the action and the end – that it is either no way of getting what he wants (or doing what he wants to do) or not the most eligible among possible means. The use of 'should' and 'ought' in moral contexts is, however, quite different. When we say that a man should do something and intend a moral judgement we do not have to back up what we say by considerations about his interests or his desires; if no such connexion can be found the 'should' need not be withdrawn. It follows that the agent cannot rebut an assertion about what, morally speaking, he should do by showing that the action is not ancillary to his interests or desires. Without such a connexion the 'should' does not stand unsupported and in need of support; the support that *it* requires is of another kind.

There is, then, one clear difference between moral judgements and the class of 'hypothetical imperatives' so far discussed. In the latter 'should' is 'used hypothetically', in the sense defined, and if Kant were merely drawing attention to this piece of linguistic usage his point would easily be proved. But obviously Kant meant more than this; in describing moral judgements as non-hypothetical – that is, categorical imperatives – he is ascribing to them a special dignity and necessity which this usage cannot give. Modern philosophers follow

---

[4] According to the position sketched here we have three forms of hypothetical imperative: 'If you want x you should do y', 'Because you want x you should do y', and 'Because x is in your interest you should do y'. For Kant the third would automatically be covered by the second.

[5] To say that at that moment one wants to be a respectable philosopher would be another matter. Such a statement requires a special connexion between the desire and the moment.

Kant in talking, for example, about the 'uncondi-tional requirement' expressed in moral judge-ments. These, they say, tell us what we have to do whatever our interests or desires, and by their inescapability they are distinguished from hypo-thetical imperatives.

The problem is to find proof for this further feature of moral judgements. If anyone fails to see the gap that has to be filled it will be useful to point out to him that we find 'should' used non-hypothetically in some non-moral statements to which no one attributes the special dignity and necessity conveyed by the description 'categorical imperative'. For instance, we find this non-hypothetical use of 'should' in sentences enunciat-ing rules of etiquette, as, for example, that an invitation in the third person should be answered in the third person, where the rule does not *fail to apply* to someone who has his own good reasons for ignoring this piece of nonsense, or who simply does not care about what, from the point of view of eti-quette, he should do. Similarly, there is a non-hypothetical use of 'should' in contexts where something like a club rule is in question. The club secretary who has told a member that he should not bring ladies into the smoking-room does not say, 'Sorry, I was mistaken' when informed that this member is resigning tomorrow and cares nothing about his reputation in the club. Lacking a con-nexion with the agent's desires or interests, this 'should' does not stand 'unsupported and in need of support'; it requires only the backing of the rule. The use of 'should' is therefore 'non-hypothetical' in the sense defined.

It follows that if a hypothetical use of 'should' gave a hypothetical imperative, and a non-hypothetical use of 'should' a categorical im-perative, then 'should' statements based on rules of etiquette, or rules of a club would be categori-cal imperatives. Since this would not be accepted by defenders of the categorical imperative in

ethics, who would insist that these other 'should' statements give hypothetical imperatives, they must be using this expression in some other sense. We must therefore ask what they mean when they say that 'You should answer . . . in the third person' is a hypothetical imperative. Very roughly the idea seems to be that one may reasonably ask why anyone should bother about what should (from the point of view of etiquette) be done, and that such considerations deserve no notice unless reason is shown. So although people give as their reason for doing something the fact that it is required by etiquette, we do not take this consid-eration as *in itself giving us reason to act*. Consider-ations of etiquette do not have any automatic reason-giving force, and a man might be right if he denied that he had reason to do 'what's done'.

This seems to take us to the heart of the matter, for, by contrast, it is supposed that moral consid-erations necessarily give reasons for acting to any man. The difficulty is, of course, to defend this proposition which is more often repeated than explained. Unless it is said, implausibly, that all 'should' or 'ought' statements give reasons for acting, which leaves the old problem of assigning a special categorical status to moral judgement, we must be told what it is that makes the moral 'should' relevantly different from the 'shoulds' appearing in normative statements of other kinds.[6] Attempts have sometimes been made to show that some kind of irrationality is involved in ignoring the 'should' of morality: in saying 'Immoral – so what?' as one says 'Not *comme il faut* – so what?' But as far as I can see these have all rested on some illegitimate assumption, as, for instance, of think-ing that the amoral man, who agrees that some piece of conduct is immoral but takes no notice of that, is inconsistently disregarding a rule of conduct that he has accepted; or again of thinking it inconsistent to desire that others will not do to one what one proposes to do to them. The fact is

---

[6] To say that moral considerations are *called* reasons is blatantly to ignore the problem.

In the case of etiquette or club rules it is obvious that the non-hypothetical use of 'should' has resulted in the loss of the usual connexion between what one should do and what one has reason to do. Someone who objects that in the moral case a man cannot be justified in restricting his practical reasoning in this way, since every moral 'should' gives reasons for acting, must face the following dilemma. Either it is possible to create reasons for acting simply by putting together any silly rules and introducing a non-hypothetical 'should', or else the non-hypothetical 'should' does not necessarily imply reasons for acting. If it does not necessarily imply reasons for acting we may ask why it is supposed to do so in the case of morality. Why cannot the indifferent amoral man say that for him 'should$_m$' gives no reason for acting, treating 'should$_m$' as most of us treat 'should$_e$'? Those who insist that 'should$_m$' is categorical in this second 'reason-giving' sense do not seem to realise that they never prove this to be so. They sometimes say that moral considerations 'just do' give reasons for acting, without explaining why some devotee of etiquette could not say the same about the rules of etiquette.

that the man who rejects morality because he sees no reason to obey its rules can be convicted of villainy but not of inconsistency. Nor will his action necessarily be irrational. Irrational actions are those in which a man in some way defeats his own purposes, doing what is calculated to be disadvantageous or to frustrate his ends. Immorality does not *necessarily* involve any such thing.

It is obvious that the normative character of moral judgement does not guarantee its reason-giving force. Moral judgements are normative, but so are judgements of manners, statements of club rules, and many others. Why should the first provide reasons for acting as the others do not? In every case it is because there is a background of teaching that the non-hypothetical 'should' can be used. The behaviour is required, not simply recommended, but the question remains as to why we should do what we are required to do. It is true that moral rules are often enforced much more strictly than the rules of etiquette, and our reluctance to press the non-hypothetical 'should' of etiquette may be one reason why we think of the rules of etiquette as hypothetical imperatives. But are we then to say that there is nothing behind the idea that moral judgements are categorical imperatives but the relative stringency of our moral teaching? I believe that this may have more to do with the matter than the defenders of the categorical imperative would like to admit. For if we look at the kind of thing that is said in its defence we may find ourselves puzzled about what the words can even mean unless we connect them with the feelings that this stringent teaching implants. People talk, for instance, about the 'binding force' of morality, but it is not clear what this means if not that we *feel* ourselves unable to escape. Indeed the 'inescapability' of moral requirements is often cited when they are being contrasted with hypothetical imperatives. No one, it is said, escapes the requirements of ethics by having or not having particular interests or desires. Taken in one way this only reiterates the contrast between the 'should' of morality and the hypothetical 'should', and once more places morality alongside of etiquette. Both are inescapable in that behaviour does not cease to offend against either morality or etiquette because the agent is indifferent to their purposes and to the disapproval he will incur by flouting them. But morality is supposed to be inescapable in some special way and this may turn out to be merely the reflection of the way morality is taught. Of course, we must try other ways of expressing the fugitive thought. It may be said, for instance, that moral judgements have a kind of necessity since they tell us what we 'must do' or 'have to do' whatever our interests and desires. The sense of this is, again, obscure. Sometimes when we use such expressions we are referring to physical or mental compulsion. (A man has to go along if he is pulled by strong men and he has to give in if tortured beyond endurance.) But it is only in the absence of such conditions that moral judgements apply. Another and more common sense of the words is found in sentences such as 'I caught a bad cold and had to stay in bed' where a penalty for acting otherwise is in the offing. The necessity of acting morally is not, however, supposed to depend on such penalties. Another range of examples, not necessarily having to do with penalties, is found where there is an unquestioned acceptance of some project or rôle, as when a nurse tells us that she has to make her rounds at a certain time, or we say that we have to run for a certain train.[7] But these too are irrelevant in the present context, since the acceptance condition can always be revoked.

No doubt it will be suggested that it is in some other sense of the words 'have to' or 'must' that one has to or must do what morality demands. But why should one insist that there must be such a sense when it proves so difficult to say what it is? Suppose that what we take for a puzzling thought were really no thought at all but only the reflection of our *feelings* about morality? Perhaps it makes no sense to say that we 'have to' submit to the moral law, or that morality is 'inescapable' in some special way. For just as one may feel as if one is falling without believing that one is moving downward, so one may feel as if one has to do what is morally required without believing oneself to be under physical or psychological compulsion, or about to incur a penalty if one does not comply. No one thinks that if the word 'falling' is used in a statement reporting one's sensations it must be used in a special sense. But this kind of mistake may be involved in looking for the special sense in which one 'has to' do what morality demands. There is no difficulty about the idea that we feel we *have* to

---

[7]   I am grateful to Rogers Albritton for drawing my attention to this interesting use of expressions such as 'have to' or 'must'.

behave morally, and given the psychological conditions of the learning of moral behaviour it is natural that we should have such feelings. What we cannot do is quote them in support of the doctrine of the categorical imperative. It seems, then, that in so far as it is backed up by statements to the effect that the moral law *is* inescapable, or that we *do* have to do what is morally required of us, it is uncertain whether the doctrine of the categorical imperative even makes sense.

The conclusion we should draw is that moral judgements have no better claim to be categorical imperatives than do statements about matters of etiquette. People may indeed follow either morality or etiquette without asking why they should do so, but equally well they may not. They may ask for reasons and may reasonably refuse to follow either if reasons are not to be found.

It will be said that this way of viewing moral considerations must be totally destructive of morality, because no one could ever act morally unless he accepted such considerations as in themselves sufficient reason for action. Actions that are truly moral must be done 'for their own sake', 'because they are right', and not for some ulterior purpose. This argument we must examine with care, for the doctrine of the categorical imperative has owed much to its persuasion.

Is there anything to be said for the thesis that a truly moral man acts 'out of respect for the moral law' or that he does what is morally right because it is morally right? That such propositions are not prima facie absurd depends on the fact that moral judgement concerns itself with a man's reasons for acting as well as with what he does. Law and etiquette require only that certain things are done or left undone, but no one is counted as charitable if he gives alms 'for the praise of men', and one who is honest only because it pays him to be honest does not have the virtue of honesty. This kind of consideration was crucial in shaping Kant's moral philosophy. He many times contrasts acting out of respect for the moral law with acting from an ulterior motive, and what is more from one that is self-interested. In the early *Lectures on Ethics* he gave the principle of truth-telling under a system of hypothetical imperatives as that of not lying *if it*

harms *one* to lie. In the *Metaphysics of Morals* he says that ethics cannot start from the ends which a man may propose to himself, since these are all 'selfish'.[8] In the *Critique of Practical Reason* he argues explicitly that when acting not out of respect for moral law but 'on a material maxim' men do what they do for the sake of pleasure or happiness.

> All material practical principles are, as such, of one and the same kind and belong under the general principle of self love or one's own happiness.[9]

Kant, in fact, was a psychological hedonist in respect of all actions except those done for the sake of the moral law, and this faulty theory of human nature was one of the things preventing him from seeing that moral virtue might be compatible with the rejection of the categorical imperative.

If we put this theory of human action aside, and allow as ends the things that seem to be ends, the picture changes. It will surely be allowed that quite apart from thoughts of duty a man may care about the suffering of others, having a sense of identification with them, and wanting to help if he can. Of course he must want not the reputation of charity, nor even a gratifying rôle helping others, but, quite simply, their good. If this is what he does care about, then he will be attached to the end proper to the virtue of charity and a comparison with someone acting from an ulterior motive (even a respectable ulterior motive) is out of place. Nor will the conformity of his action to the rule of charity be merely contingent. Honest action may happen to further a man's career; charitable actions do not *happen* to further the good of others.[10]

Can a man accepting only hypothetical imperatives possess other virtues besides that of charity? Could he be just or honest? This problem is more complex because there is no end related to such virtues as the good of others is related to charity. But what reason could there be for refusing to call a man a just man if he acted justly because he loved truth and liberty, and wanted every man to be treated with a certain respect? And why should the truly honest man not follow honesty for the sake of the good that honest dealing brings to men? Of course, the usual difficulties can be raised about the

---

[8]   Pt. II, Introduction, sec. II.

[9]   Immanuel Kant, *Critique of Practical Reason*, trans. L. W. Beck, p. 133.

[10]   It is not, of course, necessary that charitable actions should *succeed* in helping others; but when they do so they do not *happen* to do so, since that is necessarily their aim. (Footnote added, 1977.)

rare case in which no good is foreseen from an individual act of honesty. But it is not evident that a man's desires could not give him reason to act honestly even here. He wants to live openly and in good faith with his neighbours; it is not all the same to him to lie and conceal.

If one wants to know whether there could be a truly moral man who accepted moral principles as hypothetical rules of conduct, as many people accept rules of etiquette as hypothetical rules of conduct, one must consider the right kind of example. A man who demanded that morality should be brought under the heading of self-interest would not be a good candidate, nor would anyone who was ready to be charitable or honest only so long as he felt inclined. A cause such as justice makes strenuous demands, but this is not peculiar to morality, and men are prepared to toil to achieve many ends not endorsed by morality. That they are prepared to fight so hard for moral ends – for example, for liberty and justice – depends on the fact that these are the kinds of ends that arouse devotion. To sacrifice a great deal for the sake of etiquette one would need to be under the spell of the emphatic 'ought'. One could hardly be devoted to behaving *comme il faut*.

In spite of all that has been urged in favour of the hypothetical imperative in ethics, I am sure that many people will be unconvinced and will argue that one element essential to moral virtue is still missing. This missing feature is the recognition of a *duty* to adopt those ends which we have attributed to the moral man. We have said that he *does* care about others, and about causes such as liberty and justice; that it is on this account that he will accept a system of morality. But what if he never cared about such things, or what if he ceased to care? Is it not the case that he *ought* to care? This is exactly what Kant would say, for though at times he sounds as if he thought that morality is not concerned with ends, at others he insists that the adoption of ends such as the happiness of others is itself dictated by morality.[11] How is this proposition to be regarded by one who rejects all talk about the binding force of the moral law? He will agree that a moral man has moral ends and cannot be indifferent to matters such as suffering and injustice. Further, he will recognise in the statement that one *ought* to care about these things a correct application of the non-hypothetical moral 'ought' by which society is apt to voice its demands. He will not, however, take the fact that he ought to have certain ends as in itself reason to adopt them. If he himself is a moral man then he cares about such things, but not 'because he ought'. If he is an amoral man he may deny that he has any reason to trouble his head over this or any other moral demand. Of course he may be mistaken, and his life as well as others' lives may be most sadly spoiled by his selfishness. But this is not what is urged by those who think they can close the matter by an emphatic use of 'ought'. My argument is that they are relying on an illusion, as if trying to give the moral 'ought' a magic force.[12]

This conclusion may, as I said, appear dangerous and subversive of morality. We are apt to panic at the thought that we ourselves, or other people, might stop caring about the things we do care about, and we feel that the categorical imperative gives us some control over the situation. But it is interesting that the people of Leningrad were not struck by the thought that only the *contingent* fact that other citizens shared their loyalty and devotion to the city stood between them and the Germans during the terrible years of the siege. Perhaps we should be less troubled than we are by fear of defection from the moral cause; perhaps we should even have less reason to fear it if people thought of themselves as volunteers banded together to fight for liberty and justice and against inhumanity and oppression. It is often felt, even if obscurely, that there is an element of deception in the official line about morality. And while some have been persuaded by talk about the authority of the moral law, others have turned away with a sense of distrust.

---

[11] See, e.g., *The Metaphysics of Morals*, pt. II, sec. 30.
[12] See G. E. M. Anscombe, 'Modern Moral Philosophy', *Philosophy* (1958). My view is different from Miss Anscombe's, but I have learned from her.

Internal and External Reasons

Bernard Williams

Sentences of the forms '*A* has a reason to φ' or 'There is a reason for *A* to φ' (where 'φ' stands in for some verb of action) seem on the face of it to have two different sorts of interpretation. On the first, the truth of the sentence implies, very roughly, that *A* has some motive which will be served or furthered by his φ-ing, and if this turns out not to be so the sentence is false: there is a condition relating to the agent's aims, and if this is not satisfied it is not true to say, on this interpretation, that he has a reason to φ. On the second interpretation, there is no such condition, and the reason-sentence will not be falsified by the absence of an appropriate motive. I shall call the first the 'internal', the second the 'external', interpretation. (Given two such interpretations, and the two forms of sentence quoted, it is reasonable to suppose that the first sentence more naturally collects the internal interpretation, and the second the external, but it would be wrong to suggest that either form of words admits only one of the interpretations.)

I shall also for convenience refer sometimes to 'internal reasons' and 'external reasons', as I do in the title, but this is to be taken only as a convenience. It is a matter for investigation whether there are two sorts of reasons for action, as opposed to two sorts of statements about people's reasons for action. Indeed, as we shall eventually see,

even the interpretation in one of the cases is problematical.

I shall consider first the internal interpretation, and how far it can be taken. I shall then consider, more sceptically, what might be involved in an external interpretation. I shall end with some very brief remarks connecting all this with the issue of public goods and free-riders.

The simplest model for the internal interpretation would be this: *A* has a reason to φ iff *A* has some desire the satisfaction of which will be served by his φ-ing. Alternatively, we might say . . . some desire, the satisfaction of which *A* believes will be served by his φ-ing; this difference will concern us later. Such a model is sometimes ascribed to Hume, but since in fact Hume's own views are more complex than this, we might call it *the sub-Humean model*. The sub-Humean model is certainly too simple. My aim will be, by addition and revision, to work it up into something more adequate. In the course of trying to do this, I shall assemble four propositions which seem to me to be true of internal reason statements.

Basically, and by definition, any model for the internal interpretation must display a relativity of the reason statement to the agent's *subjective motivational set*, which I shall call the agent's *S*. the contents of *S* we shall come to, but we can say:

(i)   An internal reason statement is falsified by the absence of some appropriate element from S.

The simplest sub-Humean model claims that any element in S gives rise to an internal reason. But there are grounds for denying this, not because of regrettable, imprudent, or deviant elements in S – they raise different sorts of issues – but because of elements in S based on false belief.

The agent believes that this stuff is gin, when it is in fact petrol. He wants a gin and tonic. Has he reason, or a reason, to mix this stuff with tonic and drink it? There are two ways here (as suggested already by the two alternatives for formulating the sub-Humean model). On the one hand, it is just very odd to say that he has a reason to drink this stuff, and natural to say that he has no reason to drink it, although he thinks that he has. On the other hand, if he does drink it, we not only have an explanation of his doing so (a reason why he did it), but we have such an explanation which is of the reason-for-action form. This explanatory dimension is very important, and we shall come back to it more than once. If there are reasons for action, it must be that people sometimes act for those reasons, and if they do, their reasons must figure in some correct explanation of their action (it does not follow that they must figure in all correct explanations of their action). The difference between false and true beliefs on the agent's part cannot alter the *form* of the explanation which will be appropriate to his action. This consideration might move us to ignore the intuition which we noticed before, and lead us just to legislate that in the case of the agent who wants gin, he has a reason to drink this stuff which is petrol.

I do not think, however, that we should do this. It looks in the wrong direction, by implying in effect that the internal reason conception is only concerned with explanation, and not at all with the agent's rationality, and this may help to motivate a search for other sorts of reason which are connected with his rationality. But the internal reasons conception is concerned with the agent's rationality. What we can correctly ascribe to him in a third-personal internal reason statement is also what he can ascribe to himself as a result of deliberation, as we shall see. So I think that we should rather say:

(ii)   A member of S, D, will not give A a reason for ϕ-ing if either the existence of D is depen-

dent on false belief, or A's belief in the relevance of ϕ-ing to the satisfaction of D is false.

(This double formulation can be illustrated from the gin/petrol case: D can be taken in the first way as the desire to drink what is in this bottle, and in the second way as the desire to drink gin.) It will, all the same, be true that if he does ϕ in these circumstances, there was not only a reason why he ϕ-ed, but also that that displays him as, relative to his false belief, acting rationally.

We can note the epistemic consequence:

(iii)   (a) A may falsely believe an internal reason statement about himself, and (we can add)

(b) A may not know some true internal reason statement about himself.

(b) comes from two different sources. One is that A may be ignorant of some fact such that if he did know it he would, in virtue of some element in S, be disposed to ϕ: we can say that he has a reason to ϕ, though he does not know it. For it to be the case that he actually has such a reason, however, it seems that the relevance of the unknown fact to his actions has to be fairly close and immediate; otherwise one merely says that A would have a reason to ϕ if he knew the fact. I shall not pursue the question of the conditions for saying the one thing or the other, but it must be closely connected with the question of when the ignorance forms part of the explanation of what A actually does.

The second source of (iii) is that A may be ignorant of some element in S. But we should notice that an unknown element in S, D, will provide a reason for A to ϕ only if ϕ-ing is rationally related to D; that is to say, roughly, a project to ϕ could be the answer to a deliberative question formed in part by D. If D is unknown to A because it is in the unconscious, it may well not satisfy this condition, although of course it may provide the reason why he ϕ's, that is, may explain or help to explain his ϕ-ing. In such cases, the ϕ-ing may be related to D only symbolically.

I have already said that

(iv)   internal reason statements can be discovered in deliberative reasoning.

It is worth remarking the point, already implicit, that an internal reason statement does not apply only to that action which is the uniquely preferred result of the deliberation. 'A has reason to ϕ' does not mean 'the action which A has overall, all-in, reason to do is ϕ-ing'. He can have reason to do a lot of things which he has other and stronger reasons not to do.

The sub-Humean model supposes that ϕ-ing has to be related to some element in S as causal means to end (unless, perhaps, it is straightforwardly the carrying out of a desire which is itself that element in S). But this is only one case: indeed, the mere discovery that some course of action is the causal means to an end is not in itself a piece of practical reasoning.[1] A clear example of practical reasoning is that leading to the conclusion that one has reason to ϕ because ϕ-ing would be the most convenient, economical, pleasant etc. way of satisfying some element in S, and this of course is controlled by other elements in S, if not necessarily in a very clear or determinate way. But there are much wider possibilities for deliberation, such as: thinking how the satisfaction of elements in S can be combined, e.g. by time-ordering; where there is some irresoluble conflict among the elements of S, considering which one attaches most weight to (which, importantly, does not imply that there is some one commodity of which they provide varying amounts); or, again, finding constitutive solutions, such as deciding what would make for an entertaining evening, granted that one wants entertainment.

As a result of such processes an agent can come to see that he has reason to do something which he did not see he had reason to do at all. In this way, the deliberative process can add new actions for which there are internal reasons, just as it can also add new internal reasons for given actions. The deliberative process can also subtract elements from S. Reflection may lead the agent to see that some belief is false, and hence to realise that he has in fact no reason to do something he thought he had reason to do. More subtly, he may think he has reason to promote some development because he has not exercised his imagination enough about what it would be like if it came about. In his unaided deliberative reason, or encouraged by the persuasions of others, he may come to have some more concrete sense of what would be involved, and lose his desire for it, just as, positively, the imagination can create new possibilities and new

desires. (These are important possibilities for politics as well as for individual action.)

We should not, then, think of S as statically given. The processes of deliberation can have all sorts of effect on S, and this is a fact which a theory of internal reasons should be very happy to accommodate. So also it should be more liberal than some theorists have been about the possible elements in S. I have discussed S primarily in terms of desires, and this term can be used, formally, for all elements in S. But this terminology may make one forget that S can contain such things as dispositions of evaluation, patterns of emotional reaction, personal loyalties, and various projects, as they may be abstractly called, embodying commitments of the agent. Above all, there is of course no supposition that the desires or projects of an agent have to be egoistic; he will, one hopes, have non-egoistic projects of various kinds, and these equally can provide internal reasons for action.

There is a further question, however, about the contents of S: whether it should be taken, consistently with the general idea of internal reasons, as containing *needs*. It is certainly quite natural to say that A has a reason to pursue X, just on the ground that he needs X, but will this naturally follow in a theory of internal reasons? There is a special problem about this only if it is possible for the agent to be unmotivated to pursue what he needs. I shall not try to discuss here the nature of needs, but I take it that insofar as there are determinately recognisable needs, there can be an agent who lacks any interest in getting what he indeed needs. I take it, further, that that lack of interest can remain after deliberation, and, also that it would be wrong to say that such a lack of interest must always rest on false belief. (Insofar as it does rest on false belief, then we can accommodate it under (ii), in the way already discussed.)

If an agent really is uninterested in pursuing what he needs; and this is not the product of false belief; and he could not reach any such motive from motives he has by the kind of deliberative processes we have discussed; then I think we do have to say that in the internal sense he indeed has no reason to pursue these things. In saying this, however, we have to bear in mind how strong these assumptions are, and how seldom we are likely to think that we

[1] A point made by Aurel Kolnai: see his 'Deliberation is of Ends', in *Ethics, Value and Reality* (London and Indianapolis, 1978). See also David Wiggins, 'Deliberation and Practical Reason', *Proceedings of the Aristotelian Society*, LXXVI (1975–6); reprinted in part in *Practical Reasoning*, ed. J. Raz (Oxford, 1978).

know them to be true. When we say that a person has reason to take medicine which he needs, although he consistently and persuasively denies any interest in preserving his health, we may well still be speaking in the internal sense, with the thought that really at some level he *must* want to be well.

However, if we become clear that we have no such thought, and persist in saying that the person has this reason, then we must be speaking in another sense, and this is the external sense. People do say things that ask to be taken in the external interpretation. In James' story of Owen Wingrave, from which Britten made an opera, Owen's father urges on him the necessity and importance of his joining the army, since all his male ancestors were soldiers, and family pride requires him to do the same. Owen Wingrave has no motivation to join the army at all, and all his desires lead in another direction: he hates everything about military life and what it means. His father might have expressed himself by saying that *there was a reason for Owen to join the army*. Knowing that there was nothing in Owen's *S* which would lead, through deliberative reasoning, to his doing this would not make him withdraw the claim or admit that he made it under a misapprehension. He means it in an external sense. What is that sense?

A preliminary point is that this is not the same question as that of the status of a supposed categorical imperative, in the Kantian sense of an 'ought' which applies to an agent independently of what the agent happens to want: or rather, it is not undoubtedly the same question. First, a categorical imperative has often been taken, as by Kant, to be necessarily an imperative of morality, but external reason statements do not necessarily relate to morality. Second, it remains an obscure issue what the relation is between 'there is a reason for *A* to . . .' and '*A* ought to . . .' Some philosophers take them to be equivalent, and under that view the question of external reasons of course comes much closer to the question of a categorical imperative. However, I shall not make any assumption about such an equivalence, and shall not further discuss 'ought'.

In considering what an external reason statement might mean, we have to remember again the dimension of possible explanation, a consideration which applies to any reason for action. If something can be a reason for action, then it could be someone's reason for acting on a particular occa-

sion, and it would then figure in an explanation of that action. Now no external reason statement could *by itself* offer an explanation of anyone's action. Even if it were true (whatever that might turn out to mean) that there was a reason for Owen to join the army, that fact by itself would never explain anything that Owen did, not even his joining the army. For if it was true at all, it was true when Owen was not motivated to join the army. The whole point of external reason statements is that they can be true independently of the agent's motivations. But nothing can explain an agent's (intentional) actions except something that motivates him so to act. So something else is needed besides the truth of the external reason statement to explain action, some psychological link; and that psychological link would seem to be belief. *A*'s believing an external reason statement about himself may help to explain his action.

External reason statements have been introduced merely in the general form 'there is a reason for *A* to . . .', but we now need to go beyond that form, to specific statements of reasons. No doubt there are some cases of an agent's φ-ing because he believes that there is a reason for him to φ, while he does not have any belief about what that reason is. They would be cases of his relying on some authority whom he trusts, or, again, of his recalling that he did know of some reason for his φ-ing, but his not being able to remember what it was. In these respects, reasons for action are like reasons for belief. But, as with reasons for belief, they are evidently secondary cases. The basic case must be that in which *A* φ's, not because he believes only that there is some reason or other for him to φ, but because he believes of some determinate consideration that it constitutes a reason for him to φ. Thus Owen Wingrave might come to join the army because (now) he believes that it is a reason for him to do so that his family has a tradition of military honour.

Does believing that a particular consideration is a reason to act in a particular way provide, or indeed constitute, a motivation to act? If it does not, then we are no further on. Let us grant that it does – this claim indeed seems plausible, so long at least as the connexion between such beliefs and the disposition to act is not tightened to that unnecessary degree which excludes *akrasia*. The claim is in fact *so* plausible, that this agent, with this belief, appears to be one about whom, now, an *internal* reason statement could truly be made: he is one with an appropriate motivation in his *S*. A man who does believe that considerations of family honour constitute reasons for action is a man with a certain disposition to action, and also dispositions of approval, sentiment, emotional reaction, and so forth.

Now it does not follow from this that there is nothing in external reason statements. What does follow is that their content is not going to be revealed by considering merely the state of one who believes such a statement, nor how that state explains action, for that state is merely the state with regard to which an internal reason statement could truly be made. Rather, the content of the external type of statement will have to be revealed by considering what it is to *come to believe* such a statement – it is there, if at all, that their peculiarity will have to emerge.

We will take the case (we have implicitly been doing so already) in which an external reason statement is made about someone who, like Owen Wingrave, is not already motivated in the required way, and so is someone about whom an internal statement could not also be truly made. (Since the difference between external and internal statements turns on the implications accepted by the speaker, external statements can of course be made about agents who are already motivated; but that is not the interesting case.) The agent does not presently believe the external statement. If he comes to believe it, he will be motivated to act; so coming to believe it must, essentially, involve acquiring a new motivation. How can that be?

This is closely related to an old question, of how 'reason can give rise to a motivation', a question which has famously received from Hume a negative answer. But in that form, the question is itself unclear, and is unclearly related to the argument – for of course reason, that is to say, rational processes, can give rise to new motivations, as we have seen in the account of deliberation. Moreover, the traditional way of putting the issue also (I shall suggest) picks up an onus of proof about what is to count as a 'purely rational process' which not only should it not pick up, but which properly belongs with the critic who wants to oppose Hume's general conclusion and to make a lot out of external reason statements – someone I shall call 'the external reasons theorist'.

The basic point lies in recognising that the external reasons theorist must conceive *in a special way* the connexion between acquiring a motivation and coming to believe the reason statement. For of course there are various means by which the agent could come to have the motivation and also to believe the reason statement, but which are the wrong kind of means to interest the external reasons theorist. Owen might be so persuaded by his father's moving rhetoric that he acquired both the motivation and the belief. But this excludes an element which the external reasons theorist essentially wants, that the agent should acquire the motivation *because* he comes to believe the reason statement, and that he should do the latter, moreover, because, in some way, he is considering the matter aright. If the theorist is to hold on to these conditions, he will, I think, have to make the condition under which the agent appropriately comes to have the motivation something like this, that he should deliberate correctly; and the external reasons statement itself will have to be taken as roughly equivalent to, or at least as entailing, the claim that if the agent rationally deliberated, then, whatever motivations he originally had, he would come to be motivated to φ.

But if this is correct, there does indeed seem great force in Hume's basic point, and it is very plausible to suppose that all external reason statements are false. For, *ex hypothesi*, there is no motivation for the agent to deliberate *from*, to reach this new motivation. Given the agent's earlier existing motivations, and this new motivation, what has to hold for external reason statements to be true, on this line of interpretation, is that the new motivation could be in some way rationally arrived at, granted the earlier motivations. Yet at the same time it must not bear to the earlier motivations the kind of rational relation which we considered in the earlier discussion of deliberation – for in that case an internal reason statement would have been true in the first place. I see no reason to suppose that these conditions could possibly be met.

It might be said that the force of an external reason statement can be explained in the following way. Such a statement implies that a rational agent would be motivated to act appropriately, and it can carry this implication, because a rational agent is precisely one who has a general disposition in his *S* to do what (he believes) there is reason for him to do. So when he comes to believe that there is reason for him to φ, he is motivated to φ, even though, before, he neither had a motive to φ, nor any motive related to φ-ing in one of the ways considered in the account of deliberation.

But this reply merely puts off the problem. It reapplies the desire and belief model (roughly speaking) of explanation to the actions in question, but using a desire and a belief the content of which are in question. *What* is it that one comes to believe when he comes to believe that there is reason for him to φ, if it is not the proposition, or something that entails the proposition, that if he deliberated rationally, he would be motivated to act appropriately? We were asking how any true proposition could have that content; it cannot help, in answering that, to appeal to a supposed desire which is activated by a belief which has that very content.

These arguments about what it is to accept an external reason statement involve some idea of what is possible under the account of deliberation already given, and what is excluded by that account. But here it may be objected that the account of deliberation is very vague, and has for instance allowed the use of the imagination to extend or restrict the contents of the agent's *S*. But if that is so, then it is unclear what the limits are to what an agent might arrive at by rational deliberation from his existing *S*.

It *is* unclear, and I regard it as a basically desirable feature of a theory of practical reasoning that it should preserve and account for that unclarity. There is an essential indeterminacy in what can be counted a rational deliberative process. Practical reasoning is a heuristic process, and an imaginative one, and there are no fixed boundaries on the continuum from rational thought to inspiration and conversion. To someone who thinks that reasons for action are basically to be understood in terms of the internal reasons model, this is not a difficulty. There is indeed a vagueness about '*A* has reason to φ', in the internal sense, insofar as the deliberative processes which could lead from *A*'s present *S* to his being motivated to φ may be more or less ambitiously conceived. But this is no embarrassment to those who take as basic the internal conception of reasons for action. It merely shows that there is a wider range of states, and a less determinate one, than one might have supposed, which can be counted as *A*'s having a reason to φ.

It is the external reasons theorist who faces a problem at this point. There are of course many things that a speaker may say to one who is not disposed to φ when the speaker thinks that he should be, as that he is inconsiderate, or cruel, or selfish,

or imprudent; or that things, and he, would be a lot nicer if he were so motivated. Any of these can be sensible things to say. But one who makes a great deal out of putting the criticism in the form of an external reason statement seems concerned to say that what is particularly wrong with the agent is that he is *irrational*. It is this theorist who particularly needs to make this charge precise: in particular, because he wants any rational agent, as such, to acknowledge the requirement to do the thing in question.

Owen Wingrave's father indeed expressed himself in terms other than 'a reason', but, as we imagined, he could have used the external reasons formulation. This fact itself provides some difficulty for the external reasons theorist. This theorist, who sees the truth of an external reason statement as potentially grounding a charge of irrationality against the agent who ignores it, might well want to say that if Wingrave *père* put his complaints against Owen in this form, he would very probably be claiming something which, in this particular case, was false. What the theorist would have a harder time showing would be that the words *meant* something different as used by Wingrave from what they mean when they are, as he supposes, truly uttered. But what they mean when uttered by Wingrave is almost certainly *not* that rational deliberation would get Owen to be motivated to join the army – which is (very roughly) the meaning or implication we have found for them, if they are to bear the kind of weight such theorists wish to give them.

The sort of considerations offered here strongly suggest to me that external reason statements, when definitely isolated as such, are false, or incoherent, or really something else misleadingly expressed. It is in fact harder to isolate them in people's speech than the introduction of them at the beginning of this chapter suggested. Those who use these words often seem, rather, to be entertaining an optimistic internal reason claim, but sometimes the statement is indeed offered as standing definitely outside the agent's *S* and what he might derive from it in rational deliberation, and then there is, I suggest, a great unclarity about what is meant. Sometimes it is little more than that things would be better if the agent so acted. But the formulation in terms of reasons does have an effect, particularly in its suggestion that the agent is being irrational, and this suggestion, once the basis of an internal reason claim has been clearly laid aside, is bluff. If this is so, the only real claims about reasons for action will be internal claims.

A problem which has been thought to lie very close to the present subject is that of public goods and free riders, which concerns the situation (very roughly) in which each person has egoistic reason to want a certain good provided, but at the same time each has egoistic reason not to take part in providing it. I shall not attempt any discussion of this problem, but it may be helpful, simply in order to make clear my own view of reasons for action and to bring out contrasts with some other views, if I end by setting out a list of questions which bear on the problem, together with the answers that would be given to them by one who thinks (to put it cursorily) that the only rationality of action is the rationality of internal reasons.

1   Can we define notions of rationality which are not purely egoistic?
    Yes.
2   Can we define notions of rationality which are not purely means–end?
    Yes.
3   Can we define a notion of rationality where the action rational for A is in no way relative to A's existing motivations?
    No.
4   Can we show that a person who only has egoistic motivations is irrational in not pursuing non-egoistic ends?
    Not necessarily, though we may be able to in special cases. (The trouble with the egoistic person is not characteristically irrationality.)

Let there be some good, G, and a set of persons, P, such that each member of P has egoistic reason to want G provided, but delivering G requires action C, which involves costs, by each of some proper sub-set of P; and let A be a member of P: then

5   Has A egoistic reason to do C if he is reasonably sure either that too few members of P will do C for G to be provided, or that enough other members of P will do C, so that G will be provided?
    No.
6   Are there any circumstances of this kind in which A can have egoistic reason to do C?
    Yes, in those cases in which reaching the critical number of those doing C is sensitive to his doing C, or he has reason to think this.
7   Are there any motivations which would make it rational for A to do C, even though not in the situation just referred to?
    Yes, if he is not purely egoistic: many. For instance, there are expressive motivations – appropriate e.g. in the celebrated voting case.[2] There are also motivations which derive from the sense of fairness. This can precisely transcend the dilemma of 'either useless or unnecessary', by the form of argument 'somebody, but no reason to omit any particular body, so everybody'.
8   It is irrational for an agent to have such motivations?
    In any sense in which the question is intelligible, no.
9   Is it rational for society to bring people up with these sorts of motivations?
    Insofar as the question is intelligible, yes. And certainly we have reason to encourage people to have these dispositions – e.g. in virtue of possessing them ourselves.

I confess that I cannot see any other major questions which, at this level of generality, bear on these issues. All these questions have clear answers which are entirely compatible with a conception of practical rationality in terms of internal reasons for action, and are also, it seems to me, entirely reasonable answers.

---

[2]   A well-known treatment is by M. Olson Jr., *The Logic of Collective Action* (Cambridge, Mass., 1965). On expressive motivations in this connexion, see S. I. Benn, 'Rationality and Political Behaviour', in S. I. Benn and G. W. Mortimore, eds., *Rationality and the Social Sciences* (London, 1976).

23

Skepticism about Practical Reason

Christine Korsgaard

The Kantian approach to moral philosophy is to try to show that ethics is based on practical reason: that is, that our ethical judgments can be explained in terms of rational standards that apply directly to conduct or to deliberation. Part of the appeal of this approach lies in the way that it avoids certain sources of skepticism that some other approaches meet with inevitably. If ethically good action is simply rational action, we do not need to postulate special ethical properties in the world or faculties in the mind, in order to provide ethics with a foundation. But the Kantian approach gives rise to its own specific form of skepticism, skepticism about practical reason.

By *skepticism about practical reason*, I mean doubts about the extent to which human action is or could possibly be directed by reason. One form that such skepticism takes is doubt about the bearing of rational considerations on the activities of deliberation and choice; doubts, that is to say, about whether "formal" principles have any content and can give substantive guidance to choice and action. An example of this would be the common doubt about whether the contradiction tests associated with the first formulation of the categorical imperative succeed in ruling out any-

thing. I will refer to this as *content skepticism*. A second form taken by skepticism about practical reason is doubt about the scope of reason as a motive. I will call this *motivational skepticism*. In this paper my main concern is with motivational skepticism and with the question whether it is justified. Some people think that motivational considerations alone provide grounds for skepticism about the project of founding ethics on practical reason. I will argue, against this view, that motivational skepticism must always be based on content skepticism. I will not address the question of whether or not content skepticism is justified. I want only to establish the fact that motivational skepticism has no independent force.

I

Skepticism about practical reason gets its classical formulation in the well-known passages in the *Treatise of Human Nature* that lead Hume to the conclusion that

> Reason is, and ought only to be the slave of the passions, and can never pretend to any other office than to serve and obey them.[1]

---

[1] David Hume, *Treatise of Human Nature*, ed. L. A. Selby-Bigge (London: Oxford, 1888), p. 415. Page references to the *Treatise* will be to this edition.

According to these passages, as they are usually understood, the role of reason in action is limited to the discernment of the means to our ends. Reason can teach us how to satisfy our desires or passions, but it cannot tell us whether those desires or passions are themselves "rational"; that is, there is no sense in which desires or passions are rational or irrational. Our ends are picked out, so to speak, by our desires, and these ultimately determine what we do. Normative standards applying to conduct may come from other sources (such as a moral sense), but the only standard that comes from reason is that of effectiveness in the choice of means.

The limitation of practical reason to an instrumental role does not only prevent reason from determining ends; it even prevents reason from ranking them, except with respect to their conduciveness to some other end. Even the view that those choices and actions which are conducive to our over-all self-interest are rationally to be preferred to self-destructive ones is undermined by the instrumental limitation. Self-interest itself has no rational *authority* over even the most whimsical desires. As Hume says:

> 'Tis not contrary to reason to prefer the destruction of the whole world to the scratching of my finger. 'Tis not contrary to reason for me to chuse my total ruin, to prevent the least uneasiness of an *Indian* or person wholly unknown to me. 'Tis as little contrary to reason to prefer even my own acknowledg'd lesser good to my greater, and have a more ardent affection for the former than the latter. (*Treatise* 416)

Under the influence of self-interest [or of "a general appetite to good, and aversion to evil, consider'd merely as such" (417)] we may rank our ends, according to the amount of good that each represents for us, and determine which are, as Hume puts it, our "greatest and most valuable enjoyments" (416). But the self-interest that would make us favor the greater good need not itself be a stronger desire, or a stronger reason, than the desire for the lesser good, or than any of our more particular desires. Reason by itself neither selects nor ranks our ends.

Hume poses his argument as an argument against "the greatest part of moral philosophy, ancient and modern" (413). Moral philosophers, Hume says, have claimed that we ought to regulate our conduct by reason, and either suppress our passions or bring them into conformity with it; but

he is going to show the fallacy of all this by showing, first, that reason alone can never provide a motive to any action, and, second, that reason can never oppose passion in the direction of the will. His argument for the first point goes this way: all reasoning is concerned either with abstract relations of ideas or with relations of objects, especially causal relations, which we learn about from experience. Abstract relations of ideas are the subject of logic and mathematics, and no one supposes that those by themselves give rise to any motives. They yield no conclusions about action. We are sometimes moved by the perception of causal relations, but only when there is a pre-existing motive in the case. As Hume puts it, if there is "the prospect of pleasure or pain from some object," we are concerned with its causes and effects. The argument that reason cannot oppose a passion in the direction of the will depends on, and in fact springs directly from, the argument that reason by itself cannot give rise to a motive. It is simply that reason *could* oppose a passion only if it could give rise to an *opposing motive*.

What is important to notice in this discussion is the relation between Hume's views about the possible content of principles of reason bearing on action and the scope of its motivational efficacy. The answer to the question what sorts of operation, procedure, or judgment of reason exist is presupposed in these passages. In the first part of the argument Hume goes through what by this point in the *Treatise* is a *settled* list of the types of rational judgment. The argument is a sort of process of elimination: there are rational judgments concerning logical and mathematical relations; there are empirical connections such as cause and effect: Hume looks at each of these in turn in order to see under what circumstances it might be thought to have a bearing on decision and action. In other words, Hume's arguments against a more extensive practical employment of reason depend upon Hume's own views about what reason is – that is, about what sorts of operation and judgment are "rational." His motivational skepticism (skepticism about the scope of reason as a motive) is entirely dependent upon his content skepticism (skepticism about what reason has to *say* about choice and action).

Yet Hume's arguments may give the impression of doing something much stronger: of placing independent constraints, based solely on motivational considerations, on what might count as a principle of practical reason. Hume seems to say simply that all reasoning that has a motivational influence must start from a passion, that being the only possible source of motivation, and must proceed to the means to satisfy that passion, that being the only operation of reason that transmits motivational force. Yet these are separate points: they can be doubted, and challenged, separately. One could disagree with Hume about his list of the types of rational judgment, operation, or possible deliberation, and yet still agree with the basic point about the source of motivation: that all rational motivation must ultimately spring from some nonrational source, such as passion. At least one contemporary philosopher, Bernard Williams, has taken something like Hume's argument to have this kind of independent force, and has so argued in his essay "Internal and External Reason,"[2] which I will take up later in this paper.

The Kantian must go further, and disagree with Hume on both counts, since the Kantian supposes that there are operations of practical reason which yield conclusions about actions and which do not involve discerning relations between passions (or any pre-existing sources of motivation) and those actions. What gives rise to the difficulty about this further possibility is the question of how such operations could yield conclusions that can motivate us.

II

The problem can best be stated in some terms provided by certain recent discussions in moral philosophy. W. D. Falk, William Frankena, and Thomas Nagel, among others, have distinguished between two kinds of moral theories, which are called "internalist" and "externalist."[3] An *internalist* theory is a theory according to which the knowledge (or the truth or the acceptance) of a moral judgment implies the existence of a motive (not

necessarily overriding) for acting on that judgment. If I judge that some action is right, it is implied that I have, and acknowledge, some motive or reason for performing that action. It is part of the sense of the judgment that a motive is present: if someone agrees that an action is right, but cannot see any motive or reason for doing it, we must suppose, according to these views, that she does not quite know what she means when she agrees that the action is right. On an *externalist* theory, by contrast, such a conjunction of moral comprehension and total unmotivatedness is perfectly possible: knowledge is one thing and motivation another.

Examples of unquestionably external theories are not easy to find. As Falk points out (125–6), the simplest example would be a view according to which the motives for moral action come from something wholly separate from a grasp of the correctness of the judgments – say, an interest in obeying divine commands. In philosophical ethics the best example is John Stuart Mill (see Nagel 8–9), who firmly separates the question of the proof of the principle of utility from the question of its "sanctions". The reason why the principle of utility is true and the motive we might have for acting on it are not the same: the theoretical proof of its truth is contained in chapter IV of *Utilitarianism*, but the motives must be acquired in a utilitarian upbringing. It is Mill's view that *any* moral principle would have to be motivated by education and training and that "there is hardly anything so absurd or so mischievous" that it cannot be so motivated.[4] The "ultimate sanction" of the principle of utility is *not* that it can be proved, but that it is in accordance with our natural social feelings. Even to some who, like Mill himself, realize that the motives are acquired, "It does not present itself . . . as a superstition of education, or a law despotically imposed by the power of society, but as an attribute which it would not be well for them to be without" (Mill 36). The modern intuitionists, such as W. D. Ross and H. A. Prichard, seem also to have

---

2   This paper was originally published in Ross Harrison, ed., *Rational Action* (New York: Cambridge, 1980), and is reprinted in Williams, *Moral Luck* (New York: Cambridge, 1981), pp. 101–13. Page references to Williams are to this article, as it appears in *Moral Luck*. [Williams's essay is reprinted as chapter 23 of this volume.]

3   Actually, Falk and Frankena speak of internalist and externalist senses of 'ought'. See Falk, "'Ought' and Motivation," *Proceedings of the Aristotelian Society*, 1947/1948. Frankena's discussion, "Obligation and Motivation in Recent Moral Philosophy," was originally published in A. I. Melden, ed., *Essays in Moral Philosophy* (Seattle: University of Washington Press, 1958) and is reprinted in *Perspectives on Morality: Essays of William K. Frankena*, ed. Kenneth E. Goodpaster (Notre Dame, Ind.: University Press, 1976), pp. 49–73 (page references are to this volume). Nagel's discussion is in *The Possibility of Altruism* (New York: Oxford, 1970), part I.

4   *Utilitarianism*, in Samuel Gorovitz, ed., *Utilitarianism with Critical Essays* (Indianapolis: Bobbs-Merrill, 1971), p. 34.

been externalists, but of a rather minimal kind. They believed that there was a distinctively moral motive, a sense of right or desire to do one's duty. This motive is triggered by the news that something is your duty, and only by that news, but it is still separate from the rational intuition that constitutes the understanding of your duty. It would be possible to have that intuition and not be motivated by it.[5] The reason why the act is right and the motive you have for doing it are separate items, although it is nevertheless the case that the motive for doing it is "because it is right." This falls just short of the internalist position, which is that the reason why the act is right is the reason, and the motive, for doing it: it is a practical reason. Intuitionism is a form of rationalist ethics, but intuitionists do not believe in practical reason, properly speaking. They believe there is a branch of theoretical reason that is specifically concerned with morals, by which human beings can be motivated because of a special psychological mechanism: a desire to do one's duty. One can see the oddity of this if one considers what the analogue would be in the case of theoretical reasoning. It is as if human beings could not be convinced by arguments acknowledged to be sound without the intervention of a special psychological mechanism: a belief that the conclusions of sound arguments are true.

By contrast, an internalist believes that the reasons why an action is right and the reasons why you do it are the same. The reason that the action is right is both the reason and the motive for doing it. Nagel gives as one example of this the theory of Hobbes: the reason for the action's rightness and your motive for doing it are both that it is in your interest. The literature on this subject splits, however, on the question of whether the Kantian position is internalist or not. Falk, for instance, characterizes the difference between internalism and externalism as one of whether the moral command arises from a source outside the agent (like God or society) or from within. If the difference is described this way, Kant's attempt to derive morality from autonomy makes him a paradigmatic internalist (see Falk 125, 129). On the other hand, some have believed that Kant's view that the moral

command is indifferent to our desires, needs, and interests – that it is categorical – makes him a paradigmatic externalist.[6] Since Kant himself took the categorical character of the imperative and autonomy of the moral motive to be necessarily connected, this is a surprising difference of opinion. I will come back to Kant in section VII.

This kind of reflection about the motivational force of ethical judgments has been brought to bear by Bernard Williams on the motivational force of reason claims generally. In "Internal and External Reasons" Williams argues that there are two kinds of reason claims, or two ways of making reason claims. Suppose I say that some person P has a reason to do action A. If I intend this to imply that the person P has a motive to do the action A, the claim is of an internal reason; if not, the claim is of an external reason. Williams is concerned to argue that only internal reasons really exist. He points out (106–7) that, since an external-reason claim does not imply the existence of a motive, it cannot be used to explain anyone's action: that is, we cannot say that the person P did the action A because of reason R; for R does not provide P with a motive for doing A, and *that* is what we need to explain P's doing A: a motive. Nagel points out that if acknowledgment of a reason claim did not include acknowledgment of a motive, someone presented with a reason for action could ask: Why do what I have a reason to do? (9; see also Falk 121–2). Nagel's argument makes from the agent's perspective the same point that Williams makes from the explainer's perspective, namely, that unless reasons are motives, they cannot prompt or explain actions. And, unless reasons are motives, we cannot be said to be practically rational.

Thus, it seems to be a requirement on practical reasons, that they be capable of motivating us. This is where the difficulty arises about reasons that do not, like means/end reasons, draw on an obvious motivational source. So long as there is doubt about whether a given consideration is able to motivate a rational person, there is doubt about whether that consideration has the force of a practical *reason*. The consideration that such and such action is a means to getting what you want has a clear motivational source; so no one doubts that this is a

---

[5] See Prichard, "Duty and Interest," in *Duty and Interest* (London: Oxford, 1928). Falk's original use of the distinction between internal and external senses of ought in "'Ought' and Motivation" is in an argument responding to Prichard's paper.

[6] See Frankena, *op. cit.*, p. 63, for a discussion of this surprising view.

reason. Practical-reason claims, if they are really to present us with reasons for action. must be capable of motivating rational persons. I will call this the *internalism requirement*.

III

In this section I want to talk about how the internalism requirement functions – or, more precisely, malfunctions – in skeptical arguments. Hume winds up his argument by putting the whole thing in a quite general form. Reason is the faculty that judges of truth and falsehood, and it can judge our ideas to be true or false because they represent other things. But a passion is an original existence or modification of existence, not a copy of anything: it cannot be true or false, and therefore it cannot in itself be reasonable or unreasonable. Passions can be unreasonable, then, only if they are accompanied by judgments, and there are two cases of this kind. One is when the passion is founded on the supposition of the existence of objects that do not exist. You are outraged at the mocking things you heard me say about you, but I was talking about somebody else. You are terrified by the burglars you hear whispering in the living room, but in fact you left the radio on. It is of course only in an extended sense that Hume can think of these as cases where a passion is irrational. Judgments of irrationality, whether of belief or action, are, strictly speaking, relative to the subject's beliefs. Conclusions drawn from mistaken premises are not *irrational*.[7] The case of passions based on false beliefs seems to be of this sort.

The second kind of case in which Hume says that the passion might be called unreasonable is

> . . . when, in exerting any passion in action, we chuse means insufficient for the design'd end, and deceive ourselves in our judgment of causes and effects. (*Treatise* 416)

This is in itself an ambiguous remark. Hume might, and in fact does, mean simply that we base our action on a false belief about causal relations. So this is no more genuinely a case of irrationality than the other. Relative to the (false) causal belief, the action is not irrational. But it is important that there is something else one might mean in this case, which is that, knowing the truth about the relevant causal relations in the case, we might nevertheless choose means insufficient to our end or fail to choose obviously sufficient and readily available means to the end. This would be what I will call *true irrationality*, by which I mean a failure to respond appropriately to an available reason.

If the only possibility Hume means to be putting forward here is the possibility of action based on false belief about causes and effects, we get a curious result. Neither of the cases that Hume considers is a case of true irrationality: relative to their beliefs, people *never* act irrationally. Hume indeed says this:

> . . . the moment we perceive the falsehood of any supposition, or the insufficiency of any means, our passions yield to our reason without any opposition. (*Treatise* 416)

But it looks as if a theory of means/end rationality ought to allow for at least one form of true irrationality, namely, failure to be motivated by the consideration that the action is the means to your end. Even the skeptic about practical reason admits that human beings can be motivated by the consideration that a given action is a means to a desired end. But it is not enough, to explain this fact, that human beings can engage in causal reasoning. It is perfectly possible to imagine a sort of being who could engage in causal reasoning and who could, therefore, engage in reasoning that would point out the means to her ends, but who was not motivated by it.

Kant, in a passage early in the *Foundations*, imagines a human being in just such a condition of being able to reason, so to speak, theoretically but not practically. He is talking about what the world would have been like if nature had had our happiness as her end. Our actions would have been con-

---

[7]   I am ignoring here the more complicated case in which the passion in question is parent to the false beliefs. In my examples, for instance, there might be cases such as these: irritation at me predisposes you to think my insults are aimed at you; terror of being alone in the house makes you more likely to mistake the radio for a burglar. Hume does discuss this phenomenon (*Treatise* 120). Here, we might say that the judgment is irrational, not merely false, and that its irrationally infects the passions and actions based on the judgment. If Hume's theory allows him to say that the judgment is irrational, he will be able to say that some passions and actions are truly irrational, and not merely mistaken, although he does not do this.

trolled entirely by instincts designed to secure our happiness, and:

> ... if, over and above this, reason should have been granted to the favored creature, it would have served only to let it contemplate the happy constitution of its nature.[8]

The favored creature is portrayed as able to see that his actions are rational in the sense that they promote the means to his end (happiness); but he is not motivated by their reasonableness; he acts from instinct. Reason allows him to admire the rational appropriateness of what he does, but this is not what gets him to do it – he has the sort of attitude toward all his behavior that we in fact might have toward the involuntary well-functioning of our bodies.

Being motivated by the consideration that an action is a means to a desirable end is something beyond merely reflecting on that fact. The motive force attached to the end must be transmitted to the means in order for this to be a consideration that sets the human body in motion – and only if this is a consideration that sets the human body in motion can we say that reason has an influence on action. A practically rational person is not merely capable of performing certain rational mental operations, but capable also of transmitting motive force, so to speak, along the paths laid out by those operations. Otherwise even means/end reasoning will not meet the internalism requirement.

But the internalism requirement does not imply that nothing can interfere with this motivational transmission. And generally, this is something there seems to be no reason to believe: there seem to be plenty of things that could interfere with the motivational influence of a given rational consideration. Rage, passion, depression, distraction, grief, physical or mental illness: all these things could cause us to act irrationally, that is, to fail to be motivationally responsive to the rational considerations available to us.[9] The necessity, or the compellingness, of rational considerations lies in those considerations themselves, not in us: that is, we will not necessarily be motivated by them. Or rather, to put the point more properly and not to foreclose any metaphysical possibilities, their necessity may lie in the fact that, when they do move us – either in the realm of conviction or in that of motivation – they move us with the force of necessity. But it will still not be the case that they necessarily move us. So a person may be irrational, not merely by failing to observe rational connections – say, failing to see that the sufficient means are at hand – but also by being "willfully" blind to them, or even by being indifferent to them when they are pointed out.[10]

---

[8] Immanuel Kant, *Foundations of the Metaphysics of Morals*, Lewis White Beck, trans. (New York: Library of Liberal Arts, 1959), p. 11. Prussian Academy Edition, p.395.

[9] "Available to us" is vague, for there is a range of cases in which one might be uncertain whether or not to say that a reason was available to us. For instance there are (1) cases in which we don't know about the reason, (2) cases in which we couldn't possibly know about the reason, (3) cases in which we deceive ourselves about the reason, (4) cases in which some physical or psychological condition makes us unable to see the reason; and (5) cases in which some physical or psychological condition makes us fail to respond to the reason, even though in some sense we look it right in the eye. Now no one will want to say that reason claims involving reasons people do not know about are therefore external, but as we move down the list there will be a progressive uneasiness about whether the claim is becoming external. For toward the end of the list we will come to claim that someone is psychologically incapable of responding to the reason, and yet that it is internal: capable of motivating a rational person. I do not think there is a problem about any of these cases; for all that is necessary for the reason claim to be internal is that we can say that, if a person did know and *if nothing were interfering with her rationality*, she would respond accordingly. This does not trivialize the limitation to internal reasons as long as the notion of a psychological condition that interferes with rationality is not trivially defined.

[10] I have in mind such phenomena as self-deception, rationalization, and the various forms of weakness of will. Some of these apply to theoretical as well as practical reason, and for the former we can add the various forms of intellectual resistance or ideology (though "willful" is not a good way to characterize these). For some reason, people find the second thing that I mention – being indifferent to a reason that is pointed out to you – harder to imagine in a theoretical than in a practical case. To simply shrug in the face of the acknowledged reason seems to some to be possible in practice in a way that it is not in theory. I think part of the problem is that we can push what the practically paralyzed person accepts over into the realm of theory: he *believes* "that he ought to do such-and-such," although he is not moved to; whereas there seems to be nowhere further back (except maybe to a suspense of judgment) to push what the theoretically paralyzed person accepts. It may also be that the problem arises because we do not give enough weight to the difference between being convinced by an argument and being left without anything to say by it, or it may be just that what paralysis *is* is less visible in the case of belief than in the case of action.

In this respect practical reason is no different from theoretical reason. Many things might cause me to fail to be convinced by a good argument. For me to be a theoretically rational person is not merely for me to be capable of performing logical and inductive operations, but for me to be appropriately *convinced* by them: my conviction in the premises must carry through, so to speak, to a conviction in the conclusion. Thus, the internalism requirement for theoretical reasons is that they be capable of convincing us – insofar as we are rational. It is quite possible for me to be able to perform these operations without generating any conviction, as a sort of game, say, and then I would not be a rational person.

Aristotle describes the novice in scientific studies as being able to repeat the argument, but without the sort of conviction that it will have for him later, when he fully understands it. In order for a theoretical argument or a practical deliberation to have the status of reason, it must of course be capable of motivating or convincing a rational person, but it does not follow that it must at all times be capable of motivating or convincing any given individual. It may follow from the supposition that we are rational persons and the supposition that a given argument or deliberation is rational that, if we are not convinced or motivated, there must be some explanation of that failure. But there is no reason at all to believe that such an explanation will always show that we had mistaken reasons, which, if true, would have been good reasons. Many things can interfere with the functioning of the rational operations in a human body. Thus there is no reason to deny that human beings might be practically irrational in the sense that Hume considers impossible: that, even with the truth at our disposal, we might from one cause or another fail to be interested in the means to our ends.

IV

My speculation is that skepticism about practical reason is sometimes based on a false impression of what the internalism requirement requires. It does not require that rational considerations always succeed in motivating us. All it requires is that rational considerations succeed in motivating us insofar as we are rational. One can admit the possibility of true irrationality and yet still believe that all practical reasoning is instrumental. But

once this kind of irrationality is allowed in the means/end case, some of the grounds for skepticism about more ambitious forms of practical reasoning will seem less compelling. The case of prudence or self-interest will show what I have in mind. I have already mentioned Hume's account of this matter: he thinks that there is "a general appetite to good, and aversion to evil" and that a person will act prudently insofar as this calm and general passion remains dominant over particular passions. It is under the influence of this end that we weigh one possible satisfaction against another, trying to determine which conduces to our greater good. But if this general desire for the good does not remain predominant, not only the motive, but the reason, for doing what will conduce to one's greater good, disappears. For Hume says it is not contrary to reason to prefer an acknowledged lesser good to a greater.

Suppose, then, that you are confronted with a choice and, though informed that one option will lead to your greater good, you take the other. If true irrationality is excluded, and you fail to take the means to some end, this is evidence either that you don't really have this end or that it is not the most important thing to you. Thus, in this imagined case, where you do not choose your greater good, this is evidence either that you do not care about your greater good or that you do not care about it as much as you do about this particular lesser good. On the other hand, if you do respond to the news that one option leads to your greater good, then we have evidence that you do care about your greater good. This makes it seem as if your greater good is an end you might care about or not, and rationality is relative to what you care about. But, once we admit that one might from some other cause fail to be responsive to a rational consideration, there is no special reason to accept this analysis of the case. I do not mean that there is a reason to reject it, either, of course; my point is that whether you accept it depends on whether you *already* accept the limitation to means/end rationality. If you do, you will say that the case where the lesser good was chosen was a case where there was a stronger desire for it, and so a stronger reason; if you do not, and you think it *is* reasonable to choose the greater good (because prudence has rational authority), you will say that this is a case of true irrationality. The point is that the motivational analysis of the case *depends* upon your views of the content of rational principles of action, not the reverse. The fact that one might or might not be motivated to choose a certain course of action by the consideration that it leads to the greater good does not by itself show that the greater good is just one end among others, without special rational authority, something that some people care about and some people do not. Take the parallel case. The fact that one might or might not be motivated to choose a certain course of action by the consideration that it is the best available means to one's end does not show that taking the means to one's ends is just one end among others, an end some people care about and some people do not. In both cases, what we have is the fact that people are sometimes motivated by considerations of this sort, and that we all think in the latter case and some think in the former case that it is rational to be so motivated.

The argument about whether prudence or the greater good has any special rational authority – about whether it is a rational consideration – will have to be carried out on another plane: it will have to be made in terms of a more metaphysical argument about just what reason does, what its scope is, and what sorts of operation, procedure, and judgment are rational. This argument will usually consist in an attempt to arrive at a general notion of reason by discovering features or characteristics that theoretical and practical reason share; such characteristic features as university, sufficiency, timelessness, impersonality, or authority will be appealed to.[11] What the argument in favor of prudence would be will vary from theory to theory; here, the point is this: the fact that someone might fail to be motivated by the consideration that something will serve her greater good cannot by itself throw any doubt on the argument, whatever it is, that preferring the greater good is rational. If someone were not convinced by the logical operation of conjunction, and so could not reason with conviction from "*A*" and from "*B*" to "*A*" and "*B*", we would not be eager to conclude that conjunction was just a theory that some people believe and some people do not. Conjunction is not a theory to believe or disbelieve, but a principle of reasoning. Not everything that drives us to conclusions is a theory. Not everything that drives us to action need be a desired end (see Nagel 20–22).

V

An interesting result of admitting the possibility of true irrationality is that it follows that it will not always be possible to argue someone into rational behavior. If people are acting irrationally only because they do not know about the relevant means/end connection, they may respond properly to argument: point the connection out to them, and their behavior will be modified accordingly. In such a person the motivational path, so to speak, from end to means is open. A person in whom this path is, from some cause, blocked or nonfunctioning may not respond to argument, even if this person understands the argument in a theoretical way. Aristotle thinks of the incontinent person as being in a condition of this sort: this happens to people in fits or passion or rage, and the condition is actually physiological.[12] Now this is important; for it is sometimes thought, on the basis of the internalism requirement, that if there is a reason to do something it must be possible to argue someone into doing it: anyone who understands the argument will straightaway act. (The conclusion of a practical syllogism is an action.) Frankena, for example, argues against an internalist construal of the moral "ought" on the grounds that even after full reflection we do not always do what is right (71). But if there is a gap between understanding a reason and being motivated by it, then internalism does not imply that people can always be argued into reasonable conduct. The reason motivates someone who is capable of being motivated by the perception of a rational connection. Rationality is a condition that human beings are capable of, but it is not a condition that we are always in.

It is for this reason that some ethical theories centered on the idea of practical reason are best thought of as establishing ideals of character. A person with a good character will be, on such a view, one who responds to the available reasons in an appropriate way, one whose motivational structure is organized for rational receptivity, so that reasons motivate in accord with their proper force and necessity. It is not an accident that the two major philosophers in our tradition who thought of ethics in terms of practical reason – Aristotle and

---

[11] Universality and sufficiency are appealed to by Kant; timelessness and impersonality by Nagel, and authority by Joseph Butler.
[12] *Nicomachean Ethics*, VII. 3, 1147b 5–10.

Kant – were also the two most concerned with the methods of moral education. Human beings must be taught, or habituated, to listen to reason: we are, as Kant says, imperfectly rational.

In fact, the argument of the last section can be recast in terms of virtues. Suppose that it *is* irrational not to prefer the greater good: this need have nothing at all to do with having the greater good *among* your desired ends. It is of course true that some people are more steadily motivated by considerations of what conduces to their greater good than others: call such a person *the prudent person*. The fact that the prudent is more strongly motivated by reasons of greater good need not be taken to show that he has stronger reasons for attending to his greater good. (People have varying theoretical virtues too.[13]) We may indeed say that the prudent person "cares more" about his greater good, but that is just another way of saying that he responds more strongly to these kinds of consideration, that he has the virtue of prudence. It need not be taken to imply that his greater good is a more heavily weighted end with him and that, therefore, it really does matter more to him that he achieve his greater good than it does to another person, an imprudent person, that he achieve his. It makes more sense to say that this other person ignores reasons that he has. Again, take the parallel: some people respond much more readily and definitely to the consideration that something is an effective means to their end. We might call such a person a *determined* or *resolute* person. Presumably no one feels like saying that the determined or resolute person has a stronger reason for taking the means to her ends than anyone else does. We all have just the same reason for taking the means to our ends. The fact that people are motivated differently by the reasons they have does not show that they have different reasons. It may show that some have virtues others lack. On a practical-reason theory, the possibility of rationality sets a standard for character; but that standard will not always be met. But this is not by itself a reason for skepticism about the scope of the deliberative guidance that reason *can* provide. This is a reason for skepticism only about the extent to which that guidance will ever be taken advantage of.

VI

Nevertheless, the fact that a practical reason must be capable of motivating us might still seem to put a limitation on the scope of practical reason: it might be thought that it is a subjective matter which considerations can motivate a given individual and that, therefore, all judgments of practical reason must be conditional in form. In Hume's argument, this kind of limitation is captured in the claim that motivation must originate in a passion. In the means/end case, we are able to be motivated by the consideration that action A will promote purpose P because, and only if, we have a pre-existing motivational impulse (a passion) attached to purpose P. As Hume says, a relation between two things will not have any motivational impact on us unless one of the two things has such impact. This does not limit practical reason to the means/end variety, but it might seem to impose a limitation of this sort: practical-reason claims must be reached by something that is recognizably a rational deliberative process from interest and motives one already has. This position is advocated by Bernard Williams in "Internal and External Reasons." Williams, as I have mentioned, argues that only internal reasons exist; but he takes this to have a strong Humean implication. Williams takes it that internal reasons are by definition relative to something that he calls the agent's "subjective motivational set": this follows from the fact that they can motivate. The contents of this set are left open, but one kind of thing it will obviously contain is the agent's desires and passions. Internal reasons are reasons reached by deliberation from the subjective motivational set: they can motivate us because of their connection to that set. Means/end deliberation, where the end is in the set and the means are what we arrive at by the motivating deliberation, is the most characteristic, but not the only, source of reasons for action. Williams calls the means/end view the "sub-Humean model", and he says this:

> The sub-Humean model supposes that ø-ing [where ø-ing is some action we have a reason for doing] has to be related to some element in [the subjective

---

[13]   The comparisons I have been drawing between theoretical and practical reason now suggest that there should also be something like an ideal of good theoretical character: a receptivity to theoretical reasons. The vision of someone free of all ideology and intellectual resistance might be such an ideal.

motivational set] as causal means to end (unless perhaps it is straightforwardly the carrying out of a desire which is itself that element in [the subjective motivational set].) But this is only one case. . . . there are much wider possibilities for deliberation, such as: thinking how the satisfaction of elements in [the subjective motivational set] can be combined, e.g. by time ordering; where there is some irresoluble conflict among the elements of [the subjective motivational set] considering which one attaches most weight to . . . or again, finding constitutive solutions, such as deciding what would make for an entertaining evening, granted that one wants entertainment. (104–5)[14]

Anything reached by a process of deliberation from the subjective motivational set may be something for which there is an internal reason, one that can motivate. External reasons, by contrast, exist regardless of what is in one's subjective motivational set. In this case, Williams points out, there must be some rational process, not springing from the subjective motivational set and therefore not relative to it, which could bring you to acknowledge something to be a reason and at the same time to be motivated by it. Reason must be able to produce an entirely new motive, the thing that Hume said could not be done.

Thus, Williams takes up one part of the skeptic's argument: that a piece of practical reasoning must start from something that is capable of motivating you; and drops the other, that the only kind of reasoning is means/end. One might suppose that this limits the operations or judgments of practical reason to those functions which are natural extensions or expansions of the means/end variety, and the things Williams mentions in this passage, such as making a plan to satisfy the various elements in the set, or constitutive reasoning, are generally thought to be of that sort. But in fact this is not Williams' view, nor is it necessitated by his argument, as he points out.

The processes of deliberation can have all sorts of effect on [the subjective motivational set], and this is a fact which a theory of internal reasons should be very happy to accommodate. So also it should be more liberal than some theorists have been about the possible elements in the [subjective motivational set]. I have discussed [the subjective motivational set] pri-

marily in terms of desires, and this term can be used, formally, for all elements in [the subjective motivational set]. But this terminology may make one forget that [the subjective motivational set] can contain such things as dispositions of evaluation, patterns of emotional reaction, personal loyalties, and various projects, as they may abstractly be called, embodying commitments of the agent. (105)

Williams can accommodate the case of someone's acting for reasons of principle, and in this case the form the deliberation will take is that of applying the principle or of seeing that the principle applies to the case at hand. The advocate of the view that all deliberation is strictly of the means/end variety may claim to assimilate this case by the formal device of saying that the agent must have a desire to act on this principle, but this will not change the important fact, which is that the reasoning in this case will involve the application of the principle, which is not the same as means/end reasoning.

In this kind of case, Williams' point will be that in order for the principle to provide reasons for a given agent, acceptance of the principle must constitute part of the agent's subjective motivational set. If the principle is not accepted by the agent, its dictates are not reasons for her. Reasons are relativized to the set. If this is true, it looks at first as if all practical reasons will be relative to the individual, because they are conditioned by what is in the subjective motivational set. Reasons that apply to you regardless of what is in your subjective motivational set will not exist.

This argument, however, having been cut loose from Hume's very definite ideas about what sort of rational operations and processes exist, has a very unclear bearing on claims about pure practical reason. If one accepts the internalism requirement, it follows that pure practical reason will exist if and only if we are capable of being motivated by the conclusions of the operations of pure practical reason as such. Something in us must make us capable of being motivated by them, and this something will be part of the subjective motivational set. Williams seems to think that this is a reason for doubting that pure practical reasons exist, whereas what seems to follow from the internalism requirement is this: if we can be motivated by considerations stemming from pure practical reason, then

---

[14] Williams uses the designation 'S' for 'subjective motivational set', but I have put back the original phrase wherever it occurs; hence the brackets.

that capacity belongs to the subjective motivational set of every rational being. One cannot argue that the subjective motivational set contains only ends or desires; for that would be true only if all reasoning were of the means/end variety or its natural extensions. What sorts of items can be found in the set does not limit, but rather depends on, what kinds of reasoning are possible. Nor can one assume that the subjective motivational set consists only of individual or idiosyncratic elements; for that is to close off without argument the possibility that reason could yield conclusions that every rational being must acknowledge and be capable of being motivated by. As long as it is left open what kinds of rational operations yield conclusions about what to do and what to pursue, it must be left open whether we are capable of being motivated by them.

Consider the question of how an agent comes to accept a principle: to have it in her subjective motivational set. If we say that the agent comes to accept the principle through reasoning – through having been convinced that the principle admits of some ultimate justification – then there are grounds for saying that this principle is in the subjective motivational set of every rational person: for all rational persons could be brought to see that they have reason to act in the way required by the principle, and this is all that the internalism requirement requires. Now this is of course not Williams' view: he believes that the principles are acquired by education, training, and so forth, and that they do not admit of any ultimate justification. There are two important points to make about this.

First, consider the case of the reflective agent who, after being raised to live by a certain principle, comes to question it. Some doubt, temptation, or argument has made her consider eliminating the principle from her subjective motivational set. Now what will she think? The principle does not, we are supposing, admit of an ultimate justification, so she will not find that. But this does not necessarily mean that she will reject the principle. She may, on reflection, find that she thinks it better (where this will be relative to what other things are in her motivational set) that people should have and act on such a principle, that it is in some rough way a good idea – perhaps not the only but an excellent basis for community living, etc. – and so she may retain it and even proceed to educate those under her influence to adopt it. The odd thing to notice

is that this is almost exactly the sort of description Mill gives of the reflective utilitarian who, on realizing that his capacity to be motivated by the principle of utility is an acquirement of education, is not sorry. But Mill's position, as I mentioned earlier, is often taken to be the best example of an *externalist* ethical position.

More immediately to the point, what this kind of case shows is that for Williams, as for Hume, the motivational skepticism depends on what I have called the "content skepticism." Williams' argument does not show that if there were unconditional principles of reason applying to action we could not be motivated by them. He only thinks that there are none. But Williams' argument, like Hume's, gives the appearance of going the other way around: it looks as if the motivational point – the internalism requirement – is supposed to have some force in limiting what might count as a principle of practical reason. Whereas in fact, the real source of the skepticism is a doubt about the existence of principles of action whose content shows them to be ultimately justified.

VII

The internalism requirement is correct, but there is probably no moral theory that it excludes. I do not think that it even excludes utilitarianism or intuitionism, although it calls for a reformulation of the associated views about the influence of ethical reasoning or motivation. The force of the internalism requirement is psychological: what it does is not to refute ethical theories, but to make a psychological demand on them.

This is in fact how philosophers advocating a connection between morality and practical reason have thought of the matter. From considerations concerning the necessity that reasons be internal and capable of motivating us which are almost identical to Williams', Nagel, in the opening sections of *The Possibility of Altruism*, argues that investigations into practical reason will yield discoveries about our motivational capacities. Granting that reasons must be capable of motivating us, he thinks that if we then are able to show the existence of reasons, we will have shown something capable of motivating us. In Nagel's eyes, the internalism requirement leads not to a limitation on practical reason, but to a rather surprising increase in the power of moral philosophy: it can teach us about human motivational capacities; it can teach us psychology.[15]

As Nagel points out, this approach also characterizes the moral philosophy of Kant. By the end of the Second Section of the *Foundations*, there is in *one* sense no doubt that Kant has done what he set out to do: he has shown us what sort of demand pure reason would make on action. Working from the ideas that reasons in general (either theoretical or practical) must be universal, that reason seeks the unconditioned, and that its binding force must derive from autonomy, he has shown us what a law of pure reason applying to action would look like. But until it has been shown that we can be motivated to act according to the categorical imperative, it has not been completely shown that the categorical imperative really exists – that there really is a law of pure practical reason. And this is because of the internalism requirement. The question how the imperative is possible is equated to that of "how the constraint of the will, which the imperative expresses in the problem, can be conceived" (Beck 34; Acad. 417). Thus, what remains for proof by a "deduction" is that we are capable of being motivated by this law of reason: that we have an autonomous will. In the Third Section of the *Foundations*, Kant does try to argue that we can be motivated by the categorical imperative, appealing to the pure spontaneity of reason as evidence of our intelligible nature and so for an autonomous will (Beck 70–1; Acad. 452). In the *Critique of Practical Reason*,[16] however, Kant turns his strategy around. He argues that we know that we are capable of being motivated by the categorical imperative and therefore that we know (in a practical sense) that we have an autonomous will. Again, explorations into practical reason reveal our nature. It is important, however, that although in the *Critique of Practical Reason* Kant does not try to argue *that* pure reason can be a motive, he has detailed things to say about *how* it can be a motive – about how it functions as an incentive in combatting other incentives.[17] Something is still owed to the internalism requirement: namely, to show what psychological conclusions the moral theory implies.

It may be that we are immune to motivation by pure practical reason. But, for that matter, it may be that we are immune to motivation by means/ends connections. Perhaps our awareness of these in cases where we seem to act on them is epiphenomenal. In fact we are quite sure that we are not immune to the reasons springing from means/ends connections; and Kant maintained that, if we thought about it, we would see that we are not immune to the laws of pure practical reason: that we know we can do what we ought. But there is no guarantee of this; for our knowledge of our motives is limited. The conclusion is that, if we are rational, we will act as the categorical imperative directs. But we are not necessarily rational.

VIII

I have not attempted to show in this paper that there is such a thing as pure practical reason, or that reason has in any way a more extensive bearing on conduct than empiricism has standardly credited it with. What I have attempted to show is that this question is open in a particular way: that motivational considerations do not provide any reason, in advance of specific proposals, for skepticism about practical reason. If a philosopher can show us that something that is recognizably a law of reason has bearing on conduct, there is no special reason to doubt that human beings might be motivated by that consideration. The fact that the law might not govern conduct, even when someone understood it, is no reason for skepticism: the necessity is in the law, and not in us.

To the extent that skepticism about pure practical reason is based on the strange idea that an acknowledged reason can never fail to motivate, there is no reason to accept it. It is based on some sort of a misunderstanding, and I have suggested a misunderstanding of the internalism requirement as a possible account. To the extent that skepticism about pure practical reason is based on the idea that no process or operation of reason yielding uncon-

---

[15] *Op. cit.*, p. 13.

[16] See especially pp. 30 and 43–51 in the translation by Lewis White Beck (New York: Library of Liberal Arts, 1956) and pp. 30 and 41–50 in the Prussian Academy Edition.

[17] In chapter III of the Analytic of the *Critique of Practical Reason*, where Kant's project is "not . . . to show a priori why the moral law supplies an incentive but rather what it effects (or better, must effect) in the mind, in so far as it is an incentive" (Beck 17; Acad. 72).

ditional conclusions about action can be found, it depends on – and is not a reason for believing – the thesis that no process or operation of reason yielding unconditional conclusions about action can be found. To the extent that skepticism about pure practical reason is based on the requirement that reasons be capable of motivating us, the correct response is that if someone discovers what are recognizably reasons bearing on conduct and those reasons fail to motivate us, that only shows the limits of our rationality. Motivational skepticism about practical reason depends on, and cannot be the basis for, skepticism about the possible content of rational requirements. The extent to which people are actually moved by rational considerations, either in their conduct or in their credence, is beyond the purview of philosophy. Philosophy can at most tell us what it would be like to be rational.

Moral Reasons

Russ Shafer-Landau

The Antirealist Challenge

Antirealists, especially those who resist ethical objectivism, have always had an easier time explaining the normativity of morality. If moral judgements record or express our own normative endorsements, and if such endorsements, as is usually assumed, are intrinsically reason-giving, then we have a ready explanation of morality's ability to generate significant reasons. Since realism insists on fixing the content of moral demands in a stance-independent way, realists have encountered more difficulties in explaining how morality supplies us with reasons. Indeed, starting from some widely accepted assumptions about the nature of reasons and their link with morality, antirealists are able to craft an argument that seriously jeopardizes realism's plausibility. Call this the *Desire-Dependence Argument*:

1 Necessarily, if S is morally obligated to Φ at t, then S has a good reason to Φ at t. (*Moral Rationalism*)
2 Necessarily, if S has a good reason to Φ at t, then S can be motivated to Φ at t. (*Reasons Internalism*)
3 Necessarily, if S can be motivated to Φ at t, then S must, at t, either desire to Φ, or desire to ψ, and believe that by Φ-ing S will ψ. (*Motivational Humeanism*)
4 Therefore, necessarily, if S is morally obligated to Φ at t, then S must, at t, either desire to Φ, or desire to ψ, and believe that by Φ-ing S will ψ.

The Desire-Dependence Argument, if sound, is sufficient to make out the claim that the content of moral obligations crucially depends on an agent's desires. This is a kind of contingency that is inimical to moral realism. Since the Argument is valid, it is clear that moral realists must reject at least one of its premisses. There is no consensus on which to abandon. In fact, each premiss is so intuitively plausible that we can often explain a philosopher's rejection of a premiss by citing his or her endorsement of the two remaining ones.

Despite the initial attractiveness of each of the premisses, common sense tells us that the conclusion of the Desire-Dependence Argument is false. The conclusion implies that we must tailor the content of moral obligations to ensure that they don't outstrip our desires. [. . .] The argument tells us, in effect, that any putative moral requirement that fails, or is believed to fail, to fulfil our desires is too demanding, and so *cannot be* morally obligatory. But very few people accept this. Most believe that morality can sometimes require the greatest sacrifices of us, and this despite the fact that undertaking such sacrifices may satisfy none of our desires and may cost us our livelihood or our lives. We don't craft the contours of moral obligation to fit an individual's desires. Moral obligations instead represent standards by which we judge the fitness or suitability of a person's desires. The egoist and the sadist are not held to less demanding moral standards just because of their aberrant psychological profiles.

The common-sense view supports realism's claim that something is wrong with the Desire-Dependence Argument. Since it is logically valid, we must impugn at least one of the premises. [. . .] In what follows, I will attempt to undermine the argument's second premiss and defend its first. My aim will be to show that, necessarily, there is always good reason to do as morality says, even if such reasons cannot motivate the agents to whom they apply.

Arguments for Internalism

[*I*]nternalism about reasons, or *reasons internalism*, for short, alleges an internal or necessary connection between what reasons we have and what motivations we are capable of having. The sticking point about reasons internalism is understanding the relevant modality expressed in the locution 'can be motivated'. What sense of possibility is implied by this phrase?

The most plausible alternative is what we might call *rational possibility*. On this conception, one can be motivated to Φ if and only if one is already motivated to Φ, or one would be motivated to Φ were one to rationally deliberate in a successful fashion [. . .]

Williams's characterization of what I am calling *rational possibility* has it that a consideration can motivate only if it already does motivate, or would motivate if one were to rationally deliberate from one's existing motivations. [. . .] If Williams is right, then one has a reason to do something only if one is motivated to do it, or would be motivated to do it after rationally deliberating from one's actual motivations. I know of four arguments for thinking this correct. I believe that they all fail.

The Browbeating Argument

Let us begin with perhaps the weakest of the arguments, probably not meant by itself to be determinative in the debate between internalists and externalists. This argument for reasons internalism consists of an attack on reasons externalism. Since these are contradictories, this is a strategy as good as that which sets out to supply positive argument for internalism. The criticism of externalism is basically that it allows for 'browbeating'; for criticizing someone for failing to adhere to reasons whose existence he denies (Williams 1981a: 105–6). Externalism allows for this because it allows for the existence of reasons that have no appropriate link to an individual's motivations. Internalism is thought to prevent this, because on its view all reasons must be within deliberative reach of the agent for whom they are reasons. Externalism is implausible because only it licenses browbeating, a kind of conduct acknowledged by all to be faulty.

The first thing to say is that externalism *per se* is neutral about the merits of browbeating, and any decent normative theory (i.e., one specifying substantive reasons) would have one refrain from such conduct. Still, the relevant question isn't whether to condone browbeating, but whether the charge that is at the heart of a browbeating episode is true – namely, that the agent in question has reason to do something, even though he does not recognize it. It is objectionable to tell the truth in any number of contexts, including situations in which veracity is sure to do no good and is sure to do some harm. Browbeating is such a case. But its unattractive quality is compatible with its message being true. Externalist who insist on such behaviour are doubtless criticizable for their indulgence, but the unsavoury messenger may be telling the truth for all that. (Cf. Scanlon 1998: 371–2.)

We can sharpen the point by highlighting the fact that internalists, too, may license unproductive criticism. If internalists are right, then there must be a sound deliberative route from one's actual motivations to one's reasons. But many individuals lack the ability to take such a route – cognitive or affective deficiencies can yield or represent blindspots that render a person unable to undertake the kind of rational deliberation that would generate insight into one's reasons. When faced with this kind of blindness, it would be browbeating to confront the individual and insist that, despite her denials, she nevertheless has a reason. Yet in this case internalists would not deny the truth of the reasons claim. There can be a sound deliberative route from one's motivations to a reason even if psychological impediments prevent one from ever being able to trace such a route. The browbeating charge ignores this, and so fails to appreciate the fact that internalism too allows for the possibility that good advice will fall on deaf ears.

Williams (1989) offers us what is in effect an update of the browbeating argument, here focused on the preconditions of warranted blame. Like the browbeating argument, this argument focuses on what can be accomplished during an episode of criticism, and likewise saddles the externalist with unsavoury commitments. This argument claims that only those who accept Williams's link between reasons and motivation can adhere to the constraint that blaming be, at least in principle, an effective means of redirecting another's actions. There would be no point in blaming someone whose subjective motivational set contained nothing that would leave him anything but indifferent to the censure. But if reasons entailed a link to one's motivations, then at least in principle anyone properly blamed is within reach. The blamed individual is susceptible to suasion, because blaming will cite reasons that the agent neglected, and such reasons will, if Williams is right, implicate considerations that already motivate the subject of blame.

This sounds right if we accept that the point of blame is to redirect another's behaviour. It often is. Williams (1989) throughout understands blame in its performative mode – blame is not simply a verdict of censure, but is an act in which one communicates this verdict to another. Such communication might indeed lack a point, if the 'blamee' is beyond the pale – if he really does lack anything in his motivational set that might, after deliberation, prompt him to be moved as the critic wants. But this does not undermine the possible justice of the verdict. The judgement of censure may be true even though there be no recipient – even though, for instance, the one issuing the blame does not do so publicly, but keeps her own counsel. So long as we distinguish, as we should, between the efficacy of issuing blame and an agent's deserving blame, this criticism of externalism will not do. The externalist will insist that some agents may deserve blame, and perhaps deserve to be blamed, even if nothing in their existing motivations will generate conduct that corrects the failure that the blame is directed to.

The Action Explanation Argument (2)

The second argument for internalism starts from the view that, as Williams claims (1981a: 106–7), our reasons are linked with the possibility of explaining action. Reasons figure in action explanation, but if there were reasons that were unrelated to our subjective motivational sets, then they could not possibly explain our actions. Yet it must be possible to explain our actions by citing our reasons for performing them. Therefore reasons must be related to our subjective motivational set. Therefore internalism is true.

This argument is sound under one interpretation, but not the one that would lend support to internalism. The argument works perfectly if we assume that the relevant reasons are motivating reasons. It is impossible to explain action without citing the considerations that supplied our motivations. Such motivations, or motivating reasons, are invariably constituents in our subjective motivational set. But motivating reasons are of a different category from the sorts of reasons (justifying reasons) at the heart of the internalist thesis. Reasons internalism is a claim about *good* reasons – considerations that justify or legitimize action. Not every good reason is acted on, and not every action is prompted by a good reason. The confusion lies in using the same term, 'reason', for two distinct kinds of thing: motives, which are psychological states; and genuine (good, justifying) reasons, which are not. Considerations to do with the explanation of action are relevant to motives. Internalism is a thesis about justifying reasons. Thus this argument will not do.

Williams, in a later piece on this matter, gives the argument as follows: 'If it is true that A has a reason to Φ, then it must be possible that he should Φ for that reason; and if he does act for that reason, then that reason will be the explanation of his acting. So the claim that he has a reason to Φ – that is, the normative statement "He has a reason to Φ" – introduces the possibility of that reason being an explanation' (1989: 39).

Focus on the initial statement. The conditional gains its plausibility by implicitly assuming that the kind of possibility mentioned in the consequent is logical possibility. But that won't get Williams his conclusion. He must mean what I have called rational possibility if the argument is to go through. Yet employing this sense of possibility just begs the question – whether having a reason entails the pos-

sibility of being motivated upon rational deliberation is precisely what is at issue. So Williams's
latest words on the alleged link between justification and action explanation do not get us any
further on.

Korsgaard (1986) endorses Williams's point
linking the existence of reasons with their potential to motivate and explain action. She offers two
arguments in favour of internalism based on considerations to do with action explanation. In the
first, she claims that 'unless reasons are motives,
they cannot prompt or explain actions. And, unless
reasons are motives, we cannot be said to be practically rational' (1986: 11). But we can be said to be
practically rational. Thus 'it seems to be a requirement on practical reasons, that they be capable of
motivating us' (11). So: our being practically rational depends on our reasons being our motives.
Since we are practically rational, our reasons must
be capable of motivating us. Therefore internalism
is true.

The externalist should agree with Korsgaard in
thinking that our reasons must be capable of
moving us to the extent that we are practically
rational. But we aren't always practically rational.
So Korsgaard has not shown that reasons must be
capable of motivating us full stop, but only that
this motivational link is forged when we are practically rational. That falls short of a defence of
internalism.

In a second argument, Korsgaard insists, following Falk (1948: 121–2) and Nagel (1970: 9), that 'if
acknowledgement of a reason claim did not include
acknowledgement of a motive, someone presented
with a reason for action could ask: Why do what I
have a reason to do?' (1986: 11). In other words, if
reasons were not also motives, then acknowledged
reasons would not rationalize to an agent the
actions they support. But this is precisely the job
that reasons do. Therefore externalism fails to
explain the very nature of a reason.

This is too quick. In the first case, one *can* sensibly ask why one should do what one has a reason
to do, because one may recognize the existence of
countervailing reasons, and be puzzled as to which
reason should receive priority. In other cases, where
one recognizes a reason to be conclusive and determinative, one *cannot* sensibly ask why one should
do what one has reason to do. But in such circumstances the externalist isn't committed to thinking

this a sensible question. What the externalist will
insist on is the possibility of motivational failure in
the face of reasons believed to be determinative,
perhaps because of accidie, depression, violent
passion, etc. The agent in such a case won't ask why
she should do what she acknowledges she has most
reason to do. She knows why. But she may remain
unmoved anyway. Again, this needn't undermine
the existence of the reason.

There is a general problem with efforts that try
to forge a link between reasons and action explanation. The impetus behind the internalist insistence
on this connection is the thought that something
can be a reason only if it can potentially explain the
conduct of the agent for whom it is a reason. But
even internalism falls foul of this requirement.
Various emotional, neurotic, or phobic susceptibilities may render an agent incapable of motivation
even in cases where the actions in question are
rationally related to the agent's existing motivations. That an agent fails to make the rational connection, or succeeds in this but fails thereby to be
motivated (owing to psychological infirmities), is
not thought by internalists to entail the absence or
extinction of a reason. Yet these are cases in which
the affective disabilities, if severe enough, will
invariably prevent their agents from being motivated. In such cases, the relevant reasons will never
figure in an explanation of the agent's actions.
There is no scenario in which the agent, with her
existing motivations (including her affective
impairments), would act on the acknowledged
reason. This is a genuine break between reasons
and action explanation.[1]

This can lead us in one of two directions. We
may abandon the requirement that reasons be able
to figure in action explanation, in which case externalism's failure to satisfy the requirement is no flaw.
Or we may retain the requirement, in which case
internalism too must be rejected.

The Avoidability Argument

Williams (1989) provides us with the materials for
two further arguments, both of which focus on the
notion of blame and its relation to reasons. The
first of these is what I shall call *the Avoidability
Argument*:

---

[1]   See Cohon 1993: 271 for an argument similar to the one developed in this paragraph.

1. If one is properly to blame for Φ-ing, then one ought to have refrained from Φ-ing.
2. If one ought to have refrained from Φ-ing, then one could have refrained from Φ-ing.
3. If one could have refrained from Φ-ing, then such avoidance must be licensed by one's subjective motivational set.
4. Therefore if one is properly to blame for Φ-ing, then refraining from Φ-ing must be licensed by one's subjective motivational set.

This argument is valid and its premises are all appealing. Yet the conclusion, though not by itself a statement of internalism, is one that is difficult for an externalist to accept. To see why, consider the following argument:

1. Blameworthiness entails a failure to adhere to a good reason.
2. One's reasons needn't be rationally related to one's subjective motivational set.
3. Therefore one may be blameworthy for actions or omissions that bear no relation to one's subjective motivational set.

This argument is also valid. Its second premiss is a statement of externalism. The first premiss seems a conceptual truth. But the conclusion contradicts that of the previous argument. So externalists must either reject what appears to be a conceptual truth, or reject a premiss of the Avoidability Argument.

We might try rejecting the alleged conceptual truth. Some hard determinists and utilitarians will do this. They will claim that a person is properly to blame if blaming that person is morally acceptable, and that the moral acceptability of blaming depends not on a person's adherence to reasons, but on the good consequences that might emerge from the act of blaming. This strikes me as weak, however, since it does seem appropriate to distinguish between blameworthiness, on the one hand, and the appropriateness of expressing blame, on the other. An individual might be blameworthy for some conduct, and so be properly to blame, without it being morally acceptable to convey the condemnation. If that is so, then the hard determinist's argument fails to undermine the conceptual truth.

There might be other reasons for rejecting the link between blame and failure to adhere to good reasons, but this does not seem a promising route to a defence of externalism. Better would be a direct critique of one of the premises of the Avoidability Argument. But which one?

I think that the second premiss is vulnerable. This premiss, which expresses one version of the ought-implies-can principle, should be read to refer to rational possibility. In other words, the second premiss, in this context, should be read to say that if one ought to avoid Φ-ing, then such avoidance is possible, in the sense that such avoidance is rationally related to one's existing motivations.

On an assumption that both internalists and externalists can share, if one ought to Φ, then there is a reason for one to Φ.[2] It makes little sense to insist that one ought to Φ, though one lacks any reason at all to Φ. Alternatively, it makes good sense to excuse someone for failing to Φ by correctly stating that there was absolutely no reason to Φ. Now, if ought implies can, then the relevant inability cancels the ought. The relevant inability in this context is the inability, via rational deliberation, to be motivated. But since that is so, the assertion of the ought-implies-can principle in this context begs the question against the reasons externalist. It says that one ought to Φ, and hence that there is a reason to Φ, only if one can, through rational deliberation, be motivated to Φ. That is just an assertion of the truth of reasons internalism. That is why the externalist will reject the second premiss of the Avoidability Argument.

Such a rejection sounds implausible because of the modal assumption that ordinarily accompanies discussion of the ought-implies-can principle. The assumption is that the principle refers to *physical* possibility: it is obvious, to use familiar examples, that the explanation for why one isn't obligated to jump over skyscrapers or stop an avalanche with one's bare hands is that it is physically impossible to do so. But if physical possibility is the right way to understand the ought-implies-can principle in premiss (2), then physical possibility must be read into the third premiss as well, or else the Argument will contain a fallacy of equivocation. But read this way, the third premiss is clearly false – it is false that one's physically possible actions are limited to

---

[2] This doesn't beg any questions about the status of moral rationalism – the view that moral obligations entail reasons – because it is an open question at this point whether one ought to comply with one's moral obligations.

those that are licensed by one's subjective motivational set.

In short, if the relevant modality in premiss (2)
is physical possibility, then the validity of the argument requires that premiss (3) be read this way. But
then premiss (3) is false, rendering the argument
unsound. If the relevant modality is rational possibility, then the second premiss begs the question
against externalism. So on either reading of the
second premiss, we have good reason to think the
Avoidability Argument unsound.

The Unfair Choices Argument

Consider an act, Φ, whose omission is morally condemnable. Suppose that Φ is also rationally impossible for a person to perform; nothing in her
existing motivations is rationally related to Φ-ing.
Internalists may claim that blaming this person for
not Φ-ing is giving her an unpalatable choice:
either subject yourself to blame (for not Φ-ing), or
do something (Φ) which is irrational for you to do.
Forcing such a choice is surely unfair. Only externalists force such choices.

There are two replies available to the externalist. The first allows that forcing such choices is
indeed unfair, but denies that externalism presents
agents with such dilemmas. The second option
accepts that externalism allows agents to be faced
with such choices, but denies the unfairness of
such situations. I prefer the first route, but my
preference is supported by some controversial
views about rationality which other externalists
may wish to eschew. I will offer the more controversial strategy first. The faint of heart can avail
themselves of an argument with broader appeal if
this fails.

The internalist objection, in a nutshell, claims
that it is unfair to force a choice between blameworthiness (for failing to do right) and irrationality (for doing right, despite having no motivation
for doing so). But to think that externalism is committed to forcing such a choice is to beg the question, by assuming that doing something unrelated
to one's motives is irrational. This assumption is
not uncommon, and can derive support from a very
widely held view of irrationality. This view claims
that one's act or attitude is irrational if it fails to
comport with one's values, goals, commitments,
etc. Since such things are among the components
of one's subjective motivational set, it would follow

that doing something unrelated to one's motives is
irrational.

But this presupposes what seems to me to be an
unduly narrow concept of (ir)rationality. My view
is that to be irrational is to be insensitive, in one's
attitudes and behaviour, to sufficiently good
reasons (whatever those happen to be). If we retain
this neutral understanding of irrationality, we can
see that the internalist is simply assuming that sufficiently good reasons must be rationally related to
one's existing motives. The externalist will deny
this. For any action Φ whose omission is morally
condemnable, the real choice offered by the externalist is this: either subject yourself to blame (for
not Φ-ing), or do something (Φ) which is unrelated
to your existing motives. There doesn't appear to
be anything unfair about offering such a choice to
the intransigent bully or the committed misan-
thrope. A forced choice between irrationality and
blame is unpalatable, and any theory that subjects
agents who are otherwise blameless to such a choice
is suspect for that reason. But the internalist arguments offered thus far do not show that externalism generates any cases in which agents are faced
with such a choice.

Much more needs to be said about the operative
notion of rationality, and as it stands many will
remain unconvinced. So let us retreat to safer view.
The second externalist path accepts the possibility
of situations in which an agent may lack any motivation to do the right thing. But externalists
can avoid imposing unfair choices on agents in
such cases.

Two diagnoses are possible, depending on
whether the agent is at least partially responsible
for the cultivation of his character. If he isn't, then
he lacks control over which elements find themselves in his subjective motivational set. On that
assumption, it truly is unfair to blame him for
failing to do the right thing. But then it will be
unfair to blame him for *anything*. Agents might still
be faced with situations in which they lack motives
to do the right thing. Yet failure to act rightly will
not, under the present assumption, warrant a
judgement of blameworthiness. So, on the assumption that agents do not bear any responsibility for
their motives, externalists will *not* present agents
with forced choices between blameworthiness, on
the one hand, and action for which they entirely
lack a motive, on the other. The choice instead will
be to act as your motives allow, or to do the right
thing. This isn't itself an unfair choice, especially

if one is withholding blame from those who fail to do the right thing.

Alternatively, we might assume that agents *are* at least partially responsible for their motives. Agents may still find themselves in situations in which they lack a motive to do the right thing. But on our present assumption, their motivational failure is their responsibility. If, for instance, they have freely chosen to ally themselves with the principles of a ruthless terroristic organization, then their complete unwillingness to stay a cruel hand is *their fault*. In effect, if one is responsible for one's motivational make-up, then one can't plead innocence when left cold by the prospect of doing right. There doesn't seem anything unfair in holding people morally responsible for the situations they find themselves in, if we can hold them responsible for the motivations that got them there in the first place. So agents may sometimes be faced with a choice between being blamed (for their wrongdoing), or doing what they have no motivation to do (namely, the right thing in the circumstances). Yet under the assumption that agents are responsible for their practical judgements and other motivations, this choice is not an unfair one.

Agents either are or are not responsible for the motivations they possess. If they are responsible, then the choice between blameable and unmotivated activity is not unfair. If agents are not relevantly responsible, then such a choice is unfair, but externalists do not force it. Instead, they allow for situations in which agents must choose between doing right and doing what they are motivated to do. But in such a case, those who follow the last course are not to blame. So, again, externalists do not confront agents with unfair choices.

This concludes the defensive work to be done on behalf of reasons externalism. If I am right, the most powerful of the criticisms of externalism fail in their aims. By itself, this does not show that externalism is true. However, if we combine this defensive work with arguments that succeed in revealing internalism's weaknesses, then, since internalism and externalism are contradictories, we will have all the materials necessary for constructing a strong case for externalism. Let us turn, then, to a consideration of anti-internalist arguments. [. . .]

Two Arguments against Internalism

If internalism is true, then one's reasons are restricted to those rational extensions of one's existing motivations. This restriction is illegitimate, or so I shall argue. I will offer two sets of considerations designed to show that the restriction is ill conceived. The first proceeds via counter-example.

Consider a person whose melancholia combines with a dismal pessimism about prospects for happiness. She is effectively a shut-in, her shyness and poor self-conception proof against engagement with the larger world. She is clear-headed enough, and can imagine the experiences of mingling, social chat, and light flirtation. But she anticipates no pleasure from such activities, and the dread she experiences when imagining them is enough to prevent her from making any movement to change the status quo.

For such a person, nothing in her existing motivations would lead her to take steps to ease her into a flourishing social life. No dance lessons, no hesitant first calls that chance a titter or a put-down. Yet let us suppose that she would find new pleasure, even some delights, were she to emerge from her shell. In appraising her life, she would judge herself far better off in the world than out of it. From within, she would come to endorse the value of the experiences achievable only by extending herself, making herself vulnerable, occasionally being hurt, but more frequently finding pleasure with others. It is this *ex post* validation that makes it true to say of her, in her earlier phase, that she had a reason to extend herself.

The general point is this. It is true of many different kinds of people that if they were somehow to 'look beyond' the picture of things they have grown used to, they would find themselves with an outlook, a plan of life, and set of circumstances that they would find more valuable than they could ever have imagined. In such cases, realizing the relevant benefits often requires a change of character. Prior to this change, the prospects of the new life do not appeal, just because they are rationally unrelated to one's present outlook. But one may have reason to change that outlook. One's aspirations may be unduly cramped. One may undervalue the range of enjoyments available only to those who embody the traits that now seem unattractive or unachievable. One's preferences may have been formed under circumstances that bear little relation to the possibilities ahead. In any event, the goods available only to those who make such changes may be so valuable as to make it true that one has, despite one's present motivations, a reason to make the necessary changes.

An appeal to make such changes may fall on deaf ears; indeed, it almost certainly will, given that the example makes its point only if the appeal does not contain a rational relation to the addressee's existing motivations. Yet this is not bluff, bluster, bullying, or browbeating. Here, the value of certain experiences would have been endorsed *by the agent herself*, after she has had the benefit of those experiences. There is a reason for her to extend herself, even though nothing in her present make-up suggests the value of doing so, at least partly because she herself will recognize the value that such exertions bring.[3]

We need to be careful not to overstate the point here. The example doesn't commit us to the claim that one at present has an external reason whenever acting on it would lead to value, or to more value (either objectively considered or from the agent's own (later) point of view) than action from internal reasons. These views might be right, but they aren't vindicated by a single example.

A second argument begins with another imagined scenario. Consider a person so misanthropic, so heedless of others' regard, so bent on cruelty, that nothing in his present set of motives would prevent him from committing the worst kind of horrors. He cannot, in the relevant sense, be moved to forbear from such behaviour. But why should this unfortunate fact force us to revise our standards for appropriate conduct? Nothing we say to him will convince him to modify his behaviour. But is this intransigence a basis for holding him to different standards, or isn't it rather a justification for convicting him of a kind of blindness? It is natural to say that people have reason to refrain from behaviour that is fiendish, callous, brutal, arrogant, or craven. We don't withdraw such evaluations just because their targets fail (or would, after deliberation, fail) to find them compelling.

Internalists are in a difficult position here. If internalism is true, then the rational impossibility of Φ-ing means that there is no reason to Φ. Now if blame requires failure to adhere to good reasons, and rational impossibility entails an absence of reasons, then agents for whom avoidance of evil deeds is rationally impossible are morally blameless. The worst of the lot – the hate-mongers and misanthropes, the Streichers or the Himmlers

of the world – would thereby be immune from blame. And hence, presumably, from punishment, since proper punishment is predicated on blameworthiness.

The argument can be put more straightforwardly as follows:

1   If internalism is true, then one has no reason to do what is rationally impossible.
2   If one has no reason to Φ, then one can't be justly blamed or punished for not Φ-ing.
3   Therefore if internalism is true, then one can't be justly blamed or punished for avoiding what is rationally impossible.
4   Some agents are justly blamed or punished for their evil deeds, even though avoidance of such conduct was rationally impossible.
5   Therefore internalism is false.

Those who dislike the conclusion have just two premises to choose from, since the first premise is true by definition. The second premise is strong. It ties blameworthiness (and suitability for punishment) to the existence of reasons. To reject the second premise is to insist that agents may be blameworthy despite lacking any reason to refrain from their unseemly conduct. Such a stand commits one to the view that one could be properly blameworthy for Φ-ing even though one had no reason not to Φ; blameable for Φ-ing, though no consideration at all inclined against Φ-ing. That is quite a strange view. For we rightly suppose that whenever someone is blameworthy, there is in principle some explanation of this fact, some feature in virtue of which an agent is blameworthy. That feature must embody a failing. And this failure is best understood as a failure to appreciate or adhere to considerations that favour or oppose some attitude, choice, or action. But such considerations are just what reasons are. So rejecting the second premise leaves one with an unrecognizable view of the conditions under which agents are properly subject to blame.

The last option is to reject the fourth premiss. In this context, it helps if we focus again on various malefactors, say, the disciplined immoralist, or the single-minded, principled fanatic. These unsavoury characters find themselves without the kinds of motives that the rest of us routinely deploy to prompt our benign impulses and check

---

[3]   Millgram (1996: 203 ff.) has a good example and a fine discussion that makes the same point.

our harmful ones. Those who reject the fourth premiss must say of such agents that they oughtn't to be blamed or punished for the evil that they do. Yet these agents are not insane, or incapable of resisting their impulses. They have set out on a path of terror, or destruction, and have methodically pursued their vision. Internalism would immunize such agents from moral criticism.

So internalists are faced with the choice of withholding blame from the very worst that humanity has to offer, or embracing an unpalatable view of blameworthiness that severs its connection with sensitivity and adherence to reasons. Externalism easily avoids this dilemma, and that is good reason to prefer it to internalism.

[. . .]

Realism and Rationalism

[. . .]

In what follows, I offer a presumptive argument for rationalism, and then explore the strongest of the arguments designed to undermine it. I don't think that any of these arguments succeeds. At the end of the day, if all goes according to plan, this leaves us with good reason for endorsing rationalism, no good reason not to, and so a strong, albeit nonconclusive, case for moral rationalism. [. . .]

A Presumptive Argument for Moral Rationalism

Imagine someone doing an act because she thinks it right – she acts from the motive of duty, and, let us suppose, in this case she is on target about what duty requires. What justifies her in performing such an act? If she correctly cites an action's rightness as her reason for performing it, we don't ordinarily question the legitimacy or conceptual coherence of her doing so. But if the rightness of an act itself was no reason at all for performing it, then we would have to do just that. It could never be the case that the rightness of an act was what justified or legitimized its performance, made its performance appropriate under the circumstances. For legitimacy, appropriateness, and justification are all normative notions, and their proper application depends crucially on the existence of reasons. If the rightness of an act was itself no

reason to perform it, then even the prima facie justification of virtuous conduct would always be contingent on a showing that it (say) serves self-interest or satisfies the agent's desires. The implausibility of such a view implies that an action's rightness constitutes a good justifying reason for performing it.

We can support this view by considering immoral acts as well. When we deem someone's behaviour morally unjustified, we imply that he has violated a standard of appropriate conduct. Suppose such standards did not by themselves supply reasons for action. Then we would be forced to allow that though some actions are unjustified, immoral, improper, illegitimate, or inappropriate, there nevertheless may be no reason at all to avoid them. But this seems wrong – not only conceptually confused, but also gravely unfair. It seems a conceptual error to cite a standard as a guide to conduct and a basis for evaluation – to say, for instance, that S ought to have Φ-ed, and was wrong for having failed to Φ – and yet claim that there was no reason at all for S to have Φ-ed. And it seems unfair to criticize violations of such standards while admitting that an agent responsible for offensive conduct may have had no reason to do otherwise. The fairness and appropriateness of moral evaluation rest on an agent's attentiveness to reasons. An agent who correctly claims to have ignored no reasons for action cannot be held to have violated any moral standard. This plausible thought is true only if moral rationalism is true.

We are left, therefore, with the choice of either endorsing moral rationalism, or endorsing the idea that proper moral evaluation of an agent has nothing to do with the agent's attentiveness to reasons. Those who take the latter option must shoulder the burden of explaining just what (other than reasons) could serve as the basis for moral assessment, and just how this basis will manage to avoid the apparent unfairness of criticizing agents for conduct they had no reason to avoid.

Antirationalist Arguments

I think that the considerations just offered provide a good basis for accepting moral rationalism. We can strengthen the case if we are able to defuse the strongest arguments against it. Let me proceed with this task by focusing directly on the four antirationalist arguments that I believe to have the greatest chance of undermining moral rationalism. The first of these – the *Reasons Internalist Argument* – relies on some familiar views to do some new work:

1 Reasons Internalism is true.
2 Motivational Humeanism is true.
3 Moral obligations apply to agents independently of their desires.
4 Therefore moral rationalism is false.

This argument is logically valid. If reasons must be capable of motivating, and if motivation implicates pre-existing desires, then one has reason to Φ only if Φ-ing is properly related to one's pre-existing desires. If moral obligations apply to agents independently of such desires, then the classes of moral obligations and reasons for action are either not even extensionally equivalent, or are, but only contingently so. This is incompatible with moral rationalism. According to this argument, what reasons we have depends on our motivational capacity, which in turn depends on our pre-existing desires. What moral obligations we have does not depend on our desires. Therefore we may entirely lack reason to fulfil our moral obligations. Therefore moral rationalism is false.

If, as I have argued, reasons internalism is false, then this first argument for rejecting moral rationalism will not do. A second argument poses a greater threat, because it does not depend on internalism about reasons.

Call this second argument the *Rational Egoist Argument*:

1 Rational Egoism is true.
2 Weak Ethical Egoism is false.
3 Therefore Moral Rationalism is false.

Both premises have broad appeal. Rational egoism is the thesis that one has a reason to Φ if and only if Φ-ing will serve one's self-interest. Weak ethical egoism is the view that one is morally obligated to Φ only if Φ-ing will serve one's self-interest.[4] The falsity of weak ethical egoism entails that adherence to moral requirements may sometimes fail to serve one's self-interest. Rational egoism entails

that one lacks reason to perform actions that fail in this way. Therefore the combination of these views entails that one may be morally obligated to Φ even though one lacks a reason to Φ. Therefore this combination entails that moral rationalism is false.

[. . .]

Such an argument has only two possible points of vulnerability: its endorsement of rational egoism, or its rejection of weak ethical egoism. Moral rationalists might ambitiously offer a critique of this last claim. This would kill two birds with one stone. For if rationalists could vindicate weak ethical egoism, then, by embracing the rational egoism of the first premiss, they will have created a positive argument on behalf of moral rationalism. If rational egoism is true, and weak ethical egoism is *true*, then moral rationalism is true. If moral duties are guaranteed to promote self-interest, and one always has reason to undertake such promotion, then one has a reason whenever one has a moral obligation. That is moral rationalism.

There is a chance that this argument is sound. To show it so, one would have to vindicate weak ethical egoism, and so defend a particular conception of self-interest, a theory of the conditions under which one's self-interest is served, and a first-order moral theory that aligns these conditions with the content of moral demands. Though I favour moral rationalism, I don't want to avail myself of this route to getting there. If weak ethical egoism is true, then we have a powerful argument for moral rationalism only if rational egoism can be vindicated. If weak ethical egoism is false, we have a powerful antirationalist argument only if rational egoism can be vindicated. Both routes obviously depend for their success on the truth of rational egoism. I am unwilling to grant that assumption.

We can sidestep the difficulties associated with investigating weak ethical egoism, so long as we can raise enough doubts about the truth of rational egoism. That is what I want to do. The challenge is to show that agents might have reason to act morally even if doing so does not serve their interests. Success in this case will not amount to an argument for moral rationalism, but rather an

[4] Contrast this with a stronger version of ethical egoism: An act is morally right *if and* only if it *best* promotes one's self-interest.

Weak ethical egoism (= premiss 2) is the more plausible version, and will be the focus of subsequent discussion. The falsity of weak ethical egoism entails the falsity of the stronger version, but not vice versa.

argument that undermines a perennial anti-rationalist critique, by undermining the rational egoism that provides its essential support.

It may be that promotion of self-interest always supplies a good reason for action. But why believe that this is the only kind of good reason there is? Most of us firmly hold judgements that imply the falsity of this thesis. If I see someone distractedly crossing the street, about to be run over, I have reason to yell out and warn her. There is some consideration that favours and justifies my issuing such a warning, even if I (stand to) gain no benefit thereby. If I see a gang of men corner a young woman, taunt her and begin to drag her into a dark alley, I have reason to notify the police, immediately intervene, and call for the assistance of others to help. If I spot a seriously dehydrated hiker while in the backwoods, I have reason to offer up my canteen. Of course we can imagine situations where, all things considered, I have most reason not to perform these actions. But special circumstances aside, such cases certainly appear to provide at least defeasible reason for action, even though our interests are not served, and may only be hindered, by rendering such aid.

The appeal to our deeply held normative convictions can be supplemented by two criticisms of rational egoism. The first relies on the importance of autonomy. Autonomous choices for desired or valued ends at least sometimes supply reasons for action, even when such choices are known by the agent not to enhance (or perhaps only to damage) his self-interest. If a soldier decides to sacrifice himself for his comrades, then he has some reason to take the means necessary to saving their lives, even though such actions are condemned from the rational egoist standpoint. If, less dramatically, a person autonomously decides to bestow an anonymous charitable donation sufficiently large to do herself some harm, she nevertheless has some reason to carry through with her resolution. Reasons here, as in the soldier case, may also stem from the needs of those the agent is trying to help. But that isn't necessary to make the relevant point. All that is needed is a recognition that autonomous choices do sometimes supply reasons for action,

even though such choices may fail, and be known by the agent to fail, to promote the agent's own interests.

There are only two ways to dispute this anti-egoist conclusion. The first is simply to deny the independent value of autonomy. On this line, autonomous choice may in some cases supply reasons, but only derivatively – only because and to the extent that acting on such a choice promotes one's own welfare. As far as I am aware, however, there is no good argument for this conclusion – no sound argument that shows that autonomy is only derivatively valuable in this way.[5]

The alternative is to allow for the independent importance of autonomy, but to claim that autonomous choice and self-interest can never conflict, because autonomous choice invariably promotes self-interest: one has reason to Φ if and only if Φ-ing promotes one's self interest, and, necessarily, Φ-ing promotes one's self-interest *if* one autonomously chooses to Φ. But why think this? Why think it impossible for an agent to know that an action will damage his interests but to autonomously choose to do it anyway? It certainly seems possible that agents may, with relevantly full information and a minimum of external pressure, choose to perform actions that they believe will damage their interests. Surely the burden is on those who claim that in every such case the agent must either mistake his interests, be ignorant of relevant facts, or somehow be subject to far greater external pressure than was initially imagined.

The burden here is significant. We seem easily able to construct examples in which autonomous choice isn't attended by the relevant sorts of mistake, ignorance, or coercion. And there is a ready explanation for this. Autonomy in choice refers to the conditions under which the choice is made. Whether such choices promote self-interest is a matter of what effects ensue from these choices. Given the huge variety of factors that can influence the outcome of one's choices, it would be miraculous were there an invariant connection linking the conditions that define autonomous choice with a specific kind of effect resulting from such choice (namely, promoting self-interest).

[5]   One could clinch the argument by showing that one always has reason to do as one autonomously chooses; that, necessarily, autonomously choosing to Φ is a reason to Φ. This may be right, but I wouldn't want to rest my case on it. Even if it is false, however, one could still argue that autonomous choice is independently valuable, and that it often or usually supplies reasons for action. It would then be incumbent on the rational egoist to show that those cases in which it fails to supply reasons are precisely those in which one's welfare is sacrificed. I have not seen an argument for this conclusion that did not already presuppose the truth of rational egoism.

A second argument against rational egoism takes its inspiration from an argument against a strong form of ethical egoism, which claims that acts are right if and only if, *and because*, they (best) promote one's self-interest. The best criticism of this kind of ethical egoism points to its inability to justify its policy of preferential treatment. In effect, ethical egoism sanctions a policy in which each person gets to elevate his or her interests over all others. Such a policy is a departure from the default ethical position in which equals should receive equal treatment.

In response to the charge that ethical egoism licenses discriminatory treatment (because it sanctions treating the welfare of others as less important than one's own, without justifying this preference), egoists have two replies. The first is to accept that their theory *is* a policy of unequal treatment, but to deny that this is damaging, by citing a relevant feature that justifies such unequal treatment. The second is to argue that ethical egoism is not a policy of preferential treatment, but is perfectly egalitarian.

The second reply doesn't work. It says that egoism is egalitarian because it confers on every person the same privileges. *Everyone* gets to treat her interests as more important than anyone else's. But this is not enough to insulate the egoist from charges of undue preference. For the relevant context in which such charges are raised is one in which A has harmed B in order to benefit herself, A. B or anyone else can ask for justification. 'Because I'm me' isn't sufficient. And it won't do at such a juncture to say to B that she is permitted to do the same to A when she, B, gets the chance. A's treatment may prevent B from ever getting that chance. Further, that everyone gets to treat others abominably does not justify such treatment. Ethical egoism is egalitarian in one sense – everyone gets the same moral privileges. But it is inegalitarian in another – it allows one person to give herself complete priority over another for no reason other than the fact that she is the author of the action.

The other reply admits that ethical egoism is a policy of unequal treatment, but seeks to justify this policy by citing a relevant difference that justifies the inequality. Not all discrimination is bad – some students, for instance, deservedly get different grades from others. So long as one can cite a relevant difference that justifies the differential treatment, such treatment is completely above board. Now suppose that you've worked very hard

to earn what you have. Suppose also that I correctly judge that I would benefit by taking your goods by force. In that case, I am not only allowed to do so, but morally must do so. I am treating myself and you differently. What licenses such treatment? That I would benefit does not explain why I am allowed (or required) to give my own interests priority over yours, since you would benefit (or at least avoid harm) were I to refrain from the forcible taking.

There is a stronger and a weaker criticism of ethical egoism at work here. The stronger criticism, levelled by utilitarians, says that the fact that an act will promote one's own interests supplies no basis whatever for priority. The weaker criticism claims that this fact does give some reason for priority in some contexts, but that this priority is defeasible and is in fact often defeated by such things as other persons' deserts, needs, and interests. We need only the weaker claim to establish the anti-egoist point. We could go so far as to concede that it is just a brute fact that one is morally allowed to give some priority to oneself, while still demanding justification for the ethical egoist's claim that such priority is the only morally relevant consideration there is.

It strikes me that the rational egoist faces precisely the same objection. We might allow that it is simply a brute fact that there is always reason to promote one's self-interest. But we need an argument for thinking that this is the only non-derivative reason there could possibly be. Such a claim isn't self-evident, and it conflicts with some of our other very deeply held beliefs. The rational egoist claims that the only consideration that can support or justify an action is its conduciveness to self-interest. But why don't the like interests, needs, wants, and autonomous choices of others also constitute a basis for rationalizing action that serves them? They are different from one's own interests etc. in only one respect: that they are not one's own. Even if we concede (as many do not) that this difference makes some difference, why does it make *all* the difference? It seems instead simply to be an assertion of an unjustified policy of preferential treatment. What is it about oneself that gives one licence in every situation to give one's own concerns priority over others? That everyone has such licence does not justify it. It isn't clear what could possibly do so.

Rational egoism conflicts with many firm convictions we have about cases. It cannot accommodate a suitable role for autonomy in supplying reasons for action. And rational egoism forces us away from a default position of equality, in ways that are structurally similar to those of ethical egoism, and yet fails to justify the policy of preferential treatment that it is committed to.[6]

If in the end rational egoism is unsupported, then the Rational Egoist Argument fails to supply good grounds for rejecting moral rationalism. Consider, then, the *Analogical Argument*, which is clearly inspired by Philippa Foot's seminal article (1972).[7] Foot drew attention to a distinction between two senses in which imperatives can be said to be categorical. In the first sense, obligations or commands are categorical just in case they truly apply to an agent regardless of whether her desires are thereby satisfied or her interests thereby promoted. But, as Foot pointed out, one cannot infer from a demand's being categorical in this sense that it is also categorical in another sense – that of supplying a reason for anyone to whom it truly applies. As she argued, the demands of law or etiquette are such that they apply to an agent even if she doesn't want them to, and even if her interests aren't served by obedience to the demands. But whether one has any reason to comply with such demands is said to depend on the possible congruence between the content of the demand and one's desires or self-interest. Thus Foot: 'The fact is that the man who rejects morality because he sees no reason to obey its rules can be convicted of villainy but not of inconsistency. Nor will his action necessarily be irrational' (Foot 1972: 161–2). What we have reason to do depends on what serves our desires or interests. In some cases, neither our desires nor our interests will be promoted by acting morally. Therefore in some cases we lack reason to do as morality commands. Indifference to moral demands needn't be irrational.

As an argument from analogy, this can't be absolutely watertight, but it can shift the burden of proof to the rationalist, who, in the face of this argument, must take either of two options. The first is to argue that the demands of law and etiquette are in fact necessarily reason-giving. (I don't

find this a particular plausible direction to take.) The alternative is allow that they are not, but to point up a relevant disanalogy between moral requirements and those of law and etiquette.

[. . .]

In pursuing this latter alternative, we are conceding that there are requirements that are categorical in one sense without being categorical in another: such requirements apply to individuals regardless of their ends, but do not necessarily supply such individuals with any reason for action. It is incumbent on the moral rationalist to explain this.

The explanation, I believe, invokes the idea of jurisdiction. A jurisdiction comprises a set of standards that dictate behaviour for a defined set of members.[8] The rules of etiquette, or those of a board game, do not necessarily supply reasons for action, because they are not necessarily applicable; they are inapplicable to all who find themselves outside the relevant jurisdictions. A variety of factors can explain one's extra-jurisdictional status. An accident of birth explains why I am not subject to the civil statutes of Ethiopia. An autonomous choice explains why the code of the local Teamsters union does not apply to me. The choices of others explain why I am not bound to uphold the duties of a Prime Minister or President. For these reasons, and others, the strictures of the relevant domain (law, etiquette, fraternal societies, etc.) may fail to apply in a given case. And if such standards fail to apply to one's conduct, then a fortiori they will fail to supply one with reasons for action.

In this sense, the scope of the relevant rules is limited. As I see it, this limit is explained by the *conventional origin* of such rules. For any given convention, whether it be focused on law, etiquette, or play, one may lack reason to adhere to its rules because one is not a party to the convention. The requirements of law, etiquette, and games are all circumscribed. For any requirements of conventional origin, it is always in principle possible to

---

[6] The most plausible arguments that have been offered on behalf of rational egoism are carefully dissected and shown to be unsound in Shaver 1999. This short book is wonderfully lucid, rigorously argued, and compelling in its rejection of the principal arguments offered on behalf of rational egoism.

[7] Foot has since withdrawn her support for the central conclusions of this influential article. See Foot 2001: 60ff.

[8] The set may be defined territorially, as in the law, or may be defined by voluntary allegiance, as with a charitable association or bridge club, etc. Discussion of the different sources of membership is important for other contexts, especially political philosophy, but doesn't much matter here.

find oneself outside the jurisdiction. The reasons generated by conventional rules are therefore reasons that exist only contingently.

Morality is different. Its scope is pervasive. Every action is morally evaluable – even if the pronouncement is simply one of permissibility. There is no exiting the 'morality game'. One may renounce morality, may act without regard to the moral status of one's conduct, may in fact act with the intention of behaving immorally, but all such dissociative strategies do not free one from susceptibility to moral assessment. This distinguishes moral requirements from those in the law, etiquette, or games. Requirements of law, etiquette, etc. are only contingently applicable, and so only contingently reason-giving. Moral requirements do not exhibit this sort of contingency.

What explains this special character of moral assessment? I think it must be that morality is objective, in the sense that its true claims are correct independently of whether anyone thinks so. We don't create the principles that generate moral requirements. The principles are not constituted by, and do not apply to us in virtue of, conventional agreements. Moral requirements are inescapable because they are not of our own making.

This does not explain why moral rationalism is true. The pervasive scope of moral evaluation does not explain why moral facts are necessarily reason-giving. But it does serve as the basis for resisting the Analogical Argument, because a relevant disanalogy among kinds of desire-independent requirements has been identified. Not every categorical requirement is necessarily reason-giving, because some such requirements are conventional in origin, and so supply reasons only contingently. Morality's content is not conventionally fixed, and so we lack this basis for thinking that it supplies reasons only contingently.

This reply assumes that moral requirements are not conventional. If morality is conventional, then the Analogical Argument, so far as I can see, is sound, and moral rationalism must go by the board. But to assume that morality is conventional at this point is just to beg the question against [. . .] the moral rationalist, by supposing that his favoured reply to the Analogical Argument cannot work. By contrast, there is nothing question-begging *at this stage* about assuming the truth of moral realism, since realism by itself is neutral with respect to moral rationalism – many realists reject moral rationalism.

It would be question-begging to allow the truth of moral realism if the arguments we have been discussing were designed to prove its truth. But they have not had that aim. Instead, the focus is on defence of moral rationalism, as one part of a larger project of showing that realism does not fail to properly account for the normativity of morality. To test that hypothesis, one must assume realism's truth and examine its implications. If my argument thus far is sound, one of these important implications is that realism can, in fact, be enlisted on behalf of moral rationalism in its defence against an otherwise quite powerful argument. Moral realism is compatible with, and indeed supports, moral rationalism.

[. . .]

Partners in Crime

All of this still leaves us short of an account of why moral facts *are* intrinsically reason-giving – thus far we have attempted to display the attractions of rationalism, and have tried to undermine the critiques of rationalism, but haven't offered any concrete explanation of *why* moral facts supply reasons (for action or evaluation). The intrinsic moral rationalist does not explain the normativity of moral facts by positing a necessary connection between them and other kinds of intrinsically reason-giving considerations. But if this explanatory route is barred, what other route is available?

The worry here is the same as that which besets accounts of candidate intrinsic values. We ordinarily explain the value of something by displaying its relation to something else acknowledged to be intrinsically valuable. But when one's candidate intrinsic values are themselves questioned, this strategy must fail. Suppose one claims that any situation in which an innocent child is maimed solely to produce pleasure for his tormentor is bad, in itself. Isn't this true? But there's very little one can say to someone who understands the proposition and still doesn't believe this. The intrinsic moral rationalist is in much the same boat when defending the normativity of moral facts. According to her, there is no more fundamental kind of normative consideration from which moral facts can derive their reason-giving force. But just as the inability to cite a more fundamental consideration doesn't necessarily undermine the claim about intrinsic value, so too it needn't undermine the claim about normativity. One must recognize the limits of normative explanation.

That said, rationalists must concede that their favoured theory does not enjoy the same degree of endorsement as the verdict we reach in the example in which a child is maimed. But this shouldn't be seen as a stumbling block to acceptance of rationalism. Intrinsic moral rationalism is a much more complicated, less obviously correct, and less immediately appealing view than the one expressed in the example. Further, the parallel with defending claims of intrinsic value should alert us to the difficulty of justification in these contexts. Justification here is a matter of defusing arguments designed to undermine the relevant view, and adducing some non-conclusive considerations that favour it. In case such a strategy is thought by its nature to be too weak to establish the requisite degree of justification, we need to remind ourselves that this is all that can be hoped for even for those theories of practical reasons whose allegiance is much broader than moral rationalism. The brute inexplicability of the normativity of moral facts is not different in kind from that which bests other, familiar theories of practical reasons.

Consider both rational egoism and instrumentalism. Proponents of these theories claim, respectively, that self-interest or desire satisfaction are the sole kind of intrinsically reason-giving consideration. Defence of such views always consists in offering replies to criticisms, and evidence far short of demonstrable proof as positive support for their views. Indeed, on the assumption that self-interest is not identical with or best measured exclusively by desire satisfaction, at least one of these popular theories must be false.

Both rational egoism and instrumentalism are often favourably compared to intrinsic moral rationalism on explanatory grounds. Their preferred source of reasons – agents' contingent interests or desires – themselves pose no special metaphysical puzzles, and their content offers ready, if fallible, epistemic access. This is meant to contrast with rationalism's mysterious invocation of intrinsic reasons. Yet the central claim of each of rationalism's competitors here is nothing other than the insistence that interests or desires are themselves intrinsically normative. It is reasonable to ask how interests or desires can possess this special status. And why do only interests or desires, as opposed

to logical implications, various empirical truths, and moral facts, possess this special property? Egoists or instrumentalists about reasons also have some explaining to do. Here is a particular kind of fact – Φ-ing satisfies one's desires, or promotes one's interests. And to this we attach a very special property – that of supplying in itself a reason for action. To the extent that this property is mysterious, the mystery attaches equally to egoism or instrumentalism.

The relevant point here is that strategies for defending any such view – any candidate for intrinsically normative consideration – are similar across the board. The rational egoist will not be able to point to a kind of normative consideration more fundamental than self-interest, to which the reason-giving force of self-interest is of necessity related. The instrumentalist is likewise handicapped when trying to establish the intrinsic normativity of desire satisfaction. This kind of explanatory failure is not itself an argument against any one of these theories. In response to the charge that intrinsic moral rationalists are unable to explain the normativity of moral facts, rationalists should be prepared to point to partners in crime. They needn't look very far.

Conclusion

Moral rationalism can survive the strongest arguments designed to undermine it. The Reasons Internalist Argument, the Rational Egoist Argument, and the Analogical Argument do not, in the end, point up insuperable difficulties for the rationalist. There are strong considerations to do with the conceptual coherence and the fairness of moral evaluation that support moral rationalism. And intrinsic rationalism's insistence on the irreducibly normative character of moral facts should not be an impediment to its acceptance. Any problem that may arise in this context is one shared by rationalism's competitors – they do not deny intrinsic normativity, but rather assign it to something other than moral facts.

If I am right, one always has reason to do as morality says. Whether this is the best possible reason – whether moral considerations are invariably overriding – is another matter. One can't settle that issue without having in hand a theory of normative ethics, an inventory of non-moral reasons, and a method for measuring their relative strength.

We don't need to undertake such extensive investigations to establish the more circumscribed defence of rationalism that is the focus of the present chapter.

[. . .]

I would be remiss if I failed to note a potentially unsettling consequence of the views about moral reasons that have been advanced thus far. We were able to assess the merits of reasons internalism and moral rationalism in ways that were relatively independent of each other. Now it is time to consider how well these discussions sit with one another. It must be said that the combination of rejecting reasons internalism and endorsing moral rationalism can be bracing. This combination yields a view according to which we may have moral reasons that are inaccessible to us – there may be no sound deliberative path that could take us to such reasons from our existing outlook. There is something undemocratic about such a view. We like to think that moral wisdom is equally available to all, or at least all of those sufficiently inspired to exercise their imagination and reasoning. The above-mentioned combination gives us no guarantee that such success is possible.

This may be dispiriting, but is not by itself an adequate ground to call into doubt what has come before. The present combination of views forces us to the conclusion that some people will be blind to the moral obligations incumbent upon them. They will fail to see what they must do, even were they to reason perfectly from their present outlook. Theirs is a make-up so morally askew that nothing therein is rationally related to moral demands. I think it only unwarranted optimism to discount such a possibility.

[. . .]

What all of this boils down to is the possibility that we may have nothing convincing to say to a Gyges, or to a sufficiently cunning Thrasymachus or Foole. Even were they able to reason perfectly from the motivations they find themselves with, they might have nothing but a sneer and the back of their hands for those who counsel a moral path. Perhaps even these people are within reach, but reaching them will not be a matter of pointing out how their existing motivations are rationally related to the moral ends they at present do not share. Perhaps everyone, at some point in his or her life, was indeed capable of forming the sorts of motivations from which morality can be gained. But straitened circumstances and a history of poor choices can bring one to the point where all the rational extensions of one's outlook make morality seem a sucker's game. Some will seek to certify the edicts of such an outlook, restricting reasons to those considerations that can be vindicated by its rational extensions. Unsurprisingly, I think the preferred path is to convict such individuals of a (possibly ineliminable) blindness to the moral reasons that genuinely apply to them. The circumstances that generate such blindness, and the blindness itself, are often tragic. But we do best to see such tragedies for what they are, rather than to try to explain them away.

References

Cohon, Rachel. 1993. 'Internalism about Reasons for Action.' *Pacific Philosophical Quarterly*, 74: 265–88.

Falk, W. D. 1948. '"Ought" and Motivation.' *Proceedings of the Aristotelian Society*, 48: 111–38.

Foot, Philippa. 1972. 'Morality as a System of Hypothetical Imperatives.' In Foot 1978b.

Foot, Philippa. 1978b. *Virtues and Vices*. Berkeley and Los Angeles: University of California Press.

Foot, Philippa. 2001. *Natural Goodness*. Oxford: Oxford University Press.

Korsgaard, Christine 1986. 'Skepticism about Practical Reason.' *Journal of Philosophy*, 83: 5–25.

Millgram, Elijah. 1996. 'Williams' Argument against External Reasons.' *Noûs*, 30: 197–220.

Nagel, Thomas. 1970. *The Possibility of Altruism*. Oxford: Oxford University Press.

Scanlon, Thomas. 1998. *What We Owe to Each Other*. Cambridge, MA: Harvard University Press.

Shaver, Robert. 1999. *Rational Egoism*. Cambridge: Cambridge University Press.

Williams, Bernard. 1981a. 'Internal and External Reasons.' In Williams 1981b.

Williams, Bernard. 1981b. *Moral Luck*. Cambridge: Cambridge University Press.

Williams, Bernard. 1989. 'Internal Reasons and the Obscurity of Blame.' In Williams 1995.

Williams, Bernard. 1995. *Making Sense of Humanity*. Cambridge: Cambridge University Press.

II.3   Moral Explanations

Introduction

The claim that moral features explain things that happen in the world is not new. As far back as Plato's *Phaedo*, one can find a defense of the idea that moral features are (in some sense) causes. What is of relatively recent vintage, however, is the challenge to moral realist views that moral facts are explanatorily superfluous. As it is ordinarily formulated, this challenge is driven by a commitment to what we can call "the Explanatory Principle." According to this principle,

> We have reason to believe that moral facts exist only if such facts play explanatory roles R.

Moral antirealists have urged that moral facts would have to play a certain range of explanatory roles were they to exist – call these roles "the requisite explanatory roles" – and that moral facts fail to play these roles. Realists have ordinarily replied to this charge in two ways. Realists who offer a conciliatory response accept both the Explanatory Principle and the claim that moral facts exist only if they play the requisite explanatory roles. They deny, however, that moral facts fail to play these roles. Realists who offer a less conciliatory response also embrace the Explanatory Principle, but deny that the antirealists have identified the sorts of explanatory role that moral facts would play were they to exist. These philosophers maintain that we should expect moral facts to play explanatory roles of a different sort, and that moral facts do in fact play these roles. There is presently, then, a three-sided debate between antirealists and realists of a more and less conciliatory sort concerning the explanatory profile of putative moral facts. Given the terms of the debate, progress in it hinges on answering two questions: what are the requisite explanatory roles we should expect moral facts to play were they to exist? And do moral facts play these roles?[1]

When Gilbert Harman introduced the challenge that moral facts are explanatorily superfluous nearly thirty years ago, he did so by way of what are now two well-known cases (see Harman 1977: ch. 1, which is included in this section). Suppose, says Harman, you round a corner only to witness several hoodlums pouring gasoline on a cat and then igniting it. Upon having this experience, you immediately judge that their behavior is wrong. Your judgment, it would seem, is not the product of a fast piece of reasoning. You can, as it were, simply *see* that burning the cat is wrong. Contrast this case with a second: you're a physicist and you observe a vapor trail in a cloud chamber. Upon observing this, you immediately form the judgment "There goes a proton." Again, your judgment doesn't appear to be the result of a swift piece of reasoning; it appears to be an observation of a proton.

If Harman is right, these two cases are crucially different. The fact that you judge that the behavior of the hoodlums is wrong is best explained by ordinary features of your psychology (you've been trained to view actions of this sort as wrong) and ordinary nonmoral features of what you observe (that the hoodlums have ignited the cat). Thus, the wrongness of their behavior does not best explain why you judge as you do. By contrast, the fact that you judge that a proton has moved through the cloud chamber is not best explained by ordinary features of your psychology (say, that you've been trained to believe vapor trails in cloud chambers are indicative of the presence of protons) and ordinary features of a proton-less world. The best explanation of your observation in this case is that there *is* a proton that has moved through the cloud chamber.

Harman's argument, then, seems to be this:

1 We have reason to believe that moral facts exist only if such facts play the requisite explanatory role(s) R.
2 The requisite explanatory role of moral facts is that they best explain the formation of our moral judgments.
3 Moral facts do not best explain the formation of our moral judgments.
4 So, we do not have reason to believe there are moral facts.

However, as the ensuing debate between Harman and his critics has made evident, it is not as if moral antirealists accept the claim that moral facts fail to explain only the formation of moral judgments. Rather, the antirealist claim is that there is *nothing worth explaining* that moral facts best explain. While antirealists have offered nothing like a developed account of what is worth explaining (or, for that matter, what it is to "best" explain something), philosophers such as Crispin Wright have suggested that the following must at least be true were moral facts to exist: such facts would have to explain the existence of a sufficiently wide array of types of nonmoral fact (see Wright 1992: ch. 5). According to Wright, an ordinary descriptive fact such as *that the rocks are wet* can explain the existence of a wide array of types of fact, including the facts *that I perceive the rocks to be wet*, *that I've slipped and fallen*, and *that there is an abundance of lichen growing on the rocks*. It is precisely the failure of putative moral facts to play

this wide explanatory role, suggests Wright, that speaks against their existence. Accordingly, when Harman's argument is generalized to accommodate this point about explanatory width, it runs something like this:

1 We have reason to believe that moral facts exist only if such facts play the requisite explanatory role(s) R.
2 The requisite explanatory role of moral facts is that they best explain the existence of a sufficiently wide array of nonmoral facts of certain kinds.
3 Moral facts do not best explain the existence of a sufficiently wide array of nonmoral facts of these kinds.
4 So, we do not have reason to believe there are moral facts.

Earlier it was suggested that realists have responded to this argument in two ways. Let's consider these types of response.

The "conciliatory" realist response has come from naturalistic moral realists. Three claims define this position. First, according to these philosophers, moral facts are, or are constituted by, ordinary natural facts – facts, roughly, that pull their explanatory weight in the sciences. Second, these philosophers typically deny that our ordinary moral concepts can be defined entirely in terms of nonmoral or austerely naturalistic concepts. Unlike the moral naturalists whom G. E. Moore engaged with at the outset of the twentieth century, then, contemporary moral naturalists deny that we can satisfactorily elucidate moral concepts only in terms of those concepts employed in physics, biology, or the like. Third, these philosophers have generally assumed that the requisite explanatory roles that moral facts must play are causal. Interestingly, in this sense, moral naturalist views are often somewhat more restrictive than their antirealist counterparts, for neither Harman nor Wright claims that the requisite explanatory roles that moral facts would have to play are causal. (For more on moral naturalism, see part I.5, "Moral Realism.")

In his defense of moral naturalism, Nicholas Sturgeon has argued that we commonly offer moral explanations that attest to the causal efficacy of moral facts (see Sturgeon 1985, which is included in this section). Take, for example, a case in which

Hitler orders and oversees the execution of millions of people. It is Hitler's depraved moral character, Sturgeon suggests, that explains (at least in part) why so many went to their deaths in concentration camps in Europe during the middle of the twentieth century. Had Hitler not been morally depraved, then (all other things being equal) this would not have happened. Or take a case in which the citizens of a given country revolt against an oppressive and brutal regime to which they've been subject. It is the injustice of the regime's behavior, the suggestion is, that explains (at least in part) why the citizens revolt. Had the regime not been unjust, then (all other things being equal) the citizens would not have revolted. Or, finally, consider a case in which a young child lives a flourishing life in which she is physically healthy and mentally well adjusted to a high degree. It is because this child has been raised in a decent and humane way, the suggestion goes, that she enjoys this degree of flourishing. Had the child not been so raised, it is reasonable to think, then (all other things being equal), that the child would not thrive in this way.

These three cases are designed to show that we appeal to moral facts when trying to explain states of affairs and events in the world such as killings, revolts, and human well-being. They are, it is further suggested, easily extended to account for cases such as the one Harman himself furnished in the original presentation of his argument: the fact that Hitler was depraved explains (at least in part) why he instigated the deaths of millions of persons. And the fact that Hitler behaved in this way explains why ordinary agents believe that he was depraved. So, the fact that Hitler was depraved explains (at least in part) why ordinary agents believe that he was depraved. If this is right, moral facts do play a fairly wide explanatory role, explaining not only social events and the well-being of human agents, but also the formation of moral judgments of certain kinds. Briefly put, if the type of moral naturalism that Sturgeon defends is true, the third premise of the revised version of Harman's argument is false.

Sturgeon adds to this the following points: it is possible to object that, in each of these cases, it is not the putative moral features that explain the phenomena in question, but rather the underlying "subvenient" natural features that determine or constitute these moral features. But, Sturgeon argues, this is a dangerous strategy of response to

embrace. After all, if one were to apply this type of strategy in the natural and social sciences, it would threaten to undermine many of the types of explanation they offer. In social scientific explanations, for example, one could also claim that it is not the supervenient macro features such as beliefs and desires that explain an agent's behavior, but rather the underlying micro features such as her brain states. And, arguably, this is an unwelcome result for moral antirealists and realists alike, for adherents to both views do not wish to commit themselves to the causal indolence of those macro features referred to in social scientific explanations. Second, if this broad line of response is correct, it follows that realists have not only a plausible response to the antirealist challenge, but also independent evidence for the existence of moral facts. It is, it would seem, plausible to believe that if a putative entity figures in our best explanations of certain ordinary, natural events, we have excellent reason to believe it exists.

Needless to say, the antirealists have not been convinced. Harman's favored way of stating his discontent with the moral naturalist response is to claim that, despite its label, moral naturalism is insufficiently naturalistic. In the first place, Harman argues, if the contents of moral claims actually enter into genuine explanatory contexts, then they should be able to be tested empirically "in all the ways in which scientific claims can be tested" (Harman 1986: 64). But no scientists seem to appeal to moral facts when doing serious science. And this suggests that moral facts do not have the credentials for being genuine naturalistic facts, despite the claims of moral naturalists. Moreover, what is conspicuously missing from moral naturalism is any account of "*how* moral facts can be manifested in the world in a way that allows the relevant testing" (Harman 1986: 67; emphasis added). In Harman's view, were moral facts to exist, they would have to explain the formation of moral judgment. But it is incumbent on the naturalist, so Harman suggests, to furnish some kind of account of how they could do this. Merely putting forth arguments *that* moral facts play various explanatory roles without getting at the explanatory mechanisms is insufficient.

Harman's discontent with the naturalist response to his challenge to moral realism expresses an allegiance to a fairly robust empiricist methodology. Arguably, it is this commitment to empiricism, shared to some degree by moral antirealists and naturalists alike, that has provoked the second, less conciliatory realist response to Harman's argument. (For an example of such a response, see Shafer-Landau's contribution in chapter 16 of this volume.) This second type of response expresses the conviction that there is something fundamentally wrongheaded about the manner in which antirealists and their naturalist opponents have conducted the debate. The debate has assumed that, if moral facts exist, then fundamental to their job description is that they be causes or pull their explanatory weight in the sciences. This, according to the so-called nonnaturalist realists, seems to ask both too much and too little of moral facts.

It asks too much because our ordinary conception of moral facts has it that such facts are or imply moral *reasons* – that is, considerations that favor or justify morally appropriate responses of various kinds from us. To require that such facts also pull their explanatory weight in the sciences – disciplines not particularly concerned with how we morally ought to behave – seems to foist upon them a job description that is not theirs. The requirement asks too little because, by insisting that moral facts are nothing over and above ordinary natural facts, the moral naturalist has arguably omitted from the job description of moral facts what is essential to them, namely, their status as entities that give us moral reasons to behave in certain fashions. So, rather than reject the third premise of the revised version of Harman's argument, as do moral naturalists, moral nonnaturalists maintain that it is the second premise of the argument that should be rejected.

Rejecting the second premise of the antirealist argument, say advocates of the less conciliatory response claim, should not lead us to believe that moral facts fail to play any sorts of interesting explanatory role. If anything, we should believe that, if moral facts exist, then they play explanatory roles different from what parties to the debate between moral antirealists and moral naturalists have claimed. And what sorts of explanatory role are these? Various suggestions have been offered,

but here is one example: moral facts of certain kinds, the nonnaturalists claim, appear tailor-made to figure in justificatory explanatory contexts. For example, it would seem the fact *that giving a significant portion of one's income to aid those in poverty is just* explains why appropriately placed agents ought to give their money to institutions such as Oxfam. That acting in this way is just doesn't *cause* agents to give money to Oxfam or similar institutions; rather, it *justifies* it. If Jean Hampton is right, explanations of this sort should not be unfamiliar to philosophers, for they are simply teleological explanations of a certain kind: they assume (1) that there is a state of affairs that ought to obtain (our giving money to Oxfam), (2) that we can grasp it, and (3) that we ought to act for the sake of bringing about this state of affairs. (See Hampton 1998: 113 and chapter 15 of this volume, which includes sections from Hampton's book.) Admittedly, Hampton contends, explanations of this sort do not sit well with a thoroughgoing naturalism, since it has been a defining mark of naturalism to reject teleological explanations. But, says Hampton, this is not itself reason to be suspicious of explanations of this kind.

The three-party debate to which the controversy regarding moral explanation has given rise, then, is instructive inasmuch as it reveals the extent to which different metaethical positions are driven by antecedent commitments to broader metaphysical and epistemological positions such as naturalism, nonnaturalism, and empiricism. But lest the divisions between these different views appear overly stark, it is worth adding that a certain amount of eclecticism regarding moral explanation seems a viable option. One might hold, as Terence Cuneo does in his contribution to this section, that moral facts of certain kinds – say, the virtues and their exercise – are well suited to enter into causal explanations of the way in which agents behave. In this sense, they are plausibly viewed as being naturalistic in some sense of this term. Still, one might believe this about the virtues and also deny that moral facts of other kinds – say, basic moral standards or norms – are similarly naturalistic.

Note

1   Some philosophers, such as Shafer-Landau 2003: ch. 4, appear to reject the Explanatory Principle altogether. Arguably, however, these philosophers are best understood to reject particular versions of the principle in which the requisite explanatory roles are restricted to causal explanatory roles.

Selected Bibliography

Adams, Robert. 1999. *Finite and Infinite Goods*. Oxford: Oxford University Press, ch. 2.

Audi, Robert. 1997. "Ethical Naturalism and the Explanatory Power of Moral Concepts." In *Moral Knowledge and Ethical Character*. Oxford: Oxford University Press.

Blackburn, Simon. 1993. "Just Causes." In *Essays in Quasi-Realism*. Cambridge: Cambridge University Press.

Boyd, Richard. 1988. "How to be a Moral Realist." In Geoffrey Sayre-McCord, ed. *Essays on Moral Realism*. Ithaca: Cornell University Press.

Brink, David. 1989. *Moral Realism and the Foundations of Ethics*. Cambridge: Cambridge University Press, ch. 7.

Cohen, Joshua. 1997. "The Arc of the Moral Universe." *Philosophy and Public Affairs* 26: 91–134.

Copp, David. 1990. "Explanation and Justification in Ethics." *Ethics* 100: 237–58.

Cuneo, Terence. 2003. "Moral Explanations, Minimalism, and Cognitive Command." *The Southern Journal of Philosophy* 41: 351–65.

Cuneo, Terence. 2006. "Moral Facts as Configuring Causes." *Pacific Philosophical Quarterly* 87: 141–62.

Dworkin, Ronald. 1996. "Objectivity and Truth: You'd Better Believe It." *Philosophy and Public Affairs* 25: 87–139.

Enoch, David. 2003. "An Argument for Robust Metanormative Realism." Doctoral dissertation, New York University.

Gibbard, Allan. 1990. *Wise Choices, Apt Feelings*. Cambridge, MA: Harvard University Press, ch. 6.

Hampton, Jean. 1998. *The Authority of Reason*. Cambridge: Cambridge University Press, chs. 1 and 3.

Harman, Gilbert. 1977. *The Nature of Morality*. Oxford: Oxford University Press, ch. 1.

Harman, Gilbert, and Judith Jarvis Thomson. 1996. *Moral Relativism and Moral Objectivity*. Oxford: Blackwell.

Johnson, Robert N. 1998. "Minding One's Manners: Revisiting Moral Explanations." *Philosophical Studies* 90: 181–203.

Leiter, Brian. 2001. "Moral Facts and Best Explanations." In Ellen F. Paul, Fred D. Miller, and Jeffrey Paul, eds. *Moral Knowledge*. Cambridge: Cambridge University Press.

Loeb, Don. 2005. "Moral Explanation and Moral Beliefs." *Philosophy and Phenomenological Research* 67: 193–207.

Majors, Brad. 2003. "Moral Explanation and the Special Sciences." *Philosophical Studies* 113: 121–52.

McGinn, Colin. 1997. *Ethics, Evil, and Fiction*. Oxford: Oxford University Press, ch. 2.

Miller, Alexander. 2003. *An Introduction to Contemporary Metaethics*. Cambridge: Polity, ch. 8.

Nagel, Thomas. 1986. *The View from Nowhere*. Oxford: Oxford University Press, ch. 8.

Quinn, Warren. 1986. "Truth and Explanation in Ethics." *Ethics* 96: 524–44. Reprinted in *Morality and Action*. Cambridge: Cambridge University Press, 1993.

Railton, Peter. 1985. "Moral Realism." *Philosophical Review* 95: 163–207.

Railton, Peter. 1993. "Reply to Wiggins." In John Haldane and Crispin Wright, eds. *Reality, Representation, and Projection*. Oxford: Oxford University Press.

Sayre-McCord, Geoffrey. 1988. "Moral Theory and Explanatory Impotence." In Geoffrey Sayre-McCord, ed. *Essays on Moral Realism*. Ithaca: Cornell University Press.

Sayre-McCord, Geoffrey. 1992. "Normative Explanations." In James Tomberlin, ed. *Philosophical Perspectives 6: Ethics*. Atascadero, CA: Ridgeview Publishing.

Shafer-Landau, Russ. 2003. *Moral Realism: A Defence*. Oxford: Oxford University Press, ch. 4.

Sturgeon, Nicholas. 1985. "Moral Explanations." In David Copp and David Zimmerman, eds. *Morality, Reason and Truth*. Totowa, NJ: Rowman & Allanheld.

Sturgeon, Nicholas. 1986. "Harman on Moral Explanations of Natural Facts." *The Southern Journal of Philosophy* 24, supplement: 69–78.

Sturgeon, Nicholas. 1991. "Contents and Causes: A Reply to Blackburn." *Philosophical Studies* 61: 9–37.

Sturgeon, Nicholas. 1992. "Nonmoral Explanations." In James Tomberlin, ed. *Philosophical Perspectives, 6: Ethics*. Atascadero, CA: Ridgeview Publishing.

Sturgeon, Nicholas. 1995. "Evil and Explanation." In Jocelyne Couture and Kai Nielsen, eds. *On the Relevance of Metaethics: New Essays on Metaethics*. Calgary: University of Calgary Press.

Thomson, Judith Jarvis. 1996. "Epistemological Arguments for Moral Scepticism." In Gilbert Harman and Judith Jarvis Thomson. *Moral Relativism and Moral Objectivity*. Oxford: Blackwell.

Thomson, Judith Jarvis. 1998. "Reply to Critics." *Philosophy and Phenomenological Research* 68: 215–22.

Wedgwood, Ralph. Unpublished. "Normative Explanations."

Wiggins, David. 1990. "Moral Cognitivism, Moral Relativism, and Motivating Moral Beliefs." *Proceedings of the Aristotelian Society* 91: 61–85.

Williams, Bernard. 1985. *Ethics and the Limits of Philosophy*. Cambridge, MA: Harvard University Press, ch. 8.

Wright, Crispin. 1992. *Truth and Objectivity*. Cambridge, MA: Harvard University Press, ch. 5.

Wright, Crispin. 1995. "Truth in Ethics." *Ratio* 8: 209–26.

Yasenchuk, Ken. 1994. "Sturgeon and Brink on Moral Explanations." *The Southern Journal of Philosophy* 32: 483–501.

Zimmerman, David. 1985. "Moral Realism and Explanatory Necessity." In David Copp and David Zimmerman, eds. *Morality, Reason and Truth*. Totowa, NJ: Rowman & Allanheld.

25

Ethics and Observation

Gilbert Harman

1. The Basic Issue

Can moral principles be tested and confirmed in the way scientific principles can? Consider the principle that, if you are given a choice between five people alive and one dead or five people dead and one alive, you should always choose to have five people alive and one dead rather than the other way round. We can easily imagine examples that appear to confirm this principle. Here is one:

> You are a doctor in a hospital's emergency room when six accident victims are brought in. All six are in danger of dying but one is much worse off than the others. You can just barely save that person if you devote all of your resources to him and let the others die. Alternatively, you can save the other five if you are willing to ignore the most seriously injured person.

It would seem that in this case you, the doctor, would be right to save the five and let the other person die. So this example, taken by itself, confirms the principle under consideration. Next, consider the following case.

> You have five patients in the hospital who are dying, each in need of a separate organ. One needs a kidney, another a lung, a third a heart, and so forth. You can save all five if you take a single healthy person and remove his heart, lungs, kidneys, and so forth, to distribute to these five patients. Just such a healthy

person is in room 306. He is in the hospital for routine tests. Having seen his test results, you know that he is perfectly healthy and of the right tissue compatibility. If you do nothing, he will survive without incident; the other patients will die, however. The other five patients can be saved only if the person in Room 306 is cut up and his organs distributed. In that case, there would be one dead but five saved.

The principle in question tells us that you should cut up the patient in Room 306. But in this case, surely you must not sacrifice this innocent bystander, even to save the five other patients. Here a moral principle has been tested and disconfirmed in what may seem to be a surprising way.

This, of course, was a "thought experiment." We did not really compare a hypothesis with the world. We compared an explicit principle with our feelings about certain imagined examples. In the same way, a physicist performs thought experiments in order to compare explicit hypotheses with his "sense" of what should happen in certain situations, a "sense" that he has acquired as a result of his long working familiarity with current theory. But scientific hypotheses can also be tested in real experiments, out in the world.

Can moral principles be tested in the same way, out in the world? You can observe someone do something, but can you ever perceive the rightness or wrongness of what he does? If you round a corner and see a group of young hoodlums pour gasoline on a cat and ignite it, you do not need to *conclude* that what they are doing is wrong; you do not need to figure anything out; you can *see* that it is wrong. But is your reaction due to the actual wrongness of what you see or is it simply a reflection of your moral "sense," a "sense" that you have acquired perhaps as a result of your moral upbringing?

2.   Observation

The issue is complicated. There are no pure observations. Observations are always "theory laden." What you perceive depends to some extent on the theory you hold, consciously or unconsciously. You see some children pour gasoline on a cat and ignite it. To really see that, you have to possess a great deal of knowledge, know about a considerable number of objects, know about people: that people pass through the life stages infant, baby, child, adolescent, adult. You must know what flesh and blood animals are, and in particular, cats. You must have some idea of life. You must know what gasoline is, what burning is, and much more. In one sense, what you "see" is a pattern of light on your retina, a shifting array of splotches, although even that is theory, and you could never adequately describe what you see in that sense. In another sense, you see what you do because of the theories you hold. Change those theories and you would see something else, given the same pattern of light.

Similarly, if you hold a moral view, whether it is held consciously or unconsciously, you will be able to perceive rightness or wrongness, goodness or badness, justice or injustice. There is no difference in this respect between moral propositions and other theoretical propositions. If there is a difference, it must be found elsewhere.

Observation depends on theory because perception involves forming a belief as a fairly direct result of observing something; you can form a belief only if you understand the relevant concepts and a concept is what it is by virtue of its role in some theory or system of beliefs. To recognize a child as a child is to employ, consciously or unconsciously, a concept that is defined by its place in a framework of the stages of human life. Similarly, burning is an empty concept apart from its theoretical connections to the concepts of heat, destruction, smoke, and fire.

Moral concepts – Right and Wrong, Good and Bad, Justice and Injustice – also have a place in your theory or system of beliefs and are the concepts they are because of their context. If we say that observation has occurred whenever an opinion is a direct result of perception, we must allow that there is moral observation, because such an opinion can be a moral opinion as easily as any other sort. In this sense, observation may be used to confirm or disconfirm moral theories. The observational opinions that, in this sense, you find yourself with can be in either agreement or conflict with your consciously explicit moral principles. When they are in conflict, you must choose between your explicit theory and observation. In ethics, as in science, you sometimes opt for theory, and say that you made an error in observation or were biased or whatever, or you sometimes opt for observation, and modify your theory.

In other words, in both science and ethics, general principles are invoked to explain particular cases and, therefore, in both science and ethics, the general principles you accept can be tested by appealing to particular judgments that certain things are right or wrong, just or unjust, and so forth; and these judgments are analogous to direct perceptual judgments about facts.

3.   Observational Evidence

Nevertheless, observation plays a role in science that it does not seem to play in ethics. The difference is that you need to make assumptions about certain physical facts to explain the occurrence of the observations that support a scientific theory, but you do not seem to need to make assumptions about any moral facts to explain the occurrence of the so-called moral observations I have been talking about. In the moral case, it would seem that you need only make assumptions about the psychology or moral sensibility of the person making the moral observation. In the scientific case, theory is tested against the world.

The point is subtle but important. Consider a physicist making an observation to test a scientific theory. Seeing a vapor trail in a cloud chamber, he thinks, "There goes a proton." Let us suppose that this is an observation in the relevant sense, namely, an immediate judgment made in response to the situation without any conscious reasoning having taken place. Let us also suppose that his observation confirms his theory, a theory that helps give meaning to the very term "proton" as it occurs in his observational judgment. Such a confirmation rests on inferring an explanation. He can count his making the observation as confirming evidence for his theory only to the extent that it is reasonable to explain his making the observation by assuming that, not only is he in a certain psychological "set," given the theory he accepts and his beliefs about the experimental apparatus, but furthermore, there really was a proton going through the cloud chamber, causing the vapor trail, which he saw as a proton. (This is evidence for the theory to the extent that the theory can explain the proton's being there better than competing theories can.) But, if his having made that observation could have been equally well explained by his psychological set alone, without the need for any assumption about a proton, then the observation would not have been evidence for the existence of that proton and therefore would not have been evidence for the theory. His making the observation supports the theory only because, in order to explain his making the observation, it is reasonable to assume something about the world over and above the assumptions made about the observer's psychology. In particular, it is reasonable to assume that there was a proton going through the cloud chamber, causing the vapor trail.

Compare this case with one in which you make a moral judgment immediately and without conscious reasoning, say, that the children are wrong to set the cat on fire or that the doctor would be wrong to cut up one healthy patient to save five dying patients. In order to explain your making the first of these judgments, it would be reasonable to assume, perhaps, that the children really are pouring gasoline on a cat and you are seeing them do it. But, in neither case is there any obvious reason to assume anything about "moral facts," such as that it really is wrong to set the cat on fire or to cut up the patient in Room 306. Indeed, an assumption about moral facts would seem to be totally irrelevant to the explanation of your making the judgment you make. It would seem that all we need assume is that you have certain more or less well articulated moral principles that are reflected in the judgments you make, based on your moral sensibility. It seems to be completely irrelevant to our explanation whether your intuitive immediate judgment is true or false.

The observation of an event can provide observational evidence for or against a scientific theory in the sense that the truth of that observation can be relevant to a reasonable explanation of why that observation was made. A moral observation does not seem, in the same sense, to be observational evidence for or against any moral theory, since the truth or falsity of the moral observation seems to be completely irrelevant to any reasonable explanation of why that observation was made. The fact that an observation of an event was made at the time it was made is evidence not only about the observer but also about the physical facts. The fact that you made a particular moral observation when you did does not seem to be evidence about moral facts, only evidence about you and your moral sensibility. Facts about protons can affect what you observe, since a proton passing through the cloud chamber can cause a vapor trail that reflects light to your eye in a way that, given your scientific training and psychological set, leads you to judge that what you see is a proton. But there does not seem to be any way in which the actual rightness or wrongness of a given situation can have any effect on your perceptual apparatus. In this respect, ethics seems to differ from science.

In considering whether moral principles can help explain observations, it is therefore important to note an ambiguity in the word "observation." You see the children set the cat on fire and immediately think, "That's wrong." In one sense, your observation is that what the children are doing is wrong. In another sense, your observation is your thinking that thought. Moral observations might explain observations in the first sense but not in the second sense. Certain moral principles might help to explain why it was *wrong* of the children to set the cat on fire, but moral principles seem to be of no help in explaining *your thinking* that that is wrong. In the first sense of "observation," moral principles can be tested by observation – "That this act is wrong is evidence that causing unnecessary suffering is wrong." But in the second sense of "observation," moral principles cannot clearly be tested by observation, since they do not appear to help explain observations in this second sense of "observation." Moral principles do not seem to help explain your observing what you observe.

Of course, if you are already given the moral principle that it is wrong to cause unnecessary suffering, you can take your seeing the children setting the cat on fire as observational evidence that they are doing something wrong. Similarly, you can suppose that your seeing the vapor trail is observational evidence that a proton is going through the cloud chamber, if you are given the relevant physical theory. But there is an important apparent difference between the two cases. In the scientific case, your making that observation is itself evidence for the physical theory because the physical theory explains the proton, which explains the trail, which explains your observation. In the moral case, your making your observation does not seem to be evidence for the relevant moral principle because that principle does not seem to help explain your observation. The explanatory chain from principle to observation seems to be broken in morality. The moral principle may "explain" why it is wrong for the children to set the cat on fire. But the wrongness of that act does not appear to help explain the act, which you observe, itself. The explanatory chain appears to be broken in such a way that neither the moral principle nor the wrongness of the act can help explain why you observe what you observe.

A qualification may seem to be needed here. Perhaps the children perversely set the cat on fire simply "because it is wrong." Here it may seem at first that the actual wrongness of the act does help explain why they do it and therefore indirectly helps explain why you observe what you observe just as a physical theory, by explaining why the proton is producing a vapor trail, indirectly helps explain why the observer observes what he observes. But on reflection we must agree that this is probably an illusion. What explains the children's act is not clearly the actual wrongness of the act but, rather, their belief that the act is wrong. The actual rightness or wrongness of their act seems to have nothing to do with why they do it.

Observational evidence plays a part in science it does not appear to play in ethics, because scientific principles can be justified ultimately by their role in explaining observations, in the second sense of observation – by their explanatory role. Apparently, moral principles cannot be justified in the same way. It appears to be true that there can be no explanatory chain between moral principles and particular observings in the way that there can be such a chain between scientific principles and

particular observings. Conceived as an explanatory theory, morality, unlike science, seems to be cut off from observation.

Not that every legitimate scientific hypothesis is susceptible to direct observational testing. Certain hypotheses about "black holes" in space cannot be directly tested, for example, because no signal is emitted from within a black hole. The connection with observation in such a case is indirect. And there are many similar examples. Nevertheless, seen in the large, there is the apparent difference between science and ethics we have noted. The scientific realm is accessible to observation in a way the moral realm is not.

4.   Ethics and Mathematics

Perhaps ethics is to be compared, not with physics, but with mathematics. Perhaps such a moral principle as "You ought to keep your promises" is confirmed or disconfirmed in the way (whatever it is) in which such a mathematical principle as "$5 + 7 = 12$" is. Observation does not seem to play the role in mathematics it plays in physics. We do not and cannot perceive numbers, for example, since we cannot be in causal contact with them. We do not even understand what it would be like to be in causal contact with the number 12, say. Relations among numbers cannot have any more of an effect on our perceptual apparatus than moral facts can.

Observation, however, *is* relevant to mathematics. In explaining the observations that support a physical theory, scientists typically appeal to mathematical principles. On the other hand, one never seems to need to appeal in this way to moral principles. Since an observation is evidence for what best explains it, and since mathematics often figures in the explanations of scientific observations, there is indirect observational evidence for mathematics. There does not seem to be observational evidence, even indirectly, for basic moral principles. In explaining why certain observations have been made, we never seem to use purely moral assumptions. In this respect, then, ethics appears to differ not only from physics but also from mathematics.

26

Moral Explanations

Nicholas L. Sturgeon

There is one argument for moral skepticism that I respect even though I remain unconvinced. It has sometimes been called the argument from moral diversity or relativity, but that is somewhat misleading, for the problem arises not from the diversity of moral views, but from the apparent difficulty of *settling* moral disagreements, or even of knowing what would be required to settle them, a difficulty thought to be noticeably greater than any found in settling disagreements that arise in, for example, the sciences. This provides an argument for moral skepticism because one obviously possible explanation for our difficulty in settling moral disagreements is that they are really unsettleable, that there is no way of justifying one rather than another competing view on these issues; and a possible further explanation for the unsettleability of moral disagreements, in turn, is moral nihilism, the view that on these issues there just is no fact of the matter, that the impossibility of discovering and establishing moral truths is due to there not being any.

I am, as I say, unconvinced: partly because I think this argument exaggerates the difficulty we actually find in settling moral disagreements, partly because there are alternative explanations to be considered for the difficulty we do find. For example, it certainly matters to what extent moral disagreements depend on disagreements about

other questions which, however disputed they may be, are nevertheless regarded as having objective answers: questions such as which, if any, religion is true, which account of human psychology, which theory of human society. And it also matters to what extent consideration of moral questions is in practice skewed by distorting factors such as personal interest and social ideology. These are large issues. Although it is possible to say some useful things to put them in perspective, it appears impossible to settle them quickly or in any a priori way. Consideration of them is likely to have to be piecemeal and, in the short run at least, frustratingly indecisive.

These large issues are not my topic here. But I mention them, and the difficulty of settling them, to show why it is natural that moral skeptics have hoped to find some quicker way of establishing their thesis. I doubt that any exist, but some have of course been proposed. Verificationist attacks on ethics should no doubt be seen in this light, and J. L. Mackie's recent "argument from queerness" is a clear instance (Mackie, 1977, pp. 38–42 [this section of Mackie's book is included as chapter 1 of this volume]). The quicker argument on which I shall concentrate, however, is neither of these, but instead an argument by Gilbert Harman designed to bring out the "basic problem" about morality, which in his view is "its apparent immunity from observational testing" and "the seeming irrelevance of observational evidence" (Harman, 1977, pp. vii, viii. Parenthetical page references are to this work [an extract from which appears as the preceding chapter]). The argument is that reference to moral facts appears unnecessary for the *explanation* of our moral observations and beliefs.

Harman's view, I should say at once, is not in the end a skeptical one, and he does not view the argument I shall discuss as a decisive defense of moral skepticism or moral nihilism. Someone else might easily so regard it, however. For Harman himself regards it as creating a strong *prima facie* case for skepticism and nihilism, strong enough to justify calling it "the problem with ethics." And he believes it shows that the only recourse for someone who wishes to avoid moral skepticism is to find defensible reductive definitions for ethical terms; so skepticism would be the obvious conclusion for anyone to draw who doubted the possibility of such definitions. I believe, however, that Harman is mistaken on both counts. I shall show that his argument for skepticism either rests on claims that most people would find quite implausible (and so cannot be what constitutes, for *them*, the problem with ethics); or else it becomes just the application to ethics of a familiar *general* skeptical strategy, one which, if it works for ethics, will work equally well for unobservable theoretical entities, or for other minds, or for an external world (and so, again, can hardly be what constitutes the distinctive problem with *ethics*). In the course of my argument, moreover, I shall suggest that one can in any case be a moral realist, and indeed an ethical naturalist, without believing that we are now or ever will be in possession of reductive naturalistic definitions for ethical terms.

I.   The Problem with Ethics

Moral theories are often tested in thought experiments, against imagined examples; and, as Harman notes, trained researchers often test scientific theories in the same way. The problem, though, is that scientific theories can also be tested against the world, by observations or real experiments; and, Harman asks, "can moral principles be tested in the same way, out in the world?" (p. 4)

This would not be a very interesting or impressive challenge, of course, if it were merely a resurrection of standard verificationist worries about

whether moral assertions and theories have any testable empirical implications, implications suitable in some relatively austere "observational" vocabulary. One problem with that form of the challenge, as Harman points out, is that there are no "pure" observations, and in consequence no purely observational vocabulary either. But there is also a deeper problem that Harman does not mention, one that remains even if we shelve worries about "pure" observations and, at least for the sake of argument, grant the verificationist his observational language, pretty much as it was usually conceived: that is, as lacking at the very least any obviously theoretical terminology from any recognized science, and of course as lacking any moral terminology. For then the difficulty is that moral principles fare just as well (or just as badly) against the verificationist challenge as do typical scientific principles. For it is by now a familiar point about scientific principles – principles such as Newton's law of universal gravitation or Darwin's theory of evolution – that they are entirely devoid of empirical implications when considered in isolation. We do of course base observational predictions on such theories and so test them against experience, but that is because we do *not* consider them in isolation. For we can derive these predictions only by relying at the same time on a large background of additional assumptions, many of which are equally theoretical and equally incapable of being tested in isolation. A less familiar point, because less often spelled out, is that the relation of moral principles to observation is similar in *both* these respects. Candidate moral principles – for example, that an action is wrong just in case there is something else the agent could have done that would have produced a greater net balance of pleasure over pain – lack empirical implications when considered in isolation. But it is easy to derive empirical consequences from them, and thus to test them against experience, if we allow ourselves, as we do in the scientific case, to rely on a background of other assumptions of comparable status. Thus, if we conjoin the act-utilitarian principle I just cited with the further view, also untestable in isolation, that it is always wrong deliberately to kill a human being, we can deduce from these two premises together the consequence that deliberately killing a human being always produces a lesser balance of pleasure over pain than some available alternative act; and this claim is one any positivist would have conceded we know, in principle at least, how to test. If we found it to be false, moreover, then we would be forced by this empirical test to abandon at least one of the moral claims from which we derived it.

It might be thought a worrisome feature of this example, however, and a further opening for skepticism, that there could be controversy about which moral premise to abandon, and that we have not explained how our empirical test can provide an answer to *this* question. And this may be a problem. It should be a familiar problem, however, because the Duhemian commentary includes a precisely corresponding point about the scientific case: that if we are at all cautious in characterizing what we observe, then the requirement that our theories merely be *consistent* with observation is an astoundingly weak one. There are always many, perhaps indefinitely many, different mutually inconsistent ways to adjust our views to meet this constraint. Of course, in practice we are often confident of how to do it: If you are a freshman chemistry student, you do not conclude from your failure to obtain the predicted value in an experiment that it is all over for the atomic theory of gases. And the decision can be equally easy, one should note, in a moral case. Consider two examples. From the surprising moral thesis that Adolf Hitler was a morally admirable person, together with a modest piece of moral theory to the effect that no morally admirable person would, for example, instigate and oversee the degradation and death of millions of persons, one can derive the testable consequence that Hitler did not do this. But he did, so we must give up one of our premises; and the choice of which to abandon is neither difficult nor controversial.

Or, to take a less monumental example, contrived around one of Harman's own, suppose you have been thinking yourself lucky enough to live in a neighborhood in which no one would do anything wrong, at least not in public; and that the modest piece of theory you accept, this time, is that malicious cruelty, just for the hell of it, is wrong. Then, as in Harman's example, "you round a corner and see a group of young hoodlums pour gasoline on a cat and ignite it." At this point, either your confidence in the neighborhood or your principle about cruelty has got to give way. But the choice is easy, if dispiriting, so easy as hardly to require thought. As Harman says, "You do not need to *conclude* that what they are doing is wrong; you do not need to figure anything out; you can *see* that it is wrong"

(p. 4). But a skeptic can still wonder whether this practical confidence, or this "seeing," rests in either sort of case on anything more than deeply ingrained conventions of thought – respect for scientific experts, say, and for certain moral traditions – as opposed to anything answerable to the facts of the matter, any reliable strategy for getting it right about the world.

Now, Harman's challenge is interesting partly because it does not rest on these verificationist doubts about whether moral beliefs have observational implications, but even more because what it does rest on is a partial answer to the kind of general skepticism to which, as we have seen, reflection on the verificationist picture can lead. Many of our beliefs are justified, in Harman's view, by their providing or helping to provide a reasonable *explanation* of our observing what we do. It would be consistent with your failure, as a beginning student, to obtain the experimental result predicted by the gas laws, that the laws are mistaken. That would even be one explanation of your failure. But a better explanation, in light of your inexperience and the general success experts have had in confirming and applying these laws, is that you made some mistake in running the experiment. So our scientific beliefs can be justified by their explanatory role; and so too, in Harman's view, can mathematical beliefs and many commonsense beliefs about the world.

Not so, however, moral beliefs: They appear to have no such explanatory role. That is "the problem with ethics." Harman spells out his version of this contrast:

> You need to make assumptions about certain physical facts to explain the occurrence of the observations that support a scientific theory, but you do not seem to need to make assumptions about any moral facts to explain the occurrence of the so-called moral observations I have been talking about. In the moral case, it would seem that you need only make assumptions about the psychology or moral sensibility of the person making the moral observation. (p. 6)

More precisely, and applied to his own example, it might be reasonable, in order to explain your judging that the hoodlums are wrong to set the cat on fire, to assume "that the children really are pouring gasoline on a cat and you are seeing them do it." But there is no

> obvious reason to assume anything about "moral facts," such as that it is really wrong to set the cat on

fire. . . . Indeed, an assumption about moral facts would seem to be totally irrelevant to the explanation of your making the judgment you make. It would seem that all we need assume is that you have certain more or less well articulated moral principles that are reflected in the judgments you make, based on your moral sensibility. (p. 7)

And Harman thinks that if we accept this conclusion, suitably generalized, then, subject to a possible qualification I shall come to shortly, we must conclude that moral theories cannot be tested against the world as scientific theories can, and that we have no reason to believe that moral facts are part of the order of nature or that there is any moral knowledge (pp. 23, 35).

My own view is that Harman is quite wrong, not in thinking that the explanatory role of our beliefs is important to their justification, but in thinking that moral beliefs play no such role. I shall have to say something about the initial plausibility of Harman's thesis as applied to his own example, but part of my reason for dissenting should be apparent from the other example I just gave. We find it easy (and so does Harman [p. 108]) to conclude from the evidence not just that Hitler was not morally admirable, but that he was morally depraved. But isn't it plausible that Hitler's moral depravity – the fact of his really having been morally depraved – forms part of a reasonable explanation of why we believe he was depraved? I think so, and I shall argue concerning this and other examples that moral beliefs commonly play the explanatory role Harman denies them. Before I can press my case, however, I need to clear up several preliminary points about just what Harman is claiming and just how his argument is intended to work.

II.   Observation, Explanation, and Reduction

(1)   For there are several ways in which Harman's argument invites misunderstanding. One results from his focusing at the start on the question of whether there can be moral *observations*. But this question turns out to be a side issue, in no way central to his argument that moral principles cannot be tested against the world. There are a couple of reasons for this, of which the more

important by far is that Harman does not really require of moral facts, if belief in them is to be justified, that they figure in the explanation of moral observations. It would be enough, on the one hand, if they were needed for the explanation of moral beliefs that are not in any interesting sense observations. For example, Harman thinks belief in moral facts would be vindicated if they were needed to explain our drawing the moral conclusions we do when we reflect on hypothetical cases, but I think there is no illumination in calling these conclusions observations. It would also be enough, on the other hand, if moral facts were needed for the explanation of what were clearly observations, but not moral observations. Harman thinks mathematical beliefs are justified, but he does not suggest that there are mathematical observations; it is rather that appeal to mathematical truths helps to explain why we make the physical observations we do (p. 10). Moral beliefs would surely be justified, too, if they played such a role, whether or not there are any moral observations.

So the claim is that moral facts are not needed to explain our having any of the moral beliefs we do, whether or not those beliefs are observations, and are equally unneeded to explain any of the observations we make, whether or not those observations are moral. In fact, Harman's view appears to be that moral facts aren't needed to explain anything at all: although it would perhaps be question-begging for him to begin with this strong a claim, since he grants that if there were any moral facts, then appeal to other moral facts, more general ones, for example, might be needed to explain *them* (p. 8). But he is certainly claiming, at the very least, that moral facts aren't needed to explain any non-moral facts we have any reason to believe in.

This claim has seemed plausible even to some philosophers who wish to defend the existence of moral facts and the possibility of moral knowledge. Thus, Thomas Nagel has recently retreated to the reply that

> it begs the question to assume that *explanatory* necessity is the test of reality in this area. . . . To assume that only what has to be included in the best explanatory picture of the world is real, is to assume that there are no irreducibly normative truths.[1]

But this retreat will certainly make it more difficult to fit moral knowledge into anything like a causal

---

[1]   Nagel (1980), p. 114n. Nagel actually directs this reply to J. L. Mackie.

theory of knowledge, which seems plausible for many other cases, or to follow Hilary Putnam's suggestion that we "apply a generally causal account of reference . . . to moral terms" (Putnam, 1975, p. 290). In addition, the concession is premature in any case, for I shall argue that moral facts do fit into our explanatory view of the world, and in particular into explanations of many moral observations and beliefs.

(2) Other possible misunderstandings concern what is meant in asking whether reference to moral facts is *needed* to explain moral beliefs. One warning about this question I save for my comments on reduction below; but another, about what Harman is clearly *not* asking, and about what sort of answer I can attempt to defend to the question he is asking, can be spelled out first. For, to begin with, Harman's question is clearly not just whether there is *an* explanation of our moral beliefs that does not mention moral facts. Almost surely there is. Equally surely, however, there is *an* explanation of our commonsense nonmoral beliefs that does not mention an external world: one which cites only our sensory experience, for example, together with whatever needs to be said about our psychology to explain why with that history of experience we would form just the beliefs we do. Harman means to be asking a question that will lead to skepticism about moral facts, but not to skepticism about the existence of material bodies or about well-established scientific theories of the world.

Harman illustrates the kind of question he is asking, and the kind of answer he is seeking, with an example from physics which it will be useful to keep in mind. A physicist sees a vapor trail in a cloud chamber and thinks, "There goes a proton." What explains his thinking this? Partly, of course, his psychological set, which largely depends on his beliefs about the apparatus and all the theory he has learned; but partly also, perhaps, the hypothesis that "there really was a proton going through the cloud chamber, causing the vapor trail, which he saw as a proton." We will *not* need this latter assumption, however, "if his having made that observation could have been equally well explained by his psychological set alone, without the need for any assumption about a proton" (p. 6). So for reference to moral facts to be *needed* in the explanation of our beliefs and observations, is for this reference to be required for an explanation that is somehow *better* than competing explanations. Correspondingly, reference to moral facts will be

unnecessary to an explanation, in Harman's view, not just because we can find some explanation that does not appeal to them, but because *no* explanation that appeals to them is any better than some competing explanation that does not.

Now, fine discriminations among competing explanations of almost anything are likely to be difficult, controversial, and provisional. Fortunately, however, my discussion of Harman's argument will not require any fine discriminations. This is because Harman's thesis, as we have seen, is *not* that moral explanations lose out by a small margin; nor is it that moral explanations, although sometimes initially promising, always turn out on further examination to be inferior to nonmoral ones. It is, rather, that reference to moral facts always looks, right from the start, to be "completely irrelevant" to the explanation of any of our observations and beliefs. And my argument will be that this is mistaken: that many moral explanations appear to be good explanations, or components in good explanations, that are not obviously undermined by anything else that we know. My suspicion, in fact, is that moral facts are needed in the sense explained, that they will turn out to belong in our best overall explanatory picture of the world, even in the long run, but I shall not attempt to establish that here. Indeed, it should be clear why I could not pretend to do so. For I have explicitly put to one side the issue (which I regard as incapable in any case of quick resolution) of whether and to what extent actual moral disagreements can be settled satisfactorily. But I assume it would count as a defect in any sort of explanation to rely on claims about which rational agreement proved unattainable. So I concede that it *could* turn out, for anything I say here, that moral explanations are all defective and should be discarded. What I shall try to show is merely that many moral explanations look reasonable enough to be in the running; and, more specifically, that nothing Harman says provides any reason for thinking they are not. This claim is surely strong enough (and controversial enough) to be worth defending.

(3) It is implicit in this statement of my project, but worth noting separately, that I take Harman to be proposing an *independent* skeptical argument – independent not merely of the argument from the difficulty of settling disputed moral questions, but also of other standard arguments for moral skepticism. Otherwise his exposition is entirely misleading (and his argument, I think, not

worth independent discussion). For *any* of these more familiar skeptical arguments will of course imply that moral explanations are defective, on the reasonable assumption that it would be a defect in any explanation to rely on claims as doubtful as these arguments attempt to show all moral claims to be. But if *that* is why there is a problem with moral explanations, one should surely just cite the relevant skeptical argument, rather than this derivative difficulty about moral explanations, as the basic "problem with ethics," and it is that argument we should discuss. So I take Harman's interesting suggestion to be that there is a *different* difficulty that remains even if we put other arguments for moral skepticism aside and *assume*, for the sake of argument, that there are moral facts (for example, that what the children in his example are doing is really wrong): namely, that these assumed facts *still* seem to play no explanatory role.

This understanding of Harman's thesis crucially affects my argumentative strategy in a way to which I should alert the reader in advance. For it should be clear that assessment of this thesis not merely permits, but *requires*, that we provisionally assume the existence of moral facts. I can see no way of evaluating the claim that *even if* we assumed the existence of moral facts they would still appear explanatorily irrelevant, without assuming the existence of some, to see how they would look. So I do freely assume this in each of the examples I discuss in the next section. (I have tried to choose plausible examples, moreover, of moral facts most of us would be inclined to believe in if we did believe in moral facts, since those are the easiest to think about; but the precise examples don't matter, and anyone who would prefer others should feel free to substitute his own.) I grant, furthermore, that if Harman were right about the outcome of this thought experiment – that even after we assumed these facts they still looked irrelevant to the explanation of our moral beliefs and of other nonmoral facts – then we might conclude with him that there were, after all, no such facts. But I claim he is wrong: Once we have provisionally assumed the existence of moral facts, they *do* appear relevant, by perfectly ordinary standards, to the explanation of moral beliefs and of a good deal else besides. Does this prove that there *are* such facts? Well of course it helps support that view, but here I carefully make no claim to have shown so much. What I *show* is that any remaining reservations about the existence of moral facts must be based

on those *other* skeptical arguments, of which Harman's argument is independent. In short, there may still be a "problem with ethics," but it has *nothing* special to do with moral explanations.

(4)   A final preliminary point concerns a qualification Harman adds himself. As I have explained his argument so far, it assumes that we could have reason to believe in moral facts only if this helped us "explain why we observe what we observe" (p. 13); but, he says, this assumption is too strong, for we can have evidence for the truth of some beliefs that play no such explanatory role. We might, for example, come to be able to explain color perception without saying that objects have colors, by citing certain physical and psychological facts. But this would not show that there are no colors; it would show only that facts about color are "somehow reducible" to these physical and psychological facts. And this leaves the possibility that moral facts, too, even if they ultimately play no explanatory role themselves, might be "reducible to certain other facts that can help explain our observations" (p. 14). So a crucial question is: What would justify a belief in reducibility? What makes us think color facts might be reducible to physical (or physical and psychological) facts, and what would justify us in thinking moral facts reducible to explanatory natural facts of some kind?

Harman's answer is that it is still the *apparent* explanatory role of color facts, or of moral facts, that matters; and hence that this qualification to his argument is not so great as it might seem. We know of no precise reduction for facts of either sort. We believe even so that reduction is possible for color facts because even when we are able to explain color perception without saying that objects are colored,

> we will still *sometimes* refer to the actual colors of objects in explaining color perception, if only for the sake of simplicity. . . . We will continue to believe that objects have colors because we will continue to refer to the actual colors of objects in the explanations that we will in practice give.

But Harman thinks that no comparable point holds for moral facts. "There does not ever seem to be, even in practice, any point to explaining someone's moral observations by appeal to what is actually right or wrong, just or unjust, good or bad" (p. 22).

Now I shall argue shortly that this is just wrong: that sober people frequently offer such explanations of moral observations and beliefs, and that many of these explanations look plausible enough on the evidence to be worth taking seriously. So a quick reply to Harman, strictly adequate for my purpose, would be simply to accept his concession that this by itself should lead us to regard moral facts as (at worst) reducible to explanatory facts. Concern about the need for, and the role of, reductive definitions has been so central to meta-ethical discussion in this century, however, and has also proved enough of a sticking point in discussions I have had of the topic of this easy, that I should say a bit more.

As a philosophical naturalist, I take natural facts to be the only facts there are. If I am prepared to recognize moral facts, therefore, I must take them, too, to be natural facts: But which natural facts? It is widely thought that an ethical naturalist must answer this question by providing reductive naturalistic definitions for moral terms and, indeed, that until one has supplied such definitions one's credentials as a *naturalist* about any supposed moral facts must be in doubt. Once such definitions are in hand, however, it seems that moral explanations should be dispensable, since any such explanations can then be paraphrased in nonmoral terms; so it is hard to see why an ethical naturalist should attach any importance to them. Now, there are several problems with this reasoning, but the main one is that the widely held view on which it is based is mistaken: mistaken about where a scheme of reductive naturalistic definitions would be found, if there were to be one, but also about whether, on a naturalistic view of ethics, one should expect there to be such a thing at all. I shall take up these points in reverse order, arguing first (a) that it is a mistake to require of ethical naturalism that it even promises reductive definitions for moral terms, and then (b) that even if such definitions are to be forthcoming it is, at the very least, no special problem for ethical naturalism that we are not *now* in confident possession of them.

(a) Naturalism is in one clear sense a "reductionist" doctrine of course, for it holds that moral facts are nothing but natural facts. What I deny, however, is that from this metaphysical doctrine about what sort of facts moral facts are, anything follows about the possibility of reduction in another sense (to which I shall henceforth confine the term) more familiar from the philosophical literature: that is, about whether moral explanations can be given reductive definitions in some distinctive nonmoral vocabulary, in which any plausible

moral explanations could then be recast. The difficulty with supposing naturalism to require this can be seen by pressing the question of just what this distinctive vocabulary is supposed to be. It is common to say merely that this reducing terminology must be "factual" or "descriptive" or must designate natural properties; but unless ethical naturalism has already been ruled out, this is no help, for what naturalists of course contend is that moral discourse is *itself* factual and descriptive (although it may be other things as well), and that moral terms themselves stand for natural properties. The idea, clearly, is supposed to be that the *test* of whether these naturalistic claims about moral discourse are correct is whether this discourse is reducible to some other; but what other? I consider two possibilities.

(i) Many would agree that it is too restrictive to understand ethical naturalism as requiring that moral terms be definable in the terminology of fundamental physics. One reason it is too restrictive is that philosophical naturalism might be true even if physicalism, the view that everything is physical, is not. Some form of emergent dualism might be correct, for example. A different reason, which I find more interesting (because I think physicalism *is* true), is that physicalism entails nothing in any case about whether even biology or psychology, let alone ethics, is reducible to physics. There are a number of reasons for this, but a cardinality problem noted by Richard Boyd is sufficient to secure the point (Boyd, forthcoming a). If there are (as there appear to be) any continuous physical parameters, then there are continuum many physical states of the world, but there are at most countably many predicates in any language, including that of even ideal physics; so there are more physical properties than there are physical expressions to represent them. Thus, although physicalism certainly entails that biological and psychological properties (and ethical properties, too, if there are any) are physical, nothing follows about whether we have any but biological or psychological or ethical terminology for representing these particular physical properties.

(ii) Of course, not many discussions of ethical naturalism have focused on the possibility of reducing ethics to physics; social theory, psychology, and occasionally biology have appeared more promising possibilities. But that facts might be *physical* whether or not all the disciplines that deal with them are reducible to *physics*, helps give point to my question of why we should think that if all ethical facts are *natural* (or, for that matter, *social* or *psychological* or *biological*), it follows that they can equally well be expressed in some other, non-moral idiom; and it also returns us to the question of just what this alternative idiom is supposed to be. The answer to this latter question simply assumed in most discussions of ethical naturalism, I think, is that there are a number of disciplines that we pretty well know to deal with a single natural world, for example, physics, biology, psychology, and social theory; that it is a matter of no great concern whether any of *these* disciplines is reducible to some one of the others or to anything else; but that the test of whether ethical naturalism is true *is* whether ethics is reducible to some (non-moral) combination of *them*.

But what rationale is there for holding ethics alone to this reductive test? Perhaps there would be one if ethics appeared in some salient respect strikingly dissimilar to these other disciplines: if, for example, Harman were right what whereas physics, biology, and the rest offer plausible explanations of many obviously natural facts, including facts about our beliefs and observations, ethics never does. Perhaps ethics could then plausibly be required to earn its place by some alternative route. But I shall of course argue that Harman is wrong about this alleged dissimilarity, and I take my argument to provide part of the defense required for a naturalistic but nonreductive view of ethics.

(b) A naturalist, however, will certainly want (and a critic of naturalism will likely demand) a fuller account than this of just where moral facts are supposed to fit in the natural world. For all I have shown, moreover, this account might even provide a scheme of reduction for moral discourse: My argument has been not that ethical naturalism could not take this form, but only that it need not. So where should one look for such a fuller account or (if it is to be had) such a reduction? The answer is that the account will have to be derived from our best moral theory, together with our best theory of the natural world – exactly as, for example, any reductive account of colors will have to be based on all we know about colors, including our best optical theory together with other parts of physics and perhaps psychology. If hedonistic act-utilitarianism (and enough of its associated psychology) turns out to be true, for example, then we can define the good as pleasure and the absence of pain, and a right action as one that produces at least

as much good as any other, and that will be where the moral facts fit. If, more plausibly, some other moral theory turns out to be correct, we will get a different account and (if the theory takes the right form) different reductive definitions. It would of course be a serious objection to ethical *naturalism* if we discovered that the *only* plausible moral theories had to invoke supernatural facts of some kind, by making right and wrong depend on the will of a deity, for example, or by implying that only persons with immortal souls could have moral obligations. We would then have to choose between a naturalistic world view and a belief in moral facts. But an ethical naturalist can point out that there are familiar moral theories that lack implications of this sort and that appear defensible in the light of all we know about the natural world; and any of them, if correct, could provide a naturalistic account of moral facts and even (if one is to be had) a naturalistic reduction of moral discourse.

Many philosophers will balk at this confident talk of our discovering some moral theory to be correct. But their objection is just the familiar one whose importance I acknowledged at the outset, before putting it to one side: For I grant that the difficulty we experience in settling moral issues, including issues in moral theory, is a problem (although perhaps not an insuperable one) for any version of moral realism. All I contend here is that there is not, in addition to this acknowledged difficulty, any special further (or prior) problem of finding reductive definitions for moral terms or of figuring out where moral facts fit in the natural world. Our moral theory, if once we get it, will provide whatever reduction is to be had and will tell us where the moral facts fit. The suspicion that there must be more than this to the search for reductive definitions almost always rests, I believe, on the view that these definitions must be suited to a special epistemic role: for example, that they will have to be analytic or conceptual truths and so provide a privileged basis for the rest of our theory. But I am confident that moral reasoning, like reasoning in the sciences, is inevitably dialectical and lacks a priori foundations of this sort. I am also sure that no ethical naturalist need think otherwise.

The relevance of these points is this: It is true that if we once obtained correct reductive definitions for moral terms, moral explanations would be in principle dispensable; so if ethical naturalism had to promise such definitions, it would also have to promise the eliminability in principle of explanations couched in moral terms. But note three points. First, it should be no surprise, and should be regarded as no special difficulty for naturalism even on a reductionist conception of it, that we are not now in possession of such definitions, and so not *now* in a position to dispense with any moral explanations that seem plausible. To be confident of such definitions we would need to know just which moral theory is correct; but ethics is an area of great controversy, and I am sure we do not yet know this. Second, if some moral explanations do seem plausible, as I shall argue, then one important step toward improving this situation in ethics will be to see what sort of theory emerges if we attempt to refine these explanations in the light both of empirical evidence and theoretical criticism. So it is easy to see, again even on a reductionist understanding of naturalism that promises the eliminability of moral explanations in the long run, why any naturalist will think that for the foreseeable short run such explanations should be taken seriously on their own terms.

The third and most important point, finally, is that the eliminability of moral explanations for *this* reason, if actually demonstrated, would of course not represent a triumph of ethical skepticism but would rather derive from its defeat. So we must add one further caution, as I promised, concerning Harman's thesis that no reference to moral facts is *needed* in the explanation of moral beliefs. For there are, as we can now see, two very different reasons one might have for thinking this. One – Harman's reason, and my target in the remainder of this essay – is that no moral explanations even seem plausible, that reference to moral facts always strikes us as "completely irrelevant" to the explanation of moral beliefs. This claim, if true, would tend to support moral skepticism. The other reason – which I have just been considering, and with which I also disagree – is that any moral explanations that *do* seem plausible can be paraphrased without explanatory loss in entirely nonmoral terms. I have argued that it is a mistake to understand ethical naturalism as promising this kind of reduction even in principle; and I think it in any case absurd overconfidence to suppose that anyone can spell out an adequate reduction now. But any reader unconvinced by my arguments should note also that this *second* reason is no version of moral skep-

ticism: For what anyone convinced by it must think, is that we either are or will be able to say, in entirely nonmoral terms, exactly which natural properties moral terms refer to. So Harman is right to present reductionism as an alternative to skepticism; part of what I have tried to show is just that it is neither the only nor the most plausible such alternative, and that no ethical naturalist need be committed to it.

III. Moral Explanations

With these preliminary points aside, I turn to my arguments against Harman's thesis. I shall first add to my example of Hitler's moral character several more in which it seems plausible to cite moral facts as part of an explanation of nonmoral facts, and in particular of people's forming the moral opinions they do. I shall then argue that Harman gives us no plausible reason to reject or ignore these explanations; I shall claim, in fact, that the same is true for his own example of the children igniting the cat. I shall conclude, finally, by attempting to diagnose the source of the disagreement between Harman and me on these issues.

My Hitler example suggests a whole range of extremely common cases that appear not to have occurred to Harman, cases in which we cite someone's moral character as part of an explanation of his or her deeds, and in which that whole story is then available as a plausible further explanation of someone's arriving at a correct assessment of that moral character. Take just one other example. Bernard DeVoto, in *The Year of Decision: 1846*, describes the efforts of American emigrants already in California to rescue another party of emigrants, the Donner Party, trapped by snows in the High Sierras, once their plight became known. At a meeting in Yerba Buena (now San Francisco), the relief efforts were put under the direction of a recent arrival, Passed Midshipman Selim Woodworth, described by a previous acquaintance as "a great busybody and ambitious of taking a command among the emigrants."[2] But Woodworth not only failed to lead rescue parties into the mountains himself, where other rescuers were counting on him (leaving children to be picked up by him, for example), but had to be "shamed, threatened,

---

[2] DeVoto (1942), p. 426; a quotation from the notebooks of Francis Parkman. The account of the entire rescue effort is on pp. 424–4.

and bullied" even into organizing the efforts of others willing to take the risk; he spent time arranging comforts for himself in camp, preening himself on the importance of his position; and as a predictable result of his cowardice and his exercises in vainglory, many died who might have been saved, including four known still to be alive when he turned back for the last time in mid-March. DeVoto concludes: "Passed Mid-shipman Woodworth was just no damned good" (1942, p. 442). I cite this case partly because it has so clearly the structure of an inference to a reasonable explanation. One can think of competing explanations, but the evidence points against them. It isn't, for example, that Woodworth was a basically decent person who simply proved too weak when thrust into a situation that placed heroic demands on him. He volunteered, he put no serious effort even into tasks that required no heroism, and it seems clear that concern for his own position and reputation played a much larger role in his motivation than did any concern for the people he was expected to save. If DeVoto is right about this evidence, moreover, it seems reasonable that part of the explanation of his believing that Woodworth was no damned good is just that Woodworth *was* no damned good.

DeVoto writes of course with more moral intensity (and with more of a flourish) than academic historians usually permit themselves, but it would be difficult to find a serious work of biography, for example, in which actions are not explained by appeal to moral character: sometimes by appeal to specific virtues and vices, but often enough also by appeal to a more general assessment. A different question, and perhaps a more difficult one, concerns the sort of example on which Harman concentrates, the explanation of judgments of right and wrong. Here again Harman appears just to have overlooked explanations in terms of moral character: A judge's thinking that it would be wrong to sentence a particular offender to the maximum prison term the law allows, for example, may be due in part to her decency and fairmindedness, which I take to be moral facts if any are. But do moral features of the action or institution being judged ever play an explanatory role? Here is an example in which they appear to. An interesting historical question is why vigorous and reasonably widespread moral opposition to slavery arose for

the first time in the eighteenth and nineteenth centuries, even though slavery was a very old institution; and why this opposition arose primarily in Britain, France, and in French- and English-speaking North America, even though slavery existed throughout the New World. There is a standard answer to this question. It is that chattel slavery in British and French America, and then in the United States, was much *worse* than previous forms of slavery, and much worse than slavery in Latin America. This is, I should add, a controversial explanation. But as is often the case with historical explanations, its proponents do not claim it is the whole story, and many of its opponents grant that there may be some truth in these comparisons, and that they may after all form a small part of a larger explanation.[3] This latter concession is all I require for my example. Equally good for my purpose would be the more limited thesis that explains the growth of antislavery sentiment in the United States, between the Revolution and the Civil War, in part by saying that slavery in the United States became a more oppressive institution during that time. The appeal in these standard explanations is straightforwardly to moral facts.

What is supposed to be wrong with all these explanations? Harman says that assumptions about moral facts seem "completely irrelevant" in explaining moral observations and moral beliefs (p. 7), but on its more natural reading that claim seems pretty obviously mistaken about these examples. For it is natural to think that if a particular assumption is completely irrelevant to the explanation of a certain fact, then the fact would have obtained, and we would have explained it just as well, even if the assumption had been false. But I do not believe that Hitler would have done all he did if he had not been morally depraved, nor, on the assumption that he was not depraved, can I think of any plausible alternative explanation for his doing those things. Nor is it plausible that we would all have believed he was morally depraved even if he hadn't been. Granted, there is a tendency for writers who do not attach much weight to fascism as a social movement to want to blame its evils on a single maniacal leader, so perhaps some of them would have painted Hitler as a moral monster even if he had not been one. But this is only a tendency, and one for which many people know how to discount, so I

---

[3] For a version of what I am calling the standard view about slavery in the Americas, see Tannenbaum (1947). For an argument against both halves of the standard view, see Davis (1966), esp. pp. 60–1, 223–5, 262–3.

doubt that our moral belief really is overdetermined in this way. Nor, similarly, do I believe that Woodworth's actions were overdetermined, so that he would have done just as he did even if he had been a more admirable person. I suppose one could have doubts about DeVoto's objectivity and reliability; it is obvious he dislikes Woodworth, so perhaps he would have thought him a moral loss and convinced his readers of this no matter what the man was really like. But it is more plausible that the dislike is mostly based on the same evidence that supports DeVoto's moral view of him, and that very different evidence, at any rate, would have produced a different verdict. If so, then Woodworth's moral character is part of the explanation of DeVoto's belief about his moral character.

It is more plausible of course that serious moral opposition to slavery would have emerged in Britain, France, and the United States even if slavery hadn't been worse in the modern period than before, and worse in the United States than in Latin America, and that the American antislavery movement would have grown even if slavery had not become more oppressive as the nineteenth century progressed. But that is because these moral facts are offered as at best a partial explanation of these developments in moral opinion. And if they really *are* part of the explanation, as seems plausible, then it is also plausible that whatever effect they produced was not entirely overdetermined; that, for example, the growth of the antislavery movement in the United States would at least have been somewhat slower if slavery had been and remained less bad an institution. Here again it hardly seems "completely irrelevant" to the explanation whether or not these moral facts obtained.

It is more puzzling, I grant, to consider Harman's own example in which you see the children igniting a cat and react immediately with the thought that this is wrong. Is it true, as Harman claims, that the assumption that the children are really doing something wrong is "totally irrelevant" to any reasonable explanation of your making that judgment? Would you, for example, have reacted in just the same way, with the thought that the action is wrong, even if what they were doing *hadn't* been wrong, and could we explain your reaction equally well on this assumption? Now, there is more than one way to understand this counterfactual question, and I shall return below to a reading of it that might appear favorable to Harman's view. What I wish to point out for now is merely that

there is a natural way of taking it, parallel to the way which I have been understanding similar counterfactual questions about my own examples, on which the answer to it has to be simply: It depends. For to answer the question, I take it, we must consider a situation in which what the children are doing is not wrong, but which is otherwise as much like the actual situation as possible, and then decide what your reaction would be in that situation. But since what makes their action wrong, what its wrongness *consists* in, is presumably something like its being an act of gratuitous cruelty (or, perhaps we should add, of intense cruelty, and to a helpless victim), to imagine them not doing something wrong we are going to have to imagine their action different in this respect. More cautiously and more generally, if what they are actually doing is wrong, and if moral properties are, as many writers have held, supervenient on natural ones, then in order to imagine them not doing something wrong we are going to have to suppose their action different from the actual one in some of its natural features as well. So our question becomes: Even if the children had been doing something else, something just different enough not to be wrong, would you have taken them even so to be doing something wrong?

Surely there is no one answer to this question: It depends on a lot about you, including your moral views and how good you are at seeing at a glance what some children are doing. It probably depends also on a debatable moral issue; namely, just *how* different the children's action would have to be in order not to be wrong. (Is unkindness to animals, for example, also wrong?) I believe we can see how, in a case in which the answer was clearly affirmative, we might be tempted to agree with Harman that the wrongness of the action was no part of the explanation of your reaction. For suppose you are like this. You hate children. What you especially hate, moreover, is the sight of children enjoying themselves; so much so that whenever you see children having fun, you immediately assume they are up to no good. The more they seem to be enjoying themselves, furthermore, the readier you are to fasten on any pretext for thinking them engaged in real wickedness. Then it is that even if the children had been engaged in some robust but innocent fun, you would have thought they were doing something wrong; and Harman is perhaps right about you that the actual wrongness of the action you see is irrelevant to your thinking it wrong. This is because your reaction is due to a feature of the action that coincides only very accidentally with the ones that make it wrong. But, of course, and fortunately, many people aren't like this (nor does Harman argue that they are). It isn't true of them that, in general, if the children had been doing something similar, although different enough not to be wrong, they would still have thought the children were doing something wrong. And it isn't true either, therefore, that the wrongness of the action is irrelevant to the explanation of why they think it wrong.

Now, one might have the sense from my discussion of all these examples – but perhaps especially from my discussion of this last one, Harman's own – that I have perversely been refusing to understand his claim about the explanatory irrelevance of moral facts in the way he intends. And perhaps I have not been understanding it as he wishes. In any case, I agree, I have certainly not been understanding the crucial counterfactual question, of whether we would have drawn the same moral conclusion even if the moral facts had been different, in the way he must intend. But I am not being perverse. I believe, as I said, that my way of taking the question is the more natural one. And more important, although there is, I grant, a reading of that question on which it will always yield the answer Harman wants – namely, that a difference in the moral facts would *not* have made a difference in our judgment – I do not believe this can support his argument. I must now explain why.

It will help if I contrast my general approach with his. I am addressing questions about the justification of belief in the spirit of what Quine has called "epistemology naturalized" (Quine, 1969a, pp. 69–90. See also Quine, 1969b). I take this to mean that we have in general no a priori way of knowing which strategies for forming and refining our beliefs are likely to take us closer to the truth. The only way we have of proceeding is to assume the approximate truth of what seems to us the best overall theory we already have of what we are like and what the world is like, and to decide in the light of *that* what strategies of research and reasoning are likely to be reliable in producing a more nearly true overall theory. One result of applying these procedures, in turn, is likely to be the refinement or perhaps even the abandonment of parts of the tentative theory with which we began.

I take Harman's approach, too, to be an instance of this one. He says we are justified in believing in

those facts that we need to assume to explain why we observe what we do. But he does not think that our knowledge of this principle about justification is a priori. Furthermore, as he knows, we cannot decide whether one explanation is better than another without relying on beliefs we already have about the world. Is it really a better explanation of the vapor trail the physicist sees in the cloud chamber to suppose that a proton caused it, as Harman suggests in his example, rather than some other charged particle? Would there, for example, have been no vapor trail in the absence of that proton? There is obviously no hope of answering such questions without assuming at least the approximate truth of some quite far-reaching microphysical theory, and our knowledge of such theories is not a priori.

But my approach differs from Harman's in one crucial way. For among the beliefs which I have enough confidence to rely on in evaluating explanations, at least at the outset, are some moral beliefs. And I have been relying on them in the following way. Harman's thesis implies that the supposed moral fact of Hitler's being morally depraved is irrelevant to the explanation of Hitler's doing what he did. (For we may suppose that if it explains his doing what he did, it also helps explain, at greater remove, Harman's belief and mine in his moral depravity.) To assess this claim, we need to conceive a situation in which Hitler was *not* morally depraved and consider the question whether in that situation he would still have done what he did. My answer is that he would not, and this answer relies on a (not very controversial) moral view: that in any world at all like the actual one, only a morally depraved person could have initiated a world war, ordered the "final solution," and done any number of other things Hitler did. That is why I believe that, if Hitler hadn't been morally depraved, he wouldn't have done those things, and hence that the fact of his moral depravity is relevant to an explanation of what he did.

Harman, however, cannot want us to rely on any such moral views in answering this counterfactual question. This comes out most clearly if we return to his example of the children igniting the cat. He claims that the wrongness of this act is irrelevant to an explanation of your thinking it wrong, that you would have *thought* it wrong even if it wasn't. My reply was that in order for the action not to be wrong it would have had to lack the feature of deliberate, intense, pointless cruelty, and that if it had differed in this way you might very well *not* have thought it wrong. I also suggested a more cautious version of this reply: that since the action is in fact wrong, and since moral properties supervene on more basic natural ones, it would have had to be different in *some* further natural respect in order not to be wrong; and that we do not know whether if it had so differed you would still have thought it wrong. Both of these replies, again, reply on moral views, the latter merely on the view that there is *something* about the natural features of the action in Harman's example that makes it wrong, the former on a more specific view as to which of these features do this.

But Harman, it is fairly clear, intends for us *not* to rely on any such moral views in evaluating his counterfactual claim. His claim is not that if the action had not been one of deliberate cruelty (or had otherwise differed in whatever way would be required to remove its wrongness), you would still have thought it wrong. It is, instead, that if the action were one of deliberate, pointless cruelty, but this *did not make it wrong*, you would still have thought it was wrong. And to return to the example of Hitler's moral character, the counterfactual claim that Harman will need in order to defend a comparable conclusion about that case is not that if Hitler had been, for example, humane and fair-minded, free of nationalistic pride and racial hatred, he would still have done exactly as he did. It is, rather, that if Hitler's psychology, and anything else about his situation that could strike us as morally relevant, had been exactly as it in fact was, but this had *not constituted moral depravity*, he would still have done exactly what he did.

Now the antecedents of these two conditionals are puzzling. For one thing, both are, I believe, necessarily false. I am fairly confident, for example, that Hitler really was morally depraved; and since I also accept the view that moral features supervene on more basic natural properties I take this to imply that there is no possible world in which Hitler has just the personality he in fact did, in just the situation he was in, but is not morally depraved. Any attempt to describe such a situation, moreover, will surely run up against the limits of our moral concepts – what Harman calls our "moral sensibility" – and this is no accident. For what Harman is asking us to do, in general, is to consider cases in which absolutely *everything* about the nonmoral facts that could seem morally relevant to us, in light of whatever moral theory we accept and of the

concepts required for our understanding of that theory, is held fixed, but in which the moral judgment that our theory yields about the case is nevertheless mistaken. So it is hardly surprising that, using that theory and those concepts, we should find it difficult to conceive in any detail what such a situation would be like. It is especially not surprising when the cases in question are as paradigmatic in light of the moral outlook we in fact have as is Harman's example or as is [. . .] mine of Hitler's moral character. The only way we could be wrong about this latter case (assuming we have the nonmoral facts right) would be for our whole moral theory to be hopelessly wrong, so radically mistaken that there could be no hope of straightening it out through adjustments from within.

But I do not believe we should conclude, as we might be tempted to, that we therefore know a priori that this is not so, or that we cannot understand these conditionals that are crucial to Harman's argument. Rather, now that we have seen how we have to understand them, we should grant that they are true: that if our moral theory were somehow hopelessly mistaken, but all the nonmoral facts remained exactly as they in fact are, then, since we do *accept* that moral theory, we would still draw exactly the moral conclusions we in fact do. But we should deny that any skeptical conclusion follows from this. In particular, we should deny that it follows that moral facts play no role in explaining our moral judgments.

For consider what follows from the parallel claim about microphysics, in particular about Harman's example in which a physicist concludes from his observation of a vapor trail in a cloud chamber, and from the microphysical theory he accepts, that a free proton had passed through the chamber. The parallel claim, notice, is *not* just that if the proton had not been there the physicist would have thought it was. This claim is implausible, for we may assume that the physicist's theory is generally correct, and it follows from that theory that if there hadn't been a proton there, then there wouldn't have been a vapor trail. But in a perfectly similar way it is implausible that if Hitler hadn't been morally depraved we would still have thought he was: for we may assume that our moral theory also is at least roughly correct, and it follows from the most central features of that theory that if Hitler hadn't been morally depraved, he wouldn't have done what he did. The *parallel* claim about the microphysical example is, instead, that if there hadn't been a proton there, but there *had* been a vapor trail, the physicist would still have concluded that a proton was present. More precisely, to maintain a perfect parallel with Harman's claims about the moral cases, the antecedent must specify that although no proton is present, absolutely *all* the nonmicrophysical facts that the physicist, in light of his theory, might take to be relevant to the question of whether or not a proton is present, are exactly as in the actual case. (These macrophysical facts, as I shall for convenience call them, surely include everything one would normally think of as an observable fact.) Of course, we shall be unable to imagine this without imagining that the physicist's theory is pretty badly mistaken; but I believe we should grant that, *if* the physicist's theory were somehow this badly mistaken, but all the macrophysical facts (including all the observable facts) were held fixed, then the physicist, since he does accept that theory, would still draw all the same conclusions that he actually does. That is, this conditional claim, like Harman's parallel claims about the moral cases, is true.

But no skeptical conclusions follow; nor can Harman, since he does not intend to be a skeptic about physics, think that they do. It does not follow, in the first place, that we have any reason to think the physicist's theory *is* generally mistaken. Nor does it follow, furthermore, that the hypothesis that a proton really did pass through the cloud chamber is not part of a good explanation of the vapor trail, and hence of the physicist's thinking this has happened. This looks like a reasonable explanation, of course, only on the assumption that the physicist's theory is at least roughly true, for it is this theory that tells us, for example, what happens when charged particles pass through a supersaturated atmosphere, what other causes (if any) there might be for a similar phenomenon, and so on. But, as I say, we have not been provided with any reason for not trusting the theory to this extent.

Similarly, I conclude, we should draw no skeptical conclusions from Harman's claims about the moral cases. It is true, I grant, that if our moral theory were seriously mistaken, but we still believed it, and the nonmoral facts were held fixed, we would still make just the moral judgments we do. But *this* fact by itself provides us with no reason for thinking that our moral theory *is* generally mistaken. Nor, again, does it imply that the fact of Hitler's really having been morally depraved forms

no part of a good explanation of his doing what he did and hence, at greater remove, of our thinking him depraved. This explanation will appear reasonable, of course, only on the assumption that our accepted moral theory is at least roughly correct, for it is this theory that assures us that only a depraved person could have thought, felt, and acted as Hitler did. But, as I say, Harman's argument has provided us with no reason for not trusting our moral views to this extent, and hence with no reason for doubting that it is sometimes moral facts that explain our moral judgments.

I conclude with three comments about my argument.

(1) I have tried to show that Harman's claim – that we would have held particular moral beliefs we do even if those beliefs were untrue – admits of two readings, one of which makes it implausible, and the other of which reduces it to an application of a general skeptical strategy, which could as easily be used to produce doubt about microphysical as about moral facts. The general strategy is this. Consider any conclusion *C* we arrive at by relying both on some distinguishable "theory" *T* and on some body of evidence not being challenged, and ask whether we would have believed *C* even if it had been false. The plausible answer, *if* we are allowed to rely on *T*, will often be no: for if *C* had been false, then (according to *T*) the evidence would have had to be different, and in that case we wouldn't have believed *C*. (I have illustrated the plausibility of this sort of reply for all my moral examples, as well as for the microphysical one.) But the skeptic intends us *not* to rely on *T* in this way, and so rephrases the question: Would we have believed *C* even if it were false *but* all the evidence had been exactly as it in fact was? Now the answer has to be yes, and the skeptic concludes that *C* is doubtful. (It should be obvious how to extend this strategy to belief in other minds, or in an external world.) I am of course not convinced: I do not think answers to the rephrased question show anything interesting about what we know or justifiably believe. But it is enough for my purposes here that no such *general* skeptical strategy could pretend to reveal any problems peculiar to belief in *moral* facts.

(2) My conclusion about Harman's argument, although it is not exactly the same as, is nevertheless similar to and very much in the spirit of the Duhemian point I invoked earlier against verificationism. There the question was whether typical

moral assertions have testable implications, and the answer was that they do, so long as you include additional moral assumptions of the right sort among the background theories on which you rely in evaluating these assertions. Harman's more important question is whether we should ever regard moral facts as relevant to the explanation of nonmoral facts, and in particular of our having the moral beliefs we do. But the answer, again, is that we should, so long as we are willing to hold the right sorts of *other* moral assumptions fixed in answering counterfactual questions. Neither answer shows morality to be on any shakier ground than, say, physics: for typical microphysical hypotheses, too, have testable implications, and appear relevant to explanations, only if we are willing to assume at least the approximate truth of an elaborate microphysical theory and to hold this assumption fixed in answering counterfactual questions.

(3) Of course, this picture of how explanations depend on background theories, and moral explanations in particular on moral background theories, does show why someone already tempted toward moral skepticism on other grounds (such as those mentioned at the beginning of this essay) might find Harman's claim about moral explanations plausible. To the extent that you already have pervasive doubts about moral theories, you will also find moral facts nonexplanatory. So I grant that Harman may have located a natural symptom of moral skepticism; but I am sure he has neither traced this skepticism to its roots nor provided any independent argument for it. His claim that we do not *in fact* cite moral facts in explanation of moral beliefs and observations cannot provide such an argument, for that claim is false. So, too, is the claim that assumptions about moral facts seem irrelevant to such explanations, for many do not. The claim that we *should* not rely on such assump-

tions because they *are* irrelevant, on the other hand, unless it is supported by some independent argument for moral skepticism, will just be question-begging: for the principal test of whether they are relevant, in any situation in which it appears they might be, is a counterfactual question about what would have happened if the moral fact had not obtained, and how we answer that question depends precisely upon whether we *do* rely on moral assumptions in answering it.

A different concern, to which Harman only alludes in the passages I have discussed, is that belief in moral facts may be difficult to render consistent with a naturalistic world view. Since I share a naturalistic viewpoint, I agree that it is important to show that belief in moral facts need not be belief in anything supernatural or "nonnatural." I have of course not dealt with every argument from this direction, but I *have* argued for the important point that naturalism in ethics does not require commitment to reductive definitions for moral terms, any more than physicalism about psychology and biology requires a commitment to reductive definitions for the terminology of those sciences.

My own view I stated at the outset: that the only argument for moral skepticism with any independent weight is the argument from the difficulty of settling disputed moral questions. I have shown that anyone who finds Harman's claim about moral explanations plausible must already have been tempted toward skepticism by some other considerations, and I suspect that the other considerations will always just be the ones I sketched. So that is where discussion should focus. I also suggested that those considerations may provide less support for moral skepticism than is sometimes supposed, but I must reserve a thorough defense of that thesis for another occasion.

References

Boyd, Richard. Forthcoming a. "Materialism without Reductionism: non-Humean Causation and the Evidence for Physicalism." In *The Physical Basis of Mind*. Cambridge, MA: Harvard University Press.

Davis, David Brion. 1966. *The Problem of Slavery in Western Culture*. Ithaca, NY: Cornell University Press.

DeVoto, Bernard. 1942. *The Year of Decision: 1846*. Boston: Houghton Mifflin.

Harman, Gilbert. 1977. *The Nature of Morality*. Oxford: Oxford University Press.

Mackie, J. L. 1977. *Ethics: Inventing Right and Wrong*. New York: Penguin.

Nagel, Thomas. 1980. "The Limits of Objectivity." In Sterling M. McMurrin, ed., *The Tanner Lectures on Human Values*. Salt Lake City: University of Utah Press; Cambridge: Cambridge University Press, pp. 77–139.

Putnam, Hilary. 1975. "Language and Reality." In *Mind, Language and Reality. Philosophical Papers, Volume II*. Cambridge: Cambridge University Press.

Quine, W. V. O. 1969a. "Epistemology Naturalized." In *Ontological Relativity and Other Essays*. New York: Columbia University Press.

Quine, W. V. O. 1969b. "Natural Kinds." In *Ontological Relativity and Other Essays*. New York: Columbia University Press.

Sterling M. McMurrin, ed., *The Tanner Lectures on Human Values*. Salt Lake City: University of Utah Press; Cambridge: Cambridge University Press, pp. 77–139.

Tannenbaum, Frank. 1947. *Slave and Citizen*. New York: Alfred A. Knopf.

27

Moral Facts as Configuring Causes

Terence Cuneo

Moral antirealists frequently object that, if moral realism were true, then moral facts would be explanatorily idle.[1] In particular, some moral anti-realists complain that, if moral realism were true, then moral facts would be *causally* idle; they would not do any genuine causal explanatory work.[2] This complaint challenges the heart of what is perhaps the reigning orthodoxy among moral realists. The apparent orthodoxy among realists is that moral facts exist and are in some interesting sense "natural" facts.[3] But it is commonly assumed that natural facts are, in the paradigmatic case, causally efficacious. Accordingly, if moral facts are not causally efficacious, then they are not paradigmatic natural facts. And for those naturalists who believe that being causally efficacious is necessary and sufficient for something's being real, the causal indolence of putative moral facts establishes that moral facts don't exist.[4] It is not surprising, then, that a chief concern of those who subscribe to the appar-

ent realist orthodoxy has been to establish that moral facts are causally efficacious.

An interesting feature of the recent moral realism/antirealism debate is that some prominent moral realists have agreed with the aforementioned antirealist complaint. Ronald Dworkin, Colin McGinn, Robert Audi, and Judith Jarvis Thomson, for example, have all argued that moral facts are not causally efficacious.[5] Their claim is that the apparent orthodoxy is false: Moral facts exist, but are not paradigmatic natural facts. Although I have considerable sympathy with this non-naturalist position, my purpose in this essay is to say a word in defense of what I shall call the "causalist" position – the view that moral facts do genuine causal explanatory work in the world. My primary aim will be to develop a view according to which moral facts of a certain kind are plausibly viewed as being causally efficacious and, thus, "natural" in one sense of this term. To this end, I engage in two tasks. The first is

---

[1] See Harman 1977 [chapter 1 of this book is included as chapter 25 of this volume], Williams 1985, Gibbard 1990, Zimmerman 1985, Wright 1992 and 1995, and Blackburn 1995.

[2] That the "explanatory challenge" concerns the causal efficacy of moral facts becomes clear when one examines the realist responses to it. See, e.g., Sturgeon 1985 [included as chapter 26 of this volume] and 1986, Brink 1989, and McGinn 1997.

[3] See Brink 1989, Boyd 1988 [included as chapter 13 of this volume], Sturgeon 1985, Railton 1986 [included as chapter 14 of this volume], and Jackson 1998.

[4] The claim is made by Kim 1996 among many others. In what follows, I shall not assume this claim is true.

[5] See Dworkin 1996, McGinn 1997, Audi 1997 and 1993, and Thomson 1996.

to develop an account of the sense in which moral facts of certain kinds are causally efficacious. After having sketched the concept of what I call a "configuring" cause, I contend that the exercise of the moral virtues is plausibly viewed as a configuring cause. The second task is to argue that the causalist position I develop can withstand objections inspired by the work of Robert Audi and Jaegwon Kim. While engaging in these two tasks is not light work, there is nonetheless a sense in which the aim of this essay is fairly modest. A strategy commonly employed by philosophers who defend the causalist view is to argue that we have good reason to believe that moral realism is true because we have good reasons to believe that moral facts are causes of non-moral facts of certain kinds.[6] While this is a perfectly acceptable strategy to employ, I am not on this occasion concerned to argue that moral realism is true. Rather, I simply wish to contend, contrary to philosophers such as Dworkin, McGinn, Thomson, and Audi, that if moral realism is true, then we have good reason to believe that moral facts of a certain kind are causally efficacious.

I. Causality and Ontology: Some Assumptions

Let me begin by addressing two preliminary matters. First, any argument to the conclusion that moral facts are (or are not) causally efficacious presupposes some understanding of the notion of causal efficacy. Although I shall return to this topic, I want to make explicit several assumptions regarding the nature of causal efficacy that will shape the subsequent discussion.

In what follows, I shall accept a general account of causal efficacy that is fairly liberal in some senses and restrictive in others. The account is latitudinarian in the following four ways. First, I assume that entities of various kinds are causally efficacious. Thus, I assume that events, processes, facts, property instances, and so forth can figure in genuine causal explanations insofar as they are causally efficacious. Second, I assume that if an entity figures in a causal explanation by virtue of its being causally efficacious, it needn't be the case that there is some causal "mechanism" at work, a transfer of energy or conserved quantity, or a law (strict or otherwise) that is projected. Third, I will

assume that there is no sharp distinction between what is selected as the cause of an event (or fact) and the background conditions of what is selected as the cause of an event (or fact). What we select as the cause of an event (or fact) is ultimately a pragmatic matter that is a function of our interests, purposes, and knowledge. Finally, I shall assume that there are (perhaps irreducibly) different kinds of causal efficacy. A thing can be causally efficacious insofar as it causally intervenes, contravenes, modifies, inhibits, prevents, sustains, triggers, structures, and so forth.

The account of causal efficacy with which I will be working is not liberal in the following two ways, however. First, I assume that a realist account of causal efficacy is true. Causal features are not projected on the world nor do they consist merely in the constant conjunction of two or more events. Second, while I assume that it is a necessary condition of something's being causally efficacious that it supports counterfactuals of the relevant sort (i.e., had c not obtained, then, *ceteris paribus*, e would not have obtained), I do not assume that it is a sufficient condition. So, I shall not assume that a purely counterfactual account of causal efficacy is correct.

I will not offer any arguments for the foregoing assumptions since I believe that they have been effectively defended elsewhere.[7]

The second preliminary matter I wish to address concerns the ontology of moral facts. I assume that constitutive of *moral realism of a paradigmatic sort* is the thesis that there are moral facts and that facts of this kind can be divided into at least two subspecies. I call facts of the first kind "general" moral facts and facts of the latter kind "particular" moral facts. General moral facts are ones that have the following logical form: If x is a token of some intention, action, etc., type y (e.g., murder), then x has some moral property p. The fact *that murder is wrong* and the moral norm *that wicked deeds ought to be despised* are, according to the present view, general moral facts. Particular moral facts, by contrast, are those facts that consist in a contingently existing particular's exemplifying one or another moral property at a time. The facts *that this murder is wrong* and *that Hitler's wicked deeds ought to be despised* are particular moral facts.

I draw this distinction between types of moral fact for the purpose of making clear just what sorts

---

[6] See, e.g., Railton 1986, Sturgeon 1985, and Brink 1989.

[7] See, e.g., Dupré 1993, Cartwright 1983 and 1999, Corbí and Prades 2000, Baker 1995, and Mellor 1995.

of moral fact are plausibly viewed as being causally efficacious. For the purposes of this paper, I will assume that, if moral facts are causally efficacious, then it is only particular moral facts that play this role. My fundamental reason for assuming this is that I doubt that unrestricted general facts of *any* sort are causes.[8] On the assumption that this is correct, then it is also true that general moral facts are not causes.

II. Virtues and Causes

The various arguments against the causalist view offered by moral realists such as Dworkin, McGinn, Audi, and Thomson exhibit a familiar pattern. The first stage is to argue that moral features of a certain kind are not causally efficacious. Dworkin, for example, argues that necessary moral facts such as *that slavery is unjust* cannot be causes.[9] Thomson and Audi contend that contingent moral facts such as *that an act-token of a certain kind is just* are likewise non-causal.[10] McGinn argues, somewhat differently, that the property of goodness is not a cause.[11] Having shown that the selected kind of moral feature is not causally efficacious, the second stage consists in concluding that we have good reason to believe that moral features as such are causally impotent.

This strategy seems to me questionable for two reasons. In the first place, it is plausible to believe that the most defensible causalist positions are committed only to the thesis that moral facts of certain kinds are causally efficacious. The aforementioned strategy has force only if the types of moral feature that are claimed not to be causally efficacious are those that are most likely to be causes. Moreover – and this is the second point – I doubt that the objections to causalism raised by realists consider those kinds of moral feature that are the most plausible candidates for being causally efficacious. As a corrective to this strategy, I would like to put causalism in its best light by suggesting that it is the virtues in particular that are the best candidates among moral features for being causally efficacious.[12]

My argument begins with two scenarios. Here is the first:

> Margaret and Sam have been colleagues for some years in the same department. Although collegial, they are not good friends. One reason for this is that Margaret is not a person whom it is particularly easy to like. While highly intelligent, Margaret has the tendency to be at once a vocal and vigorous critic of the work of her colleagues and rather dismissive of their criticism of her own work. Recently, however, Sam has noticed that Margaret has seemed withdrawn. She rarely voices her views anymore in department gatherings. She regularly sits by herself in the cafeteria for lunch. This last year, moreover, has been uncharacteristically unproductive for her. While none of Margaret's other colleagues seems to take much notice of this, Sam suspects that all isn't well with Margaret. So, Sam asks Margaret to lunch. Initially, Margaret is a little stand-offish, but Sam is gently persistent and continues to check in with Margaret regularly. They develop a pattern of meeting for coffee and, after a short while, it becomes clear to Sam that, indeed, Margaret is struggling with serious personal issues. Upon learning this, Sam becomes very concerned about Margaret's well-being. Sam's concern isn't fleeting, but endures over the subsequent months – endures in spite of the fact that, on more than a few occasions, Margaret severely tries Sam's patience. The concerns endures because Sam works hard at making time for Margaret, keeps her situation in mind, and puts aside some of his projects for her sake.

The question I wish to raise about this scenario is the following: Sam's colleagues are presented with signs of various sorts – signs that consist in Margaret's behaving and "carrying" herself in certain ways over a period of time. However, Sam's colleagues either fail to notice these signs, or if they do notice them, their noticing them does not motivate them to help Margaret. With Sam it is different. Sam interprets these signs as calling for a certain range of responses and is motivated in an appropriate fashion by virtue of being aware of these signs. That is to say, by virtue of Sam's being aware of these signs, a variety of motivational states with appropriate content and strength that endure

---

[8]   See Hale 1987, p. 94.
[9]   See Dworkin 1996, p. 119.
[10]   See Thomson 1996, ch. 6, and Audi 1993.
[11]   See McGinn 1997, pp. 13–16.
[12]   Sturgeon 1985 also suggests that virtues and vices are plausibly seen as being causally efficacious. One might view the causalist position I wish to defend as elaborating upon Sturgeon's suggestion.

in different contexts over an appropriate stretch of time form in the right fashion. Why?

In a moment, I'll return to this scenario. Let's now have the second scenario before us:

> Both a scholar of obscure languages and a computer aficionado, Sam has several different types of computers in his office. Today he has brought Lyle to his office. Lyle is the son of American expatriates who live in an obscure village in the South Pacific. Since Lyle has been raised in a very isolated environment, he knows almost nothing about computers and how they work. As Lyle presses on certain keys on the keyboard of one of Sam's computers, letters of certain types appear on that computer's monitor screen. When he presses keys of the same type on a keyboard joined to another computer, letters from a different language appear on that computer's monitor. Lyle finds this puzzling.

Suppose we grant that the fact that Lyle pushes down on certain keys of a given computer is (to use Fred Dretske's term) a "triggering" cause of the fact that letters of certain types appear on that computer's monitor.[13] Had Lyle not pressed on these keys, then (all other things being equal) these letters would not have appeared on that computer's monitor. Given Lyle's puzzlement, however, there is a natural question to raise: when Lyle presses down on the keys of a keyboard joined to a particular computer, letters of certain types are displayed on that computer's monitor. And when he presses down on keys of the same type on a keyboard joined to a different computer, letters of different types are displayed on that computer's monitor. Why?

I am going to contend that there is a kind of causal explanation that answers both questions I have raised.

Begin with the second scenario. Our question in this case is what explains the fact that when Lyle presses down on the same types of keys on keyboards joined to different computers, letters of different types appear on those computers' monitors. The natural answer to offer is that it is certain features of the hardware conditions (the actual electrical connections in the computer) and programming (the software) of each computer working in a particular way that is causally respon-

sible for this. The fact that the hardware and software components of each computer are working in a certain way "configures" the informational content introduced by Lyle's pressing certain keys on a given keyboard in such a way so as to produce letters of a certain type on that computer's monitor.[14] We could put the matter thus: the fact that certain features of the hardware and software components of a given computer are manifested in a certain way is a configuring cause of the fact that letters of certain types appear on that computer's monitor.

So, take an information-processing system, S, an event or fact A that is an input into S, and an event or fact B that is an output of S. Assume that A carries information of a certain kind and is a triggering cause of B. Assume also that there is a type of causal process C occasioned by A that mediates A and B and that transmits the information carried by A. Assume, furthermore, that there is no sense in which C had to obtain. Given A, any number of subsequent types of causal process could have taken place. A configuring cause is a (concrete) fact or event F that configures (or structures) the information carried in A in such a way that C obtains and, thus, A causes B. Or as I shall say, given A, F is a configuring cause of B. In Lyle's case, the fact that he pressed on certain keys of a keyboard joined to a particular computer and the fact that letters of certain types appeared on that computer's monitor is mediated by a causal process. Had certain elements of the hardware and software components not operated in a particular way, then (all other things being equal) the fact that Lyle pressed certain keys on that keyboard would not have caused letters of certain types to appear on that computer's monitor.

Turn now to the scenario involving Sam and Margaret. In this instance, we asked what accounts for the fact that Sam is motivated in a variety of appropriate ways – or as I will simply say, motivated appropriately. An appealing suggestion is that what accounts for this fact is that Sam manifests various features of the virtue of compassion. If we think of a person's virtue as being comprised of "aspects" or capacities, we can say that Sam's behavior is the product of the manifestation of the

---

[13]   Cf. Dretske 1993.

[14]   Here and elsewhere I shall remain neutral concerning different accounts of what "informational content" consists in; I certainly don't wish the example I employ to suggest that the informational content of human cognitive systems can be satisfactorily analyzed as symbolic representations processed by automated formal symbol-manipulation systems!

various aspects or capacities that comprise Sam's compassion.[15] In noticing the presence (and absence) of certain features of Margaret's countenance and behavior, for example, Sam exercises what we might call the "perceptual" aspect of a virtue. In interpreting these features as morally relevant, and fixing upon an appropriate course of response, Sam exercises what we can call the "interpretive" aspect of a virtue. And in being moved to act appropriately in response to these features, what we can call the "motivational" aspect of Sam's virtue is actualized. Sam's behavior, then, is plausibly thought of as the product of the coordinated manifestation of various aspects of the particular way in which he instantiates the virtue of compassion.

According to the view I am elaborating, a virtue is a constellation of aspects or capacities. More exactly, it is a *stable* and *enduring* collection of aspects or capacities that ordinarily work in concert. What I should add is that it is plausible to believe that a virtue is not a higher-order property "over and above" this unified and stable constellation of capacities. There's not the unified and stable constellation of the perceptual, interpretive, and motivational capacities, and then Sam's compassion over and above that. Nor is there the manifestation of these aspects, and the higher-order property of *Sam's acting compassionately* over and above the manifestation of these capacities. We might call this a "token identity" or "constitution" view of a person's virtue and its manifestations – though I won't put much weight on which label we use. What is important to see is that the view isn't in any interesting sense reductionistic. By claiming that a person's virtue and its manifestations are

"nothing over and above" a stable and enduring collection of capacities and their manifestations, it is not as if we have reduced a person's virtue or its manifestations to a cluster of mere naturalistic descriptive properties. A person's virtue consists in the capacities to notice what is morally *salient*, to interpret these signs *correctly*, and to be motivated *appropriately*. A person's virtue, then, is a richly evaluative thing that consists in being reliably disposed to respond to reasons of various kinds appropriately.

The thesis I propose is that the mutual manifestation of the interpretive and motivational aspects of Sam's compassion is a configuring cause of the fact that he is motivated appropriately over a certain period of time.[16]

Suppose we assume the fact that Sam notices certain features of Margaret's behavior and countenance is a triggering cause of the fact that Sam is motivated appropriately. Suppose, moreover, this triggering cause introduces informational or "intuitional" content about Margaret (e.g., that Margaret appears in such-and-such way, etc.) into Sam's cognitive system. Suppose, also, there is a causal process occasioned by the fact that Sam notices certain features of Margaret's behavior and countenance that mediates between this fact and the fact that Sam is motivated appropriately. And suppose that this process did not have to obtain; any number of different causal processes could have occurred. Finally, suppose that this causal process is comprised of mental states that themselves bear intuitional content and that these states stand in causal relations of various types to one another. The exercise of the interpretive and motivational aspects of Sam's virtue, I suggest,

---

[15]   I use the term "capacity" in the same fashion that Cartwright 1999 does. Capacities are "open-ended" insofar as they are not restricted to any single type of manifestation.

[16]   Here is one worry concerning this suggestion: How could it be informative to claim that what causally accounts for the fact that Sam is motivated appropriately over some stretch of time is the fact that he has manifested the virtue of compassion – a disposition, in part, to be motivated aright? In the following two ways: first, it is important to note that there are interesting competing explanations for why Sam is motivated aright – explanations I will address in sections IV and V. One such competing explanation is that there is a configuring cause of his being motivated appropriately, but it does not involve the exercise of a virtue. Another competing explanation is that there is no configuring cause of Sam's being motivated appropriately. One reason, then, that the putative causal explanation I am broaching is informative is because it has what van Fraassen 1980 calls a relevant "contrast class." Second, it is helpful to keep in mind that the term "motivated appropriately" is being used as shorthand for a descriptively rich constellation of motivational states that are the product of a descriptively rich cluster of experiential inputs. To say that Sam is motivated appropriately is to say that, given his awareness of a variety of signs, Sam is appropriately motivated to listen carefully to what Margaret says in conversation, call upon her regularly for coffee, and so forth. And it is not trivial to say that the exercise of Sam's virtue causally accounts for the fact that this descriptively rich cluster of motivational states forms in response to a wide variety of different experiential inputs. For an elaboration of this basic idea, see Hempel 1965, p. 457ff.

"configures" the intuitional content of Sam's awareness of Margaret's behavior and countenance in such a way that Sam's awareness of these signs yields the formation (and maintenance) of a variety of appropriate motivational states. In so causally configuring this information, the exercise of these aspects of Sam's virtue doesn't merely transmit the informational content of Sam's awareness; it *interprets* it as being indicative of certain features of Sam's environment. Had these aspects of Sam's virtue not been manifested in certain ways, then (all other things being equal) the variety of motivational states that consist in Sam's being appropriately concerned for Margaret's well-being would not have been formed (and maintained).

Let me now lay bare two assumptions concerning this thesis – one that I will not defend at this point, the other which I will defend in a moment. The assumption that I will not defend at this point is the claim that there are such things as configuring causes. At this stage in the discussion, I simply recommend this assumption as a plausible claim about which a realist does not have reason to be particularly suspicious. The assumption that I will defend shortly is that there is a configuring cause of the fact that Sam is motivated appropriately. What I shall now defend is the conditional claim that, if there is a configuring cause of the fact that Sam is motivated appropriately, it is the exercise of Sam's virtue.

III. Developing the View

What we are trying to explain is a fairly unusual phenomenon. After all, among ordinary agents it is a regular occurrence that, given certain kinds of experience, they feel great concern only to have that concern evaporate shortly thereafter. It is also a regular occurrence among such agents that they fail to display appropriately compassionate behavior across different contexts. Sam's concern for Margaret, however, exhibits none of these defects. Given Sam's awareness of Margaret's countenance and behavior, he is motivated appropriately over a significant stretch of time in different contexts – even in the teeth of considerations that would

threaten to extinguish this motivation. It is this fairly unusual state of affairs for which we would like to find a configuring causal explanation. Here I should like to adduce a pair of considerations that speak in favor of the thesis I propose.

In the first place, it appears to be part of the very job description of the exercise of a virtue that it explains constancies in behavior across varying circumstances, resistance to distorting influences, and the like.[17] Since this is precisely what we are trying to explain, the fact that Sam has exercised the virtue of compassion is an excellent candidate for explaining the fact that he is motivated appropriately. Of course this alone doesn't give us reason to believe that, if there were a configuring cause of Sam's motivational state, then it is the manifestation of Sam's virtue. But, secondly, there are good reasons for affirming this latter claim as well. If what I've said is correct, paradigmatic configuring cause explanations are ones that appeal to the way in which an entity's "programming" configures informational content of certain kinds. To be a virtuous agent, however, arguably just is to be "programmed" in a certain fashion. The virtuous person is programmed in such a way that, given certain kinds of experiential inputs (and when all goes well), the manifestation of certain features of that programming configures the intuitional content of those experiential inputs so as to yield mental states and activities of certain kinds. Given the fact that Sam is programmed to interpret signs of certain kinds aright, when all goes well, his noticing those signs yields motivational states and activities of the appropriate types.

If this is right, being a configuring cause also appears to be part of the job description of the exercise of a virtue. However, the causalist presumably needs to say more than this in defense of her view. What the causalist presumably wants to claim is not merely that it is part of the job description of the exercise of Sam's compassion that it is a configuring cause. Rather, what the causalist also wishes to claim is that it is in virtue of its *normative* character that the exercise of Sam's compassion is a configuring cause. That is, the causalist presumably wants to maintain that the fact that the manifestation of Sam's virtue is an *appropriate*

---

[17] Here I echo Railton 1995, p. 276. Perhaps it is worth explicitly noting that the type of explanation in question doesn't seem to be merely a normative explanation. The exercise of a virtue doesn't serve merely to *justify* these constancies in behavior. Nor does the explanation seem teleological in character. It is not as if the exercise of the interpretive and perceptual aspects of Sam's virtue somehow detects the compelling rightness of Sam's being motivated appropriately.

response to reasons is fundamental to its being a configuring cause. What can be said in favor of this further claim?

I propose to address this question by considering an objection to the causalist position articulated by Robert Audi.[18] Audi's objection hinges on the claim that it is not moral facts, but the naturalistic/non-moral features that determine them that do all the causal work in putative moral explanations. The causalist reply to this objection should throw light on the sense in which it is the normative character of the exercise of Sam's virtue that functions as a configuring cause.

IV. Audi's Objection

Audi's objection proceeds on a pair of assumptions. First of all, says Audi, moral facts *ontologically depend* on "natural" facts. For any particular moral fact, there will be a range of natural facts on which that moral fact supervenes and with which that moral fact is not identical. Second, our awareness of moral facts *epistemically depends* on these natural facts. That is to say, being aware of a particular's having a moral property typically depends on being aware of its having a certain range of base natural properties that determine its having that moral property. This latter type of dependency, writes Audi, has ramifications for moral explanations:

> Whenever we explanatorily invoke a moral property, it will be in part on the basis of, or at least in the light of, some belief or presupposition to the effect that one or more natural properties is playing an explanatory role. We are thus in a position to rely – often unselfconsciously, for sure – on those other properties to do the explanatory work, and it is arguable that they, and not any moral property, are in fact what does it. . . . Our understanding of how the ascription of moral properties can explain (at least so far as causal explanation goes) seems wholly *derivative* from our understanding of how the relevant base properties can do so.[19]

The idea, then, is that for any putative causal explanation of a phenomenon E that appeals to the causal efficacy of some moral fact M, we can replace, without loss of explanatory power, the reference to M with the base natural facts N on which M supervenes. So, the idea is not that we can offer different *complementary* causal explanations of E in terms of M and N. Rather, it is that any putative causal explanation of E offered in terms of M can be *eliminated* in favor of an explanation in terms of N. But if this is right, then we have no need to claim that moral facts do any causal explanatory work. All the causal explanatory work is done by the natural facts on which these moral features supervene.

To see the thrust of Audi's objection more clearly, let's consider an example he furnishes. According to the example, the citizens of a particular country revolt because of governmental injustice. Audi writes of this putative explanation:

> One cannot know (and normally would not even believe) that there is such injustice except through some kind of awareness of, say, government seizure of land, arbitrary curfews, and police brutality, where these are construed behaviorally in terms of, for example, soldiers' occupying farmland, clearing streets at night, and clubbing non-protesters. But these are just the sorts of non-moral factors, that in their own right, we suppose . . . can perfectly well explain a revolt. They also seem to have causal power in a quite intuitive sense.[20]

Audi's view, then, is that our awareness of governmental injustice in the case described depends on both our awareness of the behavior of government employees and their intentions. We can, for instance, understand the police brutality in terms of their periodically clubbing and intending to severely harm some of the citizens. We can understand the administrative deceit in terms of the administration's making various statements intended to lead the citizens into believing falsehoods. It is these behavioral and non-moral "social-psychological" features of the world that are supposed to do the causal explanatory work in Audi's imagined revolt.[21] The injustice of the government's actions is simply epiphenomenal with respect to causally explaining the citizens' revolt.

---

[18] See Audi 1997 and 1993. Thomson 1996 has also formulated an objection to the causalist position that more or less mirrors Audi's. For ease of explication, I shall consider only Audi's version of the argument. What I say about Audi's view should apply to Thomson's position *mutatis mutandis*.
[19] Audi 1997, pp. 118–19. See also Audi 1993, p. 62.
[20] Audi 1997, p. 118.
[21] Cf. Audi 1993, p. 62.

What Audi says seems to me to present a powerful objection to causalist views of certain kinds, provided that the putatively social-psychological facts to which he adverts are themselves genuinely naturalistic/non-moral ones. While I think there is excellent reason to doubt this, I shall not pursue the point here. Instead I want to emphasize that there is an important difference between the scenario Audi sketches and the one that I have employed. According to Audi's scenario, what we are attempting to explain causally is why a non-moral state of affairs obtains, viz., *that the citizens revolt*. By contrast, in the case with which I have been working, what we are trying to explain causally is why a moral state of affairs of a certain kind obtains, viz., *that Sam is motivated appropriately*. This difference between the two cases is important because even if Audi were right to claim that we can handily eliminate reference to moral facts when causally explaining why non-moral facts of certain kinds obtain, it wouldn't follow that we can do the same when causally explaining why moral facts of certain kinds obtain. So, even if Audi's objection were to show that moral facts do not causally explain nonmoral ones, it wouldn't follow that moral facts *as such* are causally inefficacious. The question, then, that needs to be raised about Sam's case is this: can we fashion an adequate configuring cause explanation of the moral fact that Sam is motivated appropriately that makes no essential reference to moral facts?

Suppose we pursue this issue by sketching how a rival, non-normative configuring cause explanation of Sam's motivational state might go. One such explanation, broadly Humean in character, runs something like the following. Assume, first of all, that Sam is compassionate and that his being compassionate is constituted (in part) by the fact that he is deeply and firmly concerned about the welfare of his colleagues. Assume, furthermore, that the fact that Sam is aware of signs of certain kinds is a triggering cause that occasions a causal process that itself eventuates in the fact that Sam is motivated appropriately. However, maintain that we can explain why this awareness generates an appropriate motivation by appeal to a constellation of non-moral facts that constitute the exercise of Sam's virtue. Roughly, the suggestion is that the

intuitional content of Sam's awareness is configured by the manifestation of Sam's reliable disposition to form true moral and non-moral beliefs of certain types and his deep concern for his colleagues. These beliefs and concern hook up to form the appropriate motivational state. Most importantly, the beliefs and concern that determine this motivational state are not in any sense moral entities. Rather, they are simply non-normative features that both appear to have causal power in their own right and to be capable of doing all the requisite causal explanatory work to explain why Sam is motivated in the way he is.

As I've indicated, this rival configuring cause explanation is stated in fairly rough terms. I want now to argue, however, that it has to be stated thus, for once we start filling in the details, it becomes very difficult to fashion an adequate configuring cause explanation that is genuinely non-normative in character. Let me highlight three points.

First, the advocate of this rival style of explanation wants to explain the fact that Sam is motivated appropriately by appealing simply to (i) the manifestation of Sam's disposition to form true moral and non-moral beliefs of certain types given certain kinds of experiential input and (ii) the fact that these beliefs hook up with the relevant concern. But of this putative explanation one wants to ask: what *types* of true beliefs are supposed to be adequate to the explanatory task? A person can, after all, form either too few or too many true beliefs in a given situation. Form too few true beliefs and his grip on the situation will be inadequate; he will have too little accurate information concerning the case at hand. Form too many and he will have an excess of information that obfuscates the important issues; as a result, he may well be indecisive or motivationally paralyzed.[22] What we're trying to explain (in part) is why Sam reliably forms and maintains a sufficiently wide range of *relevant* true beliefs and, in addition, holds their content with an appropriate degree of confidence. Merely appealing to the manifestation of a disposition to form true beliefs of certain kinds, however, won't explain that.

Second, if Sam's motivational state is a manifestation of a virtue, it matters *how* Sam forms these beliefs and how they hook up with the rele-

[22]   As both Elgin 1996 and Zagzebski 2001 point out, true beliefs can actually be an impediment to understanding a situation well. Sometimes a representation of a situation that is strictly speaking false, because oversimplified, allows us a better understanding of a situation than one that is true.

vant concern. As recent discussions concerning so-called deviant causal chains have made evident, simply manifesting reliable dispositions of the types mentioned above isn't sufficient to establish that the beliefs and motivational states that are the product of such dispositions are virtuous or, for that matter, rational in any robust sense. The problem is that dispositions to form true beliefs and to be motivated in certain ways can be accidentally reliable insofar as they are the product of serious and systematic cognitive malfunction, bad habits of thinking, the meddling of cognitive scientists, and so on.[23] Accordingly, the mere fact that Sam's motivational states are the product of reliable tendencies to form true moral beliefs and be motivated in certain ways does not explain why those states are virtuous or rational in any full-bodied sense. (We can imagine cases in which Sam's moral beliefs reliably track truth, but are the product of unreflectively appropriating the beliefs of others, for example.) Appealing to normative configuring causes, however, will. For suppose we assume – as I have thus far – that different mental states are linked to each other by causal processes and that there is no sense in which these processes must obtain. Suppose, further, that we adopt the realist assumption that the states that result from these processes exhibit normative merits and demerits such as being rational, unjustified, conscientious, careless, and so forth. Suppose, finally, that in order for these resultant mental states to exhibit these normative features, they must have a certain kind of causal ancestry or, as I have been saying, be causally "configured" in certain ways. If all this is right, then normative facts would appear to have an important theoretical role to play insofar as they can help dissolve the problems of accidental reliability and deviant causal chains that have dogged reliabilist theories of justification and functionalist theories of the mind. All too briefly, inasmuch as normative facts of certain kinds configure causal processes that mediate different mental states – configure them in such a way that the appropriate mental states are formed or maintained – they are (in part) what prevent aberrations of the types mentioned above from occurring and ensure that mental states are formed or maintained in a virtuous or rational fashion.[24] Accordingly, if the causal history of the formation of a mental state determines (in part) why that mental state exhibits certain normative merits or demerits, then normative configuring causes can help explain why.

Third, and finally, it is doubtful that Sam's case can be adequately characterized in the Humean style described above because in Sam's case there is an ineliminable element of interpretation that is also present. This element of interpretation minimally involves fitting the information present into a broader situation, balancing it with other important factors, "walling off" certain considerations, and seeing patterns of particular kinds with a certain degree of vividness. Fundamental to the appropriateness of Sam's motivation, then, is the fact that he forms appropriate beliefs by way of interpreting his situation aright. But it is difficult to see how, in purely non-normative terms, we can fashion a configuring cause explanation of the fact that Sam interprets his situation aright, and thereby arrives at appropriate beliefs. This is not simply because the natural facts that determine the appropriateness of his interpretation form such a wildly heterogeneous group that we need to lump them under a normative concept. It is also because that among the facts that appear to configure the intuitional content of Sam's awareness is the manifestation of Sam's disposition to conduct himself *conscientiously*. However, it is difficult to think of a way in which we can give an account of Sam's conscientious conduct that does not appeal to the fact that Sam has conducted himself as he ought. Nor do I see how, having appealed to that fact, we can somehow isolate the naturalistic/non-normative features of Sam's conscientious conduct and claim that these features alone configure the intuitional content of Sam's awareness. It is not the mere fact that Sam has paid close attention to Margaret's behavior that accounts for the fact that his awareness yields an appropriate motivation. Rather, it is the fact that he has paid close attention to what (and when) he ought. And I think that once we see the intimate manner in which the normative and the natural are intertwined in "thick" moral facts such as *that Sam has conducted himself conscientiously*, we can't simply take it for granted that we can neatly sever the normative aspects of these facts from their natural features and claim that the former are mere causal idlers while the latter shoulder the real causal burden.

---

[23]   For more on these matters, see Plantinga 1993 and Zagzebski 1996, sect. 4.

[24]   For more on this theme, see Plantinga 1993, Zangwill 1998, and, especially, Wedgwood (unpublished).

To this last point there is perhaps a natural response. The natural response is to dig down deeper yet and attempt to isolate the natural facts on which Sam's conscientiousness and the moral reasons to which he responds supervene. The thought is we can claim that it is *these* natural facts (in tandem with other such facts) that causally explain the fact that Sam is motivated appropriately.

While this response may be natural, it seems to me unpromising, the main problem being that it is not obvious what kinds of naturalistic/non-moral fact Sam's conscientiousness and the reasons to which he responds ontologically depend on. Exactly what natural facts make it the case that Margaret's uttering a certain string of phonemes on a given occasion gives Sam moral reasons of various kinds to pay close attention to what she says? Exactly what natural facts make it the case that Sam has exercised moral conscientiousness on a given occasion? And exactly what natural facts make it the case that Sam holds his beliefs concerning Margaret's situation with an appropriate level of confidence and that his concern for her well-being has endured for an appropriate length of time? These are extremely difficult questions to answer. And the difficulty of these questions leads one to suspect that though instances of obligations, entitlements, virtues, and the like are perhaps ontologically and epistemically dependent on various naturalistic/non-moral properties, the ontological and epistemic dependence is in many respects not *epistemically transparent*. So, it is not as if the advocate of the present response can simply pick out the natural facts that determine the fact that Sam has behaved in a conscientious fashion and then claim that it is these natural facts alone that causally explain the occurrence of Sam's motivational state (or even the instantiation of the properties upon which this state supervenes). It is just not obvious what these natural facts are.

To sum up: what made Audi's objection appear to be a serious threat to the causalist position is its claim that the reference to moral facts in causal explanations could be replaced without loss of explanatory power with reference to the naturalistic/non-moral facts upon which they supervene. As I've pointed out, this objection assumes that, when furnishing these rival explanations, we can isolate these subvening non-moral features well enough so as to construct causal explanations in terms of them. I've argued that this assumption is

dubious. Even if we grant that moral facts are determined by natural ones, both the "shapelessness" and "thickness" of moral facts of certain types guarantees that we cannot construct the requisite type of configuring cause explanations only in terms of the determining natural features. The shapelessness of moral facts presents problems for Audi's objection because we are not able to isolate those features that determine moral ones without employing moral concepts and, thus, are unable to construct configuring cause explanations entirely in terms of these determining features. The thickness of moral facts presents an analogous difficulty insofar as these facts present an interesting case in which the normative and the non-normative are so entangled that there is no principled reason for claiming it is the non-normative features of thick moral facts, and not their moral ones, that do all the causal explanatory work.

Let me add to this summary a final point. I have said that we cannot offer a configuring cause explanation of why Sam is motivated appropriately by appealing simply to the naturalistic/non-moral facts upon which the exercise of Sam's virtue supervenes. However, I want also to suggest that, if what I've argued is correct, then we also have good reason to believe that we cannot offer a configuring cause explanation of the naturalistic/*non-moral* facts upon which the exercise of Sam's virtue supervenes that appeals only to other naturalistic/non-moral facts. For take a pair of naturalistic/non-moral facts N and N* and a pair of moral facts M and M* and assume that M supervenes on (i.e., ontologically depends on) N and M* on N*. Assume, further, that N (or some subset of features that constitute N) causes N*. Finally, assume that M* is identical with the fact that Sam is motivated appropriately. If M* supervenes on N*, however, then N* must be constituted by the types of feature sufficient for its determining M*. Presumably, among these features is N*'s having the right sort of causal ancestry; if N* were the product of a deviant causal chain, for example, then it would not determine the fact that Sam is motivated appropriately. But if what I've argued is right, given the myriad of possible causal ancestries that N* might have, we're simply not in a position to isolate adequately the facts that causally configure N* without recourse to normative concepts of various kinds. Accordingly, we are in no better position to furnish a configuring cause explanation of N* that appeals only to non-normative features that we are of providing such an explanation of M*. It follows that, although the causalist response to Audi's objection assumes that moral facts can be the explananda in causal explanations, it needn't; one can also employ the response to address a position that assumes otherwise.

V.   Engaging a Suspicion

Audi's objection is driven by the suspicion that putative moral explanations are not to be taken at face value. And while I've argued that the way in which Audi develops this suspicion fails to provide reason to believe that moral facts are causally inefficacious, I conjecture that the foregoing argument will not have shaken the conviction that it is only the underlying naturalistic/non-moral facts that are doing the genuine causal work in putative moral explanations. The reason for my conjecture is this: Audi's objection hinges on the claim – call it the "epistemic claim" – that we can consistently isolate the underlying naturalistic features doing the genuine causal work in putative moral explanations. But, it may be pointed out, causal explanations need not appeal only to causally efficacious features. So, even if the epistemic claim is false and we are forced to appeal to moral concepts in order to causally explain the existence of moral facts of certain kinds, it doesn't follow that the extension of these concepts does any genuine causal work. Accordingly, even if the foregoing reply to Audi is on the mark, it doesn't follow that causalism is true. Moreover, it might be continued, developing Audi's suspicion needn't involve appealing to the epistemic claim. All that is needed to vindicate the suspicion is *good reason* to believe that it is simply the naturalistic features (whatever they may be) that underlie moral facts that provide the real causal muscle in putative moral explanations.

Let me address these two concerns in order.

The appropriate response to the first concern, I think, is to deny that the considerations adduced in favor of the causalist view and against Audi's objection are supposed to entail that the exercise of Sam's virtue is a configuring cause. Rather, the claim is the following: given moral realism, the thesis that the exercise of Sam's virtue is a configuring cause *better* explains certain facts than a view that renders that exercise of his virtue epiphe-

nomenal. The explanation is better in part because a moral realist of a paradigmatic sort is committed to the existence of the virtues and it appears part of the very job description of the exercise of a virtue that it is a configuring cause. As I've emphasized, fundamental to our understanding of the moral virtues is the claim that their exercise sustains desires, beliefs, and intentions of certain appropriate kinds, inhibits acting on certain temptations, and influences the formation and maintenance of propositional attitudes and motivational states of appropriate types – where "sustaining," "inhibiting," and "influencing" are all causal terms that can be understood in light of the concept of a configuring cause. It is worth adding, moreover, that by thus appealing to the apparent functional profile of the virtues, the causalist is in good company. After all, our reason for believing that the exercise of the virtues is causally efficacious is really no different from our reason for believing that the propositional attitudes themselves are causally efficacious. It is precisely because it appears to be constitutive of the explanatory profile of propositional attitudes that they are causes that we take them to be causes. Accordingly, to deny that the exercise of the virtues or the propositional attitudes plays these causal roles is perforce to deny that our ordinary understanding of their job description is accurate.

Fundamental to the causalist view, then, is the conviction that, in the absence of sufficient reason to believe otherwise, the best option for the moral realist is to assume that the apparent functional profile of the virtues gives us genuine insight into their nature. And since the apparent functional profile of the virtues tells us that their exercise does genuine causal explanatory work, we should (all other things being equal) conclude that the exercise of the virtues is causally efficacious. To transpose what Tyler Burge says about mental causation, our best guide to moral causation lies in understanding our best means of explaining why agents of certain kinds are motivated appropriately in a wide array of different circumstances, hold beliefs of the appropriate sort, and so forth.[25]

Of course there may be good reasons to believe that the apparent functional profile of the virtues is misleading. And among these reasons may be ones that make no appeal to what I've called the

---

[25]   See Burge 1993, p. 112. See also Brink 1989, pp. 194–7.

"epistemic claim." Consider, as a case in point, so-called causal exclusion arguments so prominently discussed in the philosophy of mind.[26] As they are usually developed, versions of this type of argument purport to establish two conclusions: first, that the existence of causally efficacious *sui generis* supervenient entities of any sort implies either massive causal overdetermination, violations of the causal closure of the physical, or objectionable types of downward causation. And, second, these conclusions are sufficiently repugnant that we ought to accept that such putatively supervenient features are either epiphenomenal or type-identical with (or entirely explainable by) the physical features that ostensibly determine them.

Causal exclusion arguments arguably offer the most promising manner by which to develop Audi's suspicion without appeal to the epistemic claim. Nonetheless – and this is to address the second concern raised earlier – I doubt that moral realists should be much enamored with them. Few realists, I suspect, would be enthusiastic about a view according to which both mental and moral features are type-identical with (or entirely explainable by) the physical facts that determine them; the problem being that it is difficult to see how, according to such a view, we could account for either the phenomenal aspects of mentality or the normative aspects of morality in a materialistically acceptable way.[27] And few realists, I suspect, would be willing to believe that *both* mental and moral features are mere shadows of the subvenient physical realm. Audi, for one, *defends* the view that higher-order entities such as beliefs are causally efficacious.[28] In saying this, I don't mean to claim that reductionism or epiphenomenalism is strictly inconsistent with moral realism. I mean only to suggest that the reasons for affirming (and, alternatively, denying) causalism with respect to the virtues and mental features are so similar that it is doubtful we can affirm one and not the other. Accordingly, if one wants to affirm that mental features have the phenomenal features we ordinarily ascribe to them and are causally efficacious, then one should probably also embrace causalism. And, conversely, if one wishes to reject causalism, then one should probably be prepared to reject our ordinary understanding of the mental.

VI. A Loose Thread and a Suggestion

I would like to close by tying up a loose thread and then making a suggestion about how to extend the present argument.

First, the loose thread: Earlier I said that my aim in the last section was to defend the following conditional claim: if there is a configuring cause of the fact that Sam is motivated appropriately, then it is the exercise of Sam's compassion. But, so far forth, I have not defended the claim that there *is* a configuring cause of the fact that Sam is motivated appropriately. Is there anything further to say in its defense?

In fact, I have at this point little new to say in its defense. I don't think the claim should be rejected because there is something suspect with the notion of a configuring cause. To the contrary, if the preceding discussion has been on the mark, the concept appears to do important explanatory work insofar as it can help us to address problems such as accidentally reliable connections and deviant causal chains. Nor do I think the claim should be rejected because there is no causal explanation of the fact that Sam is motivated appropriately. For this latter claim to be sustained a version of moral epiphenomenalism would have to be true. But if what I've argued is sound, realists should no more be attracted to epiphenomenalism with respect to the virtues than to epiphenomenalism with respect to the propositional attitudes.

Still, I suspect that the argument I've developed, even if sound, may leave some of those sympathetic with causalism unsatisfied. The lack of satisfaction, I suspect, is rooted in the thought that a satisfactory causalist view should not merely defend the claim that moral facts causally explain other moral facts, but ought also to defend the thesis that moral facts causally explain non-moral facts. Although I do not see why it is incumbent upon a causalist who does not wish to argue for moral realism to argue for this latter claim – call it the "standard view" – one could view the argument in this paper as the thin wedge of an argument whose aim is to establish that some moral facts cause non-moral facts of certain kinds. The argument would attempt to establish that the causal efficacy of moral facts of

---

[26] For a development of (and ultimately a rejection of) the argument as applied to the moral realm, see Shafer-Landau 2003, ch. 4. The classic formulation of the exclusionary argument is due to Kim 1993 and 1998.

[27] Although see Jackson 1998.

[28] See Audi 1993.

certain kinds is general in character: roughly, given that we have good reasons to believe that moral facts of certain kinds cause other moral facts, and that there are also explanatory contexts in which we cite moral facts of certain kinds as the cause of non-moral facts, then, in the absence of reasons to think otherwise, we should also believe that moral facts of certain kinds cause non-moral facts of certain types. According to this strategy, we argue *to* the standard thesis from the phenomenon of causal relations between moral facts. Of course, if we implement only this strategy, the standard view cannot be used to argue for moral realism. But this may be a price we should be willing to pay, for implementing this strategy may be the most promising avenue by which we can develop a plausible moral naturalism.

References

Audi, Robert. 1993. "Mental Causation: Sustaining and Dynamic." In Heil and Mele 1993: 53–74.

Audi, Robert. 1997. "Ethical Naturalism and the Explanatory Power of Moral Concepts." In *Moral Knowledge and Ethical Character*. Oxford: Oxford University Press, 112–28.

Baker, Lynne Rudder. 1995. *Explaining Attitudes*. Cambridge: Cambridge University Press.

Blackburn, Simon. 1995. "The Flight to Reality." In Rosalind Hursthouse et al., eds., *Virtues and Reasons*. Oxford: Oxford University Press, 35–56.

Boyd, Richard. 1998. "How To Be a Moral Realist." In Sayre-McCord 1998: 181–228.

Brink, David. 1989. *Moral Realism and the Foundations of Ethics*. Cambridge: Cambridge University Press.

Burge, Tyler. 1993. "Mind–Body Causation and Explanatory Practice." In Heil and Mele 1993: 97–120.

Cartwright, Nancy. 1983. *How the Laws of Physics Lie*. Oxford: Oxford University Press.

Cartwright, Nancy. 1999. *The Dappled World*. Cambridge: Cambridge University Press.

Copp, David, and David Zimmerman, eds. 1985. *Morality, Reason and Truth*. Totowa, NJ: Rowman & Allanheld.

Corbí, Josep, and Josep Prades. 2000. *Minds, Causes and Mechanisms*. Oxford: Blackwell.

Dretske, Fred. 1993. "Mental Events as Structuring Causes of Behaviour." In Heil and Mele 1993: 121–36.

Dupré, John. 1993. *The Disorder of Things*. Cambridge, MA: Harvard University Press.

Dworkin, Ronald. 1996. Objectivity and Truth: You'd Better Believe It." *Philosophy and Public Affairs* 25: 87–139.

Elgin, Catherine. 1996. *Considered Judgment*. Princeton: Princeton University Press.

Gibbard, Allan. 1990. *Wise Choices, Apt Feelings*. Cambridge, MA: Harvard University Press.

Hale, Bob. 1987. *Abstract Entities*. Oxford: Blackwell.

Harman, Gilbert. 1977. *The Nature of Morality*. Oxford: Oxford University Press.

Harman, Gilbert, and Judith Jarvis Thomson. 1996. *Moral Relativism and Moral Objectivity*. Oxford: Blackwell.

Heil, John, and Alfred Mele, eds. 1993. *Mental Causation*. Oxford: Oxford University Press.

Hempel, Carl. 1965. *Aspects of Scientific Explanation*. New York: The Free Press.

Jackson, Frank. 1998. *From Metaphysics to Ethics*. Oxford: Oxford University Press.

Kim, Jaegwon. 1993. *Supervenience and Mind*. Cambridge: Cambridge University Press.

Kim, Jaegwon. 1996. *Philosophy of Mind*. Boulder, CO: Westview Press.

Kim, Jaegwon. 1998. *Mind in a Physical World*. Cambridge, MA: MIT Press.

McGinn, Colin. 1997. *Ethics, Evil and Fiction*. Oxford: Oxford University Press.

Mellor, D. H. 1995. *The Facts of Causation*. London: Routledge.

Plantinga, Alvin. 1993. *Warrant and Proper Function*. Oxford: Oxford University Press.

Railton, Peter. 1985. "Moral Realism." *Philosophical Review* 95: 163–207.

Railton, Peter. 1995. "Subjective and Objective." *Ratio* 8: 259–76.

Sayre-McCord, Geoffrey, ed. 1988. *Essays in Moral Realism*, Ithaca, NY: Cornell University Press.

Shafer-Landau, Russ. 2003. *Moral Realism: A Defence*. Oxford: Oxford University Press.

Sturgeon, Nicholas. 1985. "Moral Explanations." In Copp and Zimmerman 1985: 49–78.

Sturgeon, Nicholas. 1986. "Harman on Moral Explanations of Natural Facts." *Southern Journal of Philosophy* 24, supplement: 69–78.

Thomson, Judith Jarvis. 1996. "Epistemological Arguments for Moral Scepticism." In Harman and Thomson 1996: 69–94.

Van Fraassen, Bas. 1980. *The Scientific Image*. Oxford: Clarendon Press.

Wedgwood, Ralph. Unpublished. "Normative Explanations."

Williams, Bernard. 1985. *Ethics and the Limits of Philosophy*. Cambridge, MA: Harvard University Press.

Wright, Crispin. 1992. *Truth and Objectivity*. Cambridge, MA: Harvard University Press.

Wright, Crispin. 1995. "Truth in Ethics." *Ratio* 8: 209–26.

Zagzebski, Linda. 1996. *Virtues of the Mind*. Cambridge: Cambridge University Press.

Zagzebski, Linda. 2001. "Recovering Understanding." In Matthias Steup, ed., *Knowledge, Truth, and Duty*. Oxford: Oxford University Press, 235–54.

Zangwill, Nick. 1998. "Direction of Fit and Normative Functionalism." *Philosophical Studies* 91: 173–203.

Zimmerman, David. 1985. "Moral Realism and Explanatory Necessity." In Copp and Zimmerman 1985: 79–103.

II.4   Moral Disagreement

Introduction

In his so-called Argument from Relativity (which appears in the first selection in this book), John Mackie argues that ethics is not objective, because if it were, there would be far less moral disagreement than there is. Of course, there is also a good deal of ethical consensus, both within and across cultures, but anyone who has thought even a little about the subject cannot fail to be impressed by the breadth, and the depth, of moral disagreement. What to make of this is, of course, a contested matter.

Those who rely on moral disagreement to challenge the objectivity of ethics have leveled three basic arguments. The first of these says that if there is persistent moral disagreement, then ethics cannot be objective. And there is persistent moral disagreement – plenty of it. So ethics cannot be objective.

No philosopher that we know of actually endorses such an argument. Its first premise relies on the thought that persistent disagreement alone is enough to undercut objectivity. But this is false. There is persistent disagreement in other disciplines that are widely recognized as yielding objectively true discoveries. There is, at present, no agreement on a number of questions in theoretical physics, for instance, or in evolutionary biology, and yet there are objective truths about these disputed matters – we're just not sure what those

truths are yet. For all we know, things might be just the same in ethics.

A second argument begins with a comparative claim. There is much more disagreement in ethics than there is in other areas where we believe there to be objective truth. The greater difficulty of resolving ethical issues shows that moral judgments are very probably not objectively true. They might be uniformly untrue (as error theorists would claim – see part I.1). They might be true in an attenuated sense (as expressivists such as Horgan and Timmons would claim – see chapter 5 of this volume). Or they might be true only relative to certain agreements (as relativists such as Harman would claim – see chapter 7). This second argument concedes that ethics *might* be objective – moral claims might be literally and robustly true, by virtue of representing moral facts that obtain independently of what anyone actually thinks of them. And so it is at least possible that ethical objectivism is true. Yet the best evidence we have on the matter indicates otherwise. As a result, we are not justified in thinking that ethics is objective. We are justified in thinking that it is not.

This is a much stronger argument than the first. It is improved in two ways. First, it does not claim too much. It does not claim to have refuted ethical objectivism once and for all, and indeed allows that objectivism might be true. That admission, of course, comes in the context of an argument which says that the best evidence on the question decisively tilts against objectivism. The second strength of the argument is that the evidence it does rely on is not just a snapshot of disagreement about ethical matters, but rather a *comparative* assessment of disagreement in morality and other domains. We see much more disagreement in ethics than in other areas we acknowledge to be objective.

When comparing ethics with (say) physics, chemistry, or mathematics, we are immediately impressed by two things. The first is that there is much more disagreement in ethics about which claims are true and which false. The second is that there is much more disagreement in ethics about methods of discovery and justification. Natural scientists, while certainly not agreeing about everything, seem to have reached a far broader consensus about which methods are adequate for confirming hypotheses and making scientific progress. In ethics, by comparison, there is little agreement about how to confirm moral judgments, and just as little agreement about how to register progress in our moral outlooks.

When we ask how we might best explain these disparities between ethics and other fields, a solution immediately presents itself. The breadth and depth of moral disagreement is just what we should expect if moral judgments are nothing other than expressions of personal commitments. There is intractable disagreement in matters of taste, for instance, because there is no objective truth to finally settle the matter. So too in ethics. This is the view advanced by Mackie, and also by the noncognitivist C. L. Stevenson, whose central article on the topic is reprinted here. Stevenson's piece complements that of his fellow noncognitivist, A. J. Ayer, which is included as chapter 3.

There is a nice, instructive intramural debate amongst these three philosophers, and readers are encouraged to refer to their readings in order to track its details. Mackie believes that parties to moral disagreements are each intent on stating the moral truth. Because there is no such truth, each party invariably lands in error. Ayer denies that there are *any* moral disagreements – rather, all such apparent disagreement is really disagreement about the relevant nonmoral facts. Stevenson parts company with Ayer on that matter, while developing an account of moral disagreement that avoids Mackie's attribution of widespread error. Stevenson introduces the helpful notion of a disagreement *in attitude* as a way of analyzing what is going on in cases of moral disagreement. Stevenson sees such disagreement as involving expressions of conflicting emotions, rather than conflicting beliefs about the nature of an objective moral reality. What all three of these fine philosophers agree to is that there is no such reality awaiting discovery, and so no such reality that we might appeal to, or eventually correctly describe, in order to solve our moral disagreements.

There are a number of things to be said on the other side, of course. We might first draw attention to the great amount of ethical *agreement* that exists, both within any given society, and, more importantly, across societies. There is a common set of basic norms that cross social and historical divides, though we must admit that these norms (e.g., don't kill innocents; don't steal; keep your promises) are not many in number, and must be couched at levels of great generality in order for it to be the case that almost everyone accepts them.

David Brink, in an excerpt from his (1989) book that defends moral realism, proceeds from this slender beginning and here presents a large battery of replies to this second, comparative argument. To cite just two of the most important: the greater amount of disagreement in ethics than in other areas might be well explained by the difficulty of obtaining all relevant nonmoral knowledge about the situation. There is apparently intractable disagreement about social welfare programs, for instance, but there is also a large degree of ignorance about the costs and benefits associated with them. Were we to remove such ignorance, there would doubtless be much greater agreement about the morality of the various options in this area. So, too, if people reasoned better from the information they had, much moral disagreement would disappear. Prejudice, self-interest, lack of sympathy, disgust, and many other factors that impede sound reasoning are responsible for much of the moral disagreement that we witness. If we removed these barriers to accurate moral perception, perhaps we would see the same degree of consensus in ethics as in the sciences.

The third critical argument from disagreement is pessimistic about that forecast. This argument says that even if everyone were possessed of full nonmoral information and perfect reasoning abilities, there would still be disagreement in ethics. Further, and crucially, disagreement under these circumstances is said to be incompatible with ethical objectivity. If there is objective truth about some matter, then those who are perfectly rational and perfectly nonmorally informed must be able to obtain it. If idealized inquirers of this kind still fail to come to agreement about the matter, then that shows that there is no objective truth to settle the point. Since (it is claimed) even idealized inquirers will persist in their moral disagreements, that shows that morality is not objective.

The first thing to note about this argument is that its success depends upon a highly speculative prediction – namely, that even perfect inquirers will persist in their moral disagreements. Such a prediction may be true. But since we actual human beings fall so far short of being ideal inquirers, we might not be in a very good position to know whether that is so. If we are ignorant on this score, then we cannot know whether this third argument succeeds.

But suppose that we can ascertain the verdicts of ideal observers. And suppose, too, that these verdicts will sometimes conflict with one another. To take one from many possible examples, imagine two people who know all there is to know about a murderer's actions, and can reason perfectly well on the basis of that information. Is it really impossible for them to disagree about the morality of executing him? Perhaps. But the burden here, as in most cases, is on the one who asserts that something is impossible – especially since we can imagine and conceive of such a disagreement taking place.

Ethical objectivists must reply in one of two ways. First, they might try to offer an argument for the impossibility of disagreement among such ideal agents. Or, second, they might concede the existence of such disagreement, but challenge the initial assumption of this third argument. That assumption states that disagreement among ideal agents entails a lack of objectivity.

How might these options be vindicated? One possibility is to draw parallels between ethical disagreements and those in other areas that admit of objective truth. One such parallel (discussed in section III of chapter 16 in this volume) takes seriously the status of ethical inquiry as a branch of philosophical inquiry. On this line of thinking, there are objective philosophical truths – about whether there is an omnipotent God, about whether free will exists, about whether there is an

immortal soul, etc. Though we may disagree about these matters, there is a truth about them, and a truth not of our own making. Since ethics is a branch of philosophy, perhaps we should expect to see as much disagreement in the species as in the genus. And we wouldn't be disappointed in these expectations. There is as much disagreement in philosophy generally – both about which claims are true, and about how to make progress – as there is in ethics in particular.

A defender of this parallel will say that perfected inquirers either will, or won't, be unanimous in their philosophical verdicts. If they will invariably reach consensus, then we should expect the same thing for the ethical subset of philosophical questions. But if they won't – if disagreement persists, for instance, about the existence of God or the soul – then, since there are objective truths about their existence, this would show that disagreement, even among perfectly rational and informed beings, is compatible with objective truth. Vindicating either sort of reply would secure the ethical objectivist against this third argument from disagreement.

Critics will naturally want either to challenge the close analogy between ethics and philosophy, or to accept that parallel, but to deny the assumption that philosophical questions have objectively correct answers. They will augment their strategy of choice by taking a page from Mackie's book. Mackie claims, quite rightly, that the error theorist provides a simpler explanation of moral disagreements than any explanation available to the objectivist. As Mackie sees it, people feel differently about things, and moral disagreements are nothing more than projections of these conflicting feelings. The objectivist, by contrast, must say that in typical cases of moral disagreement, one side is right, and the other is wrong. But how could so many people fail to land on the truth? The objectivist must say that their moral understanding is clouded. But then the objectivist owes us an account of how correct moral perception will work (and why it fails to work for so many). The objectivist responses to the arguments from disagreement will not be secure (if ever they are) until objectivists manage to provide a plausible moral epistemology to fill out their replies. Whether such a thing is possible is discussed further in part II.5.

Selected Bibliography

Ayer, A. J. 1936. *Language, Truth and Logic*. London: Gollancz, ch. 6.

Brink, David. 1989. *Moral Realism and the Foundations of Ethics*. Cambridge: Cambridge University Press, ch. 7.

Gowans, Christopher, ed. 2000. *Moral Disagreement*. London: Routledge.

Gowans, Christopher. 2004. "A Priori Refutations of Disagreement Arguments against Moral Objectivity: Why Experience Matters." *Journal of Value Inquiry* 38: 141–57.

Hurley, Susan. 1985. "Objectivity and Disagreement." In Ted Honderich, ed. *Morality and Objectivity*. London: Routledge.

Loeb, Don. 1998. "Moral Realism and the Argument from Disagreement." *Philosophical Studies* 90: 281–303.

Mackie, John. 1977. *Ethics: Inventing Right and Wrong*. London: Penguin, pp. 36–8.

Milo, Ronald. 1986. "Moral Deadlock." *Philosophy* 61: 453–71.

Moody-Adams, Michele. 1997. *Fieldwork in Familiar Places: Morality, Culture and Philosophy*. Cambridge, MA: Harvard University Press.

Paul, Ellen Frankel, Fred Miller, Jr., and Jeffrey Paul, eds. 1994. *Cultural Pluralism and Moral Knowledge*. Cambridge: Cambridge University Press.

Scanlon, Thomas. 1995. "Moral Theory: Understanding and Disagreement." *Philosophy and Phenomenological Research* 55: 343–56.

Shafer-Landau, Russ. 2003. *Moral Realism: A Defence*. Oxford: Oxford University Press, ch. 9.

Thomson, Judith, and Gilbert Harman. 1996. *Moral Relativism and Moral Objectivity*. Oxford: Blackwell.

Tolhurst, William. 1987. "The Argument from Moral Disagreement." *Ethics* 97: 610–21.

Wellman, Carl. 1975. "Ethical Disagreement and Objective Truth." *American Philosophical Quarterly* 12: 211–21.

Williams, Bernard. 1985. *Ethics and the Limits of Philosophy*. Cambridge, MA: Harvard University Press, chs. 8 and 9.

Wong, David. 1984. *Moral Relativity*. Berkeley: University of California Press.

Wright, Crispin. 1992. *Truth and Objectivity*. Cambridge, MA: Harvard University Press, pp. 88–94 and 140–68.

28

The Nature of Ethical Disagreement

Charles L. Stevenson ✗ 1/9/22

1

When people disagree about the value of something – one saying that it is good or right and another that it is bad or wrong – by what methods of argument or inquiry can their disagreement be resolved? Can it be resolved by the methods of science, or does it require methods of some other kind, or is it open to no rational solution at all?

The question must be clarified before it can be answered. And the word that is particularly in need of clarification, as we shall see, is the word "disagreement."

Let us begin by noting that "disagreement" has two broad senses: In the first sense it refers to what ⓘ I shall call "disagreement in belief." This occurs when Mr. A believes p, when Mr. B believes $not\text{-}p$, or something incompatible with p, and when neither is content to let the belief of the other remain unchallenged. Thus doctors may disagree in belief about the causes of an illness; and friends may disagree in belief about the exact date on which they last met.

In the second sense the word refers to what I ② shall call "disagreement in attitude." This occurs when Mr. A has a favorable attitude to something, when Mr. B has an unfavorable or less favorable attitude to it, and when neither is content to let the other's attitude remain unchanged. The term "atti-

tude" is here used in much the same sense that R. B. Perry uses "interest"; it designates any psychological disposition of being *for* or *against* something. Hence love and hate are relatively specific kinds of attitudes, as are approval and disapproval, and so on.

This second sense can be illustrated in this way: Two men are planning to have dinner together. One wants to eat at a restaurant that the other doesn't like. Temporarily, then, the men cannot "agree" on where to dine. Their argument may be trivial, and perhaps only half serious; but in any case it represents a disagreement *in attitude*. The men have divergent preferences and each is trying to redirect the preference of the other – though normally, of course, each is willing to revise his own preference in the light of what the other may say.

Further examples are readily found. Mrs. Smith wishes to cultivate only the four hundred; Mr. Smith is loyal to his old poker-playing friends. They accordingly disagree, in attitude, about whom to invite to their party. The progressive mayor wants modern school buildings and large parks; the older citizens are against these "new-fangled" ways; so they disagree on civic policy. These cases differ from the one about the restaurant only in that the clash of attitudes is more serious and may lead to more vigorous argument.

371

The difference between the two senses of "disagreement" is essentially this: the first involves an opposition of beliefs, both of which cannot be true, and the second involves an opposition of attitudes, both of which cannot be satisfied.

Let us apply this distinction to a case that will sharpen it. Mr. A believes that most voters will favor a proposed tax and Mr. B disagrees with him. The disagreement concerns attitudes – those of the voters – but note that A and B are *not* disagreeing in attitude. Their disagreement is *in belief about* attitudes. It is simply a special kind of disagreement in belief, differing from disagreement in belief about head colds only with regard to subject matter. It implies not an opposition of the actual attitudes of the speakers but only of their beliefs about certain attitudes. Disagreement *in* attitude, on the other hand, implies that the very attitudes of the speakers are opposed. A and B may have opposed beliefs about attitudes without having opposed attitudes, just as they may have opposed beliefs about head colds without having opposed head colds. Hence we must not, from the fact that an argument is concerned with attitudes, infer that it necessarily involves disagreement *in* attitude.

2

We may now turn more directly to disagreement about values, with particular reference to normative ethics. When people argue about what is good, do they disagree in belief, or do they disagree in attitude? A long tradition of ethical theorists strongly suggest, whether they always intend to or not, that the disagreement is one *in belief*. Naturalistic theorists, for instance, identify an ethical judgment with some sort of scientific statement, and so make normative ethics a branch of science. Now a scientific argument typically exemplifies disagreement in belief, and if an ethical argument is simply a scientific one, then it too exemplifies disagreement in belief. The usual naturalistic theories of ethics that stress attitudes – such as those of Hume, Westermarck, Perry, Richards, and so many others – stress disagreement in belief no less than the rest. They imply, of course, that disagreement about what is good is disagreement *in belief* about attitudes; but we have seen that that is simply one sort of disagreement in belief, and by no means the same as disagreement *in* attitude.

Analyses that stress disagreement *in* attitude are extremely rare.

If ethical arguments, as we encounter them in everyday life, involved disagreement in belief exclusively – whether the beliefs were about attitudes or about something else – then I should have no quarrel with the ordinary sort of naturalistic analysis. Normative judgments could be taken as scientific statements and amenable to the usual scientific proof. But a moment's attention will readily show that disagreement in belief has not the exclusive role that theory has so repeatedly ascribed to it. It must be readily granted that ethical arguments usually involve disagreement in belief; but they *also* involve disagreement in attitude. And the conspicuous role of disagreement in attitude is what we usually take, whether we realize it or not, as the distinguishing feature of ethical arguments. For example:

Suppose that the representative of a union urges that the wage level in a given company ought to be higher – that it is only right that the workers receive more pay. The company representative urges in reply that the workers ought to receive no more than they get. Such an argument clearly represents a disagreement in attitude. The union is *for* higher wages; the company is *against* them, and neither is content to let the other's attitude remain unchanged. *In addition* to this disagreement in attitude, of course, the argument may represent no little disagreement in belief. Perhaps the parties disagree about how much the cost of living has risen and how much the workers are suffering under the present wage scale. Or perhaps they disagree about the company's earnings and the extent to which the company could raise wages and still operate at a profit. Like any typical ethical argument, then, this argument involves both disagreement in attitude and disagreement in belief.

It is easy to see, however, that the disagreement in attitude plays a unifying and predominating role in the argument. This is so in two ways:

In the first place, disagreement in attitude determines what beliefs are *relevant* to the argument. Suppose that the company affirms that the wage scale of fifty years ago was far lower than it is now. The union will immediately urge that this contention, even though true, is irrelevant. And it is irrelevant simply because information about the wage level of fifty years ago, maintained under totally different circumstances, is not likely to affect the present attitudes of either party. To be relevant, any belief that is introduced into the argument must be one that is likely to lead one side or the other to have a different attitude, and so reconcile disagreement in attitude. Attitudes are often functions of beliefs. We often change our attitudes to something when we change our beliefs about it; just as a child ceases to *want* to touch a live coal when he comes to *believe* that it will burn him. Thus in the present argument any beliefs that are at all likely to alter attitudes, such as those about the increasing cost of living or the financial state of the company, will be considered by both sides to be relevant to the argument. Agreement in belief on these matters may lead to agreement in attitude toward the wage scale. But beliefs that are likely to alter the attitudes of neither side will be declared irrelevant. They will have no bearing on the disagreement in attitude, with which both parties are primarily concerned.

In the second place, ethical argument usually terminates when disagreement in attitude terminates, even though a certain amount of disagreement in belief remains. Suppose, for instance, that the company and the union continue to disagree in belief about the increasing cost of living, but that the company, even so, ends by favoring the higher wage scale. The union will then be content to end the argument and will cease to press its point about living costs. It may bring up that point again, in some future argument of the same sort, or in urging the righteousness of its victory to the newspaper columnists; but for the moment the fact that the company has agreed in attitude is sufficient to terminate the argument. On the other hand: suppose that both parties agreed on all beliefs that were introduced into the argument, but even so continued to disagree in attitude. In that case neither party would feel that their dispute had been successfully terminated. They might look for other beliefs that could be introduced into the argument. They might use words to play on each other's emotions. They might agree (in attitude) to submit the case to arbitration, both feeling that a decision, even if strongly adverse to one party or the other, would be preferable to a continued impasse. Or, perhaps, they might abandon hope of settling their dispute by any peaceable means.

In many other cases, of course, men discuss ethical topics without having the strong, uncompromising attitudes that the present example has illustrated. They are often as much concerned with redirecting their own attitudes, in the light of

greater knowledge, as with redirecting the attitudes of others. And the attitudes involved are often altruistic rather than selfish. Yet the above example will serve, so long as that is understood, to suggest the nature of ethical disagreement. Both disagreement in attitude and disagreement in belief are involved, but the former predominates in that (1) it determines what sort of disagreement in belief is relevantly disputed in a given ethical argument, and (2) it determines by its continued presence or its resolution whether or not the argument has been settled. We may see further how intimately the two sorts of disagreement are related: since attitudes are often functions of beliefs, an agreement in belief may lead people, as a matter of psychological fact, to agree in attitude.

3

Having discussed disagreement, we may turn to the broad question that was first mentioned, namely: By what methods of argument or inquiry may disagreement about matters of value be resolved?

It will be obvious that to whatever extent an argument involves disagreement in belief, it is open to the usual methods of the sciences. If these methods are the *only* rational methods for supporting beliefs – as I believe to be so, but cannot now take time to discuss – then scientific methods are the only rational methods for resolving the disagreement in *belief* that arguments about values may include.

But if science is granted an undisputed sway in reconciling beliefs, it does not thereby acquire, without qualification, an undisputed sway in reconciling attitudes. We have seen that arguments about values include disagreement in attitude, no less than disagreement in belief, and that in certain ways the disagreement in attitude predominates. By what methods shall the latter sort of disagreement be resolved?

The methods of science are still available for that purpose, but only in an indirect way. Initially, these methods have only to do with establishing agreement in belief. If they serve further to establish agreement in attitude, that will be due simply to the psychological fact that altered beliefs may cause altered attitudes. Hence scientific methods are conclusive in ending arguments about values only to the extent that their success in obtaining agreement in belief will in turn lead to agreement in attitude.

In other words: the extent to which scientific methods can bring about agreement on values depends on the extent to which a commonly accepted body of scientific beliefs would cause us to have a commonly accepted set of attitudes.

How much is the development of science likely to achieve, then, with regard to values? To what extent *would* common beliefs lead to common attitudes? It is, perhaps, a pardonable enthusiasm to *hope* that science will do everything – to hope that in some rosy future, when all men know the consequences of their acts, they will all have common aspirations and live peaceably in complete moral accord. But if we speak not from our enthusiastic hopes but from our present knowledge, the answer must be far less exciting. We usually *do not know*, at the beginning of any argument about values, whether an agreement in belief, scientifically established, will lead to an agreement in attitude or not. It is logically possible, at least, that two men should continue to disagree in attitude even though they had all their beliefs in common, and even though neither had made any logical or inductive error, or omitted any relevant evidence. Differences in temperament, or in early training, or in social status, might make the men retain different attitudes even though both were possessed of the complete scientific truth. Whether this logical possibility is an empirical likelihood I shall not presume to say; but it is unquestionably a possibility that must not be left out of account.

To say that science can always settle arguments about value, we have seen, is to make this assumption: Agreement in attitude will always be consequent upon complete agreement in belief, and science can always bring about the latter. Taken as purely heuristic, this assumption has its usefulness. It leads people to discover the discrepancies in their beliefs and to prolong enlightening argument that *may* lead, as a matter of fact, from commonly accepted beliefs to commonly accepted attitudes. It leads people to reconcile their attitudes in a rational, permanent way, rather than by rhapsody or exhortation. But the assumption is *nothing more*, for present knowledge, than a heuristic maxim. It is wholly without any proper foundation of probability. I conclude, therefore, that scientific methods cannot be guaranteed the definite role in the so-called normative sciences that they may have in the natural sciences. Apart from a heuristic assumption to the contrary, it is possible that the growth of scientific knowledge may leave many disputes about values permanently unsolved. Should these disputes persist, there are nonrational methods for dealing with them, of course, such as impassioned, moving oratory. But the purely intellectual methods of science, and, indeed, *all* methods of reasoning, may be insufficient to settle disputes about values even though they may greatly help to do so.

For the same reasons I conclude that normative ethics is not a branch of any science. It deliberately deals with a type of disagreement that science deliberately avoids. Ethics is not psychology, for instance; for although psychologists may, of course, agree or disagree in belief about attitudes, they need not, as psychologists, be concerned with whether they agree or disagree with one another *in* attitude. Insofar as normative ethics draws from the sciences, in order to change attitudes *via* changing people's beliefs, it *draws* from *all* the sciences; but a moralist's peculiar aim – that of *redirecting* attitudes – is a type of activity, rather than knowledge, and falls within no science. Science may study that activity and may help indirectly to forward it; but is not *identical* with that activity.

4

I can take only a brief space to explain why the ethical terms, such as "good," "wrong," "ought," and so on, are so habitually used to deal with disagreement in attitude. On account of their repeated occurrence in emotional situations they have acquired a strong emotive meaning. This emotive meaning makes them serviceable in initiating changes in a hearer's attitudes. Sheer emotive impact is not likely, under many circumstances, to change attitudes in any permanent way; but it *begins* a process that can then be supported by other means.

There is no occasion for saying that the meaning of ethical terms is *purely* emotive, like that of "alas" or "hurrah." We have seen that ethical *arguments* include many expressions of *belief*, and the rough rules of ordinary language permit us to say that some of these beliefs are expressed by an ethical judgment itself. But the beliefs so expressed are by no means always the same. Ethical terms are notable for their ambiguity, and opponents in an argument may use them in different senses. Sometimes this leads to artificial issues, but it usually does not. So long as one person says "this is good" with emotive praise, and another says "no, it is bad," with emotive condemnation, a disagreement in attitude is manifest. Whether or not the beliefs that these statements express are logically incompatible may not be discovered until late in the argument; but even if they are actually compatible, disagreement in attitude will be preserved by emotive meaning; and this disagreement, so central to ethics, may lead to an argument that is certainly not artificial in its issues so long as it is taken for what it is.

The many theorists who have refused to identify ethical statements with scientific ones have much to be said in their favor. They have seen that ethical judgments mold or alter attitudes, rather than describe them, and they have seen that ethical judgments can be guaranteed no definitive scientific support. But one need not on that account provide ethics with any extramundane, sui generis *subject matter*. The distinguishing features of an ethical judgment can be preserved by a recognition of emotive meaning and disagreement in attitude, rather than by some nonnatural quality – and with far greater intelligibility. If a unique subject matter is *postulated*, as it usually is, to preserve the important distinction between normative ethics and science, it serves no purpose that is not served by the very simple analysis I have here suggested. Unless nonnatural qualities can be defended by positive arguments, rather than as an "only resort" from the acknowledged weakness of ordinary forms of naturalism, they would seem nothing more than the invisible shadows cast by emotive meaning.

1/19/22

Moral Disagreement

David Brink

[. . .]

The argument from moral diversity or disagreement has been a popular and philosophically influential source of moral skepticism.[1] Mackie's "argument from relativity" is the most perspicuous formulation of the argument from disagreement, so I shall focus on it.

> The argument from relativity has as its premise the well-known variation in moral codes from one society to another and from one period to another, and also the differences in moral beliefs between different groups and classes within a complex community. Such variation is in itself merely a truth of descriptive morality, a fact of anthropology which entails neither first order nor second order ethical views. Yet it may indirectly support second order subjectivism: radical differences between first order moral judgments make it difficult to treat those judgements as apprehensions of objective truths. (1977: 36)

As Mackie recognizes, disagreement does not entail nihilism; we do not infer from the fact that there are disagreements in the natural or social sciences that these disciplines do not concern matters of objective fact. Nor, from the fact that there is a specific dispute in some discipline, do we make what might seem to be the more modest inference that there is no fact of the matter on the particular issue in question. For example, no one concluded from the apparently quite deep disagreement among astronomers a short while ago about the existence of black holes that there was no fact of the matter concerning the existence of black holes. The argument from disagreement must claim that disagreement in ethics is somehow more fundamental than disagreement in other disciplines. Mackie's claim seems to be that realism about a discipline requires that its disputes be resolvable and that although scientific disputes do seem resolvable, many moral disputes do not. For this reason, the best explanation of the facts about moral disagreement requires the rejection of moral realism.

I think the moral realist should question the premises of this formulation of the argument from disagreement. Does realism about a discipline require that its disputes be resolvable? Certainly, realism about a discipline does not require that all

[1]   It is hard to document the extent of this argument's influence. Philosophical proponents include Sextus Empiricus *PH* I. 148–63, III. 179–82, 198–218, 232–5, *AM* XI. 68–77; Westermarck 1932: ch. 5; Stevenson 1937, 1948a, 1948b; Nowell-Smith 1957: 48–51; Williams 1975, 1985: chs. 8–9; Mackie 1977: 36–8; and Wong 1984. Nonphilosophical proponents include sociologists and anthropologists such as Benedict 1934, Sumner 1940, and Herskovits 1948.

actual cognizers eventually reach agreement. It could be reasonable to expect agreement on a set or facts only if all cognizers were fully informed and fully rational and had sufficient time for deliberation. Thus, if realism about a discipline requires that its disputes be resolvable, this must mean that its disputes must be resolvable *in principle*.

Does realism about a discipline require that its disputes be resolvable even in principle? I think that a realist should resist the assumption that it ought to be possible, in practice or even in principle, to get *any* cognizer to hold true beliefs. All of our beliefs are revisable, at least in principle, and dialectical investigation of our beliefs can identify explanatory tensions in our beliefs and force more or less drastic revision in them if it is carried out thoroughly. In this way, coherentist reasoning can, at least in principle, identify and correct significant and substantial error. But no theory of justification adequate to the task of accounting for justified but fallible belief (e.g., in an external world) can preclude the possibility of *systematic* error. We cannot demonstrate, and should not be expected to be able to demonstrate, the success of evolutionary theory to someone who holds systematically mistaken observational beliefs about the behavior and adaptation of different species. We cannot defend, and should not be expected to be able to defend, historical hypotheses to someone who holds no true psychological generalizations about human behavior. Similarly, there may be people with such hopelessly and systematically mistaken moral beliefs that we cannot, and should not be expected to be able to, convince them of true moral claims. Because the argument from disagreement alleges that the moral realist cannot adequately explain the nature of moral disagreement, we are entitled to see what could be said about moral disagreement and its resolvability on realist assumptions. And, as in these nonmoral cases, we can imagine people whose initial starting points are so badly mistaken that there should be no expectation of convincing them of the truth. We can imagine people whose view of themselves and others is so distorted by, say, self-concern or an inability to represent vividly the consequences of their actions that all of their considered moral beliefs will be badly mistaken. Even though these beliefs are revisable, the fact that they are systematically mistaken means that there may be no basis for correcting their errors.

Although this is, I think, a possibility, and one that demonstrates that the realist need not believe it possible, even in principle, to convince any cognizer of true moral claims, it does not undermine the argument from disagreement. For although a nonskeptical realist need not assume that any and every moral dispute is resolvable even in principle, he cannot treat every serious disagreement as one between interlocutors at least one of whom is systematically mistaken. I lose my claim to justified belief the more I simply dismiss opponents as systematically mistaken. It is incumbent on the moral realist, therefore, to claim that *most* moral disputes are resolvable at least in principle.

Is this claim plausible? Mackie supposes that the realist will defend it by trying to explain away apparent moral disagreements as the application by interlocutors of shared moral principles under different empirical conditions (1977: 37). This is the familiar idea that people who live in different social, economic, and environmental conditions might apply the same moral principle to justify quite different policies. An economically underdeveloped country might think that in a society in its economic condition distributive inequalities provide incentives that benefit everyone and that this justifies such inequalities. A more economically advanced country might oppose distributive inequalities on the ground that in societies at its level of affluence distributive inequalities are divisive and so work to everyone's disadvantage. The economically underdeveloped society thinks it should promote certain distributive inequalities, whereas the economically more developed society thinks it should oppose distributive inequalities. This might look like a moral disagreement, but the fact is that the disagreement is only apparent. The one society thinks that inequalities are justified *in economically backward conditions*, while the other society thinks that inequalities are unjustified *in economically favorable conditions*. Not only is there no disagreement here; a common moral principle seems to justify both beliefs. Since this sort of disagreement is only apparent, it poses no problem for the moral realist.

Mackie finds this realist explanation of moral disagreement inadequate for two reasons. First, this explanation of moral disputes commits the moral realist to treating many moral facts as contingent. The apparently conflicting moral beliefs of apparent disputants can only be contingently true, because their compatibility depends on contingent facts about their different environments. Necessity can attach only to the shared moral principles that underlie their apparent disagreement (1977: 37).

It is not entirely clear how this fact about a realist account of apparent disputes is supposed to constitute an objection to moral realism. Mackie seems to assume that the moral realist cannot accept this kind of contingency and is committed to defending the necessity of moral facts. But why?

It cannot be Mackie's view that moral facts are necessary, since he thinks that no moral statements are true (1977: 39–40). But if Mackie can reject completely belief in the necessity of moral truths, why can't the realist, if she needs to, deny that all moral truths are necessary? Perhaps Mackie thinks that the realist, but not he, is committed to defending common beliefs about morality and that it is a common belief about morality that moral truths are necessary.[2]

But there are several problems with this argument. Although my defense of coherentism commits me to the general reliability of considered moral beliefs, it does not commit me to the reliability of common nonmoral, second-order beliefs about morality. Moreover, I see no reason to think that belief in the necessity of moral truths is a common belief about morality, and, even if it were, there would be good reason to reject it. The ethical naturalist claims that moral facts are constituted by, and thus supervene on, natural and social scientific facts such as economic, social, and psychological facts. The naturalist, therefore, ought to accept happily the claim that "if things had been otherwise [in certain respects], quite different sorts of actions would have been right" (1977: 37). The contingency of many moral facts is, I think, a happy, rather than an untoward, consequence of the realist's explanation of apparent moral disagreement.

So, the realist's explanation of apparent moral disagreement commits him to the contingency of some moral facts. But this is a perfectly acceptable commitment, since many moral facts are contingent. Moreover, as Mackie recognizes, the realist's explanation of apparent disagreement allows him to treat some moral facts as necessary. Also, how many moral facts the realist must regard as contingent depends, in part, on how often the realist seeks to explain moral disagreement away as only apparent moral disagreement.

This brings us to Mackie's second reason for finding the realist explanation of apparent moral disagreement inadequate. Mackie seems to assume that the realist must offer this explanation as a general account of moral disputes, and he points out, quite rightly, that not all putative disagreements are merely apparent (1977: 38). People do disagree about what is right or wrong in a particular set of circumstances, and the realist must be able to explain why most genuine disputes are resolvable at least in principle.

But the realist can plausibly explain this; Mackie is wrong to restrict the realist to explaining moral disputes away as only apparent. We already noted that it is only *most* genuine disputes that a realist must regard as resolvable in principle. Some interlocutors may be so systematically mistaken that although our dispute with them concerns a matter of objective fact, we cannot, and should not be expected to be able to, convince them of true claims. Other genuine moral disputes are also in a certain sense not resolvable even in principle. For even a moral realist can maintain that some genuine moral disputes have no uniquely correct answers. Moral ties are possible, and considerations, each of which is objectively valuable, may be incommensurable. Disputes over moral ties and incommensurable values are resolvable in principle only in the sense that it ought to be possible in principle to show interlocutors who are not systematically mistaken that their dispute has no unique resolution. Of course, there are limits on how often we may construe disputes as tied or incommensurable and still plausibly defend the existence of objective moral facts and true moral propositions.

The moral realist can plausibly maintain that most moral disputes are genuine, have a unique solution, and can be resolved at least in principle. First, many genuine moral disagreements depend on disagreements over the nonmoral facts. Of these, some depend on culpable ignorance of fact and others do not.

Often, at least one disputant culpably fails to assess the nonmoral facts correctly by being insufficiently imaginative in weighing the consequences for various people of different actions or policies. Culpable failure to be sufficiently imaginative may result from negligence (e.g., laziness), prejudice, self-interest, or social ideology. This sort of error

---

[2]   I am told by Nick Sturgeon that Mackie confirmed this interpretation in a talk he gave at Cornell University in the spring of 1980.

is especially important in moral disputes, since thought experiments, as opposed to actual tests, play such an important part in the assessment of moral theories. Thought experiments play a larger role in moral methodology than they do in scientific methodology, both because it is often (correctly) regarded as immoral to assess moral theories by realizing the relevant counterfactuals, and because the desired test conditions for moral theories are often harder to produce (e.g., the experiments would involve too many variables to control for and the subjects would not always want to cooperate). Because moral disputes that depend on this kind of culpable ignorance of nonmoral fact turn on nonmoral issues that are supposed to be resolvable at least in principle, these moral disputes should themselves be resolvable at least in principle.

Other genuine moral disputes depend on reasonable (nonculpable) but nonetheless resolvable disagreements over the nonmoral facts. The correct answers to controversial moral questions often turn on nonmoral issues about which reasonable disagreement is possible and about which no one may know the answer. Moral disagreement can turn on nonmoral disagreement over such questions as 'What (re)distribution of goods would make the worst-off representative person in a society best-off?', 'Would public ownership of the means of production in the United States lead to an increase or decrease in the average standard of living?', 'What are the most important social determinants of personality?', 'What kind of life would Vera's severely mentally retarded child lead (if she brought her pregnancy to term and raised the child), and how would caring for him affect Vera and her family?', 'How malleable is human nature?', 'Which, if any, religious claims are true?', and 'If there is a god, how should its will be ascertained? (e.g., should scripture be read literally?)'. However difficult and controversial these issues are, disputes about them are supposed to be resolvable at least in principle. Insofar as moral disputes turn on such issues, they too are resolvable in principle.

Other genuine moral disputes do not depend on nonmoral disagreement; they represent antecedent moral disagreement. Mackie's discussion of how moral realism will explain apparent moral disagreement shows that he regards moral disagreement as resolvable if, and only if, there is *antecedent* agreement on general moral principles. But this assumption reflects a one-way view of moral justification, according to which moral principles can justify particular moral judgments but not vice versa, that our defense of a coherence theory of justification entitles us to reject. As coherentism insists, justification consists in *mutual* support between moral principles and judgments about particular cases. Agreement about general moral principles may be exploited to resolve (genuine) disagreement about particular moral cases, and agreement about particular moral cases may be exploited to resolve disagreement about general moral principles. Since no one's moral beliefs are entirely consistent, much less maximally coherent, consideration of coherence force each of us to revise our moral beliefs in particular ways. Ideally, we make trade-offs among the various levels of generality of belief in such a way as to maximize initial commitment, overall consistency, explanatory power, and so on. The fact that we disagree about some moral issues at the beginning of this process of adjustment gives no compelling reason to suppose that this process of adjustment will not, in the limit, resolve our disagreement. Indeed, the nihilist is committed to claiming that there is often no resolution of competing moral claims even in principle. But this is just one claim about what the results of a systematic dialectical moral inquiry among different interlocutors would be, which must stand alongside various nonskeptical claims about what the results would be, and enjoys no privileged a priori position in relation to its competitors (cf. Dworkin 1986: 85–6). As coherentists and realists about other things, we assume that this kind of coherentist reasoning is in principle capable of resolving quite deep antecedent disagreement in the natural sciences, the social sciences, and philosophy itself. There seems no reason to deny that most moral errors are not also resolvable at least in principle by coherentist reasoning. Certainly, given the burden of proof that the argument from disagreement must bear at this stage of the dialectic, the fact that the realist cannot produce a proof of her claim that most moral error is in principle correctable by coherentist reasoning gives us no reason to doubt this claim.

What of the diachronic character of the argument from disagreement? Does the fact that there seems to have been so little convergence of moral belief over time support the claim that many moral disputes are unresolvable? I do not think these questions raise any difficulties that we have not already addressed, but perhaps they focus issues in a certain way.

We need to distinguish, in our assessments of the amount of current moral consensus and of the prospects for convergence, between two levels of moral thought: (1) popular moral thought, and (2) reflective moral theory. Of course, according to a coherentist moral epistemology, levels (1) and (2) are connected; (2) begins with (1) and is in this respect at least continuous with (1). But coherentism also allows the dialectical investigation of our moral beliefs to force significant revision in those beliefs, and in this way (2) can come to diverge significantly from (1). This difference is important because the prospect of persistent disagreement at level (1) would seem much less troublesome if the prospects for agreement at level (2) were good or if there were plausible realist explanations for why agreement at level (2) should be hard to secure.

There certainly are realist explanations for why there is less convergence to date at level (1) than some might have expected there to be. Moral thinking, as we noted, is subject to various distorting influences such as particular conceptions of self-interest, prejudice, and other forms of social ideology. Because the subject matter of ethics concerns, among other things, the appropriate distribution of the benefits and burdens of social and personal interaction, these distorting influences often afflict moral thinking more than scientific thinking; it is just such issues on which these distorting mechanisms are most likely to operate. (I would not want to underestimate the extent to which such influences have distorted, say, social scientists' claims about the social and economic consequences of particular public policies or psychologists' and biologists' claims about the nature and hereditability of intelligence. But these are the sorts of exceptions that prove the rule, and they also help the realist explain the persistence of moral disputes.) And these sources of distortion are hardy perennials.

There are other realist explanations for why agreement should be hard to secure at both levels.

As others have suggested (e.g., Parfit 1984: 453–4), secular moral theory (level [2]) is in some ways a comparatively underdeveloped area of inquiry. In part, this reflects the influence of religious beliefs on both levels (1) and (2). This is not to say there have not been secular moralists since at least the Greeks, that religious ethics should not be taken seriously, that religious moralists do not make secularly acceptable moral claims, or that secular ethics is incompatible with theism. But it is certainly true that specifically religious doctrines and commitments have at many points shaped and constrained moral thinking. In some periods and places religious constraints on secular moral theory have been direct, taking the form of institutional censorship or sanctions. In other periods and places religious doctrines and commitments have constrained secular moral theory indirectly by affecting level (1). Religious commitments and doctrines have shaped what many people, and not just conscious adherents to these commitments and doctrines, take to be serious moral possibilities (think, for example, about Christian influences on popular views of sexual morality). And this sort of influence is important, since moral progress requires moral debate, and moral debate requires moral imagination. Moreover, insofar as such doctrines and commitments are not rationally defensible but must be held, if at all, as articles of faith, they have not just exerted disproportionate influence on the shape of moral thought but have actually distorted it. For the enterprise of moral theory is simply the attempt to find a rationally defensible system of moral beliefs. Moreover, it is a fundamental moral commitment that in morality's allocation of the benefits and burdens of social and personal interaction, the imposition of burdens on some requires rational justification in order to be morally legitimate. Specifically religious influences on ethics, therefore, have hindered moral progress at both levels (1) and (2), insofar as they have either infected moral thought with nonrational elements or artificially restricted people's moral imaginations. Science was not able to develop properly under similar religious constraints and did not really take off until, among other things, these constraints were largely shed. Perhaps moral thought would benefit from similar autonomy.

In any case, however much it may be due to religious influences, systematic, secular moral theory is a relatively underdeveloped area of inquiry. There are, of course, a number of figures in the history of philosophy who have developed fairly systematic, secular (or secularly acceptable) moral and political theories, many of which are powerful and attractive theories. But notice two things:

First, these figures sum to a very small total (they could perhaps be counted on two or three hands). The number of people who have worked full time to produce systematic moral theories does not even begin to compare with the number of those who have worked full time on theoretical issues in the natural sciences. Although, of course, there have been professional politicians and political strategists for a long time, the idea of a class of people devoting most of their time to the study of issues of moral and political theory is a comparatively recent one. Perhaps more progress is to be hoped for in ethics when systematic moral theory has flourished longer. These considerations provide a realistic explanation of why there has not yet been the right sort of convergence of moral opinion, as well as some reason to be cautiously optimistic about the prospects for convergence at least at level (2).

Second, the theories that have been developed have, with a few exceptions (e.g., Locke and Bentham), had very little and certainly imperfect impact on level (1). Lay persons are typically willing to defer to theorists or theoretical debate on matters scientific, but they seem largely uninterested in profiting from theoretical work that has been done in moral or political theory. (Public debates over abortion, affirmative action, and constitutional litigation concerning civil rights spring to mind.) Of course, it is not surprising that lay persons do not familiarize themselves with all of the philosophical details of existing moral theories. A certain amount of ignorance of theory is necessary if there are to be lay persons; this is as true in ethics as in science. But most lay persons, even those with strong moral sensibilities, seem largely unaware of, or uninterested in, even the outlines of theoretical work in ethics. Nor do I think that this popular ignorance of, or indifference to, moral theory can be justified by appeal to the state of theoretical disagreement in ethics or by appeal to an individual's obligation, as a moral agent, to decide matters for herself. Certainly, an individual's moral views can profit from exposure to ethical theory, even if, indeed, perhaps especially when, theoretical issues are in dispute. And one need not abdicate one's moral agency by consulting others who have thought systematically about the moral issues that concern one. Indeed, moral responsibility would seem to demand that one's moral decision be as informed as possible, and this would seem to argue in favor of consulting moral theory both when moral theory speaks unequivocally and when there is theoretical disagreement.

This makes one wonder how, if at all, the appropriate development in level (2) might affect level (1). Current popular neglect of the moral theory that is available might encourage skepticism about the effect that the development of moral theory might have on popular moral thought. But if this neglect is due in part to the comparatively underdeveloped state of moral theory, perhaps its development would encourage greater interest in, and respect for, the resources of moral theory. True, such development (with its demands on intellectual resources) may itself presuppose a greater interest in moral theory or moral issues. But marginally greater interest in certain moral issues could spur marginally greater interest in moral theory, which could spur moderately greater allocation of intellectual resources toward moral theory, which in turn could spur further interest in moral issues, and so on.

In any event, the prospects for the appropriate kind of convergence at level (2), given the appropriate development of systematic moral theory, would be sufficient reassurance to the moral realist. The fact, if it would be a fact, that the appropriate sort of convergence at level (2) would not produce similar convergence at level (1) should trouble us no more than the fact that agreement among biologists on some form of evolutionary theory does not secure the agreement of all lay persons (e.g., certain fundamentalist Christians).

Moreover, there are realist explanations for not expecting convergence in ethics, at level (1) or level (2), even over fairly long periods of time. To believe that there are moral facts and that moral knowledge is possible, as the realist does, involves no commitment to thinking that moral knowledge is easy to acquire. Insofar as particular moral disputes depend on complex nonmoral issues about economics, social theory, human nature, and the rationality of religious belief that have themselves been the subject of persistent diachronic dispute, realists should expect to find persistent moral disagreement at level (1). And insofar as these persistent nonmoral disputes are themselves intellectually legitimate (e.g., are not to be explained as the product of some distorting mechanism), realists should expect to find persistent moral disagreement at level (2). That is, there are persistent nonmoral disputes that not only provide the realist with replies by analogy (respectable company to keep) but are, in fact, largely responsible for the persistence of many moral disputes.

Finally, it seems false to the facts to suppose there has been no significant convergence of moral belief or moral progress over time, even at level (1). Most people no longer think that slavery, racial discrimination, rape, or child abuse is acceptable. Even those who still engage in these activities typically pay lip service to the wrongness of these activities and conceal the real nature of their activities from others and often themselves. Cultures or individuals who do not even pay lip service to these moral claims are rare, and we will typically be able to explain their moral beliefs as the product of various religious, ideological, or psychological distorting mechanisms. This will seem especially appropriate here, since the relevant changes in moral consciousness have all been changes in the same direction. That is, with each of these practices, in almost all cases where people's moral attitudes toward the practice have undergone informed and reflective change, they have changed in the same way (with these practices, from approval to disapproval and not the other way around). When changes in moral consciousness exhibit this sort of pattern, this is further reason to view the changes as progress (cf. Slote 1971). Of course, in viewing these changes in moral consciousness as progress and cultural or individual deviations as mistakes, I am relying at least in part on current moral views. But how could assessments of progress in ethics or the sciences be anything other than theory-dependent in this way? Surely, the sort of realism I have been defending is entitled to appeal to this kind of moral convergence as (defeasible) evidence of moral progress.

So nihilism is not clearly the best explanation of the nature of moral disagreement. The moral realist need only claim that *most genuine* moral disputes are *in principle* resolvable. Not all apparent moral disputes are genuine; some merely reflect the application of antecedently shared moral principles in different circumstances. Not every genuine moral dispute is even in principle resolvable, since some interlocutors may be so systematically mistaken in their moral beliefs that it is not possible to convince them of true claims. Moreover, moral ties are possible and some objective values or magnitudes may be incommensurable. Of those genuine moral disputes that moral realism is committed to regarding as resolvable in principle, some depend on disagreement over nonmoral issues, and others depend on antecedent disagreement over moral issues. Since nonmoral disagreement, whether culpable or not, is ex hypothesi resolvable in principle, moral disagreement that depends on nonmoral disagreement must itself be resolvable at least in principle. Finally, there seems no good reason to deny that genuine moral disputes (among interlocutors who are not systematically morally mistaken) that depend on antecedent moral disagreement are resolvable at least in principle on the basis of coherentist reasoning. These resources allow the realist a plausible account of the nature and significance of synchronic and diachronic moral disagreement.

References

Benedict, Ruth. 1934. *Patterns of Culture.* New York: Houghton Mifflin.

Dworkin, R. 1986. *Law's Empire.* Cambridge, MA: Harvard University Press.

Herskovits, M. 1948. *Man and his Works.* New York: Knopf.

Mackie, J. L. 1977. *Ethics: Inventing Right and Wrong.* New York: Penguin.

Nowell-Smith, P. 1957. *Ethics.* New York: Philosophical Library.

Parfit, D. 1984. *Reasons and Persons.* New York: Oxford University Press.

Sextus Empiricus. *Outlines of Pyrrhonism (PH).*

Sextus Empiricus. *Adversus Mathematicos (AM).*

Slote, M. 1971. "The Rationality of Aesthetic Value Judgments." *Journal of Philosophy* 68: 821–39.

Stevenson, C. L. 1937. "The Emotive Meaning of Ethical Terms." Reprinted in Stevenson 1963.

Stevenson, C. L. 1948a. "The Nature of Ethical Disagreement." Reprinted in Stevenson 1963.

Stevenson, C. L. 1948b. "Meaning: Descriptive and Emotive." Reprinted in Stevenson 1963.

Stevenson, C. L. 1963. *Facts and Values.* New Haven: Yale University Press.

Sumner, W. G. 1940. *Folkways.* New York: Ginn.

Westermarck, E. 1932. *Ethical Relativity.* New York: Humanities Press.

Williams, B. 1975. "The Truth in Relativism." Reprinted in Williams 1981.

Williams, B. 1981. *Moral Luck.* Cambridge: Cambridge University Press.

Williams, B. 1985. *Ethics and the Limits of Philosophy.* Cambridge, MA: Harvard University Press.

Wong, D. 1984. *Moral Relativity.* Los Angeles: University of California Press.

II.5   Moral Knowledge

Introduction

Perhaps the best way to understand the history of debates surrounding the topic of moral knowledge is to begin by considering the obstacles to gaining it. If error theorists or classic expressivists are correct, these obstacles are insurmountable. According to them, there is no truth in ethics, and so no chance of knowledge in this arena. But even if we reject these views, and accept that there are some moral truths, we might be worried about how we could know them.

There are a number of arguments that have sought to foster these worries, and to sow doubts about whether we can ever know right from wrong. These arguments are powerful. Most moral epistemologies have been developed against the backdrop of these arguments; whether they can be answered is the acid test of a moral epistemology's credibility.

When thinking about how to gain moral knowledge, it is important not to set the bar too high. A familiar skeptical refrain, heard more often in the classroom than in philosophy books, is that moral knowledge is impossible because we can never be certain of our moral beliefs. While we should admit our fallibility, this isn't enough to eliminate prospects for moral knowledge. For we lack certainty about almost everything. We might *feel* certain about many of our beliefs – that we each have a body, that there are other people inhabiting this planet, that there are such things as trees and insects on the earth, etc. – but these beliefs could all be mistaken.

The evidence we have for the existence of trees, our bodies, other people, etc. is comprised exclusively of sense perceptions and beliefs. But this evidence can be accounted for in either of two, incompatible, ways. The first is that we are caused to have such perceptions and beliefs by real things in an external world. There really is a cat over there, we see it, and we form the belief accordingly. The alternative story has it that our beliefs are all illusions created in us by a very powerful, manipulative genius, of whose existence we are unaware. We think that the first account is correct. But all of the available evidence is compatible with both accounts. We cannot be certain of even the most basic things we take for granted in our lives.

If a lack of certainty undermines knowledge, then we cannot have moral knowledge. But in that case, our ignorance would extend far beyond the moral realm. We are certain of almost nothing. If knowledge requires certainty, then we know practically nothing. We don't even know *that knowledge requires certainty*, as no one can be certain that such a claim is true.

Yet this argument – call it the *argument from certainty* – can serve as the basis of a different, though related, skeptical challenge. Call this one the *argument from relevant alternatives.* When we ask why so many have thought certainty so important, the answer may be that certainty ensures that we are able to eliminate relevant alternatives to our beliefs. And that is thought to be necessary to having knowledge: one knows something only if one is first able to eliminate competing beliefs. For instance, if you were in a field surrounded by dogs, most of whom looked and behaved just like your own, you couldn't be said to know that any particular one of them was yours. You'd have to be able to disqualify close competitors before truly knowing that that one, there, was your very own.

Applied to the moral realm, the skeptical thought is that we are not, in fact, able to disqualify competing moral beliefs – we cannot justify a preference for our own views over those of the people with whom we disagree. For, on the assumption that people are more or less open-minded and fair, if we were able to produce a better justification for our own beliefs, then others should be coming over to our side in droves. But that isn't what we see. Instead, we see only a relatively small number of minds changed, and many more cases in which people end up with just the moral views they started with.

This second argument can be applied to every moral belief: for any such belief, there will be smart, rational, thoughtful people who disagree with it. Until their views can be successfully refuted, one's own, competing views are vulnerable.[1] Though one's moral views might in fact be true, one can't know that they are until one has disposed of their competitors. And that, according to skeptics, is precisely what one cannot do.

Why not? Certainly the most influential set of answers to this question is given in the context of a third argument. This is the *regress argument*, which has its origins in ancient skepticism. The argument is sufficiently complex to merit a line-by-line presentation:

1 In order for anyone to be justified in holding a moral belief, that belief must be adequately supported.
2 Such support must be provided by other beliefs that lend credibility to the initial moral belief.
3 These other, supporting beliefs must be either moral or nonmoral ones.
4 Such supporting beliefs cannot be moral ones.
5 Such supporting beliefs cannot be nonmoral ones.

6 Therefore no one is justified in holding any moral beliefs.

It's only a short step from the conclusion of this argument to the claim that there can be no moral knowledge, since unjustified moral beliefs, even if they were true, cannot amount to knowledge.

At this point we will pause only to comment briefly on the rationales for premises (4) and (5). The fourth premise is what lends the argument its name. The idea is simple. If a moral belief is supported by another moral belief, then we can always ask, of this second belief, how *it* is to be supported. Well, if by another moral belief, then we can ask for its support, and so on, and so on. The problem is that there is no place to stop this process. There will be an infinite regress of support: any supporting moral belief will itself require support (per premise (1)), and thus there will be no end to the chain of support. But an endless chain, an infinite regress, justifies nothing – no link in the chain is justified, so long as there is no ultimate justification that can transmit itself throughout the chain.

The fifth premise is supported by a line of thinking suggested by David Hume. He famously remarked (in the opening pages of book III of his *Treatise on Human Nature*) that one cannot deduce an *ought* from an *is*, a prescription about what should be the case from a description about what is the case. Premise (5) is a restatement of Hume's maxim. And it seems very plausible.

No matter your moral views, if you seek to support them exclusively with nonmoral beliefs, you will fail to secure your view against critics. Suppose you condemn suicide bombings, for instance, and someone asks you to justify your condemnation. You claim that such bombings (1) impose great suffering, (2) kill people, (3) target noncombatants, (4) are against the law, (5) are widely denounced, etc. These claims are all true. But someone could acknowledge their truth, while remaining unconvinced of the moral verdict you seek to draw from them. Such a person would be committing no logical errors. Nor need he be making any factual errors – after all, he may agree with us about all of the (nonmoral) facts. We could say – indeed, we *would* say – that such a person was making a moral mistake. But saying such a thing begs the question – it presupposes the truth of the claim that is under consideration.

What is needed in order to answer such a person is a moral principle: *if* one kills, or targets innocents, or breaks the law, etc., *then* one is acting immorally. If this kind of principle can be justified, then, and only then, are we in a position to cite exclusively nonmoral facts to back up our moral views. But if premise (4) of the regress argument is true, we cannot, in fact, justify this, or any other, moral principle in this way.

Though these arguments can seem quite compelling, their conclusion does conflict with certain beliefs that we hold very dear. Most of us, for instance, are quite confident about the immorality of torturing children just for fun, or of killing people just because their taste in hair styles is different from our own. The soundness of skeptical arguments would undermine our hopes of knowing such things.

In an effort to vindicate at least some of our moral beliefs, philosophers have sought to answer these skeptical arguments by developing positive proposals in this area. Though there are a large number of candidate solutions to these problems, most can be grouped under one of two headings. The first is foundationalism, and the second, coherentism.

Foundationalists believe in the existence of basic beliefs. These are beliefs that are non-inferentially justified, i.e., justified without being derived from other beliefs. The role of basic beliefs is crucial in answering the skeptical arguments. Since basic beliefs, including any basic moral beliefs, do not require support from other beliefs, their existence would suffice to falsify premise (2) of the regress argument. They would also provide a reply to the relevant alternatives argument. Holding a basic belief might be sufficient to eliminate all competing beliefs. Or, if this is not so, it might be thought to undermine the requirement that one be able to eliminate relevant alternatives as a condition of justified belief. The central idea here is that holding a basic belief for the right reasons is enough, all by itself, to justify one's belief. Nothing else is needed – in particular, one doesn't need the assistance of other beliefs, and one doesn't need to eliminate competing beliefs, before being justified in one's belief.

The classic form of foundationalism for moral beliefs is known as *intuitionism*. Intuitionism (here represented by Robert Audi's article) claims that some basic beliefs are moral ones. Some of these will be *self-evident*: true, and justifiably believed provided they are held on the basis of adequately understanding the content of the belief. Different intuitionists will give different accounts of such adequate understanding, but we will leave that intramural debate aside. Intuitionists must also, of course, have something to say about the vast number of non-basic beliefs. Here, they claim that such beliefs are justified, when they are, only by virtue of being evidentially based on basic beliefs.

Though the existence of basic beliefs is controversial, let us take a possible example to fix ideas. If any moral belief is basic, the following is a good contender: genocide is immoral. Intuitionists will say that attentive consideration to the nature of genocide is enough to enable one to "see" its immorality. Though one certainly needs to *have* other beliefs in order to adequately understand what genocide is – one needs to have beliefs about what people are, the ways in which they are vulnerable, the ethnic or other classes that they have been grouped into, etc. – one does not need to *infer* the immorality of genocide from these other beliefs. Rather, these other beliefs are background beliefs that aid in the understanding of the proposition in question. Once one understands it, however, one needs nothing further to be clear about its truth.

The claim that a moral belief is basic is appealing when one finds oneself at the end of a line of argument with nothing left to say. Suppose you are engaged in an ethical debate and you reach the point where you say something like this: that's wrong because it causes a lot of needless pain. And your opponent says: what's so bad about causing such pain? Well, there's not a lot you can say at this point. Perhaps there is nothing more to say. Yet you might be justified in holding your belief anyway. That's because you might have landed on a properly basic belief – one that needs no further support.

Coherentists will have none of this. They deny the existence of basic beliefs. They insist that beliefs are justified if, and to the extent that, they are well supported by one's other beliefs. According to coherentists, there is no such thing as non-inferentially justified belief. All beliefs must derive their support from other beliefs.

Norman Daniels, in his article here, offers a very influential account of how to defend and apply coherentism in the moral realm. He develops an idea – that of reflective equilibrium – that was employed by John Rawls in his pathbreaking (1971) book. Daniels, following Rawls, defends a picture of justification according to which beliefs at different levels of generality, and with an ever-widening scope, are tested against one another and, at the limit, made to cohere with one another to yield a system of mutually reinforcing, mutually explanatory beliefs. This process, and this test of justification (obviously oversimplified here), is nowadays widely accepted as the correct one for the natural sciences. Many philosophers, following Rawls and Daniels, have been quick to appropriate it for the ethical arena.

It might seem that coherentists would be immune from the major criticism that besets intuitionism – namely, that so-called basic beliefs are just expressions of personal prejudice that cannot be defended, and so are placed in this special category as a way of improperly insulating them from criticism. Since coherentists reject the existence of basic beliefs, they are indeed, strictly speaking, free of this worry. Yet their theory has been subject to a variation of this concern, as the method of reflective equilibrium does identify a set of beliefs – so-called *considered moral judgments* – that are to serve as starting points from which to launch the method. These beliefs are not thought to be self-evident, but they are said to enjoy a presumptive epistemic justification, by virtue of having been adopted in epistemically favorable conditions. Critics of the method of reflective equilibrium, such as Singer (1974) and Brandt (1979: ch. 1), have objected to the method as being unduly conservative. They charge that the considered moral judgments that at least initially constrain the development of a coherent network of beliefs are unlikely to be anything other than popular, inherited prejudices, with no probative value.

Daniels replies to this criticism by insisting on the fallibility and revisability of all beliefs, even those that are elevated to the status of considered moral beliefs. Daniels fairly presents this criticism in his article here, and readers are thus well positioned to assess the merits of his reply for themselves. For what it is worth, most philosophers who nowadays write on ethical theory accept the method of wide reflective equilibrium as the correct one for ethical investigation.[2]

This does not insulate the coherentists who rely on it from other criticisms, however. The standard and perhaps most powerful one is that of circularity. Coherentists do not believe that the regress argument can be answered by citing a moral belief that needs no further support from other beliefs. *Every* belief needs such support. Well, if that is so,

how can they avoid an infinite regress? It seems that coherentists are forced to rely on circular reasoning – reasoning that justifies a given belief, ultimately, by invoking that very belief to support itself.

Coherentists accept that their picture of justification involves circularity. But they say that a circle of justification, if sufficiently large, need not be vicious – need not, in other words, undermine the justification of the beliefs within it. Nowadays coherentists like to invoke the metaphor of a web of beliefs. It isn't as if all of our beliefs are arranged in a single, linear chain, each one supported by just a single other belief, and each in turn lending support to just one other belief. Rather, any given justified belief receives support from many other beliefs, and in turn is relied upon to support a number of others. Coherentists answer the regress argument, therefore, by claiming that a mixture of moral and nonmoral beliefs can be enough to support any given moral belief, so long as that moral belief, in turn, lends some support to these other beliefs.

Coherentists have not spent much time directly addressing the argument from relevant alternatives. Their best response, it seems, would be to concede that the requirement to undermine relevant alternatives cannot be met, but to proceed to deny that it really is a necessary condition of moral justification. Rather, a maximally coherent network of beliefs is maximally justified, even if there are competing, equally coherent sets of beliefs. Those who have a perfectly harmonious outlook based on the Sermon on the Mount will not be able to undermine, once and for all, the beliefs of a Nietzschean who is bent on world domination. But coherentists should insist that this inability is compatible with a very highly justified set of beliefs.

A popular criticism of coherentism claims that it provides no guarantee that our network of coherent beliefs has any contact with reality. We have all heard of psychopaths who have created for themselves a highly coherent set of beliefs that is entirely off-base. If coherentism is true, then the beliefs of such people are as justified – perhaps even more so – as those of the rest of us.

Coherentists accept this implication of their views, but deny that it is an effective criticism. As they see it, we cannot secure the desired guarantee. We cannot ensure that *any* of our beliefs about the world accurately represent reality. A coherent set of beliefs doesn't infallibly protect us against the chance that we are very far from the truth. But it is the best we can do. Justification does not entail truth: being justified in one's beliefs does not ensure that one's beliefs are true. Still, the best criterion of truth that we can have is the coherence of our beliefs.

Though most of the discussion in moral epistemology has focused on theories of justification (i.e., theories that defend necessary and sufficient conditions under which a person is justified in her moral beliefs), there has always been a strand of philosophical inquiry that seeks to give us more practical advice in how to gain moral wisdom. Margaret Little's contribution to this section is squarely within this latter tradition. Though hardly a how-to primer on the subject, it concentrates on developing a general approach to acquir-

ing moral wisdom that parts company with a long line of philosophers who place (to Little's mind) far too great an emphasis on the role of reason, and far too little on that of the emotions, in gaining moral knowledge.

Consider the piece by Roderick Firth that we have included as chapter 9. In it, Firth defends the idea that moral truths are determined by the responses of an ideal observer. He characterizes such an observer as (among other things) dispassionate and disinterested. But should we really seek such detachment in our moral assessments? Or should we instead cultivate an attitude of engagement and emotional investment when making our moral appraisals? Little's piece strongly advocates the latter position. There can be no doubt that much hangs on the question of whether she is right.

Notes

1 For further discussion of whether the existence of intractable disagreement serves as a defeater of the justification of one's beliefs, see Bambrough 1979, Sher 2001, and section IV of chapter 16 in this volume.
2 Even those opposed to coherentism sometimes embrace this method, though they must deny that the emerging beliefs are epistemically justified by virtue of their coherence with other beliefs within the

network. They will see the method as serving other, perhaps related, purposes. Two important such purposes are: (1) serving as the best *method of discovery* in ethics, rather than as providing the necessary and sufficient conditions of epistemic justification; (2) providing a method that enables an individual to *justify to others* those mutually supporting beliefs located within her own coherent network of beliefs.

Selected Bibliography

Adams, Robert. 1999. *Finite and Infinite Goods*. Oxford: Oxford University Press, part IV.

Annas, Julia. 2001. "Moral Knowledge as Practical Knowledge." *Social Philosophy and Policy* 18: 236–56.

Audi, Robert. 1997. *Moral Knowledge and Ethical Character*. Oxford: Oxford University Press.

Audi, Robert. 2004. *The Good in the Right*. Princeton: Princeton University Press.

Bambrough, Renford. 1979. *Moral Skepticism and Moral Knowledge*. London: Routledge & Kegan Paul.

Bloomfield, Paul. 2001. *Moral Reality*. Oxford: Oxford University Press, ch. 2.

Brandt, Richard. 1979. *The Good and the Right*. Oxford: Oxford University Press.

Brink, David. 1989. *Moral Realism and the Foundations of Ethics*. Cambridge: Cambridge University Press, ch. 5.

Cuneo, Terence. 2005. "Signs of Value: Thomas Reid on the Evidential Role of Feelings in Moral Judgment." *British Journal for the History of Philosophy* 14: 69–91.

Cuneo, Terence. 2003. "Reidian Moral Perception." *Canadian Journal of Philosophy* 33: 229–58.

DePaul, Michael. 1993. *Balance and Refinement: Beyond Coherence Methods of Inquiry*. London: Routledge.

Goldman, Alan. 1988. *Moral Knowledge*. London: Routledge.

Greco, John. 2000. *Putting Skeptics in their Place*. Oxford: Oxford University Press, pp. 231–48.

Huemer, Michael. 2000. "Naturalism and the Problem of Moral Knowledge." *Southern Journal of Philosophy* 38: 575–97.

McGrath, Sarah. 2004. "Moral Knowledge by Perception." In John Hawthorne, ed. *Philosophical Perspectives* 18. Oxford: Blackwell.

Nussbaum, Martha. 1992. *Love's Knowledge*. Oxford: Oxford University Press, ch. 2.

Paul, Ellen Frankel, Fred Miller, Jr., and Jeffrey Paul, eds. 2001. *Moral Knowledge*. Cambridge: Cambridge University Press.

Peacocke, Christopher. 2004. "Moral Rationalism." *Journal of Philosophy* 99: 499–526.

Rawls, John. 1971. *A Theory of Justice*. Cambridge, MA: Harvard University Press.

Ross, W. D. 1930. *The Right and the Good*. Oxford: Oxford University Press, ch. 2.

Shafer-Landau, Russ. 2003. *Moral Realism: A Defence*. Oxford: Oxford University Press, chs. 10–12.

Sher, George. 2001. "But I Could Be Wrong." In Ellen Frankel Paul, Fred Miller, Jr., and Jeffrey Paul, eds. *Moral Knowledge*. Cambridge: Cambridge University Press.

Singer, Peter. 1974. "Sidgwick and Reflective Equilibrium." *Monist* 57: 490–517.

Sinnott-Armstrong, Walter. 2006. *Moral Skepticisms*. Oxford: Oxford University Press.

Sinnott-Armstrong, Walter, and Mark Timmons, eds. 1996. *Moral Knowledge?* Oxford: Oxford University Press.

Stratton-Lake, Phillip. 2003. *Ethical Intuitionism: Re-evaluations*. Oxford: Oxford University Press.

Timmons, Mark, ed. 1990. *Southern Journal of Philosophy*, supplementary volume 29: "Moral Epistemology."

Timmons, Mark. 1999. *Morality without Foundations*. Oxford: Oxford University Press, ch. 5.

Interested readers might also want to examine *Canadian Journal of Philosophy*, 2000, supplementary volume 26: "Moral Epistemology Naturalized."

Wide Reflective Equilibrium and Theory Acceptance in Ethics

Norman Daniels

There is a widely held view that a moral theory consists of a set of moral judgments plus a set of principles that account for or generate them. This two-tiered view of moral theories has helped make the problem of theory acceptance or justification[1] in ethics intractable, unless, that is, one is willing to grant privileged epistemological status to the moral judgments (calling them "intuitions") or to the moral principles (calling them "self-evident" or otherwise a priori). Neither alternative is attractive. Nor, given this view of moral theory, do we get very far with a simple coherence view of justification. To be sure, appeal to elementary coherence (here, consistency) constraints between principles and judgments sometimes allows us to clarify our moral views or to make progress in moral argument. But there must be more to moral justification of both judgments and principles than such simple coherence considerations, especially in the face of the many plausible bases for rejecting moral judgments; e.g., the judgments may only reflect class or cultural background, self-interest, or historical accident.

I shall argue that a version of what John Rawls has called the *method of wide reflective equilibrium*[2] reveals a greater complexity in the structure of moral theories than the traditional view. Consequently, it may render theory acceptance in ethics a more tractable problem. If it does, it may permit us to recast and resolve some traditional worries about objectivity in ethics. To make this suggestion at all plausible, I shall have to defend reflective equilibrium against various charges that it is really a disguised form of moral intuitionism and there-

---

[1]   Since the notion of justification is broadly used in philosophy, it is worth forestalling a confusion right at the outset. The problem I address in this paper is strictly analogous to the general and abstract problem of theory acceptance or justification posed in the philosophy of science with regard to nonmoral theories. I am not directly concerned with explaining when a particular individual is justified in, or can be held accountable for, holding a particular moral belief or performing a particular action. So, too, the philosopher of science, interested in how theory acceptance depends on the relation of one theory to another, is not directly concerned to determine whether or not a given individual is justified in believing some feature of one of the theories. Just how relevant my account of theory acceptance is to the question, Is so-and-so justified in believing *P* or in doing *A* on evidence *E* in conditions *C*, (vary *P*, *A*, *E*)? would require a detailed examination of particular cases.

[2]   The distinction between narrow and wide reflective equilibria is implicit in *A Theory of Justice* (Cambridge, MA: Harvard, 1971), p. 49, and is explicit in "The Independence of Moral Theory," *Proceedings and Addresses of the American Philosophical Association*, XLVII (1974/5), 5–22, p. 8.

fore "subjectivist." First, however, I must explain what wide equilibrium is and show why seeking it may increase our ability to choose among competing moral conceptions.

I.   Wide Reflective Equilibrium

The method of wide reflective equilibrium is an attempt to produce coherence in an ordered triple of sets of beliefs held by a particular person, namely, (a) a set of considered moral judgments, (b) a set of moral principles, and (c) a set of relevant background theories. We begin by collecting the person's initial moral judgments and filter them to include only those of which he is relatively confident and which have been made under conditions conducive to avoiding errors of judgment. For example, the person is calm and has adequate information about cases being judged. We then propose alternative sets of moral principles that have varying degrees of "fit" with the moral judgments. We do *not* simply settle for the best fit of principles with judgments, however, which would give us only a *narrow* equilibrium. Instead, we advance philosophical arguments intended to bring out the relative strengths and weaknesses of the alternative sets of principles (or competing moral conceptions). These arguments can be construed as inferences from some set of relevant background theories (I use the term loosely). Assume that some particular set of arguments wins and that the moral agent is persuaded that some set of principles is more acceptable than the others (and, perhaps, than the conception that might have emerged in narrow equilibrium). We can imagine the agent working back and forth, making adjustments to his considered judgments, his moral principles, and his background theories. In this way he arrives at an equilibrium point that consists of the ordered triple (a), (b), (c).[3]

We need to find more structure here. The background theories in (c) should show that the moral principles in (b) are more acceptable than alternative principles on grounds to some degree independent of (b)'s match with relevant considered moral judgments in (a). If they are not in this way independently supported, then there seems to be

no gain over the support the principles would have had in a corresponding narrow equilibrium, where there never was any appeal to (c). Another way to raise this point is to ask how we can be sure that the moral principles that systematize the considered moral judgments are not just "accidental generalizations" of the "moral facts," analogous to accidental generalizations which we want to distinguish from real scientific laws. In science, we have evidence that we are not dealing with accidental generalizations if we can derive the purported laws from a body of interconnected theories, provided these theories reach, in a diverse and interesting way, beyond the "facts" that the principle generalizes.

This analogy suggests one way to achieve independent support for the principles in (b) and to rule out their being mere accidental generalizations of the considered judgments. We should require that the background theories in (c) be more than reformulations of the same set of considered moral judgments involved when the principles are matched to moral judgments. The background theories should have a scope reaching beyond the range of the considered moral judgments used to "test" the moral principles. Some interesting, nontrivial portions of the set of considered moral judgments that constrains the background theories and of the set that constrains the moral principles should be disjoint.

Suppose that some set of considered *moral* judgments (a′) plays a role in constraining the background theories in (c). It is important to note that the acceptability of (c) may thus in part depend on some *moral* judgments, which means we are not in general assuming that (c) constitutes a reduction of the moral [in (b) and (a)] to the nonmoral. Then, our *independence constraint* amounts to the requirement that (a′) and (a) be to some significant degree disjoint. The background theories might, for example, not incorporate the same type of moral notions as are employed by the principles and those considered judgments relevant to "testing" the principles.

It will help to have an example of a wide equilibrium clearly in mind. Consider Rawls's theory of justice. We are led by philosophical argument, Rawls believes, to accept the contract and its

---

[3]   The fact that I describe wide equilibrium as being built up out of judgments, principles, and relevant background theories does not mean that this represents an order of epistemic priority or a natural sequence in the genesis of theories.

various constraints as a reasonable device for selecting between competing conceptions of justice (or right). These arguments, however, can be viewed as inferences from a number of relevant background theories, in particular, from a theory of the person, a theory of procedural justice, general social theory, and a theory of the role of morality in society (including the ideal of a well-ordered society). These *level* III theories, as I shall call them, are what persuade us to adopt the contract apparatus, with all its constraints (call it the *level* II apparatus). Principles chosen at level II are subject to two constraints: (i) they must match our considered moral judgments in (partial) reflective equilibrium; and (ii) they must yield a feasible, stable, well-ordered society. I will call *level* I the *partial* reflective equilibrium that holds between the moral principles and the relevant set of considered moral judgments. *Level* IV contains the body of social theory relevant to testing level I principles (and level III theories) for "feasibility."

The independence constraint previously defined for wide equilibrium in general applies in this way: the considered moral judgments [call them (a′)] which may act to constrain level III theory acceptability must to a significant extent be disjoint from the considered moral judgments [call them (a)] which act to constrain level I partial equilibrium. I argue elsewhere that Rawls's construction appears to satisfy this independence constraint, since his central level III theories of the person and of the role of morality in society are probably not just recharacterizations or systematizations of level I moral judgments. If I am right, then (supposing the soundness of Rawls's arguments!), the detour of deriving the principles from the contract adds justificatory force to them, justification not found simply in the level I matching of principles and judgments. Notice that this advantage is exactly what would be lost if the contract and its defining conditions were "rigged" just to yield the best level I equilibrium. The other side of this coin is that the level II apparatus will not be acceptable if competing theories of the person or of the role of morality in society are preferable to the theories Rawls advances. Rawls's Archimedean point is fixed only against the acceptability of particular level III theories.

This argument suggests that we abstract from the details of the Rawlsian example to find quite general features of the structure of moral theories in wide equilibrium. Alternatives to justice as fairness are likely to contain some level II device for principle selection other than the contract (say a souped-up impartial spectator). Such variation would reflect variation in the level III theories, especially the presence of alternative theories of the person or of the role of morality. Finally, developed alternatives to justice as fairness would still be likely to contain some version of the level I and level IV constraints, though the details of how these constraints function will reflect the content of component theories at the different levels.

By revealing this structural complexity, the search for wide equilibrium can benefit moral inquiry in several ways. First, philosophers have often suggested that many apparently "moral" disagreements rest on other, nonmoral disagreements. Usually these are lumped together as the "facts" of the situation. Wide equilibrium may reveal a more systematic, if complex, structure to these sources of disagreement, and, just as important, to sources of agreement as well.

Second, aside from worries about universalizability and generalizability, philosophers have not helped us to understand what factors *actually do* constrain the considerations people cite as reasons, or treat as "relevant" and "important," in moral reasoning and argument. A likely suggestion is that these features of moral reasoning depend on the *content* of underlying level III theories and level II principle selectors, or on properties of the level I and IV constraints. An adequate moral psychology, in other words, would have to incorporate features of what I am calling "wide equilibrium." Understanding these features of moral argument more clearly might lead to a better grasp of what constitutes evidence for and against moral judgments and principles. This result should not be surprising: as in science, judgments about the plausibility and acceptability of various claims are the complex result of the whole system of interconnected theories already found acceptable. My guess – I cannot undertake to confirm it here – is that the type of coherence constraint that operates in the moral and nonmoral cases functions to produce many similarities: we should find methodological conservatism in both; we will find that "simplicity" judgments in both really depend on determining how little we have to change in the interconnected background theories already accepted (not on more formal measures of simplicity); and we will find in both that apparently "intuitive" judgments about how "interesting," "important," and "relevant" puzzles or facts are, are really guided by underlying theory.

A third possible benefit of wide equilibrium is that level III disagreements about theories may be more tractable than disagreements about moral judgments and principles. Consequently, if the moral disagreements can be traced to disagreements about theory, greater moral agreement may result.

Some examples may perhaps make this claim more plausible. A traditional form of criticism against utilitarianism consists in deriving unacceptable moral judgments about punishment, desert, or distributive justice from a general utilitarian principle. Some utilitarians then may bite the bullet and reject reliance on these "pretheoretical" intuitions. Rawls has suggested an explanation for the class of examples involving distributive justice. He suggests that the utilitarian has imported into social contexts, where we distribute goods between persons, a principle acceptable only for distributing goods between life-stages of one person. Derek Parfit urges a different explanation: the utilitarian, perhaps supported by evidence from the philosophy of mind, uses a weaker criterion of personal identity than that presupposed by, say, Rawls's account of life plans. Accordingly, he treats interpersonal boundaries as metaphysically less deep and morally less important. The problem between the utilitarian and the contractarian thus becomes the (possibly) more manageable problem of determining the acceptability of competing theories of the person, and only one of many constraints on that task is the connection of the theory of the person to the resulting moral principles.[4]

A second example derives from a suggestion of Bernard Williams.[5] He argues that there may be a large discrepancy between the dictates of utilitarian theory in a particular case and what a person will be inclined to do given that he has been raised to have virtues (e.g., beneficence) that in general optimize his chances of doing utilitarian things. We may generalize Williams's point: suppose any

moral conception can be paired with an *optimal* set of virtues, those which make their bearer most likely to do what is right according to the given conception. Moral conceptions may differ significantly in the degree to which acts produced by their optimal virtues tend to differ from acts they deem right. Level III and IV theories of moral psychology and development would be needed to determine the facts here. Since we want to reduce such discrepancies (at least according to some level III and IV theories), we may have an important scale against which to compare moral conceptions.

More, and better developed, examples would be needed to show that the theory construction involved in seeking wide equilibrium increases our ability to choose rationally among competing moral conceptions. But there is a general difficulty that must be faced squarely: level III theories may, I have claimed, depend in part for their acceptability on some considered moral judgments, as in Rawls's level III theories. (If the independence constraint is satisfied, however, these are not primarily the level I considered judgments.) If the source of our disagreement about competing moral conceptions is disagreement on such level III considered judgments, then it is not clear just how much increase in tractability will result. The presence of these judgments clearly poses some disanalogy to scientific-theory acceptance. I take up this worry indirectly, by first considering the charge that reflective equilibrium is warmed-over moral intuitionism.

II.   The Revisability of Considered Moral Judgments

A number of philosophers, quite diverse in other respects, have argued that the method of reflective equilibrium is really a form of moral intuitionism, indeed of subjective intuitionism.[6] If we take moral intuitionism in its standard forms, then the charge seems unfounded. Intuitionist theories have generally been foundationalist. Some set of moral beliefs

---

[4]   Compare Derek Parfit, "Later Selves and Moral Principles," in Alan Montefiore, ed., *Philosophy and Personal Relations* (London: Routledge & Kegan Paul, 1973), pp. 149–60. See Rawls's reply in "Independence of Moral Theory," p.17 ff.

[5]   "Utilitarianism and Moral Self-Indulgence," in H. D. Lewis, *Contemporary British Philosophy*, IVth Series (New York: Humanities, 1976), pp. 306–21.

[6]   The charge is made by R. M. Hare ("Rawls' Theory of Justice," in Norman Daniels (ed.), *Reading Rawls* (Palo Alto: Stanford University Press, 1989), p. 82 ff), by Peter Singer ["Sidgwick and Reflective Equilibrium," *Monist*, LVIII, 3 (July 1974), 490–517, p. 494], and by Richard Brandt (*A Theory of the Good and the Right*, Oxford: Oxford University Press, 1979).

is picked out as basic or self-warranting. Theories differ about the nature or basis of the self-warrant. Some claim self-evidence or incorrigibility, others innateness, others some form of causal reliability. A claim of causal reliability might take, for example, the form of a perceptual account which even leaves room for perceptual error. Some intuitionists want to treat principles as basic. Others begin with particular intuitions, and then attempt to find general principles that systematize the intuitions, perhaps revealing and reducing errors among them. Still, and this is the central point, the justification for accepting such moral principles is that they systematize the intuitions, which carry the epistemological privilege.

No such foundationalism is part of wide reflective equilibrium as I have described it. Despite the care taken to filter initial judgments to avoid obvious sources of error, no special epistemological priority[7] is granted the considered moral judgments. We are missing the little story that gets told about why we should pay homage ultimately to those judgments and indirectly to the principles that systematize them. Without such a story, however, we have no foundationalism and so no standard form of moral intuitionism.

Nevertheless, it might be thought that reflective equilibrium involves an attempt to give us the *effect* of intuitionism without any fairy tales about epistemic priority. The effect is that a set of principles gets "tested" against a determinate and relatively fixed set of moral judgments. We have, as it were, foundationalism without foundations. Once the foundational claim is removed, however, we have nothing more than a person's moral opinion. It is a "considered" opinion, to be sure, but still only an opinion. Since such opinions are often the result of self-interest, self-deception, historical and cultural accident, hidden class bias, and so on, just systematizing some of them hardly seems a promising way to provide justification for them or for the principles that order them.

This objection really rests on two distinct complaints: (1) that reflective equilibrium merely systematizes some relatively determinate set of moral judgments; and (2) that the considered moral judgments are not a proper foundation for an ethical theory. I will return in section III to consider (2) in a version that abstracts from the issue of the revisability of considered judgments. Here I shall consider objection (1).

Wide reflection equilibrium does not merely systematize some determinate set of judgments. Rather, it permits extensive revision of these moral judgments. There is no set of judgments that is held more or less fixed as there would be on a foundationalist approach, even one without foundations. It will be useful to see just how far from the more traditional view of a moral intuition the considered moral judgment in wide reflective equilibrium has come.

The difference does not come at the stage at which we filter *initial* moral judgments to arrive at *considered* moral judgments. Sophisticated forms of intuitionism leave room for specifying optimal conditions for avoiding errors of judgment. Nor does the difference come at the stage at which we match principles to judgments, "smooth out" irregularities, and increase the power of the principles. Again, sophisticated intuitionism is willing to trade away some slight degree of unrevisability for the reassurance that errors of judgment are further reduced. It is because *narrow* reflective equilibrium allows no further opportunities for revision than these two that it is readily assimilated to the model of a sophisticated intuitionism.

But *wide* reflective equilibrium, as I have described it, allows far more drastic *theory-based* revisions of moral judgments. Consider the additional ways in which a considered moral judgment is subject to revision in wide equilibrium. Suppose the considered judgment is about what is right or wrong, just or unjust, in particular situations, or is a maxim that governs such situations. In that case, it is a judgment relevant to establishing partial reflective equilibrium with general moral principles. Consequently, we must revise it if background theories compel us to revise our general principles or if they lead us to conclude that our moral conception is not feasible. Suppose, in contrast, the considered moral judgment plays a role in determining the acceptability of a component level III theory. Then it is also revisable for several reasons. Feasibility testing of the background theory may lead us to reject it and therefore to revise the considered judgment. The judgment may be part of one background theory that is rendered implausible because of its failure to cohere with other, more

---

[7]   The fact that these sources of error have been minimized does give considered judgments *some* modest degree of epistemic priority, as William Lycan has reminded me.

plausible background theories, and so the considered judgment may have to be changed. The considered judgment may be part of a system of background theories that would lead us to accept principles, and consequently some other level I considered judgments, which we cannot accept. If we can trace the source of our difficulty back to a level III considered judgment that we can give up more easily than we can accept the new level I judgment, then we would probably revise the level III judgment.

In seeking wide reflective equilibrium, we are constantly making plausibility judgments about which of our considered moral judgments we should revise in light of theoretical considerations at all levels. No one type of considered moral judgment is held immune to revision. No doubt, we are not inclined to give up certain considered moral judgments unless an overwhelmingly better alternative moral conception is available and substantial dissatisfaction with our own conception at other points leads us to do so (the methodological conservatism I referred to earlier). It is in this way that we provide a sense to the notion of a "provisional fixed point" among our considered judgments. Since all considered judgments are revisable, the judgment "It is wrong to inflict pain gratuitously on another person" is, too. But we can also explain why it is so hard to imagine not accepting it, so hard that some treat it as a necessary moral truth. To imagine revising such a provisional fixed point we must imagine a vastly altered wide reflective equilibrium that nevertheless is much more acceptable than our own. For example, we might have to imagine persons quite unlike the persons we know.

Wide reflective equilibrium keeps us from taking considered moral judgments at face value, however much they may be treated as starting points in our theory construction. Rather, they are always subjected to exhaustive review and are "tested," as are the moral principles, against a relevant body of theory. At every point, we are forced to assess their acceptability relative to theories that incorporate them and relative to alternative theories incorporating different considered moral judgments.

III.   Coherence and Justification

A.   *No Justification without Credibility.* Consider now the claim (2) that wide equilibrium uses inappropriate starting points for the development of moral theory. Here the accusation of neo-intuitionism seems to take the opposite tack, suggesting that considered judgments are not foundational enough. The traditional intuitionist seemed to have more going for him. With some pomp and circumstance, the earlier intuitionist at least outfitted his intuitions with the regal garb of epistemic priority, even if this later turned out to be the emperor's clothes. The modern intuitionist, the proponent of reflective equilibrium, allows his naked opinions to streak their way into our theories without benefit of any cover story. Richard Brandt has raised this objection in a forceful way which avoids the mistake about revisability noted earlier.

Brandt characterizes the method of reflective equilibrium as follows. We begin with a set of initial moral judgments or intuitions. We assign an *initial credence level* (say from 0 to 1 on a scale from things we believe very little to things we confidently believe). We filter out judgments with low initial credence levels to form our set of considered judgments. Then we propose principles and attempt to bring the system of principles plus judgments into equilibrium, allowing modifications wherever they are necessary to produce the system with the highest over-all credence level. But why, asks Brandt, should we be impressed with the results of such a process? We should not be, he argues, unless we have some way to show that "some of the beliefs are initially *credible* – and not merely initially believed – for some reason other than their coherence" in the set of beliefs we believe the most (*op. cit.*, chapter I). For example, in the nonmoral case, Brandt suggests that an initially believed judgment is also an initially credible judgment when it states (or purports to state) a fact of observation. "In the case of normative beliefs, no reason has been offered why we should think that initial credence levels, for a person, correspond to *credibilities*" (*loc. cit.*). The result is that we have no reason to think that increasing the credence level for the system as a whole moves us closer to moral truth rather than away from it. Coherent fictions are still fictions, and we may only be reshuffling our prejudices.

If Brandt's "no credibility" complaint has force, a question I take up shortly, it has such force against wide, and not just narrow, reflective equilibrium. In my reconstruction, considered moral judgments *may* play an ineliminable role constraining the acceptance of background (level III) theories in wide reflective equilibrium. (In general, level III theories do not reduce the moral to the non-moral, and level IV constraints do not select only one feasible system.) But level III considered moral judgments seem to be as open as level I considered judgments to the objection that they have only initial credence and not initial credibility. At least it would take a special argument to show why worries that initial level I considered judgments about justice lack initial credibility fail to carry weight against initial level III judgments about fair procedures or about which features of persons are morally central or relevant. The problem is that all such initial judgments are still "our" judgments. The fact that wide equilibrium provides support for the principles independent from that provided by level I partial equilibrium does not imply that this support is based on considered judgments that escape the "no credibility" criticism. The criticism does not go away just because wide reflective equilibrium permits an intra-theory gain in justificatory force not provided by narrow equilibrium.

B.   *Credibility and Coherence*. Much of the plausibility of the "no credibility" objection derives from the contrast between nonmoral observation reports and considered moral judgments or "intuitions." A minimal version[8] of the claim that initial credibility attaches to observation reports must do two things. It must allow for the revisability of such reports. It must also treat them as generally reliable unless we have specific reasons to think they are not. Observation reports seem to satisfy these conditions because we can tell some story, perhaps a causal story, that explains why the reports are generally reliable, though still revisable. In contrast, moral judgments are more suspect. We know that even sincerely believed moral judgments made under conditions conducive to avoiding mistakes may still be biased by self-interest, self-deception, or cultural and historical influences. So, if we construe a considered moral judgment as an attempt to report a moral fact, we have no causal story to

tell about reliability[9] and many reasons to suspect unreliability.

I would like to suggest three responses to this way of contrasting considered moral judgments and observation reports. First, the assumed analogy between considered moral judgments and observation reports is itself inappropriate. A considered moral judgment, even in a particular case, is in many ways far more like a "theoretical" than an "observation" statement. (I am not assuming a principled dichotomy here, at most a continuum of degree of theory-dependence). Evidence comes from the way in which we support considered moral judgments as compared to observation reports: we readily give reasons for the moral judgments, and our appeal to theoretical considerations to support them is not mainly concerned with the conditions under which the judgments are made. Further evidence for my claim would require that we carry out the programmatic suggestion made earlier: see whether we can explain the features of reason-giving by reference to features of wide equilibrium.

On the other hand, some may cite other evidence to support the analogy between observations and moral judgments. They might point, for example, to language-learning contexts, in which children are taught to identify actions as wrong or unjust much as they are taught to identify nonmoral properties. Or they may point to the fact that we often judge certain acts as right or wrong with great *immediacy* – the "gut reaction," so called. But such evidence is not persuasive. One thing that distinguishes adult from childish moral reasoning is the ready appeal to theoretical considerations. Similarly, we are often impatient with the person who refuses to provide moral reasons or theory to support his immediate moral judgments, much more so than we are with the person who backs up "It is red" with nothing more than "It sure looks red."

Consequently, I conclude, though I have not fully argued the point here, that the comparison of moral judgments to observation reports is mis-

---

8   A stronger version can be formulated. It would treat some classes of observation reports as self-warranting or even incorrigible. I consider only the more plausible, weaker version above. On the strong version, the criticism of reflective equilibrium is just a foundationalist attack. On the weak version, it is an attempt to show that, foundationalism aside, coherence theories of moral justification fact special problems not faced by coherence theories of nonmoral justification.
9   Gilbert Harman makes a similar point when he claims that p's obtaining plays no role in explaining my making the moral judgment that p, but q's obtaining does play a role in explaining my nonmoral observation that q. Cf. *The Nature of Morality* (New York: Oxford, 1977), p. 7 ff. [Harman's discussion is included in chapter 25 of this volume. Eds.] I think Harman overdraws the contrast here, but that is a matter for another discussion.

leading. Rightness and wrongness, or justice and injustice, are unlikely to be simple properties of moral situations. Consequently, they are unlikely to play a role analogous to that played by observational properties in the causal-reliability stories we tell ourselves concerning observation reports. But the "no credibility" argument gains its plausibility from the assumption that the analogy to observation reports *should* hold and then denigrates moral judgments when it is pointed out they differ from observation reports. If they *should* and *do* function differently – because they are different kinds of judgments – that is not something we should hold against the moral judgments.

Secondly, the "no credibility" criticism is at best premature. It is plausible to think that only the development of acceptable moral theory in wide reflective equilibrium will enable us to determine what kind of "fact," if any, is involved in a considered moral judgment. In the context of such a theory, and with an answer to our puzzlement about the kind of fact (if any) a moral fact is, we might be able to provide a story about the reliability of initial considered judgments. Indeed, it seems reasonable to impose this burden on the theory that emerges in wide reflective equilibrium. It should help us answer this sort of question. If we can provide a reasonable answer, then we may have a way of distinguishing initially credible from merely initially believed types of moral judgments.

The "no credibility" criticism gains initial plausibility because we *are* able to assign initial credibility to nonmoral observation reports, but not to moral judgments. The credibility assignment, however, draws implicitly on a broadly accepted body of theory which explains why those judgments are credible. Properly understood, the credibility story about nonmoral observation reports is itself only the product of a nonmoral wide reflective equilibrium of relatively recent vintage. In contrast, we lack that level of theory development in the moral case. What follows from this difference is that the "no credibility" argument succeeds in assigning a burden of proof. *Some* answer to the question about the reliability of moral judgments must be forthcoming. But the argument is hardly a demonstration that no plausible story is possible.

Thirdly, a more positive – though still speculative – point can be made in favor of starting from considered moral judgments in our theory construction. It is commonplace, and true, to note that there is variation and disagreement about consid-

ered moral judgments among persons and cultures. It is also commonplace, and true, to note that there is much uniformity and agreement on considered moral judgments among persons and cultures. Philosophers of all persuasions cite one or the other commonplace as convenience in argument dictates. But moral philosophy should help us to *explain both* facts.

What wide equilibrium shows us about the structure of moral theories may help us explain the extensive agreement we do find. Such agreement on judgments may reflect an underlying agreement on features of the component background theories. Indeed, people may be more in agreement about the nature of persons, the role of morality in society, and so on, than is often assumed. Of course, these other points of agreement might be discounted by pointing to the influence of culture or ideology in shaping level III theories. But it may also be that the agreement is found because some of the background theories are, roughly speaking, true – at least with regard to certain important features. Moreover, widely different people may have come to learn these truths despite their culturally different experiences. The point is that moral *agreement* – at levels III and I – may not be just the result of historical accident, at least not in the way that some moral *disagreements* are. Consequently, it would be shortsighted to deny credibility to considered judgments just because there is widespread disagreement on many of them: there is also agreement on many. Here moral anthropology *is* relevant to answering questions in moral theory.

I conclude that the "no credibility" objection reduces either to a burden-of-proof argument, which is plausible but hardly conclusive, or to a general foundationalist objection to coherence accounts of theory acceptance (or justification). It becomes a burden-of-proof argument as soon as one notices that the credibility we assign to observation reports is itself based on an inference from a nonmoral reflective equilibrium. We do not yet have such an account of credibility for the moral case, but we also have no good reason to think it impossible or improbable that we can develop such an account once we know more about moral theory. On the other hand, the "no credibility" argument becomes a foundationalist objection if it is insisted that observation reports are credible independently of such coherence stories.

My reply to the "no credibility" criticism points again to a strong similarity in the way coherence constraints on theory acceptance (or justification) operate in the two domains, despite the disanalogy between observation reports and considered moral judgments. The accounts of initial credibility we accept for observation reports (say, some causal story about reliable detection) are based on inferences from various component sciences constrained by coherence considerations. Observation reports are neither self-warranting nor unrevisable, and our willingness to grant them initial credibility depends on our acceptance of various other relevant theories and beliefs. Such an account is also owed for some set of moral judgments, but it too will derive from component theories in wide equilibrium. Similarly, in rejecting the view that wide equilibrium merely systematizes a determinate set of moral judgments, and arguing instead for the revisability of these inputs, I suggest that wide equilibrium closely resembles scientific practice. Neither in science nor in ethics do we merely "test" our theories against a predetermined, relatively fixed body of data. Rather, we continually reassess and reevaluate both the plausibility and the relevance of these data against theories we are inclined to accept. The possibility thus arises that these pressures for revision will free considered moral judgments from their vulnerability to many of the *specific* objections about bias and unreliability usually directed against them.

IV.   Objectivity and Convergence

I would like to consider what implications, if any, the method of wide equilibrium may have for some traditional worries about objectivity in ethics. Of course, objectivity is a multiply ambiguous notion. Still, two senses stand out as central. First, in a given area of inquiry, claims are thought to be objective if there is some significant degree of intersubjective agreement on them. Second, claims are also said to be objective if they express truths relevant to the area of inquiry. Other important senses of "objectivity" reduce to one or both of the central uses [e.g., "free from bias" (said of methods or claims) and "reliability" or "replicability" (said of methods or procedures of inquiry)]. The two central senses are not unrelated. The typical realist, for example, hopes that methods or procedures of inquiry that tend to produce intersubjective agreement do so because they are methods that give us access to relevant truths. In contrast, there are also

eliminative approaches which try to show that one or the other notion of objectivity is either confused, reducible to the other, or irrelevant in a given area of inquiry. Thus some have suggested that knowledge of moral truths is unattainable (perhaps because there are no moral truths) and we should settle for the objectivity of intersubjective agreement (based on rational inquiry) if we can achieve it. Does the method of wide reflective equilibrium commit us to one or another of these approaches to objectivity in ethics?

One traditional worry, that moral judgments are not objective because there is insufficient agreement about them, may be laid to rest by seeking wide equilibrium. I have suggested that seeking wide equilibrium may render problems of theory acceptance in ethics more tractable and may thus produce greater moral agreement. Specifically, it may lead us to understand better the sources of moral agreement and disagreement and the constraints on what we count as relevant and important to the revision of moral judgments. It may allow us to reduce moral disagreements (about principles or judgments) to more resoluble disagreements in the relevant background (level III and IV) theories. None of these possibilities guarantees increased agreement. How much convergence results remains an empirical question. But I think I have made it at least plausible that wide equilibrium could increase agreement and do so in a *nonarbitrary* way. At least, it could provide us with a clearer picture of how much agreement we already have (I return to this point later). And if it does, then there are implications for how objective, at least in the minimal sense of intersubjective agreement, ethics is.

To be sure, many who point to the lack of intersubjective agreement on many moral issues do so to raise a more robust worry about lack of objectivity in ethics. They point to moral disagreement as if it were strong *evidence* for the deeper claim about objectivity, that there are no moral truths for us to agree about. The inference from lack of agreement to the absence of truths to be acquired is generally unpersuasive, however. Sometimes there is the buried assumption that *if* there were such truths, we would probably have enough access to them to produce more agreement than we have. I see no way, however, to formulate this assumption so that it does not rule out the existence of truths in most areas of scientific inquiry, at least at some time in their history. Sometimes there is the qualification that it is not the disagreement about moral claims that is important, but the "fact" that we cannot agree about what would produce resolution of the disagreement. This is likely to be more true in science and less true in ethics than is usually claimed. Still, there is a kernel of truth behind the inference, though it is insufficient to warrant it: agreement, *when it is produced by methods we deem appropriate in a given area of inquiry*, does appear to have some evidential relation to what is agreed on.

What has troubled critics of reflective equilibrium, however, is an opposite worry. Anyone who believes that there *are* objective moral truths will want to leave room for the possibility that there may be consensus on moral falsehoods. The worry is clearly reasonable when we suspect that the factors that led to consensus have little, if anything, to do with rational inquiry (and we need not have in mind anything so drastic as the Inquisition). And if one thought the method of wide equilibrium fell far short of rational inquiry, the worry would again be reasonable. Moreover, it is not obviously unreasonable even if one takes wide equilibrium to be the best method available but wants to acknowledge the possibility that it may lead to justified acceptance of moral falsehoods. The fear here is that intersubjective agreement will be taken as *constitutive* of moral truth or as eliminative of any full-blown (realist) notion of objective moral truth.

The worry might be put this way. Suppose that when diverse people are induced to seek the principles they would accept in wide reflective equilibrium, only one shared equilibrium point emerges. Can we still ask, Are these principles objective moral truths? Is the proponent of wide equilibrium committed to the view that such intersubjective agreement *constitutes* the principles and judgments as moral truths? Or is it at best *evidence* that we have discovered objective moral truths? Or is it any evidence at all that we have found some? I shall suggest that though convergence in wide equilibrium is neither a necessary nor a sufficient condition for claiming we have found objective moral truths, such convergence may constitute *evidence* we have found some.

To see that convergence in wide equilibrium is not a sufficient condition for claiming we have found objective moral truths, suppose we actually produced such convergence among diverse persons. Whether or not the principles and judgments they accept would count as such truths

would depend on *how* we come to explain the convergence. Suppose, for example, we find that we can *explain* the convergence by pointing to a psychological feature of human beings that plays a *causal* role in producing their agreement. Suppose, to be specific, that, under widespread conditions of child-rearing in diverse cultures, people tend to group others into "in groups" and "out groups" and that the effect of this mechanism is that moral judgments and principles in wide equilibrium turn out to be inegalitarian in certain ways. Suppose we discover, further, that these child-rearing practices are themselves changeable and not the product of any deep features of human biology and psychology. We might begin to feel that the convergence we had found in wide equilibrium was only a fortuitous result of a provincial feature of human social psychology. Convergence would thus not by itself be sufficient grounds for constituting the principles as moral truths.

We can turn the example around to question the necessity of convergence for constituting the principles as objective moral truths. Suppose we find, after attempting to produce wide equilibria among diverse persons, that there is no actual convergence in wide equilibrium. Different families of equilibria emerge. Suppose also that we can *explain* the failure of convergence by pointing again to a provincial feature of human psychology or biology. But suppose further that we can abstract from this source of divergence. We can construct a modified and *idealized* "agreement" on principles. Such an idealization might, depending on other factors, be a good candidate for containing objective moral truths, even though it is *not* accepted in any actual wide equilibrium.

Which way we should go in either of these cases will have something to do with how fundamental we think the source of divergence or convergence is. But what we count as "fundamental" is itself determined by the view of the nature of moral judgments and principles which emerges in wide equilibrium. For example, if the convergence-producing feature of human psychology turned out to be a central fact about the emotions or motivations, say, some fact about the nature of (Humean) sympathy, which proved invariant to all but the strangest (pathological) child-rearing practices, then we might think we had reached a fundamental fact (related at least to the *feasibility* of moral conceptions). Still, even here, I do not want to assume that metaethical considerations embedded in the background theories would force us to reject a more Kantian stance. To follow up our earlier discussion, we are here concerned with factors that may affect the "credibility" of initial considered judgments, leading us to discount some and favor others; how we weigh these factors will depend on complex features of our background theories.

In short, divergence among wide reflective equilibria does not imply that there are no such things as objective moral truths; nor does convergence imply that we have found them; nor need 'moral truth' be replaced by 'adopted in wide equilibrium'. How we will be motivated, or warranted, in treating the facts of divergence or convergence depends on the kinds of divergence or convergence we encounter and the kinds of explanation we can give for it. This result should not surprise us: wide reflective equilibrium embodies coherence constraints on theory acceptance or justification, not on truth.[10]

Actually, it is necessary to qualify my conclusion that wide reflective equilibrium need not be viewed as constitutive of moral truth. My argument that convergence is neither necessary nor sufficient to establish the discovery of moral truths depends on bringing theoretical considerations to bear which seem sufficient to destabilize the actual equilibrium in some way. Suppose we now throw back into the ring these destabilizing considerations and seek a new wide equilibrium. If we can soup up wide equilibrium in this way, so that it adds up to something like "total rational consideration," then perhaps we can revive in a strengthened form the constitutive view. We would have here, perhaps, the analogue of Putnam's "empirical realist" rejection of objective (metaphysical) moral truths.[11] This version of the eliminative view is not open to the most reasonable worries of those who feel simple moral agreement should not be taken to constitute moral truth. In any case, on its form of verificationism, ethics may be no worse off than science!

A more modest way of putting the same objection is this. My reply to the eliminative view is compatible with the following claim: there is a sense in which the question, Do we really have moral truth, given convergence in wide reflective equilibrium? is an *idle* worry in the absence of any *specific* research capable of destabilizing the equilibrium. In the absence of some particular, plausible way to challenge the convergence, the question is tantamount to strong and unfruitful skepticism.

Despite these qualifications, my inclination is not to treat wide reflective equilibrium as constitutive of moral truth (assuming convergence) and to leave room instead for a weaker *evidential* relation holding between agreement in wide equilibrium and moral truth. What we would need to support this possibility is reason to think that the methods of inquiry in ethics that tend to produce convergence do so *because* they bring us close to moral truth. I can offer only a highly qualified and indirect argument to this conclusion.

Consider for a moment a general argument of this form: (1) In a given area of inquiry, the methods used are successful in the sense that they produce convergence and a growth of knowledge; (2) the only plausible account of the success of these methods is that they lead us to better and better approximations to truths of the kind relevant to the inquiry; (3) therefore, we should adopt a realist account of the relevant objects of inquiry. Arguments of this form have been advanced to defend platonism with regard to mathematical objects and realism with regard to the referents of theoretical terms in the empirical sciences. To establish the second premise of such an argument, one must not only show that alternatives to the realist account (say intuitionist accounts in mathematics and verificationist or positivist accounts in science) will not explain the success of the methods used, but that the realist account has some independent plausibility of its own. Otherwise, it may simply seem to be a residual, *ad hoc* account. In mathematics, proponents of platonism, whatever the merits of their refutations of other accounts, have not provided accounts, aside from perceptual metaphors, which make it plausible that we can

---

[10]   If we construe wide reflective equilibrium as providing us with the basis for a full-blown coherence theory of moral justification, then my argument suggests that it faces the same difficulties and advantages as coherence theories of non-moral justification. I cannot here defend my view that a coherence theory of justification can be made compatible with a noncoherency account of truth.

[11]   Cf. Hilary Putnam, *Meaning and the Moral Sciences* (London: Routledge & Kegan Paul, 1978), part IV.

come to know anything about mathematical objects. In contrast, however, there are some interesting and promising arguments of this form in defense of scientific realism. In these, a version of a causal theory of knowledge and reference is used to satisfy the requirement that we lend plausibility to the realist account of methodology independent of the refutation of alternative accounts.

Suppose a version of such an argument for scientific realism is sound – a supposition I shall not defend here at all. Then we would be justified in claiming that certain central methodological features of science, including its coherence and other theory-laden constraints on theory acceptance (e.g., parsimony, simplicity, etc.), are consensus-producing *because* they are *evidential* and lead us to better approximations to the truth. I have been defending the view that coherence constraints in wide equilibrium function very much like those in science. If I am right, this suggests that we may be able to piggy-back a claim about objectivity in ethics onto the analogous claim we are assuming can be made for science. Suppose then that coherence constraints in wide equilibrium turn out to be consensus-producing. Then, since these constraints are similar to their analogues in science in other respects, they may also be *evidential*. That is, we have some reason to think that wide equilibrium involves methods that will lead us to objective moral truths *if there are any*. Notice that this conclusion does not presuppose there are such moral truths, nor does it give an account of what kind of truth such a truth would be.

My suggestion is obviously a highly tentative and programmatic route to an account of objectivity in ethics. Nor can I really defend it here. Some qualifying remarks are definitely in order, however.

(A)   Developed versions of the arguments for scientific realism do not simply talk about "convergence," but point to a variety of effects indicative of the cumulative nature or progress of scientific knowledge. For example, they may try to account for "take-off" effects indicative of the maturation of an area of inquiry, or they may point to the absence of "schools" or "sects." My supposition that convergence may emerge in wide equilibrium falls far short of specifying this sort of evidence for growth in moral knowledge. There is a related point: I am not sure we know what to count as evidence for convergence in ethics. For example, we do have moral disagreement on numerous issues; but is the level of disagreement

compatible with enough other agreement for it to count as convergence, or not? Does existing disagreement merely represent hard or novel problems at the "frontier"? Or is it the result of special social forces which systematically distort our view in areas of political or religious sensitivity? Some of the difficulty may stem from paucity of work in the history of ethics and in moral anthropology adequate to informing us whether we have experienced moral progress.

(B)   The piggy-back argument seems to rest on the assumption that, if a feature of method (a coherence constraint) is similar in one respect (it produces consensus) in two areas of inquiry, then it holds in both areas for the same reason (it leads to relevant truths). I do not think the assumption is obviously or even generally true; that is why my suggestion is only programmatic.

(C)   The arguments for scientific realism depend on some causal account of knowledge – e.g., perceptual knowledge depends on reliable detection mechanisms. We are reminded, therefore, of the burden of proof assumed in section III to provide *some* reliability account of moral judgments (at some level). Suppose we could provide no analogue in the moral case to the causal story we may be persuaded of for perceptual knowledge. If we still wanted to talk about "objective moral truths," we might *retreat* to the view that the objects of moral knowledge were "abstract," that is, more like mathematical objects than the things we can know about through the natural sciences. But our moral realism, then, is open to the worry I earlier expressed about mathematical platonism. To be sure, if our causal accounts of knowledge turn out to be unpersuasive, then the argument for scientific realism may be no better off than this in any case.

(D)   My account of wide reflective equilibrium has not provided (not explicitly at least) an obvious analogue to the role of experimentation in science. Some story about moral *practice* and what we can learn from it, and not just about moral thought experiments, seems to be needed. That is, we would need to examine the sense in which moral theories guide moral practice and result in social experimentation. But this account must be left for another project.

A final remark is directed not just at my suggestion about the implications of wide equilibrium for objectivity in ethics, but at my account of wide equilibrium itself. The account I have sketched defines a wide equilibrium for a given individual at a given time. The "convergence" I have been discussing is the (at least approximate) sharing of the same wide equilibrium by different persons; the ordered triples of sets of beliefs are the same for these persons. But there would seem to be another approach.

Suppose we begin by admitting into the set of initial considered moral judgments only those judgments on which there is substantial consensus. There seem to be two immediate advantages. First, ethics looks more like science in that the initial considered moral judgments share with observation reports the fact that there is substantial initial agreement on them. The starting point is more "objective," at least in the sense of intersubjective agreement. One *may* gain a slight edge in respect to the problem of initial credibility discussed earlier. (Revisability is, nevertheless, presumed.) Second, the approach makes the wide equilibrium that emerges (if one does) much more a collective or social product from the start than does my approach, which is a quite unnatural idealization in this regard.

Though I think this alternative merits further examination, which I cannot undertake here, I am not persuaded that it offers real advantages. For one thing, it builds into its procedure the assumption that considered judgments *ought* to function like observation reports in science, a question, I have argued, there is good reason to leave open. Its apparent advantage in making ultimate convergence seem more likely might, consequently, be based on the assumption that we ought to have *initial* convergence where there is no good reason to expect it (given all the things that make *initial* considered moral judgments *un*reliable). For another thing, I have assumed that extensive consideration of alternative background theories and sets of principles will produce reasonable pressures to revise and eliminate divergent considered judgments that there are good reasons to eliminate. The alternative method may shift, in too crude a fashion (losing too many possibilities), the intermediate conclusions of my procedure into the position of methodologically warranted starting points. A less important consideration is historical: reflective equilibrium is advanced by Rawls as a model for the process of justification in ethics. Part of what he wanted to capture is a model for how we may make progress in moral argument – where we have to accommodate initial disagreement on some moral judgments. My approach retains this attractive feature, though it sheds some of the other motivations for Rawls's version.

My remarks on objectivity are admittedly quite speculative; indeed, I think it a virtue of the method of reflective equilibrium that it leaves open metaethical considerations of this kind. Still, I think enough has been said about wide equilibrium, these speculations aside, to make its implications for theory acceptance in ethics worthy of closer study.

Intuitionism, Pluralism, and the Foundations of Ethics

Robert Audi

Ethical intuitionism is historically important, widely referred to, and generally considered a major position in the foundations of ethics. But it is not widely discussed in depth. This is in part because, although it is held by some leading philosophers, its resources are often underestimated. It is certainly conceived divergently among ethical theorists, and those who find its central elements compelling may often think it easier and better simply to argue for their position under another name than to indicate what kind of intuitionism they hold and defend their position under that rubric. My aim here is to clarify intuitionism, to bring out some of its strengths and weaknesses, and to reassess the case for giving it a more significant place in contemporary ethical theory.

[. . .]

To assess ethical intuitionism and the role of intuitions in supporting it, we need a clearer conception of what it is, an account of its relation to ethical intuitions, and a theory of how both are related to the distinction between rationalism and empiricism in moral epistemology. If this task of explication succeeds, it will yield more than a deeper understanding of intuitionism. It will provide the raw materials of a framework for moral theory that overcomes many of the difficulties con-

fronting intuitionism, accounts for the role of intuitions in moral reasoning, and provides the outline of a moral epistemology. In the light of the conception of intuitionism that emerges from the first three parts of this chapter, I will briefly develop this framework. The concluding parts will appraise intuitionism as a restricted version of this wider framework.

I.   Traditional Ethical Intuitionism

There are currently two main uses of the term 'intuitionism'. On one use, intuitionism is conceived as an overall kind of ethical theory; on the other, it is a moral epistemology held to be characteristic of such theories. My aim is in part to determine whether either of these common conceptions is adequate to the best intuitionist theories available.

In the former, overall conception, intuitionism has three main characteristics. (1) It is an ethical *pluralism*, a position affirming an irreducible plurality of basic moral principles. (2) Each principle centers on a different kind of ground, in the sense of a factor implying a prima facie moral duty, such as making a promise on noticing a person who will bleed to death without one's help. (3) Each principle is taken to be in some sense intuitively known.

(1) and (2) are structural and conceptual; they affirm a plurality of basic principles affecting different kinds of conduct, and they thus deny, against both Kantian and utilitarian theories, that there is just one basic moral principle. (3) is epistemological; it locates the basic principles with respect to knowledge.

In the second, epistemological conception of intuitionism, the view is roughly the thesis that basic moral judgments and basic moral principles are justified by the non-inferential deliverances of a rational, intuitive faculty, a mental capacity that contrasts with sense perception, clairvoyance, and other possible routes to justification. A number of writers, particularly critics of intuitionism, conceive intuitionism as implying the stronger thesis that the intuitive faculty yields indefeasible knowledge of self-evident moral truths. One concern of this essay is whether this stronger conception is justified.

Rossian intuitionism

The position of W. D. Ross is widely regarded as a version of intuitionism in both the overall and epistemological senses: as pluralist and as implying that we have intuitive moral knowledge. My chief concern is intuitionist moral epistemology. This epistemology is, however, fundamental in intuitionism as an overall ethical view, and an examination of the epistemology will ultimately lead us to a discussion of the pluralism of the view. We can best clarify this epistemology and appraise the adequacy of the formulation of it just given if we explore a representative intuitionism. Ross is at once an important moral philosopher and an excellent example of an intuitionist. We can learn much by examining the basic elements of his ethical theory. [. . .]

In what is probably his most important ethical work, *The Right and the Good* (1930), Ross proposed, as fundamental both to philosophical ethics and to everyday life, a now famous list of prima facie duties: duties of fidelity (promise-keeping, including honesty) and reparation, of justice and gratitude, of beneficence and self-improvement, and of non-injury.[1] In calling these duties prima facie, Ross meant to indicate that even when we acquire one, say by making a promise, the act in question need not be our final duty, since a competing duty, for instance to attend a sick child, might override the original duty.[2] This does not imply that a prima facie duty ever lacks *moral weight*; one should, for example, regret having to break a promise, and perhaps must make reparations for it, even when one did right in breaking it. The point is simply that a prima facie duty is not necessarily final, and to recognize such a duty as applicable to oneself is not sufficient for knowing what, all things considered, one should *do*.

[. . .]

The central idea underlying the Rossian notion of a prima facie duty, I suggest, is that of a duty which is – given the presence of its ground – *ineradicable but overridable*. The presence of its ground (a notion Ross does not explicate) is crucial. If, for example, others could not benefit from our help, there would be no prima facie duty of beneficence, since our ground for the duty would be absent. A prima facie duty that is ineradicable given the presence of its ground is nonetheless *cancelable* by removal of that ground. Consider the duty to keep a promise. Where the promisee releases one from a promise or where the fulfillment of the duty becomes impossible, say because the person one had a duty to help has died, there is no longer any such duty. But overriding conditions do not cancel the duty they override. A duty's being overridden by conflicting prima facie duties implies that its ground is outweighed, but not that it is removed. A superior counterforce blocks, but does not eliminate, the force it overpowers.

Ross stressed a number of features of his position, and at least some of these have become part of the common conception (so far as there is one) of intuitionism. First, he insisted on its irreducible pluralism: he argued that there is no one thing, such as enhancing goodness in the world, that is our only direct, overall duty. Second, he emphasized the self-evidence of the propositions expressing our prima facie duties. Here is the central passage:

> That an act *qua* fulfilling a promise, or *qua* effecting a just distribution of good . . . is *prima facie* right, is

---

[1] See Ross, *The Right and the Good* (Oxford: Oxford University Press, 1930), p. 21.
[2] Ross often used 'actual duty' where I use 'final duty', but this is misleading: as explained later, even an overridden duty is actually possessed.

self-evident; not in the sense that it is evident from the beginning of our lives, or as soon as we attend to the proposition for the first time, but in the sense that when we have reached sufficient mental maturity and have given sufficient attention to the proposition it is evident without any need of proof, or of evidence beyond itself. It is evident just as a mathematical axiom, or the validity of a form of inference, is evident. . . . In our confidence that these propositions are true there is involved the same confidence in our reason that is involved in our confidence in mathematics. . . . In both cases we are dealing with propositions that cannot be proved, but that just as certainly need no proof.[3]

Third, Ross apparently intended this claim of self-evidence to hold for certain kinds of act, not particular deeds. He says, for example, "[W]e are never certain that any particular possible act is . . . right," and, clarifying this, that "we apprehend *prima facie* rightness to belong to the nature of any fulfillment of a promise. From this we come by reflection to apprehend the self-evident *prima facie* rightness of an individual act of a particular type. . . . But no act is ever, in virtue of falling under some general description, necessarily actually right; its rightness depends on its whole nature and not any element in it."[4] His positive point, applied to promising, is in part that when one thinks clearly about what it *is* to promise a particular friend to do something, one can see that doing the deed is called for and would be right barring special circumstances, such as a medical emergency. His negative point, in the Rossian terminology just introduced, is something like this: from a general description of the grounds that yield a prima facie duty, for example from the description of an act of mine as a promise, it does not follow that the duty (here the duty to keep the promise) is not overridden, nor is it self-evident that it is not overridden, however clear that may be in many cases. It is not self-evident, for instance, that no medical emergency will intervene and override my duty to keep the promise.

The fourth and final point here is that in explaining how we apprehend the moral truths in question, Ross appealed to something like what we commonly call intuitions. He said, for example, that if someone challenges

our view that there is a special obligatoriness attaching to the keeping of promises because it is self-evident that the only duty is to produce as much good as possible, we have to ask ourselves whether we really, when we reflect, *are* convinced that [as he takes G. E. Moore to hold] this is self-evident. . . . [I]t seems self-evident that a promise simply as such, is something that *prima facie* ought to be kept. . . . [T]he moral convictions of thoughtful and well-educated people are the data of ethics, just as sense-perceptions are the data of a natural science. Just as some of the latter have to be rejected as illusory, so have some of the former; but as the latter are rejected only when they conflict with other more accurate sense-perceptions, the former are rejected only when they conflict with convictions which stand better the test of reflection.[5]

Ross does not make clear whether the imagined conflicts are ever resolvable by appeal to generalizations, such as one to the effect that promises to meet with students have priority over promises to campaign for political candidates. Suppose I discover that keeping a promise to comment on a long manuscript will take vastly more time than anyone could foresee. Something rather general may then occur to me (if I follow Ross): that I have prima facie duties of other sorts, arising, for instance, from duties of beneficence as well as from other promises, such as promises to my family or friends. As I think, in this light, about my overall duties, my sense that I must prepare the comments may conflict with my sense that I should fulfill other duties. Ross countenances this kind of conflict, but because he treats "the verdicts of the moral consciousness of the best people as the foundation on which we must build" and is thinking of judgments about concrete moral options, he seems to hold the view that ethical generalizations do not *independently* carry evidential weight in such conflicts. One should not, for example, appeal to a second-order generalization that duties of justice are stronger than duties of fidelity. Rather, one should focus on the specific facts and, in that light, determine what one's actual duty is.

The task of conflict resolution here is very much like that of using Aristotelian practical wisdom in dealing with a moral problem. It is possible, for Ross as for Aristotle, that a rule emerges *on the basis*

---

[3] Ibid., pp. 29–30. Cf. H. A. Prichard, "Does Moral Philosophy Rest on a Mistake?" (1912), in his *Moral Obligation* (Oxford: Oxford University Press, 1949). The mistake is "supposing the possibility of proving what can only be apprehended directly by an act of moral thinking" (p. 16).

[4] Ibid., pp. 31 and 33.

[5] Ibid., pp. 39–41.

of the resolution one reaches, but there is not necessarily any rule *antecedently* governing each particular case one may encounter. I may, through my reflection on such a conflict of duties, frame a rule for similar future cases; but I do not bring to every case a ready-made rule that, irrespective of my intuitive judgments about that case, will tell me what to do.

In this rejection of the view that there are always second-order generalizations available to resolve conflicts of prima facie duties, Ross seems to be, as regards judgments of overall obligation, a *particularist* rather than a generalist: he holds that we must attend to particular cases in order to determine what generalizations hold, even if it is repeatable features of those cases, such as their being acts of promising, that reveal the general truths we reach through reflection on the cases. This is a point not about what *can* be known but about the order of knowing: our basic moral knowledge – even of prima facie duties – comes from reflection on particular cases, especially those calling for moral decision, where those cases are properly conceived in terms of their repeatable features. Our basic moral knowledge does not come from reflection on abstract, universal moral propositions. We do not, for instance, grasp the Kantian categorical imperative a priori and then apply it to the issue at hand with a view to formulating, on the basis of it, a "theorem" that resolves our problem. That abstract, monistic approach is also precluded by Ross's pluralism. But pluralism is not his only demand: he would also reject even a set of mutually irreducible rules if they were abstractions imposed on particular cases in the way the categorical imperative or utilitarianism might be, rather than derived from reflection on particular cases.

An example of commitment to such a set of rules would be an a priori *hierarchism*, a view on which some of the prima facie duties automatically outweigh one or more others. Ross would reject this because for him, as for intuitionists in general, there is neither a *complete* ordering of duties in terms of moral weights (a ranking of duties from strongest to least strong) nor even any *pairwise ordering* (a ranking of some pair of the prima facie duties), as where the duty of non-maleficence, say, to avoid killing, is always said to outweigh that of beneficence, for instance to save life. These points do not entail that *no* comparisons between strengths of (prima facie) duties can be proper

objects of intuition. Given a typical pattern of facts concerning a babysitter annoyed by a cranky infant, one might have an intuition that the babysitter's duty not to flog the child to death is stronger than the duty not to give it a heavy but non-fatal dose of vodka.

Self-evidence and defeasibility

We can now compare Ross's view with the common conception of intuitionism (in moral epistemology) noted earlier. He fits that conception in holding that the basic moral truths – which he takes to be constituted by his principles of prima facie duty – are self-evident. But he does not posit a special rational faculty. He is not committed to the existence of a "part" of the mind, or even "capacity of reason," required only for moral thought. He talks, to be sure, of moral consciousness and of "apprehension" (roughly, understanding) of those self-evident truths (by 'apprehension' he often means a species of what is commonly meant by 'intuition', which will be explicated in the next section). But in presenting his moral epistemology he emphasizes that the prima facie moral duties are recognized in the same way as the truth of mathematical axioms and logical truths.

Ross also speaks (e.g., in the same passage) of our apprehending the self-evidence of the relevant moral and mathematical propositions. He does not always distinguish apprehending the truth of a proposition that *is* self-evident from apprehending *its self-evidence*. This is an important point, since (if there are self-evident propositions) it should be easy to apprehend the truth of at least some of them, whereas the epistemic *status* of propositions, for example their justification or self-evidence or apriority, is a paradigm source of disagreement. It should be noted, however, that even apprehension of the self-evidence of propositions does not require having a special faculty. But suppose it did. Does Ross's overall position commit him to our having non-inferential knowledge of the self-evidence, as opposed to the truth, of the relevant principles? I think not, and if I am correct then one apparently common view of intuitionism can be set aside as a misconception. Let me explain.

We might know that a moral principle is self-evident only on a limited basis, say from knowing the conceptual as opposed to empirical (e.g., observational) character of the grounds on which we know that principle to be true. We would know its truth *on* these grounds; we would know its self-evidence through knowledge *about* the grounds. For instance, if we take ourselves to know a moral proposition, say that there is a prima facie (moral) duty to keep promises, (1) on the basis of understanding the concepts involved in this proposition and (2) non-inferentially (roughly, without dependence on one or more premises as evidence), we may plausibly think it follows, from our having this kind of knowledge of the moral proposition, that it has the status of self-evidence. This way of knowing the status of a Rossian proposition expressing a basic prima facie duty requires having concepts of self-evidence, of non-inferentiality, and, in effect, of a priori knowledge. But *none* of these concepts is required simply to know that there is a prima facie duty to keep promises. It is, however, that first-order proposition, the principle that promise-keeping is a duty, and not the second-order thesis that this principle is self-evident, which is the fundamental thing we must be able to know intuitively if a Rossian intuitionism is to succeed. As moral agents we need intuitive knowledge of our duties; we do not need intuitive (or even other) knowledge of the status of the principles of duty.

This brings us to the last key point in the most common conception of intuitionism: the idea that it posits *indefeasible justification* – roughly, justification that cannot be undermined or overridden – for any cognition grounded in a genuine intuition. Ross is not committed to this general idea, even if he might have regarded some moral beliefs as indefeasibly justified. Once it is seen that the primary role of intuition is to give us direct, that is, non-inferential, knowledge or justified belief of the *truth*, rather than of the self-evidence, of moral propositions (especially certain moral principles), there is less reason to think that moral beliefs resting on an intuitive grasp of principles must be considered indefeasibly justified.

Indeed, even if self-evidence were the main element that is intuitively apprehended, Ross would be entitled to hold – and in fact stresses – that there can be conflicts of moral "convictions" in which some are given up "just as" in scientific inquiry some perceptions are given up as illusory (see the earlier quotation from *The Right and the Good*, pp. 39–40). If intuitions are sometimes prop-erly given up in this way – and the convictions in question are apparently a species of what are commonly called intuitions – the justification possessed by intuitions is plainly defeasible (subject to being undermined or overridden); and so, at least with respect to moral judgments of particular deeds, defeasibility is to be expected.

This brings us to something that does not seem to have been generally noticed by critics of intuitionism and is at least not emphasized by Ross. The view that the justification of moral intuitions is defeasible, even when grounded in the careful reflection Ross thought appropriate to them, is quite consistent with his claim that the self-evident truths in question do not admit of proof. That a proposition does not admit of proof is an epistemic fact about *it* and leaves open that a person might have only poor or overridden grounds for *believing* it. This logical and epistemic fact does not entail that one cannot lose one's justification for believing it, or even fail to become justified in believing it upon considering it, or fail to find it intuitive.

It must be granted, however, that by putting us in mind of the simplest logical and mathematical truths, Ross's unprovability claim easily creates the mistaken impression that genuine intuitions are either infallible or justificationally indefeasible, or both. Nonetheless, there is nothing in Ross's theory as set out in *The Right and the Good* which is inconsistent with the rather striking disclaimer made by his great intuitionist predecessor, G. E. Moore, following his sketch of what, in his view, constitutes an intuition. Moore says that in calling propositions intuitions he means

> *merely* to assert that they are incapable of proof; I imply nothing whatever as to the manner or origin of our cognition of them. Still less do I imply (as most Intuitionists have done) that any proposition whatever is true, *because* we cognise it in a particular way or by the exercise of any particular faculty: I hold, on the contrary, that in every way in which it is possible to cognise a true proposition it is also possible to cognise a false one.[6]

Apparently, for Moore as for Ross, even if the truth or self-evidence of a proposition can be apprehended by reflection, there need be no special faculty yielding the apprehensions; and whatever the basis of those apprehensions, it is of a kind that

---

[6] G. E. Moore, *Principia Ethica* (Cambridge: Cambridge University Press, 1903), p. x.

can produce mistaken beliefs, including some that one would naturally take to be apprehensions of self-evident truths. Anyone who is aware that mistaken beliefs can arise from apprehensions or intuitions (or in any other way one can "cognise" a proposition) should be willing to regard intuitions as capable of being unjustified or even false.

II.   Intuitions, Intuitionism, and Reflection

We have seen that if Ross's view is a paradigm of intuitionism, then a widely held conception of intuitionism is inadequate. Above all, he is (by his major views) committed neither to the existence of a special faculty of intuition – such as a capacity peculiar to ethical subject matter – nor to the epistemic indefeasibility of the "self-evident" judgments that reflection yields. The same seems true of Moore, for reasons I have suggested, but I cannot pursue Moore's views separately here. This section will clarify further what an intuitionist like Ross *is* committed to. I begin with a sketch of the notion of an intuition. I mean, of course, 'intuition' in the *cognitive sense*, a psychological state like (and perhaps a kind of) belief. We have not been discussing, and need not explicitly discuss, intuitions in the *propositional sense*, that is, propositions of the kind Moore (as quoted earlier) took to be unprovable, a kind supposed to be fitting objects of intuitions in the cognitive sense.

To summarize my negative points about intuitions, I have contended that they need not be infallible or indefeasibly justified deliverances of a special faculty that is distinct from our general rational capacity as manifested in grasping logical and (pure) mathematical truths, and presumably other kinds of truths, ethical and non-ethical, as well. What, then, is distinctive of an intuition? I shall suggest four main characteristics.

Four characteristics of intuitions

First, an intuition must be non-inferential, in the sense that the intuited proposition in question is not – at the time it is intuitively held – held on the basis of a premise. Call this the *non-inferentiality (or directness) requirement*. Some intuitionists have emphasized this, and it is at least implicit in Ross and Moore. If we do not grant it, we cannot explain why Ross and Moore should hold the stronger view

that what we know intuitively is not provable; for if they took intuition to be potentially inferential and thus potentially based on premises, they would surely have addressed the question whether, for at least some intuitively known propositions, there might be premises to serve as a ground or a proof of those propositions and thereby as an inferential basis of the intuitions in question. I should add that despite appearances the *ungroundability thesis*, as we might call it – the view that what is intuitively known cannot be (evidentially) grounded in premises – does *not* imply that a proposition intuitively known is a priori or necessary. Ross apparently believed, however, that the universal moral propositions in question (notably his principles of prima facie duty) are both a priori and necessary; but it is doubtful that he regarded as a priori one's apparently primitive sense that one has a prima facie duty to keep *this* promise. If he held some such aprioristic, rationalist view regarding particular cases, it would presumably have been qualified so as to avoid empirical assumptions, as does the position that one apprehends the truth of a concrete generalization like "*If* one sees someone fall off a bicycle and can easily help with what appears to be a broken arm, one has a prima facie obligation to do so." Consider, by contrast, the unconditional proposition that I actually have this obligation; this presupposes both my existence and that of the injured person(s) and hence is plainly neither a priori nor a necessary truth. The conditional generalization, on the other hand, even if one grasps it in application to an individual case, is simply not about any actual case. I emphasize this point because while Ross was doubtless a rationalist in his epistemology, his intuitionism – taken simply as a pluralist view committed to intuitive moral knowledge, at least – does not entail moral rationalism.

Second, an intuition must be a moderately firm cognition – call this the *firmness requirement*. One must come down on the matter at hand; if one is up in the air, the jury is still out. In the contexts that concern us, intuitions will typically be beliefs, including cases of knowing. But the term 'intuitions' may include (sincere) judgments or other mental events implying belief. A mere inclination to believe is not an intuition; an intuition tends to be a "conviction" (a term Ross sometimes used for an intuition) and to be relinquished only through such weighty considerations as a felt conflict with a firmly held theory or with another intuition.

[. . .]

Third, intuitions must be formed in the light of an adequate understanding of their propositional objects – call this the *comprehension requirement*. That they are formed in this light is doubtless one reason for their firmness, as is their being based on that understanding rather than on, say, inference from premises (I assume they are normally based on such an understanding). As to the required adequacy of this understanding, Ross, like Moore, insists that before one can apprehend even a self-evident moral truth, one must get precisely that true proposition before one's mind. In many passages (including one quoted earlier) Ross indicates that reflection is required to see the truth of the proposition in question. The more complicated the proposition, or the richer the concepts figuring in it – like the concept of a promise – the more is required for an adequate understanding of that proposition. Intuitions are sometimes regarded as arising quickly upon considering the proposition in question; they need not so arise and in some cases probably should not so arise.

The fourth requirement I suggest is that intuitions are pretheoretical: roughly, they are neither evidentially dependent on theories nor themselves theoretical hypotheses. If this *pretheoreticality requirement* entailed their being *preconceptual* or, more broadly, uninformed, it would undermine the comprehension requirement: without at least a minimal understanding of the concepts figuring in a proposition, one is not even in a position to find it intuitive. But clearly Ross and other intuitionists intend our "convictions" (intuitions), including those of other people, to be used as data for moral generalization somewhat in the way sense perceptions are data for scientific theorizing. Given his understanding of this idea, not only will an intuition not be an inference from a theory, it will also not be epistemically dependent on a theory even in the general sense that the theory provides one's justificatory ground (even a non-inferential ground) for the intuition. This point does *not* entail that intuition has a complete independence of theory: an intuition may be defeated and abandoned in the light of theoretical results incompatible with its truth, especially when these results are supported

by other intuitions. This is a kind of negative epistemic dependence of intuition on theory: the justification of the intuition does not derive from the impossibility of such untoward, hypothetical results, but it can be destroyed by them if they occur. Such defeasibility on the part of intuition is not a positive justificatory dependence on any actual theory; it is a negative dependence on – in the sense of a vulnerability to – disconfirmation by theories, whether actual or possible.[7]

In some ways, the perceptual analogy can mislead. For one thing, an intuition is more like a belief based on a careful observation than like an impression formed from a glimpse, though that impression is nonetheless perceptual and can produce belief. One could, however, speak of sensory intuitions in reference to cognitions that rest on observational sense experience in the way perceptual beliefs commonly do when they are formed under favorable conditions. Consider, for instance, visual beliefs, acquired in good light, about an island seen before one. From this point of view, my four conditions are probably too broad; but to build in, say, that intuitions are non-observational cognitions of a conceptual or at least classificatory kind would probably make the conditions too narrow, and the breadth of the characterization is appropriate to our purposes.

The perceptual analogy is also misleading because intuitions need not be about observables: rights are not observable, yet we have intuitions about them. We may see them in the sense of recognizing them, as where one sees a right to refuse feeding tubes, but they are not seen visually. If what is both non-observable and significantly complex is thereby theoretical, then we certainly have intuitions about theoretical entities; but such "theoretical" intuitions need not be epistemically dependent on any theory.

It is of course controversial whether, in either intuitive or perceptual cases, there *is* anything pretheoretical to appeal to. But if not – if, for instance, to have concepts sufficient for judging a theory a theory one must be biased by either that theory or another one relevant to judging the theory – then it is not only Ross who has a problem. One would hope that even if every judge has some biases, there are some judges who at least have no

---

[7] An intuition may also be caused by commitment to a theory, as where reflection on the theory leads one to explore a topic and one thereby forms intuitions about it. But this causal dependence of the intuition on the theory has no necessary bearing on the justificatory status of the former.

biases that vitiate their decisions on the cases they must resolve.

Even if no cognition is entirely pretheoretical, perhaps some may be pretheoretical *with respect to* a moral generalization needing appraisal. Granted, this would rule out only theoretical biases. Intuitionists apparently hope that no others are ineliminable, but absence of *all* bias is apparently not part of the concept of an intuition; the effects of biases may indeed help to explain how an intuition can be mistaken. Nor is it necessary, for purposes of working out a satisfactory intuitionism, that biases always be unavoidable; it is enough if, as Ross apparently thought, they are always correctable by further reflection. Such reflection may include comparison with the intuitions of others, just as in scientific inquiry one might compare one's observations with those of coinvestigators.

There are two points that may significantly clarify the sense in which intuitions might be pretheoretical. One point (implicit in what has been said) is that an intuition's being pretheoretical does not imply that it is indefeasible – not even indefeasible by judgments based on the theory we build from a set of intuitions including the one in question. Recall the case in which I see that keeping a promise is not my final duty because, reflecting on my general duties, I realize that other duties override my duty to keep the promise. Here, the basis of the other moral considerations is the same sort as that of the first duty. The second point is that an intuition that is pretheoretical at one time can evolve into a judgment grounded in a theory. A Rossian view is committed to the existence, at any time when our convictions provide the data for ethics, of pretheoretical intuitions; but it is not committed to denying that yesterday's intuitions can be today's theory-laden assumptions – or that they can be given up because they are undermined by the reflection of "thoughtful, well-educated people."

Let us suppose for the sake of argument that either there are no pretheoretical intuitions or, more likely, *some* of the intuitions needed for confirmation of basic moral principles are in some way theoretical. We can still distinguish between theories that bias the appraisal of a moral principle and theories that do not. If, for instance, a theory of the psychology of persons is needed for the capacity to have certain moral intuitions – for instance the intuition that flogging an infant to death is prima facie wrong – this need not vitiate

the appraisal. The intuition may depend on a theoretical (psychological) understanding of the pains caused by flogging and of (biological) death, but neither the kind nor the level of the relevant theory undermines the justifiability of the intuition. We might, then, distinguish between what is *relatively* and what is *absolutely* pretheoretical: the former is simply pretheoretical relative to the issue in question, say the moral status of the act-type, flogging an infant to death. Perhaps a relative notion of the pretheoretical is all that intuitionism needs in order to meet the objection that theoretical dependence vitiates the justificatory role it claims for intuitions.

Conclusions of reflection versus conclusions of inference

If intuitions are non-inferential and pretheoretical, one might wonder to what extend they represent rationality, as opposed to mere belief or even prejudice. Here it is crucial to recall Ross's requirements of adequate maturity and "sufficient attention." I propose to go further: there is a sense in which an intuition *can* be a conclusion formed through rational inquiry. Consider listening to someone complain about a task done by a coworker, where one has been asked to determine whether the work was adequate. In a way that is impersonal and ably documented, Timothy criticizes the work of Abby. One might judge, from his credible statements of deficiencies in her work, that it was shoddy. This is a response to evidential propositions. Now imagine being asked a different question: whether there might be some bias in the critique. One might now recall his narration in one's mind's eye and ear, and from a global, intuitive sense of Timothy's intonations, word choices, selection of deficiencies, and omission of certain merits, judge that he is jealous of her. This is a response to an overall impression. Let us call the first judgment – that the work is shoddy – *a conclusion of inference*: it is premised on propositions one has noted as evidence. Call the second judgment *a conclusion of reflection*: it emerges from thinking about the overall pattern of Timothy's critique in the context of his relation to Abby as a coworker, but not from one or more evidential premises. It is more like a response to viewing a painting or seeing an expressive face than to propositionally represented information. One responds to a pattern: one notices an emotional tone in the otherwise factual listing of deficiencies; one hears him compare her work to some that he once did; and so forth. The conclusion of reflection is a wrapping up of the question, similar to concluding a practical matter with a decision. One has not added up the evidences and formulated their implication; one has obtained a view of the whole and characterized it overall.

It might be objected here that one is really inferring, from the tone of Timothy's complaint and of his comparison of Abby's work with a job he once did, that he is jealous; this is not something just "seen" on the basis of a careful, overall look. To say that the case must be so described is to confuse the grounds of one's judgment with beliefs expressing those grounds. Granted, if I *articulate* my non-inferential grounds, they will then be available to me as premises. If, for instance, I say to myself that his tone was quite emotional given the factual character of the deficiencies he listed, I now have a premise for the conclusion that he was jealous of her. But if this point implied that my belief that he is jealous of her is inferential *prior* to my articulating my ground and "basing" my conclusion on it, the same would hold for perceptual beliefs based on visual impressions whose evidential force can be articulated. We would have to say that since the statement that I have a visual impression of gold-lettered buckram before me is a premise for believing there is a book before me, I concluded that there is a book before me, on the basis of this premise, even when I merely *had* the impression, had not articulated my having it, and from it spontaneously formed the belief that there is a book before me. But surely my having a ground that is *expressible* in a premise does not imply that I must *use* that ground *in* a premise in order to form a belief on the basis of the ground.[8] I suggest, then, that this kind of conclusion can be an intuition in the sense just sketched. Not all intuitions are of this sort, but it is essential to see that particularly when a case, real or hypothetical, is complicated, an intuition may not emerge until reflection proceeds for some time. Such an intuition can be a conclusion of reflection, temporally as well as epistemically; and it may be either empirical or a priori.

This example and other paradigms of intuition might suggest that intuitions are always about *cases* as opposed to generalizations. They typically are,

and arguably a generalization can be only *intuitive* – roughly, highly plausible considered in itself – as opposed to being the object of *an* intuition. The intuitive status of a proposition is consistent with its being inferentially believed, or with its being the object of an infirm cognition, or with both. But this restriction of intuitions to cases as opposed to generalizations is neither entailed by the four general conditions I have proposed as roughly necessary and sufficient for an intuition nor implicit in the history of the notion.

A generalization can be intuitive in much the way a singular proposition about an example can be; and just as some intuitions can be better grounded and firmer than others, some generalizations can be more intuitive than others. It is true that an intuitive generalization can be supported by intuitions about examples, but it does not follow that its only way of being intuitive is through such support. Kant might have found the generalization that I ought to keep my promises more intuitive than the singular proposition that I ought to keep my promise (to my sister) to educate her daughter; Ross might find the latter more intuitive (and would reject the generalization unless it is understood to refer to prima facie duty).

III. Self-Evidence and the Systematization of Intuitions

In order to appreciate the sense in which Ross's basic moral truths might be plausibly considered self-evident, it seems to me absolutely essential that we distinguish his actual case for them from his analogy to mathematics and logic. He knew full well that it takes more reflection and maturity to see the truth of the proposition that promises generate prima facie duties than to see the validity of a logical principle like the syllogistic 'If all *A*s are *B*s and all *B*s are *C*s, then all *A*s are *C*s'. On this score, the disanalogy between the moral case and that of logic and other domains of self-evidence both undermines the plausibility of Ross's view and gives ethical intuitionism a burden it need not carry. Logic can (let us assume) be axiomatized given a few self-evident propositions (e.g. that if (a) either *p* or *q* and (b) not-*q*, then *p*). Their

---

[8] To some readers this will need argument or further explanation; both are given in some detail in my *The Structure of Justification* (Cambridge and New York: Cambridge University Press, 1993), esp. ch. 4, "The Foundationalism-Coherentism Controversy: Hardened Stereotypes and Overlapping Theories."

substitution instances, for example the proposition that if either Jim is in his office or he is home, and he is not in this office, then he is home, have a similar axiomatic self-evidence. Moral principles, by contrast, seem to many reasonable people neither self-evident nor comparably simple. Ross might have pointed out that self-evidence, at least of the kind in question, should not be expected in substantially vague generalizations. He might also have done more to distinguish different kinds of self-evidence, for it seems to me that only one of them need be claimed by intuitionists as possessed by some moral truths.

Two kinds of self-evidence

Two kinds of self-evidence are especially relevant here. Let me first establish a general conception of self-evidence, and in that light we can distinguish them. I shall assume that the basic notion of self-evidence is this: a self-evident proposition is (roughly) a truth such that understanding it will meet two conditions: that understanding is (1) sufficient for one's being justified in believing it (i.e., for having justification for believing it, whether one in fact believes it or not) – this is why such a truth is evident *in itself* – and (2) sufficient for knowing the proposition provided one believes it on the *basis* of understanding it.[9] Two clarifications are needed immediately.

First, as reflected in (1), the self-evidence of a proposition does not entail that if one understands (and considers) the proposition, then one believes it. This non-belief-entailing conception of self-evidence is plausible because one can fail initially to "see" a self-evident truth and, later, grasp it in just the way one grasps the truth of a paradigmatically self-evident proposition: one that is obvious in itself the moment one considers it. Take, for

example, a self-evident proposition that is perhaps not immediately obvious: if there never have been any siblings then there never have been any first cousins. A delay in seeing something, such as the truth of this, need not change the character of what one sees. What is self-evident can indeed be justifiedly believed on its "intrinsic" merits; but they need not leap out at one immediately. In some cases one can see *what* a self-evident proposition says – and thus understand it – before seeing *that*, or how, it is true.

Second, the understanding in question must be adequate, as opposed to mistaken or partial or clouded, understanding. Adequate understanding of a proposition is more than simply getting the general sense of a sentence expressing it, as where one can parse the sentence grammatically, partially explain what it means, and perhaps translate it into another language one knows well. Adequacy here implies not only seeing what the proposition says but also being able to apply it to some appropriate cases, being able to see some of its logical implications, and comprehending its elements and some of their relations. If inadequate understanding is allowed, it will not be true that understanding a self-evident proposition provides a justification for believing it, nor that beliefs of the proposition based on understanding it constitute knowledge.

Given these points about (1) and (2), we may distinguish those self-evident propositions that are readily understood by normal adults (or by people of some relevant description, e.g. mature moral agents) and those understood by them only through reflection on the sorts of cases they concern. Call the first *immediately self-evident* and the second *mediately self-evident* since their truth can be grasped only through the mediation of reflection.[10] The reflection may involve drawing inferences, but their role is limited largely to

---

[9]   Two qualifications will help. First, if the belief is based on anything *other* than understanding the proposition, that understanding must still be a sufficient basis (in a sense I cannot explicate now). Second, there may be a non-truth-entailing use of 'self-evident', which would allow for false and hence unknowable self-evident propositions; but I assume that any such use is at best non-standard. What is more controversial about my characterization is that – apparently – only a priori propositions satisfy it. Note, however, that the analysandum is self-evidence simpliciter, not self-evidence *for S*. There is some plausibility in saying that it is self-evident, for me, that I exist. I leave open whether such cases illustrate a kind of self-evidence, but the relevant proposition asserting my existence is surely not self-evident.

[10]   Two clarifications. (1) Assuming one cannot reflect in the relevant way on the concepts in question without *some* kind of understanding of them, I take it that there is a level of understanding of mediately self-evident propositions, or at least of parts of them, not by itself sufficient for justification but capable of leading to that as the understanding develops by reflection. (2) The term 'normal adults' is vague, but that begs no questions here; the problem is largely eliminable by relativizing, making the basic notion mediately self-evident *for S*, or for adults with a certain level of conceptual sophistication.

clarifying what the proposition in question says: as self-evidence is normally understood, a self-evident proposition is knowable without inferential grounds. One may require time to get it in clear focus, but need not climb up to it on the shoulders of one or more premises.

Immediately self-evident propositions are *obvious*; roughly, their truth is apparent as soon as one considers them with understanding, which is usually as soon as one is presented with them in a natural formulation in a language in which one is competent. The obvious need not be self-evident, however. It is obvious that there exists at least one person, but this is not self-evident: the proposition is not evident in itself; but if we consider a natural formulation of it in a language we understand, we have ample ground *in that situation* for seeing its truth (at least if we know we are persons). Moreover, there are *degrees* (as well as kinds) of obviousness, but there are *kinds* rather than degrees of self-evidence.

Granted, some self-evident propositions are more readily seen to be true than others, but this is a different point. Even immediately self-evident propositions can differ in obviousness, whether for everyone or for some people or for one or more people at different times. Consider the proposition that if all *A*s are *B*s and all *B*s are *C*s, then all *A*s are *C*s. This is "very intuitive" and very obviously true, or at least that holds for its ordinary substitution instances, such as 'If all cats are furry creatures and all furry creatures are animals, then all cats are animals'. It is also, for many people, more readily seen to be true, even if perhaps not in the end more intuitive, than the proposition that if no *A*s are *B*s and all *C*s are *B*s, then no *C*s are *A*s, or the proposition if there never have been any siblings then there never have been any first cousins. As these examples suggest, mediately self-evident propositions need not be (psychologically) *compelling*: they need not produce belief the moment they are understood, nor, even after reflection on them, in everyone who understands them.

Once we distinguish between the immediately and the mediately self-evident, and appreciate that a self-evident proposition need not be obvious or even compelling, we can see clearly that an intuitionist – indeed, even a rationalist one like Ross – may be a fallibilist about the sense of self-evidence. He can thus make room for error even in thoughtful judgments to the effect that a proposition is, or is not, self-evident. He might grant, then, that a

non-self-evident (or even false) proposition may seem to someone to be self-evident. Moreover, not every self-evident proposition need be "intuitive," just as not every proposition believed on the basis of intuition need be self-evident. If there are self-evident moral truths, the sense that one has grasped such a truth can be illusory, and at least the majority can be expected to be in the mediate category.

Two further points may help here. The first is that particularly when a proposition is questioned, if only by a skeptic or by someone who wants a derivation of it in order to understand it better, then where the proposition is not obvious or immediately self-evident we may think that it is not self-evident at all, even if it is. Yet surely we can know a proposition to be true even if we cannot show it to be true, or even defend it by argument, as opposed to illustrating or explaining it. This is how it is for most people with respect to the proposition that if all *A*s are *B*s, and all *B*s are *C*s, then all *A*s are *C*s. They can explain it by example but can find no prior premises for it and may not even be able to defend it by (non-question-begging) argument if confronted by skillful objections. The second point is that as I have characterized intuitions, they not only are justificationally defeasible but need not even be prima facie justified. Still, insofar as they are like certain perceptual beliefs, for instance in being non-inferential, "natural," and pretheoretical, and (perhaps more important) insofar as they are based on an understanding of their propositional object, there is reason to consider them prima facie justified (in part because in such cases one tends to find it at best difficult to see how the proposition might be false). This may be as much as a moderate intuitionism needs to claim, and it does not entail that an intuition, as such, is prima facie justified. It leaves open that, say because one believes a proposition on a basis other than one's understanding of it, the proposition could become the object of an intuition for one, yet, at the time, that intuition might fail to be prima facie justified.

The possibility of grounds for the self-evident

In closing this section, I want to bring out the importance of the distinction between the immediately and the mediately self-evident and to introduce a special case of the former. By comparing his candidate basic moral truths to the (elementary) truths of logic and mathematics, Ross wrongly implied that the former are of the first kind. Indeed, when he went on to say that proving them is impossible, he created the impression that he would place them in a yet narrower category: that of propositions which are *strongly axiomatic*, in a sense implying not only immediate self-evidence, which is often taken to be roughly equivalent to simple axiomatic status, but also the further property of unprovability from anything epistemically *prior*. Such unprovability is, roughly, the impossibility of being proved from one or more premises that can be known or justifiedly believed without already knowing or justifiedly believing the proposition in question.

A different way to express the difference between self-evidence and strong axiomaticity is this. A self-evident proposition can function as an epistemic *unmoved* mover: it can be known, and can provide support for other propositions, without itself being seen to have (and perhaps without there even existing) a basis in something constituting evidence for it. But, unlike a strongly axiomatic proposition, it need not be an *unmovable* mover, one such that there cannot be further evidence for it, since the existence of that evidence would move it upward from the lowest possible foundational level.

These points about self-evidence have far-reaching implications for intuitionism. I believe that Ross said nothing implying that there cannot be good arguments for certain self-evident propositions, even the immediate ones. What is evident "in itself," even if immediately self-evident, need not be such that it cannot also be evident in some other way. It need not be known through premises; but this does not entail that it cannot be so known. Let us explore this point in relation to a further problem concerning his view.

What is it that makes all of Ross's principles moral, and might their truth be known in terms of the same account that explains why they are moral? Ross probably thought that even if there is an answer to the first question it provides no answer to the second. If there is just one fundamental obligation, and hence the property of being obligatory is (even if not by definition) equivalent to, say, that of optimizing happiness, then all moral principles can be seen as endorsements of behaviors that optimize – or condemnations of those that do the opposite. Ross rejected this view. Consider, by contrast, a Kantian unification of moral principles, including Ross's principles of duty. The intrinsic end formulation of Kant's categorical imperative

is suggestive. Above all, it stresses respect for persons: it says they are to be treated as ends and never merely as means. Is it not plausible to hold that in lying, breaking promises, subjugating, torturing, and the like one is using people merely as a means? And in keeping faith with people, acting benevolently toward them, and extending them justice, is one not treating them as ends, roughly in the sense of beings with intrinsic value (or whose experiences can have intrinsic value)? The point is not that Ross's principles can be deduced from the categorical imperative (though we need not rule out the possibility of an interpretation of it that permits such a deduction); rather, the intrinsic end formulation of the imperative expresses an ideal that renders the principles of duty intelligible or even expectable.

Ross apparently thought that the existence of a theoretical account of the prima facie duties is inconsistent with their self-evidence, at least if they are deducible from some more general principle. He may well have taken it to be also inconsistent with their plurality. But, to take the second point first, the existence of such an account would not entail that there really is just one duty, only that one moral principle can be a unifying ground for others. Unification of a set of principles in relation to a single one, say one that entails or explains them or both, does not imply that there is really only one principle. Nor does exhibiting several duties as serving a larger one entail that there is just one duty (as opposed to one basic duty). Regarding the first point – that unification of the Rossian principles of duty is not inconsistent with their self-evidence – the truth of a theoretical unification of the kind imagined would, to be sure, be inconsistent with the strong axiomatic self-evidence of these other principles. That, however, is not the kind of self-evidence to which Ross is committed by his account of how we know the moral principles corresponding to his prima facie duties.

If, then, we take that account, rather than Ross's analogy to logic and mathematics, as primary in understanding his intuitionism, we arrive at the surprising conclusion that a Rossian intuitionist – even construed as also a moral rationalist – can allow for *epistemically overdetermined moral knowledge*. There can be a moral theory that both explains and provides inferential grounds for moral propositions which, given sufficient reflection, can also be seen, non-inferentially, to be true. What is, at one time, only a conclusion of reflection – and in that way a candidate to be an intuition – can become a conclusion of inference. It can still derive support simultaneously from both the newly found premises for it and any remaining intuitive sense of its truth. An appropriately non-inferential, pre-theoretical sense of its truth may survive one's inferring it from premises. Seeing a thing in a new light need not prevent one's still seeing it in its own light.

To be sure, the categorical imperative is not immediately self-evident. Indeed, it may not be self-evident at all, but knowable (assuming it is true) only on the basis of a derivation from non-moral principles – or, as Ross might argue, as a generalization from more restricted, intuitively justified principles such as his own. That is not the issue here. What unifies moral principles need not be self-evident; presumably it need not even be a set of moral principles, but might come from a general theory of practical reason. The point is that once we appreciate that the kind of self-evidence to which intuitionism is committed is only mediate, we can allow that intuitive moral principles, even if they are self-evident, are knowable through premises as well as by reflection on their content. We can also see that these moral principles can be supported by their providing an account of our intuitions, and not just through a direct intuition of their truth or self-evidence.

IV. Reflection as a Basis for Moral Judgments

If anything has emerged from this study as common to all the ways of knowing that deserve to be called intuitive, it is reflection, above all reflection on the concepts figuring in, and on the necessary implications of, the moral or other propositions whose status is supposed to be knowable through intuition. The reflection may· be as brief as simply focusing clearly on the proposition, or it may require many sittings, possibly spread over many years. It turns out, however, that what is knowable in this reflective way – or can be at least justifiedly believed in this way – need not be strongly axiomatic, in a sense implying that there cannot be epistemically independent grounds for it. What can be justifiedly believed "in its own terms" is not thereby precluded from being justified by premises.

Intuitive justification and reflective equilibrium

I have already shown how, from a broad moral principle such as the categorical imperative taken as expressing respect for persons, one might try to derive the Rossian duties. Call this *justification from below* (from something plausibly held to be "deeper"). I now want to argue that intuitionism – or at least the method of inquiry that seems to be the core of it – can allow *justification from above*, in part by appeal to what philosophers commonly call intuitions. We can then begin to articulate the overall framework for moral theory that is a major concern of this essay.

In deriving intuitive moral principles from below, one does not presuppose them, even for the sake of argument, but builds them from one or another kind of supporting ground. By contrast, their justification from above proceeds by provisionally presupposing them and exploring the consequences one infers from them. Above all, we do two sorts of things. First, we deduce from them what kinds of decisions we would make, and what kinds of lives we would lead, if we took the principles to be true and regularly acted on them. Second, we reflect on, as Ross would put it, what we really think about these possibilities, that is, on our intuitions about them. We might, for instance, contemplate a life in which we recognize duties of beneficence versus one in which we do not, and consider whether, in the light of what we really think about those lives and about the beneficent social practices they would imply, the relevant duties still seem to be prima facie duties, as opposed to, say, mere charities or even meddling with others. If we are satisfied by what we find, we regard the principles as confirmed, as we do scientific hypotheses borne out by predictions derived from them. Granted, we may *now* form an argument that seems to proceed from below: namely, that since the assumption of these principles has these "intuitively appealing" consequences (or best explains them), we may take the principles as likely to be true and to that extent as justified. But this mode of argument is not a route to discovery of its conclusion, as argument from below may be; and it need not proceed, like the latter, from epistemically independent premises, since some of the judgments we make about cases may be partly based on the principle we are testing.

Argument from above can also result in revising, rather than confirming, the principles we began with. We may find that if, for example, we restrict the cases in which promising yields a prima facie duty – say, to situations in which it is fully voluntary – we get a better principle. A Rossian view can surely countenance such a procedure, and using it may result in enhancing our justification as well as in our revising our initial view, whether that was justified or not.

We are now in a position to see something else. The use of reflection made by Ross is quite consistent with – and indeed seems to anticipate – the procedure of reflective equilibrium as described by (among others) John Rawls.[11] One can compare one's intuitions with each other, with those of people one respects, and with the results of applying plausible generalizations to the situations that the moral intuitions are about; and one can strive to get all these items – revising them if necessary – into a stable, coherent whole: this is the equilibrium resulting from one's comparative reflections. The intuitionist might, to be sure, use the procedure more to refine moral principles already accepted than to discover moral principles; but this is a contingent matter that depends on what principles are accepted at the start of the process and on how many new principles or refinements of old ones it produces.

How wide the appropriate equilibrium should be is also contingent, and is quite variable: whether, for instance, non-moral considerations such as psychological facts should be in equilibrium with a body of plausible moral principles is left open. Some styles of reflection might proceed from principle to consequence and back again; others, such as Ross's, from case to principle first. One might think about individual promises and thereby frame standards for promise-keeping, or instead posit initially plausible principles governing this activity and refine them by looking at cases.

In a moral theorist whose basic method is reflection of a kind we find both in Ross and in Rawls and others, the order of discovery can diverge, as it does in science, from the order of justification. We might, for example, first discover a principle on the basis of serendipity, by simply guessing at the truth about the subject we are investigating, and might later get justification, and pass from conjecture to belief, by doing confirmatory experiments;

or we might both justify and discover a principle by deducing a new generalization from more comprehensive ones already established. But regardless of the kind of procedure by which we discover or justify moral principles, intuitions about cases should cohere with intuitions about the principles that apply to those cases. Inferential justification, moreover, can support intuitive justification regarding either cases or principles.

Ethical reflection as a justificatory method

It is no accident that I have been trying to exhibit common ground between intuitionism and some of its critics. It seems to me that when one looks closely at the best intuitionists, such as Ross, one finds something that transcends their own characterization of what they are doing. It is the *method of ethical reflection*: roughly, judiciously bringing to bear on moral questions, especially general ones such as what our duties are, careful reflection on what these questions involve. To take the case of promising as a source of moral duty, one reflects on what a promise is, on what a duty to keep it is, on what duties can conflict with that one, on what counts as a reason for action or – arguably equivalent to this – as an intrinsically good or bad thing, and on what human life would be like if we took certain kinds of acts to be duties, and regarded certain conflicts of duties as properly resolved in some particular way. Facts, then, come into the process. Such reflection is what, more than any other method, seems to yield reliable intuitions (roughly, intuitions likely to be true), or at least intuitions we can rationally hope will remain credible as we continue to reflect on them. Reliable intuitions may or may not be conclusions of reflection.

Inference of any kind, whether from below or above, can figure in the reflection that generates or tests intuitions. But the primary case of such reflection is that in which one arrives at conclusions of reflection or at (temporally) immediate intuitions, not at inferential judgments. If no such primacy of non-inferential reflection were recognized, then we would have to ask what else might serve to ground one's premises for inference. Factual assumptions can figure in such reflections

---

[11] See *A Theory of Justice*, (Cambridge, MA: Harvard University Press, 1971), e.g., pp. 46–52. It is true that Rawls suggests that reflective equilibrium is a coherentist procedure, whereas Ross is a foundationalist; but Rawls is probably taking foundationalism to posit indefeasible starting points, as Ross need not do.

– and must if the reflections concern what specific action to take under various future contingencies. But in the most basic cases, we consider what ought to be done *given* certain factual assumptions, for instance the assumption that we have made a promise which the promisee expects us to keep, or that we can help someone and we have no conflicting demands on us. For purposes of justifying general moral standards, the most important epistemic element is our intuitions regarding cases with factual assumptions built in, not those assumptions themselves. We may need to make observations to determine whether keeping a specific promise, say to return a set of car keys, will actually harm the promisee; but on the assumption that no harm will be produced, it will be intuitive that one has a prima facie duty to keep the promise.

The framework for ethical theorizing I have introduced here might be called *ethical reflectionism*. Its major thesis is that the method of reflection is and deserves to be our basic method for justifying ethical judgments, especially general moral principles or general judgments of what has intrinsic value, and among our basic methods for discovering such judgments. Discovery is, as in scientific inquiry, less constrained than justification. If tea leaves help us think up hypotheses, we may use them; but we may accept the hypotheses we thus arrive at only if they pass certain rigorous tests. By attacking the most common conception of intuitionism – the infallibilist, immoderately rationalist, special faculty view – I have tried to make intuitionism more plausible, with reflection as its chief method.

V. Modified Ethical Intuitionism

[. . .]

Ethical reflectionism is not as such a form of ethical intuitionism, but its truth provides the best explanation of what the most credible forms of ethical intuitionism are committed to. In these forms, I suggest, ethical intuitionism is, in outline, the view that we can have, in the light of appropriate reflection on the content of moral judgments and moral principles, intuitive (hence non-inferential) justification for holding them. Most of the plausible versions of intuitionism also endorse a plurality of moral principles (though Moore is notable for holding an overarching, ideal utilitarian principle

of right action), and most versions are also rationalist, holding that there are a priori moral principles. But an intuitionist could be an empiricist, taking intuition to be capable of providing an experiential ground for moral judgments or principles. Intuitionists typically hold that moral knowledge as well as moral justification can be intuitive, but the major ones are not committed to the view that this justification or knowledge is indefeasible, and they tend to deny that it is.

If the arguments of this essay indicate how intuitionism as just broadly characterized can be plausible, they also show how an overall rationalistic intuitionist theory like Ross's can be strengthened. Moreover, if what is said earlier in support of reflectionism indicates how an intuitionist view in moral epistemology is compatible with empiricism – even if it also brings out why it is natural for intuitionists to be rationalists – it also shows how a rationalist moral epistemology can be freed of the apparent dogmatism and associated arbitrariness, the implausible philosophy of mind, and the immoderate epistemic principles often attributed to it. Let me comment on each of these points and in that light proceed to some conclusions by way of overall appraisal of intuitionism conceived, as it should be given the overall views of Ross and its other major prominent proponents, as a rationalist view.

I will be stressing the rationalism of the reconstructed Rossian intuitionism developed earlier – construed as the view that we have intuitive justification both for some of our particular moral judgments and for a plurality of mediately self-evident moral principles – because the controversy between empiricism and rationalism as epistemological perspectives is apparently very much with us in ethical theory, despite how few ethical theorists are openly committed to either perspective. I believe, moreover, that most of the plausible objections to a broadly Rossian intuitionism are either motivated by empiricism or best seen as objections, not to its appeal to intuitions but to the underlying rationalism of the view: roughly, to its taking reason, as opposed to observation, to be capable of supplying justification for substantive truths, such as (if they are indeed true) Ross's moral principles of prima facie duty.

Is intuitionism dogmatic, as some have held?[12] It might well be dogmatic to claim both that we have

---

[12] See, e.g., Stephen C. Pepper, *Ethics* (New York: Appleton-Century-Crofts, 1960), p. 237.

intuitive, certain knowledge of what our prima facie duties are *and* that we cannot ground that knowledge on any kind of evidence. But I have argued that Ross, at least, is not committed to our having "certain knowledge" here – where the certainty in question implies having indefeasible justification for moral propositions. Far from it. Despite his in some ways unfortunate analogy between moral principles and, on the other side, elementary logical and mathematical ones, he provides a place for reflective equilibrium to enhance – or override – our justification for an "intuitive" moral judgment. Nor does anything he must hold, *qua* intuitionist, preclude his allowing a systematization of the moral principles he suggests in terms of something more general. If such systematization is achieved, then contrary to what the dogmatism charge would lead one to expect, that systematization might provide reasons for the principles and a possible source of correctives for certain intuitions or apparently intuitive moral judgments.

From these points about the issue of dogmatism, it should be evident that intuitionism also need not be arbitrary, in the sense that it permits simply positing, as reasonable moral standards, any that one finds "intuitive" and then claiming to know them. Intuitionism requires that before one can be intuitively justified in accepting a moral standard, one must have an adequate understanding of the proposition in question; this often requires reflection. What reflection yields as intuitive is not arbitrary; and although products of prejudice or whim may masquerade as intuitive, this does not imply that they cannot be discovered to be deceptive. Reflection can correct its own initial results – or even its repeated results. In sophisticated forms, intuitionism may also require an appeal to reflective equilibrium as a condition of justified adherence to a set of basic principles. This procedure often provides justifying reasons for, or for that matter indicates a need for revision or withdrawal of, the posited principle.

Moreover (and this is something not noted earlier), given how intuitions are understood – as deriving from the exercise of reason and as having evidential weight – it is incumbent on conscientious intuitionists to factor into their reflective equilibrium the apparent intuitions of *others*. Ross appealed repeatedly to "what we really think" and drew attention to the analogy between intuitions in ethics and perceptions in science. Intuitions, then, are not properly conceived as arbitrary. They normally have a history in human society and a genesis in reflection. Moreover, anything arbitrarily posited would be hard-pressed to survive the kind of reflection to which conscientious intuitionists will subject their basic moral standards. Thus, even if an intuition might arise as an arbitrary cognition, it would not necessarily have prima facie justification and could easily be defeated by other intuitions or those together with further elements in the reflective equilibrium a reasonable intuitionist would seek.

One might protest, in response to some of what I have said in arguing that intuitionism is not dogmatic or arbitrary, that if Moore and Ross claim strong axiomatic status for their candidate basic moral principles, one should take that claim as essential to intuitionism, at least insofar as they are paradigmatic intuitionists. I reject this principle of interpretation on the ground that the best theoretical classification of a philosopher's view comes not from simply putting together all its proffered theses but from considering its overall purposes and thrust. If, moreover, a view takes its name from a major phenomenon – such as intuition – and if, in addition, the relevant notion is pivotal throughout the development of the theory, there is some reason to take the overall operation of that notion in the theory as more important in characterizing the theory than relatively isolated theses which proponents of the theory advance about the notion. This certainly applies to what I have developed here in connection with Ross's view: a reconstruction of the theory intended to be among its most plausible versions, even if that means only strong continuity with its historical embodiments rather than a descriptive articulation thereof.

We can perhaps be briefer on the associated philosophy of mind, if only because the chief issue we encounter here applies to philosophy in general. Is there any reason to think that a rationalist epistemology, in ethics or elsewhere, entails an implausible philosophy of mind? Does the view presuppose either a mysterious mental faculty or a scientifically unlikely mode of access to entities that cannot causally affect the brain? It *may* be that there can be a priori knowledge or a priori justification only if we in some sense grasp abstract entities, such as the concept of a promise, where this grasp is conceived as something more than our having a set of behavioral tendencies, including linguistic ones, and requires some kind of apprehension of abstract entities that do not figure in causal relations. But if this is so, it is not obvious that the comprehension in question is either obscure or in any event not required for a grasp of arithmetic truths and other apparently a priori propositions essential for both everyday reasoning and scientific inquiry.

It is true that we will have a simpler philosophy of mind, at least ontologically, if we can avoid positing any "non-empirical" objects, such as numbers or propositions or concepts. But if properties are abstract entities, as many philosophers hold, then it is not clear that even empirical knowledge of generalizations about the physical world can be known apart from a grasp of abstract entities. I believe it is fair to say that there is at present no clearly adequate, thoroughly empiricist account of justification in general, applicable to logic and mathematics as well as to epistemic principles.

I turn now to the matter of epistemic principles, roughly principles indicating the bases or nature of knowledge and justification – say that if, on the basis of a clear visual impression of faces, I believe there are faces before me, then I am justified in so believing. There is no conclusive reason to think that Ross or other intuitionists are committed – by their intuitionism, at least – to implausible epistemic principles. I have already suggested that they need not, as intuitionists, hold the principle that if a proposition is self-evident, then it cannot be evidenced by anything else. I now want to suggest that Ross's basic principles of duty are at least candidates for a priori justification in the way they should be if they are mediately self-evident. Keeping in mind what constitutes a prima facie duty, consider how we would regard some native speaker of English who denied that there is (say) a prima facie duty not to injure other people and – to get the right connection with what Ross meant by 'duty' – meant by this something implying that doing it would not be even prima facie wrong. Our first thought is that there is a misunderstanding of some key term, such as 'prima facie.' Indeed, I doubt that anyone not in the grip of a competing theory would deny the proposition.

Imagine, however, a steadfast instrumentalist about practical rationality: someone who holds that one has a reason to do something only in virtue of its advancing one's basic desires, and then (let us suppose) insists that doing something can be wrong only if there is reason for one not to do it. Such a person would say that there *need* not be in anyone a basic desire advanced by not injuring others, so Ross's principle of non-maleficence is at best contingent.

Sophisticated versions of instrumentalism are quite powerful, and they are especially plausible in the current climate because they appear to be consistent both with empiricism and with naturalism, yet instrumentalists need not claim to reduce normative properties to non-normative ones. This is no place to explore instrumentalism in detail. But we should notice an implication of it: that either there is nothing intrinsically good or bad, including pleasure and pain, or, if there is, that the existence of things having intrinsic value, even things within our grasp, provides, apart from what we or someone else actually wants, no reason for action. This will seem to go against many intuitions, in the standard sense of 'intuition' that is neutral with respect to intuitionism. Is there not a reason why I should not burn a friend with a red-hot iron (and is this not an evil of some kind), even if at the moment, perhaps because my brain has been tampered with, I have no desires bearing on the matter? And even if I have lost all motivation in life, is there not reason, and indeed reason for me, not to burn myself? If the answer is, as it seems to be, affirmative, then there can be non-instrumental reasons favoring my action.

I have granted for the sake of argument something intuitionists would generally (and I think plausibly) deny: that one could justifiedly hold that there are things of intrinsic value, yet deny that they provide, independently of actual desires, even prima facie reasons for action. Imagine that an opponent of intuitionism takes this route. What would justify holding that there *is* anything of such value? It is not obvious that one could have an empirical justification of this thesis. To be sure, there are things people *value intrinsically*, for example toward which they take a positive attitude directly rather than on the basis of believing these things to be a means to something further. But this psychological fact about human *valuation* does not entail the normative conclusion that the things in question actually *have* intrinsic *value*. I believe that reflection will show that it is at least far from clear that justification for believing that there is anything of intrinsic value – including intrinsic moral value – does not have to rest at least in part on a priori considerations of the kind Ross describes. But I put this forward only as a challenge. The issue is highly debatable.

What is perhaps less controversial is that if we do not ascribe to reason the minimal power required in order for a moderate intuitionism of the kind I have described to be a plausible theory, then we face serious problems that must be solved before any instrumentalist or empiricist ethical theory is plausible. For one thing, instrumentalists must account for their fundamental principle that if, on my beliefs, an action serves a basic (roughly, non-instrumental) desire of mine, then there is a reason for me to perform the action. This principle appears to be a better candidate for mediate self-evidence than for empirical confirmation. This is not to say that a moderate intuitionism is true. The point is that unless reason has sufficient power to make that principle a plausible candidate for truth, then it is not clear that instrumentalist theories are plausible candidates either.

If I have been roughly correct in this defense of a reconstructed Rossian view, then intuitionism in moral epistemology, and in the foundations of ethics, should be a more serious contender for contemporary allegiance than it is. For many of the same reasons, there is more room for a rationalist moral epistemology than is generally realized. Once it is seen how reflection of an at least methodologically a priori kind is central in ethical theorizing, some of the major obstacles in the way of a rationalist account of the foundations of ethics are eliminated. There is much to commend a fallibilist, intuitionistic moral rationalism that uses reflection as a justificatory method in the ways described here, encompassing both intuitions as prima facie justified inputs to ethical theorizing and reflective equilibrium as a means of extending and systematizing those inputs. Whatever our verdicts on intuitionism and rationalism, however, when they are rightly understood they can be seen to carry less baggage than often attributed to them and to provide, in their best embodiments, a method of ethical inquiry that may be reasonably used in approaching any basic moral problem.

Seeing and Caring: The Role of Affect in Feminist Moral Epistemology

Margaret Olivia Little

Moral wisdom is hard to come by. It is usually a difficult and delicate job to discern the moral landscape accurately. Well we may ask, then, what is needed to make good moral judgments? What is the proper epistemic stance to adopt in our efforts to arrive at fair and reliable moral verdicts?

According to one central and influential tradition, the stance appropriate to moral wisdom is a *dispassionate* one. To make considered, sound moral judgments, we should abstract from our emotions, feelings, sentiments – what the eighteenth century would call "passions" – and from our desires, inclinations – what now go by the ungainly terms "pro" and "con" attitudes. Emotions and desires are not part of the equipment needed to discern moral answers. To be sure, their presence may be essential to our *responding* appropriately once we reach those verdicts – to act and to feel as we ought; but only trouble, it is thought, can come of their intrusion into deliberations toward the verdicts themselves. At best, they are irrelevant distractions, like so many pains and tickles. At worst, they are highly distorting influences: emotions "incite" and "provoke" us; desires "cloud" our judgment and "bias" our reasoning.

This would be a problem in any epistemic endeavor, but it is disastrous to moral judgments, whose role is precisely to serve as corrective to the narrow, partisan focus of our sentiments. According to this view, then, to be objective is to be *detached*; to be clear-sighted is to achieve *distance*; to be careful in deliberation is to be *cool* and *calm*.

In contrast to this tradition, certain feminist theorists have argued that emotion and desire are valuable aspects of the wise person's epistemic repertoire. Certainly, our passions and inclinations can mislead us and distort our perceptions, but it is a falsely narrow perspective to think that they invariably do so or that they have nothing distinctive to offer epistemological projects. Distance does not always clarify. Sometimes truth is better revealed, the landscape most clearly seen, from a position that has been called "loving perception" or "sympathetic thinking."[1]

I think that such feminist approaches to epistemology are of particular importance in the moral domain, for morality is precisely the arena in which a proper epistemic stance demands the presence of what we might call "appropriate affect."[2] In this essay, I try to tease apart and articulate as clearly as

---

[1] See, for instance, Lugones (1987), Jaggar (1989), Walker (1992).

[2] Throughout this essay, I use the term "affect" as a generic label for desires and emotions. It is a somewhat misleading label, because "affect" carries the connotation of feelings, and I mean it to include desires and motivational propensities that are not felt.

possible the epistemic roles of emotion and desire in gaining moral knowledge. I delineate two different roles, both of which are crucial, but one of which more fundamentally calls into question the traditional compartmentalization of reason and affect. I first try to isolate what it is about *caring* that makes it so helpful to our attempts to determine what, in the face of complicated circumstances, ought or ought not to be done. I then argue that possession of various emotions and desires – care, concern, love, but also anger, revulsion, indignation – is not just immensely useful to seeing the moral landscape, it is a *necessary* condition of doing so. The idea of dispassion as the paradigmatic epistemic stance seems to me a dangerous one, for there are some truths, I want to argue, that can be apprehended only from a stance of affective engagement.

The claim is an important one, for, if correct, it means we must reject the "bureaucratic model" of morality that is implicit in so many ethical theories. On that model, moral agency involves a clear division of labor: reason is responsible for coming to the moral verdicts; it then passes its report on to the will, motivation, or emotion, which then does or does not issue the appropriate response. How good a person is at rendering accurate moral verdicts is quite independent of how responsive she tends to be to those verdicts. It is possible, on this familiar model, for people to combine tremendous moral acumen with completely atrophied affect: the best moral experts can be the least moral people. In contrast, the view under consideration claims that possession of certain desires and emotions is crucial for seeing what morality requires in the first place. The moral landscape will be opaque to those who are in no way moral.

Before turning to develop the role of affect in a feminist moral epistemology, it is worth pausing to confront more directly the view that counsels dispassion. The view is, in a sense, our intellectual inheritance. It tends thereby to retain a subterranean influence in shaping discussions, determining what gets marked as a departure or as standing in need of explanation, and handing down certain themes and metaphors which, because of their familiarity, may go unarticulated and hence unevaluated. Feminist perspectives in the history of ideas give us special reason to be wary of the themes and metaphors that tacitly underwrite the persuasive feel of the doctrine.

For all the hotly disputed debates in the history of philosophy, one theme that emerges with remarkable consistency is an association of women with affect and men with reason (Lloyd 1979, 1983, and 1984; McMillan 1982; Tuana 1992). The way in which this "association" is unpacked varies from philosopher to philosopher, but it is usually an interestingly tangled combination of empirical, essentialist, and normative claims. Claims include that women as a class are *in fact* more swayed by affect and less by reason than men are; that women *by nature* have less *capacity* for reason and more for affect than men have; or again, independent of any questions of capacity, that it would be *inappropriate* to woman's role for her to cultivate and act from reason and *appropriate* to cultivate and act from emotion.[3] (Kant is especially keen on the last claim, mentioning that women who learn higher subjects such as Greek might as well have beards, such is the departure from the role proper to their sex!) These relatively direct associations are reinforced by the fact that both women and affect share, in turn, an association with nature and the corporeal (Merchant 1980; McMillan 1982; Dinnerstein 1977; Ortner 1974).

For purposes of this discussion, I want to draw attention, not to philosophy's traditional view of woman, which is obviously (though depressingly) off-kilter, but to the resultant views of reason and affect themselves. The nearly ubiquitous and multi-layered associations of affect with women, reason with men may well have influenced the ways in which affect and reason have been substantively conceived. Certain conceptions of affect and reason, that is, seem to be *gendered* conceptions: what is said about each – what functions they are capable of or supposed to play, what relationships they stand in with respect to each another, how they are each valued – seems to have been subtly shaped by their respective associations with certain narrow, distorted conceptions of female and male (a process that usually transpires by the unintentional exchange of metaphors used in each domain).

[3]   Indeed, it is often difficult to separate out which thesis is being advanced within a given philosopher's views. Philosophers who discuss the issue in depressing fashion include: Aristotle, *Politics*, 1252a ff., *Generation of Animals*, 1.20 and 2.3; Rousseau, part 5 of *Emile*; Kant, sec. 3 of *Observations on the Feeling of the Beautiful and Sublime*; Hegel, *Philosophy of the Right*.

The associations are perhaps most easily seen in the doctrines developed during the Enlightenment. We can begin by noting its themes about women and men. As many feminist scholars have noted, certain conceptions of men and women began slowly to solidify with the advent of the scientific revolution (Pateman 1989; Bordo 1986; Lloyd 1983; Okin 1979; Gatens 1991). Men and women were understood as having different appropriate spheres of functions. Man's central role was in the public sphere – economics, politics, religion, culture; woman's central role was in the private sphere – the domestic realm of caretaking for the most natural, embodied aspects of humans. The separation of spheres was understood to constitute a complementary system, in which each contributed something of value which, when combined, made an ideal whole (the marriage unit). Because the division was understood as grounded in the natures of man and woman, the separation was a rigid one: the idea that either side of the division could offer something useful to the other's realm would simply not emerge as a possibility. This picture of "fitting complementarity" was then complicated, and a deep tension introduced, by an added layer: the division did not involve halves of equal worth, for woman and the private sphere were seen as intrinsically less valuable. It is man, and what is accomplished in the public sphere, that represents the human ideal. Woman is understood as existing for man as his helpmate, and in this regard she may be valued, but in a romanticized and hence constraining way. Moreover, and very important, her association with the body and nature grounded an image of woman as a potential source of contamination, infection, and disorder (Merchant 1980; Dinnerstein 1977; Ortner 1974).

Now these are the *very* themes that arise in the views of reason and affect presented by many Enlightenment thinkers. Reason and affect have rigidly separate, complementary functions: reason reveals the way the world is; emotion and desire move us to respond to that world with action and feeling. Each is valued for its role, but the idea that they interact much or that they could contribute to the other's functions won't emerge as a serious possibility. Also, and in tension with this picture of complementary spheres, there is a tendency to view emotion and desire with deep suspicion, as something more to do with the body we have as animals than the mind we have as humans, and as something that infects, renders impure, and constantly

threatens to disrupt – particularly in the epistemic arena.

The Enlightenment conceptions of reason and affect, then, are marked by two themes. First, reason and affect will be conceptualized as radically separated in function, role, and ideal: that one should enter the sphere of the other will seem almost incomprehensible. Second, affect will show up in particularly devalued ways: it will be cast as a source of contamination, which we must control and, in the end, transcend. If such conceptions of reason and affect are assumed, one will inevitably and understandably valorize dispassion, detachment, and distance in epistemic enterprises. The question is whether the plausibility of such conceptions survives what seem to be historically gendered origins. Must we regard reason and affect as so rigidly bifurcated in function? Must we view affect solely as potential infection in moral epistemology? Leaving our ears tuned for recurrence of the metaphors discussed in this traditional view, let us turn to the positive task of addressing what the epistemic role of affect in morality is.

I want to separate out and develop two important roles for affect. To delineate the first role, let me begin with a now-familiar point about moral deliberation. Even if such deliberation is best characterized as the application of moral principles to a given situation, one obviously cannot start the enterprise unless one is aware of the salient features of the situation (that one's neighbor is in pain, for instance): one wouldn't know what to apply the principle *to*. Now, as several theorists have lately emphasized, awareness of the morally relevant features of a situation is no easy or automatic matter (Murdoch 1970 and 1956; Nussbaum 1985a and 1985b; Blum 1991). The details may be complex and subtle, and at any rate we are often obtuse creatures – it's all too easy to miss what's in front of one's own nose. Think of the workaholic spouse who is oblivious of her partner's growing despair, or whites who don't notice news reports of murder when the victim is black but always look up when the victim is white or from their neighborhood. Seeing what is important in the situations we face is not simply a matter of opening our eyes; as Iris Murdoch says, "It is a *task* to come to see the world as it is" (1970, 91). The natural question is, What is needed to achieve the type of awareness that goes into making good moral judgments?

One natural suggestion (and one Murdoch herself stresses) is that we must transcend our all-too-absorbing self-love. "The difficulty," as she puts it, "is to keep the attention fixed upon the real situation and to prevent it from returning surreptitiously to the self with consolations of self-pity, resentment, fantasy and despair" (1970, 91). But, although this is an important point to make, those immersed in Enlightenment conceptions of reason and affect are likely to pick this out as the *sole* feature of obtuseness: one is obtuse when something *obscures* one's vision, and affect is pegged as the source of obstruction. On this reading, emotion and desire once again get cast in the familiar role of contamination, here clouding what would otherwise be clear.

The view that obtuseness is caused *only* by the obscuring effect of emotion and desire, though, operates on the faulty picture that seeing is passive: were we just to clear our pathways of distorting affect, the information would come right in. This, of course, is not how it works. Think of what is really involved in seeing what is morally relevant. Often it means noticing what is *not* present: noticing that a student is not in class; spotting in a busy crowd that a child, though surrounded with adults, is not *accompanied* by any of them. Or again, noticing subtle patterns: that a patient ask for more pain medication on the nights after she has had a visit from her husband. Or again, noticing what is so pervasive that it tends to be invisible (notice how the movie *Fatal Attraction* or the actions of Lorena Bobbitt draw immediate and dramatic public moralizing, while the ubiquitous violence against women in film and reality continues with still too little comment). When Murdoch says that it is a task to see the world, she does not just mean that there is a task preliminary to seeing, like washing the windows before looking outdoors. She means that the seeing *itself* is a task – the task of being attentive to one's surroundings.

Now someone deeply wedded to a strongly bifurcated view of reason and affect might tend to interpret this task as equivalent to some consciously adopted assignment to be disciplined about gathering important information. Florence Nightingale offers an interesting example of this sort of intellectualist interpretation. A chapter of her short tract, *Notes on Nursing*, is devoted to the importance of observation (Nightingale 1969, 105–26). She notes with censure the lack of observation she sees among those who attend patients: they do not notice when food goes uneaten, whether a patient wants solitude or diversion –

indeed, she says, they don't even observe *that* they don't observe. She then offers her recommendation for solving this problem: nurses should work on memory skills, stay more disciplined in focusing on their tasks, and practice surveying their field of vision while reciting what they see (she cites with approval the method used by one father, who had his small son rehearse the contents of a toy-store window each day after they passed by).

Nightingale's method limits the scope of attentiveness to conscious *observational vigilance*. But, while such effort is helpful at times (as when you mentally shake off your torpor to confront a difficult decision), this is not the central feature of attentiveness. For there is no exhausting ahead of time what one should be on watch for. There are indefinitely many things that may be morally relevant in a situation, features that are often present in novel or subtle combinations. The morally aware person, then, is not someone who approaches each situation with some conscious grocery list of things to check *for*. The required attentiveness is a background disposition for relevant details to come into your consciousness – for them to emerge for you as salient, to come to the forefront of your attention.

Given this, it turns out that what one is attentive to is largely a function of the one thing Nightingale does not mention, namely, one's affect. What one is attentive to reflects one's interests, desires, in brief, what one *cares* about. Think, for instance, as Sara Ruddick asks us to do, of the awareness displayed in paradigmatically loving relationships, such as a healthy mother and child relationship (Ruddick 1987). It is because the mother cares for her child that she is attuned to subtle dangers, picks up on delicate signals, notices when help is needed. More generally put, if one cares about something, one is prepared to respond on its behalf, and preparedness to respond is intimately linked with awareness of opportunities to do so. How reliable one will be in accurately discerning the moral landscape and knowing what ought to be done depends, then, not just on how good one is at weighing risks and foreseeing consequences, say, but on the nature of one's emotions and desires.

What kind of affect does one need to be reliably good at making moral judgments? The question is well worth pressing. Obviously, when thinking about what it takes to *be* moral, we think that people need to care about what might be called recognizably moral objects or ends – justice, the patient's interests, one's child. But it isn't as clear that one needs to care about such ends in order to *know* what it takes to be moral. After all, the lesson so far is quite general: to make reliable, considered moral judgments, one must be aware of morally relevant facts, and what one tends to be aware of reflects what one cares about. This in itself doesn't prevent us from finding moral expertise in one whose nonmoral interests, by happy coincidence, attune them to the sorts of details that turn out to have moral significance.

But in fact it is extremely unlikely that one will be reliably sensitive to moral saliences unless one cares about recognizably moral ends. To make good moral judgments, one must be aware of a complex set of details and the shape they form (Dancy 1993, ch. 7; Friedman 1989). Operating under the influence of other interests, sooner or later (and usually sooner), the contours of what is noticed will diverge from the contours of what is morally important. A pharmaceutical company marketing a new all-purpose painkiller, for instance, certainly has a very strong desire to maximize sales. Its marketing division, though, will not reliably notice instances of pain: it will reliably notice instances of affluent or insured people's pain. A sadist who delights in knowing of others' pain, on the other hand, will be exquisitely reliable at sniffing out all instances of pain, but he will be oblivious to the myriad other details relevant to determining what morally should be done *about* that pain. A constellation of features are salient to determining the answer to that question – the cause of the pain (torture or appropriate punishment?), the preferences of the one in pain (she might prefer the pain to the stupor the medication gives her), one's relationship to the person in pain (alleviating the pain of one's alcoholic husband may count as enabling instead of as helping him). The extent to which one actually cares about and is responsive to moral ends, then, has enormous impact on how accurately and reliably one sees the moral landscape, because what one is attentive to is deeply influenced by what one cares about, and caring about other than recognizably moral ends will significantly compromise one's propensity to notice the morally relevant set of details.

Those who work in the ethics of care have advanced a further and more specific claim. The attentiveness necessary to good moral judgment is best ensured, it is argued, when we care, not simply about impersonal moral ideals such as justice, but about *people themselves* (Blum 1988; Walker 1991). In order for Nightingale to encourage her nurses to be optimally observant of salient details, on this view, she should have urged them not just to care deeply about discharging well the duties of nurse, or even promoting the interests of the patient, but to care about *the patient herself*.

Now there is no doubt that caring for a person, if the caring is healthy and mature, helps keep one attentive to details important to her situation. One might well wonder, though, why we should accept the claim that caring for people carries any particular epistemic advantage over caring for impersonal moral ends. I think the answer lies in the importance of a particular kind of receptive listening that comes with properly caring for a person. Because the features relevant to determining what one ought to do are often complex, one must be receptive to the particulars of cases, to what is different and novel in a case, and not just notice what, at a lower level of resolution, appear as broad similarities. As these important particularities often have to do with details known only to the people whose interests are at issue – their fears, hopes, worries, how they conceptualize the situation – we will gain important information by listening to their narratives. So much is obvious. But notice, now, what happens when we do this with the stance of an investigator, asking questions of the person only because we see her as the source of important data unfortunately unavailable elsewhere (such as data about her mental states). When we listen from this stance, we objectify the person in a certain way: we see her as a means to aiding our agenda, including agendas as laudable as furthering justice or diminishing suffering.

This stance of personal disengagement, however passionate one's desire to find out truths or to see interests advanced, carries with it tremendous epistemic danger. Most of us resist what is unique, and most of us have deep tendencies to project our own template of experiences onto others. We catalogue and classify others' experiences as soon as they are mentioned, eager for them to be confirming instances of our current favorite generality. (Here, ironically, we do have a desire that infects our epistemic efforts – the desire for intellectual closure.) One of the few antidotes we have against these tendencies is listening from a stance of caring for the person herself. In such a stance, we want to hear how it is for her, in a way that welcomes novelty or uniqueness, is slow to apply templates and open to changing them, is ready to reconceptualize what the agenda itself might end up being. This is not to be confused with patronizing agreement or the mindless suspension of judgment. Part of the love or caring here includes respect for the person as a responsible subject, which often entails voicing disagreement or even arguing (for more on the connections of respect and care, see Piper 1991; Dillon 1992). Indeed, to do otherwise is to view the person as an object in your agenda of "listening carefully to others."

The first lesson about affect's role in moral epistemology, then, is that from the valorized position of dispassionate detachment we are often actually less likely to pick up on what is morally salient. Emotional distance does not always clarify; disengagement is not always the most revealing stance. To see clearly what is before us, we need to cultivate certain desires, such as the desire to see justice done, and the desire to see humans flourish, but we must also, more particularly, work at developing our capacities for loving and caring about people.

The epistemic role so far outlined for affect is a deeply important one. I want now to argue that it is not the only one. It is, we can agree, extraordinarily unlikely that one will reliably tease out and notice all the disparate moral saliences of the complicated situations we face unless one has the affective propensities detailed above; but nothing said so far implies that it is impossible. After all, the features of a situation relevant to determining its moral qualities – the sociological, psychological, economic, or physical properties, say – are in *principle* available to anyone. Perhaps it is only because we are such "tawdry, inadequate epistemic creatures," to use mark Platts's phrase (Platts 1979, 247), because we are so little and so selectively aware of our surroundings, that we need special affective interests in justice, or caring engagement with people, to get us to notice what is there, available to be seen. For all that has been said so far, then, the *ideal* knower, facing no such limitations, has no epistemic need of affect.

Here the traditional conception of reason and affect resurfaces, providing now the archetype of the ideal. The ideal epistemic stance is, after all is said and done, still the detached "point of view of the universe," from which all is seen but nothing is cared for. The province of knowledge turns out in the end to be a role properly reserved for reason

alone; affect has merely a temporary role as a corrective. Affect serves as helpmate to reason as he struggles with his imperfections, but if all were right in the world, the separation appropriate to their natures would be restored. To be sure, affect is acknowledged as valuable for the aid she gives, but the value is only instrumental, and the acknowledgment is marked with the ambivalence one feels toward the crutch that is a reminder of one's defects. As far as epistemological projects are concerned, we can yearn for the day when affect will be left behind as superannuated. From a feminist perspective, of course, such a view has a depressing familiarity: once again, it is what is associated with man that defines the ideal. I want to argue now that the move is not just depressing; it is wrong. Possession of certain desires and emotions turns out to be a *necessary* condition of discerning moral properties, and hence must form part of even the ideal observer's epistemic repertoire.

On reflection, most people would agree that there is a difference between acknowledging that an action causes pain, say, and coming to see it as *cruel*, a difference between noting that a homeless person is going hungry and seeing that *charity* is called for. The first sort of judgment concerns properties that are in fact morally salient, as we've put it; that is, they are the good- and bad-making properties, those in virtue of which the actions have the moral properties they do. But one can acknowledge such properties and not see *that* they are morally relevant, or what exactly their moral relevance comes to. One could, for instance, simply lack the moral concept at issue (perhaps some animals are like this, having the concept of pain but not the concept of cruelty). Or again, if one had the relevant concept, one could fail to see its application in the present instance. One could see the relevant pieces but not the proper gestalt; one could fail to see the moral meaning the elements together carry. There is, then, an important difference between judgments concerning properties that are in fact morally relevant and judgments that actually employ moral concepts.

What is involved in ascension to the level of moral awareness? Put most generically, to conceptualize a situation in moral terms is to see it as meriting some response – one sees the situation as calling for some action, or again, as deserving some emotional response such as outrage or love (McDowell 1985; Wiggins 1987; McNaughton

425

1988). It is, in short, to see the situation in a way that is essentially *evaluative*: one who becomes morally aware has come to acknowledge the salient features of a situation as constituting a *reason* or a *justification* for some response. Thus the difference, for instance, between someone who discerns the painfulness of torture and someone who sees the *evil* of it is that the latter person has come to see the painfulness as a reason not to torture, to understand torture as meriting revulsion.

To see a situation in such light is to see it in a way that can rationally explain having the merited response. We understand why someone is angry if we learn that he believed himself the victim of grave injustice; we learn why someone performed an action if we learn she thought it her moral duty. More explicitly, the way in which the situation is conceptualized *itself* is sufficient to provide the explanation, to make it intelligible to us why the person had the merited response. While we would need to know more about an agent who rushed at an angry bull than is given by his testimony that it scared him (that he had accepted a dare to do something frightening, perhaps), we do not need similar supplementation when the agent explains his refusal to join in some teasing by saying he thought that, given the person's sensitivity, doing so would involve cruelty. With moral awareness, the very way in which the situation is conceived carries explanatory force. Thus when two people faced with the same moral requirement differ in their response, such that one has the merited response and the other has no response at all, there is some way in which their conceptions of the situation differ. They do not see it in the same light; they do not conceptualize it in the same way. Analogously, to give an example from another evaluative realm, aesthetics, a person who hears the particular beauty in jazz and the person who hears it as plain noise are not experiencing the music in the same way (McNaughton 1988, 112).

This is not to say that all moral conclusions, or even all sincere and deeply held moral conclusions, are followed by right action or displays of emotion. For one thing, the response is often overwhelmed or shunted aside by countervailing psychological forces. Overpowering sexual desire, the weight of depression, the dissonance of accommodating the full implications of a disturbing belief – all these can outweigh the moral motivations one genuinely possesses, can submerge emotional reactions to deeper recesses of one's psyche. The point is worth

underscoring, for the fact that we do not immediately experience the responses we acknowledge as appropriate does not mean that they are not there, manifesting themselves indirectly in how they structure various aspects of our lives. Thus we speak of depression as *masking* rage, for when the depressive is finally ready to feel her rage, it is accompanied by the realization that she *has been* angry at her tormentor for years.

But the further and crucial point is that where one does fail to have the appropriate response, the failure will show up in how clearly or how fully one saw the moral status of the situation (see McDowell 1978 and 1979; Platts 1979; Nussbaum 1985b; Sherman 1989). One who fails to respond takes in the case, perhaps, but the perception is cloudy, incomplete, distorted in some way. Aristotle makes the point by reference to the difference between the truly virtuous person, who responds morally without struggle, and those who must battle (successfully or not) to do so. The difference, Aristotle notes, is a difference in the *quality of perception*: it is because the virtuous person sees more clearly that her response comes easily, directly, reliably (see, for instance, *Nicomachean Ethics* 1146b30–1147a4, 1147a10–24).

Take, for instance, someone who gives change daily to the homeless person near her office but who does so to qualm her furtive feelings of guilt, to compensate for the irritation she can't help feeling at his presence, and to maintain a self-image she can tolerate. Now imagine that one day, walking toward the homeless person, she suddenly sees the situation differently. Her perspective shifts; the elements fall into place; she has fit the case into a different context. Perhaps she suddenly sees in this person the loneliness she herself has felt, and the picture resolves itself into a simple case of helping a fellow human in a bit of need. This change is a change in her apprehension of the situation. This is not to say that she necessarily came to know some new detail of the case. Seeing more clearly is often a matter of discerning a different gestalt of the individual elements one already apprehends: one sees the elements in a way that lets one recognize some further property they together fix. (Someone who sees a nose, mouth, eyes but cannot recognize them as his lover's face suffers a kind of *blindness*.) And the better apprehension brings with it a better response: in our example, a kindly response feels *of a piece* with the new, more accurate way in which the woman apprehends the situation.

If this view of moral motivation is correct, then, in order to "see" the moral landscape clearly,[4] in order to discern it fully and properly, one must have certain desires and emotions. Caring, being outraged, being moved to act – all these are part of discerning moral features clearly. The ideal epistemic agent herself would have appropriate affect, for it is needed if one is to discern all that there is to see.

I find the theory just outlined persuasive largely because it fits and makes sense of a rich array of phenomena in moral psychology, but also because I find its traditional rival deeply dissatisfying. On the rival picture of moral motivation, the affective efficacy of moral awareness is completely independent of its cognitive quality, for motivation is the province of some separate domain: depending on the particulars of the theory, it is a function of will, practical rationality, a faculty of emotions, or of independently intelligible desires. Note, now, that such a "bureaucratic model," as I have called it, leaves open the possibility that there are certain creatures who fully apprehend the moral landscape – who gaze intelligibly at the moral order, in all its glory – and yet *never* respond as merited. They have, perhaps, some persistent practical irrationality and comprehensively fail to draw the practical inferences they ought to in this area; or, again, they are creatures who do not possess any capacity for anger, love, outrage; or again, they are creatures whose desires extend only to gratifying their own most immediate felt urges for food and sex. Such beings are nonetheless held to be creatures who understand and apprehend the cruelty in the torture they witness (or perform), who discern moral obligation when they see a hungry child, who reliably detect when courage is called for.

I think this profoundly empties and distorts what is involved in grasping "the point" of morality. More fundamentally, it makes no sense of why we come to use moral concepts, and leaves aside what it is to understand them. A person who never appropriately responds at any level to what he terms cruel or obligatory, I want to argue, does not have *autonomous* understanding of the concepts he invokes. Imagine a person who tries to understand what is meant by "*valuable*," who suddenly seems to catch on and says, "Yes, now I see!" but persistently tries to destroy what we point to as examples. Or again, imagine a person who seems to understand that a set of her beliefs constitutes conclusive "justification" for a proposition and yet, with full possession of her faculties, remains completely impassive at the notion of actually drawing the conclusion. In these cases, we do not credit the people with understanding of the *evaluative* concepts involved, precisely because they miss their practical force.

Of course, even the complete amoralist may use moral words: he may tell us in exasperation that he knows perfectly well that murder is evil and that giving to the poor is good. But his use of moral terms will not be born of his independent competence with the language, of his having autonomous knowledge of "how to go on." His use of moral terms, instead, is *essentially parasitic*. An example with color may help illustrate what I mean. To use Frank Jackson's scenario, imagine a person who has lived all her life in a black and white room (Jackson 1986). If she is equipped with science textbooks on color and light waves, she can come to use the word "green" in completely appropriate ways; if she also has a light wave meter to consult alongside her science book, she would possess the ability to pick out green objects with perfect reliability. Still, it is when she finally steps out of the room into the sunlit forest that she has the concept of *green*, as opposed to having the concept of *light wavelength* and a conversion manual. In something analogous to this case, the amoralist can, as an outsider to the moral system, get a sense of how it goes. He knows empirically that we place great store by things labeled "good" and that we frown and punish when people do "bad." He can, then, begin to employ the terms himself. But, as in the case with green, the use is always a parasitic one: the amoralist is always

---

[4]   Throughout this essay, I have helped myself to the notion of "seeing" when I talk of apprehending moral truths. Lest that usage conjure worries stemming from its misuse by ethical intuitionists of previous centuries, let me say I am not positing any *sui generis* faculty of moral perception. We explain our ability to apprehend that something is cruel in the same way we explain our ability to apprehend that something is a table; not by appeal to any special sense organ, but by appeal to a much more familiar "faculty" – the capacity to apply concepts correctly. Put bluntly, we apprehend that something falls under the classification "cruel" by attending to the details at hand and making a judgment (which is not to say it is an easy skill to exercise). Of course, a full theory of moral epistemology would provide an account of how and when such judgments are justified. I do not take myself to have offered any such account in this essay.

glancing sideways, as it were, picking up on others' signals, and not responding *to* the *goodness* or *badness* in the situation. The amoralist, then, is not simply someone who fails to respond to the moral requirements he sees: rather, he does not himself autonomously see that a given situation is cruel, kind, right, or wrong.

Now, in the case of green, of course, absence of understanding does not compromise one's reliability in indicating green. Armed with your light wave meter and conversion manual, you'll get it right. If this were true of moral concepts as well, a modified version of the bureaucratic model would remain open: although an amoralist could not be said to have moral understanding or moral knowledge, he would, with proper training, be able to deliver accurate moral judgments. (He could be not a moral expert, but an expert moral consultant.)

But morality is crucially disanalogous to color here. Moral properties do not map onto nonmoral properties the way color maps onto light wavelength (see McDowell 1981; Wiggins 1987; McNaughton 1988, ch. 13; Dancy 1993). Items grouped together under moral classifications such as "cruel" do not form kinds recognizable as such at the nonmoral level. For one reason, there are infinitely many ways to be, say, cruel: there is no way to mark out in purely nonmoral terms why kicking the dog, verbal taunting, and forgetting to invite the neighbor's child to your daughter's birthday party get classified together. For another, as Jonathan Dancy and David McNaughton point out, considerations seem to carry their reason-giving force holistically in the moral domain: the contribution made by any given feature to an action's moral status depends, in a way that escapes codification, on what other features are present or absent (so, for instance, the fact that an action is fun is often reason in its favor but might be precisely what makes hunting animals morally problematic).[5]

This means that there are no conversion manuals – not even immensely complex ones – for inferring moral properties from nonmoral properties, no algorithms into which one can feed the latter to derive all and only the right moral answers.[6] Those then with merely parasitic competence in morality will go wrong. They can mimic genuine practice well in certain easy cases, for there are obvious rules of thumb to make use of. But their epistemological expertise will be compromised, and usually severely. It is no accident that amoralists, when trying to display their moral competence, tend to recite the crudest mantras about morality ("killing is wrong"; "feeding the hungry is good"); for the subtle contours displayed by the moral landscape of lived experiences will escape them.

Affect, then, has an ineliminable role in moral epistemology. For while affect is contingently (though significantly) important to our noticing the natural properties that are in fact good- and bad-making properties, appropriate affect is a necessary component of apprehending the moral properties themselves. If we were to succeed in transcending our affect and occupying a dispassionate epistemic stance, then, we would be blind to some of the most important truths there are, namely, moral truths.

The traditional partition of reason and affect shows up in one final and very important way in discussions of morality. Historically, many who have granted morality's intimate connection with affect have concluded that the connection comes at a price: it reveals that there are in fact no moral properties or moral truths. Philosophers from Hume to Mackie have argued that the necessary connection of a moral verdict to affect gives us *in-principle* and *ex ante* reason, in advance of any substantive investigation into moral systems, for concluding that those claims do not correspond to the way the world is (a short list of skeptical classics would inclued Hume 1978; Ayer 1936; Stevenson 1959; Mackie 1977; and Harman 1977).

---

[5]   The example is cited in Dancy (1993, 61); he attributes it to Roy Hattersley, who explained "slaughter should not be fun."

[6]   This is not to deny that moral properties are fixed by the nonmoral ("good-making") properties in a given situation. It is rather to agree with Aristotle that there are no principles codifying the myriad ways in which nonmoral properties can fix the moral ones. Murdoch (1970) argues that we are tempted to insist that there must be such principles in the offing, despite the enormous variations we experience in actual cases of cruelty, kindness, obligation, only out of anxiety at the complexity of the world. McDowell (1978) argues that the urge to posit such principles is born of misplaced loyalty to a falsely narrow notion of consistency: namely, one that counts us as "going on in the same way" when applying moral terms only if the sameness of situations can be seen at the nonmoral level.

If the use of moral concepts is necessarily tied to the possession of affective states, after all, then one's choice of moral concepts and the moral conclusions one arrives at turn out to be constrained, and in this sense determined, by the specific palette of emotions and desires one happens to have. This means, it is thought, that moral verdicts cannot be genuine products of reason, and hence cannot be cases of discerning the way the world is, for they do not result from proper employment of some epistemic method such as perceiving, weighing evidence, or reasoning. Thus, while it may look at first sight as though the motivational and emotional states we've discussed are cases of discerning moral properties, in fact what we "discern" is the result of projecting those affective states onto the world: our deep moral convictions reflect the nature of our own hearts rather than the nature of the world.

Such moral skeptics acknowledge (indeed, insist upon) affect's role in the production of moral verdicts, then, but they retain the view that affect's role is not an epistemological one, in any robust sense of the term, for it has no role in finding out what is true. For indeed, it is affect's presence in morality that ensures there is no truth there to be found. Here, once again, affect is cast as a contaminating factor. Its differential presence is sufficient to valorize science over morality: the former, whatever other problems it faces, can at least aspire to truth, while the latter, whatever other importance it may carry, is in the end merely a matter of taste. Anything too tightly associated with emotion and desire, it turns out, is metaphysically a second-class citizen.

Now, debates over moral realism – over whether there is knowable moral truth – are as complicated as any. I don't pretend to mount a defense of moral realism in this essay. What I do want to register is my skepticism of the claim that morality's connection to affect provides a *principled* basis for rejecting moral realism. The fact that moral verdicts sustain a necessary tie to affect does not itself force us to abandon the idea that such verdicts are products of reason, for it may be that some products of affect are also products of reason. That is, the fact that the moral views we hold are logically constrained by the affect we have does not itself obviate the possibility that the views are epistemically sound, that they are reached by our sensitivity to the way the world is, or that their best explanation lies in the fact that they are true: for it

might be that affect is revealing of truth. Why think that the connection to affect compromises the robustly cognitive status of moral verdicts, instead of thinking that such status extends in a meaningful sense to affect? In short, the skeptic needs an argument to explain and defend his premise that products of affect cannot be products of reason. And here, I think, the arguments proffered often simply beg the question. Let me give a couple of examples of the sort of problematic argumentation I have in mind.

One recent skeptical argument defends its claim that moral verdicts are not products of reason by appealing to desire's "direction of fit" (Smith 1987). The argument is aimed against the suggestion that moral conclusions can be products of reason, despite their connection to desires, because *desires* can be products of reason. The suggestion, that is, is that we can come to have intrinsic desires in response to evidence that the end in question is a morally worthy one. The skeptical argument, currently much discussed, claims to show that the very nature of desire precludes this possibility: intrinsic desires are not the *sort* of thing we can come to by sifting through evidence, for they do not have the proper direction of fit. The argument goes something like this.

Beliefs and desires, we are reminded, are each intentional mental states, in which a particular kind of attitude is directed toward a proposition (the idea is first set out in Anscombe 1957). A believing attitude, we might say, is an attitude of "regarding as true" some proposition, while a desiring attitude is one of "regarding as to be brought about." Beliefs, more specifically, have a mind-to-world direction of fit: they try to match the way the world is. This means that, in putting forward a belief, we regard ourselves as obligated to offer and respond to considerations that seem to bear on the truth of its propositional content. It also means that, to count as a belief, a mental state must display some level of counterfactual sensitivity to evidence about its propositional content – at some point, disregard for evidence about the truth of one's assertions indicates that one is not, despite first appearances, really making a claim about the world. Desires, in contrast, have a world-to-mind direction of fit: they don't try to match the world; they try to change it. They thus tend to persist, not disappear, in the face of evidence that their contents are false; and, because they aim at making the world match their propositional contents, desires ground dispositions to act in ways the agent believes will lead to their realization.

The charge is now made, on the basis of these quite neutral and perfectly acceptable characterizations, that desires cannot be the products of reason. Desires, it is claimed, are simply not held accountable to how the world actually is. While beliefs should change in the face of evidence, normative assessments of desires are insulated from such considerations: we do not appraise an agent's desires by looking at any of the evidence she has. And desires do not display even the minimum counterfactual sensitivity to evidence that beliefs must: desires do not alter according to evidence. It is concluded, then, that intrinsic desires cannot be "contrary to" or "conformable to" reason, as Hume put it, because they, like pains or tickles, are not the sort of thing we come to by sifting through evidence about how the world is.

But this argument, as it stands, does not succeed. Although analysis of desire's direction of fit isolates an important aspect in which desires have evidential immunity, the aspect is a very narrow one, and in its own right does nothing to foreclose the possibility that desires can be products of reason. The analysis makes explicit that a desire is neither sensitive to nor judged by reference to evidence about its *own* propositional content: the desire that *p* is neither responsive nor responsible to evidence about whether *p*. But nothing in that definitional point indicates that desires cannot be responsive to or judged by evidence about some *other* proposition, that its possession or rejection is immune from *any* evidential considerations. More specifically, nothing said so far bars the claim that sometimes an intrinsic desire for some end is developed as a response to genuine evidence that the end is a morally worthy one. To put it schematically, the desire that *p* may be sensitive to evidence that *p is good*. Such a mental state can be thought of, if one likes, as a state that has two directions of fit toward two different propositions, respectively: it is a believing attitude directed toward the proposition *p is good* (it is responsive to evidence about whether *p is good*), and it is a desiring attitude directed toward the proposition *p* (it grounds a disposition to perform actions the agent believes will bring it about that *p*). There is nothing in the mere definition of belief or desire that stands in the way of this suggestion: there are, for instance, no conflicting instantiation conditions involved in such a scenario. One will see in these neutral characteri-

zations an indication of desire's inherent disreputable epistemic status only if one has already started with the historically traditional tendency to segregate reason and affect – here, by assuming that no mental states instantiate features of both belief and desire.

Another recent skeptical argument is provided by Bernard Williams, who offers an argument from rational convergence to explain why, while "science has some chance of being more or less what it seems . . . ethical thought has no chance of being everything it seems" (Williams 1985, 135). In science, Williams states, we can well imagine that all suitably equipped investigators might ultimately converge on one theory, and in a way that would be best explained by the truth of that theory. But we have, he says, "no such coherent hope" in ethics (1985, 136). Precisely because of their intimate connections to our desires and motivations, ethical views are destined to remain local in a way scientific theories are not: any convergence we might witness would be serendipitous, not best explained as the result of the theorists having exercised their sensitivities to the world as it really is.

On what is this confident prediction based, though? A thought experiment is tacitly invoked, in which we are to imagine that similarly situated and suitably trained investigators – those equipped with the proper epistemic resources – will not converge onto any one ethical theory however long they investigate, or will do so only for reasons unrelated to evidence (mass brain-washing, say). But of course, this thought experiment proceeds as planned only if it is assumed that possession of certain affective states is not *part* of being properly epistemically equipped. If we regarded the capacity to respond with certain emotions and desires as part of what is needed to apprehend the world, ethics would be seen as being just as susceptible to rational convergences as any other domain (however much or little that might be).

To disqualify affect as an epistemic resource – and not simply beg the question by assuming it is not – one must have some nontendentious criteria of what things count as epistemic resources and what things do not, and none is forthcoming. In point of fact, I don't think we have *ex ante* any substantive picture of what sorts of things are properly thought of as epistemic equipment – some independent, settled list of the sorts of things that help gain access to truth. Rather, we fill in our picture of epistemic access and our picture of the way things are concomitantly, each reciprocally influencing the other. The list of epistemic equipment may be modified, then, by reference to the sorts of propositions we come to regard as true: if we have strong reason to believe that some things are good or courageous, and such beliefs are necessarily tied to desires and emotions, we will find ourselves with good reason for regarding affect as an epistemic precondition for apprehending certain truths.

Attempts to maintain divisions of labor between reason and affect have appeared in many realms. We have seen them surface in certain traditionalist views of marriage, where the man is assigned the thinking work and the woman assigned the emotional work for the two, and again in certain traditionalist views of health care roles, where the doctor is supposed to handle the curing while the nurse handles the caring. These bureaucratic divisions work out in moral epistemology no better

than they do in those other contexts. One must be someone who is at least somewhat *responsive* to moral considerations to be someone who can reliably discern moral considerations. For affect, it turns out, is crucial to moral knowledge, and in two independent ways. First, given our human epistemic limitations, caring for recognizably moral ends is crucial to being attentive to the morally salient details of the situations we face. This is an important point in its own right. For even if the ideal epistemic stance turns out to be a dispassionate one, we will not make the (oddly common) fallacy of taking features of the ideal as direct guides to what we should strive for. (Sometimes getting better means cultivating precisely those features not found in the ideal.) Second, possessing appropriate affect turns out to be a necessary precondition for seeing the moral landscape. This need not render morality some poor second cousin to science, for affect may be revealing of truth.

References

Anscombe, G. E. M. 1957. *Intention*. Oxford: Blackwell.

Aristotle. 1915. *Nicomachean Ethics*. Oxford: Oxford University Press.

Aristotle. 1943. *The Generation of Animals*. Cambridge, MA: Harvard University Press.

Aristotle. 1988. *The Politics*. New York: Cambridge University Press.

Ayer, A. J. 1936. *Language, Truth, and Logic*. New York: Oxford University Press.

Baier, Annette. 1989. Hume: The women's moral theorist? In *Women and Moral Theory*, ed. Eva Kittay and Diana Meyers. Stony Brook, NY: Rowman & Littlefield.

Blackburn, Simon. 1981. Rule-following and moral realism. In *Wittgenstein: To Follow a Rule*, ed. Steven Holtzman and Christopher Leich. London: Routledge & Kegan Paul.

Blum, Lawrence. 1988. Gilligan and Kohlberg: Implications for moral theory. *Ethics* 98(3): 472–91.

Blum, Lawrence. 1991. Moral perception and particularity. *Ethics* 101(4): 701–25.

Bordo, Susan. 1986. The Cartesian masculinization of thought. *Signs* 11(3): 439–56.

Dancy, Jonathan. 1993. *Moral Reasons*. Oxford: Blackwell.

Descartes, René. 1912. *A Discourse on Method*. New York: Dutton.

Descartes, René. 1985. The passions of the soul. In *Philosophical Writings of Descartes*, vol. 1. Cambridge: Cambridge University Press.

Dillon, Robin. 1992. Care and respect. In *Explorations in Feminist Ethics*, ed. Eve Browning Cole and Susan Coultrap-McQuinn. Bloomington: Indiana University Press.

Dinnerstein, Dorothy. 1977. *The Mermaid and the Minotaur*. New York: Harper & Row.

Friedman, Marilyn. 1989. Care and context in moral reasoning. In *Women and Moral Theory*, ed. Eva Kittay and Diana Meyers. Stony Brook, NY: Rowman & Littlefield.

Gatens, Moira. 1991. *Feminism and Philosophy*. Bloomington: Indiana University Press.

Harman, Gilbert. 1977. *The Nature of Morality*. New York: Oxford University Press.

Hegel, G. W. F. 1942. *Philosophy of Right*. Oxford: Clarendon Press.

Herman, Barbara. 1985. The practice of moral judgment. *Journal of Philosophy* 82(8): 414–36.

Hume, David. 1978. *A Treatise of Human Nature*. Oxford: Clarendon Press.

Jackson, Frank. 1986. What Mary didn't know. *Journal of Philosophy* 83(5): 291–5.

Jaggar, Alison. 1989. Love and knowledge: Emotion in feminist epistemology. In *Women, Knowledge, and Reality*, ed. Ann Garry and Marilyn Pearsall. Boston: Unwin Hyman.

Kant, Immanuel. 1960. *Observations of the Feeling of the Beautiful and Sublime*. Berkeley: University of California Press.

Kant, Immanuel. 1964. *The Doctrine of Virtue*. Philadelphia: University of Pennsylvania Press.

Keller, Evelyn Fox. 1982. Feminism and science. *Signs* 7(3): 589–602.

Lloyd, Genevieve. 1979. The man of reason. *Metaphilosophy* 10(1): 18–37.

Lloyd, Genevieve. 1983. Reason, gender, and morality in the history of philosophy. *Social Research* 50(3): 490–513.

Lloyd, Genevieve. 1984. *The Man of Reason: Male and Female in Western Philosophy*. London: Methuen.

Lugones, María. 1987. Playfulness, world-traveling, and loving perception. *Hypatia* 2(2): 3–19.

Mackie, J. L. 1977. *Ethics: Inventing Right and Wrong*. London: Penguin Books.

McDowell, John. 1978. Are moral requirements hypothetical imperatives? *Proceedings of the Aristotelian Society, Supplement* 52: 13–42.

McDowell, John. 1979. Virtue and reason. *The Monist* 62: 331–50.

McDowell, John. 1981. Non-cognitivism and rule-following. In *Wittgenstein: To Follow a Rule*, ed. Steven Holtzman and Christopher Leich. London: Routledge & Kegan Paul.

McDowell, John. 1985. Values and secondary qualities. In *Morality and Objectivity*, ed. Ted Honderich. London: Routledge.

McMillan, Carol. 1982. *Women, Reason, and Nature*. Oxford: Blackwell.

McNaughton, David. 1988. *Moral Vision: An Introduction to Ethics*. Oxford: Blackwell.

Merchant, Carolyn. 1980. *The Death of Nature*. San Francisco: Harper & Row.

Murdoch, Iris. 1956. Vision and choice in morality. *Proceedings of the Aristotelian Society, Supplement* 30: 32–58.

Murdoch, Iris. 1970. *The Sovereignty of Good*. London: Routledge.

Nightingale, Florence. 1969. *Notes on Nursing*. New York: Dover Publications.

Nussbaum, Martha. 1985a. Finely aware and richly responsible: Moral attention and the moral task of literature. *Journal of Philosophy* 82(10): 516–29.

Nussbaum, Martha. 1985b. The discernment of perception. In *Proceedings of the Boston Area Colloquium in Ancient Philosophy*, ed. J. Cleary. Washington, DC: University Press of America.

Nussbaum, Martha. 1990. *Love's Knowledge*. New York: Oxford University Press.

Okin, Susan, Miller. 1979. *Women in Western Political Thought*. Princeton: Princeton University Press.

Ortner, Sherry. 1974. Is female to nature as male is to culture? In *Women, Culture, and Society*, ed. Michelle Zimbalist and Louise Lamphere. Stanford: Stanford University Press.

Pateman, Carole. 1989. *The Disorder of Women*. Stanford: Stanford University Press.

Piper, Adrian. 1991. Impartiality, compassion, and modal imagination. *Ethics* 101(4): 726–57.

Platts, Mark. 1979. Moral reality. In *Ways of Meaning*. London: Routledge & Kegan Paul.

Rose, Hilary. 1983. Hand, brain, and heart: A feminist epistemology for the natural sciences. *Signs* 9(1): 73–90.

Rousseau, Jean-Jacques. 1974. *Emile*. London: Dent.

Ruddick, Sara. 1987. *Maternal Thinking: Towards a Politics of Peace*. New York: Ballantine Books.

Sherman, Nancy. 1989. *The Fabric of Character: Aristotle's Theory of Virtue*. Oxford: Clarendon.

Smith, Michael. 1987. The Humean theory of motivation. *Mind* 96(381): 36–61.

Spelman, Elizabeth. 1983. Aristotle and the politicization of the soul. In *Discovering Reality*, ed. Sandra Harding and Merrill Hintikka. Dordrecht, Holland: Reidel.

Stevenson, C. L. 1959. The emotive meaning of ethical terms. In *Logical Positivism*, ed. A. J. Ayer. New York: Free Press.

Tuana, Nancy. 1992. *Woman and the History of Philosophy*. New York: Paragon House.

Walker, Margaret Urban. 1991. Partial consideration. *Ethics* 101(4): 758–74.

Walker, Margaret Urban. 1992. Moral understandings: Alternative epistemology for a feminist ethics. In *Explorations in Feminist Ethics*, ed. Eve Browning Cole and Susan Coultrap-McQuinn. Bloomington: Indiana University Press.

Wiggins, David. 1987. A sensible subjectivism? In *Needs, Values, Truth*. Oxford: Backwell.

Williams, Bernard. 1985. *Ethics and the Limits of Philosophy*. Cambridge, MA: Harvard University Press.

Wollstonecraft, Mary. 1975. *A Vindication of the Rights of Woman*. New York: Norton.

II.6 Moral Supervenience

Introduction

The sometimes rarefied discussions that surround the topic of moral supervenience all grow out of a simple, very fundamental, philosophical question: how is the moral world related to the nonmoral world? An action's wrongness, or a situation's moral goodness, invariably depend on what is happening in the nonmoral world. But what, precisely, is the nature of this dependence? An act is immoral, for instance, because it involves a deliberate deception, or because it involves a killing, etc. But, to take a line from error theorist John Mackie: "just *what in the world* is signified by this 'because'?" (Mackie 1977: 41).

Mackie's answer is: nothing. There is *no* explanation of how the moral and nonmoral are connected, and this, according to Mackie, justifies us in thinking that there is no moral world – there are no moral facts. It's as if we were to ask how the ghostly world is linked to the natural world. The absence of a good answer to this question is good evidence that there is no such spiritual realm, and so we do best not to waste our time trying to explain the connection between the two worlds. There is only one realm: the one explored and explained by science.

Those who reject moral error theory cannot tell such a simple story. They want a vindication of moral thought and talk, and so need to explain how morality is related to the other facets of our world.

In particular, they need to account for two constraints on morality:

S1: necessarily, any two situations that are identical in all nonmoral respects are identical in all moral respects.

S2: necessarily, any change in the moral status of a situation is occasioned by a change in the nonmoral way things are.

The thesis of the supervenience of the moral on the nonmoral is given by the combination of S1 and S2. Almost everyone accepts both S1 and S2. Furthermore, just about everyone accepts that these are conceptual truths – propositions that are knowable a priori, and true just in virtue of the concepts employed therein. Explaining the nature of moral supervenience requires, at the least, explaining why S1 and S2 are (conceptually) true.[1]

Consider how plausible moral supervenience is: imagine two situations identical in *every* nonmoral respect. We don't confront such situations in everyday life, but this is a thought experiment designed to test our conceptual commitments. Imagine that Abe has seen a young child sobbing on the streets, alone, and is moved to offer assistance just from a feeling of pity and sympathy. He comforts the child, discovers that she is lost, and then takes steps to find her parents. Babe, in a situation we are imagining to be identical in all respects, does exactly the same thing, prompted by exactly the same motives and intentions. Suppose we commend Abe, but criticize Babe. How could that be? What could possibly justify such different assessments? Somehow, somewhere, we must be assuming that Babe's situation is different from Abe's – she's got some hidden motive, she's acted in some underhanded way, etc. If there were no such difference, it just wouldn't make sense to render different moral verdicts of Abe and Babe. Whatever we say of the one, we should say of the other. S1 explains why that very plausible thought is true.

Imagine that we've rightly judged both Abe and Babe's actions to have been morally commendable. It seems impossible for the actions to become morally neutral or bad, without any change in the nonmoral world taking place. If you think about any moral change over time – e.g., the moral corruption of a person's character, or the moral improvement of a government vis-à-vis its citizens – you'll see that any real moral change must reflect a change in what is happening in the nonmoral world. It wouldn't make sense (except perhaps as an expression of sarcasm) to say, for instance, that the government has improved a great deal over the past year, when it had made no changes at all in its actions, pronouncements, or policies. S2 explains why that is so.

The most straightforward way to account for the truth of S1 and S2 is taken up by reductive ethical naturalists – *reductionists*, for short. (For more on the details of such a view, see the introduction to part I.5.) These theorists (represented here by Frank Jackson) believe that moral and natural properties are identical. Though there is a distinctive moral vocabulary, moral and natural terms designate the very same features of the world. Jeremy Bentham's Utilitarianism is a classic example of this kind of view. For him, the property of being morally right was nothing other than the property of maximizing pleasure. Though we have two phrases in play – "morally right" and "maximizing pleasure" – there is only one feature of the world that these signify.

If reductionism is correct, then there is a quite clear explanation of how the moral world is linked to the nonmoral world – the former is identical to a subset of the latter. The reason that moral differences depend on nonmoral differences is that moral differences just are nonmoral differences –

differences in the rightness of various actions, for instance, are nothing other than differences about the relative distributions of pleasure.

On this view, the link between the moral way things are and the nonmoral way things are is just like the link between truths about water and truths about H_2O. We have different words or phrases to describe these things, and that may make us think – wrongly, according to reductionists – that these words or phrases are referring to different things. What in the world explains why the many truths about water depend on the many truths about H_2O? The fact that they are the very same thing. Reductionists will offer the same account of moral and nonmoral properties.

If reductionism were vindicated, then it really would offer a completely successful account of the relation between the moral and nonmoral worlds. S1 and S2 would be readily explained. But only a small number of philosophers nowadays endorse this sort of naturalism. There is a variety of reasons for this lack of support, but perhaps the most prominent is the fact that, thus far, no identification of a moral property with any particular nonmoral property has gained widespread acceptance. And it certainly hasn't been from lack of trying.

Ethical nonnaturalists, and nonreductive ethical naturalists, must find alternative ways to account for the truth of S1 and S2. (For more on these theories, see the introduction to part I.5.) Though they disagree about whether moral properties are natural ones (i.e., ones whose essential nature is best explained and understood scientifically), they do agree that moral properties are *sui generis*, a kind unto themselves. This means that moral properties are not identical to any other kind of natural property. And that makes it harder to account for the relation between moral and nonmoral properties.

For ease of exposition, let us paper over their differences in this context and lump ethical nonnaturalists and nonreductive ethical naturalists together into the *moral antireductionist* camp. Perhaps the challenge to moral antireductionists can be best understood by comparing their situation to that of antireductionists about the mind. According to this latter view, mental properties such as being a belief, or being a desire, are not identical to any physical property. For if they were, then they would have to share every feature, and, according to most philosophers, they don't – one has privileged access to one's own mental states, but one doesn't have such access to the physical states of one's nervous system; physical states, but not mental states, are locatable in space, etc. Most importantly, mental properties are multiply realizable – there are a number of physical ways, in principle, in which mental properties can be realized. And so the mental property, say, of being pained, cannot be identical with any one of these kinds of physical states, since there can be a pain without the correlative physical state. The kind of physical state that constitutes a pain in human beings, for instance, is the firing of c-fibers. But the pain of other beings may have nothing to do with c-fibers. Further, c-fibers, even when they exist in other beings, may play no role in the generation of pain. So *being in pain* cannot be the very same thing as *having one's c-fibers fire*.

The moral antireductionist agrees in thinking of moral properties along these very same lines. Though moral rightness can sometimes be realized, for instance, by an action's maximizing happiness, maximizing happiness is not necessary for an action to be morally right. Sometimes acts are right even if they fail to maximize happiness. This is a perfectly general point: this sort of failure will repeat itself for all moral properties, and all nonmoral ones that in a given case realize them. Moral properties are multiply realizable.[2]

If that is so, then the supervenience worry raises its head. The moral reductionist could account for supervenience by denying that there were two realms (the moral and the nonmoral) that needed connecting. But the moral antireductionist insists that there are, after all, the two, distinct, realms. And now we need to know how they are related. Well, they are related as S1 and S2, say they are. True enough. But why are S1 and S2 true? What accounts for their truth?

This question has become a pressing one in ethics largely because of the work of a single philosopher: Simon Blackburn. He first drew attention to this issue in his 1971 article, and returned to the subject in his 1985 paper, reprinted here. The basic worry can be expressed pretty simply. Consider a situation described in all of its nonmoral particulars. Call this description *NM*. Now focus on any particular moral property – say, wrongness. If moral properties are multiply realizable, then, no matter what the contents of our description NM, it should be possible for a situation to be NM without its being wrong. For if moral properties are not identical to any nonmoral

properties, then, it seems, there is no *necessary* connection between the way things are nonmorally and the way things are morally.

Now here's the catch. If there is no necessary connection between moral and nonmoral properties, then two scenarios seem possible: (1) a situation is NM without being wrong; (2) a situation is NM while also being wrong. And since that is so, it seems as if there should be no barrier to a world in which NM things are sometimes wrong, and sometimes not. But that is precisely what is impossible, according to S1 and S2. If the moral supervenes on the nonmoral, then although it is possible for a situation or an action to be NM without also being wrong, if it is once wrong, then it must always be wrong. Although there is no necessity that an action that is NM is also wrong, it is necessary that if *any other* NM action is also wrong, then it, too, must be wrong. That seems awfully mysterious.

One popular way of responding to this challenge is to deny the crucial assumption that underlies it. This assumption is that there is no necessary connection between nonmoral and moral properties. See how this assumption works to generate the worrying puzzle:

For any nonmoral property *NM*, and any moral property *M*,

1 There is no necessary connection between NM and M.

2 Therefore, it is possible for a situation to be NM without being M. (from premise 1)

3 Therefore, it is possible for a situation to be NM and also M. (from premise 1)

4 Therefore, it is possible for a world to contain situations that are NM and M, and also to contain situations that are NM and not M. (from premises 2 and 3)

5 But it is not possible for a world to contain situations that are NM and M, and also to contain situations that are NM and not M. (from S1 and S2)

6 Therefore (1) is false. (modus tollens)

This argument shows that (1) is incompatible with moral supervenience. Premise (1) entails premise (4). But premise (4) is incompatible with premise (5), and premise (5) is just a statement of the implications of S1 and S2 – i.e., a statement of moral supervenience. So if one wants to continue endorsing the supervenience of the moral on the nonmoral, then one must reject premise (1). And that means accepting that there is some necessary connection between the nonmoral and the moral worlds.

Well, suppose we accept this necessary connection. Does that force us back into the reductionist camp? No. To see why, consider two kinds of necessary relations that might obtain between any nonmoral property NM, and any moral property – say, wrongness.

> (A)   necessarily, if something is NM, then it is wrong.
>
> (B)   necessarily, if something is wrong, then it is NM.

Reductionists will say that, for every moral property, there is some true statement of form (A) *and* (B) that will establish its nonmoral identity. But their opponents could give up one of these without giving up the other, thereby allowing that there is some necessary connection between moral and nonmoral properties. And this is just what they do.

Here the idea is that particular configurations of nonmoral properties *do* necessitate a particular moral verdict, even though that moral verdict can be realized in other ways, as well. In other words, some statement of the form (A) will be true, but no statement of form (B) will be true. So, while an act can be wrong without being NM (this is entailed by the multiple realizability of wrongness), an act cannot be NM without being wrong – of necessity, if it is NM, then it is wrong. That would explain why every situation identical in all nonmoral respects must also be identical in all moral respects.

This reply is modeled on antireductionism about the mental, which says that certain nonmental states will necessitate the occurrence of particular mental states, but not the other way around. Indeed, many moral antireductionists have tried to insulate themselves from worries about supervenience by claiming, correctly, that supervenience relations occur in many areas, and (more controversially) that if we have no problem countenancing supervenient phenomena in other areas (e.g., mental facts, color facts, biological facts), then there should be no problem extending the same courtesy to moral facts. Blackburn himself is dubious about this maneuver. He sees a unique problem for moral supervenience.

Consider the supervenience of the mental on the physical, or the supervenience of colors on surface reflectance properties. Though the supervenience is real, it might have been otherwise – we can, for instance, imagine a world that has the same yellows and blues and reds as we do, but one in which those colors are produced in ways quite different from our own. By contrast, it isn't conceivable that worlds identical in all nonmoral respects are morally different. The supervenience of the moral on the nonmoral is a *conceptual* truth. That isn't the same for other, familiar cases of supervenience. We might be unsure about whether the mental supervenes on the physical without thereby failing to understand the essence of mental life. But we'd betray a lack of understanding if we thought it possible for situations identical in all nonmoral respects to differ morally.

And so the worry about ethics re-emerges. For any nonmoral property NM, and any particular moral property – say, wrongness – there is no *conceptual* necessity that NM cases are cases of wrongness. People of intelligence and good faith can differ about which nonmoral features of the world are right or wrong. One isn't contradicting oneself by assenting to a nonmoral description of the world, and yet withholding or endorsing a verdict of (im)morality. Thus, conceptually, it is possible for a situation to be NM and also wrong, and also for a situation to be NM and not be wrong. But once any NM situation is wrong, all other NM situations must be wrong as well. Why should that be?

Blackburn, of course, thinks that there is no good answer to that question. Rather than exploring further to see whether that is so, let us conclude with two questions. First, what if Blackburn were right, and there were no explanation of why, as a conceptual matter, the moral supervenes on the nonmoral? It isn't clear how damaging that would be. After all, not everything is susceptible to explanation, and that goes especially for conceptual truths. (There doesn't seem to be an explanation, for instance, of Leibniz's law, a conceptual truth that tells us that identical things are indiscernible.) Perhaps it is just a brute, inexplicable fact that the moral supervenes on the nonmoral. And so, even if Blackburn were successful in pointing out the absence of a plausible explanation of moral supervenience, this might do only minimal damage to his opponents' views.

Everyone agrees, however, that invoking such brute facts is always a path of last resort. Though we are sometimes driven to such a position, it would be ideal were we able to avoid it. And here our second question naturally arises: is Blackburn's own account of moral supervenience a plausible one? If Blackburn, and other expressivists, are right, then there aren't really any moral properties at all. There is the natural world, the one that science tells us about, and then there are our responses to such a world. And that is it; there is no moral world. So there really isn't a challenge to

show how these worlds are related. For Blackburn, moral supervenience turns out to be a constraint on the kinds of commitments we can have about a fundamentally nonmoral world. Whether Blackburn's take on moral supervenience earns our allegiance will depend, centrally, on the attractions of the expressivism that frames it. Those who are interested in pursuing this matter are encouraged to consider the materials on offer in part I.2.

Notes

1 This is the very least that is required in order to explain moral supervenience. As represented by the conjunction of S1 and S2, moral supervenience is merely a modal claim, i.e., a claim about what is possible or impossible. But we might also think of supervenience as a metaphysical relation. We might want to know, as Mackie apparently did, what the ontological relation is between nonmoral and moral facts. Nonmoral facts "underlie" moral ones; moral facts are as they are "because of," or "in virtue of," the way the nonmoral world is ordered. The readings in this section are focused on the modal relation, and our introduction will be tailored accordingly. But a full explanation of moral supervenience will ultimately have to go beyond that of accounting for the (conceptual) truth of S1 and S2.

2 Even Frank Jackson, an ethical reductionist, feels the pull of this consideration. As a reductionist, he is committed to the view that moral properties are identical to nonmoral ones. But these latter, he claims, are disjunctive – perhaps infinitely so. So it's not as if moral rightness is identical with (say) the single property of maximizing happiness. Rather, moral rightness is identical to the single property of *being* NM_1 *or* NM_2 *or* NM_3 *or* . . . NM_n, where each disjunct is a different nonmoral property. There is an ongoing debate, largely within the metaphysics literature, that focuses on determining whether such disjunctive properties really exist.

Selected Bibliography

Blackburn, Simon. 1971. "Moral Realism." In John Casey, ed. *Morality and Moral Reasoning*. London: Methuen. Reprinted in *Essays in Quasi-Realism*. Oxford: Oxford University Press.

Blackburn, Simon. 1985. "Supervenience Revisited." In Ian Hacking, ed. *Exercises in Analysis*. Cambridge: Cambridge University Press. Reprinted in *Essays in Quasi-Realism*. Oxford: Oxford University Press.

Bovens, Luc, and Dalia Drai. 1999. "Supervenience and Moral Realism." *Philosophia* 27: 241–5.

Brink, David. 1989. *Moral Realism and the Foundations of Ethics*. Cambridge: Cambridge University Press, ch. 6.

Dancy, Jonathan. 1993. *Moral Reasons*. Oxford: Blackwell, ch. 5.

DePaul, Michael. 1987. "Supervenience and Moral Dependence." *Philosophical Studies* 51: 425–39.

Dreier, James. 1992. "The Supervenience Argument against Moral Realism." *Southern Journal of Philosophy* 30: 13–38.

Gibbard, Allan. 2003. *Thinking How to Live*. Cambridge, MA: Harvard University Press, ch. 5.

Klagge, James. 1984. "An Alleged Difficulty Concerning Moral Properties." *Mind* 93: 37–380.

Mackie, John. 1977. *Ethics: Inventing Right and Wrong*. London: Penguin.

Majors, Brad. 2005. "Moral Discourse and Descriptive Properties." *Philosophical Quarterly* 55: 475–94.

McFetridge, Ian. 1985. "Supervenience, Realism, Necessity." *Philosophical Quarterly* 35: 245–58.

McNaughton, David, and Piers Rawling. 2003. "Naturalism and Normativity." *Proceedings of the Aristotelian Society*, supplementary volume 77: 23–45.

Shafer-Landau, Russ. 2003. *Moral Realism: A Defence*. Oxford: Oxford University Press, ch. 4.

Sobel, Jordan Howard. 2001. "Blackburn's Problem: On Its Not Insignificant Residue." *Philosophy and Phenomenological Research* 62: 361–82.

Wedgwood, Ralph. 1999. "The Price of Non-Reductive Moral Realism." *Ethical Theory and Moral Practice* 2: 199–215.

Zangwill, Nick. 1995. "Moral Supervenience." In Peter French, Theodore Vehling, and Howard Wettstein, eds. *Midwest Studies in Philosophy* 20: 240–61.

Supervenience Revisited

Simon Blackburn

I

A decade ago, in an article entitled 'Moral Realism' I presented an argument intended to show that two properties, which I called supervenience and lack of entailment, provided together an unpleasant mystery for moral realism (Blackburn, 1971). This argument was originally suggested to me in a discussion with Casimir Lewy, which in turn was directed at the paper of G. E. Moore, entitled 'The Conception of Intrinsic Value' (1922). The intervening decade has provided a number of reasons for revisiting my argument. First of all, it was couched in an idiom which subsequent work on modal logic – particularly the distinctions of various kinds of necessity and the general use of possible worlds as models – has made a little quaint. It would be desirable to see if the new notions allow the argument to stand. Secondly, we have seen a great deal of interest in supervenience, as a notion of importance beyond moral philosophy. Thus in conversation and correspondence I have heard it suggested that my argument must be flawed, because exactly the same combination of properties that I found mysterious occurs all over the place: for example, in the philosophy of mind, in the relationship between natural kind terms and others, in the relation between colours and primary properties, and so on. Since anti-realism in these

other areas is not attractive, this casts doubt upon my diagnosis of the moral case. Finally, moral realism is again an attractive option to some philosophers, so that although when I wrote I might have seemed to be shadow boxing, the argument is just now becoming relevant again. In any case, enough puzzles seem to me to surround a proper analysis of supervenience to warrant a fresh look at it.

Suppose we have an area of judgments, such as those involving moral commitments, or attributions of mental states. I shall call these F judgments, and I shall also talk of F truths and F facts: this is not intended to imply any view at all about whether the commitments we express in the vocabulary are beyond question genuine judgments, nor that there is a real domain of truths or facts in the area. Indeed part of the purpose of my argument was to find a way of querying just these ideas. At this stage, all this terminology is entirely neutral. Now suppose that we hold that the truths expressible in this way supervene upon the truths expressed in an underlying G vocabulary. For example, moral judgments supervene upon natural judgments, or mental descriptions of people upon physical ones (either of the people themselves or of some larger reality which includes them). This supervenience claim means that in *some* sense of 'necessary' it is necessarily true that if an F truth changes, then some G truth changes, or necessarily, if two situations are identical in point of G facts, then they are identical in terms of F facts as well. To analyse this more closely, I shall make free use of the possible worlds idiom. But it must be emphasised that this is merely a heuristic device, and implies no theory about the status of the possible worlds. Let us symbolise the kind of necessity in question by 'N' and possibility by 'P': for the present it does not matter whether these are thought of as logical, metaphysical, physical or other kinds of modalities. We are now to suppose that some truth about a thing or event or state, that it is F, supervenes upon some definite total set of G truths, which we can sum up by saying that it is $G^\star$. Of course, $G^\star$ can contain all kinds of relational truths about the subject, truths about other things, and so on. In fact, one of the difficulties of thinking about all this properly is that it rapidly becomes unclear just what can be allowed in our conception of a totality of G states. But intuitively it is whatever it is by way of natural or physical states that bring it about that the subject is F. I shall express this by talking of the set of G states which 'underlies' an F state. Belief in supervenience is then at least the belief that whenever a thing is in some F state, this is because it is in some underlying G state, or is in virtue of its being in some underlying G state. This is the minimal sense of the doctrine. But I am interested in something stronger, which ties the particular truth that a thing is F to the fact that it is in some particular G state. We can present the general form of this doctrine as characterising, the relation 'U' that holds when one 'underlies' the other:

(S) $N((\exists x) (Fx \& G^\star x \& (G^\star xUFx)) \supset$
    $(y) (G^\star y \supset Fy))$

The formula says that as a matter of necessity, if something x is F, and $G^\star$ underlies this, then anything else in the physical or natural or whatever state $G^\star$ is F as well. There is no claim that $G^\star$ provides the only way in which things can become F: intuitively something might be, say, evil in a number of different ways, and something in one given physical state might possess some mental property which it could equally have possessed by being in any of a family of related physical states. The supervenience claim (S) is thus in no opposition to doctrines which now go under the heading of 'variable realisation'. To get the claim which

these doctrines deny, we would need to convert the final conditional: . . . (y) $(Fy \supset G^\star y))$. But the resulting doctrine is not one in which we shall be interested.

I now want to contrast (S) with a much stronger necessity:

(N) $N(x) (G^\star x \supset Fx)$

Of course, (N) does not follow from (S). Formally they are merely related like this: (S) necessitates an overall conditional, and (N) necessitates the consequence of that conditional. So it would appear there is no more reason to infer (N) from (S) than there would be to infer Nq from N $(p \supset q)$. Hence also there is no inconsistency in a position which affirms (S), but also affirms:

(P) $P(\exists x) (G^\star x \& {\sim}Fx)$

At least, this is the immediate appearance. In my original paper it was the nature of theories which hold both (S) and (P) (which I shall call the (S)/(P) combination) which occupied me. Such a theory would think it possible (in some sense commensurate with that of the original claim) that any given G state which happens to underlie a certain F state, nevertheless might not have done so. In other words, even if some G set-up in our world is the very state upon which some F state supervenes, nevertheless, it might not have been *that* F state which supervened upon it. There was the possibility (again, in whatever modal dimension we are working) that the actually arising or supervening F state might not have been the one which supervened upon that particular G set-up. My instinct was that this combination provided a mystery for a realist about judgments made with the F vocabulary, and that the mystery would best be solved by embracing an anti-realist (or as I now prefer to call it, a projectivist) theory about the F judgments.

To pursue this further, we might question whether there could be any motivation for holding the (S)/(P) combination. Consider the following possible doctrine about 'underlying', and about the notion of the complete specification of an underlying state, $G^\star$:

(?) $N((\exists x) (Fx \& G^\star x \& (G^\star x \, U \, Fx)) \supset$
    $N(y) (G^\star y \supset Fy))$

The rationale for (?) would be this. Suppose there were a thing which was $G^{\star}$ and F, so that we were inclined to say that its being in the G state underlies its F-ness. But suppose there were also a thing which is $G^{\star}$ and ~F. Then would we not want to deny that it was x's being $G^{\star}$ which underlies its being F? Wouldn't it be its being $G^{\star}$ *and* its being different from this other thing in some further respect – one which explains why the other thing fails to be F? We can call that a *releasing* property, R, and then F will supervene only on $G^{\star}$ and ~R. More accurately, $G^{\star}$ would denote a set of properties which do not really deserve the star. We would be wrong to locate in them a *complete* underlying basis for F.

This raises quite complicated questions about the form of these various doctrines. Let me put aside one problem right at the beginning. Since (S) is a conditional and contains an existential clause as part of the antecedent, it will be vacuously true if nothing is $G^{\star}$ and F; the necessitation will likewise be vacuously true if nothing could be $G^{\star}$ and F. So if (S) captured all that was meant by supervenience, we would say, for instance, that being virtuous supervened upon being homogeneously made of granite. Necessarily, if one thing homogeneously made of granite were virtuous, and this underlay the virtuousness, then anything so made would be. But this is just because it is impossible that anything of this constitution should be virtuous. I am going to sidestep this problem simply by confining the scope of F and G henceforwards, to cases where it is possible that something with a set of G properties, denoted by $G^{\star}$, should be F. In fact, we are soon to deal with different strengths of necessity and possibility, and I shall suppose that this thesis is always strong enough to stop the conditional being satisfied in this vacuous way. The next problem of logical form is quite how we construe the denotation of a set of properties made by the term '$G^{\star}$'. Firstly, we do not want the supervenience thesis to be made vacuously true through it being impossible that any two distinct things should be $G^{\star}$ – it then following that if one $G^{\star}$ thing is F, they all are. And the threat here is quite real. If, for instance, $G^{\star}$ were held to include all the physical properties and relations of a thing – if it were that and nothing less which some property F supervened upon – then assuming the identity of indiscernibles, we would have (S) satisfied vacuously again. To get around this I am going to assume a *limitation* thesis. This will say that when-

ever a property F supervenes upon some basis, there is necessarily a boundary to the kind of G properties which it can depend upon. For example, the mental may supervene upon the physical, in which case the thesis asserts that necessarily there are physical properties of a thing which are not relevant to its mental ones. A plausible example might be its relations to things with which it is in no kind of causal connection (such as future things). Again, the moral supervenes upon the natural, and the thesis will tell us that there are some natural properties which necessarily have no relevance to moral ones – pure spatial position, perhaps, or date of beginning in time. Given the limitation thesis, (S) will not be trivialised by the identity of indiscernibles. The last problem of form which arises is whether '$G^{\star}$' is thought of as a name for some particular set of properties (which form a complete basis for F), or whether it is built into the sense of '$G^{\star}$' that any set of properties it denotes is complete. The difference is easily seen if we consider a very strong kind of necessity – say, conceptual (logical or analytic) necessity. It is unlikely to be thought analytic that being made of H_2O underlies being water. One reason is that it is not analytic that being made of H_2O exhausts the kind of physical basis which may affect the kind to which a substance belongs. That is a substantive scientific truth, not one guaranteed in any more *a priori* way. I am going to build it into the sense of '$G^{\star}$' that at least in one possible world, the set of properties it denotes is sufficient to underlie F. I do not want it to follow that this is true in all worlds, although that is a very delicate matter. Fortunately, so far as I can see, it does not occupy the centre of the stage I am about to set.

If we accept (?) as a condition on what it is for a set of properties to underlie another, and hence on what it is for a property to supervene upon such a set, the relationship between supervenience and (E) changes. Suppose that there is something whose $G^{\star}$-ness underlies its F-ness:

$$\text{(E)} \quad (\exists x)\,(Fx \,\&\, G^{\star}x \,\&\, (G^{\star}x \cup Fx))$$

then we can now derive (N). In other words, (?) and (E) together entail (N). And as I have already said, (?) is an attractive doctrine. But it does mean that supervenience becomes in effect nothing but a roundabout way of committing ourselves to (N); the *prima facie* simpler doctrine that some set of underlying truths necessitates the F truth. This is in fact the way that supervenience is taken by Kim (1978): it enables Kim to suppose that where we have supervenience, we also have reductionism. Another way of getting at the attractions of (?) would be to cease from mentioning the requirement that there is something which is $G^{\star}$ and F altogether. After all, surely some moral property might supervene upon a particular configuration of natural properties, regardless of whether there actually is anything with that set. Or, some mental property might supervene upon a particular physical make-up which nobody actually has. If we took this course, we would replace (S) by a doctrine:

$$(G^{\star}x \ U \ Fx) \supset (y) \ (G^{\star}y \supset Fy)$$

and then the doctrine which would give us (N) immediately would be:

$$(G^{\star}x \ U \ Fx) \supset N \ (G^{\star}x \ U \ Fx)$$

Yet supervenience claims are popular at least partly because they offer some of the metaphysical relief of reductions, without incurring the costs; I want therefore to preserve any gap that there may be for as long as possible. This is particularly important in the moral case, where supervenience is one thing, but reductionism is markedly less attractive. So I am going to stick with the original formulation, subject to the caveats already entered, and while we should remain well aware of (?), I do not want to presuppose a verdict on it.

If we put (?) into abeyance we should be left with a possible form of doctrine which accepts both (S) and (P): the (S)/(P) combination. It is this which I originally claimed to make a mystery for realism. If there is to be a mystery, it is not a formal one, and I actually think that with suitable interpretations, there are relations between F and G vocabularies which are properly characterised by (S) and (P). It is just that when this combination is to be affirmed, I believe it needs explanation. In the moral case I think that it is best explained by a projective theory of the F predicates. But in other cases, with different interpretations of the modalities, other explanations are also possible. I shall argue this later.

Here, then, is a way of modelling (S) and (P) together. In any possible world, once there is a thing which is F, and whose F-ness is underlain by $G^{\star}$, then anything else which is $G^{\star}$ is F as well. However, there are possible worlds in which things are $G^{\star}$ but not F. Call the former worlds $G^{\star}/F$ worlds, and the latter, $G^{\star}/O$ worlds. The one thing we do not have is any *mixed* world, where some things are $G^{\star}$ and F, and some are $G^{\star}$ but not F. We can call mixed worlds $G^{\star}/FvO$ worlds. These are ruled out by the supervenience claim (S): they are precisely the kind of possible world which would falsify that claim. My form of problem, or mystery, now begins to appear. Why should the possible worlds partition into only the two kinds, and not into the three kinds? It seems on the face of it to offend against a principle of plenitude with respect to possibilities, namely that we should allow any which we are not constrained to disallow. Imagine it spatially. Here is a possible world w_1 which is $G^{\star}/F$. Here is another, w_2 which we can make as much like w_1 as possible, except that it is $G^{\star}/O$. But there is no possible world anywhere which is just like one of these, except including just one element with its $G^{\star}$ and F properties conforming to the pattern found in the other. Why not? Or, to make the matter yet more graphic, imagine a time element. Suppose our possible worlds are thought of as having temporal duration. A mixed world would be brought about if w_1 starts off as a $G^{\star}/F$ world at some given time, but then at a later time becomes a $G^{\star}/O$ world. For then, overall, it would be mixed and the supervenience claim would be falsified by its existence. This kind of world then cannot happen, although there can be worlds which are like it in respect of the first part of its history, and equally worlds which are like it in respect of the second part of its history.

This is the ban on mixed worlds: it is a ban on inter-world travel by things which are, individually, at home. The problem which I posed is that of finding out the authority behind this ban. Why the embargo on travel? The difficulty is that once we have imagined a $G^{\star}/F$ world, and a $G^{\star}/O$ world, it is as if we have done enough to imagine a $G^{\star}/FvO$ world, and have implicitly denied ourselves a right to forbid its existence. At least, if we are to forbid its existence, we need some explanation of why we can do so. The positive part of my contention was that in the moral case, projectivists can do this better than realists. In the next section I rehearse briefly why this still seems to me to be so, if we make some important distinctions, and then I turn to consider related examples. And in time we have to return to the difficult claim (?), to assess its role in this part of metaphysics.

II

Necessities can range from something very strict, approximating to 'analytically true' through metaphysical and physical necessity, to something approximating to 'usually true'. Then anyone who sympathises a little with the puzzle in a (S)/(P) combination can quickly see that it will remain not only if there is one fixed sense of necessity and possibility involved, but also in a wider class of cases. For whenever the supervenience claim (S) involves a strong sense of necessity, then it will automatically entail any version with a weaker sense of necessity. Hence, we will get the same structure at the lower level, when the possibility is affirmed in that corresponding, weaker, sense. Thus if (S) took the form of claiming that it is metaphysically necessary that . . . , and (P) took the form of claiming that it is physically possible that . . . , and if we also suppose (as we surely should) that metaphysical necessity entails physical necessity, then we would have the (S)/(P) combination at the level of physical necessity. On the other hand we will not get the structure if the relation is reversed. If the possibility claim (P) is made, say, in the sense of 'possible as far as conceptual constraints go', this does not entail, say, 'metaphysically possible'. And then if (S) just reads 'metaphysically necessary' there is no mystery: we would just have it that it is metaphysically necessary that F supervenes upon $G^\star$, but not an analytic or conceptual truth; equally, it would not be an analytic or conceptual truth that any given $G^\star$ produces F, and there is no puzzle there. For the puzzle to begin to arise, we need to bring the modalities into line.

I mention this because it affects the moral case quite closely. Suppose we allow ourselves a notion of 'analytically necessary' applying to propositions which, in the traditional phrase, can be seen to be true by conceptual means alone. Denying one of these would be exhibiting a conceptual confusion: a failure to grasp the nature of the relevant vocabulary, or to follow out immediate implications of that grasp. In a slightly more modern idiom, denying one of these would be 'constitutive' of lack of competence with the vocabulary. We may contrast this with metaphysical necessity: a proposition will be this if it is true in all the possible worlds which, as a matter of metaphysics, could exist. Of course, we may be sceptical about this division, but I want to respect it at least for the sake of argument. For the (S)/(P) combination in moral phi-

losophy provides a nice example of a *prima facie* case of the difference, and one which profoundly affects my original argument. This arises because someone who holds that a particular natural state of affairs $G^\star$, underlies a moral judgment, is very likely to hold that this is true as a matter of metaphysical necessity. For example, if I hold that the fact that someone enjoys the misery of others underlies the judgment that he is evil, I should also hold that in any possible world, the fact that someone is like this is enough to make him evil. Using 'MN' for metaphysical necessity, I would have both:

$$(S_m) \quad MN((\exists x)\,(Fx \,\&\, G^\star x \,\&\, (G^\star x \: U \: Fx)) \supset (y)\,(G^\star y \supset Fy))$$

and

$$(N_m) \quad MN(x)\,(G^\star x \supset Fx)$$

and I would evade the original argument by disallowing the metaphysical possibility of a world in which people like that were not evil. This, it might be said, is part of what is involved in having a genuine standard, a belief that some natural state of affairs is sufficient to warrant the moral judgment. For, otherwise, if in some metaphysically possible worlds people like that were evil and in others not, surely this would be a sign that we hadn't yet located the natural basis for the judgment properly. For instance, if I did allow a possible world in which some people like that were not evil, it might be because (for instance) they believe that misery is so good for the soul that it is a cause of congratulation and rejoicing to find someone miserable. But then this fact becomes what I earlier called a releasing fact and the real underlying state of affairs is now not just that someone enjoys the misery of others, but that he does so not believing that misery is good for the soul.

Because of this the original puzzle does not arise at the level of metaphysical necessity. But now suppose we try analytic necessity. It seems to be a conceptual matter that moral claims supervene upon natural ones. Anyone failing to realise this, or to obey the constraint would indeed lack something constitutive of competence in the moral practice. And there is good reason for this: it would betray the whole purpose for which we moralise, which is to choose, commend, rank, approve, forbid, things on the basis of their natural properties. So we might have:

(S$_a$)   AN(($\exists x$) (Fx & $G^\star x$ & ($G^\star x\ U\ Fx$)) $\supset$
         (y) ($G^\star y \supset Fy$))

But we would be most unwise to have

(N$_a$)   AN(x) ($G^\star x \supset Fx$)

For it is not plausible to maintain that the adoption of some particular standard is 'constitutive of competence' as a moralist. People can moralise in obedience to the conceptual constraints that govern all moralising, although they adopt different standards, and come to different verdicts in the light of a complete set of natural facts. Of course, this can be denied but for the sake of this paper, I shall rely on the common view that it is mistaken. So since we deny (N$_a$) we have:

(P$_a$)   AP($\exists x$) ($G^\star x$ & Fx)

We then arrive at a (S$_a$)/(P$_a$) combination, and my mystery emerges: why the ban on mixed worlds at this level? These would be worlds possible as far as conceptual constraints go, or 'analytically possible' worlds. They conform to conceptual constraints, although there might be metaphysical or physical bars against their actual existence.

Of course, in a sense I have already proposed an answer to this question. By saying enough of what moralising is to make (S$_a$) plausible, and enough to make (P$_a$) plausible, I hope to enable us to learn to relax with their combination. It is just that this relaxation befits the anti-realist better. Because the explanation of the combination depended crucially upon the role of moralising being to guide desires and choices amongst the natural features of the world. If, as a realist ought to say, its role is to describe further, moral aspects of morality, there is no explanation at all of why it is constitutive of competence as a moralist to obey the constraint (S$_a$).

Can this argument be avoided by maintaining (?)? No, because there is no prospect of accepting (?) in a relevantly strong sense. For (?) to help, we would need it to be read so that, necessarily (in some sense) if something is F and $G^\star$, and the $G^\star$-ness underlies its being F, then it is analytically necessary that anything $G^\star$ is F. And this we will not have in the moral case, for we want to say that

there are things with natural properties underlying moral ones, but we also deny analyticities of the form (N$_a$). (?) would not help if the necessity of the consequent were interpreted in any weaker sense. For example, we might want to accept (?) in the form:

(?$_{MN}$)   MN(($\exists x$) (Fx & $G^\star x$ ($G^\star x\ U\ Fx$)) $\supset$
            MN(y) ($G^\star y \supset Fy$))

and then there will be metaphysical necessities of the form of the consequent, that is, of the form (N$_m$), but they will not help to resolve the original mystery, since that is now proceeding at the level of analytical necessity. It is the possibility, so far as conceptual constraints go, of mixed worlds, which is to be avoided.

III

The argument above works because we are careful to distinguish the status of the supervenience claim, and in this case its extremely strong status, from that of the related possibility claim. I have done that by indexing the modal operators involved: we have four different forms of modal claim: (S), (N), (P) and (?), and each of them can involve analytic or conceptual necessity, ($_a$) metaphysical necessity ($_m$), and we come now to physical necessity ($_p$). For now I want to turn to consider non-moral cases of the same kind of shape. These examples are all going to start life as examples of the joint (S)/(P) combination. They may not finish life like that: it may become obvious, if it is not so already, in the light either of the plausibility of (?) or of the difficulty over banning mixed worlds, that either supervenience is to be abandoned, or (N) accepted. But here are some test cases:

1st example   Suppose that in w_1 a physical set-up $G^\star$ underlies some particular mental state F. Suppose $G^\star$ is possession of some pattern of neurones or molecules in the head, and F is having a headache. Nowhere in w_1 is there anything unlike x, in being $G^\star$ but not F. Next door, in w_2 however, there are things which are $G^\star$ but not F. Now we are told that w_1 is acceptable, and that w_2 is acceptable. But nowhere is there a world w_3 which is like w_1 but which changes to become like w_2, or which contains some particular individuals who are like those of w_2.

2nd example Suppose that in w_1 a particular molecular constitution $G^\star$ underlies membership of a natural kind, F. $G^\star$ consists of a complete physical or chemical breakdown of the constitution of a substance (e.g. being composed of molecules of H_2O) and F is being water. Nowhere in w_1 could there be a substance with that chemistry, which is not water. In w_2 however this combination is found. Once again, although each of these possible worlds exists, there is no $G^\star/FvO$, or mixed world, in which some substances with this chemical constitution are water, and others are not.

3rd example Suppose that in w_1 a particular set of primary qualities, particularly concerning refractive properties of surfaces, $G^\star$, underlies possession of a colour F. Nowhere in w_1 could there be things with that kind of surface, without the particular colour. However, there are possible worlds where this combination is found: $G^\star/O$ worlds. Again, there are no mixed worlds, where some things with the primary, surface properties are F, and others are not.

In each of these cases we have the (S)/(P) combination. And I hope it is obvious that each case is at least *prima facie* puzzling – enough so to raise questions about whether the combination is desirable, or whether we should make severe distinctions within the kinds of necessity and possibility involved, to end up avoiding the combination altogether. How would this be done?

First example

How should we interpret the supervenience of the mental on the physical? Perhaps centrally as a metaphysical doctrine. So we shall accept (S_m). Should we accept (S_a)? We should if we can find arguments, as strong as those in the moral case, for claiming that it is constitutive of competence in the mental language that we recognise the supervenience of the mental on the physical. But I doubt if we can do this. For whether or not we are philosophically wedded to the doctrine, we can surely recognise ordinary competence in users who would not agree. One day Henry has a headache, and the next day he does not. Something mental is different. But suppose he simply denies that anything physical is different (giving voice to Cartesianism). Is this parallel to the error of someone who makes the same move in a moral case? I do not think so: Henry is not so very unusual, and if his error is

shown to be one because of the 'very meaning' of mental ascriptions, then whole cultures have been prone to denial of an analytic truth. In other words, it seems to me to be over-ambitious to claim that it follows, or follows analytically, from change in mental state, that there is change in an underlying physical state. It makes views conceptually incoherent when enough people have found them perfectly coherent (consider, for example, changes in God's mind).

Let us stick then with (S_m). It would seem to me plausible, if we accept this, to accept the correlative necessities, (N_m), and $(?_m)$. We would then be forced to deny (P_m), and we just do not get involved with the problem of banning mixed worlds. (N_m) does the work for us, by disallowing the metaphysical possibility of $G^\star$ without F. However there is the famous, or notorious, position of Davidson to consider, which accepts some form of supervenience of the mental on the physical, but also denies the existence of lawlike propositions connecting the two vocabularies (Davidson 1980). Davidson is not very explicit about the strength of necessity and possibility involved in his claims. But it can scarcely be intended to be weaker than joint acceptance of (S_m) and of (P_p): And even if supervenience is taken not as a matter of metaphysical, but just of sheer physical necessity (in our physical world, there is no mental change without physical change, even if there *could* be), it does not matter. For from (S_m) we can deduce (S_p), so we have the (S)/(P) combination, at the level of physical necessity. So according to me the position ought to be odd, and indeed it is. Why is it physically impossible for there to be a world which contains some w_1 characters, with headaches, and some w_2 characters, in the same physical state, but without them? Once we have allowed the physical possibility of the w_2 type, how can we disallow the physical possibility of them mingling with w_1 types?

It does not appear to me that light is cast on this by Davidson's reason for allowing (P_p). This reason is that in some sense the mental and the physical belong to different realms of theory: ascriptions of mental properties answer to different constraints from ascriptions of physical ones, and hence we can never be in a position to insist upon a lawlike correlation of any given physical state with any given mental state (this is *not* just the variable realisation point: here we are told not to insist upon a physically necessary physical-to-mental correlation;

prima facie we might be allowed to do that in various cases, even if we could never insist upon lawlike connections the other way around). I do not accept that this is a good argument, for there can certainly be interesting laws which connect properties whose ascriptions answer to different constraints: temperature and pressure, or colour and primary properties, for instance. However, I do not want to insist upon that. For there remains the oddity that if Davidson's reasoning is good, it should equally apply to the supervenience claim. How can we be in a position to insist upon anything as strong as (S_p), let alone as strong as (S_m)? The freedom which gives us (P_p) is just as effective here. I may coherently and effectively 'rationalise' one person as being in one mental state, and another as being in another, obeying various canonical principles of interpretation, regardless of whether they are in an identical $G^\star$ state: I might just disclaim interest in that. Of course, if (N_p) were true, it would be different, but it is precisely this which the anomalous character of the position denies.

So if the mental reality is in no lawlike connection with the physical, as (P_p) claims, I can see no basis for asserting that nevertheless it supervenes upon it. But, again, the word 'reality' matters here. *One* way of thinking that the mental just has to supervene upon the physical, in at least the sense of (S_m), is by convincing ourselves that the physical reality is at bottom the only one: molecules and neurones are all that there are. And then there might be something about the way mental vocabulary relates to this – relates to the only reality there is – which justifies both (S_p) and (P_p). Perhaps there is some argument that obeying the supervenience constraint is required for conceptual coherence, or at any rate for metaphysical coherence; and perhaps Davidson's argument for (P_p) can be put in a better light than I have allowed. I do not want to deny this possibility. But I do want to point out that once more it is bought at the cost of a highly anti-realist, even idealist, view of the mental. The 'truth' about the mental world is not a matter of how some set of facts actually falls out. It is a matter of how we have to relate this particular vocabulary to the one underlying reality. If we thought like this, then we would begin to assimilate the mental/physical case to the moral/natural case. At any rate, it provides no swift model for arguing that anti-realism is the wrong diagnosis of the (S)/(P) combination in that case.

Why do I say that this is an idealist or anti-realist direction? Because the constraint on our theorising is not explained by any constraint upon the way the facts can fall out. It is constrained by the way we 'must' use the vocabulary, but that 'must' is not itself derived from a theory according to which mental facts and events cannot happen in some given pattern; it is derived from constraints on the way in which we must react to a non-mental, physical world. I regard this as a characteristically idealist pattern: the way the facts have to be is explained ultimately by the way we have to describe them as being. Thus I would say that the explanation of moral supervenience is a paradigmatically anti-realist explanation. By way of contrast, and anticipating example 3, we can notice how there cannot be a strong, analytic, version of the doctrine that colours supervene upon primary properties, precisely because it is so obvious that the only conceptual constraint upon using the colour vocabulary is that you react to perceived colour in the right way. Somebody who thinks that a thing has changed colour, but who is perfectly indifferent to any question of whether it has changed in respect of any primary property (or even who believes that it positively has not done so) is quite within his rights. His eyesight may be defective, but his grasp of the vocabulary need not be so.

Second example

In order to avoid unnecessary complexity, I should enter a caveat here. I am going to take being composed of H_2O as a suitable example of $G^\star$; an example that is of the kind of complete physical or chemical basis which results in stuff being of a certain kind, such as water. I am going to take it that this is known to be the case. So I shall not be interested in the kind of gap, which can in principle open up, in which people might allow that something is H_2O and is water, allow that wateriness supervenes upon the chemical or the physical, but deny that some other specimen of H_2O is water. This is a possible position, because it is possible to disbelieve that the facts registered by something's being H_2O exhaust the physical or chemical facts which may be relevant to its kind. I am going to cut this corner by writing as though it is beyond question that molecular constitution is the right candidate for a complete underlying property – a $G^\star$ property. I don't think that this affects the argument, although it is a complex area and one in which it is easy to mistake one's bearings.

Once more, it is natural to take the various claims involving the relationship of H_2O and water in a metaphysical sense. It is also natural, to me at any rate, to assert (S_m) only if we also assert (N_m), and $(?_m)$. Being water supervenes upon being H_2O only because anything made of H_2O has to be water. And if we had an argument that it does not have to be water, perhaps because we imagine a world in which countervailing circumstance makes substances composed of that molecule quite unlike water at the macro-level (and more unlike it than ice or steam), then we would just change the basis for the supervenience. We would have argued for a releasing property, R, and the true basis upon which being water supervenes would be $G^\star$ (being H_2O) and being $\sim R$.

Might someone believe that the $(S)/(P)$ combination arises at some level here? The argument would have to be that in some strong sense it *must* be true that being water supervenes upon physical or chemical constitution; but it need not be true, in this equally strong sense, that H_2O is the particular underlying state. Now I do not think there is any very strong sense in which being water has to be a property underlain by a physical or chemical basis. Of course, *we* are familiar with the idea that any such property must be a matter of chemistry. But there is no good reason for saying that people who fail to realise this are incompetent with the kind term 'water'. They just know less about the true scientific picture of what it is that explains the phenomenologically important, macro-properties of kinds. They are not, in my view, in at all the same boat as persons who fail to respect the supervenience of the moral on the natural. This is because this latter fault breaks up the whole point of moralising. Whereas ignorance of the way in which wateriness is supervenient on the chemical or physical does not at all destroy the point of classifying some stuff as water and other stuff as not. Uneducated people still need to drink and wash. However, it is now commonly held that there is no absolute distinction here: Quine has taught us how fragile any division would be, between conceptual and 'merely' scientific ignorance. So someone might hold that there is an important kind of incompetence, half-conceptual but perhaps half-scientific, which someone would exhibit if he failed to realise the supervenience of being water upon chemistry or physics, and that this is a worse kind

of incompetence than any which would be shown by mere failure to realise that it is H_2O which is the relevant molecule. So we might try a notion of 'competently possible worlds' $(_c)$ meaning those which are as a competent person might describe a world as being: then we would have an $(S_c)/(P_c)$ combination. Should this tempt us to an anti-realist theory of 'being water'?

Saying that there are no mixed possible worlds in *this* sense just means that any competent person is going to deny that there are worlds in which some things of a given chemical or physical structure are water, and others are not; but that competent people might allow worlds in which things are H_2O but are not water. The first is a kind of *framework* knowledge, which we might expect everyone to possess; but competence to this degree need not require the *specialist* piece of scientific knowledge, which we might not expect of everyone, and which might even turn out to be false without affecting the framework. We might even suppose that supervenience claims have, characteristically, this framework appearance, and suggest that this is why they do not trail in their wake particular commitments of the (N) form. And now the counterattack against my argument in the case of morals and mind gathers momentum. For if an $(S_c)/(P_c)$ combination works in a harmless case like this, then the shape of that combination cannot in general suggest anti-realism, and something must be wrong in the arguments so far given.

One reaction would be to allow the parallelism, and to grasp the nettle. When I said that we could relax with the $(S_a)/(P_a)$ combination in morals, I tried to explain this by saying that the role of a moral judgment is not to describe further *moral* aspects of reality; it is because the vocabulary must fit the *natural* world in certain ways, that the combination is explicable. I might try the same move here: it is because 'wateriness' is not a further aspect of reality (beyond its containing various stuffs defined in chemical ways) that the combination is permissible at the level of 'competently possible' worlds. But I think this will strike most uncommitted readers as weak: anti-realism has to fight for a place these days even in the philosophy of morals, and is hardly likely to seem the best account of the judgment that I have water in my glass. I think a better reaction is to remember well all that is meant by the notion of a 'competently possible world'. Remembering this enables us to say that an $(S_c)/(P_c)$ combination is harmless, and implies no problem of explanation which is best met by anti-realism. This is because the 'ban on mixed possible worlds' which it gives rise to is explicable purely in terms of *beliefs* of ours – in particular, a belief which we suppose competent people to share. We believe, that is, that no two things could be identical physically without also forming the same stuff or kind and *we believe that all competent people will agree*. Whilst we suppose this, but also suppose that competent people may not agree that if a thing is H_2O then it is water (because this requires a higher level of specialised, as opposed to framework knowledge) then we have 'competently possible' worlds of the two kinds, and the ban on mixed worlds. But this has now been explained purely by the structure of beliefs which can coexist with competence. There is indeed no further inference to a metaphysical conclusion about the status of wateriness, because the explanation which, in the other cases, that inference helps to provide, is here provided without it. To put it another way, we could say that in the moral case as well, when we deal with analytically possible worlds, we are dealing with beliefs we have about competence: in this case the belief that the competent person will not flout supervenience. But this belief is only explained by the further, anti-realist, nature of moralising. If moralising were depicting further, moral aspects of reality, there would be no explanation of the conceptual constraint, and hence of our belief about the shape of a competent morality.

It cannot be overemphasised that my original problem is one of *explanation*. So it does not matter if sometimes an (S)/(P) combination is explained in some ways, and sometimes in others. I do not suppose that there is one uniform pattern of explanation, suitable for all examples and for all strengths of modality (particularly if we flirt with hybrids like the present one). The explanation demanded in the moral case is, according to me, best met by recognising that moralising is an activity which cannot proceed successfully without recognition of the supervenience constraint, but this in turn is best explained by projectivism. In the present case the best explanation of why competent people recognise the supervenience of kinds upon physical or chemical structure is that we live in a culture in which science has found this out. I don't for a moment believe that *this* suggests any metaphysical conclusions. If this is right it carries a small bonus. It means that the argument in the

moral case does not depend upon drawing a hard and controversial distinction between 'conceptual' and other kinds of incompetence. It merely requires us to realise that there can be good explanations of our beliefs about the things which reveal incompetence. Anti-realism is one of them, in the case of morals, and awareness of the difference between framework scientific beliefs, and specific realisations of them, is another and works in the case of natural kinds.

Third example

The previous case posed the only real challenge which I know to the original mystery. By contrast the case of colours reinforces the peculiarity in the case of morals. For it would be highly implausible to aim for colour/primary property supervenience as an analytic truth, or one constitutive of competence with a colour vocabulary. Intuitively we feel that it is very nice and satisfying that colours do indeed supervene upon primary properties, and that there would be scientific havoc if they did not. But anybody who believes that they do not (mightn't God live in a world where displays reveal different colours to him, although there are no physical properties of surfaces of the things displayed?) can recognise colours and achieve all the point and subtlety of colour classification for all that.

Recent empirical work casts doubt even on the fact that 'everybody knows', that colours of surfaces are caused by the wavelength of reflected light. Other relational properties may matter. So it is wise to be cautious before putting any advanced modal status on supervenience or necessitation claims in this area. Certainly we expect there to be *some* complete primary property story, $G^\star$, upon which colour supervenes as a matter of physical necessity. But then we would also immediately accept the corresponding thesis (N_p), and there is no problem about mixed worlds. Similarly if we bravely elevated the supervenience (S) into a metaphysical thesis, there would be no good reason why (N) should not follow suit. (N) will not rise into the realms of analytic necessity, but then neither will (S). So at no level is there a mystery parallel to the one which arose with morals, and with Davidson's position on the mental and the physical. Of course, an (S)/(P) combination could be manufactured at the level of 'competently possible worlds', as in the last example, but once more it would avail nothing, because it would be explained simply by the shape of the beliefs which we have deemed necessary for competence.

IV

I have now said enough by way of exploring the original argument and its near neighbours. It would be nice to conclude with an estimate of the importance of supervenience claims in metaphysics. Here I confess I am pessimistic. It seems to me that (?) is a plausible doctrine, and in every case in which we are dealing with metaphysical or physical necessity, it seems to me that we could cut

through talk of supervenience, and talk directly of propositions of the form (N). This makes it clear, for example, that we may be dealing with 'nomological danglers' or necessities which connect together properties of very different kinds, and it may lessen our metaphysical pride to remember that it is one thing to assert such necessities, but quite another thing to have a theory about why we can do so. Like many philosophers, I believe many supervenience claims in varying strengths; perhaps unlike them I see them as part of the problem – in the philosophy of mind, or of secondary properties, or of morals or kinds – and not part of the solution.

References

Blackburn, S. 1971. 'Moral Realism.' In *Morality and Moral Reasoning*, ed. J. Casey. London: Methuen.

Davidson, D. 1980. 'Mental Events.' In *Essays on Actions and Events*. Oxford: Clarendon Press.

Kim, J. 1978. 'Supervenience and Nomological Incom-

mensurables.' *American Philosophical Quarterly* 15: 149–56.

Moore, G. E. 1922. 'The Conception of Intrinsic Value.' In *Philosophical Studies*. London: Routledge & Kegan Paul.

34

The Supervenience of the Ethical on the Descriptive

Frank Jackson

The Supervenience of the Ethical on the Descriptive

The most salient and least controversial part of folk moral theory is that moral properties supervene on descriptive properties, that the ethical way things are supervenes on the descriptive way things are.[1] I will start by arguing that the nature of the supervenience of the ethical on the descriptive tells us that ethical properties are descriptive properties in the sense of properties ascribed by language that falls on the descriptive side of the famous is–ought divide.

The supervenience of the ethical on the descriptive is sometimes stated in an *intra*-world supervenience thesis: for all w, if x and y are descriptively exactly alike in w, they are ethically exactly alike in w. However, it is the global supervenience of the ethical on the descriptive that is important for us here. For we are concerned with how the descriptive nature of complete ways things might be settles ethical nature; and it is global supervenience theses that give us a handle on this question, pre-

cisely because they quantify over complete ways things might be.

We noted in Chapter 1 [Omitted here. Eds.] that it is a restricted, contingent, a posteriori global supervenience thesis that was called for to capture the sense in which it is at all plausible that the psychological globally supervenes on the physical. A global supervenience thesis like

> For all w and w^*, if w and w^* are exactly alike physically, then w and w^* are exactly alike psychologically

is non-controversially false. The most that is plausible is that for any world physically exactly like our world, and which satisfies a certain additional constraint, roughly, a 'no gratuitous extras' constraint, is psychologically exactly like ours. However, the global supervenience of the ethical on the descriptive is special in that an unrestricted form, namely

> (S) For all w and w^*, if w and w^* are exactly alike descriptively then they are exactly alike ethically.

is both a priori true and necessary.

[1] Or, rather, that is how to state the least controversial part of folk theory assuming cognitivism. Non-congitivists insist, of course, that supervenience must be stated as some kind of constraint on those prescriptions, expressions of attitude, and the like, that count as moral judgements in their scheme.

Thesis (S) is compatible with the idea that ethical nature, the ethical way things are, is in part determined by facts about our responses and attitudes, with the appealing idea that, in Mark Johnston's terminology, value is response-dependent. For included in the global descriptive supervenience base will be facts about our responses, both actual and hypothetical, and both first- and higher-order, as described in purely descriptive terms (as wanting a glass of milk, say, and not as wanting something good).

A fair question is how precisely to identify the purely descriptive terms. All I said earlier was that I meant what people have in mind by the 'is' side of the is–ought divide, or that they have in mind when they speak of factual or descriptive vocabulary, and factual and descriptive properties. My experience is that people either find the notion under any of its various names relatively unproblematic, in which case further explanation is unnecessary, or else no amount of explanation is of any use. But perhaps the following remarks will make matters clearer. Because I will be defending a descriptive analysis of ethical terms, I cannot hold that there is a sharp *semantic* divide between ethical and descriptive terms. I have to regard the purely descriptive terms as essentially given by a big list of terms that would generally be classified as such, and see the aim of the exercise as the analysis of ethical terms in some way or another in terms of this big list. Moreover, I need not assume that there is a sharp divide between descriptive and ethical vocabulary, any more than there is between being bald and not being bald. I can allow that it is vague whether the word 'honest', for example, should be classed as purely descriptive or as partly normative. For our purposes here, we can follow a play-safe strategy. If it is unclear whether a term is or is not purely descriptive, then we can take it off the list of the purely descriptive. For the supervenience thesis (S), on which the argument to follow turns, is plausible even after culling the terms about which there might reasonably be controversy as to their purely descriptive status. Finally, even if you belong to the party that thinks that the division between ethical and descriptive vocabulary is a hopeless confusion, and that the culling operation I just described could not be carried out in any

principled way, there is still a question of interest in this area. We can ask, for any two lists of terms, with one designated 'descriptive' and the other 'ethical', independently of whether these labels are happy labels and of how we assigned the various terms to the two lists, whether or not (S) is true relative to the two lists.

Approaching the notion of a descriptive property in this way enables us to address a famous problem about what G. E. Moore means, or should mean, when he says that goodness is a *nonnatural* property.[2] He does not mean that (moral) goodness is an ethical property; everyone who thinks that goodness is a property thinks that, and he is saying something intended to *differentiate* his view from that of many who hold that goodness is a property. He does not mean that goodness is not a property of happenings in the space-time world; it is a central part of his view that goodness is a property of such happenings. He does not mean that goodness is not the kind of property that figures in the physical sciences. It is clear that his arguments are as much directed to dualists as to physicalists: when he argues that goodness is not pleasure, his case does not rest on physicalism about pleasant sensations.[3] What he really wants to insist on, I think, is an *inadequacy* claim: what is left of language after we cull the ethical terms is in principle inadequate to the task of ascribing the properties we ascribe using the ethical terms. He wants to object to exactly the claim I will be making.

We noted in Chapter 1 that the restricted, contingent, a posteriori global supervenience of the psychological on the physical implies that the full physical account of our world entails the full psychological account of our world. But the full psychological account does not entail the full physical account – no psychological account of our world, no matter how rich, entails each and every detail about where all the electrons are; and nor, on most views, does any and every psychological account of how things are entail some physical account of how things are – psychology might be realized in non-physical stuff. There is, thus, no logical equivalence in general between the physical and psychological way things are. However, because of the special nature of the global supervenience of the ethical on the natural, there is a familiar argument

[2] For Moore's worries about what he means, see 'A Reply to My Critics', in P. A. Schilpp, ed., *The Philosophy of G. E. Moore* (Chicago, Ill.: Northwestern University Press, 1942), 533–677, esp. 581–92.
[3] G. E. Moore, *Principia Ethica* (Cambridge: Cambridge University Press, 1929), 9.

(though I do not know who first advanced it) that shows that (S) has the consequence that any claim about how things are ethically is equivalent to some claim about how things are frameable in purely descriptive terms.

Let E be a sentence about ethical nature in the following sense: (a) E is framed in ethical terms and descriptive terms; (b) every world at which E is true has some ethical nature; and (c) for all w and w^*, if E is true at w and false at w^*, then w and w^* differ ethically. Intuitively, the idea is that E counts as being about ethical nature by virtue of the fact that there must be some ethical nature for it to be true, together with the fact that the only way to change its truth-value is by changing ethical nature; the worlds must, that is, differ somehow in the distribution of ethical properties and relations.[4] Now each world at which E is true will have some descriptive nature: ethical nature without descriptive nature is impossible (an evil act, for example, must involve death or pain or . . .). And, for each such world, there will be a sentence containing only descriptive terms that gives that nature in full. Now let w_1, w_2, etc. be the worlds where E is true, and let D_1, D_2, etc. be purely descriptive sentences true at w_1, w_2, etc., respectively, which give the full descriptive nature of w_1, w_2, etc. Then the disjunction of D_1, D_2, etc., will also be a purely descriptive sentence, call it D. But then E entails and is entailed by D. For every world where E is true is a world where one or other of the D_i is true, so E entails D. Moreover, every world where one or other of the D_i are true is a world where E is true, as otherwise we would have a violation of (S): we would have descriptively exactly alike worlds differing in ethical nature. Therefore, D entails E. The same line of argument can be applied *mutatis mutandis* to ethical and descriptive predicates and open sentences: for any ethical predicate there is a purely descriptive one that is necessarily co-extensive with it.

It follows that ethical properties are descriptive properties. For it is a consequence of the way the ethical supervenes on the descriptive that any claim about how things are made in ethical vocabulary makes no distinctions among the possibilities that cannot in principle be made in purely descriptive vocabulary. The result is stronger than the one we obtained for the relation between the physical

account of our world and the psychological account of our world under the assumption of physicalism in Chapter 1. [Omitted here. Eds.] Even if physicalism is true, psychological vocabulary marks distinctions among the possibilities that cannot be marked in physical vocabulary. There are similarities between our world on the physicalists' conception of what our world is like, and the world according to Descartes, that cannot be captured in physical terms; and, of course, the point is even more marked for worlds that are quite unlike ours – two worlds made of different brands of ectoplasm might have all sorts of psychological similarities that could not be captured in physical terms. By contrast, ethical ways of partitioning the possibilities make no distinctions that are not mirrored in descriptive ways of partitioning them.

To avoid misunderstanding, I should emphasize two points at this stage. First, although for every ethical sentence, there is some equivalent purely descriptive sentence, it does *not* follow that there is no asymmetry between the ethical and descriptive accounts of how things are. A rich account of descriptive nature highly constrains ethical nature, and the full account of descriptive nature constrains ethical nature without remainder. This follows from the supervenience of the ethical on the descriptive. But a rich account of ethical nature leaves open many very different possibilities concerning descriptive nature. Even the full story about the ethical nature of a world w – in the sense of a story such that any world at which it is true is ethically exactly like w – is consistent with indefinitely many different descriptive natures, concerning, say, how certain distant and ethically insignificant electrons are moving. The relation between ethical nature and descriptive nature is in this regard like that between tallness and individual heights: 'x is tall' is logically equivalent to some sentence about individual heights, but it is a hugely (and infinitely) disjunctive sentence about individual heights that it is equivalent to. Facts about individual heights typically highly constrain facts about who is tall, but not conversely, as we observed in the first chapter.

Secondly, it does not follow from the equivalence between E and D that ethical vocabulary is dispensable in practice. The disjunctive descriptive story D that is equivalent to the ethical story E may be an

---

[4] We thus rule out a sentence like 'There have been at least one hundred evil acts or tea-drinking is common'. Some worlds at which this sentence has different truth-values differ only in how common tea-drinking is.

infinite disjunction we need ethical terms to handle. Consider the infinity of ways of having one's hair distributed that can make up being bald. You can impart the concept of baldness by exhibiting examples – perhaps by pointing to one or another of one's acquaintances, or holding up photographs – but you cannot capture the feature that we pick out with the word 'bald' solely in terms of the language of hair distribution. You have at some stage to say that to be bald is to be *like* these exemplars in the 'bald' way, hoping that one's hearers have latched onto the relevant similarity and can go on in the right way. All the same, it does not follow that baldness is anything more than the relevant infinite disjunction of hair distributions. Moreover, we do not gain the mastery of the term 'bald' that we manifestly have by magic: there must be a similarity among the hair distributions – not a relation to some further property (what baldness 'really' is) – that we finite beings latch onto. Likewise, ethical language may be needed in practice to capture the similarities among the various descriptive ways that (S) tells us constitute ethical nature, but ethical properties are, nevertheless, possibly infinitely disjunctive descriptive properties – there is nothing more 'there' other than the relevant similarities among those descriptive ways. There is no 'extra' feature that the ethical terms are fastening onto, and we could in principle say it all in descriptive language (counting talk of similarities, including similarities made salient through a relation to we who use the ethical terms, as descriptive, of course).

Many, but Simon Blackburn in particular, have properly demanded an explanation of the supervenience of the ethical on the descriptive.[5] The answer, it seems to me, is given by the a priori nature of the supervenience: it tells us that it is part of our very understanding of ethical vocabulary that we use it to mark distinctions among the descriptive ways things are. If someone asks: Why does baldness supervene on hair distribution? the answer is that the a priori nature of the supervenience tells us that the explanation is that 'bald' *is* a word for marking a distinction among kinds of hair distributions. I think we should say the same for the ethical vocabulary: it is an implicit part (if it were explicit, the matter would not be philosophically controversial) of our understanding of ethical terms and sentences that they serve to mark distinctions among the descriptive ways things are.

The Objection from the Possibility of Logically Equivalent Predicates Picking Out Distinct Properties

I now digress to consider an objection that turns on the possibility of logically equivalent predicates picking out different properties. As we noted in Chapter 1, some hold that the property of being an equilateral triangle and the property of being an equiangular triangle are distinct properties, despite the logical equivalence of '*x* is an equiangular triangle' and '*x* is an equilateral triangle'. They argue, for example, from the fact that we can think that a triangle is equilateral but fail to think that it is equiangular that they are distinct properties. Thus, it might be objected that the equivalence of the ethical and descriptive sentences and terms we derived from (S) leaves open the possibility that ethical properties and descriptive properties are related in something like the way that being an equiangular triangle and being an equilateral one are: they are necessarily co-extensive but distinct all the same.

However, on the conception of property we are working with – the conception of a way things might be, an aspect of the world, not an aspect of our discourse or thought about it – we should insist that we have here one property and not two. Cases where we think that a triangle is equiangular while failing to think that it is equilateral are ones where we have a separation in modes of representation in thought for that is, all the same, one and the same property in our sense of 'property'. We have two ways of singling out or representing to ourselves what is one and the same potential feature of reality.

A different argument sometimes offered for distinguishing being an equilateral triangle from being an equiangular one is that we could design a machine to detect whether something is an equilateral triangle without designing it to detect whether it is an equiangular one. And in such a case could not, it is argued, the flashing of a light on the machine be causally explained by an object's being an equilateral triangle but not by its being an

[5]   See e.g. Simon Blackburn, 'Supervenience Revisited', in Ian Hacking, ed., *Exercises in Analysis: Essays by Students of Casimir Lewy* (Cambridge: Cambridge University Press, 1985) [Included in this volume as chapter 33].

equiangular triangle?[6] Here, it seems, we have reason to make a distinction *in re* between being an equilateral triangle and being an equiangular one, not just a distinction between our ways of representing how things are *in re*, for we have a difference in explanatory role with respect to what happens.

However, when we consider the detail of how such a machine might operate, the force of the example evaporates. The machine, we may suppose, takes triangles and in turn measures their sides, determines whether they are all equal, and if they are, trips a circuit that leads to the light's flashing. It is plausible in this kind of case that a triangle's being equilateral explains the light's flashing, but the triangle's being equiangular does not. After all, the machine never even gets to measure the angles, so how could the angles' all being equal be what does the explaining? But the force of the example derives from the fact that we have a segmented process, one part of which especially involves the sides rather than the angles. The reason it is correct, or anyway more intuitive, to explain the light's flashing in terms of the triangle's being equilateral is that sides play a causal role along the way to the light's flashing that angles do not. But this only bears on the common ground doctrine that sides are distinct from angles. It is irrelevant to the issue about whether being an equilateral triangle is distinct from being an equiangular triangle.

This argument is essentially negative. I have explained why I find a certain alleged example of distinct but necessarily co-extensive properties unconvincing. Let me now add some positive considerations against holding that ethical properties are distinct from, though necessarily co-extensive with, descriptive properties.

First, it is hard to see how we could ever be justified in interpreting a language user's use of, say, 'right' as picking out a property distinct from that which the relevant purely descriptive predicates pick out, for we know that the complete story about how and when the language user produces the word 'right' can be given descriptively.

Secondly, it is hard to see how the further properties could be of any ethical significance. Are we supposed to take seriously someone who says, 'I see

that this action will kill many and save no-one, but that is not enough to justify my not doing it; what really matters is that the action has an extra property that only ethical terms are suited to pick out'? In short, the extra properties would be ethical 'idlers'.

And, finally, we can distinguish a more and a less extreme view. The extreme view says that for every (contingent) descriptive way there is, there is a quite distinct, necessarily co-extensive non-descriptive – ethical as it might be – way there is. This extreme version is hard to take seriously. It seems an absurdly anti-Occamist multiplication of properties: for *every* descriptive property, we have a corresponding non-descriptive one! But if the idea is that the duplication only happens occasionally, where is the principled basis for saying when it happens and when it does not? What is special about the descriptive properties that have twins from those that do not? It is hard to give a non-arbitrary answer to this question. What is more, it is hard to see how we could be assured that the twinning occurs when and only when we use ethical terms. Even if twinning does sometimes occur, how could we be confident that our use of ethical language coincides with those occasions?

Arguing from Supervenience versus Arguing from Metaphysical Fantasy

It might be wondered why I bother to argue from the supervenience thesis, (S), to the conclusion that cognitivists must identify ethical properties with descriptive ones. Can't we reject Moore's style of cognitivism as a metaphysical fantasy, as Allan Gibbard, A. J. Ayer, and Gilbert Harman, for instance, do?[7] However, what is plausible as a thesis in metaphysics concerns the kinds of properties that are *instantiated*. It is plausible that the kinds of things we morally evaluate lack any non-natural properties in Moore's sense: given that we know about what our world is like, it is hard to believe that there are instantiated properties that, as a

[6]   The example is a variant on one discussed in Elliott Sober, 'Why Logically Equivalent Properties May Pick Out Different Properties', *American Philosophical Quarterly*, 19 (1982); 183–90.

[7]   A. J. Ayer, 'On the Analysis of Moral Judgements', repr. in *Philosophical Essays* (London: Macmillan, 1959), 231–49, see 235; Allan Gibbard, *Wise Choices, Apt Feelings* (Cambridge, MA: Harvard University Press, 1990); and Gilbert Harman, *The Nature of Morality* (New York: Oxford University Press, 1977).

matter of principle, cannot be ascribed by descriptive language. Indeed, many will go further and insist if ethical properties are to be instantiated, we had better identify them with *physical* properties.[8] *Realists* – that is, cognitivists who take the extra step of holding that the ethical properties are instantiated, that the relevant truth-apt sentences are on occasion true – cannot identify ethical properties with Moorean non-natural properties. The importance of the argument from supervenience is that it shows that cognitivists should identify ethical properties with descriptive ones independently of their metaphysical views about what things are like, and, in particular, independently of whether they hold that the ethical properties are in fact possessed by anything.

This means that there is a further important difference between the supervenience of the psychological on the physical and the supervenience of the ethical on the descriptive. You could have no good reason to accept the supervenience of the psychological on the physical unless you held certain metaphysical views. The supervenience of the ethical on the descriptive is, by contrast, *prior* to metaphysics. It tells us what the possibilities are for the kinds of properties ethical properties might be – for, that is, the kinds of ways things might be marked out by ethical language – and leaves it as a further question whether the properties in question are in fact instantiated.

---

[8] See. e.g. Gibbard, *Wise Choices, Apt Feelings*, 123.

II.7 Semantic Puzzles

Introduction

As with so many areas in contemporary Anglo-American philosophy, contemporary metaethics is driven by puzzles in the philosophy of language and logic. This section concerns three such puzzles that have received a great deal of attention from moral philosophers. The first puzzle is one for moral naturalists. It asks how, given the nature of moral concepts, such concepts and the properties for which they stand could be in any substantive sense naturalistic. The second puzzle is addressed to expressivists. It asks how, if moral discourse is non-assertoric, moral sentences could figure in ordinary truth-functional contexts such as valid arguments. The third puzzle is also directed toward moral naturalists. It asks how, given that the meaning of moral terms is causally regulated by natural properties, could we account for genuine moral disagreement. What follows is a brief treatment of the main issues these puzzles raise.

The Open Question Argument

Over one hundred years ago, G. E. Moore launched an assault on moral naturalism whose central component is "the Open Question Argument." For present purposes, we can divide this argument into two stages.

The first stage purports to establish that moral concepts are not naturalistic. For consider a moral concept M such as 'being good' or 'being just.' Now consider a naturalistic concept such as 'being desired' or 'being approved by a given society.' We can now ask: is M identical in sense with N? Moore thought that we have better reason than not to believe the two types of concept could not be identical in sense, for if M were identical in sense with N, then it would not be possible coherently to claim that something satisfies M but not N. But it is possible coherently to claim that something satisfies M but not N. For example, there is no incoherence involved if Fred agrees that giving to the poor is just, but denies that it is approved by a given society. It is thus an "open question" as to whether these two expressions are identical in meaning. Now, of course, adducing examples of this kind doesn't imply that there is no moral concept M that is identical with some natural concept N. But given the fact that all the naturalistic candidates offered fail to be identical in sense with moral ones, we have better reason than not to believe there is no moral concept that is identical in sense with a naturalistic concept.

So, the first stage of the Open Question Argument endeavors to establish nonnaturalism with respect to moral concepts. The second stage of the argument is concerned to argue for nonnaturalism with respect to moral properties. In this second stage, Moore (according to the standard interpretation) tacitly accepts what is sometimes called "the synonymy criterion for property identity," which tells us that two property-candidates are identical only if the concepts that pick them out are identical in sense. But since the first stage of the Open Question Argument tells us that moral and naturalistic concepts are not identical in sense, it follows that moral properties are not identical with natural ones.

It is difficult to exaggerate the influence the Open Question Argument has exerted in the debates in ethical theory since the publication of Moore's *Principia Ethica*. In effect, it has shaped the three-party debate among expressivists, naturalists, and nonnaturalists for the last hundred years.

Expressivists have ordinarily taken the first stage of Moore's argument to be compelling; they agree that moral concepts are not naturalistic. In this sense, there is significant commonality between nonnaturalist realists and expressivists. But expressivists have typically also wanted to fit moral thought and practice into a world described naturalistically, for they have claimed that the ontological price tag of accepting moral nonnaturalism is far too high. In this sense, there is significant commonality between naturalist realists and expressivists. Accordingly, rather than say that the first stage of Moore's argument supports moral nonnaturalism, expressivists claim that it supports expressivism. Given that we have good reason not to accept both nonnaturalism and naturalism about moral features, it's best, say the expressivists, to think of moral discourse as not even being in the business of purporting to refer to moral features. Rather, expressivists claim, we should view moral discourse as discourse wherein agents purport to express attitudes of condemnation, praise, approval, and the like toward nonmoral reality. (For more on this view, see part I.2, "Expressivism.")

Far less impressed by Moore's argument, naturalistic realists have objected to both its stages. Against the argument's first stage, some naturalists have urged that, contrary to what Moore seems to assume, the meaning of moral concepts may not be transparent even to those competent with them. It may take substantial effort on our part, then, to capture accurately the sense of concepts such as 'being just' or 'being good' even for competent users of these concepts. And, for all we reasonably believe, once the effort has been expended, we will discover that moral and naturalistic concepts are identical. Indeed, some naturalists have urged, it is possible that the first stage of the Open Question Argument establishes not that moral and naturalistic concepts fail to be identical in sense, but that our moral concepts are unusually opaque. If this were true, the task is to clarify moral thought to the degree to which we can agree on the meaning of moral concepts. And, for all we reasonably believe, this might require identifying moral with naturalistic concepts of a certain kind.

Against the argument's second stage, naturalists have pointed out that the key assumption upon which it rests, namely, the synonymy criterion of property identity, is false. After all, we have plenty of examples in which distinct concepts stand for the same thing – 'being water' and 'being H_2O' being among the favorite examples cited by philosophers. Years ago, competent users of these concepts could have coherently disagreed with the claim that water is H_2O. If so, the two concepts are not identical in sense. And yet science has revealed to us that water and H_2O are the same stuff. If this is right, there is conceptual space for a view that accepts the argument's first stage but rejects its second. So, even if our moral concepts are not identical in sense with naturalistic ones, moral properties may be natural. Indeed, the process of ascertaining whether moral features are natural might be like the process of discovering that water is H_2O – an empirical one driven by our best science.

Needless to say, contemporary nonnaturalists are ordinarily sympathetic with Moore's argument, claiming that even if it isn't correct in every detail, it points us to an important truth about the moral realm, namely, that any attempt to identify moral features with naturalistic ones faces significant difficulties. Somewhat more precisely, nonnaturalists have been inclined to accept the first stage of Moore's argument: at the very least, these philosophers claim, we have a presumptive case that moral and naturalistic concepts are not identical. And, as for the second stage, nonnaturalists have emphasized that, when it comes to naturalistic concepts such as 'being water,' it is best to view these concepts as picking out something – usually a natural kind – that plays a certain range of causal explanatory roles. (Philosophers use the term "natural kind" to stand for a kind of thing the instances of which play genuine explanatory roles in the sciences.) The concept of 'being heat,' for example, stands for whatever it is that produces certain kinds of sensations in us, that explains why wax melts when placed near fire, and so forth. In this sense, the concept is fairly superficial; modern science is needed to tell us what exactly it is that plays these causal explanatory roles.

But moral concepts, nonnaturalists have urged, are not plausibly viewed as standing for natural kinds. If moral features were natural, philosophers such as Frank Jackson have argued, they would probably be radically disjunctive in nature, and natural kinds are presumably not disjunctive in this way. (For Jackson's view, see chapter 34 in this volume.) Moreover, moral concepts do not seem superficial in the way that natural kind concepts are. They don't seem, at least at first glance, to be the sort of thing whose aim it is to pick out something that plays a certain range of causal explanatory roles. According to nonnaturalists, when a person tells another that an act is wrong, she does not merely intend to refer to whatever property it is that explains why someone was harmed or caused someone to be convicted of a crime. Rather, she intends to refer to a feature of an act that indicates that we *should* disapprove of it, should do our best to prevent it from happening again, and so on. If this is right, the nature of moral concepts provides us with good reason to believe that the entities for which they stand are not naturalistic.

The Frege–Geach Problem

The second puzzle with which this section is concerned – the so-called Frege–Geach problem – has not shaped the contemporary discussion in metaethics in the way that Moore's open-question argument has. Still, this puzzle (or family of puzzles) has been at the forefront of the debate between expressivists and their rivals. Given the attention the puzzle has received, both expressivists and their rivals view it as the most pressing challenge for expressivist positions to address.

The Frege–Geach challenge was first articulated by Peter Geach some forty years ago in a pair of seminal articles (see Geach 1960 and 1965). In its initial form, the challenge begins by noting that moral sentences figure in what appear to be valid argument schemata. For example, consider the following case of modus ponens:

If Jones stole Brown's Ford, then Jones should apologize to Brown.

Jones stole Brown's Ford.

So, Jones should apologize to Brown.

Those who hold that moral sentences express moral propositions have no difficulty maintaining that this argument is valid. It is valid for the same reason that any instance of modus ponens is valid: it is impossible for its premises to be true and its conclusion false. Fundamental to this cognitivist position is the following pair of assumptions: first, that an argument is an ordered set of sentences with truth-values and, second, that the sentences that constitute the above argument have truth-values. But, according to classical expressivists at least, moral sentences do not have truth-values. So, contrary to appearances, expressivists of this sort appear forced to deny that the sequence of sentences stated above is a valid argument, because it is not even an argument in the first place.

The expressivist response to this initial formulation of the challenge, developed over the last twenty years primarily by Simon Blackburn and Allan Gibbard, has been to work out an expressivistic logic, or a "logic of attitudes," that mimics traditional truth-functional logic. (For Blackburn's position, see the essay of his included in this section.) According to its advocates, an expressivistic logic is not a variant of ordinary truth-functional logic but is, for all intents and purposes, just as good. Philosophers who develop this response agree that it is implausible simply to claim that moral sentences do not figure in anything like valid argument schemata; expressivism, after all, is supposed to save the appearances of ordinary moral thought and practice as best as possible. Moreover, philosophers such as Blackburn and Gibbard agree that simply claiming that the sentences that figure in the argument stated above are truth-apt in some deflationary sense of "true" is also an unsatisfactory response to the Frege–Geach problem. As James Dreier points out, simply stipulating that a given expression is truth-apt in some deflationary sense does not ensure that that expression makes sense or is amenable to logical operations such as negation, combination, and the like (see Dreier 1996). (For more on deflationary views of truth, see the introduction to part I.2, "Expressivism.") To use Dreier's example, suppose we invent the predicate "hiyo" and use it in such a way as to *accost* people. Accordingly, rather than yell "Hey Bob!" to accost

Bob, we utter "Bob is hiyo." However, even though a sentence such as "Bob is hiyo" looks and behaves like an ordinary truth-apt sentence, *what* the sentence expresses – an accosting – does not appear to be amenable to anything like ordinary truth-functional operations. We simply don't know how to understand a conditional such as "If Bob is hiyo, then Jones stole Brown's Ford." If this is right – as Walter Sinnott-Armstrong emphasizes in his contribution to this section – then an expressivist logic of attitudes must ensure that the content of moral sentences does not function like the content of sentences that express accostings and, thus, that it makes sense to subject them to something like ordinary truth-functional logical operations.

Expressivist attempts to develop a logic of attitudes tend to be quite technical, requiring competence with sophisticated strategies in philosophical logic. Although the details of these attempts vary, they have been met by a common response from critics, which can be stated as a dilemma: if, on the one hand, moral sentences function as expressivists say and do not express moral propositions, but attitudes, then an expressivist logic does not sufficiently mimic ordinary truth-functional logic. If, on the other hand, an expressivist logic does sufficiently mimic ordinary truth-functional logic, then it is not a genuinely expressivist view, for it fails to explain on expressivist grounds why moral sentences behave like ordinary assertions. To see in a little more detail how this dilemma plays out, consider (in a considerably simplified form) the expressivist position offered by Allan Gibbard in his book *Thinking How to Live*.[1]

Gibbard proposes that, at the outset of inquiry at least, we maintain that "ought judgments" do not express moral propositions, but decisions or action-plans. Plans are determinations of what to do. As such, they can be combined with factual content. So, for example, we can say that the plan to apologize to Smith can be combined with the belief that Smith is not dead. Assume, further, that we assume that combinations of plans and factual content – call them "factual-practical worlds" – are the objects of acceptance and rejection. (Gibbard takes such worlds to be "maximally complete," like ordinary possible worlds.) Now consider the following argument:

> Either Jones ought to apologize to Brown for having wrecked his Ford, or Jones ought to repay Brown for having wrecked his Ford.

> It is not the case that Jones ought to apologize to Brown for having wrecked his Ford.

> So, Jones ought to repay Brown for having wrecked his Ford.

According to Gibbard, we can make sense of why this argument is valid – in a perfectly respectable use of this term – even though its component sentences express not moral propositions but plans. Accepting the first sentence is a matter of ruling out every factual-practical world in which Jones neither plans to apologize to Brown for having wrecked his Ford, nor to repay Brown for having wrecked his Ford. Accepting the second sentence is tantamount to rejecting or ruling out every factual-practical world in which Jones plans to apologize to Brown for having wrecked his Ford. But were we to accept the ruling out of all the worlds of these kinds, the only worlds left to accept would be those in which Jones plans to repay Brown. There is, then, no factual-practical world that is allowed by all its premises, but not its conclusion.

Two features of this way of developing an expressivist logic are attractive. First, this strategy is not ad hoc. According to Gibbard, we can explain any inference – whether the content of that inference be factual-practical worlds or ordinary propositions – by way of maneuvers such as ruling out and allowing. Second, it is plausible to believe that plans are not like accostings, for we can agree and disagree with them over time. If this is right, factual-practical worlds appear amenable to something like truth-functional operations, and Gibbard's proposal avoids the worries raised by Dreier, which we canvassed above.

Still, there are worries about Gibbard's strategy. Here is one: fundamental to Gibbard's attempt to fashion a logic of attitudes is to appeal only to factual-practical worlds and the allowing or the ruling out thereof. Put differently, the goal is to explain inferences such as those made in the argument just stated by appeal only to mental states (planning states) and the allowing or the rejection of such states. (Gibbard maintains that we can talk of the objects of operations such as ruling out and allowing as being either worlds or mental states.) But, as Nicholas Unwin has urged, an expressivist must be able to account for two different ways in which one can fail to accept a plan: one can either flat out reject a plan or withhold accepting or rejecting it.[2] (As a comparison, think of the different attitudes that atheists and agnostics have toward the proposition *that God exists*. The atheist flat out rejects the proposition, while the agnostic withholds assent from it.) So, take the plan "I plan to apologize to Brown." One can fail to accept this plan by accepting either:

(a) I plan not to apologize to Brown

or

(b) It is not the case that I plan to apologize to Brown.

To accept the content of (a) is simply to reject a plan, namely, to apologize to Brown. Not so for (b), however. To accept the content of (b) is not necessarily to reject a plan. Rather, it is in some sense (at least in a wide range of cases) not to commit to a plan. Gibbard's view offers us a straightforward account of what it is to accept the content of (a). But how should we understand what it is to accept the content of (b)?

There are two ways to understand the acceptance of the content of (b). According to one understanding, to accept (b) is to accept the negation of a plan (or, more accurately, some combination of such plans). In this case, plan-negations are taken as primitives. However, if this is Gibbard's claim, then we do not have an expressivist explanation of claims such as those expressed in (b). For fundamental to the expressivist project is to "explain negation by explaining the state of mind of accepting a negation" (Gibbard 2003: 72). But to take plan-negations as a primitive in one's theory is not to explain them at all.

According to the second understanding, to accept the content of (b) is to disagree in some sense with a planning state, viz., to apologize to Brown. So, suppose we distinguish two types of negative attitude we can have toward planning states or factual-practical worlds: rejection and disagreement. Rejecting a planning state is what I do when I accept the content of (a). Disagreeing with a planning state is what I do when I accept the content of (b). In this case, we explain the difference between what it is to accept the content of (a), on the one hand, and the content of (b), on the other, by appealing to different types of negative attitude.

If this is Gibbard's view, the worry is that it is unclear that we really have an explanation of what it is to accept the content of (b). Simply helping ourselves to the supposition that to accept the content of (b) is at bottom to disagree with a plan does not appear to shed much light on the phenomenon of plan-negation. (We need to know more, for example, about what distinguishes rejection from disagreement and how these two attitudes are logically related to one another.) That this is so gains some support from reflecting on the case of the agnostic once again. Distinctive of the agnostic's attitude toward the proposition *that God exists* is that he withholds assent from it. If we are to characterize the agnostic's attitude in terms of disagreement with plans, then presumably we should say that his attitude consists in accepting both (i) that it is not the case that he plans to accept that God exists and (ii) that it is not the case that he plans to accept that God does not exist. He is indecisive on the matter. Suppose, then, we understand disagreement to be a species of indecision. If so, then my disagreeing with the plan to apologize to Brown is presumably not simply a matter of accepting the content of (b). Rather, it is a matter of accepting both (i) that it is not the case that I plan to apologize to Brown and (ii) that it is not the case that I plan not to apologize to Brown. But now it appears that disagreement has not been explicated in a genuinely expressivist fashion. After all, according to the present proposal, disagreeing with a plan involves accepting the negations of plans, and the negation of a plan is precisely the concept we are trying to explain.

Assuming that this is genuinely a problem, why has it arisen? Well, recall that the expressivist's project is to develop an alternate logic that functions pretty much like ordinary logic. Ordinary logic is, however, bivalent; the propositions that figure in argument forms such as modus ponens are only either true or false. Accordingly, to negate a proposition is either to represent that proposition as being false (e.g., not-p) or true (e.g., not-not-p, which is identical in truth value to "p"). In this sense, negation is, according to ordinary logic, an "on-off," two-valued logical operation: when applied to a proposition, it can represent that proposition as only being either true or false. However, at the heart of the expressivist project is the attempt to explicate logical notions such as negation entirely in terms of mental attitudes such as "ruling out" and disagreement. But attitudes such as these, as we have seen, can take various forms. To disagree with the plan to apologize to Brown (where disagreement is understood broadly), for example, might be to accept the content of (a) or (b). And to accept one of these contents can be totally to reject it, to be undecided about it, or to be indifferent to it. Disagreement, as we might put it, is a more-than-two-valued phenomenon. This raises the suspicion that attempts to solve the Frege–Geach problem encounter problems (in part) because they attempt to explicate logical operations such as negation (with respect to normative thought at least), which are two-valued, in terms of concepts such as disagreement, which are not. (Granted, this worry might dissolve were normative thought not bivalent.) At any rate, it appears that the challenge remains of how to understand what it is to accept a claim such as that expressed in (b) in a way that is both consistent with expressivism and also ensures that such claims can figure in the types of inference we make in something like ordinary truth-functional logic.

Moral Twin Earth

While the first two puzzles we've considered have occupied the attention of moral philosophers for some time, our third puzzle is of relatively recent origin. First introduced into the literature in a series of papers by Terence Horgan and Mark Timmons (one of which is included in this section), this challenge is directed toward naturalist versions of moral realism and borrows from so-called Twin Earth thought experiments made popular by Hilary Putnam in the mid-1970s.

According to Putnam's original thought experiment, we are to imagine a place – so-called Twin Earth – in which there is a clear, odorless, potable liquid that behaves just like what we earthlings call "water." In fact, the people on Twin Earth use the term we use – viz., "water" – to talk about this very stuff. The difference between earth and Twin Earth, however, is that the stuff we call "water" is H_2O and the stuff they call "water" is XYZ. On the assumption that we can refer to these different liquids, it follows that earthlings and Twin-earthlings refer to different things with the use of the term "water." But if this is true, Putnam asked, does our term "water" nonetheless mean the same as theirs?

Not according to Putnam. For imagine an earthling who knows that his use of the term "water" refers to H_2O and a Twin-earthling who knows that his use of the term "water" refers to XYZ. Now imagine that a Twin-earthling travels to earth.

While on earth, the earthling and the Twin-earthling visit Niagara Falls. The earthling points to the wet, cold stuff cascading through the air and shouts "This is water!" The Twin-earthling responds by shaking his head, pointing to the same stuff and replying "That is not water." Is there a genuine disagreement between the earthling and the Twin-earthling? Putnam suggests not. The earthling and the Twin-earthling are talking past one another. What explains the fact that there is no disagreement in this case, however? Putnam contends that what explains it is that a so-called referential theory of meaning is true: the meaning of our term "water" is determined by the stuff that it designates, viz., H_2O and the meaning of the Twin-earthling's term "water" is determined by the stuff that it designates, viz., XYZ. If this is so, then the meaning of a natural kind term such as "water" is determined by the stuff that it designates at a given world. (Because the term "water" designates H_2O and H_2O plays explanatory roles in the sciences, "water" is a natural kind term.) In fact, suggests Putnam, our term "water" is what Saul Kripke has dubbed a "rigid designator": it designates H_2O at our world and, if it is used by us to designate anything at any other world, it designates something at that world if and only if it designates H_2O at that world.

Many philosophers have found Putnam's views about the meaning of natural kind terms congenial. The core intuition behind the Moral Twin Earth objection to naturalist versions of moral realism is that Putnam's widely accepted views about the way in which natural kind terms function spell trouble for naturalistic forms of moral realism, such as those defended by Peter Railton, Richard Boyd, Nicholas Sturgeon, and others. (For Railton's and Boyd's positions, see chapters 13 and 14; for Sturgeon's view, see chapter 26.)

In its contemporary forms, moral naturalism is typically committed to two theses – one concerning moral ontology, the other concerning the semantics of moral terms. The naturalist's ontological thesis is that moral properties are (or are constituted by) natural features. The naturalist's semantic thesis is that moral terms function in a way very similar to natural kind terms such as "water." This implies that moral terms are not definite descriptions, but are rigid designators of natural properties of a certain type. According to this view, then, when we refer to the property of, say, *being right* (i.e., *being morally obligatory*), we thereby refer to a natural property N. But we do not do so by the predicative use of a descriptive phrase such as "that property that J. S. Mill believed to consist in the maximization of happiness." Rather, we do so by the predicative use of a term (in the paradigmatic case) whose use is in some way appropriately causally hooked up with or "causally regulated" by the property N. (Think about "water" as a comparison: this term refers to H_2O because our use of it bears some sort of appropriate causal connection with H_2O.) This implies that the term "rightness" is also a rigid designator: genuinely referential use of the term in our world designates N and, if it is used by us to designate anything at any other world, it designates something at that world if and only if it designates N at that world.

According to the challenge we are now considering, these two commitments of moral naturalism generate the following problem: consider two places – earth and a place we can call "Moral Twin Earth." Suppose, for argument's sake, that on earth consequentialism is true. For earthlings, the property of *being right* just is the property of *being such as to maximize happiness*. If moral naturalism is true, then, on earth our use of the term "right" is causally regulated by the natural property N, which by hypothesis is the property of *being such as to maximize happiness*. Suppose, however, that Moral Twin Earth is such that a so-called "ideal observer" position is true. At Moral Twin Earth, the property of being right just is the property of *being approved by a community of rational agents*. If moral naturalism is true, then the Twin-earthlings' use of the term "right" at this world is causally regulated by some other natural property N*, which by hypothesis is the property of *being approved by a community of rational agents*. (Let's assume these properties are not even extensionally equivalent.)

Imagine, now, that an earthling were to claim that giving a quarter of one's income to the needy is right, since doing so maximizes happiness. Imagine, also, that a Twin-earthling were to claim that it's false that giving a quarter of one's income is right, since, by hypothesis, doing so would not be approved by a community of rational agents. Is there a disagreement between the earthling and the Twin-earthling? We have strong intuitions that the answer is "Yes." In this case, the two parties are not simply talking past one another, but are genuinely disagreeing with one another. But if moral naturalism is true, it is difficult to see how this could

be. Since the earthling's use of the term "right" is causally regulated by N and the Twin-earthling's use of the term is causally regulated by N*, their terms mean different things. And, thus, they appear to be talking past one another in much the same way that the earthling and the Twin-earthling talked past one another when discussing whether or not it was water that was cascading over Niagara Falls. If this is right, naturalist moral realism cannot explain why, when there appears to be genuine moral debate and disagreement, the moral debate and disagreement is genuine.

To this challenge one might reply, in a non-conciliatory mode, that the Moral Twin Earth challenge misses the mark. For suppose, on the one hand, that both the earthlings and Twin-earthlings know what causally regulates their respective uses of the term "right." In this case, it is difficult to see why we should think that our intuition that there is genuine moral disagreement between them is accurate. By contrast, suppose, on the other hand, that the earthlings and Twin-earthlings do not know what property causally regulates the respective use of their term "right." In both worlds, it looks as if the term "right" fails to track any unique property – the sorts of thing being labeled "right" comprising a heterogeneous grab-bag of things. In this scenario, the proper response to the question of whether our intuition that there is genuine disagreement is correct appears to be: who knows? Unlike Putnam's case, in this case, it is difficult to ascertain anything about the nature of the thing we're supposed to be disagreeing about. And, accordingly, it is difficult to know whether our inclination to believe that there is genuine moral disagreement between the earthling and the Twin-earthling is reliable.

A more conciliatory response to the argument would be to concede that the Moral Twin Earth scenario exposes a problem not with naturalistic realist views as such, but with certain views about reference defended by moral naturalists. These views about reference – the response continues – can be supplemented and corrected in a way wholly amenable to naturalism. For example, suppose we agree that rightness is a functional property that has a certain functional profile. For example, rightness would have to provide reasons to act, it would have to provide reasons that trump reasons of other sorts, and so forth. Call this the "functional-role profile" of the property of *being right*. Now suppose we call any property that fulfills this functional role a "functional essence" of the property. If consequentialists are right, the functional essence of the property of *being right* is *being such as to maximize happiness*. (A comparison: the functional-role profile of water will include features such as freezing at 32 degrees Fahrenheit, being potable by humans in proper conditions, and so on. Its functional essence is H_2O.)

If we assume that anyone who is sufficiently competent with the concept of rightness grasps important features of the functional-role profile of rightness, then we can agree that, in the scenario described, there really is disagreement between the earthlings and the Twin-earthlings about rightness. The disagreement concerns what the functional

essence of rightness consists in (or perhaps it concerns what should be admitted into its functional role). The earthlings believe it is the property of *being such as to maximize happiness*, while the Twin-earthlings believe it is *being approved by a community of rational agents*. If this is correct, naturalists can agree that genuine moral disagreement is possible in Twin Earth-type scenarios. After all, it may be that, although the earthling's and Twin-earthling's use of the term "right" is causally regulated by different properties, there can be genuine disagreement about whether either of these properties genuinely satisfies the functional-role profile of rightness.

Notes

1   Gibbard indicates (2003: 60 n. 1) that this position shares some important similarities with the one developed by Blackburn in "Attitudes and Contents," which is included in this section.
2   See Unwin (2001) and Gibbard's response in Gibbard

2003: ch. 4. It should be noted that Unwin's article is concerned with Gibbard 1990's view, which is different from the view defended in Gibbard 2003. Gibbard, however, takes the worry to apply to his latest view as well.

Selected Bibliography

The Open Question argument

Ball, Stephen. 1988. "Reductionism in Ethics and Science: A Contemporary Look at G. E. Moore's Open Question Argument." *American Philosophical Quarterly* 25: 197–213.

Brink, David. 1989. *Moral Realism and the Foundations of Ethics*. Cambridge: Cambridge University Press, ch. 6.

Crisp, Roger. 1996. "Naturalism and Non-Naturalism in Ethics." In Sabina Lovibond and S. G. Williams, eds. *Identity, Truth, and Value*. Malden, MA: Blackwell.

Darwall, Stephen, Allan Gibbard, and Peter Railton. 1992. "Toward Fin de Siècle Ethics: Some Trends." *Philosophical Review* 101: 115–89.

Feldman, Fred. "The Open Question Argument: What It Isn't; and What It Is." In Ernest Sosa and Enrique Villanueva, eds. *Philosophical Issues 15: Normativity*. Oxford: Blackwell.

Frankena, William. 1939. "The Naturalistic Fallacy." *Mind* 48: 464–77.

Gampell, Eric. 1996. "A Defense of the Autonomy of Ethics: Why Value Is Not Like Water." *Canadian Journal of Philosophy* 26: 191–201.

Gibbard, Allan. 2003. *Thinking How to Live*. Cambridge, MA: Harvard University Press, ch. 2.

Horgan, Terence, and Mark Timmons, eds. 2006. *Metaethics after Moore*. Oxford: Oxford University Press.

Lewis, David. 1989. "Dispositional Theories of Value." *Proceedings of the Aristotelian Society*, supplementary volume 72: 113–37.

McGinn, Colin. 1997. *Ethics, Evil, and Fiction*. Oxford: Oxford University Press, ch. 2.

Miller, Alexander. 2003. *An Introduction to Contemporary Metaethics*. Cambridge: Polity, chs. 2 and 10.

Parfit, Derek. Unpublished. "Rediscovering Reasons."

Ridge, Michael. 2003. "Moral Non-Naturalism." Available online at <http://plato.stanford.edu/entries/moral-non-naturalism/>.

Rosati, Connie. 1995. "Naturalism, Normativity, and the Open Question Argument." *Noûs* 29: 46–70.

Shafer-Landau, Russ. 2003. *Moral Realism: A Defence*. Oxford: Oxford University Press, ch. 3.

Stratton-Lake, Philip. 2003. "Introduction." In Philip Stratton-Lake, ed. *Ethical Intuitionism*. Oxford: Oxford University Press.

Thomson, Judith Jarvis. 2003. "The Legacy of *Principia*." *The Southern Journal of Philosophy* 41: 62–82.

Wiggins, David. 1993. "A Neglected Position?" In Crispin Wright and John Haldane, eds. *Reality, Representation, and Projection*. Oxford: Oxford University Press.

Interested readers may also want to consult the following two journal volumes dedicated to G. E. Moore's legacy:

Ethics 113 (2003): *Centenary Symposium on G. E. Moore's Principia Ethica*.

The Southern Journal of Philosophy 41 (2003): *The Legacy of G. E. Moore: 100 Years of Metaethics*.

The Frege–Geach problem

Blackburn, Simon. 1984. *Spreading the Word*. Oxford: Oxford University Press, ch. 6.

Blackburn, Simon. 1993a. "Realism: Quasi or Queasy?" In Crispin Wright and John Haldane, eds. *Reality, Representation, and Projection*. Oxford: Oxford University Press.

Blackburn, Simon. 1993b. *Essays in Quasi-Realism*. Oxford: Oxford University Press, chs. 6 and 10.

Blackburn, Simon. 1998. *Ruling Passions*. Oxford: Oxford University Press, ch. 3.

Dreier, James. 1996. "Expressivist Embeddings and Minimalist Truth." *Philosophical Studies* 83: 29–51.

Dreier, James. 1999. "Transforming Expressivism." *Noûs* 33: 558–72.

Dreier, James. 2006. "Negation for Expressivists: A Collection of Problems with a Suggestion for their Solution." In Russ Shafer-Landau, ed. *Oxford Studies in Metaethics* 1. Oxford: Oxford University Press.

Geach, Peter. 1960. "Ascriptivism." *Philosophical Review* 69: 221–5.

Geach, Peter. 1965. "Assertion." *Philosophical Review* 74: 449–65.

Gibbard, Allan. 1990. *Wise Choices, Apt Feelings*. Cambridge, MA: Harvard University Press, ch. 5.

Gibbard, Allan. 2003. *Thinking How to Live*. Cambridge, MA: Harvard University Press, chs. 3–4.

Hale, Bob. 1986. "The Compleat Projectivist." *The Philosophical Quarterly* 36: 65–84.

Hale, Bob. 1993. "Can There Be a Logic of Attitudes?" In Crispin Wright and John Haldane, eds. *Reality, Representation, and Projection*. Oxford: Oxford University Press.

Hale, Bob. 2002. "Can Arboreal Knotwork Help Blackburn out of Frege's Abyss?" *Philosophy and Phenomenological Research* 65: 144–9.

Hare, Richard. 1970. "Meaning and Speech Acts." *Philosophical Review* 79: 3–24.

Hawthorne, John. 2002. "Practical Realism?" *Philosophy and Phenomenological Research* 64: 169–78.

Horwich, Paul. 1994. "The Essence of Expressivism." *Analysis* 54: 19–20.

Kölbel, Max. 2002. *Truth without Objectivity*. London: Routledge, ch. 4.

Miller, Alexander. 2003. *An Introduction to Contemporary Metaethics*. Cambridge: Polity, chs. 3–5.

Searle, John. 1962. "Meaning and Speech Acts." *Philosophical Review* 71: 423–32.

Stoljar, Daniel. 1993. "Emotivism and Truth Conditions." *Philosophical Studies* 70: 81–101.

Unwin, Nicholas. 1999. "Quasi-Realism, Negation and the Frege–Geach Problem." *The Philosophical Quarterly* 49: 337–52.

Unwin, Nicholas. 2001. "Norms and Negation: A Problem for Gibbard's Logic." *The Philosophical Quarterly* 51: 60–75.

Van Roojen, Mark. 1996. "Expressivism and Irrationality." *Philosophical Review* 105: 311–35.

Wedgwood, Ralph. 1997. "Non-Cognitivism, Truth and Logic." *Philosophical Studies* 86: 73–91.

Wright, Crispin. 1988. "Realism, Antirealism, Irrealism, Quasi-Realism." In Peter French, Theodore Uehling, and Howard Wettstein, eds. *Midwest Studies in Philosophy* 12: 25–49.

Zangwill, Nick. 1992. "Moral Modus Ponens." *Ratio* 5: 177–93.

Moral Twin Earth

Bloomfield, Paul. 2003. "The Rules of Goodness: An Essay on Moral Semantics." *American Philosophical Quarterly* 40: 197–213.

Boyd, Richard. 1988. "How To Be a Moral Realist." In Geoffrey Sayre-McCord, ed. *Essays on Moral Realism*. Ithaca: Cornell University Press.

Brink, David. 2001. "Realism, Naturalism, and Moral Semantics." In Ellen Paul, Fred Miller, and Jeffrey Paul, eds. *Moral Knowledge*. Cambridge: Cambridge University Press.

Copp, David. 2000. "Milk, Honey, and the Good Life on Moral Twin Earth." *Synthese* 124: 113–37.

Gampel Eric. 1997. "Ethics, Reference, and Natural Kinds." *Philosophical Papers* 26: 147–63.

Gibbard, Allan. 2003. *Thinking How to Live*. Cambridge, MA: Harvard University Press, ch. 8.

Horgan, Terence, and Mark Timmons. 1991. "New Wave Moral Realism Meets Moral Twin Earth." *Journal of Philosophical Research* 16: 447–65.

Horgan, Terence, and Mark Timmons. 1992a. "Troubles on Moral Twin Earth: Moral Queerness Revived." *Synthese* 92: 221–60.

Horgan, Terence, and Mark Timmons. 1992b. "Troubles for New Wave Moral Semantics: The 'Open Question Argument' Revived." *Philosophical Papers* 21: 153–75.

Horgan, Terence, and Mark Timmons. 2000. "Copping Out on Moral Twin Earth." *Synthese* 124: 139–52.

Laurence, Stephen, Eric Margolis, and Angus Dawson. 1999. "Moral Realism and Twin Earth." *Facta Philosophica* 1: 135–65.

Merli, David. 2002. "Return to Moral Twin Earth." *Canadian Journal of Philosophy* 32: 207–40.

Miller, Alexander. 2003. *An Introduction to Contemporary Metaethics*. Cambridge: Polity, ch. 8.

Sayre-McCord, Geoffrey. 1997. "'Good' on Twin Earth." In Enrique Villanueva, ed. *Philosophical Issues 8: Truth*. Oxford: Blackwell.

Timmons, Mark. 1999. *Morality without Foundations*. Oxford: Oxford University Press, ch. 2.

Van Roojen, Mark. 2006. "A New Response to the Moral Twin Earth Argument." In Russ Shafer-Landau, ed. *Oxford Studies in Metaethics* 1. Oxford: Oxford University Press.

35

The Subject-Matter of Ethics

G. E. Moore

1. It is very easy to point out some among our every-day judgments, with the truth of which Ethics is undoubtedly concerned. Whenever we say, 'So and so is a good man,' or 'That fellow is a villain'; whenever we ask, 'What ought I to do?' or 'Is it wrong for me to do like this?'; whenever we hazard such remarks as 'Temperance is a virtue and drunkenness a vice' – it is undoubtedly the business of Ethics to discuss such questions and such statements; to argue what is the true answer when we ask what it is right to do, and to give reasons for thinking that our statements about the character of persons or the morality of actions are true or false. In the vast majority of cases, where we make statements involving any of the terms 'virtue,' 'vice,' 'duty,' 'right,' 'ought,' 'good,' 'bad,' we are making ethical judgments; and if we wish to discuss their truth, we shall be discussing a point of Ethics.

So much as this is not disputed; but it falls very far short of defining the province of Ethics. That province may indeed be defined as the whole truth about that which is at the same time common to all such judgments and peculiar to them. But we have still to ask the question: What is it that is thus common and peculiar? And this is a question to which very different answers have been given by ethical philosophers of acknowledged reputation, and none of them, perhaps, completely satisfactory.

2. If we take such examples as those given above, we shall not be far wrong in saying that they are all of them concerned with the question of 'conduct' – with the question, what, in the conduct of us, human beings, is good, and what is bad, what is right, and what is wrong. For when we say that a man is good, we commonly mean that he acts rightly; when we say that drunkenness is a vice, we commonly mean that to get drunk is a wrong or wicked action. And this discussion of human conduct is, in fact, that with which the name 'Ethics' is most intimately associated. It is so associated by derivation; and conduct is undoubtedly by far the commonest and most generally interesting object of ethical judgments.

Accordingly, we find that many ethical philosophers are disposed to accept as an adequate definition of 'Ethics' the statement that it deals with the question what is good or bad in human conduct. They hold that its enquiries are properly confined to 'conduct' or to 'practice'; they hold that the name 'practical philosophy' covers all the matter with which it has to do. Now, without discussing the proper meaning of the word (for verbal questions are properly left to the writers of dictionaries and other persons interested in literature; philosophy, as we shall see, has no concern with them), I may say that I intend to use 'Ethics' to cover more than this – a usage, for which there is,

I think, quite sufficient authority. I am using it to cover an enquiry for which, at all events, there is no other word: the general enquiry into what is good.

Ethics is undoubtedly concerned with the question what good conduct is; but, being concerned with this, it obviously does not start at the beginning, unless it is prepared to tell us what is good as well as what is conduct. For 'good conduct' is a complex notion: all conduct is not good; for some is certainly bad and some may be indifferent. And on the other hand, other things, beside conduct, may be good; and if they are so, then, 'good' denotes some property, that is common to them and conduct; and if we examine good conduct alone of all good things, then we shall be in danger of mistaking for this property, some property which is not shared by those other things: and thus we shall have made a mistake about Ethics even in this limited sense; for we shall not know what good conduct really is. This is a mistake which many writers have actually made, from limiting their enquiry to conduct. And hence I shall try to avoid it by considering first what is good in general; hoping, that if we can arrive at any certainty about this, it will be much easier to settle the question of good conduct: for we all know pretty well what 'conduct' is. This, then, is our first question: What is good? and What is bad? and to the discussion of this question (or these questions) I give the name of Ethics, since that science must, at all events, include it.

3.   But this is a question which may have many meanings. If, for example, each of us were to say 'I am doing good now' or 'I had a good dinner yesterday,' these statements would each of them be some sort of answer to our question, although perhaps a false one. So, too, when A asks B what school he ought to send his son to, B's answer will certainly be an ethical judgment. And similarly all distribution of praise or blame to any personage or thing that has existed, now exists, or will exist, does give some answer to the question 'What is good?' In all such cases some particular thing is judged to be good or bad: the question 'What?' is answered by 'This.' But this is not the sense in which a scientific Ethics asks the question. Not one, of all the many million answers of this kind, which must be true, can form a part of an ethical system; although that science must contain reasons and principles sufficient for deciding on the truth of all of them. There are far too many persons, things and events

in the world, past, present, or to come, for a discussion of their individual merits to be embraced in any science. Ethics, therefore, does not deal at all with facts of this nature, facts that are unique, individual, absolutely particular; facts with which such studies as history, geography, astronomy, are compelled, in part at least, to deal. And, for this reason, it is not the business of the ethical philosopher to give personal advice or exhortation.

[. . .]

5.   But our question 'What is good?' may have still another meaning. We may, in the third place, mean to ask, not what thing or things are good, but how 'good' is to be defined. This is an enquiry which belongs only to Ethics, not to Casuistry; and this is the enquiry which will occupy us first.

It is an enquiry to which most special attention should be directed; since this question, how 'good' is to be defined, is the most fundamental question in all Ethics. That which is meant by 'good' is, in fact, except its converse 'bad,' the *only* simple object of thought which is peculiar to Ethics. Its definition is, therefore, the most essential point in the definition of Ethics; and moreover a mistake with regard to it entails a far larger number of erroneous ethical judgments than any other. Unless this first question be fully understood, and its true answer clearly recognised, the rest of Ethics is as good as useless from the point of view of systematic knowledge. True ethical judgments, of the two kinds last dealt with, may indeed be made by those who do not know the answer to this question as well as by those who do; and it goes without saying that the two classes of people may lead equally good lives. But it is extremely unlikely that the *most general* ethical judgments will be equally valid, in the absence of a true answer to this question: I shall presently try to shew that the gravest errors have been largely due to beliefs in a false answer. And, in any case, it is impossible that, till the answer to this question be known, any one should know *what is the evidence* for any ethical judgment whatsoever. But the main object of Ethics, as a systematic science, is to give correct *reasons* for thinking that this or that is good; and, unless this question be answered, such reasons cannot be given. Even, therefore, apart from the fact that a false answer leads to false conclusions, the present enquiry is a most necessary and important part of the science of Ethics.

6.   What, then, is good? How is good to be defined? Now, it may be thought that this is a verbal question. A definition does indeed often mean the expressing of one word's meaning in other words. But this is not the sort of definition I am asking for. Such a definition can never be of ultimate importance in any study except lexicography. If I wanted that kind of definition I should have to consider in the first place how people generally used the word 'good'; but my business is not with its proper usage, as established by custom. I should, indeed, be foolish, if I tried to use it for something which it did not usually denote: if, for instance, I were to announce that, whenever I used the word 'good,' I must be understood to be thinking of that object which is usually denoted by the word 'table.' I shall, therefore, use the word in the sense in which I think it is ordinarily used; but at the same time I am not anxious to discuss whether I am right in thinking that it is so used. My business is solely with that object or idea, which I hold, rightly or wrongly, that the word is generally used to stand for. What I want to discover is the nature of that object or idea, and about this I am extremely anxious to arrive at an agreement.

But, if we understand the question in this sense, my answer to it may seem a very disappointing one. If I am asked 'What is good?' my answer is that good is good, and that is the end of the matter. Or if I am asked 'How is good to be defined?' my answer is that it cannot be defined, and that is all I have to say about it. But disappointing as these answers may appear, they are of the very last importance. To readers who are familiar with philosophic terminology, I can express their importance by saying that they amount to this: That propositions about the good are all of them synthetic and never analytic; and that is plainly no trivial matter. And the same thing may be expressed more popularly, by saying that, if I am right, then nobody can foist upon us such an axiom as that 'Pleasure is the only good' or that 'The good is the desired' on the pretence that this is 'the very meaning of the word.'

7.   Let us, then, consider this position. My point is that 'good' is a simple notion, just as 'yellow' is a simple notion; that, just as you cannot, by any manner of means, explain to any one who does not already know it, what yellow is, so you cannot explain what good is. Definitions of the kind that I was asking for, definitions which describe the real nature of the object or notion denoted by a word, and which do not merely tell us what the word is used to mean, are only possible when the object or notion in question is something complex. You can give a definition of a horse, because a horse has many different properties and qualities, all of which you can enumerate. But when you have enumerated them all, when you have reduced a horse to his simplest terms, then you can no longer define those terms. They are simply something which you think of or perceive, and to any one who cannot think of or perceive them, you can never, by any definition, make their nature known. It may perhaps be objected to this that we are able to describe to others, objects which they have never seen or thought of. We can, for instance, make a man understand what a chimaera is, although he has never heard of one or seen one. You can tell him that it is an animal with a lioness's head and body, with a goat's head growing from the middle of its back, and with a snake in place of a tail. But here the object which you are describing is a complex object; it is entirely composed of parts, with which we are all perfectly familiar – a snake, a goat, a lioness; and we know, too, the manner in which those parts are to be put together, because we know what is meant by the middle of a lioness's back, and where her tail is wont to grow. And so it is with all objects, not previously known, which we are able to define: they are all complex; all composed of parts, which may themselves, in the first instance, be capable of similar definition, but which must in the end be reducible to simplest parts, which can no longer be defined. But yellow and good, we say, are not complex: they are notions of that simple kind, out of which definitions are composed and with which the power of further defining ceases.

8.   When we say, as Webster says, 'The definition of horse is "A hoofed quadruped of the genus Equus,"' we may, in fact, mean three different things. (1) We may mean merely: 'When I say "horse," you are to understand that I am talking about a hoofed quadruped of the genus Equus.' This might be called the arbitrary verbal definition: and I do not mean that good is indefinable in that sense. (2) We may mean, as Webster ought to mean: 'When most English people say "horse," they mean a hoofed quadruped of the genus Equus.' This may be called the verbal definition proper, and I do not say that good is indefinable in this sense either; for it is certainly possible to discover how people use a word: otherwise, we could never have known that

'good' may be translated by 'gut' in German and by 'bon' in French. But (3) we may, when we define horse, mean something much more important. We may mean that a certain object, which we all of us know, is composed in a certain manner: that it has four legs, a head, a heart, a liver, etc., etc., all of them arranged in definite relations to one another. It is in this sense that I deny good to be definable. I say that it is not composed of any parts, which we can substitute for it in our minds when we are thinking of it. We might think just as clearly and correctly about a horse, if we thought of all its parts and their arrangement instead of thinking of the whole: we could, I say, think how a horse differed from a donkey just as well, just as truly, in this way, as now we do, only not so easily; but there is nothing whatsoever which we could so substitute for good; and that is what I mean, when I say that good is indefinable.

9. But I am afraid I have still not removed the chief difficulty which may prevent acceptance of the proposition that good is indefinable. I do not mean to say that *the* good, that which is good, is thus indefinable; if I did think so, I should not be writing on Ethics, for my main object is to help towards discovering that definition. It is just because I think there will be less risk of error in our search for a definition of 'the good,' that I am now insisting that *good* is indefinable. I must try to explain the difference between these two. I suppose it may be granted that 'good' is an adjective. Well 'the good,' 'that which is good,' must therefore be the substantive to which the adjective 'good' will apply: it must be the whole of that to which the adjective will apply, and the adjective must *always* truly apply to it. But if it is that to which the adjective will apply, it must be something different from that adjective itself; and the whole of that something different, whatever it is, will be our definition of *the* good. Now it may be that this something will have other adjectives, beside 'good,' that will apply to it. It may be full of pleasure, for example; it may be intelligent: and if these two adjectives are really part of its definition, then it will certainly be true, that pleasure and intelligence are good. And many people appear to think that, if we say 'Pleasure and intelligence are good,' or if we say 'Only pleasure and intelligence are good,' we are defining 'good.' Well, I cannot deny that propositions of this nature may sometimes be called definitions; I do not know well enough how the word is generally used to decide upon this point. I only wish it to be under-

stood that that is not what I mean when I say there is no possible definition of good, and that I shall not mean this if I use the word again. I do most fully believe that some true proposition of the form 'Intelligence is good and intelligence alone is good' can be found; if none could be found, our definition of *the* good would be impossible. As it is, I believe *the* good to be definable; and yet I still say that good itself is indefinable.

10. 'Good,' then, if we mean by it that quality which we assert to belong to a thing, when we say that the thing is good, is incapable of any definition, in the most important sense of that word. The most important sense of 'definition' is that in which a definition states what are the parts which invariably compose a certain whole; and in this sense 'good' has no definition because it is simple and has no parts. It is one of those innumerable objects of thought which are themselves incapable of definition, because they are the ultimate terms by reference to which whatever *is* capable of definition must be defined. That there must be an indefinite number of such terms is obvious, on reflection; since we cannot define anything except by an analysis, which, when carried as far as it will go, refers us to something, which is simply different from anything else, and which by that ultimate difference explains the peculiarity of the whole which we are defining: for every whole contains some parts which are common to other wholes also. There is, therefore, no intrinsic difficulty in the contention that 'good' denotes a simple and indefinable quality. There are many other instances of such qualities.

Consider yellow, for example. We may try to define it, by describing its physical equivalent; we may state what kind of light-vibrations must stimulate the normal eye, in order that we may perceive it. But a moment's reflection is sufficient to shew that those light-vibrations are not themselves what me mean by yellow. *They* are not what we perceive. Indeed we should never have been able to discover their existence, unless we had first been struck by the patent difference of quality between the different colours. The most we can be entitled to say of those vibrations is that they are what corresponds in space to the yellow which we actually perceive.

Yet a mistake of this simple kind has commonly been made about 'good.' It may be true that all things which are good are *also* something else, just as it is true that all things which are yellow produce a certain kind of vibration in the light. And it is a fact, that Ethics aims at discovering what are those other properties belonging to all things which are good. But far too many philosophers have thought that when they named those other properties they were actually defining good; that these properties, in fact, were simply not 'other,' but absolutely and entirely the same with goodness. This view I propose to call the 'naturalistic fallacy' and of it I shall now endeavour to dispose.

11.   Let us consider what it is such philosophers say. And first it is to be noticed that they do not agree among themselves. They not only say that they are right as to what good is, but they endeavour to prove that other people who say that it is something else, are wrong. One, for instance, will affirm that good is pleasure, another, perhaps, that good is that which is desired; and each of these will argue eagerly to prove that the other is wrong. But how is that possible? One of them says that good is nothing but the object of desire, and at the same time tries to prove that it is not pleasure. But from his first assertion, that good just means the object of desire, one of two things must follow as regards his proof:

(1)   He may be trying to prove that the object of desire is not pleasure. But, if this be all, where is his Ethics? The position he is maintaining is merely a psychological one. Desire is something which occurs in our minds, and pleasure is something else which so occurs; and our would-be ethical philosopher is merely holding that the latter is not the object of the former. But what has that to do with the question in dispute? His opponent held the ethical proposition that pleasure was the good, and although he should prove a million times over the psychological proposition that pleasure is not the object of desire, he is no nearer proving his opponent to be wrong. The position is like this. One man says a triangle is a circle: another replies 'A triangle is a straight line, and I will prove to you that I am right: *for*' (this is the only argument) 'a straight line is not a circle.' 'That is quite true,' the other may reply; 'but nevertheless a triangle is a circle, and you have said nothing whatever to prove the contrary. What is proved is that one of us is wrong, for we agree that a triangle cannot be both a straight line and a circle: but which is wrong, there can be no earthly means of proving, since you define triangle as straight line and I define it as circle.' – Well, that is one alternative which any naturalistic Ethics has to face; if good is *defined* as

something else, it is then impossible either to prove that any other definition is wrong or even to deny such definition.

(2)   The other alternative will scarcely be more welcome. It is that the discussion is after all a verbal one. When A says 'Good means pleasant' and B says 'Good means desired,' they may merely wish to assert that most people have used the word for what is pleasant and for what is desired respectively. And this is quite an interesting subject for discussion: only it is not a whit more an ethical discussion than the last was. Nor do I think that any exponent of naturalistic Ethics would be willing to allow that this was all he meant. They are all so anxious to persuade us that what they call the good is what we really ought to do. 'Do, pray, act so, because the word "good" is generally used to denote actions of this nature': such, on this view, would be the substance of their teaching. And in so far as they tell us how we ought to act, their teaching is truly ethical, as they mean it to be. But how perfectly absurd is the reason they would give for it! 'You are to do this, because most people use a certain word to denote conduct such as this.' 'You are to say the thing which is not, because most people call it lying.' That is an argument just as good! – My dear sirs, what we want to know from you as ethical teachers, is not how people use a word; it is not even, what kind of actions they approve, which the use of this word 'good' may certainly imply: what we want to know is simply what *is* good. We may indeed agree that what most people do think good, is actually so; we shall at all events be glad to know their opinions: but when we say their opinions about what *is* good, we do mean what we say; we do not care whether they call that thing which they mean 'horse' or 'table' or 'chair,' 'gut' or 'bon' or 'ἀγαθός'; we want to know what it is that they so call. When they say 'Pleasure is good,' we cannot believe that they merely mean 'Pleasure is pleasure' and nothing more than that.

12.   Suppose a man says 'I am pleased'; and suppose that is not a lie or a mistake but the truth. Well, if it is true, what does that mean? It means that his mind, a certain definite mind, distinguished by certain definite marks from all others, has at this moment a certain definite feeling called pleasure. 'Pleased' *means* nothing but having pleasure, and though we may be more pleased or less pleased, and even, we may admit for the present, have one or another kind of pleasure; yet in so far as it is pleasure we have, whether there be more or less of it, and whether it be of one kind or another, what we have is one definite thing, absolutely indefinable, some one thing that is the same in all the various degrees and in all the various kinds of it that there may be. We may be able to say how it is related to other things: that, for example, it is in the mind, that it causes desire, that we are conscious of it, etc., etc. We can, I say, describe its relations to other things, but define it we can *not*. And if anybody tried to define pleasure for us as being any other natural object; if anybody were to say, for instance, that pleasure *means* the sensation of red, and were to proceed to deduce from that that pleasure is a colour, we should be entitled to laugh at him and to distrust his future statements about pleasure. Well, that would be the same fallacy which I have called the naturalistic fallacy. That 'pleased' does not mean 'having the sensation of red,' or anything else whatever, does not prevent us from understanding what it does mean. It is enough for us to know that 'pleased' does mean 'having the sensation of pleasure,' and though pleasure is absolutely indefinable, though pleasure is pleasure and nothing else whatever, yet we feel no difficulty in saying that we are pleased. The reason is, of course, that when I say 'I am pleased,' I do *not* mean that 'I am the same thing as 'having pleasure.' And similarly no difficulty need be found in my saying that 'pleasure is good' and yet not meaning that 'pleasure' is the same thing as 'good,' that pleasure *means* good, and that good *means* pleasure. If I were to imagine that when I said 'I am pleased,' I meant that I was exactly the same thing as 'pleased,' I should not indeed call that a naturalistic fallacy, although it would be the same fallacy as I have called naturalistic with reference to Ethics. The reason of this is obvious enough. When a man confuses two natural objects with one another, defining the one by the other, if for instance, he confuses himself, who is one natural object, with 'pleased' or with 'pleasure' which are others, then there is no reason to call the fallacy naturalistic. But if he confuses 'good,' which is not in the same sense a natural object, with any natural object whatever, then there is a reason for calling that a naturalistic fallacy; its being made with regard to 'good' marks it as something quite specific, and this specific mistake deserves a name because it is so common. As for the reasons why good is not to be considered a natural object, they may be reserved for discussion in another place.

But, for the present, it is sufficient to notice this: Even if it were a natural object, that would not alter the nature of the fallacy nor diminish its importance one whit. All that I have said about it would remain quite equally true: only the name which I have called it would not be so appropriate as I think it is. And I do not care about the name: what I do care about is the fallacy. It does not matter what we call it, provided we recognise it when we meet with it. It is to be met with in almost every book on Ethics; and yet it is not recognised: and that is why it is necessary to multiply illustrations of it, and convenient to give it a name. It is a very simple fallacy indeed. When we say that an orange is yellow, we do not think our statement binds us to hold that 'orange' means nothing else than 'yellow,' or that nothing can be yellow but an orange. Supposing the orange is also sweet! Does that bind us to say that the 'sweet' is exactly the same thing as 'yellow,' that 'sweet' must be defined as 'yellow'? And supposing it be recognised that 'yellow' just means 'yellow' and nothing else whatever, does that make it any more difficult to hold that oranges are yellow? Most certainly it does not: on the contrary, it would be absolutely meaningless to say that oranges were yellow, unless yellow did in the end mean just 'yellow' and nothing else whatever – unless it was absolutely indefinable. We should not get any very clear notion about things, which are yellow – we should not get very far with our science, if we were bound to hold that everything which was yellow, *meant* exactly the same thing as yellow. We should find we had to hold that an orange was exactly the same thing as a stool, a piece of paper, a lemon, anything you like. We could prove any number of absurdities; but should we be the nearer to the truth? Why, then, should it be different with 'good'? Why, if good is good and indefinable, should I be held to deny that pleasure is good? Is there any difficulty in holding both to be true at once? On the contrary, there is no meaning in saying that pleasure is good, unless good is something different from pleasure. It is absolutely useless, so far as Ethics is concerned, to prove, as Mr Spencer tries to do, that increase of pleasure coincides with increase of life, unless good *means* something different from either life or pleasure. He might just as well try to prove that an orange is yellow by shewing that it always is wrapped up in paper.

13. In fact, if it is not the case that 'good' denotes something simple and indefinable, only

two alternatives are possible: either it is a complex, a given whole, about the correct analysis of which there may be disagreement; or else it means nothing at all, and there is no such subject as Ethics. In general, however, ethical philosophers have attempted to define good, without recognising what such an attempt must mean. They actually use arguments which involve one or both of the absurdities considered in §11. We are, therefore, justified in concluding that the attempt to define good is chiefly due to want of clearness as to the possible nature of definition. There are, in fact, only two serious alternatives to be considered, in order to establish the conclusion that 'good' does denote a simple and indefinable notion. It might possibly denote a complex, as 'horse' does; or it might have no meaning at all. Neither of these possibilities has, however, been clearly conceived and seriously maintained, as such, by those who presume to define good; and both may be dismissed by a simple appeal to facts.

(1)   The hypothesis that disagreement about the meaning of good is disagreement with regard to the correct analysis of a given whole, may be most plainly seen to be incorrect by consideration of the fact that, whatever definition be offered, it may be always asked, with significance, of the complex so defined, whether it is itself good. To take, for instance, one of the more plausible, because one of the more complicated, of such proposed definitions, it may easily be thought, at first sight, that to be good may mean to be that which we desire to desire. Thus if we apply this definition to a particular instance and say 'When we think that A is good, we are thinking that A is one of the things which we desire to desire,' our proposition may seem quite plausible. But, if we carry the investigation further, and ask ourselves 'Is it good to desire to desire A?' it is apparent, on a little reflection, that this question is itself as intelligible, as the original question 'Is A good?' – that we are, in fact, now asking for exactly the same information about the desire to desire A, for which we formerly asked with regard to A itself. But it is also apparent that the meaning of this second question cannot be correctly analysed into 'Is the desire to desire A one of the things which we desire to desire?': we have not before our minds anything so complicated as the question 'Do we desire to desire to desire to desire A?' Moreover any one can easily convince himself by inspection that the predicate of this proposition – 'good' – is positively different

from the notion of 'desiring to desire' which enters into its subject: 'That we should desire to desire A is good' is *not* merely equivalent to 'That A should be good is good.' It may indeed be true that what we desire to desire is always also good; perhaps, even the converse may be true: but it is very doubtful whether this is the case, and the mere fact that we understand very well what is meant by doubting it, shews clearly that we have two different notions before our minds.

(2)   And the same consideration is sufficient to dismiss the hypothesis that 'good' has no meaning whatsoever. It is very natural to make the mistake of supposing that what is universally true is of such a nature that its negation would be self-contradictory: the importance which has been assigned to analytic propositions in the history of philosophy shews how easy such a mistake is. And thus it is very easy to conclude that what seems to be a universal ethical principle is in fact an identical proposition; that, if, for example, whatever is called 'good' seems to be pleasant, the proposition 'Pleasure is the good' does not assert a connection between two different notions, but involves only one, that of pleasure, which is easily recognised as a distinct entity. But whoever will attentively consider with himself what is actually before his mind when he asks the question 'Is pleasure (or whatever it may be) after all good?' can easily satisfy himself that he is not merely wondering whether pleasure is pleasant. And if he will try this experiment with each suggested definition in succession, he may become expert enough to recognise that in every case he has before his mind a unique object, with regard to the connection of which with any other object, a distinct question may be asked. Every one does in fact understand the question 'Is this good?' When he thinks of it, his state of mind is different from what it would be, were he asked 'Is this pleasant, or desired, or approved?' It has a distinct meaning for him, even though he may not recognise in what respect it is distinct. Whenever he thinks of 'intrinsic value,' or 'intrinsic worth,' or says that a thing 'ought to exist,' he has before his mind the unique object – the unique property of things – which I mean by 'good.' Everybody is constantly aware of this notion, although he may never become aware at all that it is different from other notions of which he is also aware. But, for correct ethical reasoning, it is extremely important that he should become aware of this fact; and, as soon as the nature of the problem is clearly understood,

there should be little difficulty in advancing so far in analysis.

14. 'Good,' then, is indefinable; and yet, so far as I know, there is only one ethical writer, Prof. Henry Sidgwick, who has clearly recognised and stated this fact. We shall see, indeed, how far many of the most reputed ethical systems fall short of drawing the conclusions which follow from such a recognition. At present I will only quote one instance, which will serve to illustrate the meaning and importance of this principle that 'good' is indefinable, or, as Prof. Sidgwick says, an 'unanalysable notion.' It is an instance to which Prof. Sidgwick himself refers in a note on the passage, in which he argues that 'ought' is unanalysable.[1]

'Bentham,' says Sidgwick, 'explains that his fundamental principle "states the greatest happiness of all those whose interest is in question as being the right and proper end of human action"'; and yet 'his language in other passages of the same chapter would seem to imply' that he *means* by the word 'right' 'conducive to the general happiness.' Prof. Sidgwick sees that, if you take these two statements together, you get the absurd result that 'greatest happiness is the end of human action, which is conducive to the general happiness'; and so absurd does it seem to him to call this result, as Bentham calls it, 'the fundamental principle of a moral system,' that he suggests that Bentham cannot have meant it. Yet Prof. Sidgwick himself states elsewhere[2] that Psychological Hedonism is 'not seldom confounded with Egoistic Hedonism'; and that confusion, as we shall see, rests chiefly on that same fallacy, the naturalistic fallacy, which is implied in Bentham's statements. Prof. Sidgwick admits therefore that this fallacy is sometimes committed, absurd as it is; and I am inclined to think that Bentham may really have been one of those who committed it. Mill, as we shall see, certainly did commit it. In any case, whether Bentham committed it or not, his doctrine, as above quoted, will serve as a very good illustration of this fallacy, and of the importance of the contrary proposition that good is indefinable.

Let us consider this doctrine. Bentham seems to imply, so Prof. Sidgwick says, that the word 'right' *means* 'conducive to general happiness.' Now this, by itself, need not necessarily involve the naturalis-

tic fallacy. For the word 'right' is very commonly appropriated to actions which lead to the attainment of what is good; which are regarded as *means* to the ideal and not as ends-in-themselves. This use of 'right,' as denoting what is good as a means, whether or not it be also good as an end, is indeed the use to which I shall confine the word. Had Bentham been using 'right' in this sense, it might be perfectly consistent for him to *define* right as 'conducive to the general happiness,' *provided only* (and notice this proviso) he had already proved, or laid down as an axiom, that general happiness was *the* good, or (what is equivalent to this) that general happiness alone was good. For in that case he would have already defined *the* good as general happiness (a position perfectly consistent, as we have seen, with the contention that 'good' is indefinable), and since right was to be defined as 'conducive to *the* good,' it would actually *mean* 'conducive to general happiness.' But this method of escape from the charge of having committed the naturalistic fallacy has been closed by Bentham himself. For his fundamental principle is, we see, that the greatest happiness of all concerned is the *right* and proper *end* of human action. He applies the word 'right,' therefore, to the end, as such, not only to the means which are conducive to it; and, that being so, right can no longer be defined as 'conducive to the general happiness,' without involving the fallacy in question. For now it is obvious that the definition of right as conducive to general happiness can be used by him in support of the fundamental principle that general happiness is the right end; instead of being itself derived from that principle. If right, by definition, means conducive to general happiness, then it is obvious that general happiness is the right end. It is not necessary now first to prove or assert that general happiness is the right end, before right is defined as conducive to general happiness – a perfectly valid procedure; but on the contrary the definition of right as conducive to general happiness proves general happiness to be the right end – a perfectly invalid procedure, since in this case the statement that 'general happiness is the right end of human action' is not an ethical principle at all, but either, as we have seen, a proposition about the meaning of words, or else a proposition about the *nature* of general happiness, not about its rightness or goodness.

---

[1] *Methods of Ethics*, bk. 1, ch. iii, §1 (6th edition).
[2] *Methods of Ethics*, bk. 1, ch. iv, §1.

Now, I do not wish the importance I assign to this fallacy to be misunderstood. The discovery of it does not at all refute Bentham's contention that greatest happiness is the proper end of human action, if that be understood as an ethical proposition, as he undoubtedly intended it. That principle may be true all the same; we shall consider whether it is so in succeeding chapters. Bentham might have maintained it, as Prof. Sidgwick does, even if the fallacy had been pointed out to him. What I am maintaining is that the *reasons* which he actually gives for his ethical proposition are fallacious ones so far as they consist in a definition of right. What I suggest is that he did not perceive them to be fallacious; that, if he had done so, he would have been led to seek for other reasons in support of his Utilitarianism; and that, had he sought for other reasons, he *might* have found none which he thought to be sufficient. In that case he would have changed his whole system – a most important consequence. It is undoubtedly also possible that he would have thought other reasons to be sufficient, and in that case his ethical system, in its main results, would still have stood. But, even in this latter case, his use of the fallacy would be a serious objection to him as an ethical philosopher. For it is the business of Ethics, I must insist, not only to obtain true results, but also to find valid reasons for them. The direct object of Ethics is knowledge and not practice; and any one who uses the naturalistic fallacy has certainly not fulfilled this first object, however correct his practical principles may be.

My objections to Naturalism are then, in the first place, that it offers no reason at all, far less any valid reason, for any ethical principle whatever; and in this it already fails to satisfy the requirements of Ethics, as a scientific study. But in the second place I contend that, though it gives a reason for no ethical principle, it is a *cause* of the acceptance of false principles – it deludes the mind into accepting ethical principles, which are false; and in this it is contrary to every aim of Ethics. It is easy to see

that if we start with a definition of right conduct as conduct conducive to general happiness; then, knowing that right conduct is universally conduct conducive to the good, we very easily arrive at the result that the good is general happiness. If, on the other hand, we once recognise that we must start our Ethics without a definition, we shall be much more apt to look about us, before we adopt any ethical principle whatever; and the more we look about us, the less likely are we to adopt a false one. It may be replied to this: Yes, but we shall look about us just as much, before we settle on our definition, and are therefore just as likely to be right. But I will try to shew that this is not the case. If we start with the conviction that a definition of good can be found, we start with the conviction that good *can mean* nothing else than some one property of things; and our only business will then be to discover what that property is. But if we recognise that, so far as the meaning of good goes, anything whatever may be good, we start with a much more open mind. Moreover, apart from the fact that, when we think we have a definition, we cannot logically defend our ethical principles in any way whatever, we shall also be much less apt to defend them well, even if illogically. For we shall start with the conviction that good must mean so and so, and shall therefore be inclined either to misunderstand our opponent's arguments or to cut them short with the reply, 'This is not an open question: the very meaning of the word decides it; no one can think otherwise except through confusion.'

15.   Our first conclusion as to the subject-matter of Ethics is, then, that there is a simple, indefinable, unanalysable object of thought by reference to which it must be defined. By what name we call this unique object is a matter of indifference, so long as we clearly recognise what it is and that it does differ from other objects. The words which are commonly taken as the signs of ethical judgments all do refer to it; and they are expressions of ethical judgments solely because they do so refer.

Attitudes and Contents

Simon Blackburn

General Considerations

G. F. Schueler's paper puts in a forceful way various reservations about my treatment of indirect contexts, on behalf of the position I have called "quasi-realism."[1] His opposition is, I think, as complete as could be: it is not only that my treatment has been incomplete, which I happily concede, or that its formulation has been defective, which I am prepared to believe, but also that nothing like it could possibly succeed. That at least is the proper consequence of some of his views – on logical form, and on validity, and on the nature of commitment. For example, if to show that an inference has "the logical form" or "is an instance" of modus ponens involves taking it as "the realist picture" has it, then no attempt to explain it in other terms will be compatible with its having that form. Again, if validity is ("as it is used in logic") defined in terms of the impossibility of premises being true and conclusions false, then persons reluctant to apply truth and falsity to any of the elements of an inference will have to admit that the inference is not valid, as the term is used in logic. Third, if "talk of 'commitments' is problematic for the antirealist" then antirealism will make no

headway by thinking of a more general class of commitments than those with representative or realistic truth conditions. Fortunately, none of these contentions seems to me correct. Since the survival of quasi-realism even in spirit demands their rebuttal, I shall start by considering them in turn.

1. It is not too clear what it is for an argument to have the logical form of modus ponens. If that is a remark about syntactical form, then obviously having that logical form is compatible with any number of deep and different semantics for the components. To show this compare "P, $P{\rightarrow}Q$, so Q" with the implication taken as truth-functional, with the same seeming argument taken as some suppose the English take it: $P{\rightarrow}Q$ is the commitment of one who attributes a high probability to Q conditional upon P. Which is the true modus ponens? If we plump for either exclusively, we face the uncomfortable consequence that it becomes controversial whether natural English contains any inferences of the form. If we embrace both, then being of the form modus ponens is compatible with any number of deep and different *explanations* of the semantics of the components: how it comes about that we have here elements describable as

---

[1] G. F. Schueler, "Modus Ponens and Moral Realism." *Ethics* 98 (Apr. 1988).

true or false, or a connective properly represented by some → or other. The same point could be made with any connective: knowing even when to interpret the negation sign of a logic as meaning negation is no easy matter.[2] If quasi-realism, in the form in which I tried to develop it, is right, the "deep" semantics of a surface example of modus ponens is to be explained in a particular, and perhaps initially surprising, way. But it is modus ponens, for all that. Or, if we say it is not, then we have no effective procedure for telling when anything is.

2.   Perhaps the best way to answer the restrictive view of validity is by appeal to authority. One might cite imperative logic. Or, one might cite the approach to propositional inference in terms of coherent subjective probability functions, where validity corresponds to there being no coherent function attributing a lesser probability to the conclusion than to the premises, and coherence is defined in terms of immunity to Dutch book.[3] (This is the approach which would best marry with the probabilistic view of conditionals above.) Or one could cite the view of Stig Kanger, that in interpreting a deontic logic the extension of the truth predicate to the formulae, which could equally be regarded as imperatives or expressions of attitude, is a conventional matter.[4] A further reply would draw the usual distinction between an algebraic, mathematical, pure, or uninterpreted semantics – itself sufficient to yield notions of satisfaction, validity, and completeness – versus an applied or interpreted semantics, in which the valuation clauses reflect something about the use or meaning of the connectives.[5] Formal studies are content with the first, so that truth-in-a-structure, or satisfiability defined in terms of (for instance) sets of open sets in the topology of the real line defines validity.[6] But even when we turn to the second, the question of priorities still arises. It does not go without saying that we interpret the propositional connectives by drawing on an antecedent understanding of (classical) truth and falsity. Falsity and negation go hand in hand, and

it should not be obvious which is the dominant partner. The view that it is by knowing how to *use* the connectives in proofs that we come to understand them, and hence gain what understanding we have of the truth tables, is perfectly open. In Prawitz's words: "Presumably, the observational consequences that can be drawn from the assumption that a person knows the condition for the truth of a sentence can also be drawn from the assumption that he knows how to use the sentence in proofs."[7] The whole philosophy of intuitionistic interpretations of the logical constants and of those who give priority to sequent calculi and natural deduction systems opposes the simple assumption that an antecedent understanding of "representative" truth and falsity affords the only road to understanding validity. A more plausible view and one which nicely fits quasi-realism is that attributions of validity and application of the truth predicate go hand in hand: I expand on this below.

3.   Schueler finds the very notion of a commitment "problematic for the anti-realist." His argument that it is one of "those terms which seem to entail a realist picture" is this: "If I am committed to, say, paying my nephew's way through school, or to the claim that a Republican succeeded Carter, then this seems something objective, forced on me by a promise I have made or other views I hold." Well it might be, if we could suitably cash the metaphor of forcing, and suitably interpret objectivity – although whether the objectivity forced by, say, promises has anything to do with realism is another matter. But equally, the commitment might not be forced by anything, like the commitment to go for a jog once a week or to improve one's golf. It does not matter, because 'commitment' I simply use as a general term to cover mental states which may be beliefs, but also those which gain expression in propositional form, but which for various reasons philosophers such as Hume, Ramsey, Wittgenstein, Stevenson, Ayer, Hare, and I have seen in terms of such things as acceptance of rules, changes in disposition, possession of

---

[2]   B. J. Copeland, "What Is a Semantics for Classical Negation?" *Mind* 95 (1986).

[3]   Hartry Field, "Logic, Meaning and Conceptual Role." *Journal of Philosophy* 74 (1977).

[4]   Stig Kanger, "New Foundations for Ethical Theory," in *Deontic Logic: Introductory and Systematic Readings*, ed. R. Hilpinen (Dordrecht: Reidel, 1971), pp. 55–6.

[5]   M. Dummett, "The Justification of Deduction," in *Truth and Other Enigmas* (London: Duckworth, 1978), p. 293; A. Plantinga, *The Nature of Necessity* (London: Oxford University Press, 1974), pp. 126 ff.

[6]   H. Weyl, "The Ghost of Modality," in *Philosophical Essays in Memory of Edmund Husserl* (Cambridge, MA: Harvard University Press, 1940).

[7]   D. Prawitz, "Meaning and Proofs: On the Conflict between Classical and Intuitionistic Logic." *Theoria* 43 (1977).

attitudes, which are worth separating from beliefs. Some commitments will have nothing to do with approval: these include the change in one who accepts a rule of inference, or treats a proposition as necessary, or accords a high subjective probability to Q upon P, and so on, as well as Schueler's example of his belief that a Republican succeeded Carter. In the sphere of ethics, approval and attitude are natural terms to work with, but it would not matter if neither fitted exactly, or if better terms for the state in question existed. What is important is the theoretical issue of whether and why the state is worth distinguishing from belief, or at least from belief with representational truth conditions thought of realistically, but since I have written extensively on this elsewhere, I shall pass that over.[8]

Fast-Track and Slow-Track Quasi-Realism

So far I have simply dissented from Schueler's reasons for general pessimism about the approach, intending to show that the ideas behind quasi-realism survive his onslaught. But he is on stronger ground in attacking the detail of my treatment. I shall turn to that after taking stock for a moment.

The problem is that of embedding of sentences which primarily express attitude, in contexts which might appear to admit only sentences which, in some contrasting way express propositions. When I say that these sentences primarily express attitude I have never intended to deny that they can be regarded as expressing beliefs or propositions. This opposition would be going beyond anything I embrace. But I do mean that the right way of theorizing about them identifies them, in the first instance, as expressing states of mind whose function is not to represent anything about the world. They express something more to do with attitudes, practices, emotions, feelings arising in contemplating some kinds of conduct, with goal seeking, with insistence upon normative constraints on conduct, and nothing to do with representing the world. In the familiar metaphor, their "direction of fit" with the world is active – to have the world conform to them, rather than descriptive or representational. I call someone who approves both of this contrast, and with this direction of theorizing, a projectivist. Projectivism may seem to be automatically opposed to the view that in saying that something is good (etc.) we give voice to a real belief about it, and it is often so introduced (as labels like 'noncognitivism' suggest). But this opposition is not automatic. Subtlety with the concept of belief, or with the concept of truth or fact, may enable the expressivist to soften this opposition. Theory may enable us to understand how a commitment with its center in the expression of subjective determinations of the mind can also function as expressing belief, or be capable of sustaining the truth predicate – properly called 'true' or 'false.' I tried to herald this development with the notion of a "propositional reflection" in the older paper "Moral Realism," and it was the point of the last pages of chapter 6, and of chapter 7, of *Spreading the Word*.[9] It means separating truth (in this application at least) from 'represents' and its allies, but nobody has ever pointed out the harm in that.

It did, however, seem to me that, before this happy result could be secured, work had to be done. It had to be shown *why* a sentence with this role could *properly* function in the ways ethical sentences do – why it sustains a fully propositional role. I now think we should distinguish a slow track to this result and a fast track. The slow track involves patiently construing each propositional context as it comes along. This is the line I took in trying to meet Geach's problem. Its advantage is that of honest toil over what might seem like theft; its disadvantage if Schueler is right is that it does not work. But before judging that I should admit not only that it threatens to look Ptolemaic but also that it seems not to correspond to any obvious cognitive processes we go through. It is not as though construing (say) conditionals with evaluative components comes harder to us than construing them with ordinary components, and this will need explanation.

Fast-track quasi-realism would get there in better style. It would make sufficient remarks about truth to suggest that we need a comparable notion to regulate evaluative discourse (even although that is nonrepresentational) and then say that our adherence to propositional forms needs no further explanation than that. The adoption of propositional form and style meets a need because we need

---

[8] A recent statement is my "Morals and Modals," in *Fact, Science and Value*, ed. G. MacDonald and C. Wright (London: Blackwell, 1986).

[9] Simon Blackburn, *Spreading the Word* (London: Oxford University Press, 1984).

to share and discuss and dissent from attitudes or other stances. It involves only philosophers in error, and little more need be said. That sounds cavalier, but it was the line of, for instance, Kant and Nietzsche and probably Wittgenstein,[10] none of whom found any particular trouble in imagining the emergence of a predicate with a nondescriptive role. Nietzsche puts it roundly:

> The pathos of nobility and distance, as aforesaid, the protracted and domineering fundamental total feeling on the part of a higher ruling order in relation to a lower order, to a *below* – *that* is the origin of the antithesis "good" and "bad" (the lordly right of giving names extends so far that one should allow oneself to conceive the origin of language itself as an expression of power on the part of the rulers: they say "this *is* this and this," they seal every thing and event with a sound, and, as it were, take possession of it).

Perhaps our general propensity to seal things with sounds needs no detailed explanation or justification (cf. "this is nice" as a way of voicing pleasure, and immediately giving rise to compounds "if it's nice, two would be nicer," etc.). But compromises are possible: the fast track can benefit from some of the security achieved on the slow, and the slow track can make use of some of the short cuts of the fast. Or so I shall argue. Notice that, whichever track we favor, the point is to *earn* our right to propositional forms – including the use of a truth predicate. If this is done, any conventional concept of validity tags along – there is a level of analysis at which modus ponens and the rest are no different when their components are evaluative and when they are not.

Embedding

A parallel to the idea that a certain sentence expresses an attitude – "Hooray for the Bears" – would be the obvious truth that some others express commands – "Go to see the Bears" – and questions – "Are the Bears doing well?" Now when imperatives and questions give rise to subordinate clauses, the linguistic forms typically maintain an indication of the original mood, even if there is

another syntactic change: "he told me *to* go to see the Bears, he asked me *whether* the Bears are doing well, if *I am to* go to see the Bears, I had better have some tea first." Here the right thing to say is that the subordinate clause maintains the mood of the original, but that it is not uttered with the *force* that a direct utterance of the sentence has (nothing is commanded or questioned). Nevertheless, mood is in some sense primarily an indicator of force. It is only by understanding what a question or command is that one understands the function of the interrogative or imperative mood.

There is a prima facie puzzle here. Mood is primarily an indicator of force, force is lost in subordinate clauses, but mood is not.

I do not think, however, that the puzzle is very deep, although its formal representation can be difficult. The subordinate clause in "He said that *P*" identifies which proposition he asserted; the clauses in "he told me to go to see the Bears" or "he asked whether the Bears are doing well" identify which order he gave or which question he asked. Mood indicates that a question or command is still part of the topic, even when the overall communication is not itself a question or command. Technically, I therefore agree with Michael Pendlebury that mood (or at least the presence of the indicator "to go . . . ," "whether . . .") affects the sense of such clauses: the embedding does not cancel the semantic significance of the mood indicator, which is to maintain some connection with an original command or question.[11] It can matter that a question or command is still in this sense part of the *topic*. Perhaps the nicest illustration of this is the difference between "he knew that the Bears had won" and "he knew whether the Bears had won" where the first simply gives us the content of his knowledge, but the mood in the second shows that what he is said to have known is the answer to a question – which might have been yes or no. Of course, saying that in this way a command or question is part of the topic is not implying that one was ever actually uttered – one can know the answer to questions that have never been asked.

We do not have a mood which in this way indicates that an attitude is part of the topic. The

[10]   I. Kant, *The Critique of Judgement*, trans. J. C. Meredith (London: Oxford University Press). [. . .] Nietzsche, *The Genealogy of Morals*, first essay, II; L. Wittgenstein, *Remarks on the Foundations of Mathematics* (Oxford: Blackwell, 1956), p. 163, contains a particularly clear statement of the view that statements of mathematics mislead philosophers by their descriptive form.
[11]   M. Pendlebury, "Against the Power of Force: Reflections on the Meaning of Mood." *Mind* 95 (1986), 361–73.

nearest approximation is in indirect reportage of wishes expressed in the optative: "would I were in Grantchester!" can perhaps be reported: he said that he would be in Grantchester, but there is at least a slight sense of strain. Normally, if I make plain to you what I feel, say about the Bears, I will most probably do so using a sentence with an "expressive" predicate: "the Bears are great!" The report of what I said in indirect speech is then easy: he said that the Bears are great. According to projectivism, the item of vocabulary shows that the original utterance was expressive of attitude. In the subordinate clause, it remains to make attitude the topic just as overt mood indicators do. The person who said that the Bears are great expressed just that attitude about the Bears. Saying that this is what he did is not of course endorsing or subscribing to the view, any more than reporting a command or question involves reissuing it in propria persona.

Suppose we spoke an "emotivist" language, in which expressions of attitude wore this function on their faces. We would not have the predicative form, to keep such expressions in the indicative mood, but an ejaculatory mood, corresponding to that of "Hooray for the Bears." It would then be necessary to have a construction of subordinate clauses corresponding to words such as "that . . . ," "to . . . ," and "whether . . . ," which marks the original attitude as the topic. There seems no problem of semantic principle about this; "that!" "whether!" and so on might be introduced, so that "he said that! hooray for the Bears" tells us which attitude he expressed, "he wondered whether! hooray for the Bears" tells us which attitude he was pondering, and so on.

If natural languages have chosen not to register expressive force by a particular mood, they may have chosen to do it in other ways. And taking other cases of mood and force as our model, there might be no great difficulty about imagining it done by an expressive mood and yielding a smooth interpretation of at least some subordinate clauses. Here there is room for the compromise between fast- and slow-track quasi-realism: see how far you get in imagining an overtly expressive language developed in such ways, and diminish (even if not to zero) the gap between what it achieves and what we do with predication, and talk of truth.

A Logic

Geach concentrated upon the special case of the antecedent of conditionals in his original article. My suggestion involved first describing what we are up to in embedding what is primarily an expression of attitude in a context, making it intelligible that the context should have a function. Second, it involved giving sufficient semantic theory to show why we have the way we do of meeting that need. Thus in the case of Geach's original conditional, my suggestion of what we are up to involved taking up an attitude to an involvement of attitude with attitude, or attitude with belief. Such "second-order" stances seemed to me both needed in themselves and plausible candidates for the import of a conditional with evaluative elements. If we use '$\Rightarrow$' to signify the *involvement* of one mental state with another, the result was that a simple conditional "if lying is wrong, then getting your little brother to lie is wrong" came out as:

$$H! \, (\backslash B!L\backslash \Rightarrow \backslash B'GBL\backslash),$$

where the \ . . . \ notation shows that our topic is the attitude or belief whose normal expression occurs within the slashes. Involvement is not a logical notion, but neither should it seem mysterious. I tried to explain it by introducing the idea of a sensibility as a function from belief to attitude, attitude to attitude, and so on: it is what we would overtly talk about by saying things like "I really approve of *making* approval of an action depend on its consequences" or "believing that *should* increase your approval of this." Endorsing or rejecting such an involvement of commitments one with another is an important thing to do; it is therefore not surprising that we have a simple English form with which to do it.

Let us now consider modus ponens. We have

$$B!L$$
$$H!(\backslash B!L\backslash \Rightarrow \backslash B!GBL\backslash)$$
$$\text{So: } B!GBL.$$

Schueler and others rightly raise doubts about the kind of inconsistency in avowing the two initial attitudes and refusing endorsement of the conclusion.[12] In *Spreading the Word* I talked of a "frac-

---

[12]   Bob Hale, "The Compleat Projectivist." *Philosophical Quarterly* 36 (1986), 65–85, anticipates the difficulties with validity.

tured sensibility" which could not be a proper object of approval. Schueler reasonably asks why it could not be an object of approval and whether in any case this smacks more of a moral or evaluative problem than of a logical one. Yet modus ponens with these components is surely logically valid, and a proper semantics for expressions of attitude ought to explain why.

How do attitudes become things which enter into logical relationships, which *matter* in the theory of inference? It is well known that logical relationships between imperatives can be studied by thinking of joint satisfiability – seeing whether there is a consistent world in which each of a set of imperatives is obeyed. Similarly deductive relationships between norms can be studied by thinking of ideal or relatively ideal worlds in which the norms are met. If we have here the basis for a logic, it extends to attitude. For $H!p$ can be seen as expressing the view that p is to be a goal, to be realized in any perfect world. A world in which $\sim p$ is less than ideal, according to this commitment. The contrary attitude $B!p$ would rule p out of any perfect world, and corresponding to permission we can have $T!p$, which is equivalent to not hooraying $\sim p$, that is, not booing p.

Putting attitude to the fore, instead of the more usual obligations and permissions of deontic logic, promises two gains. The first is that writers on deontic logic usually interpret "Op" and "Pp" as purely propositional by making them describe what is obligated or permitted by some supposed background set of norms (the most notable exception to this generalization is Hector-Neri Castañeda).[13] But this divorces them from their ordinary expressive use, which is not to describe what some (possibly alien) system of norms yields but to insist upon or permit various things. If the apparatus of deontic logic can be taken over while this use is kept primary, so much the better. But there is another gain in taking the portmanteau term "attitude" rather than the particular, restricted notion of "obligation" and "permission." This is that the logical apparatus should apply wherever we have the idea of a goal or aim, and corresponding idea of something to be avoided, or not to be avoided. We need not be in the realm of the obligatory, or of *requirements*, but merely in that of the needed or even just the desirable. Consistency in goals is still a desideratum whose logic needs development.

And in fact the deductive apparatus of deontic logic does not depend in any way on taking obligations and permissions as fully fledged deontic notions. The same structure exists if "Op" is interpreted as any kind of view that p be true ideally and "Pp" as any kind of toleration of p.

There is nothing surprising about using realization of goals or ideals as the final test for consistency. The ordinary notion of finding whether recommendations are consistent just is to imagine them carried out and see if that can be consistently done. But Schueler rightly raises a problem which might affect the extension to attitude. This is that consistency in attitude is not a particular virtue. I may wish that p and wish that $\sim p$ without particular shame. I may desire that p, and desire that q, but not desire that p & q: I want to spend the evening at the theater, and I want to read my book, but I do not want to read my book at the theater. There is a sense in which my goals are inconsistent – they cannot all be realized – but, if this does not matter, then it is not sufficiently *like* the vice of inconsistency in belief to form the basis of a logic.

My comment on this is threefold. First of all, I think part of the objection comes from confusing desires with wishes. Inconsistent wishes may not matter because in wishing or daydreaming we are spinning fictions, and inconsistent fictions do not matter. This is because there is no connection with action. But for all that, inconsistency in real desire may matter. Incompatible and therefore unrealizable goals are bad in a way quite analogous to that in which inconsistent beliefs are. The latter cannot represent the world properly. But the former cannot represent how to behave in the world properly: they cannot mate together with beliefs, in the usual belief-desire psychological framework, to direct effective action. The man who believes that it is raining and that it is not is badly placed to act if he wants, say, to avoid getting wet. But so is the man who believes that it is raining but wants to get wet and not to get wet.

The second point to notice is that attitude and desire are capable of qualification. I may be subject to some desires, or some pressures (tiredness, mood) which suggest reading a book and others which suggest visiting the theater. Do I both want to read a book and want to go to the theater? It is a crude way of representing my state. Perhaps I want to read a book *inasumuch as* I am tired, want to go to

---

[13]   H.-N. Castañeda, *Thinking and Doing* (Dordrecht: Reidel. 1975). esp. ch. 2.

the theater *inasmuch as* I like company. I feel the different pressures, but it is at least as natural to say that I don't know what I want to do as it is to say that I want to do both. I can indeed say that I would like to do both, but that takes us back to the realm of wishes (I would like them not to conflict somehow). So one way of diminishing the attraction of inconsistent desires is to remember the difference between full-scale, all-in desires, and attractions or pressures which are not yet resolved.

Even if this point were contested, a third defense is waiting. Although I have urged the advantage of thinking in terms of a catholic conception of attitude rather than of strict deontological notions, we could restrict ourselves to concepts of being for or against or neither for nor against things where consistency *does* matter. If this is a more limited range than the full spectrum of desire, this need not matter. If, for instance, it embraced only desires which one was inclined to submit to public scrutiny, or translate into practical advice, then there would be a corresponding restriction of the interpretion of notions such as 'goal' or 'ideal.' That is fine, provided the relevant attitudes satisfy the constraints when it comes to interpreting the logic in a domain such as ethics. Since ethics is at bottom a practical subject, this is to be expected.

In the usual metaphor, the direction of fit between desires and the world is opposite to that between beliefs and the world. The desire that p dictates action if it is deemed likely, but avoidable, that $\sim p$, whereas the belief that p needs abandoning if it is deemed likely that $\sim p$.[14] But since belief and desire do each have a direction of fit and a content, then each should be fitted to play a role in a logic of consistency. A person may flout the demand of consistency in complicated or demanding situations, but only at the cost of tension: his goals cannot be realized, or if he has inconsistent beliefs, the world cannot be as he represents it. It may be admirable that we sometimes get into states where we feel that tension, but this is so for belief as well as desire. It could not be admirable in general, and it could not be true in general, for these states are essentially characterized by responsibility either to the world, in the case of beliefs, or in our response to the world, in the case of attitude.

I therefore reject Schueler's contention that there is no legitimate notion of inconsistency. But it remains to be seen whether it ratifies my assault on modus ponens, or any other natural inference pattern. Meanwhile, there is another natural worry about my proposal. As it stands it yields no smooth extension to other propositional contexts. For instance, simple disjunction with an evaluative component does not yield an obvious second-order attitude. "Either Johnny has done something wrong, or Freddy has" is not well represented as $H!(\backslash B!\mathcal{J}\backslash\ OR\ \backslash B!F\backslash)$ where "OR" introduces a kind of disjunctive relation between attitudes. Because even if the idea of a disjunctive relation between attitudes makes sense, one might know that one of them has done something wrong but quite disapprove of taking up a negative attitude to *either* of them – if neither has yet been proved guilty, for instance. The stance that $H!\ (\backslash B!\mathcal{J}\backslash\ OR\ \backslash B!F\backslash)$ expresses seems to be that of someone who endorses only psychologies which contain at least one of the embedded attitudes (this would be the natural interpretation of disjunction), but this is not at all the same as the stance of someone who thinks that either Johnny has done something wrong or Freddy has. One could interpret disjunction by first translating it into the associated conditional and then using the account of conditionals on that. But there is something ad hoc about such procedures. They take the theory too far from anything which seems necessary for the ordinary truth-functional disjunction, and their very unnaturalness raises again the question of adequacy. Even if the notion of involvement gives a reasonable surrogate for implication, there may be no such notion naturally available in each case of potential embedding.

Suppose then we take the theory of inference as primary. If we ask what these embeddings are *for*, the immediate answer is that they mediate inference. They show us the deductive relationships between our commitments, and between our commitments and our beliefs. So rather than *replace* logical constants, as in the approach I just gave, we might try to *retain* them and to provide an interpretation of embeddings of attitude in the contexts the deductive system is to treat: in the first place, contexts provided by the truth functors.

We know, or think we know, what the negation, disjunction, and conjunction of an ordinary proposition is. It needs showing that we have any right to extend those notions to cover expressions of a different kind. Thus in the language to come $H!p$

---

[14] Michael Smith, "The Humean Theory of Motivation." *Mind* 96 (1987), 36–61.

is to be treated as a well-formed formula capable of entering the same embeddings as p. Even if this provides a language which is formally workable, it still needs showing that it provides one which is interpretable – in which $H!p$ can still be regarded as fundamentally expressive of attitude.

Consider first negation. What can $\sim H!A$ mean? Schueler might say: nothing much to do with truth or falsity, and since that reversal is the fundamental effect of negation, it cannot mean anything to apply the notion here. But I have already remarked that it might go the other way round: falsity of p is the truth of the negation of p. Ordinary negation is expressive of denial: $\sim p$ is that proposition whose expression denies p. There is a clear corresponding relation between attitudes: there exists that attitude which 'denies,' or rejects, having p as an aim or goal. If $H!p$ expresses the attitude of endorsing the goal p, $\sim H!p$ then expresses that of opposition: tolerating $\sim p$ or allowing it as consistent with an ideal world. So we can say that $T!A$ is substitutable for $\sim H!A$, and $H!A$ for $\sim T!A$. Such a conversion drives external 'negations' on attitudes inward. So even if the original occurrence of the external negation made us uneasy, *formally* the unease is dissipated by the conversion, and *philosophically* dissipated by recognizing sufficient analogy between conflict of attitude and conflict of belief.

What of other truth functional contexts? It is an important feature of inference using propositional calculus embeddings that they can all be represented by the normal forms of conjunction and disjunction. In a tableau development each move either adds to the string (as when A, B, are appended under $A \& B$) or divides the string (as when A makes one branch, and B another, under A v B). Now let us suppose that we are involved with an evaluative commitment, $H!A$ or $T!A$ in a propositional calculus embedding. We can see what this means if we can interpret the strings in which it issues. This reduces then to the problem of interpreting these two elements in a tree structure. But it is easy to see what a string represents if, underneath this embedding, we get $H!p$ occurring alone (e.g., under $p \& H!p$ we get $H!p$). This means that the initial complex commits us to the attitude, and this is not hard to interpret. Being against clergymen and for free love commits one to being against clergymen, and the notion of consistent realization of aims or goals shows us why.

There remains the case in which a tableau under a complex branches and $H!p$ belongs to one of the branches. The interpretation is that one potential route to drawing out the consequences of the complex involves this commitment, although another may not. Thus p v $H!q$ issues in a branch; it is the commitment of one who is what I shall call *tied to a tree*. That is, tied to (*either* accepting that p, or endorsing q), where the brackets show that this is not the same as (being tied to accepting p) or (being tied to endorsing q). Rather, the commitment is to accepting the one branch should the other prove untenable. The essential point is that this is a quite intelligible state to be in. Philosophically we justify the procedure by analogy with the ordinary notion of accepting a disjunction, which similarly ties one to a tree of possibilities, and formally the language admits of identical deductive procedures.

How does this relate to the original proposal for treating the conditional? Under a material conditional $A \rightarrow B$ we get the tree with $\sim A$ in one branch and B in the other. Suppose then we treat Geach's conditional "if lying yourself is wrong getting your little brother to lie is wrong" this way. Someone asserting it is tied to the tree of (either assenting to "lying yourself is not wrong" or to "getting your little brother to lie is wrong"). What was right about my original proposal is that being so tied is in this case characteristic of a particular value system or set of attitudes. Only someone with a certain view of the relation between doing things directly and doing them indirectly is apt to assent to the conditional. This represents the reason for his being tied. What was inelegant about the original proposal, I now think, was putting that directly into the content of the conditional itself. The assent to the conditional itself does not tell us why someone is tying himself to that tree – it only tells us that he is tied and that we can use this fact in assessing the consistency of his position. I return to this below, after detailing the logic a little.

I do not want to claim finality for the semantics I shall now sketch, but it illustrates how a logic might be developed, and it shows that notions of inconsistency and satisfiability can be defined (it also bears out Kanger's remarks mentioned above). It uses Hintikka's notion of a set of "deontic alternatives."[15] In Hintikka's semantics the central notion is that of norms obtaining in a possible

---

[15] J. Hintikka, "Deontic Logic and Its Philosophical Morals," in *Models for Modalities* (Dordrecht: Reidel, 1969).

world, and of the deontic alternatives to that world being the possible worlds which are in accordance with those norms. Hintikka compares this notion to Kant's "Kingdom of Ends" (*Reich der Zwecke*): it represents a "mere ideal" (Kant: "freilich nur ein Ideal") which is not realized but which we nevertheless must be able to think of consistently.

In Hintikka's development we work in terms of a model system or set of model sets. A model set is a partial description of a possible world or alternative. A set of sentences including oughts and permissions will be satisfiable if it is embeddable in such a set. This means that a set of sentences L is satisfiable if and only if there is a model system S and a model set $m \in S$, such that L is a subset of m. Logical truth of A is unsatisfiability of the negation of A; B is a logical consequence of A if and only if $A \rightarrow B$ is valid, that is, $(A \,\&\, {\sim}B)$ is unsatisfiable.

Where we are not concerned with attitudes the notion of a model set m is defined in a standard way:

> If $p \in m$, then not ${\sim}p \in m$;
> if $p \,\&\, q \in m$, then $p \in m$ and $q \in m$;
> if $p \lor q \in m$, then $p \in m$ or $q \in m$ or both;
> if $(Ex)p \in m$, then $p\,(a/x) \in m$ for some individual constant a;
> if $(Ax)p \in m$ and if the free singular term b occurs in the sentences of m, then $p\,(b/x) \in m$;
> $p\,(a/x)$ is the result of replacing the variable x by the singular term z everywhere in p.

Henceforward I shall depart somewhat from Hintikka's terminology, in order to separate some of the main ideas more obviously. Suppose we add to a standard first-order language operators $H!$ and $T!$ subject to the condition that if A is a well-formed formula $H!A$ is well formed and $T!A$ is well formed. Suppose now we start with a set of sentences L, which may contain sentences with these operators among them. We begin by defining a *next approximation to the ideal, L^* of L.*

> (Ii)   If $H!A \in L$, then $H!A \in L^*$;
> (Iii) If $H!A \in L$, then $A \in L^*$;
> (Iiii) If $T!p \in L$, then a set L^* containing p is to be added to the set of next approximations for L.

> (Iiv) If L^* is a next approximation to the ideal relative to some set of sentences L, then, if $A \in L^*$, $A \in$ subsequent approximations to the ideal L^{**}, L^{***} ...

We can say that a set of *final ideals*, $\{L^{***} \ldots\}$ of L is obtained when further use of these rules produces no new sentence not already in the members $L^{***} \ldots$ of the set.

The set of sentences L may contain disjunctions or conditionals ready to be treated as disjunctions in the deductive apparatus. We can say that to each branch of a disjunction there corresponds a *route* to an ideal.

We can then define:

> A set of sentences L is unsatisfiable iff each route to a set of final ideals S results in a set of sentences S one of whose members contains both a formula and its negation.

These rules need a little gloss. Obviously Iii embodies the aim that an ideal relative to a starting set of attitudes is obtained by specifying that the goals expressed are met. Rules Ii and Iii merely ensure that the attitudes specified originally remain in the subsequent realizations (if it is good that people are kind, it remains good in a world in which they are kind). The statement $T!A$ gets handled slightly differently. It sees A as compatible with perfection, but not mandatory. When tolerations are in play we have to consider both developments in which they are realized, but also developments in which they are not. One next approximation for $(T!p \,\&\, T!{\sim}p)$ should contain p, and another ${\sim}p$, but the fact that they are inconsistent with each other does not reflect back on the original sentence. So to assess consistency we need to think of formulae as producing a *set* of next approximations. The rule is that if $T!A$ is present in a set, there must be *a* next set in which A is present, although it is not to be in all. This means that we shall have to consider sets of next approximations to the ideal and sets of final idealizations. Intuitively, what is to matter is whether each such set is consistent.

It may be that modifications of Iiv would be desirable. What is obtained by realizing a toleration might not automatically feed through to subsequent approximations. The intuitive idea would be that something may be tolerated now, whereas were some ideal to become realized, it would no longer be tolerable: in that case Iiv would need qualification.

We want to iterate the procedure of generating a next ideal. This can be done by repeated use of these rules. If L^* is already a next approximation to the ideal and contains a sentence A, then except where A derives from realization of a toleration, it must transfer to further approximations to the ideal L^{**}. . . . This is not so in general if A belongs to an original set L (for it may be a pity that $A: A$ & $H! \sim A$ is consistent). Here the idea is that once we are following out what is so in the progressive approximations to a perfect world, any realized ideal remains realized. The denizens of paradise do not move.

To get a feel for such a semantics consider the formula $H!p \rightarrow p$. This is not valid: $\{H!p, \sim p\}$ is satisfiable. The next approximation is $\{H!p, p\}^*$, and this is a final ideal and is consistent. (As the gloss of Iiv showed, p does *not* transfer through to L^* – as far as the original set goes, p may be a pity, and this is reflected in its absence from the final ideal.) Now however consider $H! (H!p \rightarrow p)$. This is valid, for $T! (H!p$ & $\sim p)$ is not satisfiable. By Iv $(H!p, \sim p)^*$ must be added as a next ideal. But the ideal under that is $\{H!p, p, \sim p\}^{**}$ which is inconsistent. Here is the operation of Iiii: it was already in this working out of the ideal that $\sim p$, so it stays there when we further consider the ideal obtained by realizing $H!p$ and generates inconsistency.

Transferred to these terms Hintikka's main worked example is this. Prior once took it as a "quite plain truth" of logic that

$$H!p \ \& \ (p \rightarrow H!q) \rightarrow H!q.$$

But $\{H!p, p \rightarrow H!q, T! \sim q\}$ is perfectly satisfiable. In tree form and using the notion $=0\Rightarrow$ to signify adding the next approximation to the ideal, we get:

$$H!p$$
$$T! \sim q$$

The right-hand route is bound to contain the inconsistent set, but the left yields none – reflecting the fact that if something which ought to be so is not, obligations or norms or goals consequential on its being so need not be held either. As in the first example, something here is a pity, and

this is reflected by the fact that $H! \ [H!p$ & $(p \rightarrow H!q) \rightarrow H!q]$ is indeed valid.

The possibility of valid formulae with wide scope $H!$ suggests a notion of "deontic validity" (Hintikka's term): in other words, although A may be consistent, $H!A$ need not be. In turn this gives us a needed notion: a person may be something worse than "immoral," or possessing contingently defective attitudes, but not be "inconsistent" in the sense of believing anything logically false. He may simply have ideals or goals which admit of no consistent realization.

This logic yields one reduction principle immediately: $H!H!p$ yields $H!p$. What about $T!T! \rightarrow T!p$? $\{T!T!p$ & $H! \sim p\} =0 \Rightarrow \{T!p$ & $H! \sim p\}$ and this too is inconsistent. This reflects the "one-dimensional" way in which realizations of goals are treated: we look through $H!$ and $T!$ to see what happens when they are realized, and this transparency extends to iterations of them. Many complexities could be introduced at this point and in connection with iterations generally.

The semantics also generates interesting sidelights on the original proposal for treating modus ponens. Suppose we took as an example "X is good, if X is good Y is good, so Y is good." Then a treatment like my original might render it:

$$H!p; H! \ (H!p \rightarrow H!q) \ \text{so} \ H!q.$$

And this is indeed valid. But the satisfaction is short lived, for if we turn instead to 'Giving makes happiness; if giving makes happiness then Christmas is a good thing, so Christmas is a good thing' a parallel treatment renders it:

$$p; H! \ (p \rightarrow H!q) \ \text{so} \ H!q.$$

This argument is invalid. There is no way of reimporting the original p into the set of final ideals. Clearly a treatment which makes a big asymmetry between these two arguments is suspicious. However, my old proposal did not quite have this form – it involved no propositional calculus embedding of $H!p$. Now that such a form is available, obviously we shortcircuit these proposals simply to get $H!p$, $H!p \rightarrow H!q$, so $H!q$, and similarly for the second version. Each of these is valid.

So is Schueler right that my original proposal fails to show any inconsistency in the set containing the premises of a modus ponens inference, but a denial of the conclusion? As I mentioned, the original proposal for conditionals took seriously the idea that they create an indirect context – one where the propositions or attitudes normally expressed become, in some sense, the reference or topic of the utterance. In the present development conditionals are treated as disjunctions and broken open for example by tableau methods. Is there essential opposition here? Not necessarily. The issue is whether we can interpret endorsement of $(\backslash A \backslash \Rightarrow \backslash C \backslash)$ – the original interpretation – as equivalent in strength to $(\sim A \vee C)$ – the place conditionals now have in the logic. Only a little leeway with 'endorsement' and 'involves' ('$\Rightarrow$') is needed; as much in fact as gives the material implication its usual right to be thought of as rendering a conditional. Say: endorsing the involvement is tying oneself to the tree. In other words tying oneself to restricting admissible alternatives to those in which $\sim A$, and those in which C. You have one or the other. And the effect of this on the theory of inference, when A or C or both are evaluative, is brought out in the model theory.

Conclusion

Slow-track quasi-realism will want to say that these proposals analyze or give us the logical form of the arguments we are considering. Fast-track quasi-realism need not say this. It can say: "all this is very interesting." It shows how *little* is involved if we imagine us jumping ship – changing from an expressivist language to our normal forms. But it is unnecessary to claim that we make no jump at all. That would involve, for instance, defending the claim that negation is absolutely univocal as it occurs in $\sim H! p$ and in $\sim p$, and similarly for the other constants. But this need not be claimed. All we have is sufficient similarity of logical role to make the temptation to exploit *ordinary* propositional logic quite irresistible – and that is what we naturally do. The expressivist language serves as a model showing us why what we do is legitimate – but that may be all. This is what I meant by saying that fast-track quasi-realism can benefit from the security provided by the slow. I like this methodology. We bootstrap our way into appreciating how propositional expression, the arrival of indirect contexts, and the arrival of the truth predicate meet our needs, without in any way betraying the original, economical, metaphysical vision. At times we may have taken steps, benefiting from what are only analogies between these kinds of commitments and beliefs in order to treat the former as we treat the latter. But if so these steps are little and natural.

37

Expressivism and Embedding

Walter Sinnott-Armstrong

The problem of embedding is often seen as the most difficult problem for expressivists. However, Daniel Stoljar recently argued that expressivists can solve this problem simply by admitting that evaluative assertions[1] have minimal or deflationary truth conditions.[2] Jamie Dreier responded that the problem of embedding cannot be solved so easily, but still might be solved in a more complex way.[3] I will argue that both Stoljar and Dreier are right, because there is more than one problem of embedding, and some but not all of them can be solved simply by acknowledging minimal truth aptness. I will also argue that Dreier's arguments to show that the deepest problem of embedding cannot be solved so easily and also show that it cannot be solved in the more complex ways, developed by Gibbard[4] and Blackburn,[5] with which Dreier has more sympathy. So these expressivists have not yet solved the deepest problem of embedding.

1. Expressivism

Expressivists typically make three claims.[6] The first claim is that evaluative language is not used to assert propositions with truth values. The second claim is that evaluative assertions do not describe the world. The third claim is that evaluative assertions do express emotions or other non-cognitive states, such as attitudes or desires. The first two claims are negative, while the third claim is positive. The first claim is about semantics, while the second two claims are about pragmatics in a broad sense.

These three claims, together with an account of the expressed non-cognitive state, are supposed to

---

[1] Asserting something contrasts here with denying it, hypothesizing it (as in the antecedent of a conditional), disjoining it, questioning it, etc. Assertion in this grammatical sense does not necessarily imply any claim to truth, so my reference to asserting evaluative sentences does not beg the question against expressivists who deny that evaluative language makes any claims to truth.

[2] D. Stoljar, "Emotivism and Truth Conditions." *Philosophical Studies* 70 (1993), pp. 81–101.

[3] J. Dreier, "Expressivist Embeddings and Minimalist Truth." *Philosophical Studies* 83 (1996), pp. 29–51.

[4] A. Gibbard, *Wise Choices, Apt Feelings* (Cambridge, MA: Harvard University Press, 1990).

[5] S. Blackburn, "Attitudes and Contents." Reprinted in *Essays in Quasi-Realism* (New York: Oxford University Press, 1993), pp. 182–97 [Included as chapter 36 of this volume.]

[6] Distinguished by Stoljar, "Emotivism and Truth Conditions", p. 81.

specify the meanings of evaluative assertions. It is partly because the first claim rules out truth conditions that expressivists turn to an expressive function to explain the meanings of evaluative assertions. This expressive function is supposed to be all there is to those meanings because evaluative assertions are not used to describe or to state true propositions. So the three claims are related.

Nonetheless, these three claims are logically independent. One could consistently accept the third claim while denying the first two claims if one held that evaluative language is used both to express emotions or desires and also to describe truths. Conversely, one could consistently accept the first two claims while denying the third claim if one held that evaluative language is used to perform some other speech act incompatible with truth, description, and expression. One could also accept the first claim without the second if one held that some descriptions lack truth values, or the second claim without the first if one held that some non-descriptive assertions can be true.[7] Despite their logical independence, these three claims are often conjoined into a single theory of expressivism.

Different kinds of expressivism claim that different things are expressed by evaluative assertions. Traditional emotivists hold that emotions or attitudes are expressed. Recent expressivists often instead refer to expression of desires or motivations. These are all states of mind, but prescriptivists can also be seen as expressivists if prescriptions can also be expressed. Despite their differences, all expressivists hold that what is expressed is neither cognitive nor doxastic, and they all share the three central claims listed above, so they also all face the same basic problem of embedding. That is why I will treat them all together.

2. The Problem of Embedding

The problem of embedding in unassertive contexts was suggested by Frege and developed by Geach and Searle.[8] The standard version begins with an instance of the argument form *modus ponens*, such as this:

1. Lying is wrong.
2. If lying is wrong, then getting one's little brother to lie is wrong.
∴ 3. Getting one's little brother to lie is wrong.

It is obvious that (1)–(3) is a valid argument. The initial problem is that this obvious fact seems inconsistent with expressivism. The argument (1)–(3) would not be valid if the sentence "Lying is wrong" had different meanings in the two premises, since then the argument would commit a fallacy of equivocation. However, expressivism appears to imply that "Lying is wrong" does have different meanings in premise (1) and in the antecedent of premise (2).

One reason for this appearance is that expressivism explains the meanings of evaluative sentences by saying that assertions of them express emotions or other non-cognitive states. The sentence "Lying is wrong" is asserted in premise (1), so expressivists would analyze premise (1) in terms of expressing something like disapproval of lying. In contrast, "Lying is wrong" is not asserted when premise (2) is asserted, so an utterance of (2) and thereby of its antecedent need not and does not seem to express disapproval of lying. One could believe and assert premise (2) whether or not one disapproves of lying. Thus, expressivism seems to imply that premise (1) is used to express something that the antecedent of premise (2) is not used to express. This suggests that, according to expressivism, (1) does not mean the same as the antecedent of (2), so (1)–(3) equivocates and is invalid.

A similar problem emerges when we move from the positive pragmatic claim to the negative semantic claim of expressivism. Expressivists deny that (1) has a truth value. In contrast, the antecedent of the conditional premise (2) must have a truth value, if the conditional connective in (2) is understood in the most natural way. Even if this conditional connective is not interpreted as a material condi-

[7] As does M. Timmons, *Morality without Foundations* (New York: Oxford University Press, 1999). But see my "An Argument for Descriptivism." *Southern Journal of Philosophy* (1999).

[8] P. T. Geach, "Ascriptivism." *Philosophical Review* 69 (1960), pp. 221–5; and "Assertion." *Philosophical Review* 74 (1965), pp. 449–65. J. Searle, "Meaning and Speech Acts." *Philosophical Review* 71 (1962), pp. 423–32, and *Speech Acts* (Cambridge: Cambridge University Press, 1969), pp. 136–41. Geach cites Frege's distinction between predication and assertion as a source.

tional or as truth-functional, this conditional still seems to claim some relation between the truth values of its antecedent and its consequent.

An expressivist might respond by analyzing conditionals in some way that does not require its components to be truth apt. Such analyses are often supported by conditionals that embed questions (as in "If he's not home, where is he?") and imperatives (as in "If you can't stand the heat, get out of the kitchen"). Despite such examples, however, a conditional with indicative components can still claim some relation between the truth values of the antecedent and of the consequent, just as a conjunction of indicatives claims a relation between its conjuncts' truth values despite examples like "I'm not moving, and what are you going to do about it?". Indeed, some account that requires components of indicative conditionals to be truth apt seems necessary to fit the common logical intuition that (1)–(3) is valid, since validity is most naturally explained in terms of truth values. Moreover, the connective "If . . . , then . . ." seems to have the same meaning regardless of whether or not its antecedent or consequent is evaluative. When its components are not evaluative but are indicative and do have truth values, then a conditional does seem to claim some relation between the truth values of those components. This makes it seem that conditionals also operate on truth values when their components are evaluative indicatives. For such reasons, the antecedent of premise (2) seems to have a truth value. But the negative semantic claim of expressivism seems to imply that premise (1) has no truth value. This suggests, again, that (1) does not mean the same as the antecedent of (2), so (1)–(3) equivocates and is invalid, according to expressivism.

The problem is that, as I said, argument (1)–(3) is obviously valid. If the invalidity of this argument is implied by expressivism, then expressivism is inadequate to capture a central feature of evaluative language.

3.   Expressivist Responses to the Initial Problem of Embedding

Despite this appearance, expressivists can deny that any of their claims entails that argument

(1)–(3) is invalid. Consider, first, the positive pragmatic claim that evaluative assertions are used to express emotions (or other non-cognitive states). This claim is just about assertions. It is not about utterances in non-assertive contexts. Consequently, this positive pragmatic claim does not imply that, when a speaker asserts (2) and thereby utters its antecedent, which is (1), this utterance does not express the same emotion as an assertion of (1). Nor does it imply the opposite. Neither implication holds, because the positive pragmatic claim does not even try to give an account of unassertive contexts.

A critic of expressivism might counter that expressivism is at best incomplete if it gives no account of unassertive contexts. Since coherence requires not only consistency but also connectedness and comprehensiveness, expressivism lacks coherence if its positive pragmatic claim about assertive contexts is not connected in some way with a positive pragmatic claim about unassertive contexts. In response, expressivists can maintain several connections between assertive and unassertive contexts. Expressivists might, for example, hold that it is essential to the meaning of the antecedent of a conditional that, whenever the same sentence is asserted with the same meaning, its assertion does express emotions or other non-cognitive states. Expressivists also might hold that the meaning and/or pragmatic force of asserting a whole unassertive context, such as a whole conditional, needs to be explained in terms of the pragmatic force of asserting its parts.[9] Such claims can add coherence to the overall theory that covers both assertive and unassertive contexts.

Even if expressivism is extended in some such way, the positive pragmatic claim of expressivists still would not imply the invalidity of argument (1)–(3). To see this, suppose I assert the non-evaluative sentence "You lied to me" and thereby also express my anger at or disapproval of you or your lie. When this same sentence occurs in the antecedent of a conditional, such as "If you lied to me, then you are no friend of mine", no anger or disapproval is expressed, but this sentence still has the same meaning in any sense that is necessary for the validity of an argument with these sentences. This is shown by the fact that these two

---

[9]   For example, S. Blackburn, *Spreading the Word* (Oxford: Clarendon Press, 1984), pp. 191–6, claims that to assert (2) is to express a second-order attitude towards a combination of first-order attitudes that includes the attitude expressed when its antecedent (1) is asserted alone.

non-evaluative sentences logically imply "You are no friend of mine." The general point is that a change in the pragmatic force of an utterance is not always a change in the kind of meaning that affects validity. Since this point applies as well to evaluative utterances, no difference in the pragmatic force of "Lying is wrong" when it is asserted, as in (1), and when it is not asserted, as in (2), can show that argument (1)–(3) is invalid. Thus, the positive pragmatic claim by expressivists does not create this problem of embedding.

What about expressivists' negative pragmatic claim that moral assertions or utterances are not descriptive? That does not even seem to create any problem. If an assertion of (1) does not describe lying, neither does the non-assertive utterance of the same sentence in the antecedent of (2), so the negative pragmatic claim provides no reason to believe in any equivocation or invalidity.

The final central claim by expressivists is their negative semantic claim that evaluative sentences lack truth values (or truth conditions or truth aptness).[10] This claim might seem more troublesome, because it concerns truth and the kind of meaning that does affect validity. Nonetheless, this negative semantic claim also does not entail that argument (1)–(3) is invalid. To see this, we need to distinguish between different kinds of truth aptness.[11]

A sentence has maximal truth aptness only when it is or can be either true or false by virtue of corresponding or conflicting in a substantive way with a mind independent fact or state of affairs or reality. When there is no such fact, or when correspondence or conflict with such a fact is not what makes the sentence true or false, then the sentence lacks maximal truth aptness. Expressivists deny that evaluative sentences have such maximal truth aptness.

Other kinds of truth aptness are less demanding. A sentence is minimally truth apt whenever it is

grammatical to embed that sentence in the context "It is true that . . ." or "It is false that . . .". For example, an imperative such as "Close the door" and a question such as "Where are you?" lack minimal truth aptness, but an indicative such as "Shaquille is tall" has minimal truth aptness. Do evaluative sentences have minimal truth aptness? Obviously so, since it is not ungrammatical to call moral sentences true or false. People often say things like "It is true in general that I ought not to lie, but surprise parties are exceptions." If anything is wrong with calling moral sentences true or false, the problem is not grammar. Therefore, moral sentences have minimal truth aptness, and expressivists are mistaken if they say otherwise. The obviousness of this point is a reason to suppose that expressivists do not or should not intend to deny that evaluative sentences have minimal truth aptness.

If so, that is, if expressivists deny maximal truth aptness but not minimal truth aptness, then their negative semantic claim does not entail that argument (1)–(3) is invalid. If premise (1) and the antecedent of premise (2) both have minimal truth aptness, then their lack of maximal truth aptness does not entail that they have different meanings in any way that is relevant to validity, since the relevant kind of meaning might concern minimal truth and not maximal truth, for all we have seen so far.

4.   The Basic Problem of Embedding and its Solution

Mere consistency with the validity of (1)–(3) is not enough to save expressivism. To be complete, expressivism needs a positive explanation of the validity of argument (1)–(3) in particular and of evaluative instances of modus ponens in general. If the initial problem of embedding is to show that expressivism does not entail the invalidity of argument (1)–(3), the basic problem of embedding is

---

[10]   These notions are different. For example, even if "The present King of France is bald" lacks any truth *value* when there is no present King of France, it is still truth *apt*, because it is the right kind of thing to be true, and it would be either true or false if there were a present King of France who is not a borderline case of baldness. Similarly, even if a particular utterance of "It is noon" has a truth value and is truth apt, one might claim that it has no specifiable invariant truth *conditions*. This claim is controversial, but my point is just that the issues of truth conditions and of truth values are distinct. In any case, expressivists do not claim that evaluative sentences lack truth values either because their terms always lack referents or are too vague or because the conditions under which they are true or false are not specifiable or invariant. So the differences among truth values, truth conditions, and truth aptness do not affect the issues here about expressivism, which are most precisely described in terms of truth aptness.

[11]   Following Stoljar, "Emotivism and Truth Conditions", pp. 83–4, who uses "deflationary truth conditions" in place of "minimal truth aptness".

for expressivists to explain why evaluative instances of modus ponens are valid.

Expressivists can solve this basic problem by citing minimal truth aptness again. All sentences with minimal truth aptness fit grammatically into the antecedents of conditionals. In other words, if a sentence fits into the context "It is true that . . .", then it also fits into the antecedent of "If . . . , then . . .". Having a truth value is not necessary, since, even if "The present King of France is bald" lacks any truth value, it is still grammatical to say "If the present King of France is bald, then he is not hairy." Thus, all expressivists need to cite is minimal truth aptness in order to explain why evaluative sentences fit grammatically into conditionals.

Whenever a sentence fits into the antecedent of a conditional, a modus ponens argument whose premises are this sentence and an appropriate conditional is valid. The reason is that arguments with the form modus ponens are valid by virtue of the properties of the connective "if . . . , then . . .", not by virtue of any properties of the components that are connected by "if . . . , then . . .". Philosophers hold many views of the truth conditions of the connective "if . . . , then . . .". I do not need or want to commit myself to any controversial view of conditionals here. All that is essential here is that no analysis of the conditional connective in an instance of modus ponens can do justice to our logical intuitions unless it makes that argument formally valid. An argument is formally valid only if any argument with the same form is valid regardless of the content of its components. Thus, an instance of modus ponens is valid regardless of whether or not its components are evaluative in content.

Overall, then, expressivists can cite minimal truth aptness to explain why evaluative sentences fit grammatically into antecedents of conditionals, and they can cite the logical properties of conditionals to explain why all instances of modus ponens are valid. These two steps are enough for expressivists to explain the validity of all instances of modus ponens with an evaluative premise and to solve the basic problem of embedding. To this extent, Stoljar is right.

5.   The Deeper Problem of Embedding

This explanation of the validity of modus ponens as a general form of argument is still not quite enough to explain the validity of any particular argument, such as (1)–(3). To explain that, one still needs to show that the particular argument is an instance of the general form. This might seem easy. Just look at the words in the argument. But it is not so easy. (1)–(3) is not an instance of the form modus ponens if the sentence "Lying is wrong" has a different meaning in premise (1) than it has in the antecedent of premise (2). If "lying" in (1) refers to intentional falsehoods but "lying" throughout (2) and (3) refers to remaining horizontal ("lying down"), then argument (1)–(3) does not really have the form modus ponens (p, p ⊃ q, ∴ q), but instead has a different form (p, q ⊃ r, ∴ r); and it is not valid. Consequently, in order to complete the explanation of the validity of (1)–(3), one also needs to show that the meaning of "Lying is wrong" does not change between (1) and the antecedent of (2).

This need cannot be satisfied simply by saying that evaluative sentences have minimal truth aptness. Even if it is grammatical to call evaluative sentences "true" and "false" and put them into the antecedents of conditionals, that does not show that they do not change their meanings when they are put in those contexts, nor does it show what the resulting conditional means. To solve these deeper problems and thereby to complete the explanation of the validity of (1)–(3), we need some larger semantic theory. To this extent, Dreier is right.

Such a semantic theory is available to explain the validity of non-evaluative instances of modus ponens. Consider "Socrates is a man. If Socrates is a man, then Socrates is mortal. Therefore, Socrates is mortal." This argument's validity can be explained by saying that the intersection of the set of possible worlds in which Socrates is a man with the set of possible worlds in which, if Socrates is a man, then Socrates is mortal (that is, with the complement of the intersection of (a) the set of possible worlds in which Socrates is a man with (b) the complement of the set of possible worlds in which Socrates is mortal) is included in the set of possible worlds in which Socrates is mortal. This semantic theory thus explains why the premises cannot both be true without the conclusion also being true, which is just what it is for the argument to be valid. It also explains why "Socrates is a man" has the same content in both premises, since the content of the conditional premise is specified by reference to (a) the set of worlds where the non-conditional premise is true.

The question is whether anything like this is available for evaluative sentences. Many expressivists try to avoid possible worlds, because a possible world is usually defined in terms of what is true in that world. The negative semantic claim by expressivists might seem to deny that evaluative sentences have the needed kind of truth. Indeed, most expressivists do not give any kind of truth conditions for evaluative utterances. Without giving these truth conditions in some way, expressivists cannot provide any deeper explanation of the validity of particular arguments like (1)–(3).

One prominent exception is Alan Gibbard, who provides formal semantics to explain the validity of evaluative modus ponens.[12] Gibbard represents the content of an evaluative utterance as a set of factual-normative worlds or as ruling out the complement of that set. A factual-normative world is just a combination of a possible world with a set of general norms of the form "Do this" or "Don't do that". An evaluative sentence holds in a factual-normative world just in case the facts in the possible world plus the norms that are also in the factual-normative world logically imply the evaluative sentence. The content of a conditional is then the complement of the intersection of (a) the set of normative-factual worlds that gives the content of the antecedent with (b) the complement of the set of normative-factual worlds that gives the content of the consequent. In other words, a conditional rules out the intersection of (a) and (b).

This semantic apparatus is supposed to explain the validity of arguments like (1)–(3) as follows. Premise (1) rules out the set of all normative-factual worlds in which lying is not wrong. Premise (2) then rules out the intersection of the set of normative-factual worlds in which lying is wrong with the set of normative-factual worlds in which it is not wrong to get your little brother to lie. Together, premises (1)–(2) rule out the whole set of normative-factual worlds in which it is not wrong to get your little brother to lie. This includes every normative-factual world that the conclusion (3) rules out. Thus, this apparatus explains why argument (1)–(3) is valid. It also explains why the meaning of (1) does not change when it is placed in the antecedent of (2), since the sentence in both locations refers to the set of normative-factual worlds in which lying is wrong. This apparatus also explains the meaning of the whole conditional

premise (2) in terms of another set of normative-factual worlds. So it might seem that expressivists could not ask or be asked for more.

I do not deny that Gibbard's semantic apparatus implies and to that extent explains the validity of (1)–(3). Indeed, it works as well for all other instances of evaluative modus ponens.

It is not clear, however, that all of this apparatus is *necessary* to explain the validity of evaluative instances of modus ponens. To see this, consider this non-evaluative argument:

> 1*   I lie.
> 2*   If I lie, then my little brother lies.
> ∴ 3*   My little brother lies.

The first premise (1*) rules out all of those possible worlds where I do not lie. The second premise (2*) rules out all of those possible worlds where I lie but my little brother does not lie. Together the premises rule out all of the possible worlds where my little brother does not lie. That explains why the argument is valid. However, we do not *need* to go through all of this to explain why (1*)–(3*) is valid. Possible worlds might explain the content of the premises, but not all of that content is essential to the validity of the argument. In order to know that the argument is valid, we do not need to know whether "I lie" in (1*) and (2*) refers to my utterance of an intentional falsehood or to my being in a horizontal position (lying down). All we need to know (other than the references of "I" and "my little brother") is that "lie" in (1*) has the same meaning as it does in the antecedent of (2*), and that "lie" in the conclusion has the same meaning as it does in the consequent of (2*). The term "lie" might even have different meanings in the antecedent and in the consequent of (2*). In any case, we do not need to know what the meanings are, as long as we know that they match up in the right way with other components of the argument. We can even explain why "Toths are slithy. If toths are slithy, then t'was brillig. So t'was brillig." is a valid argument, as long as there is no change in the meanings of "toths", "slithy", etc. We still need to know the logical properties of the conditional connective in (2*), but, once we know that, we do not need any semantic theory to tell us the meanings of the terms in the components of that conditional.

---

[12]   Gibbard, *Wise Choices, Apt Feelings*, pp. 94–102.

The reason, again, is that instances of modus ponens are formally valid, and formal validity holds regardless of the contents of the components. Moreover, modus ponens is valid within propositional logic, and propositional logic can be developed completely without referring to possible worlds. Possible worlds might be needed to define validity and to explain the validity of some arguments within modal logic, but possible worlds are not needed at all to specify the features that make arguments formally valid within propositional logic.

The same point applies to instances of modus ponens with an evaluative premise. We do not need to know what (1) means or what (3) means in order to know that (1)–(3) is valid. All we need to know is that (1) and the antecedent of (2) have the same meaning (in the relevant sense of "meaning"), and that (3) and the consequent of (2) have the same meaning (in the relevant sense of "meaning"), along with the logical properties of the conditional connective in (2) and the minimal truth aptness of (1) and (3). None of this requires any reference to normative-factual worlds or any full-blown semantic theory. So Gibbard's theory is not needed.

Still, Gibbard's theory does accomplish something. By providing a way to represent the content of (1)–(3), Gibbard can specify the meaning that is shared by (1) and the antecedent of (2) as well as the meaning that is shared by (3) and the consequent of (2). One way to show that these sentences have the same meaning is to show what they both mean. But this is still not necessary. If expressivists can argue that these sentences have the same meaning without specifying what that meaning is, then they can explain the validity of this instance of modus ponens without any semantic theory like Gibbard's. One way for expressivists to do this is to appeal to linguistic intuition. In many contexts, it seems obvious that (1) and the antecedent of (2) have the same meaning in any way that is relevant to validity. Any semantic theory will have to accommodate this fact in order to be adequate. So expressivists need not commit themselves to a specific semantic theory in order to argue that any adequate semantics will imply that (1) and the antecedent of (2) have the same meaning. This also applies to (3) and the consequent of (2). Consequently, expressivists do not have to provide any specific semantic

theory in order to explain why the particular argument (1)–(3) is valid and, thereby, to solve the deeper problem of embedding.

6. The Deepest Problem of Embedding

Philosophers still won't be satisfied. They will want to know what (1), (2), and (3) mean. Although this is not necessary to explain the validity of argument (1)–(3), there still seems to be a gap in expressivism if it does not tell any adequate story about the meanings of (1), (3), and especially (2). This problem arises apart from unassertive contexts, but those contexts raise this problem with a special focus and urgency, so to fill this gap can be called the deepest problem of embedding.

Some semantic theory like Gibbard's might seem necessary to solve this deepest problem by explaining the meanings of conditionals with evaluative components. Of course, if the conditional connective is understood, one can say something about what any conditional sentence means. For example, if the conditional connective is a material conditional, then "If lying is wrong, then getting one's little brother to lie is wrong" means "Either lying is not wrong or getting one's little brother to lie is wrong." However, this does not tell us what the whole conditional means unless we already know what its components mean. When we cannot assume the meanings of components, something like Gibbard's theory might be needed to specify the meanings of evaluative sentences along with compounds including those evaluative sentences.

More generally, if expressivists make only the negative and positive pragmatic claims and the negative semantic claim, but they do not go on to make any positive semantic claim, then expressivists have not yet given any positive account of the meanings of (2) or of its components in the relevant sense of "meaning". Merely claiming minimal truth aptness for a sentence does not tell us what that sentence means, even if we also know its pragmatic force. This is one gap in expressivism that Gibbard's semantic theory might be needed to fill.

This problem is pressed forcefully by Dreier.[13] Dreier imagines an accostivist, who tell us that the

---

[13] Dreier, "Expressivist Embeddings and Minimalist Truth", pp. 42–4.

expression "Hiyo, Bob" is used to accost Bob. It is not used to describe Bob, and it has no truth value. In contrast, the indicative variation "Bob is hiyo" is also used to accost Bob, but it has minimal truth aptness by virtue of its grammatical form, so it can be used in valid arguments, such as "Bob is hiyo". If Bob is hiyo, then so is his little brother. Therefore, his little brother is hiyo." Dreier's point is that none of this stipulation gives us any idea what "Bob is hiyo" means. It does not mean "Bob is accosted" or "The speaker accosts Bob." Accostivists can say that to assert "Bob is hiyo" is to accost, but that does not help us understand a conditional with "Bob is hiyo" in its antecedent. This lack of understanding shows that merely saying that a sentence is used for a certain speech act and also has minimal truth aptness and so fits grammatically into conditionals is not enough to explain what the sentence means. But that is all that expressivism tells us about evaluative sentences before adding any positive semantics like that of Gibbard. Dreier concludes that the three central claims of expressivism plus minimal truth aptness are not enough for expressivists to explain the meanings of evaluative sentences alone and in compounds and thereby to solve the deepest problem of embedding.

I accept this negative conclusion by Dreier. It also seems that something like Gibbard's (or Blackburn's) semantics is necessary to fill out expressivism. However, Dreier goes on to suggest that something like Gibbard's semantic theory is sufficient to solve this deepest problem for expressivism.[14] I doubt that even this is sufficient. Dreier's ingenious argument creates more problems for expressivism than Dreier realizes, because it shows that Gibbard's semantic theory is not enough, even when added to the three central claims of expressivism and minimal truth.

To see this, let's construct Gibbardian semantics for "hiyo." We could introduce generalizations called "hiyorms", such as "Hiyo, everyone here" or "Everyone here is hiyo" (analogous to Gibbard's norms). Next we construct a logic of "hiyo" in terms of "hiyormative-factual worlds", which are combinations of possible worlds with hiyorms (analogous to Gibbard's "normative-factual worlds"). The content of the sentence "Bob is hiyo" can then be represented as a set of hiyorma-tive-factual worlds or as ruling out all other hiyor-mative-factual worlds. The content of the conditional "If Bob is hiyo, so is his little brother" rules out the intersection of the set of hiyormative-factual worlds where Bob is hiyo and the complement of the set of hiyormative-factual worlds where Bob's little brother is hiyo. The validity of the argument "Bob is hiyo. If Bob is hiyo, so is his little brother. So his little brother is hiyo." can then be explained by showing that every hiyormative-factual world that is ruled out by the conclusion is already ruled out by the premises. Nonetheless, this semantic story does not help us to understand "Bob is hiyo" any better than we did before going through all of this rigmarole. This lack of understanding shows that such formal semantics is not enough to explain what "Bob is hiyo" means. Consequently, analogous moves by expressivists are also not enough. When expressivists add a formal semantics like Gibbard's on top of the three central claims of expressivism plus some story about minimal truth aptness, they still do not succeed in analyzing the meanings of evaluative sentences. It might not be clear what more is needed, but my extension of Dreier's argument shows that something more is needed.

Expressivists might respond that all they need is to specify the non-cognitive state that is expressed. Gibbard does, after all, go to great lengths to explain acceptance of norms and the emotions that are expressed by assertions of evaluative sentences.[15] This is still not enough. "Hiyo, Bob" and "Bob is hiyo" are used to accost, which is to approach and speak to in an aggressive or hostile manner, so these assertions are also used to express aggression or hostility. But no analysis of aggression or hostility will make us understand "If Bob is hiyo, so is his little brother", even if added to a logic of hiyormative worlds. What we do not understand is the claim that Bob is hiyo, not just the non-cognitive state that is expressed when "Bob is hiyo" is asserted. Analogously, then, no analysis of the non-cognitive state expressed by evaluative assertions can sufficiently fill out the expressivist theory. In neither case can meanings be adequately explained by a non-cognitive state, a logic, and central claims like those of expressivism.

Another likely response is that I demand too much. Although Gibbardian semantics is not

---

[14]   Ibid., pp. 44–5.
[15]   Gibbard, *Wise Choices, Apt Feelings*, pp. 55–82 and 126–50.

enough to explain what "Bob is hiyo" means, that is because "hiyo" is unfamiliar. Gibbard's theory still might suffice to explain evaluative assertions, if we can assume a common understanding of evaluative assertions. But we can't. If the expressivist account depends on a prior understanding of evaluative terms, then it is not sufficient in itself to explain the meanings of those evaluative terms. The only reason expressivism seems to do a better job than accostivism is that we already have some sense of what evaluative sentences mean, and we take that prior sense for granted in interpreting theories like expressivism. This dependence on prior understanding, however, shows that expressivism by itself is not enough to specify those meanings.

Although I have focused so far on Gibbard, similar problems arise for Blackburn. Blackburn has changed his position several times. First, he explained unassertive contexts by propositional reflections.[16] Next, he employed meta-attitudes.[17] Blackburn's current view uses a variation on Hintikka's semantics for deontic logic.[18] This new approach treats evaluative and normative terms as operators on sentences. Corresponding to "It ought to be the case that p" is "H!p" which "can be seen as expressing the view that p is to be a goal, to be realized in any perfect world – a world in which ~p is less than ideal, according to this commitment." The contrary "It ought not to be that p" then gets expressed as "B!p" which "would rule p out of any perfect world."[19] For example, I ought not to lie in this world roughly if I do not lie in any world that is a closer approximation to the ideal. What gives content to normative claims about this world is then the assignment of certain worlds as next approximations to the ideal relative to this world.

Perfect worlds or deontic alternatives (in Hintikka's terminology) or approximations to the ideal (in Blackburn's terminology) must then meet certain formal restrictions, the most important of which are roughly that, if p ought to be the case in world W, then p is true and also ought to be the

case in each next approximation to the ideal relative to W. These restrictions do seem to explain the validity of evaluative instances of modus ponens, such as (1)–(3). Premise (1) ensures that lying does not occur in any next approximation to the ideal relative to this world. Premise (2) is then interpreted as "B!L→B!GBL",[20] which ensures that, if lying does not occur in any next approximation to the ideal relative to this world, then neither does getting your little brother to lie. It follows that getting your little brother to lie does not occur in any next approximation to the ideal relative to this world. So (1)–(3) is valid. This is how Blackburn, like Gibbard, can solve the deeper problem of embedding.

These restrictions and assignments might also seem to supply the missing element that expressivists need to explain the meanings of evaluative sentences and thereby solve the deepest problem of embedding. In addition, Blackburn's proposal might seem immune from the problems created by Dreier's accostivist, since "is hiyo" is a predicate, whereas Hintikka's logic treats evaluative and normative terms as operators on sentences. Nonetheless, analogous to Dreier's accostivist, we can imagine a betivist who introduces "Bet, Bob will quit" as a way of betting that Bob will quit. The betivist then adds that "Bet is betted to quit" is another way of making the same bet, but this way has minimal truth, even though it is not used to state that Bob will quit or that the speaker bets that Bob will quit. Formal semantics for "Bob is betted to quit" can then define this sentence as true in this world only if Bob quits in all worlds that are winners relative to this world, that is, in all worlds where the speaker wins the bet (just as Hintikka's semantics makes "Bob ought to quit" true if Bob quits in all ideal worlds). These semantics can then explain the validity of "Bob is betted to quit. If Bob is betted to quit, then so is his little brother. So Bob's little brother is betted to quit." The first premise ensures that Bob quits in all winning worlds; and the second premise ensures that, if Bob quits in all winning worlds, then Bob's little

---

[16]   Blackburn, "Moral Realism", reprinted in *Essays in Quasi-Realism*, pp. 125–9. Originally published in 1973.

[17]   See Blackburn, *Spreading the Word*, pp. 191–6 and my note 9. Blackburn's reasons for dropping meta-attitudes from his analysis of conditionals are given in his "Attitudes and Contents", pp. 191 and 196–7.

[18]   Blackburn, "Attitudes and Contents", p. 193, citing J. Hintikka, "Deontic Logic and its Philosophical Morals" in *Models for Modalities* (Dordrecht: Reidel, 1969) [included in this volume as chapter 36].

[19]   Blackburn, "Attitudes and Contents", p. 189.

[20]   Ibid., p. 197.

brother quits in all winning worlds; so together these premises ensure that Bob's little brother quits in all winning worlds. Nonetheless, this new theory still does not seem to tell us the meaning of "Bob is betted to quit" any more than the Gibbardian semantics gave the meaning of "Bob is hiyo". We still do not know what "Bob is betted to quit" means. It does not mean either "Bob will (probably) quit" or "The speaker (or someone) bets that Bob will quit." A betivist can say that to assert that Bob is betted to quit is to bet that Bob will quit, but that does not help us understand a conditional with "Bob is betted to quit" in its antecedent. Adding a logic like Hintikka's does not help either.

Perhaps some will disagree and think that they do know what "Bob is betted to quit" means. However, it is even more clear that we do not know what this sentence means when it is in the antecedent of a conditional. Suppose someone says, "If Bob is betted to quit, then you will be in trouble." According to betivism, this does not mean either "If I bet that Bob will quit, then you will be in trouble" or "If Bob quits, then you will be in trouble." So what does it mean? We just don't know. Yet the betivist has told us everything about these sentences that Blackburn has told us so far about evaluative sentences, even with Hintikka's help. Since betivist semantics is not enough to specify what betivist sentences mean, what Blackburn has told us is not enough to give the meanings of evaluative sentences either.

The general point is that formal logic cannot do the work of semantics at least for non-logical terms. This is a serious problem for expressivists, because expressivists need to claim that their theory is complete in the sense that it includes everything necessary to understand the meanings of (at least some) evaluative sentences. My extensions of Dreier's hiyo argument show that it is not sufficient for expressivists to say just that evaluative assertions are minimally truth apt and not descriptive but expressive, even if expressivists add formal semantics for these sentences. If this is all they say, the claims of expressivism do not amount to a complete theory.

But then we cannot be sure that an expressivist theory could ever be completed without referring to maximal moral truths or something else that is incompatible with the very core of expressivism. Indeed, it is hard to see how to solve the deepest problem of embedding without giving truth conditions along the lines proposed by moral realists. Moreover, it seems natural to fill the gap in expressivism by supplying realistic truth conditions for evaluative judgments, and such truth conditions do seem to solve the deepest problem of embedding. This will remain a reason to favor moral realism over expressivism until expressivists solve all of the problems of embedding, including the deepest one.

So expressivists still have a lot of serious work to do. I do not claim that expressivists cannot accomplish this task, but I would like to see them try.

38

New Wave Moral Realism Meets Moral Twin Earth

Terry Horgan and Mark Timmons

1. Introduction

There have been times in the history of ethical theory, especially in this century, when moral realism was down, but it was never out. The appeal of this doctrine for many moral philosophers is apparently so strong that there are always supporters in its corner who seek to resuscitate the view. The attraction is obvious: moral realism purports to provide a precious philosophical good, viz., objectivity and all that this involves, including right answers to (most) moral questions, and the possibility of knowing those answers. In the last decade, moral realism has re-entered the philosophical ring in powerful-looking naturalistic form. Developments in other areas of philosophical inquiry have helped rejuvenate this position, by apparently providing for a strain of naturalism which is immune to the blows that decked older versions of moral realism, including traditional versions of ethical naturalism. This new wave moral realism has come to dominate recent work in metaethics.

However, despite any advantages this new strain of naturalistic moral realism enjoys over previous versions of realism, we maintain that it is destined to travel the same road as its predecessors. In a series of papers (Horgan and Timmons 1991, 1992; Timmons 1990) we have made our case for this pessimistic prediction, investigating at some length the difficulties faced by new wave moral realism. In this paper we provide a dialectical overview: we situate the new wave position itself, and also our objections to it, in the context of the evolving program of philosophical naturalism in 20th century analytic philosophy. We seek to show that although this new contender might initially look like championship material, it succumbs to punches surprisingly similar to those that knocked out the old-fashioned versions of naturalist moral realism. New wave realism too has a glass jaw.

2. Philosophical Naturalism

Moral realism faces well-known, serious philosophical obstacles – obstacles that seem particularly difficult given a thoroughgoing philosophical naturalism. So we begin the saga of ethical naturalism with some remarks about philosophical naturalism.

We take the naturalist outlook in philosophy to be at bottom a metaphysical view about the nature of what exists. The vague, pre-theoretic idea that this view attempts to articulate and defend is simply the idea that all that exists – including any particulars, events, properties, etc., – is part of the natural physical world that science investigates. This core idea can be precisified in various ways, but common to most variants is what we'll call the *thesis of physical ontic primacy:*

> (N1)   The ontologically primary or fundamental entities (particulars, properties, facts, etc.) in the world are all part of the subject matter of physics.

There is more to metaphysical naturalism than thesis (N1), however. Common sense, and ordinary discourse, recognize all sorts of entities that seem, at least prima facie, not to be literally identical with entities that are *narrowly physical*, i.e., explicitly countenanced by physics. And this fact generates a broad project for the philosophical naturalist: *viz.,* to somehow accommodate, within a broadly naturalistic metaphysical/epistemological framework, *all* particulars, properties, facts, etc. as part of the "natural order." The operative notion of accommodation is itself vague and pre-theoretic. It too can be precisified in various ways, but the leading idea is what we'll call the thesis of *explainability*:

> (N2)   All truths are ultimately explainable on the basis of facts involving ontologically primary entities.

It is this second thesis that mainly drives the naturalist's program. And as views have changed about the kind of explainability that constitutes ontological accommodation, so has the entire program of metaphysical naturalism.

Additionally, the metaphysical viewpoint embodied in (N1) and (N2) has typically been accompanied by a nonskeptical outlook in epistemology, according to which we have access to – and can come to have knowledge of – the phenomena that comprise the natural order. If one combines this nonskeptical outlook with metaphysical naturalism, then one has an overall philosophical package – call it *philosophical naturalism* – that imposes the following metaphysical and epistemological constraints on any nonskeptical version of moral realism:

> (C1)   If there are any moral properties or facts, they must be naturalistically accommodated.

> (C2)   If moral knowledge is possible our access to and knowledge of moral properties and facts must be explainable according to epistemological principles we use to explain our knowledge of the natural world generally.

Failure of the moral realist to meet these constraints would evidently have quite a high price tag. The price for non-accommodation is metaphysical queerness of moral properties and facts, plus all the epistemological problems that come with trying to plausibly explain how we have epistemic access to such oddball entities. Certainly these constraints on an acceptable version of moral realism impose quite demanding burdens on the moral realist, but ones well worth shouldering in light of the consequences of failure to do so.

Of course, this particular problematic for metaethics is driven by philosophical naturalism, and there have been those who don't buy that picture and so don't feel constrained by (C1) and (C2). But despite one's global metaphysical and epistemological proclivities, wouldn't it be nice if moral realism could meet these constraints? It would remove most of the metaphysical and epistemological worries about ethics.

3.   Remembrance of Things Past

Those who take their philosophical naturalism seriously either have to go the eliminativist route and argue against the presumption that there are moral properties and facts to be somehow naturalistically accommodated, or get down to business and do some accommodating. How might the latter approach be implemented? I.e., if there are indeed objective moral truths, then how might these truths be explainable on the basis of lower-order, nonmoral, facts?

Traditionally, this underwriting project was shaped by a certain, quite narrow, conception of philosophical naturalism – a strongly reductive version which took identity to be the proper relation between successive ontological levels and took some sort of reductive analysis of higher-level terms and concepts to be the only available strategy for securing the needed identities. Furthermore, it certainly appeared – at first, anyway – that about the only way to approach the reductive task was by way of showing that higher-level terms and expressions had the same meaning as lower-level terms and expressions. So, for instance, a synonymy criterion of property identity was thought to undergird legitimate reductions of one property to another.

The particular reductivist program, applied to moral phenomena, meant that moral properties and facts were to be reductively identified with more basic properties and facts, perhaps psychological or even biological ones. Moreover, the reduction was to proceed by way of analytic meaning connections between moral terms and expressions on the one hand, and non-moral terms and expressions on the other. In short, moral terms were supposed to have analytic naturalistic definitions, and these were to provide the ultimate basis of the ontological accommodation of the moral to the natural. Call this version of ethical naturalism, *analytic ethical naturalism.*

Of course, if the analytic ethical naturalist could provide the desired meaning reductions, then the two naturalist constraints would be satisfied and moral realism would be in good shape. But we all know what happened: in the early part of this century, G. E. Moore's Open Question Argument lowered the boom on analytical ethical naturalism. Consider any proposed analytic definition of a moral term M by means of a non-moral term or expression N, and consider a corresponding question of the form 'Entity x is N, but is x M?' If the putative definition is correct, then the answer to this question should be knowable simply by reflection on its meaning, and in this sense closed; but invariably, such questions are open.

In light of the Open Question Argument, it appeared that analytic naturalism was simply false. This, in turn, seemed to show that the philosophical naturalist's constraints could not be satisfied vis a vis moral properties and facts. So the available alternatives, apparently, were (i) non-naturalist moral realism (Moore's position), or (ii) irrealism about matters moral. Since non-naturalism seemed so philosophically unpalpable, irrealism – in the form of noncognitivist accounts of language – proliferated in the decades following Moore. Moore's Open Question Agument had evidently put ethical naturalism down for the count, and things looked bleak for moral realism.

4.   That Was Then, This Is Now

Times have certainly changed, even in philosophy. A number of recent developments have considerably altered the program of philosophical naturalism, and consequently made possible the re-emergence of a new and improved version of ethical naturalism. Although the naturalistic outlook still reigns supreme, philosophers have lightened up about the constraints a respectable philosophical naturalism must satisfy. In particular, those wedded to the naturalist program no longer view (N2) as requiring *reduction* of higher-order terms, concepts, theories, or properties to lower-order ones – not in the narrow sense involving inter-level analytic meaning equivalences between terms and expressions of different ontological levels, and also not in the somewhat wider sense involving type/type "bridge laws" involving inter-level *nomic* equivalences. This relaxing of constraints has emerged in the wake of a number of interrelated developments in metaphysics, epistemology, philosophy of language, and philosophy of mind in the 1960s and 1970s.

First, there has been a widespread rejection of a synonymy criterion of property identity, in light of numerous apparent counterexamples. For instance, the (sortal) property *being water* is identical with the property *being composed of H₂O molecules*; heat is identical with molecular motion; temperature is identical with mean molecular kinetic energy; and so on. But no one supposes that 'being water' is synonymous with 'being composed of H₂O molecules,' or that 'temperature' is synonymous with 'mean molecular kinetic energy,' and so forth for many other scientific identities.

Second, ever since the pioneering work of Kripke (1972) and Putnam (1975), there has been articulation and widespread acceptance of the idea that names and natural kind terms are *rigid designators*; i.e., such expressions designate the same entity with respect to every possible world in which that entity exists. Two important consequences result: (i) identity statements involving rigid designators flanking the identity sign, as in 'Water = H₂O,' are necessarily true without being analytic; and (ii) such statements constitute *definitions* – not the kind that express meaning connections and are thus analytic, but rather *synthetic definitions* that give the real essence of the particular, property, or kind designated by a certain term. Thus, if true, 'Water = H₂O' is a non-analytic necessary truth that expresses the real, underlying, essence of water and thus provides a (synthetically true) definition of 'water.'

Third, ever since the pioneering work of Putnam (1967a, 1967b), there has been articulation and widespread acceptance of the idea that mental state-types (properties), except perhaps phenomenal properties ("qualia"), are *functional* properties

– i.e., their essence consists not in any intrinsic features, but rather in a certain syndrome of *typical causal relations* to other state types, in particular to sensory states, actions, and other mental states which themselves are also functional properties. Functional properties are potentially "physically realizable" quite differently from one occasion of instantiation to another – depending, perhaps, upon the specific physical composition of the cognizer in which they are instantiated.

Fourth, largely because of the influence of functionalism in philosophy of mind, philosophers have increasingly repudiated their earlier tendency to cash out constraint C2 of philosophical naturalism as requiring that the entities (particulars, properties, kinds, facts, ect.) cited by higher-order forms of discourse be *identical* to entities posited by natural science, and ultimately by physics. A more relaxed, California-style, attitude has emerged that counts certain higher-order, multiply realizable, entities as naturalistically respectable – functional properties being the paradigm case. "Naturalness" – i.e., naturalistic respectability – of these higher-order properties and facts consists in (i) *supervenience* upon lower-order properties and facts, and (ii) the *explainability* of specific psychophysical supervenience relations.

Fifth, in recent philosophy of language there has been widespread acceptance of so-called "causal" theories of reference for names and natural kind terms. In the simplest versions, such theories assert that the semantic property of reference is to be understood as essentially involving appropriate causal connections between speakers' uses of a term and the entity to which the term refers. Such theories propose to explain (i) how the reference of a term is originally determined (e.g., there being some sort of baptism or dubbing ceremony through which speakers in causal contact with an item acquire the ability to refer to that item by means of some expression used in the ceremony), and (ii) how the capacity to refer is spread throughout a linguistic community (again, by speakers' causally interacting with one another and with the item). This rather simple sketch can be elaborated in a number of ways, but the basic idea is clear: for some terms at least, reference is "grounded" by relevant causal hookups between speakers and the world.

Sixth, in epistemology there has been a move away from the idea that there are *a priori* constraints, of the sort associated with the traditional foundationalist program, on acceptable methods of knowledge gathering. Instead, philosophers have begun to move in the direction of "naturalized" epistemology, which recognizes the radical contingency of our methods and procedures of inquiry, especially in science. Accounts of knowledge in terms of such causal notions as the reliability of belief generating processes have begun to displace former views that rested heavily upon *a priori* epistemic principles. Moreover, essentially coherentist holistic frameworks of inquiry have largely displaced the more traditional foundationalist frameworks.

The various philosophical themes and developments just outlined all came together, in a manner highly relevant to the subsequent emergence of new wave moral realism, in one of the two major species of functionalism in philosophy of mind: so-called *psychofunctionalism*. On this view, mental properties are multiply-realizable functional properties whose relational essences are fully capturable not by the generalizations of common-sense mentalistic psychology ("folk psychology"), but instead by the generalizations of the (ideally complete) *empirical* psychological theory T that happens to be true of humans.[1] According to psychofunctionalism, mental terms refer rigidly to these properties; and this rigid reference underwrites certain synthetic definitions of mental properties – where the definitive causal role of each such property is specified by means of the empirical theory T. The reason why our mental terms refer to *these* properties is that there are suitable reference-subserving causal relations linking (instantiations of) these specific functional properties to people's uses of mental terms and concepts; i.e., the mental terms and concepts "track" the relevant functional properties, in something like the way that radar systems track flying objects, or that traces in a bubble chamber track electrons. Accordingly, it is quite possible to know that certain mental properties are instantiated by certain individuals, even if one does not know the functional essences of the attributed properties, and indeed even if one has numerous false beliefs about those properties. The true nature and essence of mental properties, says the

---

[1]   On psychofunctionalism, see Fodor (1968), and Block (1978), Field (1978), and Lycan (1981).

psychofunctionalist, is a thoroughly *empirical* question, to be answered not by *a priori* reflection but by scientific inquiry.

So although Moore's Open Question Argument at first made betting on ethical naturalism a sucker's bet, and turned some form of irrealism into an odds on metaethical favorite, with the emergence on the philosophical scene of an easygoing, nonreductive, naturalism, all bets were off.

5.   Ethical Naturalism Revived

The various trends noted above, and jointly embodied in psychofunctionalism, are evident in the recent revival of ethical naturalism of the 1980s. To begin with, David Brink, one of most prominent of the new wavers, has suggested that moral properties are functional properties of a certain kind:

> [T]he moral realist might claim that moral properties are functional properties. He might claim that what is essential to moral properties is the causal role which they play in the characteristic activities of human organisms. In particular, the realist might claim that moral properties are those which bear upon the maintenance and flourishing of human organisms. Maintenance and flourishing presumably consist in necessary conditions for survival, other needs associated with basic well-being, wants of various sorts, and distinctively human capacities. People, actions, policies, states of affairs, etc. will bear good-making properties just insofar as they contribute to the satisfaction of these needs, wants, and capacities . . . [and] will bear bad-making moral properties just insofar as they fail to promote or interfere with the satisfaction of these needs, wants, and capacities. The physical states which contribute to or interfere with these needs, wants, and capacities are the physical states upon which, on this functionalist theory, moral properties ultimately supervene. (1984: 121–2)

Brink also maintains that moral inquiry is a matter of seeking a normative theory that *coheres* best with both moral and nonmoral beliefs (Brink 1984, 1989). This coherentist methodology, usually called "reflective equilibrium," rejects any appeal to *a priori* moral truths or *a priori* constraints on moral inquiry: in ethics, as in science, our methods of knowledge-gathering are radically contingent. For Brink, moral properties are functional properties whose relational essences are captured by whatever specific normative moral theory would

emerge, for humans, as the outcome of correctly applied coherentist methodology:

> The details of the way in which moral properties supervene upon other natural properties are worked out differently by different moral theories. Determination of which account of moral supervenience is best will depend upon determination of which moral theory provided that best account of all our beliefs, both moral and non-moral (1984: 121, cf. 1989: 175).

One finds the clearest statement of the *semantic* component of new wave moral realism in the work of Richard Boyd (1988) [included as chapter 13 of this volume], whose position has three key ingredients. First, Boyd proposes to construe moral terms like 'good' and 'right' (and the concepts they express) as being semantically like natural kind (and other scientific) terms, in having natural, "synthetic" definitions that reveal the essence of the property the term expresses. This means, of course, that moral terms need not have analytic definitions of the sort that were central to more traditional versions of ethical naturalism. Second, the claim that moral terms function this way evidently requires that they are rigid. Like natural kind terms, moral terms allegedly rigidly designate the properties to which they refer. Third, Boyd maintains that for moral terms, just as for names and natural kind terms, reference is a matter of there being certain causal connections between people's uses of such terms and the relevant natural properties.

According to Boyd's own version of the causal theory of reference, reference is essentially an epistemic notion; so the relevant causal relations constituting reference are just those causal connections involved in knowledge gathering activities:

> Roughly, and for nondegenerate cases, a term *t* refers to a kind (property, relation, etc.) *k* just in case there exist causal mechanisms whose tendency is to bring it about, over time, that what is predicated of the term *t* will be approximately true of *k* (excuse the blurring of the use-mention distinction). Such mechanisms will typically include the existence of procedures which are approximately accurate for recognizing members or instances of *k* (at least for easy cases) and which relevantly govern the use of *t*, the social transmission of certain relevantly approximately true beliefs regarding *k*, formulated as claims about *t* (again excuse the slight to the use-mention distinction), a pattern of deference to experts on *k* with

respect to the use of *t*, etc. . . . When relations of this sort obtain, we may think of the properties of *k* as *regulating* the use of *t* (via such causal relations) . . . (1988: 195)

Extending this version of the causal theory to moral terms, as Boyd proposes to do, commits him to what we'll call the *causal regulation thesis*:

> CRT *Causal regulation thesis*: For each moral term t (e.g., 'good'), there is a natural property N such that N alone, and no other property, causally regulates the use of t by humans.

On Boyd's view, then, the fact that humankind's uses of moral terms are regulated in the way described by CRT is what allows one to conclude that moral terms like 'good' behave semantically like natural kind terms: they rigidly refer to certain natural properties and hence possess synthetic definitions. So we can summarize what we call new wave moral semantics (as developed by Boyd) as the following thesis:

> CSN *Causal semantic naturalism*: Each moral term t rigidly designates the natural property N that uniquely casually regulates the use of t by humans.

A corollary of CSN is that each moral term t has a synthetically true natural definition whose definiens characterizes, in purely natural terms, the unique natural property that supposedly casually regulates the use of t by humans. (CRT too is a corollary of CSN, since CSN cannot be true unless each moral term t is indeed causally regulated by some unique natural property N.)

Boyd's views and Brink's are evidently quite compatible, and in fact are nicely complementary. Brink is explicit in claiming that moral properties are functional properties whose essence is captured by a specific normative moral theory, but says rather little about the semantics of moral terms. Boyd, on the other hand, explicitly claims that moral terms work like natural-kind terms in science and that they designate natural properties, but says rather little about the nature of these properties. So the currently most plausible form of ethical naturalism is an amalgam – the Brink/Boyd view, as we shall call it.

Also an integral part of the Brink/Boyd view is their holistic moral epistemology, involving a coherentist methodology of moral inquiry. In light of CSN, this commitment to epistemological coherentism in ethics is evidently quite compatible with Brink's and Boyd's moral realism. For, if indeed the normative theory T that best coheres with humankind's moral and non-moral beliefs is true, then T will qualify as true not *by virtue* of this coherence – that would be an irrealist, "constructivist," conception of moral truth – but rather because coherentist methodology is likely, as a matter of *contingent fact*, to converge upon the very normative theory whose generalizations capture the essence of the functional properties that causally regulate the uses of moral terms by humankind, properties that are thus (according to CSN) the referents of moral terms.

This constellation of views – moral functionalism, a holistic moral epistemology, and causal semantic naturalism – together make up what we take to be the most plausible and complete version of new wave moral realism to date. It is a species of what we call *synthetic ethical naturalism,* to be distinguished from its predecessor, analytic ethical naturalism. And certainly (this version of) synthetic ethical naturalism, with its many similarities to psychofunctionalism in philosophy of mind, has a lot going for it.

Recall the naturalistically inspired metaphysical and epistemological constraints on moral realism. The Brink/Boyd view seems to satisfy them quite well. Take the metaphysical constraint C1, requiring that any moral properties and moral facts must be naturalistically accommodated. According to the Brink/Boyd view, moral properties are perfectly respectable natural properties, viz., multiply realizable functional properties. If so, then contrary to J. L. Mackie (1977), there is nothing metaphysically "queer" about the supervenience relation that obtains between certain lower-order properties and moral properties. The supervenience of moral properties is no more queer than is the supervenience of mental properties, given a functionalist position in philosophy of mind: in either case, specific supervenience connections are naturalistically explainable on the basis of (i) the correct synthetic definitions of the higher-order properties, together with (ii) relevant lower-order naturalistic facts.

The Brink/Boyd view also appears to hold the key for answering an epistemological worry about moral realism, thus satisfying the epistemological constraint C2. In answer to the question, "If there are objective moral properties, what access do we have to them?" the ethical naturalist simply replies that we have access to – and hence come to have knowledge of – such properties in much the way we come to have access to, and come to have knowledge of, other sorts of objective properties. Just as scientific inquiry relies ultimately upon observations (often informed by theoretical assumptions, when it comes to matters highly theoretical in nature), so in moral inquiry we make moral "observations" – viz., spontaneous moral judgments – that provide cognitive access to moral properties and facts, thereby providing the basis for developing an overall coherent system of moral and nonmoral beliefs constituting moral knowledge. Of course, philosophical critics (e.g., Mackie 1977) have frequently argued that facts about disagreement in moral belief, and diversity in people's moral codes, make the idea of moral observations highly suspect. But if people's spontaneous moral judgments are *causally regulated* by the very properties to which moral terms refer, as new-wave naturalism asserts, then these judgments thereby possess an epistemic status roughly comparable to that of observational judgments in science. i.e., spontaneous moral judgments provide humans with a (defeasible) form of cognitive access to objective moral truth – access that can then become substantially refined, deepened, systematized, and (as need be) corrected by means of coherentist methods of moral inquiry. Although people sometimes disagree in their specific moral judgments, in the moral codes to which they subscribe, and in their conceptions of the properties expressed by moral terms, these facts do not seriously call into question our access to, or knowledge of, moral properties and facts. For moral terms (as for scientific terms), Boyd's semantic thesis CSN explains (i) how, despite interpersonal variations in moral beliefs (or scientific beliefs), there is indeed some single objective property that is the referent of a given moral (or scientific) term; and (ii) how, by virtue of the causal-regulatory nature of this reference relation, humans have socially coordinated cognitive access to these properties and thus can acquire moral knowledge.

So, the Brink/Boyd version of synthetic ethical naturalism evidently meets very well both the metaphysical and the epistemological constraints imposed by philosophical naturalism. In doing so, this form of moral realism relies fundamentally on a certain semantic view about moral terms. Notice

that this fact reveals a parallel between analytic and synthetic ethical naturalism: each species involves a particular moral semantics that plays an absolutely fundamental role in defending the view's naturalistic moral ontology and the associated epistemology. But synthetic ethical naturalism, besides comporting nicely with the anti-reductivist trends in the naturalist's program, also (and as a result) entirely sidesteps Moore's open question argument: who cares if moral terms don't have analytic naturalistic definitions? It appears that new wave moral realism, having entered vigorously into the meta-ethical ring, has everything going for it. But so it seemed with Mike Tyson. The semantic thesis CSN, the linchpin of the Brink/Boyd view, is also its glass jaw.

6.   Enter: Moral Twin Earth

Suppose someone grants that the use of 'water' by humans is causally regulated by some specific physico-chemical natural kind, but then questions the claim that 'water' *rigidly designates* the natural kind (viz., H_2O) which happens to fill this role. (This skeptic might believe, for instance, that 'water' designates a more general physical natural kind – a genus which has H_2O as only one of its various actual or physically possible species.) What sort of evidence can be put forth to support the contention that 'water' really does rigidly designate the sortal kind-property H_2O?

When philosophers defend such semantic theses with respect to, e.g., names and physical natural kind terms, a particular type of thought experiment looms very large: the Putnam-style Twin Earth scenario. Recall how those go. In one of Putnam's stories, we are to imagine Twin Earth – a planet pretty much like Earth except that the oceans, lakes, and streams are filled with a liquid whose outward, easily observable, properties are just like those of water, but whose underlying physico-chemical nature is not H_2O, but some other molecular structure XYZ. Despite outward similarities and the fact that speakers of twin English apply the word 'water' to this liquid composed of XYZ, reflection on this scenario yields a very strong intuition that Twin Earthlings don't mean by their twin-English term 'water' what we mean by 'water,' and that their term is not translatable by our orthographically identical term. And along with this judgment come two further intuitive judgments: (i) that the English term rigidly designates H_2O, whereas the twin-English term rigidly designates XYZ; and (ii) that this fact explains why the terms differ in meaning.

Competent speakers have a strong intuitive mastery of both the syntactic and the semantic norms governing their language. Consequently, the intuitive judgments just described concerning the Twin Earth scenario constitute important (though of course defeasible) empirical evidence for the hypothesis that 'water' rigidly designates the specific physico-chemical physical kind that happens to causally regulate the use of this term by humans, viz., the kind H_2O.

The form of argument just canvassed can be called a *semantic competence argument*. Presumably, competent speakers have a comparable intuitive mastery of the semantic workings of 'good' and other fundamental moral terms. So if the Brink/Boyd thesis CSN is correct, then things should go the same way they go with 'water.' That is, if indeed the term 'good' purports to rigidly designate the unique natural property (if there is one) that causally regulates the use of 'good' by humankind in general, then it should be possible to construct a suitable Twin Earth scenario with these features: (i) reflection on this scenario generates intuitive judgments that are comparable to those concerning Putnam's original scenario; and (ii) these judgments are accompanied by the more general intuitive judgment that 'good' does indeed work semantically as CSN says it does. Conversely, if the appropriate Twin Earth scenario does *not* have these features – i.e., if the semantic intuitions of competent speakers turn out not to be what they should be if CSN is true – then this will mean that in all probability, CSN is false.

We maintain that things go the latter way – i.e., one's intuitive judgments concerning a suitable Twin Earth scenario go contrary to CSN. What is wanted is a Twin Earth where things are as similar to Earth as possible, consistent with the hypothesis that twin-moral terms are causally regulated, for twin-humans in general, by certain natural properties *distinct from* those natural properties which (as we are here granting for argument's sake) regulate the use of moral terms by humans in general.

So let's begin by supposing that, as the Brink/Boyd view maintains, human uses of 'good' and 'right' are regulated by certain *functional* properties; and that, as a matter of empirical fact, these are consequentialist properties whose functional

essence is captured by some specific consequentialist normative theory; call this theory T^c. We further suppose that there is some reliable method of moral inquiry which, if properly and thoroughly employed, would lead us to discover this fact about our uses of moral terms.

Now consider Moral Twin Earth, which, as you might expect, is just about like good old Earth: same geography and natural surroundings, people who live in the twin United States by and large speak twin English; there is a state they call 'Tennessee' that is situated directly south of a state they call 'Kentucky;' and every year a fairly large number of Twin Earthlings make a pilgrimage to Twin Memphis to visit the grave site of Twin Elvis. You get the idea. Of particular importance here is the fact that Moral Twin Earthlings have a vocabulary that works much like human moral vocabulary; they use the terms 'good' and 'bad,' 'right' and 'wrong' to evaluate actions, persons, institutions and so forth (at least those who speak twin English use these terms, whereas those who speak some other twin language use terms orthographically identical to the terms 'good,' 'right,' etc., in the corresponding Earthian dialects). In fact, were a group of explorers from Earth ever to visit Moral Twin Earth they would be strongly inclined to translate Moral Twin Earth terms 'good,' 'right' and the rest as identical in meaning to our orthographically identical English terms. After all, the uses of these terms on Moral Twin Earth bear all of the "formal" marks that we take to characterize moral vocabulary and moral practice. In particular, the terms are used to reason about considerations bearing on Moral Twin Earthling well-being; Moral Twin Earthlings are normally disposed to act in certain ways corresponding to judgments about what is 'good' and 'right;' they normally take considerations about what is 'good' and 'right' to be especially important, even of overriding importance in most cases, in deciding what to do, and so on.

Let us suppose that investigation into twin English moral discourse and associated practice reveals that their uses of twin-moral terms are causally regulated by certain natural properties distinct from those that (as we are already supposing) regulate English moral discourse. The properties tracked by twin English moral terms are also functional properties, whose essence is functionally characterizable by means of a normative moral theory. But these are *non-consequentialist* moral properties, whose functional essence is captured by some specific deontological theory; call this theory T^d. These functional properties are similar enough to those characterizable via T^c to account for the fact that twin-moral discourse operates in Twin Earth society and culture in much the manner that moral discourse operates on Earth. (We've already noted that if explorers ever visit Moral Twin Earth, they will be inclined, at least initially, to construe Moral Twin Earthlings as having beliefs about good and right, and to translate twin English uses of twin-moral terms into our orthographically identical terms.) The differences in causal regulation, we may suppose, are due at least in part to certain species-wide differences in psychological temperament that distinguish Twin Earthlings from Earthlings. (For instance, perhaps Twin Earthlings tend to experience the sentiment of *guilt* more readily and more intensively, and tend to experience *sympathy* less readily and less intensively, than do Earthlings.) In addition, suppose that if Twin Earthlings were to employ in a proper and thorough manner the same reliable method of moral inquiry which (as we are already supposing) would lead Earthlings to discover that Earthling uses of moral terms are causally regulated by functional properties whose essence is captured by the consequentialist normative theory T^c, then this method would lead the Twin Earthlings to discover that their own uses of moral terms are causally regulated by functional properties whose essence is captured by the deontological theory T^d.

Given all these assumptions and stipulations about Earth and Moral Twin Earth, what is the appropriate way to describe the differences between moral and twin-moral uses of 'good' and 'right'? Two hermeneutic options are available. On the one hand, we could say that the differences are analogous to those between Earth and Twin Earth in Putnam's original example, to wit: the moral terms used by Earthlings rigidly designate the natural properties that causally regulate their use on Earth, whereas the twin-moral terms used by Twin Earthlings rigidly designate the *distinct* natural properties that causally regulate their use on Twin Earth; hence, moral and twin-moral terms *differ in meaning*, and are not intertranslatable. On the other hand, we could say instead that moral and twin-moral terms do *not* differ in meaning or reference, and hence that any apparent moral disagreements that might arise between Earthlings and Twin Earthlings would be *genuine* disagreements – i.e., disagreements in moral belief and in normative moral theory, rather than disagreements in meaning.

We submit that by far the more natural mode of description, when one considers the Moral Twin Earth scenario, is the second. Reflection on the scenario just does not generate hermeneutical pressure to construe Moral Twin Earthling uses of 'good' and 'right' as not translatable by our orthographically identical terms. But if CSN were true, and the moral terms in question rigidly designated those natural properties that causally regulate their use, then reflection on this scenario ought to generate intuitions analogous to those generated in Putnam's original Twin Earth scenario. i.e., it should seem intuitively natural to say that here we have a difference in meaning, and that twin English "moral" terms are not translatable by English moral terms. Yet when it comes to characterizing the differences between Earthlings and twin Earthlings on this matter, the natural-seeming thing to say is that the differences involve belief and theory, not meaning.

One's intuitions work the same way if, instead of considering the Moral Twin Earth scenario from the outside looking in, one considers how things would strike Earthlings and Twin Earthlings who have encountered each other. Suppose that Earthlings visit Twin Earth (or vice versa), and both groups come to realize that different natural properties causally regulate their respective uses of 'good', 'right', and other moral terms. If CSN were true, then recognition of these differences ought to result in its seeming rather silly, to members of each group, to engage in inter-group debate about goodness – about whether it conforms to normative theory T^c or to T^d. (If, in Putnam's original scenario, the two groups learn that their respective uses of 'water' are causally regulated by different physical kind-properties, it would be silly for them to think they have differing views about the real nature of water.) But such inter-group debate would surely strike both groups not as silly but as quite appropriate, because they would regard one another as differing in moral beliefs and moral theory, not in meaning.

Since semantic norms are tapped by human linguistic competence, and since the relevant linguistic competence is presumably reflected in one's intuitive judgments concerning Twin Earth scenarios, this outcome constitutes strong empirical evidence against CSN.

The outcome also underwrites the following "open question argument," a version directed not against analytic semantic naturalism (as was Moore's original open question argument) but instead against CSN. First premise: If CSN is true, then questions of the following form are *closed*, in the sense that any competent speaker who properly exercises his competence will judge – solely on the basis of his understanding of how the relevant terms work semantically – that the answer to each question is trivially and obviously 'yes:'

> Q1   Given that the use of 'good' by humans is causally regulated by natural property N, is entity e, which has N, good?

and

> Q2   Given that the use of 'good' by humans is causally regulated by natural property N, does entity e, which is good, have N?

Second premise: Questions of the form Q1 and Q2 are *not* closed, as evidenced by one's intuitions concerning the Moral Twin Earth scenario. Conclusion: CSN is false.

7.   Down for the Count, Again

Moral Twin Earth packs a mean punch. Moral realism, having returned to the philosophical ring

in newly lean and mean naturalistic shape, has been decked again. Furthermore, Moral Twin Earth is more than a specific thought experiment directed at the specific semantic thesis CSN. It is, in addition, a *recipe* for thought experiments. For any potential version of synthetic naturalism that might be proposed, according to which (i) moral terms bear some relation R to certain natural properties that collectively satisfy some specific normative moral theory T, and (ii) moral terms supposedly *refer* to the natural properties to which they bear this relation R, it should be possible to construct a Moral Twin Earth scenario suitably analogous to the one constructed above – i.e., a scenario in which twin-moral terms bear the same relation R to certain natural properties that collectively satisfy some specific normative theory T', incompatible with T. The above reasoning against CSN should apply, *mutatis mutandis*, against the envisioned alternative version of semantic naturalism.

No doubt various attempts at resuscitation might be made, now that new wave moral realism is flat on the canvass. But in the end, we suspect, all such attempts will prove futile. Moral realism can be squared with the constraints imposed by philosophical naturalism only if CSN, or some similar form of semantic naturalism, is a viable approach to moral semantics. But synthetic semantic naturalism is down for the count.

References

Block, N. 1978. "Troubles with Functionalism." In C. Savage, ed., *Minnesota Studies in the Philosophy of Science*, IX. Minneapolis: University of Minnesota Press.

Boyd, R. 1988. "How to Be a Moral Realist." In G. Sayre-McCord, ed., *Essays in Moral Realism*. Ithaca, NY: Cornell University Press.

Brink, D. 1984. "Moral Realism and Skeptical Arguments from Disagreement and Queerness." *Australasian Journal of Philosophy* 62.

Brink, D. 1989. *Moral Realism and the Foundations of Ethics*. Cambridge: Cambridge University Press.

Field, H. 1978. "Mental Representation." *Erkenntnis* 13.

Fodor, J. 1968. "Propositional Attitudes." *The Monist* 61.

Horgan, T. and M. Timmons. 1991. "Troubles on Moral Twin Earth: Moral Queerness Revived." *Synthese* 66.

Horgan, T. and M. Timmons. 1992. "Troubles for New Wave Moral Semantics: The 'Open Question Argument' Revived." *Philosophical Papers* 21: 153–75.

Kripke, S. 1972. "Naming and Necessity." In D. Davidson and G. Harman, eds., *Semantics of Natural Language*. Dordrecht: Reidel.

Lycan, W. 1981. "Toward a Homuncular Theory of Believing." *Cognition and Brain Theory* 4.

Mackie, J. L. 1977. *Ethics: Inventing Right and Wrong*. New York: Penguin Books.

Putnam, H. 1967a. "The Mental Life of Some Machines." In H. Castañeda, ed., *Intentionality, Minds, and Perception*. Detroit: Wayne State University Press.

Putnam, H. 1967b. "Psychological Predicates." In W. H. Capitan and D. D. Merrill, eds., *Art, Mind, and Religion*. Pittsburgh: University of Pittsburgh Press.

Putnam, H. 1975. "The Meaning of 'Meaning'." In K. Gunderson, ed., *Minnesota Studies in the Philosophy of Science*, VII. Minneapolis: University of Minnesota Press.

Timmons, M. 1990. "On the Epistemic Status of Considered Moral Judgments." *Southern Journal of Philosophy* 29, Spindel Conference Supplement.